Federal Revenues, Expenditures, and Budget Balances, 1967–1986
(percentage of GDP, national accounts basis)

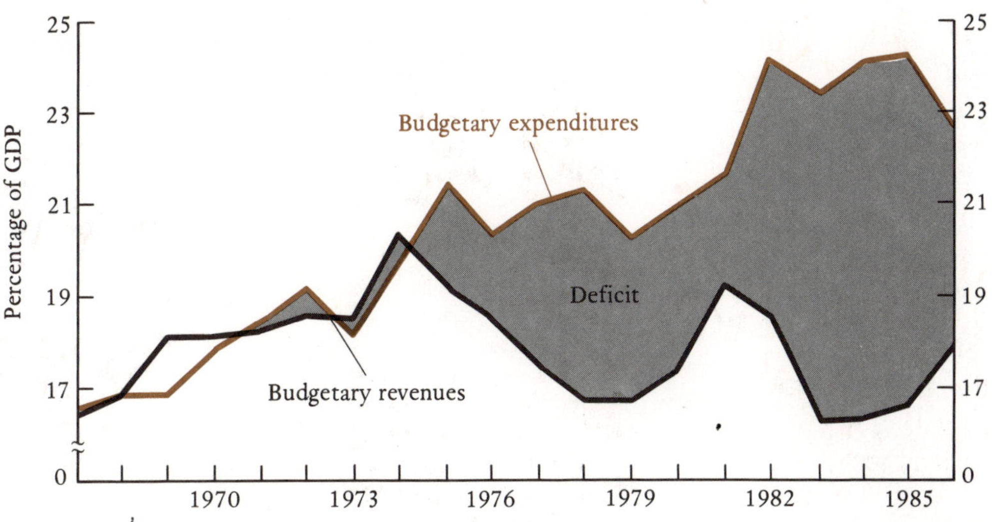

(i) Revenues and expenditures

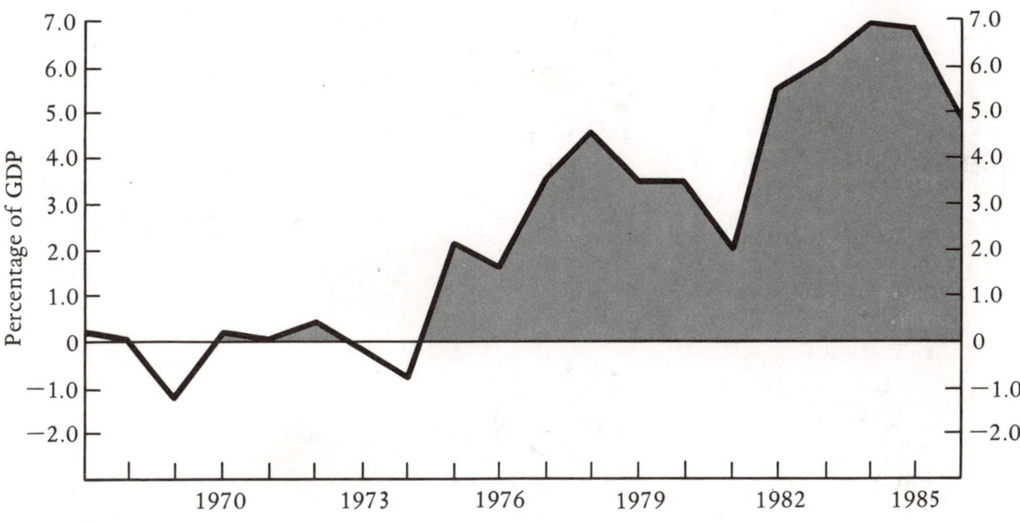

(ii) The budgetary deficit

ECONOMICS

Sixth Edition

ECONOMICS

Richard G. Lipsey
C.D. Howe Institute

Douglas D. Purvis
Queen's University

Peter O. Steiner
The University of Michigan

1817

HARPER & ROW, PUBLISHERS, New York
Cambridge, Philadelphia, San Francisco, Washington,
London, Mexico City, São Paulo, Singapore, Sydney

Sponsoring Editor: John Greenman
Development Editor: Mary Lou Mosher
Project Editor: Lenore Bonnie Biller
Text Design: Leon Bolognese
Cover Design: Lucy Krikorian
Cover Photos: Front—Grain harvest, Alberta, Canada, © 1984, Gary Crallé, The Image Bank. Back—Burrard Inlet, Vancouver, B.C., Thomas Kitchin, Valan Photos.
Text Art: Vantage Art, Inc.
Production Manager: Kewal Sharma
Compositor: Ruttle, Shaw & Wetherill, Inc.
Printer and Binder: Arcata Graphics/Kingsport Press
Cover Printer: Arcata Graphics/Kingsport Press

Economics, Sixth Edition

Library of Congress Cataloging in Publication Data

Lipsey, Richard G., 1928–
Economics / Richard G. Lipsey, Douglas D. Purvis, Peter O. Steiner.—6th ed.
p. cm.
Includes index.
ISBN 0-06-043912-2
1. Economics. I. Purvis, Douglas D. II. Steiner, Peter Otto, 1922– . III. Title.
HB171.5.L733 1988
330—dc19

87-30525
CIP

ISBN 0-06-043912-2

89 90 91 9 8 7 6 5 4 3

Brief Contents

Detailed Contents

Preface

Economics is a living discipline. Through six editions of *Economics,* our basic motivation has been to provide a text that reflects the tremendous changes in that discipline over the decades.

The first major theme of this book is to reflect the gradual movement of economics today toward becoming a science, exhibiting the key characteristic that marks any science: the systematic confrontation of theory with observation. Today most economists agree that their subject is more than a stage for parading pet theories. Nor is economics just a container for collecting masses of unrelated institutional and statistical material. Economists are expanding the frontiers of knowledge about the economic environment and learning to understand and often to control it. But new problems and new events are always challenging existing knowledge. Economists are therefore continually concerned with how theory, institutions, and facts relate to each other. Every theory is subject to empirical challenge.

A second major theme of this book concerns the relations between economic theory and economic policy. Decades of systematic observations have provided an ever-growing understanding of how things relate to one another quantitatively. This knowledge has increased economists' ability to make sensible and relevant statements about public policy. True, there remain many areas where economists' knowledge is painfully sparse, as current debates about supply-side economics and the nature of an appropriate monetary policy remind us.

The third major feature of the book has to do with the way we view students. We have tried to be as honest with them as possible within the limits of an introductory textbook. No subject worth studying is always easy, and we do not approve of slipping particularly hard bits of analysis past students without letting them see what is happening and what has been assumed, nor do we approve of teaching them things they will have to unlearn if they go on in economics (a practice sometimes justified on the grounds that it is important to get to the big issues quickly). In short, we have tried to follow Albert Einstein's advice: Make things as simple as possible, but not simpler.

Effective criticism of existing ideas is the springboard to progress in science. We believe that introductory economics should introduce students to methods for testing, criticizing, and evaluating the present state of the subject. We do not believe that it is wrong to suggest to students the possibility of criticizing current economic theory. Students will always criticize and evaluate their course content, and their criticisms are more likely to be informed and relevant if they are given practice and instruction in how to challenge what they have been taught in an effective, constructive manner.

Major Revisions in This Edition

Our main theme in this revision has been teachability. Every sentence, the structure of every argument, and every figure has been reviewed. Minor inconsistencies, and passages that our own and other teachers' experiences have told us are unnecessarily difficult, qualifications that belong only in more advanced treatments, unnecessary variations in the labelling of graphs, and a host of other smaller but significant problems have all received our attention. We hope that the result is a smoother and more teachable treatment throughout.

Some dramatic content changes have been made. The most important are listed below.

Changes in Microeconomics

1. Our surveys show that instructors split into three groups: (1) those who would argue the negative

slope of demand curves on purely intuitive grounds in an introductory course; (2) those who would teach marginal utility theory for its great insight into the distinction between value in total and value at the margin; and (3) those who feel that indifference curves are indispensable, even in a first-year course. For the first time we have tried to accommodate all three groups. The text now distinguishes between the income and the substitution effects using the budget line only (the graphical equivalent of the Slutsky equation). It also rescues some of the great insights of marginal utility theory from the oblivion of an appendix by stating them without the formal apparatus of a utility function and its first and second partial derivatives. Two appendixes now provide formal analysis of marginal utility and indifference curve theory, making it easy for instructors to teach either, neither, or both.

2. We have introduced Chapter 15 on oligopoly with an illustrative discussion of the rise and fall of OPEC. The rest of the chapter has been reworked to reflect many of the changes in economists' views about oligopoly that are being developed in the literature on the "new industrial organization theory."

3. The chapter on barriers to trade has been wholly rewritten to reflect the changing nature of trade barriers in the real world. The last half of the chapter gives a greatly expanded treatment of Canadian commercial policy, concluding with the signing of the Trade Agreement with the United States and the Great Free Trade Debate that surrounded it.

4. The micro half of the book concludes with a wholly new chapter on social policy. Few wish to dismantle Canada's social policies, but a growing chorus calls for reform to make those policies deliver more where need is greatest. The political process, however, encourages politicians to accept the "sacred trust" of preserving existing policies even where help goes to some privileged groups and misses some of those most in need. For this reason, debate on reform of the social envelope will continue, we believe, at least until the end of the century. We believe that it is important for a first-year student to come away with a view of how economists approach an evaluation of social policy. We also believe that students will find this new material interesting and rewarding, as it provides a chance to think as an economist about a very relevant current issue.

Changes in Macroeconomics

This is now the third edition in which the material on macroeconomics has relied mainly on the tools of aggregate demand and aggregate supply. Our emphasis in this revision has been on improving the teachability of the material. We have simplified the discussion in several places and restructured the material in a couple of chapters to provide flexibility to the instructor. Perhaps most important, we have introduced and developed the *AD* and *AS* curves only as they are needed; this gives rise to a simpler presentation of the basic theory.

Macroeconomic theory is now developed in three key chapters, Chapters 28, 29, and 30. The first chapter develops the fixed price model, the second allows for variations in the price level but maintains the assumption of fixed wages, while the third introduces the role of wage adjustments.

1. The introduction of the *AD* and *AS* curves that previously occurred in the introductory macro chapter, Chapter 26, has been dropped. This simplifies the introduction to macroeconomics and means that the student no longer meets *AD* and *AS* only to put them aside for several chapters.

2. The detailed treatment of index numbers has been combined with national income accounting in one chapter, Chapter 27. The treatment of both topics is both simpler and more comprehensive than in previous editions. The discussion of the national income accounts has been restructured to reflect the switch from GNP to GDP as the central measure of national income.

3. Chapter 28 develops the fixed-price model in detail. It combines the material from Chapters 28 and 29 in the fifth edition. First the *AE* function is developed and the equilibrium level of income is determined. We then turn to the comparative statics of the fixed-price model, and the development of the simple multiplier.

4. Chapter 29 then develops the model with a variable price level under the assumption of fixed factor prices. In keeping with standard terminology

we refer to this as the "short-run" model of the price level and national income. We start by analysing the effects of an exogenous price change in the fixed-price model. This allows us to derive the *AD* curve. We then add the *SRAS* curve in order to allow for an endogenous determination of the price level. The Keynesian flat *AS* curve is mentioned only in passing in the text as a qualification to the general presumption that the *SRAS* has a positive slope. Its historical importance is developed in a box.

5. Chapter 30 allows for factor price adjustments in response to the output gap. (We have moved the box introducing the Phillips curve to this chapter from the inflation chapter.) The implications of wage-price adjustment for the *SRAS* curve are then analysed, and the vertical *LRAS* curve is derived. The treatment of *LRAS* has been thoroughly revised and, where possible, simplified. The distinction, important for most of the remaining chapters, between the *SRAS* and *LRAS* curves is stressed.

We feel that it is worth making the effort required to establish this distinction because, as economists, we are concerned about the many textbooks that carry out the bulk of their analysis with a single, stable *AS* curve. This simplifies teaching, but it risks serious confusion. The alert student faced with a fixed *AS* curve and an *AD* curve that can be shifted by policy will wonder why anyone would hesitate to pay the price of a once-and-for-all increase in the price level in order to obtain a permanent increase in output and employment. And who would hesitate, faced with such a trade-off? To avoid such serious confusions, we introduce the shifting, short-run *AS* curve and the vertical, long-run *AS* curve at the outset.

6. The structure of Chapter 32, "Fiscal Policy," is mostly unchanged from the last edition, but the material has been rewritten to increase its relevance and teachability. The *AD/AS* apparatus is now fully integrated into the chapter. The historical discussion of fiscal policy in action has been shortened to make room for an extended discussion of the implications of persistent government budget deficits.

7. The chapter on inflation has been reworked and simplified. The emphasis is now more on long-term inflation control and less on the issue—important at the time of writing the previous edition—of how to break an entrenched inflation.

Teaching Aids

Tag lines and captions for figures and tables. The boldface tag line below or next to a figure or table states briefly the central conclusion to be drawn from the illustration; the lightface caption gives information needed to reach that conclusion. Each title, tag line, and caption, along with the figure or table, form a self-contained unit, useful for reviewing.

Boxes. The "boxes" contain examples or materials that are relevant extensions of the main text but need not be read as part of the text sequence. They are all optional. Some have further theoretical material. Others contain expansions and applications of points already covered in the text. The boxes give flexibility in expanding or contracting the coverage of specific chapters.

End-of-chapter material. Each chapter has a Summary, a list of Topics for Review, and Discussion Questions. The questions are designed for class discussion or for "quiz sections." Answers appear in the Instructor's Manual.

Appendixes. For several editions, the appendixes that give more detailed discussion of certain topics have been gathered in a separate section at the back of the text. In this present edition, for ease of use, we have placed the appendixes directly following the chapters to which they are related.

Mathematical notes. Mathematical notes are collected in a separate section at the end of the book. Since mathematical notation and derivation is not necessary to understand the principles of economics, but is helpful in more advanced work, this segregation seems to be a sensible arrangement. Mathematical notes provide clues to the uses of mathematics for the increasing number of students who have some background in math, without loading the text with notes that are useless and offputting to other readers.

Students with a mathematical background have often told us they find the notes helpful.

Glossary. The glossary covers widely used definitions of economic terms. Because some users treat micro- and macroeconomics in that order, and others in the reverse order, words in the glossary are printed in boldface type when they are first mentioned in *either half* of the text.

Endpapers. Inside the front cover on the left is a list of the most commonly used abbreviations in the text; on the right appears a figure representing the evolution of the federal deficit and the national debt. Inside the back cover on the left is an illustration representing the labor force, employment, and unemployment. At the right is a table of selected time series, useful data on the Canadian economy since 1926.

Supplements

Our book is accompanied by a workbook, *Study Guide and Problems,* prepared by Professors William Furlong, Kenneth Grant, and Fredric Menz. The workbook is designed to be used either in the classroom or by the students working on their own.

An *Instructor's Manual,* prepared by us, and a *Test Bank,* prepared by Delbert Ogden, are available to instructors adopting the book. The Test Bank is also available in a computerized form; contact the publisher for details.

New to this edition are 50 key theory diagrams reproduced from the text in the form of 2-color acetate transparencies; free to adopters. There are also over 100 transparency masters of important text figures available for classroom use.

Using the Book

Needs of students differ; some want material that goes beyond the average class level, but others have gaps in their backgrounds. To accommodate the former, we have included more material than we would assign to every student. Also, because there are many different kinds of first-year economics courses in colleges and universities, we have included more material than normally would be included in any single course.

Although teachers can best design their own courses, it may help if we indicate certain views of our own as to how this book *might* be adapted to difference courses.

Sequence

The choice of macro first or micro first is partly a personal one that cannot be decided solely by objective criteria. We believe, however, that there are good reasons for preferring the micro-macro order. The thrust over the last 20 years has been to examine the micro underpinnings of macro functions and to erect macroeconomics on a firmer base of micro behaviorial relations. Virtually every current macro controversy turns on some micro underpinning. For "micro-firsters" this poses no problem. For "macro-firsters" it is often hard to explain what is at issue.

Changes occur not only in economic theory but in the problems that excite students. Many of today's problems that students find most challenging—discrimination, social policy, equal-pay legislation, poverty, pollution, and free trade with the United States—are microeconomic in character. The micro-macro order, moreover, reflects the historical evolution of the subject. A century of classical and neoclassical development of microeconomics preceded the Keynesian development of macroeconomics.

For those who prefer the macro-micro order, we have attempted to make reversibility easy. The overview chapter that ends Part One provides a base on which to build either the microeconomics of Part Two or the macroeconomics of Part Seven. Chapter 4 should be assigned after Chapter 3, even in macro-first courses. Where further microeconomic concepts are required—as in the macro investment chapter—we have added brief sections to make the treatment self-contained, while providing review material for those who have covered the microeconomic section.

One-Term Courses

Thorough coverage of the bulk of the book supposes a two-term course in economics. A number of first courses in economics are only one term (or equivalent) in length and our book can be easily adapted to such courses. Suggestions for use of this book for such courses are given on page xxv. We recognize that for any one-term course a choice must be made among emphases. Most one-term survey courses give some coverage to theory and to policy, to micro- and to macroeconomics, but the relative weights vary. Instructors will wish to choose the topics to be included or excluded and to vary the order to suit their own preferences.

Acknowledgments

The starting point for this book was *Economics,* Eighth Edition, by Richard G. Lipsey, Peter O. Steiner, and Douglas D. Purvis. It would be impossible to acknowledge here all the teachers, colleagues, and students who contributed to that book. Hundreds of users have written to us with specific suggested improvements, and much of the credit for the fact that the book does become more and more teachable belongs to them. We can no longer list them individually but we thank them all most sincerely.

David Farnes and Gillian Hamilton provided excellent research assistance. A number of individuals provided reviews of the fifth edition that were most helpful in preparing the present edition. These are Torben Andersen, Red Deer College; Ronald G. Bodkin, University of Ottawa; Chris Clark, British Columbia Institute of Technology; Barry Cozier, Concordia University; M. H. I. Dore, Brock University; C. M. Fellows, Mount Royal College; S. W. Kardasz, University of Waterloo; George Kondor, Lakehead University; Victor Olshevski, University of Winnipeg; and P. L. Siklos, Wilfred Laurier University. In addition, the key micro chapters of this revision were read by Trudy Ann Cameron, UCLA; Vernon Dow, Cambrian College; and A. Gyasi Nimarko, Vanier College. The core macro chapters were seen by Sohrab Abizadeh, University of Winnipeg; G. C. Church, University of Regina; Geoffrey B. Hainsworth, University of British Columbia; Peter Howitt, University of Western Ontario; and Nicholas Rowe, Carleton University. William Furlong and Kenneth Grant, two of our study guide authors, have contributed to this edition as well.

Special thanks are due to Elaine Fitzpatrick, Patricia Casey-Purvis, Ellen McKay, and Dana Miltchen for careful and efficient handling of the manuscript at all stages.

Finally, this edition is dedicated to Clinton T. Purvis, who celebrates his ninetieth birthday as we go to press.

Richard G. Lipsey
Douglas D. Purvis
Peter O. Steiner

Suggested Outline for a One-Term Course

Note: A one-term course can cover about 20 to 22 full chapters. The core consists of about 18 chapters. Selections from other chapters, as listed below or according to the instructor's own preferences, can produce courses with various emphases.

Basic core chapters for courses covering both micro and macro

INTRODUCTION

1 The Economic Problem
2 Economics As a Social Science
3 An Overview of the Economy

MICROECONOMICS

4 Demand, Supply, and Price
5 Elasticity of Demand and Supply
9 The Role of the Firm
10 Production and Cost in the Short Run
11 Production and Cost in the Long and Very Long Run
12 Competitive Markets
13 Monopolistic Markets
17 Factor Mobility and Factor Pricing
20 The Gains from Trade
23 Benefits and Costs of Government Intervention

MACROECONOMICS

26 An Introduction to Macroeconomics
27 Measuring Macroeconomic Variables
28 National Income and Aggregate Expenditure
29 National Income and the Price Level in the Short Run
30 National Income and the Price Level in the Long Run
32 Fiscal Policy
33 The Nature of Money and Monetary Institutions
34 The Role of Money in Macroeconomics

Chapters that can be added to give different emphases to different courses[1]

MICROECONOMICS

* 6 Supply and Demand in Action: Price Controls and Agriculture
14 Oligopolistic Markets
*15 The Theory and Practice of Competition Policy
18 More on Factor Demand and Supply
*19 Wages, Unions, and Discrimination
*21 Barriers to Free Trade
*24 Taxation and Public Expenditure
*25 Social Policy

MACROECONOMICS

35 Monetary Policy
36 Inflation
37 Employment and Unemployment
38 Economic Growth
*39 Macroeconomic Controversies (First half only)
40 Exchange Rates and the Balance of Payments
*41 Alternative Exchange Rate Systems

[1] Chapters shown with an * are particularly appropriate for courses with a heavy policy orientation. Chapters not listed here, or in the core, seem to us to be lower priority in a one-term course, but they are not necessarily too difficult.

To the Student

A good course in economics will give you insight into how an economy functions and into some currently debated policy issues. Like all rewarding subjects, economics will not be mastered without effort. A book on economics must be worked at. It cannot be read like a novel.

Each of you must develop an individual technique for studying, but the following suggestions may prove helpful. It is usually a good idea to read a chapter quickly in order to get the general run of the argument. At this first reading you may want to skip the "boxes" of text material and any footnotes. Then, after reading the Topics for Review and the Discussion Questions, reread the chapter more slowly, making sure that you understand each step of the argument. With respect to the figures and tables, be sure you understand how the conclusions stated in the brief tag lines with each table or figure have been reached. You should be prepared to spend time on difficult sections; occasionally, you may spend an hour on only a few pages. Paper and a pencil are indispensable equipment in your reading. It is best to follow a difficult argument by building your own diagram while the argument unfolds rather than by relying on the finished diagram as it appears in the book. It is often helpful to invent numerical examples to illustrate general propositions. The end-of-chapter questions require you to apply what you have studied. We advise you to outline answers to some of the questions. In short, you should seek to understand economics, not merely to memorize it.

After you have read each part in detail, reread it quickly from beginning to end. It is often difficult to understand why certain things are done when they are viewed as isolated points, but when you reread a whole part, much that did not seem relevant or entirely comprehensible will fall into place in the analysis.

We call your attention to the glossary at the end of the book. Any time you run into a concept that seems vaguely familiar but is not clear to you, check the glossary. The chances are that it will be there, and its definition will remind you of what you once understood. If you are still in doubt, check the index entry to find where the concept is discussed more fully. Incidentally, the glossary, along with the captions that accompany figures and tables and the end-of-chapter summaries, may prove very helpful when reviewing for examinations.

The bracketed colored numbers in the text itself refer to a series of 54 mathematical notes that are found starting on page M-1. For those of you who like mathematics or prefer mathematical argument to verbal or geometric exposition, these may prove useful. Others may ignore them.

We hope that you will find the book rewarding and stimulating. Students who used earlier editions made some of the most helpful suggestions for revision, and we hope you will carry on the tradition. If you are moved to write to us, please do.

Einstein Started from Facts

The Morly-Michelson measurements of light, the movements of the planet Mercury, the unexplained aberrancies of the moon from its predicted place. Einstein went back to facts or told others where they should go to confirm or to reject his theory—by observation of stellar positions during a total eclipse. . . .

. . . It is not necessary, of course, for the verification of a new theory to be done personally by its propounder. Theoretical reasoning from facts is as essential a part of economic science as of other sciences, and in a wise division of labour there is room, in economics, as elsewhere, for the theoretician pure and simple, for one who leaves the technical business of verification to those who have acquired a special technique of observation. No one demanded of Einstein that he should visit the South Seas in person, and look through a telescope; but he told others what he expected them to see, if they looked, and he was prepared to stand or fall by the result. It is the duty of the propounder of every new theory, if he has not himself the equipment for observation, to indicate where verification of his theory is to be sought in facts—what may be expected to happen or to have happened if his theory is true, what will not happen if it is false.

[Now consider by way of contrast the behaviour of the participants in a current controversy in economics.] . . . None of them takes the point that the truth or falsehood of . . . [a] theory cannot be established except by appeal to facts; none of them tests it by facts himself. The distinguishing mark of economic science, as illustrated by this debate, is that it is a science in which verification of generalisations by reference to facts is neglected as irrelevant.

. . . I do not see how . . . [members of the public who survey the controversy] can avoid the conclusion that economics is not a science concerned with phenomena, but a survival of medieval logic, and that economists are persons who earn their livings by taking in one another's definitions for mangling. . . .

I know that in speaking thus I make enemies. I challenge a tradition of a hundred years of political economy, in which facts have been treated, not as controls of theory, but as illustrations. I shall be told that in the Social Sciences verification can never be clean enough to be decisive. I may be told that, in these sciences, observation has been tried and has failed, has led to shapeless accumulations of facts which themselves lead nowhere. I do not believe for a moment that this charge of barrenness of past enquiries can be sustained; to make it is to ignore many achievements of the past and to decry much solid work that is being done at this School and elsewhere. But if the charge of barrenness of realistic economics in the past were justified completely, that would not be a reason for giving up observation and verification. It would only be a reason for making our observations more exact and more numerous. If, in the Social Sciences, we cannot yet run or fly, we ought to be content to walk, or to creep on all fours as infants. . . . For economic and political theorising not based on facts and not controlled by facts assuredly does lead nowhere. . . .

There can be no science of society till the facts about society are available. Till 130 years ago we had no census, no knowledge even of the numbers and growth of the people; till fifteen years ago we had no comprehensive records about unemployment even in this country, and other countries are still where we were a generation or more ago; social statistics of every kind—about trade, wages, consumption—are everywhere in their infancy. . . .

From Copernicus to Newton is 150 years. Today, 150 years from the *Wealth of Nations*, we have not found, and should not expect to find, the Newton of economics. If we have traveled as far as Tycho Brahe we may be content. Tycho was both a theorist and an observer. As a theorist, he believed to his last day in the year 1601 that the planets went round the sun and that the sun and the stars went round the earth as the fixed centre of the universe. As an observer, he made with infinite patience and integrity thousands of records of the stars and planets; upon these records Kepler, in due course, based his laws and brought the truth to light. If we will take Tycho Brahe for our example, we may find encouragement also. It matters little how wrong we are with our theories, if we are honest and careful with our observations.

Extracts from Lord William Beveridge's farewell address as Director of the London School of Economics, June 24, 1937. Published in *POLITICA*, September 1937.

ECONOMICS

PART ONE

The Nature of Economics

1

The Economic Problem

Many of the world's most pressing problems are economic. The dominant problem of the 1930s was the massive unemployment of workers and resources known as the Great Depression. The wartime economy of the 1940s solved that problem but created new ones, especially how to reallocate scarce resources quickly between military and civilian needs. The postwar period from 1945 to 1955 was a time of world-wide economic growth, but with major imbalances as European nations tried to rebuild their war-shattered economies and export to Canada and the United States enough to pay for all that they needed to import. The period from 1955 to 1965 was a time of unparalleled growth and prosperity as the world completed its recovery from the Second World War and entered a period of expanding output and trade. Unemployment was a concern during some years in the decade, as was the inability of most of the world's economies to combine full employment with zero inflation.

From 1965 to 1975 a slowdown in growth and rising inflation became matters for serious concern. The central problems of the period from 1975 to 1985 were the rising cost of energy—oil prices increased tenfold over the decade—and the disturbing combination of rising unemployment and rising inflation, called **stagflation.**[1] By the second half of the 1980s, inflation had fallen to a low level, and the central manufacturing area of Canada was booming. The rest of the country, heavily dependent on resource-based industries whose world markets were shrinking, had severe unemployment problems. Not since the 1930s had Canada seemed so much like two economic nations, the prosperous centre and the stagnant periphery. Thus we see that the world's economic problems change over the decades, yet there are always problems.

Of course, not all the world's problems are primarily economic. Political, biological, social, cultural, and philosophical issues often predominate. But no matter how "noneconomic" a particular problem may seem, it will almost always have a significant economic dimension.

The crises that lead to wars often have economic roots. Nations fight for oil and rice and land to live on, although the rhetoric of their leaders evokes God, Glory, and the Fatherland. The current rate of world population growth is 2.2 persons a second, or about 70 million a year; the economic consequences are steady pressures on the available natural resources, especially arable land. Unless the human race can find ways to increase its food supply as fast as its numbers, increasing millions face starvation.

[1] The definitions of the terms in boldface are gathered together in the glossary at the end of the book.

Current Economic Problems

Unemployment and Inflation

Virtually every minister of finance in recent history has included in his budget speeches a statement establishing full employment and low inflation as important goals of economic policy. Reasonable as that may sound, the fact is that we have seldom had both full employment and low inflation at the same time, and in the 10-year period from the mid 1970s to the mid 1980s we had neither. Inflation was reduced to about 4 percent by 1985, but unemployment stayed disturbingly high. By 1987, inflation remained near a 4-percent plateau while the unemployment rate had crept slowly downward to below 9 percent.

If economists are right in saying that zero unemployment is an unattainable goal, what is an "acceptable" level of unemployment? Can we be sure that we will never again experience the trauma of the 1930s, when up to a quarter of all people who sought work were unable to find it? If a completely stable price level is difficult to achieve, what then is an "acceptable" amount of inflation? Why do prices in some countries rise 30 percent or 40 percent a year, while in others they rise at a rate of only 2 percent or 3 percent? Why did inflation accelerate dramatically over most of the world in the 1970s and then fall equally dramatically in the mid 1980s?

Productivity and Growth

Canadians pride themselves on having one of the highest standards of living in the world and a rapid rate of growth in their output of goods and services. During the 1970s the annual rate of growth of total Canadian output averaged 4.2 percent, down from the 5.2 percent average of the 1960s. And although the 1960s witnessed one of the longest periods of *sustained* growth in the nation's history, growth since the 1970s has been sporadic. From 1980 to 1986 the Canadian growth rate averaged 2.5 percent.

Growth in output per person employed, often called **productivity,** slowed dramatically during the seventies. Whereas productivity grew at an average annual rate of 2.7 percent between 1947 and 1973, during the last half of the seventies it averaged less than 1 percent annually. In the 1980s productivity growth increased slightly, averaging just over 1 percent per year for the first six years of the decade. Since productivity growth accounts for much of the growth in Canadian living standards, this slowdown is a matter of major significance.

What causes such a loss of momentum in the economy? Is it the uncertain state of today's economy? Is it the burden of high taxes on both individuals and business? Is it the heavy drain imposed on the economy by the government's regulation of business to provide cleaner, safer working conditions, bigger unemployment benefits, and more generous pensions and medical care? Or is it the absence of needed government intervention in the form of an industrial policy and other government incentives for growth?

Will the slowdown in our nation's economic growth be reversed? Do we *want* another century of rapid growth and industrialization? Without the automobile, the airplane, and electricity, ours would be a different and less comfortable world. But because of them, air pollution has not only become a major inconvenience but may also be dangerously harming the earth's atmosphere. The coal burned to create the electricity that does so much in homes and factories is a major cause of the acid rain that is polluting lakes and killing trees. Is large-scale pollution the inevitable companion of economic growth? If it is, how can we achieve growth with less pollution?

Two Worlds

By the late 1980s Canada's manufacturing industries were booming—largely as a result of heavy sales to the United States. Unemployment was well below 6 percent in Ontario. But the rest of the country was in difficult straits with unemployment rates of 15 percent in the Atlantic provinces, 13 percent in B.C., 11 percent in Quebec, and 9 percent in the Prairie provinces. The lumber industry was suffering, as were the mining and oil industries. Agriculture's outlook was bleak as a result of world gluts of many products and rising protectionism in many markets. Was Canada splitting into two separate worlds—the two central "have" provinces and the other eight "have nots"?

International Trade and Protectionism

The issue of free trade versus protectionism has been prominent throughout Canada's history because of the crucial role of external trade in the nation's economic development. According to the widely accepted "staples theory," early Canadian economic growth was based on the exploitation of comparative advantages in products with large natural-resource contents. This made Canadian prosperity depend on the strength of export markets for a succession of staples—fish, fur, timber, and wheat—each of which dominated a particular period of Canadian history.

The transcontinental railway was completed in 1855 as a precondition for Confederation. In 1878 Sir John A. MacDonald introduced his National Policy. After Confederation, the protective tariff—a major element in the National Policy—was adopted as a means of fostering domestic manufacturing industries. These two measures, the railway and the tariff, were the key elements in a program of economic nationalism that sought to reduce the country's dependence on unstable export markets for raw materials and to promote an east-west flow of trade that would consolidate the political union of the provinces.

Although a century of industrialization and a series of tariff reductions begun in 1936 have greatly reduced the proportion of the labor force directly engaged in working with raw materials, the issues raised by the National Policy are still at the forefront of public debate. Should Canada continue to reduce the degree of protection that it affords domestic industries from foreign competition? What would be the consequences of another major round of world trade liberalization? If that cannot be achieved, should Canada have free trade with the United States? Would Canadian industries survive and prosper? Would new ones emerge? Or would Canadians resort to being "hewers of wood and drawers of water"?

Government Deficits and the National Debt

Deficits and the national debt were things that governments had talked about for two decades, particularly before elections, but done little about, particularly after elections. Yet by the mid 1980s economists, bankers, and businesspeople were speaking in alarming terms of the present fiscal position being unsustainable. When the newly elected Conservative government heeded these warnings, it found that major efforts were needed just to stop the deficit from growing. This effort left the deficit still large—it was $32.5 billion in 1986—and the national debt growing rapidly—from 49 percent of national income in 1986 it was projected to grow to 60 percent around 1990. Since the Canadian electorate appeared to reject major cuts in government expenditures, and since most existing taxes were already levied at rates that appeared unproductively high, the only remaining alternative for reducing the debt was finding new tax sources.

How serious was the debt problem? Was there reason to accept the view of the few remaining economists who were willing to argue that the national debt is no problem at all since it is money that we owe to ourselves? Or were the majority of economists right in agreeing that the burden of raising sufficient tax revenues merely to pay the interest on the debt was becoming serious and, if the rise in the debt were not halted, would cause a drastic curtailment in other government expenditures?

Energy

Energy is vital to an industrial economy. Over the past 200 years, North America's output has grown and with it our demand for the earth's limited fossil fuels.

Throughout most of our history, the increase in energy consumption caused no serious problems because new supplies were discovered as rapidly as old ones were exhausted. In the 1970s a dramatic change occurred. The world price of oil rose sharply, and prices of other sources of energy followed suit. By 1976 Canada had become a net importer of oil and natural gas. For a while in the late 1970s and early 1980s talk of an energy crisis was common; many spoke of the need to restore Canada's "energy self-sufficiency." In the last half of the 1980s oil prices plummeted. The end of the oil boom spelled serious economic loss for the oil-producing provinces. Many Canadian workers who had gone west to share in the oil boom joined the reverse trek back to the East, where the jobs were.

Are we cured of our addiction to petroleum, or is the present easing of the energy crisis only apparent, due more to temporarily improved supplies than to our learning to live with less? Are the world's supplies of oil and gas adequate to meet its demands for energy? Can nuclear or solar energy render oil and gas as unnecessary as oil and gas rendered whale oil? What is the appropriate rate at which to deplete our petroleum reserves?

Social Policies

Canadians are both proud and protective of their social policies. These policies help such groups as the poor, the elderly, the sick, the unemployed, and parents with dependent children. Calls for reform have, however, increasingly been heard from those who argue that many existing policies cost too much to deliver too little to those who really need help.

Much of the debate has centred on the so-called principle of universality. Is the universal availability of social policies an essential part of our society that should be maintained whatever the cost? Or is universality a costly frill that should be abandoned if sufficient funds are to remain available to help people in real need?

What Is Economics?

The discussion so far has presented only a handful of the important current issues on which economic analysis is designed to shed light. One way to define the scope of economics is to say that it is the social science that deals with such problems. Another, perhaps better known, is the great English economist Alfred Marshall's: "Economics is a study of mankind in the ordinary business of life." A more penetrating definition is the following:

Economics is the study of the use of scarce resources to satisfy unlimited human wants.

Scarcity is inevitable and is central to economic problems. What are society's resources? Why is scarcity inevitable? What are the consequences of scarcity?

Resources and Commodities

A society's resources consist of natural gifts such as land, forests, and minerals; human resources, both mental and physical; and manufactured aids to production such as tools, machinery, and buildings. Economists call such resources **factors of production** because they are used to produce things that people desire. The things produced are called **commodities.** Commodities may be divided into goods and services. **Goods** are tangible (e.g., cars or shoes), and **services** are intangible (e.g., haircuts or education). Notice the implication of positive value contained in the terms *goods* and *services.* (Compare the terms *bads* and *disservices.*)

People use goods and services to satisfy many of their wants. The act of making goods and services is called **production,** and the act of using them to satisfy wants is called **consumption.** Goods are valued for the services they provide. An automobile, for example, helps to satisfy its owner's desires for transportation, mobility, and possibly status.

Scarcity

For most of the world's 4 billion human beings, scarcity is real and ever present. In relation to desires (for more and better food, clothing, housing, schooling, entertainment, and so forth), existing resources are woefully inadequate; there are enough to produce only a small fraction of the goods and services that are wanted.

Are not Canada and the United States rich enough that scarcity is nearly banished? After all, they have been characterized as affluent societies. Whatever affluence may mean, it does not mean the end of the problem of scarcity. The small proportion of Canadian households that earn $50,000 a year (a princely amount by world standards) have no trouble spending their after-tax incomes on things that seem useful to them. Yet it would take more than three times the present output of the Canadian economy to produce enough to allow all Canadian households to consume that amount.

Choice

Because resources are scarce, all societies face the problem of deciding what to produce and how to divide the products among their members. Societies differ in who makes the choices and how they are made, but the need to choose is common to all. Just as scarcity implies the need for choice, so choice implies the existence of cost.

Opportunity Cost

A decision to have more of one thing requires a decision to have less of something else. It is this fact that makes the first decision costly. We look first at a trivial example and then at one that vitally affects all of us; both examples involve precisely the same fundamental principles.

Consider the choice that must be made by a small boy who has 10 cents to spend and who is determined to spend it all on candy. For him there are only two kinds of candy in the world: gumdrops, which sell for 1 cent each, and chocolates, which sell for 2 cents. The boy would like to buy 10 gumdrops and 10 chocolates, but he knows (or will soon discover) that this is not possible. (In technical language it is not an *attainable combination* given his scarce resources.) There are, however, several attainable combinations that he might buy: 8 gumdrops and 1 chocolate, 4 gumdrops and 3 chocolates, 2 gumdrops and 1 chocolate, and so on. Some of these combinations leave him with money unspent, and he is not interested in them. Only six combinations (as shown in Figure 1-1) are both attainable and use all his money.

FIGURE 1-1 A Choice Between Gumdrops and Chocolates

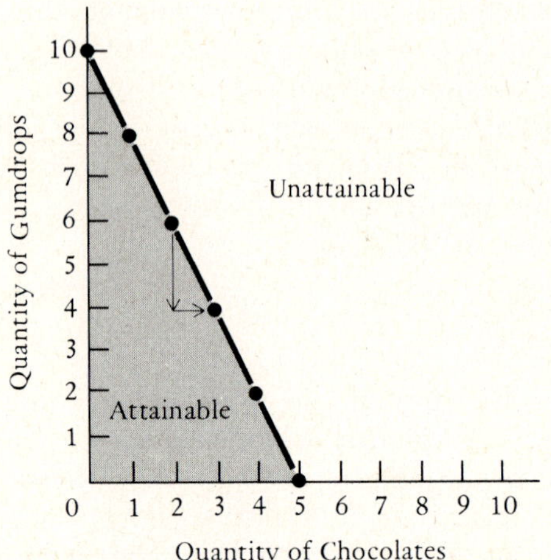

A limited amount of money forces a choice among alternatives. Six combinations of gumdrops and chocolates are attainable and use all of the boy's money. The downward-sloping line provides a boundary between attainable and unattainable combinations. The arrows show that the opportunity cost of 1 more chocolate is 2 gumdrops. In this example the opportunity cost is constant and therefore the boundary is a straight line.

After careful thought, the boy has almost decided to buy 6 gumdrops and 2 chocolates, but at the last moment he decides that he simply must have 3 chocolates. What will it cost him to get this extra chocolate? One answer is 2 gumdrops. As seen in the figure, this is the number of gumdrops he must give up to get the extra chocolate. Economists would describe the 2 gumdrops as the *opportunity cost* of the third chocolate.

Another answer is that the cost of the third chocolate is 2 cents. But given the boy's budget and his intentions, this answer is less revealing than the first one. Where the real choice is between more of this and more of that, the cost of "this" is fruitfully looked at as what you cannot have of "that." The idea of opportunity cost is one of the central insights of economics.

The **opportunity cost** is the cost of using resources for a certain purpose, measured in terms of the benefit given up by not using them in an alternative way, that is, measured in terms of other commodities that could have been obtained instead.

Every time scarcity forces one to make a choice, one is incurring opportunity costs. These costs are measured in terms of forgone alternatives.

Production Possibilities

Although the choice between gumdrops and chocolates is a minor consumption decision, the essential nature of the decision is the same whatever the choice being made. Consider, for example, the important social choice between military and civilian goods. Such a choice is similar in form to the one facing the boy deciding what candies to buy with his dime. It is not possible to produce an unlimited quantity of both military and civilian goods. If resources are fully employed and the government wishes to produce more arms, then less civilian goods must be produced. The opportunity cost of increased arms production is forgone production of civilian goods.

The choice is illustrated in Figure 1-2. Because resources are limited, some combinations—those that would require more than the total available supply of resources for their production—cannot be attained. The downward-sloping curve on the graph divides the combinations that can be attained from those that cannot. Points above and to the right of this curve cannot be attained because there are not enough resources; points below and to the left of the curve can be attained without using all of the available resources; and points on the curve can just be attained if all the available resources are used. The curve is called the **production possibility boundary.** It slopes downward because, when all resources are being used, having more of one good requires having less of some other good.

FIGURE 1-2 A Production Possibility Boundary

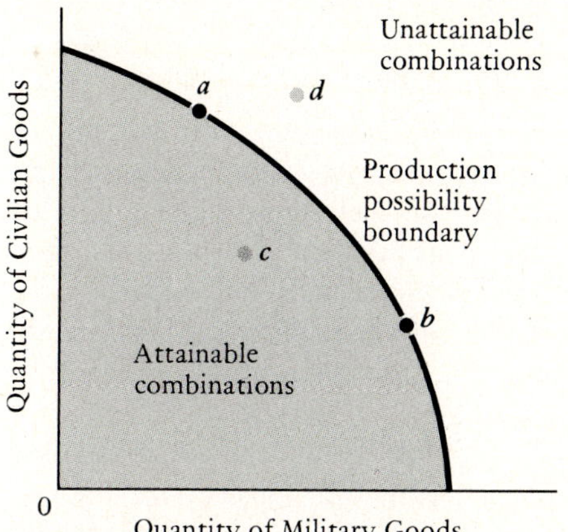

The downward-sloping boundary shows the combinations that are just attainable when all of the society's resources are efficiently employed. The quantity of military goods produced is measured along the horizontal axis, the quantity of civilian goods along the vertical axis. Thus any point on the diagram indicates some amount of each kind of good produced. The production possibility boundary separates the attainable combinations of goods such as *a, b,* and *c* from unattainable combinations such as *d*. It slopes downward because resources are scarce: In a fully employed economy, more of one good can be produced only if resources are freed by producing less of the other goods. Points *a* and *b* represent efficient use of society's resources. Point *c* represents either inefficient use of resources or failure to use all the available resources.

A production possibility boundary illustrates three concepts: scarcity, choice, and opportunity cost. Scarcity is indicated by the unattainable combinations above the boundary, choice by the need to choose among the alternative attainable points along the boundary, and opportunity cost by the downward slope of the boundary.

The shape of the production possibility boundary in Figure 1–2 implies that more and more civilian goods must be given up to achieve equal successive increases in military goods. This shape, referred to as *concave* to the origin, indicates that the opportunity cost of either good grows larger and larger as we increase the amount produced of the other. A slope that forms a straight line, as in Figure 1-1, indicates that the opportunity cost of one good in terms of the other stays constant, no matter how much of it is produced. As we shall see, there are reasons to believe that the case of rising opportunity cost applies to many important choices.[2]

Four Key Economic Questions

While modern economies are complex, many basic decisions that must be made by consumers and pro-

[2] The importance of scarcity, choice, and opportunity cost has led some people to define economics as the problem of allocating scarce resources among alternative and competing ends. The issues emphasized by this definition are important, but, as will be seen in the next section, there are also other important issues.

ducers are not very different from those made in a primitive economy in which people work with few tools and barter with their neighbors. Nor do capitalist, socialist, and communist economies differ in their need to solve the same basic problems, although they do differ, of course, in how they solve them. Most problems studied by economists can be grouped under four main headings.

1. What Is Produced and How?

The allocation of scarce resources among alternative uses, called **resource allocation,** determines the quantities of various goods that are produced. Choosing to produce a particular combination of goods means choosing a particular allocation of resources among the industries or regions producing the goods because, for example, producing a lot of one good requires that a lot of resources be allocated to its production.

Further, because resources are scarce, it is desirable that they be used efficiently. Hence it matters which of the available methods of production is used to produce each of the goods that is to be produced.

2. What Is Consumed and by Whom?

What is the relation between the economy's production of commodities and the consumption enjoyed by its citizens? Economists want to understand what determines the distribution of a nation's total output among its population. Who gets a lot, who gets a little, and why? What role does international trade play in this?

Questions 1 and 2 fall within **microeconomics,** the study of the allocation of resources and the distribution of income as they are affected by the workings of the price system and government policies.

3. How Much Unemployment and Inflation Exist?

When an economy is in a recession, unemployed workers would like to have jobs, the factories in which they could work are available, the managers and owners would like to be able to operate their factories, raw materials are available in abundance, and the goods that could be produced by these resources are needed by individuals in the community. But for some reason resources remain unemployed. This forces the economy within its production possibility boundary, at a point such as *c* in Figure 1-2.

The world's economies have often experienced bouts of prolonged and substantial changes in price levels. In recent decades the course of prices has almost always been upward. The 1970s was a period of accelerating inflation not only in North America but in most of the world. Inflation slowed in the early 1980s while unemployment soared. Were these two events related?

Why do governments worry that short-run reductions in either unemployment or inflation will be at the cost of increasing the other?

4. Is Productive Capacity Growing?

The capacity to produce commodities to satisfy human wants grows rapidly in some countries, grows slowly in others, and actually declines in still others. Growth in productive capacity can be represented by a pushing outward of the production possibility boundary, as shown in Figure 1-3. If an economy's capacity to produce goods and services is growing, combinations that are unattainable today will become attainable tomorrow. Growth makes it possible to have more of all goods.

Questions 3 and 4 fall within **macroeconomics,** the study of the determination of economic aggregates such as total output, total employment, the price level, and the rate of economic growth.

Alternative Economic Systems

This book examines the four basic questions just outlined in the context of a market economy in which private firms and households interact in markets with some assistance (and interference) from the government. We study the market economy for several reasons. First, this is the kind of economy we live in. Second, it is the economic environment in which the serious study of economics was born and has grown.

FIGURE 1-3 The Effect of Economic Growth on the Production Possibility Boundary

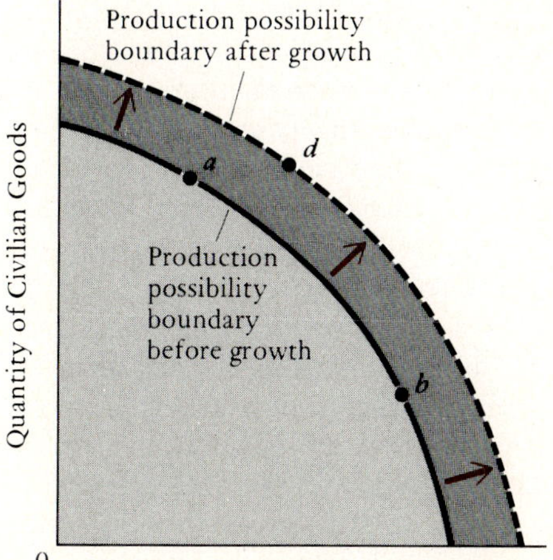

Economic growth shifts the boundary outward and makes it possible to produce more of all commodities. Before growth in productive capacity, points *a* and *b* were on the production possibility boundary and point *d* was an unattainable combination. After growth, as shown by the dark shaded band, point *d* and many other previously unattainable combinations are attainable.

Today, however, a third of the world's population lives in the Soviet Union and China, countries that reject important elements of our kind of economic system. They rely heavily on centrally planned actions to deal with the four basic questions. At least another third of the world's population lives in countries whose economies have not yet developed to the point where they could accurately be described as either *market* or *planned* economies.

To the extent that economics deals with the ways in which people respond to incentives and mobilize scarce means to given ends, the same economic principles are applicable under a variety of institutional, political, and social arrangements.

All economies face scarcity, and all must decide how to allocate scarce resources and distribute goods and services; all may face problems of inflation, unemployment, and unsatisfactory rates of growth.

Because all economies face many common problems, economic analysis can contribute valuable insights even where familiar institutions are modified or absent.

Differences Among Economies

It is common to speak of only two economic systems, capitalism (or a market-oriented system) and socialism (or a centrally planned system). But this is at best a simplification and at worst a confusion.

There are dozens of economic systems in existence today, not just two. Just as there are many differences among Canada, the United States, the United Kingdom, Germany, Sweden, Japan, and Brazil, so are there differences among the Soviet Union, China, Poland, Cuba, Czechoslovakia, and Yugoslavia. Countries are dissimilar in many respects, including who owns resources, who makes decisions, and the nature of the incentives offered to people. These three aspects are discussed in the next three sections.

Ownership of Resources

Who owns a nation's farms and factories, its coal mines and forests? Who owns its railways, its streams and golf courses? Who owns its houses and hotels?

One characteristic of capitalism is that the basic raw materials, the productive assets of the society, and the goods produced in the economy are predominantly privately owned. By this standard Canada is predominantly a capitalist economy. However, even in Canada public ownership extends beyond the usual basic services such as schools and local transport systems to include other activities such as electric power utilities and housing projects.

In contrast, in a socialist society the productive assets are predominantly publicly owned. Although the Soviets officially designate their economy as socialist, there are three sectors—agriculture, retail trade, and housing—in which some private ownership exists. However, even though the USSR is not a pure socialist economy, public ownership is sufficiently widespread to place the USSR at one end of a spectrum with predominant public ownership, and the United States at the other end. While Canada lies closer to the United States than to the USSR, it is more of a mixed economy than is the United States.

Other countries fall between them on the spectrum. Great Britain has six times in this century elected Labour governments that have been officially committed to socialism to the point of nationalizing key industries, including railroads, steel, coal, electricity, postal services, and telephones. However, the bulk of industries that produce goods and services for household consumption and machinery and equipment for firms remains privately owned. Furthermore, a major thrust for privatization, or the return of publicly owned firms to private ownership, has been under way since 1980.

Ownership patterns are generally mixed and variable rather than exclusive and unchanging. To give some idea of this variability, Figure 1-4 shows the division of investment between public and private sectors in 11 countries.

The Decision Process (Coordinating Principles)

A distinction is sometimes made between two kinds of systems: a *market system*, in which decisions are made impersonally and in a decentralized way by the interaction of individuals in markets, and a *command system*, in which centralized decision makers decide what is to be done and issue appropriate commands to achieve the desired results.

Again, no country offers an example of either system working alone. But it is true that some economies, such as those of Canada, the United States, France, and Yugoslavia, rely much more heavily on market decisions than do others, such as the economies of East Germany, the Soviet Union, and Cuba. Yet even in Canada the command principle has some sway. Minimum wages, quotas on some agricultural outputs, and quotas on clothing imports are obvious examples. More subtle examples are public expenditures and taxes that in effect transfer command of some resources from private individuals to public officials.

In the planned economies of the Soviet bloc, where targets, quotas, and directives are important aspects of the decision-making system, the command principle dominates. But the market principle also operates. For example, at the retail level people have considerable discretion in how they spend their income on a wide variety of goods.

Much economic behavior depends more on the decision pattern than on the ownership pattern. Thus in the United Kingdom, while many key industries are publicly owned, their control is vested in semiautonomous boards over which Parliament exerts little control. By and large, the boards try to make their enterprises profitable, and to the extent that

FIGURE 1-4 An Indicator of Differences in Ownership Patterns for Selected Countries

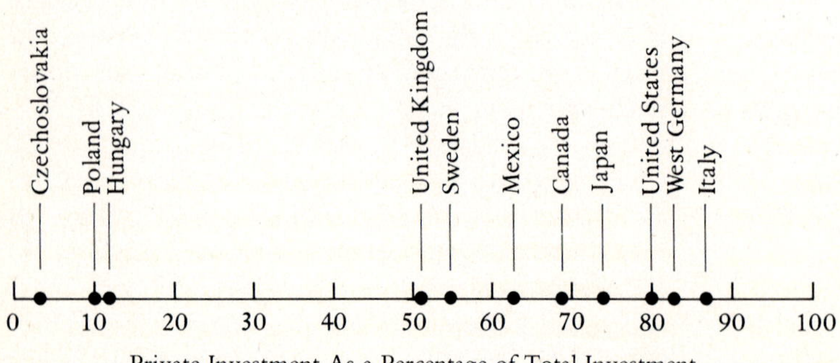

Actual economies never rely solely on private or solely on public investment. These estimates are based on the percentage of gross fixed investment accounted for by the private sector. Such investment provides additions to the stock of productive capital. Private capital investment plays a role even in communist countries; public capital is a significant part of investment in all countries. (*Source*: World Book, *World Tables.*)

TABLE 1-1 Comparative Economic Systems: Ownership and Decision Patterns

	Ownership pattern	
Decision pattern	Predominantly private	Predominantly public
Predominantly decentralized with use of market principle	Canada	Yugoslavia
Predominantly centralized with use of command principle	Nazi Germany	USSR

Each of these combinations of private and public ownership and centralized and decentralized control has occurred in practice. This table is a simplification that highlights differences among economic systems. It would be an interesting exercise to use a grid that gives several, rather than just two, gradations for each variable and then attempt to place current and past economies in the appropriate cells.

they succeed, their behavior will be similar to that of profit-seeking, privately owned firms. In contrast, firms in Hitler's Germany were under a high degree of state control, even though they were privately owned. The behavior of these firms was no doubt very different from that of privately owned firms that are managed in order to earn profits for their owners.

Table 1-1, though it makes no subtle distinctions, gives one simple classification of some twentieth century economies according to ownership and decision patterns. Such a classification suggests how communist countries such as the USSR and Yugoslavia differ significantly from one another as well as from Canada.

Incentive Systems

Psychologists know that people (and most other living creatures) respond to incentives. Incentives may be positive or negative—the carrot or the stick—and of almost infinite variety. Among positive incentives, direct monetary rewards, in the form of wages or profits or bribes, are well understood. Indirect monetary rewards, such as special housing, vacations, or subsidized education, are not always as readily identified, but they can be effective. Nonmonetary "carrots" include praise, medals, certificates, and applause. All societies use negative incentives—prison terms, public ridicule, and other penalties—to discourage aberrant behavior; in some societies indirect negative incentives, such as coercion, fear, and threat of punishment, provide as strong motivation as direct incentives.

Capitalist economies tend to rely heavily on direct monetary rewards. Socialist economies rely more heavily on indirect rewards. Both use negative incentives, but because the command system is relied on in socialist economies, negative nonmonetary incentives are prevalent. In capitalist economies, a major negative monetary incentive that is used is taxation.

Alternative Systems: A Final Word

Perhaps the most important empirical observation about different economies is that a wide variety of economic systems seem able to coexist and to be successful. Three basic points are worth remembering:

1. **All countries have "mixed" economies.**
2. **Among countries, the mixture differs in ways that are appreciable and significant.**
3. **Over time, the mixture changes.**

No economic system seems to do everything better than any major competing system; indeed, each has its strengths and weaknesses. To talk of "better" and "worse" in this context may itself be misleading.

Differences of opinion about which system is best may simply reflect differences in emphasis on particular outcomes. Canadians and Americans may view their economies as being the reason for their high standard of living and see in their well-stocked stores proof of the superiority of free enterprise capitalism. Soviet citizens may look at their economy and see the absence of urban unemployment and the availability of comprehensive welfare services as proof of its superiority to the North American economies. Sweden's slum-free public housing, nationalized medicine, and high productivity in private industry lead many Swedes to regard their "mixed" economy as more desirable than others.

Ends and means. In many less-developed countries, ordinary people often put more importance on the ends—higher living standards—than on the means of achieving them. They may regard a change of means as unimportant. The choice between a market and a planned economy may seem to be simply a choice of which group will exploit them—government officials or powerful monopoly interests. If a highly planned socialist economy offers them a good chance of a 4 percent growth rate while a market-oriented democratic society offers 2 percent, they may well choose the planned society. To warn them that in so choosing they may throw away their freedom is likely to evoke the reply: What has freedom meant to us in the past but the freedom to be hungry and exploited?

But many people in Western industrialized societies value the means of the free market and democratic processes even more highly than they value the ends of high and rising living standards. Most Canadians distrust the agglomeration of central power and the loss of democratic institutions that accompany a high degree of socialism. Markets are less personal than bureaucrats, and this makes markets more acceptable to many people because they are less arbitrary and less subject to autocratic abuse.

How many Canadians would decide to go over to Russian-style socialism, even if there were *proof* that it would produce higher material living standards than the free-market system? In the 1930s some believed that Fascist dictatorships were more efficient than democracies. Mussolini, it was said, "made the Italian trains run on time." It is debatable that the belief was correct, but many people accepted it. Yet few Canadians advocated that Canada become a Fascist dictatorship.

Of course, many Canadians and citizens of other Western societies believe there is no need to choose. They feel that free markets and democracy produce better results than do alternative systems in terms of both means and ends.

Summary

1. Every generation faces important economic problems. A common feature of such problems is that they concern the use of limited resources to satisfy virtually unlimited human wants.
2. Scarcity is a fundamental problem faced by all economies. Not enough resources are available to produce all the goods and services that people would like to consume. Scarcity makes it necessary to choose. All societies must have a mechanism for choosing what commodities will be produced and in what quantities.
3. The concept of opportunity cost emphasizes the problem of scarcity and choice by measuring the cost of obtaining a unit of one commodity in terms of the number of units of other commodities that could have been obtained instead.
4. Four basic questions must be answered in all economies: What commodities are being produced and how? What commodities are being

consumed and by whom? What are the unemployment and inflation rates? Is productive capacity changing?

5. Not all economies resolve these questions in the same ways or equally satisfactorily. Economists study how these problems are addressed in various societies and the consequences of using one method rather than another to provide solutions.
6. Economies can differ in many ways, and such capsule classifications as "capitalism" and "socialism" represent simplifications of complex matters.
7. Among the important dimensions in which economies can differ are (a) the pattern of ownership of goods and resources, (b) the decision process used, with a particularly important distinction between command and market coordinating principles, and (c) the incentive systems used.
8. All countries have mixed economies in that they exhibit a mixture of public and private ownership, of market and command decision-making systems, and of incentive mechanisms used. The mixtures differ among countries and change over time.

Topics for Review

Scarcity and the need for choice
Choice and opportunity cost
Production possibility boundary
Resource allocation
Unemployed resources
Growth in productive capacity
Alternative economic systems
Public versus private ownership
Market versus command systems

Discussion Questions

1. What does each of the following quotations tell you about the policy conflicts perceived by the person making the statement and about how he or she has resolved them?
   a. "It is an industry worth several hundred jobs to our province; we cannot afford to forgo it." British Columbia Premier William Van der Zam explaining the decision to organize a killing of wolves in northern British Columbia so that more game animals could grow up to be shot by hunters.
   b. "The annual seal hunt must be stopped even if it destroys the livelihood of the seal hunters." An animal rights advocate opposing the seal hunt in the Gulf of St. Lawrence.
   c. "Considering our limited energy resources and the growing demand for electricity, Canada really has no choice but to use all of its possible domestic energy sources, including nuclear energy. Despite possible environmental and safety hazards, nuclear power is a necessity." A representative of the electricity industry replying to criticisms from *Energy Probe*.

2. What is the difference between scarcity and poverty? If everyone in the world had enough to eat, could we say that food was no longer scarce?
3. Consider the right to free speech in political campaigns. Suppose that the Flat Earth Society and the Communist, NDP, Liberal, and Conservative parties all demand equal time on network television in a federal election. What economic questions are involved? Can there be freedom of speech without free access to the scarce resources needed to make one's speech heard?
4. Evidence accumulates that the use of chemical fertilizers, which increases agricultural production greatly, causes damage to water quality. Show the choice involved between more food and cleaner water in using such fertilizers. Use a production possibility curve with agricultural output on the vertical axis and water quality on the horizontal axis. In what ways does this production possibility curve reflect scarcity, choice, and opportunity cost? How would an improved fertilizer that increased agricultural output without further worsening water quality affect the curve? Suppose a pollution-free fertilizer were developed; would this mean there would no longer be any opportunity cost in using it?
5. "What the world of economics needs is an end to ideology and *isms*. If there is a best system of economic organization, it will prove its superiority in its superior ability to solve economic problems." Do you agree with this statement? Would you expect that if the world survives for another hundred years, a single form of economic system would be found superior to all others? Why or why not?
6. Identify the coordinating principle and the incentive system suggested by each of the following:
   a. Taxes on tobacco and alcohol
   b. Production targets assigned to a Russian factory manager by the state planning agency
   c. Legislation establishing minimum wages to be paid
   d. A provincial government directing its agencies to use local suppliers of goods rather than buying from other provinces
   e. Legislation prohibiting the sale and use of cocaine
   f. Rent controls combined with government subsidizing of the building of rental accommodation in Ontario

2

Economics As a Social Science

Economics is generally regarded as a social science. What exactly does it mean to be scientific? Can economics ever hope to be "scientific" in its study of the aspects of human behavior with which it is concerned?

A Scientific Study of Human Behavior

The Distinction Between Positive and Normative

The success of modern science rests partly on the ability of scientists to separate their views on *what does happen* from their views on *what they would like to happen*. For example, until the nineteenth century most people in the Western world believed that the earth was only a few thousand years old. About 200 years ago evidence that some existing rocks were millions or even billions of years old began to accumulate. Most people found this hard to accept: It forced them to rethink their religious beliefs. Many wanted the evidence to be wrong; they wanted rocks to be only a few thousand years old. Nevertheless, the evidence accumulated until today most people accept that the earth is neither thousands, nor millions, but 4 or 5 billion years old.

This advance in our knowledge came because the question "How old are observable rocks?" could be separated from the feelings of scientists (many of them devoutly religious) about the age they would have liked the rocks to be. Distinguishing what *is* true from what we would *like* to be true depends on recognizing the difference between positive and normative statements.

Positive statements concern what is, was, or will be. **Normative statements** concern what one believes ought to be. Positive statements, assertions, or theories may be simple or complex, but they are basically about matters of fact.

Disagreements over positive statements are appropriately handled by an appeal to the facts.

Normative statements, because they concern what ought to be, are inextricably bound up with philosophical, cultural, and religious systems. A normative statement is one that makes, or is based on, a *value judgment*—a judgment about what is good and what is bad.

Disagreements over normative statements cannot be handled merely by an appeal to facts.

Some related issues about disagreements among economists are taken up in Box 2-1.

The Distinction Illustrated

The statement "It is impossible to break up atoms" is a positive statement that can quite definitely be (and of course has been) refuted by empirical observations, while the statement "Scientists ought not to break up atoms" is a normative statement that involves ethical judgments. The questions "What government policies will reduce unemployment?" and "What policies will prevent inflation?" are positive ones, while the question "Ought we to be more concerned about unemployment than about inflation?" is normative.

The Importance of the Distinction

If we think something ought to be done, we can deduce other things that, if we wish to be consistent, ought to be done, but we can deduce nothing about what is done (i.e., is true). Similarly, if we know that two things are true, we can deduce other things that must be true, but we can deduce nothing about what is desirable (i.e., *ought* to be).

It is logically impossible to deduce normative statements from only positive statements or positive statements from only normative ones.

As an example of the importance of this distinction in the social sciences, consider the question "Has the payment of generous unemployment benefits increased the amount of unemployment?" This positive question can be turned into a testable hypothesis such as "The higher the benefits paid to the unemployed, the higher will be the total amount of unemployment." If we are not careful, however, our attitudes and value judgments may get in the way of our study of this hypothesis. Some people are opposed to the welfare state and believe in an individualist, self-help ethic. They may hope that the hypothesis will be found correct because its truth could then be used as an argument against welfare measures in general. Others feel that the welfare state is a good thing, reducing misery and contributing to human dignity. They may hope that the hypothesis is wrong because they do not want any welfare measures to come under attack. In spite of different value judgments and social attitudes, however, evidence is accumulating on this particular hypothesis. As a result, we have much more knowledge than we had 10 years ago of why, where, and by how much unemployment benefits increase unemployment. This evidence could never have been accumulated or accepted if investigators had not been able to distinguish their feelings on how they wanted the answer to turn out from their assessment of evidence on how people actually behaved.

Positive statements assert things about the world. If it is possible for a statement to be proved wrong by empirical evidence, we call it a *testable statement*. Many positive statements are testable, and disagreements over them are appropriately handled by an appeal to the facts.

In contrast to positive statements, which are often testable, normative statements are never testable. Disagreements over such normative statements as "It is wrong to steal" or "It is immoral to have sexual relations out of wedlock" cannot be settled by an appeal to empirical observations. Thus, for a rational consideration of normative questions, different techniques are needed from those used for a rational consideration of positive questions. Because of this, it is convenient to separate normative and positive inquiries. We do this not because we think the former are less important than the latter but merely because they must be handled in different ways.

The distinction between positive and normative allows us to keep our views on how we would like the world to work separate from our views on how the world actually does work. We may be interested in both. It can only obscure the truth, however, if we let our views on what we would like to be bias our investigations of what actually is. It is for this reason that the separation of the positive from the normative is one of the foundation stones of science and that scientific inquiry, as it is normally understood, is usually confined to positive questions. Some important limitations on the distinction be-

BOX 2-1

Why Economists Disagree

If you listen to a discussion among economists on *As It Happens* or *Sunday Morning* or if you read about their debates in the daily press or weekly magazines, you will find economists constantly disagreeing among themselves. Indeed, one widespread reason for rejecting economists' advice is that they seldom completely agree on any issue. Why do economists disagree, and what should we make of this fact?

In a recent column in *Newsweek,* Charles Wolf, Jr., suggests four reasons for the disagreement among economists: (1) Different economists use different benchmarks: Inflation is *down* compared with last year, but *up* compared with the 1950s. (2) Economists fail to make it clear to their listeners whether they are talking about short-term or long-term consequences: Tax cuts will stimulate consumption in the short run and investment in the long run. (3) Economists often fail to acknowledge the full extent of their ignorance. (4) Different economists have different values, and these normative views play a large part in their public discussions.

There is surely some truth in each of these assessments. But there is also a fifth reason: the public's *demand for disagreement.* For example, suppose that all economists were in fact agreed on the proposition that unions are not a major cause of inflation. This view would be unpalatable to some individuals. Those who are hostile to unions, for instance, would like to blame inflation on them and would be looking for an intellectual champion. Fame and fortune would await the economist who espoused their cause, and a champion would soon be found.

Disagreement will always exist. It is also true that by the very nature of reporting this disagreement tends to get exaggerated in the media. This is not necessarily intentional; indeed, it is hard to see how it might be avoided. When the media cover an issue, they naturally wish to give both sides of it. Normally, the public will hear one or two economists for each side of a debate, regardless of whether the profession is divided right down the middle or is nearly unanimous in its support of one side. Thus the public will not know that in one case a reporter could have chosen from dozens of economists to present each side, while in a second case the reporter had to spend three days trying to locate someone willing to take a particular side because nearly all economists contacted thought it was wrong. On many issues, the profession overwhelmingly supports one side. In their desire to show both sides of the case, however, the media present the public with the appearance of a profession equally split over all matters.

Thus anyone seeking to discredit the economists' advice by showing that they disagree will have no trouble finding evidence to support his or her case. But those who wish to know if there is a majority view or even a strong consensus will find one on a surprisingly large number of issues, such as the housing shortages caused by rent control laws and the unemployment caused by minimum-wage laws. Of course, there are also genuine disagreements among economists on many issues, especially those that involve recent and incompletely understood events, and there will always be controversies at the frontiers of current research. But there is no evidence to suggest that disagreements among economists are more common now than they have been in the past.

---

tween positive and normative are discussed in Box 2-2.

Positive and Normative Statements in Economics

Economics, like other sciences, is concerned with questions, statements, and hypotheses that could conceivably be shown to be false by actual observations of the world. It is not necessary to show them to be either consistent or inconsistent with the facts tomorrow or the next day; it is only necessary to be able to imagine evidence that could show them to be false. Normative questions cannot be settled by a mere appeal to facts. Of course, this does not mean that they are unimportant. Such questions as "Should

BOX 2-2

Limits on the Positive-Normative Distinction

While the distinction between positive and normative is useful, it has certain specific limitations.

The classification is not exhaustive. The classifications *positive* and *normative* do not cover all statements that can be made. For example, there is an important class, called *analytic statements,* whose validity depends only on the rules of logic. Thus the sentence "If all humans are immortal and if you are a human, then you are immortal" is a valid analytic statement. It tells us that *if* two things are true, *then* a third thing must be true. The validity of this statement is not dependent on whether or not its individual parts are in fact true. Indeed, the sentence "All humans are immortal" is a positive statement that has been decisively refuted. Yet no amount of empirical evidence on the mortality of humans can upset the truth of the "if-then" sentence quoted above. Analytic statements—which proceed by logical analysis—play an important role in scientific research and form the basis for much of our ability to theorize.

Not all positive statements are testable. A positive statement asserts something about the universe. It may be empirically true or false in the sense that what it asserts may or may not be true of the universe. If it is true, it adds to our knowledge of what can and cannot happen. Many positive statements are refutable: If they are wrong, this can be ascertained (within a margin for error of observation) by checking them against data. For example, the positive statement that the earth is less than 5,000 years old was tested and refuted by a mass of evidence accumulated in the nineteenth century.

The statement "Extraterrestrials exist and frequently visit the earth in visible form" is also a positive statement. It asserts something about the universe. But we could never refute this statement with evidence because, no matter how hard we searched, believers could argue that we did not look in the right places or in the right way, or that E.T.s do not reveal themselves to nonbelievers, or any one of a host of other alibis. Thus some positive statements are irrefutable.

The distinction is not unerringly applied. Because the positive-normative distinction helps the advancement of knowledge, it does not follow that all scientists automatically and unerringly apply it. Scientists are human beings. Many have strongly held values, and they may let their value judgments get in the way of their assessment of evidence. For example, many scientists are not prepared to consider evidence that there may be differences in intelligence among races because as good liberals they feel that all races ought to be equal. Nonetheless, the desire to separate what is from what we would like to be is a guiding light, an ideal, of science. The ability to do so, albeit imperfectly, is attested to by the acceptance, first by scientists and then by the general public, of many ideas that were initially extremely unpalatable—ideas such as the extreme age of the earth and the theory of evolution.

---

we subsidize higher education?" and "Should we send food to Afghanistan?" must still be decided somehow. In democracies, such questions are often settled by voting.

Economists need not confine their discussions to positive, testable statements. Economists can usefully hold and discuss value judgments as long as they do not confuse such judgments with evaluations of testable statements.

Indeed, the pursuit of what appears to be a normative statement will often turn up positive hypotheses on which the *ought* conclusion depends. For example, there are probably relatively few people who believe that government control of industry is in itself good or bad. Their advocacy or opposition will be based on beliefs that can be stated as positive rather than normative hypotheses. For example: "Government control reduces efficiency, changes the distribution of income, and leads to an increase of state control in other spheres." A careful study of this subject would reveal enough positive economic questions to keep a research team of economists occupied for many years.

The Scientific Approach

An important aspect of the scientific approach consists of relating questions to evidence. When presented with a controversial issue, scientists will look for all relevant evidence. If they find that the issue is framed in terms that make it impossible to gather evidence for or against it, they will then usually try to recast the question so that it can be answered by an appeal to evidence.

In some fields scientists are able to generate observations that will provide evidence against which to test their hypotheses. Experimental sciences such as chemistry and some branches of psychology have an advantage because it is possible for them to produce relevant evidence through controlled laboratory experiments.

Other sciences such as astronomy and economics cannot do this. They must wait for natural events to produce observations that can be used as evidence in testing their theories. The evidence that then arises does not come from laboratory conditions where everything is held constant except the forces being studied. Instead, it arises from situations where many things are changing at the same time and great care is therefore needed in drawing conclusions from what is observed.

The ease or difficulty with which one can collect evidence does not determine whether a subject is scientific or nonscientific.

Later in this chapter, we shall consider some of the problems that arise when analyzing evidence that is not generated under controlled laboratory conditions. For the moment, however, we shall consider some general problems that are more or less common to all sciences and are particularly important in the social sciences.

Is Human Behavior Predictable?

Social scientists seek to understand and to predict human behavior. A scientific prediction is based on discovering stable response patterns. But are such patterns possible with anything so complex as human beings? Sometimes this question is answered "no" on the basis of the following argument. While the natural sciences deal with inanimate matter that is subject to natural laws, the social sciences deal with human beings who have free will and therefore cannot be subject to such laws.

This view implies that inanimate matter will show stable response patterns but human beings will not. For example, so goes this argument, if you put a match to a piece of dry paper, the paper will burn, whereas if you subject human beings to torture, some will break down and do what you want them to do and others will not. Even more confusing, the same individual may react differently to torture at different times.

Does human behavior show sufficiently stable responses to factors influencing it to be predictable within an acceptable margin of error? This is a positive question that can be settled only by an appeal to evidence and not by a priori speculation. (**A priori** may be defined as the use of knowledge that is prior to actual experience.) The question itself might concern either the behavior of groups or that of isolated individuals.

Group Behavior Versus Individual Behavior

There are many situations in which group behavior can be predicted accurately without certain knowledge of individual behavior. The warmer the weather, for example, the more people visit the beach and the higher the sales of ice cream. It may be hard to say if or when one individual will buy an ice cream cone, but a stable response pattern from a large group of individuals can be seen. Although social scientists cannot predict what particular individuals will be killed in auto accidents in the next holiday weekend, they can come very close to knowing the total number who will die. The more objectively measurable data they have (for example, the state of the weather on the days in question and the trend in gasoline prices), the more closely they will be able to predict total deaths.

The well-known fact that pollsters usually do a good job of predicting elections on the basis of surveys provides evidence that human attitudes do not change capriciously. If group behavior were truly capricious, there would be no point in trying to predict anything on the basis of such surveys. The fact that 80 percent of the voters who were surveyed said they intended to vote for a certain candidate would give no information about the probable outcome of the election. Today's information would commonly be reversed tomorrow.

The difference between predicting individual and group behavior is illustrated by the fact that economists can predict with fair accuracy what households as a group will do when their take-home pay is increased. Some individuals may do surprising and unpredictable things, but the total response of all households to a permanent change in tax rates that leaves more money in their hands is predictable within quite a narrow margin of error. This stability in the response of households' spending to a change in their available income is the basis of economists' ability to predict successfully the outcome of major revisions in the tax laws.

This does not mean that people never change their minds or that future events can be foretold by a casual study of the past. The stability discussed here is a stable response to causal factors (e.g., next time it gets warm, ice cream sales will rise) and not merely inertia (e.g., ice cream sales will go on rising in the future because they have risen in the past).

The "Law" of Large Numbers

Successfully predicting the behavior of large groups is made possible by the "law" of large numbers. Broadly speaking, this law asserts that random movements of many individual items tend to offset one another. The law is based on one of the most beautiful constants of behavior in the whole of science, and yet it can be derived from the fact that human beings make errors! The law is based on the statistical relation called *normal curve of error.*

What is implied by this law? Ask any one person to measure the length of a room and it will be almost impossible to predict in advance what sort of error of measurement will be made. Dozens of things will affect the accuracy of the measurement, and, furthermore, the person may make one error today and quite a different one tomorrow. But ask a thousand people to measure the length of the same room, and we can predict within a small margin just how this *group* will make its errors. We can assert with confidence that more people will make small errors than will make large errors, that the larger the error the fewer will be the number making it, that roughly the same number of people will overstate as will understate the distance, and that the larger the number of people that we have making the measurement, the smaller will their *average* error tend to be.

If a common cause should act on each member of the group, the average behavior of the group can be predicted even though any one member may act in a surprising fashion. If, for example, each of the thousand individuals is given a tape measure that understates "actual" distances, it can be predicted that, on the average, the group will understate the length of the room. It is, of course, quite possible that one member who had in the past been consistently undermeasuring distance because of psychological depression will now overmeasure the distance because the state of his health has changed. But some other event may happen to another individual that will turn her from an overmeasurer into an undermeasurer. Individuals may act strangely for inexplicable reasons. But the group's behavior, when the inaccurate tape is substituted for the accurate one, will be predictable precisely because the odd things that one individual does will tend to cancel out the odd things some other individual does.

Irregularities in individual behavior tend to cancel one another out, and the regularities tend to show up in repeated observations.

The Nature of Scientific Theories

When some regularity between two or more things is observed, we may ask why this should be so. A *theory* is an attempt to answer this question, and by providing an explanation for the regularity, it enables us to predict as yet unobserved events. For example, national income theory predicts that a reduction in tax rates will reduce the unemployment rate. The simple theory of market behavior predicts that under specified conditions, a partial failure of the potato crop will cause an increase in the incomes of potato farmers.

Theories are used in explaining observed phenomena. A successful theory enables us to predict behavior.

Any explanation whatsoever of how given observations are linked together is a theoretical construction. Theories are used to impose order on our observations, to explain how what we see is linked together. Without theories there would be only a shapeless mass of meaningless observations.

The choice is not between theory and observation but between better or worse theories to explain observations.

Misunderstanding about the place of theories in scientific explanation gives rise to many misconceptions. One of these is illustrated by the phrase "True in theory, but not in practice." The next time you hear someone say this (or, indeed, the next time you say it yourself) you should immediately reply, "All right, then, tell me what does happen in practice." Usually you will not be told mere facts, but you will be given an alternative theory—a different explanation of the facts. The speaker should have said, "The theory in question provides a poor explanation of the facts (that is, it is contradicted by some factual observations). I have a different theory that does a much better job."

A theory consists of (1) a set of definitions that clearly define the *variables* to be used, (2) a set of *assumptions* that outline the conditions under which the theory is to apply, (3) one or more *hypotheses* about the relationships among the variables, and (4) *predictions* that are deduced from the assumptions of the theory and can be tested against actual empirical observations. We consider these four elements in the following four sections.

Variables

A **variable** is a magnitude that can take on different possible values. Variables are the basic elements of theories, and each one needs to be carefully defined.

Price is an example of an important economic variable. The price of a commodity is the amount of money that must be given up to purchase one unit of that commodity. To define a price we must first define the commodity to which it attaches. Such a commodity might be one dozen grade A large eggs. The price of such eggs sold in, say, supermarkets in Prince Albert, Saskatchewan, defines a variable. The particular values taken on by that variable might be \$0.98 on July 1, 1987, \$1.02 on July 8, 1988, and \$0.99 on July 15, 1989.

There are many distinctions between kinds of variables; two of the most important are discussed below.

Endogenous and exogenous variables. An **endogenous variable** is a variable that is explained within a theory. An **exogenous variable** influences endogenous variables but is itself determined by factors outside the theory.

For example, consider the theory that the price of apples in Nanaimo, British Columbia, on a particular day is a function of several things, one of which is the weather in the Okanagan Valley during the previous apple-growing season. We can safely assume that the state of the weather is not determined by economic conditions. The price of apples in this case is an endogenous variable—something determined within the framework of the theory. The state of the weather in the Okanagan Valley is an exogenous variable; changes in it influence prices because the changes affect the output of apples, but the state of the weather is not influenced by the prices.

Other words are sometimes used for the same distinction. One frequently used pair is *induced* for endogenous and *autonomous* for exogenous; another is *dependent* and *independent*.

Stock and flow variables. A flow variable has a time dimension; it is so much per unit of time. The quantity of grade A large eggs purchased in Prince Albert is a flow variable. No useful information is conveyed if we are told that the number purchased was 2,000 dozen eggs unless we are also told the period of time over which these purchases occurred. Two thousand dozen per hour would indicate an active market in eggs, while 2,000 dozen per month would indicate a sluggish market.

A stock variable has no time dimension; it is just so much. Thus if the egg marketing board has 2 million dozen eggs in warehouses around some province that quantity is a stock. All those eggs are there at one time, and they remain there until something happens to change the stock level. The stock variable is just a number, not a rate of flow of so much per day or per month.

Economic theories use both flow variables and stock variables, and it takes a little practice to keep them straight. The amount of income earned is a flow; there is so much per year or per month or per hour. The amount of a household's expenditure is also a flow—so much spent per week or per month. The amount of money in a bank account or a miser's hoard (earned, perhaps, in the past, but unspent) is a stock—just so many thousands of dollars. The key test is always whether a time dimension is required to give the variable meaning.

Assumptions

Assumptions are essential to theorizing. Students are often greatly concerned about the justification of assumptions, particularly if they seem unrealistic.

An example will illustrate some of the issues involved in this question of realism. Much of the theory that we are going to study in this book uses the assumption that the sole motive of all those who run firms is to make as much money as they possibly can, or, as economists put it, firms are assumed to be run so as to *maximize their profits*. The assumption of profit maximization allows economists to make predictions about the behavior of firms. They study the effects that alternatives open to firms would have on profits, and then predict that the alternative selected will be the one that produces the most profits.

But profit maximization may seem like a rather crude assumption. Surely the managers of firms sometimes have philanthropic or political motives. Does this not discredit the assumption of profit maximization by showing it to be unrealistic?

To make successful predictions, however, the theory does not require that managers are solely and always motivated by the desire to maximize profits. All that is required is that profits are a sufficiently important consideration that a theory based on the assumption of profit maximization will produce predictions that are substantially correct.

This illustration shows that it is not always appropriate to criticize a theory because its assumptions seem unrealistic. All theory is an abstraction from reality. If it were not, it would merely duplicate the world and would add nothing to our understanding of it. A good theory abstracts in a useful way; a poor theory does not. If a theory has ignored some really important factors, then its predictions will be contradicted by the evidence—at least where the factor ignored exerts an important influence on the outcome.

Hypotheses

Relations among variables. The critical step in theorizing is formulating hypotheses. A hypothesis is a statement about how two or more variables are related to each other. For example, it is a basic hypothesis of economics that the quantity produced of any commodity depends on its own price in such a way that the higher the price, the larger the quantity produced. To illustrate, the higher the price of eggs, the larger the quantity of eggs that the farmers will produce. Stated in more formal terms, the hypothesis is that the two variables, price of eggs and quantity of eggs, are positively related to each other.[1]

Functional relations. A **function,** or a functional relation, is a formal expression of a relation among variables.[2]

The particular hypothesis that the quantity of eggs produced is related to the price of eggs is an example of a functional relation in economics. In its most general form, it merely says that quantity produced is related to price. The more specific hypothesis is that as the price of eggs rises, the quantity produced also rises.

In the case of many hypotheses of this kind, econ-

[1] When two variables are related in such a way that an increase in one is associated with an increase in the other, they are said to be *positively related.* When two variables are related in such a way that an increase in one is associated with a decrease in the other, they are said to be *negatively related.*

[2] The appendix to this chapter gives a more detailed discussion of functional relations and the use of graphs in economics.

omists can be even more specific about the nature of the functional relation. On the basis of detailed factual studies, economists often have a pretty good idea of how much the quantity produced will change as a result of specified changes in price; that is, they can predict magnitude as well as direction.

Predictions

A theory's predictions are the propositions that can be deduced from that theory. An example of a prediction would be a deduction that *if* firms maximize their profits, and *if* certain other assumptions and hypotheses of the theory hold true, *then* a rise in the rate of corporate tax will cause a reduction in the amount of investment that firms make in new plant and equipment. The prediction is that the rise in the tax rate will be accompanied by a fall in investment. The reasons that lie behind the prediction are contained in the assumptions and hypotheses that constitute the theory in question.

It should be apparent from this discussion that a scientific prediction is not the same thing as a prophecy.

A scientific prediction is a conditional statement that takes the form: *If* you do this, *then* such and such will follow.

If hydrogen and oxygen are combined under specified conditions, *then* water will be the result. *If* the government cuts taxes, *then* the rate of unemployment will decrease. It is important to realize that this prediction is very different from the statement "I prophesy that in two years' time there will be a large reduction in unemployment because I believe the government will decide to cut tax rates." The government's decision to cut tax rates in two years' time will be the outcome of many influences, both economic and political. If the economist's prophecy about unemployment turns out to be wrong because in two years' time the government does not cut tax rates, then all that has been learned is that the economist is not good at guessing the future behavior of the government. However, *if* the government does cut tax rates (in two years' time or at any other time) and *then* the rate of unemployment does not decrease, a conditional scientific prediction in economic theory has been contradicted.

Testing Theories

A theory is tested by confronting its predictions with evidence. It is necessary to discover if certain events are followed by the consequences predicted by the theory. For example, is an increase in the corporate tax rate followed by a decline in business investment? (Box 2-3 gives further discussion of what can be learned from testing theories.)

Generally, theories tend to be abandoned when they are no longer useful. And theories cease to be useful when they cannot predict the consequences of actions in which one is interested better than the next best alternative. When a theory consistently fails to predict better than the available alternatives, it is either modified or replaced. Figure 2-1 (p. 25) summarizes the discussion of theories and their testing.

Refutation or confirmation. The scientific approach to any issue consists in setting up a theory that will explain it and then seeing if that theory can be refuted by evidence.

The alternative to this approach is to set up a theory and then look for confirming evidence. Such an approach is hazardous because the world is sufficiently complex that *some* confirming evidence can be found for any theory, no matter how unlikely the theory may be. For example, the advocates of conspiracy theories, such as the theory that U.S. President John Kennedy's assassination was a plot involving many persons and at least two gunmen, can always find some confirming evidence. The scientific way to deal with such questions is to set up the simplest theory—in this case that the president was assassinated by Lee Harvey Oswald acting alone—and then see if the evidence can refute it.

An example of the unfruitful approach of seeking confirmation is frequently seen when a leader, elected or self-appointed, surrounds himself with yes-sayers who feed him only evidence that confirms his existing views. This approach is usually a road to disaster because the leader's decisions become more and more out of touch with reality.

A wise leader adopts a scientific approach instinctively; he constantly checks the realism of his views

BOX 2-3

Can Hypotheses Be Proven or Refuted?

Most hypotheses in economics are universal. They say that whenever certain specified conditions are fulfilled, cause X will always produce effect Y. Such universal hypotheses cannot be proven correct with certainty. No matter how many observations are collected that agree with the hypothesis, there is always some chance that a long series of untypical observations has been made or that there have been systematic errors of observation. After all, the mass of well-documented evidence accumulated several centuries ago on the existence of the power of witches is no longer accepted, even though it fully satisfied most contemporary observers. The existence of observational errors, even on a vast scale, has been shown to be possible, although (one fervently hopes) it is not very frequent. Observations that disagree with the theory may begin to accumulate, and after some time a theory that looked nearly certain may begin to look rather shaky.

By the same token a universal hypothesis can never be proven false with certainty. Even when current observations consistently conflict with the theory, it is still possible that a large number of untypical cases has been selected or systematic errors of observation have been made. For instance, evidence was once gathered "disproving" the theory that high income taxes tend to discourage work. More recent research suggests that economists may have been wrong to reject this theory. As a result of measurement errors and bad experimental design, the conflicting evidence may not have been as decisive as was once thought.

There is no absolute certainty in any knowledge. No doubt some of the things we now think true will eventually turn out to be false, and some of the things we currently think false will eventually turn out to be true. Yet while we can never be certain, we can assess the balance of evidence. Some hypotheses are so unlikely to be true, given current evidence, that for all practical purposes we may regard them as false. Other hypotheses are so unlikely to be false, given current evidence, that for all practical purposes we may regard them as true. This kind of practical decision must always be regarded as tentative. Every once in a while we will find that we have to change our mind: Something that looked right will begin to look doubtful, or something that looked wrong will begin to look possible.

---

by encouraging subordinates to criticize them. This tests how far the leader's existing views correspond to all available evidence and encourages amendment in the light of evidence that conflicts with the current views.

Measurement and Testing of Economic Relations

So far we have given an outline of the main elements of theories. Because measurement and testing are so important in evaluating theories, we now present a more detailed discussion of these topics in relation to economic principles.

It is one thing for economists to theorize that two or more variables are related to each other; it is quite another for them to be able to say how these variables are related. Economists might generalize on the basis of a casual observation that when households receive more income, they are likely to buy more of most commodities. But precisely how much will the consumption of a particular commodity rise as household incomes rise? Are there exceptions to the rule that the purchase of a commodity rises as income rises? For estimating precise magnitudes and for testing general rules or hypotheses, common sense, intuition, and casual observation do not take us very far. More systematic statistical analysis is required.

Statistical analysis is used to test the hypothesis that two things are related and to estimate the numerical values of the function that describes the relation.

FIGURE 2-1 The Interaction of Deduction and Measurement in Theorizing

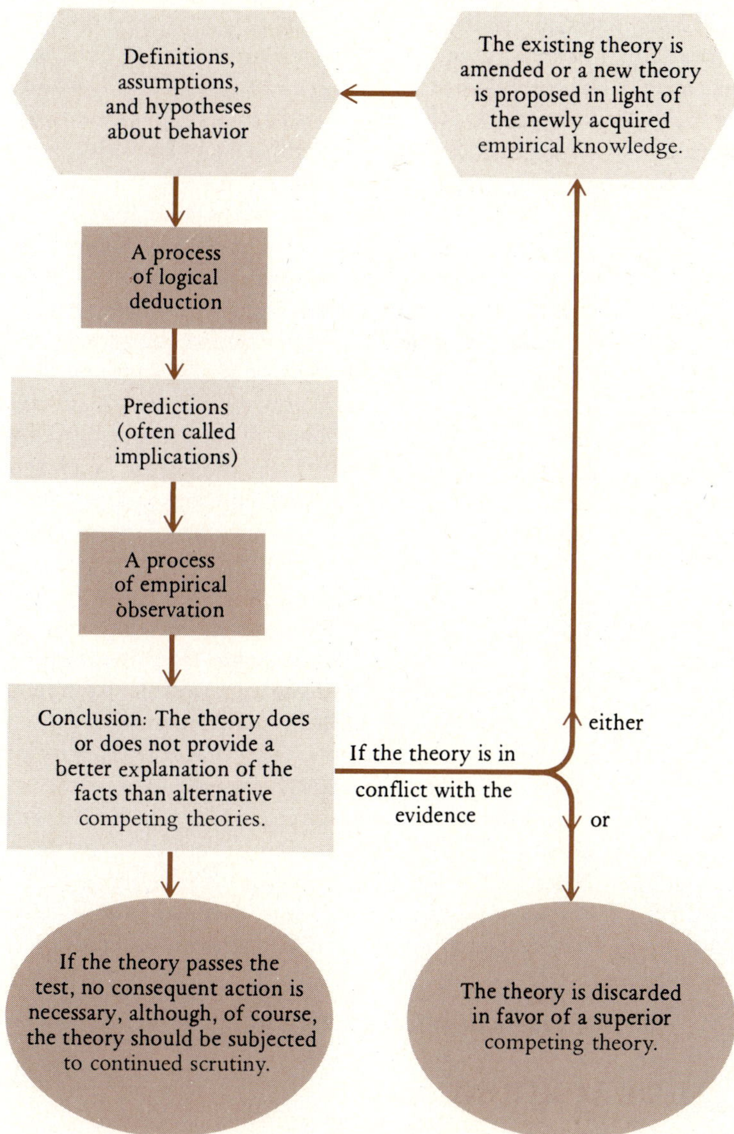

Theory and observation are in continuous interaction. Starting (at the top left) with the assumptions of a theory and the definitions of relevant terms, the theorist deduces by logical analysis everything that is implied by the assumptions. These implications are the predictions of the theory. The theory is then tested by confronting its predictions with evidence. If the theory is in conflict with facts, it will usually be amended to make it consistent with those facts (thereby making it a better theory); in extreme cases it will be discarded, to be replaced by a superior alternative. The process then begins again: The new or amended theory is subjected first to logical analysis and then to empirical testing.

In practice, the same data can be used simultaneously to test whether a relationship exists and, when it does exist, to provide a measure of it.

We have seen that economics is a nonlaboratory science. It is rarely possible to conduct controlled experiments with the economy. However, millions of uncontrolled experiments are going on every day. Households are deciding what to purchase given changing prices and incomes; firms are deciding what to produce and how to produce it; and the government is involved in the economy by its various taxes, subsidies, and controls. Because all these activities can be observed and recorded, a mass of data is continually produced by the economy.

The variables that interest economists, such as the volume of unemployment, the price of wheat, and the share of income going to wage earners, are generally influenced by many factors, all of which vary simultaneously. If economists are to test their theories about relations among variables in the economy, they must use statistical techniques designed for situations in which other things cannot be held constant.

An Example of Statistical Testing

To illustrate how data may be used to test theories even while other things are not held constant, we take the very simple and intuitively plausible hypothesis that the federal income taxes paid by households increase as their incomes increase.

A Sample

To begin with, observations must be made of family income and tax payments. It is not practical to do so for all households, so a small number (called a *sample*) are studied on the assumption that these households are typical of the entire group.

It is important that the sample be what is called a random sample. A **random sample** is chosen according to a rigidly defined set of conditions guaranteeing, among other things, that every member of the group from which we are selecting the sample has an equal chance of being selected. Choosing the sample in a random fashion has two important consequences.

First, it reduces the chance that the sample will be unrepresentative of the population from which it is selected. Second, and more important, it allows us to calculate just how likely it is that the sample will be unrepresentative by any specified amount. For example, if the average amount of income tax paid by the households in our sample is $2,000, then it is most likely that the average tax paid by all households in the country is in the vicinity of $2,000. But that is not necessarily so. The sample might be so unrepresentative that the actual figure for average tax paid by all households is only $1,500, or it might be $2,750. If the sample is random, we are able to calculate the probability that the actual data for the whole population differ from the data in our sample by any stated amount.

The reason for the predictability of random samples is that such samples are chosen by chance, and chance events are predictable.

That chance events are predictable may sound surprising, but consider these questions. If you pick a card from a deck of ordinary playing cards, how likely is it that you will pick a heart? An ace? An ace of hearts? You play a game in which you pick a card and win if it is a heart and lose if it is anything else; a friend offers you $5 if you win against $1 if you lose. Who will make money if the game is played a large number of times? The same game is played again, but now you get $3 if you win and pay $1 if you lose. Who will make money over a large number of draws? If you can answer these questions (we will bet that most of you can), you must believe that chance events are in some sense predictable.

To test the hypothesis about taxes we require relevant data. One set of readily available data refers to a random sample of 212 American families chosen by the Survey Research Center of the University of Michigan. For each family the survey records its income and the federal income tax it pays—as well as some other data that will be useful to us later. Since we are interested in methods rather than in the results at this stage, there is no problem in using data for American rather than Canadian households.

Graphical and Tabular Analysis

There are several ways in which the data may be used to evaluate the hypothesis.

Scatter diagram. One is the **scatter diagram.**[3] Figure 2-2 is a scatter diagram that relates family income to federal income tax payments. The pattern of the dots suggests that there is a strong tendency

[3] The second half of the appendix to this chapter outlines the elements of graphs and the graphical analysis of economic data. If you find graphical analysis baffling, you might read this appendix now.

FIGURE 2-2 A Scatter Diagram Relating Taxes Paid to Family Income in the United States

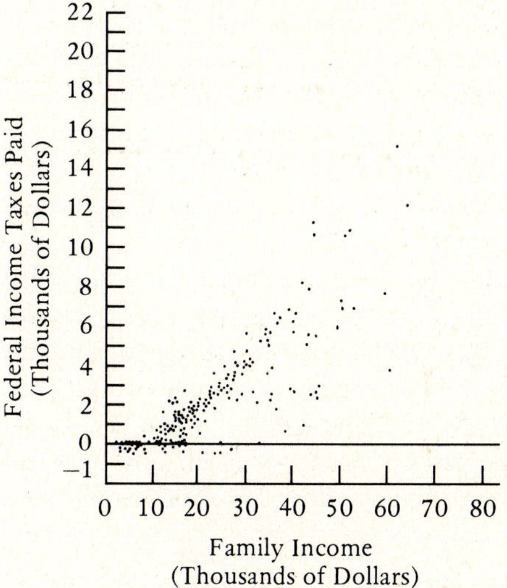

The scatter pattern shows a clear tendency for taxes paid to rise with family income. Family income is measured along the horizontal axis, and federal income taxes paid are measured along the vertical axis. Each dot represents a single family in the sample and is located on the graph according to the family's income and taxes paid. The dots fall mainly within a narrow, rising band, suggesting the existence of a systematic relationship between income and taxes paid. But they do not fall along a single line, which suggests that things other than family income affect taxes paid. The data are for 1979. (Negative amounts of tax liability arise because of such things as capital losses that may be carried forward.)

TABLE 2-1 Federal Tax Payments Cross-Classified by Family Income

Annual family income	Average income tax payment	Number of families
Less than $10,000	$ 70	38
$ 10,000–19,999	893	76
20,000–29,999	2,470	42
30,000–39,999	4,205	28
40,000–99,999	7,755	28
100,000 or more	—	0

Tax payments tend to increase as family income increases. The data on 212 families are grouped into the income classes shown in the first column. The average tax payment for families in each income group is calculated and listed in the second column. When we read down this second column, we find an unbroken rise in tax payments. This cross-classification reduces 212 individual observations to a mere 5. More (or less) detail could have been preserved by varying the size of the income classes used in the first column.

for tax payments to be higher when family income is higher. It thus supports the hypothesis.

There is some scattering of the dots because the relationship is not "perfect"; in other words, there is some variation in tax payments that cannot be associated with variations in family income. These variations in tax payments occur mainly for two reasons. First, factors other than income influence tax payments, and some of these other factors will undoubtedly have varied among the families in the sample. Second, there will inevitably be some errors in measurement. For example, a family might have incorrectly reported its tax payments to the person who collected the data.

Cross-classification table. A cross-classification table provides another way to examine the hypothesis that tax payments vary directly with income. Table 2-1 cross-classifies families by their income and their average tax payments. At the loss of considerable detail, the table makes clear the general tendency for tax payments to rise as income rises.

Regression Analysis

While both the scatter diagram and the cross-classification table reflect the general relationship between federal income tax payments and family income, neither characterizes what the precise relationship is. **Regression analysis,** a widely used technique, provides quantitative measures of the relationship between two variables and how closely it holds.[4] It employs a **regression equation** that represents the best estimate of the *average* relationship between the variables being tested. The equation can be used in

[4] Detailed discussion of techniques and conditions that must hold for the technique to be valid is left to courses in statistics and econometrics.

this case to describe the tendency for higher family income to be associated with higher tax payments.[5]

A measure of how closely the relationship holds can be obtained by calculating the percentage of the variance in federal tax payments that can be accounted for by variations in household income.[6] This measure is called the **coefficient of determination** (r^2). For our sample $r^2 = 0.734$. This number tells us that in this case 73.4 percent of the variance in tax payments can be "explained" by associating it with variations in family incomes.

A *significance test* can be applied to determine the odds that the relation discovered in the sample does not exist for the whole population but has arisen by chance because the families selected happen not to be representative of the entire set of American families. It turns out that in this example there is less than one chance in a million that the rising pattern of dots shown in Figure 2-2 would have been observed if there were no positive association between income and tax payments for U.S. families. We conclude with less than one chance in a million of being wrong that the hypothesis that tax payments and family income are positively related is correct. Statistically the relationship is said to be *significant*.

Extending the Analysis to Three Variables

The scatter diagram and the regression equation show that *all* the variation in income tax payments cannot be accounted for by observed variations in family income. If it could, all the dots would lie on a line, and r^2 would equal 1.0. Since these criteria are not met, some other factors must influence tax payments. Why might one family with an income of $12,000 pay 20 percent more in income taxes than another family with the same income?

One reason is difference in family size, for American tax laws provide exemptions based on the number of family members. (There will be other reasons too, such as differences in itemized deductions for medical expenses or charitable donations.) We anticipate that family size will be an important second reason. The survey also collected data on family size, which we now use.

There are now *three* observations for each of the 212 families: annual income, federal income tax payments, and family size. How should these data be handled? The scatter diagram technique is not available because the relation among three sets of data cannot conveniently be shown on a two-dimensional graph.

The data may, however, be classified into groups once again. This time we are testing two variables that are thought to influence tax payments, and the data have to be cross-classified in a more complicated manner, as shown in Table 2-2.

The table can be used to hold one variable roughly constant while allowing another to vary. Reading across each row, we see that income is held

TABLE 2-2 Federal Tax Payments Cross-Classified by Family Income and Family Size

Annual family income	Number of family members: 3 or less	4 or 5	6 or more
$ 0–9,999	$ 175	$ 142	$ 26
10,000–19,999	1,028	995	507
20,000–29,999	2,950	2,491	935
30,000–39,999	5,349	3,802	2,372
40,000–99,999	9,459	8,624	4,193
100,000 or more	None in the sample		

Tax payments tend to vary positively with family income and negatively with family size. Each row in the table shows the effect of family size on tax payments for a given level of income. For example, reading across the second row shows that families with incomes between $10,000 and $20,000 paid an average of $1,028 if the family had less than 4 members, $995 if the family had 4 or 5 members, and $507 if the family had 6 or more members. The declining numbers across each row show that for each income group tax payments tend to decline as family size increases. Each column in the table shows the effect of income on tax payments for a given family size. The increase in taxes paid as we move down each column shows that tax payments increase with family income.

[5] The equation of a straight line fitted to the data shown in Figure 2-2 is $T = -1{,}924 + 0.19Y$, where T is taxes paid and Y is income in thousands of dollars per year. The equation shows that for every increase of $1,000 in family income, taxes paid tend to increase by $190.

[6] *Variance* is a precise statistical measure of the amount of variability (dispersion) in a set of data.

constant within a specified range and family size is varied; reading down each column, we see that size of family is held constant within a specified range and income is varied.

To estimate a numerical relation among family income, family size, and tax payments, **multiple regression analysis** is used.[7] This type of analysis allows estimation of both the separate and joint effects on tax payments of variations in family size and variations in income by fitting to the data an equation that "best" describes them. It also permits the measurement of the proportion of the total variation in tax payments that can be explained by associating it with variations in both income and family size. Finally, it permits the use of significance tests to determine how likely it is that the relations found in the sample are the result of chance and thus do not reflect a similar relationship for all U.S. families. Chance plays a role because by bad luck an unrepresentative sample of families might have been chosen.

The Decision to Reject or Accept

In general, a hypothesis can never be proven or refuted with absolute certainty, no matter how many observations are made. Those who are interested in pursuing this matter will find further discussion in Box 2-3.

Although we can never be certain, we do have to make decisions. To do so it is necessary to accept some hypotheses (to act as if they were proven) and reject some hypotheses (to act as if they were refuted). Just as a jury can make two kinds of errors (finding an innocent person guilty or letting a guilty person go free), so can statistical decision makers make two kinds of errors. They can reject hypotheses that are true, and they can accept hypotheses that are false. Luckily, like a jury, they can also make correct decisions—and indeed they expect to do so most of the time.

Although the possibility of error cannot be eliminated in statistics, it can be controlled.

The method of control is to decide in advance how large a risk to take of accepting a hypothesis that is in fact false.[8] Conventionally in statistics this risk is often set at 5 percent or 1 percent. When the 5 percent cutoff point is used, we will accept the hypothesis if the results that appear to establish it could have happened by chance no more than 1 time in 20. Using the 1 percent decision rule gives the hypothesis a sterner test. A hypothesis is accepted only if the results that appear to establish it could have happened by chance no more than 1 time in 100.

Consider the hypothesis that a certain coin is "loaded," favoring heads over tails. The coin is flipped 100 times and comes up heads 53 times. While this result is not inconsistent with the hypothesis, such an unbalanced result could happen by chance more than 22 percent of the time. Thus the hypothesis of a head-biased coin would not be accepted using either a 1 percent or a 5 percent cutoff. Had the experiment produced 65 heads and 35 tails, a result that would occur by chance less than 1 percent of the time, we would (given a 1 percent or a 5 percent cutoff) accept the hypothesis of a loaded coin.[9]

When action must be taken, some rule of thumb is necessary. But it is important to understand, first, that no one can ever be certain about being right in rejecting any hypothesis and, second, that there is nothing magical about arbitrary cutoff points. Some cutoff point must be used whenever decisions have to be made.

Finally, recall that the rejection of a hypothesis is seldom the end of inquiry. Decisions can be reversed should new evidence come to light. Often the result of a statistical test of a theory is to suggest a new hypothesis that "fits the facts" better than the old one. Indeed, in some cases just looking at a scatter

[7] Details must be left to a course in statistics. The regression equation for our example is $T = -733 + 0.197Y - 344F$, where F is the number of family members. On average, an additional family member decreases taxes paid by \$344. R^2, the coefficient of determination in multiple regression analysis, is 0.774. Comparison with the previous $r^2 = 0.734$ shows that adding family size to the analysis increased the percentage of variance explained from 73.4 percent to 77.4 percent.

[8] Return to the jury analogy: Our notion of a person's being innocent unless the jury is persuaded of guilt "beyond a reasonable doubt" rests on our wishing to take only a small risk of accepting the hypothesis of guilt if the person being tried is in fact innocent.

[9] The actual statistical testing process is more complex than this example suggests but must be left to a course in statistics.

diagram or making a regression analysis uncovers apparent relations that no one anticipated and leads economists to formulate a new hypothesis.

Economics As a Developing Science

Economics is like other sciences in at least two respects. First, there are many observations of the world for which there are, at the moment, no fully satisfactory theoretical explanations. Second, there are many predictions that no one has yet satisfactorily tested. Serious students of economics must not expect to find a set of answers to all their questions as they progress in their study. Often they must expect to encounter nothing more than a set of problems that provides an agenda for further research. Even when they do find answers to problems, they should accept these answers as tentative and ask even of the most time-honored theory, "What observations would be in conflict with this theory?"

Economics is still a young science. On the one hand, economists know a good deal about the behavior of the economy. On the other hand, many problems are almost untouched. Students who decide to specialize in economics may find themselves, only a few years from now, publishing a theory to account for some of the problems mentioned in this book; or they may end up making a set of observations that will upset some venerable theory described in these pages.

A final word of warning: Having counseled a constructive disrespect for the authority of accepted theory, it is necessary to warn against adopting an approach that is too cavalier. No respect attaches to the person who says, "This theory is for the birds; it is *obviously* wrong." This is too cheap. To criticize a theory effectively on empirical grounds, one must demonstrate, by a careful set of observations, that some aspect of the theory is contradicted by the facts. This is a task worth attempting, but it is seldom easily accomplished.

Summary

1. It is possible, and fruitful, to distinguish between positive and normative statements. Positive statements concern what is, was, or will be, while normative statements concern what ought to be. Disagreements over positive, testable statements are appropriately settled by an appeal to the facts. Disagreements over normative statements can never be settled in this way.
2. The success of scientific inquiry depends on separating positive questions about the way the world works from normative questions about how one would like the world to work, formulating positive questions precisely enough so that they can be settled by an appeal to evidence, and then finding means of gathering the necessary evidence.
3. Some people feel that although natural phenomena can be subject to scientific inquiry and "laws" of behavior, human phenomena cannot. The evidence, however, is otherwise. Social scientists have observed many stable human behavior patterns. These form the basis for successful predictions of how people will behave under certain conditions.
4. The fact that people sometimes act strangely, even capriciously, does not destroy the possibility of scientific study of group behavior. The odd and inexplicable things that one person does will tend to cancel out the odd and inexplicable things that another person does.
5. Theories are designed to give meaning and coherence to observed

sequences of events. A theory consists of a set of definitions of the variables to be employed, a set of assumptions under which the theory is meant to apply, and a set of hypotheses about how things behave. Any theory has certain logical implications that must be true if the theory is true. These are the theory's predictions.

6. A theory provides predictions of the type "*if* one event occurs, *then* another event will also occur." An important method of testing theories is to confront their predictions with evidence. The progress of any science lies in finding better explanations of events than are now available. Thus in any developing science one must expect to discard present theories and replace them with demonstrably superior alternatives.
7. Theories are tested by checking their predictions against evidence. In some sciences these tests can be conducted under laboratory conditions where only one thing changes at a time. In other sciences testing must be done using the data produced by the world of ordinary events. Modern statistical analysis is designed to test hypotheses when many variables are changing at once.
8. Sample data are often used in testing economic theories. If the sample is random, the probability that the measured characteristics of the sample will be misleading (because of the unlucky choice of a nonrepresentative sample) can be calculated.
9. Scatter diagrams or simple cross-classification tables are devices for discovering systematic relationships between two variables. Regression analysis permits more specific measurement of the relationship: what it is, how closely it holds, and whether or not it is "significant."
10. Hypotheses involving several variables require more sophisticated statistical techniques such as the use of complex cross-classification tables and multiple regression analysis. These techniques attempt to identify the separate and joint effects of several variables on one another.
11. Methods of graphing economic observations and the use of functional relations are discussed in more detail in the appendix to this chapter.

Topics for Review

Positive and normative statements
Testable statements
The law of large numbers and the predictability of human behavior
Variables, hypotheses, assumptions, and predictions in theorizing
Endogenous and exogenous variables
Stock and flow variables
Functional relations
Prediction versus prophecy
The scientific approach
Role of statistical analysis: measurement and testing

Scatter diagrams
Cross-classification tables
Rejection and acceptance of hypotheses

Discussion Questions

1. A baby doesn't "know" of the theory of gravity, yet in walking and eating the child soon learns to use its principles. Distinguish between behavior and the explanation of behavior. Does a business executive or a farmer have to understand economic theory to behave in a pattern consistent with economic theory?
2. "If human behavior were completely capricious and unpredictable, life insurance could not be a profitable business." Explain. Can you think of any businesses that do *not* depend on predictable human behavior?
3. Write five statements about unemployment in Canada. (It does not matter whether the statements are correct, but you should confine yourself to those you think might be correct.) Classify each statement as positive or normative. If your list contains only one type of statement, try to add a sixth statement of the other type.
4. Each of the following unrealistic assumptions is sometimes made. See if you can visualize situations in which each of them might be useful.
   a. The earth is a plane.
   b. There are no differences between men and women.
   c. There is no tomorrow.
   d. People are wholly selfish.
5. Polls of voters' intentions are usually based on interviews with a very few thousand voters, yet they are remarkably accurate most of the time. Why can the answers of no more than a thousand or so voters allow us to predict the outcome of elections involving many millions of voters? Why are the predictions based on such data often wrong by a small margin and occasionally wrong by a large margin?
6. What may at first appear to be untestable statements can often be reworded so that they can be tested by an appeal to evidence. How might you do that with respect to each of the following assertions?
   a. The Canadian economic system is the best in the world.
   b. Unemployment insurance is eroding the work ethic and encouraging people to become wards of the state rather than productive workers.
   c. Robotics ought to be outlawed, because it will destroy the future of the working classes.
   d. Laws requiring equal pay for work of equal value will spell disaster for women.
7. "The simplest way to see that capital punishment is a strong deterrent to murder is to ask yourself whether you might be more inclined to commit murder if you knew in advance that you ran no risk of ending in the electric chair, in the gas chamber, or on the gallows." Comment on the methodology of social investigation implied by this statement. What alternative approach would you suggest?

8. Since 1979, when the data used in Figure 2-2 were collected, American tax laws have changed, lowering the tax rates that apply to higher incomes. How would you expect this development to change a scatter diagram of income and tax payments? Would you expect it to change the regression results? Do these changes lead you to reject the conclusions of the analysis of the 1979 data?
9. There are hundreds of eyewitnesses to the existence of flying saucers and other UFOs. There are films and eyewitness accounts of Nessie, the Loch Ness monster. Are you convinced of their existence? If not, what would it take to persuade you? If so, what would it take to make you change your mind?
10. Relate the role of the law of large numbers to the statistical idea that one can test hypotheses by using average relationships based on random samples.

Appendix to Chapter 2

Expressing and Graphing Relations Among Variables

The idea of relationships among variables is one of the basic notions behind all science. Many such relations are found in economics.

Expressing Relations: Correspondences and Functions

When mathematicians want to say that there is a relation between two variables, let us call them X and Y, they say that there is a correspondence between them. When the relation is such that for every value of X there is one and only one value of Y, mathematicians say that Y is a function of X. In what follows we confine ourselves to the subclass of correspondences that are functions.

Consider two examples, one from a natural science and one from economics. The gravitational attraction of two bodies depends on their mass and on the distance separating them, attraction increasing with size and diminishing with distance; the amount of a commodity that people would like to buy depends on (among other things) the price of the commodity, purchases increasing as price falls. Thus gravitational attraction is a function of the mass of the two bodies concerned and the distance between them, and the quantity of a product demanded is a function of the price of the product.

One of the virtues of mathematics is that it permits the concise expression of ideas that would otherwise require long, drawn-out verbal statements. There are two steps in giving compact symbolic expression to functional relations. First, each variable is given a symbol. Second, a symbol is designated to express the idea of one variable's dependence on another. Thus if G equals gravitational attraction, M equals the mass of two bodies, and d equals the distance between the two bodies, we may write

$$G = f(M, d)$$

where f is read "is a function of" and means "is uniquely related to." The whole equation states a hypothesis and is read "gravitational attraction is a function of the mass of the two bodies concerned and the distance between them." The same hypothesis can be written as

$$G = G(M, d)$$

This is read in exactly the same way and means the same thing as the previous expression. Instead of using f to represent "a function of," the left-hand symbol, G, is repeated.[1]

The hypothesis about desired purchases and price can be written

$$q = f(p)$$

or

$$q = q(p)$$

where q stands for the quantity people wish to purchase of some commodity and p is the price of the commodity. The expression says that the quantity of some commodity that people desire to purchase is a function of its price. The alternative way of writing this merely uses a different letter to stand for the same functional relation between p and q.

Functional Forms: Precise Relations Among Variables

The expression $Y = Y(X)$ merely states that the variables Y and X are related; it says nothing about the form that this relation takes. Usually the hypothesis to be expressed says more than that. Does

[1] Any convenient symbol may be used on the right-hand side before the parenthesis to mean "a function of." The repetition of the left-hand symbol may be convenient in reminding us of what is a function of what.

Y increase as X increases? Does Y decrease as X increases? Or is the relation more complicated? Take a very simple example, where Y is the length of a board in feet, and X is the length of the same board in yards. Quite clearly, $Y = Y(X)$. Further, in this case the exact form of the function is known, for length in feet (Y) is exactly three times the length in yards (X), so we may write $Y = 3X$.

This relation is a definitional one, for the length of something measured in feet is defined to be three times its length measured in yards. It is nonetheless useful to have a way of writing relationships that are definitionally true. The expression $Y = 3X$ specifies the exact form of the relation between Y and X and provides a rule whereby, if we have the value of one, we can calculate the value of the other.

Now consider a second example. Let C stand for consumption expenditure, the total amount spent on purchasing goods and services by all American households during a year. Let Y_d stand for the total amount of income that these households had available to spend during the year. We might state the hypothesis that

$$C = f(Y_d)$$

and, even more specifically,

$$C = 0.8Y_d$$

The first expression gives the hypothesis that the total consumption expenditure of households depends on their income. The second expression says, more specifically, that total consumption expenditure is 80 percent of the total available for spending. The second equation expresses a specific hypothesis about the relation between two observable magnitudes. There is no reason why it *must* be true; it may be consistent or inconsistent with the facts. This is a matter for testing. However, the equation is a concise statement of a particular hypothesis.

Thus the general view that there is a functional relation between Y and X is denoted by $Y = f(X)$, whereas any precise relation is expressed by a particular equation such as $Y = 2X$, $Y = 4X^2$, or $Y = X + 2.0X^2 + 0.5X^3$.

If Y increases as X increases (e.g., $Y = 10 + 2X$), we say that Y is an *increasing function* of X or that Y and X *vary positively* with each other. If Y decreases as X increases (e.g., $Y = 10 - 2X$), we say that Y is a *decreasing function* of X or that Y and X *vary negatively* with each other. Y varying negatively with X merely means that Y changes in the opposite direction from X.

Error Terms in Economic Hypotheses

Expressing hypotheses in the form of functions is misleading in one respect. When we say that the world behaves so that $Y = f(X)$, we do not expect that knowing X will tell us *exactly* what Y will be, only that it will tell us what Y will be *within some margin of error.*

This error in predicting Y from a knowledge of X arises for two distinct reasons. First, there may be other variables that also affect Y. When, for example, we say that the quantity of butter people wish to purchase is a function of the price of butter, $q_b = f(p_b)$, we know that other factors will also influence this demand. A change in the price of margarine will certainly affect the demand for butter, even though the price of butter does not change. Thus we do not expect to find a perfect relation between q_b and p_b that will allow us to predict q_b exactly from a knowledge of p_b.

Second, variables can never be measured exactly. Even if X is the only cause of Y, measurements will give various Ys corresponding to the same X. In the case of the demand for butter, errors of measurement might not be large. In other cases, errors can be substantial—as, for example, in the case of a relation between the total consumption expenditure of all American households and their total income. The measurements of consumption and income may be subject to quite wide margins of error, and various values of consumption associated with the same measured value of income may be observed, not because consumption is varying independently of income but because the error of measurement is varying from period to period.

When we say Y is a function of X, we appear to say Y is completely determined by X. Instead of the deterministic formulation

$$Y = f(X)$$

it would be more accurate to write

$$Y = f(X, \epsilon)$$

FIGURE 2A-1 A Coordinate Graph

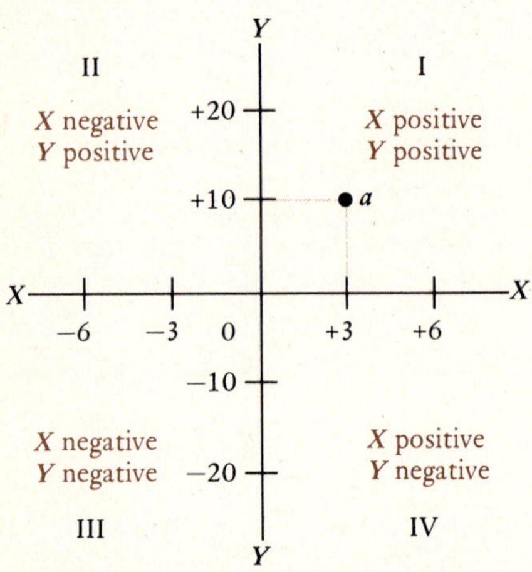

The axes divide the total space into four quadrants according to the signs of the variables. In the upper right-hand quadrant, both X and Y are greater than zero; this is usually called the *positive quadrant*. Point a has *coordinates* $Y = 10$ and $X = 3$ in the coordinate graph. These coordinates *define* point a.

where ϵ, the Greek letter epsilon, represents an **error term.**[2] Such a term indicates that the observed value of Y will differ from the value predicted by the functional relation between Y and X. Divergences will occur both because of observational errors and because of neglected variables. While economists always mean this, they usually do not say so.

The deterministic formulation is a simplification; an error term is really present in all assumed and observed functional relations in economics.

Graphing Relations Among Variables

The popular saying "The facts speak for themselves" is almost always wrong when there are many facts. Theories are needed to explain how facts are linked together, and summary measures are needed to assist in sorting out what it is that facts show in relation to theories. The simplest means of providing compact summaries of a large number of observations is the use of tables and graphs. Graphs play important roles in economics by representing geometrically both observed data and the correspondence among variables that are the subject of economic theory.

Because the surface of a piece of paper is two-dimensional, a graph may readily be used to represent pictorially any correspondence between two variables. Flip through this book and you will see dozens of examples. Figure 2A-1 shows generally how a coordinate grid can permit the representation of any two measurable variables.[3]

Representing Theories on Graphs

Figure 2A-2 shows a simple two-variable graph, which will be analyzed in detail in Chapter 4. For now it is sufficient to notice that the graph permits us to show the relationship between two variables, the *price* of carrots on the vertical axis and the *quantity* of carrots per month on the horizontal axis.[4] The downward-sloping curve, labeled D for a *demand curve*, shows the relationship between the price of carrots and the quantity of carrots buyers wish to purchase.

Figure 2A-3 is very much like Figure 2A-2, with one difference. It generalizes from the specific example of carrots to an unspecified commodity and focuses on the slope of the demand curve rather than on specific numerical values. Note that the quantity labeled q_0 is associated with the price p_0, while the quantity q_1 is associated with the price p_1.

Straight Lines and Their Slopes

Figure 2A-4 illustrates a variety of straight lines. They differ according to their slopes. **Slope** is defined as the ratio of the vertical change to the corresponding horizontal change as one moves along a curve.

[2] The relationship with the error term in it is frequently written $Y = f(X) + \epsilon$.

[3] Economics is often concerned only with the positive values of variables, and the graph is confined to the upper right-hand (or "positive") quadrant. Whenever a variable has a negative value, one or more of the other quadrants must be included.

[4] The choice of which variable to put on which axis is discussed in footnote 2 on page 91 and in math note 8 on page M-2.

FIGURE 2A-2 The Relationship Between the Price of Carrots and the Quantity of Carrots That Purchasers Wish to Buy: A Numerical Illustration

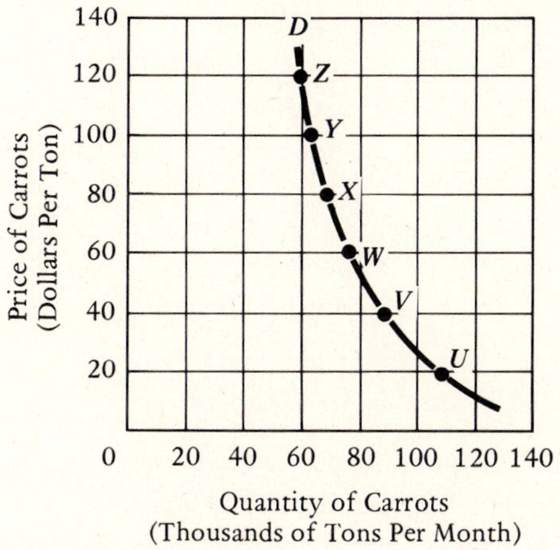

A two-dimensional graph can show how two variables are related. The two variables, the price of carrots and the quantity people wish to purchase, are shown by the downward-sloping curve labeled *D*. Particular points on the curve are labeled *U* through *Z*. For example, *Z* shows that at a price of \$120, the demand to purchase carrots is 60,000 tons per month.

FIGURE 2A-3 The Relationship Between the Price of a Commodity and the Quantity of the Commodity That Purchasers Wish to Buy

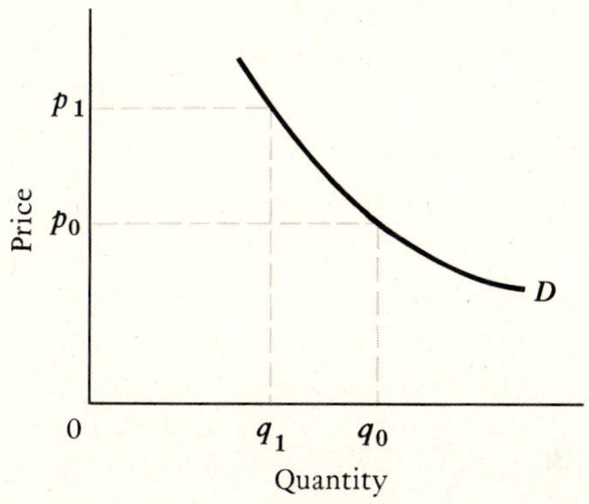

Graphs can illustrate general relationships between variables as well as between specific quantities. Here, in contrast to Figure 2A-2, price and quantity are shown as general variables. The demand curve illustrates a quantitatively unspecified *negative* relationship between price and quantity. For example, at the price p_0 the quantity that purchasers demand is q_0, while at the higher price of p_1 purchasers demand the lower quantity of q_0.

FIGURE 2A-4 Four Straight Lines with Different Slopes

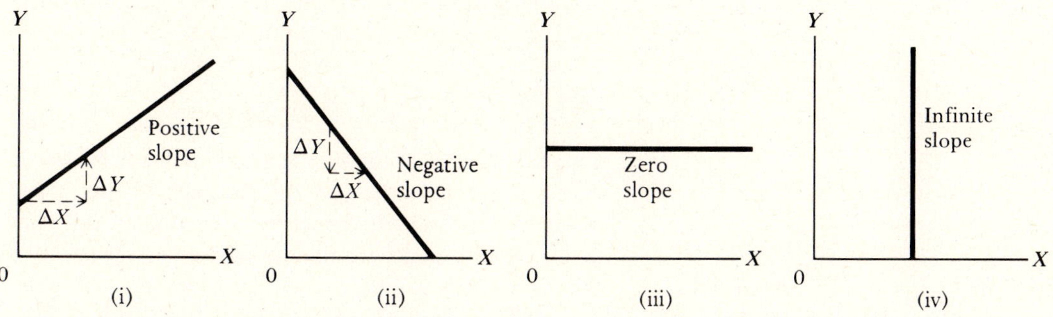

The slope of a straight line is constant but can vary from one line to another. The direction of slope of a straight line is characterized by the signs of the ratio $\Delta Y/\Delta X$. In (i) that ratio is positive because *X* and *Y* vary in the same direction; in (ii) the ratio is negative because *X* and *Y* vary in opposite directions; in (iii) it is zero because *Y* does not change as *X* increases; in (iv) it is infinite.

The symbol Δ is used to indicate a change in any variable. Thus ΔX means the change in X, and ΔY means the change in Y. The ratio $\Delta Y/\Delta X$ is the slope of a straight line. Where both increase or decrease together, the ratio is positive and the line slopes upward to the right, as in part (i) of Figure 2A-4. Where ΔY and ΔX have the opposite sign, that is, one increases while the other decreases, the ratio is negative and the line slopes downward to the right, as in part (ii). Where ΔY does not change, the line is horizontal, as in part (iii), and the slope is zero. Where ΔX is zero, the line is vertical, as in part (iv), and the slope is often said to be infinite, although the ratio $\Delta Y/\Delta X$ is indeterminate. **[1]**[5]

Slope is a quantitative measure, not merely a qualitative one. For example, in Figure 2A-5 two upward-sloping straight lines have different slopes. Line A has a slope of 2 ($\Delta Y/\Delta X = 2.0$); line B has a slope of 1/2 ($\Delta Y/\Delta X = 0.5$).

FIGURE 2A-5 Two Straight Lines with Different Slopes

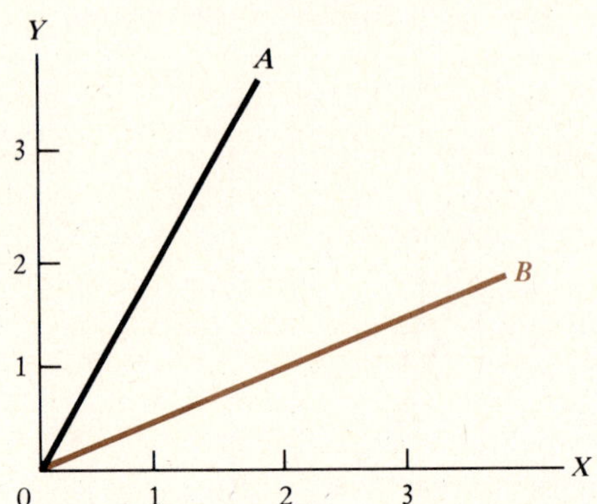

Slope is a quantitative measure. Both lines have positive slopes and thus are similar to Figure 2A-4(i). But curve A is steeper (i.e., has a greater slope) than curve B. For each 1-unit increase in X, the value of Y increases by 2 units along curve A, but by only 1/2 unit along curve B. The ratio $\Delta Y/\Delta X$ is 2 for curve A and 1/2 for curve B.

Curved Lines and Their Slopes

Figure 2A-6 shows four curved lines. The line in part (i) is plainly upward sloping and in part (ii) downward sloping. The other two change from one to the other, as the labels indicate. Unlike straight lines, whose slope is the same at every point on the line, the slope of a curve changes. The slope of a curve must be measured at a particular point and is defined as the slope of a straight line that just touches (is tangent to) the straight line at that point. This is illustrated in Figure 2A-7. The slope at point A is measured by the slope of the tangent line a. The slope at point B is measured by the slope of the tangent line b.

Graphing Observations

A coordinate space such as shown in Figure 2A-1 can be used to graph the observed values of two variables as well as the theoretical relationships between them. For example, curve D in Figure 2A-2 might have arisen as a freehand line drawn to generalize actual observations of the points labeled U, V, W, X, Y, Z. Although that graph was not constructed from actual observations, many graphs are. Two of the most important kinds are called *scatter diagrams* and *time-series graphs*.

Scatter Diagrams

Scatter diagrams provide a method of graphing any number of *paired* observations made on two variables. In Chapter 2 data for family income and taxes paid for a sample of 212 American families were studied. Figure 2-2 on page 27 shows these data on a scatter diagram. Income is measured on the horizontal axis and taxes paid on the vertical axis. Any point in the diagram represents a particular family's income combined with the tax payment of that family. Thus each family for which there are observations can be represented on the diagram by a dot, the coordinates of which indicate the family's income and the amount of taxes it paid in 1979.

The scatter diagram is useful because if there is a simple relation between the two variables, it will be

[5] Notes giving mathematical demonstrations of the concepts presented in the text are designated by colored reference numbers. These notes can be found beginning on page M-1.

FIGURE 2A-6 Four Curved Lines

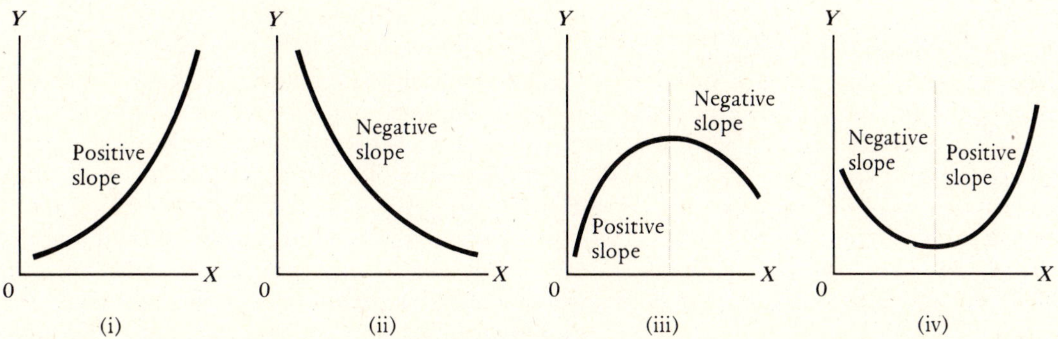

The slope of a curved line is not constant and may change direction. The slopes of the curves in (i) and (ii) change in size but not direction, whereas those in (iii) and (iv) change in both size and direction. Unlike that of a straight line, the slope of a curved line cannot be defined by a single number because it changes as the value of X changes.

apparent to the eye once the data are plotted. Figure 2-2, for example, makes it apparent that more taxes tend to be paid as income rises. It also made it apparent that the relation between taxes and income is approximately linear. A rising straight line fits the data reasonably well between about $10,000 and $40,000 of income. Above $40,000 and below $10,000 the line does not fit the data as well, but since more than two-thirds of the families sampled had incomes in the $10,000 to $40,000 range, the straight line provides a fairly good description of the basic relationship for middle income families.

FIGURE 2A-7 Defining the Slope of a Curve

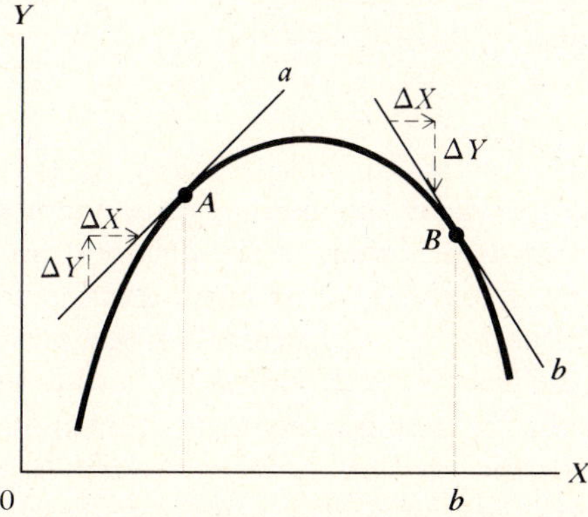

The slope of a curve at any point on the curve is defined by the slope of the straight line that is tangent to the curve at that point. The slope of the curve at point A is defined by the slope of the line a, which is tangent to the curve at point A. The slope of the curve at point B is defined by the slope of the tangent line b.

The diagram also gives some idea of the strength of the relation. If income were the only determinant of taxes paid, all the dots would cluster closely around a line or a smooth curve; as it is, the points are somewhat scattered, and particular incomes are often represented by several households, each with different amounts of taxes paid.

Time-Series Data

The data used in the example of Figure 2–2 are **cross-sectional data.** The incomes and taxes paid of different households are compared over a single period of time—the year 1979. Scatter diagrams may also be drawn for a number of observations taken on two variables at successive periods of time.

For example, if one wanted to know whether there was any simple relation between personal in-

TABLE 2A-1 Income and Consumption in the United States, 1955–1985 (*1982 dollars*)

Year	Disposable personal income per capita	Personal consumption expenditures per capita
1955	$ 5,714	$5,287
1956	5,881	5,349
1957	5,909	5,370
1958	5,908	5,357
1959	6,027	5,531
1960	6,036	5,561
1961	6,113	5,579
1962	6,271	5,729
1963	6,378	5,855
1964	6,727	6,099
1965	7,027	6,362
1966	7,280	6,607
1967	7,513	6,730
1968	7,728	7,003
1969	7,891	7,185
1970	8,134	7,275
1971	8,322	7,409
1972	8,562	7,726
1973	9,042	7,972
1974	8,867	7,826
1975	8,944	7,926
1976	9,175	8,272
1977	9,381	8,551
1978	9,735	8,808
1979	9,829	8,904
1980	9,723	8,784
1981	9,773	8,798
1982	9,732	8,825
1983	9,952	9,148
1984	10,427	9,462
1985	10,504	9,682

Source: Economic Report of the President, 1986.

come and personal consumption in the United States between 1950 and 1985, data would be collected for the levels of personal income and expenditure per capita in each year from 1950 to 1985, as is done in Table 2A-1. This information could be plotted on a scatter diagram, with income on the X axis and consumption on the Y axis. The data are plotted in Figure 2A-8, and they do indeed suggest a systematic linear relation.

Figure 2A-8 is a scatter diagram of observations taken over successive periods of time. Such data are called **time-series data,** and plotting them on a scatter diagram involves no new technique. When cross-sectional data are plotted, each point gives the values of two variables for a particular unit (say, a family); when time-series data are plotted, each point tells the values of two variables for a particular year.

Instead of studying the relation between income and consumption suggested in the preceding paragraph, a study of the pattern of the changes in either one of these variables over time could be made. Figure 2A-9 shows this information for consumption. Time is one variable, consumption expenditure the other. But time is a special variable; the order in which successive events happen is important. The year 1985 followed 1984; they were not two independent and unrelated years. In contrast, two randomly selected households are independent and unrelated. For this reason it is customary to draw in the line segments connecting the successive points, as has been done in Figure 2A-9.

Such a figure is called a *time-series graph* or a *time series.* This kind of graph makes it easy to see if the variable being considered has varied in a systematic way over the years or if its behavior has been more or less erratic.

Ratio (Logarithmic) Scales

All the foregoing graphs use axes that plot numbers on a natural arithmetic scale, with distances between two values shown by the size of the numerical difference. If *proportionate* rather than *absolute* changes in variables are important, it is more revealing to use a ratio scale rather than a natural scale. On a **natural scale** the distance between numbers is proportionate to the absolute difference between those numbers. Thus 200 is placed halfway between 100 and 300. On a **ratio scale** the distance between numbers is proportionate to the percentage difference between the two numbers (which can also be measured as the absolute difference between their logarithms). Equal distances anywhere on a ratio scale represent equal percentage changes rather than equal absolute changes. On a ratio scale the distance between 100 and 200 is the same as the distance between 200 and 400, between 1,000 and 2,000, and between any two numbers that stand in the ratio 1:2 to each other. For

FIGURE 2A-8 A Scatter Diagram Relating Consumption and Disposable Income

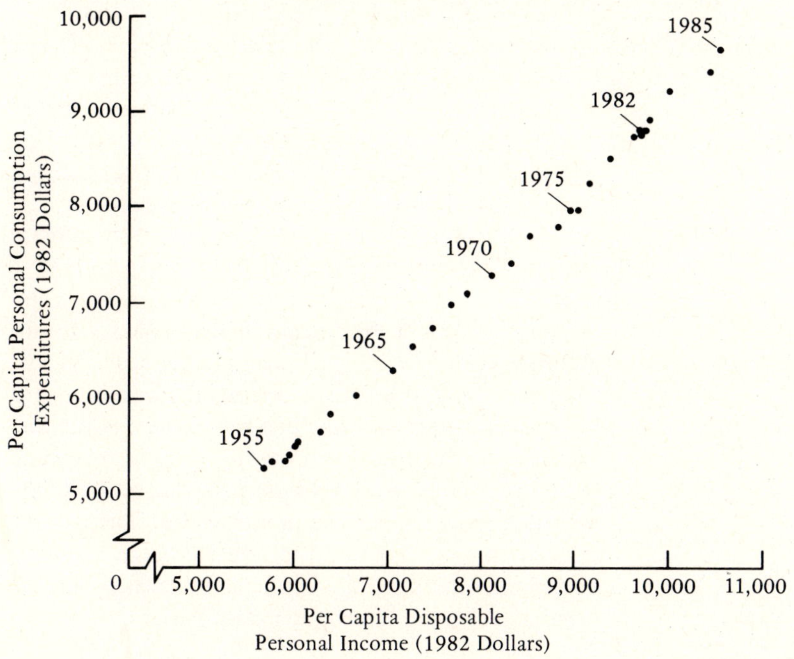

This scatter diagram shows paired values of two variables. The data of Table 2A-1 are plotted here. Each dot shows the values of per capita personal consumption expenditures and per capita disposable personal income for a given year. A close, positive, linear relationship between the two variables is established. Note that in this diagram the axes are shown with a break in them to indicate that not all the values of the variables between $4,000 and zero are given. Since no *observations* occurred in those ranges, it was unnecessary to provide space for them.

FIGURE 2A-9 A Time Series of Consumption Expenditures, 1955–1985

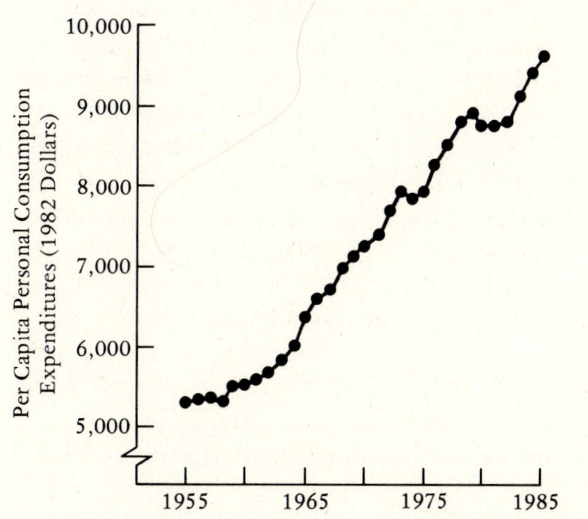

A time series plots values of a single variable in chronological order. The graph shows that, with only minor interruptions, consumption measured in 1982 dollars rose from 1955 to 1985. The data are given in the last column of Table 2A-1.

FIGURE 2A-10 The Difference Between Natural and Ratio Scales

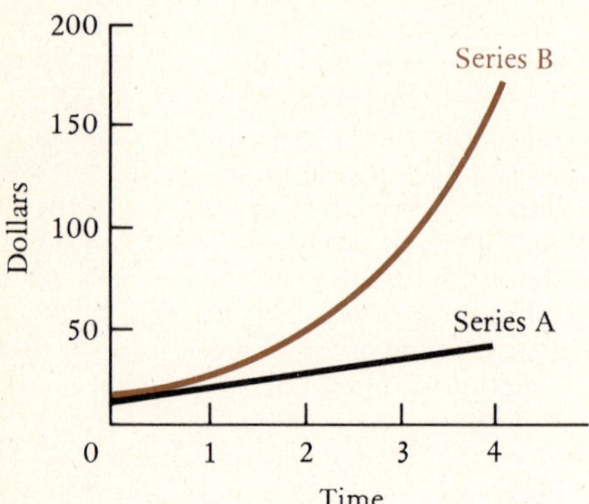

(i) A natural scale

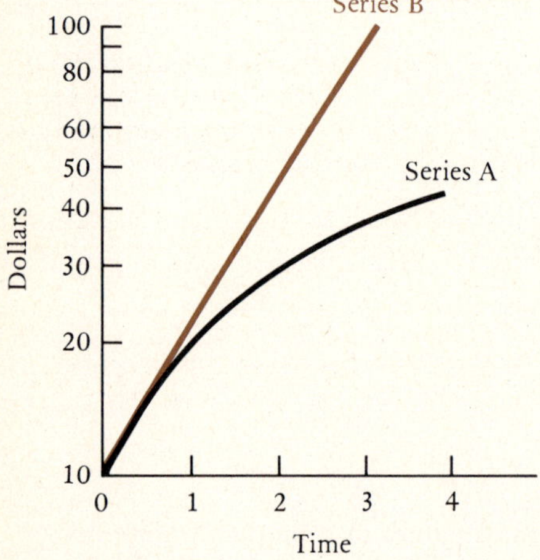

(ii) A ratio scale

On a natural scale equal distances represent equal amounts; on a ratio scale equal distances represent equal percentage changes. The two series in Table 2A-2 are plotted in each chart. Series A, which grows by a constant absolute amount, is shown by a straight line on a natural scale but by a curve of diminishing slope on a ratio scale because the same absolute growth represents a decreasing percentage growth. Series B, which grows at a rising absolute rate but a constant percentage rate, is shown by a curve of increasing slope on a natural scale but by a straight line on a ratio scale.

TABLE 2A-2 Two Series

Time period	Series A	Series B
0	$10	$ 10
1	18	20
2	26	40
3	34	80
4	42	160

Series A shows constant absolute growth ($8 per period) but declining percentage growth. Series B shows constant percentage growth (100 percent per period) but rising absolute growth.

obvious reasons a ratio scale is also called a **logarithmic scale.**

Table 2A-2 shows two series, one growing at a constant absolute amount of 8 units per period and the other growing at a constant rate of 100 percent per period. In Figure 2A-10 the series are plotted first on a natural scale, then on a ratio scale. The natural scale makes it easy for the eye to judge absolute variations, and the logarithmic scale makes it easy for the eye to judge proportionate variations.[6]

Graphing Three Variables in Two Dimensions

Often we want to show graphically more than two dimensions. For example, a topographic map seeks to show latitude, longitude, and altitude on a two-dimensional page. This is done by using contour lines, as in Figure 2A-11. Now consider the function $XY = a$, where X, Y, and a are variables. Figure 2A-12 plots this function for three different values of a. The variables X and Y are represented on the two axes. The variable a is represented by the labels on the curves. Several examples of this procedure occur throughout the book (see, for example, the discussion of indifference curves in Appendix 7B and isoquants in the appendix to Chapter 11).

[6] Graphs with a ratio scale on one axis and a natural scale on the other are frequently encountered in economics. In the cases just illustrated there is a ratio scale on the vertical axis and a natural scale on the horizontal (or time) axis. Such graphs are often called *semi-log* graphs. In scientific work graphs with ratio scales on both axes are frequently encountered. Such graphs are often referred to as *double-log* graphs.

FIGURE 2A-11 A Contour Map of a Small Mountain

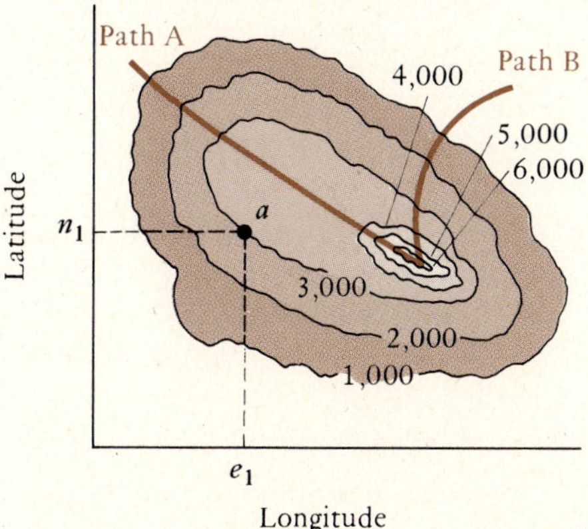

A contour map shows three variables in two-dimensional space. This familiar kind of three-variable graph shows latitude and longitude on the axes and altitude on the contour lines. The contour line labeled 1,000 connects all locations with an altitude of 1,000 feet, that labeled 2,000 connects those with an altitude of 2,000 feet, and so forth. Point a, for example, has a latitude n_1, a longitude e_1, and an altitude of 3,000 feet. Where the lines are closely bunched, they represent a steep ascent; where they are far apart, a gradual one. Clearly, path A is a gentler climb from 3,000 to 4,000 feet on this mountain than path B.

FIGURE 2A-12 Three Variables Shown in Two Dimensions

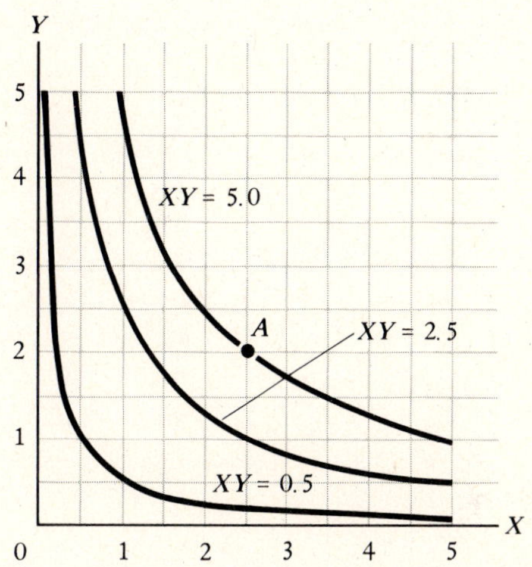

This chart illustrates examples of the three-variable function $XY = a$. The function $XY = a$ is called a *rectangular hyperbola*. The figure shows three members of the family. For example, point A represents $Y = 2.0$, $X = 2.5$, and $a = 5.0$.

3

An Overview of the Economy

The Evolution of Market Economies

The central economic problem of our times—choice under conditions of scarcity—has been with us about 10,000 years. It began with the original agricultural revolution, when human beings first found it possible to stay in one place and survive. Gradually abandoning their nomadic life of hunting and food gathering, people settled down to tend crops that they had learned to plant and animals that they had learned to domesticate. Since that time all societies have faced the problem of choice under conditions of scarcity.

Surplus, Specialization, and Trade

Along with permanent settlement, the agricultural revolution brought surplus production. Farmers could produce substantially more than they needed for survival. The agricultural surplus allowed the creation of new occupations and thus new economic and social classes such as artisans, soldiers, priests, and government officials. Freed from having to grow their own food, these new classes turned their talents to performing specialized services and producing goods other than food. They also produced more than they themselves needed, so they traded the excess to obtain whatever other goods they required.

The allocation of different jobs to different people is called **specialization of labor.** Specialization has proven extraordinarily efficient compared with self-sufficiency for at least two reasons. First, individual talents and abilities differ, and specialization allows each person to do the job he or she can do relatively best, while leaving everything else to be done by others. Second, a person who concentrates on one activity becomes better at it than could a jack-of-all-trades.

The exchange of goods and services in early societies commonly took place by simple mutual agreement among neighbors. In the course of time, however, trading became centered in particular gathering places called markets. Today we use the term **market economy** to refer to a society in which people specialize in productive activities and meet most of their material wants through exchanges voluntarily agreed on by the contracting parties.

Specialization must be accompanied by trade. People who produce only one thing must trade most of it to obtain all the other things they require.

The earliest market economies depended on **barter,** the trading of goods directly for other goods. But barter can be a costly process in terms of time spent searching out satisfactory exchanges. The evolution of money made trade easier. Money eliminates the inconvenience of barter by allowing the two sides of the barter transaction to be separated. If a farmer has wheat and wants a hammer, he does not have to search for an individual who has a hammer and wants wheat. He merely has to find someone who wants wheat. The farmer takes money in exchange, then finds another person who wishes to trade a hammer and swaps the money for the hammer.

By eliminating the need for barter, money greatly facilitates trade and specialization.

The Division of Labor

Market transactions in early economies mainly involved consumption goods. Producers specialized in making a commodity and then traded it for the other products they needed. The labor services required to make the product would usually be provided by the makers themselves, by apprentices learning to be craftsmen, or by slaves. Over the past several hundred years, many technical advances in methods of production have made it efficient to organize agriculture and industry on a large scale. These technical developments have made use of what is called the **division of labor,** which is a further step in the specialization of labor. This term refers to specialization within the production process of a particular commodity. The labor involved is divided into a series of repetitive tasks, and each individual does a single task that may be just one of hundreds of tasks necessary to produce the commodity. Today it is possible for an individual to work on a production line without knowing what commodity emerges at the end of that line!

To gain the advantages of the division of labor, it became necessary to organize production in large factories. With this development urban workers lost their status as craftsmen and became members of the working class, wholly dependent on their ability to sell their labor to factory owners and lacking a plot of land to fall back on for subsistence in times of need. The day of small craftsmen who made and sold their own goods was over. Today's typical workers do not earn their incomes by selling commodities they personally have produced; rather, they sell their labor services to firms and receive money wages in return. They have increasingly become cogs in a machine they do not fully understand or control. Adam Smith, the eighteenth century Scottish political economist, was the first to develop the idea of the division of labor, as discussed in Box 3-1 (p. 47).

Markets and Resource Allocation

The term **resource allocation** refers to the distribution of the available factors of production among the various uses to which they might be put. There are not enough resources to produce all the goods and services that could be consumed. It is therefore necessary to allocate the available resources among their various possible uses and in so doing to choose what to produce and what not to produce. In a market economy millions of consumers decide what commodities to buy and in what quantities, a vast number of firms produce these commodities and buy the factor services that are needed to make them, and millions of factor owners decide to whom they will sell these services. These individual decisions collectively determine the economy's allocation of resources.

In a market economy the allocation of resources is the outcome of countless independent decisions made by consumers and producers, all acting through the medium of markets.

Our main objective in this chapter is to provide an overview of this market mechanism.

The Decision Makers

Economics is about the behavior of people. Much that we observe in the world and that economists assume in their theories can be traced back to decisions made by individuals. There are millions of individuals in most economies. To make a systematic study of their behavior more manageable, we categorize them into three important groups: households, firms, and the government.[1] These groups are economic theory's cast of characters, and the market is the stage on which their play is enacted.

Households

A **household** is defined as all the people who live under one roof and who make, or are subject to others making for them, joint financial decisions. The members of households are often referred to as consumers. Economic theory gives households a number of attributes.

First, economists assume that each household makes consistent decisions, as though it were composed of a single individual. Thus economists ignore many interesting problems of how the household reaches its decisions. Family conflicts and the moral and legal problems concerning parental control over minors are dealt with by other social sciences.[2] These problems are avoided in economics by the assumption that the household is the basic decision-making atom of consumption behavior.

Second, economists assume that each household is consistently attempting to achieve *maximum satisfaction* or *well-being* or *utility,* as the concept is variously called. The household tries to do this within the limitations of its available resources.

Third, economists assume that households are the principal owners of factors of production. They sell the services of these factors to firms and receive their incomes in return. It is assumed that in making these decisions on how much to sell and to whom to sell it, each household seeks to maximize its utility.

[1] Although in basic economic theory we can get away with three sets of decision makers, it is worth noting that there are others. Probably the most important are such nonprofit organizations as private universities and hospitals, charities such as the Canadian Cancer Society, and funding organizations such as the Niagara Institute. These bodies are responsible for allocating some of the economy's resources.

[2] In academic work, as elsewhere, a division of labor is useful. However, it is important to remember that when economists speak of "the" consumer or "the" individual, they are in fact referring to the group of individuals composing the household. Thus, for example, the commonly heard phrase *consumer sovereignty* really means *household sovereignty.*

Firms

A **firm** is defined as a unit that employs factors of production to produce commodities that it sells to other firms, to households, or to government. For obvious reasons a firm is often called a *producer.* Economic theory gives firms several attributes.

First, economists assume that each firm makes consistent decisions, as though it were composed of a single individual. Thus economics ignores the internal problems of how particular decisions are reached. In doing this, economists assume that the firm's internal organization is irrelevant to its decisions. This allows them to treat the firm as the atom of behavior on the production or supply side of commodity markets, just as the household is treated as the atom of behavior on the consumption or demand side.

Second, economists assume that most firms make their decisions with a single goal in mind: to make as much profit as possible. This goal of *profit maximization* is analogous to the household's goal of utility maximization.

Third, economists assume that in their role as producers, firms are the principal users of the services of factors of production. In markets where factor services are bought and sold, the roles of firms and households are thus reversed from what they are in commodity markets: In factor markets firms do the buying and households do the selling.

Government

The term **government** is used in economics in a broad sense to include all public officials, agencies, government bodies, and other organizations belonging to or under the direct control of federal, provincial, and municipal governments. For example, in Canada the term *government* includes the prime minister and his cabinet, the Bank of Canada, provincial premiers and legislators, mayors and city councils, commissions and regulatory bodies, income tax inspectors, judges, the military, and the police force. It is not important to draw up a comprehensive list, but one should have in mind a general idea of the organizations that have legal and political power to exert control over individual decision makers and over markets.

BOX 3-1

The Division of Labor

Adam Smith begins *The Wealth of Nations* (1776) with a long study of the division of labor.

> The greatest improvements in the productive powers of labour . . . have been the effects of the division of labour.
>
> To take an example . . . the trade of the pinmaker; a workman not educated to this business (which the division of labour has rendered a distinct trade), nor acquainted with the use of the machinery employed in it could scarce, perhaps, with his utmost industry, make one pin in a day, and certainly could not make twenty. But in the way in which this business is now carried on . . . it is divided into a number of branches. . . . One man draws out the wire, another straightens it, a third cuts it, a fourth points it, a fifth grinds it at the top for receiving the head; to make the head requires two or three distinct operations; to put it on, is a peculiar business, to whiten the pins is another; it is even a trade by itself to put them into the paper; and the important business of making a pin is, in this manner, divided into about eighteen distinct operations, which, in some manufactories, are all performed by distinct hands, though in others the same man will sometimes perform two or three of them.

Smith observes that even in smallish factories, where the division of labor is exploited only in part, output is as high as 4,800 pins per person per day!

Later Smith discusses the general importance of the division of labor and the forces that limit its application.

> Each animal is still obliged to support and defend itself, separately and independently, and derives no sort of advantage from that variety of talents with which nature has distinguished its fellows. Among men, on the contrary, the most dissimilar geniuses are of use to one another; the different produces of their respective talents, by the general disposition to truck, barter, and exchange, being brought, as it were, into a common stock, where every man may purchase whatever part of the produce of other men's talents he has occasion for.
>
> As it is the power of exchanging that gives occasion to the division of labour, so the extent of this division must always be limited by the extent of that power, or, in other words, by the extent of the market. When the market is very small, no person can have any encouragement to dedicate himself entirely to one employment for want of the power to exchange all that surplus part of the produce of his own labour, which is over and above his own consumption, for such parts of the produce of other men's labour as he has occasion for.

Smith notes that there is no point in specializing to produce a large quantity of pins, or anything else, unless there are enough persons making other commodities to provide a market for all the pins that are produced. Thus the larger the market, the greater the scope for the division of labor and the higher the resulting opportunities for efficient production.

It is *not* a basic assumption of economics that the government always acts in a consistent fashion. Several important reasons for this may be mentioned here. First, the mayor of Montreal, an Alberta MLA, and the minister of finance in Ottawa represent different constituencies, and therefore they may express different and conflicting views and objectives.

Second, individual public servants, whether elected or appointed, have personal objectives (such as staying in office, achieving higher office, power, prestige, and personal aggrandizement) as well as public service objectives. Although the balance of importance given to the two types of objectives will vary among persons and among types of office, both will almost always have some importance. It would be a rare MP, for example, who would vote against a measure that slightly reduced the "public good" if this vote almost guaranteed his defeat at the next election. ("After all," he could reason, "if I am defeated, I won't be around to vote against *really* bad measures.")

Decisions on interrelated issues of policy are made by many different bodies. Federal and provincial legislatures pass laws, the courts interpret laws, the governments decide which laws to enforce with vigor and which not to enforce, the Department of Finance and the Bank of Canada influence monetary conditions, and a host of other agencies and semiautonomous bodies determine actions in respect to different aspects of policy goals. Because of the multiplicity of decision makers, it would be truly amazing if fully consistent behavior resulted.

Another problem arises from the fact that in a democracy legislators and political officials have as important goals their own and their leader's re-election. This means, for example, that any measure that imposes large costs and few benefits obvious to the electorate over the short run is unlikely to find favor, no matter how large the long-term benefits are. There is a strong bias toward shortsightedness in an elective system. Although much of this bias stems from an inability to grasp long-run consequences or a selfish unwillingness to look beyond the present, some of it reflects genuine uncertainty about the future. The further into the future that the economist calculates, the wider the margin of possible error. It is not surprising that politicians, who must worry about the next election, often tend to worry less about the long-term effect of their actions. "After all," they may argue, "who can tell what will happen 20 years hence?"

Markets and Economies

We have seen that households, firms, and the government are the main actors in the economic drama. Their action takes place in individual markets.

Markets

The word *market* originally designated a place where goods were traded. The St. Lawrence Market in Toronto is a modern example of a market in the everyday sense, and most cities have fruit and vegetable markets. Much early economic theory attempted to explain price behavior in just such markets. Why, for example, can you sometimes obtain great bargains at the end of the day and at other times get what you want only at prices that appear exorbitant in relation to prices quoted only a few hours before?

As theories of market behavior were developed, they were extended to cover commodities such as wheat. Wheat produced anywhere in the world can be purchased almost anywhere else in the world, and the price of a given grade of wheat tends to be nearly uniform the world over. When we talk about the wheat market, the concept of a market has been extended well beyond the idea of a single place to which the producer, the storekeeper, and the homemaker go to sell and buy.

Economists distinguish two broad types of markets: **product markets,** in which outputs of goods and services are sold, and **factor markets,** in which services of factors of production are sold.

Economies

An **economy** is rather loosely defined as a set of interrelated production and consumption activities. It may refer to this activity in a region of one country (for example, the economy of the Maritimes), in a country (the Canadian economy), or in a group of countries (the economy of Western Europe). In any economy the allocation of resources is determined by the production, sales, and purchase decisions made by firms, households, and the government.

A **free-market economy** is an economy in which the decisions of individual households and firms (as distinct from the government) exert the major influence over the allocation of resources.

The opposite of a free-market economy is a **command economy,** in which the major decisions about the allocation of resources are made by the government and in which firms and households produce and consume only as they are ordered.

As we saw in Chapter 1, the terms *free-market* and *command economy* are often used to describe economies. No real economies rely solely on either free markets or commands. In practice all economies are **mixed economies** in the sense that some decisions are made by firms, households, and the government acting through markets and some are made by the government using the command principle.

Sectors of an Economy

Parts of an economy are usually referred to as **sectors** of that economy. For example, the agricultural sector is the part of the economy that produces agricultural commodities.

Market and Nonmarket Sectors

Producers make commodities. Consumers use them. Commodities may pass from one group to the other in two ways: They may be sold by producers and bought by consumers through markets, or they may be given away.

When commodities are bought and sold, producers expect to cover their costs with the revenue they obtain from selling the product. We call this type of production *marketed production,* and we refer to this part of the economy's activity as belonging to the **market sector.**

When the product is given away, the costs of production must be covered from some source other than sales revenue. We call this *nonmarketed production,* and we refer to this part of the economy's activity as belonging to the **nonmarket sector.** In the case of private charities the money required to pay for factor services may be raised from the public by voluntary contributions. In the case of production by the government—which accounts for the bulk of nonmarketed production—the money is provided from government revenue, which in turn comes mainly from taxes.

Whenever a government enterprise *sells* its output, its production is in the market sector. But much state output is in the nonmarket sector by the very nature of the product provided. For example, one could hardly expect the criminal to pay the judge for providing the service of criminal justice. Other products are in the nonmarket sector because governments have decided that there are advantages to removing them from the market sector. This is the case, for example, with much of Canadian education. Public policy places it in the nonmarket sector even though much of it could be provided by the market sector.

Private and Public Sectors

An alternative division of an economy's productive activity is between private and public sectors. The **private sector** refers to all production that is in private hands and the **public sector** to all production that is in public hands. The distinction between the two sectors depends on the legal distinction of ownership. In the private sector the organization that does the producing is owned by households or other firms; in the public sector it is owned by the state. The public sector includes all production of goods and services by the government plus all production by government-operated industries that is sold to consumers through ordinary markets.

The distinction between market and nonmarket sectors is economic; it depends on whether or not the producer earns revenue by selling output to users. The distinction between the private and the public sectors is legal; it depends on whether the producing organizations are privately or publicly owned.

Microeconomics and Macroeconomics

As we saw in Chapter 1, there are two different but complementary ways of viewing the economy. The first, *microeconomics,* studies the detailed workings of individual markets and interrelations between markets. The second, *macroeconomics,* suppresses much of the detail and concentrates on the behavior of broad aggregates.[3]

An Overview of Microeconomics

Early economists observed the market economy with wonder. They saw that most commodities were made by a large number of independent producers and yet in approximately the quantities that people wanted to purchase. Natural disasters aside, there were neither vast surpluses nor severe shortages of products. They also saw that in spite of the ever-changing geographic, industrial, and occupational patterns of demand for labor services, most laborers were able to sell their services to employers most of the time.

How does the market produce this order in the absence of conscious coordination? It is one thing to have the same good produced year in and year out

[3] The prefixes *micro-* and *macro-* derive, respectively, from the Greek words *mikros,* "small," and *makro,* "large."

when people's wants and incomes do not change; it is quite another thing to have production adjusting continually to changing wants, incomes, and techniques of production. Yet this adjustment is accomplished relatively smoothly by the market—albeit with occasional, and sometimes serious, interruptions.

A major discovery of eighteenth century economists was that the price system is a social control mechanism.

Adam Smith, in his classic *The Wealth of Nations*, published in 1776, spoke of the price system as "the invisible hand." It allows decision making to be decentralized under the control of millions of individual producers and consumers but nonetheless to be coordinated. Two examples may help to illustrate how this coordination occurs.

A Change in Demand

For the first example, assume that households wish to purchase more of some commodity than previously. To see the market's reaction to such a change, imagine a situation in which farmers find it equally profitable to produce either of two crops, carrots or brussels sprouts, and so are willing to produce some of both commodities, thereby satisfying the demands of households who wish to consume both. Now imagine that consumers develop a greatly increased desire for brussels sprouts and a diminished desire for carrots. This change might have occurred because of the discovery of hitherto unsuspected nutritive or curative powers of brussels sprouts.

When consumers buy more brussels sprouts and fewer carrots, a shortage of brussels sprouts and a glut of carrots develop. To unload their surplus stocks of carrots, merchants reduce the price of carrots—in the belief that it is better to sell them at a reduced price than not to sell them at all. Sellers of brussels sprouts, however, find that they are unable to satisfy all their customers' demands for that product. Sprouts have become scarce, so merchants charge more for them. As the price rises, fewer people are willing and able to purchase sprouts. Thus making them more expensive limits the quantity demanded to the available supply.

Farmers see a rise in the price of brussels sprouts and a fall in the price of carrots. Brussels sprout production has become more profitable than in the past; the costs of producing sprouts remain unchanged while their market price has risen. Similarly, carrot production is less profitable than in the past because costs are unchanged while the price has fallen. Attracted by high profits in brussels sprouts and deterred by low profits or potential losses in carrots, farmers expand the production of sprouts and curtail carrot production. Thus the change in consumers' tastes, working through the price system, causes a reallocation of resources—land and labor—out of carrot production and into brussels sprout production.

As the production of carrots declines, the glut of carrots on the market diminishes and their price begins to rise. On the other hand, the expansion in brussels sprout production reduces the shortage and the price begins to fall. These price movements will continue until it no longer pays farmers to reduce carrot production and to expand brussels sprout production. When all of the adjustments have occurred, the price of sprouts is higher than it was originally but lower than it was when the shortage sent the price soaring before output could be adjusted, and the price of carrots is lower than it was originally but higher than when the initial glut sent the price tumbling before output could be adjusted.

The reaction of the market to a change in demand leads to a transfer of resources. Carrot producers reduce their production; they will therefore be laying off workers and generally demanding fewer factors of production. Brussels sprout producers expand production; they will therefore be hiring workers and generally increasing their demand for factors of production.

Labor can probably switch from carrot to sprout production without much difficulty. Certain types of land, however, may be better suited for growing one crop than the other. When farmers increase their sprout production, their demands for those factors especially suited to sprout growing also increase—and this creates a shortage of these resources and a consequent rise in their prices. Meanwhile, with carrot production falling, the demand for land and other factors of production especially suited to carrot growing is reduced. A surplus results, and the prices of these factors are forced down.

Thus factors particularly suited to sprout production will earn more and will obtain a higher share of total national income than before. Factors particularly suited to carrot production, however, will earn less and will obtain a smaller share of the total national income than before.

Changes of this kind will be studied more fully later; the important thing to notice now is how a change in demand causes a reallocation of resources in the direction required to cater to the new, higher level of demand.

A Change in Supply

For a second example, consider a change originating with producers. Begin as before with a situation in which farmers find it equally profitable to produce either brussels sprouts or carrots and in which consumers are willing to buy, at prevailing prices, the quantities of these two commodities that are being produced. Now imagine that, at existing prices, farmers become more willing to produce sprouts than in the past and less willing to produce carrots. This shift might be caused, for example, by a change in the costs of producing the two goods—a rise in carrot costs and a fall in sprout costs that would raise the profitability of sprout production and lower that of carrot production.

What will happen now? For a short time, nothing at all; the existing supply of sprouts and carrots on the market is the result of decisions made by farmers at some time in the past. But farmers now begin to plant fewer carrots and more sprouts, and soon the quantities on the market begin to change. The quantity of sprouts available for sale rises, and the quantity of carrots falls. A shortage of carrots and a glut of sprouts result. The price of carrots consequently rises, and the price of sprouts falls. This provides the incentive for two types of adjustments. First, households will buy fewer carrots and more sprouts. Second, farmers will move back into carrot production and out of sprouts.

This example began with a situation in which a shortage of carrots caused the price of carrots to rise. The rise in the price of carrots removed the shortage in two ways: It reduced the quantity of carrots demanded, and it increased the quantity offered for sale (in response to the rise in the profitability of carrot production). Remember that there was also a surplus of brussels sprouts that caused the price to fall. The fall in price removed the surplus in two ways: It encouraged consumers to buy more of this commodity, and it reduced the quantity of sprouts produced and offered for sale (in response to a fall in the profitability of sprout production).

These examples illustrate a general point:

The price system is a mechanism that coordinates individual, decentralized decisions.

The existence of such a control mechanism is beyond dispute. How well it works in comparison with alternative coordinating systems has been in serious dispute for over a hundred years. It remains today a major unsettled social question.

Microeconomics and Macroeconomics Compared

Microeconomics and macroeconomics differ in the questions each asks and in the level of aggregation each uses. Microeconomics deals with the determination of prices and quantities in individual markets and with the relations among these markets. Thus it looks at the details of the market economy. It asks, for example, how much labor is employed in the fast food industry and why the amount is increasing. It asks about the determinants of the output of brussels sprouts, pocket calculators, automobiles, and Mother's Pizzas. It asks, too, about the prices of these things—why some prices go up and others down. Economists interested in microeconomics analyze how prices and outputs respond to exogenous shocks caused by events in other markets or by government policy. They ask, for example, how a technical innovation, a government subsidy, or a drought will affect the price and output of beet sugar and the employment of farm workers.

In contrast, macroeconomics focuses on much broader aggregates. It looks at such things as the total number of people employed and unemployed, the average level of prices and how it changes over time, national output, and aggregate consumption. Macroeconomics asks what determines these aggregates and how they respond to changing conditions. Whereas microeconomics looks at demand and supply with regard to particular commodities, macroeconomics looks at aggregate demand and aggregate supply.

An Overview of Macroeconomics

We can group together all the buyers of the nation's output and call their total desired purchases **aggregate demand.** We can also group together all the producers of the nation's output and call their total desired sales **aggregate supply.** Determining the magnitude of these and explaining why they change are among the major problems of macroeconomics.

Major changes in aggregate demand are called *demand shocks,* and major changes in aggregate supply are called *supply shocks.* Such shocks will cause important changes in the broad averages and aggregates that are the concern of macroeconomics, including total output, total employment, and average levels of prices and wages. Sometimes government actions are the cause of demand or supply shocks, while at other times they are reactions to such shocks and are used in an attempt to cushion or change the effects of such shocks.

The Circular Flow of Income

One way to gain insight into aggregate demand and aggregate supply is to view the economy as a giant set of flows. A major part of aggregate demand arises from the purchases of consumption commodities by the nation's households. These purchases generate income for the firms that produce and sell commodities for consumption. A major part of aggregate supply arises from the production and sale of consumption goods by the nation's firms. This production generates income for all the factors that are employed in making these goods.

The grey arrows in Figure 3-1 show the interaction between firms and households in two sets of markets—factor markets and product markets—through which their decisions are coordinated. Consider households first. The members of households want commodities to keep themselves fed, clothed, housed, entertained, healthy, and secure. They also want commodities to educate, edify, beautify, stupefy, and otherwise amuse themselves. Households have resources with which to attempt to satisfy these wants. But not all their wants can be satisfied with the resources available. Households are forced, therefore, to make choices as to which goods and services to buy in product markets that offer them myriad ways to spend their incomes.

Now consider firms. They must choose among the products they might produce and sell, among the ways of producing them, and among the various quantities (and qualities) they can supply. Firms must also buy factors of production. Payments by firms to factor owners provide the factor owners with incomes. The recipients of these incomes are households whose members want commodities to keep themselves fed, clothed, housed, and entertained.

We have now come full circle! The action of this drama involves firms and households interacting with one another.

Payments flow from households to firms through product markets and back to households again through factor markets.

If the economy consisted only of households and firms, if households spent all the income they received on buying goods and services produced by firms, and if firms distributed all their receipts to households either by purchasing factor services or by distributing profits to owners, the circular flow would be simple indeed. Everything received by households would be passed on to firms, and everything received by firms would be passed back to households. The circular flow would be a completely closed system, aggregate demand and aggregate supply would consist only of consumption goods, and macroeconomics would involve little more than measuring the flows of production of and expenditure on consumption goods.

The circular flow is not, however, a completely closed system. First, households do not spend all

FIGURE 3-1 The Circular Flow of Expenditures and Income

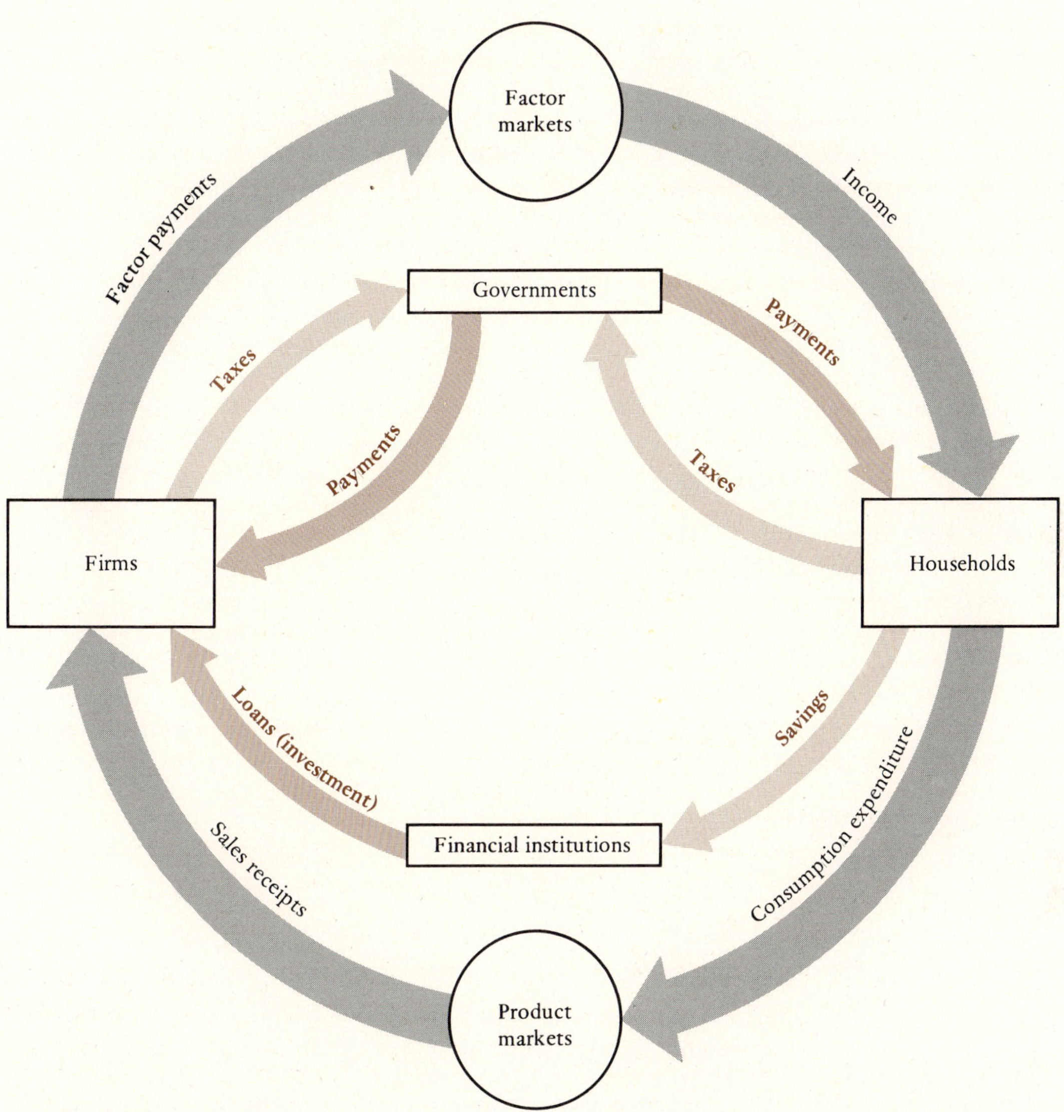

The interaction of firms and households in product and factor markets generates a flow of expenditure and income. These flows are also influenced by other institutions such as governments and the financial system. Factor services are sold by households through factor markets, which leads to a flow of income from firms to households. Commodities are sold by firms through product markets, which leads to a flow of receipts from households to firms. If these primary flows, shown by the grey arrows, were the only flows, the circular flow would be a closed system. But other institutions, such as governments and financial institutions, play roles. For example, governments may inject funds in the form of government payments to households and firms, and banks may inject funds in the form of loans to firms for investment expenditures. Such additions or injections are illustrated by the dark-colored arrows. Similarly, governments may withdraw funds in the form of taxes, and financial institutions may do so by accepting funds that households wish to save. Such leakages or withdrawals are illustrated by the light-colored arrows.

their income. Some of their income is saved, and some goes to governments as taxes. As a result, total household demand for consumption goods and services falls short of total household income. These two *leakages* from the circular flow are shown by the light-colored arrows flowing out of the households in Figure 3-1. As shown in the figure, a third leakage occurs because firms also pay taxes. (Of course, firms may also save, but this leakage is omitted from the figure for simplicity.)[4]

A second reason why the circular flow is not a closed system is that there are elements of aggregate demand that do not arise from household spending. The two main additional elements are investment and government expenditure. A major component of aggregate demand stems from firms that borrow in order to purchase such investment goods as plant and equipment. A further major component of aggregate demand comes from governments—federal, provincial, and municipal. They add to total expenditure on the nation's output by spending on a whole range of goods and services from national defense through the provision of justice to the building of roads and schools. These two major additions to the circular flow of income are shown by the dark-colored arrows flowing into the firms in Figure 3-1. As shown in the figure, a third addition arises because households also receive payments from government. (Of course, households may also borrow from financial institutions to finance current consumption expenditure, but for simplicity this fourth addition is omitted from the figure.)

When any of these elements of aggregate demand changes, aggregate output and total income earned by households are likely to change as a result. Thus studying the determinants of total consumption, investment, and government spending is crucial to understanding the causes of changes both in the nation's total output and in the employment generated by the production of that output.

[4] Additional elements related to international trade are discussed later in the book.

The Next Step

Soon you will be going on to study micro- or macroeconomics. Whichever branch of the subject you study first, it is important to remember that microeconomics and macroeconomics are complementary, not competing, views of the economy. Both are needed for a full understanding of the functioning of a modern economy.

Summary

1. This chapter provides an overview of the workings of the market economy. Modern economies are based on the specialization and division of labor, which necessitate the exchange of goods and services. Exchange takes place in markets and is facilitated by the use of money. Much of economics is devoted to a study of how markets work to coordinate millions of individual, decentralized decisions.
2. In economic theory three kinds of decision makers—households, firms, and government—interact in markets. Households are assumed to maximize their satisfaction and firms to maximize their profits. Government may have multiple objectives.
3. A free-market economy is one in which the allocation of resources is determined by the production, sales, and purchase decisions made by firms and households acting in response to such market signals as prices and profits.
4. Subdivisions of an economy are called sectors. Economies are commonly divided into market and nonmarket sectors and into public and private sectors. These divisions cut across each other; the first is

based on the economic distinction of how costs are covered, and the second is based on a legal distinction of ownership.

5. A key difference between micro- and macroeconomics is in the level of aggregation to which attention is directed. Microeconomics looks at prices and quantities in individual markets and how they respond to various shocks that impinge on those markets. Macroeconomics looks at broader aggregates such as aggregate consumption, employment and unemployment, and rate of change of the price level.
6. The questions asked in micro- and macroeconomics differ, but they are complementary parts of economic theory. They study different aspects of a single economic system, and both are needed for an understanding of the whole.
7. Microeconomics deals with the determination of prices and quantities in individual markets and the relations among those markets. It shows how the price system provides signals that reflect changes in demand and supply and to which producers and consumers react in an individual but nonetheless coordinated manner.
8. The microeconomic interactions between households and firms through markets may be illustrated in a circular flow diagram that traces money flows between households and firms. These flows are the starting point for studying the circular flows of aggregate income that are key elements of macroeconomics.
9. Household purchases of consumption goods generate income for firms whose payments to factors then flow back to the households as income. This circular flow is not a simple closed system because not all income received by households is spent for the output of firms and some receipts of firms are not paid out to households. Also, some payments to firms do not result from the spending of households and some payments to households do not result from the spending of firms. The flows of expenditure in the economy determine total output, total income, and total employment.

Topics for Review

Specialization and division of labor
Economic decision makers
Markets and market economies
Market and nonmarket sectors
Private and public sectors
The price system as a social control mechanism
Relation between microeconomics and macroeconomics

Discussion Questions

1. Suggest some examples of specialization and division of labor among people you know.
2. There is a greater variety of specialists and specialty stores in large cities than in small towns having populations with the same average income. Explain this in economic terms.

3. Define the household of which you are a member. Consider your household's income last year. What proportion of it came from the sale of factor services? Identify other sources of income. Approximately what proportion of the expenditures by your household became income for firms?
4. "It is not from the benevolence of the butcher, the brewer, or the baker that we expect our dinner, but from their regard to their own self-interest. We address ourselves, not to their humanity, but to their self-love, and never talk to them of our necessities, but of their advantages." Do you agree with this quotation from *The Wealth of Nations*? How are "their self-love" and "our dinner" related to the price system? What are assumed to be the motives of firms and of households?
5. Trace the effect of a sharp change in consumer demand away from cigarettes and toward chewing gum as a result of continuing reports linking smoking with lung cancer and heart disease.
6. List some of the decision makers not mentioned in the text that do not fit into the categories of firm, household, and government. Are you sure that the concept of a firm will not stretch sufficiently to cover some of the items on your list?
7. Trace out some significant microeconomic and macroeconomic effects of the enormous increase in the proportion of women choosing to work rather than to stay at home that has occurred over the past two decades.
8. Which, if any, of the arrows in Figure 3-1 would each of the following events affect first?
   a. Households increase their consumption expenditures by reducing saving.
   b. The government lowers income tax rates.
   c. In view of a recession, firms decide to postpone production of some new products.
   d. Consumers like the new model cars and borrow money from the banking system to buy them in record numbers.

PART TWO

A General View of the Price System

4

Demand, Supply, and Price

Some people believe that economics begins and ends with the "law" of supply and demand. It is, of course, too much to hope for "economics in one lesson." (An unkind critic of a book with that title remarked that the author needed a second lesson.) Still, the so-called laws of supply and demand are an important part of our understanding of the market system.

First we need to understand what determines the demands for commodities and the supplies of them. Then we can see how demand and supply together determine price and how the price system as a whole allows the economy to respond to changes in demand and in supply. Demand and supply help us in understanding the price system's successes and its failures, as well as the consequences of such government interventions as price controls, minimum-wage laws, and sales taxes.

Demand

Canadian consumers spent about $300 billion on goods and services in 1986. Table 4-1 shows the composition of this expenditure and how it has changed over 35 years. Economists ask many questions about the pattern of consumer expenditure: Why is it what it is at any moment? Why does it change in the way it does? Why do consumers spend a higher proportion of their incomes on durable goods and a lower proportion on nondurables than they did 35 years ago? Why has the proportion spent on services risen only slightly (from 40 to 42½ percent) in Canada while in the United States it has increased by nearly 50 percent over the same period? Why do Canadians now heat their homes with electricity, oil, and natural gas when 30 years ago they used coal? How have they reacted to the large changes in fuel prices that occurred in the late 1970s and early 1980s? Why do people who build houses in Norway and the Canadian West rarely use brick, while it is commonly used in England and eastern Canada? Why have the maid and the washerwoman been replaced by the vacuum cleaner and the washing machine?

Quantity Demanded

The total amount of a commodity that all households wish to purchase is called the **quantity demanded** of that commodity.[1] It is important

[1] In this chapter we concentrate on the demand of *all* households for commodities. Of course, what all households do is only the sum of what each individual household does, and in Chapters 7 and 8 we shall study the behavior of individual households in greater detail.

TABLE 4-1 Composition of Personal Consumption Expenditures, 1951 and 1986 ***(percentages)***

	1951		1986	
Durable goods		9.2		14.6
Automobile and parts	5.4		7.6	
Furniture and household equipment	2.8		2.9	
Other	1.0		4.1	
Semidurable goods		16.0		10.4
Clothing and footwear	9.1		6.1	
Other	6.9		4.3	
Nondurable goods		34.7		28.2
Food	27.1		11.9	
Electricity, gas, and other fuels	3.0		3.2	
Gasoline, oil, and grease	2.0		3.6	
Other	2.6		9.5	
Services		40.1		46.8
Housing and household services	13.6		18.6	
Health services	2.6		4.9	
Other	23.9		23.3	

Source: Statistics Canada, 13–001, 13–20; Department of Finance, *Economic Review*.

Nondurable and semidurables have declined in relative importance, while durables and services have increased.

to notice three things about this concept. First, quantity demanded is a *desired* quantity. It is how much households wish to purchase, given the price of the commodity, other prices, their incomes, tastes, and so on. This may be different from the amount that households actually succeed in purchasing. If sufficient quantities are not available, the amount households wish to purchase may exceed the amount they actually do purchase. To distinguish these two concepts, the term *quantity demanded* is used to refer to desired purchases, and a phrase such as **quantity actually bought** is used to refer to actual purchases.

Second, *desired* does not refer to idle dreams but to effective demands, that is, to the amounts people are willing to buy given the price they must pay for the commodity.

Third, quantity demanded refers to a continuous *flow* of purchases. It must therefore be expressed as so much per period of time: 1 million oranges per day, 7 million per week, or 365 million per year. For example, being told that the quantity of new television sets demanded (at current prices) in Canada is 10,000 means nothing unless you are also told the period of time involved. Ten thousand television sets demanded per day would be an enormous rate of demand; 10,000 per year would be a very small rate. (The important distinction between stocks and flows was discussed on pages 21–22.)

What Determines Quantity Demanded?

The amount of some commodity that all households are willing to buy in a given time period is influenced by the following important variables. **[2]**[2]

Commodity's own price
Average household income
Prices of related commodities
Tastes
Distribution of income among households
Size of the population

We cannot understand the separate influence of each of these variables if we try to consider what happens when everything changes at once. Instead, we consider the influence of the variables one at a time. To do this, we hold all but one of them constant. Then we let that one selected variable vary and study how it affects quantity demanded. We can do the same for each of the other variables in turn, and in this way we can come to understand the importance of each.[3] Once this is done, we can aggregate the separate influences of the variables to discover what would happen if several things changed at the same time—as they often do in practice.

Holding all other influencing variables constant is often described by the words "other things being equal" or by the equivalent Latin phrase, ***ceteris paribus.*** When economists speak of the influence of the

[2] Notes giving mathematical demonstrations of the concepts presented in the text are designated by colored reference numbers. These notes can be found beginning on page M-1.

[3] A relation in which many variables—in this case average income, population, tastes, and many prices—influence a single variable—in this case quantity demanded—is called a *multivariate* relation. The technique of studying the effect of each of the influencing variables one at a time while holding the others constant is common in mathematics, and there is a specific concept, the *partial derivative*, designed to do so.

price of wheat on the quantity of wheat demanded *ceteris paribus,* they refer to what a change in the price of wheat would do to the quantity demanded if all other factors that influence the demand for wheat did not change.

Demand and Price

We are interested in developing a theory of how commodities get priced. To do this we need to study the relation between the quantity demanded of each commodity and that commodity's own price. This requires that we hold all other influences constant and ask: How will the quantity of a commodity demanded vary as its own price varies?

A basic economic hypothesis is that the lower the price of a commodity, the larger the quantity that will be demanded, other things being equal.

Why might this be so? Commodities are used to satisfy desires and needs, and there is almost always more than one commodity that will satisfy any given desire or need. Such commodities compete with one another for the purchasers' attention. Hunger may be satisfied by meat or vegetables, a desire for green vegetables by broccoli or spinach. The need to keep warm at night may be satisfied by several woolen blankets or one electric blanket or a sheet and a lot of oil burned in the furnace. The desire for a vacation may be satisfied by a trip to the seashore or to the mountains, the need to get there by different airlines, a bus, a car, a train. And so it goes. Name any general desire or need, and there will be at least two and often dozens of different commodities that will satisfy it.

Now consider what happens if we hold income, tastes, population, and the prices of all other commodities constant and vary only the price of one commodity. As that price goes up, the commodity becomes an increasingly expensive way to satisfy a want. Some households will stop buying it altogether; others will buy smaller amounts; still others may continue to buy the same quantity. Because many households will switch wholly or partially to other commodities to satisfy the same want, less will be bought of the commodity whose price has risen. As meat becomes more expensive, for example, households may switch to some extent to meat substitutes; they may also forgo meat at some meals and eat less meat at others.

Alternatively, a fall in a commodity's price makes it a cheaper method of satisfying a want. Households will buy more of it. Consequently, they will buy less of similar commodities whose prices have not fallen and which as a result have become expensive *relative to* the commodity in question. When a bumper tomato harvest drives prices down, shoppers switch to tomatoes and cut their purchases of many other vegetables that now look relatively more expensive.

The Demand Schedule and the Demand Curve

A **demand schedule** is one way of showing the relationship between quantity demanded and price. It is a numerical tabulation showing the quantity that is demanded at selected prices.

Table 4-2 is a hypothetical demand schedule for carrots. It lists the quantity of carrots that would be demanded at various prices on the assumption that all other influences on quantity demanded are held constant. We note in particular that average household income is fixed at $20,000 because later we will wish to see what happens when income changes. The table gives the quantities demanded for six selected prices, but actually a separate quantity would be demanded at each possible price from one cent to several hundreds of dollars.

A second method of showing the relation between quantity demanded and price is to draw a graph. The six price-quantity combinations shown in Table 4-2 are plotted on the graph shown in Figure 4-1. Price is plotted on the vertical axis and quantity on the horizontal axis. The smooth curve drawn through these points is called a **demand curve.** It shows the quantity that purchasers would like to buy at each price. The slope of the curve, downward to the right, indicates that the quantity demanded increases as the price falls.

Each point on the demand curve indicates a single price-quantity combination. The demand curve as a whole shows more.

TABLE 4-2 A Demand Schedule for Carrots

	Price per ton	Quantity demanded when income is $20,000 per year (thousands of tons per months)
U	$ 20	110.0
V	40	90.0
W	60	77.5
X	80	67.5
Y	100	62.5
Z	120	60.0

The table shows the quantity of carrots that would be demanded at various prices, *ceteris paribus*. For example, row *W* indicates that if the price of carrots were $60 per ton, consumers would desire to purchase 77,500 tons of carrots per month, given the values of the other variables that affect quantity demanded, including average household income.

The demand curve shows the relation between quantity demanded and price, other things being equal.

When economists speak of the conditions of demand in a particular market as being given or known, they are referring not just to the particular quantity being demanded at the moment (i.e., not just to one point on the demand curve). Instead, they are referring to the entire demand curve—to the relation between desired purchases and all the possible alternative prices of the commodity.

Thus the term **demand** refers to the entire relation between price and quantity (as shown, for example, by the schedule in Table 4-2 or the curve in Figure 4-1). In contrast, a single point on a demand schedule or curve is the *quantity demanded* at that point (for example, at point *W* in Figure 4-1, 77,500 tons of carrots a month are demanded at a price of $60 a ton).

Shifts in the Demand Curve

The demand schedule is constructed and the demand curve plotted on the assumption of *ceteris paribus*. But what if other things change, as surely they must? What if, for example, households find themselves with more income? If they spend their extra income, they will buy additional quantities of many commodities *even though their prices are unchanged.*

But if households increase their purchases of any one commodity whose price has not changed, the purchases cannot be represented on the original demand curve. They must be represented on a new demand curve, which is to the right of the old curve. Thus the rise in household income shifts the demand curve to the right as shown in Figure 4-2. This illustrates the operation of an important general rule.

A demand curve is drawn on the assumption that everything except the commodity's own price is held constant. A change in any of the variables previously held constant will shift the demand curve to a new position.

A demand curve can shift in many ways; two of them are particularly important. In the first case more is bought at *each* price, and the demand curve

FIGURE 4-1 A Demand Curve for Carrots

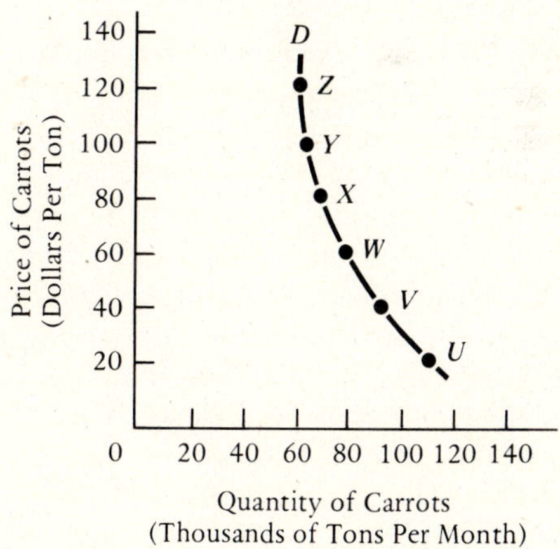

This demand curve relates quantity of carrots demanded to the price of carrots; its downward slope indicates that quantity demanded increases as price falls. The six points correspond to the price-quantity combinations shown in Table 4-2. Each row in the table defines a point on the demand curve. The smooth curve drawn through all of the points and labeled *D* is the demand curve.

TABLE 4-3 Two Alternative Demand Schedules for Carrots

Price per ton p	Quantity demanded when average household income is $20,000 per year (thousands of tons per month) D_0		Quantity demanded when average income is $24,000 per year (thousands of tons per month) D_1	
$ 20	110.0	U	140.0	U'
40	90.0	V	116.0	V'
60	77.5	W	100.8	W'
80	67.5	X	87.5	X'
100	62.5	Y	81.3	Y'
120	60.0	Z	78.0	Z'

An increase in average household income increases the quantity demanded at each price. When average income rises from $20,000 to $24,000 per year, quantity demanded at a price of $60 per ton rises from 77,500 tons per month to 100,800 tons per month. A similar rise occurs at every other price. Thus the demand schedule relating columns p and D_0 is replaced by one relating columns p and D_1. The graphical representations of these two functions are labeled D_0 and D_1 in Figure 4-2.

shifts right so that each price corresponds to a higher quantity than it did before. In the second case less is bought at *each* price, and the demand curve shifts left so that each price corresponds to a lower quantity than it did before.

The influence of changes in variables other than price may be studied by determining how changes in each variable shift the demand curve. Any change will shift the demand curve to the right if it increases the amount people wish to buy, other things remaining equal, and to the left if it decreases the amount households wish to buy, other things remaining equal.

Average household income. If households receive more income on average, they can be expected to purchase more of most commodities even though commodity prices remain the same.[4] Considering all households, we expect that no matter what price we pick, more of any commodity will be demanded than was previously demanded at the same price. This shift is illustrated in Table 4-3 and Figure 4-2.

A rise in average household income shifts the demand curve for most commodities to the right. This indicates that more will be demanded at each possible price.

Other prices. We saw that the downward slope of a commodity's demand curve occurs because the lower its price, the cheaper the commodity is relative to other commodities that can satisfy the same needs or desires. Those other commodities are called **substitutes.** Another way for the same change to come about is for the price of the substitute commodity to rise. For example, carrots can become cheap relative to cabbage either because the price of carrots falls or because the price of cabbage rises. Either change will increase the amount of carrots households are prepared to buy.

FIGURE 4-2 Two Demand Curves for Carrots

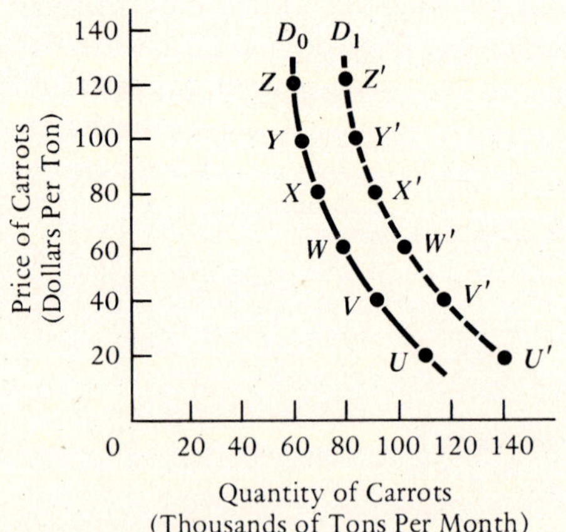

The rightward shift in the demand curve from D_0 to D_1 indicates an increase in the quantity demanded at each price. The lettered points correspond to those in Table 4-3. A rightward shift in the demand curve indicates an increase in demand in the sense that more is demanded at each price and that a higher price would be paid for each quantity.

[4] Such commodities are called *normal goods*. Commodities for which the amount purchased falls as income rises are called *inferior goods*. These concepts are defined and discussed in Chapter 5.

A rise in the price of a substitute for a commodity shifts the demand curve for the commodity to the right. More will be purchased at each price.

For example, a rise in the price of cabbage would shift the demand curve for carrots to the right in Figure 4-2.

Complements are commodities that tend to be used jointly with each other. Cars and gasoline are complements; so are golf clubs and golf balls, electric stoves and electricity, an airplane trip to Calgary and lift tickets at Banff. Since complements tend to be consumed together, a fall in the price of either will increase the demand for both.

A fall in the price of a complementary commodity will shift a commodity's demand curve to the right. More will be purchased at each price.

For example, a fall in the price of airplane trips to Calgary may lead to a rise in the demand for lift tickets at Banff even though their price is unchanged.

Tastes. Tastes have a large effect on people's desired purchases. A change in tastes may be long lasting, such as the shift from fountain pens to ball-point pens or from slide rules to pocket calculators. Or it may be a short-lived fad such as hula hoops. In either case a change in tastes in favor of a commodity shifts the demand curve to the right. More will be bought at each price.

Distribution of income. If a constant total of income is redistributed among the population, demands may change. If, for example, the government increases the deductions that may be taken for children on income tax returns and compensates by raising basic tax rates, income will be transferred from childless persons to households with large families. Demands for commodities more heavily bought by the childless will decline, while demands for commodities more heavily bought by those with large families will increase.

A change in the distribution of income will shift to the right the demand curves for commodities bought most by those gaining income, and it will shift to the left the demand curves for commodities bought most by people losing income.

Population. Population growth does not by itself create new demand. The additional people must have purchasing power before demand is changed. Extra people of working age who are employed, however, will earn new income. When this happens, the demands for all the commodities purchased by the new income earners will rise. Thus it is usually true that:

A rise in population will shift the demand curves for commodities to the right, indicating that more will be bought at each price.

The reasons that demand curves shift are summarized in Figure 4-3.

Movements Along the Demand Curve Versus Shifts of the Whole Curve

Suppose you read in today's newspaper that a soaring price of carrots has been caused by a greatly increased demand for that commodity. Then tomorrow you read that the rising price of carrots is greatly reducing the typical household's purchases of carrots as shoppers switch to potatoes, yams, and peas. The two statements appear to contradict each other. The first associates a rising price with a rising demand; the second associates a rising price with a declining demand. Can both statements be true? The answer is that they can be because they refer to different things. The first describes a shift in the demand curve; the second describes a movement along a demand curve in response to a change in price.

Consider first the statement that the increase in the price of carrots has been caused by an increased demand for carrots. This statement refers to a shift in the demand curve for carrots. In this case the demand curve must have shifted to the right, indicating more carrots demanded *at each price*. This shift will, as we shall see later in this chapter, increase the price of carrots.

Now consider the statement that fewer carrots

FIGURE 4-3 Shifts in the Demand Curve

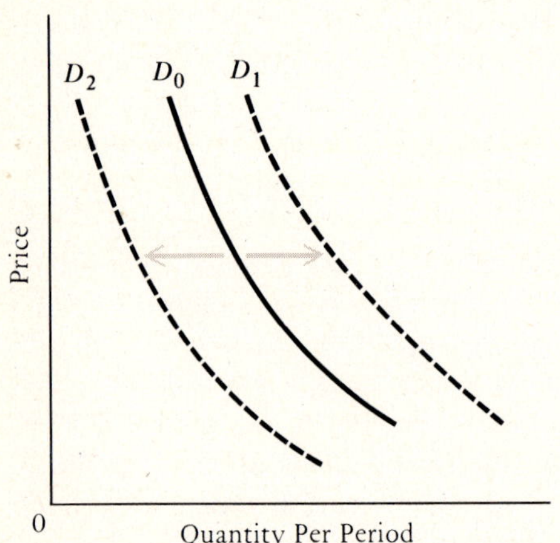

A shift in the demand curve from D_0 to D_1 indicates an increase in demand; a shift from D_0 to D_2 indicates a decrease in demand. An increase in demand means that more is demanded at each price. Such a rightward shift can be caused by a rise in income, a rise in the price of a substitute, a fall in the price of a complement, a change in tastes that favors the commodity, an increase in population, or a redistribution of income toward groups who favor the commodity.

A decrease in demand means that less is demanded at each price. Such a leftward shift can be caused by a fall in income, a fall in the price of a substitute, a rise in the price of a complement, a change in tastes that disfavors the commodity, a decrease in population, or a redistribution of income away from groups who favor the commodity.

are being bought because carrots have become more expensive. This refers to a movement along a given demand curve and reflects a change between two specific quantities being bought, one before the price rose and one afterward.

So what lay behind the two stories might have been something like the following.

1. A rise in the population is shifting the demand curve for carrots to the right as more and more are demanded at each price. This in turn is raising the price of carrots (for reasons we will soon study in detail). This was the first newspaper story.
2. The rising price of carrots is causing each individual household to cut back on its purchase of carrots. This causes a movement upward to the left along any particular demand curve for carrots. This was the second newspaper story.

To prevent the type of confusion caused by our two newspaper stories, economists have developed a specialized vocabulary to distinguish shifts of curves from movements along curves.

We have seen that *demand* refers to the *whole* demand curve. Economists reserve the term **change in demand** to describe a shift in the whole curve, that is, a change in the amount that will be bought at *every* price.

An increase in demand means that the whole demand curve has shifted to the right; a decrease in demand means that the whole demand curve has shifted to the left.

Any one point on a demand curve represents a specific amount being bought at a specified price. It represents, therefore, a particular quantity demanded. A movement along a demand curve is referred to as a **change in the quantity demanded. [3]**

A movement down a demand curve is called an increase (or a rise) in the quantity demanded; a movement up the demand curve is called a decrease (or a fall) in the quantity demanded.

To illustrate this terminology, look again at Table 4-3. When average income is $20,000, an increase in price from $60 to $80 decreases the *quantity demanded* from 77.5 to 67.5 thousand tons a month. An increase in average income from $20,000 to $24,000 increases *demand* from D_0 to D_1.

Figure 4-4 shows the combined effect of a rise in demand, shown by a rightward shift in the whole demand curve, and a fall in the quantity demanded, shown by a movement upward to the left along a given demand curve in response to a change in price.

FIGURE 4-4 Shifts of and Movements Along the Demand Curve

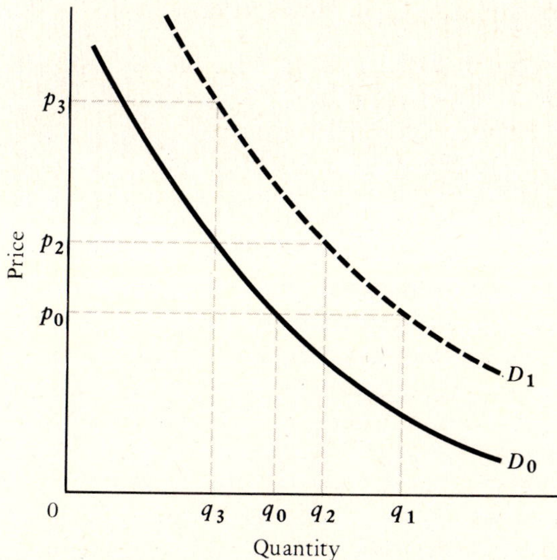

A rise in demand means that more will be bought at each price, but it does not mean that more will be bought under all circumstances. The demand curve is originally D_0 and price is p_0 at which q_0 is bought. Demand then increases to D_1, which implies that at the old price of p_0, there is a larger quantity demanded, q_1. Now assume the price rises above p_0. This causes quantity demanded to fall below q_1. *The shift in the demand curve means that more is bought at each price. A movement upward along the demand curve causes less to be bought in response to a rise in price.* The net effect of these two shifts can be either an increase or a decrease in the quantity demanded. In the figure a rise in price to p_2 leaves the quantity demanded of q_2 still in excess of the original quantity q_0, whereas a rise in price to p_3 leaves the final quantity of q_3 below the original quantity of q_0.

Supply

Canada's private sector produced goods and services worth nearly $300 billion in 1986. A broad classification of what was produced is given in Table 4-4. Economists have as many questions to ask about production and its changing compositions as they do about consumption. The percentages shown in Table 4-4 reflect some of the changes in 35 years.

The table shows the growth of services and the relative decline of primary industries as well as the relatively stable proportion accounted for by manufacturing. Much more dramatic changes have occurred within each of the categories shown in the table.

Economists want to know why. Why did the aluminum industry grow faster than the steel industry? Why, even within a single industry, did some firms prosper and grow, others hold their own, and still others decline and fail? Why and how do firms and industries come into being? All these questions and many others are aspects of a single question: *What determines the quantities of commodities that will be produced and offered for sale?*

Full discussion of these questions of supply will come later (in Part Four). For now it is enough to develop the basic relation between the price of a commodity and the quantity that will be produced

TABLE 4-4 Domestic Product by Industry of Origin, 1951 and 1986 (*percentage distribution*)

Industry group[a]	1951	1986
Agriculture, forestry, fishing, and trapping	15.5	4.9
Mining, quarrying, and oil wells	4.4	6.4
Manufacturing	31.2	22.4
Construction	5.4	8.3
Transportation, storage, and communication	10.0	9.0
Utilities	2.2	3.7
Wholesale and retail trade	11.5	13.9
Finance, insurance, and real estate	9.5	18.1
Other services	10.3	13.3
	100	100

Source: Statistics Canada, 11–003, 13–201.
[a] Excluding government and government enterprises.

Since 1951 agriculture, mining, and manufacturing have all declined in relative importance, while utilities, finance, and services have gained. Construction, transportation, and trade show considerable fluctuation with no evident trend.

and offered for sale by firms and to understand what forces lead to shifts in this relationship.

Quantity Supplied

The amount of a commodity that firms wish to sell is called the **quantity supplied** of that commodity. Quantity supplied is a flow; it is so much per unit of time. Note that this is the amount that firms are willing to offer for sale; it is not necessarily the amount they succeed in selling. The term **quantity actually sold** indicates what they succeed in selling.

When we look at desired purchases and sales, it is clear that households may desire to purchase an amount that differs from what sellers desire to sell. Households cannot, however, succeed in buying what someone else does not sell. A purchase and a sale are merely two sides of the same transaction. Looked at from the buyer's side, there is a purchase; looked at from the seller's side, there is a sale.

Since desired purchases do not have to equal desired sales, quantity demanded does not have to equal quantity supplied. But because no one can buy what someone does not sell, the quantity actually purchased must equal the quantity actually sold.

What Determines Quantity Supplied?

The amount of a commodity that firms will be willing to produce and offer for sale is influenced by the following important variables. **[4]**

Commodity's own price
Prices of inputs
Goals of firms
State of technology

The situation is the same here as it is on the demand side. The list of influencing variables is long, and we will not get far if we try to discover what happens when they all change at the same time. So again we use the convenient *ceteris paribus* technique to study the influence of the variables one at a time.

Supply and Price

Since we want to develop a theory of how commodities get priced, we study the relation between the quantity supplied of each commodity and that commodity's own price. We start by holding all other influences constant and asking: How do we expect the quantity of a commodity supplied to vary with its own price?

A basic economic hypothesis is that, for many commodities, the higher the price of the commodity, the larger the quantity that will be supplied, other things being equal.

Why might this be so? It is because the profits that can be earned from producing a commodity are almost certain to increase if the price of that commodity rises while the costs of inputs used to produce it remain unchanged. This will make firms, which are in business to earn profits, wish to produce more of the commodity whose price has risen and less of other commodities.[5]

The Supply Schedule and the Supply Curve

The general relationship just discussed can be illustrated by a **supply schedule,** which shows the quantities that producers would wish to sell at alternative prices of the commodity. A supply schedule is analogous to a demand schedule; the former shows what producers would be willing to sell, while the latter shows what households would be willing to buy at alternative prices of the commodity. Table 4-5 presents a hypothetical supply schedule for carrots.

A **supply curve,** the graphical representation of the supply schedule, is illustrated in Figure 4-5. While each point on the supply curve represents a specific price-quantity combination, the whole curve shows more.

The supply curve represents the relation between quantity supplied and price, other things being equal.

[5] Notice, however, the qualifying word *many* in the hypothesis. It is used because, as we shall see in Part Four, there are exceptions to this rule. Although the rule states the usual case, a rise in price (*ceteris paribus*) is not always necessary to call forth an increase in quantity in the case of all commodities.

TABLE 4-5 A Supply Schedule for Carrots

	Price per ton	Quantity supplied (thousands of tons per month)
u	$ 20	5.0
v	40	46.0
w	60	77.5
x	80	100.0
y	100	115.0
z	120	122.5

The table shows the quantities that producers wish to sell at various prices, *ceteris paribus*. For example, row *y* indicates that if the price were $100 per ton, producers would wish to sell 115,000 tons of carrots per month.

When economists speak of the conditions of supply as being given or known, they refer not just to the particular quantity being supplied at the moment, that is, not to just one point on the supply curve. Instead, they are referring to the entire supply curve, to the complete relation between desired sales and all possible alternative prices of the commodity.

Supply refers to the entire relation between supply and price. A single point on the supply curve refers to the *quantity supplied* at that price.

Shifts in the Supply Curve

A shift in the supply curve means that at each price a different quantity will be supplied than previously. An increase in the quantity supplied at each price is shown in Table 4-6 and graphed in Figure 4-6. This change appears as a rightward shift in the supply curve. In contrast, a decrease in the quantity supplied at each price would appear as a leftward shift. A shift in the supply curve must be the result of a change in one of the factors that influence the quantity supplied other than the commodity's own price. The major possible causes of such shifts are summarized in the caption of Figure 4-7 (p. 69) and are considered briefly below.

For supply, as for demand, there is an important general rule.

A change in any of the variables (other than the commodity's own price) that affects the amount of a commodity that firms are willing to produce and sell will shift the whole supply curve for that commodity.

Prices of inputs. All things that a firm uses to produce its outputs—such as materials, labor, and machines—are called the firm's inputs. Other things being equal, the higher the price of any input used to make a commodity, the less will be the profit from making that commodity. We expect, therefore, that the higher the price of any input used by a firm, the lower will be the amount that the firm will produce and offer for sale at any given price of the commodity.

A rise in the price of inputs shifts the supply curve to the left, indicating that less will be

FIGURE 4-5 A Supply Curve for Carrots

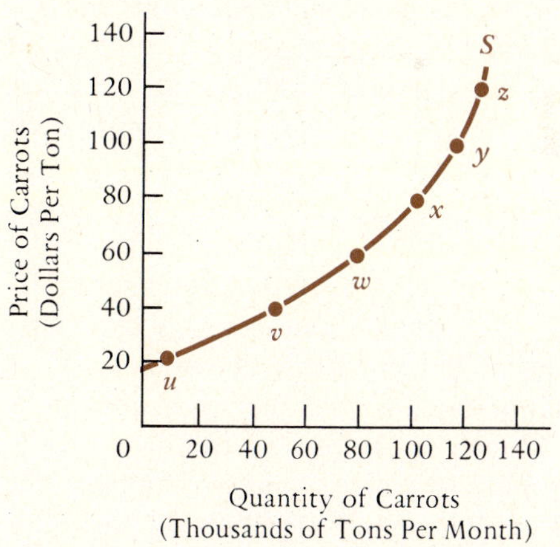

This supply curve relates quantity of carrots supplied to the price of carrots; its upward slope indicates that quantity supplied increases as price increases. The six points correspond to the price-quantity combinations shown in Table 4-5. Each row in the table defines a point on the supply curve. The smooth curve drawn through all of the points and labeled *S* is the supply curve.

TABLE 4-6 Two Alternative Supply Schedules for Carrots

Price per ton p	Quantity supplied before cost-saving innovation (thousands of tons per month) S_0		Quantity supplied after innovation (thousands of tons per month) S_1	
$ 20	5.0	u	28.0	u'
40	46.0	v	76.0	v'
60	77.5	w	102.0	w'
80	100.0	x	120.0	x'
100	115.0	y	132.0	y'
120	122.5	z	140.0	z'

A cost-saving innovation increases the quantity supplied at each price. As a result of a cost-saving innovation, the quantity that is supplied at $100 per ton rises from 115,000 to 132,000 tons per month. A similar rise occurs at every price. Thus the supply schedule relating p and S_0 is replaced by one relating p and S_1.

FIGURE 4-6 Two Supply Curves for Carrots

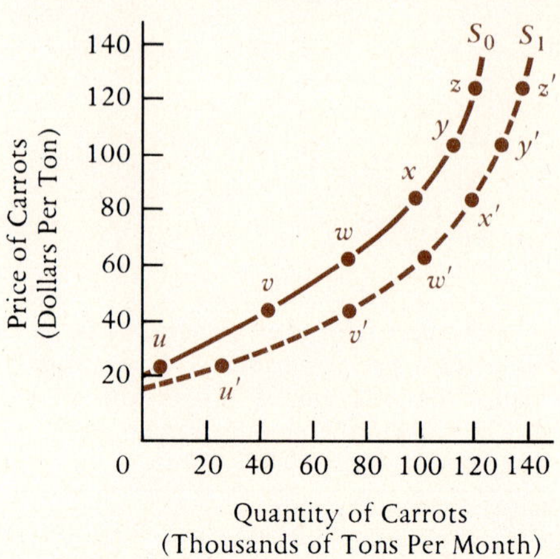

The rightward shift in the supply curve from S_0 to S_1 indicates an increase in the quantity supplied at each price. The lettered points correspond to those in Table 4-6. A rightward shift in the supply curve indicates an increase in supply in the sense that more carrots are supplied at each price.

supplied at any given price; a fall in the cost of inputs shifts the supply curve to the right.

Goals of the firm. In elementary economic theory, the firm is assumed to have the single goal of profit maximization. Firms might, however, have other goals either in addition to or as substitutes for profit maximization. If the firm worries about risk, it will pursue safer lines of activity even though they promise lower probable profits. If the firm values size, it may produce and sell more than the profit-maximizing quantities. If it worries about its image in society, it may forsake highly profitable activities (such as the production of dioxin) when there is major public disapproval. However, as long as the firm prefers more profits to less, it will respond to changes in the profitabilities of alternative lines of action, and supply curves will slope upward.

A change in the importance that firms give to other goals will shift the supply curve one way or the other, indicating a changed willingness to supply the quantity at any given price and hence a changed level of profitability.

Technology. At any time what is produced and how it is produced depend on what is known. Over time knowledge changes; so do the quantities of individual commodities supplied. The enormous increase in production per worker that has been going on in industrial societies for about 200 years is largely due to improved methods of production. Yet the Industrial Revolution is more than a historical event; it is a present reality. Discoveries in chemistry have led to lower costs of production of well-established products, such as paints, and to a large variety of new products made of plastics and synthetic fibers. The invention of transistors and silicon chips has radically changed products such as computers, audiovisual equipment, and guidance-control systems, and the consequent development of compact computers is revolutionizing the production of countless other nonelectronic products.

Any technological change that decreases production costs will increase the profits that can be earned at any given price of the commodity. Since increased profitability lead to increased production, this change shifts the supply curve to the right, indicating an

FIGURE 4-7 Shifts in the Supply Curve

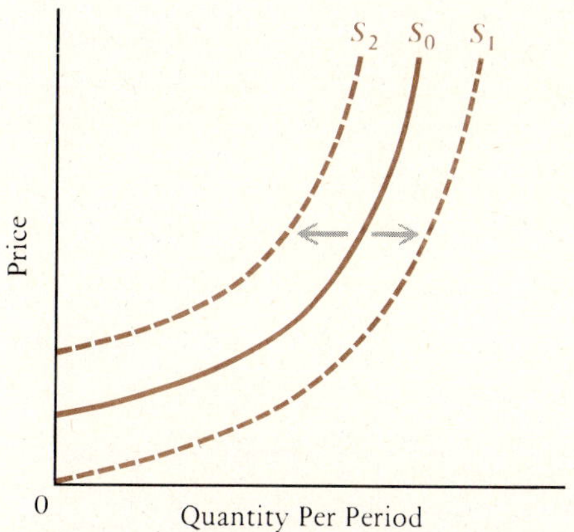

A shift in the supply curve from S_0 to S_1 indicates an increase in supply; a shift from S_0 to S_2 indicates a decrease in supply. An increase in supply means that more is supplied at each price. Such a rightward shift can be caused by certain changes in producers' goals, improvements in technology, or decreases in the costs of inputs that are important in producing the commodity.

A decrease in supply means that less is supplied at each price. Such a leftward shift can be caused by certain changes in producers' goals, or increases in the costs of inputs that are important in producing the commodity.

increased willingness to produce the commodity and offer it for sale at each possible price.

Movements Along the Supply Curve Versus Shifts of the Whole Curve

As with demand, it is important to distinguish movements along supply curves from shifts of the whole curve. The term **change in supply** is reserved for a shift of the whole supply curve. This means a change in the quantity supplied at each price of the commodity. A movement along the supply curve indicates a *change in the quantity supplied* in response to a change in the price of the commodity. Thus an increase in supply means that the whole supply curve has shifted to the right; an increase in the quantity supplied means a movement upward to the right along a given supply curve.

Determination of Price by Demand and Supply

So far demand and supply have been considered separately. The next question is this: How do the two forces interact to determine price in a competitive market? Table 4-7 brings together the demand and supply schedules from Tables 4-2 and 4-5. The quantities of carrots demanded and supplied at each price may now be compared.

There is only one price, $60 a ton, at which the quantity of carrots demanded equals the quantity supplied. At prices of less than $60 a ton there is a shortage of carrots because the quantity demanded exceeds the quantity supplied. This is often called a situation of **excess demand.** At prices greater than $60 a ton there is a surplus of carrots because the quantity supplied exceeds the quantity demanded. This is called a situation of **excess supply.**

To discuss the determination of market price, suppose first that the price is $100 a ton. At this price 115,000 tons would be offered for sale, but only 62,500 tons would be demanded. There would be an excess supply of 52,500 tons a month. We assume that sellers will then cut their prices to get rid of this surplus and that purchasers, observing the stock of unsold carrots, will offer less for what they are prepared to buy.

Excess supply causes a downward pressure on price.

Next consider the price of $20 a ton. At this price there is excess demand. The 5,000 tons produced each month are snapped up quickly, and 105,000 tons of desired purchases cannot be made. Rivalry between would-be purchasers may lead to their offering more than the prevailing price to outbid other purchasers. Also, perceiving that they could have sold their available supplies many times over, sellers may begin to ask a higher price for the quantities that they do have to sell.

Excess demand causes an upward pressure on price.

TABLE 4-7 Demand and Supply Schedules for Carrots and Equilibrium Price

(1) Price per ton p	(2) Quantity demanded (thousands of tons per month) D	(3) Quantity supplied (thousands of tons per month) S	(4) Excess demand (+) or excess supply (−) (thousands of tons per month) $D - S$
$ 20	110.0	5.0	+105.0
40	90.0	46.0	+ 44.0
60	77.5	77.5	0.0
80	67.5	100.0	− 32.5
100	62.5	115.0	− 52.5
120	60.0	122.5	− 62.5

Equilibrium occurs where quantity demanded equals quantity supplied—where there is neither excess demand nor excess supply. These schedules are those of Tables 4-2 and 4-5. The equilibrium price is $60. For lower prices there is excess demand; for higher prices there is excess supply.

Finally, consider a price of $60. At this price producers wish to sell 77,500 tons a month and purchasers wish to buy that quantity. There is neither a shortage nor a surplus of carrots. There are no unsatisfied buyers to bid the price up, nor are there unsatisfied sellers to force the price down. Once the price of $60 has been reached, therefore, there will be no tendency for it to change.

An equilibrium implies a state of rest, or balance, between opposing forces. The **equilibrium price** is the one toward which the actual market price will tend. It will persist once established, unless it is disturbed by some change in market conditions.

The price at which the quantity demanded equals the quantity supplied is called the equilibrium price.

Any other price is called a **disequilibrium price:** the price at which quantity demanded does not equal quantity supplied, and price will be changing. A market that exhibits either excess demand or excess supply is said to be in a state of **disequilibrium.**

Anything that must be true if equilibrium is to be obtained is called an **equilibrium condition.** In the competitive market, the equality of quantity demanded and quantity supplied is an equilibrium condition. **[5]**

This same story is told in graphical terms in Figure 4-8. The quantities demanded and supplied at any price can be read off the two curves; the magnitude of the shortage or surplus is shown by the horizontal distance between the curves at each price. The figure makes it clear that the equilibrium price occurs where the demand and supply curves intersect. Below that price there will be a shortage and hence an upward pressure on the existing price. Above it there will be a surplus and hence a downward pressure on price. These pressures are represented by the vertical arrows in the figure.

The Laws of Demand and Supply

Changes in any of the variables other than price that influence quantity demanded or supplied will cause a shift in the supply curve or the demand curve or both. There are four possible shifts: (1) a rise in demand (a rightward shift in the demand curve), (2) a fall in demand (a leftward shift in the demand curve), (3) a rise in supply (a rightward shift in the supply curve), and (4) a fall in supply (a leftward shift in the supply curve).

Each of these shifts causes changes that are described by one of the four "laws" of demand and supply. Each of the laws summarizes what happens when an initial position of equilibrium is upset by

FIGURE 4-8 Determination of the Equilibrium Price of Carrots

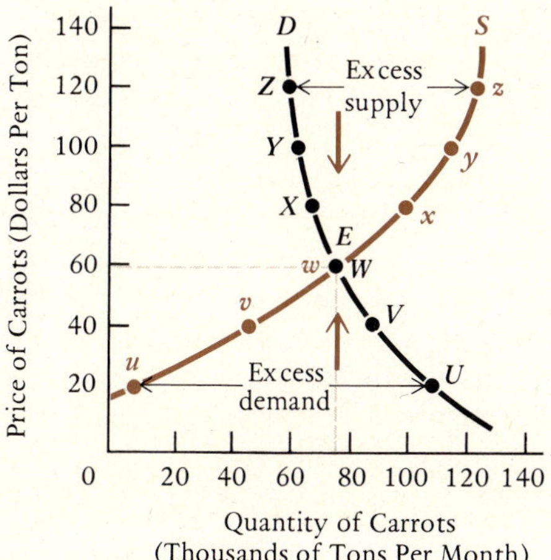

The equilibrium price corresponds to the intersection of the demand and supply curves. Equilibrium is indicated by *E*, which is point *W* on the demand curve and point *w* on the supply curve. At a price of $60 quantity demanded equals quantity supplied. At prices above equilibrium there is excess supply and downward pressure on price. At prices below equilibrium there is excess demand and upward pressure on price. The pressures on price are represented by the vertical arrows.

some shift in either the demand or the supply curve and a new equilibrium position is then established. The sense in which it is correct to call these propositions "laws" is discussed in Box 4-1.

To discover the effects of each of the curve shifts that we wish to study, we use the method known as **comparative statics.**[6] We start from a position of equilibrium and then introduce the change to be studied. The new equilibrium position is determined and compared with the original one. The differences between the two positions of equilibrium must result from changes in the data that were introduced, for everything else has been held constant.

The four laws of demand and supply are derived in Figure 4-9 (p. 73), which generalizes our specific discussion about carrots. Previously, we had given the axes specific labels, but from here on we will simplify. Because it is intended to apply to any commodity, the horizontal axis is simply labeled *Quantity.* This should be understood to mean quantity per period in whatever units output is measured. *Price,* the vertical axis, should be understood to mean the price measured as dollars per unit of quantity for the same commodity. The laws of supply and demand are as follows:

1. **A rise in demand causes an increase in both the equilibrium price and the equilibrium quantity exchanged.**
2. **A fall in demand causes a decrease in both the equilibrium price and the equilibrium quantity exchanged.**
3. **A rise in supply causes a decrease in the equilibrium price and an increase in the equilibrium quantity exchanged.**
4. **A fall in supply causes an increase in the equilibrium price and a decrease in the equilibrium quantity exchanged.**

In this chapter we have studied many forces that can cause demand or supply curves to shift. These were summarized in Figures 4-3 and 4-7. By combining this analysis with the four laws, we can link many real-world events that cause demand or supply curves to shift with changes in market prices and quantities.

The theory of the determination of price by demand and supply is beautiful in its simplicity. Yet, as we shall see, it is powerful in its wide range of applications.[7] The usefulness of this theory in interpreting what we see in the world around us is further discussed in Box 4-2 (p. 74), while its application in an open economy in which international trade is important is discussed in the appendix to this chapter.

[6] The term *statics* is used because we are not concerned about the actual path by which the market goes from the first equilibrium position to the second. Analysis of that path would be described as dynamic analysis.

[7] The laws of demand and supply apply in competitive markets where a supply curve exists and slopes upward. As we shall see later, not all markets satisfy these conditions.

BOX 4-1

Laws, Predictions, Hypotheses

In what sense can the four propositions developed for supply and demand be called "laws"? They are not like acts passed by Congress, interpreted by courts, and enforced by the police; they cannot be repealed if people do not like their effects. Nor are they like the laws of Moses, revealed to man by the voice of God. Are they natural laws similar to Newton's law of gravity? In labeling them *laws*, classical economists clearly had in mind Newton's laws as analogies.

The term *law* is used in science to describe a theory that has stood up to substantial testing. A law of this kind is not something that has been proven to be true for all times and all circumstances, nor is it regarded as immutable. As observations accumulate, laws may often be modified or the range of phenomena to which they apply may be restricted or redefined. Einstein's theory of relativity, for one example, forced such amendments and restrictions on Newton's laws.

The laws of supply and demand have stood up well to many empirical tests, but no one believes that they explain all market behavior. Indeed, the range of markets over which they seem to meet the test of providing accurate predictions is now much smaller than it was 80 years ago. It is possible—though most economists would think it unlikely—that at some future time they would no longer apply to any real markets. They are thus laws in the sense that they predict certain kinds of behavior in certain situations and the predicted behavior occurs sufficiently often to lead people to continue to have confidence in the predictions of the theory. They are not laws—any more than are the laws of natural science—that are beyond being challenged by present or future observations that may cast their predictions in doubt. Nor is it a heresy to question their applicability to any particular situation.

Laws, then, are hypotheses that have led to predictions that account for observed behavior. They are theories that, in some circumstances at least, have survived attempts to refute them and have proven useful. It is possible, in economics as in the natural sciences, to be impressed both with the "laws" we do have and with their limitations: to be impressed, that is, both with the power of what we know and with the magnitude of what we have yet to understand.

Prices in Inflation

Up to now we have developed the theory of the prices of individual commodities under the assumption that all other prices remained constant. Does this mean that the theory is inapplicable to an inflationary world when almost all prices are rising? Fortunately the answer is no.

The key lies in what are called relative prices. We have mentioned several times that what matters for demand and supply is the price of the commodity in question relative to the prices of other commodities. This is called a **relative price.**

In an inflationary world we are often interested in the price of a given commodity as it relates to the average price of all other commodities. If, during a period when the general price level rose by 40 percent, the price of oranges rose by 60 percent, then the price of oranges rose relative to the price level as a whole. Oranges became *relatively* expensive. However, if oranges had risen in price by only 30 percent when the general price level rose by 40 percent, then the relative price of oranges would have fallen. Although the money price of oranges rose substantially, oranges became *relatively* cheap.

In Lewis Carroll's famous story *Through the Looking-Glass,* Alice finds a country where you have to run in order to stay still. So it is with inflation. A commodity's price must rise as fast as the general level of prices just to keep its relative price constant.

It has been convenient in this chapter to analyze a change in a particular price in the context of a constant price level. The analysis is easily extended to an inflationary period by remembering that any

FIGURE 4-9 The "Laws" of Demand and Supply

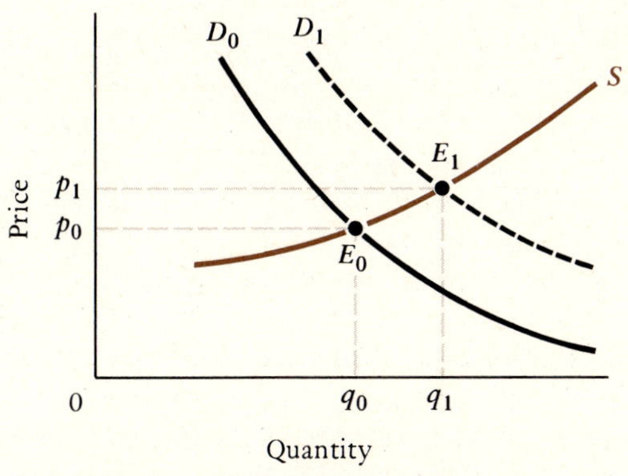

(i) The effect of shifts in the demand curve

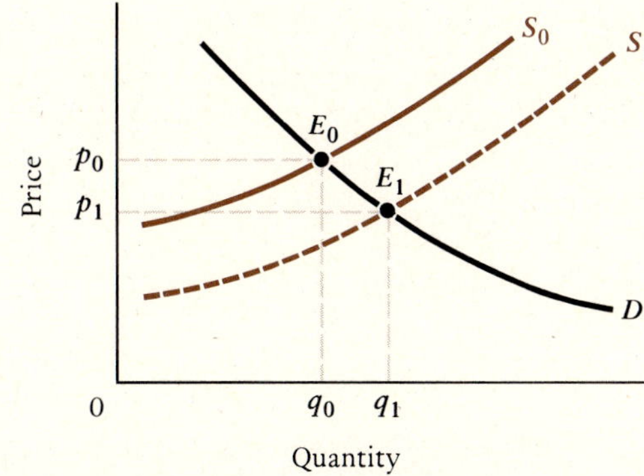

(ii) The effect of shifts in the supply curve

The effects on equilibrium price and quantity of shifts in either demand or supply are called the laws of demand and supply.

A rise in demand. In (i) assume that the original demand and supply curves are D_0 and S, which intersect to produce equilibrium at E_0, with a price of p_0 and a quantity of q_0. An increase in demand shifts the demand curve to D_1, taking the new equilibrium to E_1. Price rises to p_1 and quantity rises to q_1.

A fall in demand. In (i) assume that the original demand and supply curves are D_1 and S, which intersect to produce equilibrium at E_1, with a price of p_1 and a quantity of q_1. A decrease in demand shifts the demand curve to D_0, taking the new equilibrium to E_0. Price falls to p_0 and quantity falls to q_0.

A rise in supply. In (ii) assume that the original demand and supply curves are D and S_0, which intersect to produce an equilibrium at E_0, with a price of p_0 and a quantity of q_0. An increase in supply shifts the supply curve to S_1, taking the new equilibrium to E_1. Price falls to p_1 and quantity rises to q_1.

A fall in supply. In (ii) assume that the original demand and supply curves are D and S_1, which intersect to produce an equilibrium at E_1, with a price of p_1 and a quantity of q_1. A decrease in supply shifts the supply curve to S_0, taking the new equilibrium to E_0. Price rises to p_0 and quantity falls to q_0.

force that raises the price of one commodity when other prices remain constant will, given general inflation, raise the price of that commodity faster than the price level is rising. For example, a change in tastes in favor of carrots that would raise their price by 20 percent when other prices were constant would raise their price by 32 percent if at the same time the general price level goes up by 10 percent.[8] In each case the price of carrots rises 20 percent *relative to the average of all prices*.

In price theory, whenever we talk of a change in the price of one commodity, we mean a change relative to other prices.

If the price level is constant, this change requires only that the money price of the commodity in question rise. If the price level is itself rising, this change requires that the money price of the commodity in question rise faster than the price level.

[8] Let the price level be 100 in the first case and 110 in the second. Let the price of carrots be 120 in the first case and x in the second. To preserve the same relative price we need x such that $120/100 = x/110$, which makes $x = 132$.

BOX 4-2

Demand and Supply: What Really Happens

"The theory of supply and demand is neat enough," said the skeptic, "but tell me what really happens."

"What really happens," said the economist, "is that first, demand curves slope downward; second, supply curves slope upward; third, prices rise in response to excess demand; and fourth, prices fall in response to excess supply."

"But that's theory," insisted the skeptic. "What about reality?"

"That is reality as well," said the economist.

"Show me," said the skeptic.

The economist produced the following passages from recent newspaper articles.

As fiber optics substitute for copper wire, Canadian copper mines cut back output in the face of falling world copper prices.

* * *

The continuing housing boom in Toronto causes soaring costs of accommodation and attracts construction workers back from Alberta.

* * *

Increased demand for macadamia nuts causes price to rise above competing nuts. Major producer now plans to double the size of its orchards during the next five years.

* * *

OPEC countries once again fail to agree on output quotas. Output soars and prices plummet. (1985)

OPEC and allied countries agree on quotas, and prices rise gently. (1987)

* * *

Last summer, Rhode Island officials reopened the northern third of Narragansett Bay, a 9,500-acre fishing ground that had been closed since 1978 because of pollution. Suddenly clam prices dropped, thanks to an underwater population explosion that had transformed the Narragansett area into a clam harvester's dream.

* * *

Increasing third world agricultural production threatens the stability of North American agriculture. In the 1970s North American farm prosperity was built on rising demand due to world prosperity and on falling output in Eastern Europe. Farm experts now worry that the propensity will prove fragile in the face of major increases in world output.

The skeptic's response is not recorded, but you will have no trouble telling which clippings illustrate which of the economist's four statements about "what really happens."

Summary

1. The amount of a commodity that households wish to purchase is called the *quantity demanded.* It is a flow expressed as so much per period of time. It is determined by the commodity's own price, average household income, the prices of related commodities, tastes, the distribution of income among households, and the size of the population.
2. Quantity demanded is assumed to increase as the price of the commodity falls, *ceteris paribus.* The relationship between quantity demanded and price is represented graphically by a demand curve that shows how much will be demanded at each market price. A movement along a demand curve indicates a change in the quantity demanded in response to a change in the price of the commodity.
3. A shift in a demand curve represents a change in the quantity demanded at each price and is referred to as a *change in demand.* The demand curve shifts to the right (an increase in demand) if average income rises, if the price of a substitute rises, if the price of a complement falls, if population rises, or if there is a change in tastes

in favor of the product. The opposite changes shift the demand curve to the left (a decrease in demand).

4. The amount of a commodity that firms wish to sell is called the *quantity supplied.* It is a flow expressed as so much per period of time. It depends on the commodity's own price, the costs of inputs, the goals of the firm, and the state of technology.
5. Quantity supplied is assumed to increase as the price of the commodity increases, *ceteris paribus.* The relationship between quantity supplied and price is represented graphically by a supply curve that shows how much will be supplied at each market price. A movement along a supply curve indicates a change in the quantity supplied in response to a change in price.
6. A shift in the supply curve indicates a change in the quantity supplied at each price and is referred to as a *change in supply*. The supply curve shifts to the right (an increase in supply) if the costs of producing the commodity fall or if, for any reason, producers become more willing to produce the commodity. The opposite changes shift the supply curve to the left (a decrease in supply).
7. The *equilibrium price* is the one at which the quantity demanded equals the quantity supplied. At any price below equilibrium there will be excess demand; at any price above equilibrium there will be excess supply. Graphically, equilibrium occurs where demand and supply curves intersect.
8. Price is assumed to rise when there is a shortage and to fall when there is a surplus. Thus the actual market price will be pushed toward the equilibrium price, and when it is reached, there will be neither shortage nor surplus and price will not change until either the supply curve or the demand curve shifts.
9. Using the method of comparative statics, the effects of a shift in either demand or supply can be determined. A rise in demand raises both equilibrium price and quantity; a fall in demand lowers both. A rise in supply raises equilibrium quantity but lowers equilibrium price; a fall in supply lowers equilibrium quantity but raises equilibrium price. These are the so-called laws of supply and demand.
10. Price theory is most simply developed in the context of a constant price level. Price changes discussed in the theory are changes relative to the average level of all prices. In an inflationary period a rise in the *relative price* of one commodity means that its price rises by more than the rise in the price level; a fall in its relative price means that its price rises by less than the rise in the price level.

Topics for Review

Quantity demanded and quantity exchanged
Demand schedule and demand curve
Quantity supplied and quantity exchanged
Supply schedule and supply curve
Movement along a curve and shift of a whole curve

Change in quantity demanded and change in demand
Change in quantity supplied and change in supply
Equilibrium, equilibrium price, and disequilibrium
Comparative statics
Laws of supply and demand
Relative price

Discussion Questions

1. What shifts in demand or supply curves would produce the following results? (Assume that only one of the two curves has shifted.)
   a. The price of pocket calculators has fallen over the past few years and the quantity exchanged has risen greatly.
   b. As the Canadian standard of living rose over the past three decades, both the prices and the consumption of prime cuts of beef rose steadily.
   c. Summer sublets in Kensington, Ontario, are at rents well below the regular rentals.
   d. Style changes cause the sale of jeans to decline.
   e. Potato blight causes spud prices to soar.
   f. "Gourmet food market grows as affluent shoppers indulge."
   g. Du Pont increased the price of synthetic fibers, although it acknowledged demand was weak.
   h. The Edsel was a lemon when produced in 1958–1960 but is now a best-seller among cars of its vintage.
   i. Some of the first $10 coins minted in Canada to commemorate the Olympics were imperfectly stamped. These flawed pieces are currently worth as much as $1,000.
   j. Do the same for all the examples given in Box 4-2.
2. Recently the U.S. Department of Agriculture predicted that this spring's excellent weather would result in larger crops of corn and wheat than farmers had expected. But its chief economist warned consumers not to expect prices to decrease since the costs of production were rising and foreign demand for American crops was increasing. "The classic pattern of supply and demand won't work this time," the economist said. Discuss his observation.
3. Suppose that compact disk producers find that they are selling more at the same price than they did two years ago. Is this a shift of the demand curve or a movement along the curve? Suggest at least four reasons why this rise in sales at an unchanged price might occur.
4. What would be the effect on the equilibrium price and quantity of marijuana if its sale were legalized?
5. The relative price of personal computers has dropped drastically over time. Would you explain this falling price in terms of demand or supply changes? What factors are likely to have caused the demand or supply shifts that did occur?
6. Classify the effect of each of the following as (i) a decrease in the demand for fish, (ii) a decrease in the quantity of fish demanded, or (iii) other. Illustrate each diagrammatically.
   a. The government of Iceland bars fishermen of other nations from its waters.
   b. People buy less fish because of a rise in fish prices.

c. The Roman Catholic Church relaxes its ban on eating meat on Fridays.
d. The price of beef falls and as a result households buy more beef and less fish.
e. Fears of mercury pollution leads locals to shun fish caught in nearby lakes.
f. It is discovered that eating fish is better for one's health than eating meat.

7. Predict the effect on the price of at least one commodity of each of the following:
   a. Winter snowfall is at a record high in Quebec, but drought continues in Rocky Mountain ski areas.
   b. A recession decreases employment in Windsor automobile factories.
   c. The French grape harvest is the smallest in 20 years.
   d. The state of New York cancels permission for citizens to cut firewood in state parks.
8. Are the following two observations inconsistent? (a) Rising demand for housing causes prices of new homes to soar. (b) Many families refuse to buy homes as prices become prohibitive for them.

Appendix to Chapter 4

The Laws of Demand and Supply in an Open Economy

So far in this chapter we have discussed the determination of price in a single domestic market. But what about all those goods that are traded internationally? A brief look at these may be a useful exercise at this point.

To start we need to define a few terms. An economy that engages in international trade is called an **open economy.** One that does not is called a **closed economy,** and a situation with no international trade is called **autarky.** In this section we examine the simple case of a **small open economy (SOE),** which is an economy whose exports and imports are small enough in relation to the total volume of world trade that changes in the quantities it imports or exports do not influence the prices of goods established in world markets. For many countries and commodities, this is an empirically applicable assumption.

FIGURE 4A-1 **The Domestic Supply and Demand for Wheat (a Typical Exported Good)**

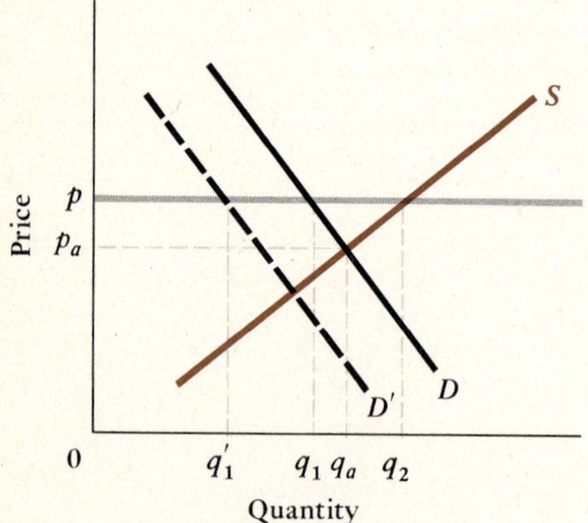

Exports are determined by the domestic excess supply of a tradable good at the world price. D and S are the domestic demand and supply schedules. In autarky, the domestic price would be p_a, and quantity q_a would be produced and consumed domestically. If the world price of wheat, p, exceeds the autarky price, p_a, the country will export wheat. At the world price p, quantity supplied will be q_2, domestic consumption will be q_1, and q_1q_2 will be exported. A fall in domestic demand to D' increases the quantity exported to $q_1'q_2$.

We also divide all goods into two types. **Nontradables** are goods and services that are produced and sold domestically and do not enter into international trade. Their prices are set on domestic markets by domestic supply and demand. **Tradables** are goods and services that enter into international trade. For a small open economy, the prices of tradables, whether the economy imports or exports them, are given, since they are set on international markets.

Nontraded Goods

Equilibrium is where the quantity demanded by domestic purchasers is equal to the quantity supplied by domestic producers. In effect, the pricing of nontraded goods is what we discussed in Chapter 4. Price of nontradables is set by the forces of domestic demand and domestic supply.

Traded Goods

Traded goods prices are set on international markets, while domestic demand and supply determine the quantities that are consumed, produced, and traded at that price.

Exports. Domestic demand and supply would establish a domestic price in the absence of world trade. If, however, the given world price exceeds that domestic price, the good will be exported. Since the small open economy's exports are an insignificant fraction of total world production and consumption of the commodity, the world price will dominate, and the excess of domestic quantity supplied over domestic quantity demanded at that price will be exported. This is analyzed in detail in Figure 4A-1.

Notice that trade raises the price of the exported good above its autarky level. Notice also that the equilibrium is no longer where domestic quantity demanded equals domestic quantity supplied; instead, the equilibrium price is the given world price, and the excess of domestic quantity supplied over domestic quantity demanded is exported.

Imports. If the world price is less than the autarky price, the good will be imported, as shown in Figure 4A-2. Notice that trade lowers the price of the imported good below its autarky level. Notice also that the equilibrium is once again not where domestic quantity demanded equals domestic quantity supplied; price is given by the world price, and the excess of domestic quantity demanded over domestic quantity supplied is met by imports.

For an open economy, equilibrium in markets for traded goods is consistent with domestic demand for those goods being different from domestic supply. If at the world price quantity demanded domestically exceeds quantity supplied domestically, the good will be imported; if quantity supplied domestically exceeds quantity demanded domestically, the good will be exported.

FIGURE 4A-2 The Domestic Supply and Demand for Cotton (a Typical Imported Good)

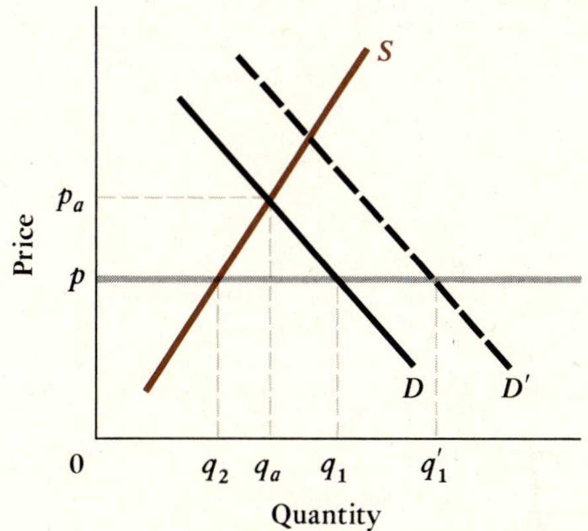

Imports are determined by the excess domestic demand for a tradable good at the world price. *D* and *S* are the domestic demand and supply schedules. In autarky, the domestic price would be p_a, and quantity q_a would be produced and consumed domestically. If the world price of cotton, p, is less than the autarky price, p_a, the country will import cotton. At the world price p, quantity supplied will be q_2, domestic consumption will be q_1, and q_2q_1 will be imported. A rise in domestic demand to D' increases the quantity imported to q_2q_1'.

Effects of Changes in Domestic Supply and Demand

Suppose that domestic residents experience a change in tastes. At the same prices, and values of other variables that influence quantity demanded, they decide to consume less of the exported good and more of the imported good. This decision is illustrated in Figure 4A-1, where the demand for the exported good shifts to the left, and in Figure 4A-2, where the demand for imported goods shifts to the right. At the prevailing world prices, these shifts lead to an increase in the quantity of exports and also to an increase in the quantity of imports.

The effects of a change in domestic supply can also be studied. For example, an increase in domestic wages would increase the cost of producing both the imported and the exported good. This would reduce the quantity that would be supplied domestically at each price; that is, the supply curves shift upward. The reader can verify that *ceteris paribus* this would lead to an increase in the quantity of imports and a decrease in the quantity of exports.

In a small open economy, other things being equal, shifts in domestic supply and demand lead to changes in quantities imported and exported rather than to changes in prices.

Since the economy we are studying is assumed to be small relative to the whole world, these changes in domestic demand or supply do not have a noticeable effect on world prices. The result of shifts in domestic demand or supply is a change in the *quantities* of imports and exports. The assumption that world prices are constant means that, in effect, the domestic economy can buy or sell any quantities of tradable goods it wants on world markets.

Note in conclusion that the laws of supply and demand derived in Chapter 4 still apply, but they need modification to cover the case of the horizontal demand curve faced by the tradable goods produced by a small open economy. Shifts in demand have the effects given in the text, while shifts in supply have all of their effects concentrated on quantities and none on prices.

5

Elasticity of Demand and Supply

The laws of demand and supply predict the direction of changes in price and quantity in response to various shifts in demand and supply. But often it is not enough to know merely whether quantity rises or falls in response to a change in price; it is also important to know by how much.

When flood damage led to major destruction of the onion crop, onion prices rose dramatically. Not surprisingly, overall consumption fell. The press reported that many consumers stopped using onions altogether and substituted onion salt, sauerkraut, cabbage, and other products. Other consumers still bought onions, but in reduced quantities. Were aggregate dollar sales of onions (price times quantity) higher or lower? The data given do not tell, but this is the sort of information that may matter a good deal. A government concerned with the effect of a bad crop on farm income will not be satisfied with being told that prices will rise and quantities consumed will fall; it will need to know by approximately how much they will change if it is to assess the effects on farmers.

Measuring and describing the extent of the responsiveness of quantities to changes in prices and other variables is often essential if we are to understand the significance of these changes. This is what the concept of elasticity does.

Price Elasticity of Demand

Suppose there is an increase in a farm crop, that is, a rightward shift in the supply curve. The two parts of Figure 5-1 show the same rightward shift. Because the demand curves are different, the magnitude of the effects on equilibrium price and quantity are different.

A shift in supply will have different quantitative effects depending on the shape of the demand curve.

The difference may have great policy significance. Consider what would happen if the rightward shift of the supply curve shown in Figure 5-1 occurs because the government has persuaded farmers to produce more of a certain crop. (It might, for example, have paid a subsidy to farmers for producing this crop.)

Figure 5-1(i) illustrates a case in which the quantity that consumers

FIGURE 5-1 **The Effect of the Shape of the Demand Curve**

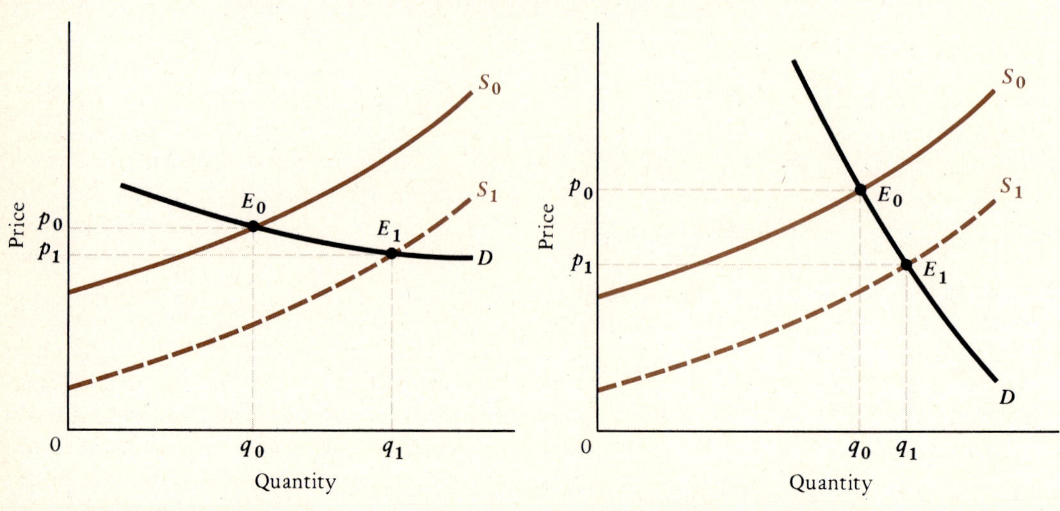

(i) A relatively flat demand curve.

(ii) A relatively steep demand curve.

The flatter the demand curve, the less the change in price and the greater the change in quantity. Both parts of the figure show the same shift in the supply curve. In each part initial equilibrium is at price p_0 and output q_0 and the new equilibrium is at p_1 and q_1. In (i) the effect of the shift in supply from S_0 to S_1 is a slight fall in the price and a large increase in quantity. In (ii) the effect of the identical shift in the supply curve from S_0 to S_1 is a large fall in the price and a relatively small increase in quantity.

demand is very sensitive to price changes. The extra production brings down price, but because the quantity demanded is quite responsive, only a small change in price is necessary to restore equilibrium. The effect of the government's policy, therefore, is to achieve a large increase in the production and sales of this commodity and only a small decrease in price.

Figure 5-1(ii) shows a case in which the quantity demanded is quite unresponsive to price changes. As before, the increase in supply at the original price causes a surplus that brings the price down. But this time the quantity demanded by consumers does not increase much in response to the fall in price. Thus the price continues to drop until, discouraged by lower and lower prices, farmers reduce the quantity supplied nearly to the level attained before they received the increased incentive to produce. The effect of the government's policy is to bring about a large fall in the price and only a small increase in the quantity produced and sold.

In both of the cases shown in Figure 5-1, it can be seen that the government's policy has exactly the same effectiveness as far as farmers' willingness to supply the commodity is concerned (the supply curve shifts are identical). But the effects on the equilibrium price and quantity are very different because of the different degrees to which the quantity demanded by consumers responds to price changes. If the purpose of the policy is to increase the quantity of this commodity produced and consumed, the policy will be a great success when the demand curve is similar to the one shown in Figure 5-1(i), but it will be a failure when the demand curve is similar to the one shown in Figure 5-1(ii). If, however, the main purpose of the policy is to achieve a large reduction in the price of the commodity, the policy will be a failure when demand is as shown in (i), but it will be a great success when demand is as shown in (ii).

The Measurement of Price Elasticity

In Figure 5-1 a measure of demand responsiveness to a change in price could be obtained by comparing the geometrical steepness of the two demand curves because they were both drawn on the same scale. Thus, for any given price change, the quantity changes more on the flatter curve than it does on the steeper one. However, it can be misleading to inspect a *single* curve and to conclude from its general appearance something about the degree of responsiveness of quantity demanded to price changes. You can make a curve appear as steep or as flat as you like by changing the scales. For example, a curve that looks steep when the horizontal scale is 1 inch = 100 units will look much flatter when the horizontal scale is 1 inch = 1 unit as long as the same vertical scale is used in each case.

Instead of gaining a vague general impression from the shape of demand curves, one could note the actual change in quantity demanded in response to a certain price change. But it would still be impossible to compare degrees of responsiveness for different commodities.

Assume that we have the information shown in Table 5-1. Should we conclude that the demand for radios is not as responsive to price changes as the demand for beef? After all, price cuts of $.20 cause quite a large increase in the quantity of beef demanded but only a small increase in radios.

There are two problems here. First, a reduction of price of $.20 will be a large price cut for a low-priced commodity and an insignificant price cut for a high-priced commodity. The price reductions listed in Table 5-1 represent different fractions of the total prices. It is usually more revealing to know the percentage change in the prices of the various commodities. Second, by an analogous argument, knowing the quantity by which demand changes is not very revealing unless the level of demand is also known. An increase of 7,500 pounds is quite a significant reaction of demand if the quantity formerly bought was 15,000 pounds, but it is only a drop in the bucket if the quantity formerly demanded was 10 million pounds.

Table 5-2 shows the original and new levels of price and quantity. Changes in price and quantity expressed as percentages of the average prices and quantities are shown in the first two columns of Table 5-3.[1] **Elasticity of demand,** the measure of responsiveness of quantity demanded to price changes, is symbolized by the Greek letter eta, η. It is defined as follows: **[6]**

$$\eta = \frac{\text{percentage change in quantity demanded}}{\text{percentage change in price}}$$

This measure is frequently called *demand elasticity*. When it is necessary to distinguish it from other related concepts, it may, however, be called **price elasticity of demand,** since the variable causing the change in quantity demanded is the commodity's own price.

Interpreting Numerical Elasticities

Because demand curves slope downward, an *increase* in price is associated with a *decrease* in quantity demanded and vice versa. Since the percentage changes in price and quantity have opposite signs, demand

TABLE 5-1 Price Reductions and Corresponding Increases in Quantity Demanded

Commodity	Reduction in price	Increase in quantity demanded
Beef	$.20 per pound	7,500 pounds
Men's shirts	.20 per shirt	5,000 shirts
Radios	.20 per radio	100 radios

[1] The use of averages is designed to avoid the ambiguity caused by the fact that, for example, the $.20 change in the price of beef is a different percentage of the original price, $1.70, than it is of the new price, $1.50 (11.8 percent versus 13.3 percent). We want the elasticity of demand between any two points (*A* and *B*) to be independent of whether we move from *A* to *B* or from *B* to *A*; as a result, using either original prices and quantities or new prices and quantities would be less satisfactory than using averages. In this illustration $.20 is unambiguously 12.5 percent of $1.60 and applies to a price increase from $1.50 to $1.70, as well as to the decrease discussed in the text. Further discussion is found in the appendix to this chapter.

TABLE 5-2 Price and Quantity Information Underlying the Data of Table 5-1

Commodity	Unit	Original price	New price	Average price	Original quantity	New quantity	Average quantity
Beef	per pound	$ 1.70	$ 1.50	$ 1.60	116,250	123,750	120,000
Men's shirts	per shirt	8.10	7.90	8.00	197,500	202,500	200,000
Radios	per radio	40.10	39.90	40.00	9,950	10,050	10,000

These data provide the appropriate context of the data given in Table 5-1. The table relates the $.20 per unit price reduction of each commodity to the actual prices and quantities demanded.

elasticity is a negative number. (We shall follow the usual practice of ignoring the minus sign and speak of the measure as a positive number, as we have done in the illustrative calculations in Table 5-3.) Thus the more responsive the quantity demanded, for example, radios relative to beef, the greater the elasticity of demand and the higher the measure: 2.0 compared to 0.5.

The numerical value of elasticity can vary from zero to infinity. Elasticity is zero when quantity demanded does not respond at all to a price change. As long as the percentage change in quantity is less than the percentage change in price, the elasticity of demand has a value of less than unity (i.e., less than one). When the two percentage changes are equal to each other, elasticity is equal to unity. When the percentage change in quantity exceeds the percentage change in price, the value for the elasticity of demand is greater than unity.

TABLE 5-3 Calculation of Demand Elasticities

Commodity	(1) Percentage decrease in price	(2) Percentage increase in quantity	(3) Elasticity of demand (2) ÷ (1)
Beef	12.5	6.25	0.5
Men's shirts	2.5	2.5	1.0
Radios	0.5	1.0	2.0

Elasticity of demand is the percentage change in quantity divided by the percentage change in price. The percentage changes are based on average prices and quantities shown in Table 5-2. For example, the $.20 per pound decrease in the price of beef is 12.5 percent of $1.60. A $.20 change in the price of radios is only 0.5 percent of the average price per radio of $40.

When the percentage change in quantity is less than the percentage change in price (elasticity less than one), the demand is said to be **inelastic.** When the percentage change in quantity is greater than the percentage change in price (elasticity greater than one), the demand is said to be **elastic.** This terminology is important, and you should become familiar with it. It is summarized in the first half of Box 5-1.

A demand curve need not, and usually does not, have the same elasticity over every part of the curve. Figure 5-2 (p. 86) shows that a downward-sloping, straight-line demand curve does not have a constant elasticity. A straight line has constant elasticity only when it is vertical or when it is horizontal. Figure 5-3 (p. 87) illustrates three special cases of demand curves with constant elasticities.

Price Elasticity and Changes in Total Expenditure

The total amount spent by purchasers is also the total revenue received by the sellers. How does this revenue react when the price of a product is changed? The simplest example will show that it may rise or fall in response to a decrease in price. Suppose 100 units of a commodity are being sold at a unit price of $1. The price is then cut to $.90. If the quantity sold rises to 110, the total revenue of the sellers falls from $100 to $99; but if quantity sold rises to 120, total revenue rises from $100 to $108.

What happens to total revenue depends on the price elasticity of demand. If elasticity is less than unity, the percentage change in price exceeds the percentage change in quantity. The price change will then dominate so that total revenue will change in the same direction as the price changes. If, however,

BOX 5-1

Terminology of Elasticity

Term	Symbol	Numerical measure of elasticity	Verbal description
A. Price elasticity of demand (supply)	$\eta(\eta_S)$		
Perfectly or completely inelastic		Zero	Quantity demanded [supplied] does not change as price changes.
Inelastic		Greater than zero, less than one	Quantity demanded [supplied] changes by a smaller percentage than does price.
Unit elasticity		One	Quantity demanded [supplied] changes by exactly the same percentage as does price.
Elastic		Greater than one, less than infinity	Quantity demanded [supplied] changes by a larger percentage than does price.
Perfectly, completely, or infinitely elastic		Infinity	Purchasers [sellers] are prepared to buy [sell] all they can at some price and none at all at an even slightly higher [lower] price.
B. Income elasticity of demand	η_y		
Inferior good		Negative	Quantity demanded decreases as income increases.
Normal good		Positive	Quantity demanded increases as income increases:
Income-inelastic		Greater than zero, less than one	less than in proportion to income increase
Income-elastic		Greater than one	more than in proportion to income increase
C. Cross-elasticity of demand	η_{xy}		
Substitute		Positive	Price increase of a substitute leads to an increase in quantity demanded of this good (and less of the substitute).
Complement		Negative	Price increase of a complement leads to a decrease in quantity demanded of this good (as well as less of the complement).

FIGURE 5-2 **Elasticity Along a Straight-Line Demand Curve**

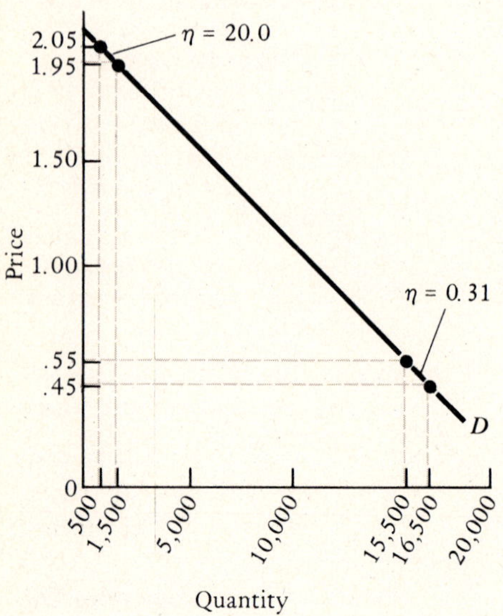

Moving down a straight-line demand curve, elasticity falls continuously. On this straight line a reduction in price of $.10 always leads to the same increase (1,000 units) in quantity. Near the upper end of the curve, however, where price is $2.00 and quantity is 1,000 units, a reduction in price of $.10 (from $2.05 to $1.95) is only a 5 percent price reduction, but the 1,000-unit increase in quantity is a 100 percent quantity increase. Here, elasticity (η) is 20. At the price of $.50 and quantity of 16,000 units, a price reduction of $.10 (from $.55 to $.45) leads to the same 1,000-unit increase in demand. The 20 percent price decrease combines with the 6.25 percent quantity increase to give an elasticity of 0.31.

elasticity exceeds unity, the percentage change in quantity exceeds the percentage change in price. The quantity change will then dominate so that total revenue will change in the same direction as quantity changes (that is, in the opposite direction to the change in price).

Notice what happened to total revenue when the prices of radios, shirts, and beef fell in our example. (The calculations are shown in Table 5-4.) In the case of beef the demand is inelastic, and a cut in price lowers the sellers' revenue; in the case of radios the demand is elastic, and a cut in price raises revenue. The borderline case is men's shirts; here the elasticity is unity, and the cut in price leaves revenue unchanged.

The general relations between elasticity and change in price can be summarized as follows:

1. **If demand is elastic, a fall in price increases total revenue and a rise in price reduces it.**
2. **If demand is inelastic, a fall in price reduces total revenue and a rise in price increases it.**
3. **If elasticity of demand is unity, a rise or a fall in price leaves total revenue unaffected. [7]**

Consider two real examples. When a bumper potato crop in the United States sent prices down 50 percent, quantity sold increased only 15 percent, and potato farmers found their revenues falling sharply. Demand was clearly inelastic. Some years ago, when Salt Lake City's transit authority cut its bus fares by 40 percent for the average journey, the volume of passenger traffic increased from 4.4 million to 14 million journeys within two years, and revenues rose sharply. Demand was clearly elastic.

What Determines Elasticity of Demand?

Table 5-5 (p. 88) shows some measured elasticities of demand. Evidently, they can vary considerably. The main determinant of elasticity is the availability of substitutes. Some commodities, such as margarine, cabbage, lamb, and Fords, have quite close substitutes—butter, other green vegetables, beef, and similar makes of cars. A change in the price of these commodities, *the prices of the substitutes remaining constant,* can be expected to cause much substitution. A fall in price leads consumers to buy more of the commodity and less of the substitutes, and a rise in price leads consumers to buy less of the commodity and more of the substitutes. More broadly defined commodities, such as all foods, all clothing, cigarettes, and gasoline, have few if any satisfactory substitutes. A rise in their price can be expected to cause a smaller fall in quantity demanded than would be the case if close substitutes were available.

FIGURE 5-3 Three Demand Curves

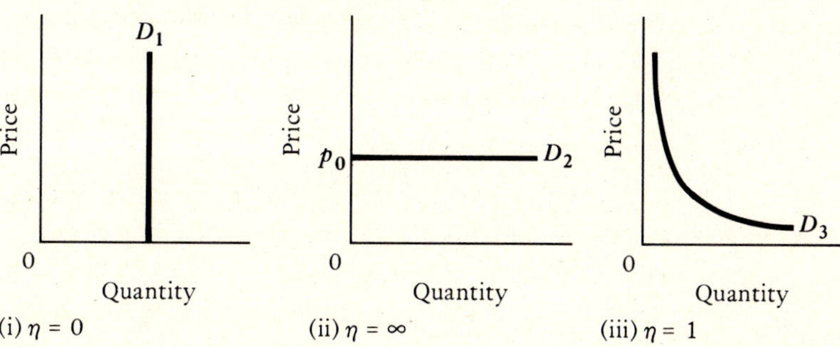

Each of these demand curves has constant elasticity. D_1 has *zero elasticity:* The quantity demanded does not change at all when price changes. D_2 has *infinite elasticity at the price* p_0: A small price increase from p_0 decreases quantity demanded from an indefinitely large amount to zero. D_3 has *unit elasticity:* A given percentage increase in price brings an equal percentage decrease in quantity demanded at all points on the curve.

A commodity with close substitutes tends to have an elastic demand, one with no close substitutes an inelastic demand.

Closeness of substitutes—and thus measured elasticity—depends both on how the commodity is defined and on the time period. This is explored in the following sections.

Definition of the Commodity

Food is a necessity of life. Thus, for food taken as a whole, demand is inelastic over a large price range. It does not follow, however, that any one food, such as white bread or beef, is a necessity in the same sense. Individual foods can have quite elastic demands, and they frequently do. This is because any one food product usually has many other closely related food products that can easily be substituted for it on most households' menus.

Durable goods provide a similar example. Durables as a whole are less elastic than individual kinds of durable goods. For example, when the price of television sets rises, many households may replace their lawnmower or their vacuum cleaner instead of buying that extra television set. Thus, while their purchases of television sets fall, their total purchases of durables do not.

Because most specific manufactured goods have close substitutes, studies show they tend to have price-elastic demand. Millinery, for example, has been estimated to have an elasticity of 3.0. In contrast, clothing in general tends to be inelastic.

TABLE 5-4 Changes in Total Revenue (Total Expenditure) for the Example of Table 5-2

Commodity	Price × quantity (original prices and quantities)	Price × quantity (new prices and quantities)	Change in revenue (expenditure)	Elasticity of demand from Table 5-3
Beef	$ 197,625	$ 185,625	−$12,000	0.5
Men's shirts	1,599,750	1,599,750	0	1.0
Radios	398,995	400,995	+ 2,000	2.0

Whether revenue increases or decreases in response to a price cut depends on whether demand is elastic or inelastic. The $197,625 figure is the product of the original price of beef ($1.70) and the original quantity (116,250 pounds); $185,625 is the product of the new price ($1.50) and quantity (123,750), and so on.

TABLE 5-5 Estimated Price Elasticities of Demand[a] ***(selected commodities)***

Demand significantly inelastic (less than 0.9)	
Apples (Canada)	0.1
Potatoes	0.3
Sugar	0.3
Public transportation	0.4
All foods	0.4
Cigarettes	0.5
Gasoline	0.6
All clothing	0.6
Consumer durables	0.8
Demand of close to unit elasticity (between 0.9 and 1.1)	
Beef	
Beer	
Marijuana	
Demand significantly elastic (more than 1.1)	
Furniture	1.2
Electricity	1.3
Lamb and mutton (U.K.)	1.5
Automobiles	2.1
Millinery	3.0

[a] For the United States except where noted.

The wide range of price elasticities is illustrated by these selected measures. These elasticities, from various studies, are representative of literally hundreds of existing estimates. Explanations of some of the differences are discussed in the text.

Any one of a group of related products will tend to have an elastic demand, even though the demand for the group as a whole may be inelastic.

Long-Run and Short-Run Elasticity of Demand

Because it takes time to develop satisfactory substitutes, a demand that is inelastic in the short run may prove elastic when enough time has passed. For example, when cheap electric power was first brought to many rural areas in the 1930s, few households were wired for electricity. The initial measurements showed demand for electricity to be very inelastic. Some commentators even argued that it was foolish to invest so much money in bringing cheap electricity to farmers because they did not buy it even at low prices. But gradually rural households and farms became electrified and purchased appliances, and elasticity steadily increased.

Petroleum provides a more recent example. When the first OPEC oil price shock occurred in the mid 1970s, the short-run demand for oil proved highly inelastic. Large price increases were met in the short run by very small reductions in quantity demanded. In this case the short run lasted for several years. Gradually, however, the high price of petroleum products led to such adjustments as the development of smaller, more fuel-efficient cars, economizing on heating oil by installing more efficient insulation, and replacement of fuel oil in many industrial processes by such other power sources as coal and hydroelectricity. The long-run elasticity of demand, relating the change in price to the change in quantity demanded after all adjustments were made, turned out to be well in excess of one, although the long-run adjustments took as much as a decade to work out.

The degree of response to a price change, and thus the measured price elasticity of demand, will tend to be greater the longer the time span over which adjustments can take place.

Because the elasticity of demand for a commodity varies over time as consumers adjust their habits and substitutes are developed, the demand curve also changes; hence a distinction can be made between short-run and long-run demand curves. Every demand curve shows the response of consumer demand to a change in price. For such commodities as cornflakes and pillowcases, the full response occurs quickly, and there is little reason to worry about longer-term effects. But other commodities are typically used in connection with highly durable appliances or machines. A change in price of, say, electricity and gasoline may not have its major effect until the stock of appliances and machines using these commodities has been adjusted. This adjustment may take a long time to occur.

For commodities whose substitutes are developed over a period of time, it is helpful to identify two kinds of demand curve. A *short-run demand curve* shows the response of quantity demanded to a change in price for a given structure of the durable goods that use the commodity and for the existing sets of substitute commodities. A different short-run demand curve will exist for each such structure.

The *long-run demand curve* shows the response of quantity demanded to a change in price after enough time has passed to assure that all adjustments to the changed price have occurred. The relation between long-run and short-run demand curves is shown in Figure 5-4. Suggested in the discussion of elasticity is the principal conclusion:

The long-run demand curve for a commodity will tend to be substantially more elastic than any of the short-run demand curves.

The importance of this distinction will be evident in the chapters that follow.

FIGURE 5-4 Short-Run and Long-Run Demand Curves

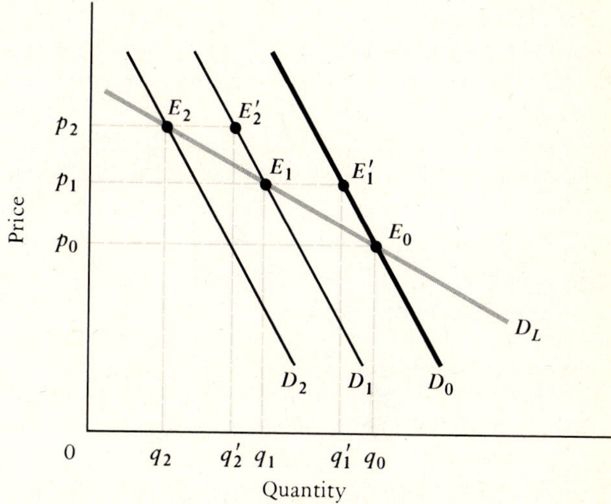

The long-run demand curve is more elastic than the short-run curves. D_L is a long-run demand curve. Suppose consumers are fully adjusted to price p_0. Equilibrium is then at E_0, with quantity demanded q_0. Now suppose price rises to p_1. In the short run consumers will react along the short-run demand curve D_0 and reduce consumption to q_1'. Once time has permitted the full range of adjustments to price p_1, however, a new equilibrium at E_1 will be reached with quantity q_1, leading to a new short-run demand curve D_1. A further rise in price to p_2 would lead first to a short-run equilibrium at E_2' but eventually to a new long-run equilibrium at E_2. The screened long-run demand curve is more elastic than the short-run curves.

Other Demand Elasticities

Income Elasticity of Demand

One of the most important determinants of demand is the income of the potential customers. When the Food and Agricultural Organization (FAO) of the United Nations wants to estimate the future demand for some crop, it needs to know by how much world income will grow and how much of that additional income will be spent on the particular foodstuff. For example, as a nation gets richer, its consumption patterns change, with relatively more being spent on meat and relatively less on staples such as rice and potatoes.

The responsiveness of demand to changes in income is termed **income elasticity of demand** and may be symbolized η_y.

$$\eta_y = \frac{\textbf{percentage change in quantity demanded}}{\textbf{percentage change in income}}$$

For most goods, increases in income lead to increases in demand, and income elasticity will be positive. These are called **normal goods.** Goods for which consumption decreases in response to a rise in income have negative income elasticities and are called **inferior goods.**

The income elasticity of normal goods may be greater than unity (elastic) or less than unity (inelastic), depending on whether the percentage change in the quantity demanded is greater or less than the percentage change in income that brought it about. It is also common to use the terms *income-elastic* and *income-inelastic* to refer to income elasticities of greater or less than unity. (See Box 5-1 for further discussion of elasticity terminology.)

The reaction of demand to changes in income is extremely important. We know that in most Western countries economic growth has caused the level of income to double every 20 to 30 years over a sustained period of at least a century. This rise in income is shared to some extent by most citizens. As they find their incomes increasing, they increase their demands for most commodities. But the demands for some commodities, such as food and basic clothing, will not increase much, while the demands for other commodities increase rapidly. In developing countries, such as Ireland and Mexico, the demand for durable goods is increasing most rapidly as household incomes rise, while in the United States for some time it is the demand for services that has been rising most rapidly. Canada now seems to be entering the stage where the largest percentage responses to income increases occur in the demand for services rather than for durables. The uneven impact of the growth of income on the demands for different commodities has important effects on the economy and groups in it, and these will be studied at several different points in this book, beginning with the discussion of agriculture in Chapter 6.

TABLE 5-6 Estimated Income Elasticities of Demand[a] *(selected commodities)*

Inferior goods (negative income elasticities)	
Whole milk	−0.3
Starchy roots	−0.2
Inelastic normal goods (0.0 to 1.0)	
Coffee (U.S.)	0.0
Wine (France)	0.1
Vegetables	0.2
All food (U.S.)	0.2
Poultry	0.3
Beef and veal	0.4
Housing (U.S.)	0.6
Cigarettes (U.S.)	0.8
Elastic normal goods (greater than 1.0)	
Gasoline (U.S.)	1.1
Wine (U.S.)	1.4
Cream (U.K.)	1.7
Wine	1.8
Consumer durables	1.8
Poultry (Sri Lanka)	2.0
Restaurant meals (U.K.)	2.4

[a] For Canada except where noted.

Income elasticities vary widely across commodities and sometimes across countries. The basic source of food estimates by country is the FAO, but many individual studies have been made. Explanations of some of the differences are discussed in the text.

What Determines Income Elasticity?

The variations in income elasticities shown in Table 5-6 suggest that the more basic or staple a commodity, the lower its income elasticity. Food as a whole has an income elasticity of 0.2, consumer durables of 1.8. In Canada such starchy roots as potatoes are inferior goods; their quantity consumed falls as income rises.

Does the distinction between luxuries and necessities help to explain differences in income elasticities? The table suggests that it does. The case of meals eaten away from home is one example. Such meals are almost always more expensive, calorie for calorie, than meals prepared at home. It would thus be expected that at lower ranges of income restaurant meals would be regarded as an expensive luxury, but the demand for them would expand substantially as households became richer. This is in fact what happens.

Does this mean that the market demand for the foodstuffs that appear on restaurant menus will also have high income elasticities? Generally the answer is no. When a household eats out rather than preparing meals at home, the main change is not in what is eaten but in who prepares it. The additional expenditure on "food" goes mainly to pay cooks and waiters and to yield a return on the restaurateur's capital. Thus when a household expands its expenditure on restaurant food by 2.4 percent in response to a 1 percent rise in its income, most of the extra expenditure on "food" goes to workers in service industries; little, if any, finds its way into the pockets of farmers. Here is a striking example of the general tendency for households to spend a rising proportion of their incomes on services as their incomes rise and a lower proportion on foodstuffs.

The more basic an item in the consumption pattern of households, the lower its income elasticity.

So far we have focused on differences in income elasticities among commodities. However, income elasticities for any one commodity also vary with the level of a household's income. When incomes are low, households may eat almost no meat and consume lots of starchy foods such as bread and potatoes; at higher income levels they may eat the cheaper cuts of meat and more green vegetables along with their bread and potatoes; at yet higher levels they are likely to eat more (and more expensive) meat, to substitute frozen for canned vegetables, and to eat a greater variety of foods.

What is true of individual households is also true of countries. Empirical studies show that for different countries at comparable stages of economic development, income elasticities are similar. But the countries of the world are at various stages of economic development and so have widely different income elasticities for the same products. Notice in Table 5-6 the different income elasticity of poultry in Canada, where it is a standard item of consumption, and in Sri Lanka, where it is a luxury.

Graphical Representation

Increases in income shift the demand curve for a normal good to the right and for an inferior good to the left. Figure 5-5 shows a different kind of graph, an **income-consumption curve.** The curve resembles an ordinary demand curve in one respect: It shows the relation of quantity demanded to one variable, *ceteris paribus*. The variable, however, is not price but household income. (An increase in the price of the commodity, incomes remaining constant, would shift the curves shown in Figure 5-5 downward.)

The figure shows three different patterns of income elasticity. Goods that consumers regard as necessities will have high income elasticities at low levels of income, but their income elasticities will become low beyond some income level. The obvious reason is that as incomes rise, households are able to devote a smaller proportion of their incomes to meeting basic needs and a larger proportion to buying things they have always wanted but could not afford. Some of the commodities that were necessities at low income levels may even become inferior goods at higher incomes. So-called luxury goods will not tend to be purchased at low levels of income but will have high income elasticities once incomes rise enough to permit households to sample the better things of life available to them.[2]

Cross-Elasticity of Demand

The responsiveness of demand to changes in the prices of other commodities is called **cross-elasticity of demand.** It is often denoted η_{xy} and defined as

$$\eta_{xy} = \frac{\text{percentage change in quantity demanded of one good (X)}}{\text{percentage change in price of another good (Y)}}$$

Cross-elasticity can vary from minus infinity to plus infinity. Complementary commodities such as cars and gasoline have negative cross-elasticities. A large rise in the price of gasoline will lead (as it did in Canada in the 1970s) to a decline in the demand for cars as some people decided to do without a car and others decided not to buy a second (or third) car. Substitute commodities, such as cars and public transport, have positive cross-elasticities. A large rise in the price of cars (relative to public transport) would lead to a rise in the demand for public transport as some people shifted from cars to public transport.

Measures of cross-elasticity sometimes prove helpful in defining whether producers of similar products are in competition with each other. For example, glass bottles and tin cans have a high cross-elasticity of demand. The producer of bottles is thus in competition with the producer of cans. If the bottle company raises its price, it will lose substantial sales to the can producer. Men's shoes and women's

[2] In Figure 5-5, in contrast to the ordinary demand curve, quantity demanded is on the vertical axis. This follows the usual practice of putting the to-be-explained variable (called the *dependent variable*) on the vertical axis and the explanatory variable (called the *independent variable*) on the horizontal axis. It is the ordinary demand curve that has the axes "backward." This practice dates to Alfred Marshall's *Principles of Economics* (1890), the classic that is one of the foundation stones of modern price theory. [8] For better or worse, Marshall's scheme is now used by everybody, although mathematicians never fail to wonder at this further example of the odd ways of economists.

FIGURE 5-5 Curves Relating Income to Consumption of Different Commodities

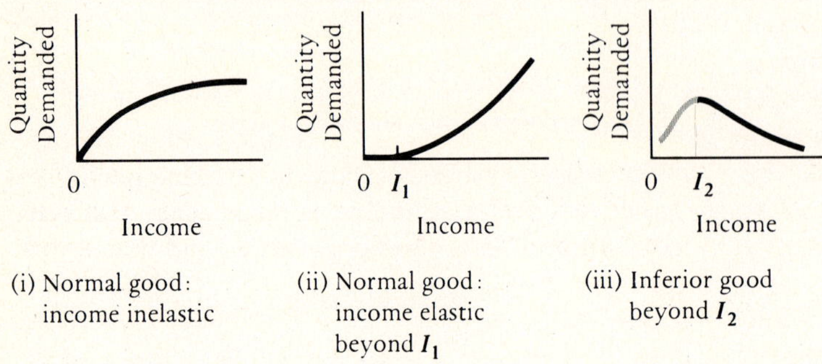

Different shapes of the curve relating quantity demanded to income correspond to different ranges of income elasticity. Normal goods have rising curves; inferior goods have falling curves. Many different patterns of income elasticity have been observed. The good in (i) is a typical normal good that is a necessity. It is purchased at all levels of income; even at high levels some fraction of extra income is spent on it, although this fraction steadily decreases. The good in (ii) is a luxury good that is income-elastic beyond income I_1. The good in (iii) is a necessity at low incomes that becomes an inferior good for incomes beyond I_2.

shoes have a low cross-elasticity. A producer of men's shoes is not in close competition with a producer of women's shoes. If the former raises its price, it will not lose many sales to the latter. This kind of knowledge has been important in anticombines investigations where the issue was whether a firm in one industry was or was not in active competition with firms in another industry. Whether waxed paper and plastic wrap or aluminum cable and copper cable are or are not substitutes may determine questions of monopoly under the law. The positive or negative sign and the size of cross-elasticities tell us whether or not goods are substitutes.

Elasticity of Supply

The concept of elasticity can be applied to supply as well as to demand. Just as elasticity of demand measures the response of quantity demanded to changes in any of the forces that influence it, so elasticity of supply measures the response of quantity supplied to changes in any of the forces that influence it. We will focus on the commodity's own price as a factor influencing supply.

Elasticity of supply measures the responsiveness of the quantity supplied to a change in the commodity's own price. It is denoted η_S and defined as

$$\eta_S = \frac{\text{percentage change in quantity supplied}}{\text{percentage change in price}}$$

The supply curves considered in this chapter all have positive slopes: An increase in price causes an increase in quantity sold. Such supply curves all have positive elasticities.

There are important special cases. If the supply curve is vertical—the quantity supplied does not change as price changes—elasticity of supply is zero. This would be the case, for example, if suppliers produced a given quantity and dumped it on the market for whatever it would bring. A horizontal supply curve has an infinitely high elasticity of supply: A small drop in price would reduce the quantity producers are willing to supply from an indefinitely large amount to zero. Between these two extremes elasticity of supply will vary with the shape of the supply curve.[3]

What Determines Elasticity of Supply?

Supply elasticities are important for many problems in economics. We shall discuss them only briefly here

[3] Steepness, which is related to absolute rather than percentage changes, is *not* always a reliable guide. As is shown in the appendix to this chapter, any upward-sloping straight line passing through the origin has an elasticity of +1.0 over its entire range.

for two reasons. First, much of the treatment of demand elasticity carries over to supply elasticity and does not need repeating. For example, the ease of substitution can vary in production as well as in consumption. If the price of a commodity rises, how much more can be produced profitably? This depends in part on whether it is easy to shift from the production of other commodities to the one whose price has risen. If agricultural land and labor can be readily shifted from one crop to another, the supply of any one crop will be more elastic than if they cannot. Here also, as with demand, length of time for response is critical. It may be difficult to change quantities supplied in response to a price increase in a matter of weeks or months but easy to do so over a period of years. An obvious example concerns the planting cycle of crops. Also, new oil fields can be discovered, wells drilled, and pipelines built over a period of years, but not in a few months. Thus elasticity of oil supply is much greater over five years than over one year.

The second reason for brevity of treatment is that supply elasticity depends to a great extent on how costs behave as output is varied, an issue that will be treated at length in Part Three. If costs of production rise rapidly as output rises, then the stimulus to expand production in response to a price rise will quickly be choked off by increases in costs. In this case supply will tend to be rather inelastic. If, however, costs rise only slowly as production increases, a rise in price that raises profits will elicit a large increase in quantity supplied before the rise in costs puts a halt to the expansion in output. In this case supply will tend to be rather elastic.

Summary

1. *Elasticity of demand* (also called *price elasticity of demand*) is a measure of the extent to which the quantity demanded of a commodity responds to a change in its price. It is defined as the percentage change in quantity divided by the percentage change in price that brought it about. Elasticity is defined to be a positive number, and it can vary from zero to infinity.
2. When the numerical measure of elasticity is less than unity, demand is *inelastic*. This means that the percentage change in quantity is less than the percentage change in price that brought it about. When the numerical measure exceeds unity, demand is *elastic*. This means that the percentage change in quantity is greater than the percentage change in price that brought it about.
3. Elasticity and total revenue of sellers are related in the following way: If elasticity is less than unity, a fall in price lowers total revenue; if elasticity is greater than unity, a fall in price raises total revenue; and if elasticity is unity, total revenue does not change as price changes.
4. The main determinant of the price elasticity of demand is the availability of substitutes for the commodity. Any one of a group of close substitutes will tend to have an elastic demand even though the group as a whole may have a highly inelastic demand.
5. Elasticity of demand tends to be greater the longer the time over which adjustment occurs. Items that have few substitutes in the short run may develop ample substitutes when consumers and producers have time to adapt.
6. *Income elasticity* is the percentage change in quantity demanded divided by the percentage change in income that brought it about. Luxuries tend to have higher income elasticities than necessities. The income elasticity of demand for a commodity will usually change as

income varies. For example, a commodity that has a high income elasticity at a low income (because increases in income bring it within reach of the typical household) may have a low or negative income elasticity at higher incomes (because with further rises in incomes it can be replaced by a superior substitute).

7. *Cross-elasticity* is the percentage change in quantity demanded divided by the percentage change in the price of some other commodity that brought it about. It is used to define commodities that are substitutes for one another (positive cross-elasticity) and commodities that complement one another (negative cross-elasticity).
8. *Elasticity of supply* is an important concept in economics. It measures the ratio of the percentage change in the quantity supplied of a commodity to the percentage change in its price. It is the analogue on the supply side to the elasticity of demand.
9. An appendix to this chapter, for students with some mathematics training, extends the analysis.

Topics for Review

Elasticity of demand
Significance of elastic and inelastic demands
Relation between demand elasticity and total expenditure
Income elasticity of demand
Short-run and long-run demand curves
Income-elastic and income-inelastic demands
Normal goods and inferior goods
Cross-elasticity of demand
Substitutes and complements
Elasticity of supply

Discussion Questions

1. From the following quotations what (if anything) can you conclude about elasticity of demand?
   a. "Good weather resulted in record corn harvests and sent corn prices tumbling. For many corn farmers the result has been calamitous."
   b. "Ridership always went up when bus fares came down, but the increased patronage never was enough to prevent a decrease in overall revenue."
   c. "As price of compact disk players fell, producers found their revenues soaring."
   d. "Coffee to me is an essential—you've gotta have it no matter what the price."
   e. "Soaring price of condominiums does little to curb the strong demand in Toronto."
2. Advocates of minimal charges for people using doctors' services in Canada hope that this will greatly reduce the cost to the provinces while not denying essential medical services to anyone. Opponents argue that even minimal charges will deny critical services to lower-

income Canadians. Use elasticity terminology to restate the views of each of these groups.

3. What would you predict about the relative price elasticity of demand of (a) food, (b) meat, (c) beef, (d) chuck roast, (e) chuck roast sold at the local supermarket? What would you predict about their relative income elasticities?
4. "Avocados have a limited market, not greatly affected by price until the price falls to less than $.25 a pound. Then they are much demanded by manufacturers of dog food." Interpret this statement in terms of price elasticity.
5. "Home computers were a leader in sales appeal through much of the 1980s. But per capita sales are much lower in Puerto Rico than in Canada and lower in New Brunswick than in Ontario. Manufacturers are puzzled by the big differences." Can you offer an explanation in terms of elasticity?
6. What elasticity measure or measures would be useful in answering the following questions?
   a. Will cheaper transport into the central city help keep downtown shopping centers profitable?
   b. Will raising the bulk-rate postage rate increase or decrease the postal deficit?
   c. Are producers of toothpaste and mouthwash in competition with each other?
   d. What effect will falling gasoline prices have on the sale of cars that use propane gas?
7. Interpret the following statements in terms of the relevant elasticity concept:
   a. "As fuel for tractors has gotten more expensive, many farmers have shifted from plowing their fields to no-till farming. No-till acreage increased from 30 million acres in 1972 to 95 million acres in 1982."
   b. "Fertilizer makers brace for dismal year as fertilizer prices soar."
   c. "When farmers are hurting, small towns feel the pain."
8. It has been observed recently that obesity is a more frequent medical problem for the relatively poor than for the middle-income classes. Can you use the theory of demand to shed light on this observation?
9. Suggest commodities that you think might have the following patterns of elasticity of demand.
   a. High income elasticity, high price elasticity
   b. High income elasticity, low price elasticity
   c. Low income elasticity, low price elasticity
   d. Low income elasticity, high price elasticity
10. When the New York City Opera was faced with a growing deficit, it cut its ticket prices by 20 percent, hoping to attract more customers. At the same time the New York Transit Authority raised subway fares to reduce its growing deficit. Was one of these two opposite approaches to reducing a deficit necessarily wrong?

Appendix to Chapter 5

Elasticity: A Formal Analysis

The verbal definition of elasticity used in the text may be written symbolically in the following form:

$$\eta = \frac{\Delta q}{\Delta p} \times \frac{\text{average } p}{\text{average } q}$$

where the averages are over the arc of the demand curve being considered. This is called **arc elasticity,** and it measures the average responsiveness of quantity to price over an interval of the demand curve.

Most theoretical treatments use a different but related concept called **point elasticity.** This is the responsiveness of quantity to price at a particular point on the demand curve. The precise definition of point elasticity uses the concept of a derivative, which is drawn from differential calculus.

In this appendix we first study arc elasticity, which may be regarded as an approximation to point elasticity. Then we study point elasticity.

Before proceeding, we should notice one further change. In the chapter text we multiplied all our calculations of demand elasticities by −1, thereby defining elasticity of demand as a positive number. In theoretical work it is more convenient to retain the concept's natural sign. Thus normal demand curves will have negative signs, and statements about "more" or "less" elastic must be understood to refer to the absolute, not the algebraic, value of demand elasticity.

The following symbols will be used throughout.

$\eta \equiv$ elasticity of demand
$\eta_s \equiv$ elasticity of supply
$q \equiv$ the original quantity
$\Delta q \equiv$ the change in quantity
$p \equiv$ the original price
$\Delta p \equiv$ the change in price

Arc Elasticity As an Approximation of Point Elasticity

Point elasticity measures elasticity at some point (p, q). In the approximate definition, however, the responsiveness is measured over a small range starting from that point. For example, in Figure 5A-1 the elasticity at point 1 can be measured by the responsiveness of quantity demanded to a change in price that takes price and quantity from point 1 to point 2. The algebraic formula for this elasticity concept is

$$\eta = \frac{\Delta q}{\Delta p} \times \frac{p}{q} \qquad [1]$$

This is similar to the definition of arc elasticity used in the text except that since elasticity is being measured at a point, the p and q corresponding to that point are used (rather than the average p and q over an arc of the curve).

Equation 1 splits elasticity into two parts: $\Delta q/\Delta p$, the ratio of the change in quantity to the change in price, which is related to the *slope* of the demand curve, and p/q, which is related to the *point* on the curve at which the measurement is made.

Figure 5A-1 shows a straight-line demand curve. To measure the elasticity at point 1, take p and q at

FIGURE 5A-1 A Straight-Line Demand Curve

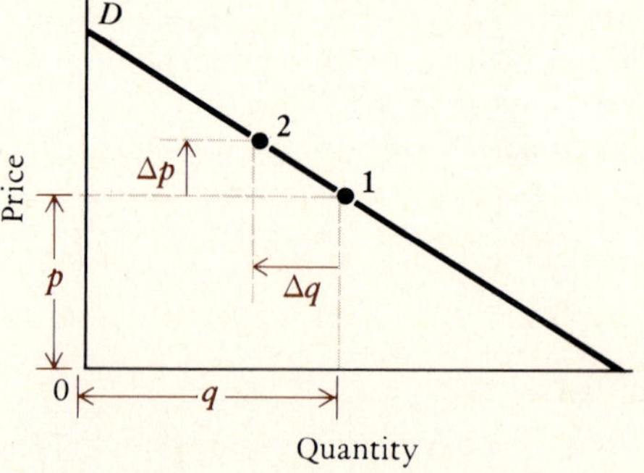

Because p/q varies with $\Delta q/\Delta p$ constant, the elasticity varies along this demand curve, being high at the left and low at the right.

that point and then consider a price change, say, to point 2, and measure Δp and Δq as indicated. The slope of the straight line joining points 1 and 2 is $\Delta p/\Delta q$. The term in Equation 1 is $\Delta q/\Delta p$, which is the reciprocal of $\Delta p/\Delta q$. Therefore the first term in the elasticity formula is the reciprocal of the slope of the straight line joining the two price-quantity positions under consideration.

Although point elasticity of demand refers to a point (p, q) on the demand curve, the first term in Equation 1 still refers to changes over an arc of the curve. This is the part of the formula that involves approximation, and, as we shall see, it has some unsatisfactory results. Nonetheless some interesting theorems can be derived using this formula as long as we confine ourselves to straight-line demand and supply curves.

1. *The elasticity of a downward-sloping straight-line demand curve varies from zero at the quantity axis to infinity at the price axis.* First notice that a straight line has a constant slope, so the ratio $\Delta p/\Delta q$ is the same everywhere on the line. Therefore its reciprocal, $\Delta q/\Delta p$, must also be constant. The changes in η can now be inferred by inspecting the ratio p/q. Where the line cuts the quantity axis, price is zero, so the ratio p/q is zero; thus $\eta = 0$. Moving up the line, p rises and q falls, so the ratio p/q rises; thus elasticity rises. Approaching the top of the line, q approaches zero, so the ratio becomes very large. Thus elasticity increases without limit as the price axis is approached.

2. *Where there are two straight-line demand curves of the same slope, the one farther from the origin is less elastic at each price than the one closer to the origin.* Figure 5A-2 shows two parallel straight-line demand curves. Compare the elasticities of the two curves at any price, say, p_0. Since the curves are parallel, the ratio $\Delta q/\Delta p$ is the same on both curves. Since elasticities at the same price are being compared on both curves, p is the same, and the only factor left to vary is q. On the curve farther from the origin, quantity is larger (i.e., $q_1 > q_0$) and hence p_0/q_1 is smaller than p_0/q_0; thus η is smaller.

It follows from theorem 2 that parallel shifts of a straight-line demand curve lower elasticity (at each price) when the line shifts outward and raise elasticity when the line shifts inward.

FIGURE 5A-2 Two Parallel Straight-Line Demand Curves

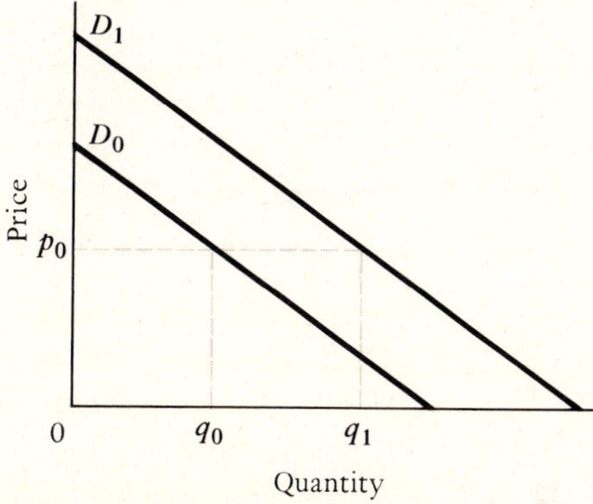

For any given price the quantities are different on these two parallel curves; thus the elasticities are different, being higher on D_0 than on D_1.

3. *The elasticities of two intersecting straight-line demand curves can be compared at the point of intersection merely by comparing slopes, the steeper curve being the less elastic.* In Figure 5A-3 there are two intersecting curves. At the point of intersection, p and q are common to both curves and hence the ratio p/q is the same. Therefore η varies only with $\Delta p/\Delta q$. On the steeper curve, $\Delta q/\Delta p$ is smaller than on the flatter curve, so elasticity is lower.

4. *If the slope of a straight-line demand curve changes while the price intercept remains constant, elasticity at any given price is unchanged.* This is an interesting case for at least two reasons. First, when more customers having similar tastes to those already in the market enter the market, the demand curve pivots outward in this way. Second, when more firms enter a market that is shared proportionally among all firms, each firm's demand curve shifts inward in this way.

Consider, in Figure 5A-4, the elasticities at point b on demand curve D_0 and at point c on demand curve D_1. We shall focus on the two triangles abp_0 on D_0 and acp_0 on D_1, formed by the two straight-line demand curves emanating from point a and by the price p_0.

FIGURE 5A-3 **Two Intersecting Straight-Line Demand Curves**

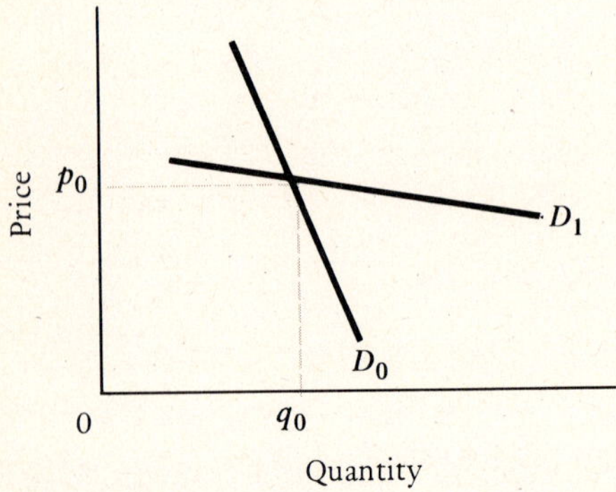

Elasticities are different at the point of intersection of these demand curves because the slopes are different, being higher on D_0 than on D_1. D_1 is more elastic at p_0.

FIGURE 5A-4 **Two Straight-Line Demand Curves from the Same Price Intercept**

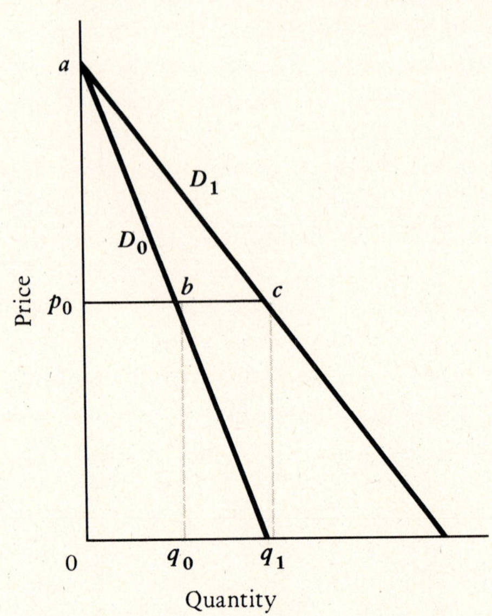

The elasticity is the same on D_0 and D_1 at any price p_0. This situation occurs because the steeper slope of D_0 is exactly offset by the smaller quantity demanded at any price.

The price p_0 is the line segment $0p_0$. The quantities q_0 and q_1 are the line segments p_0b and p_0c, respectively. The slope of D_0 is $\Delta p/\Delta q = ap_0/p_0b$ and the slope of D_1 is $\Delta p/\Delta q = ap_0/p_0c$.

From Equation 1 we can represent the elasticities of D_0 and D_1 at the points b and c respectively as

$$\eta \text{ at point } b = \frac{p_0b}{ap_0} \times \frac{0p_0}{p_0b} = \frac{0p_0}{ap_0}$$

$$\eta \text{ at point } c = \frac{p_0c}{ap_0} \times \frac{0p_0}{p_0c} = \frac{0p_0}{ap_0}$$

The two are the same. The reason is that the distance corresponding to the quantity demanded at p_0 appears in both the numerator and denominator and thus cancels out.

Put differently, if the straight-line demand curve D_0 is twice as steep as D_1, it has half the quantity demanded at p_0. Therefore in the expression

$$\eta = \frac{\Delta q}{q} \times \frac{p}{\Delta p}$$

the steeper slope (a smaller Δq for the same Δp) is exactly offset by the smaller quantity demanded (a smaller q for the same p).

FIGURE 5A-5 **A Straight-Line Supply Curve Through the Origin**

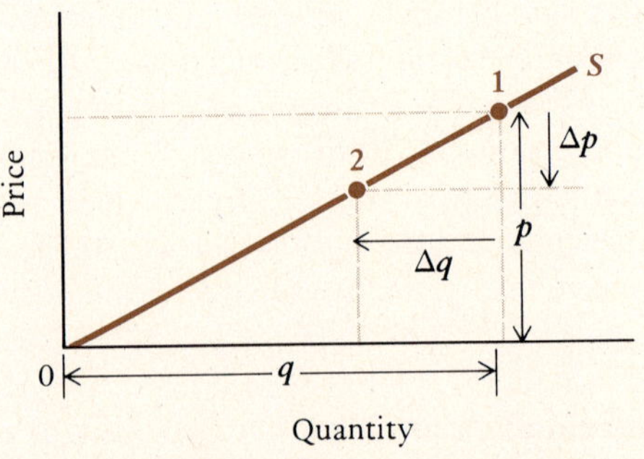

At every point on the curve, p/q equals $\Delta p/\Delta q$; thus elasticity equals unity at every point.

5. *Any straight-line supply curve through the origin has an elasticity of one.* Such a supply curve is shown in Figure 5A-5. Consider the two triangles with the sides p, q, and the S curve and Δp, Δq, and the S curve. Clearly, these are similar triangles. Therefore, the ratios of their sides are equal, that is,

$$\frac{p}{q} = \frac{\Delta p}{\Delta q} \qquad [2]$$

Elasticity of supply is defined as

$$\eta_s = \frac{\Delta q}{\Delta p} \times \frac{p}{q}$$

which, by substitution from Equation 2, gives

$$\eta_s = \frac{q}{p} \times \frac{p}{q} \equiv 1$$

6. *The elasticity measured from any point p, q, according to Equation 1, is dependent on the direction and magnitude of the change in price and quantity.* Except for a straight line (for which the slope does not change), the ratio $\Delta q/\Delta p$ will not be the same at different points on a curve. Figure 5A-6 shows a demand curve that is not a straight line. To measure the elasticity from point 1, the ratio $\Delta q/\Delta p$—and thus η—will vary according to the size and the direction of the price change.

Theorem 6 yields a result that is very inconvenient and is avoided by use of a different definition of point elasticity.

Point Elasticity According to the Precise Definition

To measure the elasticity at a point exactly, it is necessary to know the reaction of quantity to a change in price *at that point*, not over a range of the curve.

The reaction of quantity to price change at a point is called dq/dp, and this is defined to be the reciprocal of the slope of the straight line tangent to the demand curve at the point in question. In Figure 5A-7 the

FIGURE 5A-6 Point Elasticity of Demand Measured by the Approximate Formula

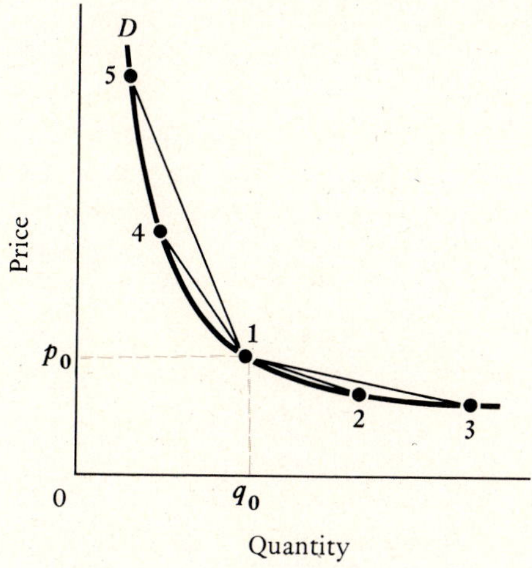

When the approximation of $\eta = \frac{\Delta q}{\Delta p} \times \frac{p}{q}$ is used, many elasticities are measured from point 1 because the slope of the chord between 1 and every other point on the curve varies.

FIGURE 5A-7 Point Elasticity of Demand Measured by the Exact Formula

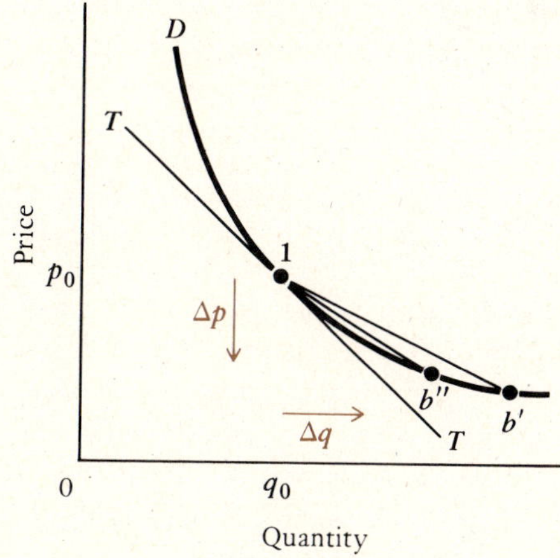

When the exact definition $\eta = \frac{dq}{dp} \times \frac{p}{q}$ is used, only one elasticity is measured from point 1 because there is only one tangent to the demand curve at that point.

elasticity of demand at point 1 is the ratio p/q (as it has been in all previous measures), now multiplied by the ratio of $\Delta q/\Delta p$ measured along the straight line T, tangent to the curve at 1, that is, by dq/dp.

Thus the exact definition of point elasticity is

$$\eta = \frac{dq}{dp} \times \frac{p}{q} \qquad [3]$$

The ratio dq/dp, as defined, is in fact the differential calculus concept of the *derivative* of quantity with respect to price.

This definition of point elasticity is the one normally used in economic theory. Equation 1 is mathematically only an approximation of this expression. It is obvious from Figure 5A-7 that arc elasticity will come closer to point elasticity the smaller the price change used to calculate the arc elasticity. The $\Delta q/\Delta p$ in Equation 1 is the reciprocal of the slope of the chord connecting the two points being compared. As the chord becomes shorter, its slope gets closer to that of the tangent T. (Compare the chords connecting point 1 to b' and b'' in Figure 5A-7.) Thus the error in using Equation 1 as an approximation of Equation 3 tends to diminish as the size of Δp diminishes.

6

Supply and Demand in Action: Price Controls and Agriculture

The theory of supply and demand has application to many real-world problems. In this chapter we illustrate these applications by studying government policies that involve intervention into competitive markets. In the first half of the chapter we study the general problems involved in the setting of both minimum and maximum prices and then go on to a case study of rent controls. In the second half we study the problems of government intervention in markets for agricultural commodities.

We use the method of comparative statics, first encountered on page 71. The method, you will recall, is to start from a position of equilibrium in the market and then introduce the change to be studied. The new position is then determined and compared with the original one. The difference between the two positions can be attributed to the change introduced, because this is the only change that we have allowed to occur. Notice that the new position may or may not be one of equilibrium—it will not be if the change being studied is one that prevents the attainment of equilibrium.

Controlled Prices

Equilibrium in a free market occurs when the quantity demanded equals the quantity supplied. Government **price control policies** are designed to hold the actual price at some disequilibrium value that could not be maintained in the absence of the government's intervention. Some price control policies hold the market price below equilibrium. In so doing they cause quantity demanded to exceed quantity supplied at the controlled price, creating shortages. Other price control policies are designed to hold prices above equilibrium. In so doing they cause quantity supplied to exceed quantity demanded at the controlled price, creating surpluses.

Disequilibrium Prices

In competitive markets price tends to change whenever quantity supplied does not equal quantity demanded. Thus price will move toward its equilibrium value, at which there are neither unsatisfied suppliers nor unsatisfied demanders.

When price controls hold price at some disequilibrium value, what determines the quantity actually traded on the market? The key to the answer to this question is the simple fact that any voluntary market transaction requires both a willing buyer and a willing seller. This means that if quantity demanded is less than quantity supplied, demand will determine the amount actually exchanged, while the rest of the quantity supplied will remain in the hands of the unsuccessful sellers. On the other hand, if quantity demanded exceeds quantity supplied, supply will determine the amount actually exchanged, while the rest of the quantity demanded will represent desired purchases of unsuccessful buyers. This argument is spelled out in more detail in Figure 6-1, which establishes the general conclusion that:

At any disequilibrium price, quantity exchanged is determined by the *lesser* of quantity demanded or quantity supplied.

FIGURE 6-1 The Determination of Quantity Exchanged in Disequilibrium

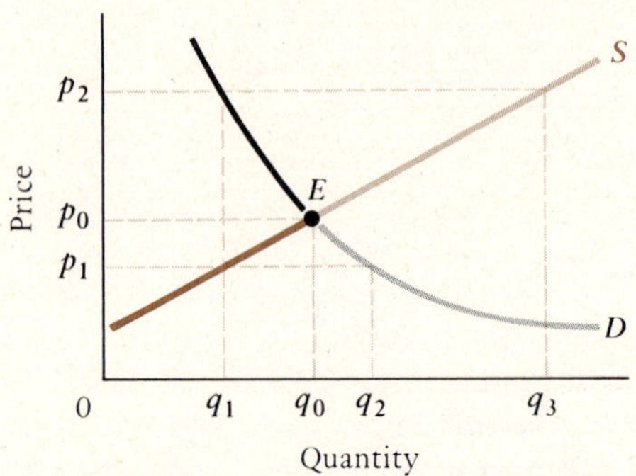

In disequilibrium, quantity exchanged is determined by the *lesser* of quantity demanded or quantity supplied. At p_0 the market is in equilibrium, with quantity demanded equal to quantity supplied at q_0. For prices below p_0, such as p_1, the quantity exchanged will be determined by the supply curve. For example, the quantity q_1 will be exchanged at the disequilibrium price p_1 in spite of the excess demand of q_1q_2. For prices above p_0, such as p_2, the quantity exchanged will be determined by the demand curve. For example, the quantity q_1 will be exchanged at the disequilibrium price p_2 in spite of the excess supply of q_1q_3. Thus the darker portions of the S and D curves show the actual quantities exchanged at different prices.

Price Floors

The government sometimes establishes a minimum price, or **price floor,** for a good or service. Minimum wages for labor and guaranteed prices for some agricultural commodities are well-known examples.

A price floor that is set at or below the equilibrium price has no effect, because equilibrium remains attainable and will not be inconsistent with the legal price floor. If, however, the price floor is set above the equilibrium price, it is said to be *binding* or *effective.*

Price floors may be established by rules that make it illegal to sell the commodity below the prescribed price, as in the case of the minimum wage (examined in Chapter 19). Or the government may establish a floor by announcing that it will guarantee a certain price by buying any excess supply of the product that emerges at that price.

The key result of price floors is illustrated in Figure 6-2.

Effective price floors lead to excess supply. Either an unsold surplus will exist or someone must step in and buy the excess production.

The consequences of excess supply will, of course, differ from commodity to commodity. If the commodity is labor, subject to a minimum wage, excess supply translates into people without jobs. If the commodity is wheat, and more is produced than can be sold, the surplus wheat must accumulate in grain elevators or government warehouses. These consequences may or may not be "worthwhile" in terms of the other goals achieved. But, in the absence of further offsetting policies, these consequences are inevitable whenever the price floor is set above the market-clearing, equilibrium price.

Why might the government wish to incur these consequences? One reason is that those who actually succeed in selling their commodities at the price floor are better off than if they had to accept the lower equilibrium price. Workers and farmers are among those who have sometimes persuaded the government to establish floor prices and so help them raise the prices of what they sell.

FIGURE 6-2 A Price Floor

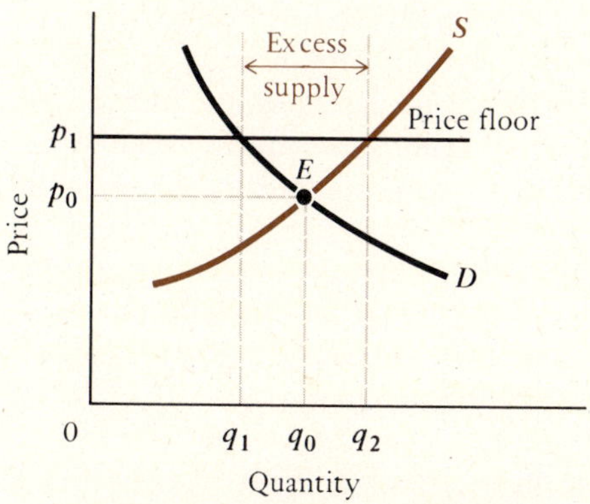

If a price floor is above the equilibrium price, quantity supplied will exceed quantity demanded. The free-market equilibrium is at E, with price p_0 and quantity q_0. If the government makes it illegal for the price to fall below p_1, it has established an effective price floor. Quantity supplied will exceed quantity demanded by q_1q_2. If the government does nothing, this excess supply will be in private hands and will either go to waste or accumulate in inventories. If the government buys the excess supply, sellers will get rid of the full quantity they wish to produce, q_2, but the government will have the quantity q_1q_2 to store or dispose of.

FIGURE 6-3 A Price Ceiling and Black Market Pricing

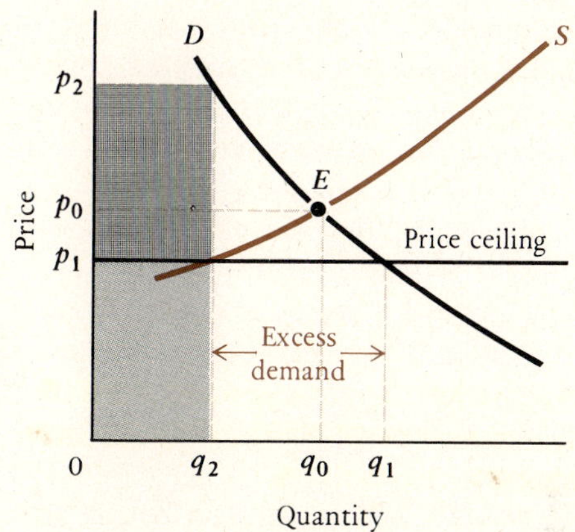

A price ceiling set below the equilibrium price causes excess demand and invites a black market. Equilibrium price is at p_0. If a price ceiling is set at p_1, the quantity demanded will rise to q_1 and the quantity supplied will fall to q_2. Quantity actually exchanged will be q_2. Although excess demand is q_2q_1, price may not rise legally to restore equilibrium. If all the available supply of q_2 were sold on a black market, price to consumers would rise to p_2, with black marketeers earning receipts shown by the shaded areas. The dark shaded area shows the profit of those who buy at the price ceiling and sell at the black market price.

Price Ceilings

It is common in wartime, and not unknown in peacetime, for the government to fix the *maximum prices* at which certain goods and services may be sold. Price controls on oil, natural gas, and rental housing have been features of the Canadian scene at various times since World War II.

Although frequently referred to as *fixed* or *frozen prices,* most price controls actually specify the highest permissible price that producers may legally charge. This maximum is often called a **price ceiling.** If the ceiling is set above the equilibrium price, it has no effect, since the equilibrium remains attainable. If, however, the ceiling is set below the equilibrium price, the ceiling is binding or effective. The key result for price ceilings is established in Figure 6-3.

Effective price ceilings lead to excess demand, and the quantity exchanged falls below its equilibrium amount.

Allocating a Commodity in Short Supply

The free market eliminates excess demand by allowing prices to rise, thereby allocating the available supply among would-be purchasers. Since this does not happen under price ceilings, some other method of allocation must be adopted. Experience shows that certain alternatives are likely.

If stores sell their available supplies on a first-come, first-served basis, people will rush to those stores that are said to have stocks of any commodity in short supply. In many Eastern European and African countries where prices of "essentials" are subject to effective price ceilings, even the rumor that a shop is selling supplies of a scarce commodity can cause a local stampede. Buyers may wait hours to get into the shop, only to find that supplies are exhausted before they can be served. This is why standing in lines is often a way of life in command economies.

Instead of first come, first served, storekeepers may use a different system of allocation of a scarce commodity. They may decide to keep goods "under the counter" and sell only to customers of their own choosing. When sellers decide to whom they will (and will not) sell scarce supplies, allocation is by **sellers' preferences.**

If the government dislikes the distribution that results from sellers' preferences, it can do at least two things. First, it can pass laws requiring suppliers to sell on a first-come, first-served basis. To the extent that this legislation is effective, it leads to allocation according to willingness to stand in line.

Second and more drastic, the government can ration the commodity. To do so, it prints only enough ration coupons to match the available supply and then distributes the coupons to purchasers, who need both money and coupons to buy the commodity. The coupons may be distributed equally among the population or on the basis of some criterion such as age, family status, or occupation.

Rationing substitutes the government's preferences for the sellers' preferences in allocating a commodity that is in excess demand because of an effective price ceiling.

Black Markets

Price ceilings, with or without rationing, usually give rise to black markets. A **black market** is any market in which goods are sold illegally at prices above a legal price ceiling.

Many manufactured products are produced by only a few firms but sold by many retailers. Thus, although it may be easy to police the few producers, it is often impossible to enforce the price at which the many retailers sell to the general public. If the government can control the price received by producers but not retailers, production remains at a level consistent with the price ceiling because the producers receive the controlled price for their product. At the retail level, however, the opportunity for a black market arises because purchasers are willing to pay more than the price ceiling in order to acquire the limited amounts of the commodity that are available.

Effective price ceilings always create the potential for a black market, because a profit can be made by buying at the controlled price and selling at the black market price.

Figure 6-3 also illustrates the extreme case in which all the available supply is sold on a black market.[1]

Does the existence of a black market mean that the goals sought by imposing price ceilings have been thwarted? The answer depends on the goals. A government might be interested mainly in (1) restricting production (perhaps to release resources for war production), (2) keeping prices down, or (3) satisfying notions of equity in the consumption of a commodity that is temporarily in short supply. When price ceilings are accompanied by a black market, only the first objective is achieved. When goods find their way onto the black market, the second objective is frustrated. Effective price ceilings on manufacturers plus an extensive black market at the retail level may produce the opposite of the third goal. There will be less to go around than if there were no controls, and the available quantities will tend to go to those with the most money or the least social conscience.

Rent Controls: A Case Study of Price Ceilings

A widespread use of price ceilings in North America today relates to the rental of houses and apartments

[1] This case is extreme because there are honest people in every society and because governments ordinarily have considerable power to enforce their price ceilings. Although *some* of a commodity subject to an effective price ceiling will be sold on the black market, it is very unlikely that *all* of that commodity will be so sold.

for private occupancy. Rent controls have been used the world over, with similar consequences: severe housing shortages, private allocation systems, and black markets.

Controls have existed in New York City, London, Paris, and many other large cities at least since World War II. In Sweden and Britain, where rent controls on unfurnished apartments have existed for decades, housing shortages are chronic. In 1914, when British rent controls were first instituted, almost 50 percent of the population lived in privately supplied rental accommodation. By 1985 the number had fallen to less than 8 percent, mostly in aging buildings nearing the end of their useful lives. Rent controls are to a very great extent responsible for virtually eliminating the market of privately supplied, unfurnished rental accommodation. When British controls were extended to furnished apartments in 1973, the supply of such accommodations dried up, at least until loopholes were found in the law. When rent controls were initiated in Rome in 1978, a housing shortage developed virtually overnight. This kind of induced shortage led University of Chicago professors George Stigler and Milton Friedman to point to the conflict between "ceilings" and "roofs."

Rent controls exist in many parts of Canada and the United States today. Though of recent vintage in Canada, their effects are already becoming apparent. Economic theory is useful in understanding the current experience with rent controls and in predicting the consequences. Rent controls are just a special case of price ceilings, and Figure 6-3 can be applied to them. It allows us to derive the following predictions, which are straightforward applications to housing of results that apply to any commodity subject to *binding* price ceilings.

1. There will be a housing shortage in the sense that quantity demanded will exceed quantity supplied.
2. The actual quantity of rental accommodation will be less than if free-market rents had been charged.
3. The shortage will lead to alternative allocation schemes. Landlords may allocate by sellers' preferences, or the government may intervene. (In the housing market government intervention usually takes the form of security-of-tenure laws, which protect the tenant from eviction and thus give existing tenants priority over potential new tenants.)
4. Black markets will appear. For example, landlords may require large "entrance fees" from new tenants. In general, the greater the housing shortage, the larger the amount the landlord can obtain. In the absence of security-of-tenure laws, landlords may force tenants out when their leases expire, and they may even try to evict them to extract a large entrance fee from new tenants.

Special Features of the Housing Market

Housing has unusual features that make the analysis of rent controls somewhat special. The most important is the nature of the commodity itself. Housing is an example of a **durable good,** a good that yields its services gradually over an extended period of time. Once built, an apartment can be used for decades or even centuries.

The supply of rental accommodation depends on the *stock* of rental housing available, which in any year is composed mainly of buildings built in the past. The stock is augmented by conversions of housing from other uses and construction of new buildings, and it is diminished by conversions to other uses and demolition or abandonment of existing buildings whose economic life is over. The stock usually changes slowly from year to year.

These considerations mean we can draw more than one supply curve for rental accommodation, depending on how much time is allowed for reactions to occur to any given level of rents. We shall distinguish just two such curves. The *long-run supply curve* relates rents to the quantity of rental accommodation that will be supplied after sufficient time has passed for all adjustments to be made. The *short-run supply curve* relates rents to quantity supplied when only a short time—say, a few months—is allowed for adjustments to be made in response to a change in rents.

The Long-Run Supply Curve of Rental Accommodation

In the long run, the supply of apartments is normally highly elastic as long as the going rate of profit that is being earned on comparable investments in other lines of activity can also be earned on investments in apartments. If more than that rate can be earned, new apartments will be built until the increasing supply forces rentals down to the level where only the going rate is earned. If less than the going rate of return is earned, new investment will go elsewhere. Apartment construction will stop, and old apartments will not be replaced as they wear out. The quantity will fall until the reduced supply forces rentals up high enough that the remaining supply of apartments can earn the going rate of return. At that time further apartments that wear out will be replaced and the overall quantity will remain constant.

The long-run supply curve of apartments tends to be quite elastic.

The Short-Run Supply Curve of Rental Accommodation

Now consider the supply response over a few months. What if rents rise? Even though investing in new apartments immediately becomes profitable, years may pass before land is obtained, plans drawn up, and construction completed. Of course, some existing housing can be more quickly converted to rental uses, but in many cases even this will take more than a few months. Thus a long time may pass between the decision to create more apartments and the occupancy of those apartments by tenants.

What if rents fall? New construction will fall off, which will surely decrease the supply at some time in the future. It will, however, pay the owners of existing apartments with no attractive alternative use of their rental units to rent them for whatever they will earn, providing that the rentals at least cover current out-of-pocket costs such as taxes and heating. Some rental housing can be converted to other uses, but, again, this will not usually happen very quickly.

The short-run supply curve tends to be inelastic at the level of the quantity currently supplied.

The longer the time allowed for adjustment, the less inelastic the supply curve will be. For the very short run, however, it is likely to be almost completely inelastic.

Supply Response to Changes in Rents

If rents rise due to a housing shortage, the quantity will initially remain more or less the same because the short-run supply curve is inelastic. For a while existing landlords will make **windfall profits,** profits that bear no relation to current or historical costs. These profits, however, serve as a spur to the long-run allocation of resources. New construction and conversions will begin, and after a year or two new rental units will begin to come onto the market. The quantity will continue to expand until a new point on the long-run supply curve has been attained and all windfall profits have been eliminated.

If rents decrease, the quantity supplied will also remain more or less unchanged because of the inelastic short-run supply curve. Landlords who were breaking even will now make *windfall losses.* As the profitability of rental accommodations falls, new construction will be curtailed. But it will take time before the stock of rental housing shrinks to its new point on the long-run supply curve. Only then will it again pay to maintain the remaining stock of rental housing.

Short-run windfall profits or losses provide the signals that bring about long-run supply adjustments in a free market.

Because houses are durable, they do not disappear quickly. But owners of rental properties can speed the shrinkage in various ways. Some apartments can be converted into cooperatives or condominiums. Some apartment buildings occupy land with valuable alternative uses. If rents fall far enough, owners may find it profitable to demolish those apartments and use the land for something else.

Many existing apartment buildings have no real alternative uses and stand on land that is worth less than the cost of demolishing the building. These will continue to provide rental accommodation until they are abandoned as useless. The less spent on maintenance and repairs, the shorter the structure's effective life. The lower the rents, the less it will pay landlords to spend on upkeep and thus the faster the apartment will "wear out."

If rental revenues fall below the minimum costs of operation (which include such things as taxes and heating), the owner may simply abandon the apartment. Although this may sound extreme, it has happened repeatedly. When it happens, a stock of housing that might have lasted decades or even centuries is dissipated within a few years.

Having seen how supply responds to price changes we can analyze the supply-side effects of rent control. An effective ceiling on rents drives them below their free-market equilibrium value. As shown in Figure 6-4, the controls lead to a growing housing shortage.

Rent controls that remain in force for a sustained period inevitably lead to a large reduction in the quantity of rental housing available.

FIGURE 6-4 Effects of Rent Control in the Short and Long Run

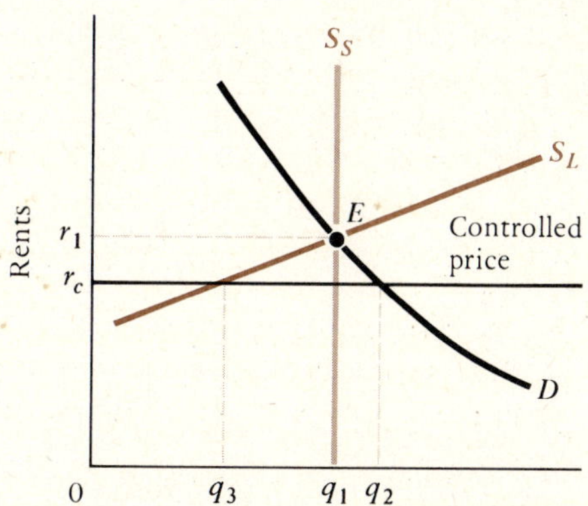

Rent control causes housing shortages that worsen as time passes. The controlled rent of r_c forces rents below their free-market equilibrium value of r_1. The short-run supply of housing is shown by the inelastic curve S_S. Thus quantity supplied remains at q_1 in the short run, and the housing shortage is q_1q_2. Over time, the quantity supplied shrinks, as shown by the long-run supply curve S_L. In long-run equilibrium there are only q_3 units of rental accommodation, far fewer than when controls were instituted. Since the long-run supply is quite elastic, the housing shortage of q_3q_2, which occurs after supply has fully adjusted, ends up being much larger than the initial shortage of q_1q_2.

Demand Response to Changes in Rents

There are many reasons to expect the demand for apartments and other forms of rental housing to be quite elastic. As the relative price of rental accommodation in an area rises, four things occur:

1. Some people stop renting and buy instead.
2. Some move to where rental housing is cheaper.
3. Some economize on the amount of housing they consume by renting smaller, cheaper accommodations or renting out to others a room or two in their present accommodations.
4. Some double up and others do not "undouble" (for example, young adults do not move out of parental homes as quickly as they might otherwise do).

Such occurrences contribute to an elastic demand for rental housing: Increases in rents will sharply decrease the quantity demanded.

Rent controls prevent such increases in rents from occurring. Thus, even while the supply of rental housing is shrinking for the reasons discussed above, the signal to economize on rental accommodation is *not* given through rising rentals. The housing shortage grows as the stock of rental accommodation shrinks, while nothing decreases the quantity demanded.

When Rent Controls May Work: Short-Term Shortages

Pressure for rent controls often arises in response to rapidly rising rents for housing. The case for controlling rising rentals is strongest when the shortages causing the increasing rents are temporary.

Sometimes there is a temporary influx of population into an area. Possibly an army camp is established in wartime, or a pipeline or a power complex is being built, and many workers are required for the time being even though few will remain behind. When the temporary population floods in, market rents will rise. New construction of apartments will not occur, however, because investors recognize the rise in demand and the rise in rentals as temporary. In such a situation rent controls may stop existing owners from gaining windfall profits with few harmful supply effects since a long-run supply response is not expected in any case. After the boom is over, demand will fall and free-market rents will return to the controlled level (their original level). Controls may then be removed with little further effect.

Even when rent controls have no long-run adverse effect, there will be some disadvantages. At controlled rents there will be a severe housing shortage but no incentive for existing tenants to economize on housing and no incentive for potential suppliers to find ways to provide extra short-run accommodation. If rents rise on the free market, existing tenants will economize and some tenants and owners will find it profitable to rent out rooms. Even though the supply of permanent apartments does not change, the supply of casual temporary accommodation (mobile homes and rooms in other people's houses, for example) will increase. Such reactions are induced by the signal of rising rents but inhibited by controls.

Temporary controls are also disadvantageous because political pressures to make them permanent may prove irresistible. For example, many of the provincial rent controls introduced in 1975 and 1976 as a temporary anti-inflationary policy are still in place in the majority of Canadian provinces more than a decade after the remainder of the anti-inflationary controls were removed.

When Rent Controls Fail: Long-Term Shortages

Long-Run Increases in Demand

Consider a long-term increase in the demand for rental accommodation. An example is provided by the Sunbelt states of the United States, where rapidly increasing population is creating severe local housing shortages and forcing up rents. Such increases in rents give the signal that apartments are highly profitable investments. A consequent building boom has led to increases in the quantity supplied, and it will continue to do so as long as windfall profits can be enjoyed.

If rent controls are imposed in the face of such long-term increases in demand, as they have been in Ontario, they will prevent short-run windfalls, but they will also prevent the needed long-run construc-

FIGURE 6-5 Rent Controls in Response to Increasing Demand

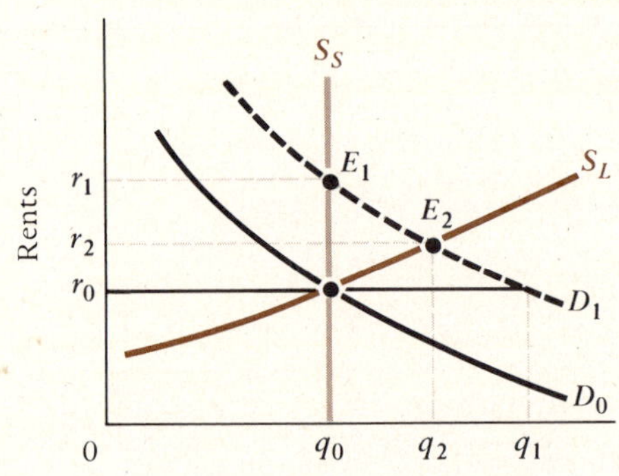

Rent controls prevent a temporary skyrocketing of rents when demand rises but also prevent the long-term supply adjustment to demand increases.

Temporary demand fluctuations. The short-run supply curve S_S applies. In the free market a temporary rise in demand from D_0 to D_1 and then back to D_0 will change rents from r_0 to r_1 and then back to r_0. Rent control would hold rents at r_0 throughout; there would be a housing shortage of q_0q_1 due to excess demand as long as demand was D_1, but rent control would not affect the quantity of housing available.

Permanent changes in demand. The long-run supply curve S_L applies. A permanent rise in demand from D_0 to D_1 will cause free-market rents to rise temporarily from r_0 to r_1 and then to fall to r_2 as the quantity of accommodation supplied grows from q_0 to q_2. Controlling the rent at r_0 to prevent windfall profits produces a permanent housing shortage of q_0q_1.

tion boom from occurring. Thus controls will convert a temporary shortage in the rapidly expanding areas of the province into a permanent one. This is illustrated in Figure 6-5.

Inflation in Housing Costs

Rent controls also fail when they are introduced to protect tenants from rent increases in an inflationary world. Inflation raises both the costs of construction of new housing and the costs of operating and maintaining existing housing. As we saw in Chapter 4, a rise in costs shifts the supply curve upward and to the left. Rent ceilings in an economy that is experiencing a steady inflation will produce a housing shortage that grows over time. If inflation is combined with growth in demand, the growth in the housing shortage becomes large, as shown in Figure 6-6.

Of course, the housing shortage need not grow if the controlled rent is allowed to rise as fast as the equilibrium rent. But since the usual purpose of controls is to hold rents down in the face of rapid increases in costs and demand, controlled rents have usually been allowed to rise more slowly than market-determined rents. Thus housing shortages grow over the years, although not as fast as they would if controlled rents were *never* changed.

Box 6-1 takes up the interesting question of why, if the consequences are so bad, rent controls are so often resorted to in today's world.

FIGURE 6-6 An Ever-growing Housing Shortage

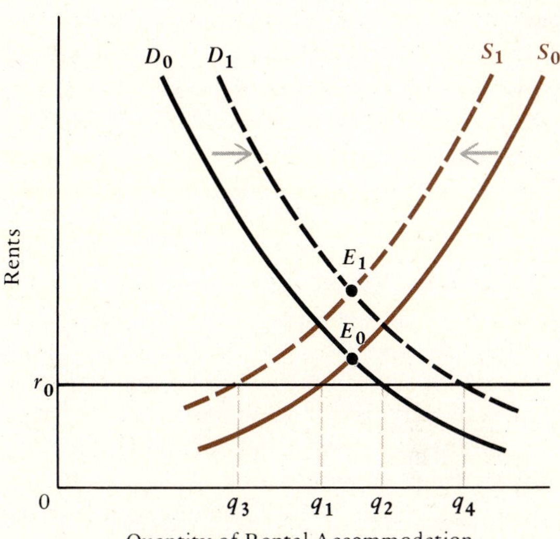

In a growing, inflation-prone economy, rent control will cause the housing shortage to worsen year by year. In a growing economy the demand curve is continually shifting rightward as more people with higher real incomes demand more housing. In an inflationary economy the supply curve is continually shifting leftward because construction, maintenance, and operating costs are rising. Such shifts, when combined with rent control, cause the housing shortage to grow over time. For example, when the curves are D_0 and S_0, rent control at r_0 is accompanied by a housing shortage of q_1q_2. When the curves have shifted to D_1 and S_1, however, the same controlled rent causes an overall housing shortage of q_3q_4.

Alternative Responses to the Rising Cost of Housing

Most rent controls today are meant to protect lower-income tenants not only against profiteering by landlords in the face of severe local shortages but also against the steadily rising cost of housing.

The free-market solution is to let rents rise sufficiently to cover the rising costs. If ordinary people (and others) really decide they cannot afford the market price of apartments and will not rent them, construction will cease. Given what we know about past consumer behavior, however, it is more likely that agonizing choices will be made to economize on housing or to spend a higher proportion of total income on it.

If the government does not wish to accept this free-market solution, what alternatives are open to it?

One alternative is to control rents below the cost of new building, with the inevitable consequence of a housing shortage that grows as the stock of rental accommodation wears out and is not replaced.

A second alternative is for government to fill the gap between total demand and private supply with subsidized public housing, financed at the taxpayers' expense (since the high costs of housing must be paid by someone).

BOX 6-1

The Call for Rent Control

In the face of the predicted and observed consequences, why do rent controls persist and even grow? The answer is largely that the primary victims of rent control do not identify themselves as such, while the primary beneficiaries do.

Tenants constitute an important and sympathetic political constituency for rent controls. Renting families include a disproportionate fraction of the aged, the unemployed, welfare recipients, students, and members of minority groups. For some of these people the free-market rents could absorb up to half of their money incomes. Whatever the long-term consequences of rent control, all tenants, rich and poor, know that the immediate effect is to hold down the cost of existing housing.

In contrast, landlords are less important and less sympathetic as a group. Many are wealthy individuals and rich companies, and they are certainly much less numerous than are tenants.

Of course, many tenants are well off; after all, there are middle-range and luxury apartments, as well as low-rent ones. Also, many landlords are neither rich nor powerful. At the other end of the spectrum are those who have put their savings into one or two small apartments, and those who rent out a room or a floor in the family home now that the kids have moved out.

If the beneficiaries of rent control are existing tenants, who are the victims? The housing shortage hurts those who will want rental housing that will not be available in the future. The elderly couples who fight to keep rent control on the apartments they occupy are behaving in their own best interest. But if they succeed they are making life more difficult for the next generation of aged couples, many of whom will not find housing of the same quality if rent controls are kept. The welfare family protected today will have a hard time finding housing if it moves when the opportunity for a job arises or when its present apartment house is abandoned. Minority groups will find that their members are hurt in the long run by the steadily shrinking quantity and quality of available rental housing.

Those who are hurt also include those landlords who bought apartments in anticipation of a certain return and who now find that much less can be earned. The loss is taken by those who held the apartments when controls were instituted or unexpectedly changed. Once the existence of controls is known, their effect is felt in a lower sale price of an apartment building. Anyone buying an existing apartment building will insist on receiving the going rate of return, and so the resale price of apartments will be low enough to ensure that new investors receive this amount.

Why do so many people favor rent controls when control-induced shortages will make it more difficult for them to find a suitable apartment? The answer, when it is not an ideological dislike of landlords, seems to be that they do not recognize the link between the lower rents they will pay—if they are lucky enough to find a rent-controlled apartment where they want it—and the decreased chance of finding such an apartment.

The call for rent control comes both from existing tenants, who gain at the expense of those who do not have secured leases in rental housing, and from potential tenants, who underestimate the adverse effects control-induced housing shortages may have on them. In contrast, the articulate opposition is the much smaller group of landlords (who are viewed less sympathetically by the press and the general public). The silent victims, who are the future unsuccessful searchers for rental units, may never realize the causal link between rent controls and the housing shortage from which they suffer.

That many individuals are either selfish or myopic in calling for rent control is understandable. That their leaders and public representatives do not fully appreciate the long-term consequences is less comprehensible except in political terms. Perhaps the politicians are selfish and myopic, too, judging next year's election (and today's constituency) to be more important than adverse long-run effects.

A third alternative is to subsidize the housing of the less-well-off citizens by providing them with housing vouchers good for paying so much rent and redeemable by landlords in cash paid by the government. A reason for using methods such as the second or third rather than rent control is that controlling the price paid by all buyers in order to help the minority of buyers who have low incomes is a clumsy and costly method of assistance. Furthermore, in the not uncommon case where tenants are better off than their landlords, the controls act perversely to redistribute income from poor to rich. Also, those who suffer most when the control-induced housing shortage becomes acute are the low-income groups. When more and more housing becomes owner-occupied rather than rented, the very people who find it hardest to raise the initial down payment for a house, to say nothing of meeting monthly mortgage payments, are the low-income groups.

Note that whenever housing is built, its resource cost must be met by someone. Either the tenant pays in higher rents, or the taxpayer pays in subsidies to government housing that is rented at less than cost or to finance a scheme of housing ventures. The only way the cost can be avoided is when, under effective rent control, the housing that costs more than is yielded by the controlled rents is not built at all (which is why a housing shortage develops under this arrangement).

The costs of providing additional housing cannot be voted out of existence; they can only be transferred from one set of persons to another.

Rent Controls: The Future Outlook

Several European countries have been through the whole process of imposing rent controls to protect tenants and ending up with excess demand and an increasingly expensive program of subsidized public housing. In the face of other public needs, they are now trying to give more scope to private markets for housing, but policies of rent controls often remain politically popular. Only time will tell how far Canada is to travel the same path. Economics cannot tell society which hard choice to make, but it can show what the choices are. The greatest danger is that the long-run costs will be neglected in making the choice.

Box 6-2 discusses some of the already visible effects of rent control on the Toronto housing market, less than five years after Ontario rent controls were extended to cover all rental accommodation.

The Problems of Agriculture

For decades the "farm problem" has plagued most nations in the non-Communist world. Left to operate on its own, the price system produces two characteristic problems in agriculture. First, prices fluctuate widely from year to year, causing much uncertainty about farm income. Second, there is a long-run tendency for farm incomes to be depressed below urban incomes in spite of both an extremely rapid rise in agricultural productivity and a long-term shift of labor from the farms. This latter movement has been dramatic. In 1900 over 40 percent of the Canadian labor force worked in agriculture; by 1930 it was down to 29 percent, and today it has fallen below 5 percent.

To deal with the farm problem, governments have tried a variety of techniques including price supports, crop insurance, transportation and storage subsidies, and marketing boards. But each of these "solutions" seems to bring problems of its own, sometimes more serious than the original problem they were meant to solve.

Long-Term Trends

The causes of agriculture's long-term problems have come from both the demand and the supply sides of agricultural markets.

Domestic demand. In this century output per worker in Canada has increased at an average annual rate of almost 2 percent. Such increases in productivity lead to increases in the real incomes enjoyed by Canadians. How did Canadians choose to consume their extra incomes?

The relevant measure is income elasticity of demand, which shows the effect of increases in income

BOX 6-2

Rent Control in Toronto

Controlling rents causes no great problems in areas that are not growing. In those areas free-market housing prices and rental values are not rising, and rent controls may have little effect (because they do not keep rents far below their free-market values). In rapidly growing areas, such as the city of Toronto, the effects are significant, and over a decade or two they become dramatic.

The original Ontario rent-control legislation did not apply to new housing or to higher-priced rentals and so threatened only the stock of older and cheaper rental housing. In 1984, however, the Liberal-NDP coalition government extended the controls to all rental housing. Very quickly new apartment construction dwindled. There was also a rush to convert rental accommodation to condominiums. Within a very few years the vacancy rate for apartments fell below 0.5 percent (compared with 3.0 percent in Vancouver), and the "Toronto housing crisis" became a commonplace term.

A series of schemes—responding to the original legislation—gave grants to property developers in order to increase the supply (and thereby showed that the purpose of the controls was not to hold rents to the levels of reasonable rates of return on investment). The existing stock of housing was protected by laws preventing conversions to owner-occupied status, but the slow erosion of the housing stock continued. As housing prices soared due to the rapid growth of the city, the shortage of rental accommodation worsened. Condominium construction boomed, while the construction of apartments came to a virtual standstill.

Until 1987 rent increases were allowed only at 4 percent per year. Since that time the formula has been altered to allow rent increases to cover increases in the landlords' costs. This formula may prevent the existing stock of housing from decaying by preserving a sufficient profit margin for landlords to continue maintenance and repairs. It does not appear, however, to restore the return on new rental accommodation to high enough levels to make the building of rental accommodation competitive with other uses of scarce land such as condominium construction.

The gap between the free-market price and the controlled price was a valuable asset that people scrambled to appropriate. Key money—the price charged by landlords to gain access to a rent-controlled flat—became prevalent, and the press reported payments running into many thousands of dollars. (Such lump-sum payments are most burdensome on the low-income persons that the policy is supposed to be aiding.) Subletting became common: A tenant pays the landlord the controlled rent and then sublets at the market rent. This is the worst of both worlds as analyzed in Figure 6-3: The supplier gets the controlled price and hence supplies only a small quantity, while the ultimate user pays the market price, which, because of the control-induced shortage, is higher than the uncontrolled free-market price would have been. The windfall to the original tenant serves no allocative purpose since that person is responsible neither for maintaining the existing building nor for erecting new ones.

The growing housing shortage leads to more and more frantic searches for the available space. A feature article in the *Toronto Star* in early 1987 told of searches involving bribing of caretakers, hunting through obituary columns, and finding elderly tenants in the hope of being first on the scene when death makes a flat available. Younger people, particularly in less skilled jobs, told of landlord preferences for middle-class tenants holding white-collar jobs and earning higher incomes—a predictable allocation by sellers' preferences that tended to discriminate against the very groups the policy was supposed to help.

None of these events is a surprise to anyone who has studied the effects of rent controls elsewhere in the world. They are the all-too-predictable consequences of the system. City and provincial politicians and many other rent-control advocates, however, express surprise at these events—being understandably unwilling to accept the responsibility that they actually bear for them. Efforts continue to be made to avoid the worst effects that have occurred elsewhere, but as long as rents are held below their long-term market equilibrium level—and there would be no point in having controls otherwise—the consequences analyzed in this chapter will continue to be felt.

on the demands for various goods. At the levels of income existing in Canada and other advanced industrial nations over the past 50 years, most foodstuffs have low income elasticities because most people are already well fed. When people get extra income, they tend to spend much of it on consumer durables and on such services as entertainment and travel. Thus the influence of income growth is only a small increase in the demand for agricultural goods. (Large increases in the demand for agricultural goods depend on population growth because all new citizens must spend a significant proportion of their incomes on food.)

If productivity were expanding uniformly among industries, the demands for goods with low income elasticities would be expanding more slowly than output. In such industries excess supplies would develop, prices and profits would be depressed, and resources would be induced to move elsewhere. Exactly the reverse would happen for industries producing goods with high income elasticities. Demands would expand faster than supplies, prices and profits would tend to rise, and resources would move into the industries producing these goods.

Domestic supply. Our discussion of the effects of increases in real income on the demands for various commodities shows what would happen if there were an equal rate of growth of productivity in all industries. In fact, growth in agricultural productivity has been well *above* the average for the economy. Encouraged by government-financed research, by subsidies, and by a government-assured demand for farm output at relatively stable prices, agricultural productivity has increased enormously in this century. Since 1947, for example, Canadian farm output per agricultural worker has grown at the rate of about 5 percent per year, nearly twice the rate of growth of total output per worker. These productivity increases shift the supply curves of agricultural goods rapidly to the right, indicating a greatly increased ability and willingness to produce at each price.

Exports. The explosive growth of world population in the past half century has provided an expanding export market for North American agriculture that tended to alleviate the domestic pressures just discussed. In recent years, however, many less-developed countries have succeeded in dramatically increasing their own food production while the European agricultural supports have turned the countries of the European Community into exporters of agricultural products, rather than importers, which they had been for the previous 100 years. So now, instead of alleviating the domestic problem, recent international developments have tended to exacerbate it.

Resource reallocation. We have seen that demand has been increasing only slowly while supply has been increasing rapidly. If resources had not been reallocated out of farming, there would have been enormous increases in output, resulting in production that could hardly have been sold within Canada or exported at any price that would cover its costs.

Reallocations of resources in a free-market economy take place under the incentives of low prices, low wages, and depressed incomes in the declining sector and high prices, wages, and incomes in the expanding sector. But incentives of this kind prove painful—indeed, pain is the spur—to people who live and work on farms, especially when resources move slowly in response to depressed incomes. It is one thing for the farmer's son or daughter to move to the city; it is quite another for the farmer and the farmer's parents, who are more set in their ways, to do so. Because farmers are people—and voters—governments tend to respond when asked to help in overcoming the depressed conditions that free markets often produce.

Notice that analogous problems arise in any industry where growth in demand is low while productivity growth is high. For example, the rapid rise in productivity in automobile production, combined with government subsidies to auto producers, threatens to produce severe excess capacity in the North American auto industry in the 1990s.

Short-Term Fluctuations

Why is short-term price volatility typical of many agricultural markets? Farm crops are subject to variations in output because of many factors completely beyond farmers' control. For example, pests, floods,

FIGURE 6-7 The Effect on Price of Unplanned Variations in Output Depends on Elasticity of Demand

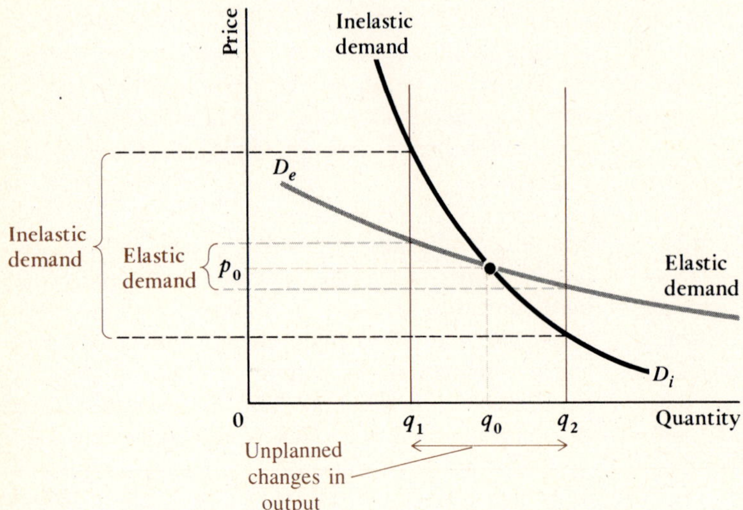

An unplanned fluctuation in output of a given size leads to a much sharper fluctuation in price if the demand curve is inelastic than if it is elastic. Suppose that the expected price is p_0 and the planned output is q_0. The two curves D_i and D_e are *alternative* demand curves. If actual production always equaled planned production, the equilibrium price and quantity would be p_0 and q_0 with either demand curve. Unplanned variations in output, however, cause quantity to fluctuate year by year between q_1 (a bad harvest) and q_2 (a good harvest). When demand is inelastic (shown by the black curve), prices will show large fluctuations. When demand is elastic (shown by the gray curve), price fluctuations will be much smaller.

and lack of rain can drastically reduce output, and exceptionally favorable conditions can cause production to exceed expectations. By now you should not be surprised to hear that such unplanned fluctuations in output cause fluctuations in farm prices. There are other, less obvious consequences that shed light on farmers' problems.

Fluctuating Supply with Inelastic Demand

The basic behavior is illustrated in Figure 6-7. Variations in farm output cause price fluctuations in the direction opposite to crop sizes. A bumper crop sends prices down; a small crop sends them up. The price change will be larger, the less elastic the demand curve.

Because farm products typically have inelastic demands, price fluctuations tend to be large in response to unplanned changes in production.

What are the effects on the receipts of farmers? If the commodity in question has an elastic demand, increases in the quantity supplied will raise farmers' receipts. If the demand is inelastic, increases in quantity supplied will reduce farmers' receipts. (What is received from the sale of some crop provides income not just for the farmers who produced it but also for those who produced every input used by farmers.)

Wherever demands are inelastic, good harvests will bring reductions in total farm receipts and bad harvests will bring increases.

Most farm products do have inelastic demands. When nature is bountiful and produces a bumper crop, farmers' receipts dwindle; when nature is moderately unkind and output falls unexpectedly, their receipts rise. The interests of the farmer and the consumer are exactly opposed in such cases. This conflict is dramatically illustrated every time a partial crop failure sends food prices soaring but raises farm incomes and whenever a bumper crop that brings relief to consumers evokes a cry for help from farmers, whose incomes are shrinking.

Fluctuating Demand with Inelastic Supply

As the tide of business activity flows and ebbs, demand curves for all commodities rise and fall. The

FIGURE 6-8 The Effect on Receipts of a Decrease in Demand

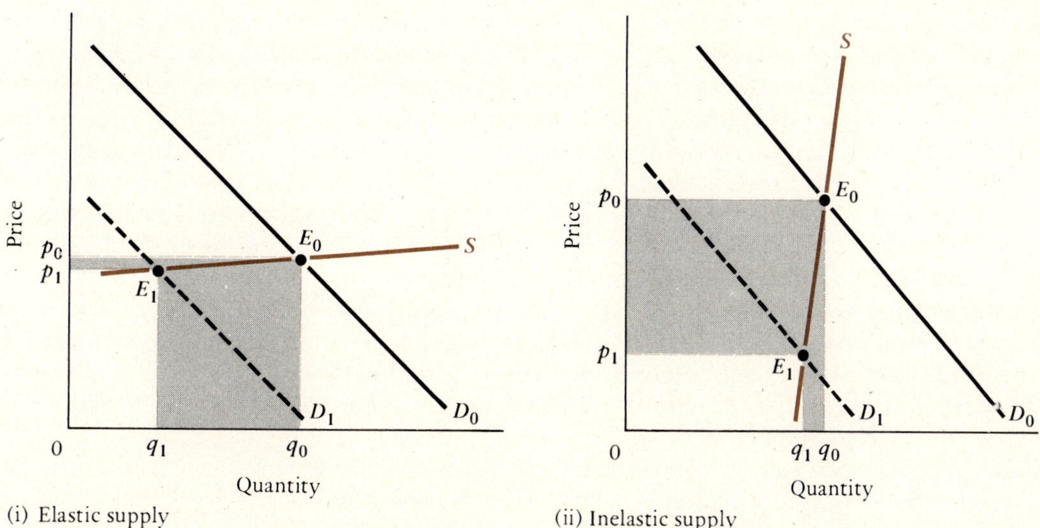

Both elastic and inelastic supply curves can lead to sharp decreases in receipts, but the effects on prices are very different in the two cases. In each part of the figure, when demand decreases from D_0 to D_1, price and quantity decrease to p_1 and q_1 and total receipts decline by the shaded area. In (i) the symptom is primarily the sharp decrease in quantity. Employment and total profits earned fall drastically, though wage rates and profit margins on what is produced may remain close to their former level. In (ii) the symptom is mainly the sharp decrease in price. Output and employment remain high, but the drastic fall in price will reduce or eliminate profits and put downward pressure on wages.

magnitude of the effects on prices and outputs depend on the elasticity of *supply*. Industrial products typically have rather elastic supply curves, so shifts in demand cause fairly large changes in outputs but only small changes in prices as Figure 6-8(i) illustrates.

Agricultural commodities typically have rather inelastic supply curves because land, labor, and machinery devoted to agricultural uses is neither quickly transferred to non-agricultural uses when demand falls nor quickly returned to agriculture when demand rises. Given an inelastic supply curve for most agricultural products, farm prices, farm receipts, and farm income will be sensitive to demand shifts, as Figure 6-8(ii) illustrates. A sharp drop in demand (a leftward shift of the demand curve) will cause hardship among those whose income depends on farm crops.

Agricultural Stabilization in Theory

Governments throughout the world intervene in agricultural markets in attempts to stabilize agricultural prices and incomes in the face of short-term and uncontrollable fluctuations in supply and cyclical fluctuations in demand. Box 6-3 discusses some of the political consequences of food stabilization schemes. In the text we consider the economics of several of the most common types of schemes.

To start, assume that the supply curve in each case refers to planned (or average) production per year but that actual production fluctuates around that level. In a free market, as we have seen, this causes both prices and farmers' receipts to fluctuate widely from year to year.

We deal with two cases that are relevant to much of Canadian agriculture. In the first case, an agricul-

BOX 6-3

The Political Economy of Food Subsidies

Many governments in diverse parts of the world have adopted policies to hold food prices below their costs of production. These policies typically involve price controls in retail markets and subsidies to producers. Low food prices are understandably popular with ordinary people, particularly in poorer countries where food takes up a large percentage of total household expenditure.

The governments' motivations are not always clear. To some extent they may be motivated by a genuine but misguided feeling that holding food prices low is the best way to raise the welfare of ordinary citizens. To some extent, however, governments may be making the short-term political calculation that low food prices are the way to court popular support. Whatever the motives involved, the long-term consequences are usually disastrous, not only for the economy, but also for the body politic.

When the state holds food prices below their costs of production, which include what farmers must be paid for producing the food, the difference must be made up by a state-financed subsidy. The revenue to pay the subsidy must come from one of two sources. First, it may come from the public, either in the form of tax revenue or (unlikely in poor countries) government borrowing. Second, it may come from government creation of new money. In this case the result is inflation because the state pays its subsidy by giving out new purchasing power that has no counterpart in the form of new production available to be purchased.*

Most countries, including communist ones, have suffered some inflation over the last two decades. As inflation proceeds, the temptation is to hold the rate of increase in food prices below the rate of inflation. As a result, the price of food typically rises at a rate below the overall rate of inflation. This increases the amount of the state's food subsidy as the gap between costs of production and selling prices is widened. Furthermore, as food becomes relatively cheaper and cheaper—since food prices are not rising as fast as other prices—people are induced to buy more food than they would if the prices covered the full costs of production. This also increases the total subsidy that the state must pay.

These forces cause the total subsidy bill to grow continuously until the state's finances cannot support it. At this point a food crisis arises, and the state has no choice but to raise the price of food. Having postponed the decision until the last possible moment, the price increases that will make any real dent in the total subsidy bill are dramatic. Typically, prices will be raised from 50 to 100 percent.

This is the real shock to consumers. They could have adjusted, although with pain, to prices that rose, say, 7 percent every year, and so raised food prices by just over 100 percent over 10 years. But to be faced with stable prices for 10 years and then see a sudden doubling of prices can be traumatic. In these circumstances food riots commonly break out, and existing governments—whether dictatorial or democratic—are sometimes toppled.

Governments in the Eastern bloc (most notably Poland), Africa (including Ghana and Nigeria), and Asia (including Burma and China) have found themselves in such predicaments. Economic analysis helps us understand their problems by showing what happens when real costs are ignored by state planners. The next time you read of a food riot accompanying some sudden government-legislated increase in food prices, congratulate yourself that you probably understand more economics than the policymakers involved. You might also wish that you could share your knowledge with them.

*The details of how the state creates new money and how new money creates inflation are discused in Part Nine.

tural product is produced mainly for export at prices that are determined on international markets. These prices are largely independent of the amount sold by domestic producers because these producers contribute only a small proportion of total world supply. This is the case discussed in the Appendix to Chapter 4. In the second case, an agricultural product is sold mainly on the domestic market, where the price is determined mainly by domestic demand and supply because high transport costs or trade barriers keep out imports.

Exports at World Market Prices

When Canadian production is sold on world markets at prices largely beyond Canadian control, domestic producers face a perfectly elastic demand curve indicating that they can sell all that they wish at the given world price. A government stabilization policy then faces two key problems: first, how to cope with short-term supply fluctuations at home and, second, how to react to fluctuations in world prices.

FIGURE 6-9 Exports at a Given World Price

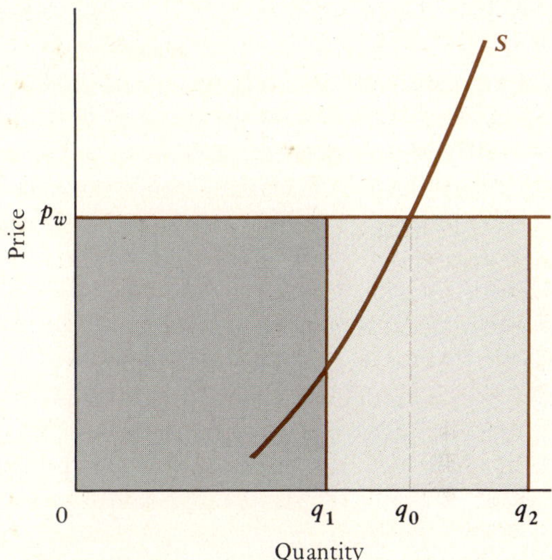

A country that exports only a small portion of the world's supply of some commodity faces a perfectly elastic demand because the price is not affected by its volume of sales. The given world price is p_W. The domestic supply curve shows that intended output is q_0 at that price. Unintended fluctuations cause output to vary between q_1 and q_2. When output is at q_1, farm income is given by the dark shaded area. When output is q_2, farm income is given by the total of the light and the dark shaded areas.

Output fluctuations at given world prices. Figure 6-9 illustrates fluctuations in domestic output. It considers sales over several years at a given world price. If the government does nothing in the face of supply fluctuations, farmers will find their incomes fluctuating positively with their outputs. In years of bumper crops sales will rise, and price will not be driven down, so incomes will rise. In years of poor crops sales will fall, but price will not rise, so incomes will fall.

Note the contrast with the case where demand is inelastic, so that farm incomes fluctuate in the direction opposite to output. Good harvests depress incomes and bad harvests raise them. The effect of selling on the international market and being only a small part of total world supply is to make the demand curve facing domestic producers perfectly elastic (even though the world demand curve is inelastic). This reverses the direction of income fluctuations.

When domestic farmers sell at a given world price that is unaffected by their own volume of sales, their incomes fluctuate in the same direction as their short-term fluctuations in output.

The incomes of farmers who produce nonperishable crops could be stabilized if the government develops a scheme allowing farmers to store their outputs in years of bumper crops and to sell from stocks in years of poor crops. Effectively, sales would always be equal to planned output. Any unplanned excess of production is stored, and any shortfall is made up out of sales from stocks.

This would certainly stabilize farmers' receipts, but it would not be a desirable policy. Consider two alternatives. One is to store the crop. But storage costs money and postpones the receipt of revenue until the sales occur. The other alternative is to sell all the crop each year and then save the extra money received in good years to spend in bad years. In that case the extra receipts in good years are received immediately and can be invested to earn interest until they are needed in bad years.

Fluctuations in world prices. When world prices fluctuate it may pay to hold stocks. When the government judges that this year's price is unusually low, it can store some of the output in the hope of selling it later at a better price. When the government judges that this year's price is unusually high, it can sell some of the stocks that it put aside in years when the price was low.

In a world in which future prices were known with certainty the government would have a simple calculation to make. It would merely calculate the extra revenue that could be obtained by selling at some future price higher than the present one and subtract the costs of storage to see if the crop should be sold now or held.[2] In practice the future is not known, and the government must use its knowledge of market conditions to guess its best policy. The government will be inclined to store a larger amount this year the more it expects prices to rise in future years and to sell more from stocks the more it expects prices to fall in future years.

Governments employ agricultural economists who monitor weather conditions and trends in world demands and supplies. Economists in university departments of agriculture have developed sophisticated data for analyzing such data and predicting the behavior of world markets of foodstuffs. If the government is good at predicting the future state of the market, it will increase farmers' revenues by selling less when prices are low and more when prices are high, as compared with a policy of selling the whole crop each year. If the government's market predictions are wrong, however, the scheme can bring losses. Consider an example. Say the market price falls this year and the government thinks the low price will not last, so it stores some of this year's crop. Next year, however, prices are even lower. But the government remains optimistic about the future, so it adds further to its stocks in storage. This continues for several years until the government finally concludes that the downward drift in prices is a long-term trend that will not be reversed in the foreseeable future. The government must now try to unload its excess stocks, and the holdings will be sold at much lower prices than would have been achieved if the whole crop had been sold each year.

[2] Since the money from selling the crop now could be invested, the profit from waiting to sell at a future date must exceed the revenue that could be earned by selling now and investing the money until that later date.

Sales on the Domestic Market Only

We now study commodities that are sold mainly on the domestic market where the main supply comes from domestic production. The difference between this case and the one just considered is that the demand for the domestic product is now negatively sloped and inelastic. Market price is determined by domestic demand and supply, and if nothing is done, the analysis of Figure 6-7 will apply, and farm income will fluctuate in the direction opposite to output. Can farm income be stabilized in this case?

Price stabilization. Suppose the government enters the market, buying and thereby adding to its own stocks when there is a surplus and selling and thereby reducing its stocks when there is a shortage. If it had enough grain elevators and warehouses, and if its support price were set at a realistic level, the government could stabilize *prices* indefinitely. But this would not stabilize farmers' revenues, which would be high with bumper crops and low with poor crops.

In effect, the government policy imposes a demand curve that is perfectly elastic at the support price. The situation is then the same as the one analyzed in Figure 6-9, a product is exported at a given world price and income fluctuates in the same direction as output.

Government price supports at the equilibrium price would not stabilize revenues. They would, however, reverse the pattern of revenue fluctuation.

Revenue stabilization. Obviously, there must be a government buying and selling policy that will stabilize farmers' receipts. What are its characteristics? As has been seen, too much price stability causes receipts to vary directly with production, and too little price stability causes receipts to vary inversely with production. It appears that the government should aim at some intermediate degree of price stability. If the government allows prices to vary in inverse proportion to variations in production, receipts will be stabilized. A 10 percent rise in production should be met by a 10 percent fall in price, and a 10 percent fall in production by a 10 percent rise in price.

To stabilize farmers' receipts, the government must make the demand curve facing the farmers one of unit elasticity. It must buy in periods of high output and sell in periods of low output, but only enough to let prices change in inverse proportion to farmers' output.

Long-term effects. In practice stabilization plans, whether they seek to fix prices completely or merely to dampen free-market fluctuations, often seek to set an average price *above* the average free-market equilibrium level. This is due to the fact that stabilization is not the only goal; there is also a desire to assure farmers of a standard of living comparable with that of city dwellers. This involves attempting to *raise* farm incomes in addition to stabilizing them.

Here, too, the government buys in periods of high output and sells in periods of low output, but on average it buys much more than it sells, with the result that unsold surpluses accumulate (see Figure 6-10). Taxpayers will generally be paying farmers for producing goods that no one is willing to purchase at prices that come near to covering costs. This is the route taken by the European Community with its Common Agricultural Policy (CAP). This policy has supported the existing farm population of Europe by guaranteeing them stable and high prices. It has also turned Western Europe from a net importer of agricultural products—which it would still be under free-market determination—into a net exporter. When Spain recently entered the EC and had to adopt the CAP, the United States complained bitterly because Spanish purchases of efficiently produced, cheap American agricultural imports were largely replaced by expensive but protected production from the rest of the Community.

As a result of the CAP, the EC is now faced with mounting stockpiles of many agricultural products. Periodically, it seeks to sell some of the surpluses to outside countries, particularly those in Eastern Europe, charging prices well below costs of production. The net result is that taxpayers in Western Europe are subsidizing consumers in Eastern Europe by allowing them to buy goods at prices much below their cost of production. Payments under the CAP now account for over half of the EC's entire budget. Concern is mounting that the ever-growing payments to farmers may soon outrun the EC's ability to pay the required payments.

FIGURE 6-10 Price Supports Above the Equilibrium Price

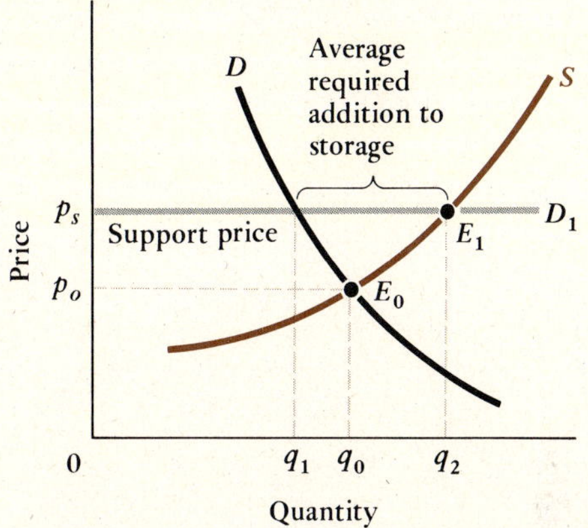

The support price becomes a price floor, and the government must purchase the excess supply at that price. Average annual demand and supply are D and S, respectively. The free-market equilibrium is at E_0. If the government will buy any quantity at p_s, the demand curve becomes the gray curve D_1 and equilibrium shifts to E_1. The average addition to storage is the quantity q_1q_2. The government purchases add to farmers' receipts and to government expenditures.

Government quotas. Another way of holding the price above its free-market equilibrium level is to reduce the supply through quotas. Under this system no one can produce the product without having a government-issued quota. Sufficient quotas are is-

FIGURE 6-11 **Price Support Through the Use of Quotas**

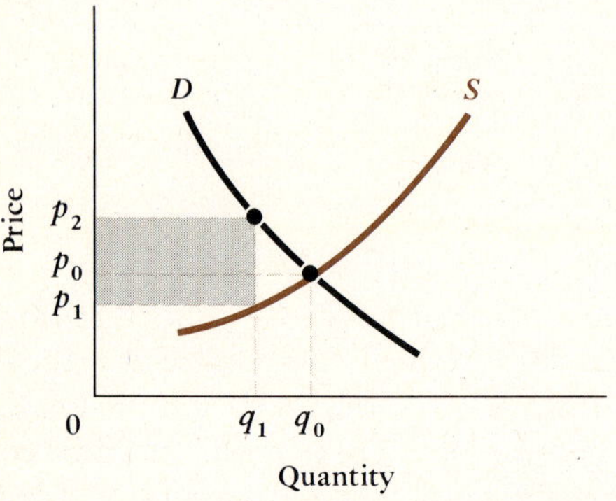

A quota below the equilibrium quantity maintains the price above the equilibrium level without generating surpluses. If a total quota of q_1 is enforced, the price will rise to p_2. Since the supply curve indicates that in a free market producers would be willing to supply q_1 at a lower price p_1, the effect is to provide holders of quotas with additional revenues, represented by the shaded areas.

sued to hold production at any desired level below the free-market output. This drives prices above their free-market level. This quota system, which is analyzed in Figure 6-11, has the advantage of not causing the accumulation of massive unsold surpluses. It is widely used in Canada.

The quota system affects both the short-term and the long-term behavior of agricultural markets. Consider short-term fluctuations first. There will still be good crops and poor crops, and other natural disturbances such as outbreaks of disease, that will cause short-term fluctuations in output. A shortfall of output below the quota will drive price upwards. Farmers with no crop to sell will lose, but those farmers whose outputs fall proportionally less than the price rise will gain. Since most agricultural products have inelastic demands, the typical farmer must gain—the percentage increase in market price will exceed the percentage fall in the aggregate crop.

What about unplanned extra output due to favorable conditions? The farmer is allowed to sell only the amount covered by the quota. The rest must be either destroyed or sold on some secondary market not covered by the quota system. (For example, milk quotas usually do not cover the sale of milk for manufacturing into cheese and other products, so surpluses are sold—at a greatly reduced price—on these markets.) Farm income is stabilized. The quota output is sold at the market price for that output even when there is surplus output (and the rest goes for what it can get). In a free-market system, given the typical inelastic demand, price would fall more, proportionally, than output would rise, and producers' incomes would shrink drastically.

A quota system guarantees that farmers will always get the free-market price of the total quota output whenever output equals or exceeds the quota and more when output falls short of the quota.

Thus the quota system is superior to many of the systems mentioned earlier in that it really does remove the downside risks caused by unexpected increases in output, and it does not, like the CAP, lead to accumulating stockpiles of unsalable output. The main cost is met by consumers, who on average pay a price that is higher, and consume an output that is lower, than would occur under free-market conditions.

Now consider the long term. We have seen that the quota drives price above its free-market level by restricting output. For purposes of illustration let us say that the quota is on eggs. Those who are producing eggs when the system is first instituted must gain. Since production falls, total costs must fall; since demand is inelastic, total revenue must rise. Therefore egg producers find their profits rising, since they spend less to earn more revenue. No wonder quotas are popular among the original producers!

But do quotas really increase farm income in the long run? Because people leave the industry for such reasons as death and retirement and new people must enter to replace them, the quotas are made transferable. Existing holders can transfer their quotas to new, would-be egg producers. But the quota is valuable since it confers the right to produce eggs that earn a large profit as a result of the supply restriction. Therefore the quota commands a price. The price turns out to be the value of the extra profits that the quota system has produced.[3] The reasons why this is so are spelled out in detail in Chapter 12, where we consider entry into a competitive industry. But to show the common sense of the result now we argue as follows.

People have alternative ways of investing their money. For example, someone with money to invest could buy an egg farm, a small factory, a share in a large corporation, or a government bond. When returns are relatively high in one line of activity, people will rush to invest funds in it; when returns are relatively low, people will be reluctant to invest in that activity. This search of investors for the most profitable use for their funds tends to force an equality in the rates of return in alternative investments that are open to investors (making due allowances for differences in risk).

When the quota system makes production of eggs unusually profitable, there will be a rush to invest in egg production. But to produce eggs one must have a quota. The result is that the rush to enter the egg industry will bid up the price of the egg quota until egg production is no more profitable than other investments with similar risks.

The free-market price of a quota to produce some good will be such that the profitability of that good's production will be no more than the profitability of other lines of activity carrying similar risks.

In other words, the whole extra profitability created by the quota system becomes embodied in the price of the quota. The extra profits created by the quota will just provide an acceptable return on the money invested in buying the quota—if it provided more, the price of the quota would be bid up; if it provided less, the price of the quota would fall.

[3] The profits are an ongoing flow that will come to the farmer every year, whereas the price paid for the quota is a once-and-for-all payment. In Chapter 17 we will see how to calculate what is called the *discounted present value* of a flow of future receipts. This is what determines the exact price of the quota. In principle, it is the value to someone today of the claim to the flow of profits that will be received over the future.

For this reason new entrants to the industry will earn no more than the return available in other lines of production. Since that would also be the case under market-determined prices and outputs, the quota does not raise the profitability of producing eggs. What it does do is reduce some of the uncertainty due to unexpected short-term fluctuations of output. Farming becomes a somewhat less risky operation than before.

One other long-run effect needs to be mentioned. If demand keeps rising after the new producer has bought a quota while the number of quotas is not increased correspondingly, profitability of egg production will rise. Producers will sell the same amount of eggs at a higher price. As a result, the market price of a quota will rise. Thus all producers who bought their quotas before the demand rise was foreseen will gain from an increase in quota prices. They will find that when they come to retire they can sell out for more than they paid to buy in. This is the typical case in most real-world quota systems, and it gives existing producers, even those who bought in recently, some long-term gain from the system—once again bought at the expense of consumers who pay more for their eggs than under a free-market system.

Economics cannot tell us whether such a system is good or bad. What it can do is show us who will gain and who will lose and also which alleged sources of gain are effective and which are illusory.

Agricultural Policy in Canada

Marketing Boards and the Use of Quotas

The primary method by which agricultural stabilization is attempted in Canada is through the operation of marketing boards. Sales through them account for about half of all farm cash receipts.

Basically there are two types of government marketing boards. The first seeks to influence prices. This requires that a significant part of total supply be controlled. Most provincial marketing boards are of this "supply management" variety.

The second type of marketing board accepts prices as set on world markets and acts as a selling agency for producers. The benefits such boards offer to producers need not be at the cost of consumers. The most important example of this type in Canada is the Canadian Wheat Board.

Supply Management

The supply management schemes typically are provincially administered systems restricting output through quotas issued by provincial marketing boards. They vary from province to province but often cover milk, eggs, cheese, butter, and poultry. The monopoly profits created by these schemes are enormous and can be accurately measured by the prices farmers must pay to purchase quotas. For example, it currently costs $0.8 million to buy the minimum-sized quota needed to operate one family-sized chicken farm in Ontario and it costs $0.75 million to buy the quota needed to operate an average-sized dairy farm in the Fraser Valley.

All such supply management schemes require federal cooperation to limit imports. Otherwise the high prices would attract a flood of imports. This is the type of scheme analyzed in Figure 6-11.

The schemes are successful in reducing short-term fluctuations. They also greatly increase the cost of becoming a producer because a quota must be purchased in addition to the physical capital needed for production. The schemes are popular among farmers because they reduce risk in the short term and because the value of the quotas rises over the long term.

The political appeal of these schemes is evidence of the strong power of a small number of concentrated and well-organized producers, who gain, in relation to the lack of power of the large number of organized consumers, who foot the bill.

Orderly Marketing Schemes

The prime example here is the Canadian Wheat Board, which markets Canadian wheat at prices set on the world wheat market. The origins of government involvement in the marketing of Canadian wheat can be traced back to the early 1900s, when disparities in bargaining power emerged between western farmers and grain buyers. The growers' associations protested that unfair practices and control of prices were carried out by the companies controlling the elevators to which the farmers delivered their grain. The government's response was limited; except for the World War I period, government intervention before 1930 was confined to regulation of marketing procedures (such as grading, inspection, and provision of railway facilities), and provincial government participation in the subsidization of cooperative elevator companies. Pressures to establish a national marketing board built up during the 1920s, when the growers' vulnerability to the vagaries of the international wheat situation became the dominant concern, the proportion of output exported having grown to more than 70 percent. Heavy involvement by the government of Canada in the marketing of wheat finally came as a response to the disruptions of the Great Depression.

Under the Canadian Wheat Board Act of 1935, each year the government estimates the average price at which it expects the wheat crop to be sold. Seventy-five percent of that price is then paid to each farmer on delivery of the wheat. After the board sells the wheat, any proceeds in excess of the initial payments are distributed to the producers in proportion to the amount of wheat supplied by each. Should the sales revenue be less than the initial payments, the loss is absorbed by the government. But such a disastrous mistake—value of sales less than 75 percent of estimated value—rarely occurs, so the board's activities are largely self-financing.

The goals of the Wheat Board are not to influence world prices. Instead, by paying farmers 75 percent of the estimated average selling price over the year, the board provides farmers with a secure cash flow early in the selling period. The board also serves to secure farmers' incomes against intra-year fluctuations in wheat prices. It does this by pooling all its receipts and paying them out to farmers according to the amount of wheat delivered by each farmer but irrespective of the date within the year of that delivery. So the farmer is relieved of worry about what the spot price of wheat may be on the day of delivery. These functions of the board appear to be in the farmers' interests and not to be disadvantageous to consumers. Most farmers like the annual averaging of receipts, most find the information provided by an early estimate of this year's price useful, and most like the early cash flow of 75 percent of the estimated selling price provided on delivery.

Stocks. The board still has to decide whether to sell all of this year's crop or to carry some over as stocks until next year. The amounts held have varied dramatically with the state of the world wheat market. During some periods stocks have risen dramatically—to the extent that acreage reduction schemes were used temporarily at the end of the 1960s; during other periods stocks have stayed at quite low levels. Recently oversupply in the wheat market has led to the accumulation of stocks that in 1987 reached the record level of 8.3 million tons of wheat (which is 36 percent of a typical year's Canadian output).

The Outlook

Canada has two quite different agricultural sectors. The first serves mainly the local market. Some products, including many vegetables, compete on substantially free markets. Others, such as eggs, milk, cheese, and poultry, are supply-managed and sell in markets protected from foreign competition and stabilized by government management. Although problems arise from time to time, these producers are relatively successful and reasonably profitable when good years and bad years are taken together.

The second sector relies on exports for much of its earnings. The interests of this sector are to reduce protectionism—of the very sort that supply-managed industries wish to perpetuate—and their fortunes are tied to world market conditions. Fortunes differ dramatically from product to product in this sector. Producers of beef have competed well in the United States and have resisted suggestions for a supply management scheme. Wheat producers, by contrast, have been in great difficulty during the latter half of the 1980s and have received billions of dollars in both statutory and discretionary government aid.

After a decade of booming international markets from the early 1970s to the early 1980s, market conditions have taken a dramatic turn for the worse. World agricultural markets have been suffering from sagging prices due to a more rapid expansion of supply than demand. Very large subsidies and similar payments cushion the farmers in the United States and the EC, while farmers in Canada and such other countries as Australia depend more on market prices for their prosperity.

Agriculture Minister John Wise said in January 1987 that Canada provides direct subsidies of $34 a metric ton to wheat farmers, compared with $130 in the EC and the United States. Other studies suggest, however, that indirect subsidies to Canadian farmers close that gap substantially, making Canadian farmers depend heavily on massive public aid. The *Toronto Globe & Mail* recently reported that subsidies accounted for one-third of total Canadian farm revenue in 1986!

On the demand side, the world's population continues to grow and is projected to reach 6 billion by the end of the century. Although this will provide some new demand, much of the growth will be in countries where incomes, and hence demands, are the lowest. On the supply side, the so-called Green Revolution of the 1970s vastly expanded agricultural output in third world countries. This, plus the large quantities produced by subsidized farmers in the United States and the EC, suggests troubled times ahead for Canadian farmers who depend on export markets for their major source of income.

Five General Lessons About Resource Allocation

Our discussion of government intervention in markets that might have been left unregulated suggests four widely applicable lessons.

1. Costs May Be Shifted, but They Cannot Be Avoided

Production, whether in response to free-market signals or to government controls, uses resources; thus it involves costs to members of society. If it takes 5 percent of the nation's resources to provide housing at some stated average standard, those resources will not be available to produce other commodities. If resources are used to produce unwanted food products, those resources will not be available to produce other commodities. For society there is no such thing as free housing or free food.

The average standard of living depends on the amounts of resources available to the economy and the efficiency with which these resources are used. It follows that *costs are real* and are incurred no matter who provides the goods. Rent controls or subsidies to agriculture can change the share of the costs paid by particular individuals or groups, lowering the share for some and raising the share for others, but they cannot make the costs go away.

Different ways of *allocating* the costs may also affect the total amount of resources used and thus the amount of costs incurred. For example, controls that keep prices and profits of some commodity below free-market levels will lead to increased quantities demanded and decreased quantities supplied. Unless government steps in to provide additional supplies, fewer resources will be allocated to producing the commodity. If government chooses to supply all the demand at the controlled prices, more resources will be allocated to it, which means fewer resources will be devoted to other kinds of goods and services.

2. Free-Market Prices and Profits Encourage Economical Use of Resources

Prices and profits in a market economy provide signals to both demanders and suppliers. Prices that are high and rising (relative to other prices) provide an incentive to purchasers to economize on the commodity. They may choose to satisfy the want in question with substitutes whose prices have not risen so much (because they are less costly to provide) or to satisfy less of that want by shifting expenditure to the satisfaction of other wants.

On the supply side, rising prices tend to produce rising profits. Short-term windfall profits that bear no relation to current costs repeatedly occur in market economies. They attract resources that continue to move into the industry until profits fall to levels that can be earned elsewhere in the economy.

Falling prices and falling profits provide the opposite motivations. Purchasers are inclined to buy more; sellers are inclined to produce less and to move resources out of the industry and into more profitable undertakings.

The price system coordinates individual decisions that cause the allocation of resources to change in response to such events as the loss of a source of a raw material or the outbreak of a war. Changing relative prices and profits signal the need for change to which consumers and producers respond.

3. Government Intervention Affects Resource Allocation

Governments intervene in the price system sometimes to satisfy generally agreed social goals and sometimes to help politically influential interest groups. Government intervention changes the allocation of resources that the price system would achieve.

Interventions have allocative consequences because they inhibit the free-market allocative mechanism. Some controls, such as rent controls, prevent prices from rising (in response, say, to an increase in demand with no change in supply). If the price is held down, the signal is not given to consumers to economize on a commodity that is in short supply. On the supply side, when prices and profits are prevented from rising, the profit signals that would attract new resources into the industry are never given. The shortage continues, and the movements of demand and supply that would resolve it are not set in motion.

Other controls, such as agricultural price supports, prevent prices from falling (in response, say, to an increase in supply with no increase in demand). This leads to excess supply, and the signal is not given to producers to produce less or to buyers to increase their purchases. Surpluses continue, and the movements of demand and supply that would eliminate them are not set in motion.

4. Intervention Requires Alternative Allocative Mechanisms

Intervention typically requires alternative allocative mechanisms. During times of shortages allocation will be by sellers' preferences, on a first-come, first-

BOX 6-4

The Price of Haircuts and the Profits of Barbers

Assume that there are many barber shops and freedom of entry into barbering: anyone who qualifies can set up as a barber. Assume that the going price for haircuts is $10 and that at this price all barbers believe their income is too low. The barbers hold a meeting and decide to form a trade association. They agree on the following points: First, all barbers in the city must join the association and abide by its rules; second, any new barbers who meet certain professional qualifications will be required to join the association before they are allowed to practice their trade; third, the association will recommend a price for haircuts that no barber shall undercut.

The barbers intend to raise the price of haircuts in order to raise their incomes. You are called in as a consulting economist to advise them of the probable success of their plan. Suppose you are persuaded that the organization does have the requisite strength to enforce a price rise to, say, $14. What are your predictions about the consequences?

You now need to distinguish between the short-run and the long-run effects of an increase in the price of haircuts. In the short run the number of barbers is fixed. Thus, in the short run the answer depends only on the elasticity of the demand for haircuts.

If the demand elasticity is less than one, total expenditure on haircuts will rise and so will the incomes of barbers; if demand elasticity exceeds one, the barbers' revenues will fall. Thus you need some empirical knowledge about the elasticity of demand for haircuts.

Suppose on the basis of the best available evidence you estimate the elasticity of demand over the relevant price range to be 0.45. You then predict that barbers will be successful in raising incomes in the short run. A 40 percent rise in price will be met by an 18 percent fall in business, so the total revenue of the typical barber will rise by about 15 percent.*

* Let p and q be the price and quantity before the price increase. Total revenue after the increase is $TR = (1.40p)(.82q) = 1.148pq$.

Now what about the long run? If barbers were just covering costs before the price change, they will now be earning profits. Barbering will become an attractive trade relative to others requiring equal skill and training, and there will be a flow of barbers into the industry. As the number of barbers rises, the same amount of business must be shared among more and more barbers, so the typical barber will find business—and thus profits—decreasing. Profits may also be squeezed from another direction. With fewer customers coming their way, barbers may compete against one another for the limited number of customers. The association does not allow them to compete through price cuts, but they can compete in service. They may spruce up their shops, offer their customers expensive magazines to read, and so forth. This kind of competition will raise operating costs.

These changes will continue until barbers are just covering their opportunity costs, at which time the attraction for new entrants will vanish. The industry will settle down in a new long-run equilibrium in which individual barbers make incomes only as large as they did before the price rise. There will be more barbers than there were in the original situation, but each barber will be working for a smaller fraction of the day and will be idle for a larger fraction (the industry will have excess capacity). Barbers may prefer this situation; they will have more leisure. Customers may or may not prefer it: They will have shorter waits even at peak periods, and they will get to read a wide choice of magazines, but they will pay more for haircuts.

But you were hired to report to the barbers with respect to the effect on their incomes, not the effect on their leisure. The report that you finally present will thus say: "You will succeed in the short run (because you face a demand curve that is inelastic), but your plan is bound to be self-defeating in the long run unless you are able to prevent the entry of new barbers."

served basis, or under some system of government rationing. During periods of surplus there will be unsold supplies unless the government buys and stores the surpluses. Since long-run changes in demand and costs do not induce resource reallocations through private decisions, the government will have to step in. It will have to force resources out of industries where prices are held too high, as it has tried to do in agriculture, and into industries where prices are held too low, as it can do, for example, by providing public housing.

Intervention almost always has both benefits and costs. Economics cannot answer the questions of whether a particular intervention with free markets is desirable, but it can clarify the issues by identifying benefits and costs and who will enjoy or bear them. In doing so it can identify the competing values involved. This will be discussed in detail in Chapter 23.

5. Intervention Can Control Prices and Quantities but Unless Entry Can Also Be Controlled It Cannot Control Incomes

For example, output restraints by existing producers reduce quantity and drive up price. But if farmers' incomes are increased, entry will occur. The supplies of new farmers will drive down prices until farmers earn the same incomes as can be earned in other comparable occupations. Similarly, if prices are pushed up as a result of public policy, incomes may increase initially but, once again, entry will occur until incomes return to normal. Box 6-4 (p. 125) illustrates this conclusion with a further example.

Summary

1. The elementary theory of supply, demand, and price provides powerful tools for analyzing and understanding some real-world problems and policies. The chapter illustrates a few of them.
2. Effective price floors lead to excess supply. Either the potential seller is left with quantities that cannot be sold, or the government must step in and buy the surplus. Effective price ceilings lead to excess demand and provide a strong incentive for black marketeers to buy at the controlled price and sell at the higher free-market price.
3. Rent controls are a form of price ceiling. The major consequence of effective rent control is a shortage of rental accommodation that gets worse due to a slow but inexorable decline in the quantity of rental housing.
4. Rent controls can be an effective response to temporary situations in which there is a ban on building or a transitory increase in demand. They will almost surely fail when they are introduced as a response to a long-run increase in demand or to inflation in the costs of providing rental housing.
5. The long-term problems of agriculture arise from a high rate of productivity growth on the supply side and a low income elasticity on the demand side. This means that unless many resources are being transferred out of agriculture, quantity supplied increases faster than quantity demanded year after year.
6. Many agricultural prices and incomes are depressed by chronic surpluses in agricultural markets. At various times and places, government policies to protect farm incomes have included buying farmers' output at above free-market prices, limiting production and acreage by quotas, and paying farmers to leave crops unpro-

duced. Such policies tend to inhibit the reallocation mechanism and thus to increase farm surpluses above what they would otherwise be and lead to accumulating stocks.

7. Agricultural commodities are subject to wide fluctuations in market prices, which cause fluctuations in producers' incomes. This is because of year-to-year unplanned fluctuations in supplies combined with inelastic demand and because of cyclical fluctuations in demand combined with inelastic supplies. Where demand is inelastic, large crops tend to be associated with low total receipts and small crops with high total receipts.
8. Canadian government stabilization policies operate in two types of markets. In the first, which covers products such as wheat, the bulk of production is exported at prices set in world markets. In this case there is little that the government can usefully do to stabilize prices or to insulate revenues from fluctuating in response to unplanned fluctuations in output. The government can, however, seek to mitigate fluctuations in revenue that stem from fluctuations in world prices. This is done by storing some of the crop when prices are thought to be unusually low and selling out of stocks when prices are thought to be unusually high.
9. In the second type of market, which includes many products such as milk, eggs, cheese, and chickens, the product is sold on a domestic market that is protected from foreign competition either by natural factors or by government restrictions on imports. This is the case with most provincial supply management schemes. These seek to reduce output by issuing quotas. The effect is that price is not driven down when there is an unplanned increase in supply (because the extra output cannot be sold on the market covered by the quota scheme), and thus actual price exceeds the free-market equilibrium price. Farmers gain by the reduction in short-term price fluctuations and by any increase in the values of their quotas after they have purchased them. Since the quota price reflects the additional profits brought about by supply restriction, new entrants into the industry do not earn higher returns on their investments than they could earn in other lines bearing similar risks or that they would have earned if the good were produced under free-market conditions.

Topics for Review

Price floor and price ceiling
Allocation by sellers' preferences, rationing, and black market
Windfall profits and their allocative function
Short-run and long-run supply curves
Effects of high productivity growth and low income elasticity
Importance of export demand
Price supports at and above the level of free-market equilibrium
Supply management in domestic markets

Discussion Questions

1. "When a controlled item is vital to everyone, it is easier to start controlling the price than to stop controlling it. Such controls are popular with consumers, regardless of their harmful consequences." Explain why it may be inefficient to have such controls, why they may be popular, and why, if they are popular, the government might nevertheless choose to decontrol these prices.
2. A law school has 1,000 qualified applicants for 200 places in the first-year class. It is debating a number of alternative admission criteria: (a) a lottery, (b) examination grades, (c) recommendations from alumni, and (d) place of residence of applicant. An economist on the faculty determined that if the tuition level is doubled, the excess demand will disappear. Argue for (or against) using the tuition rate to replace each of the other suggested criteria.
3. It is sometimes asserted that the rising costs of construction are putting housing out of the reach of ordinary citizens. Who bears the heaviest cost when rentals are kept down by (a) rent controls, (b) a subsidy to tenants equal to some fraction of their rent payments, and (c) low-cost public housing?
4. Discuss the following extract from a story that appeared in the *Toronto Star* in October 1986. Toronto landlord Lawrence Smither "says he won't rent his empty apartments until the [Rent Control] Commission gives him permission to charge $400.40 for all his two-bedroom units. Rent review officer Robert Sutherland agrees $400.40 is a 'reasonable rent' for those units, but he says the commission won't give Smither permission to charge higher rents because they would exceed the allowable annual rent increases."
5. The press recently reported that "Angry [Toronto city] council members said the Rental Housing Protection Act, passed last summer to thwart demolitions, luxury renovations and condominium conversions of affordable rental housing, is flawed because it does not apply to vacant buildings." What do you think landlords had been doing to provoke this anger from council members? Why would they want to do this? Why is such an act apparently needed in Ontario but not in several other Canadian provinces including Alberta and British Columbia? If current landlords have to be prevented by law from converting their apartments to other uses, what kinds of buildings would you expect to find being newly constructed?
6. Recently several Liberal and Conservative Ontario politicians were quoted as saying that they did not intend to keep their provinces' rent controls indefinitely; they went on to say that controls would be removed as soon as the vacancy rate for apartments rose to reasonable levels, signaling an end to the housing crisis. Given this condition for their removal, how long would you expect rent controls to persist?
7. "This year the weather smiled on us, God smiled on us, and we made a crop," says Don Marble, a grain and cotton farmer in South Plains, Texas. "But just as we made a crop, the economic situation changed." This quotation brings to mind the old saying, "If you are a farmer, the weather is always bad." Discuss the sense in which this saying might be true.

8. The Kenya Meat Commission (KMC) decided it was undemocratic to allow meat prices to be out of the reach of the ordinary citizen. It decided to freeze meat prices. Six months later, in a press interview, the managing commissioner of the KMC made the following statements. Do the facts alleged make sense given KMC's policy?
   a. "The price of almost everything in Kenya has gone up, but we have not increased the price of meat. The price of meat in this country is still the lowest in the world."
   b. "Cattle are scarce in the country, but I do not know why."
   c. "People are eating too much beef, and unless they diversify their eating habits and eat other foodstuffs, the shortage of beef will continue."
9. Discuss the following statement by University of Saskatchewan professor of agricultural economics Gary Storey, recently quoted in the press. "One of the sad truths of the agricultural policies in Europe and the United States is that they do very little for the future generations of farmers. Most of the subsidies get capitalized into higher land prices, creating windfall gains for current landowners. It creates a situation where the next generation of farmers require, and ask for, increased government support."
10. Compare the following two headlines that appeared within a week of each other in the early 1980s.
    a. "Bumper potato crop dashes farmers' hopes."
    b. "Record high wheat crop leaves farmers smiling."
11. Discuss the following two statements, each made in 1987. Do you see a relation between them?
    a. "The current financial crisis is so large that it may be beyond the fiscal capability of governments to solve by subsidies and public assistance. Government assistance has not been able to prevent farm financial problems."—George Brinkman, professor of agricultural economics, University of Guelph
    b. "Ironically, the industry is a victim of its own success. Programs (to increase agricultural production in many countries in the 1970s) were so successful that the world is now awash with surplus food. There are mountains of grain, cheese, and beef in storage around the world, and lakes of milk, wine, and olive oil."—Oliver Bertin, journalist
12. Discuss the following recent headlines in terms of the analysis of this chapter.
    a. "Huge grain stockpiles blunt price upturn, economist says."
    b. "Farm children plan for careers off the family land."
    c. "Subsidies for farmers may be intractable dilemma."
    d. "If wheat falls, so do land prices."

PART THREE

Consumption, Production, and Cost

7

Household Consumption Behavior

In Part Two we saw that demand is an important part of the explanation of market prices and that the shapes of demand curves influence how markets behave. But why do market demand curves have the shapes they do? To address this question, we need to study the behavior of individual households since that behavior underlies market demand curves.

We start by studying the choices that face every household that has money to spend and commodities it would like to buy. Later in the chapter we go on to develop theories of how households make their choices.

The Choices Households Face

To begin, let us reduce our problem to its basics by considering a household that has a specific income that it must spend on just two commodities, food and clothing. (Simplifying by considering only two goods allows us to see the essential points in their simplest context.) Suppose that the household has a money income of $360 a week and that the prices for food and clothing are $12 a unit for food and $6 a unit for clothing. For the purpose of our example, further suppose that the household does not save; its only choice is in deciding how much of its $360 to spend on food (*F*) and how much to spend on clothing (*C*).

The Budget Line

The household's alternatives are described by the solid line *ab* in Figure 7-1. That line, which is called a **budget line,** shows all the combinations of food and clothing that the household can buy. It indicates all the combinations of commodities available to the household if it spends a fixed amount of money, in this case all its income, at fixed prices of the commodities. (It is also sometimes called an *isocost line* since all points on it represent bundles of goods with the same total cost.) The budget line has several important properties.

1. Points on the budget line indicate bundles of commodities that use up the household's entire income. (Try, for example, the point 20*C*, 20*F*.)
2. Points between the budget line and the origin indicate bundles

FIGURE 7-1 A Budget Line

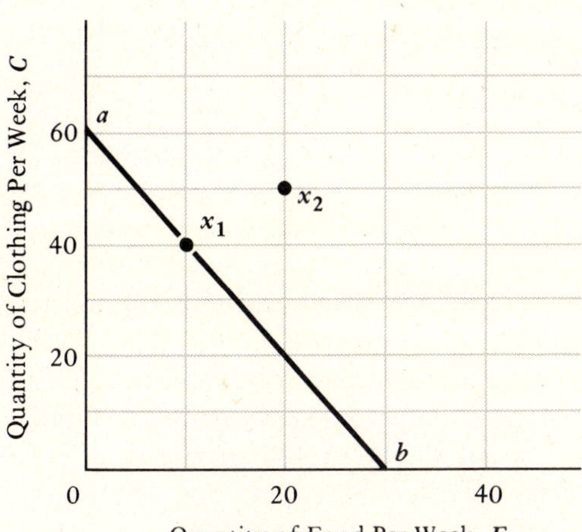

The budget line shows the quantities of goods available to a household given its money income and the prices of goods it buys. Any point in this diagram indicates a combination (or bundle) of so much food and so much clothing. Point x_2, for example, indicates 50 units of clothing and 20 units of food per week. With an income of $360 a week and prices of $12 for food and $6 for clothing, respectively, the household's budget line is *ab*. This line shows all the combinations of *F* and *C* available to a household spending that income at those prices. The household could spend all of its income on clothing and obtain 60 units of clothing and zero food each week. It could also go to the other extreme and purchase only food, buying 30 units of *F* and zero of *C*. Or it could choose an intermediate position and consume some of both goods; for example, it could spend $120 to buy 10 units of *F* and $240 to buy 40 units of *C* (point x_1). Points above the budget line such as x_2 are not available.

of commodities that cost less than the household's income. (Try, for example, the point 20*C*, 10*F*.)

3. Points above the budget line indicate combinations of commodities that cost more than the household's income. (Try, for example, the point 30*C*, 40*F*.)

The budget line shows all combinations of commodities that are available to the household given its money income and the prices of the goods that it purchases.

Shifts in the Budget Line

Change in Money Income

What happens to the budget line when money income changes? If the household's money income is halved from $360 to $180 per week, while prices remain unchanged at $12 for food and $6 for clothing, the amount of goods the household can buy will also be halved. This causes the budget line to shift inward toward the origin as shown in Figure 7-2. All possible combinations now open to the household appear on budget line *cd*, which is closer to the origin than the original budget line *ab*.

If the household's income rises to $540 while the prices of food and clothing remain unchanged, it will be able to increase its purchases of both commodities. The budget line shifts outward as shown by the line *ef* in Figure 7-2.

Variations in the household's money income, with prices constant, shift the budget line parallel to itself. It shifts outward (away from the origin) when income rises and inward (toward the origin) when income falls.

Proportional Changes in All Prices

Now return to the initial situation where the household has an income of $360 and faces prices of $12 for food and $6 for clothing. Let the prices of food and clothing double to $24 and $12, respectively. This halves the quantities of food and clothing that can be bought and so shifts the budget line inward parallel to itself. These price changes have exactly the same effect as when prices remain constant at $12 and $6, but money income falls from $360 to $180. Similarly, a proportional reduction of both prices causes the budget line to shift outward in exactly the same manner that an increase in money income does.

Proportional changes in the money prices of all goods, with money income constant, shift the budget line parallel to itself. It shifts outward (away from the origin) when prices fall and inward (toward the origin) when prices rise.

FIGURE 7-2 The Effect on the Budget Line of Changes in Money Income

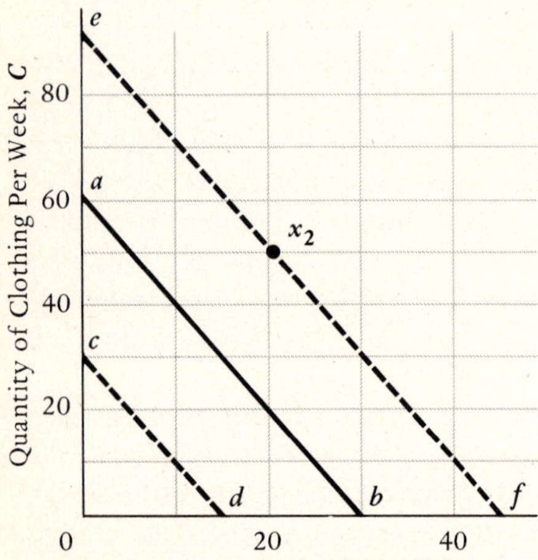

Changes in the household's income shift the budget line outward when income rises and inward when income falls. The original budget line *ab* refers to a money income of $360 and prices of $12 for *F* and $6 for *C*. If the household's money income is halved from $360 to $180 per week, while prices remain unchanged, the amount of goods the household can buy will also be halved. This causes the budget line to shift inward (toward the origin) to *cd*. If the household spends all its income on clothing, it will now get 30 units of clothing and zero units of food (point *c* in the figure). If it spends all its income on food, it will get 15 food and zero clothing (point *d*).

If the household's income rises to $540 while the prices of food and clothing remain unchanged, the budget line shifts outward to *ef*. If the household buys only clothing, it can have 90 units of clothing; if it buys only food, it can have 45 units of food. Point x_2, indicating 50 units of *C* and 20 of *F*, is now available, as shown by the fact that it lies on the new budget line *ef*.

Money Income and Real Income

Clearly, there can be exactly offsetting changes in prices and money incomes, which leave the real choices available to the household unchanged. For example, if money income and prices all rise by 10 percent, the position of the budget line is unchanged.

A proportional change in money income and in all money prices leaves the household neither better nor worse off in terms of its ability to purchase commodities.

The foregoing observations lead us to make the important distinction between money income and real income. A household's **money income** is its income measured in money units—so many dollars and cents per week or per year. A household's **real income** is the *purchasing power* of its money income; it is the quantity of goods and services that can be purchased with that money income.

If prices remain constant, any change in money income will cause a corresponding change in purchasing power. If the household's money income rises by 10 percent (say, from $10,000 to $11,000), the household is able to buy 10 percent more of all commodities—its real income has also risen by 10 percent.

If prices change, purchasing power and money incomes will not change in the same proportion; indeed, they can easily change in *opposite* directions. Consider a situation in which all prices rise by 10 percent. If money income rises by any amount less than 10 percent, real income falls. If money income also rises by 10 percent, real income will be unchanged. Only if money income rises by more than 10 percent will real income also rise.

Changes in real income are shown graphically by shifts in the budget line. When the budget line in Figure 7-2 shifts away from the origin, real income rises. When the line shifts toward the origin, real income falls.

A household's ability to purchase goods and services is measured by real income, not by money income.

Changes in Relative Prices

The price of a commodity usually refers to the amount of money that must be spent to acquire one unit of the commodity. This is called the **absolute price** or *money price*. A **relative price** is the ratio of two absolute prices. The statement "The price of *F* is \$12" refers to an absolute price; the statement "The price of *F* is twice the price *C*" refers to a relative price.

A change in the relative price can be accomplished by changing both of the absolute prices in different proportions or by holding one absolute price constant and changing the other. The points we wish to make can be established by studying the case in which changes in relative prices are accomplished by holding one money price constant and changing the other.

Return, for example, to the original illustration where a household with an income of \$360 faced prices of \$12 for food and \$6 for clothing. Now let the price of food fall to \$6. This lowers the price of food *relative* to the price of clothing and, as shown in Figure 7-3, changes the slope of the budget line.

FIGURE 7-3 The Effect on the Budget Line of Changes in the Price of Food

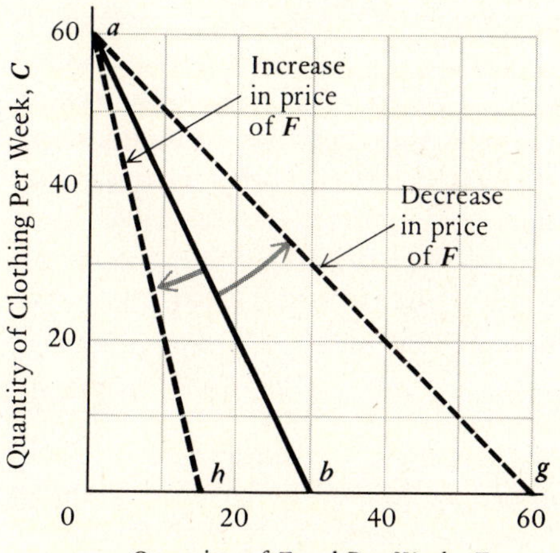

A change in the absolute price of one commodity changes relative prices and thus changes the slope of the budget line. The original budget line *ab* occurred with a money income of \$360, with units of *C* priced at \$6 and units of *F* at \$12. A fall in the price of *F* to \$6 doubles the quantity of *F* obtainable for any given quantity of *C* purchased and pivots the budget line outward to *ag*. A rise in the price of *F* to \$24 reduces the quantity of *F* obtainable and pivots the budget line inward to *ah*.

The important conclusion is this:

A change in relative prices alters the slope of the budget line.

The significance of the slope of the budget line for food and clothing is that it reflects the opportunity cost of food in terms of clothing. This is because, as we have just seen, the slope of the budget line reflects the relative prices of the two commodities. In order to increase food consumption while maintaining expenditure constant, one must move along the budget line and therefore consume less clothing.

Return for the moment to the original situation where the price of food (p_F) is \$12 and the price of clothing (p_C) is \$6. With income fixed, it is necessary to forgo the purchase of two units of clothing to acquire one unit extra of food. The opportunity cost of a unit of food is thus two units of clothing. This opportunity cost can also be stated as p_F/p_C, which is the relative price of food in terms of clothing.

Notice that the relative price (in our example $p_F/p_C = 2$) is consistent with an infinite number of absolute prices. If $p_F = \$40$ and $p_C = \$20$, it still takes the sacrifice of two units of clothing to acquire one unit of food. This shows that it is relative, not absolute, prices that determine opportunity cost.

The opportunity cost of food in terms of clothing is measured by the slope of the budget line and also by the relative price ratio, p_F/p_C. [9]

The Choices Households Make

The combination that the household chooses will depend on both what it can do and what it wants to do. What it can do is shown by the budget line it faces, which we have just studied; what it wants to do is determined by its tastes. Given its budget line and its tastes, what will the household do?[1]

[1] In the two appendixes to this chapter we develop two theories of household choice. In the text we show how far we can get using the budget line alone plus the simple assumption that households are consistent in their decision making.

The key assumption about household behavior is that *households maximize what is variously called their satisfactions, their welfare, their well-being or their utility.* In Appendix 7A you will find this assumption worded in the form that households seek to maximize utility. In Appendix 7B this assumption is worded in the form that households seek to maximize welfare by reaching the highest attainable indifference curve: However it is worded, and whatever the theory used to develop it, the important thing is that households are assumed to try to do as well for themselves as they can. Faced with a choice between two alternative consumption bundles, each household is assumed to choose the bundle that it prefers—which is the same thing as saying that the household makes its choices so as to maximize its satisfactions or its welfare. The popular but misguided criticism that this assumption is to be rejected because it is "unrealistic" is considered in Box 7-1.

Income and Substitution Effects

How does the household react to a change in the price of one good? (For purposes of illustration we consider a fall in price.) A fall in the price of one good affects the consumer in two ways. First, relative prices change, providing an incentive to buy *more of the good in question* because it is cheaper. Second, the household's real income increases, because it can buy more of all commodities (as can be seen, for example, by comparing budget lines *ab* and *ag* in Figure 7-3). This rise in real income provides an incentive to buy *different amounts of all goods.* (Recall from Chapter 5 that when its income rises the household buys more of all normal goods and less of all inferior goods.)

These two effects are illustrated in Table 7-1 and Figure 7-4, both of which continue the example used earlier in this chapter. The household initially has a money income of $360 and faces prices of food and clothing of $12 and $6, respectively. The data are shown in the table, and the budget line is shown in the figure. Given the household's tastes, it will prefer a combination of goods shown by some particular point on this line. For our purposes it does not matter which particular point is chosen, so we let it be the point shown by row (2) of the table, indicated by the point E_0 in part (i) of Figure 7-4.

The price of food then falls to $6, making it possible for the household to buy more of both commodities—which is why we say its real income has risen. The household chooses its preferred position on the new budget line, which we assume to be the one indicated in row (9) of the table and by point E_1 in the figure. The shift in consumption is partly a response to the change in the *slope* of the budget line, reflecting the change in relative prices. It is also partly a response to an *outward shift* in the budget line, reflecting the increase in the household's real income due to the fall in one money price with money income and all other money prices remaining constant.

To isolate the effect of the change in relative price, when the price of food falls, we also reduce the household's money income to its original purchasing power. To do this we reduce income until the original bundle of food and clothing can just be bought at the new prices. Facing the household with the new prices, and the reduced money income that just allows it to purchase its original bundle of goods, isolates the effects of the change in relative prices when the purchasing power of income is held constant. The household's reaction is the **substitution effect.** Whatever the household now does is a result of a change in relative prices with the purchasing power of income held constant. As shown by both row (5) of the table and part (ii) of the figure, the household buys more food, whose relative price has fallen, and less clothing, whose relative price has risen.

Next we restore the household's money income, which shifts the budget line outward parallel to itself. Assuming that we are dealing with a normal good, the household will increase its consumption of food. (It will also increase its consumption of clothing.) The household's reaction to this shift of its budget line is called its **income effect.** It is shown by the change between rows (5) and (9) in the table and points E_i and E_1 in part (iii) of the figure.

We have now broken down the reaction to a fall in the price of a commodity (food in our example) into a substitution effect and an income effect. In our numerical example the substitution effect raises the consumption of food by 6 and the income effect

BOX 7-1

Does Demand Theory Require That Households Always Act Rationally?

The theory of household behavior uses the key assumption that households always act rationally in the maximization of their satisfaction. This rationality assumption appears in slightly different form in various theories, but it always amounts to assuming that each household assesses any choices it faces and consistently chooses its preferred alternative.

It is tempting to dismiss demand theory with the objection that consumer rationality is an unrealistic assumption. After all, most of us know people who occasionally buy strawberries in spite of, even because of, a rise in their price and others who sometimes spend a week's pay on a binge or a frivolous purchase that they afterward regret.

To assess the significance of such observed "irrationalities" it is helpful to distinguish three possible uses of demand theory. The first is to study the aggregate behavior of all households—as illustrated, for example, by the market demand curve for gasoline or carrots. The second use is to make statements about an individual household's probable actions. The third is to make statements about what each household will certainly do.

The criticism that the assumption of rationality is not realistic applies primarily to the third use of demand theory. Observations of unusual or irrational behavior refute only the prediction that *all* households *always* behave as assumed by the theory. To predict the existence of a relatively stable, negatively sloped market demand curve (the first use) or to predict what an individual household will probably do (the second use), we do *not* require that *all* households behave as assumed by the theory all of the time. Consider two illustrations.

First, some households may always behave in a manner not assumed by the theory. Households whose members have serious emotional disturbances are one obvious example. The inconsistent or erratic behavior of such households will not cause market demand curves to depart from their downward slope, provided these households account for a minority of total purchasers of any product. Their erratic behavior will be swamped by the normal behavior of the majority of households.

Second, an occasional spurt of impulse buying or of downright irrationality on the part of every household will not upset the downward slope of the market demand curve so long as these isolated inconsistencies do not occur at the same time and in the same way in all households. As long as such inconsistencies are unrelated across households, occurring now in one and now in another, their effects will be offset by the normal behavior of the majority of households.

The downward slope of the demand curve requires only that at any moment of time most households are behaving as predicted by the theory. This is compatible with inconsistent behavior on the part of some households all of the time and on the part of all households some of the time.

Long ago the great U.S. president Abraham Lincoln said, "You can fool some of the people all of the time and all of the people some of the time, but you cannot fool all of the people all of the time." The same thought holds for irrational behavior: Most people may behave irrationally some of the time, some people behave irrationally all of the time, but all people will not be irrational all of the time. Lincoln's observation helps make clear why the assumption of rationality yields correct predictions about the slope of market demand curves.

raises it by 4, making the overall response to the fall in price of food an increase of 10 units. Of course, when the price of food falls, the household moves directly from its initial position to its final position, buying 10 more units of food. By breaking this movement into two parts, however, we are able to study the response to a change in relative prices and to a change in real income.

TABLE 7-1 Calculation of the Income and Substitution Effects: A Numerical Example

	FOOD	CLOTHING	TOTAL
I. Initial position			
(1) Price	$ 12	$ 6	
(2) Quantity	15	30	
(3) Expenditure	$180	$180	$360
II. The price of food falls to $6 while money income is reduced to $270 so that the initial bundle can still just be purchased at the new prices.			
(4) Price	$ 6	$ 6	
(5) Quantity	21	24	
(6) Expenditure	$126	$144	$270
(7) Substitution effect: Line (5) − line (2) = 6			

	FOOD	CLOTHING	TOTAL
III. Money income is returned to $360.			
(8) Price	$ 6	$ 6	
(9) Quantity	25	35	
(10) Expenditure	$150	$210	$360
(11) Income effect: Line (9) − line (5) = 4			

IV. Total effect on food purchases of a change in the price of food

Substitution effect (from row 7):	6
plus: Income effect (from row 11):	4
Total effect	10
Or, what is the same thing.	
Final quantity purchased (from row 9):	25
minus: Initial quantity purchased (from row 2):	−15
Total effect	10

The substitution effect measures the response to a change in relative prices when purchasing power of income is held constant; the income effect measures the response to a change in purchasing power when relative prices are held constant. In the initial position shown in panel I, a consumer with a money income of $360 faces prices of $12 for food and $6 for clothing, buying 15*F* and 30*C*. As shown in panel II, the money price of food then falls to $6. Initially, money income is reduced to $270, so the initial bundle of 15*F* and 30*C* can just be bought at the new prices of $6 each. In this example the household now purchases 21*F* and 24*C*. This change is a result of the substitution effect. As shown in panel III, income is then returned to its original level of $360. As a result, the consumption of *F* and *C* both rise. In this example, *F* rises to 25 and *C* to 35. As shown in panel IV, the total effect is the sum of the income and the substitution effects, so a fall in the price of *F* from $12 to $6 leads to an increase of 10 units in the quantity of *F* demanded, from 15 to 25 units per week.

Notice that the size of the income effect depends on the amount of income spent on the good whose price changes and on the amount by which the price changes. In our simple example, where the household was spending half its income on food, a 50 percent fall in the food price was equivalent (at the new prices) to a 25 percent increase in income. Now consider a different case. Assume that the price of petroleum falls by 20 percent. For a household that was spending only 5 percent of its income on gas and oil, this is equivalent (at the new prices) to only a 1 percent increase in purchasing power.

The Slope of the Demand Curve

The demand curve relates the quantity of a particular quantity demanded to the commodity's price. Its negative slope shows that a fall in price leads to an increase in the quantity demanded. Earlier in the book we merely assumed this slope, but the analysis underlying Figure 7-4 allows us to explain it. As drawn in Figure 7-4, the substitution effect leads the household to buy more food, which is the commodity whose price has fallen.

We now ask a fundamental question. Could the substitution effect of a fall in the price of food have led the household to buy less food? Graphically, this would mean that the household would select some bundle that had less food and more clothing than its initial bundle. An example would be the bundle indicated by the point *x* on budget line *de* in part (ii) of Figure 7-4. But when the household was faced with its original budget line, *ab*, it could have gone to *x* (by not spending all of its income). But it chose

FIGURE 7-4 The Income and the Substitution Effects

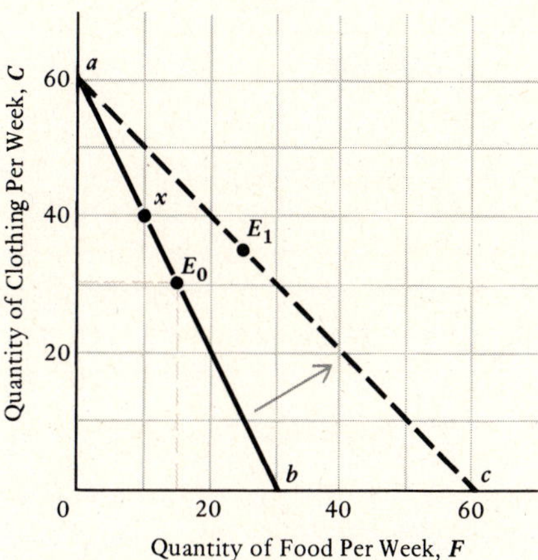

(i) A fall in the price of food

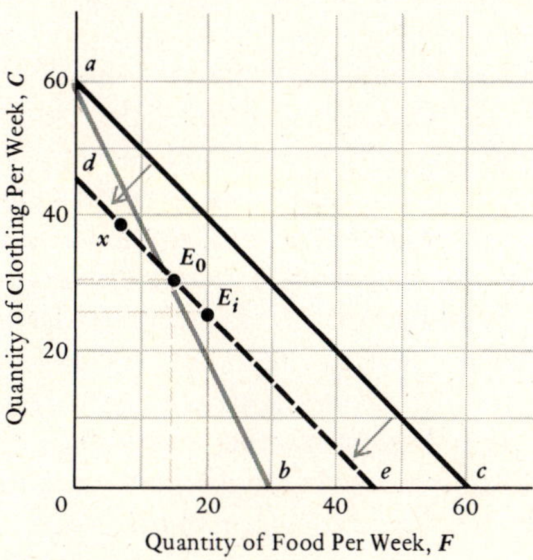

(ii) The substitution effect

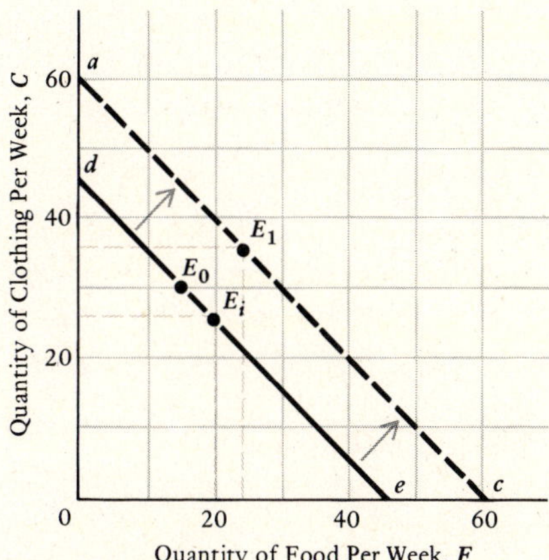

(iii) The income effect

The effect of a change in price can be broken into a substitution effect measuring the response to a change in relative prices, with purchasing power held constant, and an income effect measuring the response to the change in purchasing power caused by the price change. (i) The initial budget line is *ab*, and the household's chosen position is E_0 (row 2 of Table 7-1). The price of food then falls, taking the budget line to *ac* and consumption to the bundle indicated by E_1 (row 9 of the table). (ii) The pure substitution effect is shown by reducing money income so that the original bundle can just be bought at the new prices. Graphically, this shifts the budget line to *de*, where it is parallel to *ac* but passes through E_0. The household would choose point E_i on *de*, making the substitution effect the movement from E_0 to E_i. (iii) The income effect is measured by restoring money income to its original level. Graphically, this shifts the budget line from *de* to *ac*. The income effect is the change in consumption from E_i to E_1.

Could the substitution effect ever lead the household to buy less food when its price falls? Such an outcome would mean that the household had chosen a bundle such as x, which lies to the left of E_0 on budget line *de* in part (ii). But when the household had budget line *ab*, it could have chosen x (by not spending all its income). Instead it rejected x in favor of E_0. If the household is consistent, it will not now choose a rejected combination; instead it will choose some position on *de* at, or to the right of, E_0, which points were not available to it when it chose E_0 on budget line *ab*. *Any* point on *de* to the right of E_0 indicates more consumption of food, the good whose price has fallen.

BOX 7-2

More About the Slope of Demand Curves

This box gives a more precise treatment of the discussion in the text and then discusses the implication of the negative income effects that arise with inferior goods. The basic assumption about tastes that is used in this approach is called the *consistency assumption.* It states that if the household chose some bundle of goods that we call *A* over some other bundle that we call *B* in one situation, it will never choose *B* over *A* in some subsequent situation in which *A* and *B* are both available to it.

Normal Sloped Demand Curves

Let the initial budget line be *ab* and the chosen position be E_0. This means that the household has chosen the combination indicated by E_0 over all other attainable combinations. The rejected combinations are indicated by the points in the shaded triangle between *ab* and the origin. (Note that when faced with the budget line *ab* the household can reach any point on *ab* by spending all of its income and can reach any point lying in the shaded area below *ab* by spending less than all its income.) If the household is consistent, it will never choose another bundle within that area when the bundle indicated by E_0 is also available.

Now let the price of *F* fall, taking the budget line to *ac*. To isolate the substitution effect, we also reduce money income so that the budget line becomes *de*. This new budget line is parallel to *ac*, indicating that the household faces the new relative price. The new budget line also passes through E_0, indicating that the household has only its original purchasing power.

Consistency requires that the household cannot choose any point to the left of E_0 on the new budget line *de* since those points lie within the shaded area that was rejected when E_0 was chosen on the budget line *ab*. The household either stays at E_0 or moves to some point to the right of E_0—let us say it goes to E_i.

The foregoing argument shows that the substitution effect cannot be positive; when the price of food falls, the household cannot buy less food.

Now consider the income effect. Begin by drawing a vertical and a horizontal line from E_i to cut *ac* at *j* and *k*. Points on *ac* between *j* and *k* indicate an increase in the consumption of both commodities when the budget line goes from *de* to *ac*. This is what must happen if both goods are normal goods. This shows that the income effect of a fall in the price of food must lead to an increase in the demand for food assuming only that it is a normal (non-inferior) good.

So we know if the price of some product falls the

---

not to do so, going to E_0 instead. So as long as its preferences are unchanged, the household will not now go to *x*.

This argument, which is laid out more fully in Box 7-2, leads us to an important conclusion:

The substitution effect can *never* lead a household to purchase less of a commodity whose price has fallen.

Now consider the second half of the household's adjustment to the fall in price, the income effect. A rise in income leads the household to buy more of all normal goods. This leads to the second conclusion:

The income effect leads the household to buy more of the commodity whose price has fallen, provided that it is a normal commodity.

Putting these two effects together gives the following conclusion:

Because of the combined operation of the substitution and income effects, the demand curve for any normal commodity will be negatively

substitution effect cannot lead to less of it being consumed if the good is normal, and the income effect leads to more of it being consumed. A fall in the price of any normal good must lead to an increase in its demand; that is, its demand curve has a negative slope.

Positively Sloped Demand Curves

Could the demand curve for F ever be positively sloped? This can happen only if F is an inferior good (a necessary condition). The figure illustrates two cases where F is inferior. In the first case, the movement of the budget line from *de* to *ac* takes the equilibrium position along the arrow I' to E_1'. In this case the income effect leads to a fall in the demand for F, but the substitution effect is stronger than the income effect. Hence the overall change in the quantity of F is an increase as the chosen position goes from E_0 to E_1'. In the second case the negative income effect is stronger, and the equilibrium follows the path I'' from E_i to E_1''. In this case the income effect of the inferior good outweighs the substitution effect, and the quantity of F demanded falls from that indicated by E_0 to that indicated by E_1'', as a result of a fall in the price of F.

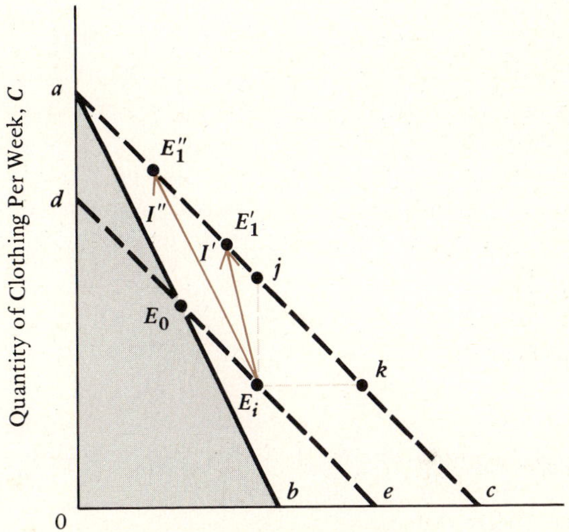

We can now conclude the following:

1. **All normal goods have negatively sloped demand curves.**
2. **All inferior goods for which the substitution effect outweighs the income effect have negatively sloped demand curves.**
3. **A positively sloped demand curve requires an inferior good for which the income effect outweighs the substitution effect.**

sloped, indicating that a fall in price will lead to an increase in quantity demanded.

The Role of Tastes

Earlier we observed that what the household can do depends on its budget line, while what it does depends on its tastes. Yet we appear to have studied the household's reactions to a change in price without saying much about the household's tastes. In fact, we did make use of a simple assumption about tastes. We assumed that households were consistent in the sense that if once they chose bundle of goods A over bundle B, they would not subsequently choose bundle B over bundle A. This is what allowed us to say that when the price of food fell and income was adjusted so that the original bundle could just be purchased, the household would never choose a new bundle containing less food because any such bundle could have been chosen in the initial situation. This consistency assumption is laid out in more detail in Box 7-2 for readers who would like to study it further. The box also considers the possibility of the unusual case where the demand curve for an inferior good could be positively sloped.

Do Demand Curves Really Have Negative Slopes?

What the great English economist Alfred Marshall called the **law of demand** asserts that the price of a product and the quantity demanded are negatively associated with each other. Criticisms of the law have taken various forms, focusing on Giffen goods, conspicuous consumption goods, and goods whose demands are perfectly inelastic. Let us consider each of these in turn.

Giffen Goods

Great interest was attached to the nineteenth century English economist Sir Robert Giffen's apparent refutation of the law of demand. He is alleged to have observed that when a rise in the price of imported wheat led to an increase in the price of bread, members of the British working class *increased* their consumption of bread. This meant that their demand curve for bread was positively sloped.

Modern theory shows that such an exception to the law of demand could occur. There are two requisites: (1) The good must be an inferior good, and (2) the good must take a large proportion of total household expenditure; that is, its income effect must be large. Bread was indeed a dietary staple of the British working classes in the nineteenth century. A rise in the price of bread would cause a large reduction in their real income. This could lead to increased consumption of bread as households cut out their few luxuries in order to be able to consume enough bread to keep alive. Though possible, such cases are all but unknown in the modern world. The reason is that in all but the poorest societies, typical households do not spend large proportions of their incomes on a single inferior good. (See Box 7-2 for further discussion.)

Conspicuous Consumption Goods

Thorstein Veblen in *The Theory of the Leisure Class* noted that some commodities were consumed not for their intrinsic qualities but because they carried a snob appeal. He suggested that the more expensive such a commodity became, the *greater* might be its ability to confer status on its purchaser.

Consumers might buy diamonds, for example, not because they particularly like diamonds per se but because they wish to show off their wealth in an ostentatious but socially acceptable way. They are assumed to value diamonds precisely because diamonds are expensive. Thus a fall in price might lead them to stop buying diamonds and to switch to a more satisfactory object of conspicuous consumption. They may behave in the same way with respect to luxury cars, buying them *because* they are expensive.

Households that behave in this way will have positively sloped *individual* demand curves for diamonds and cars. However, no one has ever observed a positively sloped *market* demand curve for such commodities. The reason for this is easy to discover. Consideration of the countless lower-income consumers who would be glad to buy diamonds or Cadillacs if these commodities were sufficiently inexpensive suggests that upward-sloping demand curves for a few individual wealthy households are much more likely than is a positively sloped market demand curve for the same commodity.

Perfectly Inelastic Demand Curves

Even if demand curves do not have positive slopes as suggested in the foregoing cases, the substantial insight provided by the law of demand would be diminished if there were important commodities for which changes in price had virtually no effect on quantity demanded.

It is surprising how often the assumption of a vertical demand curve is implicit. A common response of urban bus or subway systems to financial difficulties is to propose a percentage increase in fares equal to the percentage increase that they require in their revenues. Even professors are not immune. At a meeting of the American Association of University Professors, a motion was introduced "to raise annual dues by 20 percent in order to raise revenues by 20 percent"—in spite of the empirical evidence that a previous increase in dues had led (as theory would predict) to a significant drop in membership.

It was once widely argued that the demand for

gasoline was almost perfectly inelastic on the grounds that people who had paid thousands of dollars for cars would not balk at a few cents extra for gas. The events of the past 15 years have proven how wrong that argument was: Higher gas prices in the 1970s led to smaller cars, to more car pools, to more economical driving speeds, and to less pleasure driving. Falling gas prices in the mid-1980s led to a reversal of these trends.

In summary, there is a mass of accumulated evidence confirming that most demand curves do in fact have a negative slope.

The hypothesis that demand curves are negatively sloped is strongly supported by the evidence.

A Preview

This chapter has presented the demand theory that is needed for the rest of this book. The next chapter presents a number of applications. The two appendixes to this chapter present more formal theories of household tastes that lead to the prediction of negatively sloped demand curves. Some of you will skip both of these appendixes; others will read one or both. Whatever you do, remember that although very abstract in its current presentation, modern demand theory grew up to handle a number of real and interesting problems. We shall see how the theory can be applied to real issues both in the next chapter and later in this book.

Summary

1. The budget line shows all combinations of commodities that are available to the household given its money income and the prices of the goods it purchases.
2. The budget line is shifted parallel to itself by either a change in money income with all money prices held constant or a proportionate change in all money prices with money income held constant.
3. Changes in relative prices change the slope of the budget line.
4. While the budget line describes what the household *can* purchase, what it does purchase depends on its tastes.
5. A change in one money price has an income effect and a substitution effect. The substitution effect is the reaction of the household to the change in relative prices with purchasing power of income held constant. It is measured by allowing price to change and then altering money income until the original bundle can just be purchased. In this situation a consistent household would never reduce its purchases of the commodity whose relative price has fallen. The income effect is then measured by a parallel shift of the budget line to restore its initial money income. The income effect of a fall in one money price will lead to an increase in the purchases of all normal commodities.
6. The combined effect of the income and the substitution effect ensure that the quantity demanded of any normal good will increase when its money price falls, other things being equal. This means that normal goods have negatively sloped demand curves.
7. Three conceivable exceptions to the law of negatively sloped demand curves are a Giffen good, which is an inferior good on which a household spends much of its income; conspicuous consumption goods, which are goods consumed *because* they are expensive; and

goods with perfectly inelastic demands. Examples of any of these possible exceptions are rarely, if ever, observed.

Topics for Review

Causes of shifts in the budget line
Real income and money income
Absolute (or money) prices and relative prices
Income effect and substitution effect
The law of demand and its possible exceptions

Discussion Questions

1. Is a household relatively better off if its money income is decreased by 10 percent or if the prices of all the goods it buys are increased by 10 percent? Does it matter in answering this question whether the household spends all its income?
2. Look at Figure 7-4 and see what happened to the quantity of clothing demanded when the price of food fell. Could that change in the quantity of clothing consumed have been in the opposite direction from the one you determine? What would that have implied about the change in the quantity of food? Can you use the figure to discover a relationship between the price elasticity of demand for food and the change in the quantity of clothing bought when the price of food changes.
3. A middle-aged business executive reports that he now drinks a lot more French wine than he used to when he first started with the company, even though imported wine is now much more expensive than it used to be. Do you think he has a positively sloped demand curve for French wine?
4. The measured elasticity of demand for salt is quite low. Why do you think this is so? Does this low elasticity imply that if one firm were to monopolize the sales of salt in the whole country, it could go on raising its revenues indefinitely by continually increasing the price of salt?
5. From 1977 to 1987 the cost of purchasing a representative bundle of consumers' goods rose by just over 100 percent, as measured by the consumers' price index. What else would you need to know to find out what had happened to the average Canadian's real income?
6. When the price of fuel oil and gasoline rose drastically in the early 1980s, many Canadians reported that they felt worse off. Did this feeling have anything to do with the income and/or the substitution effect? What do you think the income and the substitution effects of these price rises were?
7. Compare and contrast the consequences of the income effect of a drastic fall in food prices with the consequences of a rise in money incomes when money prices are constant.
8. In recent years, the cost of housing has increased dramatically in Toronto and Vancouver and only slightly in Halifax and Winnipeg. What income and substitution effects would you expect from these changes?

Marginal Utility Theory

The history of demand theory has seen two major breakthroughs. The first was the marginal utility theory, which assumed that the utility people got from consuming commodities could be measured objectively. By distinguishing total and marginal values, this theory explained why what seemed like a paradox—necessary goods that cannot be dispensed with often have low market values, while luxury goods that could easily be dispensed often have high market values—was not a paradox at all. (See further discussion of this so-called paradox of value in Chapter 8.)

The second breakthrough came with indifference theory, which showed that demand theory could dispense with the dubious assumption of measurable utility on which marginal utility theory was based. All that was needed in this new theory was to assume that households could say which of two consumption bundles they preferred without having to say by how much.

Appendix A develops marginal utility theory, and Appendix B deals with the more modern indifference theory.

Marginal and Total Utility

We confine our attention for the moment to the consumption of a single commodity. The satisfaction a household receives from consuming that commodity is called its **utility. Total utility** refers to the total satisfaction from the amount of that commodity consumed. **Marginal utility** refers to the change in satisfaction resulting from consuming a little more or a little less of that commodity. For example, the total utility of consuming 14 eggs a week is the total satisfaction that those 14 eggs provide. The marginal utility of the fourteenth egg consumed is the additional satisfaction provided by the consumption of that unit. Thus marginal utility is the difference in total utility gained by consuming 13 eggs and by consuming 14.[1]

The Hypothesis of Diminishing Marginal Utility

The basic hypothesis of utility theory, sometimes called the *law of diminishing marginal utility,* is as follows:

The utility any household derives from successive units of a particular commodity diminishes as total consumption of the commodity increases while the consumption of all other commodities remains constant.

Consider water. Some minimum quantity is essential to sustain life, and a person would, if necessary, give up all his or her income to obtain that quantity of water. Thus the marginal utility of that much water is extremely high. More than this bare minimum will be drunk, but the marginal utility of successive glasses of water drunk over a period will decline steadily.

Evidence for this hypothesis will be considered later, but you can convince yourself that it is at least reasonable by asking a few questions. How much money would induce you to cut your consumption of water by one glass per week? The answer is very little. How much would induce you to cut it by a second glass? By a third glass? To only one glass consumed per week? The answer to the last question is quite a bit. The fewer glasses you are consuming

[1] Here and elsewhere in elementary economics it is common to use interchangeably two concepts that mathematicians distinguish. Technically, *incremental* utility is measured over a discrete interval; such as from 9 to 10, whereas *marginal* utility is a rate of change measured over an infinitesimal interval. But common usage applies the word *marginal* when the last unit is involved, even if a one-unit change is not infinitesimal. **[10]**

already, the higher the marginal utility of one more or one less glass of water.

But water has many uses other than for drinking. A fairly high marginal utility will be attached to some minimum quantity for bathing, but much more than this minimum will be used only for more frequent baths or for having a water level in the tub higher than is absolutely necessary. The last weekly gallon used for bathing is likely to have a low marginal utility. Again, some small quantity of water is necessary for tooth brushing, but many people leave the water running while they brush. The water going down the drain between wetting and rinsing the brush surely has a low utility. When all the extravagant uses of water by the modern consumer are considered, it is certain that the marginal utility of the last, say, 30 percent of all units consumed is very low, even though the total utility of *all* the units consumed is extremely high.

Utility Schedules and Graphs

The schedule in Table 7A-1 is hypothetical. It is constructed to illustrate the assumptions that have been made about utility, using movie attendance as an example. The table shows that total utility rises as the number of movies attended each month rises. Everything else being equal, the more movies the household attends each month, the more satisfaction it gets—at least over the range shown in the table. But the marginal utility of each additional movie per month is less than that of the previous one even though each movie adds something to the household's satisfaction. The schedule shows that marginal utility declines as quantity consumed rises. [11] The same data are shown graphically in the two parts of Figure 7A-1.

TABLE 7A-1 Total and Marginal Utility Schedules

Number of movies attended per month	Total utility	Marginal utility
0	0	
1	30	30
2	50	20
3	65	15
4	75	10
5	83	8
6	89	6
7	93	4
8	96	3
9	98	2
10	99	1

Total utility rises, but marginal utility declines as this household's consumption increases. The marginal utility of 20, shown as the second entry in the last column, arises because total utility increases from 30 to 50—a difference of 20—with attendance at the second movie. To indicate that the marginal utility is associated with the change from one rate of movie attendances to another, the figures in the third column are recorded between the rows of the figures in the second column. When plotting marginal utility on a graph, it is plotted at the midpoint of the interval over which it is computed.

Maximizing Utility

A basic assumption of the economic theory of household behavior is that households try to make themselves as well off as they possibly can in the circumstances in which they find themselves. In other words, the members of a household seek to maximize their total utility.

The Equilibrium of a Household

How can a household adjust its expenditure so as to maximize its total utility? Should it go to the point at which the marginal utility of each commodity is the same, that is, the point at which it would value equally the last unit of each commodity consumed? This would make sense only if each commodity had the same price per unit. But if a household must spend $3 to buy an additional unit of one commodity and only $1 for a unit of another, the first commodity would represent a poor use of its money if the marginal utility of each were equal. The household would be spending $3 to get satisfaction it could have acquired for only $1.

The household maximizing its utility will allocate its expenditure among commodities so that the utility of the last dollar spent on each is equal.

FIGURE 7A-1 Total and Marginal Utility Curves

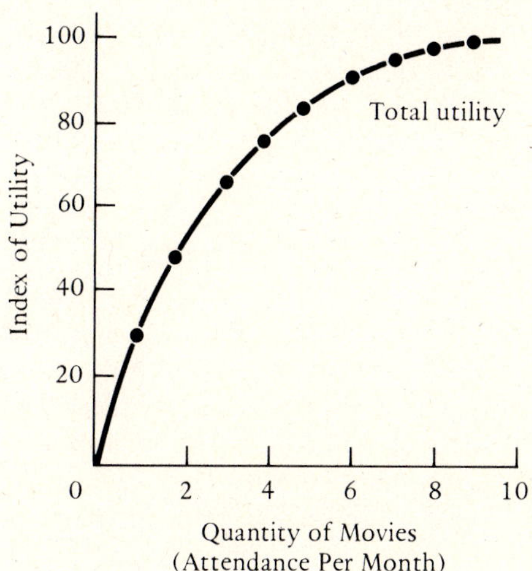

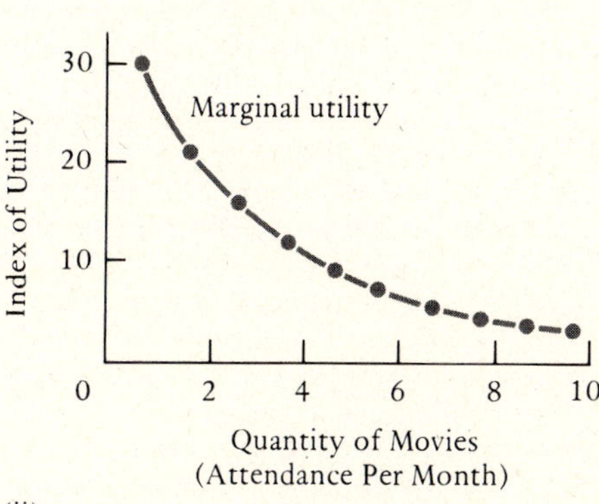

The total utility curve rises, but the marginal utility curve falls as the quantity consumed rises. The dots correspond to the points listed in Table 7A-1; smooth curves have been drawn through them.

Imagine that the household is in a position in which the utility of the last dollar spent on carrots yields three times the utility of the last dollar spent on brussels sprouts. In this case total utility can be increased by switching a dollar of expenditure from sprouts to carrots and gaining the difference between the utilities of a dollar spent on each.

The utility-maximizing household will continue to switch its expenditure from sprouts to carrots as long as a dollar spent on carrots yields more utility than a dollar spent on sprouts. But this switching reduces the quantity of sprouts consumed and, given the law of diminishing marginal utility, raises the marginal utility of sprouts; at the same time the switching increases the quantity of carrots consumed and thereby lowers the marginal utility of carrots.

Eventually the marginal utilities will have changed enough so that the utility of a dollar spent on carrots is just equal to the utility of a dollar spent on sprouts. At this point there is nothing to be gained by a further switch of expenditure from sprouts to carrots. If the household persists in reallocating its expenditure, it will further reduce the marginal utility of carrots (by consuming more of them) and raise the marginal utility of sprouts (by consuming less of them). Total utility will no longer be at its maximum because the utility of a dollar spent on sprouts will exceed the utility of a dollar spent on carrots.

Let us now consider the conditions for maximizing utility in a more general way. Denote the marginal utility of the last unit of commodity X by MU_x and its price by p_x. Let MU_y and p_y refer, respectively, to the marginal utility of a second commodity Y and its price. The marginal utility per dollar of X will be MU_x/p_x. For example, if the last unit adds 30 units to utility and costs \$2, its marginal utility per dollar is 30/2 = 15.

The condition required for a household to maximize its utility is, for any pair of commodities,

$$\frac{MU_x}{p_x} = \frac{MU_y}{p_y} \qquad [1]$$

This says that the household will allocate its expenditure so that the utility gained from the last dollar spent on each commodity is equal.

This is the fundamental equation of the utility theory of demand. Each household demands each good (for example, movie attendance) up to the point at which the marginal utility per dollar spent on it is the same as the marginal utility of a dollar spent on another good (for example, water). When this condition is met, the household cannot shift a dollar of expenditure from one commodity to another and increase its utility.

An Alternative Interpretation of Household Equilibrium

If we rearrange the terms in Equation 1 we can gain additional insight into household behavior.

$$\frac{MU_x}{MU_y} = \frac{p_x}{p_y} \quad [2]$$

The right side of this equation states the *relative* price of the two goods. It is determined by the market and is outside the control of individual household; the household reacts to these market prices but is powerless to change them. The left side states the relative ability of the goods to add to the household's satisfaction and is within the control of the household. In determining the quantities of different goods it buys, the household determines also their marginal utilities. (If you have difficulty seeing why, look again at Figure 7A-1(ii).)

If the two sides of Equation 2 are not equal, the household can increase its total satisfaction by rearranging its purchases. Assume, for example, that the price of a unit of X is twice the price of a unit of Y ($p_x/p_y = 2$), while the marginal utility of a unit of X is three times that of a unit of Y ($MU_x/MU_y = 3$). Under these conditions it pays the household to buy more X and less Y. For example, reducing its purchases of Y by two units frees enough purchasing power to buy a unit of X. Since one extra unit of X bought yields 1.5 times the satisfaction of two units of Y forgone, the switch is worth making. What about a further switch of X for Y? As the household buys more X and less Y, the marginal utility of X falls and the marginal utility of Y rises. The household will go on rearranging its purchases—reducing Y consumption and increasing X consumption—until, in this example, the marginal utility of X is only twice that of Y. At this point total satisfaction cannot be further increased by rearranging purchases between the two commodities.

Now consider what the household is doing. It is faced with a set of prices that it cannot change. The household responds to these prices and maximizes its satisfaction by adjusting the things it can change—the quantities of the various goods it purchases—until Equation 2 is satisfied for all pairs of commodities.

This sort of equation—one side representing the choices the outside world gives decision makers and the other side representing the effect of those choices on their welfare—recurs in economics. It reflects the equilibrium position reached when decision makers have made the best adjustment they can to the external forces that limit their choices.

When it enters the market, every household faces the same set of market prices. When all households are fully adjusted to these prices, each will have identical ratios of its marginal utilities for each pair of goods. Of course, a rich household may consume more of each commodity than a poor household. However, the rich and the poor households (and every other household) will adjust their *relative* purchases of each commodity so that the relative marginal utilities are the same for all. Thus, if the price of X is twice the price of Y, each household will purchase X and Y to the point at which the household's marginal utility of X is twice its marginal utility of Y. Households with different tastes will, however, have different marginal utility schedules and so may consume differing relative quantities of commodities, even though the ratios of their marginal utilities are the same for all households.

Derivation of the Household's Demand Curve

To derive the household's demand curve for a commodity, it is only necessary to ask what happens when there is a change in the price of that commodity. To do this for candy, take Equation 2 and let X stand for candy and Y for all other commodities. What will happen if, with all other prices constant, the price of candy rises? The household that started from a position of equilibrium will now find itself in a position in which[2]

$$\frac{MU \text{ of candy}}{MU \text{ of } Y} < \frac{\text{price of candy}}{\text{price of } Y} \quad [3]$$

[2] The inequality sign (<) points to the smaller of two magnitudes. When the price of candy rises, the right side of Equation 2 increases. Until the household adjusts its consumption patterns, the left side will stay the same. Thus Equation 2 is replaced by Inequality 3.

To restore equilibrium, it must buy less candy, thereby raising its marginal utility until once again Equation 2 (where *X* is candy) is satisfied.[3] The common sense of this is that the marginal utility of candy *per dollar* falls when its price rises. The household began with the utility of the last dollar spent on candy equal to the utility of the last dollar spent on all other goods, but the rise in candy prices changes this. The household buys less candy (and more of other goods) until the marginal utility of candy rises enough to make the utility of a dollar spent on candy the same as it was originally.

[3] For most consumers candy absorbs only a small proportion of total expenditure. If, in response to a change in its price, expenditure on candy changes by $5 per month, this represents a large change in candy consumption but only a negligible change in the consumption of other commodities. Hence in the text we proceed by assuming that the marginal utilities of other commodities do not change when the price and consumption of candy change.

This analysis leads to the basic prediction of demand theory.

A rise in the price of a commodity (with income and the prices of all other commodities held constant) will lead to a decrease in the quantity of the commodity demanded by each household.

If this is what each household does, it is also what all households taken together do. Thus the theory predicts a downward-sloping market demand curve.

Summary

1. Marginal utility theory distinguishes between the total utility gained from the consumption of all units of some commodity and the marginal utility resulting from the consumption of one more unit of the commodity.
2. The basic assumption made in utility theory is that the utility the household derives from the consumption of successive units of a commodity per period of time diminishes as the consumption of that commodity increases.
3. Households are assumed to maximize utility and thus reach equilibrium when the utility derived from the last dollar spent on each commodity is equal. Another way of putting this is that the marginal utilities derived from the last unit of each commodity consumed will be proportional to their prices.
4. Here is why demand curves slope downward. When the price of one commodity, *X*, falls, each household restores equilibrium by increasing its purchases of *X*. This restores the ratio of *x*'s marginal utility to its new price (MU_x/p_x) to the same level as the household has achieved for all other commodities.

Appendix B to Chapter 7

Indifference Theory

In this second appendix to Chapter 7 we study the modern theory of household behavior, which is based on what are called indifference curves.

An Indifference Curve

Start with an imaginary household that currently has available to it some specific bundle of goods. Say that bundle is 18 units of clothing and 10 units of food. Now offer the household an alternative bundle, say, 13 units of clothing and 15 units of food. This alternative combination of goods has 5 fewer units of clothing and 5 more units of food than the first one. Whether the household prefers this bundle depends on the relative valuation that it places on 5 more units of food and 5 fewer units of clothing. If it values the extra food more than the forgone clothing, it will prefer the new bundle to the original one. If it values the food less than the clothing, it will prefer the original bundle. If the household values the extra food the same as it values the forgone clothing, it is said to be *indifferent between* the two bundles.

Assume that after much trial and error we have identified several bundles among which the household is indifferent. In other words, each bundle gives the household equal satisfaction. They are shown in Table 7B-1.

There will, of course, be combinations of the two commodities other than those enumerated in the table that will give the same level of satisfaction to the household. All these combinations are shown in Figure 7B-1 by the smooth curve that passes through the points plotted from the table. This curve is an indifference curve. In general, an **indifference curve** shows all combinations of goods that yield the same satisfaction to the household. A household is indifferent between the combinations indicated by any two points on one indifference curve.

Any points above the curve show combinations of food and clothing that the household would prefer to combinations indicated by points on the curve. Consider, for example, the combination of 20 food and 18 clothing, represented by point *g* in the figure. Although it may not be obvious that this bundle must be preferred to bundle *a* (which has more clothing but less food), it is obvious that it will be preferred to bundle *c* because there is both less clothing and less food represented at *c* than at *g*. Inspection of the graph shows that *any* point above the curve will be obviously superior to *some* points on the curve in the sense that it will contain both more food and more clothing than those points on the curve. But since all points on the curve are equal in the household's eyes, the point above the curve must be superior to *all* points on the curve. By a similar argument, points below and to the left of the curve represent bundles that are inferior to bundles represented by points on the curve.

The Hypothesis of Diminishing Marginal Rate of Substitution

How much clothing would the household be prepared to give up to get one more unit of food? The answer to this question measures what is called the marginal rate of substitution of clothing for food. The **marginal rate of substitution (*MRS*)** is the amount of one commodity a consumer would be prepared to give up to get one more unit of another commodity.

The first basic assumption of indifference theory is that the algebraic value of the *MRS* is always negative.

This means that to gain a positive change in its consumption of one commodity, the household is prepared to incur a negative change in its consumption

TABLE 7B-1 Alternative Bundles Giving a Household Equal Satisfaction

Bundle	Clothing	Food
a	30	5
b	18	10
c	13	15
d	10	20
e	8	25
f	7	30

These bundles all lie on a single indifference curve. Since all of these bundles of food and clothing give equal satisfaction, the household is "indifferent" among them.

of a second. The negative marginal rate of substitution is indicated in graphical representations by the downward slope of all indifference curves. (See, for example, the curve in Figure 7B-1.)

The second basic assumption of indifference theory is that the marginal rate of substitution between any two commodities depends on the amounts of the commodities currently being consumed by the household.

Consider a case in which the household has a lot of clothing and only a little food. Common sense suggests that the household might be willing to give up quite a bit of its plentiful clothing to get one unit more of scarce food. It suggests as well that the household with a little clothing and a lot of food would be willing to give up only a little of its scarce clothing to get one more unit of already plentiful food.

This example illustrates the hypothesis of diminishing marginal rate of substitution. The less of one commodity, *A*, and the more of a second commodity, *B*, the household has already, the smaller will be the amount of *A* it will be willing to give up to get one further unit of *B*. The hypothesis says that the marginal rate of substitution changes systematically as the amounts of two commodities presently consumed vary. The graphical expression of this is that the slope of any indifference curve becomes flatter as the household moves downward and to the right along the curve. In Figure 7B-1 a movement downward to the right means that less clothing and more food is being consumed. The decreasing steepness of the curve means that the household is willing to sacrifice less and less clothing to get each further unit of food. [12]

FIGURE 7B-1 An Indifference Curve

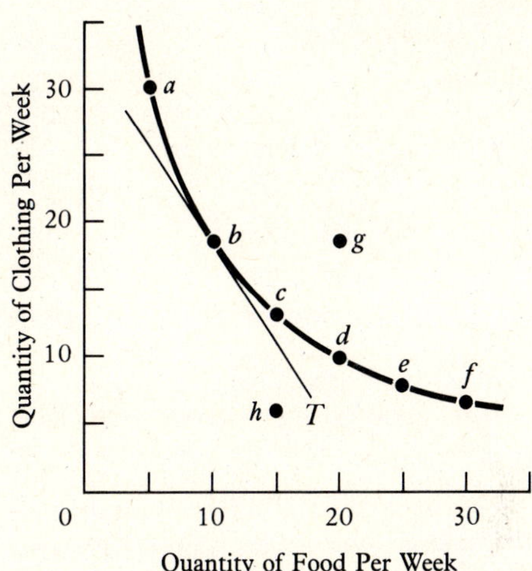

This indifference curve shows combinations of food and clothing that yield equal satisfaction and among which the household is indifferent. Points *a* to *f* are plotted from Table 7B-1. The smooth curve through them is an indifference curve; each combination on it gives equal satisfaction to the household. Point *g* above the line is a preferred combination to any point on the line; point *h* below the line is an inferior combination to any point on the line. The slope of the line *T* gives the marginal rate of substitution at point *b*. Moving down the curve from *b* to *f*, the slope flattens, showing that the more food and the less clothing the household has, the less willing it will be to sacrifice further clothing to get more food.

The hypothesis is illustrated in Table 7B-2, which is based on the example of food and clothing in Table 7B-1. The last column of the table shows the rate at which the household is prepared to sacrifice units of clothing per unit of food obtained. At first the household will sacrifice 2.4 units of clothing to get 1 unit more of food, but as its consumption of cloth-

TABLE 7B-2 The Marginal Rate of Substitution Between Clothing and Food

Movement	(1) Change in clothing	(2) Change in food	(3) Marginal rate of substitution (1) ÷ (2)
From *a* to *b*	−12	5	−2.4
From *b* to *c*	− 5	5	−1.0
From *c* to *d*	− 3	5	−0.6
From *d* to *e*	− 2	5	−0.4
From *e* to *f*	− 1	5	−0.2

The marginal rate of substitution of clothing for food declines as the quantity of food increases. This table is based on Table 7B-1. When the household moves from *a* to *b*, it gives up 12 units of clothing and gains 5 units of food; it remains at the same level of overall satisfaction. The household at point *a* was prepared to sacrifice 12 clothing for 5 food (i.e., 12/5 = 2.4 units of clothing per unit of food obtained). When the household moves from *b* to *c*, it sacrifices 5 clothing units for 5 food units (a rate of substitution of 1 unit of clothing for each unit of food).

ing diminishes and that of food increases, the household becomes less and less willing to sacrifice further clothing for more food.[1]

The Indifference Map

So far we have constructed only a single indifference curve. However, starting at any other point in Figure 7B-1, such as *g*, there will be other combinations that will yield equal satisfaction to the household. If the points indicating all of these combinations are connected, they will form another indifference curve. This exercise can be repeated as many times as we wish, and as many indifference curves as we wish can be generated. The farther any indifference curve is from the origin, the higher will be the level of satisfaction given by any of the combinations of goods indicated by points on the curve.

A set of indifference curves is called an **indifference map,** an example of which is shown in Figure 7B-2. It specifies the household's tastes by showing its rate of substitution between the two commodities for every level of current consumption of these commodities. When economists say that a household's tastes are *given,* they do not mean that the household's current consumption pattern is given; rather, they mean that the household's entire indifference map is given.

The Equilibrium of the Household

Indifference maps describe the preferences of households. Budget lines describe the possibilities open to

FIGURE 7B-2 An Indifference Map

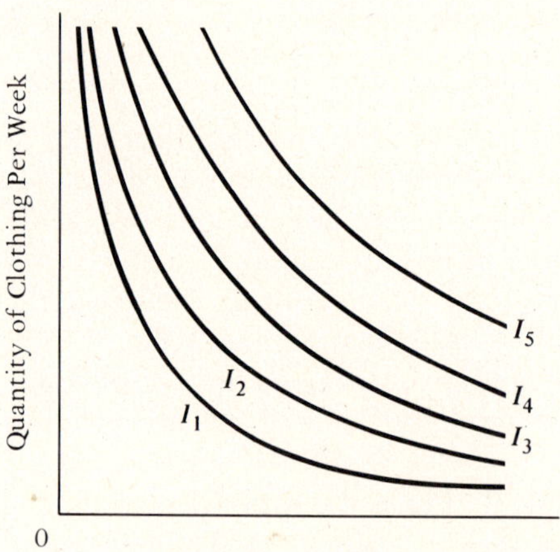

An indifference map consists of a set of indifference curves. All points on a particular curve indicate alternative combinations of food and clothing that give the household equal satisfaction. The further the curve from the origin, the higher the level of satisfaction it represents. For example, I_5 is a higher indifference curve than I_4, which means that all the points on I_5 yield a higher level of satisfaction than do the points on I_4.

[1] Movements between widely separated points on the indifference curve have been examined. In terms of a small movement from any of the points on the curve, the rate at which the household will give up clothing to get food is shown by the slope of the tangent to the curve at that point. The slope of the line *T,* which is a tangent to the curve at point *b* in Figure 7B-1, may thus be thought of as the slope of the curve at that precise point. It tells us the rate at which the household will sacrifice clothing per unit of food obtained when it is currently consuming 18 clothing and 10 food (the coordinates of point *b*).

each household. To predict what households will actually do, both sets of information must be put together. This is done in Figure 7-B3. The household's budget line is shown by the straight line in the figure, and the curves from the indifference map are also shown. Any point on the budget line is attainable. But which point will actually be chosen by the household?

Since the household wishes to maximize its satisfactions, it wishes to reach its highest attainable indifference curve. Inspection of the figure shows that if the household purchases any bundle on its budget line at a point cut by an indifference curve, a higher indifference curve can be reached. Only when the bundle purchased is such that the indifference curve is tangent to the budget line is it impossible for the household to alter its purchases and reach a higher curve.

The household's satisfaction is maximized at the point where an indifference curve is tangent to the budget line.

At such a tangency position the slope of the indifference curve (the household's marginal rate of substitution of the goods) is the same as the slope of the budget line (the relative prices of the goods in the market).

The common sense of this result is that if the household values goods differently than the market does, there is room for profitable exchange. The household can give up some of the good it values relatively less than the market and take in return some of the good it values relatively more than the market does. When the household is prepared to swap goods at the same rate as they can be traded on the market, there is no further opportunity for it to raise its satisfaction by substituting one commodity for the other.

The household is presented with market prices that it cannot change. It adjusts to these prices by choosing a bundle of goods such that, at the margin, its own subjective evaluation of the goods conforms with the valuations given by market prices.

FIGURE 7B-3 The Equilibrium of a Household

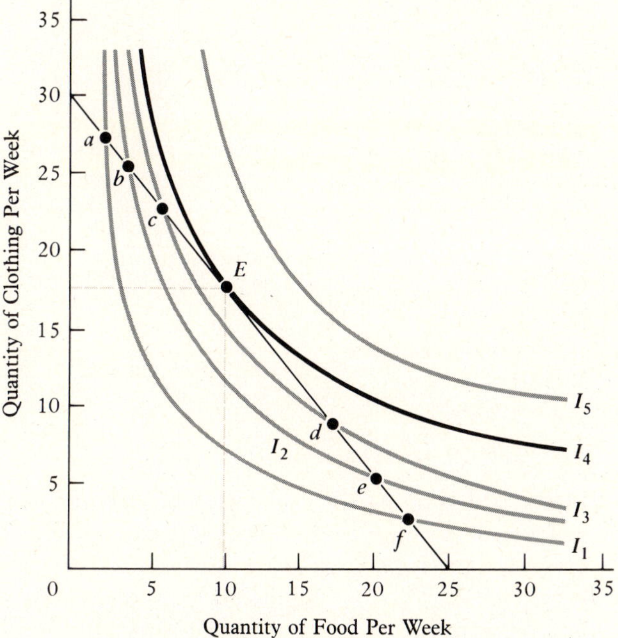

Equilibrium occurs at *E*, where an indifference curve is tangent to the budget line. The household has an income of $750 a week and faces prices of $25 a unit for clothing and $30 a unit for food. A combination of units of clothing and food indicated by point *a* is attainable, but by moving along the budget line, higher indifference curves can be reached. The same is true at *b* and *c*. At *E*, however, where an indifference curve is tangent to the budget line, it is impossible to reach a higher curve by moving along the budget line. If the household did alter its consumption bundle by moving from *E* to *d*, for example, it would move to the lower indifference curve I_3 and thus to a lower level of satisfaction.

The Household's Reaction to a Change in Income

We have seen that a change in income leads to parallel shifts of the budget line—toward the origin when income falls and away from the origin when income rises. For each level of income there will be an equilibrium position at which an indifference curve is tangent to the relevant budget line. Each such equilibrium position means that the household is doing as well as it possibly can for that level of income. If we move the budget line through all possible levels of income, and if we join up all the points of equilibrium, we will trace out what is called an **income-consumption line,** an example of which is shown in Figure 7B-4. This line shows how consumption bundles change as income changes, with relative prices held constant.

The Household's Reaction to a Change in Price

We already know that a change in the relative price of the two goods changes the slope of the budget line. Given a price of clothing, for each possible price of food there is an equilibrium consumption position for the household. Connecting these positions traces out a **price-consumption line,** as is shown in Figure 7B-5. Notice that as the relative price of food and clothing changes, the relative quantities of food and clothing purchased also change. In particular, as the price of food falls, the household buys more food.

FIGURE 7B-4 The Income-Consumption Line

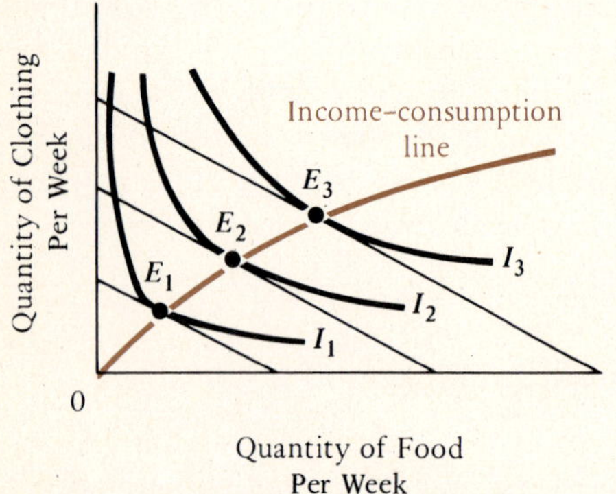

The income-consumption line shows how the household's purchases react to a change in income with relative prices held constant. Increases in income shift the budget line out parallel to itself, moving the equilibrium from E_1 to E_2 to E_3. By joining up all the points of equilibrium, an income-consumption line is traced out.

FIGURE 7B-5 The Price-Consumption Line

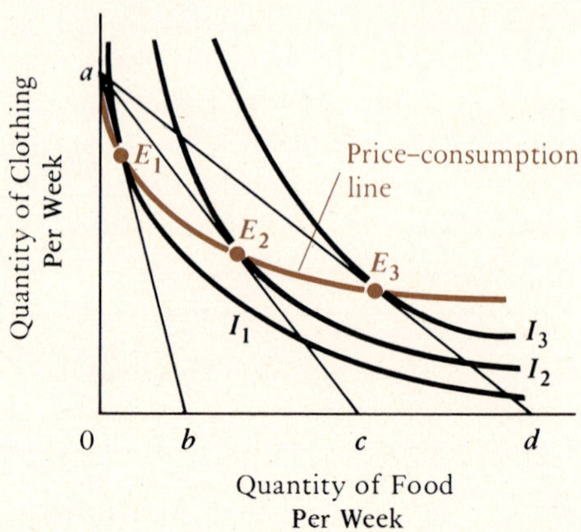

The price-consumption line shows how the household's purchases react to a change in one price with money income and other prices held constant. Decreases in the price of food (with money income and the price of clothing constant) pivot the budget line from *ab* to *ac* to *ad*. The equilibrium position moves from E_1 to E_2 to E_3. By joining up all the points of equilibrium, a price-consumption line is traced out.

Derivation of the Demand Curve

If food and clothing were the only two commodities purchased by households, we could derive a demand curve for food from the price-consumption line of Figure 7B-5. That line represents how the quantity of food demanded varies as the price of food changes, with the price of clothing unchanged. This is what we did in Chapter 7 to explain the general idea. Now, however, we wish to be more precise. To use indifference theory to derive the type of demand curve introduced in Chapter 4, it is necessary to depart from the world of two commodities.

What happens to the household's demand for some commodity, say, gasoline, as the price of that commodity changes, *all other prices being held constant?* In part (i) of Figure 7B-6 a new type of indifference map is plotted in which gallons of gas are measured on the horizontal axis and the value of all other goods consumed is plotted on the vertical axis. We have in effect used *everything but gasoline* as the second com-

FIGURE 7B-6 Derivation of a Household's Demand Curve

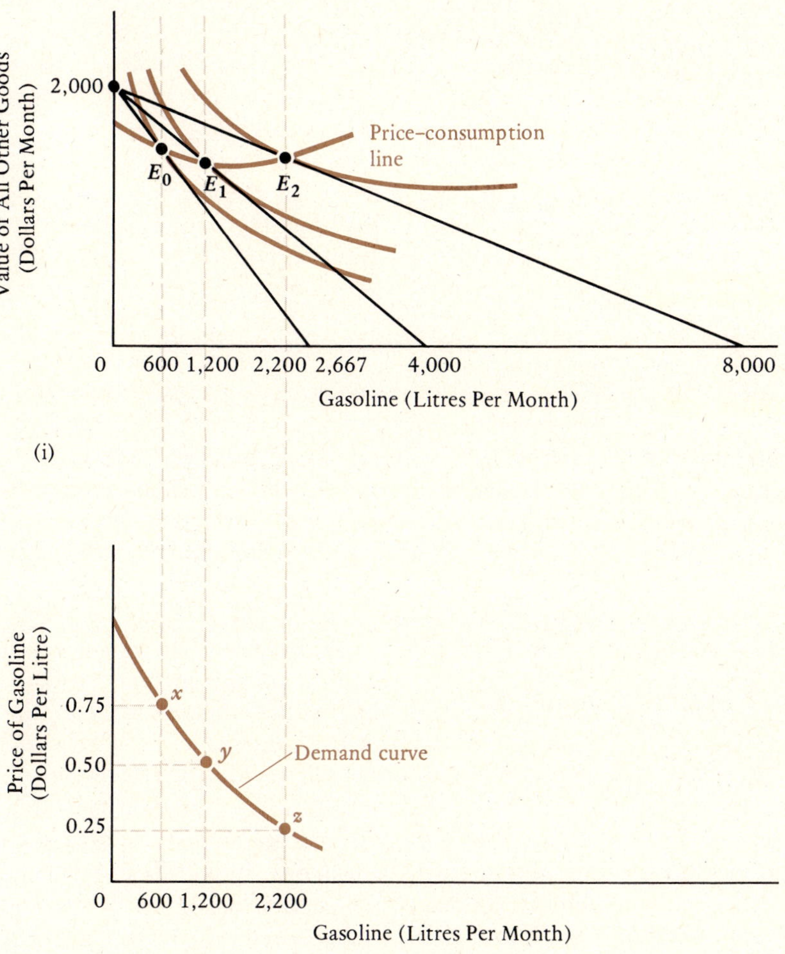

Every point on the price-consumption line corresponds to both a price of the commodity and a quantity demanded; this is the information required for a demand curve. In part (i) the household has an income of $2,000 and alternatively faces prices of $0.75, $0.50, and $0.25 per litre of gas, choosing positions E_0, E_1, and E_2 at each price. The information for litres demanded at each price is then plotted in part (ii) to yield the household's demand curve. The three points x, y, and z in part (ii) correspond to the three equilibrium positions E_0, E_1, and E_2 in part (i).

modity. The indifference curves give the rate at which the household is prepared to substitute gas for money (which allows it to buy all other goods) at each level of consumption of gas and of all other goods.

To illustrate the derivation of demand curves, we use the numerical example shown in Figure 7B-6. The household is assumed to have an after-tax income of $2,000 per month. This income is plotted on the vertical axis, showing that if the household consumes no gas, it can consume $2,000 worth of other goods each month. When gas costs $0.75 a litre the household could buy a maximum of 2,667 litres per month. This gives rise to the innermost budget line. Given its tastes, the household reaches equilibrium at point E_0, consuming 600 litres of gasoline and $1,550 worth of other commodities.[2] Next let the price of gasoline fall to $0.50 a litre. Now the

[2] Our household must do a lot of traveling! If we chose more realistic figures for its consumption of gas, however, the various equilibrium positions would all be so close to the horizontal axis that the graph would be difficult to read.

maximum possible consumption of gas is 4,000 litres per month, giving rise to the middle budget line in the figure. The household's equilibrium is, as always, at the point where the new budget line is tangent to an indifference curve. At this point, E_1, the household is consuming 1,200 litres a month and spending \$1,400 on all other goods. Finally, let the price fall to \$0.25 per litre. The household can now buy a maximum of 8,000 litres per month, giving rise to the outermost of the three budget lines. The household reaches equilibrium by consuming 2,200 litres a month and spending \$1,450 on other commodities.

If we let the price vary over all possible amounts, we will trace out a complete price-consumption line as shown in the figure. The points derived in the preceding paragraph are merely three points in this line.

We have now derived all that we need to plot the household's demand curve for gas, since we know how much the household will purchase at each price. To draw the curve we merely replot the data from part (i) for Figure 7B-6 onto a demand graph, as shown in part (ii) of Figure 7B-6.

Like part (i), part (ii) has quantity of gas on the horizontal axis. By placing the two graphs one under the other, we can directly transcribe the quantity determined on the upper graphs to the lower one. We first do this for the 600 litres consumed on the innermost budget line. We now note that the price of gas that gives rise to that budget line is \$0.75. Plotting 600 litres against \$.75 in part (ii) produces the point *a*, derived from point E_0 in part (i). This is one point on the household's demand curve. Next we consider the middle budget line, which occurs when the price of gas is \$0.50. We take the figure of 1,200 litres from point E_1 in part (i) and transfer it to part (ii). We then plot this quantity against the price of \$0.50 to get the point *b* on the demand curve. Doing the same thing for point E_2 yields the point *c* in part (ii): price \$0.25, quantity 2,200 litres.

Repeating the operation for all prices yields the demand curve in part (ii). Note that the two parts of the figure describe the same behavior. Both parts measure the quantity of gas on the horizontal axes; the only difference is that in part (i) the price of gas determines the slope of the budget line, while in part (ii) the price of gas is plotted explicitly on the vertical axis.

The Slope of the Demand Curve

The price-consumption line in part (i) of Figure 7B-6 indicates that as price decreases, quantity of gasoline demanded increases. But one can draw the indifference curves in such a way that the response to a given decrease in price is for less to be consumed rather than more. This possibility gives rise to the positively sloped demand curve, referred to as a Giffen good, that was briefly discussed in the text of Chapter 7. Let us see how the conditions leading to this case are analyzed using indifference curves.

Income and Substitution Effects

The key, as we saw in the text, is to distinguish between the income effect and the substitution effect of a change in price. In the text of Chapter 7 we eliminated the income effect by changing money income *until the original bundle of goods could just be consumed.* This is the approach used in the famous Slutsky equation, which is a major tool in empirical studies of demand.

In indifference theory, however, the income effect is removed by changing money income until the original level of satisfaction—the original indifference curve—can just be achieved.

The separation of the two effects according to indifference theory is shown in Figure 7B-7. The figure shows in greater detail part of the price-consumption line first drawn in Figure 7B-6. Points E_0 and E_2 are on the price-consumption line for carrots. We can think of the separation occurring in the following way. After the price of the good has fallen, we reduce money income *until the original indifference curve can just be obtained.* This leads the household to move from point E_0 to an imaginary point E_1, and this response is defined as the substitution effect. Then, to measure the income effect, we restore money income. The household moves from the point E_1 to the final point E_2, and this response is defined as the income effect.

Now compare this indifference theory definition with the Slutsky definition used in the text of Chapter 7. In the text we measure the substitution effect of any price change by altering money income until the original bundle of goods can just be purchased. In this appendix we measure the substitution effect

FIGURE 7B-7 The Income Effect and the Substitution Effect in Indifference Theory

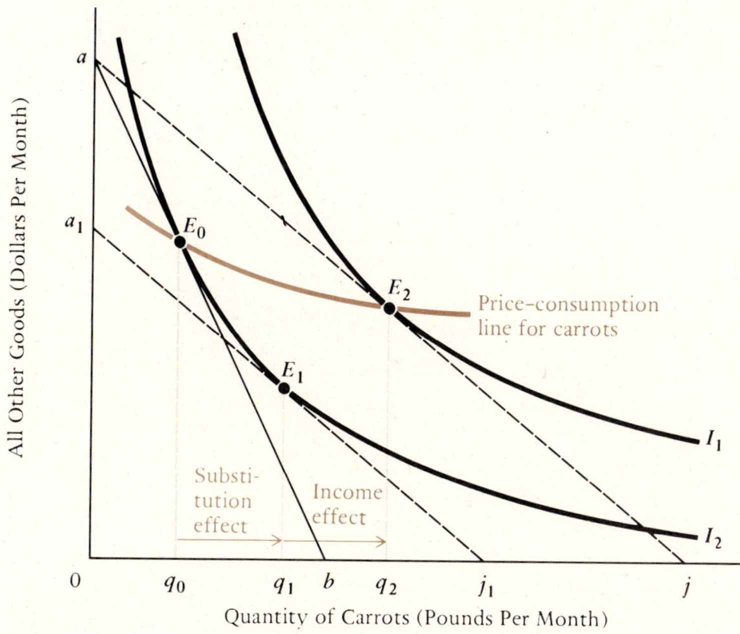

The substitution effect is defined by sliding the budget line around a fixed indifference curve; the income effect is defined by a parallel shift of the budget line. The original budget line is at *ab* and a fall in the price of carrots takes it to *aj*. The original equilibrium is at E_0 with q_0 of carrots consumed, and the final equilibrium is at E_2 with q_2 of carrots consumed. To remove the income effect, imagine reducing the household's income until it is just able to attain its original indifference curve. We do this by shifting the line *aj* to a parallel line nearer the origin that just touches the indifference curve that passes through E_0. The intermediate point E_1 divides the quantity change into a substitution effect q_0q_1 and an income effect q_1q_2. It can also be obtained by sliding the original budget line *ab* around the indifference curve until its slope reflects the new relative prices.

by altering money income until the original level of satisfaction—the original indifference curve—can just be attained.

The advantage of the Slutsky definition is that it is operational; the change in income required to allow the original bundle to be purchased at the new prices is simply calculated. The disadvantage is that this change does not leave unchanged the household's real income, defined as its level of satisfaction. The advantage of the indifference curve approach is that the change does leave the household's level of satisfaction unchanged and hence defines the substitution effect as the response to changes in relative prices with real satisfaction unchanged. The disadvantage is that the measurement is not easily made operational; we have to know each household's tastes to be able to make the required change in income.

In Figure 7B-7, the income and substitution effects are in the same direction, both tending to increase quantity demanded when price falls. Is this necessarily the case? The answer is no. While it follows from the convex shape of indifference curves that the substitution effect is always in the same direction, income effects can be in either direction. The direction depends on the distinction we drew earlier between normal and inferior goods.

The Slope of the Demand Curve for a Normal Good

For a normal good, an increase in real income due to a decrease in the price of the commodity leads to its increased consumption, reinforcing the substitution effect. Because quantity demanded increases, the demand curve slopes downward.

The Slope of the Demand Curve for an Inferior Good

Figure 7B-8 shows indifference curves for inferior goods. The income effect is negative in each part of the diagram. This follows from the nature of an

FIGURE 7B-8 Income and Substitution Effects for Inferior Goods

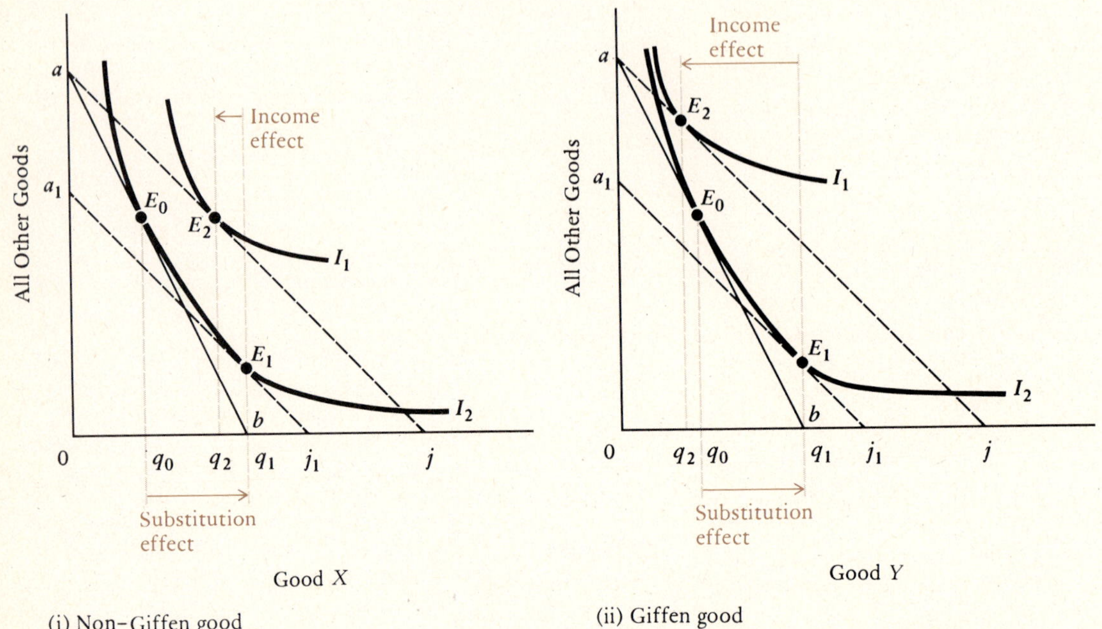

Inferior goods have negative income effects. A large enough negative income effect can outweigh the substitution effect and lead to a decrease in consumption in response to a fall in price. In each part of the diagram the household is in equilibrium at E_0, consuming a quantity q_0 of the good in question. The price then decreases and the budget line shifts to *aj*, with a new equilibrium at E_2 and quantity consumed q_2. In each case the substitution effect is to increase consumption from q_0 to q_1. In (i) there is a negative income effect of q_1q_2. Because this is less than the substitution effect, the latter dominates, so good *X* has a normal, downward-sloping demand curve. In (ii) the negative income effect q_1q_2 is larger than the substitution effect, and quantity consumed actually decreases. Good *Y* is thus a Giffen good.

inferior good: As income rises, less of the good is consumed. In each case the substitution effect serves to increase the quantity demanded as price decreases and is offset to some degree by the negative income effect. The final result depends on the relative strengths of the two effects. In part (i) the negative income effect only partially offsets the substitution effect, and thus quantity demanded increases as a result of the price decrease, though not as much as for a normal good. This is the typical pattern for inferior goods, and it too leads to downward-sloping demand curves, often relatively inelastic ones.

In part (ii) the negative income effect actually outweighs the substitution effect and thus leads to an upward-sloping demand curve. This is the Giffen case. For this to happen the good must be inferior. But that is not enough; the change in price must have a negative income effect *strong enough* to offset the substitution effect. A combination of circumstances that makes this possible is not often expected, and therefore an upward-sloping market demand curve is at most an infrequent exception to the rule that demand curves slope downward.

Summary

1. While the budget line describes what the household *can* purchase, indifference curves describe the household's tastes and, therefore, refer to what it *would like* to purchase. A single indifference curve joins combinations of commodities that give the household equal satisfaction and among which it is therefore indifferent. An indifference map is a set of indifference curves.
2. The basic hypothesis about tastes is that of a diminishing marginal rate of substitution. This hypothesis states that the less of one good and the more of another the household has, the less willing it will be to give up some of the first good to get a further unit of the second. This means indifference curves are downward sloping and convex to the origin.
3. The household achieves an equilibrium that maximizes its satisfactions given its budget line at the point at which an indifference curve is tangent to its budget line.
4. The income-consumption line shows how quantity consumed changes as income changes with relative prices constant.
5. The price-consumption line shows how quantity consumed changes as relative prices change. When prices change, the household will consume more of the commodity whose relative price falls.
6. The price-consumption line relating the purchases of one particular commodity and all other commodities contains the same information as an ordinary demand curve. The horizontal axis measures quantity, and the slope of budget line measures price. Transferring this price-quantity information to a diagram whose axes represent price and quantity leads to a conventional demand curve.
7. The effect of a change in price of one commodity, all other prices and money income constant, changes not only relative prices, but also real incomes. A price decrease can affect consumption both through the substitution effect and the income effect.
8. Demand curves for normal goods slope downward because both income and substitution effects work in the same direction, a decrease in price leading to increased consumption.
9. For an inferior good a decrease in price leads to more consumption via the substitution effect and less consumption via the income effect. In the extreme case of a Giffen good the negative income effect more than offsets the substitution effect, and the consumption of the commodity decreases as a result of a price decrease. This is a theoretical possibility that has seldom if ever been observed in fact.

8

Using Demand Theory

In Chapter 7 we covered some difficult material on the theory of demand. In this chapter we get a return on that investment by developing some important applications. We start by showing the link between the household demand curves that we discussed in Chapter 7 and the market demand curves that were discussed in earlier chapters.

Market and Individual Demand Curves

Market demand curves tell how much is demanded by all purchasers. For example, in Figure 4-1 (page 61) the market demand for carrots is 90,000 tons when the price is $40 per ton. This 90,000 tons is the sum of the quantities demanded by millions of different households. It may be made up of 4 pounds for the Tremblays, 7 pounds for the Chows, 1.5 pounds for the Smiths, and so on. The demand curve in that earlier figure also tells us that when the price rises to $60, aggregate quantity demanded falls to 77,500 tons per month. This quantity too can be traced back to individual households. The Tremblays might buy only 3 pounds, the Chows 6.5 pounds, and the Smiths none at all. Notice that we have now described two points not only on the market demand curve but also on the demand curves of each of these households.

The market demand curve is the horizontal sum of the demand curves of the individual households.

It is the horizontal sum because we wish to add quantities demanded at a given price, and quantities are measured in the horizontal direction on a conventional demand curve diagram. This is illustrated in Figure 8-1.

Consumers' Surplus

Imagine yourself faced with an either-or choice concerning some particular commodity: You can have the amount you are now consuming or you can have none of it. Assume that you would be willing to pay as much as $100 a month for that amount rather than do without it. Further assume that you actually buy that amount of the commodity for $60 instead of $100. What a bargain! You have paid $40 less than the top figure you were willing to pay. Yet this sort of bargain is not rare; it occurs every day in any economy where prices do the rationing. Indeed, it is so common that the $40 "saved" in this example has been given a

FIGURE 8-1 The Relation Between Household and Market Demand Curves

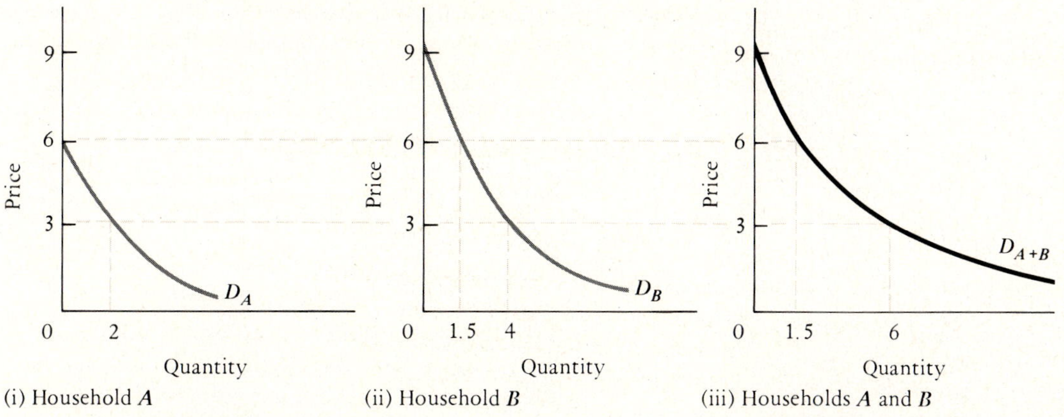

An aggregate demand curve is the horizontal sum of the individual demand curves of all households in the market. The figure illustrates aggregation over only two households. At a price of \$3, household A purchases 2 units and household B purchases 4 units; thus together they purchase 6 units. No matter how many households are involved, the process is the same.

name: *consumers' surplus.* We will define the term later; first let us look at how this surplus arises.

Consumers' surplus is a direct consequence of downward-sloping demand curves. To illustrate the connection, suppose that we have collected the information in Table 8-1 on the basis of an interview with Mrs. Swartz. Our first question to Mrs. Swartz is, "If you were getting no milk at all, how much would you be willing to pay for one glass per week?" With no hesitation she replies \$3.00. We then ask, "If you had already consumed that one glass, how much would you pay for a second glass per week?" After a bit of thought she answers \$1.50. Adding one glass per week with each question, we discover that she would be willing to pay \$1.00 to get a third glass per week and \$.80, \$.60, \$.50, \$.40, \$.30, \$.25, and \$.20 for successive glasses from the fourth to the tenth glass per week.

The sum of the values that she places on each glass of milk gives us the **total value** that she places on all ten glasses. In this case, Mrs. Swartz values ten glasses of milk per week at \$8.55. This is the amount she would be willing to pay if faced with the either-or choice of ten glasses or none. This is also the amount she would be willing to pay if she were offered the milk one glass at a time, and charged the maximum she was willing to pay for each.

But Mrs. Swartz does not have to pay a different price for each glass of milk she consumes each week; she can buy all she wants at the prevailing market price. Suppose the price is \$.30. She will buy eight glasses per week (one each weekday and two on Sunday) because she values the eighth glass just at the market price, while valuing all earlier glasses at higher amounts. Because she values the first glass at \$3.00 but gets it for \$.30, she makes a "profit" of \$2.70 on that glass. Between her \$1.50 valuation of the second glass and what she has to pay for it she clears a "profit" of \$1.20. She clears \$.70 on the third glass, and so on. These "profits" are called her consumer's surpluses on each glass. They are shown in column 3 of the table; the total surplus is \$5.70 per week.

In the table we arrive at her consumer's surplus by summing her surpluses on each glass. We arrive at the same total by first summing what she would pay for all eight glasses, which is \$8.10, and then subtracting the \$2.40 that she does pay.

TABLE 8-1 Consumers' Surplus on Milk Consumption by One Consumer

(1) Glasses of milk consumed per week	(2) Amount the consumer would pay to get this glass	(3) Consumers' surplus on each glass if milk costs $.30 per glass
First	$3.00	$2.70
Second	1.50	1.20
Third	1.00	.70
Fourth	.80	.50
Fifth	.60	.30
Sixth	.50	.20
Seventh	.40	.10
Eighth	.30	.00
Ninth	.25	—
Tenth	.20	—

Consumers' surplus on each unit consumed is the difference between the market price and the maximum price the consumer would pay to obtain that unit. The table shows the value that one consumer, Mrs. Swartz, puts on successive glasses of milk consumed each week. Her negatively sloped demand curve shows that she would be willing to pay progressively smaller amounts for each additional unit consumed. As long as she would be willing to pay more than the market price for any unit, she obtains a consumers' surplus on it when she buys it. The marginal unit is the one valued just at the market price and on which no consumers' surplus is earned.

The value placed by each household on its total consumption of some commodity can be estimated in at least two ways: The valuation that the household places on each successive unit may be summed, or the household may be asked how much it would pay to consume the amount in question if the alternative were to have none.[1]

Although other households would put different numerical values into Table 8-1, the negative slope of the demand curve implies that the figures in column 2 would be declining for each household. Since a household will go on buying additional units until the value placed on the last unit equals the market price, it follows that there will be a consumers' surplus on every unit consumed except the last one.

In general, **consumers' surplus** is the difference between the total value households place on all the units consumed of some commodity and the payment they must make to purchase that amount of the commodity.

The data in columns 1 and 2 of Table 8-1 give Mrs. Swartz's demand curve for milk. It is her demand curve because she will go on buying glasses of milk as long as she values each glass at least as much as the market price she must pay for it. When the market price is $3.00 per glass, she will buy only one glass; when it is $1.50, she will buy two glasses; and so on. The total valuation is the area below her demand curve, and consumer's surplus is the part of the area that lies above the price line. This is shown in Figure 8-2.

Figure 8-3 shows that the same relation holds for the smooth market demand curve that indicates the total amount all consumers would buy at each price.[2]

Some Applications of Consumers' Surplus

In subsequent chapters we will find many uses for the concept of consumers' surplus. In this chapter we show how it can be used to resolve some very old problems.

The Paradox of Value

Early economists, struggling with the problem of what determines the relative prices of commodities,

[1] This is only an approximation, but it is good enough for our purposes. More advanced theory shows that the calculations presented here overestimate consumers' surplus because they ignore the income effect. Although it is sometimes necessary to correct for this bias, no amount of refinement upsets the general result that we establish here: When consumers can buy all units they require at a single market price they pay much less than they would be willing to pay if faced with the choice between having the quantity they consume and having none.

[2] Figure 8-2 is a bar chart because we only allowed Mrs. Swartz to vary her consumption in discrete units of one glass at a time. Had we allowed her to vary her consumption of milk a drop at a time, we could have traced out a continuous curve similar to the one shown in Figure 8-3.

FIGURE 8-2 Consumers' Surplus for an Individual

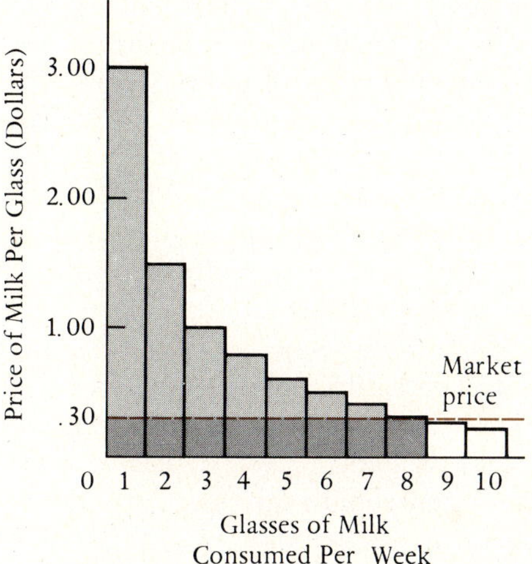

Consumers' surplus is the sum of the extra valuations placed on each unit above the market price paid for each. This figure is based on the data in Table 8-1. Mrs. Swartz will pay the dark shaded area for the eight glasses of milk she will consume per week when the market price is $.30 a glass. The total value she places on these eight glasses is the entire shaded area. Hence her consumers' surplus is the light shaded area.

FIGURE 8-3 Consumers' Surplus for the Market

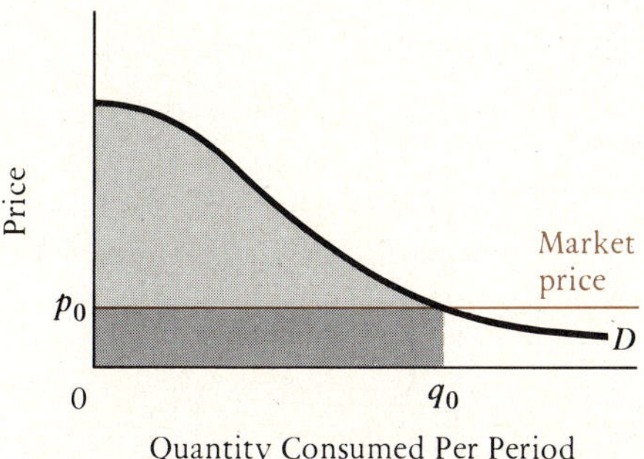

Total consumers' surplus is the area under the demand curve and above the price line. The demand curve shows the amount consumers would pay for each unit of the commodity if they had to buy their units one at a time. The area under the demand curve shows the total valuation consumers place on all units consumed. For example, the total value that consumers place on q_0 units is the entire shaded area under the demand curve up to q_0. At a market price of p_0 the amount paid for q_0 units is the dark shaded area. Hence consumers' surplus is the light shaded area.

encountered what they called the *paradox of value:* Many necessary commodities, such as water, have prices that are low compared with the prices of luxury commodities, such as diamonds. Water is necessary to our existence, while high-quality diamonds are mostly used for frivolous purposes and could disappear from the face of the earth tomorrow without causing any real hardship. Does it not seem odd, then, these economists asked, that water is so cheap and diamonds are so expensive? It took a long time to resolve this apparent paradox, so it is not surprising that even today analogous confusions cloud many policy discussions.

The key to solving the "paradox" lies in the important distinction between what one would pay to avoid having one's consumption of a commodity reduced to zero and what one would pay to gain the use of one more unit of the commodity. This point involves a distinction between total and marginal values that is frequently encountered in many branches of economics, and which was studied in detail in Appendix 7A.

We have already seen that the area under the demand curve shows what the household would pay for the commodity if it had to purchase it unit by unit. It is thus a measure of the total value that the household places on *all* of the units it consumes. In Figure 8-3 the *total* value of q_0 units is the entire shaded area (light and dark) under the demand curve.

What about the **marginal value** that the household places on one more, or one less, than the q_0 units it is currently consuming? This is given by the commodity's market price, which is p_0 in this case. Faced with a market price of p_0, the household buys all the units that it values at p_0 or greater but does not purchase any units that it values at less than p_0. It follows that the household places on the last unit consumed of any commodity a value that is measured by the commodity's price.[3]

Now look at the total market value of the commodity. This is the amount everyone spends to purchase it. It is price multiplied by quantity. In Figure 8-3 this is the dark shaded rectangle with sides p_0 and q_0.

We have seen that the total value consumers place on a given amount of a commodity, as measured by the relevant area under the demand curve, is different from the total market value of a commodity as given by the commodity's price multiplied by the quantity consumed. Being different, the two values do not have to be related to each other. Figure 8-4 illustrates a case where a good with a total high value has a low market value and vice versa.

The resolution of the paradox of value is that a good that is very plentiful, such as water, will have a low price and will thus be consumed to the point where all households place a low value on the last unit consumed, whether or not they place a high value on their total consumption of the commodity. By contrast, a commodity that is relatively scarce will have a high market price, and consumption will therefore stop at a point where consumers place a high value on the last unit consumed regardless of the value they place on their total consumption of the good.

We have now reached an important conclusion:

Because the market price of a commodity depends on demand and supply, there is nothing paradoxical in a commodity on which consumers place a high total value selling for a low price and hence having only a low amount spent on it.

Necessities, Luxuries, and Elasticity

In ordinary discussion people often distinguish between necessities and luxuries, necessities being commodities that are difficult to do without and luxuries being commodities that could be fairly easily dispensed with. The distinction is somewhat arbitrary; for example, are eggs a necessity or a luxury? Nonetheless, some sense can be made of the distinction by understanding it to compare the *total* values that households place on their consumptions of different commodities. Earlier in this chapter we learned to measure these total values by the areas under demand curves. Using this terminology we would say that a necessity has a very large area under its demand curve; a luxury has a smaller area.

A frequent error occurs when people try to use knowledge of total values to predict demand elasticities. It is sometimes argued that since luxuries can be given up, they have highly elastic demands; when their prices rise, households can stop purchasing them. It is likewise argued that necessities have highly inelastic demands because when prices rise, households have no choice but to continue to buy them.

But elasticity of demand depends on how consumers value commodities at the margin, not on how much they value the total consumption of the commodity. The relevant question for the determination of elasticity is, "How much do households value a bit more of some commodity?" not "How much do they value *all* of the commodity that they are now consuming?"

Demand theory leads to the prediction that when the price of a commodity rises, each household will reduce its purchases of that commodity until it values the last unit consumed at the price that it must pay for that unit. Will the reduction in quantity required to raise the valuation be a little or a lot? This depends on the shape of the demand curve in the relevant range. If the demand curve is flat, a large change in quantity is required, and demand will be elastic. If the curve is steep, a small change will suffice, and demand will be inelastic. Figure 8-5 (p. 166) presents two possible responses to a doubling in price. It leads to this important conclusion:

The size of the response of quantity demanded to a change in price depends on the value households place on a bit more or a bit less of the commodity and has no necessary relation to the

[3] In terms of utility theory (Appendix 7A) the price measures the marginal utility of the last unit that the household purchases. In terms of indifference theory (Appendix 7B) the price measures the rate at which the household is prepared to substitute the good in question for money—that is, the slope, at the equilibrium point, of the indifference curve drawn with the quantity of the good on one axis and consumption of all other goods, measured in money units, on the other axis.

FIGURE 8-4 Total Value Versus Market Value

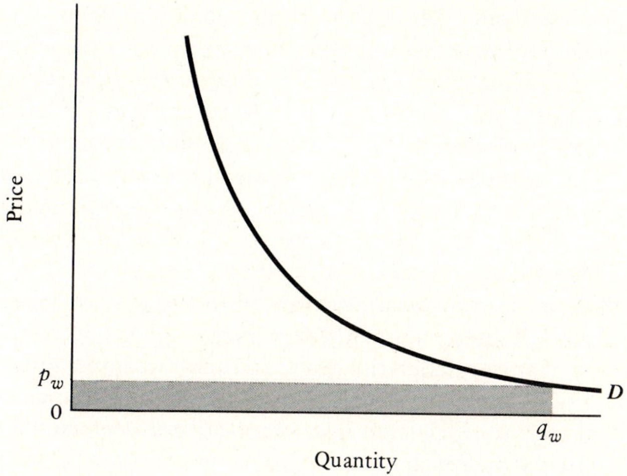

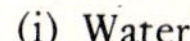
(i) Water

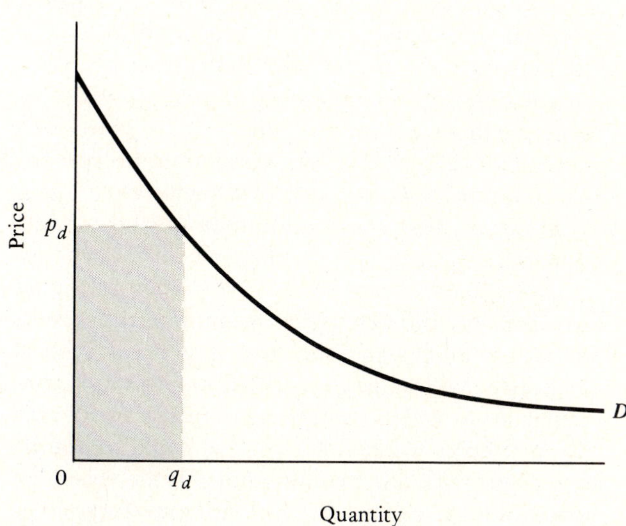

(ii) Diamonds

The market value of the amount of some commodity bears no necessary relation to the total value consumers place on that amount. The diagram presents hypothetical demand curves for water and diamonds that are meant to be stylized versions of the real curves. The total value that households place on water, as shown by the area under the demand curve, is great—indeed, we do not even show the curve for very small quantities because people would pay all they had rather than be deprived completely of water. The total valuation that households place on diamonds is shown by the area under the demand curve for diamonds. This is clearly less than the total value placed on water.

The low supply of diamonds makes diamonds scarce and keeps diamonds high in price, as shown by p_d in the figure. Thus the total market value of diamonds sold, indicated by the dark shaded area of $p_d q_d$, is high.

The large supply of water makes water plentiful and makes water low in price, as shown by p_w in the figure. Thus the total market value of water consumed, indicated by the dark shaded area of $p_w q_w$, is low.

value they place on their total consumption of the quantity in question.

Box 8-1 (p. 167) provides an example from outside the field of economics of the importance of distinguishing between the total value that people get from some activity and the value they would place on doing a bit more or a bit less of it.

Free, Scarce, and Freely Provided Goods

A **free good** is one for which the quantity supplied exceeds the quantity demanded at a price of zero. Such goods will therefore not command positive prices in a market economy. A household can make itself better off by increasing its consumption of free

FIGURE 8-5 The Relation of Elasticity of Demand to Total Value

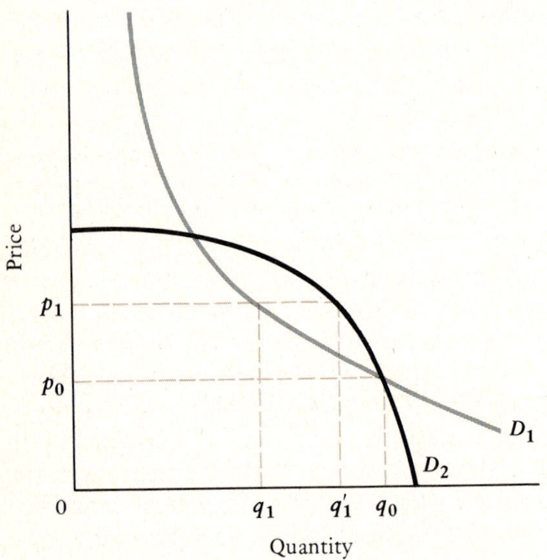

Elasticity of demand is determined by marginal valuation in the relevant range, not total value. Consider two alternative demand curves for a commodity, D_1 and D_2. Suppose price is p_0. Given either demand curve the household consumes the quantity q_0, where the last unit consumed is valued at p_0. When the price rises to p_1, households cut their consumption.

If the black line D_2 is the demand curve, consumption only falls to q_1' and the demand for the product is quite inelastic. If, however, the grey line D_1 is the demand curve, consumption falls to q_1 and the demand for the product is less inelastic.

Although the shape of the demand curve in the relevant range is important, its shape outside of this range is irrelevant for determining elasticity. But total value depends on the whole area under the curve. Depending on the shape of the curve up to q_0, either curve can show more or less total value than the other. Thus total value has no influence on market behavior in response to a change in price from p_0 to p_1.

goods as long as it places any positive value on the extra units consumed. It follows that free goods will be consumed up to the point at which the value households place on another unit consumed is zero. At some times in some places, air, water, salt, sand, and wild fruit have been free goods. Note that a good may be free at one time or place but not at another.

A **scarce good** is one for which the quantity demanded exceeds the quantity supplied at a price of zero. If all such goods had zero prices, the total amount that people would want to consume would greatly exceed the amount that could be produced. Such goods will therefore command positive prices in a market economy. Most goods are scarce goods.

Many people have strong views about the prices charged for certain commodities. These views are often an emotional reaction to the total values of goods rather than to their marginal values. Here is an example: "Because water is such a complete necessity of life to rich and to poor, it is wrong to make people pay for water. Instead the government should provide free water for everyone."

When deciding between a zero price and a modest price for water, the relevant question is, "Are the marginal uses of water so important that we are willing to use scarce resources to provide the necessary quantities?" The question is not, "Is water so necessary that we want everyone to be provided with some of it?" The distinction is important because the two questions will have different answers.

Evidence about the consumption of water at various prices suggests that the demand curve for water is shaped like the curve shown in part (i) of Figure 8-4. If so, the difference in consumption that results from providing water free and charging a modest price for it will be large. The additional water consumed, however, is costly to provide, and its provision requires scarce resources that could have been used to produce other commodities. If the value that households place on the commodities forgone is higher than the value they place on the extra water consumed, households are worse off as a result of receiving water free. A charge for water would release resources from water production to produce commodities that households value more highly at the margin. Of course, some minimum quantity of water could be provided free to every household, but the effects of this would be quite different from the effects of making all water free.

It follows that neither the gain to consumers of

BOX 8-1

What Do Attitude Surveys Measure?

Consider a type of survey that is popular both in the daily newspapers and in sociology and political science. These surveys take the form of asking such questions as these:

"Do you like the PC more than the Liberals?"
"In deciding to live in area *A* rather than area *B*, what factors influenced your choice? List the following in order of importance: neighbors, schools, closeness to swimming area, price and quality of housing available, play areas for children, general amenities."
"In choosing a university, what factors were important to you? List in order of importance: environment, academic excellence, residential facilities, parents' opinion, school opinion, athletic facilities, tuition."

You should be able to add other examples to this list. The three survey questions cited, and most of those you might add, attempt to measure the *total* valuation households place on some activity rather than the *marginal* valuation they would place on a little more or a little less consumption.

The total value being asked about includes the consumers' surplus. There is, of course, nothing illegal or immoral about this. People are free to measure anything that interests them, and in some cases knowledge of total valuation may be useful. But in most cases actual behavior is determined by marginal valuations, and anyone who attempts to predict such behavior from a knowledge of total valuations, even a correct knowledge, will be hopelessly in error.

Where the behavior being predicted involves an either-or decision, such as a vote for the Conservative or the Liberal in a two-party contest, total value attached to each choice will indeed be what matters because the voters are choosing one or the other. But where the decision is marginal, between a little more and a little less, total value is not what will determine behavior.

A recent newspaper poll in a large U.S. city showed that two-thirds of the city's voters rated its excellent school system as an important asset. Yet in a subsequent election the voters turned down a school bond issue. Is this irrational behavior, as the newspaper editorials charged? Does it show a biased sample in the poll? It demonstrates neither. The poll measured the people's assessment of the total value derived from the school system (high), whereas the bond issue vote depended on the people's assessment of the marginal value of a little more money spent on the school system (low). There is nothing contradictory in anyone's feeling that the total value of the city's fine school system is high but that the city (or the taxpayer) has other needs that have a higher value at the margin than further money spent on schools.

A recent survey showed—paradoxically, it claimed—that many Canadians are getting more pleasure from their families just at the time they are electing to have smaller families. There is nothing paradoxical about a shift in tastes that increases the marginal value of the first one or two children and reduces the marginal value of each additional child. Nor is there any paradox in a parent's getting a high total value from the total time spent with the children but assigning a low marginal value to the prospect of spending additional time with them each evening.

---

encouraging a little more consumption of some commodity nor the loss from inducing a little less can be inferred from a knowledge of the total value placed on all of the consumption of that commodity.

Similar considerations apply to food, medical services, and a host of other commodities that are necessities of life but also have numerous low-value uses that will be encouraged if a scarce commodity is provided at a zero price.

Summary

1. Market demand curves reflect the aggregate of the consumption behavior of the millions of households in the economy.
2. Consumers' surplus arises because a household can purchase every unit of a commodity at a price equal to the value it places on the last unit purchased. The negative slope of demand curves implies that the value that households place on all other units purchased exceeds the value of the last unit purchased and hence that all but the last unit purchased yield a consumers' surplus.
3. It is important to distinguish between total marginal values because choices concerning a bit more and a bit less cannot be predicted from a knowledge of total values.
4. The total value that consumers place on some quantity of one commodity consumed is given by the area under the demand curve up to that quantity. The market value is given by an area below the market price up to that quantity. Consumers' surplus is the difference between the two.
5. The paradox of value involves a confusion between total value and market value.
6. Elasticity of demand is related to the marginal value that households place on having a bit more or a bit less of some commodity; it bears no necessary relation to the total value that households place on all of the units consumed of that commodity.
7. Households will consume any good that has a zero price up to the points where the marginal value that they place on further consumption is zero.

Topics for Review

Market demand and individual household demand curves
Consumers' surplus
The paradox of value
Total value versus marginal value
Necessities and luxuries
Free goods and scarce goods

Discussion Questions

1. Why is market demand the horizontal sum of individual demand curves? Is the vertical sum different? What would a vertical sum of individual demand curves show? Can you imagine any use of vertical summation of demand curves?
2. Which of the choices implied below involve a consideration of marginal values and which total values?
   a. Parliament debates whether 17-year-olds should be given the vote.
   b. A diet calls for precisely 1,200 calories per day.
   c. My doctor says I must give up smoking and drinking or else accept an increased chance of heart attack.

d. When Armand Hammer decided to buy the Rembrandt painting *Juno* for $3.25 million, he called it the "crown jewel of my collection."

e. I enjoyed my golf game today, but I was so tired that I decided to stop at the seventeenth hole.

3. Explain the transactions described in the following quotations in terms of the value of the commodity. Interpret "worthless" and "priceless" as used here.

a. "Bob Koppang has made a business of selling jars of shredded U.S. currency. The money is worthless, and yet he's sold 53,000 jars already and has orders for 40,000 more—at $5 a jar. Each jar contains about $10,000 in shredded bills."

b. "In February 1987 Vincent Van Gogh's priceless painting *Sunflowers* sold at auction for $39 million."

4. The *New York Times* called it the great liver crisis. Chopped liver is a delicacy on the table, particularly the kosher table, but not long ago it was a glut on the market. Prices had sunk to a 20-year low as supplies had risen to an all-time high due to a high cattle slaughter. What do the following quotations from the *Times* tell you about the marginal and total value of liver?

a. "Grade A-1 liver is being used for cats and dogs instead of people. It's unheard of, it's a waste," says the manager of Kosher King Meat Products. "Even Israel is drowning in chopped liver."

b. "They're falling all over their feet to sell to me," said the president of Mrs. Weinberg's Kosher Chopped Liver Co., which uses 3,500 pounds of liver daily. "I've been offered prices so low I can't believe them."

c. "The nature of people being what they are, even though they like a good bargain, they're not going to eat something that doesn't agree with their taste."

5. Mary is willing to pay $10 for the first widget she purchases each year, $9 for the second, $8 for the third, and so on down to $1 for the tenth and nothing for the eleventh. How many widgets will she buy and what will be her consumer's surplus if widgets cost $3 each? What will happen if the price of widgets rises to $5. Can you state a generalization about the relation between consumers' surplus obtained and price of a commodity?

9

The Role of the Firm

Ask almost anyone you know to name 10 North American business firms. The odds are overwhelming that the lists will include some of these firms: General Motors Corporation, Bombardier, General Electric, Bell Canada, Dow Chemical, the T. D. Bank, Dome Petroleum, Du Pont, Canadian Pacific, Canadaire, Air Canada, London Life, the CBC, and B.C. Forest Products. Drive around Gananoque, Ontario, and note at random 10 firms that come into view. They will probably include Dominion supermarket, Harding's Drugstore, a PetroCan service station, Donevan's Hardware, the Modern Cafe, and the Bank of Montreal. Drive through Manitoba or Saskatchewan and look around you: Every farm is a business firm as well as a home.

Firms develop and survive because they are efficient institutions for organizing resources to produce goods and services and for organizing their sale and distribution. It is not hard to count ways in which Bell Canada, the Modern Cafe, and the Saskatchewan wheat farm are different. But insight can be gained in treating them all under a single heading, that is, seeing what they have in common. This is what economic theory does. Economists usually assume that the firm's behavior can be understood in terms of a common motivation. Whether the firm is Ma and Pa's Bar and Grill or the Ford Motor Company and whether a particular decision is made by the board of directors, the third vice-president in charge of advertising, or the owner-manager is regarded as irrelevant to predicting what decisions are made. Criticisms that economic theory neglects differences among firms will be considered in Chapter 16.

Before studying how the firm is treated in economic theory, we shall examine more closely the firm in North America today.

The Organization of Production

Forms of Business Organization

There are three major forms of business organization: the single proprietorship, the partnership, and the corporation. In the **single proprietorship,** a single owner makes all decisions and is personally responsible for everything done by the business. In the **partnership,** there are two or more joint owners. Either may make binding decisions, and each partner is personally responsible for everything done by the business. In the **corporation,** the firm has a legal identity of its own. The owners (the stockholders) are not each personally responsible for everything that is done by the business. Owners elect a board of directors who hire managers to run the firm under the board's supervision.

In most sections of the Canadian economy the corporation is the dominant form of organization. In 1986 about 70 percent of manufacturing firms were incorporated; their share of employees was about 90 percent and their share of the value of shipments about 95 percent. Only in agriculture and in services (such as hair styling, medicine, and accounting) is the corporation relatively unimportant, yet even here its share of the business is steadily rising.

The Proprietorship and the Partnership

The major advantage of the single proprietorship is that the owner can maintain full control over the firm. The owner is the boss. The disadvantages are, first, that the size of the firm is limited by the capital the owner can personally raise and, second, that the owner is personally responsible in law for all debts of the firm.

The ordinary (or general) partnership overcomes to some extent the first disadvantage of the proprietorship but not the second. Ten partners may be able to finance a much bigger enterprise than one owner could, but they are still subject to unlimited liability. Each partner is fully liable for all the debts of the firm.

Because of this unlimited liability, people with substantial personal assets will be unwilling to enter a partnership unless they have complete trust in the other partners and a full knowledge of all the obligations of the firm. Also, it is difficult to raise money from persons who wish to invest but not be active in the business. Investors may be willing to put up $1,000 but unwilling to jeopardize their entire fortune; if, however, they join a partnership in order to do the former, they may also do the latter.

The **limited partnership** is designed to avoid some of these difficulties. General partners in a firm continue to have unlimited liability, but there are also limited partners. The limited partner's liability is restricted to the amount he or she has invested in the firm. Such partners do not participate in the management of the firm or engage in agreements on behalf of the partnership. In effect, the limited partnership permits some division of the functions of decision making, provision of capital, and risk taking.

In most respects this division of responsibility is more effectively achieved through the corporation. But there are certain professions in which general partnership is traditional. These include law, medicine, and (until recently) brokerage. Partnerships survive in these fields partly because they all depend heavily on a relationship of trust with their clients, and the partners' unlimited liability for one another's actions is thought to enhance public confidence in the firm.

The Corporation

The corporation is regarded in law as an entity separate from the individuals who own it. It can enter into contracts, it can sue and be sued, it can own property, it can contract debts, and it can generally incur obligations that are the legal obligations of the corporation *but not of its owners*. The right of the corporation to be sued may not seem to be an advantage, but it is, because it makes it possible for others to enter into enforceable contracts with the corporation.

Although some corporations are owned by just a few stockholders who also manage the business, the most important type of corporation is one that sells shares to the general public. The company raises the funds it needs for the business by the sale of stock, and the stockholders become the company's owners. They are entitled to share in corporate profits. When paid out, profits are called **dividends. Undistributed profits** also belong to the owners, but they are usually reinvested in the firm's operations. If the corporation is liquidated, stockholders share any assets that remain after all debts are paid.

Diffuse ownership of corporate shares means that the owners cannot all be managers. Stockholders, who are entitled to one vote for each share they own, elect a board of directors. The board defines general policy and hires senior managers who are supposed to translate this general policy into detailed decisions.

Should the company go bankrupt, the personal liability of any one shareholder is limited to whatever money that shareholder has actually invested in the firm. This is called **limited liability.**

From a shareholder's viewpoint, the most important aspect of the corporation is limited liability.

The corporation's advantage is that it can raise capital from a large number of individuals. Each investor shares in the firm's profits but has no liability for corporate action beyond risking the loss of the amount invested. Thus investors know their exact maximum risk and may simply collect dividends without needing to know anything about the policy or operation of the firm they own collectively. Because shares are easily transferred from one person to another, a corporation has a continuity of life unaffected by frequent changes in owners.

From the individual owner's point of view, there are disadvantages in investing in a corporation. First, the owner may have little to say about the management of the firm. For example, if those who hold a majority of the shares decide that the corporation should not pay dividends, an individual investor cannot compel the payment of his or her share of the earnings. Second, the income of the corporation is taxed twice. Corporations are taxed on their income before dividends are paid. Dividends are paid out of the after-tax income. Then individual stockholders are also taxed on any dividends paid to them. This "double taxation" of corporate income is viewed by some as unfair and discriminatory; others see it as the price to be paid for the advantage of incorporation. Judging from the continuing importance of the corporation in Canada the price has not been prohibitive, despite combined federal and provincial corporate tax rates that have long been between 40 and 50 percent depending on the corporation's size and provincial location.

The Rise of the Modern Corporation

The corporate form of organization is employed today wherever large enterprises are found. The principal reason is that it has decisive advantages over any other form in raising the vast sums of capital required for major enterprises. Historically, wherever and whenever large accumulations of capital in a single firm were required, the limited liability company developed. In recent times the corporate form has spread to the service industries and agriculture, as firms in these industries grew in size.

The direct predecessor of the modern corporation was the English chartered company of the sixteenth century. The Muscovy Company, granted a charter in 1555, the East India Company, first chartered in 1600, and the Hudson's Bay Company, chartered in 1609 and still going strong 380 years later, are famous examples of early joint-stock ventures with limited liability. Their special needs for many investors to finance a ship that would not return with its cargo for years—if it returned at all—made this exceptional form of organization seem desirable.

In the next three centuries the trading company's needs (large capital requirements, the need to diversify risk, the need for long-term investment) were seen to exist in other fields, and charters were granted in the fields of insurance, turnpikes and canals, and banking, as well as foreign trade. The new techniques introduced during the Industrial Revolution made the large firm efficient and so extended the needs for large amounts of capital committed over long periods of time to many more fields. During the nineteenth century the demand for a basis for incorporation other than special privilege became strong. General laws permitting incorporation with limited liability *as a matter of right rather than special grant of privilege* became common in England and Canada during the late nineteenth century.

Today incorporation is relatively routine, although it is subject to a variety of provincial laws. Moderate fees are charged for the privilege of incorporation, and a company can choose to incorporate either federally or under the regulations of one of the provinces.

Financing of Firms

The money a firm raises for carrying on its business is sometimes called its **financial** (or money) **capital** as distinct from its **real capital** (or *physical capital*), the physical assets that constitute plant, equipment, and inventories. Money capital may be broken down into **equity capital,** provided by the owners, and **debt,** which consists of the funds borrowed from persons and institutions who are not owners of the firm.

The use of the term *capital* to refer to both an amount of money and a quantity of goods can be confusing, but it is usually clear from the context which is being referred to. The two uses are not independent, for much of the money capital raised by a firm will be used to purchase the capital goods the firm requires for production.

There are two basic methods by which a firm raises financial capital: equity financing and debt financing.

Equity Financing

The owners of the firm are its **stockholders,** people who have put up money to purchase shares in the firm. They make their money available to the firm and risk losing it in return for a share of any profits the firm makes.

Stockholders usually have voting rights and have only a residual claim on the firm's revenues. After all other claims have been met, the remaining funds, if any, belong to the stockholders. There is no legal limit to the profits that may be earned by the company and therefore no limit to potential dividends that may be paid out to common stockholders. Firms are not obliged by law to pay out any fixed portion of profits as dividends, and in fact practices among corporations vary enormously. Firms sometimes pay out a large fraction and hold back only enough to meet contingencies; at other times they pay small or no dividends in order to reinvest retained funds in the enterprise.

As this suggests, there are two ways for the firm to raise equity. One is to issue and sell new shares. The other is to reinvest, or plow back, some or all of its own profits, thus increasing the stake that existing shareholders have in the firm.

Reinvestment has become an extremely important source of funds in modern times. In Canada over $15 billion per year is obtained for investment in this fashion. The shareholder who does not wish his or her profits to be reinvested can do little about it except to sell the stock and invest in a company with a policy of paying out a larger fraction of its earnings as dividends.

Debt Financing

Firms can also raise money by issuing debt, either by selling bonds or by borrowing from banks and other financial institutions. Debtholders are creditors, not owners, of the firm. They have loaned money to the firm in return for a promise to pay interest on the loan and, of course, a promise to repay the principal. Bank loans are often short-term; sometimes the firm even commits to repay the principal *on demand.* A **bond** is a promise to pay interest each year and to repay the principal at a stated time in the future (say, 20 years hence). In either case the promise to pay is a legal obligation on the firm's part whether or not profits have been made. If these payments cannot be met, the debtholders can force the firm into bankruptcy. Should this happen, the debtholders have a prior claim on the firm's assets. Only when the debtholders and all other creditors have been repaid in full can the stockholders attempt to recover anything for themselves.

Much of the firm's short-term and some of its long-term monetary needs are met through bank loans. This is often true of giant corporations and is particularly the case for small businesses. Banks, however, limit the amounts they are willing to lend companies, typically to specified fractions of the companies' total financial needs.

A major disadvantage to the corporation of raising capital through issuing debt is that interest payments must be met whether or not there are profits. Many a firm that would have survived a temporary crisis had all its capital been equity-financed has been forced into bankruptcy because it could not meet its contractual obligations to pay interest to its debtholders.

The Firm in Economic Theory

IBM and the Main Street Deli certainly make decisions in different ways. Indeed, within a single large corporation not all decisions are made by the same people or in the same way. To take an example, someone at IBM decided to introduce a small com-

BOX 9-1

Different Kinds of Firms

In economic theory the firm is defined as the unit that makes decisions with respect to the production and sale of commodities. This single definition covers a variety of business organizations from the single proprietorship to the corporation and a variety of business sizes from the inventor operating in his garage and financed by whatever he can extract from a reluctant bank manager to vast undertakings with tens of thousands of shareholders and creditors. We know that in large firms decisions are actually made by many different individuals. We can nonetheless regard the firm as a single consistent decision-making unit because of the assumption that all decisions are made to achieve the common goal of maximizing the firm's profits.

Whether a decision is made by a small independent proprietor, a plant manager, or a board of directors, that person or group is the firm for the purpose of that decision. This is a truly heroic assumption; it amounts to saying that for purposes of predicting the aspects of their behavior that interest us, we can treat a farm, a corner grocery, a department store, a small law partnership, B.C. Telephone, and a giant multinational corporation all under the umbrella of a single theory of the behavior of the firm. If this turns out to be even partially correct, it will prove enormously valuable in revealing some unity of behavior where to the casual observer there is only bewildering diversity.

You should not be surprised, therefore, if at first encounter the theory appears rather abstract and out of touch with reality. To generalize over such a wide variety of behavior, the theory must ignore many familiar features that distinguish the farmer from the grocer and each of them from the Stelco Corporation. Any theory that generalizes over a wide variety of apparently diverse behavior necessarily has this characteristic because it ignores the factors that are most obvious to us and create the appearance of diversity. If it were not possible to do this, it would be necessary to have dozens of different theories, one for each type of firm. The task of learning economics would then be much more complex than it now is!

---

puter in 1981. Someone else decided to call it the IBM personal computer and market it for home use. Someone else decided how and where to produce it. Someone else decided its price. Someone else decided how best to promote its sales. The common aspect of these decisions is that all were in pursuit of the same goal—the manufacture and sale of products to earn profits for IBM.

Economic theory assumes that the same principles underlie each decision made within a firm and that the decision is uninfluenced by who makes it. The assumption that all firms are the same is further discussed in Box 9-1.

Motivation: Profit Maximization

It is assumed that the firm makes decisions in such a way that its profits will be as large as possible. In other words, the firm is assumed to *maximize its profits*. The concept of profits requires careful definition, which will be given later in this chapter. For now we may treat it in the everyday sense of the difference between the value of the firm's sales and the costs to the firm of producing what is sold.

The assumption of profit maximization provides a principle by which a firm's decisions can be predicted.

Economists predict the firm's behavior by studying the effect that making each choice would have on the firm's profits. They then predict that from these alternatives the firm will select the one that produces the largest profits.

At this point you may well ask if it is sensible to build a theory on such a simple assumption about the motives of business people. Of course, some business people are inspired by motives other than a desire to make as much money as possible. Cases in which they use their positions to seek political influence or pursue charitable objectives are not difficult to document.

This theory does not say, however, that profit is the *only* factor that influences business people. It says only that profits are so important that a theory that assumes profit maximization to be the firm's sole motive will produce predictions that are substantially correct.

Why is this assumption made? First, it is necessary to make *some* assumption about what motivates decision makers if the theory is to predict how they will act. Second, a great many of the predictions of theories based on this assumption have been confirmed by observation. Third, no alternative assumption has yet been shown to yield more accurate predictions. However, the assumption has been criticized, and alternatives have been suggested (see Chapter 16).

Factors of Production

Firms seek profits by producing and selling commodities. Production may be compared to a sausage machine. Certain elements, such as raw materials and the services of capital and labor, are fed in at one end, and a product emerges at the other. The materials and factor services used in the production process are called **inputs,** and the products that emerge are called **outputs.** One way of looking at the process is to regard the inputs as being combined to produce the output. Another equally useful way is to regard the inputs as being used up, or sacrificed, to gain the output.

Hundreds of inputs enter into the output of a specific good. Among the inputs entering into automobile production are, to name only a few, sheet steel, rubber, spark plugs, electricity, machinists, cost accountants, forklift operators, managers, and painters. These inputs can be grouped into four broad classes: (1) those that are inputs to the automobile manufacturer but outputs to some other manufacturer, such as spark plugs, electricity, and sheet steel; (2) those that are provided directly by nature, such as soil and minerals; (3) those that are provided directly by households, such as the services of workers; and (4) those that are provided by the machines used for manufacturing automobiles.

The first class of inputs is made up of goods produced by other firms. These products, which may be called *intermediate products*, appear as inputs only because the stages of production are divided among different firms so that, at any one stage, a firm is using as inputs goods produced by other firms. If these products are traced back to their sources, all production can be accounted for by the services of only three kinds of inputs, which are called *factors of production*. Economists call all gifts of nature, such as land and raw materials, **land.** All physical and mental efforts provided by people are called **labor** services. All machines and other production equipment are grouped in a category called **capital,** defined as manufactured aids to further production.

Extensive use of capital—the services of machines and other capital goods—is one distinguishing feature of modern as opposed to primitive production. Instead of making consumer goods directly with only the aid of simple natural tools, productive effort goes into the manufacture of tools, machines, and other goods that are desired not in themselves but as aids to making further goods. The use of capital goods renders the production processes *roundabout*. Instead of making what is wanted directly, productive effort first goes to making tools that will subsequently be used to make what is finally wanted.

Economic Efficiency

There is usually more than one way to produce a given product. For example, it is possible to produce agricultural commodities by farming a small quantity of land, combining a great deal of labor and capital with each acre of land, as is done in Belgium. It is also possible to produce the same commodities by farming a great deal of land, using only a small amount of labor and capital per acre of land, as is done in Australia.

Faced with alternative production processes, how does the firm decide which process is best? The firm could choose the process that uses the fewest inputs for producing a given output, that is, the one that is technically most efficient. Alternatively, the firm might choose the process that costs the least for producing a given output, that is, the one that is economically most efficient. **Technological efficiency** (or *technical efficiency*) measures use of inputs in physical terms; **economic efficiency** measures use in terms of costs.[1] An example distinguishing the concepts is given in Box 9-2.

The economically most efficient method of producing a given output is the one that minimizes costs. Economic efficiency depends on factor prices and on technological efficiency.

Cost and Profit to the Firm

The Meaning of Cost

Economic efficiency is defined in terms of cost. But what is cost? **Cost,** to the producing firm, is the value of inputs used in producing its output.

Notice the use of the word *value* in the definition. A given output produced by a given technique, say, 6,000 cars produced each week by General Motors with its present production methods, has a given set of inputs associated with it—so many working hours of various types of laborers, supervisors, managers, and technicians, so many tons of steel, glass, and aluminum, so many kilowatt hours of electricity, and so many hours of the time of various machines. The cost of each can be calculated, and the sum of these separate costs is the total cost to G.M. of producing 6,000 cars per week.

Purpose in Assigning Costs

Costs are an important element in business decisions because profit from production is the difference between revenue from the sale of outputs and the cost of inputs. To understand the behavior of profit-maximizing firms, we need to understand how costs change as the firm's production changes.

There are several reasons why an economist may be interested in the behavior of firms: (1) to *describe* actual behavior of firms, (2) to *predict* how the behavior of firms will respond to specified changes in the conditions they face, (3) to *help* firms make the best decisions they can in achieving their goals, and (4) to *evaluate* how well firms use scarce resources.

The same measure of cost need not be correct for all of these purposes. For example, a firm behaves according to the information it has, but that information may be wrong or incomplete. In describing or predicting that firm's behavior, economists should use the information the firm actually uses, even if they know it is incorrect. But in helping the firm to achieve its goals, economists should substitute the correct information.

Economists use a well-established definition of costs in solving problems that involve helping and evaluating firms. If business people use the same definition and have the same information, the economists' definition will be appropriate for problems of description and prediction as well. This will be assumed for the moment.

Opportunity Cost

Although the details of economic costing vary, they are governed by a common principle that is sometimes called *user cost* but is more commonly called *opportunity cost.* We met this concept first in Chapter 1.

The cost of using something in a particular venture is the benefit forgone (or opportunity lost) by not using it in its best alternative use.

An old Chinese merchant's proverb says: "Where there is no gain, the loss is obvious." The sense of this proverb is that the merchant who shows no gain has wasted time, time that could have been used in some other venture. The merchant has neglected the opportunity cost of his time. Box 9-3 considers opportunity cost more generally.

The Measurement of Opportunity Cost by the Firm

To measure opportunity cost, the firm must assign to each input that it has used a monetary value equal to what it has sacrificed to use the input. Applying

[1] Efficiency plays an important role in economic discussions. We shall discuss it at greater length in later chapters.

BOX 9-2

Technological Versus Economic Efficiency: An Example

Suppose, given the state of technology, there are only four known ways to produce 100 widgets per month.

	Quantity of inputs received	
	Capital	Labor
Method A	6	200
Method B	10	250
Method C	10	150
Method D	40	50

Method B is technologically inefficient because it uses more of both inputs than method A. Among the other three methods, method A uses the least capital but uses the most labor.* Method D conserves labor but uses much more capital. Method C is intermediate between them. (If you consider method D technologically most efficient because it uses only 90 units of all resources, think again.)

* There is yet a third concept of efficiency, "engineering efficiency," which involves the least use of a particular factor. When engineers speak of the efficiency of an engine, they may mean how much of the fuel it turns into power.

Methods A, C, and D are all technologically efficient because no one of them uses more of both resources than either of the others.

Which one is the least costly—that is, which is economically efficient? We cannot tell without knowing the costs of capital and of labor. Economic efficiency depends on factor prices. Consider the three cases shown in the table below. As we move from case I to II to III, a unit of labor becomes increasingly expensive *relative to* a unit of capital.

Method A is economically efficient when labor is cheap relative to capital. Method C becomes efficient when labor gets somewhat more expensive relative to capital. Finally, when labor gets very expensive relative to capital, method D, which uses the least labor per unit of capital, becomes economically efficient.

To test your understanding, answer these questions:

1. Can a technologically inefficient method ever be economically efficient?
2. Is there a set of factor prices for which both method C and method D will be economically efficient?

	Factor prices per unit		*Total cost of factors*		
	Capital	Labor	Method A	Method C	Method D
Case I	$50	$3	$ 900	$950	$2,150
Case II	20	5	1,120	950	1,050
Case III	15	5	1,090	900	850

this principle to specific cases, however, reveals some tough problems.

Purchased and Hired Factors

Assigning costs is a straightforward process when inputs purchased in one period are used up in the same period and when the price the firm pays is determined by forces outside the firm. Many raw material and intermediate product purchases fall into this category. If the firm pays $110 per ton for coal delivered to its factory, it has sacrificed its claims to whatever else $110 can buy, and thus the purchase price is a reasonable measure of the opportunity cost to it of using one ton of coal.

For hired factors of production, where the rental price is the full price, the situation is identical. Borrowed money is paid for by **interest.** An **interest rate** is the money price paid to use $1 for one year. Interest payments measure the opportunity cost of

BOX 9-3

Opportunity Cost More Generally

Opportunity cost plays a vital role in economic analysis, but it is also a fundamental principle that applies to a wide range of situations. It is one of the great insights of economics. Consider some examples:

- George Bernard Shaw, on reaching his ninetieth birthday, was asked how he liked being 90. He is reputed to have said, "It's fine, when you consider the alternative."
- Llewelyn Formed likes to hear both Knowlton Nash and Lloyd Robertson. If he finally settles on Nash, what is the opportunity cost of this decision?
- Link Heartthrob, a 31-year-old bachelor, is thinking about marrying. But although he thinks Miss Jones is a lovely girl, he figures that if he marries her, he will give up the chance of wedded bliss with another girl he may meet next year. So he decides to wait awhile. What other information do you need to determine the opportunity cost of the decision?
- Serge Ginn, M.D., complains that now that he is earning large fees, he can no longer afford to take the time for a vacation trip to Europe. In what way does it make sense to say that the opportunity cost of his vacation depends on his fees?
- In 1987 retired General William Russ, who was married to a wealthy woman, decided to contribute $5,000 to a political candidate. His lawyer pointed out to him that since he was in the 50 percent tax bracket and since political contributions are not deductible from income, the real cost of his contribution would be the same as giving an extra $10,000 to his favorite charity, the General Russ Foundation. Was the opportunity cost of the political contribution $5,000 or $10,000, or some other figure?

borrowed funds. Most labor services are hired, and the cost includes the wages paid and any related expenses such as contributions to pension funds, unemployment and disability insurance, and other fringe benefits.

Imputed Costs

Cost must also be assessed for inputs that the firm uses but neither purchases nor hires for current use. Since no payment is made to anyone outside the firm, these costs are not so obvious. They are called **imputed costs.** To discover the most profitable lines of production, the opportunity cost of these factors should be assessed as the value the firm might earn from the factors if it shifted them to their next best use. The following examples all involve imputed costs.

Using the firm's own money. Consider a firm that uses $100,000 of its own money that it could instead have loaned out at 10 percent per year.

Thus $10,000 (at least) should be deducted from the firm's revenue as the cost of funds used in production. If, to continue the example, the firm makes only $6,000 over all other costs, one should say not that the firm made a profit of $6,000 by producing but that it lost $4,000, for if it had closed down completely and merely loaned out its money to someone else, it could have earned $10,000.

Costs of durable assets. The costs of using assets owned by the firm, such as buildings, equipment, and machinery, consist of the cost of the money tied up in them and a charge, called **depreciation,** for the loss in value of the asset because of its use in production. Depreciation includes the loss in value due to physical wear and tear and to obsolescence. The economic cost of owning an asset for a year is the loss in value of the asset during the year.

Accountants use several conventional methods of depreciation based on the price originally paid for the asset. One of the most common is *straight-line depreciation,* in which the same amount of historical cost is deducted in every year of useful life of the asset. While historical costs are often useful approximations, they may in some cases differ seriously from the depreciation required by the opportunity cost principle. Consider two examples.

Assets that may be resold. A woman buys a new

automobile for $12,000. She intends to use it for six years and then sell it for $6,000. She may think that, using straight-line depreciation, this will cost her $1,000 per year. But if after one year the value of her car on the used-car market is $10,000, it has cost her $2,000 to use the car during the first year. Why should she charge herself $2,000 depreciation during the first year? After all, *she* does not intend to sell the car for six years. The answer is that one of the purchaser's alternatives is to buy a one-year-old car and operate it for five years. Indeed, that is the position she is in after the first year. Whether she likes it or not, she has paid $2,000 for the use of the car during the first year of its life. If the market had valued her car at $11,500 after one year (instead of $10,000), the correct depreciation would have been only $500.

Sunk costs. In the previous example, an active used-asset market was considered. At the other extreme, consider an asset that has no alternative use. This is sometimes called a *sunk cost.* Assume that a firm has a set of machines it purchased a few years ago for $100,000. These machines were expected to last 10 years, and the firm's accountant calculates the depreciation costs of these machines by the straight-line method at $10,000 per year. Assume also that the machines can be used to make one product and nothing else. Suppose, too, that they are installed in the firm's plant, they cannot be leased to any other firm, and their scrap value is negligible. In other words, the machines have no value except to this firm in its current operation. Assume that if the machines are used to produce the one product, the cost of all other factors used will amount to $25,000, while the goods produced can be sold for $29,000.

Now, if the accountant's depreciation "costs" of running the machines are added in, the total cost of operation comes to $35,000; with revenues at $29,000, this yields an annual loss of $6,000 per year. It appears that the goods should not be made!

The fallacy in this argument lies in adding in a charge based on the sunk cost of the machines as one of the costs of current operation. The machines have no alternative uses whatsoever. Clearly, their *opportunity cost* is *zero.* The total costs of producing this line of goods is thus only $25,000 per year (assuming all other costs have been correctly assessed), and the line of production shows an annual return over all relevant costs of $4,000, not a loss of $6,000.

To see why the second calculation leads to the correct decision, notice that if the firm abandons this line of production as unprofitable, it will have no money to pay out and no revenue received on this account. If the firm takes the economist's advice and pursues the line of production, it will pay out $25,000 and receive $29,000, thus making it $4,000 per year richer than if it had not done so. Clearly, production is worth undertaking. The amount the firm happened to have paid out for the machines in the past has no bearing whatever on deciding the correct use of the machines once they are installed on the premises.

Because they involve neither current nor future costs, sunk costs should have no influence on deciding what is currently the most profitable thing to do.

The "bygones are bygones" principle extends well beyond economics and is often ignored in poker, in war, and perhaps in love. Because you have invested heavily in a poker hand, a battle, or a courtship does not mean you should stick with it if the prospects of winning become very small. At every moment of decision, you should be concerned with how benefits from this time forward compare with current and future costs.

Risk taking. One difficulty in imputing costs is the evaluation of the service of risk taking. Business enterprise is often a risky affair. The risk is borne by the owners of the firm, who, if the enterprise fails, may lose the money they have invested in the firm.

Risk taking is a service that must be provided if the firm is to carry on production, and it must be paid for by the firm. If a firm does not yield a return sufficient to compensate for the risks involved, the firm will not be able to persuade people to contribute money to it in return for a part ownership in the firm. The owners will not take this risk unless they receive compensation. They expect a return that exceeds what they could have obtained by investing their money in a virtually riskless manner, say, by buying a government bond.

Suppose, in investing $100,000 in a class of risky ventures, a businesswoman expects that most of the ventures will be successful but some will fail. In fact, she expects about $10,000 worth to be a total loss. (She does not know which specific projects will be the losers, of course.) Suppose further that she requires a 20 percent return on her total investment. To earn a $20,000 profit and recover the $10,000 expected loss, she needs to earn a $30,000 profit on the $90,000 of successful investment. This is a rate of return of 33⅓ percent. She charges 20 percent for the use of the capital plus 13⅓ percent for the risk she takes.

TABLE 9-1 The Calculation of Economic Profits: An Example

Gross revenue from sales	$1,000
Less: direct cost of production (materials, labor, electricity, etc.)	650
"Gross profits" (or "contributions to overhead")	350
Less: indirect costs (depreciation, overhead, management salaries, interest on debt, etc.)	140
"Net profits"	210
Less: normal profits, i.e., imputed charges for own capital used and for risk taking	100
Economic profits before income taxes	110
Less: income taxes payable	100
Economic profits after income taxes	$ 10

Economic profits are less than net profits. The main difference between economic profits and net profits is the subtraction of normal profits, or imputed charges for use of capital owned by the firm and for risk taking. Income tax is levied on whatever definition of profits the taxing authorities choose, usually closely related to net profits. Although economic profits are less than net profits, they can be greater or less than normal profits. (In this example they are much less.)

Patents, trademarks, and other special advantages. Suppose a firm owns a valuable patent or a highly desirable location or produces a popular brand-name product such as Coca-Cola or Labatts' Blue. Each of these involves an opportunity cost to the firm in production (even if it was acquired free) because if the firm does not choose to use the special advantage itself, it could sell or lease it to others. Typically, the value of these advantages will differ from their historical cost. Indeed, typically several alternative uses will be open to the owner. The opportunity cost in any one is the value forgone in the *best* alternative use.

The Meaning and Significance of Profits

Economic profits on goods sold, sometimes also called *pure profits,* are the difference between the revenues received from the sale and the opportunity cost of the resources used to make them. If costs are greater than revenues, such "negative profits" are called *losses.* This definition includes in costs (and thus excludes from profits) the imputed returns to capital and to risk taking.

This definition of the words *profits* and *losses* gives specialized meaning to words that are in everyday use. It is therefore a potential source of confusion to the student who has used the words in a more general sense before. Table 9-1 may help clarify terms used in connection with this specific definition.

Some economists, while following substantially the same definitions, label as **normal profits** the imputed returns to capital and risk taking just necessary to prevent the owners from withdrawing from the industry. These normal profits are, of course, what has been defined as the opportunity costs of risk taking and capital. Whatever they are called, they are costs that have to be covered if the firm is to stay in operation in the long run.

Other Definitions of Profits

Business firms define profits as the excess of revenues over the costs with which accountants provide them. We explore in the appendix to this chapter some of the differences between accountants' and economists' views of business transactions. Some of these differences affect the meaning of profits. Accountants do not include as costs charges for risk taking and use of owners' own capital, and thus these items are recorded by businesses as part of their profits. When a business says it *needs* profits of such and such an amount to stay in business, it is making sense within its definition, for its "profits" must be large enough to pay for the factors of production that it uses but the accounting profession does not include as costs.

Economists would express the same notion by saying that the business needs to cover *all* its costs, including those not employed in accounting conventions. If the firm is covering all its opportunity costs, it could not do better by using its resources in any other line of activity than the current one.

A situation in which revenues equal costs (economic profits of zero) is a satisfactory one—because all factors, hidden as well as visible, are being rewarded at least as well as in their *best* alternative uses.

With zero economic profits, then, you can do no better, although you might do worse. To reverse the Chinese proverb cited earlier, "Where there is no loss compared to the best alternative use of every input, the gain is obvious."

The income tax authorities have yet another definition of profits, which is implicit in the thousands of rules as to what may and may not be included as a deduction from revenue in arriving at taxable income. In some cases the taxing authorities allow more for cost than accountants recommend; in other cases they allow less.

It is important to be clear about different meanings of the term *profits* not only to avoid fruitless semantic arguments but also because a theory that predicts that certain behavior is a function of profits defined in one way will not necessarily predict behavior accurately given some other definition. For example, if economists predict that new firms will seek to enter an industry whenever profits are earned, this prediction will frequently be wrong if the accountants' definition is used to determine profits. The definition of profits as an excess over all opportunity costs is for many purposes the most useful, but in order to apply it to business behavior or to tax policy, appropriate adjustments must be made. And to apply accounting or tax data to particular theories, the data must be rectified. Henceforth, when we use the word *profits*, unless otherwise noted, we mean *economic* profits.

Profits and Resource Allocation

When resources are valued by the opportunity-cost principle, their costs show how much these resources would earn if used in their best alternative uses. If there is an industry in which all firms' revenues exceed opportunity costs, all the firms in the industry will be earning profits. Thus the owners of factors of production will want to move resources into this industry because the earnings potentially available to them are greater there than in alternative uses of the resources. If in some other industry firms are incurring losses, some or all of this industry's resources are more highly valued in other uses. Owners of the resources will want to move them to those other uses.

Profits and losses play a crucial signaling role in the workings of a free-market system.

Profits in an industry are the signal that resources can profitably be moved into the industry. Losses are the signal that the resources can profitably be moved elsewhere. Only if there are zero economic profits is there no incentive for resources to move into or out of an industry.

Summary

1. The firm is the economic unit that produces and sells commodities. The economist's definition of the firm abstracts from real-life differences in size and form of organization of firms.
2. The single proprietorship, the partnership, and the corporation are the major forms of business organization in Canada today. The corporation is by far the most common wherever large-scale production is required. The corporation is recognized as a legal entity;

its owners, or shareholders, have a liability that is limited to the amount of money they have actually invested in the organization. Corporate ownership is readily transferred by sale of shares of the company's stock in securities markets.

3. Firms can raise money through equity financing or debt financing. A firm's owners provide equity capital either by purchasing newly issued shares or when the firm reinvests its profits. The firm obtains debt financing from creditors either by borrowing from financial institutions or by selling bonds.
4. Economic theory assumes that the same principles underlie each decision made within the firm and that the actual decision is uninfluenced by who makes it. The key behavioral assumption is that the firm seeks to maximize its profit.
5. Production consists of transforming inputs (factors of production) into outputs (goods and services). It is often convenient to divide factors of production into categories. One common classification is land, labor, and capital. Land includes all primary products (land and natural resources), labor means all human services, and capital denotes all manufactured aids to further production. An outstanding feature of modern production is the use of capital goods and roundabout methods of production.
6. Because there is more than one way to produce a commodity, the firm must decide *how* to produce. Efficiency measures are based on the relative amounts of inputs necessary to produce a given output. Technological efficiency evaluates units of input in physical terms. Economic efficiency evaluates them in terms of costs.
7. The opportunity cost of using a resource is the value of that resource in its best alternative use. If the opportunity cost of using a resource in one way is less than or equal to the gain from using the resource in this way, there is no superior way of using it.
8. Measuring opportunity cost to the firm requires some difficult imputations in cases involving resources not purchased or hired for current use. Among these imputed costs are those for use of owners' money, depreciation, risk taking, and any special advantages that the firm may possess.
9. A firm that is maximizing profits, defined as the difference between revenue and opportunity cost, is making the best allocation of the resources under its control, according to the firm's evaluation of its alternatives.
10. Economic profits and losses provide important signals concerning the reallocation of resources. Profits earned in an industry provide a signal that more resources can profitably move into the industry. Losses show that some resources have more profitable uses elsewhere and serve as a signal for them to move out of that industry.
11. The appendix to this chapter introduces balance sheets and profit and loss statements and uses them to discuss some of the differences between the concept of profits used by accountants and that used by economists.

Topics for Review

Role of profit maximization
Single proprietorship, partnership, and corporation
Advantages of the corporation
Debt and equity financing
Inputs and factors of production
Economic efficiency
Opportunity costs
Economic profits and normal profits
Profits and resource allocation

Discussion Questions

1. Can the economic theory of the firm be of any help in analyzing the productive decisions of such nonprofit organizations as governments, churches, and colleges? What role, if any, does the notion of opportunity cost play for them?
2. In *The Engineers and the Price System,* Thorstein Veblen argued that businessmen who made decisions about financing, pricing, and the like were largely superfluous to the operation of a business. In his view, knowledge of the technology would be sufficient to ensure efficient operation of firms. Discuss Veblen's contention.
3. "There is no such thing as a free lunch." Can anything be costless? Until the mid 1970s gas stations always provided free services, including windshield cleaning, air pumps for tire inflation, and road maps. Now most free services have been discontinued. Indeed, self-service stations are becoming increasingly popular with motorists who like the lower gas prices at those stations. Under what conditions will profit-maximizing behavior lead to the coexistence of full-service and self-service gas stations? What would determine the proportions in which each occurred?
4. What is the opportunity cost of the following?
   a. Fining a politician $10,000 and sending him to prison for one year
   b. Lending $500 to a friend
   c. Not permitting a $116-million electric power dam to be built because it would destroy the snail darter, a rare 3-inch-long fish found only in that particular river
   d. Towing icebergs to Saudi Arabia to provide drinking water at the cost of $.50 per cubic meter
5. Is straight-line depreciation an appropriate method of assessing the annual cost to the typical Canadian household of using a passenger automobile? Some firms that use trucks allocate the cost on a per-mile basis. Why might this method be more appropriate for trucks than for automobiles owned by households?
6. Having bought a used car from Smiling Sam for $900, you drive it two days and it stops. You now find that it requires an extra $500 before it will run. Assuming that the car is not worth $1,400 fixed, should you make the repairs?
7. "To meet a legislated standard of 3.4 grams of carbon monoxide per mile driven, General Motors has calculated that it will cost $100 million and prolong 200 lives by one year each, thus costing $500,000

per year of extra life. It has been estimated that the installation of special cardiac-care units in ambulances could prevent premature deaths each year at an average cost of only $200 for each year of extra life." Assume that the facts in this quotation are correct. If the money spent on carbon monoxide control would have been spent on cardiac-care units instead, what is the opportunity cost of the carbon monoxide requirement? If the money would not have been so spent but simply reduced automobile companies' costs, what is the opportunity cost? In either case, do the facts tell us whether the regulation of carbon monoxide to the 3.4-gram level is desirable or undesirable?

8. Which concept of profits is implied in each of the following quotations?
   a. "Profits are necessary if firms are to stay in business."
   b. "Profits are signals for firms to expand production and investment."
   c. "More rapid depreciation write-offs allowed by Revenue Canada lowers taxable profits and thus benefits the company's owners."

Balance Sheets, Income Statements, and Costs of Production: Two Views

Accounting is a major branch of study in and of itself. Many students of economics will want to study accounting at some stage in their careers. It is not our intention to give a short course in accounting in this appendix but rather to acquaint you with the kinds of summary statements that are used by both economists and accountants. **Balance sheets** report the status of a firm at a particular time. They balance in the sense that they show the assets (or valuable things) owned by the firm on one side and the claims against those assets on the other side. **Income statements** summarize the flows of resources through the firm in the course of its operations over a specified period of time (for example, a year). Balance sheets thus measure a stock; income statements measure a flow.

To illustrate what balance sheets and income statements are, the same example will be treated from two points of view: that of the accountant and that of the economist.

An Example

Late in 1986, James Maykby, the second vice-president of Acme Artificial Flower Corporation (at a salary of $50,000 per year), decided he would go into business for himself. He quit his job and organized the Maykby Leaf Company. He purchased suitable plant and equipment for $160,000 and acquired some raw materials and supplies. By December 31, 1986, he was in a position to start manufacturing. The funds for his enterprise were $80,000 raised as a bank loan on the factory (on which he is obligated to pay interest of $10,000 per year) and $110,000 of his own funds, which had previously been invested in common stocks. He also owed $10,000 to certain firms that had provided him with supplies.

Maykby, who is a trained accountant, drew up a statement of his company's position as of December 31, 1986 (see Table 9A-1).

Maykby showed this balance sheet to his brother-in-law, an economist, and was pleased and surprised to find that he agreed that this was a fair and accurate statement of the position of the company as it prepared to start operation.[1]

During 1987, the company had a busy year hiring factors, producing and selling goods, and so on. The following points summarize these activities of the 12-month period.

1. The firm hired labor and purchased additional raw materials in the amount of $115,000, of which it still owed $20,000 at the end of the year.[2]

[1] He was surprised because he and his brother-in-law usually disagree about everything.

[2] In this example all purchased and hired factors are treated in a single category.

TABLE 9A-1 Maykby Leaf Company, Balance Sheet, December 31, 1986

Assets		Liabilities and equity	
Cash in bank	$ 10,000	Owed to suppliers of factors	$ 10,000
Plant and equipment	160,000	Bank loan	80,000
Raw materials and supplies	30,000	Equity	110,000
Total assets	$200,000	Total liabilities and equity	$200,000

2. The firm manufactured artificial leaves and flowers whose sale value was $200,000. At year's end it had sold all of these and still had on hand $30,000 worth of raw materials.
3. The firm paid off the $10,000 owed to suppliers at the beginning of the year.
4. At the very end of 1987, the company purchased a new machine for $10,000 and paid cash for it.
5. The company paid the bank $10,000 interest on the loan.
6. Maykby paid himself $20,000 "instead of salary."

An Accountant's Balance Sheet and Income Statement

Taking account of all these things and also recognizing that he had depreciation on his plant and equipment,[3] Maykby spent New Year's Day 1988 preparing three financial reports (see Tables 9A-2, 9A-3, and 9A-4). These reports reflect the operations of the firm as described above. The bookkeeping procedure by which these various activities are made to yield both the year-end balance sheet and the income statement need not concern you at this time, but you should notice several things.

1. Some transactions affect the balance sheet but do not enter into the current income statement. Examples of these are the purchase of a machine, which is an exchange of assets—cash for plant and equipment—and will be entered as a cost in the income statements of some future periods as depreciation is charged; and the payment of past debts, which entered the income statements in the period in which the things purchased were used in production.[4]
2. The net profit from operations increased the owner's equity, since it was not "paid out" to him. A loss would have decreased his equity.
3. The income statement, covering a year's operation, provides a link between the opening balance sheet (the assets and the claims against assets at the beginning of the year) and the closing balance sheet.
4. Every change in a balance sheet between two dates can be accounted for by events that occurred during the year. (See the exhibits to the balance sheet, Table 9A-3.)

After studying these records, Maykby felt that it had been a good year. The company had money in the bank, it had shown a profit, and it was able to sell the goods it produced. He was bothered, however, by the fact that he and his wife felt poorer than in the past years. Probably the cost of living had gone up!

An Economist's Balance Sheet and Income Statement

When Maykby's brother-in-law reviewed the December 31, 1987 balance sheet and the 1987 income statement, he criticized them in three respects.

[3] The tax people told him he could charge 15 percent of the cost of his equipment as depreciation during 1987, and he decided to use this amount in his own books as well. No depreciation was charged on the new machine.

[4] Beginning students often have difficulty with the distinction between *cash* flows and *income* flows. If you do, analyze item by item the entries in Exhibit 1 in Table 9A-3 and in Table 9A-4, the income statement.

TABLE 9A-2 Maykby Leaf Company, Accountant's Balance Sheet, December 31, 1987

Assets		Liabilities and equity	
Cash in bank (See Exhibit 1)*	$ 65,000	Owed to suppliers of factors (See Exhibit 4)*	$ 20,000
Plant and equipment (See Exhibit 2)*	146,000	Bank loan	80,000
Raw materials and supplies (See Exhibit 3)*	30,000	Equity (See Exhibit 5)*	141,000
Total assets	$241,000	Total liabilities and equity	$241,000

* All exhibits are in Table 9A-3.

TABLE 9A-3 Maykby Leaf Company, Exhibits to Balance Sheet of December 31, 1987

Exhibit 1. Cash			
Balance, January 1, 1987	$ 10,000		
+Deposits			
Proceeds of sales of goods	200,000		$210,000
−Payments			
Payments to suppliers (1987 bills)	10,000		
Payments for labor and additional raw materials	95,000		
"Salary" of Mr. Maykby	20,000		
Purchase of new machine	10,000		
Interest payment to bank	10,000		−145,000
Balance, December 31, 1987			65,000
Exhibit 2. Plant and Equipment			
Balance, January 1, 1987	$160,000		
+New machine purchased	10,000		170,000
−Depreciation charged			− 24,000
Balance, December 31, 1987			146,000
Exhibit 3. Raw Materials and Supplies			
On hand, January 1, 1987	$ 30,000		
Purchases in 1987	115,000		145,000
Used for production during 1987			−115,000
On hand, December 31, 1987			30,000
Exhibit 4. Owed to Suppliers			
Balance, January 1, 1987	$ 10,000		
New purchases, 1987	115,000		125,000
Paid on old accounts	10,000		
Paid on new accounts	95,000		−105,000
Balance, December 31, 1987			$ 20,000
Exhibit 5. Equity			
Original investment		$110,000	
+Income earned during year (See income statement)		31,000	
Balance, December 31, 1987		$141,000	

TABLE 9A-4 Maykby Leaf Company, Accountant's Income Statement for the Year 1987

Sales		$200,000
Costs of operation		
Hired services and raw materials	$115,000	
Depreciation	24,000	
Mr. Maykby	20,000	
Interest to bank	10,000	−169,000
Profit		$ 31,000

1. Maykby should have charged the company $50,000 for his services, since that is what he could have earned outside.
2. Maykby should have charged the company for the use of the $110,000 of his funds. He computes that had Maykby left these funds in the stock market, he would have earned $11,000 in dividends and capital gains.
3. Maykby's depreciation figure is arbitrary. The plant and equipment purchased for $160,000 a year ago now has a *market value* of only $124,000. (Assume he is correct about this fact.)

The brother-in-law prepared three revised statements (see Tables 9A-5, 9A-6, and 9A-7).

It was not hard for Maykby to understand the difference between the accounting profit of $31,000 and the reported economist's loss of $22,000. The difference of $53,000 is made up as follows:

Extra salary	$30,000
Imputed cost of capital	11,000
Extra depreciation	12,000
	$53,000

What Maykby did *not* understand was in what sense he *lost* $22,000 during the year. To explain this, his brother-in-law prepared the report shown in Table 9A-8.

Although Maykby spent the afternoon muttering to himself and telling his wife that his brother-in-law was not only totally lacking in any business sense but unpleasant as well, he was observed that evening at the public library asking the librarian whether there was a good "teach yourself economics" book. (We do not know what reply he was given.)

The next day Maykby suggested to the economist that they work out together the expected economic profits for next year. "After all," he said, "dwelling on what might have been doesn't really help decide whether I should continue the Maykby Leaf Company next year." The economist agreed. Because of expected sales increases, they concluded, the prospects were good enough to continue for at least another year. They dipped deep in the bowl of New Year's cheer to toast those stalwart pillars of society, the independent business person and the economist.

TABLE 9A-5 Maykby Leaf Company, Economist's Income Statement for the Year 1987

Sales		$200,000
Cost of operations		
Hired services and raw materials	$115,000	
Depreciation[a]	36,000	
Interest to bank[b]	10,000	
Imputed cost of capital	11,000	
Services of Maykby	50,000	−222,000
Loss		$(22,000)

[a] Market value on January 1 less market value on December 31.
[b] Because the bank loan is secured by the factory, its opportunity cost seems to the economist as properly measured by the interest payment.

TABLE 9A-6 Maykby Leaf Company Economist's Balance Sheet, December 31, 1987

Assets		Liabilities and equity	
Cash	$ 65,000	Owed to suppliers of factors	$ 20,000
Plant and equipment	134,000	Bank loan	80,000
Raw materials and supplies	30,000	Equity (see Table 9A-7)	129,000
	$229,000		$229,000

TABLE 9A-7 Exhibit to Balance Sheet, December 31, 1987: Equity to Mr. Maykby

Original investment		$110,000
New investment by Mr. Maykby		
Salary not collected	$30,000	
Return on capital not collected	11,000	41,000
		151,000
Less loss from operations		22,000
Equity		$129,000

TABLE 9A-8 Maykby's Situation Before and After

	(1) As second vice-president of Acme Flower Company	(2) As owner-manager of Maykby Leaf Company	(3) Difference (2) − (1)
Salary paid	$ 50,000	$ 20,000	−$30,000
Earnings on capital, invested in stocks	11,000	0	− 11,000
Assets owned	110,000 (stocks)	129,000 (equity in Maykby Leaf Co.)	+ 19,000
Net change			−$22,000

10

Production and Cost in the Short Run

Several decades ago, firms in the Canadian paper industry produced the full line of paper products—over 300 different varieties. They sold these on the Canadian market, which was protected against imports by high tariffs. Subsequently, Canadian and American tariffs were removed from paper products. In response, Canadian firms eliminated many of their lines of production to specialize in a reduced range of products. They sold these product lines on the domestic market and also exported them. American firms did the same. As a result, both the exports and the imports of paper products increased in both countries; each plant's volume of output rose in each of its remaining lines of production, which now served both the export and the home market; and the cost of production per unit of product fell in both countries. Similar adaptations occurred in many other industries that were affected by the tariff cuts. The range of product lines fell, the volume of production in the remaining lines rose, and unit costs fell.

What this experience illustrates is that costs of producing each unit of production can, and usually do, vary with the level of output. In the case of paper, unit costs fell as output rose, but the opposite is also possible: Unit costs may rise as output rises.

Another aspect of costs relates to factor prices. For example, when rising feed prices reached the point at which the cost of feeding chickens as they grew exceeded the price of fully grown chickens, farmers killed off their stocks and chicken production fell drastically. Similarly, during a period when price controls were in effect, meat packers were squeezed between the legal maximum price at which they could sell and the rising cost of the livestock they bought. Some of them suspended production.

In Chapter 9 we defined costs of production. In this chapter we see how and why costs vary with the level of production and with changes in factor prices.

Choices Open to the Firm

Consider a firm producing a single product in a number of different plants. If its rate of sales has fallen off, should production be reduced correspondingly? Or should production be held at the old rate and the unsold amounts stored up against an anticipated future rise in sales? If production is to be reduced, should a single plant be closed or should some plants be put on short time? Such decisions concern how best to use *existing* plant and equipment. They involve time periods too short to build new plants or to install more equipment.

Rather different decisions must be made when managers do long-range planning. Should the firm adopt a highly automated process that will greatly reduce its wage bill, even though it must borrow large sums of money to buy the equipment? Or should it continue to build new plants that use the same techniques it is now using? Should it build new plants in an area where labor is plentiful but that is distant from its sources of raw materials? These matters concern what a firm should do when it is changing or replacing its plant and equipment. Such decisions may take a long time to put into effect.

In the examples just given, managers make decisions from known possibilities. Large firms also have research and development (R&D) staffs whose job is to discover new methods of production. But the firm must decide how much money to devote to R&D and in what areas the payoff for new development will be largest. If, for example, a shortage of a particular labor skill or raw material is anticipated, the research staff can be told to try to find ways to economize on that input or even eliminate it from the production process.

Time Horizons for Decision Making

Economists organize the decisions firms are constantly making into three theoretical groups: (1) how best to employ existing plant and equipment—the *short run;* (2) what new plant and equipment and production processes to select, given the framework of known technical possibilities—the *long run;* (3) how to encourage or adapt to the invention of new techniques—the *very long run.*

The Short Run

The **short run** is a time period in which the quantity of some inputs cannot be varied. A **fixed factor** is one that cannot be increased in the short run.[1] The firm cannot get more of the fixed factors than it has on hand, and it is committed to make any money payments that are associated with these fixed factors. A fixed factor is usually an element of capital (such as plant and equipment), but it might be land, the services of management, or even the supply of skilled labor. Inputs that can be varied in the short run are called **variable factors.**

The short run does not correspond to a specific number of months or years. In some industries it may extend over many years; in others it may be only a matter of months or even weeks. Furthermore, it may last a different period of time when an industry is expanding than when it is contracting.

In the electric power industry, for example, it takes three or more years to acquire and install a steam turbine generator. An unforeseen increase in demand will involve a long period during which the extra demand must be met as best it can with the existing capital equipment. In contrast, a machine shop can acquire new equipment or sell existing equipment in a few weeks. An increase in demand will have to be met with the existing stock of capital for only a brief time, after which it will be possible to adjust the stock of equipment to the level made desirable by the higher demand.

The Long Run

The **long run** is a time period in which all inputs may be varied but the basic technology of production cannot be changed. As with the short run, the long run does not correspond to a specific length of time.

The special importance of the long run in production theory is that it corresponds to the situation facing the firm when it is planning to go into busi-

[1] Sometimes it is physically impossible to increase the quantity of a fixed factor in a short time. For instance, there is no way to build a hydroelectric dam or a nuclear power plant in a few months. Other times it might be physically possible, but prohibitively expensive, to increase the quantity. For example, a suit-manufacturing firm could conceivably rent a building, buy and install new sewing machines, and hire a trained labor force in a few days if money were no consideration. Economists regard prohibitive cost along with physical impossibility as a source of fixed factors.

ness, to expand the scale of its operations, to branch out into new products or new areas, or to modernize, replace, or reorganize its method of production.

The firm's *planning decisions* are characteristically made with fixed technological possibilities, but with freedom to choose from a variety of production processes that will use factor inputs in different proportions.

The Very Long Run

Unlike the short and long run, the **very long run** is a time period in which the technological possibilities available to a firm may change. A central characteristic of modern industrial society has been the continuously changing technology that leads to new and improved products and production methods.

Some of these technological advances arise from within the firm as part of its own research and development efforts. For example, much of the innovation in cameras and films has been due to the efforts of the Kodak and Polaroid companies. Other firms adopt technological changes developed elsewhere. For example, the transistor and the electronic chip have revolutionized dozens of industries that had nothing to do with developing them. The firm must regularly decide how much to spend in its efforts to change its technology either by developing new techniques or by adapting techniques developed by others.

Connecting the Runs: The Production Function

The various "runs" are simply different aspects of the same basic problem: getting output from inputs efficiently. They differ in terms of what the firm is able to change.

The relation between inputs into the production process and the quantity of output obtained is called the **production function.** A simplified production function in which there are only two factors of production, labor and capital, will be considered here, but the conclusions apply equally when there are many factors. The variation of output and cost under the assumption that one of the two factors is fixed is examined. (Capital is taken to be the fixed factor and labor the variable one.) The long-run situation in which both factors can be varied is covered in the next chapter.

Short-Run Choices

Total, Average, and Marginal Products

Assume that a firm starts with a fixed amount of capital (say, 4 units) and contemplates applying various amounts of labor to it. Table 10-1 shows three different ways of looking at how output varies with the quantity of the variable factor. As a first step, some terms need to be defined.

Total product (*TP*) means the total amount produced during a given period of time. If the inputs of all but one factor are held constant, total product will change as more or less of the variable factor is

TABLE 10-1 Variation of Output with Capital Fixed and Labor Variable

(1) Quantity of labor (*L*)	(2) Total product (*TP*)	(3) Average product (*AP*)	(4) Marginal product (*MP*)
0	0	—	
			15
1	15	15.0	
			19
2	34	17.0	
			14
3	48	16.0	
			12
4	60	15.0	
			2
5	62	12.4	

The relation between output and changes in the quantity of labor can be looked at in three different ways.

Capital is assumed to be fixed at 4 units. As the quantity of labor increases, the level of output (the total product) increases. Average product increases at first and then declines. The same is true of marginal product.

Marginal product is shown between the lines because it refers to the *change* in output from one level of labor input to another. When graphing the schedule, *MP*s of this kind should be plotted at the midpoint of the interval. Thus, graphically, the marginal product of 12 would be plotted to correspond to quantity of labor of 3.5.

used. This variation is shown in columns 1 and 2 of Table 10-1, which gives a total product schedule. Figure 10-1(i) shows such a schedule graphically. (The shape of the curve will be discussed shortly.)

Average product (*AP*) is the total product per unit of the variable factor, labor. The number of units of labor is denoted by *L*.

$$AP = \frac{TP}{L}$$

Notice in column 3 of Table 10-1 that as more of the variable factor is used, average product first rises and then falls. The level of output where average product reaches a maximum (34 units in the example) is called the **point of diminishing average productivity.** Up to that point, average productivity is increasing; beyond that point, average productivity is decreasing.

Marginal product (*MP*), sometimes called **incremental product,** or **marginal physical product (*MPP*),** is the change in total product resulting from the use of one unit more of the variable factor. **[13]**

$$MP = \frac{\Delta TP}{\Delta L}$$

Computed values of marginal product are shown in column 4 of Table 10-1.[2] The figures in this column are placed between the other lines of the table to stress that the concept refers to the *change* in output caused by the *change* in quantity of the variable factor. For example, the increase in labor from 3 to 4 units ($\Delta L = 1$) raises output by 12 from 48 to 60 ($\Delta TP = 12$). Thus the *MP* equals 12, and it is recorded between 3 and 4 units of labor. Note that the *MP* in the example first rises and then falls as output increases. The level of output at which marginal product reaches a maximum is called the **point of diminishing marginal productivity.**

Figure 10-1(ii) plots average product and marginal product curves. Although three different schedules are shown in Table 10-1 and three different curves are shown in Figure 10-1, they are all aspects of the same single relationship described by the production function. As we vary the quantity of labor,

[2] Δ is read "change in." For example ΔL is read "change in quantity of labor."

FIGURE 10-1 Total Product, Average Product, and Marginal Product Curves

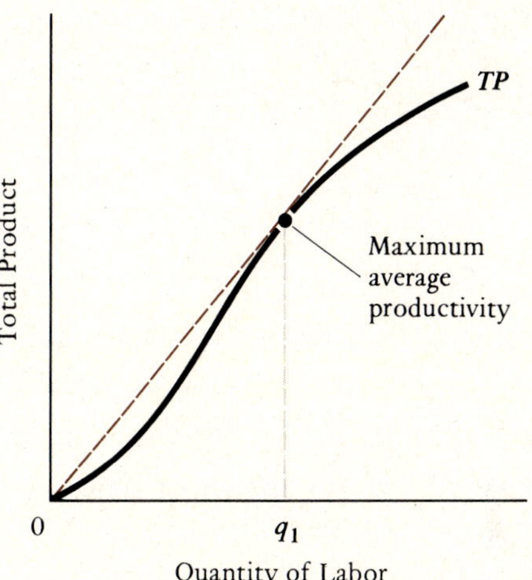

(i) Total product curve

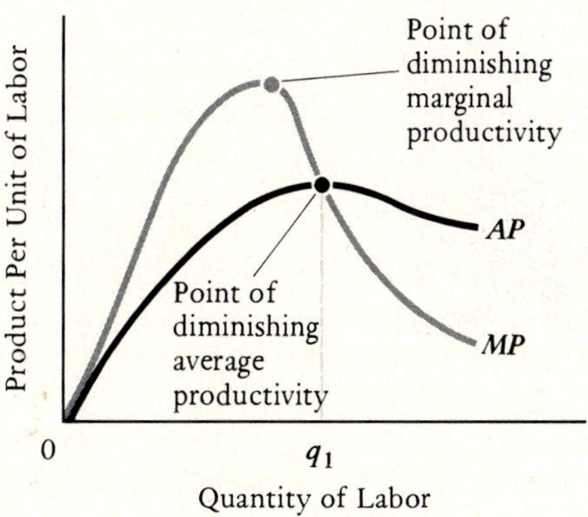

(ii) Average and marginal product curves

Total product (*TP*), average product (*AP*), and marginal product (*MP*) curves often have the shapes shown here. (i) The total product curve shows the total product steadily rising, first at an increasing rate, then at a decreasing rate. This causes both the average and the marginal product curves in (ii) to rise at first and then decline. The point of maximum average productivity (also called the point of diminishing average productivity) is q_1. At this point $MP = AP$.

with capital fixed, output changes. Sometimes it is interesting to look at total output, sometimes at the average output, and sometimes at the marginal change in output.

Finally, bear in mind that the schedules of Table 10-1 and the curves of Figure 10-1 all assume a specified quantity of the fixed factor. If the quantity of capital had been, say, 6 or 10 instead of the 4 units that were assumed, there would be a different set of total product, average product, and marginal product curves. The reason for this is that if any specified amount of labor has more capital to work with, it can produce more output; that is, its total product will be greater.

The Shape of Marginal Product and Average Product Curves

The Hypothesis of Diminishing Returns

The variations in output that result from applying more or less of a variable factor to a given quantity of a fixed factor are the subject of a famous economic hypothesis. Usually it is called the **hypothesis of diminishing returns** (it is sometimes also called the *law of diminishing returns* or the *law of variable proportions*).

The hypothesis of diminishing returns states that if increasing amounts of a variable factor are applied to a given amount of a fixed factor, eventually a situation will be reached in which each additional unit of the variable factor adds less to total product than did the previous unit.

The common sense of diminishing marginal product is that the fixed factor limits the amount of additional output that can be realized by adding more of the variable factor. The hypothesis of diminishing returns predicts only that sooner or later the marginal product will decline. It is conceivable that marginal product might diminish from the outset, so that the first unit of labor contributes most to total production and each successive unit contributes less than the previous unit. (This is the case in what is known as the Cobb-Douglas production function.)

It is also possible for the marginal product to rise at first and decline later. Thus what is called the law of diminishing marginal returns might more accurately be described as the law of *eventually* diminishing marginal returns. The reason for such a rise and decline is clear when seen in the context of the organization of production.

Consider the use of a variable number of workers in a manufacturing operation. If there is only one worker, that worker must do all the tasks, shifting from one to another and becoming competent in each. As a second, third, and subsequent workers are added, it is often possible to break the tasks into a large number of separate jobs, with each laborer specializing in one job and becoming expert at it. This process, as we noted in Chapter 1, is called the *division of labor.* If additional workers permit more and more efficient divisions of labor, marginal product will rise. But (according to the hypothesis of diminishing returns) the scope for such economies must eventually disappear and sooner or later the marginal products of additional workers must decline. When this happens, each additional worker will increase total output by less than the previous worker increased it. This sort of case, where marginal product rises at first and then declines, is illustrated in Figure 10-1.

Eventually, marginal product may reach zero and become negative. It is not hard to see why, when you consider the extreme case where there are so many workers in a limited space that additional workers simply get in the way.

The hypothesis is usually described in terms of diminishing marginal returns, but it can equally well be stated in terms of diminishing average returns. The law of diminishing *average* returns states that if increasing quantities of a variable factor are applied to a given quantity of fixed factors, the average product of the variable factor will eventually decrease. **[14]**

The Significance of the Hypothesis of Diminishing Returns

Empirical confirmation of both diminishing marginal and diminishing average returns occurs fre-

BOX 10-1

Diminishing Returns

The law of diminishing returns applies in a wide range of circumstances. Here are three examples.

When Southern California Edison was required to modify its Mojave power plant to reduce the amount of fly ash emitted into the atmosphere, it discovered that a series of filters applied to the smokestacks could do the job. A single filter eliminated half the discharge. Five filters in series reduced the fly ash discharge to the 3 percent allowed by law. When a state senator proposed a new standard that would permit no more than 1 percent fly ash emission, the company brought in experts who testified that such a requirement would require at least 15 filters per stack and would triple the cost.

British Columbia's Campbell River, a noted sport fishing area, has become the center of a thriving, well-promoted tourist trade. As fishing has increased, the total number of fish caught has steadily increased, but the number of fish per person fishing has decreased and the average hours fished for each fish caught has increased.

Public opinion pollsters, as well as all students of statistics, know that you can use a sample to estimate characteristics of a very large population. Even a relatively small sample can provide a useful estimate—at a tiny fraction of the cost of a complete enumeration of the population. However, sample estimates are subject to sampling error. If, for example, 38 percent of a sample approves of a certain policy, the percentage of the population that approves of it is likely to be close to 38 percent, but it might well be anywhere from 36 to 40 percent. The theory of statistics shows that the size of the expected sampling error can always be reduced by increasing the sample size. The 4 percent interval (in the example above) could be cut in half—to 2 percent—by *quadrupling* the sample size. That is, if the original sample had been 400, a new sample of 1,600 would halve the chance of an error of any given size from occurring. To reduce the interval to 1 percent, the new sample would have to be quadrupled again—to 6,400. In other words, increasing the sample size diminishes marginal returns in terms of accuracy.

quently. Some examples are illustrated in Box 10-1. One might wish that it were not so. There would then be no reason to fear that the world population explosion will bring with it a food crisis. If the marginal product of additional workers applied to a fixed quantity of land were constant, world food production could be expanded in proportion to the population merely by keeping a constant fraction of the population on farms. But with fixed techniques, diminishing returns dictate an inexorable decline in the marginal product of each additional laborer because an expanding population has a fixed world supply of agricultural land.

Thus unless there is a continual improvement in the techniques of production, continuous population growth will bring with it, according to the hypothesis of diminishing returns, declining average living standards and eventually widespread famine. This gloomy prediction of the nineteenth century English economist Thomas Malthus is discussed further in Box 11-1 on page 209.

The Relation Between Marginal and Average Curves

Notice that in Figure 10-1(ii) the *MP* curve cuts the *AP* curve at the *AP*'s maximum point. Although the relation between marginal and average curves is a mathematical one and not a matter of economics, it is important to understand how these curves are related. [15]

The average product curve slopes upward as long as the marginal product curve is above it; it makes no difference whether the marginal product curve is itself sloping upward or downward. The common sense of this relation is that if an additional worker is to raise the average product of all workers, his or her output must be greater than the average output of all other workers. It is immaterial whether the new worker's contribution to output is greater or less than the contribution of the worker hired immediately before; all that matters is that his or her contribution to output exceeds the average output of *all* workers hired previously. (The relation between marginal and average measures is illustrated further in Box 10-2.)

Short-Run Variations in Cost

We now shift our attention from the firm's production function to its costs. We consider firms that are not in a position to influence the prices of the inputs they employ. These firms must pay the going market price for all inputs.[3] Given these prices and the physical returns summarized by the product curves, the costs of different levels of output can be calculated.

Cost Concepts Defined

The following brief definitions of several cost concepts are closely related to the product concepts just introduced.

Total cost (*TC*) is the total cost of producing any given level of output. Total cost is divided into two parts, **total fixed costs (*TFC*)** and **total variable costs (*TVC*)**. A **fixed cost** is one that does not vary with output; it will be the same if output is one unit or a million units. Such a cost is also referred to as an *overhead cost* or *unavoidable cost.* A cost that varies directly with output, rising as more is produced and falling as less is produced, is called a **variable cost** (also a *direct* or *avoidable cost*). In the example of Table 10-1, since labor was the variable factor of production, the wage bill is a variable cost.

Average total cost (*ATC*), also called **average cost (*AC*),** is the total cost of producing any given output divided by that output. Average total cost may be divided into **average fixed costs (*AFC*)** and **average variable costs (*AVC*)** in the same way that total costs were.

Although average *variable* costs may rise or fall as production is increased (depending on whether output rises more rapidly or more slowly than total variable costs), it is clear that average *fixed* costs decline continuously as output increases. A doubling of output always leads to a halving of fixed costs per unit of output. This is a process popularly known as *spreading one's overhead.*

Marginal cost (*MC*), sometimes called **incremental cost,** is the increase in total cost resulting from raising the rate of production by one unit. Because fixed costs do not vary with output, marginal fixed costs are always zero. Therefore, marginal costs are necessarily marginal variable costs, and a change in fixed costs will leave marginal costs unaffected. For example, the marginal cost of producing a few more potatoes by farming a given amount of land more intensively is the same, whatever the rent paid for the land. [16]

Short-Run Cost Curves

Take the production relationships in Table 10-1. Assume that the price of labor is $10 per unit and the price of capital is $25 per unit. The cost schedules for these values are shown in Table 10-2[4] (p. 198).

Figure 10-2 plots cost curves that are similar in shape to those arising from the data in Table 10-2. Notice that the marginal cost curve cuts the average total cost curve and the average variable cost curve at their lowest points. This is another example of the relation between a marginal and an average curve. The *ATC* curve, for example, slopes downward as long as the *MC* curve is below it; it makes no difference whether the *MC* curve is itself sloping upward or downward.

Short-run average variable cost. In Figure 10-2 (p. 198) the average variable cost curve reaches a minimum and then rises. With fixed factor prices, when average product per worker is a maximum, average variable cost is a minimum. [17] The common sense of this proposition is that each additional worker adds the same amount to cost but a different amount to output, and when output per worker is rising, the cost per unit of output must be falling and vice versa.

The hypothesis of eventually diminishing average productivity implies eventually increasing average variable costs.

[3] The important problems that arise when the firm is in a position to influence the prices it pays for its factors of production are considered in Chapter 19.

[4] If you do not see where any of the numbers come from, review Table 10-1 and the definitions of cost just given.

BOX 10-2

George Bell's Batting Statistics

The relationship between the concepts of marginal and average measures is very general. An illuminating example comes from the Toronto Blue Jays' *Scorebook Magazine*. The table shows the average batting percentage—number of hits (output) divided by number of official at bats (input)—of Blue Jays star outfielder George Bell during the first five years of his baseball career. For each year column 1 gives his lifetime batting percentage as of the start of that year's baseball season. Column 2 gives his batting percentage during that year. Column 3 gives his lifetime batting percentage at the end of the season. This, of course, is also the entry in column 1 for the next year.

An interesting relationship exists among these columns:

Whenever his performance during a season is better than his lifetime average at the start of the season, his lifetime average rises. This occurred (trivially) in his first season, 1982; in 1983, when he batted .268, thus raising his lifetime average from .233 to .247; and again in 1984 and 1986.

Whenever his performance during a season is worse than his lifetime average at the start of the season, his lifetime average falls. This occurred in 1985 when he had a below-average year and as a result saw his lifetime average fall (slightly).

This illustrates an important relationship between marginal (in this case, current year) and average (in this case, lifetime) measures.

If the average is to rise, all that matters is that the marginal is above the average; if the average is to fall, all that matters is that the marginal is below the average.

George Bell's Batting Record

Year	*Old average* **(Lifetime batting percentage at start of season)**	*Marginal* **(Batting percentage during the season)**	*New average* **(Lifetime batting percentage at end of season)**
1982	.000	.233	.233
1983	.233	.268	.247
1984	.247	.292	.278
1985	.278	.275	.277
1986	.277	.309	.287

Short-run average total cost curve. Short-run *ATC* curves are often U-shaped. This reflects the assumptions that (1) average productivity is increasing when output is low, but (2) at some level of output average productivity begins to fall fast enough to cause average variable costs to increase faster than average fixed costs fall. When this happens, *ATC* increases.

Marginal cost curves. In Figure 10-2(ii) the marginal cost curve is shown as a declining curve that reaches a minimum and then rises. This is the reverse of the usual shape of the marginal product curve as seen in Figure 10-1(ii). The reason for the reversal is as follows. With a fixed price per unit of the variable factor, if extra units of the variable factor produce increasing quantities of output (marginal *product* rising), the cost per unit of extra output must be falling (marginal *cost* falling). If marginal product is falling, marginal cost will be rising. Thus the hypothesis of eventually diminishing marginal product implies eventually increasing marginal cost. **[18]**

TABLE 10-2 Variation of Costs with Capital Fixed and Labor Variable

		Total cost ($)			Marginal cost ($ per unit)	Average cost ($ per unit)		
(1) Labor (*L*)	(2) Output (*q*)	(3) Fixed (*TFC*)	(4) Variable (*TVC*)	(5) Total (*TC*)	(6) (*MC*)	(7) Fixed (*AFC*)	(8) Variable (*AVC*)	(9) Total (*ATC*)
0	0	100	0	100		—	—	—
					0.67			
1	15	100	10	110		6.67	0.67	7.33
					0.53			
2	34	100	20	120		2.94	0.59	3.53
					0.71			
3	48	100	30	130		2.08	0.62	2.71
					0.83			
4	60	100	40	140		1.67	0.67	2.33
					5.00			
5	62	100	50	150		1.61	0.81	2.42

The relation of cost to level of output can be looked at in several ways. These cost schedules are computed from the product curves of Table 10-1, given the price of capital of $25 per unit and the price of labor of $10 per unit. Marginal cost (in column 6) is shown between the lines of total cost because it refers to the *change* in cost divided by the *change* in output that brought it about. For example, the *MC* of $.71 is the $10 increase in total cost (from $120 to $130) divided by the 14-unit increase in output (from 34 to 48). In constructing a graph, marginal costs should be plotted midway in the interval over which they are computed. The *MC* of $.71 would be plotted at output 41.

FIGURE 10-2 Total Cost, Average Cost, and Marginal Cost Curves

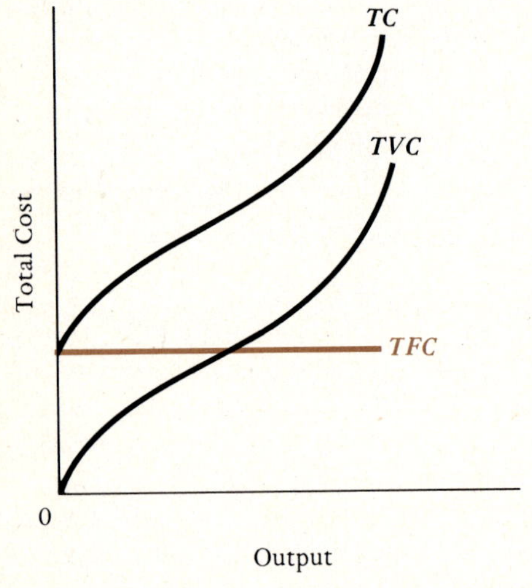

(i) Total cost curves

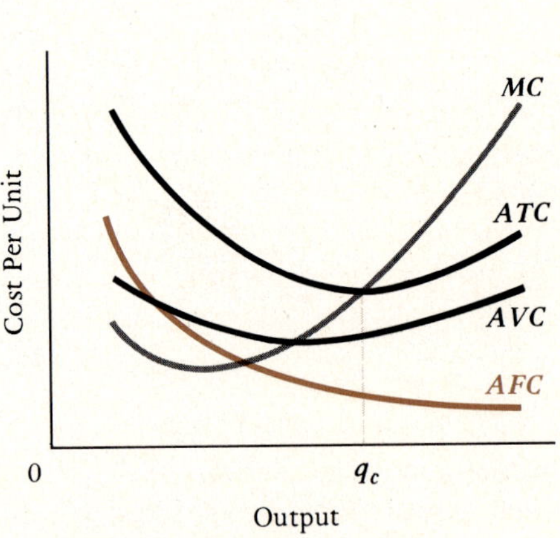

(ii) Marginal and average cost curves

Total cost (*TC*), average cost (*AC*), and marginal cost (*MC*) curves often have the shapes shown here. (i) Total fixed cost does not vary with output. Total variable cost and the total of all costs ($TC = TVC + TFC$) rise with output, first at a decreasing rate, then at an increasing rate. The total cost curves in (i) give rise to the average and marginal curves in (ii). Average fixed cost (*AFC*) declines as output increases. Average variable cost (*AVC*) and average total cost (*ATC*) fall and then rise as output increases. Marginal cost (*MC*) does the same, intersecting *ATC* and *AVC* at their minimum points. Capacity output is q_c, the minimum point on the *ATC* curve.

Total variable cost. In Figure 10-2(i) total variable cost is shown as a positively sloped curve, indicating that total variable cost rises with the level of output. This is true as long as marginal cost is positive, since the total variable cost of producing any given level of output is just the area under the marginal cost curve up to that level of output. **[19]**

Definition of Capacity

The output that corresponds to the minimum short-run average total cost is often called by economists and business people the **capacity** of the firm. Capacity in this sense is not an upper limit on what can be produced. Instead, it is the largest output that can be produced without encountering rising average costs per unit. In Figure 10-2(ii) capacity output is q_c units, but higher outputs can be achieved, provided the firm is willing to accept the higher per unit costs that accompany output "above capacity." A firm producing with **excess capacity** is producing at an output smaller than the point of minimum average total cost.

The technical definition gives the word *capacity* a meaning different from that in everyday speech; it is a useful concept that is widely used in economic and business discussions.

A Family of Short-Run Cost Curves

A short-run cost curve shows how costs vary with output for a given quantity of the fixed factor, say, a given size of plant.

There is a different short-run cost curve for each given quantity of the fixed factor.

A small plant for manufacturing nuts and bolts will have its own short-run cost curve. A medium-size plant and a large plant will each have its own short-run cost curve. If a firm expands and replaces its small plant with a medium-size plant, it will move from one short-run cost curve to another. This change from one plant size to another is a long-run change. How short-run cost curves of plants of different size are related to each other is studied in the next chapter.

Summary

1. The firm's production decisions can be classified into three groups: (a) how best to employ existing plant and equipment—the short run, (b) what new plant and equipment and production processes to select, given the framework of known technical possibilities—the long run, and (c) how to encourage or adapt to technological changes—the very long run.
2. The short run involves decisions in which one or more factors of production are fixed. The long run involves decisions in which all factors are variable but technology is given. The very long run involves decisions in which technology can change.
3. The production function describes the ways in which different inputs may be combined to produce different quantities of output. Short-run and long-run situations can be interpreted as implying different kinds of constraints on the production function. In the short run the firm is constrained to use no more than a given quantity of some fixed factor; in the long run it is constrained only by the available techniques of production.
4. The theory of short-run behavior depends on the productivity of variable factors when combined with fixed factors. The concepts of total, average, and marginal product represent alternative ways of

looking at the relation between output and the quantity of the variable factor of production.

5. The hypothesis of diminishing returns asserts that if increasing quantities of a variable factor are combined with a given quantity of fixed factors, the marginal and the average products of the variable factor will eventually decrease. This hypothesis leads directly to implications of eventually rising marginal and average costs.
6. Given physical productivity schedules and the costs per unit of factors, it is a matter of simple arithmetic to develop the whole family of short-run cost curves, one for each quantity of the fixed factor.
7. Short-run average total cost curves are drawn as U-shaped to reflect the expectation that average productivity increases for small outputs but eventually declines sufficiently rapidly to offset advantages of spreading overheads. The output corresponding to the minimum point of a short-run average total cost curve is called the plant's capacity.

Topics for Review

Short run, long run, and very long run
Total product, average product, and marginal product
The hypothesis of diminishing returns
Marginal product curves and average product curves
Relation between productivity and cost
Total cost, marginal cost, and average cost
Short-run cost curves
Capacity and excess capacity

Discussion Questions

1. Is the short run the same number of months for increasing output as for decreasing it? Must the short run in an industry be the same length for all firms in the industry? Under what circumstances might the short run actually involve a longer time span than even the very long run for one particular firm?
2. Use the distinction between long and short run to discuss each of the following.
   a. A guaranteed annual employment contract of at least forty-eight 40-hour weeks of work for all employees
   b. A major economic depression during which there is substantial unemployment of labor and in which equipment is being used at well below capacity levels of production
   c. A speeding up of delivery dates for new easy-to-install equipment
3. Experimenters with chemical fertilizers at the Rothampsted Experimental Station, an agricultural research institute in Hertfordshire, England, in 1921 applied different amounts of a particular fertilizer to 10 apparently identical quarter-acre plots of land. The results for one test, using identical seed grain, are listed in the table. Compute the average and marginal product of fertilizer and identify the (approximate) points of diminishing average and marginal productivity.

Plot	Fertilizer dose	Yield index*
1	15	104.2
2	30	110.4
3	45	118.0
4	60	125.3
5	75	130.2
6	90	132.4
7	105	131.9
8	120	132.3
9	135	132.5
10	150	132.8

*Yield without fertilizer = 100

4. Indicate whether each of the following conforms to the hypothesis of diminishing returns and, if so, whether it refers to marginal or average returns or both.

a. "The bigger they are, the harder they fall."

b. As more and more of the population receive smallpox vaccinations, the reduction in the smallpox disease rate for each additional 100,000 vaccinations becomes smaller.

c. Five workers produce twice as much today as 10 workers did 40 years ago.

5. Consider the education of a human being as a process of production. Regard years of schooling as one variable factor of production. What are the other factors? What factors are fixed? At what point would you expect diminishing returns to set in? For an Einstein, would it set in during his lifetime?

6. Suppose that each of the following news items is correct. Discuss each in terms of its effects on cost. (You will have to decide which concept of cost is most likely to be affected.)

a. The Quebec Ministry of Education reports that the increasing level of education of youth has led both to higher productivity and to increases in the general level of wages.

b. During the winter of 1977 many factories were forced by fuel shortages to reduce production and to operate at levels of production far below capacity.

c. NASA, the U.S. space agency, reports that the space program has led to development of electronic devices that have brought innovations to many industries.

7. "Because overhead costs are fixed, increasing production lowers costs. Thus small business is sure to be inefficient. This is a dilemma of modern society, which values both smallness *and* efficiency." Discuss.

11

Production and Cost in the Long and Very Long Run

Analyzing the short-run behavior of the firm helps us understand how markets work to allocate resources, but it cannot deal with longer-run phenomena. In this chapter we first look at the firm's *long-run* behavior, when it is free to vary all factors of production. Should the firm use a great deal of capital and only a small amount of labor? Should it use less capital and more labor? What do these decisions mean in terms of the firm's costs?

In the second part of the chapter we examine what we have called the *very long run*. This discussion deals with the improvements in technology and productivity that have dramatically increased output and incomes in all industrial countries during the past 100 years.

The Long Run: No Fixed Factors

In the short run, in which only one factor varies, the only way to produce a given output is to adjust the input of the variable factor until the desired level of output is achieved. Thus in the short run the firm must make a decision about its desired output, but once it has decided on a rate of output, there is only one technically possible way of achieving it. In the long run, all factors may be varied, so there are numerous technically possible ways to produce output. Thus the firm must decide on a level of output and also on which method to employ. More specifically this means that firms in the long run must choose the nature and amount of plant and equipment.

Long-run planning decisions are important. Today's variable factors are tomorrow's fixed factors. A firm deciding on a new steel mill and the machinery to go into it will choose among many alternatives. But once installed, that equipment is fixed for a long time. If the firm makes a wrong choice now, its survival may be threatened; if it estimates shrewdly, it may reward both owners and farsighted managers with large profits and bonuses.

Long-run decisions are difficult because the firm must anticipate what methods of production will be efficient not only today but also in the years ahead, when costs of labor and raw materials may have changed. The decisions are difficult, too, because the firm must estimate how much output it will want to produce. Is the industry of which it is a part growing or declining? Will new products emerge to render its typewriters or LP records less useful than an extrapolation of past sales suggests?

Profit Maximization and Cost Minimization

Any firm that is trying to maximize its profits should in the long run select the method that produces its output at the lowest possible cost. This implication of the hypothesis of profit maximization is called **cost minimization.** From the alternatives open to it, the firm chooses the least costly ways of achieving any specific output.

What can a firm do in the long run to make its costs as low as possible? The firm does not have the least costly method of production if it is possible to substitute one factor for another so as to keep its output constant while reducing its total cost.

Choice of factor mix. The firm should substitute one factor (for example, capital) for another factor (for example, labor) as long as the marginal product of the one factor *per dollar expended on it* is greater than the marginal product of the other factor *per dollar expended on it.* The firm cannot have minimized its costs as long as these two magnitudes are unequal. Using K to represent capital, L labor, and p the price of a unit of the factor, the necessary condition of cost minimization may be stated as follows:

$$\frac{MP_K}{p_K} = \frac{MP_L}{p_L} \qquad [1]$$

Whenever the two sides of Equation 1 are not equal, there are possibilities for factor substitutions that will reduce costs.[1]

To see why this equation needs to be satisfied if costs of production are to be minimized, suppose that the left side of Equation 1 is equal to 10, showing that the last dollar spent on capital added 10 units to output, while the right side is equal to 4, showing that the last dollar spent on labor added only 4 units to output. In such a case the firm, by using \$2.50 less of labor, would reduce output by 10 units. But it could regain that lost output by spending \$1.00 more on capital.[2] Making such a substitution of capital for labor would leave output unchanged and reduce cost by \$1.50. Thus the original position was not the cost-minimizing one.

By rearranging terms in Equation 1 we can look at the cost-minimizing condition a bit differently.

$$\frac{MP_K}{MP_L} = \frac{p_K}{p_L} \qquad [2]$$

The ratio of the marginal products on the left side compares the contribution to output of the last unit of capital and the last unit of labor. If the ratio is 4, this means one unit more of capital will add four times as much to output as one unit more of labor. The right side of the equation shows how the cost of one unit more of capital compares to the cost of one unit more of labor. If it is also 4, it does not pay the firm to substitute capital for labor or vice versa. But suppose the right side is 2. Capital, although twice as expensive, is four times as productive. It will pay the firm to switch to a method of production that uses more capital and less labor. If, however, the right side is 6 (or *any* number more than 4), it will pay to substitute labor for capital.

How much should inputs be changed? We have seen that when the ratio MP_K/MP_L is 4, while the ratio p_K/p_L is 2, the firm will substitute capital for labor. But how far does the firm go in making this substitution? There is a limit because as the firm uses more capital, its marginal product falls, while as it uses less labor, the marginal product of labor rises. Thus the ratio MP_K/MP_L falls. When it reaches 2, the firm need substitute no further. The ratio of the marginal products is equal to the ratio of the prices.[3]

This formulation shows how the firm can adjust the elements over which it has control (the quantities

[1] Readers who read Appendix 7A should notice that Equation 1 is analogous to the condition for the utility-maximizing household, given on page 148, in which the household equated the ratio of the marginal utilities of each pair of goods with the ratio of their prices.

[2] The argument in the two preceding sentences assumes that the marginal products do not change when expenditure is changed by a few dollars.

[3] The appendix to this chapter provides a graphic analysis of this condition, which is similar to the analysis of household behavior in Appendix B to Chapter 7.

of factors used, and thus the marginal products of the factors) to the prices or opportunity costs of the factors given by the market.

Long-run equilibrium of the firm. The firm will have achieved long-run equilibrium factor proportions when there is no opportunity for cost-reducing substitutions. This occurs when the marginal product per dollar spent on each factor is the same (Equation 1) or, equivalently, when the ratio of the marginal products of factors is equal to the ratio of their prices (Equation 2).

The Principle of Substitution

Suppose that a firm is producing by a method that meets the cost-minimizing conditions shown in Equations 1 and 2 but that the cost of labor increases while the cost of capital remains unchanged. The least-cost method of producing any output will now use less labor and more capital than was required to produce the same output before the factor prices changed.

Methods of production will change if the relative prices of factors change. Relatively more of the cheaper factor and relatively less of the more expensive one will be used.

This prediction, called the **principle of substitution,** follows from the assumption that firms minimize their costs.

The principle of substitution plays a central role in resource allocation in a market economy since it relates to the way the individual firm will respond to changes in relative factor prices that are caused by the changing relative scarcity of factors to the economy as a whole. The individual firm is thus motivated to use less of factors that have become scarcer to the economy.

For example, as construction workers' wages have risen sharply relative to the wages of factory labor and the cost of machinery, many home builders have shifted from on-site construction to panelization. Panelization is a method of building standardized modules with wiring, plumbing, insulation, and painting done at the factory. The bulk of the work is performed by machinery and by assembly line workers, whose wages are only half those of on-site construction workers.

Consider another example. One country has a great deal of land and a small population. The price of land will be low, and, because labor is in short supply, the wage rate will be high. Producers of agricultural goods will tend to make lavish use of the cheap land while economizing on expensive labor; thus a production process will be adopted that uses a low ratio of labor to land. Suppose a second country is small in area and has a large population. Here the demand for land will be high relative to its supply, and land will be relatively expensive while labor will be relatively cheap. Firms producing agricultural goods will tend to economize on land by using a great deal of labor per unit of land; thus a productive process will be adopted that uses a high ratio of labor to land.

Once again we see the price system functioning as an automatic control system. No single firm needs to be aware of national factor surpluses and scarcities. These are reflected by market prices, so individual firms that never look beyond their own private profit are led to economize on factors that are scarce to the nation as a whole.

This discussion suggests why methods of producing the same commodity differ among countries. In Canada, where labor is highly skilled and expensive, a large-scale farmer may use elaborate machinery to economize on labor. In China, where labor is abundant and capital scarce, a much less mechanized method of production is appropriate. The Western engineer who believes that the Chinese are inefficient because they are using methods dismissed in the West long ago may be missing the truth about economic efficiency in the use of resources. The notion that to aid underdeveloped countries we have only to export Western "know-how" is misleading.

Cost Curves in the Long Run

There is a best (least-cost) method of producing each level of output when all factors are free to be varied. In general, this method will not be the same for different levels of output. If factor prices are given, a minimum achievable cost can be found for each possible level of output; if this cost is expressed as an amount per unit of output, we can obtain the long-run average cost of producing each level of output. When this information is plotted on a graph, the result is called a **long-run average cost (*LRAC*) curve.** Figure 11-1 shows such a curve.

This cost curve is determined by the technology of the industry (which is assumed to be fixed) and by the prices of the factors of production. It is a "boundary" in the sense that points below the curve are unattainable; points on or above the curve are attainable if sufficient time elapses for all inputs to be adjusted.

The *LRAC* curve is the boundary between those cost levels that are attainable with known technology and given factor prices and those that are unattainable.

The Shape of the Long-Run Average Cost Curve

The long-run average cost curve shown in Figure 11-1 first falls and then rises. This curve is often described as U-shaped, although "saucer-shaped" might be more accurate.

Decreasing costs. Over the range of output from zero to q_m the firm has falling long-run average costs. An expansion of output permits a reduction of costs per unit of output. These are referred to as **economies of scale.** (Of course, such economies will be realized only after enough time has elapsed to allow changes in the methods of production.) Since the prices of factors are assumed to be constant, the reason for the decline in long-run average cost must be that output increases faster than inputs as the scale of the firm's production expands. Over this range of output the firm is often said to enjoy long-run **increasing returns.**[4]

Increasing returns may arise as a result of increased opportunities for specialization of tasks made possible by the division of labor. Adam Smith's classic discussion of this important point is given in Box 3-1 on page 47. Even the most casual observation of the differences in production technique used in large and small plants shows the greater specialization that larger plants use.

These differences arise because large, specialized

[4] Economists shift back and forth between speaking in physical terms (i.e., *increasing returns* to scale) and cost terms (i.e., *decreasing costs* of production). As we have seen in the text, the same relation can be expressed in either terms.

FIGURE 11-1 A Long-Run Average Cost Curve

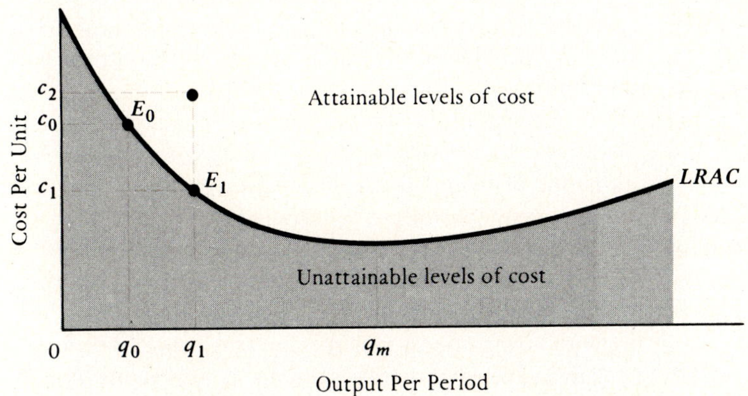

The long-run average cost (*LRAC*) curve provides a boundary between attainable and unattainable levels of cost. If the firm wishes to produce output q_0, the lowest attainable cost level is c_0 per unit. Thus point E_0 is on the *LRAC* curve. E_1 represents the least-cost method of producing q_1. Suppose a firm is producing at E_0 and desires to increase output to q_1. In the short run it will not be able to vary all factors, and thus costs above c_1, say, c_2, must be accepted. In the long run a plant optimal for output q_1 can be built and cost of c_1 can be attained. At output q_m the firm attains its lowest possible per unit cost of production for the given technology and factor prices.

equipment is useful only when the volume of output that the firm can sell justifies its employment. For example, assembly line techniques, body-stamping machinery, and multiple-boring engine-block machines in automobile production are economically efficient only when individual operations are repeated thousands of times. Using elaborate harvesting equipment (which combines many individual tasks that would otherwise be done by hand and by tractor) provides the least-cost method of production on a big farm but not on a few acres.

Increasing returns may also arise because of substitution of one input for another. Typically, as the level of planned output increases, capital is substituted for labor and complex machines for simpler machines. Robotics is a contemporary example. Electronic devices can handle huge numbers of operations quickly, but unless the level of production requires such a large volume of operations, it does not make sense to use robotics or other forms of automation.

Increasing costs. Over the range of outputs greater than q_m the firm encounters rising costs. An expansion in production, even after sufficient time has elapsed for all adjustments to be made, will be accompanied by a rise in average costs per unit of output. If costs per unit of input are constant, this rise in costs must be the result of an expansion in output less than in proportion to the expansion in inputs. A firm experiencing this phenomenon is said to encounter long-run **decreasing returns.**[5] Decreasing returns imply that the firm suffers some diseconomy of scale. As its scale of operations increases, diseconomies, say, of management, are encountered that increase its per unit costs of production.

Constant returns. In Figure 11-1 the firm's long-run average costs fall to output q_m and rise thereafter. Another possibility should be noted. The firm's *LRAC* curve might have a flat portion over a range of output around q_m. With such a flat portion, the firm would be encountering constant costs over the relevant range of output. This would mean that the firm's long-run average costs per unit of output do not change as its output changes. Since factor prices are assumed to be fixed, this must mean that the firm's output is increasing exactly as fast as its inputs are increasing. Such a firm is said to be encountering **constant returns.**

Relation Between Long-Run and Short-Run Costs

The family of short-run cost curves mentioned at the conclusion of Chapter 10 and the long-run curve studied in this chapter are all derived from the same production function. Each short-run curve assumes given prices for all factor inputs. In the long run all factors can be varied; in the short run some must remain fixed. The long-run average cost (*LRAC*) curve shows the lowest cost of producing any output when all factors are variable. Each short-run average cost (*SRAC*) curve shows the lowest cost of producing any output when one or more factors are held constant at some specific level.

No short-run cost curve can fall below the long-run curve because the *LRAC* curve represents the *lowest* attainable cost for each possible output. As the level of output is changed, a different size plant is normally required to achieve the lowest attainable costs. This is shown in Figure 11-2, where the *SRAC* curve lies above the *LRAC* curve at all outputs except q_0.

As we observed at the end of Chapter 10, an *SRAC* curve such as the one shown in Figure 11-2 is one of many such curves. Each curve shows how costs vary as output is varied from a base output, holding some factors fixed at the quantities most appropriate to the base output. Figure 11-3 shows a family of short-run average cost curves, along with a single long-run average cost curve. The long-run curve is sometimes called an **envelope curve** because it encloses the whole family of short-run curves. Each short-run cost curve is tangent to (touches) the long-run curve at the level of output

[5] Long-run decreasing returns differ from the short-run diminishing returns. In the short run at least one factor is fixed, and the law of diminishing returns ensures that returns to the variable factor will eventually diminish. In the long run all factors are variable, and it is possible that physically diminishing returns would never be encountered—at least as long as it was genuinely possible to increase inputs of all factors.

FIGURE 11-2 Long-Run Average Cost and Short-Run Average Cost Curves

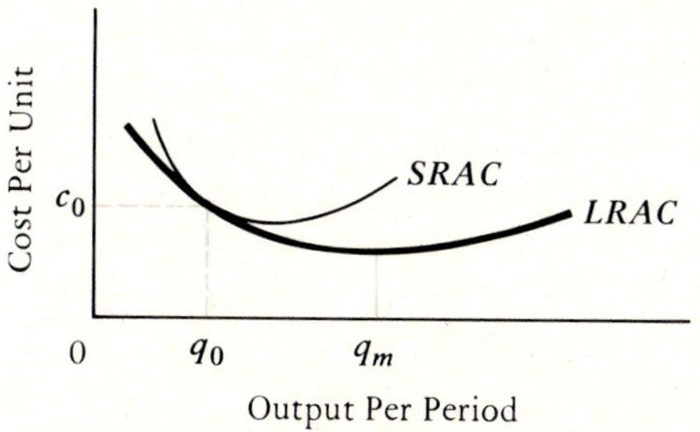

The short-run average cost (*SRAC*) curve is tangent to the long-run average cost (*LRAC*) curve at the output for which the quantity of the fixed factors is optimal. If output is varied around q_0 units with plant and equipment fixed at the optimal level for producing q_0, costs will follow the short-run cost curve. Whereas *SRAC* and *LRAC* are at the same level for output q_0 where the fixed plant is optimal for that level, for all other outputs there is too little or too much plant and equipment and *SRAC* lies above *LRAC*. If some output other than q_0 is to be sustained, costs can be reduced to the level of the long-run curve when sufficient time has elapsed to adjust the plant and equipment.

for which the quantity of the fixed factor is optimal and lies above it for all other levels of output.

Shifts in Cost Curves

The cost curves derived so far show how cost varies with output, given constant factor prices and fixed technology. Changes in either technological knowledge or factor prices will cause the entire family of short-run and long-run cost curves to shift. Loss of existing technological knowledge is rare, so technological change normally works in only one direction, to shift cost curves downward. Improved ways of making existing commodities will mean that lower-cost methods of production become available. (Technological change is discussed in more detail in the next section of this chapter.)

Factor price changes can exert an influence in either direction. If a firm has to pay more for any factor that it uses, the cost of producing each level of output will rise; if the firm has to pay less, costs will fall.

A rise in factor prices shifts the family of short-run and long-run cost curves upward. A fall in factor prices or a technological advance shifts the entire family of cost curves downward.

Although factor prices usually change gradually, they sometimes change suddenly and drastically. For example, in the mid 1980s oil prices fell dramatically; the effect was to shift downward the cost curves of all users of oil and oil-related products.

The Very Long Run

In the long run the nation's producers are assumed to do the best they can to produce known products with the techniques and the resources currently available. The best they can do is to be on, rather than above, their long-run cost curves. *In the very long run the techniques and resources that are available change.* Such changes cause shifts in long-run cost curves. These, along with the development of new products, are major sources of economic growth, the long-run rise in output that accounts for rising living standards.

The decrease in cost levels that can be achieved by choosing wisely among available factors of production, known techniques, and alternative levels of output is necessarily limited, since a firm can never do better in the long run than select the best available technique. But improvements by invention and innovation are potentially limitless. For this reason, the long-term struggle to get ever more from the world's limited resources is critically linked to technological change.

Kinds of Technological Change

Three kinds of change tend to dominate production and cost in the very long run. All are related to technology, broadly defined.

New techniques. Over an average lifetime in the twentieth century, changes in the techniques available

FIGURE 11-3 The Envelope Relation Between the Long-Run Average Cost Curve and All the Short-Run Average Cost Curves

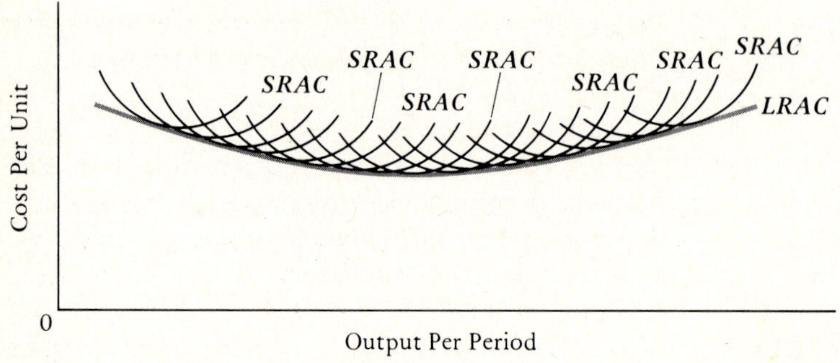

To every point on the long-run average cost (*LRAC*) curve there is an associated short-run average cost (*SRAC*) curve tangent at that point. Each short-run curve shows how costs vary if output varies, with the fixed factor held constant at the level that is optimal for the output at the point of tangency.

for producing existing products have been dramatic. About the same amount of coal is produced in North America today as 50 years ago, but the number of coal miners is less than one-tenth of what it was then. Eighty years ago roads and railways were built by gangs of workers using buckets, spades, and draft horses. Today bulldozers, steam shovels, giant trucks, and other specialized equipment have completely banished the workhorse from construction sites and to a great extent have displaced the pick-and-shovel worker. Generally, capital has been substituted for labor.

New products. Changes in available goods and services are constantly occurring. Television, polio vaccine, nylon, personal computers, and many other current consumer products did not exist three generations ago. Other products are so changed that the only connection they have with the "same" commodity produced in the past is the name. A 1989 Ford automobile is very different from a 1929 Ford. It is even different from a 1979 Ford in size, safety, and gasoline consumption. Modern jets are revolutionary compared with the DC-3, which itself barely resembled the Vickers bomber in which Alcock and Brown were the first to fly the Atlantic travelling from Newfoundland to Ireland in 1919.

Improved inputs. Improvements in such intangibles as health and education raise the quality of labor services. Today's workers and managers are healthier and better educated than their grandparents. Even unskilled workers today tend to be literate and competent in arithmetic, and their managers are apt to be trained in modern scientific methods of business control and computer science.

Similarly, improvements in raw materials occur. For example, the type and quality of metals have changed. Steel replaces iron, and aluminum substitutes for steel in a process of change that makes a statistical category such as "primary metals" seem unsatisfactory and obsolete. Even for a given category, say, steel, today's product is lighter, stronger, and more flexible than the product manufactured only 15 years ago.

Sources of Technological Change

To measure the extent of technological change, economists use the notion of **productivity,** defined as a measure of output per unit of resource input. One widely used measure of productivity is output *per hour of labor.*[6] The rate of increase in productivity provides a measure of the progress caused by technical change. The concept of productivity highlights

[6] This is the measure we shall use. Other possible measures include output *per worker*, output *per person*, and output *per unit of inputs*, measured by an index number.

BOX 11-1

The Significance of Productivity Growth

Economics used to be known as the dismal science because some of its predictions were dismal. Malthus and other classical economists predicted that the pressure of more and more people on the world's limited resources would cause a decline in output per person. Human history would see more and more people living less and less well, with the surplus population that could not be supported dying off from hunger and disease.

This prediction has proven wrong for the industrial countries for two main reasons. First, the population has not expanded as rapidly as foreseen by early economists writing before birth control techniques were widely used. Second, pure knowledge and its applied techniques have expanded so rapidly during the past 150 years that our ability to squeeze more out of limited resources has expanded faster than the population; that is, we have experienced growth in productivity.

Growth in productivity permits increases in output per person and thus contributes to rising standards of living.

Productivity increases are a powerful force for increasing living standards. Our great-grandparents would have regarded today's standard of living in most industrialized countries as unattainable. An apparently modest rate of increase in productivity of 2.0 percent per year leads to a doubling of output per hour of labor every 35 years. Productivity in Canada increased at a rate somewhat greater than this in every decade from 1900 to 1970.

In other countries growth rates have been even higher. Since World War II productivity in Germany has increased at 5 percent per year, doubling output every 14 years. In Japan it has increased at more than 9 percent per year, a rate that doubles output per hour of labor approximately every 8 years! In many countries, productivity growth at a stable rate came to be taken for granted as an automatic source of ever-increasing living standards.

Then in the late 1960s productivity increases dropped sharply below their historical trends. This slowdown happened worldwide to some degree but was particularly acute in the United States and Canada. Indeed, from 1977 to 1982 North American nonagricultural productivity did not increase at all. Since 1982 productivity growth has resumed at about 2 percent per year in the United States and 1.5 percent in Canada. It remains to be seen whether the 1965 to 1982 slowdown was a one-time occurrence or whether the accustomed doubling every generation is a thing of the past.

It matters a great deal. A permanent slowdown in productivity growth would have severe consequences. Lower productivity growth combined with a stable level of employment leads to a lower rate of increase of real output. Combined with declining employment, it may actually contribute to declining output per person. Declining productivity growth surely means that living standards rise more slowly or actually decline.

Decreases in rates of productivity growth also contribute to inflation. For example, if productivity increases at 3 percent per year, all factor prices, and profits, too, can increase 3 percent per year on average without leading to product price increases. But factor price increases in excess of productivity growth become inflationary. Thus lower rates of productivity growth make a given rate of factor price increases more inflationary.

---

society's ability to get more and better output from the basic resources of the economy. The significance of such changes is explored further in Box 11-1.

Productivity is increased by anything that increases output while maintaining the number of hours worked or that decreases the hours required to attain the same output. Here are some of the major historical sources of productivity increase.

Substitution of Capital for Labor

In manufacturing, transportation, communications, mining, and agriculture, capital has been substituted for labor to a major extent. This substitution can be measured by the **capital-labor ratio,** which determines changes in the amount of capital per worker. The capital-labor ratio increased continually over more than 100 years.

Three reasons for this substitution can be identified. First, the price of labor rose relative to capital goods. As predicted by the principle of substitution, this led to the use of more capital and less labor per unit of output. Second, more productive machines were developed to replace older ones. Third, the opportunity provided by both population growth and growth in demand enabled businesses to produce larger outputs by using more capital, thereby taking advantage of economies of scale.

Energy Substitution

Related to the substitution of capital for labor has been the increasing reliance on inanimate energy for production. Energy to plow fields, to turn machines, to move goods, to provide heat, and to transform natural resources is a major determinant of the productive power of an economy. In 1900 more than half of all Canadian energy requirements was supplied by human beings, horses, mules, and oxen. By 1985 human and animal power provided less than 10 percent of all energy; they have been replaced by coal, oil, gas, nuclear, and hydroelectric power.

Invention and Innovation

Invention is the discovery of something new, such as a production technique or a product. **Innovation** is the introduction of an invention into use. Invention is thus a necessary precondition to innovation.

Invention is cumulative in effect. A useful invention is adopted, a useless one discarded. The cumulative impact of many small, useful devices and techniques may be fully as great as or greater than the impact of the occasional dramatic mechanism such as the steam engine, the cotton gin, or the sewing machine. Indeed, none of these famous inventions represented a single act of creative inspiration. Each depended on the contributions of prior inventors. The backlog of past inventions constitutes society's technical knowledge, and that backlog in turn feeds innovation.

Innovation depends on a steady supply of new inventions. However, new methods, machines, materials, and products do not come into use simply "because they are there." They are introduced if and when it appears *profitable* to do so.

The Endogenous Nature of Technical Change

Technical change was once thought to be mainly a random process, brought about by inventions made by crackpots and mad scientists working in garages or basements. We now know better.

Changes in technology are to a major degree *endogenous* responses to changing economic signals; that is, they are responses to the same things that induce the substitution of one factor for another with a given technology. In our discussion of long-run demand curves in Chapter 5, we looked at just such technological changes in response to rising relative prices when we spoke of the development of smaller, more fuel-efficient cars in the wake of rising gasoline prices. Similarly, much of the move to substitute capital for labor in North American industry in response to rising wage rates has taken the form of developing labor-saving methods of production.

Even invention can frequently be produced on demand. The development of the atomic bomb in the 1940s is a very dramatic example of this fact. Money can buy invention. Major changes in the store of technical knowledge are often the result of expenditures on research and development (R&D). In proportion to its GDP, Canada spends less on this activity than do many other industrial countries. This is due partly to Canada's specialization in many industries that do not typically do a lot of R&D, and partly to the fact that Canadian subsidiaries of multinational corporations have direct access to the R&D done by their companies in other countries. When these and other similar factors are allowed for, the question of whether Canada still does less R&D than is needed for good very long run growth prospects is the subject of a controversy that we take up in a later chapter.

Innovation has an unmistakably endogenous component, rising as profit incentives increase, declining as they fall. Profit incentives are in turn affected by many aspects of the economic climate, among them the rate of growth of the economy, the level of capacity utilization, the cost and availability of money for investment, and all sorts of government policies from taxes to regulations.

How Much Productivity Growth Do We Want?

There remains an important question about social values. Progress, as measured by productivity growth, is no longer an unquestioned overriding goal of society. Progress has come to mean growth, and growth has meant industrialization. Applied to the economy as a whole, industrialization and its accompanying changes in productivity have vastly increased our material well-being and permitted ever more people to escape the ravages of hunger and poverty. Clearly, we do not wish to remain permanently an economy whose productivity growth is absent. But not all slowdowns in productivity growth are unwanted. The shift to the provision of services with high income elasticities but low productivity levels is the most obvious example. The population evidently does not want more manufactured goods if it means less police protection, or more food at the cost of less recreation, even though such shifts would increase productivity growth.

Moreover, growth in productivity has often been accompanied by increased pollution and more industrial accidents. Nothing is without its cost. In the case of growth this fact is increasingly being recognized. The gasoline engine, the steel mill, the jet airplane, DDT, plastics, and the skyscraper with its hundreds of thousands of electric lights are the artifacts of our progress over the past century. In some ways they may have lowered the quality of life even while raising the standard of living.

Just as members of a society can benefit (at some stage in economic development) from more luxuries and fewer basic necessities, so, too, may they sometimes benefit from more amenities and lower productivity growth. To the extent that they can, a somewhat reduced rate of productivity growth may bring about a better life, not a worse one. The debate over the pros and cons of a rapid growth rate is discussed in much more detail in Chapter 38.

Summary

1. There are no fixed factors in the long run. The profit-maximizing firm chooses, from the alternatives open to it, the least costly way of achieving any specific output. A long-run cost curve represents the boundary between attainable and unattainable levels of cost for the given technology.
2. The principle of substitution says that efficient production will substitute cheaper factors for more expensive ones. If the relative prices of factors change, relatively more of cheaper factors and relatively less of more expensive ones will be used.
3. The shape of the long-run cost curve depends on the relationship of inputs to outputs as the whole scale of a firm's operations changes. Increasing, constant, and decreasing returns lead to decreasing, constant, and increasing long-run average costs.
4. The long-run and short-run cost curves are related. Every long-run cost corresponds to *some* quantity of each factor and is thus on some short-run cost curve. The short-run cost curve shows how costs vary when that particular quantity of a fixed factor is used to produce outputs greater than or less than that for which it is optimal.

5. Cost curves shift upward or downward in response to changes in the prices of factors or the introduction of changed technology. Increases in factor prices shift the cost curves upward. Decreases in factor prices or technological advances that make it possible to produce the same amount of output with lower quantities of all inputs shift cost curves downward.
6. Over extended periods, the most important influence on costs of production and the standard of living has been the increases in output made possible by new technology, which has led to new techniques, new products, and improved inputs. These considerations involve the so-called very long run.
7. Major sources of productivity growth in industrializing countries include the substitution of capital for labor (an increasing capital-labor ratio), increased energy use, and invention and innovation.
8. Innovation in one form or another is the key to productivity growth. It requires invention, but also profitable opportunities for the introduction of available knowledge. Thus innovation and the changes in technology it brings are to a major degree endogenous. The economic climate (its growth and level of capacity utilization), institutional climate, and differences in technological possibilities in sectors where demand is growing and declining all affect the opportunities for innovation.

Topics for Review

Implication of cost minimization
Interpretation of $MP_K/MP_L = p_K/p_L$ and $MP_K/p_K = MP_L/p_L$
The principle of substitution
Increasing, decreasing, and constant returns
Economies of scale
Envelope curve
Distinction between production and productivity
Level of productivity and rate of growth of productivity
Sources of increasing productivity
Invention and innovation
Determinants of innovation

Discussion Questions

1. Why does the profit-maximizing firm choose the least costly way of producing any given output? Might a non-profit-maximizing organization such as a university, church, or government intentionally choose a method of production other than the least costly one?
2. Use the principle of substitution to predict the effect of each of the following:
   a. During the 1960s salaries of professors rose much more rapidly than those of teaching assistants. During the 1970s salaries of teaching assistants rose more than those of professors.

b. The cost of land in big cities increases more than the cost of high-rise construction.
c. Gold leaf is produced by pounding gold with a hammer. The thinner it is, the more valuable. The price of gold is set on a world market, but the price of labor varies among countries.
d. Wages of textile workers and shoe machinery operators rise more in Ontario than in Quebec.

3. The long-run average cost curve can be thought of as consisting of points from each of a number of short-run average cost curves. Explain in what sense any point on the long-run curve is also on some short-run curve. What is the meaning of a move from one point on a long-run cost curve to another point on the same curve? Contrast this with a movement along a short-run curve.
4. Israel, a small country, imports the "insides" of its automobiles but manufactures the bodies. If this makes economic sense, what does it tell us about cost conditions of automobile manufacture?
5. Look at one of the many available pictures of gangs working on the building of the CPR and compare it with what you see in any modern road or railway construction site. What does your comparison suggest about the type of factor substitution that has occurred? What do you think was the effect on the productivity of road and railway construction workers?
6. Name five important modern products that were not available when you were in grade school. Make a list of major products that you think have increased their sales at least tenfold in the past 40 years. Consider to what extent the growth in each may reflect product or process innovation.
7. Each of the following is a means of increasing productivity. Discuss which groups in the society might oppose each one.
   a. A labor-saving invention that permits all goods to be manufactured with less labor than before
   b. Rapidly increasing growth of population in the economy
   c. Removal of all government production safety rules
   d. Reduction in corporate income taxes
   e. Reduction in production of services and increase in agricultural production
8. The chairman of an American multinational oil company recently said, "Our government has adopted a gratuitously hostile attitude. Industry has been compelled to spend more and more of its research dollars to comply with environmental, health, and safety regulations—and to move away from longer-term efforts aimed at major scientific advance." Suppose this is true. Is it necessarily a sign that government policies are misguided?

Appendix to Chapter 11

Isoquants: An Alternative Analysis of the Firm's Input Decisions

The production function gives the relation between the factor inputs that the firm uses and the output that it obtains. In the long run the firm can choose among many different combinations of inputs that will yield the same output. The production function and the choices open to the firm can be represented graphically using the concept of an isoquant.

A Single Isoquant

Table 11A-1 illustrates a hypothetical example in which different combinations of two inputs (labor and capital) that produce a given quantity of output. The data from Table 11A-1 are plotted in Figure 11A-1. A smooth curve is drawn through the points to indicate that there are additional ways, not listed in the table, of producing six units.

This curve is called an **isoquant.** It shows the whole set of technologically efficient possibilities for producing a given level of output—6 units in this case. This is an example of graphing a three-variable function in two dimensions. It is analogous to the contour line on a map that shows all points of equal

TABLE 11A-1 Alternative Methods of Producing 6 Units of Output: Points on an Isoquant

Method	K	L	ΔK	ΔL	Rate of substitution $\Delta K/\Delta L$
a	18	2			
			−6	1	−6.0
b	12	3			
			−3	1	−3.0
c	9	4			
			−3	2	−1.5
d	6	6			
			−2	3	−0.67
e	4	9			
			−1	3	−0.33
f	3	12			
			−1	6	−0.17
g	2	18			

An isoquant describes the firm's alternative methods for producing a given output. The table lists some of the methods indicated by a production function as being available to produce 6 units of output. The first combination uses a great deal of capital (K) and very little labor (L). As we move down the table, labor is substituted for capital in such a way as to keep output constant. Finally, at the bottom, most of the capital has been replaced by labor. The rate of substitution between the two factors is calculated in the last three columns of the table. Note that as we move down the table, the absolute value of the rate of substitution declines.

FIGURE 11A-1 An Isoquant for Output of 6 Units

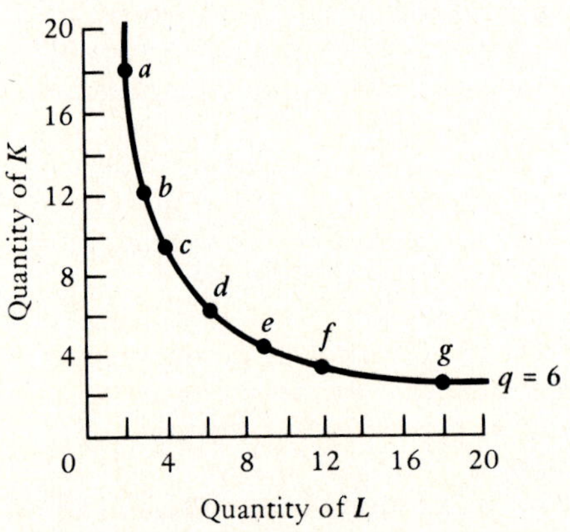

Isoquants are downward-sloping and convex. The downward slope reflects the requirement of technological efficiency. A method that uses more of one factor must use less of the other factor if it is to be technologically efficient. The convex shape of the isoquant reflects a diminishing marginal rate of substitution. The lettered points on the graph are plotted from the data in Table 11A-1. Starting from point *a*, which uses relatively little labor and much capital, and moving to point *b*, 1 additional unit of labor can substitute for 6 units of capital (while holding production constant). But from *b* to *c*, 1 unit of labor substitutes for only 3 units of capital. This diminishing rate is expressed geometrically by the flattening of the slope of the isoquant.

altitude and to an indifference curve that shows all combinations of commodities that yield an equal utility.

As we move from one point on an isoquant to another, we are *substituting one factor for another* while holding output constant. If we move from point *b* to point *c,* we are substituting 1 unit of labor for 3 units of capital. The marginal rate of substitution measures the rate at which one factor is substituted for another with output held constant. Graphically, the marginal rate of substitution is measured by the slope of the isoquant at a particular point. Table 11A-1 shows the calculation of some rates of substitution between various points of the isoquant. [20]

The marginal rate of substitution is related to the marginal products of the factors of production. To see how, consider an example. Assume that at the present level of inputs of labor and capital the marginal product of 1 unit of labor is 2 units of output, while the marginal product of capital is 1 unit of output. If the firm reduces its use of capital and increases its use of labor to keep output constant, it needs to add only 0.5 unit of labor for each unit of capital given up. If, at another point on the isoquant with more labor and less capital, the marginal products are 2 for capital and 1 for labor, the firm will have to add 2 units of labor for every unit of capital it gives up. The general proposition is as follows:

The marginal rate of substitution between two factors of production is equal to the ratio of their marginal products.

Isoquants satisfy two important conditions: They are downward-sloping, and they are convex viewed from the origin. What is the economic meaning of these conditions?

The downward slope indicates that each factor input has a positive marginal product. If the input of one factor is reduced and that of the other is held constant, output will be reduced. Thus if one input is decreased, production can be held constant only if the other factor input is increased. The marginal rate of substitution has a negative value. Decreases in one factor must be balanced by increases in the other factor if output is to be held constant.

To understand convexity, consider what happens as the firm moves along the isoquant of Figure 11A-1 downward and to the right. Labor is being added and capital reduced to keep output constant. If labor is added in increments of exactly 1 unit, how much capital may be dispensed with each time? The key to the answer is that both factors are assumed to be subject to the law of diminishing returns. Thus the gain in output associated with each additional unit of labor added is *diminishing* while the loss of output associated with each additional unit of capital forgone is *increasing.* It therefore takes ever-smaller reductions in capital to compensate for equal increases in labor. This implies that the isoquant is convex viewed from the origin.

An Isoquant Map

The isoquant of Figure 11A-1 referred to 6 units of output. There is another isoquant for 7 units, another for 7,000 units, and a different one for every other rate of output. Each isoquant refers to a specific output and connects combinations of factors that are technologically efficient methods of achieving that output. If we plot a representative set of these isoquants on a single graph, we get an **isoquant map** like that in Figure 11A-2. The higher the level of

FIGURE 11A-2 An Isoquant Map

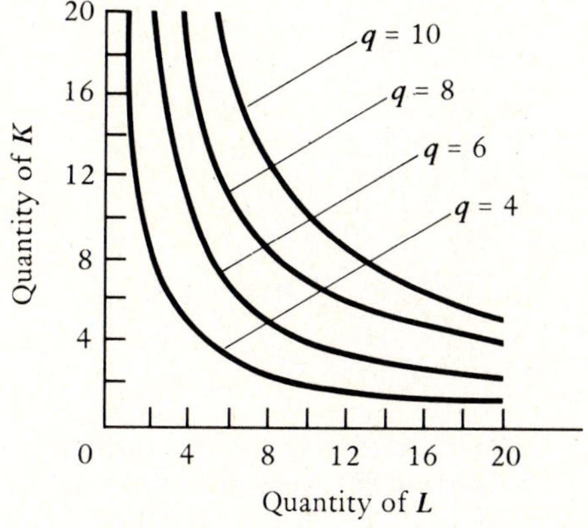

An isoquant map shows a set of isoquants, one for each level of output. The figure shows four isoquants drawn from the production function and corresponding to 4, 6, 8, and 10 units of production.

output along a particular isoquant, the farther the isoquant is from the origin.

Conditions for Cost Minimization

Finding the efficient way of producing any output requires finding the least-cost factor combination. To find this combination when both factors are variable, factor prices need to be known. Suppose, to continue the example, that capital is priced at $4 per unit and labor at $1. In Chapter 7 a budget line was used to show the alternative combinations of goods a household could buy; here an *isocost line* is used to show alternative combinations of factors a firm can buy for a given outlay. Four different isocost lines appear in Figure 11A-3. The slope of each reflects *relative* factor prices, just as the slope of the budget line in Chapter 7 represented relative product prices. For given factor prices a series of parallel isocost lines will reflect the alternative levels of expenditure on factor purchases that are open to the firm. The higher the level of expenditure, the farther the isocost line is from the origin.

FIGURE 11A-3 Isocost Lines

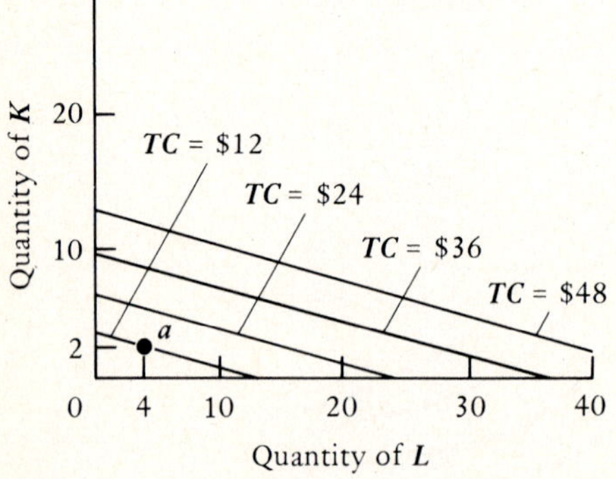

Each isocost line shows alternative factor combinations that can be purchased for a given outlay. The graph shows the four isocost lines that result when labor costs $1 a unit and capital $4 a unit and expenditure is held constant at $12, $24, $36, and $48, respectively. The line labeled $TC = \$12$ represents all combinations of the two factors that the firm could buy for $12. Point *a* represents 2 units of *K* and 4 units of *L*.

In Figure 11A-4 the isoquant and isocost maps are brought together. The economically most efficient method of production must be a point on an isoquant that just touches (i.e., is tangent to) an isocost line. If the isoquant cuts the isocost line, it is possible to move along the isoquant and reach a lower level of cost. Only at a point of tangency is a movement in either direction along the isoquant a movement to a higher cost level. The lowest attainable cost of producing 6 units is $24. This cost level can be achieved only by operating at *A*, the point where the $24 isocost line is tangent to the 6-unit isoquant. The lowest average cost of producing 6 units is thus $24/6 = $4 per unit of output.

The least-cost position is given graphically by the tangency point between the isoquant and the isocost lines.

Notice that point *A* in Figure 11A-4 indicates not only the lowest level of cost for 6 units of output but also the highest level of output for $24 of cost. Thus we find the same solution if we set out *either* to minimize the cost of producing 6 units of output *or* to maximize the output that can be obtained for $24. One problem is said to be the "dual" of the other.

The slope of the isocost line is given by the ratio of the prices of the two factors of production. The slope of the isoquant is given by the ratio of their marginal products. When the firm reaches its least-cost position, it has equated the price ratio (which is given to it by the market prices) with the ratio of the marginal products (which it can adjust by varying the proportions in which it hires the factors). In symbols,

$$\frac{MP_K}{MP_L} = \frac{p_K}{p_L}$$

This is equivalent to Equation 2 on page 203. We have now derived this result by use of the isoquant analysis of the firm's decisions. [21]

The Principle of Substitution

Suppose that with technology unchanged, that is, with the isoquant map fixed, the price of one factor changes. Suppose that with the price of capital un-

FIGURE 11A-4 The Determination of the Least-Cost Method of Output

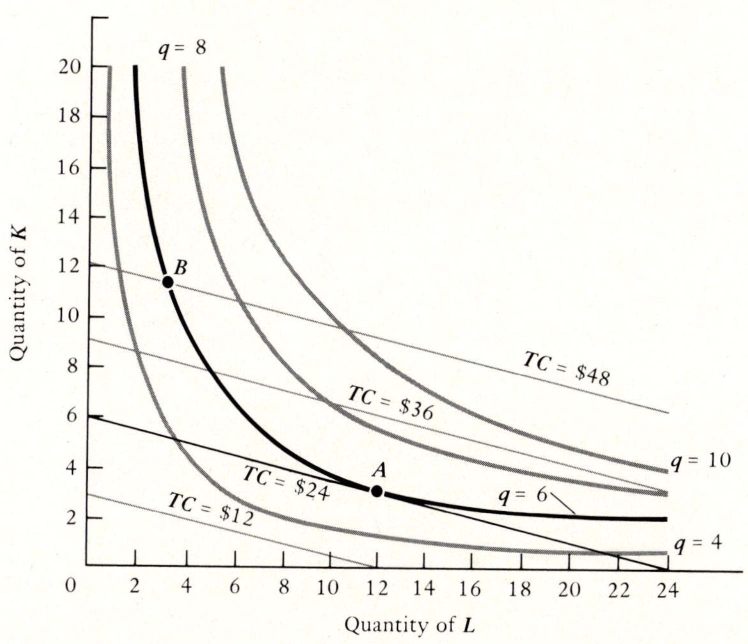

Least-cost methods are represented by points of tangency between isoquant and isocost lines. The isoquant map of Figure 11A-2 and the isocost lines of Figure 11A-3 are brought together. Consider point *A*. It is on the 6-unit isoquant and the $24 isocost line. Thus it is possible to achieve the output $q = 6$ for a total cost of $24. There are other ways to achieve this output, for example, at point *B*, where $TC =$ $48. Moving along the isoquant from point *A* in either direction increases cost. Similarly, moving along the isocost line from point *A* in either direction lowers output. Thus either move would raise cost per unit.

FIGURE 11A-5 The Effects of a Change in Factor Prices on Costs and Factor Proportions

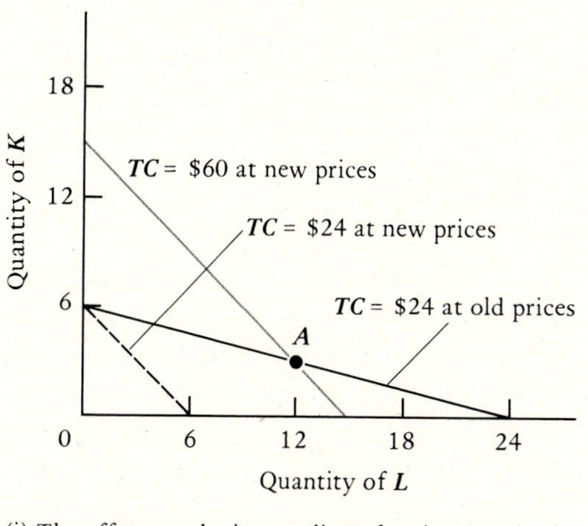

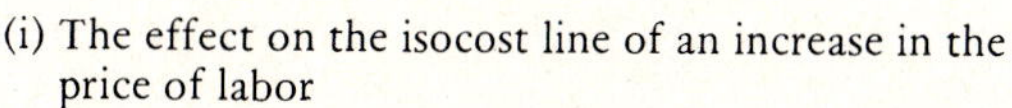
(i) The effect on the isocost line of an increase in the price of labor

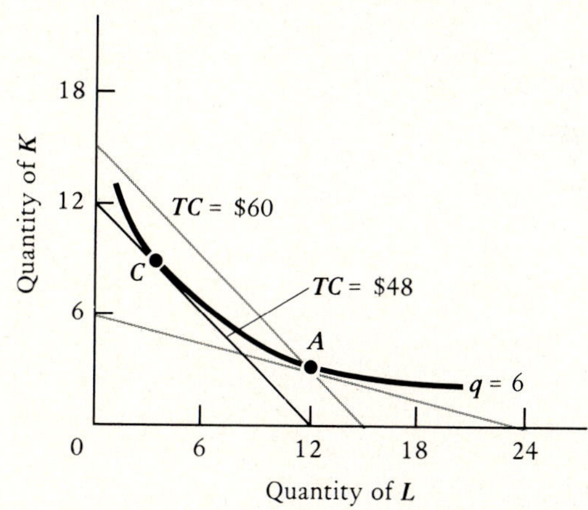

(ii) Substitution of capital for labor resulting from an increase in the price of labor

An increase in the price of labor pivots the isocost line inward and thus increases the cost of producing any output. It also changes the slope of the isocost line and thus changes the least-cost method of producing. (i) The rise in price of *L* from $1 to $4 a unit (with price of *K* constant at $4) pivots the $24 isocost line inward to the dashed line. Any output previously produced for $24 will cost more at the new prices if it uses any amount of labor. The new cost of producing *A* rises from $24 to $60. (ii) The steeper isocost line is tangent to the isoquant at *C*, not *A*. Costs at *C* are $48, higher than they were before the price increase, but not as high as they would be if the factor substitution had not occurred.

changed at $4 per unit, the price of labor rises from $1 to $4 per unit. Originally, the efficient factor combination for producing 6 units was 12 units of labor and 3 units of capital. It cost $24. To produce that same output in the same way would now cost $60 at the new factor prices. Figure 11A-5 (p. 217) shows why that is not efficient. The slope of the isocost line has changed, which makes it efficient to substitute the now relatively cheaper capital for the relatively more expensive labor. This illustrates the principle of substitution.

Changes in relative factor prices will cause a partial replacement of factors that have become relatively more expensive by factors that have become relatively cheaper.

Of course, substitution of capital for labor cannot fully offset the effects of a rise in cost of labor, as Figure 11A-5(i) shows. Consider the output attainable for $24. In the figure there are two isocost lines representing $24 of outlay—at the old price and the new price of labor. The new isocost line for $24 lies inside the old one (except where no labor is used). The isocost line must therefore be tangent to a lower isoquant. This means that if production is to be held constant, higher costs must be accepted. However, because of substitution, it is not necessary to accept costs as high as would accompany an unchanged factor proportion. In the example 6 units can be produced for $48 rather than the $60 that would be required if no change in factor proportions were made.

This leads to the following predictions:

A rise in the price of one factor with all other factor prices constant will (1) shift upward the cost curves of commodities that use that factor and (2) lead to a substitution of factors that are now relatively cheaper for the factor whose price has risen.

Both these predictions were stated in Chapter 11; now they have been derived formally using the isoquant technique.

PART FOUR

Markets and Pricing

12

Competitive Markets

Market Structure and Firm Behavior

Does Holiday Inn compete with Relax Inn? Does Eatons compete with Simpsons? Does a wheat farmer from Biggar, Saskatchewan, compete with a wheat farmer from Brandon, Manitoba? In the ordinary meaning of the word *compete*, the answers to the first two questions are plainly yes, and the answer to the third question is probably no.

Holiday Inn and Relax Inn both advertise extensively to persuade travelers to stop at their hotels. Simpsons and Eatons watch each other closely, and many comparison shoppers check both firms' prices and product qualities before making a purchase. But nothing the Saskatchewan farmer can do will affect either the sales or the profits of the Manitoba farmer.

Competitive Behavior and Competitive Market Structure

To sort out the questions of who is competing with whom and in what sense, it is useful to distinguish between the *behavior* of individual firms and the *type of market* in which the firms operate. In everyday use the word *competition* usually refers only to competitive behavior; economists, however, are interested both in the competitive behavior of individual firms and in a quite distinct concept, competitive market structure.

The term *market structure* refers to all aspects of a market, such as the number of firms and the type of product sold, that may affect the behavior and performance of the firms in that market.

Competitive market structure. The competitiveness of the market refers to the extent to which individual firms have power over that market—power to influence the price or other terms on which their product is sold. The less power an individual firm has to influence the market in which it sells its product, the more competitive is that market.

The extreme form of competitiveness occurs when each firm has zero power because there are so many firms that each must accept the price set by the forces of market demand and supply. This extreme is called the *perfectly competitive market structure*. In it there is no need for individual firms to compete actively with one another since none has any power over the market. One firm's ability to sell its product does not depend on the behavior of any other firm.

For example, the Saskatchewan and Manitoba wheat farmers do not engage in active *competitive behavior* with each other. They operate in a perfectly competitive market over which they have no power. Neither has significant power to change the market price for its wheat by altering its own behavior.

Competitive behavior. In everyday language the term *competitive behavior* refers to the degree to which individual firms actively compete with one another. For example, Holiday Inns and Relax Inns certainly engage in competitive behavior.

It is also true, however, that both chains have some power over their markets. Either chain could raise its prices and still continue to attract customers. Each has the power to decide, within limits set by buyers' tastes and the prices of competing motels and hotels, what price travelers will pay for their own accommodation. Thus, although they compete actively with each other, they do not do so within the confines of a perfectly competitive market structure.

Behavior versus structure. The distinction just made explains why firms in perfectly competitive markets (e.g., the Saskatchewan and Manitoba wheat farms) do not actively compete with each other, while firms that do compete actively with each other (e.g., Simpsons and Eatons) do not operate in perfectly competitive markets.

The Significance of Market Structure

From the point of view of a buyer, the **market** consists of the firms from which a well-defined product can be purchased; from the point of view of a firm, the market consists of the buyers to whom a well-defined product can be sold. A group of firms that sells a well-defined product or closely related set of products is said to constitute an **industry.** The market demand curve is the demand curve for an industry's product.[1]

Consider a firm that produces a specific product for sale in a particular market and competes for customers with other firms in the same industry. If the firm knows the demand curve it faces, it knows the price it could charge for each rate of sales and thus knows its potential revenues. If it also knows its costs, the firm can calculate the profits that would be associated with each rate of output and can choose the rate that maximizes its profits.

But what if the firm knows only its costs and the *market* demand curve for its industry's product? Because it does not know its *own* demand curve, it does not know what its own sales would be at any price that it might charge. To know how its own demand would change as its own price changes, the firm needs to know how other firms will respond to its change in price. If it reduces its price by 10 percent, will other sellers leave their prices unchanged, or will they also reduce them? If so, by how much? Obviously, these responses will have an effect on the firm's sales and thus on its revenues and profits.

We have seen that economists define market structure to mean the characteristics that affect the behavior and performance of firms that sell in that market. These characteristics are many of the ones that determine the relation between the market demand curve for the industry's product and the demand curve facing each firm in that industry.

The number of sellers and the nature of the product are highly significant dimensions of market structure. There are others as well, such as the ease of entering the industry, the nature and number of the purchasers of the firm's products, and the firm's ability to influence demand by advertising. To reduce these aspects to manageable proportions, economists have focused on a few theoretical market structures that they believe represent a high proportion of the cases actually encountered in market economies. In this and the following chapters, we shall look at four market structures: perfect competition, monopoly, monopolistic competition, and oligopoly.

Before considering any of these, it is useful to deal with the rules of behavior common to all firms that seek to maximize profits.

Profit-maximizing Behavior

Marginal revenue. A firm interested in maximizing its profits must pay attention to both its costs and its revenues. In Chapter 10 we defined *marginal cost* as

[1] An industry typically sells many different products and sells them in many different markets. For our elementary treatment, we shall focus attention on the single-product industry and the market (or markets) in which that product is sold.

the addition to the firm's total cost caused by increasing its rate of production by one unit. It is now helpful to define a parallel revenue concept. **Marginal revenue (*MR*)** is the change in the firm's total revenue caused by a change in its sales by one unit. At any level of sales, marginal revenue shows what the firm would gain on the revenue side by selling a bit more and what revenue it would lose by selling a bit less.

Should the firm produce at all? The firm always has the option of producing nothing. If it exercises that option, it will have an operating loss equal to its fixed costs. If it decides to produce, it will add the variable cost of production to its costs and the receipts from the sale of its product to its revenue. Therefore, if there is some level of output for which revenue exceeds variable cost, it will pay the firm to produce; if, however, revenue is less than variable cost at every level of output, the firm will actually lose more by producing than by not producing.[2]

***Rule 1:* A firm should not produce at all if the total revenue from selling its product does not equal or exceed the total variable cost of producing it.** [22]

How much should the firm produce? If a firm decides that according to Rule 1, production is worth undertaking, it must decide how much to produce. Common sense dictates that on a unit-by-unit basis, if any unit of production adds more to revenue than it does to cost, that unit will increase profits; if it adds more to cost than to revenue, it will decrease profits. If a further unit of production will increase the firm's profits, the firm should expand output. However, if the last unit produced will reduce profits, the firm should contract output. From this it follows that the only time the firm should leave its output unaltered is when the last unit produced adds the same amount to costs as it does to revenue.

***Rule 2:* Assuming that it pays the firm to produce at all, the firm should produce where marginal revenue equals marginal cost.** [23]

[2] Formal proofs of the propositions discussed in the text are given in the Mathematical Notes.

These rules refer to each firm's own costs and revenues, and they apply to all profit-maximizing firms, whatever the market structure in which they operate.[3] Before we can apply the rules, however, we need to consider particular market structures in order to relate the demand curve for an industry's product to the demand curves facing individual firms.

Elements of the Theory of Perfect Competition

The theory of the perfectly competitive market structure applies directly to a number of real-world markets. It also provides a benchmark for comparison with other market structures.

Assumptions of Perfect Competition

The theory of **perfect competition** is built on two critical assumptions, one about the behavior of the individual firm and one about the nature of the industry in which it operates.

The *firm* is assumed to be a **price taker**; that is, the firm is assumed to be able to alter its production and sales output greatly without significantly affecting the price of its product. Thus, as stated earlier, a firm operating in a perfectly competitive market has no power to influence that market through its own individual actions. It must passively accept whatever price happens to be ruling.

The *industry* is assumed to be characterized by **freedom of entry and exit**; that is, any new firm is free to set up production if it so wishes, and any existing firm is free to cease production and leave the industry. Existing firms cannot bar the entry of new firms, and there are no legal prohibitions on entry or exit.

The ultimate test of the theory based on these assumptions will be the usefulness of its predictions,

[3] There is also a third rule that is needed to distinguish between profit-*maximizing* and profit-*minimizing* positions: The marginal cost curve must cut the marginal revenue curve from below. [24] This rule is not, however, needed in what follows, so we say nothing further about it.

but because students are often bothered by the first assumption, it is worth examining whether it is in any way reasonable. To do this, we contrast the demands for the products of an automobile manufacturer and a wheat farmer.

An automobile manufacturer. General Motors is aware that it has market power. If it increases its prices substantially, sales will fall off; if it lowers prices substantially, it will sell more of its products. If GM decides on a large increase in production that is not a response to a known or anticipated rise in demand, it will have to reduce prices in order to sell the extra output. General Motors is *not* a price taker. The quantity that it is able to sell will depend on the price it charges, but it does not have to accept passively whatever price is set by the market. In other words, an auto manufacturing firm such as GM is faced with a downward-sloping demand curve for its product. It may select any price-quantity combination consistent with that demand curve.

A wheat farmer. In contrast, an individual firm producing wheat is just one of a very large number of firms all growing the same product; one firm's contribution to the total production of wheat will be a tiny drop in an extremely large bucket. Ordinarily, the firm will assume that it has no effect on price and will think of its own demand curve as being horizontal. Of course, the firm can have *some* effect on price, but a straightforward calculation will show that the effect is small enough that the firm can justifiably ignore it.

The market elasticity of demand for wheat is approximately 0.25. This means that if the quantity of wheat supplied in the world increased by 1 percent, the price would have to fall by 4 percent to induce the world's wheat buyers to purchase the whole crop. Even huge farms produce a small fraction of the total crop. In a recent year an extremely large Canadian wheat farm produced about 50,000 tons, only about 1/4,000 of total world production of 200 million tons. Suppose a large wheat farm increased its production by 20,000 tons, say, from 40,000 to 60,000 tons. This would be a big percentage increase in its own production but an increase of only 1/100 of 1 percent in world production. Table 12-1 shows that this increase would lead to a decrease in the world price of 4/100 of 1 percent (4¢ in $100) and give the firm an elasticity of demand of 1,000! This is a very high elasticity of demand; the farm would have to increase its output 1,000 percent to bring about a 1 percent decrease in the price of wheat. Because the firm's output cannot be varied this much, it is not surprising that the firm regards the price of wheat as unaffected by any change in output that it could conceivably make. In other words, the firm is faced with a perfectly elastic demand curve for its product—*it is a price taker.*

The difference between General Motors and the wheat farmer is one of degree of market power. The firm producing wheat, as an insignificant part of the whole market, has no power to influence the world price of wheat. The automobile firm does have power to influence the price of automobiles because its own production represents a significant part of the total supply of automobiles.

Demand and Revenue for the Perfectly Competitive Firm

The demand curve facing a single firm in perfect competition is horizontal because variations in its production over the range that we need to consider for all practical purposes will have a negligible effect on price. Of course, if the single firm increased its production by a vast amount, a thousandfold, say, this might well cause a significant increase in supply, and the firm would be unable to sell all it produced at the going price. The horizontal (perfectly elastic) demand curve does not mean that the firm could actually sell an infinite amount at the going price; rather, the variations in production *that it will normally be practicable for the firm to make* will leave price virtually unaffected. Figure 12-1 contrasts the demand curve for a competitive industry and for a single firm in that industry.

Total, average, and marginal revenue. The notions of total, average, and marginal revenue are the demand counterparts of the notions of total, average, and marginal cost that we considered in Chapter 10. We focus now on the receipts to a seller from the sale of a product.

TABLE 12-1 Calculation of a Firm's Elasticity of Demand (η_F) from Market Elasticity of Demand (η_M)

Given

$\eta_M = 0.25$

World output = 200 million tons

Firm's output increases from 40,000 to 60,000 tons, a 40% increase over the average quantity of 50,000 tons

Step 1. Find the percentage change in world price.

$$\eta_M = -\frac{\text{percentage change in world output}}{\text{percentage change in world price}}$$

$$\text{Percentage change in world price} = -\frac{\text{percentage change in world output}}{\eta_M} = -\frac{1/100 \text{ of } 1\%}{0.25} = -4/100 \text{ of } 1\%$$

Step 2. Compute the firm's elasticity of demand.

$$\eta_F = -\frac{\text{percentage change in firm's output}}{\text{percentage change in world price}} = -\frac{+40\%}{-4/100 \text{ of } 1\%} = +1{,}000$$

Because even a large change in output to the firm is a minute change in world wheat production, the effect on world price is small. Thus the firm's elasticity of demand is high. This table relies on the concept of elasticity of demand developed in Chapter 5. Step 1 shows that a 40 percent increase in the firm's output leads to only a tiny decrease in the world's price. Thus, as step 2 shows, the firm's elasticity of demand is very high: 1,000.

The arithmetic is not important, but understanding why the wheat farm will be a price taker in these circumstances is vital.

FIGURE 12-1 Demand Curve for a Competitive Industry and for One Firm in the Industry

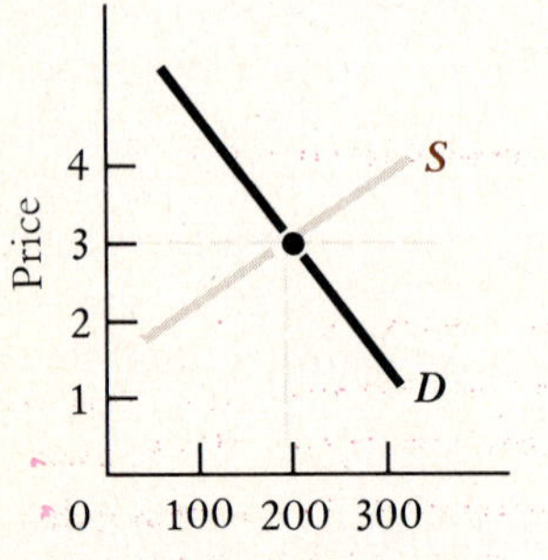

(i) Competitive industry's demand curve

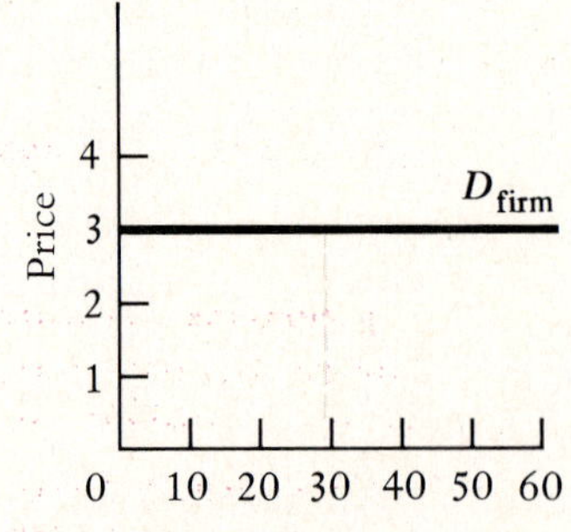

(ii) Competitive firm's demand curve

The industry's demand curve is downward-sloping; the firm's demand curve is virtually horizontal. Notice the difference in the quantities shown on the horizontal scale in each part of the figure. The competitive industry has a price of $3 and an output of 200 million tons. The individual firm takes that market price as given to it and considers producing up to 60,000 tons. The firm's demand curve in part (ii) appears horizontal because of the change in the quantity scale compared to the industry's demand curve in part (i). The firm's output variation has only a tiny percentage effect on industry output. If one plotted the industry demand curve from 199,970,000 tons to 200,030,000 tons on the scale used in part (ii), the *D* curve would appear virtually horizontal.

Total revenue (TR) is the total amount received by the seller. If q units are sold at p dollars each, $TR = p \cdot q$.[4]

Average revenue (AR) is the amount of revenue *per unit* sold. This is the price of the product.

Marginal revenue (MR), sometimes called incremental revenue, has already been defined. It is the change in total revenue resulting from a change in the firm's rate of sales by one unit. **[25]**

Calculations of these revenue concepts for a price-taking firm are illustrated in Table 12-2. The table shows that as long as the firm's output does not affect the price of the product it sells, both average and marginal revenue will be equal to price at all levels of output. Thus, graphically, as shown in part (i) of Figure 12-2, average revenue and marginal revenue are both horizontal lines at the level of market price. Since the firm can sell any quantity it wishes at this price, the same horizontal line is also the *firm's* demand curve.

If the market price is unaffected by variations in the firm's output, the firm's demand curve, the average revenue curve, and the marginal revenue curve coincide in the same horizontal line. Thus for a firm in perfect competition, price equals marginal revenue.

Total revenue, of course, does vary with output; since price is constant, it follows that total revenue rises in direct proportion to output, as shown in part (ii) of Figure 12-2.

TABLE 12-2 Revenue Concepts for a Price-taking Firm

Price p	Quantity q	$TR = p \cdot q$	$AR = TR/q$	$MR = \Delta TR/\Delta q$
$3	10	$30	$3	
				$3
3	11	33	3	
				3
3	12	36	3	
				3
3	13	39	3	

When price is fixed, $AR = MR = p$. Marginal revenue is shown between the lines because it represents the change in total revenue (e.g., from $33 to $36) in response to a change in quantity (from 11 to 12 units): $MR = (36-33)/(12-11) = \$3$ per unit.

Short-Run Equilibrium

The Firm's Equilibrium Output

In perfect competition the firm is a price taker and can adjust to varying market conditions only by changing the quantity it produces. In the short run it has one or more fixed factors, and the only way to vary its output is by using more or less of the factors that it can vary. Thus the firm's short-run cost curves are relevant to its output decision.

We saw earlier that *any* profit-maximizing firm will seek to produce at the level of output at which marginal cost equals marginal revenue. We also saw that a perfectly competitive firm's demand and marginal revenue curves coincide in the same horizontal line, the height of which represents the price of the product. It follows that a firm operating in a perfectly competitive market will equate its marginal cost of production to the market price of its product (as long as price exceeds average variable cost).

The market determines the price at which the firm sells its product. The firm picks the quantity of output that maximizes its profits. This is the output for which $p = MC$. When the firm is maximizing profits, it has no incentive to change its output. Therefore, unless prices or costs change, the firm will continue producing this output because it is doing as well as it can do, given the situation. The firm is said to be in **short-run equilibrium,** which is illustrated in Figure 12-3.

In a perfectly competitive market, each firm is a mere quantity adjuster. It pursues its goal of profit maximization by increasing or decreasing quantity until it equates its short-run marginal cost with the prevailing price of its product—a price that is given to it by the market.

In a perfectly competitive market the firm responds to a price that is set by the forces of demand

[4] Three common ways of indicating that two variables, p and q in this case, are to be multiplied together are $p \cdot q$, $p \times q$, and pq.

FIGURE 12-2 Revenue Curves for a Price-taking Firm

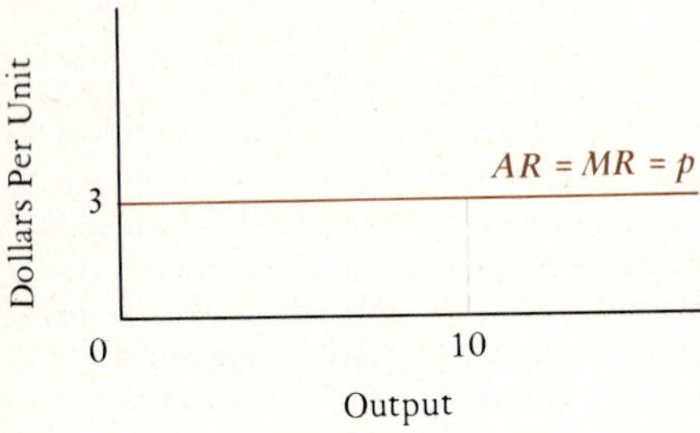

(i) Average and marginal revenue

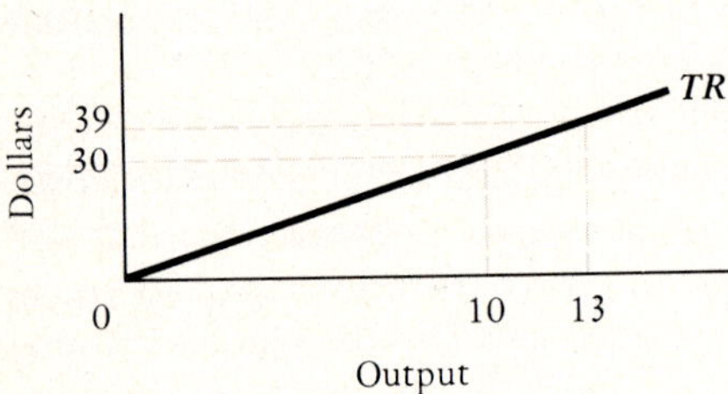

(ii) Total revenue

This is a graphic representation of the revenue concepts of Table 12-2. Because price does not change, neither marginal nor average revenue varies with output. When price is constant, total revenue is an upward-sloping straight line from the origin.

FIGURE 12-3 Short-Run Equilibrium of a Competitive Firm

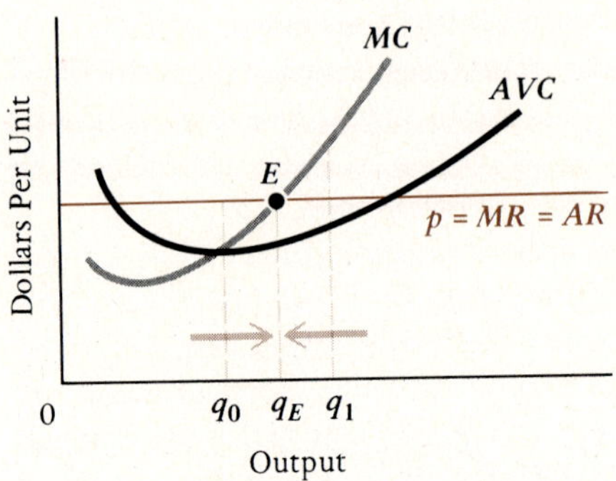

The firm chooses the output for which $p = MC$ above the level of *AVC*. When $p = MC$ as at q_E, the firm would decrease its profits if it either increased or decreased its output. At any point to the left of q_E, say, q_0, price is greater than the marginal cost, and it pays to increase output (as indicated by the arrow on the left). At any point to the right of q_E, say, q_1, price is less than the marginal cost, and it pays to reduce output (as indicated by the arrow on the right). The short-run equilibrium output for the firm is q_E.

and supply. By adjusting the quantity it produces in response to the current market price, the firm helps to determine market supply. The link between the behavior of the firm and the behavior of the competitive market is provided by the market supply curve.

Short-Run Supply Curves

The supply curve for one firm. Figure 12-4(i) shows a firm's marginal cost curve and four alternative prices. The horizontal line at each price is the firm's demand curve when the market price is at that level. The firm's marginal cost curve gives the marginal cost corresponding to each level of output. We require a supply curve that shows the quantity the firm will supply at every price. For prices below average variable cost, the firm will supply zero units (Rule 1). For prices above *AVC*, the firm will equate price and marginal cost (Rule 2 modified by the proposition that $MR = p$ in perfect competition). This leads to the following conclusion:

In perfect competition the firm's supply curve has the identical shape as the firm's marginal cost curve above average variable cost.

The supply curve of an industry. Figure 12-5 illustrates the derivation of an industry supply curve for an example of only two firms. The general result is as follows:

In perfect competition the industry supply curve is the horizontal sum of the marginal cost curves (above the level of average variable cost) of all firms in the industry.

FIGURE 12-4 Derivation of the Supply Curve for a Price-taking Firm

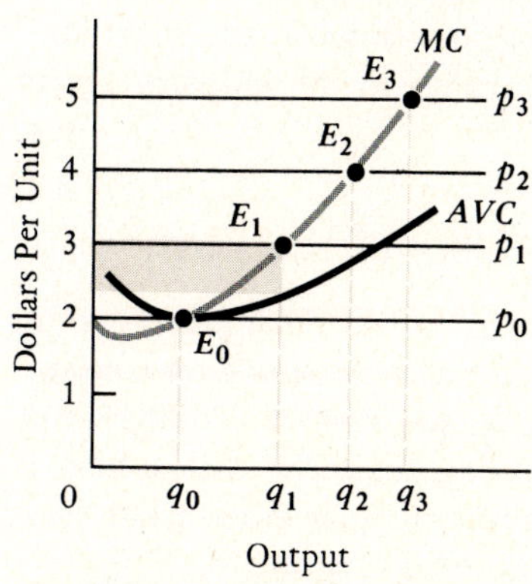

(i) Marginal cost and average variable cost curves

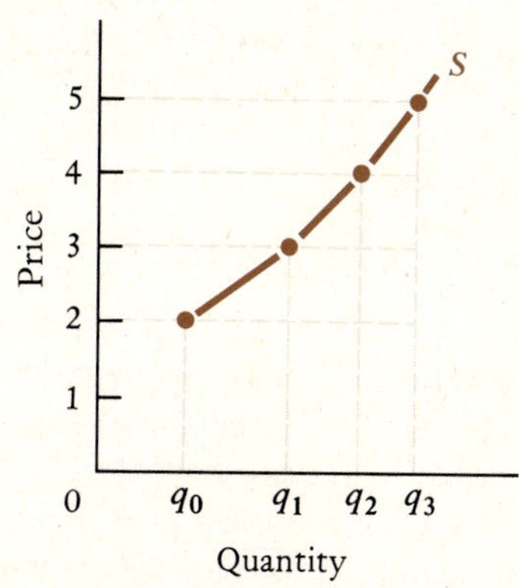

(ii) Supply curve

For a price-taking firm, the supply curve (ii) has the same shape as its *MC* curve above the level of *AVC* (i). As prices rise from \$2 to \$3 to \$4 to \$5, the firm wishes to increase its production from q_0 to q_1 to q_2 to q_3. For prices below \$2, output would be zero because there is no positive output at which *AVC* can be covered. The point E_0, where price equals *AVC*, is the shutdown point. If price were \$3, the firm would produce output q_1 rather than zero because that output would be making a contribution to fixed costs, as shown by the shaded rectangle.

The reason for this is that each firm's marginal cost curve tells us how much that firm will supply at each given market price, and the industry supply curve is the sum of what each firm will supply. This supply curve, based on the short-run marginal cost curves of the firms in the industry, is the industry's supply curve of the kind introduced in Chapter 4 and used as an important part of our analysis. It is sometimes

FIGURE 12-5 Derivation of the Supply Curve for an Industry

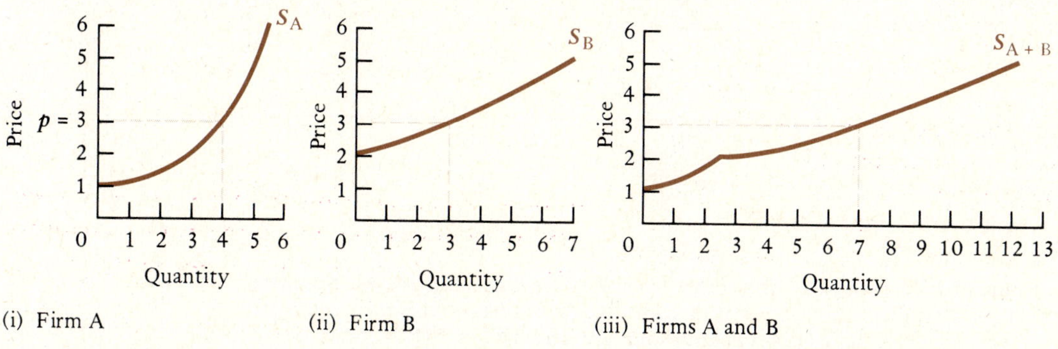

(i) Firm A (ii) Firm B (iii) Firms A and B

The industry supply curve is the horizontal sum of the supply curves of each of the firms in the industry. At a price of \$3, firm A would supply 4 units and firm B would supply 3 units. Together, as shown in part (iii), they would supply 7 units. If there are hundreds of firms, the process is the same. Each firm's supply curve (derived in the manner shown in Figure 12-4) shows what the firm will produce at any given price *p*. The industry supply curve relates the price to the sum of the quantities produced by each firm. In this example, because firm B does not enter the market at prices below \$2, the supply curve S_{A+B} is identical to S_A up to price \$2 and is the sum of $S_A + S_B$ above \$2.

called a **short-run supply curve** to distinguish it from a long-run supply curve, which is used in more advanced analysis that concerns the relation of long-run equilibrium price and quantities supplied.

Short-Run Equilibrium Price

The market price of a product sold in a perfectly competitive market is determined by the interaction of the industry's short-run supply curve and the market demand curve. Although no one firm can influence market price significantly, the collective actions of all firms in the industry (as shown by the industry supply curve) and the collective actions of households (as shown by the market demand curve) together determine the equilibrium price at the point where the demand and supply curves intersect.

At the equilibrium price each firm is producing and selling a quantity for which its marginal cost equals price. No firm is motivated to change its output in the short run. Since total quantity demanded equals total quantity supplied, there is no reason for market price to change in the short run; the market and all the firms in the industry are in short-run equilibrium.

Short-Run Profitability of the Firm

Although we know that when the industry is in short-run equilibrium the competitive firm is maximizing its profits, we do not know *how large* these profits are. It is one thing to know that a firm is doing as well as it can in particular circumstances; it is another to know how well it is doing.

Figure 12-6 shows three possible positions for a firm in short-run equilibrium. In all cases the firm is

FIGURE 12-6 Alternative Short-Run Equilibrium Positions of a Competitive Firm

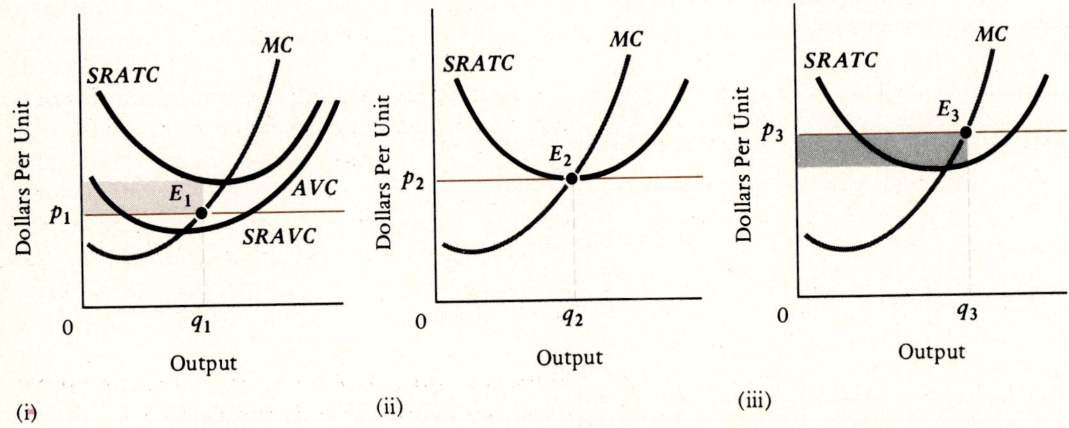

When it is in short-run equilibrium, a competitive firm may be suffering losses, breaking even, or making profits. The diagrams show a firm with given costs faced with three alternative prices p_1, p_2, and p_3. In each part of the diagram equilibrium is where $MC = MR =$ price. Since in all three cases price exceeds AVC, the firm is in short-run equilibrium at E_1, E_2, and E_3, respectively, in part (i), part (ii), and part (iii).

In part (i) price is p_1 and the firm is suffering losses, shown by the color shaded area, because price is below average total cost. Since price exceeds average variable cost, it pays the firm to keep producing, but it does *not* pay it to replace its capital equipment as it wears out.

In part (ii) price is p_2 and the firm is just covering its total costs. It pays the firm to replace its capital as it wears out since it is covering the full opportunity cost of its capital.

In part (iii) price is p_3 and the firm is earning profits, shown by the gray shaded area, in excess of all its costs.

maximizing its profits by producing where $p = MC$, but in part (i) the firm is making losses, in part (ii) it is just covering all costs, and in part (iii) it is making profits in excess of all costs. In (i) it might be better to say that the firm is minimizing its losses rather than maximizing its profits, but both statements mean the same thing. The firm is doing as well as it can, given its costs and prices.

FIGURE 12-7 Effect of New Entrants on the Supply Curve

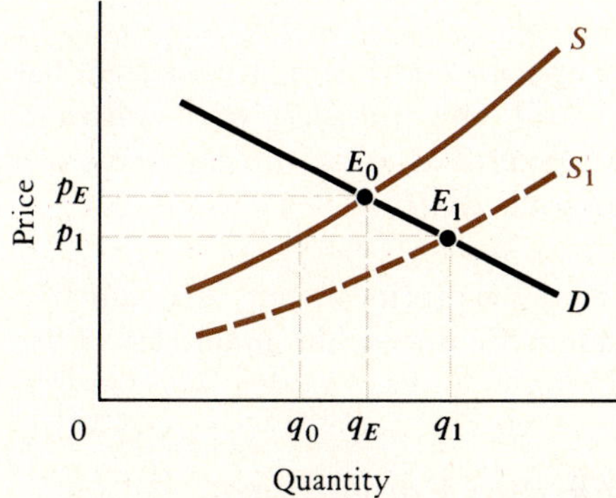

New entrants shift the supply curve to the right and lower the equilibrium price. Initial equilibrium is at E_0. If the supply curve shifts to S_1 by virtue of entry, the equilibrium price must fall to p_1 while output rises to q_1. At this price only q_0 is produced by the firms who were originally in the industry. The extra output is supplied by new firms.

Long-Run Equilibrium

Although Figure 12-6 shows three possible short-run equilibrium positions for the profit-maximizing firm in perfect competition, not all of them are possible equilibrium positions in the long run.

The Effect of Entry and Exit

The key to long-run equilibrium under perfect competition is entry and exit. We have seen that when firms are in *short-run* equilibrium, they may be making profits or losses or just breaking even. Since costs include the opportunity cost of capital, firms that are just breaking even are doing as well as they could do by investing their capital elsewhere. Thus there will be no incentive for existing firms to leave the industry; neither will there be an incentive for new firms to enter the industry, for capital can earn the same return elsewhere in the economy. If, however, existing firms are earning profits over all costs, including the opportunity cost of capital, new capital will enter the industry to share in these profits. If existing firms are making losses, capital will leave the industry because a better return can be obtained elsewhere in the economy. Let us consider the process in a little more detail.

If all firms in the competitive industry are in the position of the firm in Figure 12-6(iii), new firms will enter the industry, attracted by the profitability of existing firms. Suppose that in response to high profits for 100 existing firms, 20 new firms enter. The market supply curve that formerly added up the outputs of 100 firms now must add up the outputs of 120 firms. At any price more will be supplied because there are more producers.

This shift in the short-run supply curve, with an unchanged market demand curve, means that the previous equilibrium price will no longer prevail. The shift in supply will lower the equilibrium price, and both new and old firms will have to adjust their output to this new price. This is illustrated in Figure 12-7. New firms will continue to enter and equilibrium price will continue to fall until all firms in the industry are just covering their total costs. Firms will then be in the position of the firm in Figure 12-6(ii), which is called a *zero-profit equilibrium*.

Profits in a competitive industry are a signal for the entry of new capital; the industry will expand, forcing price down until the profits fall to zero.

If the firms in the industry are in the position of the firm in Figure 12-6(i), they are suffering losses. They are covering their variable costs, but the return on their capital is less than the opportunity cost of this capital; the firms are not covering their total costs. This is a signal for the exit of firms. As plant and equipment are discarded, they will not be replaced. As a result, the industry's short-run supply curve shifts left, and market price rises. Firms will continue to exit and price will continue to rise until the remaining firms can cover their total costs, that is, until they are all in the zero-profit equilibrium illustrated in Figure 12-6(ii). Exit then ceases.

Losses in a competitive industry are a signal for the exit of capital; the industry will contract, driving price up until the remaining firms are covering their total costs.

In all of this we see profits serving their function of allocating resources among the industries of the economy.

Cost in Long-Run Equilibrium

There are four major conditions for a competitive industry to be in long-run equilibrium.

First, existing firms must be doing as well as they can, given their existing plants. This means that marginal costs of production must be equal to market price.

Second, existing firms must not be making losses. If they are making losses, they will not replace their capital. In this case the size of the industry will be shrinking over time.

Third, there must be no incentive for new firms to enter the industry. The absence of an incentive for entry requires that existing firms are not earning profits on their existing plants; if they were, new entrants could duplicate these facilities and earn profits themselves.

Fourth, existing firms must not be able to increase their profits by building plants of a different size. This implies that each existing firm must be at the minimum point of its long-run cost curve. This is a new condition; to understand it, assume that it does not hold and see that firms could then increase their profits. This is shown in Figure 12-8. Here the firm is in short-run equilibrium and just covering all costs. But there are unexploited economies of scale. By increasing its size, for example, by building a new plant with a larger capacity than its existing plant, the firm can reduce its average cost. Since in its present position average cost is just equal to price, any reduction in average cost must yield profits.

To summarize, the conditions for long-run equilibrium for a competitive industry are as follows: (1) existing firms produce where marginal cost equals price, (2) existing firms have no incentive to exit (existing firms are not making losses), (3) new firms have no incentive to enter (existing firms are not making profits), and (4) existing firms produce at the minimum point on their long-run average cost curve.[5] This is the position shown in Figure 12-9. (Note that conditions 2 and 3 can be collapsed into

FIGURE 12-8 Short-Run Versus Long-Run Equilibrium of a Competitive Firm

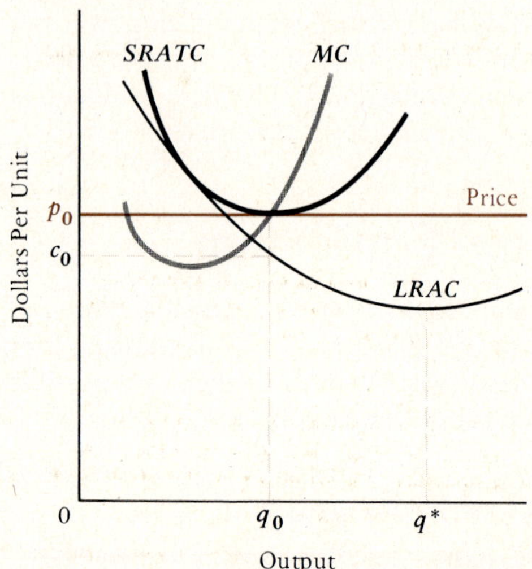

A competitive firm that is not at the minimum point on its *LRAC* curve cannot be in long-run equilibrium. A competitive firm with short-run cost curves *SRATC* and *MC* faces a market price of p_0. The firm produces q_0 where *MC* equals price and total costs are just being covered. However, the firm's long-run cost curve lies below its short-run curve at output q_0. The firm could produce output q_0 at cost c_0 by building a larger plant so as to take advantage of economies of scale. Profits would rise because average total costs of c_0 would then be less than price p_0. The firm cannot be in long-run equilibrium at any output below q^* because with any such output, average total costs can be reduced by building a larger plant. The output q^* is the *minimum efficient scale* of the firm.

[5] Since all costs are variable in the long run, there is no need to distinguish long-run average variable costs (*LRAVC*) from long-run average total cost (*LRATC*). They are identical, and we refer to them merely as long-run average costs (*LRAC*).

FIGURE 12-9 Equilibrium of a Firm When the Industry Is in Long-Run Equilibrium

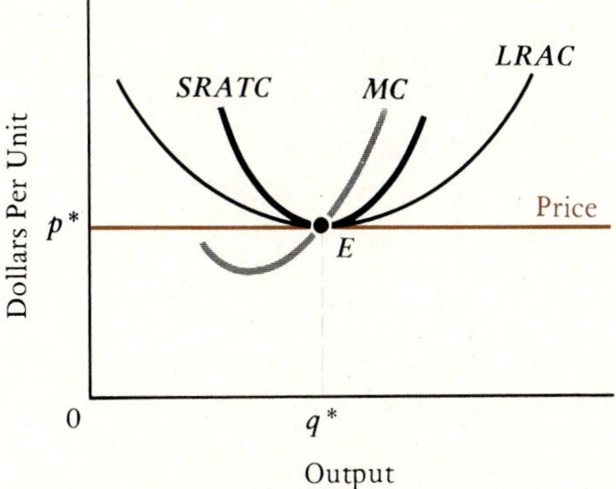

In long-run competitive equilibrium the firm is operating at the minimum point on its *LRAC* curve. In long-run equilibrium each firm must be (1) maximizing short-run profits, $MC = p$; (2) earning profits of zero on its existing plant, $SRATC = p$; and (3) unable to increase its profits by altering the size of plant. These three conditions can be met only when the firm is at E, the minimum point on its *LRAC* curve, with price p^* and output q^*.

the single condition that the total revenue of existing firms should exactly equal their total cost.)

The only way in which a price-taking firm can be in long-run equilibrium with respect to its size is by producing at the minimum point on its *LRAC* curve.

The level of output where *LRAC* is a minimum is thus known as the **minimum efficient scale (MES)** or *minimal optimal scale (MOS)* of the firm.

When all firms in the industry are producing at the minimum point of their long-run average cost curve and just covering costs (i.e., are in a position shown in Figure 12-9), the whole industry is in equilibrium. Because marginal cost equals price, no firm can improve its profits by varying its output in the short run. Because *LRAC* is above price at all possible outputs except the current one, where it is equal to the price, and because there are no profits to be earned above opportunity costs, there is no incentive for entry into the industry.

In long-run competitive equilibrium the firm's cost is the lowest attainable cost, given the limits of known technology and factor prices.

We can now use our long-run theory to understand two commonly encountered but often misunderstood real-world situations.

Changes in Technology

Consider an industry in long-run equilibrium. Since the industry is in equilibrium, each firm must be in zero-profit equilibrium. Now assume that some technological development lowers the cost curves of newly built plants. Since price is just equal to the average total cost for the old plants, new plants will now be able to earn profits, and more of them will now be built. But this expansion in capacity shifts the short-run supply curve to the right and drives price down.

The expansion in capacity and the fall in price will continue until price is equal to the short-run average total cost of the *new* plants. At this price old plants will not be covering their long-run costs. As long as price exceeds their average variable cost, however, such plants will continue in production. As the outmoded plants wear out, they will gradually disappear. Eventually a new long-run equilibrium will be established in which all plants use the new technology.

What happens in a competitive industry in which technological change occurs not as a single isolated event but more or less continuously? Plants built in any one year will tend to have lower costs than plants built in any previous year.[6] This common occurrence is illustrated in Figure 12-10 (p. 233).

Industries subject to continuous technological change have a number of interesting characteristics. One is that plants of different ages and different levels of efficiency exist side by side. This characteristic is

[6] This statement refers to real resource costs, which tend to fall due to technological change. Of course, in times of general inflation, *money* costs of plants may well be rising. In the comparisons made here, we are assuming that costs have been adjusted for changes in the general price level.

dramatically illustrated by the variety of vintages of steam turbine generators found in any long-established electricity utility. Critics who observe the continued use of older, less efficient plants and urge that "something be done to eliminate these wasteful practices" miss the point of economic efficiency.

If the plant is already there, the plant can be profitably operated as long as it can do anything more than cover its variable costs. As long as a plant can produce goods that are valued by consumers at an amount above the value of the resources currently used up for their production (variable costs), the value of society's total output is increased by using that plant to produce goods.

A second characteristic of a competitive industry subject to continuous technological change is that price is governed by the *minimum ATC of the most efficient plants.*[7] Entry will continue until plants of the latest vintage are just expected to earn normal profits over their lifetimes. The benefits of the new technology are passed on to consumers because all units of the commodity, whether produced by new or old plants, are sold at a price that is related solely to the *ATC* of the new plants. Owners of older plants find their returns over variable costs falling steadily as more and more efficient plants drive the price of the product down.

A third characteristic is that old plants are discarded (or "mothballed") when the price falls below their *AVC*. This may occur well before the plants are physically worn out. In industries with continuous technical progress, capital is usually discarded because it is *economically obsolete,* not because it has physically worn out. Old capital is obsolete when its average variable cost exceeds the average total cost of new capital.

Declining Industries

What happens when a competitive industry in long-run equilibrium begins to suffer losses due to a permanent and continuing decrease in the demand for its products? As demand declines, price falls and firms that were previously covering average total costs are no longer able to do so. They find themselves in the position shown in Figure 12-6(i). Firms suffer losses instead of breaking even, and the signal for exit of capital is given. But exit takes time.

The economically correct response to a steadily declining demand is not to replace old equipment and to continue to operate with existing equipment as long as variable costs of production can be covered. As equipment breaks down and is not repaired or replaced, the capacity of the industry will gradually shrink, slowly at first. If demand keeps declining, capacity must keep shrinking.

Declining industries typically present a sorry sight to the observer. Revenues are below long-run total costs, and as a result new equipment is not brought in to replace old equipment as it wears out. The average age of equipment in use thus rises steadily. The untrained observer, seeing the industry's plight, is likely to blame it on the old equipment.

The antiquated equipment in a declining industry is often the effect rather than the cause of the industry's decline.

It would not usually make sense for firms to modernize in the face of steadily falling demand even if new, improved equipment is available. To do so would increase the industry's capacity and its output, thereby making its overall plight still worse. Price would fall even more rapidly, adding further to the losses of existing firms.

Some of the issues involved in government support of declining industries are discussed in Box 12-1 (p. 234).

A striking example of the confusion of cause and effect in a declining industry occurred during the debate over the nationalization of the coal industry in Great Britain in the period between the two world wars. The view that public control was needed to save the industry from the dead hand of third-rate, unenterprising private owners was commonly held and was undoubtedly a factor leading to its nationalization in 1946. Sir Roy Harrod, a leading British economist from the 1920s to the 1960s, shocked

[7] Price will not necessarily equal minimum *ATC*. If firms anticipate the future changes, they will install new capital only when they expect to cover costs over the lifetime of the capital. This means that there must be sufficient profits in early years to match the losses in later years. Thus price will exceed average costs of the most efficient plants.

FIGURE 12-10 Plants of Different Vintages in an Industry with Continuing Technical Progress

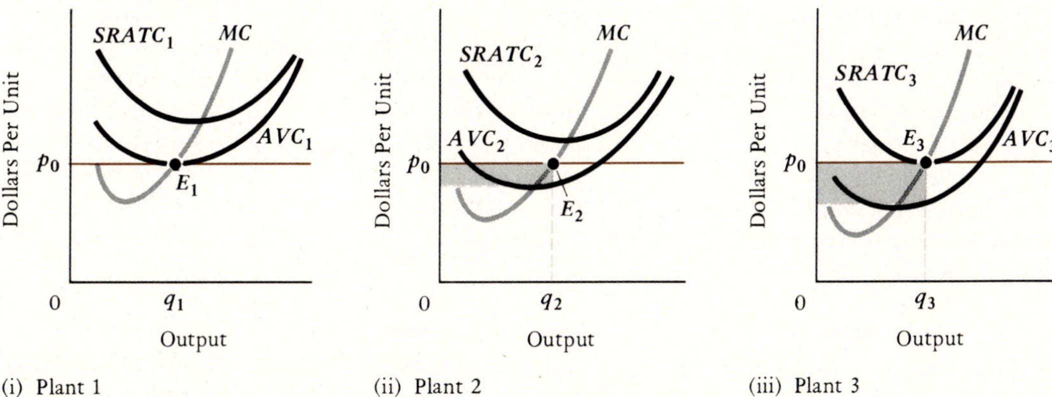

(i) Plant 1 (ii) Plant 2 (iii) Plant 3

Entry of progressively lower-cost firms forces price down, but older plants with higher costs remain in the industry as long as price covers average variable cost. Plant 3 is the newest plant with the lowest costs. Long-run equilibrium price will be determined by the average total costs of plants of this type since entry will continue as long as the owners of the newest plants expect to earn profits from them. Plant 1 is the oldest plant in operation. It is just covering its *AVC*, and if the price falls any further it will be closed down. Plant 2 is a plant of intermediate age. It is covering its variable costs and earning some contribution toward its fixed costs. In (ii) and (iii), the excess of revenues over variable costs is indicated by the shaded area.

many by taking the opposite view, arguing that the run-down state of the coal industry in some parts of England represented the correct response of the owners to the signals of the market.

> Economic efficiency does not consist in always introducing the most up-to-date equipment that an engineer can think of. . . . In not introducing new equipment, the managements may have been wise, not only from the point of view of their own interest, but from that of national interest, which requires the most profitable application of available capital. . . . It is right that as much should be extracted from the inferior mines as can be done by old-fashioned methods [i.e., with equipment already installed], and that they should gradually go out of action.[8]

[8] Roy Harrod, *The British Economy* (New York: McGraw-Hill, 1963), p. 54.

Harrod's general point is extremely important. Capital resources are scarce; to install new plant and equipment in a genuinely declining industry is to use scarce resources where they will not lead to the largest possible increases in the value of national output. It is in the public and the private interest that what appear to be antiquated methods be employed in declining industries.

The Appeal of Perfect Competition

The theory of perfect competition shows that profit-maximizing, price-taking firms, responding to prices set by the impersonal forces of supply and demand, will be motivated to provide all commodities for which total revenues are equal to or greater than total costs. They will be motivated to produce every unit for which price is greater than marginal cost, and they will thus expand production up to the point

BOX 12-1

Government Support of Threatened Firms

Troubled industrial giants pose serious concerns for policymakers. Whether it be Dome Petroleum, Massey Ferguson, or a large textile firm, the threatened bankruptcy of such a company often calls forth a government policy to support that company. Bankruptcy means that the firm has not been able to meet its financial obligations, and its creditors—both its suppliers and those who have lent it money—foreclose. In considering potential government support, it is useful to distinguish three different cases.

Firms That Can Cover Variable Costs

What is often forgotten is that real capital equipment does not crumble away just because a firm goes bankrupt. A company may get into financial difficulties for many reasons. It may have been mismanaged, or the demand for its product may have declined. It may be able to cover its variable costs but be unable to meet its debt obligations. As long as the real capital can cover its variable costs of operation, someone will find its operation profitable.

If such a firm goes bankrupt, its shareholders—and possibly also its creditors—will suffer the initial losses. The firm, however, will be reorganized. Its capital will continue to operate, and it will continue to employ workers. Some cutbacks and firings may be involved in making the firm once again viable. As long as it can earn anything above its variable costs, the firm's creditors can operate it and regain some of what the firm owes them.

When the government steps in to save such a firm from bankruptcy, it is common for policymakers to say they are doing this to save jobs. Often, however, the government is really saving the investments of the owners and creditors of the firm, not the jobs of the work force.

Firms That Cannot Cover Variable Costs

Sometimes firms that go bankrupt find they are no longer able to cover even their variable costs of production. They will then go out of business, and all their employees will lose their jobs.

As growth proceeds, the pattern of demands and costs shifts; some industries decline and others expand. So we can always expect to find declining industries, and in them firms that are closing their doors and creating unemployment. However, we can also expect to find expanding industries, and in them growing firms that are seeking to expand their employment.

When the government steps in and supports the declining industries, the consequences can be serious. The nation's scarce resources are wasted when they are used to produce goods that consumers value less than the cost of the variable inputs that make up those goods.

To prop up declining industries is to reduce the

where price equals marginal cost. The entry and exit of firms will, in long-run equilibrium, push prices to the level of minimum average total costs, that is, to the lowest level attainable for the given technology and factor prices.

Consider an economy in which every industry is perfectly competitive. For the nineteenth century liberal economists, such a world was more than a theoretical model; it was a most attractive ideal. One of them, Bascom, glowingly characterized such an economic system as "more provocative of virtue than virtue herself." The appeal of a competitive economy has both noneconomic and economic aspects. The noneconomic aspects are considered briefly below. The economic aspects are discussed in detail in Chapter 15.

In a perfectly competitive economy there are many firms and many households. Each is a price taker, responding as it sees fit, freely and without coercion, to signals sent to it by the market. For growth rate by preventing the factors of production—labor and capital—from moving to sectors that are growing. To attempt to freeze a particular industrial pattern in a changing world is to impose heavy and growing costs on the economy and in the end to attempt an impossible task.

Regional Policy

A common reason for supporting industries that are unable to stand on their own relates to regional policy. Industries are sometimes subsidized because policymakers believe that living standards in these areas would otherwise be too low. In effect this represents a transfer of income in the form of a subsidy from wealthier areas to poorer areas.

Insofar as the subsidy slows, or even stops, the adjustment process whereby old industries give way to new ones, the policy may in the long run be harmful to the very region it seeks to help. Insofar as the alternative is more or less permanent unemployment—because other rigidities have already prevented the adjustment process from working—the policy of subsidizing jobs may be preferred to the policy of subsidizing consumption through direct grants to households in need.

It is quite possible for a well-to-do major part of the country to subsidize a less well-to-do smaller part of the country (small in terms of population and resources)—as, for example, when central Canada subsidizes industries in the Atlantic Provinces. Whether or not this is efficient, the policy will not "break the bank." But if a major part of the country's industry, such as the industrial sector of Quebec and Ontario, were to be subsidized in the same way, the burden would quickly become intolerable.

Conclusion

Experience shows that propping up genuinely declining industries in the end succeeds not in saving them but only in delaying their demise—at large national costs. And when the government finally withdraws its support, the decline is much more abrupt and hence more difficult to adjust to than it would have been had the industry been allowed to decline gradually under the market force of steadily declining demand.

One can only hope that governments come to recognize the decay of certain industries and the collapse of certain firms as an inevitable part of growth. The appropriate response is to provide welfare and retraining schemes that cushion the blow of change, moderating the effects on the incomes of workers who lose their jobs and making it easier for them to transfer to expanding sectors of the economy. Intervention intended to increase mobility and reduce the social and personal costs of mobility is an appropriate long-run policy. Trying to freeze the existing structure by shoring up an inevitably declining industry is not.

someone who believes in the freedom of individuals to make decisions and who distrusts all power groups, the perfectly competitive model is almost too good to be true. No single firm has power over the market, nor has any single consumer. Individual consumers and producers are quantity adjusters who respond to market signals.

Yet the impersonal force of the market produces an appropriate response to all changes. If tastes change, for example, prices will change, and the allocation of resources will change in the appropriate direction. Throughout the entire process, no one will have any power over anyone else. Dozens of firms will react to the same price changes, and if one firm refuses to react, there will be countless other profit-maximizing firms eager to make the appropriate changes.

Because the perfectly competitive market mechanism works efficiently, it is not necessary for the government to intervene. There is no need for regulatory agencies or bureaucrats to make arbitrary decisions about who may produce what, how to produce it, or how much it is permissible to charge for the product. If there are no government officials to make such decisions, there will be no one to bribe to make one decision rather than another.

In the impersonal decision-making world of perfect competition, neither private firms nor public officials wield economic power. The market mechanism, like an invisible hand, determines the allocation of resources among competing uses.

It is a noble model: No one has power over anyone, yet the system behaves in a systematic and purposeful way. Many people regret that the model corresponds so imperfectly to economic reality as we know it today. Not surprisingly, some people still cling tenaciously to the belief that the perfectly competitive model describes the world in which we live; so many problems would disappear if only it did.

Summary

1. Market behavior is concerned with whether and how individual firms compete against one another; market structure is concerned with the type of market in which firms operate. Market structure affects the degree of power that individual firms have to influence such market variables as the price of the product. Under the market structure known as perfect competition, individual firms are price takers.
2. A profit-maximizing firm will produce at a level of output where (a) price is at least as great as average variable cost and (b) marginal cost equals marginal revenue.
3. The two critical assumptions of the theory of perfect competition are that firms are price takers and that the industry displays freedom of entry and exit. A firm that is a price taker will adjust to different market conditions by varying its output.
4. Under perfect competition each firm's short-run supply curve is identical in shape to its marginal cost curve above average variable cost. The perfectly competitive industry's short-run supply curve is the horizontal sum of its firms' supply curves (i.e., the horizontal sum of the firms' marginal cost curves).
5. If any profit-maximizing firm is to produce at all, it must be able to cover its variable cost. But such a firm may be making losses (price less than average total cost), making profits (price greater than average total cost), or just breaking even (price equal to average total cost).
6. In the long run, profits or losses will lead to the entry or exit of capital from the industry. Entry or exit will push a competitive industry to a long-run zero-profit equilibrium and move production to the level where market price equals minimum average total cost.
7. The long-run response of a growing, perfectly competitive industry to steadily changing technology is the gradual replacement of less efficient plants and machines by more efficient ones. Older plant and equipment will be used as long as price exceeds average variable cost; only when average variable costs rise above price will they be discarded and replaced by more modern ones. The long-run response

of a declining industry will be to continue to satisfy demand from its existing machinery as long as price exceeds *AVC*. Despite the appearance of being antiquated, this is an efficient response to steadily falling demand.

The great appeal of perfect competition as a means of organizing production lies in the decentralized decision making of myriad firms and households. No individual exercises power over the market. At the same time it is not necessary for the government to intervene to determine resource allocation and prices.

Topics for Review

Competitive behavior and competitive market structure
Behavioral rules for the profit-maximizing firm
Price taking and a horizontal demand curve
Average revenue, marginal revenue, and price under perfect competition
Relation of the industry supply curve to firms' marginal cost curves
Entry and exit in achieving equilibrium
Short-run and long-run equilibrium of firms and industries

Discussion Questions

1. A number of agricultural products, such as milk, eggs, and chickens, were once produced in Canada under conditions coming close to perfect competition. What were the main features of these industries that made them perfectly competitive? Use the theory you have learned in this chapter to predict the consequences of the introduction of provincial marketing boards that attempted to raise farmers' incomes by restricting total output through a system of quotas.
2. Consider the suppliers of the following commodities. What elements of market structure might you invoke to account for differences in their market behavior? Could any of these be characterized as perfectly competitive industries?
   a. Television broadcasting
   b. Automobiles
   c. Sand and gravel
   d. Insurance services
   e. Mortgage loans
   f. Retail fruits and vegetables
   g. Copper
3. Which of the following observed facts about an industry are inconsistent with its being a perfectly competitive industry?
   a. Different firms use different methods of production.
   b. There is extensive advertising of the industry's product by a trade association.
   c. Individual firms devote 5 percent of sales receipts to advertising their own product brand.
   d. There are 24 firms in the industry.
   e. The largest firm in the industry makes 40 percent of the sales and

the next largest firm makes 20 percent, but the products are identical and there are 61 other firms.
f. All firms made large profits in 1980.

4. In which of the following sectors of the Canadian economy might you expect to find competitive behavior? In which might you expect to find industries that are classified as operating under perfectly competitive market structures?
   a. Manufacturing
   b. Agriculture
   c. Transportation and public utilities
   d. Wholesale and retail trade
   e. Illegal drugs
5. In the 1930s the U.S. coal industry was characterized by easy entry and price taking. Because of large fixed costs in mine shafts and fixed equipment, however, exit was slow. With declining demand, many firms were barely covering their variable costs, but not their total costs. As a result of a series of mine accidents, the federal government began to enforce mine safety standards, which forced most firms to invest in new capital if they were to remain in production. What predictions would competitive theory make about market behavior and the quantity of coal produced? Would coal miners approve or disapprove of the new enforcement program?
6. Suppose that entry into an industry is not artificially restricted but takes time because of the need to build plants, acquire know-how, and establish a marketing organization. Can such an industry be characterized as perfectly competitive? Does ease of entry imply ease of exit, and vice versa?
7. What, if anything, does each one of the following tell you about ease of entry or exit in an industry?
   a. Profits have been very high for two decades.
   b. No new firms have entered the industry for 20 years.
   c. The average age of the firms in a 40-year-old industry is less than 7 years.
   d. Most existing firms are using obsolete equipment alongside newer, more modern equipment.
   e. Profits are low or negative; many firms are still producing, but from steadily aging equipment.
8. In the 1970s prices obtained for Canadian wheat rose substantially relative to other agricultural products. Explain how each of the following may have contributed to this result.
   a. Crop failures caused by unusually bad weather around the world in several years
   b. Rising demand for beef and chickens because of rising population and rising per capita income
   c. Great scarcities in fishmeal, a substitute for grain in animal diets, because of a mysterious decline in the anchovy harvest off Peru
   d. Increased Soviet purchases of grain on the world market
9. In the late 1980s the prices obtained for Canadian wheat fell dramatically. Explain how each of the following may have contributed to the result.

a. The green revolution has made more and more countries self-sufficient in food.
b. Reforms in Russian agricultural production led to bumper harvests in the late 1980s.
c. Agricultural subsidies in the European Community (EC) have turned it from a net importer to a net exporter of agricultural produce.

13

Monopolistic Markets

Is Québec Hydro a monopoly? How about IBM, Stelco, the National Hockey League, or the Coca-Cola Company? The word *monopoly* comes from the Greek words *monos polein*, which mean "alone to sell." Economists say that a **monopoly** occurs when the output of an entire industry is controlled by a single seller. This seller is called a *monopolist* or a monopoly firm.

Because the monopoly firm is the only producer of a particular product, its demand curve is identical to the market demand curve for that product. The market demand curve, which shows the aggregate quantity that buyers will purchase at every price, also shows the quantity that the monopolist will be able to sell at any price it sets. The importance of this is that the monopoly, unlike the firm in perfect competition, faces a downward-sloping demand curve. The monopolist therefore faces a trade-off between price and quantity: Sales can be increased only if price is reduced, while price can be increased only if sales are reduced.

Through most of this chapter we look at the price and output decisions of pure monopolists. In the final section, however, we look at data for the Canadian economy and discover that we need theories for cases between the two extremes of perfect competition and complete monopoly.

A Single-Price Monopolist

At the outset we confine ourselves to a monopolist that charges a single price for all units of the product that are sold.

Monopoly Revenue

Given the market demand curve, the firm's average revenue and marginal revenue curves can be readily deduced. When the monopoly seller charges a single price for all units sold, average revenue per unit is identical with price. Thus the market demand curve is also the firm's average revenue curve. But marginal revenue is less than price because the firm has to lower the price it charges on *all* units in order to sell a single *extra* unit. **[26]** This is an important difference from the case of perfect competition; it is explored numerically in Table 13-1 and graphically in Figure 13-1.

The top part of Figure 13-2 (p. 242) illustrates the average and

TABLE 13-1 Relation of Average Revenue and Marginal Revenue: A Numerical Illustration

Price $p = AR$	Quantity q	$TR = p \times q$	$MR = \Delta TR/\Delta q$
$9.10	9	$81.90	
			$8.10
9.00	10	90.00	
			7.90
8.90	11	97.90	

Marginal revenue is less than price because price must be lowered to sell an extra unit. A monopolist can choose either the price or the quantity to be sold. But choosing one determines the other. In this example, to increase sales from 10 to 11 units, it is necessary to reduce the price on all units sold from $9.00 to $8.90. The extra unit sold brings in $8.90, but the firm sacrifices $.10 on each of the 10 units that it could have sold at $9.00 had it not wanted to increase sales. The net addition to revenue is the $8.90 minus $.10 times 10 units, or $1.00, making $7.90 altogether. Thus the marginal revenue resulting from the increase in sales by 1 unit is $7.90, which is less than the price at which the units are sold.

Marginal revenue is shown displaced by half a line to emphasize that it represents the effect on revenue of the *change* in output.

FIGURE 13-1 Effect on Revenue of an Increase in Quantity Sold

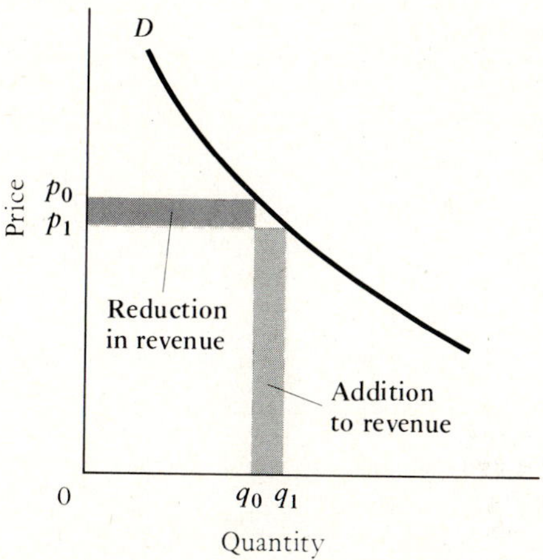

For a downward-sloping demand curve, marginal revenue is less than price. A reduction of price from p_0 to p_1 increases sales from q_0 to q_1 units. The revenue from the extra amount sold is shown as the lighter shaded area. But to sell this extra amount, it is necessary to reduce the price on all of the q_0 units previously sold. The loss in revenue is shown as the darker shaded area. Marginal revenue of the extra amount is equal to the *difference* between the two areas.

marginal revenue curves for a monopolist, based on a downward-sloping straight-line demand curve.[1] In Chapter 5 we discussed the relation between elasticity of demand and total revenue. Figure 13-2 summarizes this earlier discussion and extends it to cover marginal revenue. When the demand curve is elastic, total revenue rises as quantity rises; marginal revenue must therefore be positive. When the demand curve is inelastic, total revenue falls as quantity rises; marginal revenue must therefore be negative.

Short-Run Monopoly Equilibrium

To describe the profit-maximizing position of a monopolist, we need only bring together information about the monopolist's revenues and its costs and apply the rules developed in Chapter 12 (page 222). The key difference between firms in these two types of market structure lies in the demand conditions.[2] The firm that sells in a perfectly competitive market is faced with a perfectly elastic demand curve. This not only sets its price but also implies that price equals marginal revenue. The firm that sells in a monopolized market faces a downward-sloping de-

[1] It is helpful for sketching these curves to remember that if the demand curve is a downward-sloping straight line, the *MR* curve also slopes downward and is twice as steep. Its price intercept (where $q = 0$) is the same as that of the demand curve, and it cuts the quantity axis (where $p = 0$) at just half the output that the demand curve does. **[27]**

Although the *MR* curve is always negatively sloped when the demand curve is linear, it can be positively sloped over part of its range when the demand curve is nonlinear. This possibility affects nothing that we do here, and we therefore leave it to be considered in more advanced courses.

[2] A monopoly firm is subject to the law of diminishing returns in just the same way as a firm that operates in a perfectly competitive market. Thus the monopoly firm will have the same type of U-shaped cost curve as a competitive firm.

FIGURE 13-2 Relation of Total, Average, and Marginal Revenue to Elasticity of Demand

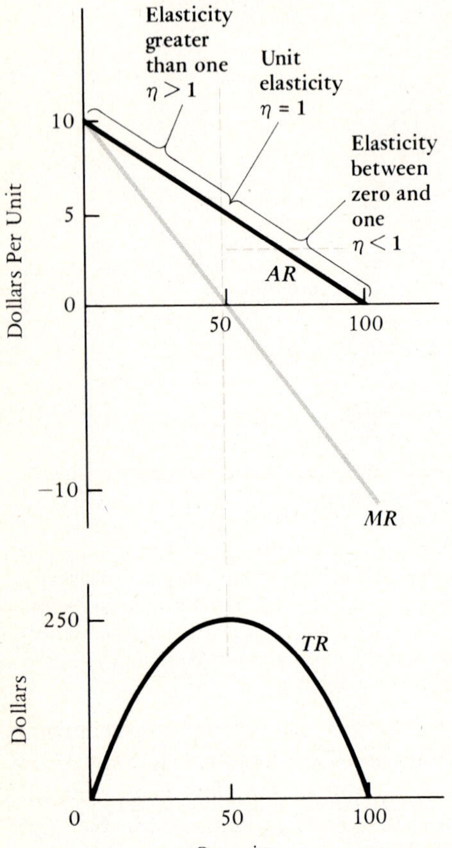

For a monopolist *MR* is always less than price; when *TR* is rising, *MR* is greater than zero and elasticity is greater than one. The monopoly firm's demand curve is its *AR* curve; the *MR* curve is below and steeper than the *AR* curve because the demand curve has a negative slope.

In the example shown, for outputs from 0 to 50, marginal revenue is positive, elasticity is greater than one, and total revenue is rising. For outputs from 50 to 100, marginal revenue is negative, elasticity is less than one, and total revenue is falling.

mand curve. Hence its actions influence its price. This causes the firm's marginal revenue to differ from price; as we have seen, marginal revenue is less than price. Thus when the monopoly firm follows the profit-maximizing rule of equating marginal revenue to marginal cost, it reaches the equilibrium shown in Figure 13-3, where marginal cost is less than price.

The monopoly firm produces where marginal revenue equals marginal cost. The price corresponding to that output is given by the demand curve.

Note one key respect in which the equilibrium of a monopoly differs from that of a firm in perfect competition. While a competitive firm produces at an output where $p = MC$, the monopoly firm produces at an output where p is greater than MC. We shall discuss some implications of this later.

Our earlier discussion of the relation between elasticity and revenue has one interesting implication for the monopoly equilibrium that we have just developed. Since marginal cost is always greater than zero, the profit-maximizing monopoly (which produces where $MR = MC$) will produce where marginal revenue is positive, that is, where demand is elastic. If the firm were producing where demand were inelastic, it could both increase its revenue and reduce its costs by reducing its sales.

A profit-maximizing monopoly will never push its sales of a commodity into the range over which the demand curve becomes inelastic.

Monopoly profits. The fact that a profit-maximizing monopoly produces at an output where $MR = MC$ says nothing about how large profits will be in the short run or even whether there will be monopoly profits. Profits may exist, as shown in Figure 13-3(i), and indeed they may persist for a long time because as long as the firm retains its monopoly, entry of new firms does not push price down to the level of average total cost.

But as Figure 13-3(ii) shows, the profit-maximizing monopolist might just be able to cover costs or

FIGURE 13-3 Profit-maximizing Position of a Monopolist

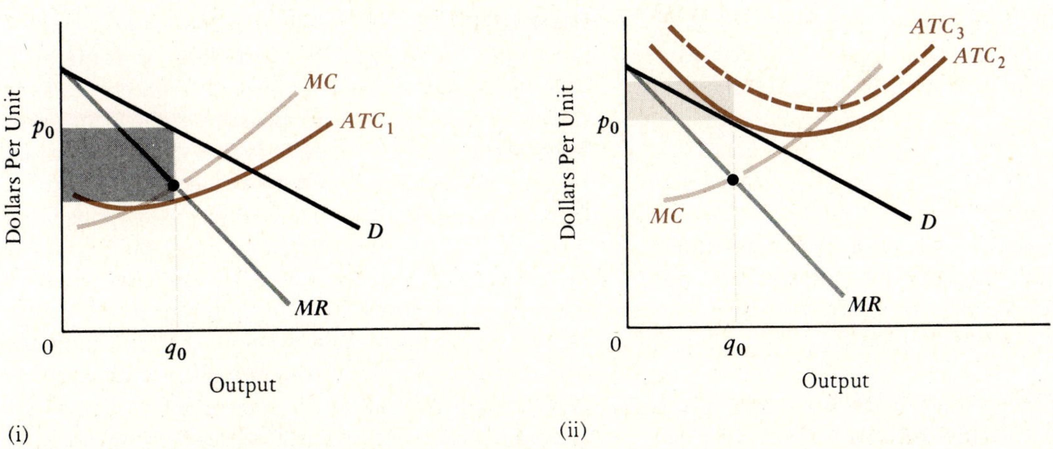

Profit-maximizing output is q_0, where $MR = MC$; price is p_0, which is above MC at that output. The rules for profit maximization require $MR = MC$ and $p > AVC$. (AVC is not shown in the diagram, but it must be below ATC.)

Whether or not there are profits depends on the position of the ATC curve. In part (i), where average total cost is ATC_1, there are profits, as shown by the gray shaded area. In part (ii), where average total cost is ATC_2, profits are zero. If average total costs rose to ATC_3, the monopolist would suffer losses, as shown by the color shaded area.

it might even suffer losses. Nothing guarantees that a monopolist will make profits, and if it cannot eliminate its losses, the firm will eventually fail.

The supply curve under monopoly. In describing the monopolist's profit-maximizing behavior, we did not introduce the concept of a supply curve, as we did in the discussion of perfect competition. A supply curve relates the quantity supplied to the price offered. In perfect competition the industry short-run supply curve is known as soon as the marginal cost curves of the individual firms are known. This is because under perfect competition profit-maximizing firms equate marginal cost to price. Given marginal costs, it is possible to know how much will be produced at each price.

This is not the case, however, with monopoly.

In monopoly there is no unique relation between market price and quantity supplied.

Let us see why this is so. Like all profit-maximizing firms, a monopoly equates marginal cost with marginal revenue; but unlike firms in perfect competition, for the monopolist marginal revenue does not equal price. Because the monopolist does *not* equate marginal cost to price, it is possible for demand curves of different shapes to give rise to the same output but to differing prices. If the same output can be associated with different prices, there is no unique relation between price and output that is required for a supply curve.

Long-Run Equilibrium of the Firm and Industry

When a monopolist is the only producer in an industry, there is no need for separate theories of the firm and the industry, as is necessary with perfect competition. The monopolist *is* the industry. Thus the profit-maximizing position of the firm shown in

Figure 13-3 is the short-run equilibrium of the industry.

In a monopolized industry, as in a perfectly competitive one, profits provide an incentive for new firms to enter. If such entry occurs, the equilibrium position will change, and the firm will no longer be a monopolist.

Entry Barriers

A monopoly will persist only if entry of new firms does not occur. Impediments that prevent entry are called **entry barriers**; they may be either natural or created.

If a monopoly is to persist in the long run, there must be barriers to entry of other firms into the industry.

Natural barriers. Natural barriers commonly arise as a result of economies of scale. If the long-run average cost declines over a large range of output, big firms will have significantly lower average total costs than small firms.

Recall from Chapter 12 that the *minimum efficient scale* (*MES*) is the smallest size of firm that can reap all of the economies of large-scale production. It occurs at the level of output where the firm's long-run average total cost curve reaches a minimum.

Now suppose the technology of an industry is such that the typical firm's minimum efficient scale is 10,000 units a week at an average total cost of $10 per unit. Further assume that at a price of $10, the total quantity demanded is 11,000 units per week. In these circumstances there is room for only one firm operating at or near its minimum efficient scale.

A natural monopoly results when, as in the example just given, the industry's demand conditions are such that only one firm can operate at the minimum efficient scale. In these circumstances, if a second firm tried to enter the industry, it could not achieve sales large enough to obtain costs that were competitive with the existing firm.

Another type of natural barrier is *set-up cost*. If a firm could be catapulted full-grown into the market, it might be able to compete effectively with the existing firm. But the cost to the new firm of entering the market, developing its products, and establishing such things as its brand image and its dealer network may be such that entry is rendered unprofitable.

Created barriers. Barriers to entry may be created by the conscious action of participants in some markets. Some are created by the government and are therefore condoned by it. Patent laws, for instance, may prevent entry by conferring on the patent holder the sole right to produce a particular commodity. A firm may also be granted a charter or a franchise that prohibits competition by law.

Other barriers are created by the existing firm itself. We shall study these in more detail in Chapter 14, but in the meantime we note that anything the existing firm can do to increase the set-up costs of new entrants will act as a barrier to entry. Of course, activities such as the threats of force, sabotage, or a price war can also deter entry, if the existing firm can make such threats credible. (The most transparent entry barriers are seen in the field of organized crime, where legal prohibitions do not prevent the use of a whole battery of crude but potent barriers to new entrants.)

Significance of entry barriers. If there are no entry barriers, a firm would enter an industry whenever it judged the market sufficient to support at least one more firm. Thus in perfect competition, where there are no entry barriers, profits cannot persist in the long run. Entry will continue until profits are no longer being earned.

Profits may persist in monopoly even in the long run, but only if there are natural or created barriers to the entry of new firms. Otherwise the existence of monopoly profits will attract new firms until the profits of the original firm are eliminated. This process will of course eliminate the monopoly situation.

This analysis of profits and entry provides a basic insight into a two-edged driving force of the market economy:

Entry always erodes profits, and profits always attract entry.

Cartels As Monopolies

So far in this chapter we have talked about monopoly as a situation in which one firm is the single seller in an industry. A second way in which a monopoly can arise is for the firms in an industry to agree to cooperate with one another, to behave *as if* they were a single firm, and thus to eliminate competitive behavior among themselves. Such a group of firms is called a **cartel.** A cartel that includes *all* the firms in the industry can behave in just the same way as would a single-firm monopoly that owned all these firms. The firms can agree among themselves to restrict their total output to the level that maximizes their joint profits.

When firms agree to cooperate in order to restrict output and raise profits, their behavior is called **collusion.** Collusive behavior may occur with or without an actual agreement to collude. Where explicit agreement occurs and a cartel is formed, economists speak of *overt* or *covert collusion,* depending on whether the agreement is open or secret. Where no agreement actually occurs, economists speak of **tacit collusion** (while lawyers speak of *conscious parallel action*). In this case all firms behave as if they were a single monopolist without an explicit agreement to do so. They merely understand that it is in their mutual interest to restrict output and not to cheat by trying to increase their sales and so drive prices downward.

Effects of Cartelization

To study the incentive to form a cartel, we will consider markets free from any form of government regulation and control. These circumstances lead to one basic result:

It is always possible for the firms in perfectly competitive equilibrium to increase their profits through an output-restricting agreement.

The reason is that the equilibrium of a perfectly competitive industry is *invariably* one in which a restriction of output, and a consequent increase in price, would raise the profits of all producers. At any competitive equilibrium each firm is producing where marginal cost equals price. (See, for example, Figure 12-3.) But as we have seen, marginal revenue for the industry is less than price and therefore also less than marginal cost. Thus in competitive equilibrium the last unit sold necessarily contributes less to the industry's revenue than to its costs. Clearly, restricting the industry's output must raise the industry's profits. The effect of cartelizing a perfectly competitive industry is shown in more detail in Figure 13-4.

Problems of Cartel Enforcement

Consider a cartel that includes all the firms in a formerly competitive industry. Since before the cartel

FIGURE 13-4 Effect of Cartelizing an Industry in Perfectly Competitive Equilibrium

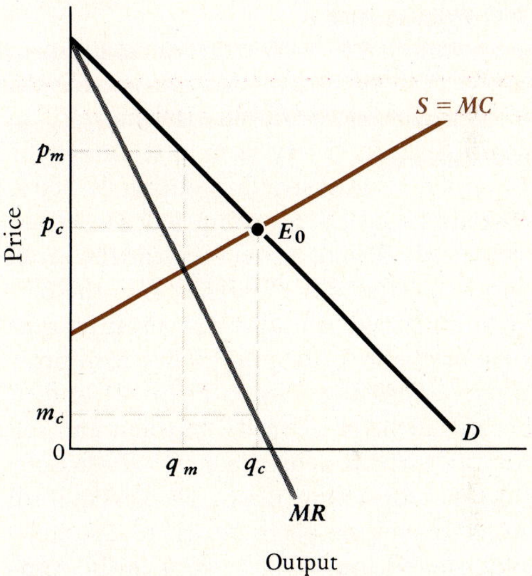

Cartelization of a perfectly competitive industry can always increase that industry's profits. Equilibrium for a perfectly competitive industry occurs at E_0, where the supply and demand curves intersect. Equilibrium price and output are at p_c and q_c. Because the industry demand curve slopes downward, marginal revenue is necessarily less than price. In the diagram, marginal revenue is m_c at the competitive equilibrium output of q_c.

If the industry is cartelized, profits can be increased by reducing output. All units between q_m and q_c add less to revenue than to cost—the marginal revenue curve lies below the marginal cost curve. (Recall from Figure 12-5 that the industry's supply curve is the sum of the marginal cost curves of the firms in the industry.) If the units between q_m and q_c are not produced, output is reduced to q_m and price rises to p_m. This price-output combination maximizes the industry's profits because it is where marginal revenue equals marginal cost.

was formed the members were separate firms in the one industry, we infer that the industry contains no overriding natural entry barriers. Thus the cartel, just like a single-firm monopoly in an industry with weak natural entry barriers, must create and maintain barriers to prevent the entry of new firms attracted by the profits that cartelization makes possible.

In addition, cartels have some special problems of their own. One key problem is how to secure cartel membership by all the firms in the industry so as to establish what is, in effect, monopoly behavior. A second problem is how to prevent the cartel's members from cheating by departing from their joint agreement to restrict output.

Self-interest motivates individual firms to remain outside the cartel or to cheat if they are inside the cartel, but their joint interest provides them with an incentive to cooperate. Every firm that enters the cartel and cooperates in restricting output is better off than it would be if all firms competed. However, if firm X is the only firm to remain outside the cartel or if it is inside but the only cheater, it is in the best of all possible situations. All other firms restrict output and drive up the industry price. They earn profits, but only by restricting output. Firm X can then reap the benefit of the other firms' restraint and sell all that it wishes at the price that is set by the actions of all the other cooperating firms. However, if all firms cheat, price will be pushed back to the competitive level, and all firms will be back in the zero-profit position.

Cartels tend to be unstable because of the incentives for individual firms to violate the output quotas that are needed to enforce the monopoly price.

The conflict between cooperation and independent action is analyzed in more detail in Figure 13-5.

Cartels and similar output-restricting arrangements have a long history. For example, schemes to raise farm incomes by limiting crops through cooperative action bear ample testimony to the accuracy of the predicted instability of cartels. Crop restriction agreements often break down and prices fall as individuals exceed their quotas. The great bitterness and occasional violence that are sometimes exhibited against cheaters by members of crop restriction plans are readily understandable. This instability is why crop restriction schemes that are successful in the long run are usually those that are run by the state, such as provincial marketing boards in Canada. The state has the coercive power to force monopoly behavior on producers where private cooperatives can only rely on voluntary cooperation.

In Chapter 15 we shall study the behavior of one of the classic cartels of modern times, the Organization of Petroleum Exporting Countries (OPEC).

A Multiprice Monopolist: Price Discrimination

So far in this chapter we have assumed that the monopoly firm charges the same price for every unit of product no matter to whom or where it sells. But other situations are common. Raw milk is often sold at one price when it is to go into fluid milk but at a lower price when it is to be used to make ice cream or cheese. Lawyers sometimes charge for their services according to the incomes of their clients. Movie theaters may have lower admission prices for children and senior citizens than for adults. Railroads charge different rates per ton-mile for different products. Utilities sell electricity at lower rates for industrial than for home use. Many Canadian universities charge foreign students higher tuition than residents. The Canadian Wheat Board sells wheat more cheaply to foreign consumers than to Canadians.

Price discrimination occurs when a producer sells different units of a specific commodity to buyers at two or more different prices for reasons not associated with differences in cost. Not all price *differences* represent price *discrimination*. Quantity discounts, differences between wholesale and retail prices, and prices that vary with the time of day or the season of the year may not indicate price discrimination because the same physical product sold at a different time or place or in different quantities may have different costs. If an electricity utility has un-

FIGURE 13-5 Conflicting Forces Affecting Cartels

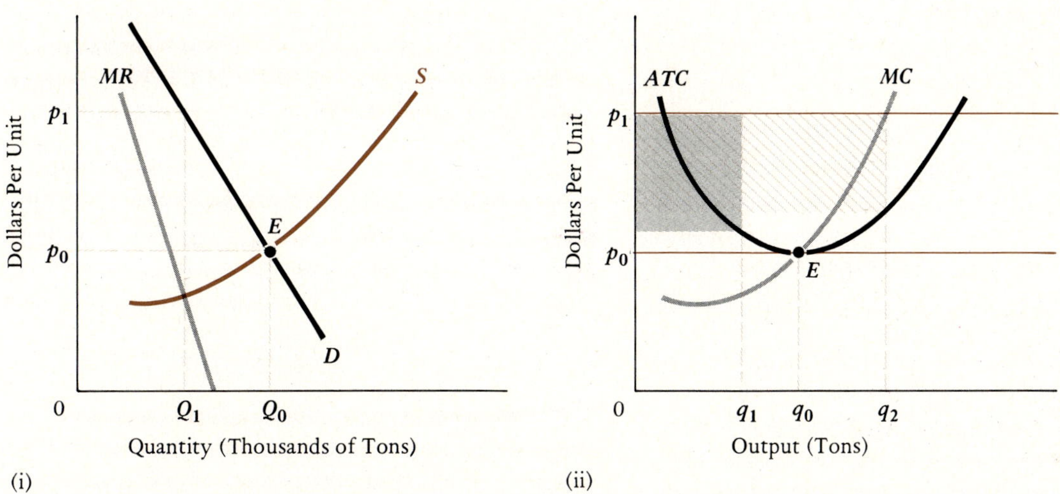

Cooperation leads to the monopoly price, but individual self-interest may lead to production in excess of the monopoly output. Market conditions are shown in part (i) and the situation of a typical firm in part (ii). (Note the change of scale between the two graphs.) Initially, the market is in competitive equilibrium with price p_0 and quantity Q_0. The individual firm is producing output q_0 and is just covering its total costs.

The cartel is formed and then enforces quotas on individual firms sufficient to reduce the industry's output to Q_1, the output where the supply curve cuts the marginal revenue curve. Q_1 is thus the output that maximizes the joint profits of the cartel members. Price rises to p_1 as a result. The typical firm's quota is q_1. The firm's profits rise from zero to the amount shown by the gray shaded area. Once price is raised to p_1, however, the individual firm would like to increase output to q_2, where marginal cost is equal to the price set by the cartel. This would allow the firm to earn profits shown by the diagonally striped area. But if all firms increase their outputs above their quotas, industry output will increase beyond Q_1, and the profits earned by all firms will fall.

used capacity at certain times of day, it may charge a lower price for electricity consumed during those hours than at peak demand hours. If the price differences reflect cost differences, they are nondiscriminatory.

However, when price differences depend on different buyers' valuations of the same product, they are discriminatory. It does not cost a movie theater operator or Air Canada less to fill a seat with a child than an adult, but each may charge children less nonetheless.

Why should a firm want to sell some units of output at a price well below the price it gets for other units? In other words, why is price discrimination profitable?

Why Price Discrimination Pays

Persistent price discrimination comes about either because different buyers are willing to pay different amounts for the same commodity or because one buyer is willing to pay different amounts for different units of the same commodity. The basic point about price discrimination is that in either of these circumstances sellers may be able to capture some of the consumers' surplus that would otherwise go to buyers. (Review the discussion of consumers' surplus on pages 160–162.)

Discrimination among units. Look back to Table 8-2 on page 162, which shows the consumers' surplus received by one consumer if she bought eight glasses of milk at a single price. If the firm could sell her each glass separately, it could capture this consumers' surplus. It would sell the first unit for $3.00, the second for $1.50, the third for $1.00, and so on until the eighth was sold for $.30. The firm would get total revenues of $8.10 rather than the $2.40 received by selling at the single price. In this example, the firm has been able to discriminate perfectly and extract every bit of the consumers' surplus.

Of course, such perfect price discrimination may not be possible. But suppose the firm could charge two different prices, one for the first four units sold and one for the next four sold. If it sold the first four for $.80 and the next four for $.30, it would receive $4.40—less than if it could discriminate perfectly, but more than it would receive from the sale of all units at any single price.

Discrimination among buyers. Think of the demand curve in a market containing individual buyers, each of whom has indicated the maximum price he or she is prepared to pay for a single unit. Suppose for simplicity that there are only four buyers, the first of whom is prepared to pay any price up to $4, the second $3, the third $2, and the fourth $1. Suppose the product has a marginal cost of production of $1 per unit for all units. If the seller is limited to a single price, it will maximize its profits by charging $3, sell two units, and earn profits of $4. If the seller can discriminate between units, it could charge the first buyer $4 and the second $3, thus increasing profits from the first two units to $5. Moreover, it could also sell the third unit for $2 and the fourth unit for $1. Its profits would increase to $6.

Price discrimination more generally. Demand curves have negative slopes because the same individual values different units differently and because different individuals value the same unit (e.g., the first unit each consumes) differently. The downward slope of the demand curve, combined with a single price, gives rise to consumers' surplus.

The ability to charge multiple prices gives a seller the opportunity to capture some of the consumers' surplus.

In general, the more prices that can be charged, the greater the seller's ability to increase its revenue at the expense of consumers. This is illustrated in Figure 13-6.

It follows, for any given output, that if a seller is able to discriminate by price, it can increase revenues received (and thus also profits) from the sale of those units. **[28]** But price discrimination is not always possible, even if there are no legal barriers to its use.

When Is Price Discrimination Possible?

Discrimination among units of output sold to the same buyer requires that the seller be able to keep track of the units a buyer consumes in each period. Thus the tenth unit purchased by a given buyer in a given month can be sold at a different price from the fifth unit *only* if the seller can keep track of who buys what. This can be done by the electricity utility through its meter readings or by the magazine publishers' distinguishing between renewals and new subscriptions. It can also be done by an establishment's giving a certificate or coupon providing, for example, a reduced-price car wash for a return visit.

Discrimination among buyers is possible only if the goods cannot be resold by the buyer who faces the low price to the buyer who faces the high price. However much the local butcher might like to charge the banker's wife twice as much for hamburger as he charges the taxi driver, he cannot succeed in doing so. Madame Banker can always shop for meat in the supermarket, where her husband's occupation is not known. Even if the butcher and the supermarket agreed to charge her twice as much, she could hire the taxi driver to shop for her. The surgeon in private practice, however, may succeed in discriminating (if all reputable surgeons will do the same) because it will not do the banker's wife much good to hire the taxi driver to have her operations for her.

Price discrimination is possible if the seller can either distinguish individual units bought by a single buyer or separate buyers into classes such that resale among classes is impossible.

FIGURE 13-6 Price Discrimination

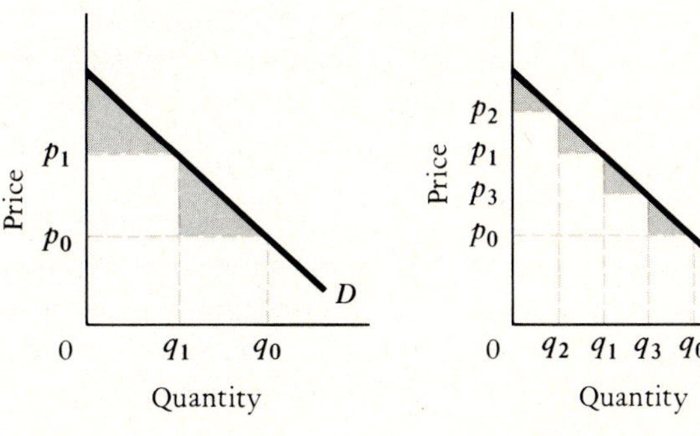

(i) Two prices charged

(ii) Four prices charged

Multiple prices permit a seller to capture consumers' surplus. Suppose in either graph that if a single price were charged, it would be the price p_0. Quantity q_0 would be sold, and consumers' surplus would be the entire area above p_0 and below the demand curve. In part (i) two prices are charged: p_1 for the first q_1 units and p_0 for the remaining units. Consumers' surplus is reduced to the two shaded areas, and the seller's revenue is increased accordingly. In part (ii) four prices are charged: p_2 for the first q_2 units, p_1 for the units between q_2 and q_1, and so on. Consumers' surplus is further reduced to the shaded areas, and the seller's revenue is increased accordingly. At the extreme, if a different price could be charged for each unit, producers could extract every bit of the consumers' surplus, and the price discrimination would be perfect.

Ability to prevent resale tends to be associated with the character of the product or the ability to classify buyers into readily identifiable groups. Services are less easily resold than goods; goods that require installation by the manufacturer (e.g., heavy equipment) are less easily resold than movable goods such as household appliances. An interesting example of nonresalability occurs in the case of plate glass. Small pieces are much cheaper per square foot than bigger pieces, but the person who needs glass for a 6′ × 10′ picture window cannot use four pieces of 3′ × 5′ glass. Transportation costs, tariff barriers, and import quotas separate classes of buyers geographically and may make discrimination possible.

It is, of course, not enough to be able to separate buyers or units into separate classes. The seller must be able to control the supply to each group. This is what makes price discrimination an aspect of the theory of monopoly.[3] For readers who wish to study it in more detail, price discrimination is analyzed graphically in Box 13-1.

For example, the Canadian Wheat Board sells wheat on foreign markets at the world price—as it must if it is to sell any at all. It sells on the Canadian market at a higher price, thus allowing Canadian farmers to make some monopoly profits at the expense of Canadian consumers. This price discrimination is made possible by Canadian government restrictions on importing foreign wheat, which could otherwise be bought at the world price and sold for a profit at the higher Canadian price.

Positive Aspects of Price Discrimination

The positive consequences of price discrimination are summarized in two propositions.

1. **For any given level of output, there will always be some system of discriminatory prices that will provide higher total revenue to the firm than the profit-maximizing single price.**

This proposition was illustrated in Figure 13-5. All it requires is a downward-sloping demand curve.

[3] For price discrimination to be profitable, the different groups must have different degrees of willingness to pay. The hypothesis of diminishing marginal utility would lead to the prediction that different valuations are placed by an individual on different units, and differences in income and tastes would lead to the prediction that different subgroups will have different elasticities of demand for a given commodity. Thus the potential for profitable price discrimination is usually present.

BOX 13-1

A Graphic Analysis of Price Discrimination

A monopolist who can discriminate between markets will allocate output between them so that marginal revenues in each will be equal. Total output will be such that marginal cost equals overall marginal revenue.

Consider a monopoly firm that sells a single product in two distinct markets, A and B. Customers in one market cannot buy in the other because the two markets are completely insulated from each other. The demand and marginal revenue curves for each market are shown in parts (i) and (ii) of the figure.

Allocation of a Given Total Output

How will a profit-maximizing monopolist behave in each market? To begin, imagine the firm deciding how best to allocate *any* given output, q^*, between the two markets. Because output is fixed (arbitrarily

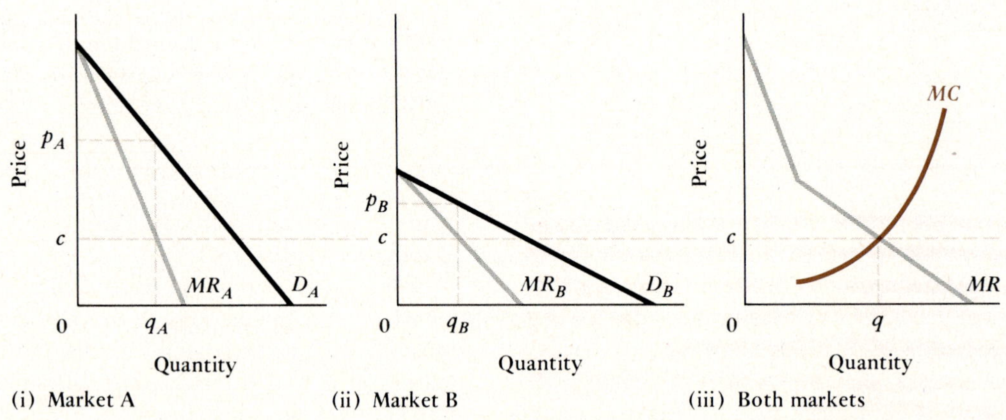

(i) Market A (ii) Market B (iii) Both markets

To see that this is reasonable, remember that a monopolist with the power to discriminate *could* produce exactly the same quantity as a single-price monopolist and charge everyone the same price. Therefore, it need never get *less* revenue, and it can do better if it can raise the price on even one unit sold.

2. **Output under price discrimination will generally be larger than under single-price monopoly.**

Remember that a monopoly firm that must charge a single price produces less than the perfectly competitive industry because producing and selling more would drive down the price against itself. Price discrimination allows it to avoid this disincentive. To the extent that the firm can sell its output in separate blocks, it can sell another block without spoiling the market for the block already being sold. In the case of *perfect* price discrimination, where every unit of output is sold at a different price, the profit-maximizing firm will produce every unit for which the price charged can be greater than or equal to its marginal cost. It will therefore produce the same output as the firm in perfect competition.

Normative Aspects of Price Discrimination

The predicted combination of higher average revenue and higher output does not in itself have any *normative* significance. It will typically lead to a different distribution of income and a different level of at q^*), there is nothing the firm can do about costs. The best thing to do therefore is to maximize the total revenue that is received from selling q^* in the two markets. *To do this, the firm will allocate sales between the markets until the marginal revenues of the last unit sold in each are the same.*

Consider what would happen if this strategy were not followed. If the marginal revenue of the last unit sold in market A exceeded the marginal revenue of the last unit sold in market B, the firm could keep overall output constant at q^* but reallocate a unit of sales from market B to market A, thereby gaining a net addition in revenue equal to the difference between the marginal revenues in the two markets. It therefore pays the firm to reallocate a given total output between markets whenever marginal revenues are not equal in the two markets.

Choosing Total Output

The determination of profit-maximizing output and prices is shown in the figure. The firm's marginal cost varies with its total output, as shown in part (iii). Thus we cannot just put the *MC* curve onto the diagram for each market, for the marginal cost of producing another unit for sale in market A will depend on how much is being produced for sale in market B, and vice versa. To determine what overall production should be, we need to know overall *marginal revenue.* To find this we merely sum the separate quantities in each market that correspond to each particular marginal revenue. The appropriateness of this procedure follows from the argument that at any value of total production, sales will be allocated to equate marginal revenues in the two markets. If, for example, the tenth unit sold in market A and the fifteenth unit sold in market B each have a marginal revenue of c in their separate markets, then the marginal revenue of c corresponds to overall sales of q units (divided into q_A units in market A and q_B in market B). This is shown in the figure by the *MR* curve in part (iii).

Profit-maximizing total output is at q in part (iii), where *MR* and *MC* intersect. Because marginal revenue is c in each market, market outputs are q_A and q_B, respectively. Although marginal revenue is equal in the two markets, the prices P_A and P_B (read off the demand curves) are not.

output than when the seller is limited to a single price. The ability of the discriminating monopolist to capture some of the consumers' surplus will seem undesirable to consumers but not to the monopolist. How outsiders view the transfer may depend on who gains and who loses. For instance, when railroads discriminated against small farmers, the results aroused public anger; when doctors, in the days before provincial medical insurance, discriminated by giving low-priced service to poor patients, it was taken to be necessary since the poor would not be able to afford medical care if doctors charged all their patients the same fees.

Price discrimination, we have seen, tends to lead to larger output than is produced by a single-price monopoly. That price discrimination may produce a result that is closer to what would happen in perfect competition than in monopoly may seem paradoxical. After all, price discrimination has a bad reputation among many economists and lawyers. To many people *discrimination* of any sort has odious connotations. Laws make certain kinds of price discrimination illegal. But is discrimination by airlines in giving senior citizens lower fares really bad? Some further examples are explored in Box 13-2.

There are two quite separate questions involved in evaluating a particular example of price discrimination. One is a question of the level of output produced; the other is a question of the distribution of income. Economists can identify both kinds of effects, and the desirability of each can be debated. Whether an individual judges price discrimination as bad or good depends on the details of the particular example as well as on personal value judgments.

BOX 13-2

Is Price Discrimination Bad?

The consequences of price discrimination differ from case to case. No matter what an individual's values are, he or she is almost bound to evaluate individual cases differently from one another.

Secret rebates. A large oil-refining firm agrees to ship its product to market on a given railroad, provided that the railroad gives the firm a secret rebate on the transportation cost and does not give a similar concession to rival refiners. The railroad agrees and is thereby charging discriminatory prices. This rebate gives the oil company a cost advantage that it uses to drive its rivals out of business or to force them into a merger on dictated terms. (John D. Rockefeller was accused of using such tactics in the early years of the Standard Oil Company.)

Use of product. When the Aluminum Company of America had a virtual monopoly on the production of aluminum ingots, it sold both the raw ingots and aluminum cable made from the ingots. At one time ALCOA sold cable at a price 20 percent *below* its price for ingots. (Of course, the cable price was above ALCOA's cost of producing cable.) It did so because users of cable could substitute copper cable, but many users of ingot had no substitute for aluminum. In return for its "bargain price" for cable, ALCOA made the purchasers of cable agree to use it only for transmission purposes. (Without such an agreement, any demander of aluminum might have bought cable and melted it down.)

Covering costs. A product that many people want to purchase has a demand and cost structure such that there is no single price at which a producing firm can cover total costs. However, if the firm is allowed to charge discriminatory prices, it will be willing to produce the product and it may make a profit. This is illustrated in the figure.

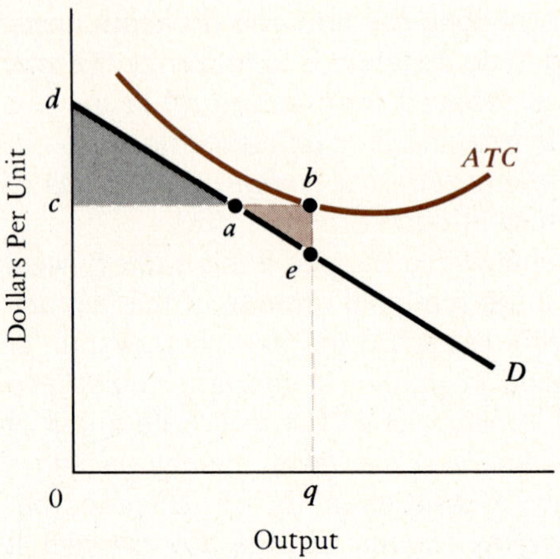

Because the average total cost (*ATC*) curve is everywhere higher than the demand curve (*D*), no single price would lead to revenues equal to costs. A price-discriminating monopolist may be able to cover cost. The total cost of output *q* is the area 0*cbq*. The maximum revenue attainable at any output by perfect discrimination is the area under the demand curve. For output *q* that area, shaded gray, exceeds total cost since the gray shaded triangle *cda* is greater than the color shaded triangle *abe*.

Equitable fares. For many years British railways were not allowed to discriminate among passengers in different regions. To prevent discrimination, a fixed fare per passenger mile was specified and charged on all lines, whatever their passenger traffic and whatever the elasticity of demand for the services of the particular line. In the interests of economy, branch lines that could not cover costs closed down. Some lines stopped operating even though their users preferred rail transport to any alternatives and the strength of their preference was such that they would have willingly paid a price sufficient for the line to yield a profit. But the lines were closed because it was thought inequitable to discriminate against the passengers on these lines.

Often it is the income redistribution caused by price discrimination that accounts for the strong emotional reactions to price discrimination. When it transfers income from poor to rich, price discrimination may seem bad, even if it increases total output; when it transfers income from rich to poor, it may seem good independent of its effect on output.

Systematic and Unsystematic Price Discrimination

The discussion so far has been concerned with systematic and persistent price discrimination. Systematic price discrimination most often consists of classifying buyers according to age, location, industry, income, or the use they intend to make of the product and then charging different prices for the different "classes" of buyers. It may also take other forms, such as charging more for the first unit bought than for subsequent units, or vice versa.

Another sort of price discrimination is common. Any firm that occasionally gives a favorite customer a few cents off or shaves its price to land a new account is also engaged in price discrimination. If these practices are used irregularly, they are called *unsystematic discrimination*. Such discrimination is not really part of the price structure but is instead the consequence of rivalrous behavior. Since we are here concerned with the consequences of market structure, we have ignored such unsystematic discrimination. This does not mean that it is unimportant; on the contrary, unsystematic price discrimination plays a major role in the dynamic process by which prices change in response to changing conditions of supply and demand.

The causes and consequences of systematic price discrimination are very different from those of unsystematic price discrimination.

The law, however, is generally unable to distinguish between the two kinds of price discrimination and so hits at both. Legislation, motivated solely by a desire to attack systematic discrimination, may have unforeseen and possibly undesired effects on unsystematic discrimination. Because unsystematic price discrimination is important for the working of competition, prohibiting it may aid the maintenance of monopoly power.

Structure of the Canadian Economy

Do we need more theories than monopoly and perfect competition in order to understand the real world? Gulf, Shell, and PetroCan are three of the "major" oil companies. They are not, singly or collectively, monopolists, nor are they firms in perfect competition. Yet they are typical of many real firms in our economy. Similar comments apply to the companies that manufacture Coca-Cola and Pepsi-Cola. We now look at some statistics to see how well the assumptions about monopoly and competition describe the Canadian economy.[4] Today most economists believe that although the models of monopoly and perfect competition are clearly useful, there is a need for other models as well.

Concentration ratios. When measuring whether an industry has power concentrated in the hands of only a few firms or dispersed over many, it is not sufficient just to count the number of firms. For example, an industry with one enormous firm and 29 minute ones is more concentrated in any meaningful sense than an industry with only five firms, all of which are of equal power. To get around the problem that number of firms is not a good criterion, economists calculate what is called a **concentration ratio,** which shows the fraction of total market sales controlled by the largest group of sellers. Common types of concentration ratios cite the share of total market sales made by the largest four or eight firms.

A problem in using concentration ratios is to define the market with reasonable accuracy. On the one hand the market may be much smaller than the

[4] Description is not the whole of the matter, for it is the purpose of theories to abstract from the complexity of reality. Even descriptively unrealistic models may be adequate to make predictions that are confirmed by observations. But poor descriptions make one cautious.

whole country. For example, concentration ratios in national cement sales are low, but they understate the market power of cement companies because heavy transportation costs divide the cement *industry* into a series of regional *markets*, in each of which there are relatively few firms. On the other hand the market may be larger than one country. This is a particularly important consideration in a small trading country such as Canada. For example, a single Canadian firm in one industry does not have a monopoly if it is in competition with five U.S. firms that can easily sell into the Canadian market. When appropriately used, however, concentration ratios tell us how much production for a given market is concentrated in the hands of a few firms.

Two Groupings of Canadian Industries

It is relatively easy to divide much of Canadian industry into two broad groups, those with low concentration ratios and hence a large number of relatively small firms and those with high concentration ratios and hence a small number of relatively large firms. If these two groups are described by the two market forms we have studied so far, perfect competition would characterize the first group and monopoly the second.

Sectors with Many Small Firms

Just under 50 percent of the national product is produced by industries made up of a large number of small firms. This includes most agricultural production, most services (travel agents, lawyers, plumbers, television technicians, etc.), most retail trade, most wholesale trade, most construction, and industries whose major business is exchange (real estate agents, stockbrokers, etc.).

The competitive model, with the addition of government intervention where necessary, does quite well in describing many of these industries. This is obviously so where the business of the industry is exchange rather than production. Foreign-exchange markets and stock exchanges are notable examples. Agriculture also fits fairly well in most ways; the individual farmer is clearly a price taker, entry into farming is easy, and exit is possible, though not in fact very rapid.[5] Many basic raw materials such as iron ore, tin, and copper are sold on world markets where prices fluctuate continually in response to changes in demand and supply.

Many other industries, however, are not described by the perfectly competitive model even though they contain many firms. In retail trade and services, for example, most firms have some influence over prices. The local grocery, supermarket, discount house, and department store not only consider weekend specials and periodic sales important to business success, but they also spend a good deal of money advertising them. Moreover, each store in these industries has a unique location that may give it some local monopoly power over nearby customers. In wholesaling the sales representative is regarded as a key figure—which would not be true if the firm could sell all it wished at a given market price. We are, as Professor R. L. Bishop has observed, "a race of eager sellers and coy buyers, with purchasing agents getting the Christmas presents from the salesmen rather than the other way around."

The first group of industries therefore contains some that are clearly described by the model of perfect competition and many others that are not.

Sectors with a Few Large Firms

About half of the national product is produced by industries dominated by a few large firms. The names of these firms are part of the average citizen's vocabulary. In this category fall most transportation firms (e.g., C.A.I., Wardair, Voyageur Colonial Coach Lines), communications (CTV, McLean Hunter, B.C. Tel), public utilities (Québec Hydro, Canadian Post Office), and much of the largest sector of the economy, manufacturing.

A casual look at the manufacturing sector can be misleading if one does not distinguish between products and firms. In some manufacturing industries many differentiated products are produced by only a few firms. In breakfast foods, for example, a vast

[5] Although, as we saw in Chapter 6, the size of Canadian farms has increased dramatically in recent years, even the largest farm is small in relation to total market demand. Thus even the largest farmer is a price taker, not a price setter.

variety of products is produced by a mere three firms. Similar circumstances exist in chemicals, cigarettes, and numerous other industries where many more or less competing products are in each case produced by a very few firms. Clearly, these industries are not perfectly competitive. Yet neither do they appear to be monopolies, for the few firms typically compete energetically against one another.

Throughout Canadian history, there have been few cases of single-firm monopolies outside the regulated industries. They include the Eddy Match Company, which was virtually the sole producer of wooden matches in Canada between 1927 and 1940, and Canada Cement Limited, which produced nearly all the output of cement until the 1950s. At the time of the Royal Commission on Price Spreads (1935), Canadian Industries Limited produced all ammunition and explosives, the Consolidated Mining and Smelting Company produced over 90 percent of lead and over 70 percent of zinc, and 70 percent of the nickel used in Canada was refined by the International Nickel Company.

Many of the large companies no longer hold such dominant positions in their respective markets. Imperial Oil Company refined approximately 80 percent of all gasoline sold in Canada in 1921, but the company's percentage of total output had fallen to 55 percent by 1932 and 38 percent in 1968. In the mid 1930s approximatley 70 percent of tobacco output was accounted for by the Imperial Tobacco Company; by the 1970s the company's sales represented less than 40 percent of industry output.

The most striking cases of monopoly in today's economy are in transportation and public utilities. All railway rates in Canada are regulated by the Railway Transport Committee of the Canadian Transport Commission. Telephone rates of the two federally chartered companies, Bell Canada and British Columbia Telephone, are also subject to the regulation of the Canadian Transport Commission, and the rates of companies operating in the Atlantic and Prairie provinces fall under provincial regulation.

Even here, however, the monopoly sometimes exists only because of government regulation. For example, if a legal monopoly were not enforced by the government, postal delivery services would be fiercely competitive. In other cases a monopoly that seems quite unassailable will not persist over the decades. Technological breakthroughs have already been made that will make voice communication a competitive industry in the foreseeable future. The days of the monopoly of the telephone company are clearly numbered.

Monopoly and perfect competition together do not *describe* much of the economy. Many industries with numerous firms depart from some of the conditions of perfect competition; most industries with no more than a few firms depart from the conditions of monopoly.

Patterns of Concentration in Manufacturing

Table 13-2 shows four-firm concentration ratios in selected Canadian manufacturing industries. Many of these industries approximate neither pure competition nor single-firm monopoly.

The competitive model conceivably fits a few of the industries near the bottom of the list, but even here there are doubts. Manufacturers of women's clothing have some control over price, contrary to the conditions of perfect competition, because of style and fashion. Metal stamping firms, print shops, and soft drink bottlers, while numerous nationally, operate in small regional and local markets in which a small number of sellers, in direct rivalry with one another, do not regard themselves as price takers.

Concentration ratios have long been used in the United States as indicators of the degree of competition in an industry. Whatever the validity of this use of concentration ratios in the United States, there is little justification for doing so in Canada because the Canadian economy is different from the American economy in some key respects. The population of Canada is only about 10 percent of the population of the United States. Canadian GDP is slightly less than 10 percent of the U.S. total. Foreign trade is of greater importance in the Canadian economy than in the American.

Although similarities in standard of living, consumption patterns, and education in the two countries have caused many similarities in industrial structure, the Canadian manufacturing sector is

TABLE 13-2 Concentration Ratios in Selected Manufacturing Industries, 1980

Industry	Four-firm concentration ratio (percentage)
Breweries	99
Motor vehicles	93.7
Cane and beet sugar procedures	92.0[a,b]
Aluminum rolling, casting, etc.	88.1
Cement	84.4
Iron and steel mills	77.9
Radio and television sets	77.1[a]
Distilleries	74.9
Agricultural implements	61.9
Petroleum refining	61.7
Soft drinks	48.2
Motor vehicle parts	44.6
Dairy products	37.0
Bakeries	33.5
Sporting goods	31.8
Pulp and paper mills	30.9
Pharmaceuticals and medicines	27.1
Shoes	25.5[a]
Men's clothing	20.6
Women's clothing	6.4

Source: Statistics Canada, 31-402.

[a] Figure given is for 1978; figure for 1980 is secret.
[b] Six-firm concentration ratio is 100.0

Concentration varies greatly among manufacturing industries. The concentration ratios show the share of the industry's sales accounted for by the four largest firms. These data are revised infrequently and although a revision of the data presented here was due, it had not yet been published when this book went to press.

substantially more concentrated than the American. This is partly because the small size of the economy leaves room for fewer firms operating at minimum efficient scale than the larger American economy does. But the Canadian economy is a very open economy, and for many industries the relevant market is the combined Canadian-American market.

Three economists, John Baldwin of Queen's University, Paul Gorecki of the Economic Council of Canada, and John McVey of Statistics Canada, have taken up this point, arguing that Canadian concentration ratios significantly overstate the amount of effective concentration in Canadian manufacturing industries. They suggest a number of corrections to the published data. First, the published data assign all of the output of each plant to the industry to which the largest proportion of its output belongs. They separate output streams from multiple output plants and assign each to its appropriate industry. Second, no account is taken of imports in the published concentration ratios. The authors correct for this fault by adding to each firm's output any imports that it brings in for sale in Canada, and by adding to the size of the Canadian market any sales made by firms that only import. Thus the market size is estimated on the basis of what is sold, whether or not it is produced in Canada, and the importance of one firm in that market is estimated on the basis of what it sells in that market no matter where these goods were produced.

Table 13-3 gives the results based on the published four-firm concentration ratios for Canada and the corrected figures derived by the three authors. It shows that when the corrections are made, the number of Canadian industries that have low concentration ratios rises while the number that have high ratios falls.

Table 13-3 shows that even with the corrected data, in about 70 percent of Canadian manufacturing industries, the four largest firms control over 25 percent of the value of sales. Such industries are not monopolies because there are several firms in the industry, and these firms engage in rivalrous behavior. Residents even of small towns will find more than one drugstore, garage, barber, and dress shop competing for their patronage. Similarly, manufacturers of computers, television sets, and chemicals belong to industries in which there are several close domestic rivals (and often foreign competitors). But neither are these firms in perfectly competitive markets. Often there are only a few major rival firms in an industry, but even when there are many, *they are not price takers.* Virtually all consumer goods are differentiated products. Any one firm will typically have several lines of a product that differ more or less from one another and from competing lines produced by other firms. There is no market setting a single price for razor blades or television sets that equates overall demand to overall supply. Instead, it

TABLE 13-3 Distribution of Concentration Ratios for 140 Canadian Manufacturing Industries

Concentration ratio categories	Industry count	
	Unadjusted ratio	Adjusted ratio
0–24.9	17	41
25–49.9	50	58
50–74.9	45	34
75–100	28	7
All Industries	140	140

The standard concentration ratios overstate the degree of concentration in Canadian industries. The first column shows the four-firm concentration ratio. For example 0–24.9 indicates a low degree of concentration since the four largest firms account for less than 25 percent of the sales, while 75–100 indicates a high level of concentration with the four largest firms accounting for more than 75 percent of all sales. The second column gives the number of industries in each concentration ratio class according to the standard figures. The last column gives the distribution of the same industries when corrections are made for plants with multi-industry outputs and for the importance of imports in the Canadian market. When the corrected figures are substituted for the usual ones, the fall in measured concentration of the typical Canadian industry is striking.

is in the nature of such products that *sellers must state a price at which they are willing to sell.*

The Importance of Administered Prices

Rivalrous behavior among firms that are not price takers immediately takes us out of the domain of either perfect competition or monopoly. We thus require additional market structures if we wish to explain the behavior.

In perfect competition firms face a market price that they are quite unable to influence, and they set their quantities in respect to that price. Changes in market conditions are signaled to firms by changes in the market prices that they face, and firms respond by changing the quantities that they produce.

In perfect competition firms are price takers and quantity adjusters.

In all other market structures firms face downward-sloping demand curves and thus know that they have a choice of what price to charge for their product. Whenever different firms' products are not perfect substitutes for other products that consumers may purchase instead, firms must decide on a price to quote. If they are unsatisfied with the sales they achieve at that price, they can change their quote, but quote a price they must. In such circumstances we say that the firm *administers its price.* The term **administered price** refers to a price set by the decisions of an individual firm rather than by impersonal market forces.

When a firm sets its price, the amount that it sells is determined by its demand curve. Changes in market conditions change the amount that can be sold at its administered price. The changed conditions may or may not lead the firm to change the price that it charges.

In market structures other than perfect competition, firms set their prices and then let demand determine their sales. Changes in market conditions are signaled to the firm by changes in the quantity it can sell at its administered price.

Monopolistic Competition

We have seen that the perfect competition and monopoly models do not accurately describe the Canadian economy and that their elements do not provide all that is needed to analyze market behavior. The two theories do, however, identify key variables. One of these is the firm's view of the demand curve it faces. In monopoly the firm faces the market demand curve; in perfect competition it faces a horizontal line at the level of market price. But what of situations where firms are not strictly price takers but their administered prices are not independent of what other firms in the industry do? What if firms think about their rivals' reactions before setting prices? Another key variable is entry. In perfect competition entry is unimpeded, while in classic monopoly there are barriers that make entry impossible. But what of situations where entry is neither free nor totally blockaded, just more or less difficult, more or less slow to occur?

Recognition that these additional relevant dimensions of market structure are potentially important has led economists to formulate additional theoretical market structures, one of which is discussed here and others in the next chapter.

The theory we are about to consider evolved in response to an empirical challenge. Shortly after the theory of perfect competition was developed by the great English economist Alfred Marshall, concern arose over an inconsistency. According to the theory, firms in long-run, perfectly competitive equilibrium must be at the minimum point on their average total cost curves, but common empirical observations showed that most English manufacturing firms of that time had unexploited economies of scale.

This point was made most forceably by the Italian economist Pierro Sraffa, and Sraffa's challenge was taken up by two economists, Joan Robinson and Joseph Chamberlin. Robinson, of Cambridge University in England, made the assumption that all manufacturing industries were monopolies. Although her work helped greatly in developing the modern theory of monopoly, it proved a dead end in responding to Sraffa's challenge. Chamberlin, of Harvard University in the United States, produced ideas that were seminal in the development of theories of market structures intermediate between perfect competition and monopoly. Chamberlin's theory concerned a market structure that he called **monopolistic competition.**[6]

The market envisaged in this theory is similar to perfect competition in that there are many firms with relatively easy entry and exit. But it differs in one important respect: Each firm has some power over price because each sells a product that is differentiated significantly from those of its competitors. One firm's soap might be similar to another firm's soap, but it differs in chemical composition, color, smell, softness, brand name, reputation, and a host of other characteristics that matter to customers. This is the phenomenon of **product differentiation.** It implies that each firm has a certain degree of local monopoly power over its own product. It could raise its price, even if its competitors did not, and not lose all of its sales. This is the "monopolistic" part of the theory. The monopoly power is severely restricted, however, by the presence of similar products sold by many competing firms and by easy entry and exit. As a result, the monopolistically competitive firm's demand curve is very much flatter than the industry demand curve. This is the "competition" part of the theory.

From a theoretical point of view the major difference between perfect and monopolistic competition lies in the respective assumptions of homogeneous and differentiated products. Firms in perfect competition sell a **homogeneous product,** a product similar enough across the industry that no one firm has any power over price because consumers regard different firms' products as perfect substitutes for one another. Firms in monopolistic competition sell a **differentiated product,** a group of commodities similar enough to be called the same product but dissimilar enough that the producer of each has some power over its own price. This dissimilarity leads to, and is enhanced by, establishment of brand names and advertising.

Assumptions of the Theory

The theory of monopolistic competition has four key assumptions. First, each firm is not a price taker. Instead, each firm faces a negatively sloped demand curve. However, the curve is highly elastic because similar products sold by other firms provide many close substitutes. The negative slope of the demand curve provides the potential for monopoly profits in the short run.

Second, the industry contains so many firms, each of which is in close competition with many others, that each ignores the possible reactions of its many competitors when it sets its own price.

Third, there is freedom of entry and exit. This forces profits to zero in the long run. If profits are being earned by existing firms in the industry, new firms will enter. Their entry will mean that the demand for the product must be shared among more

[6] Since the term *monopolistic competition* is now often used in a broader sense than Chamberlin used it, it is necessary to add the qualification that we are here considering the large-group case of monopolistic competition. The small-group case is considered in Chapter 15.

brands. Thus the demand curve for any one firm's brand will shift to the left. Entry continues until profits fall to zero.

Fourth, any new firm that entered the industry would take equal amounts of sales from all existing firms. This is the so-called *symmetry assumption.*[7]

Predictions of the Theory

An important prediction of the theory is that in an industry with differentiated products and free entry, each firm will, in equilibrium, produce an output smaller than the one that would minimize its costs of production. This prediction, called the **excess capacity theorem,** is illustrated and discussed more fully in Box 13-3. In a monopolistically competitive industry there are many brands of the product, each produced in smaller quantities and priced at a higher level than if the industry produced a homogeneous product and was perfectly competitive

The excess capacity theorem once aroused passionate debate. It seemed to suggest that industries selling differentiated products are *inefficient* because they have excess capacity in long-run equilibrium and thus have a higher level of costs of production than is necessary. More modern analysis has shown that the inefficiency charge is not proven. The "excess capacity" of monopolistic competition does not necessarily indicate inefficiency or waste of resources because price is not the only relevant aspect of a differentiated product. People care about which brand of a product they buy. Differentiated products provide a choice of brands to consumers. Clearly, people have different tastes; some prefer one brand and some another. Each brand has its devotees. This creates a trade-off, from the point of view of consumer welfare, between producing more brands to satisfy diverse tastes and producing fewer at a lower cost per unit.

[7] Although it does not need to concern us greatly here, it proved to be the Achilles' heel of the theory because it denied that any new entrant would have some near substitutes that would be heavily affected by the new product's entry and some more distant substitutes that would be less affected. For example, according to the symmetry assumption, the entry of a new brand of low-tar cigarette would take sales equally from all other cigarettes whether they were low-tar, medium-tar, or high-tar. In reality, we would expect the effect of the new product to be mainly on the sales of other low-tar products, less on medium-tar products, and even less on high-tar ones.

Monopolistic competition produces a wider range of products, but at a somewhat higher cost per unit, than perfect competition.

We cannot conclude that consumers are better off with 10 brands of a differentiated product than with one standard brand, or vice versa. If consumers value variety, the extra cost that variety imposes must be matched against the benefits. Only if the costs exceed the benefits is the variety wasteful. To maximize consumers' satisfaction, the number of brands of a differentiated product should be increased until the gain from adding one more equals the loss from having to produce each existing brand at a higher cost, because less of each is produced.

Ironically, the prediction of excess capacity outlasted the theory that first gave rise to it. Extensive debate over several decades showed, among other things, that once advertising, distribution, and other nonproduction costs were allowed for, Chamberlin's theory no longer predicted the necessity of unexploited scale economies in production. Nonetheless, empirical observations of the rounds of tariff reductions that have occurred over the past several decades revealed the importance of differentiated commodities and of unexploited economies of scale. When tariffs were cut, firms in each country reduced the number of differentiated products that they produced and achieved lower costs on their remaining product lines.

Thus, for example, when tariffs were cut on Canadian-American trade as a result of two major rounds of international bargaining, Canadian companies reduced the number of product lines that they were producing and increased the outputs of their remaining lines, experiencing lower unit costs as a result. American firms did the same. The overall result was more specialization among differentiated products in each country, more trade between the two countries, and lower costs all around, as a result of expanded output of each of the product lines that any one firm continued to produce. Similar observations were made in Europe after the formation in

BOX 13-3

The Excess Capacity Theorem

The excess capacity theorem of monopolistic competition is an implication of two of the assumptions of the theory: first, downward-sloping demand curves for each of the firms due to product differentiation and, second, free entry, which pushes profits to zero at long-run equilibrium. Thus average revenue must equal average cost at some level of output but exceed it at none. In other words, free entry pushes firms to the point at which the demand curve is tangent to the average total cost curve.

Two curves that are tangent at a point have the same slope at that point. Thus when a downward-sloping demand curve is tangent to the average total cost curve, the latter must also be downward sloping at the point of tangency. In such a situation each firm is producing an output less than the one for which its average total cost reaches its minimum point; that is, it has excess capacity.

This is illustrated in the figure. Equilibrium is at point E_0, price is p_0, and quantity is q_0. Price is greater and quantity is less than the purely competitive equilibrium price and quantity (p_1 and q_1). At equilibrium the monopolistically competitive firm has *excess capacity* of q_0q_1. The excess capacity theorem can be formally stated as follows:

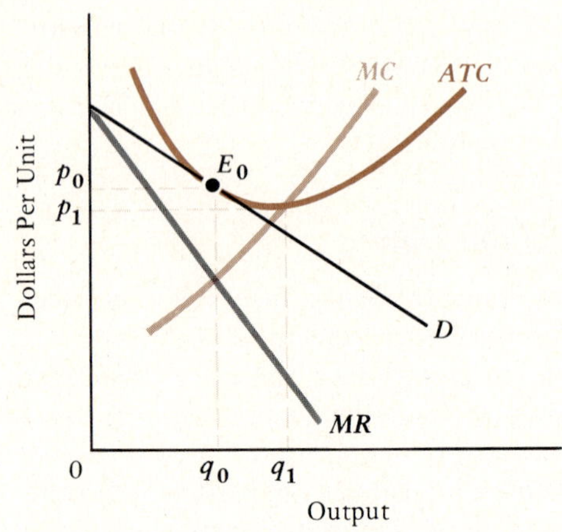

The zero-profit equilibrium of a monopolistically competitive firm occurs at an output less than the one at which average total cost is a minimum.

1958 of the European Common Market (now called the European Community or EC). (This is discussed further in Chapter 21.)

The modern explanation of these events is, as we shall see, not quite the one that Chamberlin provided, but his insights into the importance of product differentiation in modern economies were crucial in directing economists to new paths that have proven fruitful.

The Lasting Contribution of Monopolistic Competition

The theory of monopolistic competition recognized the facts of product differentiation, the ability of firms to influence prices, and the presence of brand names and advertising. The incorporation of these factors into a new theory encouraged economists to consider the question of their effects on the operation of the price system. It rekindled economists' interest in such things as how and when firms took each other's reactions into account, what made for easy or restricted entry, and the significance to competition of differentiated products that were similar to one another.

The reason it has not become one of the main market forms used to understand market economies is that, as economists came to realize gradually, the large-group case of monopolistic competition is rarely, if ever, found in the economy.

This claim may sound surprising at first because there are many industries in which a large number of slightly differentiated products compete for the buyers' attention. The catch, however, is that in most such cases the industries have only a few firms, each of which sells a large number of products.

Consider the soap and detergent industry. Among the well-known brands currently on sale in Canada are Cheer, Oxydol, Tide, Dreft, Ivory Snow,

Ivory Liquid, Joy, Cascade, Camay, Bounce, Bold, Zest, Mr. Clean, Spic and Span, Comet, and Downey. Surely this is impressive differentiation among a large number of products. This list of products might appear to provide a perfect example of monopolistic competition. But *every one* of the products is manufactured by a single company, Procter & Gamble, which is one of the very few major firms selling soaps, cleansers, and detergents in Canada. Clearly, such industries are not the large-group case envisaged by Chamberlin. Today, product differentiation is recognized to occur mainly where a small group rather than a large group of firms compete.[8]

The modern theory of product differentiation is a direct descendant of the earlier theories of monopolistic competition. The focus remains on product differentiation and on industrial structures thought to describe the nature of the modern economy. But it is the small-group case of firms with differentiated products rather than the large-group case of monopolistic competition that seems relevant.

In the last half of the 1970s there was a great outburst of theorizing about all aspects of product differentiation.[9] In these theories, just as in the earlier ones, it pays firms to differentiate their products, to advertise heavily, and to engage in other forms of non-price competition. These are characteristics to be found in their world, but not in perfect competition. Most of the modern theory of product differentiation relates to industries with a small number of firms, such as soaps and detergents, breakfast foods, and automobiles. This is the province of "competition among the few."

[8] At first sight, retailing may appear to be closer to the conditions of monopolistic competition than manufacturing. Certainly every city has a large number of retailers selling any one commodity. The problem is that they are differentiated from each other mainly by their geographical location, each firm having only a few competing close neighbors. Thus a model with every firm in close competition with only a few neighbors seems to be a better model for retailing than the large-group monopolistic competition model, in which every firm competes directly with a large number of other firms.

[9] It is one of those regrettable confusions of life that the theory that studies market structures where a *small* number of firms compete to sell a large number of differentiated products has also taken the name *monopolistic competition*. The term now refers to any industry in which more than one firm sells differentiated products.

A Preview of "Imperfect Competition Among the Few"

As the data in Tables 13-1 and 13-2 showed, much of Canadian industry is characterized by small groups of firms accounting for a large fraction of an industry's production. In most of these industries a relatively small number of firms have enough market power that they may not be regarded as price takers (as in perfect competition) but are subject to enough rivalry that they cannot consider the market demand curve as their own (as they can in monopoly). In most of these cases entry is neither perfectly easy nor wholly prevented. In many industries a small number of firms—between three and a dozen—tend to dominate the industry, and newcomers find it hard to establish themselves. The market structure that embraces such industries is called **oligopoly,** from the Greek words *oligos polein,* meaning "few to sell."

Oligopoly is an important market structure. It applies wherever concentration ratios are high and may apply even in nationally unconcentrated industries, such as cement. A national concentration ratio is relevant where there is one national market. But if transport costs split the country into numerous regional markets, each one may contain a small number of oligopolistic firms.

Oligopolistic industries are of many types. In some there are only a few firms in the entire industry. In others there are many firms, but only a few dominate the market. For example, in the United States there are 282 petroleum refiners, but the 232 smallest firms together account for only 7 percent of the aggregate value of output. There are 108 tire and tube manufacturing companies, of which the 100 smallest supply less than 14 percent of the market. Oligopoly is not inconsistent with a large number of small sellers, called a "competitive fringe," when the "big few" dominate the decision making in the industry.

In oligopolistic industries prices are typically administered. Products are usually, but not necessarily, differentiated. The intensity and nature of rivalrous behavior varies greatly from industry to industry and from one period of time to another. This variety has invited extensive theoretical speculation and empirical study. It is the topic of the next chapter.

Summary

1. In the simplest possible theory of monopoly, an entire industry is supplied by a single firm that sets a single price for its product.
2. The monopoly firm's own demand curve is identical with the market demand curve for the product. The market demand curve is the monopoly firm's average revenue curve, while its marginal revenue curve always lies below its average revenue curve.
3. When the monopoly is maximizing profits, marginal revenue is positive, and thus elasticity of demand is greater than unity. The amount of profits a monopoly earns may be large, small, zero, or negative in the short run, depending on the relation between demand and cost. For monopoly profits to persist in the long run, there must be effective barriers to the entry of other firms. Entry barriers can be natural or created.
4. Monopoly power is limited by the presence of substitute products, the development of new products, and the entry of new firms.
5. A single firm is not the only way a monopoly can occur. A group of firms may form a cartel by agreeing to restrict output and eliminate competitive behavior among themselves. If effective such a cartel becomes a monopoly. But cartels tend to be unstable because there are strong incentives for firms to violate cartel agreements.
6. Price discrimination occurs when different buyers are charged different prices or when the same buyer is charged different prices on different units of the commodity purchased for reasons not associated with differences in costs. A successful price discriminator captures some of the consumers' surplus that would exist at a single price.
7. The conditions under which a firm can succeed in charging discriminatory prices are, first, that it can control the supply of the product offered to particular buyers and, second, that it can prevent the resale of the commodity from one buyer to another.
8. Two predictions about price discrimination are (a) for any given level of output, the best system of discriminatory prices will provide higher total revenue to the firm than the best single price, and (b) output will usually be larger than under a single-price monopoly.
9. Price discrimination affects the distribution of income and the allocation of resources. Any individual is almost certain to evaluate individual cases differently, according to his or her personal set of values and the circumstances of each case. Further, there are important differences in the effects of systematic and unsystematic price discrimination.
10. A review of the structure of the Canadian economy shows that while there are both large-firm and small-firm sectors, most of the industries involved have important features that differ from those assumed in the models of either perfect competition or monopoly.
11. In market structures other than perfect competition, firms tend to administer prices and sell the quantities demanded at those prices.

Changes in market conditions are signaled not by changes in the price firms' quote or face but by changes in the quantities they can sell.

12. Monopolistic competition is a market structure in which firms sell a differentiated product. Large-group monopolistic competition does not apply to a significant number of industries in today's world. Differentiated products abound, but generally they are produced in industries that contain a small number of firms, each one of which sells many such products. This is one form of oligopoly.

Topics for Review

Relationship between price and marginal revenue for a monopolist
Relationships among marginal revenue, total revenue, and elasticity for a monopolist
Potential monopoly profits in any perfectly competitive equilibrium
Minimum efficient scale (*MES*)
Natural and created entry barriers
Cartels
Price discrimination and price differences
Systematic and unsystematic price discrimination
Administered prices
Product differentiation
Monopolistic competition

Discussion Questions

1. Suppose that only one professor teaches economics at your school. Would you say this professor is a monopolist who can exact any "price" from students in the form of readings assigned, tests given, and material covered? Suppose that two additional professors are hired; has the original professor's monopoly power been decreased?
2. Imagine a monopoly firm with fixed costs but no variable or marginal costs—for example, a firm owning a spring of water that produces indefinitely, once certain pipes are installed, in an area where no other source of water is available. What would be the firm's profit-maximizing price? What elasticity of demand would you expect at that price? Would this seem to be an appropriate pricing policy if the water monopoly were municipally owned?
3. Consider the following practices of many Canadian airlines. Do they represent price discrimination?
   a. Fares to Europe are higher in the summer than in the winter.
   b. You often pay more if you book shortly before your flight than if you book well in advance.
   c. You can often get a lower fare if you stay over a weekend than if you do not.
   d. Tour companies often pay less for the seat they include in your package tour than you would have to pay if you booked the seat yourself.
4. Which of these industries—licorice candy, copper wire, outboard motors, coal, local newspapers—would you most like to monopo-

lize? Why? Does your answer depend on several factors or just one or two? Which would you as a consumer least like to have monopolized by someone else? If your answers to the two questions are different, explain why.

5. A movie exhibitor, Aristotle Murphy, owns movie theaters in two towns of roughly the same size, 50 miles apart. In Monopolia he owns the only chain of theaters; in Competitia there is no theater chain, and he is but one of a number of independent operators. Would you expect movie prices to be higher in Monopolia than in Competitia in the short run? In the long run? If differences occur in his prices, would Mr. Murphy be discriminating in price?
6. Fashion clothing can often be bought at a much lower price at the end of the season than at the beginning. Some transportation companies charge lower fares during the week than on weekends. Electricity companies charge consumers lower rates, the more electricity they use. Are these all examples of price discrimination? What additional information would you like to have before answering?
7. Discuss whether each of the following represents price discrimination. In your view, which are the most socially harmful?
   a. Standby fares on airlines that are less than full fare
   b. Standby fares available only to bona fide students under 22 years of age
   c. First-class fares that are 50 percent greater than tourist fares, recognizing that two first class seats use the space of three tourist seats
   d. Negotiated discounts from list price, where sales personnel are authorized to bargain hard and get as much in each transaction as the traffic will bear
   e. Higher tuition for foreign university students than for local students
   f. Higher tuition for medical students than for history students
8. It is sometimes said that there are more drugstores and gasoline stations than are needed. In what sense might that be correct? Does the consumer gain anything from this plethora of retail outlets?
9. Are any of the following industries monopolistically competitive? Explain your answer.
   a. Textbook publishing (*Fact:* Over 50 elementary economics textbooks are in use somewhere in North America this year.)
   b. Post-secondary education
   c. Cigarette manufacture
   d. Restaurant operation
   e. Automobile retailing

14

Oligopolistic Markets

We saw in Chapter 13 that many Canadian industries are oligopolies. Such industries have three major characteristics:

1. There are two or more competing firms—thus the industry is not a monopoly.
2. Each firm faces a downward-sloping demand curve for its own product—thus the industry is not perfectly competitive.
3. There is at least one firm large enough to know that its competitors will react to any move it makes—thus the industry is not monopolistically competitive.

In this chapter we will look at the general behavior of firms in oligopolistic industries, but first we can learn quite a bit by considering the behavior of one real-world oligopoly.

OPEC

In Chapter 13 we saw how an industry-wide cartel could result in monopoly behavior even though the firms retained their separate legal identities. The formation of a cartel that includes a substantial portion, but not all, of the producers in an industry is one way in which an oligopoly can arise.

The Organization of Petroleum Exporting Countries (OPEC) is an example of the attempted cartelization of a formerly competitive industry. It illustrates many of the problems of oligopolistic industries, and it is these aspects that we wish to emphasize now.

The Pre-OPEC Energy Binge

During the half century before 1973, North Americans increased their consumption of energy at a rate of about 5 percent per year, enough to double consumption every 14 years. That energy came increasingly from oil and gas.

Much of the long-term surge in energy consumption resulted from the growing use of automobiles. As North American households became richer, they tended to buy larger numbers of ever faster, bigger, and more lavishly equipped cars, to say nothing of trailers and recreational vehicles. Year by year the demand for gasoline to power their internal combustion engines rose. Yet the price of gasoline remained low—so low that until the 1970s the cost of fuel remained a minor part of the cost of owning and operating a car. (In 1970, the gasoline cost of running the average car was less than \$.04 per mile, measured in 1988 prices.)

This epoch of ever-increasing demand at a constant price is analyzed in Figure 14-1. The long-run supply curve seemed to be almost perfectly elastic at a low price. For every barrel of oil produced, another was discovered.

The fact that the demand curve shifted to the right year after year seemed no cause for alarm. After all, energy fueled the increasing productivity that led to ever-rising material standards of living. Canada and the United States rode the crest of a wave of prosperity based on cheap and plentiful energy provided to a great extent by oil.

Canadians and Americans traveling abroad were amused by the small, cramped cars they saw and rented, and they were appalled by the high cost of gasoline. The high prices abroad were due to high taxes on gasoline and led to lower gasoline consumption. Europeans drove smaller cars, waited until they reached a higher level of income before buying a car (or buying a second car), and relied more on bicycles and public transportation. The European situation during this period is also shown in Figure 14-1.

FIGURE 14-1 Gasoline Prices in an Era of Unlimited Supply

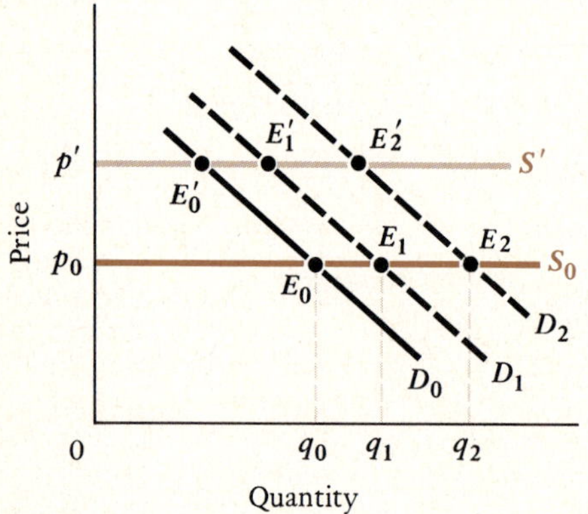

With a horizontal long-run supply curve, demand can increase year by year with no increase in price. S_0 is a long-run supply curve that is perfectly elastic at price p_0. Suppose S_0 applies to the North American market in the early 1960s. The various demand curves refer to different years: D_0 for the early 1960s, D_1 for the late 1960s, and D_2 for the early 1970s. As gasoline consumption increases, the demand curve shifts to the right from D_0 to D_1 to D_2 and so on. The equilibrium shifts from E_0 to E_1 to E_2. Consumption continues to grow, but this leads to no increase in price above p_0.

The supply curve S' is also perfectly elastic, at the higher price p'. Suppose it reflects the supply in European countries that have levied a high tax on gasoline. For the same set of demand curves, equilibrium consumption is much lower in European countries than in North America, yet there, too, it increases over time with no increase in price, as shown by E_0', E_1', and E_2'.

The OPEC Cartel

The oil industry in the years before 1973 was not perfectly competitive. However, there were many oil-producing countries, so many, indeed, that no one of them could significantly influence the world price of oil by withholding its own output from the market. They were price takers in the market in which they sold their oil.

OPEC did not attract world attention until 1973. In that year, however, its members placed a temporary embargo on the export of Middle Eastern oil. (The embargo was in retaliation for Western support for Israel in the Arab-Israeli war that broke out in that year.)

After the embargo ended, the OPEC members voluntarily restricted their output by negotiating quotas among themselves. At the time OPEC countries accounted for about 70 percent of the world's supply of crude oil and 87 percent of world oil exports. So, although it was not quite a complete monopoly, the cartel had substantial monopoly power. The world oil market contained one large oligopolistic producers' organization surrounded by a competitive fringe of many smaller producing countries.

Success of the Cartel

OPEC's policy of output restriction succeeded for several reasons. First, the member countries provided a large part of the total world supply of oil;

second, other producing countries could not quickly increase their outputs in response to price increases; third, world demand for oil was expanding rapidly; and fourth, world demand for oil proved to be highly inelastic in the short term.

As a result of these factors, OPEC was able to cause a substantial increase in the world price of oil. OPEC's oil production was about 31 million barrels a day in 1973; to raise prices within a year from an average of $3.37 per barrel to an average of $11.25 a barrel, exports had only to be restricted to 28.5 million barrels a day. To get a better idea of the significance of these price changes we can express them in 1988 dollars. When this is done we see the price going from about $10 a barrel to just over $30 a barrel. What happened is analyzed in more detail in Figure 14-2.

A reduction in OPEC's exports of less than 10 percent was sufficient to more than triple the world price. The higher prices were more or less maintained for the remainder of the decade. As a result OPEC countries found themselves suddenly enjoying vast wealth, while oil-importing countries found their real incomes greatly diminished. For some underdeveloped countries the rise in prices threatened disaster, and they managed to maintain needed oil imports only through loans that became an increasing burden on their economies as time went by.

The incentive for members to cheat on their output quotas (which we studied in Chapter 13) was not present during the early stages of OPEC. So great was the increase in the wealth of the member countries that the temptation to cheat in order to gain even more was small.

There was only so much that Arab sheiks and princes could spend on themselves, and there was only so much that could be spent on their countries' economic development. Indeed, the development programs of many OPEC countries were constrained not by funds but by limited physical facilities. For example, ships with supplies to build roads, warehouses, and other basic facilities often lay in harbor for months because of insufficient port facilities. Even when they were unloaded, supplies often sat at the harbor site for further months because of inadequate internal transport facilities. Because further funds were not urgently needed by OPEC members, the enforcement of OPEC's output quotas was an easy matter.

OPEC's ability to restrict output and keep prices high made its operation successful, but longer-term forces were working against OPEC, both from the supply side and from the demand side of the market.

FIGURE 14-2 OPEC As a Successful Cartel

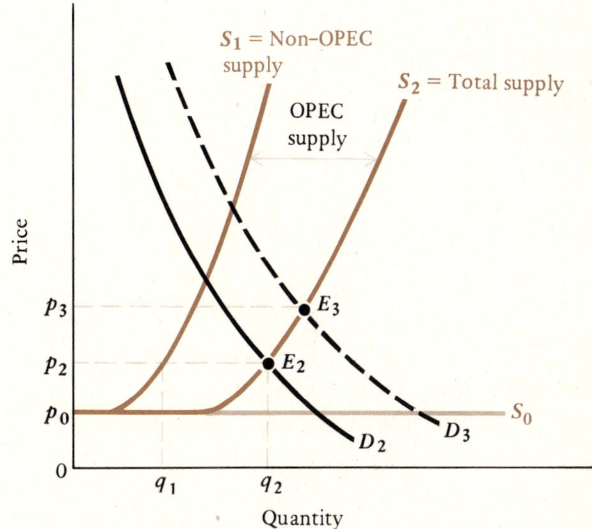

Given a rising non-OPEC supply curve of oil, the members of OPEC can determine equilibrium prices by choosing their contribution to total supply. The curve S_1 represents the non-OPEC supply of the product. If OPEC were prepared to supply unlimited quantities at p_0, the supply curve would be S_0 and the situation shown in Figure 14-1 would be restored. But by fixing its production, OPEC can determine the new total (OPEC + non-OPEC) supply curve S_2. OPEC can, for a given demand curve and non-OPEC supply curve, pick a price (such as p_2) and determine what quantity to supply (q_1q_2) to make that the equilibrium price. If demand is increasing, as from D_2 to D_3, while OPEC holds its supply constant, price will increase, in this case from p_2 to p_3.

Pressure on the Cartel

Monopolistic producers always face a dilemma. The closer their prices are to the profit-maximizing level, the greater their short-term profits but also the greater the incentive for market reactions that will reduce their profits in the longer term.

Increasing World Supply

The high prices and high profits achieved by the OPEC cartel spurred major additions to the world's oil supply by non-OPEC suppliers. This was, in effect, new entry. In 1973 OPEC produced more than 70 percent of the world's oil; by 1979 its share was less than 60 percent and by 1985 only 30 percent. North Sea oil, Mexican oil, Soviet oil, and increased Canadian and American production gradually replaced output that had been withdrawn from the market by OPEC. Higher prices made additional oil exploration and increased production from already proven reserves profitable. In the United States this production trend was greatly speeded by the deregulation of oil and gas prices that occurred at the end of the 1970s. As the supply of non-OPEC oil increased, the amount of OPEC production that was consistent with maintaining a given total world supply shrank.

Declining World Demand

The response of demand to the price rise was slow in coming for two distinct reasons, one related to government policy and the other to the long time required for a full adjustment to be made in the case of petroleum.

First consider government policy. The governments of many countries held their domestic price of oil down to shield consumers from the price shock. Canadians felt that as major producers of cheap oil, they should not have to pay the high world price. Indeed, a major cause of the defeat of the freshly elected Conservative government in 1980 was its plan to raise the domestic price toward the world price. Shortly after opposing the price rise and winning the 1981 election, the Liberals accepted the inevitable and raised the domestic price toward the world price. Most other countries, including the United States, had already done the same. In the 1970s the American government had tried to bypass price incentives by exhorting people to engage in such energy-saving behavior as turning down their thermostats and forming car pools. The response was predictably limited until domestic prices were allowed to rise, after which the response eventually became dramatic.

Next consider the natural lag in response of petroleum demand to a rise in its price. Even after government policies allowed prices to rise, the full response took years to develop. At the outset the response to rising domestic prices was small.

Any demand curve shows how purchases will vary as the price of a commodity varies, *other things being equal*. But other things being equal, there was little that users could do to reduce their consumption of petroleum products in response to the initial price rise. Car drivers took fewer Sunday trips, and some took a bus to work when gas prices soared. Homeowners and office managers turned their thermostats down a bit. Factories tried to economize on their fuel consumption. But overall, the response of world demand to the price increase was modest—a reduction in rate of growth of demand rather than a decrease in demand. The reason was that the scope for short-run economizing in the use of oil was limited because so much existing machinery ran on oil products. Over a longer period of time, however, major reductions in oil consumption proved possible—as they almost always do for any product whose relative price rises greatly.

When it came time to replace the family car, many households responded to the high price of gasoline by buying smaller, more fuel-efficient cars. (Indeed, the subsequent troubles in the North American automobile industry stemmed partly from the fact that this shift in consumer demand gave sales to foreign car firms who had decades of experience in producing small cars under the incentive of high gasoline taxes in those countries.) Homeowners and office managers found that they could greatly reduce their fuel bills by properly insulating their buildings or by turning to such alternative sources of heating as natural gas. New factories were able to use newly designed power plants that economized on fuel oil or used alternative fuels. These and a host of other longer-term adaptations that economized on petroleum products within known technology were gradually made.

Furthermore, even more potent very long run forces were unleashed. The high price of petroleum led to a burst of scientific research to develop more petroleum-efficient technologies and alternatives to petroleum. Solar heating technology was advanced, as was technology for longer-term alternatives such as harnessing tidal power and capturing heat from the earth's interior. Had the price of petroleum remained at the high levels of the early 1980s, this research would have continued at an intense pace and in all likelihood would have borne increasing fruits in the decades that followed.

As a result of these developments, other things did not remain equal over the long term, and the demand curve for petroleum products began to shift to the left.

The combined effect of decreasing demand and increasing supply is illustrated in Figure 14-3. The shrinking market for OPEC oil at the high OPEC price necessitated ever-stiffer production limitations if the cartel was to maintain its prices. By 1981 OPEC exports were only 18 million barrels a day, two-thirds of the 1973 level, and by 1985 it was estimated that OPEC could maintain prices only if production were cut to 15 million barrels a day. This created increasing problems and led, at the end of 1985, to a complete collapse of OPEC's agreements to limit the output of its members.

FIGURE 14-3 OPEC in Trouble

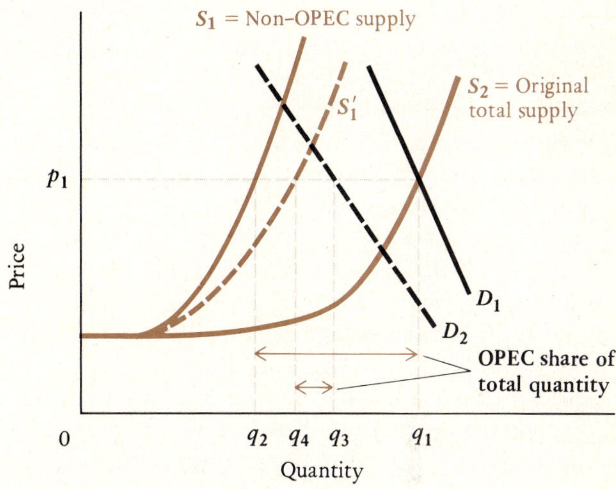

As demand declines and non-OPEC oil supply increases, declining OPEC production is required to maintain the cartel price. Total supply is originally S_2, of which S_1 is from non-OPEC sources and the quantity q_2q_1 from OPEC. Demand is originally D_1, and the cartel price p_1 prevails. Total quantity sold is q_1.

Now suppose demand decreases to D_2 and non-OPEC supply increases to S_1'. If the cartel wishes to maintain the price at p_1, it must limit total supply to q_3. Since non-OPEC supply will be q_4, this means restricting its own supply to q_4q_3, much less than before the shifts occurred.

Pressure to Cheat

We have seen that as world output of oil grew, OPEC output had to be reduced substantially to hold prices high. As a result, incomes in OPEC countries declined sharply. But many OPEC countries had become used to their new wealth, and the instabilities inherent in any cartel began to be felt seriously. In 1981 the cartel price reached its peak of $35 a barrel. In real terms this was about five times as high as the 1972 price, but production quotas were less than half of OPEC's capacity. Eager to increase their oil revenues, many individual OPEC members gave in to the pressure to cheat by producing in excess of their production quotas.

OPEC members met every few months to debate quotas, deplore cheating, and argue about strategy. Saudi Arabia, the giant of OPEC with 40 percent of all OPEC oil reserves, maintained a semblance of order after 1981 by a combination of threats to flood the market with oil if cheating continued and willingness to take a lion's share of the additional cuts required to keep prices high. Between 1981 and 1983 Saudi Arabia cut its production from 9.8 to 5.1 million barrels a day, accounting for virtually all of the reduction in total OPEC production during those years.

Disagreements About Strategy

The primary strategy question concerned the tradeoff between present production and future production. Oil taken out of the ground today is not available for sale in the future, while oil conserved for the future does not generate income now. But oil saved for the future will be valuable only as long as oil is still in heavy demand and has not been displaced—as sooner or later it will be—by some other source of energy. Deciding on the best strategy, even for a single country, is a difficult problem, for it involves a trade-off between a known present and an uncertain future. The problem is not merely one of guessing the future but also of affecting it. The higher the price charged for using oil today, the greater will be buyers' incentive to find permanent substitutes for it.

OPEC members, representing 13 countries, did not see eye to eye on these questions because of vast differences among the countries, both in their needs for current oil revenues and in their proven oil reserves. Libya, Nigeria, Algeria, and Venezuela had relatively small reserves and a great need for immediate cash. The war between Iran and Iraq created pressing needs for cash in both countries. Only Saudi Arabia's willingness to reduce its own production maintained any order in the OPEC cartel after 1981. Its huge reserves, small population, and high per capita income gave it the incentive to preserve the role of oil in the future and to discourage both the development of oil substitutes and the use of high-cost oil from other sources. Thus it did not regard falling prices as an unmixed disaster, although plainly it did not wish to see prices fall to the levels that prevailed before 1973.

By late 1985 Saudi Arabia indicated it would not tolerate further cheating by its partners and demanded that others share equally in quota reductions. But agreement proved impossible. In December 1985 OPEC decided to eliminate production quotas and let each member make its own output decision.

OPEC's collapse as a cartel produced a major reduction in world oil prices. Early in 1986 the price reached $20 a barrel and fell to $11 later in the year. This was just a fraction over the real price that prevailed just before OPEC began its adventure in oligopolistic behavior in 1973. Prices were extremely volatile throughout 1986, but gradually all oil-producing countries came to realize that a very low price was in the interest of no one. Gradually the price stabilized in the range of $18 to $20 a barrel. This was $8–10 above the price that would have emerged if all producers regarded themselves as mere quantity setters reacting to a given world price. It was also only half of the price that the OPEC countries had once managed to impose. It remained to be seen whether even that modest markup over the fully competitive price could be maintained in the face of the pressures on each country to produce its own profit-maximizing output at the world price.

Relevance of the OPEC Experience to Oligopoly

OPEC's experience illustrates nicely the traditional problems of cartels, which OPEC did well to keep under control for most of a decade. The experience also illustrates many of the aspects of oligopoly, even when there is no formal agreement among the members of the industry. Four aspects are worthy of closer inspection.

1. Restriction of output below the competitive level can lead to immense profits in the short term.

This is particularly so if the demand curve turns out to be highly inelastic in the short term. There is thus substantial incentive for a group of producers to cooperate in exercising their collective market power.

2. Maintaining market power becomes increasingly difficult as time passes.

Supply is likely to increase as new producers find ways of overcoming entry barriers in order to share in the large profits. Demand is likely to decrease as new substitutes are invented and put into production.

3. Producers with market power face a basic trade-off between profits in the short term and profits in the longer term.

The closer a group of producers gets price to the monopolistic level, the higher are its short-run profits, but the greater is the incentive for longer-term market reactions from both the supply side—entry of new sources of supply—and the demand side—invention of substitutes.

4. **Output restriction by voluntary agreement among several firms is difficult to maintain in the long run.**

This is particularly so if declining demand and increasing competition from new sources or new products lead to a steadily shrinking share of the market and falling levels of profits.

OPEC illustrates many problems that are typical of oligopolies whose individual producers exercise market power. But OPEC did not face some of the problems typical of many oligopolies both because it had the power of national governments behind its output-restriction agreements and because at the outset it was the only producer with significant market power, being surrounded as it was by a host of other producing countries, each with an output that was small relative to the industry's total output.

Because OPEC is somewhat atypical, we must shift our focus for the remainder of our discussion to the classic oligopoly, an industry containing only a few firms manufacturing consumer goods such as cars, cameras, refrigerators, soap, washing machines, or cigarettes.

Economists have devoted much effort to studying the behavior of all types of oligopolistic industries over the years. We shall discuss three of the most important questions arising out of these studies. First, what accounts for the observed short-run stickiness of prices set by firms in oligopolistic industries? Second, how do oligopolists make longer-term price and output decisions in the face of the interdependence among firms that typifies such industries? Third, how do oligopolists seek to protect their long-term profits by creating barriers to entry?

Short-Run Price-Output Decisions

One of the most striking contrasts between perfectly competitive markets and oligopolistic markets concerns the behavior of prices. In perfect competition prices change continually in response to changes in demand and supply. In oligopoly prices change less frequently. Prices for radios, automobiles, television sets, and men's suits do not change with anything like the frequency that prices change in markets for basic materials or stocks and bonds. Of course, prices in oligopolistic industries do change, but usually by significant amounts at discrete intervals of time. The basic empirical finding is this:

Oligopolistic firms do not alter their prices every time demand shifts. Instead, they fix prices and let the quantity sold adjust in the short term.

This phenomenon is often referred to as the *stickiness* of oligopolistic prices. Before considering possible explanations of why prices may be sticky, it is important to recognize how and when oligopolistic prices do change.

Changing prices. Oligopolistic prices ordinarily change when there are major changes in costs of production. Rises in raw material prices or wage rates are passed on fairly quickly by rises in product prices.[1] Also, major reductions in costs, as when a new product, such as the home computer, is being developed, are usually followed by reductions in prices. This is because of the rivalry among oligopolistic firms. If one firm fails to cut price when costs fall, another firm will do so, seeking thereby to increase its market share.

Oligopoly prices also often change in response to large unexpected shifts in demand. If an industry finds itself faced with an apparently permanent and unexpected downward shift in demand, firms will often cut prices in an attempt to retain their markets

[1] Oligopolistic pricing may convert more or less continuous changes in input prices into discrete changes in output prices. Say that inflation is steadily raising the prices of industrial raw materials as determined in perfectly competitive markets. Firms find it expensive to change list prices every day or every week. They will therefore make discrete jumps in the prices they charge every few months, first getting output prices ahead of input prices, then slowly falling behind until a further adjustment of output prices is necessary.

until longer-term adjustments can be made. For example, the North American auto industry was faced with declining demand from 1980 to 1982 due to its lag in developing small, fuel-efficient cars that were competitive with Japanese imports. It offered big rebates that slashed prices to levels that could not have been maintained in the long run.

Sticky prices. The rigidity of oligopolistic prices occurs mainly in the face of cyclical and seasonal fluctuations in demand. The existence of business cycles—alternating periods of high and low demand for output—is well known to firms, even if the precise course of each cycle cannot be predicted in advance. Oligopolistic firms tend to hold their prices fairly constant through cyclical fluctuations in demand while allowing output to vary.

Price stickiness is short-term behavior that need not affect our longer-term view of how the economy functions. Nonetheless, the stickiness is an interesting problem in its own right, and it has important implications for macroeconomics.[2] The modern explanation of this pricing behavior has two parts. The first concerns the nature of short-run cost curves in industries that are typically oligopolistic; the second concerns the costs of changing prices.

FIGURE 14-4 Saucer-shaped Average Variable and Marginal Cost Curves

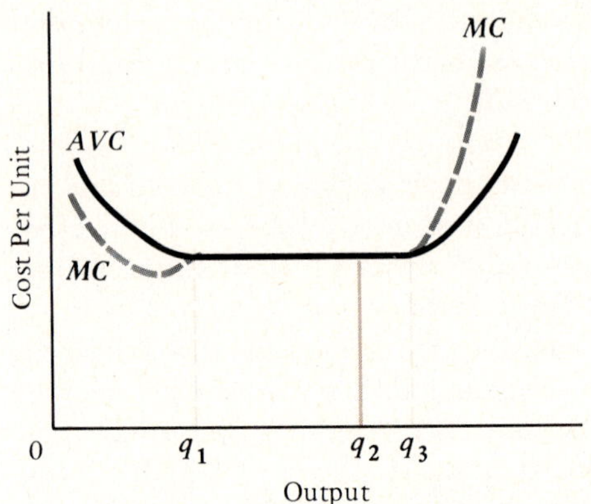

Where the *AVC* curve is horizontal, marginal costs coincide with average variable costs and are likewise constant per unit of output. It is possible to design a plant that achieves roughly constant variable and marginal costs over a large range of output. Such a curve is shown here. While average variable costs decrease for outputs up to q_1 and increase beyond q_3, they are constant over the large range q_1 to q_3. The level of output q_2 is normal capacity output, which is the average output the firm hopes to achieve. This is less than the highest level of output at which *AVC* is a minimum. With this cost curve, the firm can vary production over the whole interval from q_1 to q_3 and have constant marginal costs per unit.

Short-Run Costs

Saucer-shaped cost curves. Ever since economists began measuring the cost curves of manufacturing firms, they have reported flat short-run variable cost curves. The evidence is now overwhelming that in manufacturing, and in some other sectors, cost curves are shaped like the black curve in Figure 14-4, with a long, flat, middle portion and sharply rising sections at each end. For such a cost curve, which may be described as saucer-shaped, there is a large range of output over which average variable costs are constant. Over that range marginal costs are equal to average variable costs, and thus they too are constant per unit of output.

Given a saucer-shaped cost curve, there is no single output where average costs are minimized (in Chapter 10 we called the output that minimizes average total cost *capacity output*). Instead, we distinguish two new concepts.

Full-capacity output, which is shown as q_3 in Figure 14-4, is the maximum output that can be produced before average and marginal costs start to rise.

Normal-capacity output, a somewhat lower level shown by q_2 in Figure 14-4, is the output that the firm hopes to maintain on average. The margin between normal-capacity output and full-capacity output is available to meet unexpected, seasonal, or

[2] A major issue in macroeconomics is to understand why in the short run it is mainly output, rather than prices, that responds to changes in the total demand for goods and services across the whole economy. The oligopolistic behavior studied in this section provides an important part of the explanation of this phenomenon.

cyclical peaks in demand. The firm expects to use it in periods of peak demand but not in periods of average or slack demand.

Explaining the saucer shape. Why are many cost curves saucer-shaped rather than U-shaped? The answer is that firms design plants to have this property so that they can accommodate the inevitable seasonal and cyclical swings in demand for their products. As Professor George Stigler (the 1982 Nobel Laureate in Economics) was the first to point out, a firm faced with two possible average variable cost curves, such as those shown in Figure 14-5, might well prefer to build a plant that results in the flat-bottomed curve if it anticipates widely fluctuating demand. The saucer-shaped curve then leads on average to lower costs, even though at some output the U-shaped cost curve dips below it.

FIGURE 14-5 U-shaped Versus Saucer-shaped Cost Curves

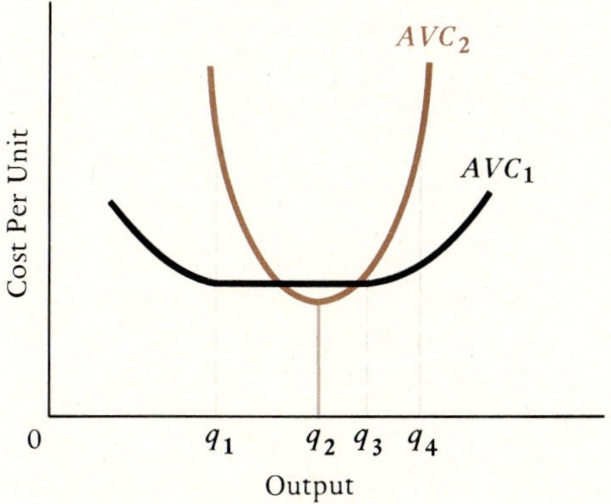

A firm anticipating fluctuating output may choose a plant with a flat-bottomed cost curve. AVC_1 and AVC_2 are alternatives based on how a plant is designed and built. While AVC_2 achieves lower unit costs than AVC_1 if output is very close to q_2, it is much less adaptable to either higher or lower outputs. If the firm could count on producing q_2 every period, it would prefer the plant with the cost curve AVC_2. But if it anticipated outputs ranging from q_1 to q_4, it would prefer the plant with AVC_1.

How does it happen that the firm has a choice of the shape of its short-run average cost curve? Consider again the law of diminishing returns first encountered in Chapter 10. The U-shaped short-run cost curve arises when a variable amount of one factor, say, labor, is applied to a fixed amount of a second factor, say, capital. Starting from zero output and zero use of the variable factor, as more of that factor is used, a more nearly optimal combination with the fixed factor is achieved. Once the optimal combination is arrived at, the use of further units of the variable factor leads to too much of the variable factor being used in combination with the fixed factor and thus to rising average variable costs. Only one quantity of labor leads to the least-cost factor proportions.

The changing combinations of fixed and variable factors must occur in the short run whenever all of the fixed factor must be used all of the time—in other words, when the fixed factor is *indivisible*. But this is not always the case. Even though the firm's plant and equipment may be fixed in the short run so that no more than what exists is available, it is often possible to use less than all the fixed capital. For that reason the flat cost curve is not inconsistent with the law of diminishing returns. The divisibility of the "fixed factor" means that diminishing returns does not apply because variations in output below full capacity are accomplished by reducing the input of both labor and capital.

Consider as a simple example a factory that consists of 10 sewing machines in a shed, each with a productive capacity of 20 units per day when operated by 1 operator for 1 shift. If 200 units per day are required, then all 10 machines are operated by 10 workers on a normal shift. If demand falls to 180, then 1 operator can be laid off. But there is no benefit to have the 9 remaining operators dashing about trying to work 10 machines. Clearly, 1 machine can be "laid off" as well and the ratio of *employed* labor to *employed* machines held constant. Production can go from 20 to 40 to 60 all the way to 200 without any change in factor proportions for the factors in use. In this case we would expect the factory to have constant marginal and average variable costs from 20 to 200 units and only then to encounter rising costs, as production must be extended by overtime and other means of combining more labor with the maximum available supply of 10 machines.

In such a case the fixed factor is *divisible.* Since some of it can be left unemployed, there is no need to depart from the most efficient ratio of *labor used* to *capital used* as production is decreased. Thus average variable costs can be constant over a large range, up to the point at which all of the fixed factor is used.

The existence of plants with divisible physical capital can account for the observed saucer shape of many cost curves at the plant level.

A similar situation occurs when a firm has many plants. For example, a plywood manufacturer with 10 or more plants may choose to reduce its output by temporarily closing one or more plants while operating the rest at normal-capacity output. The *firm's* short-run variable costs tend to be constant over a large range of output because there is no need to depart from the optimal combination of labor and capital in the plants that are kept in operation.

Cost of Changing Prices

The second part of the explanation of sticky prices concerns the high costs of changing administered prices. Such costs include the costs of printing new list prices for the many products of a typical multiproduct firm, the costs of notifying all customers, the accounting and billing difficulty of keeping track of frequently changing prices, and the loss of customer and retailer loyalty and goodwill due to the uncertainty caused by frequent changes in prices.

Sticky Price Behavior

The composite explanation of sticky prices is illustrated in Figure 14-6. Firms estimate their *normal demand curve,* that is, the average of what they can expect to sell at each price over booms and slumps. Having built a plant consistent with this normal demand and with the expected fluctuations in output, they then pick the profit-maximizing price derived from their normal demand curve as their "normal price." Short-run fluctuations in demand are met by holding price constant and varying output. This avoids all the costs involved in repeated changes of prices.

The behavior just described is consistent with profit maximization. Because the cost of changing prices is high, often the best thing a firm can do is set the price that maximizes profits for average demand and then adjust output rather than price as demand varies over the cycle.

Note, however, that this behavior is profitable only with a saucer-shaped cost curve, such as AVC_1 in Figure 14-5. If the curve were U-shaped, such as AVC_2 in that figure, the firm's losses would be unacceptable when costs soared at the extremes of lower and higher than normal output.

Holding price constant in the face of short-term fluctuations in demand can be the profit-maximizing course of action only if costs remain relatively stable over the range of output fluctuations normally encountered.

Implications of the theory. The theory that oligopolistic firms have saucer-shaped cost curves and that it is costly for oligopolists to change prices has a number of important implications.

1. As long as output remains within the range over which the average cost curve is flat, the price charged tends to be a relatively fixed markup over the constant level of average cost.
2. Cyclical fluctuations in demand are met by quantity adjustments rather than price adjustments.
3. Cost changes in either an upward or a downward direction are passed on through price changes (although possibly with a lag because oligopolistic firms find it costly to make continual price changes).
4. Oligopolistic firms receive signals from the economy just as do perfectly competitive firms, but the form the signals take is different. Perfect competitors receive their signals about market conditions from a price change; oligopolies receive their signals from a change in their volume of sales.

The second and the third implications are especially important when we study some current controversies in macroeconomics. We shall return to them in Chapter 39.

FIGURE 14-6 A Theory of Sticky Prices in the Face of Fluctuating Demand

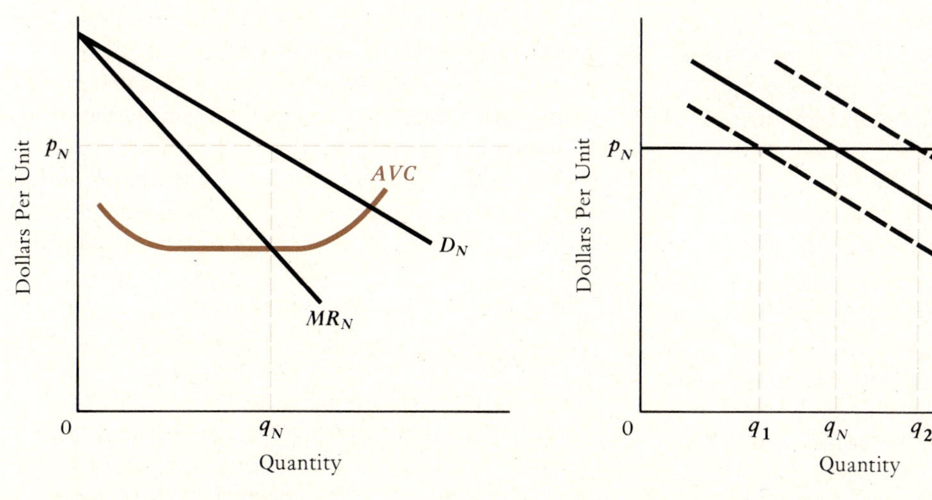

If it is costly to make price changes, a profit-maximizing firm may fix a price based on average sales and vary quantity in the face of fluctuating demand. In part (i) the firm with normal capacity q_N and a normal (average) demand curve D_N with a marginal revenue curve MR_N sets p_N as the profit-maximizing price, where $MR_N = MC$. This price becomes its normal price. As shown in part (ii), when demand slumps to D_1, the firm reduces output to q_1 but keeps price unchanged. When demand peaks at D_2, it also maintains price and increases output to q_2.

Long-Run Price-Output Decisions

While oligopolistic firms tend to hold prices constant in the face of expected short-term fluctuations in demand, prices do change in response to longer-term forces. How, then, are prices set in oligopolistic industries? In competitive industries prices are set by the impersonal forces of demand and supply. But as we have already observed, oligopolists must administer their prices. What price to charge is a decision that must be made by each individual firm and cannot be left to impersonal forces external to the firm.

Interdependence of decisions. There is one key problem facing most oligopolistic firms that the OPEC experience did not illustrate. While there were many non-OPEC producers of oil, no one of them had anything like the output of OPEC during the 1970s. Thus the cartel did not face another producer with substantial power to influence the world's price in response to OPEC's own decisions. Instead, OPEC was the only unified group with a large enough proportion of the total output to have real power to influence that price.

A more typical oligopolistic industry contains a few large firms, each of which is aware that it has market power. Thus asking how prices are set under oligopoly raises a critical aspect of oligopoly theory.

The few large firms in a typical oligopolistic industry have identifiable rivals whose behavior they cannot afford to ignore.

Eatons watches Simpsons, and Simpsons watches Eatons, and each firm *knows* it is being carefully watched by the other. When one makes some pricing decision, it is likely to take into account how it thinks the other will react. So what Eatons does may depend on what it *thinks* Simpsons will do, and the outcome of Eatons' actions will depend on what Simpsons *actually* does. To deal with this complexity, economists have sometimes proposed simplifying models and sometimes turned to empirical findings to suggest generalizations. We shall look at each of these approaches.

Model-based Approaches

The first model of price setting we consider avoids the complexity of interdependence by assuming that each firm will ignore the other firms' reactions to its decision making. The second model includes interdependence and assumes that a firm considers the reactions that it expects from its competitors when making its decisions.

Cournot-Nash Equilibrium

An important breakthrough in dealing with the oligopoly problem was made in 1838 by the French economist A. A. Cournot. He dealt with the special case of an industry containing only two firms, called a **duopoly.**

Cournot assumed that the two firms sold an identical product and that each chose its profit-maximizing output on the assumption that *the other firm would hold its output constant.* A pair of quantities would not represent equilibrium if at least one firm wished to change its quantity *given* the other firm's quantity. Cournot's great discovery was the existence of an equilibrium at which each firm's profit-maximizing quantity was its existing quantity *given* the existing quantity of the other firm. This equilibrium has two key characteristics:

1. The market is divided in a determinate way between the two firms. (It is shared equally if the two firms have identical cost curves.)
2. The resulting price is higher than the competitive price but lower than the price a monopolist would charge.

These results established oligopoly as not just a mixture of competition and monopoly but as a truly separate market form. The equilibrium Cournot analyzed has survived in modern theorizing. It is now often called the **Cournot-Nash equilibrium.** It is the equilibrium that results when each firm makes its output decisions on the assumption that all other firms' outputs will be unchanged.

Because this equilibrium may occur when firms do not take their competitors' reactions into account, it arises when there is no collusion among firms. For this reason it is often called a *non-cooperative equilibrium.* It is also a *self-policing* equilibrium in that no single firm has a profit incentive to depart from the equilibrium.

Conjectural Variations

The assumption that each firm takes its rival's behavior as given seems wrong in many small-group situations. The Ford Motor Company knows (or quickly learns) that if it slashes the prices on some of its cars, GM and Chrysler will react in some way, usually by adjusting their prices on comparable models. Similar considerations apply when de Haviland considers altering the price of one of its commuter aircraft or Domtar the prices of its paper products.

One way to deal with this interdependence is to assume that when it makes its decisions, an oligopolistic firm takes into account what are called *conjectural variations.* This model assumes that when making price or output decisions, each firm conjectures variations its choices will induce its rivals to make in their prices or outputs. The firm then takes these variations into account when making its decisions. For example, firm A might assume that whatever price or output it sets, its rivals will set the same price or output. Or the firm might assume that if it raises prices, its rivals will also raise their prices, but only by half as much.

From the point of view of a simple theory, the problem with conjectural variations is that there are so many possible different ones. Thus they lead not to a single prediction but to a variety of market outcomes. Conjectural variations are not a single theory of oligopoly but a great number of possible theories.

Differentiated products. All the complexity just described arises even when oligopolists sell a homogeneous product, as Cournot assumed they did. But most oligopolies sell a wide range of differentiated products. For example, one brand of running shoes sold by Nike differs not only from all other brands it sells but also from all brands sold by Adidas and other competing companies. In such cases oligopolies face an additional set of problems. With differentiated products, each product is distinct from every other product. As a result, firms do not need to compete only by means of price; they can also use quality, advertising, and the nature of their whole product line as competitive weapons. This adds yet further to the complexity and multiplicity of model-based theories of oligopoly behavior.

Empirical Approaches

Because the problem of price-output behavior under oligopoly is so complex, some economists have sought to build a theory by generalizing from observations of the behavior of oligopolistic firms. These economists believe that we need to begin with detailed knowledge of the actual behavior of such firms. This knowledge is then used to narrow the range of theoretically possible cases by selecting those that actually occur.

Such empirically based approaches to the problem start by recognizing two limits to oligopolistic prices and profits. First, if there is no recognition of interdependence at all, a non-cooperative equilibrium will be established, and profits will be much lower than they would be under a monopoly. They might even be pushed to the zero-profit position that occurs under perfect competition. Second, if the firms collude to maximize their joint profits, they might reach the upper limit and establish a monopoly price.

Although the upper limit can be attained through explicit agreement, as in the case of OPEC, such agreements are illegal for firms producing in Canada. Such a position might also arise, however, through tacit agreement based on mutual recognition of interdependence. If all firms assume that their competitors will match their own price, they will each be motivated to establish the joint profit-maximizing price and output. Because such an equilibrium can result from either actual or tacit cooperation, it is often called the *cooperative equilibrium*.

As we have already seen, however, there are forces at work to upset such a cooperative solution. Even if joint profits are maximized, there is the problem of market shares. How is the profit-maximizing level of sales to be divided among the competing firms? Competition for market shares may upset the tacit agreement to hold to joint maximizing behavior. In an industry with many differentiated products and where sales are often by contract between buyers and sellers, cheating may be covert rather than overt. Secret discounts and rebates can allow a firm to increase its sales at the expense of its competitors while appearing to hold to the tacitly agreed monopoly price.

Another reason why the monopoly level of profits may not be achieved, even if the monopoly price is maintained, is that firms often compete for market shares by various forms of non-price competition such as advertising. Such competition is costly, and it may reduce the industry's profits.

These considerations suggest that we look at an oligopolistic industry in terms of the conflicting pressures of cooperation and competition that act on it. First, the recognition of interdependence is a force leading firms toward the monopoly price and the cooperative equilibrium of joint profit maximization. Second, the possibility of gaining at the expense of one's rivals is a force pushing toward competitive behavior that leads firms away from the cooperative equilibrium and in the direction of a non-cooperative equilibrium.

These considerations lead to the *hypothesis of qualified joint profit maximization*, first stated by Professor William Fellner.

The hypothesis of qualified joint profit maximization is that the relative strength of the tendencies toward and away from joint profit maximization varies from industry to industry in a systematic way that is associated with observable characteristics of firms, markets, and products.

Here are some of the characteristics that are hypothesized to affect the strength of the two tendencies.

1. *The tendency toward joint maximization is greater for small numbers of sellers than for larger numbers.* This characteristic involves both motivation and ability. When there are few firms, they will know

that one of them cannot gain sales without inducing retaliation by its rivals. Also, a few firms can tacitly coordinate their policies with less difficulty than can many firms.

2. *The tendency toward joint maximization is greater for producers of similar products than for producers of sharply differentiated products.* The argument here is that the more nearly identical the products of sellers, the closer will be the direct rivalry for customers and the less the ability of one firm to gain a lasting advantage over its rivals. Such sellers will tend to prefer joint efforts to achieve a larger pie to individual attempts to increase their own shares.
3. *The tendency toward joint maximization is greater in a growing market than in a contracting market.* The argument here is that when demand is growing, firms can use their capacity fully without resorting to attempts to "steal" their rivals' customers. When firms have excess capacity, they are tempted to give price concessions to attract customers, but when their rivals retaliate, price cuts become general.
4. *The tendency toward joint maximization is greater when the industry contains a dominant firm rather than a set of more or less equal competitors.* A dominant firm may become a *price leader*, that is, a firm that sets the industry's price while all other firms fall into line. Even if a dominant firm is not automatically a price leader, other firms may look to it for judgment about market conditions, and its decisions may become a tentative focus for tacit agreement.
5. *The tendency toward joint profit maximization is greater when non-price rivalry is absent or limited.* If non-price competition is not limited, tacit price fixing to maximize joint profits will cause non-price competition that will take the industry away from its joint maximizing position. The argument here is that when firms seek to suppress their basic rivalry by avoiding price competition, rivalry will break out in other forms. Firms may seek to increase their market shares through extra advertising, quality changes, the establishment of new products, giveaways, and a host of similar schemes that leave their prices unchanged but increase their costs.
6. *The tendency toward joint profit maximization is greater when the barriers to entry of new firms are greater.* The high profits of existing firms attract new entrants, who will drive down price and reduce profits. The greater the barriers to entry, the less this will occur. Thus the greater the entry barriers, the closer the profits of existing firms can be to their joint maximizing level without being reduced by new entry.

The Importance of Entry Barriers

Point 6 has taken us beyond price and output decisions and into considerations of entry. Perhaps the most important empirical observation about actual behavior of firms in oligopoly is what Professor Joe S. Bain called the *condition of entry,* which relates to what we have called entry barriers.

Suppose firms in an oligopolistic industry succeed in raising prices above long-run average total costs and earn substantial profits that are not completely eliminated by non-price competition. Why do these profits not cause other firms to enter the industry, increase output, and force prices down to the zero-profit level? The answer lies in barriers to entry.

Natural barriers were discussed in Chapter 13 (see page 244). If natural barriers to entry do not exist, oligopolistic firms can earn profits in the long run only if they can create entry barriers. To the extent to which this can be done, existing firms can move toward joint profit maximization without fear of new entrants attracted by the high profits. We discuss next a few types of created barriers.

Brand Proliferation

Many products have several characteristics, which can be varied over a wide range. Thus it is possible to have many similar products, each with a somewhat different mix of characteristics. Consider the many kinds of breakfast cereals or cars. Although the multiplicity of brands is no doubt partly a response to consumers' tastes, it may also be partly an attempt to discourage the entry of new firms. When the existing firms sell a wide array of differentiated products, entry on a small scale by a new firm is difficult.

To illustrate why brand proliferation may be a formidable barrier to a small potential entrant, assume that the product is subject to substantial brand switching by consumers. In this case the larger the number of brands sold by existing firms, the smaller the expected sales of a new entrant. Say that an industry contains three large firms, each selling one brand of cigarettes, and say that 30 percent of all smokers change brands in a random fashion each year. If a new firm enters the industry, it can expect to pick up 25 percent of the smokers who change brands (it has one out of the new total of four available brands). This would give it 7.5 percent (25 percent of 30 percent) of the total market the first year merely as a result of picking up its share of the random switchers, and it would keep increasing its share year by year thereafter.[3] If, however, the existing three firms have 5 brands each, there would be 15 brands already available, and a new firm selling 1 new brand could expect to pick up only one-sixteenth of the brand switchers, giving it less than 2 percent of the total market the first year and smaller gains in subsequent years also. This is an extreme case, but it illustrates a general result.

The larger the number of differentiated products sold by existing oligopolists, the smaller the market available to a new firm entering with a single new product.

Set-up Costs

Existing firms can create entry barriers by imposing on new entrants significant fixed costs of setting up operations in that market. This is particularly important if the minimum efficient scale occurs at an output that is low relative to total industry output, that is, if there are only weak natural barriers to entry.

Advertising is one means by which existing firms can impose heavy set-up costs on new entrants. Advertising, of course, serves purposes other than creating barriers to entry. Among them, it may perform the useful function of informing buyers about their alternatives, thereby making markets work more smoothly. Indeed, a new firm may find that advertising is essential, even when existing firms do not advertise at all, simply to call attention to its entry into an industry where it is unknown.

Nonetheless, advertising can also operate as a potent entry barrier by increasing the set-up costs of new entrants. Where there is much effective brand-image advertising, a new firm will have to spend a great deal on advertising its product in order to bring the product to the public's attention. If the firm's sales are small, advertising costs *per unit sold* will be correspondingly large. Large sales allow the fixed advertising costs needed to break into the market to be spread over a large number of units. This may reduce costs per unit enough so as not to confer a significant competitive disadvantage on the new firm.

Figure 14-7 illustrates how heavy advertising can shift the cost curves of a firm with a low minimun

FIGURE 14-7 Advertising Cost As a Barrier to Entry

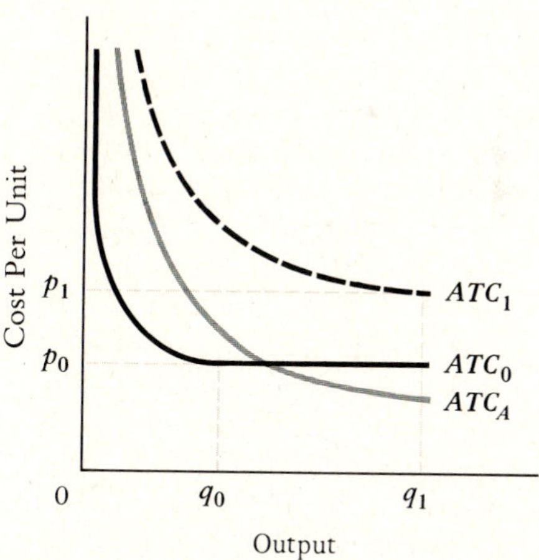

Large advertising costs can increase the minimum efficient scale (*MES*) of production and thereby increase entry barriers. The ATC_0 curve shows that the *MES* without advertising is at q_0. The curve ATC_A shows that advertising cost per unit falls as output rises. Advertising increases total cost to ATC_1, which is downward sloping over its entire range. Advertising has given a scale advantage to large sellers and has thus created a barrier to entry.

[3] Because it is smaller than its rivals, it would lose fewer customers to them by random switching than it would gain from them.

efficient scale to make it one with a high *MES*. In essence, what happens is that a scale advantage of advertising is added to a low *MES* of production with the result that the overall *MES* is raised.

A new entrant with small sales but large set-up costs finds itself at a substantial cost disadvantage relative to its established rivals.

Any once-and-for-all cost of entering a market has the same effect as a large, initial advertising expenditure. For example, with many consumer goods the cost of developing a new product that is similar but not identical to existing products may be quite substantial. Even if there are few economies of scale in the production of the product, its large fixed development cost can lead to a falling long-run average total cost curve over a wide range of output.

An application. We have seen that brand proliferation and advertising can act as entry barriers. The combined use of the two help to explain one apparent paradox of everyday life—the fact that one firm often sells multiple brands of the same product, which compete directly against one another as well as against the products of other firms.

The soap and cigarette industries provide classic examples of this behavior. Since all available scale economies can be realized by quite small plants, both industries have few natural barriers to entry. Both contain a few large firms, each of which produces an array of heavily advertised products. The array of products makes it harder for a new entrant to obtain a large market niche with one new product. The heavy advertising, though directed against existing products, creates an entry barrier by increasing the set-up costs of a new product that seeks to gain the attention of consumers and establish its own brand image. Together multiple products and heavy advertising may provide a formidable entry barrier to any new firm.

Predatory Pricing

A firm that is considering entry will not do so if faced with certain losses after entry. One way existing firms can create such a situation is to cut prices to—or below—cost whenever entry occurs and keep them there until the entrant goes bankrupt. The existing firms sacrifice profits while doing so, but they send a discouraging message to future as well as present potential rivals.

There is much controversy concerning predatory pricing. Some economists argue that pricing policies that appear to be predatory can be explained by other motives and that existing firms only hurt themselves when they engage in such practices instead of reaching an accommodation with new entrants. Others argue that predatory pricing seems to have been observed and that it is in the long-run interests of existing firms to punish new entrants even when it is costly to do so in the short run. The reason is that the reputation the firm earns may persuade future potential entrants not to try entering. Hence the firm can earn large profits in the future without attracting entry.

Oligopoly and the Functioning of the Economy

Oligopoly is the most commonly encountered market structure in large sectors of the Canadian and American economies. What does the recognition of the impossibility of achieving perfect competition and of the necessity for oligopoly over a large part of the economy do to our views of the working of the price system?

Resource Allocation

We have seen that under perfect competition prices are set by the impersonal forces of demand and supply. Firms in oligopolistic markets administer their prices. The market signaling system works slightly differently when prices are administered rather than determined by the market. Changes in the market conditions for both inputs and outputs are signaled to the perfectly competitive firm by changes in the prices of its inputs and its outputs. Changes in the market conditions for inputs are signaled to the oligopolistic firm by changes in the prices of its inputs. Changes in the market conditions for the oligopolist's output are typically signaled, however, by a change in sales at the administered price.

Increases in costs of inputs will shift cost curves upward, and oligopolistic firms will be led to raise prices and lower output. Increases in demand will cause the sales of oligopolistic firms to rise. Firms will then respond by increasing output, thereby increasing the quantities of society's resources that are allocated to producing that commodity.

The market system reallocates resources in response to changes in demand and costs in roughly the same way under oligopoly as it does under perfect competition.

Some oligopolies succeed in coming close to joint profit maximization. Others compete so intensely among themselves that they come close to competitive prices and outputs. The consequences for the behavior of the economic system vary accordingly.

Innovation

Although oligopolies do not fulfill the technical conditions of allocative efficiency, an important issue is how much they contribute to economic growth by engaging in innovative activity in the very long run.

An important defense of oligopoly relates to Schumpeter's concept of creative destruction (see page 296). Some economists have theorized that intermediate market structures, such as oligopoly, would lead to more innovation than would occur in either competitive or monopolistic industries. They argue that the oligopolist is faced with clear and present competition from existing rivals and cannot afford the more relaxed life of the monopolist. At the same time, however, the oligopoly firm expects to keep a good share of the profits that it earns because of the barriers to entry and its ability to avoid excessive price competition with existing rivals.

The empirical evidence is broadly consistent with this hypothesis. Professor Jesse Markham of Harvard University concluded a survey of empirical findings by saying:

> If technological change and innovational activity are, as we generally assume, in some important way a product of organized R&D activities financed and executed by business companies, it is clear that the welfare payoffs that flow from them can to some measurable extent be traced to the doorsteps of large firms operating in oligopolistic markets.

Everyday observation provides some confirmation of this finding. Leading North American firms that operate in highly concentrated industries, such as Bombardier, Kodak, IBM, Northern Telecom, du Pont, CIL, Xerox, General Electric, and Noranda, have been highly innovative over many years.

A Final Word

Oligopoly is an important market structure in today's economy because there are many industries where the minimum efficient scale is simply too large to support a large group of competing firms. Although oligopoly will not usually achieve the same efficiency as perfect competition, rivalrous oligopoly may produce more satisfactory results than monopoly. Oligopoly may also be effective in producing very long run adaptations that develop both new products and cost-reducing methods of producing old ones.

The defense of oligopoly as a market form is that it may be the best of the available alternatives when minimum efficient scale is large. The challenge to public policy is to keep oligopolists competing and using their competitive energies to improve products and to lower costs rather than merely to erect entry barriers.

Summary

1. The OPEC cartel provides insights into the problems of oligopolies. It proved remarkably successful during the 1970s in raising the prices of oil above the previous, approximately competitive level. At the time OPEC included a large fraction of the world's oil-exporting

countries, and it succeeded for almost 10 years in holding prices high and limiting output to maintain these prices. Its initial success was due partly to the facts that many governments prevented the price signals from reaching their domestic markets and, when the price changes were finally allowed, neither demand nor alternative sources of supply could change quickly.

2. In the era before OPEC, demand for oil products rose steadily in response to rising incomes, sustained low prices, and a highly elastic long-run supply. OPEC changed the supply situation overnight by means of an effective cartel. Using a strategy of restricting output, it converted a horizontal supply curve into a steeply rising one. From 1973 until the early 1980s OPEC managed the world price of oil and received enormous monopoly profits from its own sales.
3. OPEC's ability to control the oil market was weakened as oil-consuming countries decreased their reliance on oil and as non-OPEC sources of energy steadily expanded. In the early 1980s OPEC members found it necessary to accept ever-larger reductions in their production and in their shares of world markets in order to maintain the high oil prices. Unable to agree on quotas or on how to enforce them, the cartel collapsed at the end of 1985 and prices tumbled toward the competitive level.
4. There are several important lessons in the OPEC experience: (a) Restriction of output can lead to large short-run profits, (b) the required output restrictions become larger over time due to reductions in demand and development of other supplies, and (c) as the cartel's market shrinks, it becomes increasingly difficult to maintain output restriction agreements.
5. An important empirical finding is the relative short-run stickiness of oligopoly prices in response to seasonal and cyclical fluctuations in demand. This stickiness results from the combined influence of the flat short-run cost curves and the high costs involved in changing administered prices frequently. While prices are changed when the firms' costs change or in response to permanent shifts in demand, oligopolistic firms find it profitable to vary output, keeping prices fixed, as demand fluctuates around its normal level.
6. A key empirical finding about oligopolistic industries, particularly in the manufacturing sector, is that short-run cost curves tend to be saucer-shaped rather than U-shaped. This reflects the decision of firms to build plants capable of being operated over a range of outputs at roughly constant marginal cost so as to keep average costs low in the face of fluctuating output. The flat cost curve does not violate the law of diminishing returns as long as the proportion in which capital and labor are used in production can be held constant for outputs below full capacity.
7. There is no simple set of predictions about the long-term outcome of oligopolistic competition. The final outcome depends on the strategies adopted by the individual firms. Therefore, instead of a single

theory, there are many possible patterns of behavior. The general hypothesis of qualified joint profit maximization says that firms that recognize they are rivals will be motivated by two sets of opposing forces, one set moving them toward joint profit maximization and the other moving them away from it.

8. Oligopoly profits persist in the long run because of barriers to entry, which may be natural or created. Firm-created barriers include brand proliferation and various types of set-up costs. They may also include the threat of predatory pricing.
9. Under oligopoly the price system works to reallocate resources in response to changes in demand and costs in qualitatively the same way as it does under perfect competition. Oligopoly does not, however, fulfill the technical conditions for efficiency that are fulfilled by perfect competition. Some economists argue that oligopoly (and monopoly) profits are conducive to rapid growth because they encourage highly competitive behavior.

Topics for Review

Effects of OPEC cartelization
Sticky short-term prices
Saucer-shaped short-run average cost curves
Cooperative and non-cooperative equilibria
Conjectural variations
Hypothesis of qualified joint profit maximization
Created barriers to entry
Resource allocation under oligopoly

Discussion Questions

1. What bearing did each of the following have on the eventual inability of OPEC to maintain a monopoly price for oil?
   a. Between 1979 and 1985 OPEC's share of the world oil supply decreased by half.
   b. "Saudi Arabia's interest lies in extending the life span of oil to the longest possible period," said Sheik Yamani.
   c. The Soviet Union, in order to earn Western currency to pay for grain, increased its oil exports to the West during the late 1970s, becoming the world's second largest oil exporter.
   d. The Iran-Iraq war decreased oil production in the Middle East from 1979 to 1981 by 4.5 million barrels a day.
   e. Government policies during the 1970s protected consumers from oil price shocks by holding domestic prices well below OPEC levels.
   f. In the late 1980s, Iran became increasingly concerned to maximize its oil revenues in order to pay for its war with Iraq.
2. How did these headlines, all from 1985, foreshadow the collapse of OPEC?
   a. "Saudis threaten to double oil production if OPEC does not accept its terms"

b. "Britain's price cut adds to OPEC's predicament"
c. "Saudi economy is ailing after three years of recession"
d. "New oil discovery adds Colombia to world's producers"
e. "OPEC oil ministers meet amid discord on pricing policy"

3. Do the following groups stand to gain or to lose if oil prices fall further over the next five years?
   a. Canadian consumers
   b. Coal miners in North America
   c. People who have invested in companies developing synthetic fuels
   d. Indonesia, an oil-exporting country with small oil reserves and a large population
   e. U.S. drillers of wildcat oil wells
   f. Saudi Arabia
4. "The decade from 1975 to 1985 proved to the world that there were many available substitutes for gasoline, among them bicycles, car pools, moving closer to work, cable TV, and Japanese cars." Discuss how each of these may be a substitute for gasoline.
5. It has been estimated that if automobile companies did not change models for 10 years, the cost of production would be reduced by approximately 30 percent. In view of this, why are there annual model changes? Which, if any, of the reasons you have suggested depend on the industry's being oligopolistic? Should frequent model changes be forbidden by law?
6. Compare the effects on the automobile and the wheat industries of each of the following. In the light of your answers discuss general ways in which oligopolistic industries fulfill the same general functions as perfectly competitive industries.
   a. Large rise in demand
   b. Large rise in costs of production
   c. Temporary cut in supplies coming to market due to a three-month rail strike
   d. Rush of cheap foreign imports
7. Most Canadian provinces have laws requiring a company to produce beer in the Province if it wishes to sell there. What do you think this does to the price of beer? What would be the consequences of repealing these laws? Why can small, high-cost local beers exist in open competition with large, low-cost, nationally sold beers?
8. Evidence suggests that the profits earned by all the firms in many oligopolistic industries are less than the profits that would be earned if the industry were monopolized. What are some reasons why this might be so?

15

The Theory and Practice of Competition Policy

In this chapter we look first at the concepts of efficiency and inefficiency as they have been traditionally used by economists, assuming that technology is fixed and that there is nothing that prevents a competitive market economy from existing. These assumptions lead to a preference for perfect competition over monopoly. Second, we look at considerations that may lead to a modification of the previous conclusions, including the possibility that technology requires oligopoly rather than perfect competition. Third, we look at competition policy as it is practiced in Canada.

Economic Efficiency in the Evaluation of Competition and Monopoly

Monopoly has long been regarded with suspicion. In *The Wealth of Nations* (1776), Adam Smith developed a ringing attack on monopolists. Since then most economists have criticized monopoly and advocated freer competition. Part of the appeal of competition and distrust of monopoly is noneconomic and was discussed in Chapter 12. But much of it has to do with the allegation that competition is efficient in ways that monopoly is not. This constitutes the classic case against monopoly. To understand it, we must first carefully define efficiency.

Efficiency and Inefficiency with Known Technology

Efficiency requires avoiding the waste of resources. When labor is unemployed and factories lie idle (as occurs in serious recessions), their potential current output is lost. If these resources could be employed, total output would be increased and hence everyone could be made better off.

But full employment of resources by itself is not enough to prevent the waste of resources. Even when resources are being fully used, they may be used inefficiently. Let us look at three examples of inefficiency in resource use.

1. If firms do not use the least costly method of producing their chosen outputs, they waste resources. For example, a firm that produces

30,000 pairs of shoes at a resource cost of $400,000 when it could be done at a cost of only $350,000 is using resources inefficiently. The lower-cost method would allow $50,000 worth of resources to be transferred to productive uses.
2. If some firms produce at high cost while other firms produce at low cost, the industry's overall cost of producing its output is higher than necessary.
3. If too much of one product and too little of another is produced, resources are being used inefficiently. To take an extreme example, say that so many shoes are produced that the marginal utility of shoes is zero for every consumer, while the marginal utility of coats remains high at the current level of output. Since no one places any value on the last pair of shoes produced but people place a high value on an additional coat, no consumer will be made worse off by a reduction of the output of shoes by one or two pairs, yet some consumer will be made better off by using the resources to increase the production of coats.

These examples suggest that we must refine our ideas of the waste of resources beyond the simple notion of ensuring that all resources are used. Economists define rather precisely what is meant by efficiency and inefficiency in resource use.

Resources are said to be used *inefficiently* when it would be *possible* by using them differently to make at least one household better off without making any household worse off. Conversely, resources are said to be used *efficiently* when it is *impossible* by using them differently to make any one household better off without making at least one other household worse off.

Efficiency in the use of resources is often called **Pareto-optimality** or **Pareto-efficiency** in honor of the great Italian economist Vilfredo Pareto (1848–1923), who pioneered in the study of efficiency.

How does an economy achieve efficiency in this sense? The three sources of inefficiency given earlier suggest important conditions that must be fulfilled if economic efficiency is to be attained. These conditions are conveniently collected into two categories, productive efficiency and allocative efficiency.

Conditions for Productive Efficiency

Productive efficiency requires that whatever output is being produced is being produced at the lowest attainable cost. When this is true, the output of any one commodity entails the lowest possible opportunity cost in terms of forgone outputs of other commodities. When this is not true, an unnecessary sacrifice of other commodities is being incurred; costs could be reduced and more resources spared for the production of other commodities. (Recall that opportunity cost reflects the value of the resources in their best alternative uses.) Two specific conditions must be fulfilled if productive efficiency is to be achieved.

Firms must be on their relevant cost curves. The first condition is that firms be on, rather than above, their relevant cost curve. If the firm is making a short-run decision, it must be on its short-run cost curve rather than above it. If the firm is making a long-run decision, it must choose the lowest achievable long-run cost for the output it wishes to select. If this condition is not met, there is (by definition) a less costly way for a firm to produce its present output.

This condition is met if firms are maximizing profits. Any firm that incurs more cost than is necessary will be making less profit than is possible. So it is in the interest of *all* profit-maximizing firms, no matter what type of market they sell in, to minimize their costs. This means producing on, not above, their relevant cost curve.

Though easy to state, this condition is often difficult to fulfill in practice. We know that existing firms sometimes, perhaps often, do not take advantage of all of the cost-reducing opportunities available to them. This may be so, for example, if the opportunities arise out of some new technology that existing managers have not learned about or are not trained to use. Or it may be due to inability to raise sufficient financial capital.

One major reason for firms being taken over by

other firms is that the existing management is not achieving the lowest costs and the acquiring firm sees a chance to raise profits by cutting costs.

All firms in an industry must have the same level of marginal cost. The second condition for productive efficiency ensures that production of any given total industry output be distributed among the producing firms so as to minimize total industry costs. This condition is fulfilled if the marginal cost of producing the last unit of output by each firm in the industry is the same for every other firm.

To see the importance of this condition, assume that it is not fulfilled. Suppose that the Jones Brothers shoe manufacturing firm has a marginal cost of $40 for the last shoe of some standard type that it produces, while Tremblay Ltd., has a marginal cost of only $35 for the same type of shoe. If the Jones plant produces one less pair of shoes and the Tremblay plant produces one more, total shoe output is unchanged, but total industry costs are reduced by $5. Thus $5 worth of resources will be freed to increase the production of other commodities.

Clearly, this cost saving can go on as long as the two firms have different marginal costs. But as the Tremblay firm produces more shoes, its marginal cost rises, while as the Jones firm produces fewer shoes, its marginal cost falls. (In producing more, the Tremblay firm is moving upward to the right along its given *MC* curve, whereas in producing less, the Jones firm is moving downward to the left along its given *MC* curve.) Say, for example, that after Tremblay Ltd., increases its production by 1,000 shoes per month, its marginal cost has *risen* to $37, whereas by the time Jones Brothers has reduced its output by the same amount, its marginal cost has *fallen* to $37. Now there is no further cost saving to be obtained by reallocating production between the two firms.

Conditions for Allocative Efficiency

Productive efficiency ensures that any given volume of output is produced at the lowest possible cost. Allocative efficiency concerns the appropriate mix of products. Resources must be allocated among the various goods that can be produced. **Allocative efficiency** ensures that the bundle of goods produced is an efficient bundle. If allocative efficiency is not achieved, resources can be reallocated to produce a different bundle of goods that will allow someone to be made better off while no one is made worse off.

To understand the conditions for allocative efficiency, we need to recall our analysis of consumers' choice in Chapter 8. There we saw that a consumer would buy all the units that he or she valued as much as or more than the market price for these units.[1] Faced with a single price of all units of some commodity bought, a consumer would go on buying units until the last unit was valued the same as its price. Consumers' surplus arises because the consumer would be willing to pay more than the given price for all but the last unit bought. This is another way of saying that the consumer values all other units bought more than the last unit. Thus a consumers' surplus is gained on all units except the marginal one. On the last marginal unit, however, the consumer only "breaks even" because the valuation placed on it is just equal to its price.

Price must equal marginal cost for all products. What is the right production mix? For example, how many shoes should be produced for allocative efficiency? How many dresses? How many hats? The answer is that the economy's allocation of resources is efficient when for every good produced, marginal cost of production is equated to its price.

To understand the significance of this condition, assume that shoes sell for $30 a pair but have a marginal cost of $40. If one less pair of shoes were produced, the value that households place on the pair of shoes not produced would be $30. But by the

[1] In Chapter 8 we took the household's valuation of consuming another unit of the commodity per period of time as being simply revealed by how much it was prepared to pay to consume another unit of the commodity per period of time. In Appendix A to Chapter 7 marginal utility theory made the household's valuation measurable by its marginal utility from consuming another unit of the commodity per unit of time. In Appendix B to Chapter 7 indifference theory made the household's valuation measurable by the marginal rate of substitution between purchasing power in general and another unit of the good in question. In all cases what we are measuring is the valuation that the household places on the marginal unit of a commodity in terms of money.

meaning of opportunity cost, the resources that would have been used to produce that pair of shoes could instead produce other goods (say, a coat) valued at $40. If society can give up something its members value at $30 and get in return something its members value at $40, the original allocation of resources is inefficient. Someone can be made better off, and no one need be worse off.

This is easy to see when the same household gives up the shoes and gets the coat. But it follows even when different households are involved, for the gaining household could compensate the losing household and still come out ahead.

Assume next that shoe production is cut back until the price of a pair of shoes rises from $30 to $35, while its marginal cost falls from $40 to $35. The efficiency condition is now fulfilled in shoe production because $p = MC = \$35$. Now if one less pair of shoes were produced, $35 worth of shoes would be sacrificed, while at most $35 worth of other commodities could be produced with the freed resources.

In this situation the allocation of resources to shoe production is efficient because it is not possible to change it so as to make someone better off without making someone else worse off. If one household were to sacrifice the pair of shoes, it would give up goods worth $35 and would then have to obtain for itself all of the new production of the alternative commodity produced just to break even. It cannot gain without making another household worse off. The same argument can be repeated for every commodity, and it leads to this conclusion:

The allocation of resources is efficient when each commodity's price equals its marginal cost.

Allocative efficiency is thus assured if $p = MC$ in all industries.

Efficiency in Perfect Competition and Monopoly

How do the market structures of perfect competition and monopoly affect the ability to achieve productive and allocative efficiency?

Productive Efficiency

The monopolist's output will be different from a competitive industry's output because the monopoly restricts output to raise its price. But in either situation a firm that wishes to maximize its profits will wish to produce *whatever output it produces* at the lowest possible cost. Not to do so would be to sacrifice profits by having higher costs than necessary. Thus profit maximization ensures that firms in either monopoly or competition will be motivated to satisfy the first condition of productive efficiency by producing on, rather than above, their relevant cost curves.

What about allocating output among plants? If the monopoly had more than one plant, it will wish to ensure that its production is divided efficiently among these plants. The efficient allocation among plants becomes a matter of internal organization with a monopoly that owns all of the plants. The profit-maximizing monopolist will allocate production so that all plants produce with the same marginal cost. There is no inherent barrier to doing so.

In perfect competition this allocation occurs automatically. Since all firms are faced with the same market price and all maximize their profits by equating marginal costs to price, all firms end up having the same marginal cost. For example, if the price of the type of shoe we have been considering is $37 a pair, all perfectly competitive, profit-maximizing firms will produce that type of shoe until the marginal cost of the last pair that they produce is $37.

Profit-maximizing behavior is sufficient to assure productive efficiency in a market economy.

Allocative Efficiency

We have already seen that perfectly competitive firms maximize their profits by equating marginal cost to price. Thus when perfect competition is the prevailing market structure across the whole economy, price is equal to marginal cost for all production, and allocative efficiency is assured.

As we have seen, the monopolist chooses an output at which the price charged is greater than marginal cost. This violates the conditions for allocative efficiency because the amount that consumers pay for the last unit exceeds the opportunity cost of producing it.

Consumers would be prepared to buy additional units for an amount greater than the cost of producing these units. Some consumers could be made better off, and none need be made worse off, by shifting extra resources into production of the monopolized commodity, thus increasing production of the product. As a consequence the monopoly produces an output that is *not* allocatively efficient.

From this follows at once the classic, efficiency-based preference for competition over monopoly:

An economy in which any output is produced under monopoly conditions will not be allocatively efficient.

This result has had important policy implications for economists and political leaders, as we shall see later in this chapter.

Note also that this result extends beyond the case of a simple monopoly. Whenever a firm has any power over the market in the sense that it faces a downward-sloping rather than a horizontal demand curve, its profit-maximizing behavior will lead it to produce where *MC* equals *MR*, *not* where *MC* equals price.

Contrasts with a Command Economy

We have seen that in a free-market economy perfect competition achieves allocative efficiency by the decentralized decisions of millions of independent households and firms each responding to prices given to them by the market. We have also seen that both monopolists and perfect competitors are motivated to achieve productive efficiency by the profit motive. There are thus powerful decentralized forces pushing the economy toward efficient results.

Where a centrally planned (command) economy replaces the market mechanism and the profit motive, it must find ways to allocate resources across different products and industries and to allocate production across plants in the same industry. It must also find ways to motivate producers to minimize costs of whatever output they do produce.

These are not impossible tasks, but they have proven among the most difficult to do well in the Soviet Union, Yugoslavia, China, and other countries that have, to some degree, rejected the profit motive and the price system.

Allocative Efficiency: An Elaboration

A fuller interpretation of the normative significance of allocative efficiency can be given using the concepts of consumers' and producers' surplus.[2]

Consumers' and Producers' Surplus

We have seen that consumers' surplus is the difference between the total value consumers place on all the units consumed of some commodity and the payment consumers must make for purchase of that commodity. Consumers' surplus is shown in Figure 15-1.

Producers' surplus is analogous to consumers' surplus. It occurs because all units of each firm's output are sold at the same market price while, given a rising supply curve, each unit but the last is produced at a marginal cost less than the market price.

Producers' surplus is defined as the amount producers are paid for a commodity less their total variable cost of producing the commodity. As we saw on page 199, the total variable cost of producing any output is shown by the area under the supply curve up to that output. Thus producers' surplus is the area above the supply curve and below the line giving market price. Producers' surplus is also shown in Figure 15-1.

The Allocative Efficiency of Perfect Competition Revisited

If the sum of the consumers' and producers' surplus is not maximized, the industry could be moved to the point where it was, and the extra surplus available

[2] The brief discussion of allocative efficiency in the previous section is all that is strictly required for the rest of this book. The importance of the concept, however, leads us to present a fuller exposition. This section, including Figures 15-1 to 15-3, may be omitted without loss of continuity.

FIGURE 15-1 Consumers' Surplus and Producers' Surplus

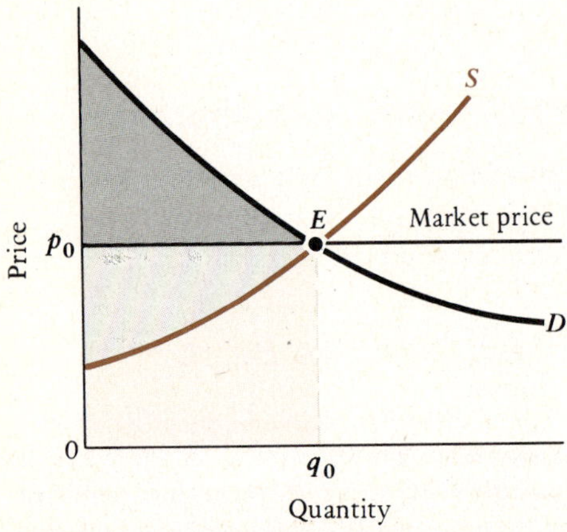

Consumers' surplus is the area under the demand curve and above the price line. Producers' surplus is the area above the supply curve and below the price line. The equilibrium price and quantity in this competitive market are p_0 and q_0. The total value consumers place on q_0 of the commodity is given by the sum of the three shaded areas. The amount they pay is p_0q_0, the rectangle consisting of the two lighter shaded areas. The difference, shown as the dark shaded area, is *consumers' surplus.*

The receipts to producers from the sale of q_0 units are also p_0q_0. The area under the supply curve, the color shaded area, is total variable cost, the minimum amount producers require to supply the output. The difference, shown as the light gray shaded area, is *producers' surplus.*

could be used to make some household better off without making anyone worse off.

Allocative efficiency occurs at the point where the sum of consumers' plus producers' surplus is maximized.

The point where the sum of consumers' plus producers' surplus is maximized is where the demand curve intersects the supply curve, that is, the point of equilibrium in a competitive market. This is shown graphically in Figure 15-2. For any output less than the competitive output, the demand curve is above the supply curve, which means that consumers value the last unit at an amount greater than its marginal cost of production. Suppose, for example, that the current output of shoes is such that consumers value at $45 an additional pair of shoes that adds $35 to costs. If it is sold at any price between $35 and $45, both producers and consumers gain; there is $10 of potential surplus to be divided between the two groups. In contrast, the last unit produced and sold at competitive equilibrium adds nothing to either consumers' or producers' surplus, since consumers value it at exactly its market price, and it adds the full amount of the market price to producers' costs.

If production were pushed beyond the competitive equilibrium, the sum of the two surpluses would be diminished. Assume, for example, that firms were forced to produce and sell further units of output at the competitive market price and that consumers were forced to buy these extra units at that price. (Note that neither group would do so voluntarily.) Firms would lose producers' surplus on those extra units because their marginal costs of producing the extra output would be above the price they received for it. Purchasers would lose consumers' surplus because the valuation that they placed on these extra units, as shown by the demand curve, would be less than the price they would have to pay.

The sum of producers' and consumers' surplus is maximized *only* at the competitive output, which is thus the only output that is allocatively efficient.

If the government of some command economy wanted to "maximize the sum of producers' and consumers' surplus," it could order firms to produce every unit up to the point where the cost of making the last unit was just equal to the valuation the purchasers placed on that last unit. The perfectly competitive market price provides exactly that signal!

The Allocative Inefficiency of Monopoly Revisited

Since, as we have just seen in Figure 15-2, the perfectly competitive equilibrium output maximizes the

FIGURE 15-2 The Allocative Efficiency of Perfect Competition

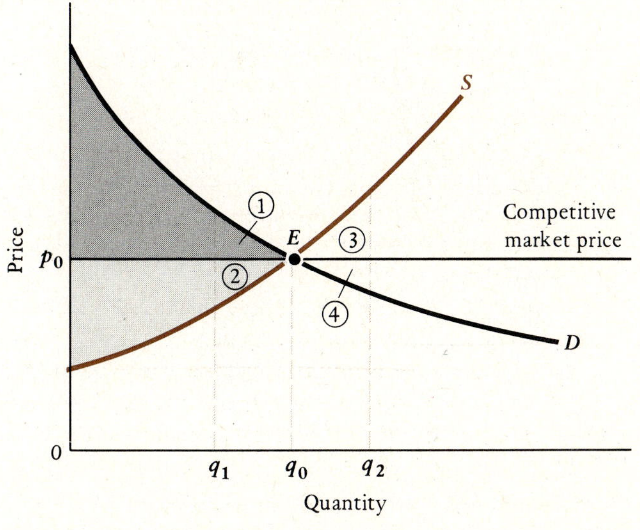

Competitive equilibrium is allocatively efficient because it maximizes the sum of consumers' plus producers' surplus. The competitive equilibrium occurs at the price-output combination, p_0q_0. At that equilibrium consumers' surplus is the dark shaded area above the price line, while producers' surplus is the light shaded area below the price line.

For any output less than q_0 the sum of the two surpluses is less than at q_0. For example, reducing output to q_1 but keeping price p_0 lowers consumers' surplus by area 1 and lowers producers' surplus by area 2.

For any output greater than q_0 the sum of the surpluses is also less than at q_0. For example, if producers are forced to produce output q_2 and sell it to consumers, who are forced to buy it at price p_0, producers' surplus is reduced by area 3 (the amount by which variable costs exceed revenue on those units), while the amount of consumers' surplus is reduced by area 4 (the amount by which expenditure exceeds consumers' satisfactions on those units).

Only the competitive output, q_0, maximizes the sum of the two surpluses.

sum of consumers' and producers' surplus, it follows immediately that the lower monopoly output must result in a smaller total of consumers' plus producers' surplus.

Why would producers and consumers agree to reduce their surpluses? The answer is that the monopoly equilibrium is not the outcome of voluntary agreement between the one producer and the many consumers. Instead it is imposed by the monopolist by virtue of the power it has over the market. When the monopolist reduces output below the competitive level, market price rises. As a result, consumers' surplus is diminished and producers' surplus is increased. In this way the monopoly firm gains at the expense of its customers. But that is not the whole story.

When output is lowered from the competitive level, there is always a *net* loss of surplus. More is given up by consumers than is gained by the monopolist. Some surplus is lost because output between the monopolistic and competitive levels is not produced. This loss of surplus is called the *deadweight loss of monopoly*. This is illustrated in Figure 15-3.

To recapitulate, there are two effects when a monopoly replaces competition. By reducing output below the competitive level, a smaller total of consumers' plus producers' surplus is available to be shared between the consumers and the producer. But by raising price the monopolist gets a larger share of this smaller pie for itself. As a result, the monopolist is better off, consumers are worse off, but the two groups taken together are worse off.

Beyond Allocative Efficiency in the Evaluation of Market Structure

Why Perfect Competition May Not Be Ideal

Having seen that an economy that consisted of perfectly competitive industries would achieve allocative efficiency, it would be a mistake to jump to the conclusion that perfect competition is the best of all possible worlds and that government policy ought to do everything possible to achieve it. Let us note four important reasons why this would be a mistake.

FIGURE 15-3 **The Allocative Inefficiency of Monopoly**

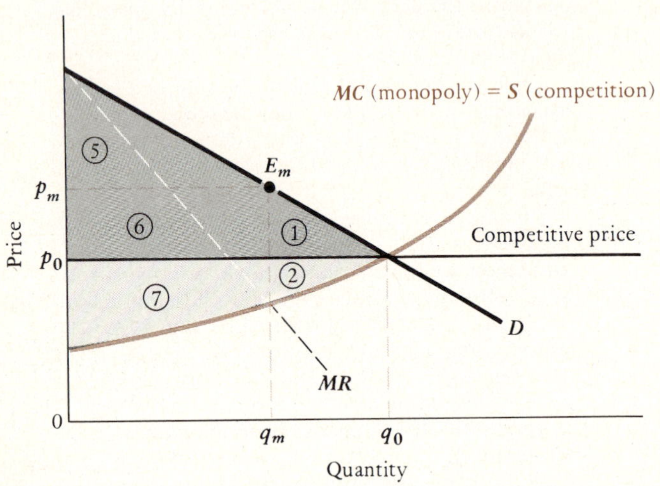

Monopoly is allocatively inefficient because it produces less than the competitive output and thus does not maximize the sum of consumers' and producers' surplus. If this market were perfectly competitive, price would be p_0, output would be q_0, and consumers' surplus would be the sum of areas 1, 5, and 6 (the dark shaded area). When the industry is monopolized, price rises to p_m, and consumers' surplus falls to area 5. Consumers lose area 1 because that output is not produced; they lose area 6 because the price rise has transferred it to the monopolist.

Producers' surplus in a competitive equilibrium would be the sum of areas 7 and 2 (the light shaded area). When the market is monopolized and price rises to p_m, the surplus area 2 is lost because the output is not produced. But the monopolist gains the area 6 from consumers (6 is known to be greater than 2 because p_m maximizes profits).

While area 6 is transferred from consumers' to producers' surplus by the price rise, *areas 1 and 2 are lost.* They represent the deadweight loss resulting from monopoly and account for its allocative inefficiency.

Efficiency is not the only goal. A competitive economy distributes output as well as produces it. Though unlikely, a freely functioning competitive economy could conceivably produce a distribution of income consisting of 1 millionaire and 999 paupers. Such an economy may be more efficient than an economy with 1,000 persons of roughly equal income. Before one can speak of a competitive economy as being unambiguously desirable, one must consider goals other than efficiency. This matter is discussed further in Chapter 23.

Private costs may be poor measures of society's costs. Producing a good up to the point at which the price just equals the *firms'* marginal cost is efficient from society's point of view only if the firms' private costs reflect the opportunity costs to society of using the resources. As we shall see in Chapter 23, this is often not the case because of what are called *externalities.* For example, if the firms in a competitive industry use resources they do not pay for (such as the clean air around the factories), the industry may produce too much output and too much pollution to be efficient. It does so because *its marginal costs fail to include the value that members of society place on some of the resources (clean air) the industry uses up.*

Perfect competition throughout the economy may not be compatible with productive efficiency. The argument for the allocative efficiency of perfect competition requires that price equal marginal cost for all firms in the economy. If price does not equal marginal cost *everywhere,* there is no presumption about the effects of making price equal marginal cost *somewhere* in the economy. Thus, for example, if price does not equal marginal cost in industry A, making price equal to marginal cost in industry B may not increase the economy's allocative efficiency.

This proposition illustrates what is known as the "theory of the second best": We may know how to identify the best of all possible worlds (from the limited point of view of the optimum we are discussing), but we have a much harder task when attempting to rank two imperfect situations.

This result is significant because there are many industries in which market forces will ensure that price does not equal marginal cost. These are industries in which technology makes perfect competition unattainable. If scale economies are not exhausted until firms are large in relation to total market demand, there will be room for only a few firms in the industry. In the extreme case of natural monopoly, there is room for only one. Whenever scale effects mean that oligopoly or monopoly is the natural outcome of market forces, price will not equal marginal cost. Instead the firms that survive in the industry will face downward-sloping demand curves and by equating marginal cost to marginal revenue, they will ensure that price exceeds marginal cost.

Innovation may be more rapid in one market structure than another. In a perfectly competitive industry, production occurs at the lowest level of cost attainable by the competitive firm using known technology. But it is possible that firms in a perfectly competitive industry may not innovate as rapidly as firms in another market structure. If so, cost curves will not be shifting downward in the very long run as much as they would under a more monopolistic market structure. Thus, although the competitive industry will appear productively efficient by virtue of producing on its cost curves, the cost curves themselves will not be as low as they could be. Put differently, productive efficiency in the very long run may be different from productive efficiency with given technology.

Conditions Where Cost Determines Market Structure

The classic comparison of monopoly and competition assumed that market structure and level of cost were independent. But that need not be the case.

Economies of scale. In Chapter 11 we encountered a downward-sloping long-run average cost curve, that is, a situation in which there are economies of scale. The shape of the *LRAC* curve meant that firms had to achieve a certain minimum scale of production (which was defined in Chapter 12 as minimum efficient scale, *MES*) to reach the lowest unit costs of production. If the *MES* for a plant is sufficiently large, there may not be room in the industry for many efficient plants; at the extreme of *natural monopoly* there may be room for only one. If so, perfect competition will not persist because there will not be enough firms to have each one behave as a price taker.

If a competitive industry did exist, with each firm producing with "too small" a plant, it would pay one of them (or a new entrant) to build a bigger plant, achieve lower costs, and find itself in a position to price below the costs of the other firms (see Figure 12-8 on page 230). Its profits would attract other firms to do the same. Eventually the competitive industry would be replaced by one with a smaller number of firms, each of which had achieved minimum efficient scale.

When minimum efficient scale is large, productive efficiency will be improved, rather than worsened, by a shift from perfect competition to a market structure with fewer firms.

Economies of scope. Even beyond any advantages of large-scale *plants,* large *firms* may be able to achieve economies, and thus lower costs, by multiproduct production and associated large-scale distribution, national advertising, and large-scale purchasing. Such economies are called **economies of scope** rather than economies of scale.

Economies of scope cause the cost curves of large, integrated firms to be lower than the cost curves of many small firms producing the same output. In such a case the few large firms will be more productively efficient than the many small firms.

Effect of Economies of Scale or Scope

The existence of significant economies of scale or scope may mean that perfect competition will not continue to be attainable because the remaining number of firms would not continue to be price takers. If the resulting noncompetitive industry's firms use their power to raise price above marginal cost, the industry will no longer be allocatively efficient. Looked at somewhat differently, allocative efficiency is now unattainable in a free market because cost minimization leads to a market structure where price exceeds marginal cost. Will consumers necessarily be worse off than if the economies of scope and scale were never achieved?

The answer is no. For example, consider a monopoly replacing a competitive industry where there are unexploited advantages of large scale or scope. The monopolist shuts some plants, reorganizes production and distribution, and thus lowers costs. The monopolist also changes price until marginal revenue equals the new (lower) level of marginal cost. If the cost savings are large enough, output may be larger and price lower than under perfect competition. This is illustrated in Figure 15-4, which shows a situation where consumers benefit from the monopolization of the industry in spite of the emergence of some monopoly profits. The reason is that cost savings are large enough so that both producers and consumers can gain.

FIGURE 15-4 A Case in Which Monopolization Leads to Lower Prices

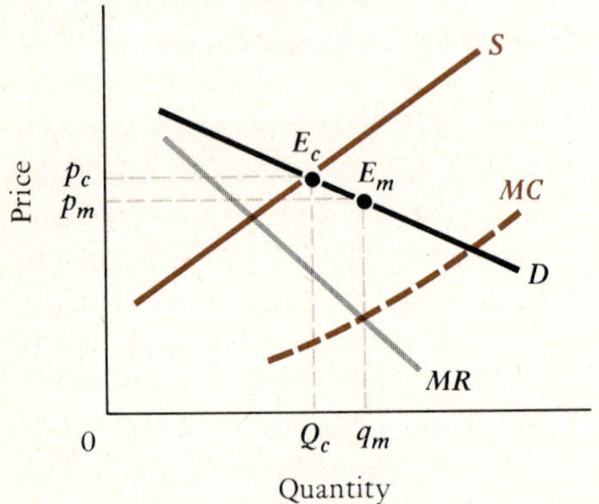

If monopolization lowers costs sufficiently, it may lead to greater output and lower price than competition. D and S are the demand and supply curves of a competitive industry that is in equilibrium at E_c with price p_c and output Q_c. If costs are unaffected by monopolization, S will become the monopolist's marginal cost curve and the monopolist will restrict output and raise price. However, if the monopolization reduces costs to MC, the equilibrium will be at E_m, with p_m less than p_c and q_m greater than Q_c.

Saying that monopolization of a competitive industry *may* lead to lower costs and prices does not mean that departures from competition usually or always lead to lower costs and prices. If there is a reduction in costs, but it is relatively small, the cost decrease may be outweighed by the increase in price due to the monopolist's reduction in output. Moreover, a monopolist protected from competition may become careless and costs may actually rise. (There may be a grain of truth in Judge Learned Hand's observation that the monopolist's greatest reward is an easy life.)

While survival of perfect competition is, in any case, unlikely once large economies of scale and scope are recognized to exist, there is still a question of whether in general we should struggle hard to maintain as much competition as possible. The key question is factual: In what circumstances do a few large firms in less competitive market structures achieve significantly lower levels of cost than many smaller firms in a more competitive market structure?

The answer to this question is affected by economies of scale and scope, but it is affected much more by the effect of market structure on innovation.

Very Long-Run Considerations

In what we have called the very long run, attention shifts from given products and a fixed technology to new products and new methods of production (see Chapter 11). Our attention shifts from operating on given cost curves to asking how rapidly the cost curves shift downward. This has two not unrelated aspects. One is the effect of market structure on innovation; the other is the effect of monopoly profits as an incentive to new entrepreneurs.

Market Structure and Innovation

Does market structure affect the rate of innovation? Many economists believe it does, but they do not all agree on which way.

Incentive to introduce cost-saving innovations. Both the monopolist and the perfect competitor have a profit incentive to introduce cost-reducing innovations. A monopoly can always increase its profits if it can reduce its costs. We have seen that a cost reduction will cause the monopoly to produce more, to sell at a lower price, and to increase its profits. Furthermore, since it is able to prevent the entry of new firms into the industry, these additional profits will persist into the long run. Thus, from the standpoint of maximizing profits, a monopoly has both a short- and a long-run incentive to reduce its costs.

The firm in perfect competition has the same incentive in the short run but not in the long run. In the short run a reduction in costs will allow a firm that was just covering costs to earn profits. In the long run other firms will be attracted into the industry by these profits. Existing firms will copy the cost-saving innovation, and new firms will enter the industry using the new techniques. This will go on until the profits of the innovator have been eliminated.

The effectiveness of profits as an incentive to reduce costs for a firm in competition will thus depend on the magnitude of the extra profits and on how long they persist. If, for example, it takes only a few months for existing firms and new entrants to copy and install the new invention, the original innovating firm will earn profits for only a few months. These may not be sufficient to compensate for the risks and the costs of developing the innovation. In such a case the incentive to innovate will be absent from a competitive industry. By contrast, if it takes several years for other firms to copy and install the cost-saving innovation, the profits earned over these years by the innovating firm may be more than sufficient to compensate for all costs and risks. In this case the incentive to innovate is present in a competitive industry.

Monopolies have both a short- and long-run incentive to innovate; competitive firms have only a short-run incentive.

Funds for research and development. So far we have considered the profit incentive to introduce new innovations. Another consideration is the availability of the resources to finance the research needed to invent new methods and new products. It is widely believed that the large profits available to firms with monopoly power provide a ready fund out of which research and development will be financed. While in principle money for research and development could come from anywhere, business practice tends to use reinvested earnings rather than borrowed funds for these purposes. To the extent that this is so, the typical competitive firm, earning only enough money to cover its costs, will have few funds to spare for research and development. If profits provide the funds for research and development, competitive firms will do little of it.

Penalties for not innovating. Skeptics about the superiority of the monopolist as innovator often argue that competitive firms *must* innovate or they will lose out to a competitor who does so, whereas monopolists do not have the same urgent need because they are insulated from potential competitors by barriers to entry. In this view innovation is essential in competition and merely optional in monopoly.

Those who disagree with this argument point out that no firm, not even a complete monopolist, is shielded from competition in the very long run. It is always possible that a new firm will be able to break into the market by developing some new, similar, but superior product that overcomes existing barriers to entry. It is also the case that a firm, even a monopoly, that fails to innovate opens itself to the threat of a takeover by another firm.

Patents and the incentive to innovate. Economists who believe that competitive market structures serve consumers best by assuring them low prices, but who worry about the possible lack of incentives to innovate under competition, believe that other institutions, such as the patent laws, can provide the necessary incentives.

Patent laws confer a temporary monopoly on the use of an easy-to-copy invention. The intent of the patent laws is to lengthen the period during which the inventor can earn profits as a reward. Once the patent expires—sometimes even before by infringement or evasion—other firms can copy the invention, and if there are no other barriers to entry, production will expand until profits are eliminated. There is little doubt that without patent laws, many inventions would be copied sooner and the original innovators would not earn as much extra revenue to compensate them for the costs and risks of development. Thus patents do increase the rewards to invention. Just how much actual extra invention occurs is a subject of substantial debate.

Because patented items *can* be imitated, the real advantage of patents to the competitive firm should not be exaggerated. Some economists have argued that patents may be of even greater advantage to a monopolistic than to a competitive firm. A monopolist, so goes the argument, has the resources to develop, patent, and "keep on the shelf" processes that might enable a potential competitor to challenge its position.

"Creative Destruction"

An early and articulate dissenter from economists' usual opposition to monopoly was the distinguished Austrian (and later American) economist Joseph A. Schumpeter. Schumpeter's theory relies on many of the forces just discussed. His basic argument has two main parts.

The first is that innovations that lower costs of production—by increasing output per head and creating economic growth—have a much larger effect on living standards than any "misallocation" of resources caused by too much production of one kind of commodity and too little of another at any one time.

Schumpeter believed that losses due to allocative inefficiency were small relative to the gains attributable to cost reductions. Modern empirical measures have tended to support Schumpeter in this contention. It appears unlikely that the losses due to misallocations caused by departures from competition have ever amounted to more than 2 or 3 percent of a country's national income.[3] But the national income of most countries was for many years growing at that rate each year. Thus if misallocation lets growth continue year after year, it is positively beneficial.

The second part of Schumpeter's argument is that only the incentive of profits leads people to take the great risks of innovation and that monopoly power is much more important than competition in providing the profits that motivate innovation. The large short-run profits of the monopolist provide the incentive for others to try to usurp some of these for themselves. If a frontal attack on the monopolist's barriers to entry is not possible, the barriers will be circumvented by such means as the development of similar products against which the monopolist will not have entry protection.

Schumpeter called the replacing of one monopoly by another through the invention of new products or new production techniques the *process of creative destruction*.

Schumpeter put part of his argument in the following words:

> What we have got to accept is that it [monopoly] has come to be the most powerful engine of progress and in particular of the long-run expansion of total output not only in spite of, but to a considerable extent through, this strategy [of creating monopolies] which looks so restrictive when viewed in the individual case and from the individual point of time. In this respect, perfect competition is not only impossible but inferior, and has no title to being set up as a model of ideal efficiency. It is hence a mistake to base the theory of government regulation of industry on the principle that big business should be made to work as the respective industry would work in perfect competition.[4]

An example of this process is discussed in Box 15-1.

Slide rules provide an example of one good product having its market destroyed by a new one, with the resulting elimination of a firm's monopoly power. Keuffel & Esser had by the 1960s achieved a dominant position in the manufacture and sale of slide rules, which at the time were an essential tool

[3] In one of the most famous of these studies, Professor Arnold Harberger of the University of Chicago put the figure at about one-tenth of 1 percent of the U.S. national income!

[4] *Capitalism, Socialism, and Democracy*, 3d ed. (New York: Harper & Row, 1950), p. 106.

BOX 15-1

Erosion of a Monopoly

The great strength of the incentive to share in a monopoly profit can be illustrated by the case of ball-point pens, where a monopoly was created by product innovation.

In 1945 Milton Reynolds developed a new type of pen that wrote with a ball bearing rather than the then conventional nib. He formed the Reynolds International Pen Company, capitalized at $26,000, and began production on October 6, 1945.

The Reynolds pen was introduced with a good deal of fanfare by Gimbels, which guaranteed that the pen would write for two years without refilling. The price was set at $12.50. Gimbels sold 10,000 pens on October 29, 1945, the first day they were on sale. In the early stages of production the cost of production was estimated to be around $.80 per pen.

The Reynolds International Pen Company quickly expanded production. By early 1946 it employed more than 800 people in its factory and was producing 30,000 pens per day. By March 1946 it had $3 million in the bank.

Macy's, Gimbels' traditional rival, introduced an imported ball-point pen from South America. Its price was $19.98 (production costs unknown).

The heavy sales quickly elicited a response from other pen manufacturers. Eversharp introduced its first model in April, priced at $15.00. In July 1946 *Fortune* magazine reported that Sheaffer was planning to put out a pen at $15.00, and Eversharp announced its plan to produce a "retractable" model priced at $25.00. Reynolds introduced a new model, but kept the price at $12.50. Costs were estimated at $.60 per pen.

The first signs of trouble emerged. The Ball Point Pen Company of Hollywood put a $9.95 model on the market, and a manufacturer named David Kahn announced plans to introduce a pen selling for less than $3.00. *Fortune* reported fears of an impending price war in view of the growing number of manufacturers and the low cost of production. In October Reynolds introduced a new model, priced at $3.85, that cost about $.30 to produce.

By Christmas 1946 approximately 100 manufacturers were in production, some of them selling pens for as little as $2.98. By February 1947 Gimbels was selling a ball-point pen made by the Continental Pen Company for $.98. Reynolds introduced a new model priced to sell at $1.69, but Gimbels sold it for $.88 in a price war with Macy's. By this time ball-point pens had become economy rather than luxury items, but they were still highly profitable.

In mid 1948 ball-point pens were selling for as little as $.39 and costing about $.10 to produce. In 1951 prices of $.25 were common. Within six years the power of the monopoly was gone forever. Ever since then the market has been saturated with a wide variety of models and prices of pens ranging from $.19 up. Their manufacture is only ordinarily profitable.

Of course there can still be strong incentives to gain monopoly power and profits, even if the effort is sure to fail eventually. The lag between an original monopoly and its subsequent erosion by competition may be long enough to ensure large profits to the monopolist. It is estimated, for example, that Milton Reynolds earned profits as high as $500,000 *in a single month*—about 20 times his original investment.

---

of the engineer and the applied scientist. Its dominant position and highly profitable operations were wiped out not by a better slide rule but by the pocket calculator. When first introduced in the early 1970s, pocket calculators were relatively expensive, often costing over $100. They were also relatively crude in their capabilities. Nonetheless they proved popular; sales and profits rose, and firms rushed to enter the lucrative new field. Competition led simultaneously to product improvement and price reduction. Today calculators that perform basic calculations can be bought for a few dollars, and sophisticated scientific and programmable pocket calculators can be bought for under $50. Few of today's college students have heard of Keuffel & Esser, but most know about Texas Instruments.

Similarly, during the 1980s microcomputers for home and office are showing signs of sweeping away the markets of many currently important products and services. For instance, in-store computers are being used to answer customer questions and decrease the need for salespeople. One day computers may even displace the college textbook.

The State of the Debate

For all of the reasons discussed in this section, there is no current consensus among economists that if only the two polar cases were available, perfect competition is always to be preferred to monopoly. The empirical evidence seems overwhelming that perfectly competitive firms have not been leading innovators. For example, none of the innovations that have vastly raised agricultural productivity over the last century were developed by the typical competitive farming unit; rather, they were developed by a few manufacturers of farm equipment and by researchers in universities and in government-financed research institutions. But not all firms with monopoly power have been dynamic innovators either. Thus Schumpeter's insight into the *potential* advantage of monopoly over competition does not lead economists to be unconcerned about monopoly.

Much more important is the difficulty in evaluating oligopoly. Scale economies mean that in most, if not all, manufacturing industries, perfect competition is an unattainable ideal. If natural monopolies are fairly rare, industries whose cost conditions would allow them to be perfectly competitive are even rarer. Oligopoly is the rule of the day given modern manufacturing technologies. What can we say about what public policy should be toward this pervasive market structure?

Whenever a firm faces a downward-sloping demand curve, the analysis of the inefficiency of monopoly, given earlier in this chapter, applies. The firm will equate marginal cost with marginal revenue and so will not produce where marginal cost equals price. Thus the normal efficiency conditions will not be fulfilled. But oligopolies are not monopolies. Oligopolistic firms usually compete with each other, often fiercely.

Competition among oligopolists may be the maximum competition that is feasible in most industries in the modern economy. The issues are (1) does such competition come close to what earlier economists referred to as "workable competition," (2) is such competition sufficient both to keep the economy adaptive to changes in tastes and technology and to hold profits to levels that could not be described as exploitive, and (3) do oligopolies, for the reasons discussed by Schumpeter, encourage dynamic change and growth in the economy? Although many people feel that the answers to these three questions are yes, such answers do not follow as theorems in the way that the optimal allocation of resources follows logically from the assumptions of perfect competition. The validity of these answers must be judgments based on a mixture of theory and observations of the way that real economists work.

This puts public policy in a difficult position. Many economists agree that monopoly is undesirable and hence that it should be broken up wherever possible and regulated where a monopoly is natural or unavoidable. But what about oligopoly? If it cannot be replaced by perfect competition, should it be regulated, or should it be left alone to carry on with whatever competition occurs naturally? If it is to be regulated, what should the regulators strive to achieve? Is a government monopoly, which would result if the industry were nationalized or taken over by a crown corporation, likely to perform better than the oligopoly itself?

Canadian Competition Policy

Although economists have not always agreed on what market structures are preferable from among those that are practicable, policymakers have had to make decisions on what public policy to adapt toward firm behavior. By and large government competition policy has sought to discourage monopolistic practices and encourage competitive behavior even when perfectly competitive market structures could not be established.

The Thrust of Canadian Policy

Canadian competition laws are called **combine laws.** These laws seek to prohibit monopolies, attempts to monopolize, and conspiracies in restraint of trade. The first such laws were proposed in the late nineteenth century. Originally adopted in 1889 and 1890, they have been changed frequently, but their basic pro-competition stance still prevails in current legislation.

Throughout the history of Canadian policy, some of the details of which are outlined in Box 15-2, legislation has been directed chiefly at the misuse and abuse of power by large associations and only rarely at combinations per se. In introducing legislation proposed in 1910, Mackenzie King, then minister of labor, stated during a debate in the House of Commons that "this measure seeks to afford the means of conserving to the public some of the benefits which arise from large organizations of capital."

This acceptance of the need for large firms in the business sector has been explained in terms of the *staples theory* of economic growth which held that much of Canada's real growth was tied to a succession of export staples such as fur, wheat, lumber, and base metals. The exploitation of these resources required not only large amounts of private capital in a country where capital was scarce but also substantial "social overhead" capital in the form of an extensive east-west transportation network. In addition, uncertainty was created by the wide price fluctuations to which these products were subject. The result was a reliance on firms with substantial monopoly power and considerable direct government support.

Canadian public policy did not condemn monopolies per se but instead accepted them as sometimes inevitable and then sought to control them to act in the public interest. In practice, it becomes difficult to determine just when an offense has been committed and whether there is a real threat to competition. Ideally the law should reflect economic analysis, but this is difficult given the problem of drafting a statute that will cover all future situations and the uncertainty concerning what interpretation the courts will place on its provisions. Further, economists are frequently not in agreement on the likely consequences of various forms of behavior of firms in imperfectly competitive markets.

Regulation of Natural Monopolies

Seemingly the simplest case for public intervention arises with a natural monopoly, an industry in which scale effects are so dominant that there is room for only one firm to operate at the minimum efficient scale. Policymakers have not wanted to compel the maintenance of several smaller, less efficient producers when a single firm would be much more efficient; neither have they wanted to give a monopolist the opportunity to restrict output, raise prices, and appropriate as profits the gains from large-scale production.

How might these values be reconciled with the view, dominant in the late nineteenth century, that government should not interfere with the free market? The answer was to identify certain natural monopoly products as *public utilities*. The products—such as water, railroad transportation, electricity, telephone, and telegraph—were considered of critical importance and therefore products whose provision ought to be supervised by the government.

The public utility concept grew out of the recognition by economists that when there are major economies of large-scale production, protection of the public interest by competition is impractical, if not impossible.

One response is for government to assume ownership of the single firm, which is then called a *nationalized* industry, or a crown corporation. The government then appoints managers who are supposed to set prices guided by their understanding of the national interest. A different response, common in Canada and the United States since the late nineteenth century, has been to allow private enterprise but to regulate its behavior.

Public utility regulation gives to appropriate public authorities (usually specially constituted regulatory commissions) control over the price and quantity of service provided by a natural monopoly. The objective is to achieve the efficiency of a single

BOX 15-2

The Development of Canadian Competition Policy

Government policy with respect to trusts and industrial combinations in Canada dates from 1888, when a select committee of the House of Commons initiated an investigation into alleged combinations in trade. Initial legislation, enacted in 1889, made it an offense to combine or agree to lessen competition unduly or to restrain trade. The Combines Investigation Act of 1910 created powers for the minister of labor to appoint a board of three commissioners to carry out a full inquiry and publish a report of its finding. In framing this legislation, the Canadian government was influenced by what was regarded as the unhappy experience of the United States with its Sherman Antitrust Act (1890). There was no inclination to copy the "trustbusting" activities that involved the American antitrust division of the Department of Justice in a large number of prosecutions during the period 1904–1911, when the courts adopted a strict interpretation of the Sherman Antitrust Act.* Instead, early Canadian legislation relied strongly on the publicity attached to an investigation as a deterrent to restrictive trade practices.

The Combines Investigation Act of 1923 provided punishment for past participation in the formation or operation of a combine. In 1935 the legislation was amended to prohibit discriminatory pricing that substantially lessened competition or eliminated a competitor, and in 1951 resale price maintenance was added to the list of proscribed practices. With these amendments, the legislation prohibited three broad classes of activity: (1) combinations such as price-fixing agreements that unduly lessen competition, (2) mergers or monopolies that may operate to the detriment of the public interest, and (3) unfair trade practices (after 1960).

A large number of cases of unfair trade practices were successfully pursued, but—compared to the U.S. enforcement experience—there was a striking paucity of merger cases. During the 60 years following the first legislation in 1910, only two full-scale cases came before the courts. Both defendants, Canadian Breweries, Ltd., and B.C. Sugar Refining Company, were acquitted by the trial courts, and neither decision was appealed. One plea of guilty was entered to a merger charge in 1970, and in 1973 the crown obtained an order, without a full trial, prohibiting a merger. In 1974 K. C. Irving, Ltd., was convicted, but this judgment was reversed on appeal.

The reason most often cited for the lack of combines enforcement in Canada was the inability of criminal legislation to cope with complex economic issues. Under criminal law the government must prove beyond a reasonable doubt that the accused has committed the offense. In the United States most antitrust cases are civil cases in which a lesser standard of proof is required to obtain a conviction. In American merger cases litigated since 1950, for example, when a substantial share of the market has been controlled, the courts have generally found that the merger restricts competition and is therefore illegal.

There is also some doubt whether the penalties imposed for violations in Canada were effective. The most common penalty, the criminal fine, which on

* This period of vigorous prosecution ended with the enunciation by the Supreme Court of the "rule of reason." In forcing Standard Oil Company and American Tobacco Company to divest themselves of a large share of their holdings of other companies, the Court stated that only *unreasonable* combinations in restraint of trade merited conviction under the Sherman Antitrust Act.

seller without the output restriction of the monopolist.

In return for allowing a company to be the sole producer, the public utility regulators reserve the right to regulate its behavior.

Although regulatory commissions were first created to deal with natural monopoly problems, most regulatory activity is no longer of that kind. In this section, however, we are concerned only with natural monopoly regulation.

Regulation of Price

The dilemma of natural monopoly is illustrated in Figure 15-5 (p. 302). To achieve low costs, a single large producer is necessary, but an unregulated, only one occasion exceeded $25,000 for a single company, may not have deterred contraventions of the act.

Canadian courts have also appeared less willing than American courts to assess economic evidence. Mr. Justice Hope in *R.* v. *Container Materials, Ltd.* (1940) expressed this reluctance with the caveat "Our Lady of the Common Law is not a professed economist," and Mr. Justice Spence in *R.* v. *Howard Smith Paper Mills* (1959) reemphasized the courts' difficulty:

> Surely the determination of whether or not an agreement to lessen competition was "undue" by a survey of one industry's profits against profits of industry generally, and a survey of the movement of the prices in that one industry against the movement of prices generally, would put the Court to the essentially non-judicial task of judging between conflicting political theories. It would entail the Court's being required to conjecture—and by a Court it would be nothing more than mere conjecture, since a Court is not trained to act as an arbitrator of economics—whether better or worse results would have occurred to the public if free and untrammelled competition had been permitted to run its course.

Competition Policy in the 1960s and 1970s

A major review of Canadian legislation was begun in 1966 by the Economic Council of Canada. Its recommendations, published in a report in 1969, together with those of a committee of experts appointed by the Department of Consumer and Corporate Affairs, formed the basis of proposed amendments to the Combines Investigation Act. The amendments were subsequently presented to Parliament in two stages.

The stage 1 amendments were proclaimed on January 1, 1976. They included provisions for extending the Combines Investigation Act to service industries, for allowing civil actions to be brought for damages resulting from contraventions of the act, and for strengthening legislation against misleading advertising. One significant feature of the stage 1 amendments is that they give the Restrictive Trade Practices Commission (RTPC) the power to order suppliers to cease certain practices. Customers were protected by prohibiting suppliers from refusing to supply, providing exclusive dealerships, restricting the way the good is sold, or requiring tied sales. As a result, the way in which many goods are retailed has changed considerably.

The sections of the amendments that deal with *misleading advertising* are extensive. Although the commission cannot act directly in such cases, the Department of Consumer and Corporate Affairs has shown itself to be quite willing to prosecute on the advice of the commission. Claims about product quality must now be based on adequate tests. Advertising a product at a bargain price when the supplier does not or cannot supply the product in reasonable quantities, and supplying a product at a price higher than the advertised price, except when the advertised price is erroneous and is immediately corrected, are explicitly prohibited.

The stage 2 amendments deal with the issues of conspiracies and of mergers and monopolization. Initially this stage proposed the transfer of certain practices from criminal to civil law and recommended the appointment of a Competition Board to replace the courts in the examination of trade practices, but more recent amendments abandoned the Competition Board in favor of a larger role for the civil courts.

profit-maximizing monopoly would restrict output and raise price, thus failing to provide the large volume of output at a low price that the technology makes possible.

What price should a regulatory commission permit? It might wish to set price equal to marginal cost in order to achieve allocative efficiency ("the way it would be in perfect competition"), but such a price and quantity would surely lead to losses, for marginal cost is necessarily below average cost when average cost is falling. This is illustrated in Figure 15-6. Such a pricing scheme would require a continuing subsidy of the resulting losses.

As an alternative, regulation has often aimed at setting prices high enough to permit firms to cover all their costs, yet low enough to achieve the large sales required to reap the scale economies that characterize natural monopoly situations. If a regulatory

FIGURE 15-5 The Problem of Natural Monopoly

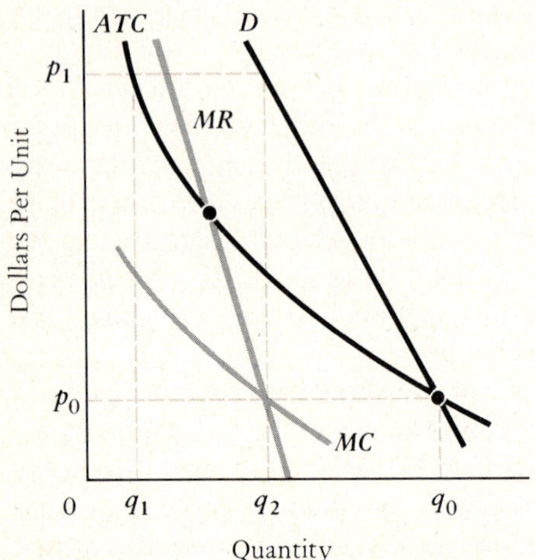

Cost conditions in a situation of natural monopoly are such that a single firm is needed to achieve the economies of scale, but a monopolist finds it profitable to restrict output to maximize profits. *ATC* and *MC* are the cost curves of an efficient firm. *D* is the market demand curve, and *MR* marginal revenue. Because *ATC* declines sharply, efficiency is served by having a single firm. Clearly, one firm producing at q_0 would be more efficient than several firms each producing q_1 at a cost of p_1 per unit. But an unregulated monopoly would restrict output to q_2 and charge price p_1, thereby depriving consumers of the advantages of large-scale production.

FIGURE 15-6 Pricing Strategy for a Regulatory Commission

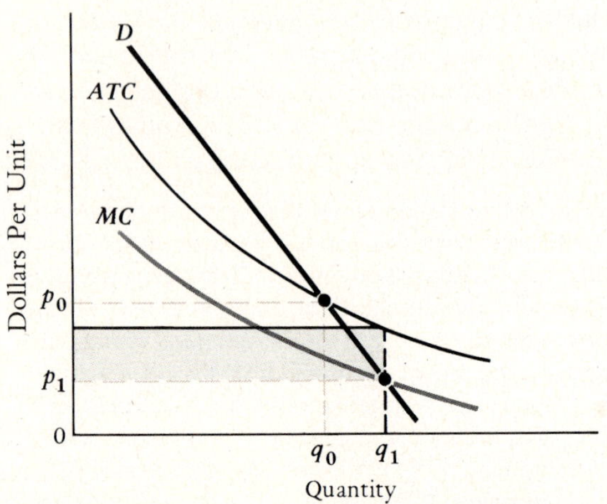

Average cost pricing is the goal of regulatory commissions that seek low prices but no losses for natural monopolies. Allocative efficiency requires a quantity q_1 where price equals marginal cost. But at the price-quantity combination p_1 and q_1, a firm would suffer losses (shown as the shaded area). A regulatory commission could not insist on price p_1 unless it was prepared to subsidize the firm. But it might require price p_0, which permits the firm to produce q_0 and cover all costs. The output q_0 achieves some, but not all, of the cost advantages of large-scale output. Pricing where demand crosses *ATC* is called average cost pricing.

commission knew the demand curve and the cost curves exactly, it could simply pick the price indicated by the intersection of the demand curve and the average total cost curve. This is called *average cost pricing*. Average cost pricing will not, in general, lead to allocative efficiency because price is not equal to marginal cost, as is also shown in Figure 15-6. But average cost pricing would give much lower prices and larger outputs than would an unrestrained monopoly.

Of course, regulators do not know exactly what demand and cost curves look like, and regulatory commissions often do not have even reasonably accurate demand and cost information. In its absence commissions have tended to judge prices according to the level of profits they produce. Generally, having set prices, regulatory agencies permit price increases when profits fall below "fair" levels and require price reductions if profits exceed such levels. Thus what started as price regulation becomes instead profit (or what is called *rate of return*) regulation.

Problems in Regulation

Charging an appropriate price ensures that only a normal rate of return will be earned; that is, profits will be zero. The reverse, however, is not necessarily true. Profits can be zero because of inefficient operation or misleading accounting. Thus commissions that rely on rate of return as their guide to pricing must also monitor other aspects of the regulated firm's behavior.

Definition of costs. If a company is to be allowed to charge a price determined as "cost plus a fair profit" (as the regulators say), and if that price is below the profit-maximizing one, it is clearly in the firm's interest to exaggerate reported costs. One major activity of regulatory commissions has been to define rules of allowable costing. Cost supervision is an important activity of public utility regulation for another reason as well. Without it, managers of the regulated industries might have little incentive to be efficient and might simply let costs drift upward.

Rate base. Average total cost includes an appropriate rate of return on the capital invested in the business. Suppose it is agreed that a firm should be allowed to earn a rate of return of 11 percent on its capital. The **rate of return** is defined as the ratio of net profits to invested capital. What is the value of the capital to which 11 percent is to be applied? The allowable amount is called the **rate base.** There has been no more controversial area than this in public utility regulation. Should the original cost or the reproduction cost of the firm's assets be used?

It does not make much difference unless prices are changing, but in an inflationary situation reproduction cost is uniformly higher than original costs. Use of reproduction cost then leads to higher rate bases, higher permitted profits, and higher prices to users. If the major concern is to generate earnings to buy replacement equipment, reproduction cost is appropriate. If the major concern is to generate a return just sufficient to compensate past capital investments, original cost may be appropriate.

The precise nature of regulatory rules is important because the rules affect the incentives of the firms regulated. Economists Harvey Averch and Leland Johnson have shown that a regulated utility has less incentive to resist excessive capital costs than an unregulated one. In some circumstances it even pays the unregulated utility to buy relatively unproductive equipment. If profits depend on the rate base, the firm can increase its base by acquiring expensive capital goods. Thus the notion of "necessary and prudent investments" enters into regulatory rules. This tendency for one regulation to lead to a need for yet further regulation has been called the *tar-baby effect,* after a fictional creature that enveloped attackers in the tar of which it was made.

Fair return. The permitted rate of return that is implicit in the theory of public utility regulation is the opportunity cost of the owners' capital, with allowances for risk. This is what economists call a position of zero profits. Regulatory commissions have paid some attention to overall earnings rates in the economy, and the level of permitted earnings has changed slightly over time. But fairness and tradition have played a much larger role than considerations of opportunity cost, and regulatory commissions have been slow to adjust permitted rates of return to changing market conditions. For decades permitted rates of return of 6 to 9 percent were employed. But when market interest rates soared to double-digit figures during the late 1970s, the traditional levels were not sufficient to induce new investment. Yet regulatory commissions were reluctant to permit the large increases in prices that would result from sharp increases in the permitted rate of return.

Curtailment of service. While regulatory commissions regulate prices with an eye on profits, they do not guarantee any minimum rate of return. A regulated utility in a declining industry may have a serious problem. If it is failing to earn the permitted rate, it may apply for permission to increase its prices, but if its demand is elastic, a rise in rates will lead to a reduction in revenues and may reduce profits. Privately owned urban transit systems and passenger rail lines have proven unprofitable because of declining demand as people shifted to substitutes: private cars and airplanes. Given elastic demand curves, when transport companies raise fares (hoping to increase revenues), they find that they only lose more customers to other means of transport.

At this point a local bus company, for example, may look to its costs to see how it can avoid losses. Often it finds that some parts of its service (such as routes to outlying neighborhoods) no longer cover even the variable costs of providing them, and it proposes to the regulatory authority that this service be dropped. Often the regulators say no. The reason is that they see other considerations in abandoning the bus service (such as increased congestion in the downtown area as even more people use their own cars) that are important to the regulators but not to the bus company.

The regulators want the regulated company to "cross-subsidize" the less popular routes with profits from the more popular routes; at the same time they do not want to force the company into bankruptcy. Thus each time a curtailment of service is proposed, regulators must make the difficult determination of whether the company is merely trying to increase its profits and is shirking its public service responsibility or whether it is truly in trouble.

The Evolution of Competition Policy

The years following the onset of the Great Depression saw a high point in the belief that the government could improve the efficiency of the economy by direct intervention into business decision making. Two important reasons were in operation. First, the prolonged depression of the 1930s spread skepticism concerning the efficacy of the private enterprise system. Second, the success of the command economy techniques used by most governments during World War II led many to conclude that governments could do many things better than private firms.

The resulting intervention took two forms. In the United Kingdom it was primarily nationalization of private industries, which were then to be run by government-appointed boards. In the United States firms were largely left in private hands, but their decisions were regulated by government-appointed bodies that set prices and oversaw many other decisions. As often happens, Canada followed a mixture of the British and the American practices. Many Canadian crown corporations, which are in effect nationalized firms, were set up, and many industries that were left in private hands were regulated.

Hopes for these changes were high. When the British mines were nationalized in 1945, workers stood, cap in hand, singing "The New Jerusalem," a famous hymn about building a utopia in Britain, as the Union Jack was run up over the pit heads. Indeed, expectations were so high that some disillusionment was inevitable.

In the event, two experiences were critical. First, the period of high employment and rapid economic growth in the two decades that followed the end of the Second World War restored people's belief in the efficacy of the private enterprise system.

Second, the record of postwar government intervention into regulated industries seemed poorer in practice than its supporters had predicted. Industrial strife did not go away just because ownership was vested in the people. Antagonism persisted between management, concerned with financial viability, and workers, concerned with take-home pay. As a result, it was not long before the unexpected became commonplace: strikes against the industries that the people themselves owned. Nor was the record of regulation unblemished. Research slowly uncovered the fact that in many cases regulatory bodies were captured by the industries they were supposed to regulate. As a result, the bodies that were meant to ensure competition often acted to enforce restrictive practices that would have been illegal if instituted by the firms themselves.

This theme, which entails the use of competition policy to protect firms from too much competition rather than to protect consumers from too little, is discussed in more detail in the next section.

Protection *Against* Competition

Whereas the main thrust of competition policy and the original purpose of the regulation of industries was the protection of *competition,* a parallel and, for a time, growing aspect of public policy in these areas was a shift to protection of *competitors* against the rigors of competition. To understand both the overall nature of competition policy and the current movement toward deregulation, it is necessary to review its protectionist aspects.

The world of perfect competition is a harsh one. The best a firm can hope for in the long run is to cover all its costs. Any competitive edge in methods of production or product characteristics it may achieve will be quickly eroded through entry of new firms or imitation by existing firms. Moreover, any failure to maintain efficiency will inexorably lead to operating losses and eventual loss of whatever investment the owner has made. Because exit from an industry typically takes longer than new entry, fluctuations in demand and supply for the industry's output are likely to be accompanied by longer periods of depressed conditions than of unusual prosperity.

Because competitive conditions are most likely to occur where there are large numbers of individual firms—in farming, in retailing, in trade—large numbers of people are affected directly. Their very numbers make them a political force to be reckoned with. and the political system has not neglected small businessmen, farmers, traders, or workers.

We have already seen, in agricultural policy, some of the devices designed to protect the incomes of such groups. There is also a temptation to see the *symptom* of their plight—the low prices of the things they sell—as the cause. The fallacy of this should be clear.

If excess capacity is driving prices down and thus signaling the need for resources to withdraw from the industry, artificially raising these prices only removes the signal without eliminating the cause.

Unless the policy also reduces output, the problems caused by excess capacity will reemerge in another form.

For example, there seems little doubt that originally U.S. railroad rates were regulated in order to keep them down. By the 1930s, however, concern had grown over the depressed economic condition of the railroads and the emerging vigorous competition from trucks and barges. The regulators then became the protectors of the railroads, permitting them to establish *minimum* rates for freight of different classes, allowing price discrimination, and encouraging other restrictive practices. Moreover, it became a leading advocate of bringing motor carriers under the regulatory umbrella.

Restricting entry into trucking and setting *minimum* rates for trucks was unmistakably protectionist. The only reason for regulating the large carriers was to control their competition with the railroads. The big carriers were limited in where they could go and how *low* a price they could quote. As a result, they became targets for small, unregulated truckers, who could cut rates and thus draw away customers without fear of retaliation. To eliminate the rate competition, regulation was extended to small truckers.

As another example consider airline regulation in Canada and the United States. When airline routes and fares were first regulated, there was arguably so little demand that competition could not have been effective. By the mid 1960s, however, the regulation was plainly protectionist and designed to shield the major carriers from competition in both countries. Supporters of regulation argued that unrestricted competition would be so intense that it might ruin the industry and even invite cost-cutting practices that endangered public safety. Critics argued that competition might destroy some existing airlines but would prepare the ground for an efficient industry.

Canadian regulation of airline prices has consistently blocked price competition. Foreign airlines wishing to cut fares between Canada and Europe have been barred from doing so. Until recently airlines other than Air Canada and C.A.I. were prevented from introducing cheap transcontinental fares. Under the circumstances, it is hard to see Canadian airline regulation as protecting the interests of passengers against the predatory behavior of the carriers.

What accounted for the turn toward protectionism by regulatory commissions whose original mandate was protection of consumers from natural monopolists? One thesis is that the regulatory commissions were gradually captured by the firms they were supposed to regulate. Another is that the protectionist policies of the 1930s really reflected the public's mood and a genuine fear of destructive competition. The depression of the 1930s deeply affected a whole generation. It shook public confidence in many long-held beliefs, including the "received wisdom" that competition was in the public's interest. Faith in competition was greatly shaken by bank and business failures and by the massive unemployment of workers and factories. With the emergence of new generations for whom the Great Depression is but another episode in history, not a remembered nightmare, some degree of faith in competition is returning. But it is fragile, as was demonstrated anew by the calls for more protectionism during the 1980s.

Deregulation and Privatization

The last decade has seen a movement in many advanced industrial nations to reduce the level of government control over industry. A number of forces have been pushing in this direction: (1) the difficulties of regulating industries to make them act competitively, (2) the experience that regulatory bodies often sought to reduce rather than increase competition, (3) the dashing of the unreasonable hopes that nationalized industries would work miracles in the areas of efficiency, productivity growth, and industrial relations by the realization that replacing a private monopoly with a publicly owned one did not greatly change performance, and (4) the increased world competition as a result of falling transportation costs and revolutions in data processing and communications.

The transformations brought about by these technological changes is nowhere more evident than in the financial sector. For example, funds no longer needed because one financial center has closed for the day are lent out in other financial centers that are still open. In this way balances held by large organizations follow the sun around the world from New York to Tokyo to London and back to New York, making one circuit in each 24-hour period. (The London market now opens at 6 A.M. so as to fit into this pattern.)

Financial institutions have been internationalized as a result of these developments, and their minimum efficient scales have grown tremendously. Country after country has had to drop restrictions against mergers and foreign ownership rather than see their financial centers disappear. For example, when in 1987 the Ontario securities commission permitted banks and brokers to merge, they did so in the knowledge that some Japanese securities firms had capital of over $5 billion U.S. and that $1 billion was thought by many to be the minimum needed to spread one's risks comfortably in the highly integrated world securities markets, while the total capital of all Canadian brokers was only $700 million.

Reducing government control of industry. This took the form of deregulation—leaving prices and entry free to be determined by private decisions—and privatization—the selling off of nationalized industries and crown corporations.

Privatization went a long way in the U.K. in the 1980s. Many giants, such as steel and telephones, have already been privatized, as well as numerous smaller companies, such as Rolls-Royce. The intention is that many others, including British Airways, and the gas companies, will have been sold by the end of the decade.

Once a government decides to sell off a crown corporation or a nationalized industry, a decision has to be made between short-run and long-run benefits. The industry can earn the most profits, and thus will sell for the highest price, if it is sold as a monopoly. But the government may then face renewed regulation pressures when the monopoly position is exploited by the private owners. Competition can be encouraged if the industry is sold to different owners in as many parts as possible. But the sale price will then be less because a competitive industry will earn lower profits than the monopolized one. Many economists urged governments to enhance the long-run social interest by selling off their industries in as competitive a form as possible. The U.K. government has not done this and has often elected to get the maximum revenue—which can be used to generate a temporary reduction in its budget deficit—by selling off industries in a monopolized form. In deciding to offer British Airways for sale as a single unit, the government ignored its own committee's recommendations that the organization be broken up before sale. It remains to be seen if the Canadian government will be more farsighted or whether it will give in to the temptation to get the maximum sale price when it comes to privatize some of its own large crown corporations.

In the United States the movement to reduce government intervention took the form of deregulation. Airlines, motor carriers, banks, natural gas producers, and long-distance telephone companies are among those that have been substantially unleashed from close regulatory supervision of both prices and entry. The effects, and thus the wisdom of these changes, will be the subject of both economic analysis and political debate for years to come. For one thing, a considerable lapse of time is needed before the industry settles into a stable post-regulation pattern. For example, when the airline industry was first deregulated, competition became fierce as many small entrants challenged the existing giants. Fares fell and travelers enjoyed numerous bargains.

Slowly, however, a series of mergers produced larger and larger companies, and the lowest cut-rate fares gradually disappeared. Where the industry will finally settle, and whether that position will be judged to be more in the consumers' interests than the prederegulation situation, remains to be seen.

Deregulation has already gone some way in Canada and plans exist to go much further. For example, airlines have seen substantial deregulation of fares and entry. A large number of small commuter airlines have sprung up as a result, but changes are not restricted to the small firms: Pacific Western Airlines took over Canadian Pacific Air Lines to become Canadian Air International (C.A.I.), and Wardair introduced low-priced transcontinental services. More is involved in the deregulatory movement than just reversing protectionist policies for producers. It concerns, more basically, the whole question of how much interference with private decision making is desirable. Much of the regulation that is targeted for review in the United States is "social regulation" that is concerned with protection of consumers, not from high prices or monopolistic exploitation but from other kinds of hazards. The targets of this deregulation include many agencies that were designed to protect consumers from health hazards, fraud, pollution, and occupational and product dangers rather than from excessive prices. Although the deregulation movement has not gone so far in Canada, similar agencies exist, and similar questions about how will they really serve the public interest are being asked.

Changes in regulation in some form or another seem likely to continue over the next decade. Some people favor rapid deregulation and reliance on market forces. Others believe that the deficiencies lie in the structure of regulation and that changing the way regulation is carried out will improve matters. Still others think that the failures of regulation require nationalization or new legislation defining a novel approach to what regulators should do.

Summary

1. Resources are said to be used efficiently when it is impossible, by using them differently, to make any one household better off without making at least one other household worse off. We distinguish two kinds of efficiency: productive and allocative.
2. Productive efficiency exists for given technology when whatever output is being produced is being produced at the lowest attainable cost for that level of output. This requires, first, that firms be on, rather than above, their relevant cost curves and, second, that all firms have the same marginal cost. Profit-maximizing behavior assures achieving productive efficiency.
3. Allocative efficiency is achieved when it is impossible to change the mix of production in such a way as to make someone better off without making someone else worse off. The allocation of resources will be efficient when each commodity's price equals its marginal cost.
4. Whereas either an economy of monopoly or of perfect competition can be productively efficient, allocative efficiency would be achieved in an economy of perfect competition but not in an economy with monopolies.
5. The classical economic appeal of perfect competition is that it achieves both productive and allocative efficiency. Productive efficiency is achieved because the same forces that lead to long-run equilibrium lead to production at the lowest attainable cost. Allo-

cative efficiency is achieved because in competitive equilibrium price equals marginal cost for every product. The classical economic case against monopoly rests on its allocative inefficiency, which arises because price exceeds marginal cost.

6. The classical belief in the superiority of perfect competition should be interpreted with four qualifications in mind: (a) Efficiency is not the only goal, (b) private costs may be poor measures of society's costs, (c) perfect competition throughout the economy may be incompatible with productive efficiency, and (d) in the very long run, cost curves may shift downward faster in market structures other than competition.
7. Levels of cost are not independent of market structures. If there are advantages of scale or scope, the minimum efficient size of the firm may be too large to be compatible with conditions of perfect competition. In such cases a shift from competition to a more concentrated market structure may lead to lower costs and increased efficiency.
8. Very long run considerations, such as the effect of market structure on innovation and the incentive effect of monopoly profits, are important in evaluating market structures. Joseph Schumpeter advocated the view that the incentive to innovate is so much greater under monopoly that monopoly is to be preferred to perfect competition, despite its allocative inefficiency. Though few modern economists go that far, the empirical evidence suggests that technological change and innovation can to a measurable extent be traced to the efforts of large firms in concentrated industries.
9. The policy implications of the classical view of monopoly and competition led policy in two directions: public utility regulation to deal with natural monopoly and competition policy to deal with other kinds of monopoly.
10. The original philosophy of public utility regulation was to grant a monopoly where necessary to achieve the advantages of large-scale production but to prevent the monopolist from restricting output and raising price. The most common regulatory approach has been to regulate prices. This is done by watching profits, allowing price increases only if necessary to permit the regulated utility to earn a fair return on its capital and requiring price decreases if profits rise above the approved level.
11. Implementation of this straightforward theory encounters difficulties because any set of rules becomes a set of signals that induces patterns of response from the firms regulated. Natural utility regulation appears to most observers not to have been an unqualified success. To some this is because the regulators have not made much difference. To others it is because regulators have tended to shift their focus from protection of consumers to protection of the firms being regulated.

12. Historically, Canada has not pursued an aggressive competition policy, particularly in comparison with the United States. Early legislation relied strongly on public disclosure rather than penalties as a deterrent to illegal practices. The new Competition Act promises stricter enforcement through the use of civil review procedures rather than criminal prosecution.
13. The entire regulatory apparatus has come under close scrutiny in recent years. In the United States major bills have been passed deregulating airlines and motor carriers. Canadian deregulation has been slower and is likely to remain a major political issue of the next several years.

Topics for Review

Productive and allocative efficiency
Consumers' and producers' surplus
Classical preference for competition over monopoly
Pareto-optimality
Economies of scale and scope
Effect of cost on market structure
Effect of market structure on costs
Creative destruction
Deregulation
Privatization

Discussion Questions

1. "Suppose that allocative inefficiency of some economy amounts to 5 percent of the value of production." What does that statement mean? If it is true, would consumers be better off if policy measures succeeded in eliminating the allocative inefficiency? Why or why not?
2. If the many plants producing a given product were built at different times, have different levels of capacity, and have different cost curves, is it possible that producing the industry's output using all of them is productively efficient? Show why or why not.
3. Consider an innovation that lowers the marginal cost of production by the same amount in two industries, one of which is perfectly competitive and the other a single-firm monopoly. Show that prices will fall as a response to a change in marginal costs in each industry but that prices and quantities will change less in monopoly than in competition.
4. "Productive efficiency or inefficiency can be evaluated at the level of an individual plant, firm, or industry. Allocative efficiency or inefficiency can be evaluated only for the economy as a whole." Discuss.
5. Is the consumer benefited by lower prices, by higher quality, by more product variety, by advertising? If trade-offs are necessary

(more of one means less of another), how would you evaluate their relative importance with respect to the following products?

a. Vitamin pills
b. Beer
c. Cement
d. Bath soap
e. Women's dresses
f. Television programs

6. White sidewall tires cost only about $1 per tire more to manufacture than black sidewall tires, and they lower somewhat the durability of tires. At the retail level the extra cost of a white sidewall tire is at least $5 per tire. Yet 70 percent of all passenger car tires manufactured in 1986 were white sidewalls. What, if anything, do these facts tell you about the market structure of the manufacture, distribution, or marketing of automobile tires? If white sidewalls are found to be somewhat more likely to suffer blowouts, should their use be prohibited by law?
7. Would anti-combines laws be necessary in an economy of perfect competition? Would they be beneficial in an economy of natural monopoly?
8. What are the arguments for and against exemption from anti-combines prosecution of the following?
   a. Labor unions
   b. Farmers
   c. Professional baseball teams (but not professional football teams)
9. Price-fixing agreements are (with some specific exemptions) violations of federal laws. Consider the effects of the following. In what way, if at all, should they be viewed as being similar to price-fixing agreements?
   a. A manufacturer "recommends" minimum prices to its dealers.
   b. A manufacturer publishes a product price list that is changed only every three months.
   c. A trade association publishes "average industry total costs of production" every month.
10. "In a competitive market the least-cost production techniques are revealed by entry and exit, while in public utility regulation they are revealed by commission rate hearings. It is easier to fool the commission than the market. Therefore, wherever possible, competition should be permitted." Discuss.

16

Who Runs the Firm and for What Ends?

Does the continuing success of the economies of the industrialized nations depend on the initiative of healthy, independent, private firms? Does it depend instead on increased public scrutiny and control of the behavior of these firms? Does it require subsidization or protection of domestic firms from foreign competition?

What light does the theory we have studied so far shed on these important questions? In standard economic theory firms are users of factors of production and producers of commodities. They face cost and demand curves that are largely determined by forces beyond their control. They seek to maximize their profits by keeping their costs as low as possible and producing to satisfy consumers' demands. They care only about profits, and their decisions are uninfluenced by their internal structure. Thus they contribute to our high living standards by producing, as cheaply as possible, goods that satisfy consumers' demands.

The ultimate source of all profits, even monopoly profits, is consumers' willingness to buy. Thus the firms that succeed are the ones that best satisfy consumers' demands, while firms that consistently do not satisfy them will eventually fail. The need for firms to respond to consumers' desires is an important part of any argument for a free enterprise system. If firms did not so respond, there would be little justification in allowing them to exert major influences on the allocation of the country's resources.

An important body of criticism disputes this standard theory of the firm. It says instead that firms have the power to control market conditions. They manipulate demand by advertising, and they do not face strong competitive pressure to produce efficiently by holding costs down. Firms, the critics continue, do not even seek to maximize profits. Instead they seek other goals that are determined by their internal structure, and these goals often cause them to behave in ways that are socially undesirable.

If true, such criticisms would support the view that firms hinder rather than advance consumer welfare and that firms need to be forced by government to act in the social interest. In this chapter we will study some of these criticisms. We begin with those that strike at the very core of the standard microeconomic theory.

Do Firms Control the Market? The Galbraith Hypothesis

John Kenneth Galbraith and consumer advocate Ralph Nader argue that it is *not* consumers' wants that create the market signals that in turn provide the profit opportunities that motivate business behavior. Instead, large corporations have the power to create and manipulate demand. Firms must plan and invest for an uncertain future, and the profitability of the enormous investments they make is threatened by the unpredictability of events. Firms try to make the future less unpredictable by actively manipulating market demand and by co-opting government agencies that are supposed to control their activities.

Manipulation of demand. The most important unpredictable events that may jeopardize corporate investments are unexpected shifts in market demand curves. To guard against unexpected declines in demand, corporations spend vast amounts on advertising to allow them to sell what they want to produce rather than what consumers want to buy. At the same time, corporations decide not to produce some products that consumers would like to buy. This reduces the risks inherent in investing in new and untried products and avoids the possibility that successful new products might spoil the market for existing products.

According to this hypothesis, consumers are the victims of the corporations; they are pushed around at the corporate whim, persuaded to buy things they do not really want and denied products they would like to have.

Corruption of public authorities. A second threat to the long-range plans and investments of corporations comes from uncontrollable and often unpredictable changes in the nature of government interference with the freedom of the corporation. According to the theory, this political threat is met by co-opting or corrupting the members of Parliament, who pass laws affecting corporations, and the government agencies that are supposed to be regulating them. Corporation managers indirectly subvert public institutions, from universities to regulatory agencies.

Government, instead of regulating business and protecting the public interest, has become the servant of the corporation. It supplies the corporate sector with such essential inputs as educated, trained, healthy, socially secure workers. Government also serves the giant corporation through policies concerning tariffs, import quotas, tax rules, subsidies, and research and development. These policies protect the industrial establishment from competitive pressures and reinforce its dominance and profitability.

Corruption of our value system. Galbraith distinguishes between the owners of the firm, who are capitalists, and the people who run it, who are technically trained managers. He calls the latter technicians or technocrats and points out that they have great power. The corporations they manage earn large profits that can be reinvested to further the achievement of the values of the ruling group, a group that Galbraith calls the *technostructure*. The values of this "ruling class" emphasize industrial production, rapid growth, and materialistic aspirations at the expense of the better things of life (such as cultural and aesthetic values) and the quality of the environment.

More important, the industrial managers join with the military in a military-industrial complex that uses, trains, and elevates the technicians to positions of power and prestige not only in industry but in the armed services, in the defense establishment, and in the highest positions of government. In so doing, the corporations and their managers threaten to dominate, if not subvert, our foreign as well as our domestic policies.[1]

[1] Dwight D. Eisenhower also warned of the dangers of the military-industrial complex. Eisenhower had commanded the Allied armies in the 1944 invasion of Hitler's Europe and went on to become the president of the United States from 1953 to 1960. In his retirement speech he warned Americans of the power of this alliance between the military and the large private firms that produced arms for them. A military-industrial complex had never seemed a problem in Canada until in the White Paper on Defense Policy of 1987 the government seemed consciously to be attempting to create one.

The new industrial state. The foregoing is an outline of what Galbraith calls the *new industrial state*.[2] If Galbraith's thesis were substantially correct, we would have to make major revisions in our ideas of how free-market economies work.

In Galbraith's new industrial state the largest corporations (1) largely control market demand rather than being controlled by it, (2) co-opt government processes rather than being constrained by them, and (3) use their substantial discretionary power against the interests of society.

Many facts lend superficial support to Galbraith's hypothesis. The corporate giants are well known. Leading the *Financial Post*'s list of the top 200 Canadian industrial companies is General Motors of Canada, with annual sales in excess of $5 billion. Other companies with sales above $2 billion include Imperial Oil, Canadian Pacific, Bell Canada, Massey-Ferguson, Alcan, and International Nickel. If power comes with size, a "few" people—perhaps 200 or 300 strategically placed executives of the country's leading corporations—have great power over economic affairs. Moreover, this corporate elite forms in many ways a close-knit group with common values and a (small "c") conservative point of view.[3] They exercise political influence through lobbying, contributions to political parties, and direct participation in the process of governing.

It is also true, as the hypothesis predicts, that the great corporations, along with many smaller firms, spend vast amounts on advertising. These expenditures are obviously designed to influence consumers' demand, and there is little doubt that if firms such as Lever Brothers, Gulf Oil, Molson's, and GM cut their advertising, they would lose sales to their competitors.

Similarly, it is true that much of the pollution of our environment is associated with industries that consist of well-known large firms. If automobiles, steel, oil, industrial chemicals, detergents, and paper are the primary sources of our pollution, surely Ford, Stelco, Dow Chemical, Texaco, Procter & Gamble, and Abitibi Paper are significantly to blame.

Doubts About the Hypothesis

Sensitivity to Market Pressures

Even the largest, most powerful industries are not immune to market pressures. Ford's Edsel was a classic example of the market's rejecting a product. The penetration of small foreign cars into the North American market forced the automobile industry into first the compact car and then the still cheaper subcompacts. In spite of this, massive losses were suffered by North American automobile manufacturers as consumers turned in large numbers, even in the face of heavy advertising of North American cars, to foreign cars whose low cost and high gas mileage they preferred. The decline of railroads for passenger travel is manifest in many ways, as the troubled financial history of Via Rail amply illustrates.

Changes in demand and in taste can be sudden and dramatic, but mostly they are gradual, continual, and less noticeable month by month than decade by decade. On the average, about two new firms enter the top 100 every year, and as a consequence two others leave. This means a significant change over a decade.

Turnover in the list of leading companies is revealing. In the United States only two, U.S. Steel and Standard Oil of New Jersey (Exxon), were in the top 10 both in 1910 and in 1985. Today's giants include automobile, oil, airline, computer, and electricity utilities—for the obvious reason that demand for these products is strong.

Are these demand shifts explained by the corpo-

[2] These views did not originate with the publication in 1967 of Galbraith's book by that title or with the formation of "Nader's raiders." Much earlier James Burnham wrote *The Managerial Revolution* and Robert Brady sounded an alarm in *Business As a System of Power.* Thorstein Veblen had predicted the technocratic takeover of society in *The Engineers and the Price System* in 1921, and Karl Marx predicted the subversion of the government bureaucrat by the businessman more than a century ago.

[3] See Peter C. Newman, *The Canadian Establishment,* vol. 1 (Toronto: McClelland & Stewart, 1975).

rate manipulation of consumers' tastes through advertising or by more basic changes? Advertising has two major aspects: It seeks to inform consumers about available products, and it seeks to influence consumers by altering their demands. The first aspect, informative advertising, plays an important part in the efficient operation of any free-market system; the second aspect is one through which firms seek to control, rather than be controlled by, the market.

Clearly, advertising does influence consumers' demand. If GM were to stop advertising, it would surely lose sales to Ford, Chrysler, and foreign imports, but it is hard to believe that the automotive society was conjured up by advertisers. When you are persuaded to take advantage of Wardair's new low-priced services, your real alternative is not a covered wagon, a bicycle, or even a Greyhound bus; more likely you are forgoing Air Canada or C.A.I.

Careful promotion can influence the success of one rock group over another, but could it sell the waltz to today's teenager? Taste making through advertising unquestionably plays a role in shaping demand, but so do more basic human attitudes, psychological needs, and technological opportunities.

Certainly, advertising shifts demands among similar products. It is hard to believe, however, that the Canadian economy or the average Canadian's system of values would be fundamentally changed if there were available one more or one less make of automobile or television set or brand of shoes. A look at products that have brought basic changes to the economy—and perhaps to our value systems—suggests that these products succeeded *because consumers wanted them,* not because advertisers brainwashed people into buying them. Consider a few major examples.

The automobile transformed North American society and is in demand everywhere, even in Communist countries where only informative advertising exists. The Hollywood movie had an enormous influence in shaping our world and in changing some of our values; it was, and still is, eagerly attended throughout the world, whether or not it is accompanied by advertising. The jet airplane has shrunk the world. It has allowed major league sports to expand beyond cities that could be reached by an overnight bus or rail journey; it has made the international conference a commonplace; and it has made European, Pacific, and Caribbean vacations a reality for many. For better or worse, the birth control pill has revolutionized many aspects of behavior in spite of the fact that it has never been advertised in the mass media. Television has changed the activities of children (and adults) in fundamental ways and has created national rather than regional markets in dozens of commodities. The word processor has revolutionized writing procedures, and computers have transformed our banking practices and will soon do the same for shopping.

The new products that have significantly influenced the allocation of resources and social attitudes have succeeded because consumers wanted them. Most of those that failed did so because they were not wanted—at least not at prices that would cover their costs of production. Box 16-1 deals with a case study of a giant firm that found out the hard way just how little control it could exert over the market.

The evidence suggests that the allocation of resources owes more to the tastes and values of consumers than it does to corporate advertising and related activities.

Who Controls the Government?

Is government subservient to big business? Lobbying is a legal activity engaged in on a large scale by many groups. Big business has its influence, but so do farmers, labor unions, and small business.

Cases of corrupt behavior have been documented at all levels of government. It does not follow, however, that government is usually subservient to the corporations and that decision making by the former is *dominated* by the wishes of the latter.

On the one hand, tobacco companies have seen government agencies first publicize the hazards of their principal product and then restrict their advertising. On the other hand, governments have resisted pressure from medical groups to strengthen their anti-tobacco campaigns. Airlines finally lost their decades-long battle to prevent the introduction of cheap transatlantic air fares and have now lost virtually all regulatory bolstering of fare structures and

BOX 16-1

The Market Controls the Firm: The A&P Story

The Great Atlantic and Pacific Tea Company (A&P) was the world's first grocery chain store. In 1859 A&P opened 100 stores in New York City, and their large-scale purchasing and low-price policies led the company and the concept to prosper. By 1912 A&P was running a national chain of economy stores whose central policy was described as "cash and carry, no deliveries, no credit, no advertising, no telephone."

Although widely copied—Kroger's was formed in 1887 and Safeway in 1915, among many others—A&P was dominant, with over 50 percent of the chain food sales all through the 1920s and into the 1930s. The firm was so dominant in the 1930s that antitrust authorities tried to restrain it, and legislation was introduced to limit its ability to compete so effectively.

Did A&P control the market? Many people in and out of the company believed that it did, but events were to show that it did not. Its first big mistake occurred in the early 1930s, when it made the decision to neglect an innovation in marketing, the supermarket. Supermarkets consisted of several departments (meat, produce, baked goods, groceries) under one roof and relied on self-service. A&P was a *grocery* chain and used clerks. Scale efficiencies and lower labor costs enabled the supermarkets to operate much more economically than traditional clerk-operated chain grocery stores. "King Kullen the Price Wrecker" opened the first supermarket in 1930 and was extremely successful. Supermarkets spread rapidly. A&P believed that supermarkets were a passing fad, and it refused to go along. Part of this was its feeling of loyalty to its clerks, who would surely have had a difficult time finding new jobs during the depression.

But A&P's policy, whatever the motivation, meant higher labor costs and higher prices than its supermarket competitors. In 1937 John Hartford, the company president, belatedly and reluctantly decided that A&P should enter the supermarket business seriously. By then, however, A&P had lost more than half its market share.

Though A&P never regained the 50 percent market share it had in the early 1930s, its profit levels and rates rebounded as the depression ended and A&P supermarkets were opened. By the early 1950s it had secured roughly 33 percent of the chain grocery market. Although less dominant than in its heyday, it was still the leading chain.

The second crisis of A&P's existence was the opening in the 1950s and 1960s of suburban shopping malls. A&P resisted this trend because traditional company policy had been against signing long-term leases for store locations. Long-term leases were, however, necessary to secure stores in suburban malls. Company policy clashed with market necessity, and the latter won. By the time A&P realized its mistake, the prime locations had been taken by the company's competitors.

A&P had believed that it was big and powerful enough to continue attracting customers without moving to giant stores in high-rent suburban shopping malls. In later years, as gasoline costs rose and large numbers of women entered the work force, the demand for one-stop shopping grew. When other stores increased brand coverage and started stocking nonfood items, A&P's shelves in its smaller stores were already full. Between 1953 and 1971, A&P's gross sales stayed roughly constant at between $5 and $6 billion, but its market share slid from 30 to 12 percent. By 1972 it was losing money, and over the decade of the 1970s its losses continued. Late in the 1970s the question was not whether A&P was too powerful but whether it would survive.

As the 1980s began, A&P was once again rebuilding—by closing many of its too small, badly located stores and by employing new marketing techniques copied from its competitors. Today it appears to have won its battle for survival. Its market share is stable, but nowhere is it still the dominant firm.

Does the firm control the market? A&P thought so and found out that it was wrong.

limitation of competition on routes in the United States and seem likely to suffer similar losses in Canada.

These examples show that while business often succeeds in attempts to protect its commercial interests through political activity, it does so within limits. Where the truth lies between the extremes of "no influence" and "no limits" is a subject of current research. Yet it does seem safe to say that, first, corporations have much political influence and, second, there are some serious constraints on the ability of corporations to exert political influence over all levels of American government.

Neglect of the Public Interest?

One aspect of the Galbraithian critique has found a receptive public: the apparent disregard by large corporations of the adverse effects of productive activities on the environment. The problems of pollution, which we will discuss in Chapter 23, arise from the activities of both small and large corporations and the activities of government units and citizens.

Consumerism is a movement that asserts a conflict between the interests of firms and the public interest. Consumerists hold that the conflict should be removed by pressuring firms to be motivated by the public interest rather than by their stockholders' desires for maximum profits.

Consumerists believe, for example, that GM's directors must be made to recognize that automobiles pollute and cause accidents and that GM's resources should be invested in the development and installation of safety and antipollution devices. This, they argue, is proper use of GM's funds, even if GM's stockholders do not see it that way and even if automobile purchasers do not want to pay for the extra safety and antipollution devices.

What are the main arguments *for* this view? First, only the company can know the potentially adverse effects of its actions. Second, by virtue of holding a corporate charter, the corporation assumes the responsibility to protect the general welfare while pursuing private profits.

What are the main arguments *against* the consumerist view? Managers of companies have neither the knowledge nor the ability to represent the general public interest; they are largely selected, judged, and promoted according to their ability to run a profit-oriented enterprise, and the assumption that they are especially competent to decide broader *public* questions is unjustified. Moral, as distinct from economic, decisions—such as whether to use nuclear power, to make or use internal combustion engines, to manufacture or smoke cigarettes, and to manufacture or use DDT or aerosol sprays—cannot properly be delegated to corporations or their executives. Some are individual decisions; others require either the expertise or the authority of a public regulatory agency. Whoever makes decisions on behalf of the public must be potentially responsible to the public.

Opponents of the consumerist view hold that most required changes in corporate behavior should be accomplished not by exhorting business leaders to behave responsibly or by placing consumer representatives on the corporation's board of directors but by regulations or incentives that force or induce the desired corporate behavior. Let corporations pursue their profits—subject to public laws. Let governments change these laws where the results of current corporate behavior are unacceptable. For example, Parliament can require that all cars have seat belts or air bags or antipollution valves or meet specific standards of emission levels. Another alternative is to open the way for lawsuits that would either enjoin certain behavior or force corporations to pay for the damages their products cause.

The controversy is important, and much of the credit for initiating and continuing it belongs to Galbraith and Nader. Should policies attempt to alter the behavior of corporations, and if so, what changes are desirable? These are major questions, whether corporations are primarily responding to market signals or are impervious to them.

What Do Firms Maximize?

Most critics of the theory of firm behavior accept what Galbraith denies: Industries face market demand curves that the firms can influence only slightly. The critics then go on to suggest that firms will behave in ways different from those suggested by profit maximization. In effect, these theories view firms as maximizers of something other than profits.

The view that many firms maximize something other than profits is made more plausible by the changing nature of the firm. One hundred years ago the single-proprietor firm, whose manager was its owner, was common in many branches of industry. In such firms the single-minded pursuit of profits would be expected. Today, however, ownership is commonly diversified among thousands of stockholders, and the firm's managers are rarely its owners. The two theories considered in this section use these changes to suggest reasons why firms may no longer be profit maximizers.

The Hypothesis of Minority Control

It is quite possible for the owners of a minority of the stock to control a majority of the shares that are voted and thus to exercise effective control over the decisions of the corporation. This possibility arises because not all shares are actually voted.

Each share of common stock has one vote in a corporation. Shares must be voted at the annual meeting of stockholders, either in person or by assigning a **proxy** to someone attending. (The proxy authorizes the person attending to cast the shareholder's vote.) Any individual or group controlling 51 percent of the stock clearly controls a majority of the votes. But suppose one group owns 30 percent of the stock, and the remaining 70 percent is distributed so widely that few of the dispersed group even bother to vote; in this event 30 percent may be the overwhelming majority of the shares *actually voted.* In general, a small fraction (sometimes as little as 5 percent) of the shares may exercise dominant influence at meetings of stockholders.

The hypothesis of minority control is that a well-organized minority often controls the destiny of the corporation against the wishes of the majority.

Dispersed ownership and minority control are well established in the corporate sector. But the hypothesis requires more than that a minority control the voting shares; it requires that stockholders be able to exert a significant influence on the firm's behavior *and* that the controlling minority have interests and motives different from the holders of the majority of the firm's stock. If all stockholders are mainly interested in having the firm maximize its profits, it does not matter, as far as market behavior is concerned, which set of stockholders actually influences the firm's policy.

There is no accepted evidence to show that controlling groups of stockholders generally seek objectives different from those sought by the holders of the majority of the firm's stock. Of course, disagreements between stockholder groups sometimes arise. A colorful phenomenon in corporation history is the **proxy fight,** in which competing factions of stockholders (or management) attempt to collect the voting rights of the dispersed and generally disinterested stockholders.

The Hypothesis of the Separation of Ownership from Control

A different consequence of diversified ownership was suggested by A. A. Berle and Gardiner Means. They hypothesized that because of diversified ownership and the difficulty of assembling stockholders or gathering proxies, the managers rather than the stockholders or the directors exercise effective control over the corporation.

The hypothesis of the separation of ownership from control is that managerial control occurs and leads to different behavior than stockholder control would.

In the modern corporation the stockholders elect directors, who appoint managers. Directors are supposed to represent stockholders' interests and to determine broad policies that the managers will carry out. In order to conduct the complicated business of running a large firm, a full-time professional management group must be given broad powers of decision. Although managerial decisions can be reviewed from time to time, they cannot be supervised in detail. The links between the directors and the managers are typically weak enough that top management often truly controls the corporation over long periods of time.

As long as directors have confidence in the managerial group, they accept and ratify their proposals, and stockholders elect and re-elect directors who are proposed to them. If the managerial group does not satisfy the directors' expectations, it may be removed and replaced, but this disruptive and drastic action is infrequently employed.

Within wide limits, then, effective control of the corporation's activities resides with the managers. Although the managers are legally employed by the stockholders, they remain largely unaffected by them. Indeed, the management group typically asks for, and gets, the proxies of enough stockholders to elect directors who will reappoint it—and thus it perpetuates itself in office.

The hypothesis of the separation of ownership from control requires not only that the managers be able to exert effective control over business decisions but also that they wish to act differently from the way the stockholders and directors wish to act. One such view is found in the sales maximization theory.

Sales maximization. This theory uses the separation of management and ownership in the large corporation. The managers need to make some minimum level of profits to keep the stockholders satisfied; after that they are free to seek growth unhampered by profit considerations. This is a sensible policy on the part of management, the argument runs, because salary, power, and prestige all rise with the size of a firm as much as with its profits. Generally, the manager of a large, normally profitable corporation will earn a salary considerably higher than that earned by the manager of a small but highly profitable corporation.

The sales maximization hypothesis says that managers of firms seek to maximize their sales revenue, subject to a profit constraint.

Sales maximization subject to a profit constraint leads to the prediction that firms will sacrifice some profits by setting price below and output above their profit-maximizing levels (see Figure 16-1).

FIGURE 16-1 Output of the Firm Under Profit Maximizing, Sales Maximizing, and Satisficing

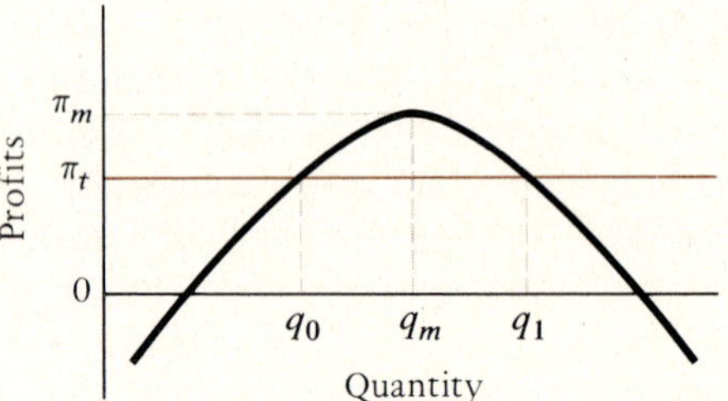

The "best" level of output depends on the motivation of the firm. The curve shows the level of profits associated with each level of output. A profit-maximizing firm produces output q_m and earns profits of π_m. A sales-maximizing firm, with a minimum profit constraint of π_t produces outpr+ q_1.

A satisficing firm, with a target level of profits of π_t, is willing to produce any output between q_0 and q_1. Thus satisficing allows a range of outputs on either side of the profit-maximizing level, while sales maximizing results in a higher output than does profit maximizing.

Nonmaximizing Theories of the Firm

Many students of large firms have been critical of economic theory for regarding modern corporations as "simple profit-maximizing computers." They believe that such firms are profit-oriented in the sense that, other things being equal, more profits are preferred to less. They do not believe, however, that firms are profit maximizers.

Nonmaximization Due to Ignorance

One group of critics says that profit-maximizing theory is inadequate because firms, however hard they may try, cannot reach decisions in the way the theory predicts. We consider two such criticisms, one crude, the other more sophisticated.

Failure to understand marginal concepts. One of the crudest criticisms is based on the observation that business people do not calculate in the manner assumed by the theory. When business people are interviewed, it is sometimes discovered (apparently to the surprise of the interviewer) that they are unaware of the concepts of marginal cost and marginal revenue. It is then argued that (1) the theory assumes that firms equate marginal cost to marginal revenue; (2) empirical observations show that many managers have not heard of marginal cost and marginal revenue; (3) therefore, the theory is refuted, because managers cannot be employing concepts of which they are unaware.

This observation, assuming it to be correct, does refute the theory that managers of firms make decisions by calculating marginal values and consciously equating them. But it does not refute the theory that firms maximize profits.

The mathematical concepts of marginal cost and marginal revenue are used by economic theorists to discover what will happen as long as, by one means or another—be it guess, clairvoyance, luck, or good judgment—firms do succeed in maximizing their profits. If firms are maximizing their profits, the tools of economic theory allow economists to predict how firms will react to certain changes (e.g., the introduction of a tax), and these predictions are independent of the thought process by which firms actually reach their decisions.

Inadequate information. More sophisticated critics point out that the information available to decision makers is often not adequate to permit them to reach the decisions economists predict they will reach. This argument generally takes one of three forms: that firms are the victims of their accountants and base their decisions on accounting concepts, which differ from economic ones; that the natural lag between accumulating and processing data is such that important decisions must be made on fragmentary and partially out-of-date information; or that firms cannot afford to acquire as much information as economists assume them to have.

Nonmaximization by Choice

Alternatives to maximizing theories are usually based on observations of actual firms. The observations, and the theories built on them, all have in common the implication that firms *choose* not to be maximizers.

Full-Cost Pricing

Most manufacturing firms are price setters: They must quote a price for the products rather than accept a price set on some impersonal competitive market. Simple profit-maximizing theory predicts that these firms will change their prices in response to every change in demand and cost that they experience. Yet students of large firms have long alleged that this much price flexibility is not observed. In the short run, prices of manufactured goods do not appear to vary in response to every shift in the firm's demand. Instead, they appear to change rather sluggishly.

This short-run behavior is consistent with the hypothesis of **full-cost pricing,** which was originally advanced in the 1930s by Robert Hall, a British economist, and Charles Hitch, an American, following a series of detailed case studies of actual pricing decisions. Case studies in the intervening decades have continued to reveal the widespread use of full-cost pricing procedures.

The full-cost pricer, instead of equating marginal revenue with marginal cost, sets price equal to average cost at normal-capacity output plus a conventional markup.

The firm changes its prices when its average costs change substantially (as a result of such events as a new union contract or a sharp change in the prices of key raw materials), and it may occasionally change its markup. However, its short-run pricing behavior is rather conventional and is not characterized even by local profit maximization.

A nonmaximizing interpretation of full-cost pricing. Some modern critics of profit-maximizing theory hold that the prevalence of conventional full-cost practices shows that prices are typically not at their profit-maximizing level. They also hold that full-cost pricing shows that firms are creatures of custom that make only occasional, profit-oriented changes at fairly infrequent intervals.

A profit-maximizing interpretation of full-cost pricing. We saw in Chapter 14 that the short-term stickiness of oligopolistic prices can be accounted for under profit-maximizing theory by saucer-shaped cost curves and by the fact that it is costly for a multi-product firm to change its list prices. The possible conflict between full-cost and profit-maximizing theory then concerns only the setting of the markup that relates prices to costs. If markups are arbitrary and only rarely revised, there is conflict. If, however, the markup is the profit-maximizing one for normal-capacity output, full-cost pricing can be consistent with profit maximization.

Organization Theory

A common criticism of profit-maximizing theory is that the behavior of firms is influenced seriously by their organizational structure. **Organization theory** argues that in big firms decisions are made after much discussion by groups and committees and that the structure of the process affects the substance of the decisions.

The central prediction of organization theory is that different decisions will result from different kinds of organizations, even when all else is unchanged.

One proposition that follows from this theory is that large and diffuse organizations find it necessary to develop standard operating procedures to help them in making decisions. These decision rules arise as compromises among competing points of view and, once adopted, are changed only reluctantly. Even if a particular compromise were the profit-maximizing strategy in the first place, it would not remain so when conditions changed. Thus it is argued that profits will not usually be maximized.

Another prediction is that decision by compromise will lead firms to adopt conservative policies that avoid large risks. Smaller firms not faced with the necessity of compromising competing views will take bigger risks than large firms.

Organization theorists have suggested an alternative to profit maximization that they call **satisficing.** Satisficing theory was first put forward by Professor Herbert Simon of Carnegie-Mellon University, who in 1978 was awarded the Nobel Prize in economics for his work on firm behavior. He wrote, "We must expect the firm's goals to be not maximizing profits but attaining a certain level or rate of profit, holding a certain share of the market or a certain level of sales."

According to the satisficing hypothesis, firms will strive to achieve certain target levels of profits, but having achieved them, they will not strive to improve their profit position further. This means that the firm could produce any one of a range of outputs that yield at least the target level of profits rather than the unique output that maximizes profits. This behavior is illustrated in Figure 16-1.

Satisficing theory predicts not a unique equilibrium output but a range of possible outputs that includes the profit-maximizing output somewhere within it and the sales-maximizing output at the upper limit.

Evolutionary Theories

The modern evolutionary theories advanced by such economists as Richard Nelson and Sidney Winter of Yale University build on the earlier theories of full-cost pricing and satisficing. Nelson and Winter argue that firms do not—indeed, could not—behave as profit-maximizing theory predicts. They see firms operating cautiously with imperfect information in an uncertain world and so making only gradual changes toward the profit-maximizing position. But since the conditions are constantly changing, firms are best seen as evolving toward a moving target that they never reach. Thus, although firms are profit-oriented, they never, except by accident, succeed in maximizing their profits.

Evolutionary theorists have gathered much evidence to show that tradition seems to be important in firms' planning. The basic effort at the early stages of planning is directed, they argue, toward the problem of performing reasonably well in established markets and maintaining established market shares. They quote evidence to show that suggestions made in preliminary planning documents to do something entirely new in some areas, even on a 10-year horizon, are usually weeded out in the reviewing process. They believe that most firms spend little effort on plans to enter entirely new markets and still less on plans to leave or even reduce their share in long-established markets. These attitudes were illustrated by one firm, faced with obviously changing circumstances, that reported nevertheless: "We have been producing on the basis of these raw materials for more than 50 years with success, and we have made it a policy to continue to do so."

The evolutionary theory of the firm draws many analogies with the biological theory of evolution. Here are two.

Genes. In biological theory some behavior patterns are transmitted by genes. Rules of behavior fulfill the same function in the evolutionary theory of the firm. In Professor Winter's words:

> A great deal of firm decision behavior is routinized. Routinized decision procedures cover decision situations from pricing practices in retail stores to such "strategic" decisions as advertising or R and D effort, or the question of whether or not to invest abroad.

Winter talks of firms "remembering by doing" according to repetitive routines. He adds that government policymakers tend to have unrealistic expectations about firms' flexibility and responsiveness to changes in market incentives. These expectations arise from the maximizing model, whose fatal flaw, Winter alleges, is to underestimate the difficulty "of the task of merely continuing the routine performance, i.e., of preventing undesired deviations."

Mutations. In the theory of biological evolution, mutations are the vehicle of change. In the evolutionary theory of the firm, this role is played by innovations. Some innovations are the introduction of new products and new production techniques. However, a further important class of innovations in evolutionary theory is the introduction of new rules of behavior. Sometimes innovations are thrust on the firm; at other times the firm consciously plans for and creates innovations.

According to maximizing theory, innovations are the result of incentives—the "carrot" of new profit opportunities. In evolutionary theory the firm is much more of a satisficer, and it usually innovates only under the incentive of the "stick" of unacceptably low profits or of some form of external prodding. Firms change routines when they get into trouble, not when they see a chance to improve an already satisfactory performance. For example, in the growing markets of the 1960s many firms continued all sorts of wasteful practices that they shed fairly easily when their profits were threatened in the more difficult economic climate of the 1970s and 1980s.

How Far Can Firms Depart from Profit-maximizing Behavior?

Many of the criticisms of modern microeconomic theory assume that firms seek to do things other than maximize their profits. Notice, however, that if the present management elects not to maximize its profits, some other management could make more money by operating the firm. A major restraint on existing management is the threat of a stockholder revolt or a takeover bid.

A management that fails to come close to achieving the profit potential of the assets it controls becomes a natural target for acquisition. The management of the acquiring firm makes a **tender offer** (or **takeover bid,** as it is sometimes called) to the stockholders of the target firm, offering them what amounts to a premium for their shares, a premium it can pay because it believes it can increase the firm's profits. Managers who wish to avoid takeover bids cannot let the profits of their firm slip far from the profit-maximizing level because their unrealized profits provide the incentives for takeovers.

The pressure of the threat of takeovers severely limits the discretion of corporate management to pursue goals other than profit maximization.

The Significance of Nonmaximizing Theories

An impressive array of evidence can be gathered in apparent support of various nonmaximizing theories.

What would be the implications if they were accepted as being better theories of the behavior of the economy than profit maximization?

If nonmaximizing theories are correct, the economic system does not perform with the delicate precision that follows from profit maximization. But the systems described by nonmaximizing theories *do* function. Firms sell more when demand goes up and less when it goes down. They also alter their prices and their input mixes when faced with sufficiently large changes in input prices.

Nonmaximizing theories do not conflict with the broad generalization that the price system coordinates the response of decentralized decision makers to changes in tastes and costs.

But profit-oriented, nonmaximizing firms will also exhibit a great deal of inertia. They will not respond quickly and precisely to small changes in market signals from either the private sector or government policy. Neither are they certain to make radical changes in their behavior even when the profit incentives to do so are large. This casts doubt over the efficacy of government policies that make relatively small changes in such market incentives as taxes and subsidies, hoping that firms will respond to these as profit maximizers.

When firms are oriented toward profits but do not try to maximize profits, the price system is sensitive to large but not to small changes in price and profit signals caused by changes in demand, costs, or public policy.

Without doubt, profits are a potent force in the life and death of firms. The resilience of profit-maximizing theory and its ability to predict the economy's reactions to many major changes (such as the dramatic variations in energy prices that have occurred since the 1970s began) suggest that firms are at least strongly motivated by the pursuit of profits.

If profit-maximizing theory should eventually give way to some more organizationally dominated theory, the new theory will still be profit-oriented. The search for profits and the avoidance of losses drive the economy even when firms are not continuously maximizing profits.

Summary

1. Galbraith, Nader, and others make a sweeping attack on the traditional theory of the behavior of the firm. Galbraith argues that large corporations manipulate markets, tastes, and governments instead of responding to market and government pressures. Although there is evidence about the influence of large corporations, there is also much evidence of market influence on corporate behavior.
2. In recent years serious concern has developed over whether corporations should represent the interests of their owners and managers or whether they should be responsible to a broader public interest. Consumerists argue for the latter point of view; others prefer to rely on markets and government control to protect the public interest.
3. The widespread ownership of the modern corporation leads to the question, Who really controls the modern corporation? Attempts to answer this question have led to alternative theories that firms maximize something other than profits. Two important hypotheses have been advanced.
   a. A minority group of stockholders often controls the corporation against the wishes of the majority. The fact of minority control is widely accepted, but there is little evidence to suggest that the minority usually coerces the majority.

   b. Because of the widespread ownership of the corporation, stockholders cannot exert effective control over the managers; thus the latter have the real control of the organization and operate it for their advantage rather than that of the stockholders. This hypothesis has some serious, but by no means universal, support.

4. These and other hypotheses suggest that firms may seek to maximize something other than profits. One alternative is the hypothesis of sales maximization: Firms seek to be as large as possible (judged by sales revenue), subject to the constraint that they achieve a minimum rate of profit.

5. An alternative set of hypotheses denies that firms seek to maximize profits in any way.

   a. Some theories hold that firms do not have sufficient information to maximize their profits. Other theories hold that firms consciously choose to do something other than maximize their profits.

   b. The full-cost hypothesis states that firms determine price by adding a customary—and infrequently changed—markup to full costs. This also makes their pricing behavior relatively insensitive to short-term fluctuations in demand.

   c. Organization theorists see firms as insensitive to short-term fluctuations in market signals. The reason lies in the decision-making structure of large organizations, which must rely on routines and rules of thumb rather than on fresh calculations of profitabilities as each new situation presents itself.

   d. Evolutionary theorists build on full-cost and organizational theories. They see the firm as a profit-oriented entity in a world of imperfect information, making small, profit-oriented changes from its present situation but being more resistant to large, "structural" changes.

6. Under both maximizing and nonmaximizing theories, profits are an important driving force in the economy, and changes in demand and costs cause changes in profits, which cause firms to reallocate resources. The speed and precision, but not the general direction of the reallocations, are what is different between maximizing and nonmaximizing theories.

Topics for Review

The new industrial state
Consumerism
Hypothesis of minority control
Hypothesis of separation of ownership from control
Sales maximization
Full-cost pricing
Organization theory
Satisficing
Evolutionary theories

Discussion Questions

1. In 1976 the automobile manufacturers introduced their 1977 models. GM and American Motors (AMC) put major emphasis on smaller, more economical cars, and Ford and Chrysler stayed with their 1976 model sizes. Read the following news headlines (which appear in chronological order) and then discuss the light they shed on the hypothesis that firms control the market.
   a. "GM's 1977 line runs ahead of the pack. The big question: Do people want small cars?"
   b. "Ford, Chrysler, beam; AMC in trouble on sales."
   c. "GM's fuel-saving Chevette: Right car at the wrong time."
   d. "Price cuts and rebates lift sales of small AMC and GM cars."
   e. "GM confirms plans to drop the subcompact Vega."
   What do these further events reveal about the same hypothesis?
   f. In 1979 auto firms sold all the small cars they could produce. But they were left with sizable unsold inventories of large cars, and as a result they are preparing to alter their production mix in favor of small cars.
   g. Throughout the 1980s North American car makers have faced growing competition from Japanese car makers, who have taken an ever-growing part of the market.
2. "Because automobile companies were interested only in profits, they would not produce the safer, less polluting, but more expensive cars that the public really wanted. Legislation was necessary, therefore, to force producers to meet consumer needs." Discuss.
3. Assume that each of the following assertions is factually correct. Taken together, what would they tell you about the prediction that big business is increasing its control of the Canadian economy?
   a. The share of total manufacturing assets owned by the 100 largest corporations has been rising over the past 25 years.
   b. The number of new firms begun each year has increased over the past 25 years.
   c. The share of manufacturing in total production has been decreasing for 40 years.
   d. Profits as a percentage of national income are no higher now than half a century ago.
4. "Our economy, like an engine, must have fuel to operate. And the fuel our economy runs on is profit. Profits keep it going—and growing. But there is strong evidence that the economy's fuel supply is running low. Profits of U.S. corporations today are about 5 percent on sales—less than the 1965 rate.

   "We Americans have become accustomed to a quality of life that can survive only through profits. For profits not only create jobs and goods, they furnish essential tax revenues. Federal, state, and local taxes finance the countless programs that our citizens demand—from paving the roads on which we drive to building our country's defense forces . . . to helping millions of Americans who need some form of assistance."

   Comment on this excerpt from an Allied Chemical Corporation advertisement.
5. "The business of the businessman is to run his business so as to make

profits. If he does so, he will serve the public interest better than if he tries to decide what is good for society. He is neither elected nor appointed to that task." Discuss.

6. "Our list prices are really set by our accounting department: They add a fixed markup to their best estimates of fully accounted cost and send these to the operating divisions. Managers of these divisions may not change those prices without permission of the board of directors, which is seldom given. Operating divisions may, however, provide special discounts if necessary to stay competitive." Does this testimony by the president of a leading manufacturing company support the full-cost pricing hypothesis?
7. The leading automobile tire manufacturers sell original equipment (OE) tires to automobile manufacturers at a price below the average total cost of all the tires they make and sell. This happens year after year. Is this consistent with profit-maximizing behavior in the short run? In the long run? If it is not consistent, what does it show? Do OE tires compete with replacement tires?

PART FIVE

The Distribution of Income

17

Factor Mobility and Factor Pricing

Are the poor getting poorer and the rich richer, as Karl Marx thought they would? Are the rich becoming relatively poorer and the poor relatively richer, as Alfred Marshall hoped they would? Is the distribution of income affected by social changes such as the increased participation of women in the labor force? Is it affected by changes in public policy toward poverty? Should we reject the view held by Italian economist Vilfredo Pareto that inequality of income is a social constant determined by forces that are possibly beyond human understanding and probably beyond human influence?

The founders of classical economics, Adam Smith and David Ricardo, were concerned with the distribution of income among what were then the three great social classes: workers, capitalists, and landowners. They defined three factors of production: labor, capital, and land. The return to each factor was treated as the income of the respective social class.

Smith and Ricardo were interested in what determined the income of each group relative to the total national income. Their theories predicted that as society progressed, landlords would become relatively better off and capitalists would become relatively worse off. Karl Marx had a different view. He predicted that as growth occurred, capitalists would become relatively better off and workers relatively worse off (at least until the whole capitalist system collapsed).

These nineteenth century debates focused on what is now called the **functional distribution of income,** defined as the distribution of total income among the major factors of production. Table 17-1 shows data for the functional distribution of income in Canada in 1985.

Although functional distribution categories (wages, rent, profits) pervade current statistics, economists have shifted to another way of looking at differences in incomes. At the beginning of the century, Pareto studied what is now called the **size distribution of income,** the distribution of income among different households without reference to the source of the income or the social class of the household. He discovered that inequality in income distribution was substantial in all countries and, more surprisingly, that the degree of inequality was quite similar from one country to another. Tables 17-2 and 17-3 show that in Canada in 1985 there was substantial inequality in the size distribution of income.

Inequality in the distribution of income is shown graphically in Figure 17-1 (p. 330). This curve of income distribution, called a **Lorenz curve,** shows how much of total income is accounted for by given proportions of the nation's families. (The farther the curve bends away

TABLE 17-1 Functional Distribution of National Income in Canada, 1985

Type of income	Billions of dollars	Percentage of total
Employee compensation	255.6	68.4
Corporate profits	47.5	12.7
Proprietor's income, including rent	30.5	8.2
Interest	40.1	10.7
Total	373.7	100.0

Source: Bank of Canada Review, January 1987.

Total income is classified here according to the nature of the factor service that earned the income. Although these data show that employee compensation is nearly 70 percent of national income, this does not mean that workers and their families receive only that proportion of national income. Many households will have income in more than one category listed in the table.

TABLE 17-3 Inequality in Family Income Distribution, 1985

Family income rank	Percentage share of aggregate income
Lowest fifth	6.3
Second fifth	12.3
Middle fifth	17.9
Fourth fifth	24.1
Highest fifth	39.4
	100.0

Source: Statistics Canada, 13–207.

Though far from showing overall equality, income distribution is relatively equal for the middle 40 percent of the distribution. If the income distribution were perfectly equal, each fifth of the families would receive 20 percent of aggregate income.

from the diagonal, the more unequal is the distribution of income.) Today the bottom 20 percent of all Canadian households receives less than 7 percent of all income earned. The present size distribution of income is virtually unchanged from what it was 20 years ago.

There are good reasons why much of the attention of modern economists is devoted to the size, rather than the functional, distribution of income. After all, some capitalists (such as the owners of small retail stores) are in the lower part of the income scale, while some wage earners (such as skilled athletes) are at the upper end of the income scale. Moreover, if someone is poor, it matters little whether that person is a landowner or a worker.

To understand the distribution of income, we must first study how the income of households is determined. Superficial explanations of differences in income, such as "People earn according to their ability," are clearly inadequate. Incomes are distributed much more unequally than any *measured* index of ability, be it IQ, physical strength, or typing skill. In what sense is Corey Pavin five times as able a golfer as Dave Barr? His average score is only 1 percent better, yet he earns five times as much. However, if answers couched in terms of worth and ability are easily refuted, so are answers such as "It's all a matter of luck" or "It's just the system."

How does economic theory explain the distribution of income more satisfactorily than these superficial explanations? In this chapter we provide an answer to this question using the basic tools of supply and demand.

TABLE 17-2 Incomes of Canadian Families, 1985

Income class	Percentage of families
Less than 9,999	5.8
10,000–19,999	18.2
20,000–29,999	18.2
30,000–39,999	18.7
40,000–49,999	14.7
50,000 and over	24.4

Source: Statistics Canada, 13–208.

The median family income was about $34,000 in 1985.

The Theory of Income Distribution

Every element of income has, in a purely arithmetical sense, two components: the quantity of the income-

FIGURE 17-1 A Lorenz Curve of Family Income in Canada

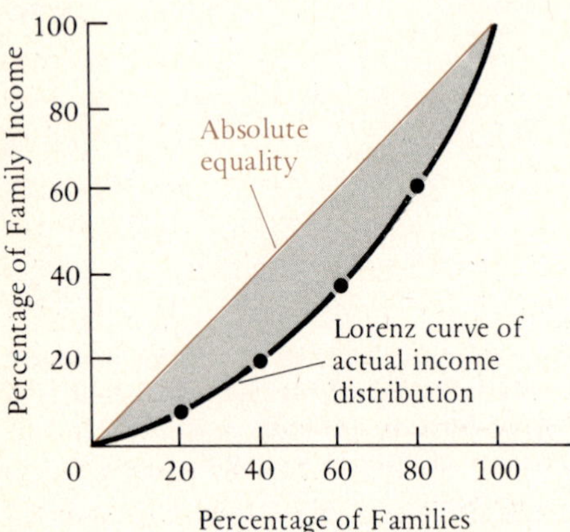

The size of the shaded area between the Lorenz curve and the diagonal is a measure of the inequality of income distribution. If there were complete income equality, the bottom 20 percent of income receivers would receive 20 percent of the income, and so forth, and the Lorenz curve would be the diagonal line. Because the lowest 20 percent receive only 6.3 percent of the income, the actual curve lies below the diagonal. The lower curve shows actual Canadian data. The extent to which it bends away from the straight line indicates the amount of inequality in the distribution of income.

earning service that is provided and the price per unit paid for it. For example, the amount a worker earns in wages depends on the number of hours worked and the hourly wage received.

Factor Income and Factor Prices

As with the market theory studied in Chapter 4, the theory of distribution is concerned with *relative* magnitudes. One factor becomes "more expensive" when its price rises relative to that of other factors. In an inflationary world most prices are rising, but not at the same rate, so some factors become relatively more expensive, some relatively cheaper. The phrase *rise in price* means a rise in relative price and the phrase *fall in price* means a fall in relative price (see pages 72–73 for a fuller discussion).

In this chapter we consider competitive markets. Microeconomic theory states that the competitive market price of any commodity or factor is determined by demand and supply. The competitive market determination of the equilibrium price and quantity, and thus the money income, of a factor of production is illustrated in Figure 17-2. (Look again at Figure 4-9, page 73, to see why this analysis is familiar.) The market equilibrium, illustrated in Figure 17-2, gives rise to what is called the *neoclassical* theory of income distribution.

According to the neoclassical theory of distribution, the problem of distribution is just a special case of the pricing of any good or service.

The theory of factor prices is absolutely general. If one is concerned with labor, one should interpret factor prices to mean wages, if thinking about land, factor prices should be interpreted to mean land rents, and so on.

FIGURE 17-2 Determination of Factor Price and Income in a Competitive Market

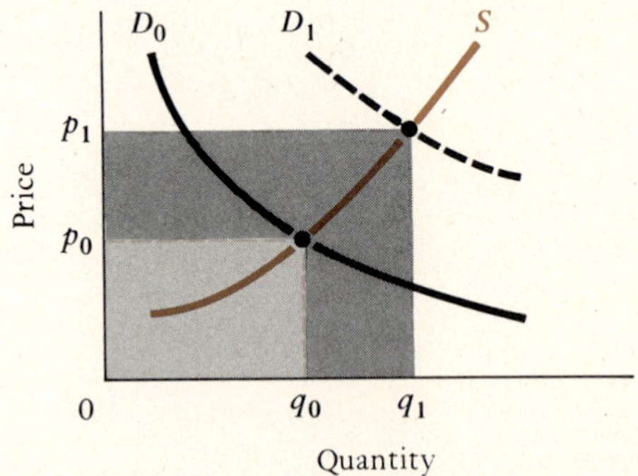

In competitive factor markets, demand and supply determine factor prices, quantities of factors used, and factor incomes. With demand and supply curves D_0 and S, the price of the factor will be p_0 and the quantity employed q_0. The total income earned by the factor is the light shaded area. A shift in demand from D_0 to D_1 raises equilibrium price and quantity to p_1 and q_1. The income earned by the factor rises by an amount equal to the dark shaded area.

The Demand for Factors

Firms require inputs not for their own sake but as a means to produce goods and services. For example, the demand for computer programmers and technicians is growing as we use more and more computers. The demand for carpenters and building materials rises or falls with the amount of housing construction. Anything that increases the demand for new housing—population growth, lower interest rates on mortgages, and so on—will increase the demand for the inputs required to build houses. The demand for any input depends on the existence of a demand for the goods or services it helps produce; the demand for a factor of production is therefore called a **derived demand.**[1] Typically, one input will be used in making many commodities. Steel is used in dozens of industries, as are the services of carpenters.

The total demand for an input will be the sum of the derived demands for it in every activity in which it is used.

The theory of income distribution rests in part on the demand for land, labor, and capital as factors of production. Firms also use as inputs products produced by other firms, such as steel, plastic, and electricity. If we trace back to the production of these inputs, we may find that they, too, are made using land, labor, capital, and other produced inputs. However, if we trace back far enough, we can net out all these produced inputs and focus on the basic inputs of the economy—land, labor, and capital.

The Supply of Factors

At any one time the total supply of each factor of production is given. For example, in each country the labor force is of such and such a size, there is so much arable land available, and there is a given known supply of petroleum. However, these supplies can and do change in response to both economic and noneconomic forces. Sometimes the change is very gradual, as when a climate change slowly turns arable land into desert or when a medical discovery lowers the rate of infant mortality and hence increases the rate of population growth and eventually increases the supply of adult labor. Sometimes the changes can be quite rapid, for example, when a boom in business activity brings retired persons back into the labor force, when a rise in the price of oil greatly encourages the discovery of new oil supplies, or when a rise in the price of agricultural produce encourages the draining of marshes to add to the supply of arable land.

In the next chapter we return to the question of the extent to which economic forces determine the *total supply* of a factor to the whole economy. In this chapter we focus on the extent to which such forces determine the *supply available to a particular industry* or use.

Most factors have many uses. A given piece of land can be used to grow any one of several crops, or it can be subdivided for a housing development. A computer programmer in Halifax can work for one of several firms, for the government, or for Dalhousie University. A lathe can be used to make many different products and requires no adaptation when it is turned from one use to another. Plainly, it is easier for any one user to acquire more of a scarce factor of production than it is for all users to do so simultaneously. One user can bid resources away from another user, even though the total supply may be fixed.

The total supply of any factor must be allocated among all the different uses to which it can possibly be put.

Factor Mobility

When considering the supply of a factor to a particular use, the most important concept is *factor mobility*. A factor that shifts easily between uses in response to small changes in incentives is said to be mobile. It will be in elastic supply in any one of its uses because a small increase in the price offered will attract many units of the factor from other uses. A factor that does not shift easily from one use to another, even in response to large changes in remu-

[1] In the next chapter we look in detail at the role of marginal productivity theory in understanding the derived demand for the services of factors of production.

neration, is said to be immobile. It will be in inelastic supply in any one of its uses because even a large increase in the price offered will attract only a small inflow from other uses. Often a factor may be immobile in the short run but mobile in the long run.

An important key to factor mobility is time. The longer the time interval, the easier it is for a factor to convert from one use to another.

Consider the mobility among particular uses of each of the three key factors of production.

Capital. While some kinds of capital equipment—lathes, trucks, and computers, for example—can be readily shifted among uses, many others are comparatively unshiftable. A great deal of machinery is utterly specific: Once built, it must be used for the purpose for which it was designed, or it cannot be used at all. (It is the immobility of much fixed capital equipment that makes the exit of firms from declining industries a slow and difficult process.)

In the long run, however, capital is highly mobile. When capital goods wear out, firms may simply replace them with identical goods. But the firm has many other options. It may buy a newly designed machine to produce the same goods; it may buy machines to produce totally different goods; or it may spend its resources in other ways. Such decisions lead to changes in the long-run allocation of a country's stock of capital among various uses.

Land. Land, which is physically the least mobile of factors, is one of the most mobile in an economic sense. Consider agricultural land. Within one year one crop can be harvested and a totally different crop planted. A farm on the outskirts of a growing city can be sold for subdivision and development on short notice.

Once land is built on, its mobility is much reduced. A site on which a hotel has been built can be converted into an office building site, but it takes a large differential in the value of land use to make it worthwhile because the hotel must be torn down.

Although land is highly mobile among alternative uses, it is completely immobile as far as location is concerned. There is only so much land within a given distance of the center of any city, and no increase in the price paid can induce further land to locate within that distance. This locational immobility has important consequences, including high prices for desirable locations and the tendency to build tall buildings to economize on the use of scarce land, as in the center of large cities.

Labor. Labor is unique as a factor of production in that the supply of the service requires the physical presence of the owner of the source of the service. Absentee landlords can obtain income from land located in remote parts of the world while continuing to live in the place of their choice. Investment can be shifted from iron mines in South Africa to mines in Labrador while the owners of the capital commute between Vancouver and Hawaii. But when a worker employed by a firm in Regina decides to supply labor service to a firm in Toronto, the worker must physically travel to Toronto. This has an important consequence.

Because of the need for physical presence, nonmonetary considerations are much more important in the allocation of labor than in the allocation of other factors of production.

People may be satisfied with or frustrated by the kind of work they do, where they do it, whom they do it with, and the social status of their occupations. Since these considerations influence their decisions about what they will do with their labor services, they will not move every time they can earn a higher wage. Nevertheless, occupational and job movement will occur when there are changes in the wage structure.

The mobility that does occur depends on many forces. For example, it is not difficult for a secretary to shift from one company to another to take a job in Penticton instead of in Vernon, but it can be difficult for a secretary to become an editor, a model, a machinist, or a doctor in a short period of time. Lack of ability, training, or inclination will stratify some people and make certain kinds of mobility difficult for them.

Some barriers may be virtually insurmountable for a person once his or her training has been completed. It may be impossible for a farmer to become a surgeon or for a truck driver to become a professional athlete, even if the relative wage rates change greatly. But the children of farmers, doctors, truck drivers, and athletes, when they are deciding how much education or training to obtain, are not nearly as limited in their choices as their parents, who have completed their education and are settled in their occupations.

Thus the labor force as a whole is more mobile than individual members of it. At one end of the age distribution people enter the labor force from school; at the other end they leave it through retirement or death. The turnover due to these causes is about 3 or 4 percent per year. Over a period of 10 years a society could create a totally different occupational distribution merely by directing new entrants to jobs other than the ones left vacant by workers leaving the labor force, without a single individual ever changing jobs. The role of education in adapting people to available jobs is great. In a society in which education is provided to all, it is possible to achieve large increases in the supply of any desired labor skill within a decade or so.

Factor Price Differentials

If all units of labor were identical and if all benefits were monetary, the price of labor would tend to be the same in all uses.[2] Workers would move from low-priced jobs to high-priced ones. The quantity of labor supplied would diminish in occupations in which wages were low, and the resulting shortage would tend to force those wages up; the quantity of labor supplied would increase in occupations in which wages were high, and the resulting surplus would force wages down. The movement would continue until there were no further incentives to change occupations, that is, until wages were equalized in all uses.

In fact, however, wage differentials commonly occur. These differentials may be divided into two distinct types: dynamic and equilibrium.

Dynamic Differentials

Some factor price differentials reflect a temporary state of disequilibrium. Such differences in factor prices, called **dynamic differentials,** or *disequilibrium differentials,* are self-correcting and disappear in equilibrium. They are brought about by circumstances such as the growth of one industry and the decline of another. The differentials themselves lead to reallocation of factors, and such reallocations in turn act to eliminate the differentials.

Consider the effect on factor prices of a rise in the demand for air transport and a decline in the demand for rail transport. There will be an increase in the airline industry's demand for factors and a decrease in the railroad industry's demand for factors. Relative factor prices will go up in airlines and down in railroading. The differential in factor prices will itself foster a net movement of factors from the railroad industry to the airline industry, and this movement will cause the dynamic differentials to lessen and eventually disappear. How long this process takes will depend on how easily factors move from one industry to the other, that is, on the degree of factor mobility.

Equilibrium Differentials

Some factor price differentials persist in equilibrium, without giving rise to forces that eliminate them. These **equilibrium differentials** can be explained by intrinsic differences in the factors themselves, by differences in the cost of acquiring skills, or by different nonmonetary advantages of different occupations.

Intrinsic differences. If various units of a factor have different characteristics, the price paid may differ among these units. If intelligence and dexterity are required to accomplish a task, intelligent and manually dexterous workers will earn more than less intelligent and less dexterous workers. If land is to be used for agricultural purposes, highly fertile land will earn more than poor land. These differences will persist even in long-run equilibrium.

Acquired differences. If the fertility of land can be increased by costly methods, that land must command a higher price than less fertile land. If it did not, landlords would not incur the costs of improving fertility. The same holds true for labor. It is costly to acquire most skills. For example, a mechanic must

[2] Similar remarks apply to all other factors of production as well.

BOX 17-1

Could Per Capita Incomes and Unemployment Rates Be Equalized Across Canadian Provinces?

The answer to the question posed in the title is almost certainly no—at least when we consider the kinds of policy tools likely to be available to any foreseeable Canadian government.

This answer comes from a simple application of the hypothesis of *equal net advantage.* As long as provinces differ in their nonmonetary attractiveness, there will be equilibrium differences in their per capita incomes and/or unemployment rates. Why is this so?

Consider low levels of income. Low incomes may be the result of strong natural economic forces that will not yield to such simple-minded policy measures as raising local demand. For example, suppose that Province A—despite strong physical, climatic, and social attractions—has a set of natural endowments that will not produce as high an income per person employed as Province B. Deficiencies in economic opportunities in a particular province might arise for many reasons: Inadequate resource base, technological backwardness, slow growth in demand for one region's products, and rapid natural growth of the labor force are just a few.

Suppose that because of migration costs, cultural and language differences, climatic advantages, or other local amenities, many people choose to live in Province A even though they earn lower incomes there. Markets can adjust to such regional differences in two basic ways.

If wages and prices are flexible, real wages and incomes will fall in Province A for the kinds of workers who are in excess supply. The falling real wages will give the province an advantage in new lines of production. Real wages will continue to fall until everyone who is willing to stay at the lower wage has a job and those who are not have migrated. In long-run equilibrium, Province A is a low-wage, low-income province, but it has no special unemployment problem. Those who do not value its amenities as much as they value the higher incomes to be earned in Province B or who are subject to lower migration costs will have left. What the price system does is equalize net advantages. It does not equalize economic advantage, because the noneconomic advantages of living in Province A exceed those of living in Province B.

The second possibility arises because we do not have these flexibilities in wages today. Minimum wage

---

train for some time, and unless the earnings of mechanics remain sufficiently above what can be earned in less skilled occupations, people will not incur the cost of training.

Nonmonetary advantages. Whenever working conditions differ among various uses for a single factor, that factor will earn different equilibrium amounts in its various uses. The difference between a test pilot's wage and a chauffeur's wage is only partly a matter of skill; the rest is compensation for the higher risk of testing new planes compared to driving a car. If they were paid the same, there would be an excess supply of chauffeurs and a shortage of test pilots.

Academic researchers commonly earn less than they could earn in the world of commerce and industry because of the substantial nonmonetary advantages of academic employment. If chemists were paid the same in both sectors, many chemists would prefer academic to industrial jobs. Excess demand for industrial chemists and excess supply of academic chemists would then force chemists' wages up in industry and down in academia until the two types of jobs seemed equally attractive on balance.

The same forces account for equilibrium differences in regional earnings of otherwise identical factors. People who work in remote logging or mining areas are paid more than people who do jobs requiring similar skills in large cities. Without higher pay, not enough people would be willing to work at sometimes dangerous jobs in unattractive or remote locations. Similarly, if enough people prefer living in the Atlantic provinces to living in Hamilton, Ontario, equilibrium wages in comparable occupations laws, national unions, and nationwide pay scales for the federal civil service put substantial restraints on possible interprovincial wage differentials. People who prefer Province A remain there, yet wages do not fall to create a wage incentive to move to B. Instead, unemployment rates in A rise until (1) the extra uncertainty of finding a job and (2) the lower lifetime income expectations because of bouts of unemployment just balance both the nonpecuniary advantages that A enjoys over B and the costs of moving from A to B. In the long run, those who are willing to stay in spite of the higher unemployment remain, and the others leave.

In these circumstances, increasing local demand, even where that is possible, will lower the rate of out-migration but *not* the unemployment rate. This is because in the long run A's unemployment rate must remain sufficiently high relative to B's to balance the relative amenity and migration-cost advantages that Province A enjoys over B.

In these circumstances trade restrictions, such as "employ local labor only" laws and labor market policies such as employment subsidies, will not reduce unemployment, although they will increase employment. As new jobs are created, the rate of out-migration slows so that the rate of unemployment is unchanged. Unless the province's policies are sufficient to create jobs for everyone entering its labor force, all that will happen when more jobs are created is that fewer people will migrate. The local supply rises as fast as the local demand for labor, and the unemployment rate is left unchanged.

The foregoing argument does not imply that nothing can be done for regions that have lower incomes or higher unemployment rates. There are many reasons why we might wish to make income transfers to poorer regions. However, it is important to realize that if the differential is an equilibrium phenomenon, no amount of policy intervention will remove it. If the policies continue to be strengthened as long as these differentials in unemployment persist, expenditures will rise and rise and rise, and the ultimate goal of equalization will continue to prove elusive.

will be lower in the Atlantic provinces than in Hamilton. Box 17-1 discusses the implications of trying to remove equilibrium differentials among Canadian provinces.

Differentials and Factor Mobility

The distinction between dynamic and equilibrium differentials is closely linked to factor mobility.

Dynamic differentials lead to, and are eroded by, factor movements; equilibrium differentials are not eliminated by factor mobility.

Dynamic differentials tend to disappear over time; equilibrium differentials persist indefinitely.

Equalizing net advantages. The removal of dynamic differentials and the persistence of equilibrium differentials leads to a generalization called the *hypothesis of equal net advantage*. The hypothesis assumes that owners of factors will choose to use their factors in a way that maximizes the net advantage to themselves, where net advantage includes both monetary and nonmonetary rewards. The **hypothesis of equal net advantage** states that in eroding dynamic differentials, factor mobility serves to equalize the net advantage earned by factors in different locations and occupations.[3]

This hypothesis plays the same role in the theory of distribution as the assumption that firms seek to

[3] Since the central idea is maximizing behavior, we might well refer to the hypothesis of "maximum net advantage." However, the terminology in the text has become standard.

maximize profits plays in the theory of production. It leads to the prediction that the units of each kind of factor of production will be allocated among various uses in such a way that their owners receive the same net return in every use.

Though nonmonetary advantages are important in explaining differences in levels of pay for labor in different occupations, they tend to be quite stable over time. As a result, monetary advantages, which vary with market conditions, lead to changes in *net* advantage. Variations in monetary advantages thus play a bigger role in reallocating resources.

A change in the relative pay of a factor between two uses will change the net advantages of the uses. It will lead to a shift of some units of that factor to the use whose rate of pay has increased.

This implies a rising supply curve for a factor in any particular use. When the price of a factor rises in that use, more will be supplied to that use. This factor supply curve (like all supply curves) can *shift* in response to changes in other variables; for example, one thing that can shift it is a change in size of nonmonetary benefits.

Policy issues. The distinction between equilibrium and dynamic factor price differentials raises an important consideration for policy. Trade unions, governments, and other bodies often have explicit policies about earnings differentials, often seeking to eliminate them in the name of equity. The wisdom (and success) of such policies depends to a great extent on the kind of differential that is being attacked.

Consider a policy that resists a dynamic differential. Only a short time ago large differentials opened up between earnings in the Prairie oil patch and those in the industrial East. These were *disequilibrium* differentials associated with an economic boom in the oil industry. Policies that sought to narrow the wage differentials may have appeared to succeed, but they would have slowed the movement of labor to the West and thus prolonged the period during which there was excess labor in the East and a shortage in the West.

Policies that attempt to eliminate equilibrium differentials will encounter even more severe difficulties. If an equilibrium differential occurs in response to nonmonetary differences and a policy resisting the monetary differential is adopted, the nonmonetary differences will change to compensate. For example, if a policy resists a wage premium that emerged for an unattractive job—say, garbage collecting—a shortage of garbage collectors would emerge. Companies and governments that hired garbage collectors but were unable to offer higher wages would develop non-wage benefits—longer holidays, shorter hours, better working conditions—to attract sufficient workers. In terms of regulating the relative attractiveness of the occupation, the policy will have failed.

Factor price differentials are a natural market consequence of conditions of supply and demand. Mobility of factors tends to establish equilibrium levels of factor prices at which dynamic differentials are eliminated and equilibrium differentials are restored. Policies that seek to eliminate factor price differentials without consideration of what caused them or how they affect the supply of the factor are likely to have perverse results.

Transfer Earnings and Economic Rent

One of the most important distinctions in economics is that between transfer earnings and economic rent. The amount that a factor must earn in its present use to prevent it from moving (i.e., transferring) to another use is called its **transfer earnings.** Any excess it earns over this amount is called its **economic rent.** The distinction is crucial in predicting the effects of changes in earnings on the movement of factors.

The concept of economic rent, the surplus of total earnings over transfer earnings, is analogous to the economists' concept of profit as a surplus over opportunity cost. The terminology is confusing because economic rent is often called, simply, rent, and *rent* also means the price paid to hire something, such as a machine or a piece of land. How the same term came to be used for these two different concepts is explored in Box 17-2.

The Division of Factor Earnings

In most cases the actual earnings of a factor of production are a composite of transfer earnings and eco-

BOX 17-2

Origin of the Concept of Economic Rent

In the early nineteenth century there was a public debate about the high price of wheat in England. The price was causing great hardship because bread was a primary food of the working class. Some argued that wheat had a high price because landlords were charging high rents to tenant farmers. To pay these land rents, the prices that farmers charged for their wheat also had to be raised to a high level. In short, it was argued that the price of wheat was high because the rents of agricultural land were high. Some people who held this view advocated restricting the rents that landlords could charge.

David Ricardo argued that the situation was exactly the reverse. The price of wheat was high, he said, because there was a shortage caused by the Napoleonic wars. Because wheat was profitable to produce, there was keen competition among farmers to obtain land on which to grow wheat. This competition in turn forced up rents on wheat land. Ricardo advocated removing the tariff so that imported wheat could come into the country, thereby increasing its supply and lowering both the price of wheat and the rent that could be charged for the land on which it was grown.

The essentials of Ricardo's argument were these: The supply of land was fixed. Land was regarded as having only one use, the growing of wheat. Nothing had to be paid to prevent land from transferring to a use other than growing wheat because it had no other use. No self-respecting landowner would leave land idle as long as he could obtain some return, no matter how small, by renting it out. Therefore, all the payment to land—that is, rent—was a surplus over and above what was necessary to keep it in its present use.

Given a fixed supply of land, the price of land depended on the demand for land, which depended on the demand for wheat. *Rent,* the term for the payment for the use of land, thus became the term for a surplus payment to a factor over and above what was necessary to keep it in its present use.

Later, two facts were realized. First, land often had alternative uses, and from the point of view of any one use, part of the payment made to land would necessarily have to be paid to keep it in that use. Second, factors of production other than land also often earn a surplus over and above what is necessary to keep them in their present use. Television stars and great athletes, for example, are in short and fairly fixed supply, and their potential earnings in other occupations are often quite moderate. But because there is a huge demand for their services as television stars or athletes, they may receive payments greatly in excess of what is needed to keep them from transferring to other occupations. This surplus is now called *economic rent,* whether the factor is land or labor or a piece of capital equipment.

---

nomic rent. It is possible, however, to imagine cases in which earnings are all one or the other. The possibilities are illustrated in Figure 17-3. When the supply curve is perfectly inelastic (vertical), the whole of the payment is an economic rent. Even a price barely above zero would not lead suppliers to decrease the quantity supplied, so transfer earnings are therefore zero. The price actually paid allocates the fixed supply to the buyers most willing to pay for it.

When the supply curve is perfectly elastic (horizontal), the whole of the price paid is a transfer earning. A purchaser who does not pay at least this price will not obtain any quantity of the factor.

The more usual situation is that of a gradually rising supply curve. A rise in the factor's price serves the allocative function of attracting more units of the factor into employment, but the same rise provides additional economic rent to all units of the factor already employed. We know this increment is an economic rent because the owners of these units were willing to supply them at a lower price. This is a general result:

If the demand for a factor in any of its uses rises relative to the supply available to that use, its price will rise in that use. This will serve the allocative function of attracting additional units

FIGURE 17-3 Division of Factor Payments Between Economic Rent and Transfer Earnings

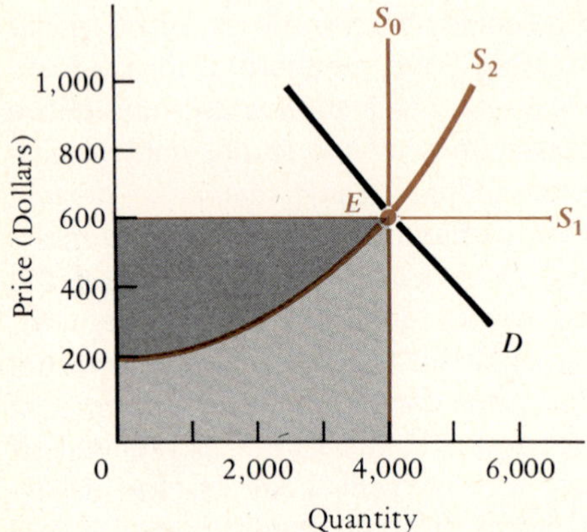

The division of total factor payments between economic rent and transfer earnings depends on the shape of the supply curve. A single demand curve is shown with three different supply curves. In each case the competitive equilibrium price is \$600, and 4,000 units of the factor are hired. The total payment (\$2.4 million) is represented by the entire shaded area.

When the supply curve is vertical (S_0), the whole payment is economic rent, because a decrease in price would not lead any unit of the factor to move elsewhere.

When the supply curve is horizontal (S_1), the whole payment is transfer earnings, because even a small decrease in price offered would lead all units of the factor to move elsewhere.

When the supply curve rises to the right (S_2), part of the payment is rent and part is transfer earnings. As shown by the height of the supply curve, at a price of \$600 the 4,000th unit of the factor is just receiving transfer earnings, but the 2,000th unit, for example, is earning well above its transfer earnings. The aggregate of economic rents is shown by the dark shaded area and the aggregate of transfer earnings by the light shaded area.

into that use. It will also increase the economic rent earned by all units of the factor already in that use, since their transfer earnings were already being covered.

Determinants of the Division

How much of a given payment to a factor is economic rent and how much is transfer earnings varies from situation to situation. We cannot point to a factor of production and assert that some fixed fraction of its income always is transfer earnings and the remainder is economic rent. The division depends on the mobility of the factor, that is, on the alternatives open to it.

The mobility of a factor depends on the perspective of our analysis. If we focus on a narrowly defined use of a given factor, say, the factor's use by a particular firm, then the factor will be highly mobile. Since it could readily move to another firm in the same industry, it has a number of alternatives open to it. Therefore, it will be necessary to make payments to keep it employed in a specific firm. Thus from the perspective of the firm, a large proportion of the factor payment is a transfer payment.

If we focus on a more broadly defined use, for example, the factor's use in an industry, then it is less mobile, because it would be more difficult for the factor to gain employment quickly outside the industry. From the perspective of the particular *industry* (rather than the specific *firm* within the industry), a larger proportion of the factor payment is economic rent and a smaller proportion is transfer payment.

From the even more general perspective of a particular *occupation*, mobility is likely to be even less and the proportion of the factor payment that is economic rent even larger.

As the perspective moves from a narrowly defined use of a factor to a broadly defined use, the mobility of the factor decreases; as mobility decreases, the share of the factor payment that is economic rent increases.

We now illustrate how these considerations apply to each of the key factors of production.

Labor. Some labor is always able to move from job to job, and therefore something must be paid to keep a given unit of labor in its present use. This amount is transfer earnings. How much has to be paid to keep labor in its present use depends on the use.

First, consider movement *among firms in one industry*. Assume, for example, that carpenters receive \$160 for working a normal eight-hour day. A construction firm will have to pay \$160 per day or it will not obtain the services of any carpenter. To that one firm, the whole $160 is a transfer payment; if it were not paid, carpenters would not remain with that firm.

Second, consider movement *among industries*. Assume that there is a decline in demand for buildings and that all construction firms reduce the wages offered to carpenters. Now carpenters cannot move to other construction firms to get more money. If they do not like the wages offered, they have to move to another industry that employs carpenters. If the best they can do elsewhere is $125 per day, they will not begin to leave the construction industry until wages in that industry fall below $125. In this case the transfer earnings of carpenters in construction is $125. When they were receiving $160 (presumably because there was a heavy demand for their services), the additional $35 was an economic rent from the point of view of the construction *industry*, even though it was a transfer earnings from the point of view of an individual firm.

Third, consider movement *among occupations*. Assume that there is a decline in the demand for carpenters in all industries. The only option a carpenter has is to move to another occupation, say, truck driving. If no carpenters are induced to leave carpentry until the wage falls to $110, then $110 is the transfer payment to carpenters in general. The wage of $110 has to be paid to persuade people to remain carpenters.

Consider how this applies to the often controversial large salaries received by some highly specialized types of labor, such as superstar singers and professional athletes. These performers have a style and talent that cannot be duplicated, whatever the training. The earnings they receive are mostly economic rent from the viewpoint of the occupation: These performers enjoy their occupations and would pursue them for much less than the high remuneration they actually receive. For example, Wayne Gretzky would choose hockey over other alternatives even at a much lower salary. However, because of Gretzky's amazing hockey skills, any team in the National Hockey League would pay handsomely to have him on its team, and he is able to command a high salary from the team he does play for. From the perspective of the firm, the Edmonton Oilers, most of Gretzky's salary is required to keep him from switching to another team and hence is properly viewed by it as a transfer payment.

Land. The analysis for land is identical to the analysis for labor. First, consider the case of an *individual wheat farmer*. In order to have the use of the land, he must pay the land's going price to prevent it from being transferred to another wheat farmer. From his point of view, therefore, the whole of the payment he makes is a transfer payment to land.

Second, consider the particular *agricultural industry* that produces wheat. To secure land for wheat production, it will be necessary to offer at least as much as the land could earn when put to other uses. From the point of view of the wheat industry, the part of the payment made for land that is equal to what it could earn in its next most remunerative use is transfer payment. If that much is not paid, the land will be transferred to the alternative use. If, however, land particularly suitable for wheat growing is scarce relative to the demand for it, then the actual payment for the use of this land may be above the transfer earnings; the additional payment is economic rent.

Third, consider the choice between *agricultural* and *urban uses*. Land is highly mobile between agricultural uses because its location is usually of little importance. For urban uses, however, location is critical. From this point of view, land is, of course, completely immobile. If there is a shortage of land in central Toronto, any land that is available will command a high price, but no matter what the price, land in rural areas will not move into central Toronto. The high payments made to urban land are thus well in excess of what is necessary to prevent it from being transferred back to agricultural uses; the payment is thus economic rent.[4]

[4] From the point of view of any particular urban use, however, high rents are transfer earnings. Movie theaters, for example, account for but a small portion of the total demand for land in central Toronto; if there were no movie theaters at all, rentals of land would be about what they are now. Thus the industry faces an elastic supply of land in central Toronto, and the whole of the price it pays for its land is a transfer payment that must be paid to keep the land from transferring to other urban uses. Thus the old examination question "Is it correct to say that the price of movie seats is high in central Toronto because the price of land is high?" should be answered in the affirmative, not in the negative, as examiners often seemed to expect. The view that the prices of *all* goods and services in central Toronto are high because rents are high should, however, be denied.

BOX 17-3

De-industrialization: From Big Steel to Big Mac

The growth of employment in services and retail trade over the past two decades has been dramatic in all industrialized nations. The growth was concentrated in several areas: transportation and communication, eating and drinking, health care, education, retail services such as hotels and entertainment, and a host of business services. In the United States in 1985, *total* employment in the manufacturing of durable goods (under 11 million persons) was less than the *increase* in employment in services over the previous two decades.

This is in one sense good news, for without these new job opportunities, overall unemployment would have been high. But many people worry that the substitution of service employment and production for industrial employment and production is a mixed blessing to the economy. High levels of productivity and the opportunities for growth in productivity have fueled high standards of living and growth. But people who worry about de-industrialization fear that productivity is lower and the opportunities for growth are much more limited in service industries than in goods-producing industries. The possibilities for substituting capital for labor, they point out, are less in selling hamburgers than in producing metal and metal products.

There are reasons to be cautious about accepting some of the popular views concerning the growth of services. First, the trend toward services has been going on for over 100 years in advanced industrial societies, although the speed of the shift seems to have accelerated since 1970. In newly industrializing countries such as Canada, the general shift towards services has been slowed by the growth of industry that is associated with their initial industrialization. But the general trend is toward de-industrialization, and Canada is following it, even if at a slightly slower pace than the average industrialized country.

Second, to a considerable extent, the decrease in the share of manufacturing in total employment is a result of that sector's dynamism. More and more manufactured goods have been produced by fewer and fewer workers, leaving more workers to produce services. Incomes earned in the service sector provide the demand to buy manufacturing goods, which have been falling in relative price because of their high productivity growth.

This movement is analogous to the one out of agriculture earlier in the century. At the turn of the century nearly 50 percent of the Canadian labor force worked on farms. Today less then 5 percent of the labor force work in farming, yet they produce more total output than did the 50 percent in 1900. The "de-agriculturalization" of Canada (and the United States) freed workers to move into manufacturing, raising our living standards and transforming our way of life. So also de-industrialization is freeing workers to move into services and, by replacing the grimy blue-collar jobs of the pollution-creating, smokestack industries with white-collar jobs in the relatively clean service

Capital. If a piece of capital equipment has several uses, the analysis of land or labor can be repeated. Much equipment, however, has only one use. For capital that is virtually immobile, any income arising from its use is rent.

Assume, for example, that when some machine was installed, it was expected to earn $5,000 per year in excess of all its operating costs, and suppose also that the machine has no scrap value. If the demand for the product falls so that the machine can earn only $2,000, it will still pay to keep it in operation rather than scrap it. Indeed, it will pay to do so as long as it yields any return at all over its operating costs.[5] Thus all the return earned by the installed machine is economic rent because it will still be allocated to its present use—it has no other—as long as it yields even $1 above its operating costs. *Once the machine has been installed,* any net income it earns is economic rent.

The machine will, however, wear out eventually, and it will not be replaced unless it is expected to earn a return over its lifetime sufficient to make it a

[5] Recall the proposition in Chapter 12, page 222, that it pays a firm to continue in operation in the short run as long as it can cover its variable costs of production.

industries, it will once again transform our way of life.

Third, to a considerable extent the decrease in the share of manufacturing in total employment also follows from consumers' tastes. Just as consumers in the first half of the century did not want to go on consuming more and more food products as their incomes rose, today's consumers do not wish to spend all of their additional incomes on manufacturing products. Households have chosen to spend a high proportion of their increased incomes on services, thus directing employment in that direction.

Fourth, although some service industries—particularly personal services and fast foods—do generate low-paying jobs, so do many manufacturing industries. Two decades ago pessimists worried that the new industrial revolution of automation and computerization was going to destroy most of the jobs for the unskilled. But the growth in the service sector fully compensated for the lost low-skilled jobs in manufacturing.

One needs to keep a sense of perspective about the low-paying service jobs. Disposable income per employed person has been rising in all of the industrialized countries, including Canada. As a nation, we are getting wealthier, not poorer. Since the size distribution of income is no more skewed than it was two decades ago, it follows that this wealth is no less evenly distributed than it was before de-industrialization became an issue.

Finally, it is easy to underestimate the scope for quality, quantity, and productivity increases in services. As one example of productivity increases, compare your local bank with what you see in a movie made in a bank no more than 20 years ago. As another, note that since 1950, output per full-time worker has grown about twice as fast in the communications industry, as it has in manufacturing.

Also, many quality improvements in services go unrecorded. Today's hotel room is vastly more luxurious than a hotel room of 40 years ago, yet this is unlikely to show up in our national income statistics as a quality improvement. All that the statistics are likely to reflect is that the price of "a hotel room" has risen.

Measuring such technological improvements is even more difficult when they take the form of entirely new products. Airline transportation, telecommunications, fast food chains, and financial services are prominent examples. The resulting increase in output is not properly captured in our existing statistics.

The moral is that it is easy to get depressed by looking at the official statistics for slow growth rates and at the low wages earned in some service jobs. If we look at the growth in real standards of living, there is little reason to think that the shift in employment from industries to services in the second half of the twentieth century—which, after all, is driven by our rising real incomes—will be any less beneficial to industrialized nations than was the shift from agriculture to manufacturing in the first half of the century.

good investment for its owner. Thus, over the long run some of the revenue earned by the machine is transfer earnings; if the revenue is not earned, a machine will not continue to be allocated to that use in the long run.

Do Factors Move in Response to Changes in Earnings?

The theory developed in this chapter predicts that factors move among uses, industries, and places, taking both monetary and nonmonetary rewards into account. It predicts they will move in such a way as to maximize the net advantages to the owners of factors.

We now ask: Does the world behave in the way theory predicts? Because there are impediments to the mobility of factors, there may be lags in the response of factors to changes in relative prices, but the question remains: Do adjustments occur even though there are impediments?

Land and Capital

The most casual observation reveals that the allocative system works pretty much as described by the theory with respect to land and capital. Land is transferred from one crop to another in response to changes in the relative profitabilities of the crops. Land on the edge of town is transferred from rural to urban uses as soon as it can earn substantially more as a building site than as a cornfield. Materials and capital goods move from use to use in response to changes in relative earnings in those uses.

This is hardly surprising. Nonmonetary benefits do not loom large for factors other than labor, and the theories of both competition and monopoly predict that quantities supplied will respond to increases in earnings generated by increased demand.

In the case of nonhuman factors—land and capital—there is strong evidence that factors move in response to earnings differentials.

Labor

Labor can be mobile in many ways. Labor can move among occupations, industries, firms, skill categories, and regions. These categories are not exclusive; to change occupation from a farm laborer to a steelworker, for example, a man will also have to change industries and probably where he lives.

There are, of course, barriers to labor mobility. Unions, pension funds, and other institutions can and do inhibit labor mobility in various ways. State governments have erected barriers to mobility in the form of occupational licensing, differential training requirements, and the like.

Nevertheless, the documented mobility of labor is impressive. When wages in manufacturing areas soared during World War II, workers flocked there to take lucrative jobs in the rapidly expanding industries producing aircraft, ships, and other materials of war. When new oil fields were discovered in northern Canada and Alaska, high wages attracted welders, riveters, and the many other types of labor the oil fields required.

During the period 1950–1970 American workers migrated steadily from the South to the North in search of jobs. During the 1970s this trend slowed, and in the late 1970s and early 1980s it was reversed as the movement of many American firms to the Sunbelt created new jobs in the South.

FIGURE 17-4 The Changing Composition of the Nonagricultural Labor Force

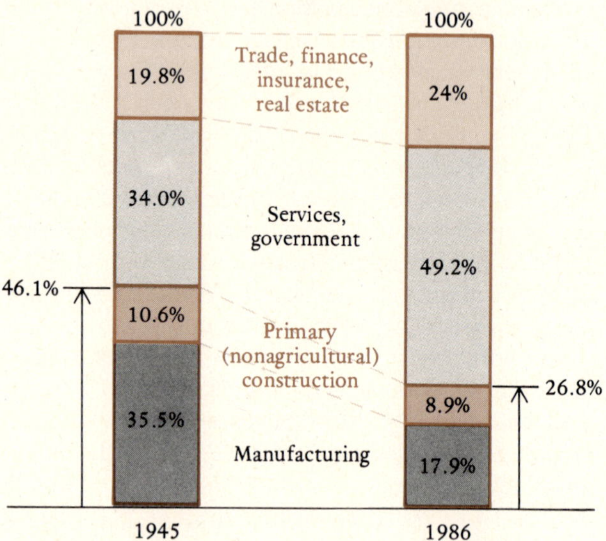

In less than half a century, a major shift has occurred in labor utilization. In 1945, 46 percent of the nonagricultural labor force was in the heavy industrial (largely blue collar) sectors. As shown by the bottom two blocks, this figure had decreased to 27 percent by 1986. The shift was to the service-oriented (largely white collar) sectors of government, trade, finance, and other services.

Figure 17-4 illustrates another dimension of labor mobility. The shifts among sectors that have occurred in the postwar period indicate the substantial adaptability of the labor force to changing patterns of demand for the outputs of various sectors. The process of "de-industrialization" evident in this figure is discussed further in Box 17-3 (p. 340).

From decade to decade, labor is highly mobile in response to changes in demand.

Of course, labor does not always move promptly and fully in response to changes in earnings. Thus not all behavior is neatly explained by the theory. For example, despite the recent relative decline in academic salaries and job opportunities, many more students persist in getting Ph.D.s in fields such as history and English than can reasonably expect to find jobs that will require or make use of their training. Economists can speculate about such behavior, for example, by saying that for many students graduate education is a consumption good as well as an investment or that the nonmonetary advantages of an academic position are large enough to be worth the gamble of finding a job. But such hypotheses go beyond elementary economics. At this stage we have to be satisfied with a theory that explains much, but not all, behavior.

Summary

1. The functional distribution of income refers to the shares of total national income going to each of the major factors of production; it focuses on sources of income. The size distribution of income refers to the shares of total national income going to various groups of households; it focuses only on the size of income, not its source.
2. The income of a factor of production is composed of two elements: the price paid per unit of the factor and the quantity of the factor used. The determination of factor prices and quantities is an application of the same price theory used to determine product prices and quantities.
3. The demand for any factor of production is a derived demand because the factor is used as an input into the production of goods and services. The total demand for a factor of production will be the sum of the individual derived demands for it in each activity where it is used. The total supply of any factor must be allocated among all the uses to which it can possibly be put.
4. Factor mobility is the ease with which a factor can move to alternative uses. Land is mobile between uses but cannot change its geographical location. Capital equipment is durable, but firms regularly replace discarded or worn-out machinery with totally different machines and so change the composition of the nation's capital stock gradually but steadily. Labor mobility is greatly affected by nonmonetary considerations. The longer the period of time, the more mobile is a factor.
5. In competitive factor markets prices are determined by demand and supply, but factor price differentials occur. Dynamic differentials in the earnings of different units of factors of production serve as signals of a disequilibrium and induce factor movements that eventually remove the differentials. Equilibrium differentials reflect differences among units of factors as well as nonmonetary benefits of different jobs; they can persist indefinitely.
6. The hypothesis of equal net advantage is a theory of the allocation of the total supply of factors to particular uses. Owners of factors will choose the use that produces the greatest net advantage, allowing for monetary and nonmonetary advantages of a particular employment. In so doing, they will cause dynamic factor price differentials to be eliminated.
7. Transfer earnings are what must be paid to a factor to prevent it from transferring to another use. Economic rent is the difference

between a factor's transfer earnings and its actual earnings. Whenever the supply curve is upward-sloping, part of the factor's total pay is transfer earnings and part is rent. The proportion of each depends on the mobility of the factor; the more narrowly defined the use, the larger the fraction that is transfer earnings and the smaller the fraction that is economic rent.

8. Factor mobility is typically greater for nonhuman factors than it is for labor. Even where impediments to mobility exist, factors (including labor) tend to move in response to persistent differences in earnings or employment opportunities.

Topics for Review

Functional distribution and size distribution of income
Derived demand
Factor mobility
Dynamic and equilibrium differentials
Hypothesis of equal net advantage
Transfer earnings and economic rent

Discussion Questions

1. Other things being equal, how would you expect each of the following to affect the size distribution of after-tax income? Do any of them lead to clear predictions about the functional distribution of income?
   a. An increase in unemployment
   b. Rapid population growth in an already crowded city
   c. An increase in food prices relative to other prices
   d. An increase in social insurance benefits and taxes
2. Consider the effects on the overall level of income inequality of each of the following.
   a. Increasing participation of women in the labor force as many women shift from work in the home to full-time jobs
   b. Increasing use by produce growers of immigrant workers who have entered the country illegally
   c. Increasing numbers of minority group members studying law and medicine
3. Distinguish between economic rent and transfer earnings in the following payments for factor services.
   a. The $750 per month a landlord receives for an apartment leased to students
   b. The salary of the prime minister
   c. The $1,000,000 annual salary of Wayne Gretzky
   d. The salary of a window cleaner who says, "It's dangerous, dirty work, but it beats driving a truck."
4. Which of the following are dynamic and which are equilibrium differentials in factor prices?
   a. Differences in earnings of hockey coaches and wrestling coaches
   b. A "bonus for signing on" offered by a construction company seeking carpenters in a tight labor market

c. Differences in monthly rental charged for three-bedroom houses in different parts of the same metropolitan area

5. Equal pay for equal work is a commonly held goal. But "equal work" is hard to define. What would be the consequences of legislation enforcing equal pay for what turned out to be unequal work?
6. Rent controls often succeed in reducing rents paid by tenants in the short run, but at the cost of a growing housing shortage in the long run. What does this tell us about the nature of the earning of landlords in the short and the long run? (Consider the categories of rent and transfer earnings.)
7. Look again at the data in Figure 17-4. What economic forces might have given rise to the labor movements described there? What would you predict about the pattern of wages in the various categories in the figure? (Check the facts to see if your predictions were correct.) For occupations that saw an increase in wages, did the increases represent increased transfer payments or economic rents?
8. During the oil boom from 1975 to 1985, workers flooded into the oil-producing areas of the Western provinces. When oil prices tumbled in 1986, the boom ended abruptly, and a reverse movement to the East set in, particularly to the booming areas around Toronto. What would you expect to be happening to relative wages and unemployment rates in the West and the East over this time period? What about rents of apartments and prices of houses in Calgary and Toronto?

18

More on Factor Demand and Supply

What determines whether the demand for a factor will be elastic? Why are the supplies of some factors highly inelastic, so that most of their earnings are economic rents, while the supplies of other factors are highly elastic, so that most of their earnings are transfer payments? Why do the supply and demand curves for some factors shift frequently, while the curves for other factors remain relatively stable? To deal with these and many related subjects, we need to inquire further into the determinants of the demand for and supply of factors of production.

The Demand for Factors

We saw in Chapter 17 that the demand for any factor depends on the demand for the goods it helps produce. For this reason the demand for a factor is called a *derived demand*. We now consider in detail the economic forces that influence that demand.

Marginal Productivity Theory

All profit-maximizing firms, whether they are selling under conditions of perfect competition, monopolistic competition, oligopoly, or monopoly, produce to the point at which marginal cost equals marginal revenue. Similarly, all profit-maximizing firms hire units of the variable factor up to the point at which the last unit employed adds as much to revenue as it does to cost. Thus it is a simple implication of profit maximization that firms hire units of a variable factor up to the point where the marginal cost of the factor (i.e., the addition to the total cost resulting from the employment of one more unit) equals the marginal revenue produced by the factor.

Because we use the term *marginal revenue* to denote the change in revenue resulting when the rate of product sales is increased by one unit, we shall use another term, **marginal revenue product (*MRP*),** to refer to the change in revenue caused by the sale of the product contributed by *an additional unit of the variable factor.* [29] Using this term, state the equilibrium condition above as

$$\text{Marginal cost of the variable factor} = \text{Marginal revenue product of that factor}$$

If the firm is unable to influence the price of the variable factor by buying more or less of it, that is, if the firm is a price taker when *buying factors*, the marginal cost of the factor is merely its price. The cost, for example, of adding an extra laborer to the firm's work force is the wage that must be paid. In these circumstances firms adjust the quantity of the variable factor they hire at the established market price, and we may state the equilibrium condition as

$$w = MRP$$

where w is the price of a unit of the factor.

A profit-maximizing firm that is a price taker in factor markets hires a factor up to the point at which the price of the factor equals the marginal revenue product.

The proposition that in equilibrium factors will be paid the value of their respective marginal products is often called the **marginal productivity theory of distribution.**[1] This is nothing more than an implication of profit maximization. Over the years, however, the theory has been the subject of many emotional attacks and defenses and without doubt has often been seriously misunderstood. Some of these issues are taken up further in Box 18-1.

Slope of the Demand Curve

What happens to quantity demanded when a factor's price rises? One influence operates through the link between a factor's price and the price of the good or service it helps to produce. Consider, for example, a rise in the wages of carpenters, which increases the cost of producing houses. The rise in cost shifts the supply curve of houses to the left. This leads to a rise in the price of houses and to a decrease in the number of houses sold. If fewer houses can be sold, fewer will be built, and smaller quantities of factors will be needed. Thus there will be a decrease in the quantity demanded of carpenters used to produce houses.

A second influence operates through the principle of substitution. When the price of one factor goes up, other relatively cheaper factors will be substituted. For example, if carpenters' wages rise relative to those of factory workers, some prefabricated door and window frames made by factory workers will be used to replace on-the-job carpenters.

Demand curves for factors slope downward because a change in a factor price influences the price of commodities that are produced using the factor and also gives rise to the substitution of relatively cheaper for relatively more expensive factors.

Elasticity of Factor Demand

The elasticity of demand for a factor measures the degree of the response of the quantity demanded to a change in its price. The three major forces that determine the elasticity of the demand curve for a factor, sometimes called the *principles of derived demand,* are elasticity of demand for the final commodity, ease of substitution, and importance of the factor.

Elasticity of demand for the final commodity. Other things being equal, the more elastic the demand for the commodity that the factor helps to make, the more elastic the demand for the factor will be. If an increase in the price of the commodity causes a large fall in the quantity demanded, that is, if the demand for the commodity is elastic, there will be a large decrease in the quantity of a factor needed to produce it in response to a rise in the factor's price. But if an increase in the price of a commodity causes only a small fall in its quantity demanded, that is, if the demand for the commodity is inelastic, there will be only a small decrease in the quantity of the factor required in response to a rise in its price.

Ease of substitution. The greater the ease with which one factor can be substituted for another in response to changes in relative factor prices, the greater the elasticity of demand for those factors. The ease of substitution depends on the substitutes available and technical conditions of production. Even in the short run it is possible to vary factor proportions in surprising ways. For example, in automobile manufacture and in building construction,

[1] The way in which marginal productivity theory can be used to derive a firm's demand curve for a factor is discussed in the appendix to this chapter.

BOX 18-1

The Marginal Productivity Theory of Distribution

The marginal productivity theory is simply an implication of profit maximization: Any firm that is maximizing its profits must hire each variable factor up to the point at which the last unit hired adds just as much to costs (the price of the factor) as it does to revenue (the marginal revenue product). Nonetheless, misconceptions about the theory exist. (Indeed, in certain quarters marginal productivity theory is almost a dirty word.) It *seems* to say that each factor, including labor, is paid exactly the value of what it produces. It has been criticized on the grounds that it is inhumane and that it falsely implies that the market leads to factor prices that, however low they might be, are "just." Both criticisms rest on misconceptions of what the theory says and implies.

Marginal productivity theory does not take into account the differences between human services and other services. Some think the theory inhumane because it treats human labor as it treats a ton of coal or a wagonload of fertilizer.

The marginal productivity theory is only a theory of the *demand* for a factor. It predicts only what profit-maximizing employers would like to buy. It predicts that desired purchases of a factor depend on the price of the factor, the technical conditions of production, and the demand for the product produced using the factor. *Supply* conditions undoubtedly differ between human and nonhuman factors, but these differences are accommodated within the theory of distribution. No evidence has been gathered to indicate that it is necessary to have separate theories of the demand for human and nonhuman factors of production.

In a world of perfectly competitive factor markets the theory predicts that in equilibrium all factors receive payment equal to the values of their marginal products. Some eminent economists in the past spoke as if this led to a just distribution because factors were rewarded according to the value of their own contributions to the national product. "From each according to his ability; to each according to his own contribution" might have been the slogan for this group. Many critics of the low levels of wages that then prevailed reacted passionately to a theory that was claimed to justify them.

According to the marginal productivity theory, each worker receives the value of what one more worker would add to production if that worker were taken on while all other factors were held constant. If 1 million similar workers are employed, each of the 1 million will receive a wage equal to the extra product that would have been contributed by the millionth worker if he or she had been hired while capital and all other factors remained unchanged. Whether such a distribution of the national product is or is not "just" may be debated. The marginal productivity theory does not, however, contribute to that debate; it does not say that each unit of a factor receives as income the value of *its own* contribution to production. Indeed, where many factors cooperate in production, it is generally impossible to divide total production into the amounts contributed by each unit of each factor of production.

It is possible both to hold that marginal productivity tends to determine how people get paid and to believe that government policies that change the distribution of income are desirable. Many economists hold both positions.

glass and steel can be substituted for each other simply by varying the dimensions of the windows. In most durable goods, materials can be substituted for maintenance labor. This is done by making the product more or less durable and more or less subject to breakdowns by using more or less expensive materials in the product's construction.

Nor are such direct short-run substitutions the end of the story. In the long run a factory that has a particular technique embodied in its equipment (and thus cannot easily vary factor proportions in the short run) can be replaced. Plant and equipment are continually being replaced, and more or less capital-intensive methods can be adopted in new plants in response to changes in factor prices. Similarly, engines that use less gasoline per mile are developed when the price of gasoline rises.

Importance of the factor. The larger the fraction of total costs that are payments to a factor, the greater the elasticity of demand for the factor. Suppose that wages are 50 percent of the costs of producing a good, while raw materials account for 15 percent. A 10 percent rise in the price of labor raises the cost of producing the commodity by 5 percent (10 percent of 50 percent), but a 10 percent rise in the price of raw materials raises the cost of the commodity by only 1.5 percent (10 percent of 15 percent). The larger the increase in cost, the larger the increase in the commodity's price, and hence the larger the decrease in the quantity demanded of the commodity and the factors used to make it.[2]

The Supply of Factors

There are two important economic questions concerning the supply of factors: To what extent do economic forces determine the *total supply* of a factor to the whole economy? To what extent do economic forces determine the *supply available to a particular industry?* In Chapter 17 we took the total supply as given and concentrated on the supply to a particular industry. In this chapter we return to the question of the role of economic forces in determining the total supply of factors.

Let us look more closely at why total supply is not fixed, even though there is plainly a finite limit to many natural resources on earth. Although people worry about depleting natural resources, actual exhaustion of resources has not arisen often. Frequently newly discovered or previously unexploited sources of a resource maintain the supply, although perhaps at higher cost than existing supplies. Ultimately, of course, there is an upper limit, and resources can be exhausted; worse, they can be contaminated or otherwise despoiled so as to be useless before they are consumed. But even when the supply of one resource is exhausted, substitutes are developed. The exhaustion of high-grade iron ore reserves in the Mesabi Range of northern Michigan did not end steel production in Canada and the United States, partly because ways to use low-grade iron ores once thought worthless were discovered and partly because new supplies in Labrador and the Caribbean were developed.

Shortages often lead to their own correction. For example, as oil becomes scarce, its price will rise; users will turn to substitutes to meet their demands, synthetic oils will be developed, and oil companies will explore for new sources. A sufficient increase in the price of oil would also make it economically worthwhile to process the vast quantities of previously unexploited shale oil.

As the discussion of dynamic differentials in Chapter 17 suggested, a factor may be immobile in the short run but mobile in the long run. Similar considerations apply to the total supply of a factor.

Time is an important element in the determination of the total supply of a factor. The longer the time period, the more responsive the total supply of any factor will be to economic forces.

Consider in turn the total supply of three key factors of production.

[2] This is necessarily true when there is only one variable factor of production. When there are many variable factors, we must also consider the ease of substitution. For example, copper tubing may be a small part of building costs, but if aluminum tubing is nearly a perfect substitute, the demand for copper tubing may be quite elastic. In contrast, the demand for tubing of some kind may be quite inelastic. The text statement is another example of something that is correct *other things being equal:* For a given degree of substitutability among factors, the demand for any factor will be more elastic the larger the proportion of total costs that are payments to that factor.

BOX 18-2

Taxes, Welfare, and the Supply of Effort

Taxes

Many people believe that high income taxes tend to reduce the supply of effort by lowering the incentive for people to work. Such objective evidence as exists, however, suggests that tax cuts do not always increase the supply of effort. Even when they do, the aggregate effect may be small.

A tax cut sets up two opposing forces, and the final effect on the amount of work done by people depends on the relative strengths of each. An example will suggest why this is so. Consider Barry Bluecollar, who has a job on an assembly line. He typically takes off 5 hours a week and so works only 35 hours, with a take-home pay of $8.50 an hour or $297.50 a week. Now suppose there is a tax cut so that his take-home pay rises to $10.00 an hour. He might elect to work a little more, since every hour he works now nets him $10.00 instead of $8.50. If he raises his average weekly hours to 37, he will raise his take-home pay by $72.50 to $370.00. Economists call the tendency to work more because the reward for an hour's work has risen the *substitution effect.*

However, Bluecollar might elect to work a little less, since with the rise in hourly take-home pay, he can have more income *and* get more leisure. Suppose he takes off an extra 3 hours a week. His take-home pay is now $320.00 a week (32 hours at $10.00 compared to 35 hours at $8.50 before the tax cut). Now he has 3 more hours of leisure a week *and* $22.50 more income. Economists call the tendency to work less because it is possible to have more income *and* more leisure the *income effect.*

If the substitution effect dominates, people respond to a tax cut by working more. If the income effect dominates, they work less. Either result is possible, so a tax cut may raise or lower the amount of work people want to do.

A good deal of research has been done on the effect of tax rate increases. It has shown that in response to a rise in taxes some people work fewer hours because the reward is less, while others feel poorer and work more to maintain their after-tax income. The most recent research, however, suggests at most a small net disincentive up to a level of marginal tax rate of 50 percent, such as existed in Canada in 1987. The sharp decrease in maximum rates, introduced by the t ; reform of 1987–8, will provide important additional evidence within a few years.

Welfare

Do welfare payments and other assistance make the poor less willing to take jobs? Though it is true that many people receiving payments are unable to find work, there is no doubt that some welfare rules discourage work by heavily taxing much or all of any income welfare recipients might earn. If a family's welfare payment of, say, $500 per month is decreased dollar for dollar by any earnings, this amounts to a 100 percent tax on the first $500 of earnings per month. The person who could earn $400 by part-time work would have no economic incentive to do so. The major disincentives that exist in the Canadian tax and welfare systems are discussed in detail in Chapter 25.

Total Supply of Capital

The supply of capital in a country consists of the stock of existing machines, plant, equipment, and so on. Capital is a manufactured factor of production, and its total supply is in no sense fixed, although it changes only slowly. Each year the stock of capital goods is diminished by the amount that becomes physically or economically obsolete and increased by the amount that is produced. On balance, the trend has been for the capital stock to grow over the decades. In the final section of this chapter we consider the theory of investment that describes how the stock of capital changes over time.

Total Supply of Arable Land

If the term *land* is used to refer to the total area of dry land, then the total supply of land in a country will be almost completely fixed. It was nineteenth century practice (following Ricardo) to define land as the *original and inexhaustible powers of the soil.* But dust bowls were a phenomenon unknown to Ricardo, who also did not know that the deserts of North Africa were once fertile plains. Clearly, the supply of fertile land is not fixed. Considerable care and effort is required to sustain the productive power of land. If the return to land is low, its fertility may be destroyed within a short time. Moreover, scarcity and high prices may make it worthwhile to increase the supply of arable land by irrigation and other forms of reclamation.

Total Supply of Labor

The total supply of labor means the total number of hours of work that the population is willing to supply. This quantity is often called the **supply of effort.** It has many obvious determinants, such as the rewards for working, the age at which people enter the labor force and retire from it, and the length of the conventional work week. It also has many less obvious ones. For example, a social trend such as the women's liberation movement affects labor force participation. For another, the whole pattern of tax rates, unemployment insurance, and welfare payments affects the relative advantages of working and not working.

The evidence is overwhelming that such things matter. What is debated, however, is how *large* their impact is. As is discussed in Box 18-2, the evidence shows some, but relatively small, adverse effects of taxes on the supply of effort. However, welfare schemes have sometimes been a severe disincentive to work. Although most people prefer working to being on welfare, it is not surprising that they respond rationally to an incentive system that severely penalizes any work done by welfare recipients.

Distribution Theory: Some Evidence

Does the theory of distribution satisfactorily explain the allocation process in our economy? In Chapter 17 we reviewed the impressive array of evidence that despite the presence of impediments to factor mobility, such as licensing and union restrictions for labor, safety requirements for capital equipment, and zoning laws for land, factors do move in response to changes in factor earnings. In the following section we examine whether market forces do in fact play the roles predicted by the theories of competition and monopoly in determining factor prices and the allocation of resources.

Do Market Conditions Determine Factor Earnings?

Some commentators have denied the relevance of the theory of distribution outlined in this and the preceding chapter. They argue that prices of products and factors bear little relation to market conditions because prices and wages are administered by oligopolies and giant unions. Entry barriers in industry and mobility barriers for factors of production, the argument continues, prevent significant movements of resources in response to product and factor price differentials that exist or develop. Should we therefore conclude that the theory of income distribution that we have developed is irrelevant to the real world? Let us see what a careful look at the evidence says.

Capital and Land

Many nonhuman factors are sold on competitive markets. The theory predicts that changes in the earnings of these factors will be associated with changes in market conditions. The evidence overwhelmingly supports this prediction, as shown by the following examples.

The prices of plywood, tin, rubber, cotton, and hundreds of other materials fluctuate daily in response to changes in their demand and supply. The responses of factor markets to the many shortages that seemed to characterize the Canadian economy in the 1970s provide dramatic confirmation. When the price of agricultural commodities shot up following a grain shortage, farm income soared. When oil became scarce, prices rose and oil producers and owners of oil properties found their profits and income rising rapidly. Not only did the relative prices of oil products rise, but so did the relative prices of commodities, such as chemical fertilizers and air travel, that make use of petroleum products. When oil became abundant in the mid 1980s, these trends were reversed.

Land in the heart of growing cities provides another example. Such land is fixed in supply, and values rise steadily in response to increasing demand for it.[3] Land values may even be high enough to make it worthwhile to destroy durable buildings in order to convert the land to more productive uses. The high-rise is a monument to the high value of urban land. The increase in the price of land on the periphery of every growing city is an observable example of the workings of the market.

Similar results occur in markets that are far from being perfectly competitive. In 1979 the price of power in virtually all forms rose sharply in response to the energy shortage caused by the doubling of the price of oil. Oligopolists producing key metals such as zinc, molybdenum, steel, and aluminum have raised prices when their costs of production rose or when demand outran production. Further examples can be found in almost every issue of the *Financial Post* and the *Financial Times,* but the point should now be clear:

The prices and earnings of nonhuman factors are successfully predicted by market theories of factor pricing.

Labor

When we apply the theory to labor, we encounter two important sets of complications. First, because labor is the human factor of production, nonmonetary considerations loom large in its incentive patterns, and thus market fluctuations may have less effect. Second, the competitive and noncompetitive elements of labor markets occur in different proportions from market to market. These complications make it harder to see if market conditions determine factor earnings. Nevertheless, there is a mass of evidence to support the view that they do.

Market fluctuations. Do earnings respond to normal fluctuations of demand and supply as the theory predicts? The evidence shows that they often do. For example, with the advent of the automobile, skilled carriage makers saw the demand for their services decline rapidly. Earnings fell, and many older workers found that they had been earning substantial economic rents for their scarce but highly specific skills. They suffered large income cuts when they moved to other industries. Workers who acquired skills wanted in the newly expanding automotive industry found that the demands for their services and their incomes rose rapidly.

More recently there has been a large increase in the earnings of premier professional athletes. In part this has resulted from rising demand due to expansion in the number of major league teams. In part it has resulted from increased revenues to the teams and leagues from televising sports, which has increased the marginal revenue product of the athletes. And in part it has resulted from athletes' acquiring the right to offer their services to more than one employer, thereby reducing the ability of employers to hold down wages by acting as single buyers, or *monopsonists.* (Monopsony is discussed in the next chapter.)

One group that has been suffering the consequences of factor price determination on competitive markets is college graduates. In recent years the earnings of college graduates have fallen relative to other workers as employment opportunities dropped sharply, especially for new graduates. The downturn is explained partly by slackening demand due to changes in industrial structure (e.g., substituting sophisticated computers for college-trained persons) and partly by continued growth of supply as the "baby-boomers" finish college.

Wage changes induced by market conditions have

[3] A friend is fond of saying, "Nobody buys land anymore; its price is much too high because everybody wants it."

little to do with abstract notions of justice or merit. If you have some literary talent, why can you make a lot of money writing copy for an advertising agency, but very little money writing poems? It is not because an economic dictator or group of philosophers has decided that advertising is more valuable than poetry. It is because in the economy there is a large demand for advertising and a small demand for poetry.

Effects of monopoly elements. A strong union—one able to bargain effectively with management and to control entry of labor into the field—can raise wages well above the competitive level. The high earnings attract others to the occupation or industry, and the privileged position can be maintained only if the supply of labor can be effectively restricted. Highly skilled plasterers, plumbers, and electricians have all managed to restrict entry into their trades and as a result maintain wages well above their transfer earnings. Many similar cases have been documented.

Not only can monopoly elements raise incomes above their competitive levels, but they can also prevent wages from falling in response to decreases in demand. (Of course, if the demand disappears more or less overnight, there is nothing any union can do to maintain incomes.)

Consider coal mining in the years just after World War II. From 1945 to 1965 the production of coal declined as oil, gas, and electricity were steadily substituted for it. The coal that was produced was mined by ever more capital-using and labor-saving techniques. Both these forces led employment to shrink steadily. Coal mining was plainly a declining labor market from 1945 until 1965. Competitive theory would predict relatively low wages and low incomes, followed by exit of the most mobile coal miners and hard times for those who decided to stick it out.

Precisely this happened in Canada. Average wages, which in 1945 had been 36 percent above those in manufacturing, fell steadily until in 1965 they were 8 percent below those in manufacturing, and employment declined to 35 percent of its previous level. In the United States, however, this was *not* the pattern. Faced with a similar decline in production, relative wages actually rose in coal mining, from 18 percent above manufacturing in 1945 to 34 percent above it in 1965. Employment did fall; indeed, by 1965 employment was only 30 percent of the 1945 level. But those who kept jobs did relatively well.

What happened was that in the United States a powerful union, the United Mine Workers, prevented wages from falling. By raising wages despite falling demand, the union actually accelerated the decline in employment. The lower employment that accompanied the "high-wage" policy of the United Mine Workers discouraged the young from waiting for jobs in the industry. As workers left the industry because of retirement, ill health, or death, they were not replaced.[4]

All these examples support the general proposition:

Earnings of labor respond to significant changes in market conditions.

Some Efficiency Implications

The theory and evidence presented in this and the preceding chapter can be summarized in two central propositions.

1. **Factors will move between alternative uses so as to maximize the net advantage to the factors' owners.**
2. **Individual profit-maximizing employers will hire any factor up to the point where the last unit hired adds as much to costs as it does to revenue.**

Together these two propositions have a powerful implication for economic efficiency. We present the argument in terms of labor, but it also applies to capital and land. The argument is developed in stages by first considering a special case that makes the proposition considerably easier to interpret and understand.

[4] After 1965 the demand for coal miners rebounded as the demand for coal to produce electricity surged. As a result, in both Canada and the United States, as theory predicts, employment *and* relative wages in coal mining rose sharply.

Absence of nonmonetary advantages. Suppose that all alternative uses for labor were alike in all respects so that none had any nonmonetary benefits or disadvantages relative to any other. In this circumstance the hypothesis of equal *net* advantage would mean that labor would move between alternative jobs and occupations until the wage rates in all were equal. When there are no nonmonetary advantages, only the monetary advantage, that is, the wage, of alternatives need be equalized.

The two propositions printed in color thus imply that in the absence of nonmonetary advantages, the marginal revenue product of labor will be equalized in all uses. When that condition holds, the value of total output cannot be increased by shifting labor from one use to another, since the increase in the value of the output of the firm labor moves to will be exactly offset by the fall in the value of the output of the firm labor is moved from.

If there are no nonmonetary advantages to alternative uses of a factor, its marginal revenue product will be equalized in all uses; as a result, the value of total output is maximized.

Effect of nonmonetary advantages. If alternative uses of labor involve differing nonmonetary advantages, the value of the marginal product of labor will differ among uses by an amount reflecting the difference in nonmonetary advantages. Hence output will not reach its maximum value; output could be increased by moving labor from a use where the value of its marginal product is low (because the use has a high nonmonetary advantage) to a use where the value is high (because that use has a low nonmonetary advantage).

But the "psychic" value of output would not go up, because the increase in output of goods and services would be offset by the "psychic" cost to the worker from moving from a less preferred activity to a more preferred one. For example, a carpenter in Victoria may earn a lower wage and have a lower marginal product than one in Dawson City. If he moves to the Yukon, the economy's value of output of carpentry services would go up. But if the initial difference in wages, and hence in marginal products, reflected the net nonmonetary advantage to the carpenter of living in Victoria, the increase in value of output of carpentry services will be exactly matched by the decrease in nonmonetary returns to the carpenter.

The message is that factor prices reflect the value of factors in alternative uses and thus play a key role in their efficient allocation. If factors are not priced according to their scarcity, there will be no easy means of allocating them efficiently among competing uses. This is not just idle speculation. In the early years of the communist experiment in Russia, interest, which is the price paid for capital, was banned for ideological reasons. This led to serious waste due to the misallocation of capital. This and related ideological issues concerning interest and capital are taken up in Box 18-3.

Capital and Interest

In this section we explore a complication that applies in some measure to all factors of production but is most clear in the case of capital goods. The complication arises because some factors of production, such as capital goods, are durable, lasting for many years, even decades. It is convenient to think of a capital good's lifetime as being divided into shorter periods that we refer to as *production periods* or, equivalently, *rental periods*.

The Stock of Capital and the Flow of Capital Services

The durability of capital goods makes it necessary to distinguish between the capital good itself and the flow of services that it provides in a given production period. This distinction is just a particular case of the general distinction between stocks and flows first encountered on page 21.

Two Prices for Capital

The distinction between stocks and flows means that we can identify two prices for capital goods, the rental price and the purchase price.

BOX 18-3

Capital, Capitalists, and Capitalism

The two most essential characteristics of capital goods are (1) that they are produced inputs into further production rather than things found in nature and (2) that they tend to be durable, lasting for many periods of production.

A capitalist is one who owns capital goods. The role of the capitalist is interpreted differently in different economic philosophies. For example, to many Marxists the capitalist is a villain; to many socialists the capitalist is at best a dispensable drone; to many conservatives the capitalist is the hero who steers the economy through the risky channels that lead to ever higher living standards.

Ideology aside, if there is capital, someone must own it. Capital may be predominantly in private hands, in which case the economy is sometimes described as *capitalist,* or it may be predominantly owned by the state, in which case the economy is described as socialist or communist. In virtually all economies ownership is mixed; some capital is owned privately and some publicly.

No matter who owns the capital goods, such goods are indispensable in the productive process. A primitive society in which there are no capital goods—no spear, no lever, no stone for grinding grain, no jug for carrying water—has never occurred in recorded human history.

Since resources must be used in the manufacture of capital goods, such goods have scarcity value. Any economic system interested in maximizing production will want to allocate scarce capital to its most productive uses. One effective way of doing this is to assign a rental price to capital that reflects its opportunity cost and to allow firms to use more capital only if the capital earns enough to cover this price. Charging producers for use of capital serves such important functions that it is hard to eliminate it without serious consequences.

Early communist rulers in Russia thought differently. Payments for the use of capital were officially barred during the years following the Russian Revolution of 1917 on the ground that a communist society should purge itself of this reminder of capitalism. But this left no way of deciding how to allocate scarce capital efficiently among its many competing uses. Indeed, prices are such an efficient allocative device that today all communist states use them for allocating scarce capital among competing uses. Furthermore, their planners give a good deal of attention to setting the correct rental price for capital.

If capital is privately owned and a price is charged for its use, the payments go to the capitalists and become their income. In communist countries capital is owned by the state, and payments for its use go to the state. The desirability of private versus public ownership of the *means of production* (the term often used in socialist and communist literature to describe capital) is still debated hotly. But the issue of ownership is quite a separate issue from that of whether to charge a rental price for the use of capital.

Rental price. The price paid to use a capital good for a period of time is called the *rental price of capital*. Renting a capital good entitles the renter to the services that the capital good generates over the rental period. Our earlier discussion of the marginal productivity theory of factor pricing relates directly to the services of capital and thus to the rental price of such services.

The rental price of capital is the amount a firm would pay to obtain the services of the capital good for a given rental period. It will equal the marginal revenue product of those capital services.

Capital goods may be owned by one firm and used by another. This is especially true for portable equipment with "specialty" uses that any given firm would need only occasionally. It is also obviously true for many dwellings and commercial properties where the owner is the landlord and the renter is the tenant. In such circumstances the term *rental price* refers to the actual payment made per period for the use of the capital good.

A capital good may also be used by the firm that owns it. In this case no rental price is actually paid, but the concept of the rental price is still a useful one. It represents the amount the firm would charge for the use of the good if in its role as owner it were to lease the capital good to another firm; it thus reflects the opportunity cost to the firm of using the capital good itself. The rental price also represents what the firm in its role as user of the capital good would pay if it were to lease it from another firm; it thus reflects the marginal revenue product of the capital good. Although a rental price is neither actually charged nor paid for the use of the good, there is nevertheless an implicit rental price that reflects the value of the services of the capital good to the firm during the period.

Purchase price. The price paid to acquire ownership of a capital good is called the *purchase price of capital*. Ownership of a capital good entitles the owner to the income generated by the services of the capital good. As we shall see, the purchase price is related to the value of the capital good as an asset and reflects the total value of the benefits that accrue to the owner over the lifetime of the capital good.

As a preliminary to understanding the relationship between the purchase price and the rental price of capital, we must define the key concept of present value.

Present Value of Future Returns

In general, **present value (PV)** refers to the value *now* of payments to be made in the future. As we have seen, a capital good is a durable factor of production that yields a stream of payments over a number of future periods. To know what a firm would be willing to pay to own such a capital good, we must be able to calculate the present value of the stream of future payments that the capital good is expected to yield. How is this present value determined?

Present value of a single future payment. How much would you be prepared to pay *now* to acquire the right to receive \$100 in one year's time? One way to answer this question is to ask how much would you have to deposit in a savings bank now in order to have \$100 a year from now? It would surely not be profitable for you to pay more than such an amount.

Suppose the interest rate is 5 percent. You have to calculate how much money *now* is equivalent to \$100 in one year's time at that rate. Letting X stand for this unknown amount, we can write $X(1.05) = \$100$, and thus $X = \$100/1.05 = \$95.24$. The value today of \$100 next year is \$95.24 if the interest rate is 5 percent. That sum is said to be the *present value* of \$100 next year.

The particular numerical value depends on the interest rate used to *discount* (i.e., reduce to its present value) the \$100 to be received one year hence. If the interest rate is 7 percent, the present value of the \$100 receivable next year is $\$100/1.07 = \$93.46$. In general, the present value of X dollars one year hence at an interest rate of i per year is

$$PV = \frac{X}{(1 + i)}$$

Note that in this expression a rate of interest of 5 percent is written $i = 0.05$, so $1 + i = 1.05$.

The present value of \$100 *two* years hence at an interest rate of 5 percent is $\$100.00/(1.05)(1.05) = \$90.70$. That is, \$90.70 put in a savings bank now would be worth \$100 in two years. In the first year the deposit would earn interest of $(0.05)(\$90.70) = \$4.54$ and hence after one year it would be worth \$95.24. In the second year interest would be earned on this entire amount; interest earned in the second year would equal $(0.05)(\$95.24) = \$4.76$. Hence in two years the deposit would be worth \$100. (The payment of interest in the second year on the interest income earned in the first year is known as *compound interest*.)

In general, the present value of X dollars after t years at i percent is

$$PV = \frac{X}{(1 + i)^t}$$

From the formula $PV = X/(1 + i)^t$ we can conclude that the present value of a given sum payable in the future will be smaller the further

away the payment date and the higher the rate of interest.

Present value of an infinite stream of payments. Now consider the present value of a stream of income that continues indefinitely. While at first glance that might seem very high, since as time passes the total received grows without reaching any limit, the far distant payments will not in fact be highly valued now. To find the present value of $100 per year, payable forever, we need only ask how much money would have to be invested now at an interest rate of i percent per year to obtain $100 each year. This is simply $i \times X = \$100$, where i is the interest rate and X the sum required. This tells us that the present value of the stream of $100 a year forever is $100 divided by i, or

$$PV = \frac{X}{i}$$

If the interest rate were 10 percent, the present value would be $1,000. Here, as before, PV is related to the rate of interest: The higher the interest rate, the less the (present) value of distant payments.

Present value of a finite stream of payments. It is also possible to obtain the present value of some finite stream of income. Consider, for example, a machine that yields the following stream of gross returns: $100 now, $275 in one year, $242 in two years, $133.10 in three years, and nothing thereafter. The present value of this flow of income, the market rate of interest is 10 percent ($1 + i = 1.1$), is

$$\begin{aligned} PV &= \$100 + (\$275/1.1) + \\ &\quad (\$242/1.1^2) + (\$133.10/1.1^3) \\ &= \$100 + \$250 + \$200 + \$100 \\ &= \$650 \end{aligned}$$

But $650 invested at 10 percent interest will yield a flow of $65 per annum in perpetuity. Thus the irregular finite flow listed above has the same present value as the smooth flow of $65 forever. So in any practical problems concerning an irregular flow, we can substitute an equivalent regular flow, which can be handled with much greater ease.

Present value in general. We have now seen how to compute the present values of amounts at specific future dates and of infinite streams of income. Any income stream can be treated as the sum or difference of such streams and amounts; thus the present value of any stream of future payments can be computed.

For example, receiving $100 per year for three years can be considered either as the present value of $100 next year, plus the PV of $100 two years hence, plus the PV of $100 three years hence or as the *difference* between the PV of $100 received each year from now to infinity and the PV of $100 received from year 4 to infinity. There are standard actuarial tables that make calculation of present value easy.

Purchase Price of a Capital Good

What then determines the market price of any existing asset? The asset might be a piece of land, a machine, a contract for a baseball player's services, or an apartment house. The asset produces a stream of income given by its future marginal revenue products. The present value of this income stream is the value of the asset to whoever purchases it and hence will determine the price that a potential buyer would be willing to pay to acquire it.

The purchase price of a capital good is related to the present value of the future stream of income that the capital good is expected to produce.

The present value of the income stream is also called the **capitalized value** of the income stream.

If the capitalized value of a machine (or other capital good) is greater than the purchase price of such machines, it will pay firms to buy additional machines. As they do, given diminishing productivity, the capitalized value of additional machines will fall. Eventually it will fall to the level of the purchase price of the machines.

The previous discussion shows how the purchase price of capital and the rental price are related. Other things being equal, the higher the rental price, the higher the purchase price; for any given rental price, the higher the interest rate, the lower the purchase price; and the further in the future the rental prices occur, the lower the purchase price.

The Rate of Interest and the Capital Stock

It is convenient to think of any firm, or indeed the economy, as having a quantity of capital that can be measured in physical units. The term **capital stock** refers to this total quantity of capital.[5] As with any other factor of production, there is a marginal and an average product of capital. (More precisely, there is a marginal and an average product of the flow of services provided by the capital stock.)

We now examine the relationship between the rate of interest in the economy and the size of its capital stock. For simplicity, in the text we consider only the case where there is no risk; Box 18-4 discusses the issues of risk and depreciation and takes up some related terminology.

Consider the simple case where an additional unit of capital gives rise to a steady stream of additional payments into the indefinite future. This makes the basic calculations simple while still conveying accurately the general principles. The purchase price of capital, which we denote by P, then equals the rental price of capital (which equals its marginal revenue product) divided by the interest rate. This condition is expressed in the equation

$$P = \frac{MRP}{i} \qquad [1]$$

If the interest rate were 5 percent, it would cost 20 times as much (i.e., 1/.05) to purchase a capital good as it would to rent it for one year. If the interest rate were 10 percent, the purchase price would be only 10 times the rental price.

Marginal efficiency of capital. *Marginal product* (*MP*) is a *physical* measure of the additional output per period resulting from an additional unit of capital. *Marginal revenue product* (*MRP*) is a mixture of physical and value measures; it gives the value per period of the additional output produced by an additional unit of capital. (As we have seen, in a competitive market the rental price of capital will be set equal to the marginal revenue product.) To obtain a *value* measure we value both the additional output and the additional capital at their market prices. The ratio gives the monetary return on the marginal dollar's worth of capital and is called the **marginal efficiency of capital (*MEC*).** The *MEC* is defined as the marginal revenue product divided by the price of capital.

$$MEC = \frac{MRP}{P} \qquad [2]$$

A schedule that relates the *MEC* to the size of the capital stock is called a **marginal efficiency of capital schedule (*MEC* schedule).** Because capital, like any other factor, is eventually subject to diminishing returns, the value of additional output produced per dollar of additional capital employed will fall. The *MEC* schedule is thus negatively sloped, as shown in Figure 18-1 (p. 360).

To derive the relationship between the stock of capital and the interest rate, we can substitute the equilibrium value of the price of capital from Equation 1 in Equation 2. This yields the important equilibrium condition:

$$MEC = \frac{MRP}{MRP/i} = i \qquad [3]$$

To see the implications of this condition that the marginal efficiency of capital equals the interest rate, it is useful to distinguish between how it applies to an individual firm and how it applies to the economy as a whole.

Equilibrium in the Individual Firm

The firm, being small relative to the economy, takes the interest rate as given. It pays a firm to purchase a capital good whenever the marginal efficiency of capital is greater than the interest rate that could be earned on the money used to buy the good.

Suppose that for \$8,000 a firm can purchase a machine that yields \$1,000 a year into the indefinite future. Also suppose that the firm can borrow (and lend) money at an interest rate of 10 percent. The present value of the income stream earned by the machine is X/i = \$1,000/0.10 = \$10,000. (The pres-

[5] The idea of a capital stock measured by a single number is a simplification. Society's stock of capital goods is made up of a diverse array of aids to production such as factories, machines, bridges, and roads.

BOX 18-4

Productivity, Risk, and Return

The Productivity of Capital

In what sense is capital productive? To be productive it must lead to higher output than would be possible without it. The use of capital renders production processes roundabout. Instead of making what is wanted directly, producers engage in the indirect process of first making capital goods that are then used to make consumer goods.

For example, a worker may be employed in a factory that makes machines that are used in mining coal; the coal may be burned by a power plant to make electricity; the electricity may provide power for a factory that makes machine tools; the tools may be used to make a tractor; the tractor may be used by a potato farmer to help in the production of potatoes, which are the final good that may ultimately be eaten by consumers. This kind of indirect production is worthwhile when the farmer, using a tractor, can produce more potatoes than could be produced by applying all the factors of production involved in the chain directly to the production of potatoes (using only such tools as were provided by nature). In fact, the roundabout capital-using method of production often leads to more output than the direct method. The difference between the flows of output that would result from the two methods is called the productivity of capital.

The Return on Capital

Take the receipts from the sale of the goods produced by a firm and subtract the appropriate costs for purchased goods and materials, for labor, for land, and for the manager's own contributed talents. Subtract also an allowance for the taxes the firm will have to pay, and what is left may be called the **gross return to capital.**

It is convenient to divide the gross return to capital into four components.

1. **Depreciation** is an allowance for the decrease in the value of a capital good as a result of using it in production.
2. The **pure return on capital** is the amount that capital could earn in a riskless investment in equilibrium.
3. The **risk premium** compensates the owners for the actual risks to the enterprise.
4. Economic profit is the residual after all other deductions have been made from the gross return. It may be positive, negative, or zero.

The **productivity of capital,** also called the *net return on capital,* is its gross return minus the depreciation.

There is an important difference between the first three components, all of which are elements of opportunity cost, and the fourth component. In a market economy positive and negative economic profits are a signal that resources should be reallocated because earnings exceed opportunity costs in some lines of production and fall short of them in other lines. Profits, defined in this way, are thus a phenomenon of disequilibrium. In equilibrium, profits will be zero and the return to capital will be equal to the opportunity cost of capital.

It is usual to deal with a rate of return *per dollar* of capital. This concept requires placing a money value on a unit of capital (the "price of capital goods") and a money value on the stream of earnings resulting from the productivity of capital. If we let X stand for the annual value of the net return on a unit of capital and P for the price of a unit of capital, the ratio X/P may be defined as the **rate of return on capital.**

---

ent value of $8,000 now is, of course, $8,000.) Clearly, it is profitable for the firm to purchase the machine.

Another way to see this is to suppose that the firm has only two uses for its money: to buy the machine or to lend out the $8,000 at 10 percent

FIGURE 18-1 Marginal Efficiency of Capital

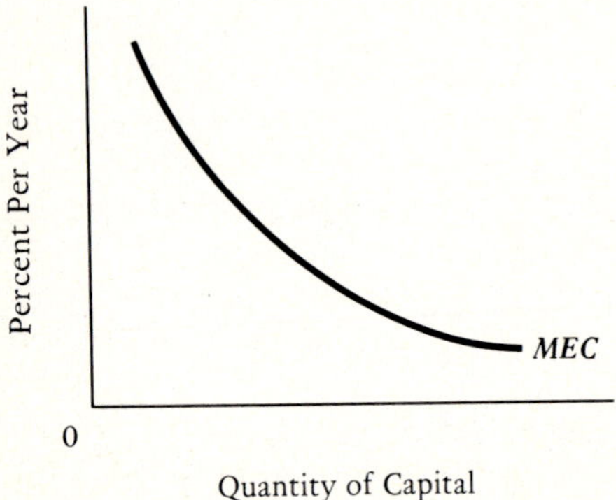

The marginal efficiency of capital (*MEC*) schedule shows the relation between the size of the capital stock and the rate of return on the marginal unit of capital. The *MEC* schedule slopes downward because of the hypothesis of diminishing returns applied to capital. Each successive unit of capital adds less to output than each previous unit. Thus the curve, which relates the value of the additional output of each additional dollar's worth of capital added to the capital stock, is downward-sloping.

FIGURE 18-2 Equilibrium Capital Stock of a Firm

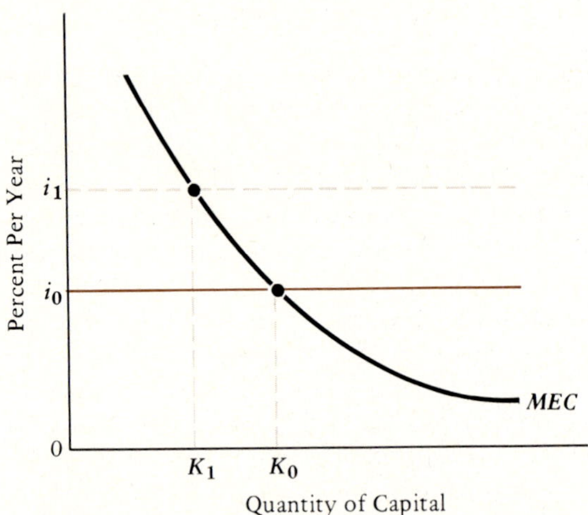

A firm's desired capital stock is negatively related to the market interest rate. The *MEC* curve is reproduced from Figure 18-1. It relates this firm's desired capital stock to the market rate of interest. Its negative slope thus reflects the diminishing marginal productivity of capital.

At an interest rate i_0 the firm's desired capital stock K_0 is that for which the *MEC* is equal to i_0. If, for example, the firm had a capital stock of only K_1, the *MEC* would exceed the interest rate and the firm would wish to expand its capital stock until it reached K_0. If the interest rate rose to, say, i_1, the firm would wish to reduce its capital stock to K_1.

interest. It will pay to buy the machine, for the firm can do so and earn $1,000 per year, while if it lends the $8,000 at 10 percent it will earn only $800 per year.

Since the *MEC* declines as the firm's capital stock rises, the firm will eventually reach an equilibrium with respect to its capital stock. Equation 3 states the condition for determining the equilibrium capital stock of an individual firm.

The equilibrium capital stock of the firm is such that the *MEC* equals the (given) interest rate.[6]

This is shown in Figure 18-2. It also follows from the negative slope of the *MEC* function that a rise in the rate of interest leads to a decrease in the firm's desired capital stock.

Equilibrium in the Economy

For the economy as a whole, the relationship between the rate of interest and the capital stock is similar to the relationship in the individual firm, with one important difference. Any firm takes the interest rate as given and determines its own desired capital stock according to the relationship between the rate of interest and the *MEC* as indicated in Equation 3. In the economy as a whole, the total capital stock

[6] In this chapter we assume that the rate of interest reflects the opportunity cost of capital to the firm. We saw in Chapter 9 that this may not always be the case. When the market rate of interest and the firm's own opportunity cost of capital diverge, the *MEC* must be equated to the latter, not the former.

can be changed only gradually through time. Hence at any point in time the capital stock, and hence the *MEC*, can be taken as given. Equation 3 then determines the interest rate in the economy.

For the economy as a whole, the condition that *MEC* = *i* determines the equilibrium interest rate.

If the market interest rate were below the *MEC*, it would pay to borrow money to invest in capital. But for the economy as a whole, the stock of capital cannot change quickly, so the effect of this demand for borrowing would be to push up the interest rate until it equaled the *MEC*. This is illustrated in Figure 18-3.

FIGURE 18-3 Equilibrium Interest Rate in an Economy

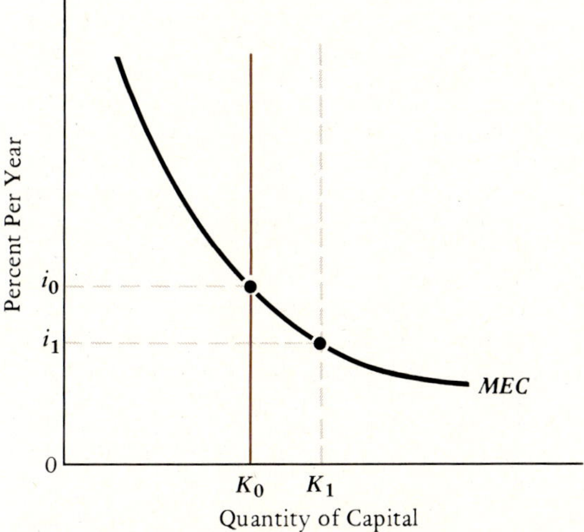

The equilibrium interest rate in an economy is negatively related to the stock of capital. The *MEC* curve is reproduced from Figure 18-2. In that figure we assumed that the rate of interest was fixed (from the point of view of the firm) and used it to determine the firm's capital stock. Here we use the *MEC* curve to determine the interest rate for a given capital stock. It relates the equilibrium interest rate in the economy to the economy's stock of capital.

If the capital stock is K_0, the equilibrium interest rate is i_0. At an interest rate below i_0 it will pay people to borrow to invest in more capital. This will drive the interest rate up. An increase in the capital stock K_1 would cause the equilibrium interest rate to fall to i_1.

Investment in Human Capital

Although capital goods are usually discussed in terms of tangible assets such as buildings or machines, the notion of a capital asset as something that produces an increase in the stream of future output suggests another sort of capital good. Consider a high school graduate who has enough schooling to get and keep a job. Instead of taking a job, however, she elects to go to university and possibly to graduate or professional school. During her university career her contribution to society's current output is small (only a summer job perhaps), but because of her education, her lifetime contribution to production may be substantially larger than it would have been had she taken a job after high school.

The choice of whether to take a job now or to continue one's education has all the basic elements of an investment decision, and it is useful to regard the student as making an investment to acquire capital. Because the value derived from such investments is embodied in a person—in terms of greater skills, more knowledge, better health, and the like—rather than in a machine, it is known as **human capital.** Major elements of human capital are health and education of all sorts. An extended education program requires, for example, that resources be withdrawn from the production of goods for current consumption. The resources include materials in the school, services of teachers, and the time and talents of pupils. The education of an individual is productive if the difference between the value of the lifetime output of the trained worker and the lifetime output of the individual without that education exceeds the value of the incremental resources used in the education process. If so, the education increases the value of total production of the economy.

The payoff to education as an investment in human capital has been studied extensively, and many investigators have concluded that investment in education pays, in the sense just defined. Of course, education also has other payoffs; it may be valued for cultural or social reasons, and it may bestow benefits or costs on individuals other than the individuals who are educated. But the fact that it may be more than a capital investment does not prevent it from being an investment.

Summary

1. The demand for any factor is derived from the demand for the commodities the factor is used to make. Factor demand curves slope downward for two reasons. First, an increase in a factor's price will raise the cost of production of goods that use the factor in their production; this will increase the price of those goods and thus reduce the amount demanded. Second, an increase in a factor price will create incentives for producers to substitute cheaper factors for more expensive ones.
2. A profit-maximizing firm will hire units of any variable factor until the last unit hired adds as much to costs as it does to revenue. If factors are bought in a competitive market, the addition to cost will be the price of a unit of a factor. From this comes the important condition that in competitive equilibrium, the price of a factor will equal its marginal revenue product. This is the marginal productivity theory of distribution.
3. The elasticity of factor demand will tend to be greater (a) the greater the elasticity of demand of the products it makes, (b) the greater the ease of substitution of one factor for another, and (c) the greater the proportion of the total cost of production accounted for by the factor.
4. The total supplies of most factors are variable over time and respond in some degree to economic influences. The most important influences are not the same for labor, or capital, or arable land and natural resources.
5. Market conditions exert a powerful influence on factor earnings. This is most evident for nonhuman factors such as raw materials and land, but it is also true for labor, despite the greater role of nonmonetary considerations and the greater importance of noncompetitive markets.
6. The marginal productivity theory of factor demands has the important implication that factors will be allocated efficiently among competing uses.
7. Because capital goods are durable, we distinguish between the stock of capital goods and the flow of services provided by them and thus between their purchase price and their rental price. The linkage between them relies on the ability to assign a present value to future returns. The present value of a future payment will be lower the more distant the payment and the higher the interest rate.
8. The rental price of capital, equal to its marginal revenue product, is the amount paid to obtain the flow of services a capital good

provides for a given period. The purchase price is the amount paid to acquire ownership of the capital and is equal to the present value of the future income stream earned by the capital.

9. The marginal efficiency of capital (*MEC*) is the ratio of the value of the additional income stream to the value of the additional capital stock that is needed to produce the increased income stream. In equilibrium, the *MEC* will equal the interest rate.
10. An individual firm will invest in capital goods as long as the *MEC* exceeds the interest rate; thus the condition that $MEC = i$ determines the firm's equilibrium capital stock. In the economy as a whole, the size of the total capital stock, and hence the *MEC*, changes only slowly; hence the condition that $MEC = i$ determines the interest rate.

Topics for Review

Derived demand
Marginal revenue product
Marginal productivity theory of distribution
Elasticity of factor demand
Total supplies of factors
Efficient allocation of factors
Rental price and purchase price of durable goods
Present value
Marginal efficiency of capital
The interest rate and the capital stock
Human capital

Discussion Questions

1. The demands listed below have been increasing rapidly in recent years. What derived demands would you predict have risen sharply? Where will the extra factors of production demanded be drawn from?
   a. Demand for electric power
   b. Demand for medical services
   c. Demand for international and interregional travel
2. Can the following factor prices be explained by the marginal productivity theory of distribution?
   a. The actor James Garner is paid $25,000 for appearing in a 10-second commercial. The model who appears in the ad with him is paid $250.
   b. The same jockey riding the same horse is paid 50 percent more money for winning a $\frac{3}{4}$-mile race with a $150,000 first prize than a $1\frac{1}{2}$-mile race with a $100,000 prize.
   c. The manager of the New York Yankees is paid *not* to manage in the third year of a three-year contract.
3. Consider the large-scale substitution of jumbo jets, each with a seating capacity of about 350, for jets with a seating capacity of about 125. What kinds of labor service would you predict to have

experienced an increase in demand and what kinds a decrease? Under what conditions would airplane pilots (as a group) be made better off economically by virtue of the switch?

4. A recent study showed that after taking full account of differences in education, age, hours worked per week, weeks worked per year, and so forth, professionally trained people earned approximately 15 percent less if they worked in universities than if they worked in government service. Can this be accounted for by the theory of distribution we have been studying?
5. Discuss the implications of the suggestion that the Canadian government should change its policy of paying all its secretaries according to the same salary scale, regardless of location, to one that adapted the salary scale to local market conditions.
6. Each of the following is sometimes described as an "investment" in everyday usage. Which represent investments in capital in the economist's sense?
   a. Building of the Aswan Dam by the government of Egypt
   b. Acquisition of a law degree at Dalhousie
   c. Purchase of a newly discovered painting by Picasso (Does it matter to your answer if the purchaser is the Art Gallery of Ontario or a private collector?)
   d. Purchase by one company of the stock or assets of another company
7. Suppose you are offered, free of charge, either one of each of the following pairs of assets. What considerations would determine your choice?
   a. A perpetuity that pays $20,000 a year forever or an annuity that pays $100,000 a year for five years
   b. An oil-drilling company that earned $100,000 after corporate taxes last year or Canada Savings Bonds that paid $100,000 interest last year
   c. A 1 percent share of a new company investing $10 million in a new cosmetic thought to appeal to middle income women or a $100,000 bond issued by the same company

The Firm's Demand for Factors

In Chapter 18 we saw that all profit-maximizing firms will hire units of the variable factor up to the point at which the marginal cost of the factor equals the marginal revenue produced by the factor. For a firm that is a price taker in factor markets, this means that it hires a factor up to the point at which the factor's price equals its marginal revenue product.

Consider a single firm with only one variable factor, labor, and one fixed factor, capital. Assume that the average and marginal revenue products of the labor are those shown in Figure 18A-1. The firm wishes to hire the quantity of labor that will maximize its profits.

FIGURE 18A-1 Demand for a Factor and Marginal Revenue Product

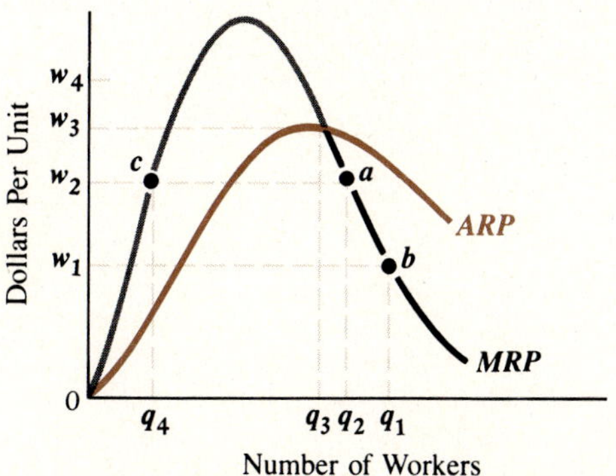

The derived demand curve for a factor is the downward-sloping portion of the *MRP* curve below the *ARP* curve as indicated by the black portion of the *MRP* curve. Suppose the factor in question is labor. The average revenue generated by a unit of labor, the average revenue product of labor, is shown by the curve *ARP*, while the revenue generated by a marginal increase in the labor force, the marginal revenue product of labor, is shown by the curve *MRP*. Only points on the black portion of the *MRP* curve are on the firm's demand curve for the factor.

The demand curve for a factor is the downward-sloping portion of the marginal revenue product curve where it is below the average revenue product curve.

To see why this statement is correct, let us ask a number of questions.

Why do points on the downward-sloping portion of *MRP*, such as *a* and *b* in the figure, belong on the demand curve? If the wage rate (the price of the variable factor) is w_2, the profit-maximizing firm will hire the factor up to the point where $w = MRP$, that is, up to q_2. This is point *a*. If the wage rate is w_1, the firm will hire up to q_1. This is point *b*. Points *a* and *b* are thus on the firm's demand curve for the factor.

What is the maximum wage rate the firm will pay? We saw in Chapter 12 that it will never pay to produce a product when its price is below the level of average variable cost. We also saw that where average product is a maximum, average variable cost is a minimum. For any wage rate above w_3, such as w_4, the average revenue generated by a unit of labor (shown by *ARP*) would be less than the variable cost of the unit of labor (its wage rate). For such a wage rate it does not pay the firm to hire any workers. In other words, w_3, where average revenue product is a maximum, is the highest factor price a firm could pay and still cover variable costs.

Why is the downward-sloping, not the upward-sloping, portion of *MRP* the demand curve? Consider the wage rate w_2. Here $w = MRP$ at both q_4 (point *c*) and q_2 (point *a*). We have already seen that point *a* is on the demand curve; what about point *c*? For every unit of labor hired up to q_4, *MRP* is less than the wage rate. In other words, each unit of labor is contributing less to revenue than to cost. Thus a profit-maximizing firm would be better off hiring zero units than q_4 units. For every unit of labor from q_4 to q_2, *MRP* exceeds the wage rate. Thus, if a firm were hiring q_4 units, it would find each additional unit beyond q_4 (up to q_2) worth hiring. Point *c*, where *MRP* is rising when it equals the wage rate, is a point of *minimum* profit, not maximum profit. **[30]** A firm at point *c* would improve its profitability by moving in either direction, to hiring zero workers or to hiring q_2 workers. (We already know that q_2 is better than zero because at that quantity *ARP* is greater than the wage rate.)

Only points where *MRP* cuts the wage rate from above, that is, where *MRP* is downward sloping, are possible profit-maximizing quantities.

Will There Be a Downward-Sloping Portion of *MRP*?

Having shown that only downward-sloping portions of *MRP* are relevant to the demand curve for the factor, we may ask whether we have any reason to believe *MRP* will slope downward. The presence of diminishing returns is sufficient to assure this result, as can be easily shown. Marginal revenue product depends on two things: (1) the physical increase in output that an additional unit of the variable factor makes possible, multiplied by (2) the increase in revenue derived from that extra output. The first of these is called the marginal product (*MP*); the second is the by now familiar concept of marginal revenue:

$$MRP = MP \times MR$$

The hypothesis of diminishing marginal returns was introduced in Chapter 8. This hypothesis says that *MP* has a declining section over some range of output. If marginal revenue is constant (as it is in perfect competition), *MRP* will have the same shape as *MP* and must also decline.

Marginal revenue, however, may not be constant. If *MR* declines as output increases (as it does in monopoly and in any other situation in which the firm's demand curve declines), *MRP* must decline even more sharply. The hypothesis of diminishing marginal productivity thus implies diminishing *MRP* and a downward-sloping demand curve for the factor.

19

Wages, Unions, and Discrimination

Why do workers in the meat-packing industry get the same pay for the same work, no matter where they work in Canada? Why do carpenters get different wages in different locations? Why do railroad employees, who work in a declining industry, get higher rates of pay than equally skilled workers in many expanding industries? How does a worker in a plant employing 5,000 people "ask for a raise"? How does a worker let her employer know that she would be glad to trade so many cents per hour in wages for a better medical insurance scheme? Why do strikes occur?

The competitive theory of factor price determination tells us a lot about factor prices, factor movements, and the distribution of income. Indeed, for the pricing of many nonhuman factors, there is little need to modify the competitive model. Much of what is observed about labor markets is also consistent with the theory. But not all of it is.

Labor is in many ways the exceptional factor of production. The owners of capital or land need not be present when the services of those factors are used; indeed, the owners need not even live close to where these factors are employed. In contrast, the owner of labor must be present when labor services are used. As a result, nonmonetary factors such as location and working conditions are likely to be more important in the labor market than in markets for other factors of production.

Considerations other than material advantage enter the relationship between employer and employee, for it is a relationship between people who look for loyalty, fairness, appreciation, and justice along with paychecks and productivity. Discrimination on the basis of sex, race, or age can further complicate labor markets.

Labor unions, employers' associations, collective bargaining, and government intervention in free-market wage determination are important features of the real world. They influence wages and working conditions and affect the levels of employment and unemployment in many industries.

The theory of factor price determination must therefore be extended somewhat before it can be applied to the full range of problems concerning the determination of wages.

Theoretical Models of Wage Determination

In a labor market firms are the buyers and workers are the sellers. Noncompetitive elements can enter on either or both sides of the market and influence the outcome of the wage bargain.

Two extreme but relevant cases are, first, the one in which there are so many employers that no one of them can influence the wage rate by varying its own demand for labor and, second, the one in which there is a single purchaser of labor, either a single firm or an association of several firms operating as a single unit in the labor market. In the former case labor is said to be purchased under competitive conditions; in the latter case, under monopsonistic conditions. **Monopsony** means a single buyer; it is the equivalent on the purchasing side of monopoly on the selling side (a single seller). What is the effect of introducing a union into the extreme situations?

A Union in a Competitive Market

Where there are many employers and many unorganized workers there is a competitive factor market of the kind discussed in Chapter 18. Under competitive conditions the wage rate and level of employment are set by supply and demand.[1]

Suppose a union enters such a market and sets a wage for the industry above the competitive level. By so doing it is establishing a minimum wage below which no one will work. This changes the supply curve of labor. The industry can hire as many units of labor as are prepared to work at the union wage but no one at a lower wage. Thus the industry (and each firm) faces a supply curve that is horizontal at the level of the union wage up to the quantity of labor willing to work at that wage.

This is shown in Figure 19-1. The intersection of this horizontal supply curve and the demand curve establishes a higher wage rate and lower level of employment than the competitive equilibrium.

There will be a group of workers who would like to obtain work in the industry or occupation but cannot. This presents a problem for the union if it seeks to represent *all* the employees in the industry or occupation. A conflict of interest has been created between serving the interests of the union's employed and unemployed members. Pressure to cut the wage rate may develop among the unemployed, but the union must resist this pressure if the higher wage is to be maintained.

An alternative way to achieve the higher wage level *without* the resulting unemployment is to shift the supply curve to the left. The union may be able to do this by restricting entry into the occupation by methods such as lengthening required apprenticeship periods and reducing openings for trainees. Or the union may be able to persuade the government to

[1] Remember that, unless otherwise specified, we are dealing with real wages, that is, wages relative to the price level. See the discussion of the theory of price in an inflationary world on page 72.

FIGURE 19-1 Union Wage Setting Above the Competitive Level

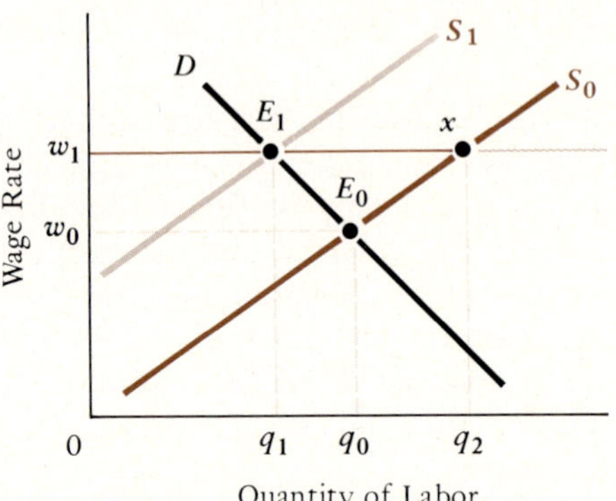

In a competitive labor market a union can raise the wages of workers who continue to be employed at the expense of the level of employment. The competitive equilibrium is at E_0, the wage is w_0, and employment is q_0. If a union enters this market and sets a wage of w_1, a new equilibrium will be established at E_1. The supply curve has become $w_1 \times S_0$. At the new wage, w_1, there will be q_1q_2 workers who would like to work but whom the industry will not hire. Employment will be q_1. The decrease in employment due to the wage increase is q_1q_0.

The wage w_1 can be achieved without generating a pool of persons seeking but unable to find work in the occupation. To do so the union must restrict entry into the occupation and shift the supply curve to the left to S_1. Employment will still be q_1.

This figure can also be used to illustrate the effect of government's imposing a minimum wage of w_1 on the market where the competitive equilibrium is at E_0. The q_1 workers who remain employed benefit by the wage increase. The q_1q_0 workers who lose their jobs in this industry suffer to the extent that they fail to find new jobs at an equivalent wage.

impose licensing or certification requirements on many who work.

Raising wages without restricting supply will lead to unemployment. Restricting supply will tend to raise wages without creating a group of workers who are unemployed in the occupation at the going wage.

Raising wages by restricting entry is not, of course, limited to unions. Consider the professions of medicine and law. Since professional standards have long been regarded as necessary to protect the public from incompetent practitioners, doctors and lawyers have found it publicly acceptable to control supply by limiting entry into their professions.

A Monopsonistic Market Without a Union

Consider a labor market in which there are many unorganized workers, but only a small number of firms. Imagine a case in which the firms form an employers' hiring association in order to act as a single unit so that there is a monopsony in the labor market.

While the employers' association can offer any wage rate that it chooses—the laborers must either work at that rate or find other jobs—the wage rate chosen will affect the profitability of its operations. For any given quantity that the monopsonist wishes to hire, the labor supply curve shows the price per unit it must offer; to the monopsonist, this is the *average cost curve* of labor. In deciding how much labor to hire, however, the monopsonist will be interested in the *marginal cost* of hiring additional workers.

Whenever the supply curve of labor slopes upward, the marginal cost of employing extra units will exceed the average cost. It exceeds the wage paid (the average cost) because the increased wage rate necessary to attract an extra worker must also be paid to everyone already employed. [31] For example, assume that 100 workers are employed at $4.00 per hour and that to attract an extra worker the wage must be raised to $4.01 per hour. The marginal cost of the 101st worker is not the $4.01 per hour paid to him but $5.01 per hour—made up of the extra $.01 per hour paid to the 100 existing workers and $4.01 paid to the new worker.

The profit-maximizing monopsonist will hire labor up to the point where the marginal cost just equals the amount the firm is willing to pay for an additional unit of labor. That amount is determined by the marginal revenue product of labor and is shown by the demand curve. This is illustrated in Figure 19-2.

Monopsonistic conditions in a factor market will result in a lower level of employment and a lower wage rate than would prevail when the factor is purchased under competitive conditions.

The common sense of this result is that the monopsonistic firm is aware that by trying to purchase more of the factor it is responsible for driving up the

FIGURE 19-2 Monopsony in a Labor Market

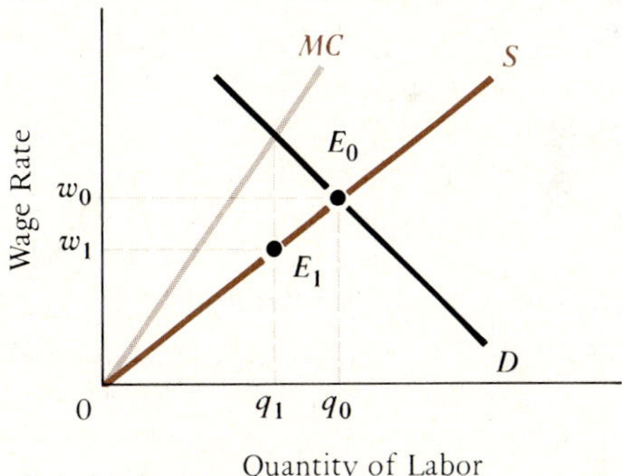

A monopsonist lowers both the wage rate and employment below their competitive levels. D and S are the competitive demand and supply curves. In competition equilibrium is at E_0, the wage rate is w_0, and the quantity of labor hired is q_0. The marginal cost of labor (MC) to the monopsonist is above the average cost. The monopsonistic firm will maximize profits at E_1. It will hire only q_1 units of labor. At q_1 the marginal cost of the last worker is just equal to the value to the firm of that worker's output, as shown by the demand curve. The wage that must be paid to get q_1 workers is only w_1.

price. It will therefore stop short of the point that is reached when the factor is purchased by many different firms, no one of which can exert an influence on the wage rate.

A Union in a Monopsonistic Market

What if a wage-setting union enters a monopsonistic market and sets a wage below which labor will not work? There will then be no point in the employer's reducing the quantity demanded in the hope of driving down the wage rate, nor will there be any point in holding off hiring for fear of driving the wage up. Here, just as in the case of a wage-setting union in a competitive market, the union presents the employer with a horizontal supply curve (up to the maximum number who will accept work at the union wage). The union raises wages and employment above the monopsony level. This result is demonstrated in Figure 19-3.

Because the union turns the firm into a price taker in the labor market, it can prevent the exercise of the firm's monopsony power and thus raise both wages and employment to competitive levels.

The union may not be content merely to neutralize the monopsonist's power. It may choose to raise wages further. If it does, the outcome will be the same as that shown in Figure 19-1. If the wage is raised above the competitive level, the employer will no longer wish to hire all the labor offered at that wage. The amount of employment will fall, and unemployment will develop. This is also shown in Figure 19-3. Notice, however, that the union can raise wages substantially above the competitive level before employment falls to a level as low as it was in the pre-union monopsonistic situation.

FIGURE 19-3 A Union Enters a Monopsonistic Labor Market

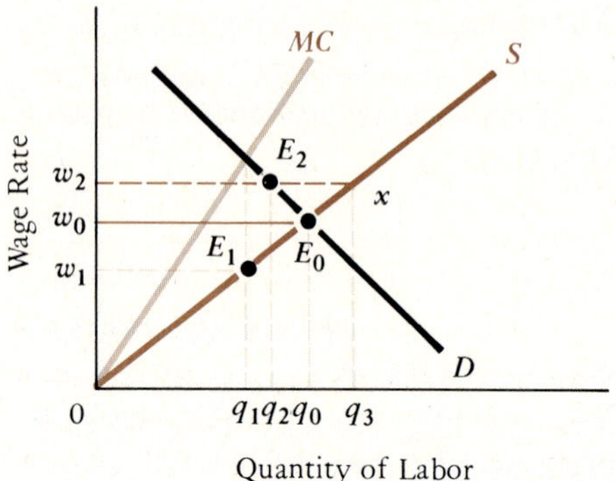

By presenting a monopsonistic employer with a fixed wage, the union can raise both wages and employment over the monopsonistic level. The monopsony position before the union enters is at E_1 (from Figure 19-2), with a wage rate of w_1 and q_1 workers hired. A union now enters and sets the wage at w_0. The supply curve of labor becomes w_0E_0S, and wages and employment rise to their competitive levels of w_0 and q_0 without creating a pool of unemployed workers. If the wage is raised further, say, to w_2, the supply curve will become w_2xS, and the quantity of employment will fall below the competitive level, to q_2, while a pool of unsuccessful job applicants of q_2q_3 will develop.

This figure can also be used to illustrate the effect of the government's imposing a minimum wage of w_0 or w_2 on a monopsonistic labor market.

Minimum-Wage Laws

When unions set wages for their members, they are in effect setting a minimum wage. Governments can cause similar effects by legislating specific **minimum wages,** wage rates that are the lowest that may legally be offered.

In Canada, industries under federal jurisdiction are subject to the Canadian Labour Code, which in 1987 set a minimum wage of $4.00 per hour. The major coverage, however, is provided by provincial legislation that in 1986 set minimum wages for adult workers ranging from $3.80 per hour in several provinces to $4.35 in Ontario and Quebec.

For a large proportion of all employment covered by the law, the minimum wage is below the actual market wage. Where this is true, the wage is said to be "not binding." But many workers are in occupations or industries where the free-market wage rate would be below the legal minimum, and there the minimum wage is said to be binding, or effective.

Whether minimum wages are effective is not always easy to determine. For example, one response of employers to minimum-wage legislation might be to reduce fringe benefits so that total compensation remains constant.

The consequences of minimum wages are controversial. To the extent that they are effective, they raise the wages of employed workers. But as our analysis in Chapter 6 indicated, an effective floor price (which is what a minimum wage is) may well lead to a market surplus—in this case, unemployment. Thus minimum wages will benefit some groups while hurting others. The effects of minimum wages have been studied extensively.[2] The problem is more complicated than the analysis of Chapter 6 would suggest both because not all labor markets are competitive and because minimum-wage laws do not cover all employment. Moreover, some groups in the labor force, especially youth and minorities, are affected more than the average worker.

A Comprehensive Minimum Wage

Suppose first that minimum-wage laws apply uniformly to all occupations. The occupations and industries in which minimum wages are effective will be the lowest-paying in the country; they usually involve unskilled or at best semiskilled labor. In most of them the workers are not members of unions. Thus the market structures in which minimum wages are likely to be effective include both those in which competitive conditions pertain and those in which employers exercise monopsony power. The employment effects of minimum wages are different in the two cases.

Competitive labor markets. The employment consequences of an effective minimum wage are unambiguous when the labor market is competitive. By raising the wage facing employers, minimum-wage legislation leads to a reduction in the quantity of labor demanded and an increase in the quantity supplied. As a result the actual level of employment falls, and unemployment is generated. This situation is exactly analogous to the one that arises when a union succeeds in setting a wage above the competitive equilibrium wage, as illustrated in Figure 19-1. The excess supply of labor at the minimum wage also creates incentives for people to evade the law by working below the legal minimum wage.

In competitive labor markets effective minimum-wage laws raise the wages of those who remain employed but also create some unemployment.

Monopsonistic labor markets. By effectively flattening out the labor supply curve, the minimum-wage law can simultaneously increase wages and employment. The circumstances in which this can be done are the same as those in which a union facing a monopsonistic employer succeeds in setting a wage above that which the employer would otherwise pay, as shown in Figure 19-3. Of course, if the minimum wage is raised above the competitive wage, employment will start to fall, as in the union case. When set at the competitive wage, however, the minimum wage can protect the worker against monopsony power and lead to increases in employment.

A Noncomprehensive Minimum Wage

Suppose that a minimum wage covers only 50 percent of all jobs and that applying the minimum wage to the covered jobs does cause some unemployment in that sector. The workers displaced can move to the uncovered sector. If they do, they will shift the supply curve in the uncovered sector to the right. This will lead to lower wages and increased employment in the uncovered sector. As a general rule the increase in employment in the uncovered sector will not be large enough to offset the decrease in the covered sector.[3]

[2] One comprehensive survey is Charles Brown, Curtis Gilroy, and Andrew Kohen, "The Effect of the Minimum Wage on Employment and Unemployment." *Journal of Economic Literature* (June 1982), pp. 487–528.

[3] Only if the demand curve in the uncovered sector is horizontal (infinitely elastic) or if the supply curve is vertical (completely inelastic) will every displaced worker from the covered sector find employment. But these are not likely circumstances.

The Overall Effect of Minimum-Wage Laws

A great deal of empirical work has been done on the actual effect of minimum wages on employment. Minimum wages cause unemployment, particularly among youths aged 16 to 19: It is estimated that the rate of youth employment is decreased from 1 percent to 3 percent for every 10 percent increase in minimum wages. For young adults (aged 20 to 24) the employment effect is also adverse but smaller. Other differences too have been documented.

Many of the adverse employment effects are borne largely by the workers who are least skilled, least experienced, and perhaps most intended to be the beneficiaries of minimum-wage policies. Several provinces responded to this kind of evidence by allowing lower minimum wages for young or inexperienced workers and for workers demonstrably in a "learning period."[4]

The adverse employment effect is, however, only one element in deciding whether, overall, minimum wages are beneficial or harmful. It is clear that minimum-wage laws raise the incomes of many workers at the very lowest levels of pay. Some of those who benefit most are members of groups that are chronically poor, whom the government is eager to aid by income redistribution. But it is not only the lowest paid who gain. Because union wage structures maintain differentials between skill classes, an increase in minimum wages also raises wages in a large number of occupations that are already above the minimum.

Given this mixed result, what explains the widespread belief in using increased minimum wages to alleviate poverty and redistribute income from the rich to the poor? Much of the explanation, we believe, rests on neglect of adverse employment effects.

Organized labor finds minimum wages beneficial to most of its employed members, and labor unions have been consistently in favor of both increasing the level of minimum wages and expanding coverage. No equally powerful political force opposes them since workers who do not find jobs because of the minimum-wage laws are unlikely to identify these laws as the cause of their unemployment.

Though many economists are critical of minimum wages, as a practical matter the minimum wage is likely to remain. It is one of the hard-won labor gains dating back to the 1930s, and it has great symbolic significance for labor.

[4] It may be objected that such exceptions are discriminatory. But labeling something "discriminatory" does not necessarily mean that it is bad. The argument favoring a lower youth wage is that it is better to be employed at a lower wage than unemployed at a higher one.

The Nature and Evolution of Modern Labor Unions

Unions today represent only about 28 percent of the workers in the private sector and less than 38 percent of all workers. But union influence is greater than these percentages suggest. One reason is the impact union wage contracts have in other labor markets. When, for example, the Canadian Auto Workers negotiate a new contract, its provisions set a pattern that directly or indirectly affects almost all the labor markets in Southern Ontario. A second reason is the major leadership role unions have played for more than half a century in the development of labor market practices and in lobbying for legislation that applies to all workers.

Labor Market Institutions

For the purposes of our discussion of labor markets, a **union** (or *trade union* or *labor union*) is an association of individual workers that speaks for them in negotiations with their employers. Unions negotiate with individual employers or employers' associations. North American unionism has developed not only its own institutions but also something of a specialized vocabulary, some of which is presented in Box 19-1 (p. 374).

The process by which unions and employers (or their representatives) arrive at and enforce their agreements is known as **collective bargaining.** This process has an important difference from the theoretical models with which we began this chapter. There we assumed that the union set the wage and the employer decided how much labor to hire. In collective bargaining the wage is negotiated. In terms of Figure 19-3 it may be that the employer wants the wage to be w_1 and the union wants w_2. Depending on each side's market power and bargaining strength, the final agreed wage may be anywhere in between. In collective bargaining there is always a substantial range over which an agreement can be reached, and the actual result in particular cases will depend on the strengths of the two bargaining parties and the skill of their negotiators.

Unionism today is accepted, especially in the heavy manufacturing industries and in government service. It was not always so. Within the lifetime of many of today's members, unions were fighting for their lives and union organizers and members were risking theirs. In the 1930s the labor movement evoked the loyalties and passions of people as a great liberal cause in ways that seem quite extraordinary today. Indeed, unions today often appear to many as conservative, even reactionary groups of hard hats. Why the change, and how did it come about?

The Urge to Organize

Trade unionism had its origin in the pitifully low standard of living of the average nineteenth century worker's family. Much of the explanation for the low standard of living throughout the world lay in the small size of the national output relative to the population. Even in the wealthiest countries an equal division of national wealth among all families in 1850 would have left each one in poverty by our present standards.

Poverty had existed for centuries. It was accentuated, however, by the twin processes of urbanization and industrialization. Immigrants and farmers who were moderately content working the land usually became restive and discontented when the family moved into a grimy, smoky, nineteenth century city, lived in crowded, unsanitary tenements, and took jobs in a sweatshop or a factory. Box 19-2 (p. 376) provides a vivid picture of factory conditions at the turn of the present century.

The focus of resentment was usually the employer. The employer set the wages, and the wages were low. Unhappy workers had, of course, the right of all free people to quit their job—and starve. If they grumbled or protested, they could be fired and, worse, blacklisted, which meant no one else would hire them.

Out of these conditions and other grievances of working men and women came the full range of radical political movements. Out of the same conditions also came a pragmatic form of collective action called **bread-and-butter unionism,** whose goals were higher wages and better working conditions rather than political reform.

The early industrial organizer saw that 10 or 100 employees acting together had more influence than one acting alone and dreamed of the day when all would stand solid against the employer. (The word *solidarity* occurs often in the literature and songs of the labor movement.) The union was the organization that would provide a basis for confronting the monopsony power of employers with the collective power of the workers. But it was easier to recognize solidarity as a solution than it was to achieve it. Organizations of workers would hurt the employer, and employers did not sit by idly; they, too, knew that in union there was strength. "Agitators" who tried to organize workers were fired and blacklisted; in some cases they were beaten and killed.

To achieve effective power over the labor market, a union had to gain control of the supply of labor and have the financial resources necessary to outlast the employer in a struggle for survival. There was no right to organize. The union had to force an employer to negotiate with it, and few employers did so willingly. Unions started in a small way among highly skilled workers and spread slowly.

Why did the union movement show its first real power among small groups of relatively skilled workers? First, it was easier to control the supply of skilled workers than unskilled ones. Organize the unskilled, and the employer could find replacements for them. But skilled workers—the coopers (barrelmakers), the bootmakers, the shipwrights—were another matter. There were few of them, and they controlled the access to their trade by apprenticeships. The original craft unions were, in effect, closed shops: One had to belong to the union to hold a job in the craft, and the union set the rules of admission.

Second, employers were vulnerable to the demands of a union of workers whose skills might be indispensable to the production process. Third, because labor in a particular skilled occupation is likely to account for a relatively low proportion of total

BOX 19-1

The Vocabulary of Unionism

Kinds of Unions

The **craft union** organized workers with a common set of skills in a common association, no matter where or for whom they work. The craft principle of organization is the hallmark of the American Federation of Labor (AFL) and its Canadian counterpart, the Trades and Labour Congress (TLC). The **industrial union** is organized along industry lines; all workers in a given plant or industry are collected into a single union. This is the pattern developed by the member unions of the Congress of Industrial Organizations (CIO) and the Canadian Congress of Labour (CCL), which existed from 1940 to 1956. Among the prominent industrial unions are the Canadian Automobile Workers and the United Steelworkers.

The two principles of unionism conflict. Should a carpenter employed in the steel industry be represented by the carpenters' union or the steelworkers' union? Disputes over which union shall have the right to *organize* (i.e., bring into their union) a particular group of workers are known as **jurisdictional disputes.** They have led to prolonged, bitter, and bloody battles of union against union.

The important level for most of the economic functions of the union is the national level. The national officers do the bargaining, set the policies, and set the tone. Individual workers, however, belong to a local to which they pay dues (a part of which goes to the national). There are about 165 national or international unions, which have over 10,000 locals. The local for a craft union is geographical, for example, the Fredericton chapter of the carpenters. The local for an industrial union is a plant or a company, for example, the Ford local of the Canadian Automobile Workers.

The **federation** is a loose organization of national unions. Most international unions operating in Canada are affiliated with the single American federation, the AFL–CIO, as well as the Canadian Labour Congress (CLC). Most of the purely Canadian national unions are affiliated with either the CLC or the Quebec-based Confederation of National Trade Unions (CNTU).

Kinds of Bargaining Arrangements

In an **open shop** a union represents its members, but does not have exclusive bargaining jurisdiction for all workers in the shop. Membership in the union is not needed to get or keep a job.

Unions vehemently oppose such an arrangement. If, on the one hand, the employer yields to union demands and raises wages, the non-members ("free riders") get the benefits of the union without paying dues or sharing the risks or responsibilities. If, on the other hand, the firm chooses to fight the union, it can run its plants with the non-union employees.

If the union succeeds in raising wages above their competitive level, there will be an excess supply of labor. With an open shop, there is nothing to prevent unemployed non-union workers from accepting a

costs, the effect on the employer's overall costs of giving in to a small group's demand for a wage increase is small.

The difficulty of substituting other factors for skilled labor and a relatively small contribution to total costs combined to create an inelastic demand. This gave the unions of skilled workers an advantage in fighting the employer not enjoyed by other groups of workers. In the early days unions needed every advantage they could get since anti-unionism was for some employers a matter of principle, a crusade, and a way of life.

Even where unions gained a foothold in a strategic trade, they had their ups and downs. When employment was full and business booming, the cost of being fired for joining a union was not great because there were other jobs. However, during periods of depression and unemployment an individual worker knew that if he or she caused trouble, unemployed members of the trade would be there wage below the union one and so undermining the union's power to maintain high wages.

In a **closed shop** only union members may be employed, and the union controls its membership as it sees fit. The union can prevent its members from accepting less than the union wage and so has the power to maintain high wages in spite of the existence of excess supply.

Employers traditionally regard this as an unwarranted limitation of their right to choose their employees. Its use has been prohibited in the United States and in most provinces in Canada.

The **union shop** is a compromise between a closed shop and an open shop. In a union shop a firm may hire anyone it chooses at the union wage, but every employee must join the union within a specified period. This leaves employers free to hire anyone they wish but gives the union the power to enforce its union wages because workers are prevented from accepting employment at lower wages. It is the most common union arrangement in Canada.

Weapons of Conflict

The **strike** is the concerted refusal to work by the members of the union. It is the strike or the threat of a strike that backs up the union's demands in the bargaining process. Workers on strike are, of course, off the payroll, so many unions set aside a portion of the dues collected to have a fund for paying striking workers. **Strikebreakers** ("scabs") are workers brought in by management to operate the plant while the union is on strike.

Picket lines are made up of striking workers who parade before the entrance to their plant or firm. Other union members will not, by time-honored convention, cross a picket line. Thus if bricklayers strike against a construction firm, carpenters will not work on the project, nor will teamsters deliver supplies to a picketed site, although they themselves may have no grievance against the firm. Pickets represent an enormous increase in the bargaining power of a small union. (Much of the bitterness against jurisdictional disputes arises from the fact that an employer may be unable to settle with either union without facing a picket line from the other union.)

A **labor boycott** is an organized attempt to persuade customers to refrain from purchasing the goods or services of a firm or industry whose employees are on strike. The boycotts organized in California by César Chávez's United Farm Workers Union against grapes, lettuce, and bananas are prominent examples.

The **lockout** is the employer's equivalent of the strike. By closing the plant, the employer locks out the workers until the dispute is settled. A **blacklist** is an employer's list of workers who have been fired for playing a role in union affairs that was regarded by the employer as undesirable. Other employers are not supposed to give jobs to blacklisted workers.

to take the job. Solidarity could yield to hunger. Membership in trade unions showed a clear cyclical pattern, rising in good times and falling in bad.

The Historical Development of Canadian Unions

The origins of the present structure of Canadian trade unionism can be traced to the latter half of the nineteenth century. Its development has been strongly dominated by the influence of what are now called international unions, which have their headquarters and an overwhelming proportion of their membership outside Canada. The creation of Canadian locals of American unions began in the 1860s.[5] The first attempts at unifying Canadian unions into a central national organization occurred in 1873, but it was

[5] In 1911, the earliest date for which figures are available, international unions had 90 percent of total union membership. In recent years the proportion has been about 60 percent.

BOX 19-2

Factory Life in 1903

Stories of workers' very real suffering during the Industrial Revolution and the years that followed could fill many volumes, but an example will at least illustrate some of the horrors that lay behind the drive for change and reform. (The quotation comes from *Poverty* by Robert Hunter, published in 1904.)

In the worst days of cotton-milling in England the conditions were hardly worse than those now existing in the South. Children—the tiniest and frailest—of five and six years of age rise in the morning and, like old men and women, go to the mills to do their day's labor; and when they return home, they wearily fling themselves on their beds, too tired to take off their clothes. Many children work all night—"in the maddening racket of the machinery, in an atmosphere insanitary and clouded with humidity and lint." It will be long before I forget the face of a little boy of six years, with his hands stretched forward to rearrange a bit of machinery, his pallid face and spare form showing already the physical effects of labor. This child, six years of age, was working twelve hours a day in a country which has established in many industries an eight-hour day for men. The twelve-hour day is almost universal in the South, and about twenty-five thousand children are now employed on twelve-hour shifts in the mills of the various Southern states. The wages of one of these children, however large, could not compensate the child for the injury this monstrous and unnatural labor does him; but the pay which the child receives is not enough, in many instances, even to feed him properly. If the children fall ill, they are docked for loss of time. . . . The mill-hands confess that they hate the mills, and no one will wonder at it. A vagrant who had worked in a textile mill for sixteen years once said to a friend of mine: "I done that [and he made a motion with his hand] for sixteen years. At last I was sick for two or three days with a fever, and when I crawled out, I made up my mind that I would rather go to hell than go back to the mill."

not until 1883 that the first body with nationwide representation, the Trades and Labour Congress of Canada (TLC), was formed. In 1956 the TLC merged with other groups to form the Canadian Labour Congress (CLC).

Two facets dominated the history of Canadian trade unionism in the first half of this century. One was the movement toward a single national federation; the other was the struggle to achieve autonomy in the face of American attempts to control the development of Canadian unions. The issues became intertwined when conflicts in the United States between craft and industrial unions became a disruptive force in Canada because of the TLC's ties with the American Federation of Labor (AFL). Until the 1930s craft unions were the characteristic form of collective action in the United States. In Canada, meanwhile, trade unionists were attracted to the principle of industrial unions that embraced unskilled workers as well as skilled craftsmen.

Because of the impossibility of establishing bargaining strength through the control of supply in the case of unskilled workers, the rise of industrial unionism in Canada was associated with political action as an alternative means of improving the lot of the membership. The classic Canadian manifestation of revolutionary industrial unionism was the One Big Union formed by western unionists who broke away from the TLC after the Winnipeg General Strike of 1919.

In general, social and political reform were given much more emphasis by Canadian unionists than by their American counterparts. Political action here extended to the development of a viable socialist political party in the form of the Cooperative Commonwealth Federation (CCF), established in 1932, and its successor, the New Democratic Party (NDP), formed in 1961. The CLC does not have a formal affiliation with the NDP; the relationship is similar to that between the British Trades Union Congress and the British Labour Party.

International Unionism

In spite of the divergent patterns of development in the two countries, at the beginning of this century the TLC lined itself up squarely on the side of international unionism because of the greater resources made available to it through its constituent unions affiliated with the AFL. Then the rise of industrial unionism in the United States in the 1930s resulted in a severe blow to labor unity in Canada. Following the leadership of John L. Lewis of the United Mine Workers, the industrial unions in steel and automobiles split from the conservative AFL and formed the Congress of Industrial Organizations (CIO). Although the TLC had always been willing to accept both kinds of unions, in 1939 the AFL forced it to expel the Canadian branches of CIO unions.

The dominance of international—that is, American—unions in the Canadian labor movement continues to be a source of public concern in Canada. Some people regard it as inconsistent with Canadian sovereignty and dangerous to Canadian interests. However, Senator Eugene Forsey, a former director of research for the CLC, views the unification of the bulk of Canadian unions under the CLC in 1956 as the beginning of virtual autonomy for Canadian locals. Unlike the TLC, the CLC has complete control over its qualifications for membership and has not hesitated to embrace unions expelled by the AFL-CIO or to expel unions affiliated with it.

Nevertheless, agitation for greater Canadian autonomy has continued. The CLC had developed guidelines for the conduct of international unions operating in Canada, and a number of groups have severed their connection with international unions and formed independent Canadian unions. Some of the defectors have affiliated with the Confederation of Canadian Unions, a small CLC rival whose main base is in British Columbia.

The distribution of Canadian union membership by affiliation in 1987 is shown in Table 19-1. International unions account for about 40 percent of the total, compared to about 70 percent in the mid 1950s. One factor in the increased share of national unions is the growth of membership in the two unions representing government workers, the Canadian Union of Public Employees and the Public Service Alliance. Public sector unions are discussed further in Box 19-3. Another major component of non-international union membership has arisen out of the distinct aspirations of French-Canadian workers. This is reflected in Table 19-1 by the 6 percent share of the Quebec-based Confederation of National Trade Unions.

TABLE 19-1 Union Membership by Type and Affiliation, 1986

Type and affiliation	Thousands of members	Percentage of total
International unions	1459	39
AFL-CIO/CLC	866	23
CLC only	147	4
Other	447	12
National unions	2131	57
Canadian Labour Congress (CLC)	1145	31
Confederation of National Trade Unions	218	6
Unaffiliated unions	621	17
(CEQ, CCU, CSD, CFL)	147	4
Directly chartered and independent local organizations	139	4
Total[a]	3730	100

[a] May not add up due to rounding off.

Source: Labour Canada, *Labour Organizations in Canada,* 1986.

The Development of Public Policy Toward Collective Bargaining

As shown in Figure 19-4 (p. 380), rapid gains in union membership occurred in the years during and immediately after World War II. This led to pressure to give Canadian unionists the legal protections provided in the United States by the Wagner Act of 1935, which guaranteed the right of workers to organize and to elect an exclusive bargaining agent. The rights were carried over into Canada through the provisions of the Wartime Labour Relations Regulations of 1944.

Government intervention in industrial disputes in Canada has a history dating back to the early years of this century. The earliest legislation applied only

BOX 19-3

Unionism in the Public Sector

Whatever the reason, the scope of union activity within the public sector has expanded rapidly since the 1960s. Indeed, the rapid growth in union membership in Canada, shown in Figure 19-4, arises primarily from this increase in union membership in the public sector.* In addition, because most public service unions are Canadian, their growth has diminished the role of international unions in Canada.

Since 1965 public-sector unions have had the right to strike, and strikes in the public sector have not been infrequent. Canadians have often been angered by interruptions in the postal service or by having to cancel holidays because of the disruption of airport services.

It is often argued that such withdrawals of services are unfair because they affect large numbers of people who are not party to the labor-management dispute. They are also unfair, some argue, precisely because government often has a monopoly in the provision of the services being withheld, and hence there are no alternatives. Not only do unions in the public sector have considerable power because of the nature of the services that strikes curtail, but public-sector employers are not restrained by market forces from conceding excessive wages. Government services are not typically sold in the marketplace but are paid for out of general tax revenues. Further, politicians have a strong incentive to avoid unpopular strikes.

Professor Morely Gunderson of the University of Toronto has estimated that during the six-year period beginning in 1965 (the year of the institution of the right to strike in the public sector), there developed a public service wage advantage of about 6 percent for males and 8 percent for females, relative to comparable jobs in the private sector. Other studies confirm the maintenance of, if not an increase in, this advantage over the next few years for all but the most senior public employees.

Many economists believe that increased public-sector wages become the standard by which private-sector wages are set; in this view the public sector has become a wage leader and a source of potential inflation in the economy. However, studies have called into question the evidence confirming a spillover, and the issue is still hotly contested.

Furthermore, many observers felt that one major reason for the introduction of wage and price controls by the federal government in 1975 was to appeal to an external force to regain control over wage settlements with their own employees. Public-sector unions, in this view, had become so powerful that the federal government was unable, or unwilling, to control wages in the federal civil service through the usual negotiating and bargaining procedures; it had to impose controls on the entire economy to control public-sector wages. In 1982 the federal government again introduced wage controls, this time only on

* Under Canadian law, municipalities are treated as private corporations and their employees governed by labor legislation applicable to the private sector.

to public utilities and coal mining, where there was a strong public interest element. It provided that before a strike or a lockout could be initiated, the parties were required to submit any dispute to a conciliation board.

This system of compulsory conciliation and compulsory delay in work stoppage was extended to a much larger segment of the economy under special emergency powers adopted by the government of Canada during World War II. In the postwar period, jurisdiction over labor policy reverted to the provinces, but the principles established have been carried over into provincial legislation.

Objectives of Modern Unions

Union constitutions are extremely democratic documents. All members have one vote, officers are wages under federal government jurisdiction, with its 6 & 5 Program. These provided guidelines for the moderation of wage demands while the inflation rate was expected to fall. After two years the program was ended and in the climate of low inflation and slack labor markets, civil service wage increases were moderate for the next several years.

In the last half of the 1980s, with increased foreign competition in the private sector and pressure to hold down costs in the public sector, the big bargaining issues became job security and the maintenance of previously won working conditions rather than wage increases. A postal strike in 1987 was a case in point. Faced with a directive from Ottawa to remove its large deficit, the post office sought concessions from unions that would reduce the number of jobs (by attrition, not by direct firing) and alter working conditions so that more of the hours actually paid for would be spent on the job. Union opposition was bitter. No doubt they opposed the proposals on their own merits, but also because they saw the post office's suggestions as the thin edge of the wedge for many further cost-reducing demands in other public-sector occupations.

A long strike over similar issues also occurred in the recently privatized de Havilland company, now a branch of the Boeing company. Here again, a company that was a habitual money loser when it was in the public sector—this time in spite of its successful Dash series of commuter aircraft—was fighting a bitter battle in an attempt to change union practices in order to turn losses into profits.

It is useful to compare the Canadian situation with that prevailing elsewhere. In the United States, federal and state government workers are prohibited from striking and are not permitted to bargain over pay. In Britain, the normal means of determining government pay levels is strict adherence to private-sector comparability guidelines. Canadian public-sector labor regulation policy is now among the most liberal in the world.

Some economists believe that government employees do not need collective bargaining or the strike weapon to ensure that they are paid adequately; in the long run the supply of labor to the public sector is a function of the price paid for labor by the public employer, relative to what workers can earn elsewhere. This offers considerable insurance that public employees, with or without collective bargaining, will not long be underpaid, at least at entry job levels. Some even advocate that bargaining for pay in the public sector be eliminated in favor of a policy in which pay scales are set by an independent agent on the basis of comparability to the private sector. This policy has much to recommend it, but it also has obvious administrative and political drawbacks; furthermore, it rules out changes in relative wages as part of a long-run adjustment to new relative demands in the two sectors.

---

elected by the vote of the membership, the rights of individual workers are fully protected, and so on. In practice, however, the relation between the members of a union and its national officers is closer to that of the relationship between stockholders and managers of a giant corporation than to that of the Canadian people and their government. Unions tend toward one-party democracy in most cases. Union leaders are highly paid professionals whose business is to run the union, while the main business of union members is to earn a living on the job. That many union members feel the need for little participation in union decision making is understandable; they are paying dues that permit the union to pay generous salaries to union leaders who are expected to look out for the rank and file's interests, and as long as the leadership "delivers," all goes well. But delivers what and to whom?

FIGURE 19-4 Union Membership in Canada, 1921–1987

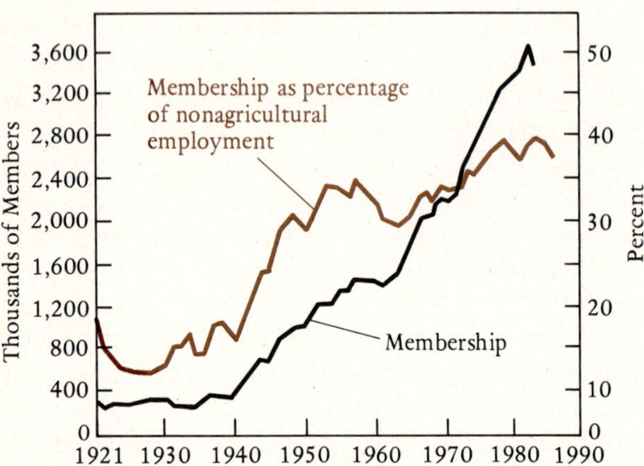

Rapid growth in unionism occurred in the period 1941–1951 and in the period 1961–1978. The growth in union membership in recent years reflects to a large extent growth in the unions representing government employees. (*Source:* Labour Canada, *Labour Organizations in Canada,* 1986.)

Wages Versus Job Security

Until the 1980s people who were in their teens during the Great Depression dominated the leadership of North American unions. Not surprisingly, they had a strong defensive attitude toward union members' jobs. They had lived through a period when unemployment was above 20 percent of the total labor force and nearer 50 percent in many of the hardest-hit areas. They had seen people grow up, marry, and raise children on relief or part-time work.

One method of seeking job security is through *seniority rules* that require employers to lay off and rehire on the basis of length of service. This protects existing workers, and many unions have been willing to accept lower wages in order to build seniority provisions into their contracts.

A second method of seeking job security is to resist the introduction of labor-saving innovations. In a period of heavy unemployment, the installation of a labor-saving machine in a factory is likely to mean unemployment for workers whose jobs are lost by the change. It is little wonder that during and after the Great Depression new machines were opposed bitterly and that job-saving restrictive practices were adhered to with tenacity.

The heritage of this fear survived in featherbedding practices such as the standby musician at the television studio and the meticulous division of tasks in the building trades that inhibit many labor-saving consolidation and reorganization of tasks.

But in the long run mechanization increases productivity and consequently the wages and profits that are earned. After World War II the attitude of many unions slowly changed from one of resisting technological change to one of collaborating with it and trying to reduce some of its costs to individuals who are adversely affected.

The return of higher unemployment rates in the 1980s again heightened American unions' interest in job security, but in more constructive ways. Elimination of some restrictive practices that raised labor costs has been accepted by unions in return for company agreement to pass on savings in lower product prices and to delay planned layoffs.

The biggest change in attitude (compared with the past) is that the current generation of American leaders sees the increased mechanization of Japanese, Korean, and German firms as the principal threat to union workers' jobs. Many of today's labor leaders seem prepared to help their American employers improve their international competitiveness.

Canadian unions have not always followed the Americans in these ways. They have sometimes put their reliance in traditional modes of behavior and have regarded flexible approaches to industries by foreign competition as unacceptable.

Wages Versus Fringe Benefits

Indirect or **fringe benefits**—such as company contributions to union pension and welfare funds, sick leave, and vacation pay, as well as required payments toward social and unemployment insurance—are estimated to make up almost a third of the total compensation of industrial workers. Why do unions and employers not simply agree to a wage and let it go at that? Why should the average employed automobile worker who earns $30,000 cost the company $45,000?

Fringe benefits appeal to employees in part because they are not subject to income taxes. Pension funds and medical benefits let employees provide for their future and that of their families more cheaply than they could by purchasing private insurance, and their benefits often protect them even when they lose their jobs. A package of fringe benefits that includes high wages and job security for the employed and unemployment benefits for those squeezed out by high wages appeals to union leaders because it provides something for everyone.

There are also advantages to employers. For example, fringe benefits such as pension funds tend to bind the worker more closely to the company, thereby decreasing the turnover rate. If employees stand to lose part of their benefits by changing jobs, they will not be so ready to move.

Wages Versus Employment

A union that sets wages above the competitive level is making a choice of higher wages for some and unemployment for others. Should the union strive to maximize the earnings of the group that remains employed? If it does, some of its members will lose their jobs and the union's membership will decline. Should it instead maximize the welfare of its present members? Or should it seek to expand employment opportunities (perhaps by a low-wage policy) so that the union membership grows? Different unions decide these questions differently.

Severe strains have recently developed between Canadian and American members of international unions as a result of different views of how to respond to the difficult economic conditions of the 1980s. Two key differences typified a range of differences in attitudes.

American unions were willing to reopen contracts and accept wage cuts when the alternative seemed to be plant closures or company liquidations. They were also willing to consider schemes designed to move away from the traditional pattern where wages are relatively stable over the cycle while employment does most of the adjusting to fluctuating demand. The alternative is to have wages vary more over the cycle in order to maintain a more stable employment pattern. One way of doing this is to move toward the Japanese arrangement whereby wages are to some extent linked to profits.

Canadian unions have been more inclined to stick with traditional approaches. First, a contract should not be reopened before it expires. Even if the agreed wages threaten to cause plant closures, the sanctity of the contract is a more important principle than the saving of specific jobs. Second, profit sharing means selling out to the bosses. The traditional system should be maintained in which wages are stable over the cycle and most of the adjustment to variations in demand occurs through variations in employment.

Under the dynamic leadership of Bob White, the Canadian auto workers split with the American auto workers over these and related issues. A separate Canadian union was set up, and its different approach to bargaining soon became apparent.

Many American union leaders tend to see their Canadian colleagues as trying to live in a world that is quickly fading. They worry that practices appropriate to the 1960s will not be in the best interests of labor in the 1990s. Many Canadian union leaders tend to see their American confreres as having sold out to management. By reopening contracts and considering profit sharing, the traditional interests of the working class have, in their view, been seriously compromised. Time should tell if the balance of experience favors either of these two views.

The Persistence of Unemployment

Labor unions and the various institutions and practices that have developed in collective bargaining have long been known to make a difference in the way in which particular markets function. Recently economists have engaged in a major debate about whether these institutions and practices affect the overall ability of the economy to cope with unemployment and if so, how. We are now in a position to look at these questions.

Neoclassical Theories of Unemployment

Competitive labor markets. In the neoclassical theory of competitive wage determination, the wage rate adjusts to equate the demand and supply of labor. This is the sort of standard supply and demand analysis that is now familiar.

If the wage rate is free to vary, the competitive wage rate will equate demand and supply and thus "clear the market." At this wage rate there is no involuntary unemployment.

Of course, given an ordinary supply curve there are more potential workers than those employed at the competitive wage, but the extra potential workers are *voluntarily* unemployed—they do not choose to work at the competitive wage rate. **Involuntary unemployment** occurs when qualified persons seek but cannot find jobs at the going wage rate. As long as the wage-quantity combination that occurs is on the supply curve, everyone who is in the market and wants to work at the going wage rate gets a job.

It follows that persistent involuntary unemployment can occur if, but only if, the real wage is held above its competitive equilibrium level. This was shown in Figure 19-1. The remedy for involuntary unemployment in the neoclassical world is thus obvious: *Reduce the real wage rate to the competitive level.* There can be no involuntary unemployment at the competitive equilibrium wage.

Noncompetitive markets. How then could economists explain the fact of unemployment? Plainly either labor unions or monopsony or both together could lead to unemployment. For example, a wage-setting union could raise the wage rate above the market-clearing level and accept the unemployment of some of its members. Similarly, monopsony could lower the level of employment below the competitive level, as was shown in Figure 19-2.

Classical economists readily accepted that either monopsony or monopoly might lead to unemployment. Thus they did not deny the existence of unemployment. *What they could not accept was that unemployment could persist in competitive markets.* Yet the evidence, accumulated in recession after recession, showed that unemployment did occur, and any doubts about its persistence were shattered during the decade of the 1930s.

New Theories of Unemployment

The Great Depression triggered a major interest in understanding the problem of persistent involuntary unemployment. For a long time economists were satisfied with the explanation offered by early Keynesian economists. Workers would fail to appreciate the link between wages and unemployment and would in a variety of ways resist a downward movement in their money wage rate. Thus, when the real wage rate was too high, competitive forces would not reduce it by forcing money wages down because workers would stubbornly resist such a fall.

Recently economists have sought alternative explanations of persistent unemployment by reexamining the determination of wages. As a result, a new set of theories has arisen. These theories question whether forces exist in actual markets that cause wages to fluctuate quickly enough to equate the current demands for and supplies of labor. If they do not, there is reason for supply and demand *not* to be equated for extended periods of time.

These theories start with the observation that labor markets are not auction markets in which prices always respond to excess demand or excess supply. When unemployed workers are looking for jobs, they do not knock on employers' doors offering to work at lower wages than are being paid to existing workers; instead, they answer want ads and hope to get the jobs offered but are often disappointed. Nor do employers, seeing an excess of applicants for the few jobs available, go to their existing workers and reduce their wages until there is no one looking for a job; instead, they pick and choose until they fill their needs and then hang out a sign saying "No help wanted."

The explanation of these familiar observations that is provided by the newer theories rests on the

FIGURE 19-5 Economic Discrimination: Wage-Level Effects

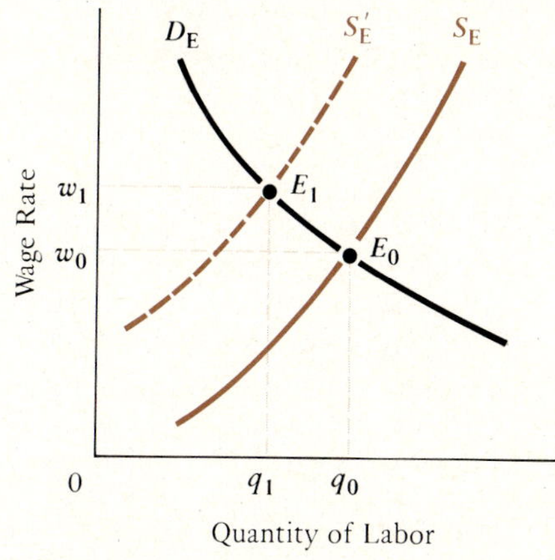

(i) Elite market (E)

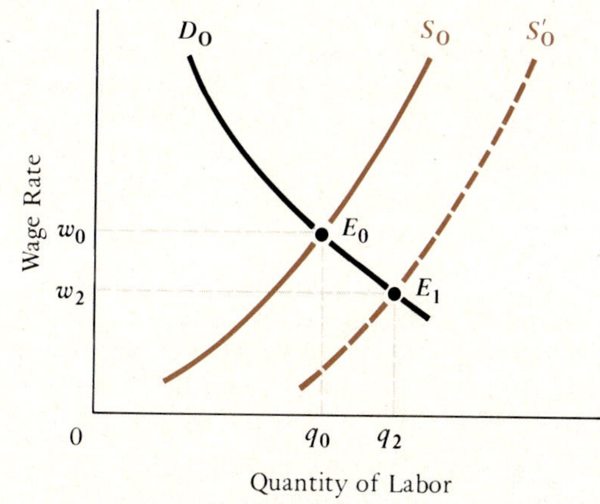

(ii) Ordinary market (O)

If market E discriminates against one group and market O does not, the supply curve will shift to the left in E and to the right in O. Market E requires above average skills, while market O requires only ordinary skills. When there is no discrimination, demands and supplies are D_E and S_E in market E and D_O and S_O in market O. Initially the wage rate is represented by w_0 and employment by q_0 in each market. (The actual wage in market E will be slightly higher than the wage in market O.) When all women are barred from E occupations, the supply curve shifts to S_E', and the wage earned by the remaining workers, all of whom are men, rises to w_1. Women put out of work in the E occupation now seek work in the O occupation. The resulting shift in the supply curve to S_O' brings down the wage to w_2 in the O occupations. Since all women are in O occupations, they have a lower wage rate than many men. The average wage for men is higher than the average for women.

who cannot move to where jobs are available become unemployed or withdraw from the labor force.

A different mechanism can produce the identical result if women who lose their E jobs as a result of discrimination withdraw from the labor force. They may do just this if they have the skill and training to do the more rewarding E jobs. Indeed, it may be less demeaning to accept unemployment compensation or even welfare than to accept the only jobs that the discriminatory society offers them.

In the long term these unemployment effects may be increased by sociological and economic forces. Female children of women who are discriminated against may take as role models women who have made a life outside the labor force. Technological changes in the economy tend to decrease the demand for less skilled labor of the kind required in O occupations, which become increasingly oversupplied. This possibility is sketched in Figure 19-6(iii).

These theoretical possibilities have their counterparts in the real world. We shall discuss them briefly.

Female-Male Differentials

Although high unemployment is often a feature of labor market discrimination, it is not the key to female-male differentials. The labor force participation of adult women increased from 28 percent in 1956 to 42 percent in 1985. This occurred without any increase in the unemployment rate of females, which is approximately equal to that of males.

Getting jobs is, of course, not the whole story. It has long been clear that women and men make, and are offered, different occupational choices. But even

FIGURE 19-6 Economic Discrimination: Employment Effects

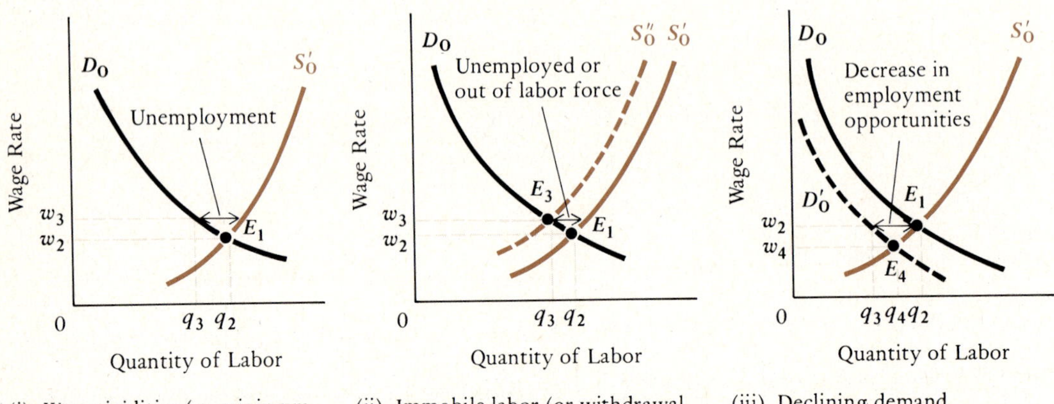

(i) Wage rigidities (or minimum wage)

(ii) Immobile labor (or withdrawal from labor force)

(iii) Declining demand

Increasing supply or decreasing demand in occupations in which those discriminated against are the major sources of labor can increase unemployment. In each part of the diagram the curves D_O and S'_O are those from Figure 19-5(ii); they show the market for O workers after the discriminatory policies are put into effect. Equilibrium is at E_1. In each case the wage w_2 would clear the market and provide employment of q_2.

(i) If the wage rate cannot fall below w_3, perhaps because of a minimum-wage law, employment will fall to q_3, and unemployment will occur in the amount shown by the arrow.

(ii) If some of the potential workers in O occupations are unable or unwilling to take employment in O jobs, the supply curve will not be S'_O but S''_O. Equilibrium will be at E_3. While O wages will rise somewhat to w_3, employment will be only q_3, and a number of workers, shown by the arrow, will not be employed. Whether they are recorded as "unemployed" or as having withdrawn from the labor force will depend on the official definitions.

(iii) If demand is declining in O occupations over time, say, from D_O to D'_O, either wages and employment will fall to the new equilibrium E_4 with w_4 and q_4, or wages will be maintained but employment will fall to q_3. The arrow illustrates the latter case, where the fall in employment is q_3q_2.

here there is notable progress. Over the past two decades women have steadily increased their participation in supposedly higher-status occupations, including managerial, sales, scientific, and technical jobs. For example, in 1966 women accounted for 16% percent of the professional labor force, and by 1985 that figure had risen to 44 percent.

Despite these rather dramatic changes, average earned income of females in the labor force is well below that of males of similar ages. Wages of females tend to be only about two-thirds those of males. The "salary gap" for females is due to a combination of causes: Women are still underrepresented in high-status occupations, proportionately fewer women than men reach higher-paying jobs in the occupations in which both work, and those who do reach higher-paying jobs do so more slowly. Do these facts reflect discrimination?

Discrimination within occupations. To what extent do differences in pay levels of men and women *within* an occupation reflect discrimination against women and to what extent do they reflect such other sex-linked characteristics as the voluntary choice of different lifetime patterns of labor force participation? The statistics show that, on average, women have fewer years of education, training, and work experience than men of the same age. The average working female is less mobile occupationally and geographically than her male counterpart. At least some of these facts reflect what is called lower *labor market attachment;* for example, many women decide to withdraw from the labor force or to work only part-time in order to have and raise children.

The extent of direct discrimination in an occupation may be measured by comparing the pay status of groups with similar characteristics. Mary Corcoran and Gregory Duncan analyzed pay differences between men and women and found that less than half (44 percent) of the difference could be explained by differences in education, work experience, and labor market attachment. Other studies show much the same thing and add up to 10 to 25 percent pay differences *not* explained by these variables. Analysts attribute this part of male-female pay differentials to direct discrimination.

Interoccupational discrimination. Women may have also suffered indirect discrimination as a result of being employed in a different set of occupations from men. They have been refused admission or discouraged from seeking entry into certain occupations; for example, they have traditionally been pushed into nursing rather than medicine, social work rather than law, and secretarial schools rather than managerial training programs. This is called *occupational segregation*. Similarly, girls raised in a culture in which their education seems less important than that of their brothers or in which they are trained to think of themselves as potential homemakers and urged to prepare themselves to attract and serve a husband are less likely to acquire the skills for many high-paying occupations that are wholly within their capabilities.

Differences in pay among occupations will, as we have seen, reflect differences in supply and demand, including nonmonetary factors. But may they not also reflect discrimination if one occupation is predominantly female and the other predominantly male? This is certainly possible, and many persons concerned about labor market discrimination have urged attention to interoccupational pay differences under the general term *pay equity*. Determining how much of observed differences reflect discrimination is extremely difficult because so many different considerations affect the pay levels of, say, firemen and librarians.

Government Policies to Remove Discrimination

Governments have long operated policies to eliminate discrimination between men and women doing the same job. These policies are relatively easy to administer. They require that a man and a women doing a job with the same job description must receive the same pay.

A much harder case arises when an attempt is made to remove alleged discrimination between jobs. If one job is primarily staffed with women and another by men, do differences between the wages paid in the two jobs represent differences in market conditions, or are they due to discrimination?

There is no doubt that some discrimination does occur. For example, psychologists have conducted many studies that suggest a bias against women that could easily lead to discriminatory pay differences. In one experiment, department heads were given identical files, one with a male name and the other a female name. They were 10 percent more likely to select the male for a job offer than the female with the identical resumé. In another experiment, female college students were asked to rank paintings on a scale from 1 to 10. The same picture consistently got a higher rating when it had a male name attached than when it was ascribed to a female artist.

Most empirical studies of male-female wage differentials show that much of the differences between jobs is due to differences in such objective factors as educational requirements and years of experience in the work force and on the job. When all such factors have been allowed for, however, there remains a residual that is consistent with some sex discrimination.

Two theories. The efficient labor market view is that markets reward people for their productivity, independent of such extraneous characteristics as sex

BOX 19-4

Equal Pay for Work of Equal Value

Equal pay for work of equal value has been in force in the federal civil service and some provincial governments for some time. Canadian provinces, who have the responsibility for regulating the workplace, are just beginning to consider extending the coverage to the private sector. Several states in the United States, however, have some longer-standing experience with equal pay legislation in both state and city governments. The following story catches the essence of some of the American experience.

The problems arise with instituting an equal pay decision and then coping with the disequilibrium situations that it creates. Of course, wherever the differentials were due to pure discrimination, eliminating them causes no further economic problems. Unfortunately, however, many differentials do reflect what we have earlier called equilibrium differentials—differences due to nonmonetary advantages, or job requirements, that imply that demand and supply can be balanced in two jobs only when their wages are unequal.

Suppose that two groups of city employees, call them librarians and firefighters, have the supply and demand curves shown below. In competitive equilibrium librarians would earn a wage w_1, firefighters w_2, that is, there is an equilibrium differential in the market-clearing wages. Now, as a result of a comparable worth study, the city is ordered to pay equal wages to the two groups.

The mayor proposes to comply by paying both groups a compromise wage, w_c, somewhat higher than the wage librarians have been receiving, but lower than that of firefighters. Librarians are pleased, and, indeed, the mayor begins to get extra applications from persons who seek to be librarians once the new wage goes into effect. (There is excess supply of librarians, q_1q_2, at w_c.) But the head of the Firemen's Union is burned up: "You can't cut our pay. We'll quit." Indeed, some of the firemen do quit. (At wage w_c there is excess demand of q_3q_4.) The fire chief warns the mayor he won't be able to fill the firehouse or meet all the calls for putting out fires. The mayor decides to go back to the court with her dilemma. The judge is unsympathetic: "All your problems come from the proposed cut in firefighters' pay. You may pay anything you like to firefighters; just be sure to pay the librarians the same."

The mayor then tells the state compensation director that he should raise librarians' pay to w_2, the firefighters' competitive rate.

In order to meet the extra wage bill, the city council orders libraries closed two days a week and lays off some librarians. While the firefighters do not complain, the laid-off librarians do, and so do the citizens who want the libraries open on Fridays and Saturdays. Meanwhile, the head of libraries is besieged with applications for the newly attractive library jobs.

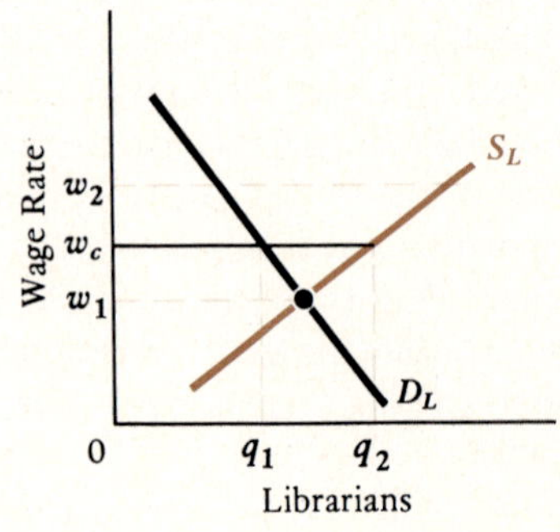

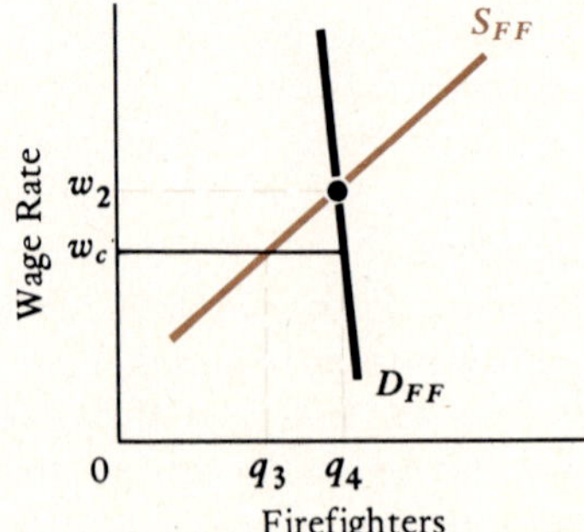

or color. Many women are low paid because they chose low-paid, low-productivity jobs, jobs that permit them to enter and leave the labor force, jobs that require little training, and jobs that are typically neither dangerous nor unduly arduous.

The institutionalist view is that custom and tradition matter greatly in determining wages. Similar jobs are paid differently because of habit, tradition, and discrimination. Even if shareholders want profit maximization, many managers and foremen may choose to exercise prejudice. They have substantial latitude to do so without making a noticeable change in total profits, and in nonprofit institutions, such as universities and government offices, the latitude is larger.

Indeed, if the majority of managers and foremen discriminate, there is no check on any one of them through relative profits. In any case, so goes this theory, no one really knows the marginal product of a librarian or a department store elevator operator.

Efficient market theory says boosting women's wages would cause employers to hire fewer women and reduce efficiency. By upsetting the allocation system, the labor market will work in a much poorer way and employers will be put at a disadvantage when competing with firms located in jurisdictions where such laws do not exist.

The institutionalist view is that employers can be persuaded to raise women's wages by accepting women in previously all-male jobs; or equalizing wages in "equal" jobs held predominantly by either sex. Since there is a big arbitrary element in wages, changing these differentials in the interest of equity will not have serious efficiency effects.

The concept of equal pay for work of equal value. To give effect to this policy, some group decides what jobs are of equal worth and equal pay is then enforced. Supporters of such a policy note that big firms operate such schemes all the time. These schemes evaluate jobs, not persons, and they typically use from 10 or 12 variables to evaluate office and production jobs. Common to both office and shop jobs are the variables for education and experience. The shop-job evaluations also look at initiative, physical demand, responsibility for equipment, hazards, etc., while office job evaluations look at complexity of duties, loss to firm from errors, supervision required, supervision of others given, working conditions, etc.

Critics of equal value legislation point out, however, that private employers can, and do, temper their equal worth decisions with market considerations. If they cannot fill all their positions in job A but can more than fill them in job B at the wage decided, they will revise their equal pay calculations. That means that equal pay calculations within firms are only guidelines to use when there are no strong market signals telling them to alter wage relatives. (Firms worry that the absence of market force allowances in binding government-imposed, equal pay decisions will cause many problems.)

In the typical government-imposed, equal pay policy these evaluations are used differently. Someone outside of the firm does the evaluations, which typically allow for a much smaller range of variables than is used in the firms' own evaluation schemes. Furthermore, the relatives imposed cannot then be varied as demand and supply conditions produce surpluses in some occupations and shortages in others. In some schemes, such as the one being instituted by the Province of Ontario now, the firm itself is left free to design its own scheme, which will be accepted unless it is challenged by labor.

All evaluation schemes contain two arbitrary elements. First, what equivalency rating scheme is to be used? There are many such schemes, and experiments show that they can give quite divergent results. Generally, the crude ones are easier to administer, but give much poorer results. The more complex methods are harder to administer, but give more satisfactory results (but none of them takes account of market conditions, since by their very nature they evaluate the job, not the market for that job).

The second arbitrary element is how to find the equivalent male job, when no two job classifications have exactly the same equivalency rating. (The smaller the firm, the greater is this problem.) To illustrate, assume that a female job class rates 55 on the scale and the closest male classes rate 50 and 62. What is the equivalent male wage for a job rated 55? The simplest solution is to fit a linear relation to the male jobs and use this to predict the wage at all job rating numbers. But why should the relation be linear? The job rating is at best an ordinal measure. There is no reason to believe that each 10 points on an arbitrary scale should be worth the same increase in wages. Experiments show that different ways of solving this problem can produce very different results.

When all the argument is finished, two basic issues remain. First, how much damage will be done to the allocative system by setting wage relatives by criteria that take no account of demand and supply? Second, is the cost in lost efficiency a price that is worth paying to gain the increase in equity, caused by reducing discriminatory differences, by a crude method that cannot distinguish between differentials caused by discrimination and many other causes? The allocative issue is further discussed in Box 19-4 (p. 388).

Who Loses from Discrimination?

Obviously, the victims lose as a result of labor market discrimination. But it is a mistake to think that they are the only losers. Society loses, too, because of the efficiency losses that discrimination causes and in other ways.

Efficiency losses arise for several reasons. If women are not given equal pay with males for equal work, the labor force will not be allocated so as to get the most out of society's resources. When people are kept from doing the jobs at which they are most productive and must instead produce goods or services that society values less, the total value of goods and services produced is reduced. And when prejudice increases unemployment, it reduces the nation's total output.

The gainers from discrimination are those who earn the higher pay that comes from limiting supply in their occupations, those who get the jobs that others might have held, and the bigots who gain pleasure from not having to work with or consume services provided by members of the discriminated-against group. But if the total output of society is less, the net losses will have to be borne by the society as a whole.

Beyond the efficiency losses that discrimination imposes on society are further economic and social costs. Increased welfare or unemployment payments may be required, and the costs of enforcing anti-discrimination laws must be paid.

Summary

1. A wage-setting union entering a competitive market can raise wages, but only at the cost of reducing employment and creating a pool of unemployed former workers and others who would like to work at the going wage but are unable to gain employment in that market.
2. If the union can limit entry into the field, it can shift the supply curve to the left and achieve a higher wage without creating unemployment in the occupation.
3. A wage-setting union entering a monopsonistic market may increase both employment and wages over some range. If, however, it sets the wage above the competitive level, it will create a pool of workers who are unable to get the jobs they want at the going wage.
4. Governments set some wages above their competitive levels by passing minimum-wage laws. The overall effects of minimum wages have now been extensively studied. It is clear that they raise the incomes of many employees, but they cause unemployment for many of those with the lowest levels of skills.
5. Labor markets have developed a wide variety of institutions, including labor unions and employers' associations. Such institutions greatly affect wage determination.

6. North American unionism developed first in the skilled trades, along craft lines, where it was possible to control supply and prevent non-union members from undercutting union wages. Widespread organization of the unskilled did not occur until later. The emergence of mature collective bargaining is a relatively recent development in the stormy and sometimes bloody history of North American labor unions.
7. Unions face a basic conflict between the goals of raising wages and preserving employment opportunities for members and potential members. Other trade-offs concern wages and job security, and wages and fringe benefits.
8. Labor market institutions can lead to labor markets that operate very differently from the competitive labor market of neoclassical economics. Unemployment may persist because of labor market practices that assure relatively long-term, stable employment relationships. Much of the market clearing in labor markets that occurs in the face of fluctuations in demand takes the form of fluctuations in employment rather than fluctuations in wage rates.
9. Discrimination has played a role in labor markets. Direct discrimination affects wages and employment opportunities by limiting the supply in the best-paying occupations and increasing it in less attractive occupations.
10. Indirect discrimination has had an effect through limiting the opportunities for education and training available to people subject to discrimination and through lowering people's aspirations in their choices of training and of careers.
11. Discrimination imposes costs on the victims of discrimination. It leads to inefficiency and loss of output and is costly in other ways.

Topics for Review

Monopsony power
Union power
Effects of minimum wages
Collective bargaining
Goals of unions
Possible causes of involuntary unemployment
Labor market attachment
Wage effects and employment effects of economic discrimination
Direct and indirect discrimination
Comparable worth

Discussion Questions

1. A union that has bargaining rights in two plants of the same company in different states almost always insists on "equal pay for equal work" in the two plants. It does not always insist on equal pay for men and women in the same jobs. Can you see any economic reasons for such a distinction?

2. Why were craft unions more successful than industrial unions in the late nineteenth century?
3. "The great increase in the number of women entering the labor force for the first time means that relatively more women than men earn beginning salaries. It is therefore not evidence of discrimination that the average wage earned by females is less than that earned by males." Discuss.
4. U.S. unions have traditionally supported laws
   a. Restricting immigration
   b. Expelling illegal aliens
   c. Raising the minimum wage and extending its coverage

   How do each of these positions benefit or hurt the following groups: consumers, workers as a whole, and unionized workers with seniority in their jobs.
5. In the past companies manufacturing dangerous chemicals often had policies of removing women of child-bearing age from, or not hiring them for, jobs that expose them to lead or other substances that could damage a fetus. Is this sex discrimination? Whether it is or not, debate whether this sort of protective hiring rule is something the government should require, encourage, or prohibit.
6. "One can judge the presence or absence of discrimination by looking at the proportion of the population in different occupations." Does such information help? Does it suffice? Consider each of the following examples. Relative to their numbers in the total population, there are
   a. Too many blacks and too few Jews among professional athletes
   b. Too few male secretaries
   c. Too few female judges
7. "About 40 percent of working women are in traditionally female occupations—secretaries, nurses, cashiers, waitresses, elementary school teachers, beauticians, maids, and sales clerks, for example. While this may result from past sex stereotyping, the notion that only women can do these jobs may also benefit women by preserving employment opportunities for them, given the high unemployment rates among black males and teenage males." Discuss this argument.
8. Consider the consequences of applying the notion of "equal pay for comparable worth" to compensation of:
   a. Football coaches and cross-country coaches
   b. University presidents and network news announcers
   c. Fashion models and poets
   d. Secretaries working inside and carpark attendants working outside Victoria B.C. and in Quebec City
9. Compare the following policies designed to reduce pay differentials due to occupational segregation of women in lower-paid jobs.
   a. Making pay adjustments based on an analysis of the "comparable worth" of occupations
   b. Removing barriers to women's employment in traditionally male jobs
   c. Setting quotas based on the relevant population statistics for minimum fractions of females in each occupation

PART SIX

International Trade

20

The Gains from Trade

Canadians buy Volkswagens, Germans take holidays in Italy, Italians buy spices from Tanzania, Africans import oil from Kuwait, Arabs buy Japanese cameras, and the Japanese buy coal from Canada. *International trade* refers to exchanges of goods and services that take place across international boundaries.

The founders of modern economics were concerned with foreign trade problems. The great eighteenth century British philosopher and economist David Hume, one of the first to work out the theory of the price system as a control mechanism, developed his concepts mainly in terms of prices in foreign trade. Adam Smith in his *Wealth of Nations* attacked government restriction of trade. David Ricardo in 1817 developed the basic theory of the gains from trade that is studied in this chapter. The repeal of the Corn Laws—tariffs on the importation of grains into Great Britain—and the transformation of that country during the nineteenth century from a country of high tariffs to one of completely free trade were to a significant extent the result of agitation by economists whose theories of the gains from trade led them to condemn all tariffs.

In this chapter we explore the fundamental question of what is gained by international trade. In Chapter 21 we will deal with the pros and cons of interfering with the free flow of such trade. In that chapter we also focus on the importance of international trade for the Canadian economy and discuss the issues that arise from Canadian policies toward such trade.

Sources of the Gains from Trade

The advantages realized as a result of trade are called the **gains from trade.** The source of such gains is most easily visualized by considering the differences between a world with trade and a world without it. Although politicians often regard foreign trade differently from domestic trade, economists from Adam Smith on have argued that the causes and consequences of international trade are simply an extension of the principles governing domestic trade. What is the advantage of trade among individuals, among groups, among regions, or among countries?

Interpersonal, Interregional, and International Trade

Consider trade among individuals. Without trade each person would have to be self-sufficient; each would have to produce all the food, clothing, shelter, medical services, entertainment, and luxuries that he or she consumed. A world of individual self-sufficiency would be a world with extremely low living standards.

Trade among individuals allows people to specialize in activities they can do well and to buy from others the goods and services they cannot easily produce. A good doctor who is a bad carpenter can provide medical services not only for his or her own family but also for an excellent carpenter without the training or the ability to practice medicine. Thus trade and specialization are intimately connected. Without trade everyone must be self-sufficient; with trade everyone can specialize in what he or she does well and satisfy other needs by trading.

The same principles apply to regions. Without interregional trade each region would be forced to be self-sufficient. With trade each region can specialize in producing commodities for which it has some natural or acquired advantage. Plains regions can specialize in growing grain, mountain regions in mining and forest products, and regions with abundant power in manufacturing. Cool regions can produce wheat and other crops that thrive in temperate climates, and hot regions can grow such tropical crops as bananas, sugar, and coffee. The living standards of the inhabitants of all regions will be higher when each region specializes in products in which it has some natural or acquired advantage and obtains other products by trade than when all regions seek to be self-sufficient.

The same principle also applies to nations. A national boundary seldom delimits an area that is naturally self-sufficient. Nations, like regions or persons, can gain from specialization and the international trade that must accompany it. Specialization means that each country produces more of some the goods than its residents wish to consume, and less of others.

International trade is necessary to achieve the gains that international specialization makes possible.

This discussion suggests one important possible gain from trade.

With trade, each individual, region, or nation is able to concentrate on producing goods and services that it produces efficiently while trading to obtain goods and services that it does not produce efficiently.

Specialization and trade go hand in hand because there is no motivation to achieve the gains from specialization without being able to trade the goods produced for goods desired. Economists use the term *gains from trade* to embrace the results of both.

We shall examine two sources of the gains from trade. The first is differences among regions of the world in climate and resource endowment that lead to advantages in producing certain goods and disadvantages in producing others. These gains occur even though each country's costs of production are unchanged by the existence of trade. The second source is the reduction in each country's costs of production that result from the greater scale of production that specialization brings.

Gains from Specialization with Given Costs

In order to focus on differences in countries' conditions of production, suppose that there are no advantages arising from either economies of large-scale production or cost reductions that are the consequence of learning new skills. In these circumstances what leads to gains from trade? To examine this question we shall use an example involving only two countries and two products, but the general principles apply as well to the real-world case of many countries and many commodities.

A Special Case: Absolute Advantage

The gains from trade are clear when there is a simple situation involving absolute advantage. **Absolute advantage** concerns the quantities of a single product that can be produced using the same quantity of resources in two different regions. One region is said to have an absolute advantage over another in the production of commodity X when an equal quantity of resources can produce more X in the first region than in the second.

Suppose region A has an absolute advantage over B in one commodity, while region B has an absolute advantage over A in another. This is a case of *reciprocal absolute advantage*: Each country has an absolute advantage in some commodity. In such a situation the total production of both regions can be increased (relative to a situation of self-sufficiency) if each specializes in the commodity in which it has the absolute advantage.

Table 20-1 provides a simple example. Total world production of both wheat and cloth increases when each country produces more of the good in which it has an absolute advantage. As a result there is more wheat *and* more cloth for the same use of resources.

The gains from *specialization* make the gains from *trade* possible. England is producing more cloth and Canada more wheat than when they were self-sufficient. Canada is producing more wheat and less cloth than Canadian consumers wish to buy, and England is producing more cloth and less wheat than English consumers wish to buy. If consumers in both countries are to get cloth and wheat in the desired proportions, Canada must export wheat to England and import cloth from England.

TABLE 20-1 Gains from Specialization with Absolute Advantage

A: Amounts of wheat and cloth that can be produced with one unit of resources in Canada and England

	Wheat (bushels)	Cloth (yards)
Canada	10	6
England	5	10

B: Changes resulting from the transfer of one unit of Canadian resources into wheat and one unit of English resources into cloth

	Wheat (bushels)	Cloth (yards)
Canada	+10	− 6
England	− 5	+10
Total	+ 5	+ 4

When there is a reciprocal absolute advantage, specialization makes it possible to produce more of both commodities. Part A shows the production of wheat and cloth that can be achieved in each country by using one unit of resources. Canada can produce 10 bushels of wheat or 6 yards of cloth; England can produce 5 bushels of wheat or 10 yards of cloth. Canada has an absolute advantage in producing wheat, England in producing cloth. Part B shows the changes in production caused by moving one unit of resources out of cloth and into wheat production in Canada and moving one unit of resources in the opposite direction in England. There is an increase in total production of 5 bushels of wheat and 4 yards of cloth; globally, there are gains from specialization. In this example the more resources transferred into wheat production in Canada and into cloth production in England, the larger the gains will be.

A First General Statement: Comparative Advantage

When each country has an absolute advantage over the other in a commodity, the gains from trade are obvious. But what if Canada can produce both wheat and cloth more efficiently than England? In essence this was David Ricardo's question, posed nearly two centuries ago. His answer underlies the theory of comparative advantage and is still accepted by economists as a valid statement of the potential gains from trade.

To start with, assume that Canadian efficiency increases tenfold above the levels recorded in the earlier example, so that a unit of Canadian resources can produce either 100 bushels of wheat or 60 yards of cloth. English efficiency remains unchanged (see Table 20-2). It might appear that Canada, which is now better at producing both wheat and cloth than is England, has nothing to gain by trading with such an inefficient foreign country. But it *does* have something to gain, as shown in Table 20-2. Even though Canada is 10 times as efficient as in the situation of Table 20-1, it is still possible to increase world production of both wheat and cloth by having Canada produce more wheat and less cloth and England produce more cloth and less wheat.

What is the source of this gain? Although Canada has an absolute advantage over England in the production of both wheat and cloth, the margin of advantage differs in the two commodities. Canada can produce 20 times as much wheat as England by using

TABLE 20-2 Gains from Specialization with Comparative Advantage

A: Amounts of wheat and cloth that can be produced with one unit of resources in Canada and England

	Wheat (bushels)	Cloth (yards)
Canada	100	60
England	5	10

B: Changes resulting from the transfer of one-tenth of one unit of Canadian resources into wheat and one unit of English resources into cloth

	Wheat (bushels)	Cloth (yards)
Canada	+10	− 6
England	− 5	+10
Total	+ 5	+ 4

When there is comparative advantage, specialization makes it possible to produce more of both commodities. The productivity of English resources is left unchanged from Table 20-1; that of Canadian resources is increased tenfold. England no longer has an absolute advantage in producing either commodity. Total production of both commodities can nonetheless be increased by specialization. Moving one-tenth of one unit of Canadian resources out of cloth and into wheat and moving one unit of resources in the opposite direction in England causes total production of wheat to rise by 5 bushels and cloth by 4 yards. Reciprocal absolute advantage is not necessary for gains from trade.

the same quantity of resources, but only 6 times as much cloth. Canada is said to have a **comparative advantage** in the production of wheat and a *comparative disadvantage* in the production of cloth. (This statement implies another: England has a comparative disadvantage in the production of wheat, in which it is 20 times less efficient than Canada, and a comparative advantage in the production of cloth, in which it is only 6 times less efficient.)

A key result is this:

The gains from specialization and trade depend on the pattern of comparative, not absolute, advantage.

A comparison of Tables 20-1 and 20-2 refutes the notion that the absolute *levels* of efficiency of two areas determine the gains from specialization. The key is that the margin of advantage one area has over the other must differ between commodities. As long as this margin differs, total world production can be increased when each area specializes in the production of the commodity in which it has a comparative advantage.

Comparative advantage is necessary as well as sufficient for gains from trade. This is illustrated in Table 20-3, showing Canada with an absolute advantage in both commodities and neither country with a comparative advantage over the other in the production of either commodity. Canada is 10 times as efficient as England in the production of wheat and in the production of cloth. Now there is no way to increase the production of both wheat and cloth

TABLE 20-3 Absence of Gains from Specialization When There Is No Comparative Advantage

A: Amounts of wheat and cloth that can be produced with one unit of resources in Canada and England

	Wheat (bushels)	Cloth (yards)
Canada	100	60
England	10	6

B: Changes resulting from the transfer of one unit of Canadian resources into wheat and 10 units of British resources into cloth

	Wheat (bushels)	Cloth (yards)
Canada	+100	−60
England	−100	+60
Total	0	0

Where there is no comparative advantage, no reallocation of resources within each country can increase the production of both commodities. In this example Canada has the same absolute advantage over England in each commodity (tenfold). There is no comparative advantage, and world production cannot be increased by reallocating resources in both countries. Therefore, specialization does not increase total output.

by reallocating resources within Canada and within England. Part B of the table provides one example of a resource shift that illustrates this.

Absolute advantage without comparative advantage does not lead to gains from trade.

A Second General Statement: Opportunity Costs

Much of the foregoing argument has used the concept of a unit of resources. It assumes that units of resources can be equated across countries, so that statements such as "Canada can produce 10 times as much wheat with the same quantity of resources as England" are meaningful. Measurement of the real resource cost of producing commodities poses many difficulties. If, for example, England uses land, labor, and capital in proportions different from those used in Canada, it may not be clear which country gets more output per unit of resource input. Fortunately, the proposition about the gains from trade can be restated without reference to so fuzzy a concept as units of resources.

To do this, go back to the examples of Tables 20-1 and 20-2. Calculate the *opportunity cost* of wheat and cloth in the two countries. When resources are assumed to be fully employed, the only way to produce more of one commodity is to reallocate resources and produce less of the other commodity. Table 20-1 shows that a unit of resources in Canada can produce 10 bushels of wheat *or* 6 yards of cloth. From this it follows that the opportunity cost of producing a unit of wheat is 0.60 units of cloth, whereas the opportunity cost of producing a unit of cloth is 1.67 units of wheat. These data are summarized in Table 20-4. The table also shows that in England the opportunity cost of a unit of wheat is 2.0 units of cloth forgone, while the opportunity cost of a unit of cloth is 0.50 units of wheat. Table 20-2 also gives rise to the opportunity costs in Table 20-4.

The sacrifice of cloth involved in producing wheat is much lower in Canada than it is in England. World wheat production can be increased if Canada rather than England produces it. Looking at cloth production, we can see that the loss of wheat involved in producing one unit of cloth is lower in England than in Canada. England is the lower (opportunity) cost producer of cloth. Total cloth production can be increased if England rather than Canada produces it. This situation is shown in Table 20-5.

TABLE 20-4 Opportunity Cost of Wheat and Cloth in Canada and England

	Wheat (bushels)	Cloth (yards)
Canada	0.60 yards cloth	1.67 bushels wheat
England	2.00 yards cloth	0.50 bushels wheat

Comparative advantages can be expressed in terms of opportunity costs that differ between countries. These opportunity costs can be obtained from Table 20-1 or Table 20-2. The English opportunity cost of one unit of wheat is obtained by dividing the cloth output of one unit of English resources by the wheat output. The result shows that 2 yards of cloth must be sacrificed for every extra unit of wheat produced by transferring English resources out of cloth production and into wheat. The other three cost figures are obtained in a similar manner.

The gains from trade arise from differing opportunity costs in the two countries.

The conclusions about the gains from trade arising from international differences may be summarized as follows:

1. Country A has a comparative advantage over country B in producing a commodity when the opportunity cost (in terms of some other commodity) of production in country A is lower. This implies, however, that it has a comparative disadvantage in the other commodity.
2. Opportunity costs depend on the relative costs of producing two commodities, not on absolute costs. (Notice that the examples in Tables 20-1 and 20-2 each give rise to the opportunity costs in Table 20-4.)
3. When opportunity costs are the same in all countries, there is no comparative advantage and thus no possibility of gains from specialization and trade. (You can illustrate this for yourself by cal-

TABLE 20-5 Gains from Specialization with Differing Opportunity Costs

Changes resulting from each country's producing one more unit of a commodity in which it has the lower opportunity cost

	Wheat (bushels)	Cloth (yards)
Canada	+1.0	−0.6
England	−0.5	+1.0
Total	+0.5	+0.4

Whenever opportunity costs differ between countries, specialization can increase the production of both commodities. These calculations show that there are gains from specialization given the opportunity costs of Table 20-4. To produce one more bushel of wheat, Canada must sacrifice 0.6 yards of cloth. To produce one more yard of cloth, England must sacrifice 0.5 bushels of wheat. Making both changes raises total production of both wheat and cloth.

culating the opportunity costs implied by the data in Table 20-3.)

4. When opportunity costs differ in any two countries and both countries are producing both commodities, it is always possible to increase production of both commodities by a suitable reallocation of resources within each country. (This proposition is illustrated in Table 20-5.)

Gains from Specialization with Variable Costs

So far we have assumed that unit costs are the same whatever the scale of output and have seen that there are gains from specialization and trade as long as there are interregional differences in opportunity costs. If costs vary with the level of output or as experience is acquired via specialization, *additional* sources of gain are possible.

Economies of Scale

Real production costs, measured in terms of resources used, generally fall as the scale of output increases over a substantial range.[1] The larger the scale of operations, the more efficiently large-scale machinery can be used and the more a detailed division of tasks among workers is possible. Smaller countries such as Canada, France, and Israel whose domestic markets are not large enough to exploit economies of scale would find it prohibitively expensive to become self-sufficient. They would have to produce a little bit of everything at very high cost.

Trade allows smaller countries to specialize and produce a few commodities at high enough levels of output to reap the available economies of scale.

Bigger countries such as the United States and the USSR have markets large enough to allow the production of most items at home at a scale of output great enough to obtain the available economies of scale. For them the gains from trade arise mainly from specializing in commodities in which they have a comparative advantage. Yet even for such countries a broadening of their markets permits achieving economies of scale in subproduct lines.

The importance of product diversity and specialization in specific subproduct lines has been one of the important lessons learned from the changing patterns of world trade since World War II. When the European Common Market (now called the European Community) was set up in the 1950s, economists expected that specialization would occur according to the classical theory of comparative advantage, with one country specializing in cars, another in refrigerators, another in fashion clothes, another in shoes, and so on. This is not the way it worked out. Today one can buy French, English, Italian, and German fashion goods, cars, shoes, appliances, and a host of other goods in London, Paris, Bonn, and Rome. Ships loaded with Swedish furniture bound for London pass ships loaded with English furniture bound for Stockholm, and so on.

What free European trade did was to allow a proliferation of differentiated products with different countries each specializing in different subproduct

[1] This effect is discussed in detail in Chapter 11. The classic discussion by Adam Smith is quoted in Box 3-1 on page 47.

lines. Consumers have shown by their expenditures that they value this enormous increase in the range of choice among differentiated products. As Asian countries have expanded into North American markets with textiles, cars, and electronic goods, North American manufacturers have increasingly specialized their production, and we now export textiles, cars, and electronics equipment to Japan even while importing similar but different products from Japan.

Learning by Doing

The discussion so far has assumed that costs vary only with the *level* of output. They may also vary with the length of time a product has been produced.

Early economists placed great importance on a factor that we now call learning by doing. They believed that as countries gained experience in particular tasks, workers and managers would become more efficient in performing them. As people acquire expertise, costs tend to fall. There is substantial evidence that such learning by doing does occur.

The distinction between this phenomenon and the gains from economies of scale is illustrated in Figure 20-1; it is one more example of the difference between a movement along a curve and a shift of the curve.

Recognition of the opportunities for learning by doing leads to an important implication: Policymakers need not accept *current* comparative advantages as given. Through such means as education and tax incentives, they can seek to develop new comparative advantages.[2] Moreover, countries cannot complacently assume that an existing comparative advantage will persist. Misguided education policies, the wrong tax incentives, or policies that discourage risk taking can lead to the rapid erosion of a country's comparative advantage in a particular product. So, too, can competitive developments elsewhere in the world.

A changing view of comparative advantage. The classical theory of the gains from trade, assumes given cost structures based largely on a country's natural endowments. This leads to a given pattern of international comparative advantage. It also leads to the policy advice that a government interested in maximizing its citizens' material standard of living should encourage production to be specialized in those goods where it currently has a comparative advantage. When all countries follow this advice, the theory predicts that each will be specialized in a relatively narrow range of distinct products. To start with Ricardo's own example, the British will produce cloth, the Portuguese wine, and, to go beyond Ricardo, the Central Americans will grow bananas.

There is today a competing view. In extreme form it says that comparative advantages are certainly there, but they are typically acquired, not nature-given—and they change. This view of comparative advantage is *dynamic* rather than static. New industries are seen to depend more on human capital than on fixed physical capital or natural resources. The skills of a computer designer, a videogame programmer, a sound mix technician, or a rock star are acquired by education and on-the-job training. Natural endowments of energy and raw materials cannot account for Britain's prominence in modern pop music nor for the leadership in ideas of Silicon Valley in California. When a country such as the United States finds its former dominance (based on comparative advantage) declining in such smokestack industries as automobiles and steel, its firms need not sit idly by. Instead they can begin to adapt by developing new areas of comparative advantage.

There are surely elements of truth in both extreme views. It would be unwise to neglect resource endowments, climate, culture, and social and institutional arrangements as sources of comparative advantages. But it would also be unwise to forget that the sources of comparative advantage are not immutable; indeed, they can be acquired, and they can be dissipated.

The Terms of Trade

So far we have seen that world production can be increased when countries specialize in the production

[2] Of course, they can, foolishly, use the same policies to develop industries in which they do not have, and will never achieve, comparative advantage. See the discussion in Chapter 21.

FIGURE 20-1 Gains from Specialization with Variable Costs

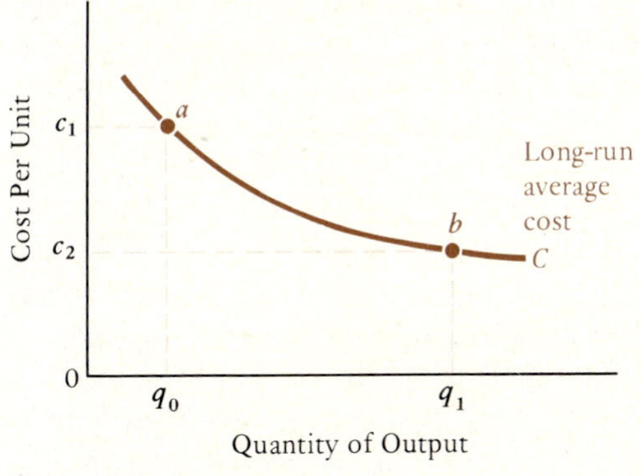

(i) Economies of scale

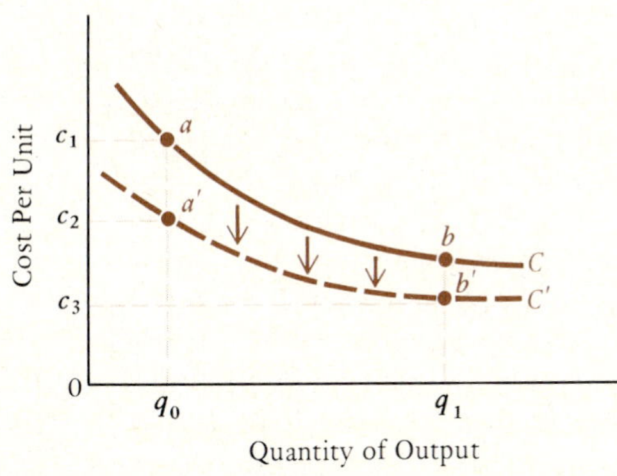

(ii) Learning by doing

Specialization may lead to gains from trade by permitting economies of larger-scale output, by leading to downward cost curves, or both. Consider a country that wishes to consume the quantity q_0. Suppose that it can produce that quantity at an average cost per unit of c_1. Suppose further that the country has a comparative advantage in producing this commodity and can export the quantity q_0q_1 if it produces q_1. This may lead to cost savings in two ways. (i) The increased level of production of q_1 compared to q_0 permits it to *move along* its cost curve, C, from a to b, thus reducing costs per unit to c_2. This is an economy of scale. (ii) As workers and managements become more experienced, they may discover means of increasing productivity that lead to a downward shift of the cost curve from C to C'. This is learning by doing. The downward *shift*, shown by the arrows, lowers the cost of producing every unit of output. At output q_1 costs per unit fall to c_3. The movement from a to b' incorporates both economies of scale and learning by doing.

of the commodities in which they have or can acquire a comparative advantage and then trade with one another. We now ask: How will these gains from specialization and trade be shared among countries? The division of the gain depends on the terms at which trade takes place. The **terms of trade** depend on the quantity of imported goods that can be obtained per unit of goods exported and are measured by the ratio of the price of exports to the price of imports.

A rise in the price of imported goods, with the price of exports unchanged, indicates a *fall in the terms of trade;* it will now take more exports to buy the same quantity of imports. Similarly, a rise in the price of exported goods, with the price of imports unchanged, indicates a *rise in the terms of trade;* it will now take fewer exports to buy the same quantity of imports. Thus the ratio of prices is a proxy for the amount of exported goods needed to acquire a given quantity of imports.

In the example of Table 20-4 the Canadian domestic opportunity cost of one unit of cloth is 1.67 bushels of wheat. In other words, if in Canada resources are transferred from wheat to cloth, 1.67 bushels of wheat are given up for every yard of cloth gained. But if Canada can obtain its cloth by trade on more favorable terms, it pays to produce and export wheat to pay for cloth imports. Suppose, for

BOX 20-1

The Gains from Trade Illustrated Graphically

International trade leads to an expansion of the set of goods that can be consumed in the economy in two ways: by allowing the bundle of goods consumed to differ from the bundle produced and by permitting a profitable change in the pattern of production. The key to these gains is that international trade allows the separation of production decisions from consumption decisions. Without international trade the choice of which bundle of goods to produce is the same thing as the choice of which bundle to consume. With international trade the consumption and production bundles can be altered independently to reflect the relative value placed on goods by international markets.

This proposition is illustrated graphically for a simplified world in which there are only two goods, X and Y. The illustration is in two stages.

Stage 1: Fixed Production

In each part of the figure the black curve is the economy's production possibility boundary (such a boundary was first introduced in Figure 1-2, page 7).

If there is no international trade, the economy must consume the same bundle of goods that it produces. Thus the production possibility boundary is also the consumption possibility boundary. Suppose the economy produces and consumes at point *a*, with q_1 of good X and q_2 of good Y, as in part (i).

Next, suppose that while production stays at point *a*, good Y can be exchanged for good X in international markets. The consumption possibilities are now enhanced, as is shown by the line *tt* drawn through point *a*. The slope of this line indicates the world terms of trade and reflects the quantity of Y that exchanges for a unit of X on the international market.

Although production is fixed at *a*, consumption can now be anywhere on the line *tt*. For example, the consumption point could be at *b*. This could be achieved by exporting *ac* units of Y and importing *cb* units of X. Since point *b* (and all others on line *tt* to the right of *a*) lies outside of the production possibility boundary, there are potential gains from trade. Consumers are no longer limited by *their* country's production possibilities. Let us suppose they prefer point *b* to point *a*. They have achieved a gain from trade by being allowed to exchange some of their production of good Y for some quantity of good X and thus to consume more of good X than is produced at home.

Stage 2: Variable Production

In stage 1 production was constant at *a*. An additional opportunity for the expansion of the country's consumption possibilities arises because, with trade, the production bundle may be profitably altered in response to international prices. The country may pro-

example, that international prices are such that 1 yard of cloth exchanges for (i.e., is equal in value to) 1 bushel of wheat. At those prices Canadians can obtain 1 yard of cloth for 1 bushel of wheat exported. They get more cloth per unit of wheat exported than they can by moving resources out of wheat into cloth production at home. Therefore, the terms of trade favor specializing in the production of wheat and trading it for cloth on international markets.

Similarly, in the example of Table 20-4 English consumers gain when they can obtain wheat abroad at any terms of trade more favorable than 2 yards of cloth per unit of wheat. If the terms of trade permit exchange of 1 bushel of wheat for 1 yard of cloth, the terms of trade favor English traders' buying wheat and selling cloth on international markets. Here both England and Canada gain from trade. Each can obtain the commodity in which it has a comparative disadvantage at a lower opportunity cost through international trade than through domestic production. The way in which the terms of trade affect the gains from trade is illustrated graphically in Box 20-1.

Because actual international trade involves many

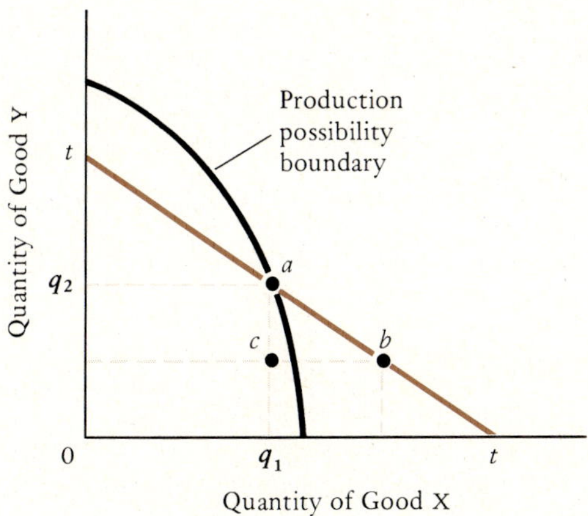

(i) Stage 1: fixed production

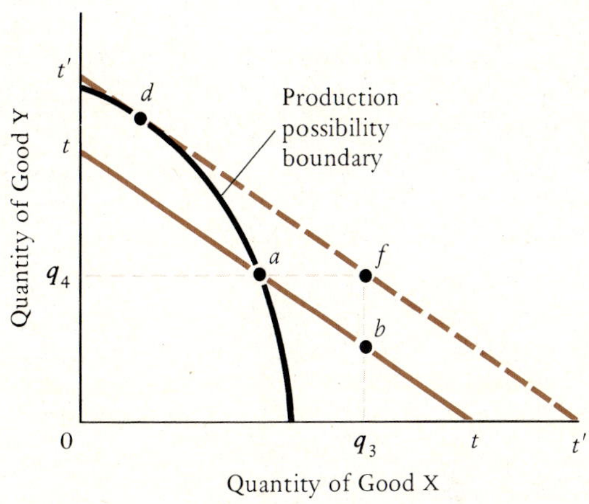

(ii) Stage 2: variable production

duce the bundle of goods that is most valuable in world markets. That is represented by the bundle *d* in part (ii). The consumption possibility set is shifted to the line *t′t′* by changing production from *a* to *d* and thereby increasing the country's degree of specialization in good Y. For every point on the original consumption possibility set, *tt*, there are points on the new set, *t′t′*, that allow more consumption of both goods. Compare, for example, points *a* and *f*. Notice also that except at the zero-trade point, *d*, the new consumption possibility set lies everywhere above the production possibility curve.

Many consumption bundles that cannot be produced domestically are made available by trade. The benefits from moving from a no-trade position, such as *a*, to a trading position, such as *b* or *f*, are the *gains from trade* to the country. When the production of good Y was increased and the production of food X decreased, the country was able to move to point *f* by producing more of good Y, in which the country has a comparative advantage, and trading the additional production for good X. Economists refer to such production changes as exploiting the country's comparative advantage.

countries and many commodities, a country's terms of trade are computed as an index number:

$$\text{Terms of trade} = \frac{\text{index of export prices}}{\text{index of import prices}} \times 100$$

A rise in the index is referred to as a *favorable* change in a country's terms of trade. A favorable change means that more can be imported per unit of goods exported than previously. For example, if the export price index rises from 100 to 120 while the import price index rises from 100 to 110, the terms of trade index rises from 100 to 109. At the new terms of trade a unit of exports will buy 9 percent more imports than at the old terms.

A decrease in the index of the terms of trade, called an *unfavorable* change, means that the country can import less in return for any given amount of exports or, what is the same, it must export more to pay for any given amount of imports. For example, the sharp rise in oil prices in the 1970s led to large unfavorable shifts in the terms of trade of oil-importing countries. When oil prices fell sharply in the mid 1980s, the terms of trade of oil-importing countries changed favorably.

Summary

1. The sources of the gains from trade between any two entities—individuals, regions, or nations—are the same.
2. One country (or region or individual) has an absolute advantage over another country (or region or individual) in the production of a commodity when, with the same input of resources in each country, it can produce more of the commodity than can the other.
3. In a situation of absolute advantage, total production of both commodities will be raised if each country specializes in the production of the commodity in which it has the absolute advantage. However, the gains from trade do not require absolute advantage on the part of each country, only comparative advantage.
4. Comparative advantage is the relative advantage one country enjoys over another in production of various commodities. Total production of all commodities can be increased if each country transfers resources into the production of the commodities in which it has a comparative advantage.
5. Comparative advantage arises from countries' having different opportunity costs of producing particular goods. This creates the opportunity for all nations to gain from trade.
6. The theory of the gains from trade is that trade allows all countries to obtain the goods in which they do not have a comparative advantage at a lower opportunity cost than they would face if they were to produce all commodities for themselves. This allows all countries to have more of all commodities than they could have if they tried to be self-sufficient.
7. As well as gaining the advantages of specialization arising from comparative advantage, a nation that engages in trade and specialization may realize the benefits of the economies of large-scale production and of learning by doing.
8. Classical theory regarded comparative advantage as largely determined by natural resource endowments and thus difficult to change. Economists now believe that comparative advantage can be acquired and thus can be changed. A country may, in this view, seek to influence its role in world production and trade.
9. The terms of trade refer to the ratio of the prices of goods exported to those imported, which determines the quantities of exports needed to pay for imports. The terms of trade determine how the gains from trade are shared. A favorable change in terms of trade, that is, a rise in export prices relative to import prices, means that one can acquire more imports per unit of exports.

Topics for Review

Interpersonal, interregional, and international specialization
Absolute advantage and comparative advantage
Gains from trade: specialization, scale economies, and learning by doing

Opportunity cost and comparative advantage
Dynamic comparative advantage
Terms of trade

Discussion Questions

1. Adam Smith saw a close connection between the wealth of a nation and its willingness "freely to engage" in foreign trade. What is the connection?
2. Suppose that the situation described in the table exists. Assume that there are no tariffs and no government intervention and that labor is the only factor of production. Let X take different values—say, \$10, \$20, \$40, and \$60. In each case, in what direction will trade have to flow in order for the gains from trade to be exploited?

	Labor cost of producing one unit of	
Country	**Artichokes**	**Bikinis**
Inland	\$20	\$40
Outland	\$20	\$$X$

3. Suppose that Canada had an absolute advantage in all manufactured products. Should it then ever import any manufactured products?
4. Suppose the Quebec referendum had gone the other way, and Canada had become two separate countries starting in 1980. What predictions would you make about the standard of living compared with what it is today? Does the fact that Canada, the United States, and Mexico are separate countries lead to a lower standard of living in the three countries than if they were united into a new country called Northica?
5. Studies of Canadian trade patterns have shown that high wage sectors of industry are among the largest and fastest-growing export sectors. Does this contradict the principle of comparative advantage?
6. Saudi Arabia has a comparative advantage over West Germany in producing oil. In what, if anything, does it have a comparative disadvantage? When Saudi Arabia lowers the price of oil, does it change the gains from trade? What does it change?
7. Predict what each of the following events would do to the terms of trade of the importing country and the exporting country, other things being equal.
   a. A blight destroys a good part of the coffee beans produced in the world.
   b. The Japanese cut the price of the steel they sell to the Canada.
   c. A general inflation of 10 percent occurs around the world.
   d. Violation of OPEC output quotas leads to a sharp fall in the price of oil.
8. Heavy Canadian borrowing abroad has several times led to a high value of the dollar and thus a rise in the ratio of export prices to import prices. Although this is called a favorable change in the terms of trade, are there any reasons why it may not have been a good thing for the Canadian economy?

21

Barriers to Free Trade

Conducting business in a foreign country is always difficult. Differences in language, in local laws and customs, and in currency all complicate transactions. Our concern in this chapter is not, however, with these difficulties but with the government's policy toward international trade, which is called its **commercial policy.** At one extreme is a policy of **free trade**, which means an absence of any form of government interference with the free flow of international trade. Any departure from free trade designed to give some protection to domestic industries from foreign competition is called **protectionism.**

The Theory of Commercial Policy

Today debates over commercial policy are as heated as they were 200 years ago when the theory of the gains from trade was still being worked out. Should a country permit the free flow of international trade, or should it seek to protect its local producers from foreign competition? Such protection may be achieved either by **tariffs,** which are taxes designed to raise the prices of foreign goods, or by **nontariff barriers,** which are devices other than tariffs that are designed to reduce the flow of imports. Examples include quotas and customs procedures that are deliberately made more cumbersome than necessary.

The Case for Free Trade

The case for free trade is based on the analysis presented in Chapter 20. We saw that whenever opportunity costs differ among countries, specialization and trade will raise world living standards. Free trade allows all countries to specialize in producing commodities in which they have a comparative advantage.

Free trade allows the maximization of world production, thus making it *possible* for every household in the world to consume more goods than it could without free trade.

This does not necessarily mean that everyone *will* be better off with free trade than without it. Protectionism could allow some people to obtain a larger share of a smaller world output so that they would benefit even though the average person would lose. If we ask whether it is *possible* for free trade to be advantageous to everyone, the answer is yes. But if we ask whether free trade is in fact *always* advantageous to everyone, the answer is not necessarily.

There is abundant evidence that significant differences in opportunity costs exist and that large gains are realized from international trade because of these differences. What needs explanation is the fact that trade is not wholly free. Why do tariffs and nontariff barriers to trade continue to exist two centuries after Adam Smith and David Ricardo stated the case for free trade? Is there a valid case for protectionism? Before addressing these questions, let us examine the methods used in protectionist policy.

Methods of Protectionism

There are three main types of protectionist policy. All three may end up affecting both the price and the quantity of exports. They differ, however, in what the policy changes in the first instance.

The first policy raises the *price* of the imported commodity. A tariff, also often called an *import duty*, is the most common price-raising device. Others are rules and regulations that are costly to comply with, that do not apply to competing domestically produced commodities, and that are more than is required to meet purposes other than trade restriction.

Tariffs come in two main forms: **specific tariffs,** which are so much money per unit of the product, and **ad valorem tariffs,** which are a percentage of the price of the product. Tariffs raise revenue as well as acting as a protective device. For some less-developed countries with limited sources of revenue, import duties can be an important revenue source. For advanced countries such as Canada the revenue-raising function is relatively unimportant. Hence it and will be ignored in what follows.

The second type of protectionist policy restricts the *quantity* of the imported commodity. A common example is the **import quota**, by which the importing country sets a maximum on the quantity of some commodity that may be imported each year. Increasingly popular, however, is the **voluntary export restriction (VER)** by which an exporting country agrees to limit the amount it sells to a second country. In 1983 Canada and the United States negotiated VERs with Japan. The Japanese government agreed to restrict total sales of Japanese cars to those two countries for 3 years. When the agreements ran out in 1986, the Japanese continued to restrain their car sales by unilateral voluntary action.

The third type consists of domestic policies that reduce the demand for imported commodities. For example, the U.S. government recently required that all imported steel pipe be marked with its country of origin, which is costly and is alleged to reduce the quality of certain types of pipe. Whatever the apparent purpose of the legislation, its effect was to reduce the demand for imported steel pipe. Other countries restrict the ability of their citizens to purchase the foreign exchange needed to pay for the imports. This shifts the demand curve for imports to the left.

Figure 21-1 illustrates the three methods of restricting trade. Although each method achieves a reduction in imports, each has different side effects. Box 21-1 (p. 410) investigates the economics of VERs in more detail.

In addition to devices designed to restrict imports for protectionist purposes, there is also a series of devices designed to prevent what are called "unfair trade practices" by foreign firms or governments. The two most common of these are *antidumping duties* and *countervailing duties*. Laws relating to these measures are often called **fair trade laws.** Although not intended as tools of protectionism, they can be used as such, and we shall consider them later in the chapter.

Nominal and Effective Rates of Tariff

The rate of tariff charged on each commodity, called the **nominal rate of tariff**, does not necessarily show the degree of protection given to that commodity. Nominal rates frequently understate the degree of protection offered to domestic manufacturing industries and a better measure is provided by what is called the effective tariff rate.

The distinction between nominal and effective rates of tariff arises whenever imported raw materials or semi-finished goods carry a lower rate of duty than imports of the final manufactured goods that embody these intermediate products. When the final good is made abroad, the duty for manufactured goods is applied to the entire price of that good, even though the price includes the values of the raw ma-

FIGURE 21-1 **Three Ways of Reducing Imports**

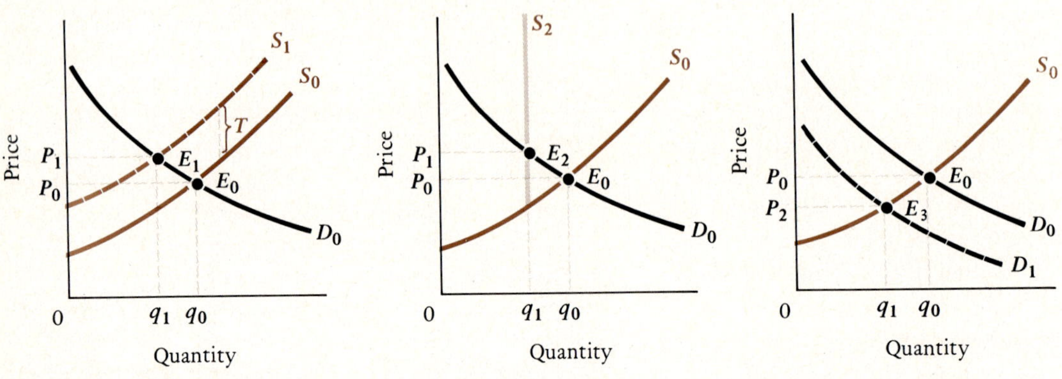

(i) An upward shift in the supply curve caused by a tariff

(ii) A shift in the supply curve caused by a quota

(iii) A shift in the demand curve caused by nontariff barriers

The government can restrict imports by policies that raise the price of the commodity, that directly reduce the quantity imported, or that reduce the demand for the commodity. In all three graphs, D_0 is the domestic demand and S_0 is the foreign supply to the domestic market of some commodity that is not produced domestically. P_0 and q_0 are the equilibrium price and quantity, but the government wishes to reduce the quantity of imports, and hence the quantity of consumption, to q_1.

In part (i) the government adopts a specific tariff that raises by T per unit the price at which any quantity will be supplied. This shifts the supply curve vertically by the amount of the tariff to S_1 and achieves a new equilibrium at E_1.

In part (ii) the government sets a maximum quantity of q_1 that can be imported. The new supply curve follows the old curve S_0 between 0 and q_1 but then follows the vertical line S_2 at quantity q_1. The new equilibrium is at E_2.

In part (iii) the government causes demand to shift leftward to D_1 by such policies as limiting importers' rights to purchase either the commodity or the foreign exchange needed to pay for it. In this case a new equilibrium occurs at E_3.

terials and semi-finished goods that it embodies. When the final good is produced domestically, the raw materials and semi-finished goods enter at the lower rate of tariff. For this reason a tariff of, say, 10 percent on the final good will protect a domestic producer that is much more than 10 percent less efficient than its foreign competitor.

To illustrate this important point, consider an example. A product is manufactured in both Canada and the United States using a Canadian raw material. The raw material is assumed to enter the United States duty free, but the manufactured good is subject to a 10 percent tariff. Further assume that when the product is manufactured in Canada, the raw material accounts for half the cost of the final product and the other half is value added by the Canadian manufacturer. Because of the 10 percent tariff, a unit of output that costs $1.00 to produce in Canada will sell in the United States for $1.10.

Now consider the position of a U.S. manufacturer who is assumed to be less efficient than the Canadian manufacturer. Let the American firm's production costs be 20 percent higher than those of the Canadian firm. Thus to produce one unit of output, the raw material costs the U.S. firm $.50, but its other costs—including the opportunity costs of its capital—are $.60 (i.e., 20 percent higher than the Canadian manufacturer's costs of $.50.) This gives the U.S. firm a final price of $1.10, which is just low enough to compete against the tariff-burdened Canadian import.

In this example, a tariff of 10 percent on the value of the final product is sufficient to protect a U.S. firm that is 20 percent less efficient than its Canadian competitor. To measure this effect, the **effective rate of tariff** expresses the tariff as a percentage of the *value added* by the exporting industry in question. Thus the effective American rate of tariff on the Canadian manufacturing industry in the example is 20 percent, whereas the nominal tariff on manufactured goods is only 10 percent.

The Case for Protectionism

Two kinds of arguments for protection are commonly offered. The first concerns national objectives other than output; the second concerns the desire to increase domestic national income, possibly at the expense of total world income.

Objectives Other Than Maximizing National Income

It is quite possible to accept the proposition that national income is higher with free trade and yet rationally oppose free trade because of a concern with policy objectives other than maximizing per capita national income. For example, comparative advantage might dictate that a country should specialize in producing a narrow range of commodities. The government might decide, however, that there are distinct social advantages to encouraging a more diverse economy. Citizens would be given a wider range of occupations, and the social and psychological advantages of diversification would more than compensate for a reduction in living standards by, say, 5 percent below what they could be with complete specialization of production according to comparative advantage.

For a very small country, specializing in the production of only a few commodities—though dictated by comparative advantage—may involve risks that a country does not wish to take. One such risk is that technological advances may render its basic product obsolete. Everyone understands this risk, but there is debate about what governments can do about it. The pro-tariff argument is that the government can encourage a more diversified economy by protecting industries that otherwise could not compete. Opponents argue that governments, being naturally influenced by political motives, are in the final analysis poor judges of what industries can be protected to produce diversification at a reasonable cost.

Another risk is cyclical fluctuations in the prices of basic commodities, which may face depressed prices for years at a time and then enjoy periods of very high prices. The national income of a country specializing in the production of such commodities will be subject to wide fluctuations. Even though the average income level over a long period might be higher if specialization in the production of a few basic commodities were allowed, the serious social problems associated with a widely fluctuating national income may make the government decide to sacrifice some income in order to reduce fluctuations. The government might use protectionist policies to encourage the expansion of several less cyclically sensitive industries.

Although most people would agree that, other things being equal, they would prefer more income to less, it can be perfectly rational for a nation to choose to sacrifice some income in order to achieve other goals. Economists can do three things when faced with such reasons for imposing tariffs. First, they can see if the proposed tariff really does achieve the ends suggested. Second, they can calculate the cost of the tariff in terms of lowered living standards. Third, they can check policy alternatives to see if there are other means of achieving the stated goal at lower cost in terms of lost output.

The Objective of Maximizing National Income

Next we consider four important arguments for the use of tariffs when the objective is to make national income as large as possible.

To alter the terms of trade. Trade restrictions can be used to turn the terms of trade in favor of countries that produce and export a large fraction of the world's supply of some commodity. They can also

BOX 21-1

Import Restrictions on Japanese Cars: Tariffs or Quotas?

In the early 1980s imports of Japanese cars seriously threatened the automobile industries of the United States, Canada, and Western Europe. While continuing to espouse relatively free trade as a long-term policy, the American and Canadian governments argued that the domestic industry needed short-term protection. This protection was to tide it over the period of transition it faced as smaller cars became the typical North American household's vehicle. Once the enormous investment needed to transform the North American auto industry had been made and new models had gained acceptance, it was hoped that free trade could be restored and the North American industry asked to stand up to foreign competition.

But how was the temporary protection to be achieved? Voluntary export restrictions (VERs) mutually agreed on by the two governments seemed the easiest route. An agreement was reached severely limiting the number of Japanese cars to be exported to Canada. (A similar agreement was reached between the Japanese and U.S. governments.)

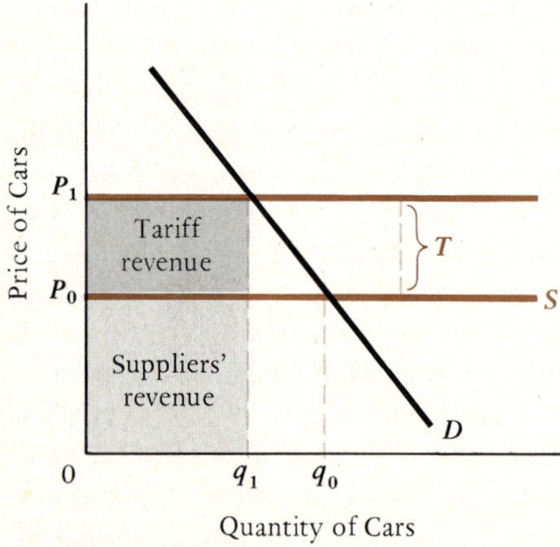

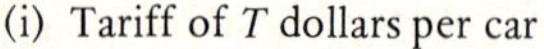

(i) Tariff of T dollars per car

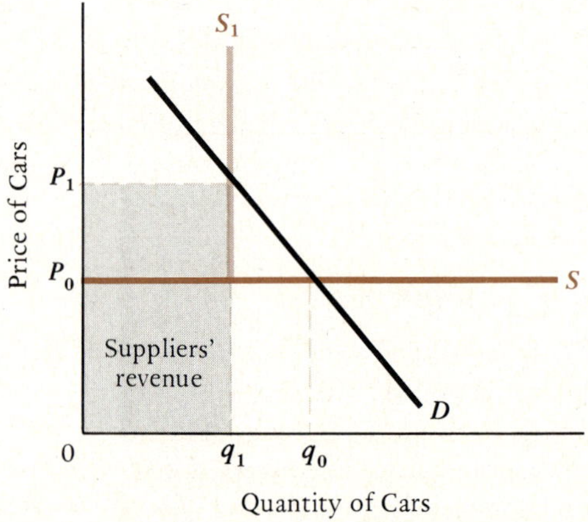

(ii) Quota of q_1 cars

be used to turn the terms of trade in favor of countries that constitute a large fraction of the world demand for some commodity that they import.

When the OPEC countries restricted their output of oil in the 1970s, they were able to drive the price of oil up relative to the prices of other traded goods. This turned the terms of trade in their favor; for every barrel of oil exported, they were able to obtain a larger quantity of imports. When the output of oil grew greatly in the mid 1980s, the relative price of oil fell dramatically, and the terms of trade turned unfavorably to the oil-exploring companies. These are illustrations of how changes in the quantities of exports can affect the terms of trade.

Now consider a country that provides a large fraction of the total demand for some product that it imports. By restricting its demand for that product through tariffs it can force the price of that product down. This turns the terms of trade in its favor because it can now get more units of imports per unit of exports.

Both of these techniques lower world output. They can, however, make it possible for a small group of countries to gain because they get a suffi-

What does theory predict to be the economic difference between VERs and tariffs? In both cases imports are restricted and the resulting scarcity supports a higher market price. With a tariff the extra market value is appropriated by the government of the importing country—in this case the Canadian government. With a VER the extra market value accrues to the goods' suppliers—in this case the Japanese car makers and their Canadian retailers.

Both cases are illustrated in the figure. We assume that the Canadian market provides a small enough part of total Japanese car sales to leave the Japanese willing to supply at their fixed list price all the cars that are demanded in Canada. This is the price P_0 in both parts of the figure. Given the Canadian demand curve for Japanese cars, D, there are q_0 cars sold before restrictions are imposed.

In part (i) Canada places a tariff of T per unit on Japanese cars, raising their price in Canada to p_1 and lowering sales to q_1. Suppliers' revenue is shown by the light shaded area. Canadian government tariff revenue is shown by the dark shaded area.

In part (ii) a VER of q_1 is imposed, making the supply curve vertical at q_1. The market-clearing price is P_1. The suppliers' revenue is the whole shaded area (P_1 times q_1).

In both cases the shortage of Japanese cars drives up their price, creating a substantial margin over costs. Under a tariff the Canadian government captures the margin. Under a VER policy, however, the margin accrues to the Japanese manufacturers.

Although this is a simplified picture, it captures the essence of what actually happened. First, while sellers of North American cars were keeping prices as low as possible and sometimes offering rebates on slow-selling models, Japanese cars were listed at healthy profit margins. Second, while it was always possible for the buyer of a North American car to negotiate a good discount off the list price, Japanese cars usually sold for their full list price. Third, since Japanese manufacturers were not allowed to supply all the cars they could sell in Canada, they had to choose which types of cars to supply. Not surprisingly, they tended to satisfy fully the demand for their more expensive cars, which have larger profit margins, and to restrict exports of the less expensive cars with lower profit margins. This change in the "product mix" of Japanese cars exported to Canada raised the average profit per car exported. The VERs were thus very costly to North American consumers and an enormous profit boon to Japanese car manufacturers. Indeed, it was estimated that North American consumers paid about $150,000 per year for each job saved in the American or Canadian car industry and that most of this went to Japanese producers.

ciently larger share of the smaller world output. However, if foreign countries retaliate by raising their tariffs, the ensuing tariff war can easily leave every country with a lowered income.

To protect against "unfair" actions by foreign firms and governments. Tariffs may be used to prevent foreign industries from gaining an advantage over domestic industries by use of predatory practices that will harm domestic industries and hence lower national income. Two common practices are subsidies paid by foreign governments to their exporters and dumping by foreign firms. Such practices are called "unfair trade practices," and the laws that deal with them are called "fair trade laws." The circumstances under which dumping and foreign subsidization provide a valid argument for tariffs are considered in detail later in this chapter.

To protect infant industries. The oldest valid argument for protectionism as a means of raising living standards concerns economies of scale. It is usually called the **infant industry argument.** If an industry has large economies of scale, costs and prices will be high when the industry is small but will fall as the industry grows. In such industries the country first in the field has a tremendous advantage. A newly developing country may find that in the early stages of development its industries are unable to compete with established foreign rivals. A trade restriction may protect these industries from foreign competition while they grow up. When they are large enough, they will be able to produce as cheaply as foreign rivals and thus be able to compete without protection.

To encourage learning by doing. Learning by doing, which we discussed in Chapter 20, suggests that the existing pattern of comparative advantage need not be taken as immutable. If a country can learn enough by producing commodities in which it currently is at a comparative disadvantage, it may gain in the long run by specializing in those commodities and developing a comparative advantage in them as the learning process lowers their costs.

Learning by doing is an example of what in Chapter 20 we called dynamic comparative advantages. The successes of such *newly industrializing countries* (the so-called NICs) as Brazil, Hong Kong, Korea, Singapore, and Taiwan seemed to many observers to be based on acquired skills and government policies that create favorable business conditions. This gave rise to the theory that comparative advantages can change and can be developed by suitable government policies.

Protecting a domestic industry from foreign competition may give its management the time to learn to be efficient and its labor force the time to acquire needed skills. If so, protection of the industry against foreign competition while a dynamic comparative advantage is being developed may pay in the very long run.

This route was followed by Canada, starting in 1879, when high tariffs were first introduced. Canadian industry grew up sheltered against foreign competition by these tariffs. It served mainly the domestic market. Then, starting in 1935, Canadian tariffs were reduced over the next 50 years. Today, although tariff protection is still substantial on some products, many Canadian manufacturing industries hold their own in world competition with minimal or nonexistent tariff protection.

Some countries have clearly succeeded in developing strong comparative advantages in targeted industries, but others have failed. One reason such policies sometimes fail is that protecting local industries from foreign competition may make the industries unadaptive and complacent. Another reason is the difficulty of identifying the industries that will be able to succeed in the long run. All too often the protected infant grows up to be a weakling requiring permanent tariff protection for its continued existence. Or else the rate of learning is slower than for similar industries in countries that do not provide protection from the chill winds of international competition. In these instances the anticipated comparative advantage never materializes.

How Much Protectionism?

So far we have seen that there is a strong case for allowing free trade in order to realize the gains from trade but that there are also some reasons for departing from completely free trade.

It is not necessary to choose between free trade on the one hand and absolute protectionism on the other. A country can have some trade and some protectionism, too.

Free Trade Versus No Trade

It would undoubtedly be possible to grow coffee beans in Canadian greenhouses and to synthesize much of the oil we require in our factories (as Germany did during the Second World War). But the cost in terms of other commodities forgone would be huge because these artificial means of production require lavish inputs of factors of production. It would likewise be possible for a tropical country, currently producing foodstuffs, to set up industries to produce all the manufactured products that it consumes. But for a small country without natural advantages in industrial production, the cost in terms of resources used could be enormous. It is thus clear that there is a large gain to all countries in having specialization and trade. The real output and consumption of all countries would be very much lower if each chose to produce domestically all the goods it consumed.

In an all-or-nothing choice, almost all countries would choose free trade over no trade.

A Little More Trade Versus a Little Less Trade

Today we have trade among nations, but that trade is not perfectly free. Table 21-1 shows the levels of tariffs on selected commodities in force today.

Would we be better off if today's barriers to trade were reduced or increased a little bit? This question shifts the focus of our discussion considerably, for it is quite a jump from the proposition that "free trade is better than no trade" to the proposition that "a little less trade restriction than we have at present is better than a little more." This question directs attention away from the essentially irrelevant issue of the cost of prohibitive tariffs toward the important issue of the cost of the present tariff.

The Cost of the Canadian Tariff

The cost of the Canadian tariff can be studied in three stages: first, the cost under the classical as-

TABLE 21-1 Current Tariffs on Industrial Products by Sector: Canada, United States, and All Industrial Countries ***(percentage)***[a]

Sector	Canada	United States	All industrial countries
Textiles	16.7	9.2	8.5
Wearing apparel	24.2	22.7	17.5
Leather products	6.3	4.2	3.0
Footwear	21.9	8.8	12.1
Wood products	3.2	1.7	1.9
Furniture and fixtures	14.3	4.1[b]	7.3
Paper and paper products	6.7	0.2	4.2
Printing and publishing	1.0	0.7	1.5
Chemicals	7.5	2.4	6.7
Rubber products	6.7	2.5	4.1
Nonmetal mineral products	6.4	5.3	4.0
Glass and glass products	7.2	6.2	7.9
Iron and steel	5.4	3.6	4.4
Nonferrous metals	2.0	0.7	1.6
Metal products	8.5	4.8	6.3
Nonelectrical machinery	4.5	3.3	4.7
Electrical machinery	5.8	4.4	7.1
Transportation equipment	1.6	2.5	6.0
Miscellaneous manufactures	5.4	4.2	4.7
All industries	5.2	4.3	5.8

Source: A. V. Deardorff and R. M. Stern, "Economic Effects of Complete Elimination of Post-Tokyo Round Tariffs," in W. R. Cline, ed., *Trade Policy in the 1980s* (Washington, D.C.: Institute for International Economics, 1983), pp. 674–675.

[a] Weighted by own-country imports, excluding petroleum.

[b] Estimated from incomplete data.

Canada remains a relatively high tariff country. In spite of having cut its tariffs significantly over the past several decades, Canada remains a relatively high tariff country compared to both the United States, its largest trading partner, and to the average of all industrial countries. Note that a few Canadian tariffs are still over 20 percent. The data show tariff rates rulling after the last round of tariff negotiations had been phased in at the end of 1986.

sumption of constant costs in all industries; second, the cost when economies of scale are allowed for; and third, the cost when certain longer-run issues are also brought into consideration.

Constant costs. Most early measurements of the cost of the Canadian tariff assumed constant costs. It was assumed that the costs of producing all commodities would remain unchanged when tariffs were removed. Under this assumption the cost of the tariff was typically measured to be somewhere between 1 and 2 percent of Canadian GDP.

To gain some insight into these figures, compare the effects of a 20 percent uniform effective rate of tariff with those of free trade. Tariffs of 20 percent will protect industries that are up to 20 percent less efficient than foreign competitors. If the costs of the various tariff-protected industries were spread out evenly, some would be 20 percent less efficient than their foreign competitors and others only 1 percent less efficient. Their average inefficiency would be about half the tariff rate, so they would be on average about 10 percent less efficient than their foreign competitors.

Suppose that as a result of tariffs, approximately 15 percent of a country's resources are allocated to industries different from the ones to which they would be allocated if there were no tariffs. If the average protected industry is 10 percent less efficient than its foreign rival, approximately 15 percent of a country's resources are producing on average about 10 percent less efficiently than they would be if there were no tariffs. This causes a reduction in national income on the order of 1.5 percent as a result of tariff protection.

Scale effects. Many industries produce a wide range of differentiated products; for example, over 300 types and grades of paper products are commonly produced by the paper industry. Furthermore, technological developments are constantly changing the products that can be produced.

Each differentiated product has associated with it fixed costs for product development and for product-specific machinery. Like all fixed costs, they give rise to a range of falling unit costs as the overheads are spread over more units when output rises. Unit costs will start to rise only when scale diseconomies are strong enough to offset the effect of these falling overheads per unit of output. As a result, each line of differentiated goods has associated with it a minimum efficient scale that is often quite large.

The consequences of this large *MES* for firms serving the Canadian market were analyzed in an important study, Professors Harry Eastman and Stephen Stykholt of the University of Toronto. They argued, as shown in Figure 21-2, that the Canadian market is often not large enough to allow each dif-

FIGURE 21-2 Product-line Specialization by Canadian Firm

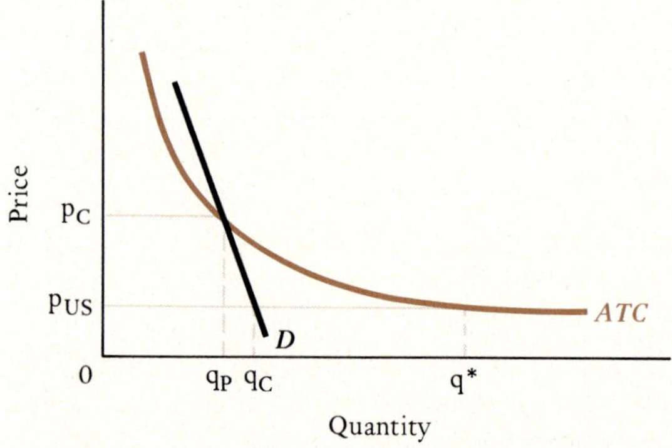

The Canadian market is often too small to allow Canadian firms to reach minimum efficient scale in a wide range of differentiated goods. The figure shows the average total cost curve for one product line in a firm producing many differentiated products. The Canadian demand curve for the product is *D*. The lowest price at which costs can be covered is p_C, where sales are q_C.

The U.S. market is so large that firms selling a range of differentiated products in that market can produce an output of each product that is at least as large as the *MES* of q^*. They thus achieve the price p_{US}.

If Canadian firms gain access to the U.S. market, they will specialize in a few product lines and produce at a volume sufficient to reach the *MES* of each. The outputs of these products will be q*, or more. This will allow cost to be covered at the price ruling in the American market, which is p_{US}.

ferentiated product to be produced at minimum efficient scale when each Canadian industry produces the whole range of products for the domestic market alone. Thus when tariffs protect Canadian firms selling solely for the home market, costs are considerably higher than they would be if the market were large enough to allow production to reach *MES* in each product line, as it often does in the large U.S. markets.

When tariffs are removed, the Canadian firms specialize in a reduced number of product lines, which they produce at their *MES*s, selling some of the output in the domestic market and exporting the rest. As a result, cost-reducing economies are achieved. Exports of some product lines go up, as do imports of other product lines. So trade increases on an intra-industry basis, and the advantages of efficiency in production are achieved without losing the advantages of diversity in consumption. This specialization in a narrowed range of product lines, with the resulting increase in intra-industry trade, is often referred to as *rationalization* of the domestic industry.

Such rationalization has occurred when tariffs have been reduced on Canadian-American trade as a result of successive rounds of negotiations under the General Agreement on Tariffs and Trade (GATT). It has often resulted from simple, profit maximizing reactions to changing market circumstances. It has sometimes resulted from conscious decisions made by multinational corporations to allow foreign subsidiaries to specialize in particular product lines, which they export to markets throughout the world. Yet other times it has resulted from international agreements, of which the best known is the Canadian-American Auto Pact of 1965. These types of rationalizations are further discussed in Box 21-2 and Box 21-3 that appear on pages 416 and 417.

Calculations allowing for these effects have been made by such Canadian economists as Richard Harris of Queen's University and David Cox of the University of Toronto. They suggest a cost of the tariff of between 5 to 10 percent of Canadian GDP.

Suppose that the cost of the Canadian tariff is 5 percent of GDP. That may not seem like a very large number, especially when one realizes that is the increase in GDP that economic growth produces on average every three or four years. Yet at 1987 prices it is $15 billion. That amount each year forever could buy a lot of hospitals, schools, medical research, and new energy supplies.

Longer-run considerations. Some people have argued that the cost of tariffs is low enough that Canada could afford to turn its back on attempts to liberalize international trade and adopt a policy of protecting many of our industries with new import restrictions. Before accepting such a conclusion, some long-run political and economic possibilities need to be considered. The world prosperity of recent decades has been built largely on a rising volume of relatively free international trade. There are real doubts that such prosperity could be maintained if the volume of trade were to shrink steadily because of growing trade barriers. Yet the pressure to use trade restrictions in troubled times is strong. If countries give in and begin to raise barriers moderately when the initial economic costs are not large, so strong are the political forces involved that there is no telling where the process, once begun, will end.

In today's world a country's products must stand up to international competition if they are to survive. Protection, by conferring a national monopoly, reduces the incentive for industries to fight to hold their own internationally. If any one country adopts high tariffs unilaterally, its domestic industries will become less competitive. Secure in their home market because of the tariff wall, they often become less and less competitive in the international market. However, as the gap between domestic and foreign industries widens, *any* tariff wall will provide less and less protection. Eventually, the domestic industries will be forced to meet the foreign competition or be eliminated by it. Meanwhile, domestic living standards will fall relative to foreign ones as an increasing productivity gap opens between domestic tariff-protected industries and foreign, internationally oriented ones.

Although restrictive policies have sometimes been pursued following a rational assessment of the approximate cost, it is hard to avoid the conclusion that more often than not, such policies are pursued for flimsy objectives or on fallacious grounds, with little idea of the actual costs involved. The very high

BOX 21-2

Rationalization by Formal Agreement: The Auto Pact

The Canadian automobile industry was established under tariff protection. The tariff caused the major U.S. automobile manufacturers to export to Canada *indirectly* by establishing branch plants within Canada.

By the late 1950s Canadian policymakers had become concerned about the structure of the Canadian automobile industry. The protection offered by the tariff was supposed to enable the industry to become efficient and to compete on its own against foreign imports. This had not happened; Canadian costs and prices remained well above their U.S. counterparts. A Royal Commission on the Automobile Industry led to the enactment of the Automobile Products Trade Act (the Auto Pact) in 1965. As a result, the Canadian automobile industry was rationalized.

Prior to the enactment of the Auto Pact, a wide range of cars was being produced in Canada. In 1964 Ford was producing 60 different models of five distinct lines at its single Canadian plant. Because this entailed short production runs, the industry was unable to achieve its *MES* and hence operated inefficiently.

The Auto Pact allowed the tariff-free importation of U.S. automobile products by Canadian *manufacturers* on a dollar-for-dollar basis with exports of Canadian products. Imports not matched by exports were subject to a "penalty" duty. As a result, Canadian plants specialized in particular product lines and exported most of the cars that they produced. In return, the manufacturers were able to import a wide variety of models for sale in Canada; the benefits of increased efficiency were gained without forsaking product variety in domestic consumption.

One problem with such a scheme is that the domestic economy becomes so narrowly specialized that it is vulnerable to swings in demand. In 1980 the Canadian auto industry was especially hard hit because it had specialized in large, fuel-inefficient models and in expensive specialty models, both of which were extremely vulnerable during the energy crunch. But when a fall in energy prices caused a revival in the demand for larger cars, Canadian producers benefited from their specialization.

In recent years the Auto Pact has been subject to much analysis. Some saw it as an example of sectorial free trade, pointing the way to a broader Canadian-American free trade agreement. Others saw it as a triumph of managed trade that was anything but free. The key aspect in this debate was the existence of safeguards that prevent the industry from transferring the bulk of its activities to one country or the other. These safeguards have never needed to be invoked in recent years, thus giving ammunition to those who argue that the pact is essentially a free trade arrangement. "No," say those on the other side, "the very existence of the safeguards, even if they are not invoked, is what holds a reasonable balance of production between the two countries." Since unit costs are significantly lower in Canadian auto plants than in U.S. ones, it is hard to believe that the auto manufacturers need government sanctions to induce them to maintain production in Canada at least under current conditions.

Another future problem for the auto pact lies in the overcapacity that is predicted for the North American industry in general, and for Canada in particular, by the 1990s. When the foreign-owned plants currently planned or under construction in Canada are completed, Canada will have to become a substantial exporter of Canadian-built foreign cars if the capacity is to be fully used. Looming excess capacity suggests layoffs and plant closures, and an economic and political debate relating to how they are to be distributed between the United States and the Canadian plants. Such issues will no doubt put heavy strains on the Auto Pact if it has not already been abrogated or superceded by some new arrangement.

BOX 21-3

Rationalization by Manufacturer's Choice: World Product Mandating

One way in which an inefficient domestic industry previously dependent on protection could survive a move to free trade would be for it to rationalize its product lines in the ways discussed on page 414. This has happened as a result of explicit policy in the auto industry. But that is not the only way it can happen. Large multinational corporations often permit foreign "branch plants" to develop particular product lines both for sale in home market and for export into world markets. This is called "world product mandating." It involves specialization in production in order to exploit economies of scale. It may also involve transferring increased managerial and marketing responsibility to the former branch plant.

In Canada product mandating has been common in the electrical products and home appliance industries (where such firms as Westinghouse and Black & Decker have led the way) and in the relatively high-technology computer and office machine industries (where such giants as IBM, NCR, and Xerox have adopted the strategy).

In the 12 years since the local management of Black & Decker Canada persuaded its parent to grant it world rights to produce the company's orbital sander, the subsidiary has increased plant capacity fivefold, sales by nearly 25 percent a year, and staff to include 24 full-time design engineers. The company has gone on to develop several other new products for worldwide distribution—including the popular Workmate handyman's bench—and export sales now account for close to half of the Canadian Company's production.

Westinghouse has operated in Canada since 1903. Until 1950, the profit ratios of the Canadian enterprise were better than those of the parent company, on the average, in three of every four years. Then Westinghouse Canada's fortunes began to slip. Earnings declined, employment levels slipped downhill, and a number of product lines were phased out.

In this situation, the parent company executives faced a choice—to make a place for Westinghouse Canada in their worldwide activities or to sell off the investment—and they chose to integrate the Canadian operation into the company's global production and marketing operations. The orientation of the Canadian operation was changed from that of a branch plant to that of a rationalized operation, with active participation in the marketing activities of the multinational company.

In the early 1980s, the company's exports grew at twice the rate of domestic sales; research and development activities for specific products destined for world markets tripled; corporate capital spending doubled; and productivity improved more rapidly than that of the parent company.

World product mandating can be beneficial. Yet the policy is not without its critics. Many believe that the narrow product specialization leaves the economy vulnerable to shifts in demand or cost conditions. Others believe that ironically, if world mandating is too successful, strong foreign subsidiaries could hinder the development of similar skills and technology by truly Canadian companies. But even critics are willing to admit that in an economy where non-Canadian companies are a fact of life, world product mandating is an excellent way to achieve the efficiency of large-scale production.

---

tariffs in the United States during the 1920s and 1930s are a conspicuous example. The current clamor for the government to do something about the competition from Japan, Korea, and other countries of the East may well be another.

Fallacious Trade Policy Arguments

We have seen that there are gains from a high volume of international trade and specialization. We have also seen that there can be valid arguments for a moderate degree of protectionism. There are also many claims that do not advance the debate. Fallacious arguments are heard on both sides, and they color much of the popular discussion. These arguments have been around for a long time, but their survival does not make them true. We will examine them now to see where their fallacies lie.

Fallacious Free Trade Arguments

Free trade always benefits all countries. This is not necessarily so. We saw earlier that a small group of countries may gain by restricting trade in order to get a sufficiently favorable shift in their terms of trade. Such countries would lose if they gave up these tariffs and adopted free trade unilaterally.

Infant industries never abandon their tariff protection. It is sometimes argued that granting protection to infant industries is a mistake because these industries seldom admit to growing up and will cling to their protection even when fully grown. But infant industry tariffs are a mistake *only* if these industries never grow up. In this case tariffs would be required permanently to protect a weak industry never able to compete on an equal footing in the international market. But if the industries do grow up and achieve the expected scale economies, the fact that like any special interest group they cling to their tariff protection is not a sufficient reason for denying protection to genuine infant industries. When economies of scale are realized, the real costs of production are reduced and resources are freed for other uses. If the tariff is retained, consumers will pay more and owners will make higher profits than if the tariff were removed. Whether or not the tariff or other trade barriers remain, however, a cost saving has been effected by the scale economies, and total GDP will be increased.

Fallacious Protectionist Arguments

Prevent exploitation. According to the exploitation theory, trade can never be mutually advantageous; one trading partner must always gain at the other's expense. Thus the weaker trading partner must protect itself by restricting its trade with the stronger partner. But by showing that it is possible for both parties to gain from trade, the principle of comparative advantage refutes the exploitation doctrine of trade. When opportunity cost ratios differ in two countries, specialization and the accompanying trade make it possible to produce more of all commodities and thus make it possible for both parties to consume more as a result of trade than they could get in its absence.

Keep the money at home. This argument says, If I buy a foreign good, I have the good and the foreigner has the money, whereas if I buy the same good locally, I have the good and our country has the money, too.

The argument is based on a misconception. It assumes that domestic money actually goes abroad physically when imports are purchased and that trade flows only in one direction. But when Canadian importers purchase Italian-made goods, they do not send dollars abroad. They (or their financial agents) buy Italian lire and use them to pay the Italian manufacturers. They purchase the lire on the foreign exchange market by giving up dollars to someone who wishes to use them for expenditure *in Canada.* Even if the money did go abroad physically—that is, if an Italian firm accepted a shipload of Canadian dollars—it would be because that firm (or someone to whom it could sell the dollars) wanted them to spend in the only country where they are legal tender, Canada.

Dollars ultimately do no one any good except as purchasing power. It would be miraculous if colored pieces of paper could be exported in return for real goods; after all, the Bank of Canada has the power to create as much new money as it wishes. It is only because Canadian money can buy Canadian commodities and assets that others want it.

Protect against low-wage foreign labor. Surely, the argument says, the products of low-wage countries will drive Canadian products from the market, and the high Canadian standard of living will be dragged down to that of its poor trading partners. Arguments of this sort have swayed many voters through the years.

As a prelude to considering them, stop and think what the argument would imply if taken out of the international context and put into a local one, where the same principles govern the gains from trade. Is it really impossible for a rich person to gain from trading with a poor person? Would the local millionaire be better off if she did all her own typing, gardening, and cooking? No one believes that a rich person cannot gain from trading with those who are less rich. Why then must a rich group of people lose from trading with a poor group? "Well," you say, "the poor group will price goods too cheaply." Does anyone believe that consumers lose from buying in a discount house or a supermarket just because the prices are lower there than at the old-fashioned corner store? Consumers gain when they can buy the same goods at a lower price. If the Koreans pay low wages and sell their goods cheaply, *Korean* labor may suffer, but we will gain because we obtain their goods at a low cost in terms of the goods that we must export in return. The cheaper our imports are, the better off we are in terms of the goods and services available for domestic consumption.

As we saw in Chapter 20, the gains from trade depend on comparative, not absolute, advantages. World production is higher when any two areas, say, Canada and Japan, specialize in the production of the goods for which they have a comparative advantage than when they both try to be self-sufficient.

Might it not be possible, however, that Japan will undersell Canada in all lines of production and thus appropriate all, or more than all, the gains for itself, leaving Canada no better off, or even worse off, than if it had no trade with Japan? The answer is no. The reason for this depends on the behavior of exchange rates, which we shall study in Chapter 41. As we shall see, equality of demand and supply on foreign exchange market ensures that trade flows in both directions.

Imports can be obtained only by spending the currency of the country that makes the imports. Claims to this currency can be obtained only by exporting goods and services or by borrowing. Thus, lending and borrowing aside, imports must equal exports. All trade must be in two directions; we can buy only if we can also sell.

In the long run trade cannot hurt a country by causing it to import without exporting.

Trade, then, always provides scope for international specialization, with each country producing and exporting goods for which it has a comparative advantage and importing goods for which it does not.

Protect against changing comparative advantage. Although there is an important grain of truth in the proposition that low-wage countries can sometimes undersell high-wage countries, this does not constitute a valid reason for tariffs. It is important to understand this grain of truth so as not to get it confused with the fallacious argument that high-wage countries cannot trade profitably with low-wage countries.

When, as has happened in recent decades, some underdeveloped countries begin to develop the skills and acquire the capital necessary for manufacturing, they will usually develop a comparative advantage in goods at the cheap end of the market; inexpensive shoes and shirts are typical examples. Industries in these developing countries will then begin to undersell similar industries in developed, higher-wage countries.

Owners and workers in these threatened industries will then call out for protection against the imports from cheap-labor countries. Often the government of the developed country will succumb to such pleas—certainly the Canadian government often has. Let us see what the result will be.

First, the government will be trying to freeze the country's industrial structure in the face of world change, an attempt that may succeed in the short term but one that becomes increasingly difficult and costly over the longer term. Second, it will be denying the benefits of economic growth to the poorer countries, which cannot develop an industrial structure unless they can sell their goods to other countries—particularly, as so often is the case, if their domestic markets are small. Third, they will be harming their own consumers by shutting out low-priced imports that are cheaper than their domestically manufactured equivalents, and the persons most hurt will be the lower-income groups, since it is usually cheap, lower-grade products that are the object of this type of protectionism. Fourth, they will also be denying markets to their efficient export industries because the developing countries can buy from the developed countries only if they can sell to them.

If instead of giving in to the pleas for protectionism the government allows the market to work, the developed country's industries producing the cheap products will decline, and resources will move into the production of more expensive products that use the skilled labor and abundant capital of the developed country. There is a good case for easing the transition with such measures as assistance for retraining and relocating labor. But a policy of accepting the change will produce higher living standards than a policy of resisting it.

Exports raise living standards; imports lower them. Exports add to aggregate demand; imports subtract from it. Thus, other things being equal, exports tend to increase national income and imports to reduce it. Surely, then, it is desirable to encourage exports and discourage imports. This is an appealing argument, but it is incorrect.

Exports raise national income by adding to the value of domestic output, but they do not add to the value of domestic consumption. In fact, exports are goods produced at home and consumed abroad, while imports are goods produced abroad and consumed at home. The standard of living in a country depends on the goods and services available for *consumption*, not on what is produced.

If exports were really good and imports really bad, a fully employed economy that managed to increase exports without a corresponding increase in imports ought to be better off. Such a change, however, would result in a reduction in current standards of living, because when more goods are sent abroad and no more are brought in from abroad, the total goods available for domestic consumption must fall.

The living standards of a country depend on the goods and services consumed in that country. The importance of exports is that they permit imports to be made. This two-way international exchange is valuable because more goods can be imported than could be obtained if the same goods were produced at home.

Create domestic jobs and reduce unemployment. It is sometimes said that an economy with substantial unemployment, such as that of Canada in the 1930s or mid-1980s, provides an exception to the case for freer trade. Suppose that tariffs or import quotas cut the imports of Japanese cars, Korean textiles, Italian shoes, and French wine. Surely, the argument maintains, this will create more employment for Oshawa auto workers, Toronto textile workers, Montreal shoe factories, and Okanagan Valley farm workers. The answer is that it will—initially. But the Japanese, Koreans, Italians, and French can buy from Canada only if they get Canadian dollars from those who have goods in Canada. The decline in their sales of autos, textiles, shoes, and wine will decrease their purchases of Canadian machinery, aircraft, grain, and vacations in Canada. Jobs will be lost in our export industries and gained in industries that formerly faced competition from imports. The likely long-term effect is that overall unemployment will not be reduced but will merely be redistributed among industries. Since the export industries that contract tend to be more efficient than the competing import industries that expand, this policy tends to reallocate resources from more to less efficient lines of production and hence to reduce overall GDP.

Industries and unions that compete with imports tend to favor protectionism, whereas those with large exports tend to favor more trade. Most economists are highly skeptical about the government's ability to reduce overall unemployment through protectionism.

To offset an overvalued exchange rate. To complete the list of fallacious arguments for protection, we must add a point that we cannot study in detail until Chapter 40, when we have learned about the forces that determine a country's exchange rate.

In the mid 1980s the U.S. dollar had an extremely high value on the foreign exchange market. This made it difficult for American firms to sell in foreign markets but easy for foreign firms to sell in the American market. The pressure on American industries led to growing pressure in Congress to alleviate the plight of American manufacturers by raising trade restrictions. As we shall see in Chapter 40, the need to import foreign capital to finance the American government's budget deficit led to the overvalued exchange rate for the U.S. dollar. Until the government's deficit is made low enough to be financed by domestic rather than foreign borrowing, no amount of tariffs can help to bring down the exchange rate and so aid American exporters.

Trade Policy in the World Today

The Use of Nontariff Barriers

We have noted that a nontariff barrier is anything other than an import duty that restricts trade. It may take any of the three forms illustrated in Figure 21-1 by raising the price of the imported good, directly restricting its quantity, or shifting the demand for imports. In recent years protectionist-minded countries have made increasing use of nontariff barriers to replace tariff barriers that have been reduced by international agreement.

While the Canadian and American governments mainly impose low or moderate tariffs, each uses many nontariff barriers to protect particular domestic industries that have been losing ground to foreign competition in the 1980s. Some of these restrictions have been negotiated; others have been imposed unilaterally.

Negotiated VERs

In the late 1950s the textile and clothing industries in many advanced industrial nations saw their market shares reduced by a rising volume of trade from Hong Kong, Korea, the Philippines, and other newly industrializing nations. In response to a United States initiative, international meetings were held in 1961. Out of these meetings came the *multi-fiber agreements* (MFAs), providing maximum annual quotas for each exporting textile-producing country for a 20-year period. Starting in 1981 many of these agreements were renegotiated, generally leading to policies that were more rather than less restrictive.

Similar "orderly marketing agreements" have been accepted by foreign countries with respect to footwear in 1977, color television sets in 1977, and citizens band radio sets in 1978. Lobbyists for many other industries have urged similar agreements for their products. One of the most recent agreements, which limited Japanese car exports to Canada and the United States, is considered in Box 21-1.

Why, one may ask, would a country such as Korea agree voluntarily to limit its profitable exports to North America when it needs the revenue and foreign exchange that its exports earn? The answer is that the United States and Canada are so needed as markets and allies that their "requests" have the weight of veiled threats.

Unilaterally Imposed Antidumping Rules

When a firm sells abroad at lower prices than it charges domestically, it is said to be *dumping*. (Occasionally *dumping* is defined as selling abroad at a price below total cost, but we shall use the conventional definition just given.) Dumping has occurred recently, for example, with exports of Japanese steel into North American markets. Not surprisingly, the North American steel industry has requested help from their respective governments.

Motives for dumping. Japanese producers dump steel in North America because it is profitable for them to do so. But there are several different reasons why dumping may prove profitable to them.

1. It may be a sensible long-term strategy because the Japanese home market is permanently too small to support an industry of efficient size. In

such circumstances, to have an efficient industry requires an export market, but to achieve that market, a low-price policy may be required. Dumping in this case, by making it possible to produce output at the lowest possible cost per unit, benefits both domestic and foreign customers.

2. It may be a sensible cyclical strategy to provide a market for output in periods when Japanese demand is low, thereby utilizing the capacity required to meet maximum Japanese demand in periods of boom and expansion. Sales in the export market simply permit Japanese production to continue on an even level over the cycle.
3. It may be a predatory strategy designed to destroy the foreign industry. After foreign plants have shut down, prices can be raised to exploit the foreigner's new dependence on imports.

Effects on the buying country. Suppose that Canada is the "beneficiary" of Japanese steel sold at less than the Japanese domestic price and (let us suppose) below the average cost of production in Canada. If such sales continue, they will either eliminate the Canadian industry or force it to become more efficient. This will benefit Canadian steel buyers for as long as they are able to buy cheaper steel.

No matter what the Japanese producers' motives, the Canadian steel industry and the United Steelworkers of America will want the government to stop this, for it threatens their profits and their jobs.

Suppose that the government chooses to look beyond the political pressures of the moment and to do what is best for the national interest. Here it matters which motivation explains the dumping. If the Japanese are prepared to supply cheap steel on a permanent basis, it would surely benefit Canadians to buy Japanese steel and use Canadian resources to produce something in which we have a comparative advantage. This is the case for doing nothing to protect the domestic steel industry.

However, if cheap Japanese steel would destroy the Canadian industry without replacing the need for it—that is, for either of the last two listed reasons—sufficient protection to preserve a viable industry may be required. This is the valid case for protectionism.

The problem for policy is to diagnose what is happening and to adopt rules that will preserve needed industries without depriving Canadian buyers of cheaper sources of supply.

Antidumping provisions. Under the Anti-Dumping Act of 1968, Canadian producers who believe that competing foreign goods are being dumped in Canada may complain to the deputy minister of national revenue. If, on the basis of an initial inquiry, the deputy minister finds that dumping that may cause material injury is occurring, he will impose a provisional duty and refer the case to the Anti-Dumping Tribunal (ADT). The ADT conducts a thorough investigation and makes a final recommendation to the minister. If material injury is found to be present (or anticipated), dumping duties will be levied at a rate to remove the effect of dumping on the Canadian price of the imported commodity.

Antidumping provisions have been increasingly applied in the 1980s. During the period starting in 1982, a number of developing countries that were under heavy pressure to export in order to earn the foreign currency needed to service their foreign debts were hit heavily by antidumping duties. These countries were forced to restrict their exports to the United States and Canada as a result of the provision that they could not sell below their average total cost even if they were doing so at home. Brazil, Argentina, and Guatemala, among other countries, were hurt by this measure.

Two features of the American antidumping system now in effect make it highly protectionist. First, *any* price discrimination is classified as dumping and thus subject to penalties. Thus the foreign prices become, in effect, minimum prices below which no foreign producer can risk selling. Thus the provisions inhibit foreign competition and serve as nontariff barriers to trade, both where dumping is beneficial to American interests and where it is not.

Second, U.S. law calculates the "margin of dumping" as the difference between the price charged in the American market and the foreign producer's "full allocated cost" (i.e., average total cost, including a normal return on capital). This means that if there is global excess demand so that the profit-maximizing price for all producers is below average total cost (but above average variable cost), foreign producers can be convicted of dumping in the U.S. market, even though their American selling prices are the same as their own domestic selling prices and even though they are not undercutting the prices charged by American producers. This latter provision makes U.S. antidumping laws highly protectionist, especially in periods of slack demand. The Canadian steel industry has been particularly hard hit by this provision.

Countervailing Duties

Countervailing duties were not designed to act as nontariff barriers, but rather as a means of creating a "level playing field" on which fair international competition could take place. North American firms often complain that they cannot compete against the bottomless purses of foreign governments. Subsidized foreign exports can be sold indefinitely in North America at prices that would guarantee losses in the absence of the subsidy. The object of countervail is to counteract the effect on price of the presence of such foreign subsidies.

If a domestic firm suspects the existence of such a subsidy and registers a complaint, the government is then required to make an investigation. For a countervailing duty to be levied, the investigation must find, first, that the foreign subsidy to the specific industry in question does exist and, second, that it is large enough to be a potential injury to competing domestic firms.

There is no doubt that countervailing duties have sometimes been used to remove the effects of "unfair" competition caused by foreign subsidies. Foreign governments complain, however, that countervail is also sometimes used as a thinly disguised barrier to trade. For example, a countervailing duty was placed on Canadian pork and hog exports to the United States after the finding that Canadian agricultural policy conferred a subsidy to Canadian producers of $.05 a pound, notwithstanding the fact that U.S. policies gave a subsidy to American producers of between $.10 and $.15 a pound. Commenting on this case, one observer said, "In allowing a countervailing duty based on the existence of any foreign subsidy, rather than on the net difference between the foreign and the American subsidy, countervail has proved itself to be a one-eyed referee."

So far countervailing duties have been used mainly by the United States. In 1986, however, when Canada placed a countervailing duty on corn imported from its neighbor to the south, this was the first time that an American export had ever been subject to countervail. There were indications that many other governments were studying the possibility of levying such duties on subsidized American exports. Observers feared the outbreak of a trade war of escalating countervailing duties.

International Agreements Concerning Trade and Tariffs

In the past any country could impose any desired set of tariffs on its imports. But when one country increases its tariffs, the action may trigger retaliatory changes by its trading partners. Just as an arms race can escalate, so can a tariff war; precisely this happened during the 1920s and early 1930s. Extended negotiations may then be required to undo the damage.

The General Agreement on Tariffs and Trade (GATT)

One of the most notable achievements of the post–World War II world in retreating from the high-water mark of protectionism in the 1930s was the General Agreement on Tariffs and Trade (GATT). Under this agreement GATT countries meet periodically to negotiate bilaterally on mutually advantageous cuts in tariffs. They agree in advance that any tariff cuts negotiated in this way will be extended to all member countries according to what is called the "most favored nation" principle. Significant tariff reductions have been effected by the member countries.

The two most recent rounds of GATT agreements have each reduced tariffs by about one-third.

The Kennedy Round negotiations were completed in 1967, and new rates were phased in over a five-year period ending in 1972. The Tokyo Round negotiations began in 1975 and were completed in 1979. The reductions began to take effect in 1981 and were completed in 1986.

Ironically, as that new round of reductions began, pressure was mounting in many countries to protect jobs at home through trade restrictions. Protectionist policies grew alarmingly in Europe. As time passed, even GATT itself came under attack. The worldwide recession that began in late 1981 was undoubtedly the main cause of this pressure. In addition, protectionist pressures in many countries were also created by the decline in the international competitiveness of traditional industries due to sharp changes in terms of trade. Also, under the impact of the high value of the U.S. dollar, protectionist pressures grew throughout the 1980s in the United States.

Although GATT has produced large reductions in *tariffs*, the results are a bit misleading in terms of the freedom of trade because of the growing use of nontariff barriers. One important feature of the Tokyo Round was the agreement, for the first time, on some very limited steps to restrict the growth of nontariff barriers.

In 1986 and 1987, preliminary meetings were held as preliminaries to a new round of GATT negotiations to take place in Uruguay. This round will grapple with two pressing issues: the growing worldwide use of nontariff barriers to trade and the need to develop rules for liberalizing trade in services, which is the most rapidly growing component of foreign trade.

Common Markets

A **common market** is an agreement among a group of countries to eliminate barriers to free trade among themselves, to present a common trading front to the rest of the world in terms of common barriers to trade, and to permit free movement of factors of production among member countries. The most important example came into being in 1957 when the Treaty of Rome brought together France, Germany, Italy, the Netherlands, Belgium, and Luxembourg in the European Economic Community (EEC). The original six were joined in 1973 by the United Kingdom, the Republic of Ireland, and Denmark; Greece entered in 1983, Portugal and Spain in 1986.

This organization, now known as the European Community (EC), is dedicated to bringing about free trade, complete mobility of factors of production, and the eventual harmonization of fiscal and monetary policies among the member countries. All tariffs for manufactured goods have been eliminated and much freedom of movement of labor and capital achieved. Movement toward the harmonization of economic and social policies and creation of a common monetary system seems once again to have gathered momentum, having been stalled for many years.

Other common markets have been formed, such as the Central American Common Market and the East African Community, but none has yet achieved the success of the EC.

Free Trade Associations

A **free trade association** allows for tariff-free trade between the member countries, but unlike a common market, it leaves each member free to levy its own tariffs on imports from other countries and to restrict the movement of factors of production among members. As a result, members must maintain customs points at their common borders (if such exist) to make sure that imports into the free trade area from the rest of the world do not all enter through the country levying the lowest tariff on each item.

The first important free trade association in the modern era was the European Free Trade Association (EFTA). It was formed in 1960 by a group of European countries unwilling to join the European Community because of the latter's all-embracing character. Not wanting to be left out of the gains from trade, they formed an association whose sole purpose was to remove tariffs among themselves and subsequently also with the members of the EC.

American interest in forming free trade associations arose in the 1980s when the United States became frustrated with what it saw as European and Japanese protectionism and as the subversion of

GATT liberalization agreements through the use of nontariff barriers. In an effort to put pressure on GATT members for further multilateral liberalization, the U.S. administration advocated negotiating bilateral trade-liberalizing agreements. In 1985 a free trade association was signed with Israel. In 1986 negotiations began over the formation of a free trade association between the United States and its largest trading partner, Canada. These historic negotiations are discussed later in this chapter.

Canadian Trade and Trade Policy

Foreign trade accounts for a large part of the Canadian economy. In 1986 exports were over 30 percent of GDP, compared to about 9 percent for the United States. The most important explanation of these figures is the relative size of the two countries. The world as a whole can do no "foreign" trade (at least until other worlds are colonized). As a general rule, the larger the country, the larger its interregional trade and the less its international trade.

Figure 21-3 shows Canadian merchandise exports and imports as a percentage of GDP for the years 1947–1983. As can be seen, both ratios have consistently been in the 20 to 30 percent range.

The data in Figure 21-3 underestimate the international exposure of the Canadian economy in two important ways. First, because government expenditure on goods and services accounts for more than 20 percent of Canadian GDP, exports represent virtually half the goods produced in the private sector. Second, the figures represent goods actually imported and exported. Many imported goods face competition in domestic markets from close substi-

FIGURE 21-3 Exports and Imports As a Percentage of GDP, 1947–1983 (figures for fourth quarter of year)

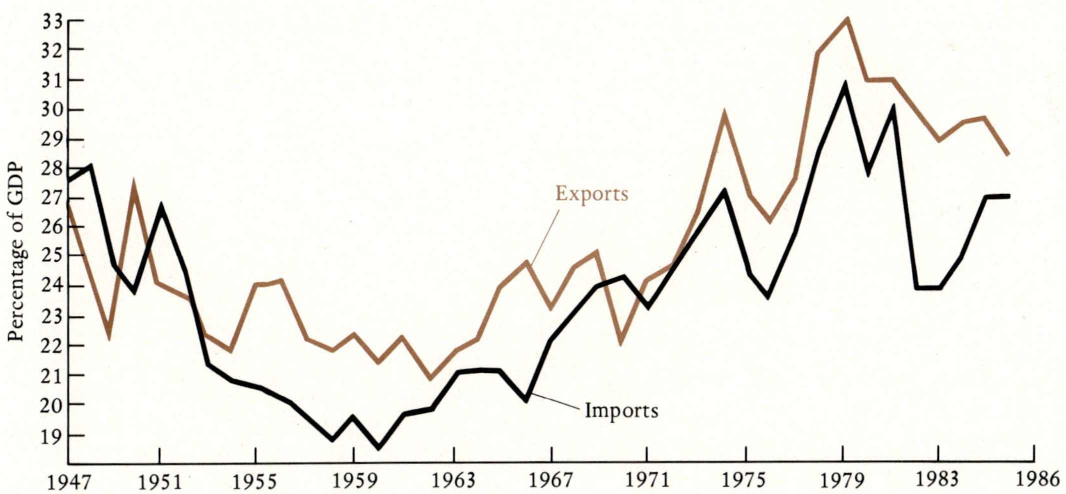

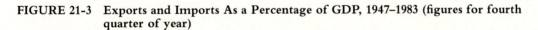

Exports and imports have each been a relatively constant fraction of GDP in the post–World War II period. Exports and imports are plotted as a percentage of national income. Although exports, imports, and GDP all fluctuate considerably, the three series tend to be fairly closely correlated, and thus their ratios are relatively stable. Fluctuations in exports cause fluctuations in GDP, so the two series tend to move together. Fluctuations in GDP cause fluctuations in expenditure on imports, so these two series tend to move together as well.

tutes produced in Canada, called import-competing goods. Similarly, goods identical or very similar to those exported are also produced and consumed in Canada. Hence the fractions of *importables* and *exportables* are much larger than the fractions of actual imports and exports.

In determining our trade patterns, Canada's climate and resource endowments also matter greatly. Severe winters cause Canadians to spend money on foreign vacations and on imports of fresh fruits and vegetables. Our large supply of natural resources relative to our population distinguishes Canada from many other developed countries and helps to determine our comparative advantages. Canada has an abundance of arable land, timber, minerals, and energy in the form of both fossil fuels and hydroelectric power. As a consequence, Canada's exports were originally concentrated in *primary products* and in commodities that require large amounts of these resources in their production. The importance of natural resources dominates the interpretation of our economic history and explanations of our economic development at least to the end of the Second World War.

A further important resource is human capital. A literate, numerate, relatively sophisticated Canadian population gives Canada a comparative advantage in many skill-intensive commodities.[1]

Trade and Trade Policy in the Past

The Staples Thesis

The central role of primary product exports in Canada's economic development is illustrated by our experience with prairie wheat, which emerged as an important export between the years 1886 and 1914. During this "wheat boom" period, real GDP increased by 150 percent and population grew from 5.1 to 7.9 million. Much of this growth was tied closely to the wheat sector. An example was the railway boom. Over 10,000 miles of railway track were laid in order to transport agricultural products from the prairies to the lakehead at Thunder Bay, Ontario, and to the west coast. With the expansion of the railways came construction of grain elevators and investment in farm equipment and food-processing industries.

Based in part on Canada's experience during the wheat boom, the late Professor Harold Innis of the University of Toronto developed the "staples thesis." According to this thesis, economic growth in Canada has been tied to a sequence of exports of staple products, which are primary products for which Canada has had a comparative advantage. The important staple industries in the seventeenth and eighteenth centuries were the fur trade and the east coast fishery; during the nineteenth century timber and wheat from Upper Canada were the important staples; and in the twentieth century it has been prairie wheat, pulp and paper, minerals, and oil and natural gas. These staples have been important not only to exports but also because they have induced additional growth through linkages to other sectors of the economy.

Reciprocity: 1854–1866

In 1854 British North America and the United States signed a reciprocity treaty, and until 1866, when the treaty was abrogated by the United States, many commodities (including all primary products) crossed the border duty free. The period was one of great prosperity, which many economists attribute to increased trade with the United States. Although there are some dissenters, the prevailing view among economic historians is that Canada's experiment with free trade in primary products was beneficial.

After Confederation, the Canadian government maintained low tariffs as it tried to persuade the United States to renew the reciprocity treaty. In the mid 1870s, however, the Canadian economy was hit with a recession, and, as often happens during recessions, manufacturers pressed for more protection.

[1] This is one reason why economists worry so much about the decline in educational standards. If the education of Canadians and Americans who become average members of the labor force declines seriously relative to what is obtained by Europeans and Japanese, Canadian and American comparative advantages will shift toward lower-skilled, lower-income-producing activities.

High Tariffs and the National Policy: 1878–1935

Partly in response to this pressure, Sir John A. MacDonald introduced his National Policy in 1878. This policy was presented as a program for long-run economic development and included subsidies for railway building, support for farm settlement, and emphasis on the export of a few primary products. However, the cornerstone was increased tariff protection for Canadian manufacturing. This protectionist policy remained essentially unchanged until 1935.

Did the National Policy help or hinder Canada's economic growth? Economic historians disagree. W. A. Easterbrook and H. G. Aitken view the effects as beneficial: "The protective tariff . . . rounded out a broad, consistent and comprehensive programme of national planning." They argue that where a tariff kept out foreign products, it encouraged domestic manufacturing, and where it did not, tariff revenue was generated to help finance railway construction. Either way, Canada was better off. John Dales, in sharp contrast, concludes that protectionism was a mistake: "We would have been better off . . . if we had never tangled with the National Policy." He argues that high tariffs prevented the full realization of the gains from our comparative advantage in natural resource industries; moreover, he points out that the 15-year period following the introduction of the National Policy was one of slow growth and unusually high emigration of Canadians to the United States.

Whatever the merits of the National Policy, many underdeveloped nations have since followed similar routes. They have adopted import substitution policies that used tariffs to protect domestic industries producing for the home market manufactured goods that could have been imported more cheaply from abroad.

In Canada the National Policy sowed the seeds of much regional discord. Manufacturing industries in Ontario and Quebec gained from tariff protection, but the remaining provinces, which mainly exported primary goods and imported manufactured goods, lost by it. The National Policy raised the prices of their manufactured goods. They either had to buy expensive, and tariff-protected, Canadian-produced goods or else pay the tariff-burdened price for imported goods.

Falling Tariffs and the GATT Period: 1935 to the Present

The enormous increase in world protectionism in the 1920s and early 1930s demonstrated how vulnerable Canadians were to trade restrictions imposed by other countries. As a result, Canadian policy switched from promoting trade restrictions to promoting trade liberalization. Canadians readily accepted an American initiative and negotiated substantial bilateral tariff reductions in 1935. Then, in 1937, a Canadian initiative brought the United States back to the bargaining table for negotiations that ended in further significant tariff reductions.

This historic shift to a policy of promoting trade liberalization that began in 1935 was confirmed in 1947 when Canada became a charter member of what is arguably the most important economic institution to emerge from the Second World War, the General Agreement on Tariffs and Trade (GATT).

As a result of the tariff cuts negotiated through the GATT, Canadian tariffs have fallen from high to mainly moderate levels. In the process, much Canadian manufacturing industry has been integrated into the world economy, and Canada has become an exporter of manufactured goods (while remaining an important exporter of primary products). Table 21-2 gives some relevant data.

Analysis of Canada's trade and industrial performance indicates that trade liberalization in the 1970s and 1980s resulted in more trade within each industry. Canadian firms rationalized by reducing the number of their product lines, attaining competitive costs on a much smaller range of products. Many of these products proved to be exportable, and the abandoned lines were now imported. The net effect was an increased amount of intra-industry foreign trade between Canada and the United States.

Some industries did experience growth in imports relative to exports, although even in these industries exports grew—they just grew less than imports. Since these industries experienced a decline in

TABLE 21-2 Commodity Composition of Canadian Exports, 1960–1986

	1960	1970	1980	1986
Food and agriculture	18.8	11.4	11.1	8.5
Crude materials	21.2	18.8	19.8	13.2
Fabricated materials	5.9	35.8	39.4	32.8
Manufactured end products	7.8	33.8	29.4	45.2
Special transactions	0.3	0.2	0.3	.3
Total	100.0	100.0	100.0	100.0

Source: Statistics Canada, *Summary of External Trade.*

net exports as a proportion of total production, some shrinkage in their relative size did occur.

In other industries the reverse happened. Resource-based industries such as wood products and paper, which were already substantial net exporters, experienced modest increases in their net exports. The most dramatic increase in exports occurred in industries such as chemicals, machinery, and rubber and plastic products, all of which had been significant net importers during the 1960s.

Thus as trade barriers have been reduced, both Canadian exports and Canadian imports have increased in virtually all sectors. Whole industries have not disappeared either in Canada or in the United States. Instead, each industry has specialized in particular product lines in each country so that both Canadian and American exports have increased in each industry. The shift in *net* export positions has been modest for most industries. This is just as it was in Europe when trade was liberalized after formation of the EC, and for just the same reason—because so much of the adjustment was intra-industry.

The foregoing discussion explains why many economists believe that a misunderstanding of the adjustment process has led some people to overestimate the difficulties of adjusting to tariff cuts. The evolution from 1935 to 1986 that took away something like three-quarters of Canadian tariff barriers created far more jobs than it destroyed. It also caused far fewer adjustment difficulties than might have been expected because so much of the reallocation of resources was intra-industry. For example, it is far easier to reallocate resources from producing one type of paper product to another type or from producing one type of fashion good to another (intra-industry shifts) than it is to reallocate resources from, say, the fashion goods industry to the paper products industry (an inter-industry shift).

The development of a competitive manufacturing sector in Canada was aided by a sectoral free trade agreement called the Auto Pact, which was discussed in detail in Box 21-2 (p. 416).

Increasing Dependence on the United States

In 1938 some 40 percent of Canada's exports went to the United Kingdom and only 23 percent to the United States. By 1960 a mere 17 percent went to the U.K. while 57 percent went to the U.S. In 1986 the figures were 2 percent to the U.K. and 78 percent to the U.S. In part the causes of this shift were beyond Canadian control. For example, the U.K.'s entry into the European Economic Community in 1973 ended any major trading relation between Canada and the U.K. In part the shift represents a major victory of Canadian business. In the 1980s, with the European economies stagnant and the less-developed countries trying to cut imports, the American market was the only growing market open to international traders. Firms from all over the world tried to sell more in that market. The great increase in Canadian exports to the United States is a measure of the success of Canadian exporters in doing what everyone was trying to do—and Canada succeeded better than almost any other country, gaining a share of the great growth in American demand. Table 21-3 tells us the story of the changes.

TABLE 21-3 Composition of Canada's Trade, Selected Years (*percentage*)

	Exports			Imports		
AREA	**1960**	**1983**	**1986**	**1960**	**1983**	**1986**
United States	57	73	78	70	72	69
United Kingdom	17	3	2	11	2	3
Other EC	8	5	4	5	6	8
Japan	3	5	5	2	6	7
All other countries	15	14	11	12	14	13

Source: Statistics Canada, *Summary of External Trade.*

Many Canadians worried about these changes; many wished that Canada was not so dependent on its enormous neighbor to the south. But no Canadian government has been able to develop an effective policy to reduce that dependence. In 1961 conservative Prime Minister John Deifenbaker announced a policy of shifting Canadian trade from the United States to Europe. When the British took him seriously and suggested a mutual reduction of tariffs, Deifenbaker changed his mind, and the initiative died. In 1975 Prime Minister Trudeau announced his "Third Option," which called for increasing trade with countries other than the United States and the EC. What was needed to effect this policy, however, was to reduce trade restrictions on textiles, cheap shoes, and the other "down-market" products that these less-developed countries produce. They would then export these products to Canada, industries producing competing products in Canada would decline, and other Canadian exports would expand to balance the increased Canadian imports. Faced with the major adjustment problems that such a policy required, successive Canadian governments, including Trudeau's, have chosen to advocate trade with third countries, but to balk at the adjustment costs that these policies would require.

The Current Setting

The current makeup of Canada's imports and exports has been shown in Table 21-2. As it always has, Canada exports far more primary products than it imports. In return, in spite of the growth of Canadian manufacturing, Canada imports more manufactured goods than it exports.

Canada is a small country with a heavy dependence on foreign trade. A great deal is made today of the fact that Canada is an anomaly among advanced industrial countries. Along with Australia, it is the only such country whose industries lack secure access to a market of at least 100 million people. Japan and the United States have enormous domestic markets, and the Western European countries are joined in a single market of over 300 million by the two institutions of the European Community (EC) and the European Free Trade Area (EFTA), both of which were discussed earlier in this chapter.

Why are economists so concerned today about Canada's security of access to foreign markets? Why did Canadians not worry about this issue 50 years ago? Before the Second World War, Canada's prosperity was heavily dependent on resource industries, with a high-cost, protected manufacturing sector mainly serving the home market. Canada was a major part of the world's supply of many primary products. For example, in 1950 the nation produced over three quarters of the world's total output of nickel. Thus Canada did not need to worry about access to the world's markets; the world beat a path to its door. By the 1980s, however, the prosperity of resource-based industries had been seriously reduced by international developments in the form of new sources of supply, particularly in the less-developed countries, and synthetic substitutes for many natural materials. For example, fiber optics was replacing copper wiring as a means of transmitting messages and so causing a fall in the world demand for Canadian copper.

As we have seen, Canada, along with the rest of the industrialized world, embarked in 1947 on a policy of tariff reduction under the newly formed GATT. As a result of these tariff reductions and of the Auto Pact, many Canadian manufacturing industries have developed to the extent that they can export successfully. Given its hard-pressed resource-based industries, Canada's future prosperity will be linked more and more to its ability to export manufactured and service-related products. But the world does not beat a path to Canada's door for its manufactured goods or its traded services. The world's markets for manufactured goods and services are fiercely competitive, and Canada's access to these markets is not assured. Policymakers are concerned not only to gain better access but simply to preserve existing access.

Canadian industry is also under competitive pressure from newly industrialized countries (the NICs), especially in lower-wage, lower-value-added commodities. Canadians need to adjust to this, just as Japan did, by reallocating resources out of lower-wage, lower-value-added lines of production and into higher-wage, higher-value-added lines.

Canada and the Rise of World Protectionism

The slowness of the world recovery from the deep recession of the early 1980s has made many governments more protectionist-minded than they were a decade earlier. An important feature of the recent rise in protectionism is that nontariff barriers (NTBs), rather than tariffs, have been raised. GATT rules constrain the use of tariffs and also codify (as a result of negotiations in the 1970s) the circumstances under which NTBs can be used. The GATT authorities have, however, had little success in constraining the growing use of NTBs. This unfortunate development means that the GATT can no longer be fully relied on to play its traditional role of preventing the erection of barriers to trade.

To this general worldwide drift toward protectionism was added a powerful American thrust. Throughout the post–Second World War era, the United States had been a major force pushing for trade liberalization. In the 1980s, however, an ominous change occurred in the American policy stance. As most economists see it, the causes ran from American domestic policy to effects on its foreign trade. During the 1980s the Reagan administration presided over the growth of an enormous federal budget deficit, which at its peak rose to nearly $200 billion. To finance this deficit the government had to borrow enormous sums, and domestic sources proved inadequate. Foreign capital was inevitably drawn in to fill the gap between domestic savings and domestic borrowing requirements. The demand on the part of foreign investors to buy U.S. dollars in order to invest in the United States bid up the price of the U.S. dollar on foreign exchange markets. This in turn made it hard for Americans to sell abroad and easy for foreigners to sell in the United States. The result was a trade deficit that was nearly as large as the budget deficit. Standard trade theory predicts that the trade deficit cannot be removed until the domestic budget deficit is substantially reduced.[2]

The trade deficit meant falling employment and rising bankruptcies in the export- and import-competing sectors of U.S. manufacturers. Not surprisingly, employees and employers in these affected sectors were upset—and rightly so. Not surprisingly, the political arm was responsive to this concern—and rightly so. Not surprisingly, in searching for the cause of the intense competition that was eliminating many U.S. firms and U.S. jobs, most people focused on foreign sources of U.S. imports—and wrongly so.

Instead of seeing the U.S. trade deficit as a result of bad internal macro policies, Americans blamed it on unfair trading practices of foreign countries. This diagnosis sparked off a series of measures, among them the aggressive use of countervailing duties designed to reduce foreign sales in the U.S. market. Many Canadian products such as fish, pork and hogs, softwood lumber, and potash were countervailed.

Growing U.S. protectionism not only threatened the access to the American market of many of Can-

[2] The theory on which this paragraph is based is discussed in detail in Chapters 40 and 41.

ada's exports, but it also threatened to cause an exodus of Canadian capital to the United States. Many successful Canadian exporters were motivated to set up plants in the United States in order to avoid existing trade barriers and threatened new ones. Under present arrangements the only way to avoid these barriers is to relocate in the United States. Such relocations are already occurring in large numbers, and surveys of investment intentions, conducted by Canadian economists Don Daly and D.C. McCharles, show that unless something changes, relocation to the United States will increase greatly over the next decade.

Canada's Trade Options

As awareness grew that Canada's current position was a very difficult one, most people agreed that policy changes were required. In the debate that ensued throughout the second half of the 1980s major differences of opinion became apparent on what changes were desirable. The most important difference was between those who would maintain the outward-looking stance of Canada's trade policy that began in 1935 and those who would seek to turn inward by returning to some modernized version of Sir John A. MacDonald's National Policy.

The Inward-looking Option

A few economists—and many more people from other academic disciplines, organized labor, and some political parties—have been attracted to a policy of reducing the Canadian economy's degree of dependence on foreign trade. They would seek to use government procurement regulations, subsidies, and other policies to favor domestic purchases of domestically produced manufactured goods. Professor Abraham Rothstein advocates such an *import substitution policy* when he calls for (1) "strong government support . . . to enhance Canadian capabilities that would increase the range of products over which an import substitution program could function," (2) "a comprehensive government program . . . to determine the domestic availability of goods already being imported," (3) using the \$60 billion of government purchases at all three levels of government as "an effective instrument for decreasing imports and encouraging production from Canadian manufacturers," and (4) "influencing private-sector purchasing behaviour by publishing Canadian content guidelines."[3]

Many economists feel that Canada is too small to build a high living standard based on industry producing mainly for the home market. They feel that to gain the benefit of scale effects Canada must specialize in, and export, a relatively small number of product lines and import the rest. They also argue that far from creating new income and employment, the policy of import substitution merely replaces employment in efficient high-income-creating export industries with employment in inefficient low-income-creating industries that need protectionism to survive against imports.

Outward-looking Options

Those who look outward seek to preserve the policy that seems to them to have served Canada successfully for over half a century. They believe that Canada's future lies in secure access to the world's trading markets. They hope to increase that access while recognizing that strong efforts are needed to preserve even the access that Canadian exports now have. Those who accepted the outward-looking option split, however, into a group who would pursue only the multilateral approach and a group who would combine it with a bilateral approach to the United States.

The exclusively multilateral approach. One group would rely solely on the multilateral route. They would use the GATT rules and regulations as Canada's means of protecting the market access Canada now has, and they would use the upcoming round of GATT negotiations as the means of further liberalizing trade so as to increase Canada's existing market access.

Many observers worry, however, about the continued effectiveness of the GATT. First, they worry that the GATT will be unable to protect Canada's

[3] Abraham Rothstein, *Rebuilding from Within* (Toronto: Canadian Institute for Public Policy, 1984), pp. 50–54.

existing markets against the rising tide of world protectionism, preserving even the access Canadian exporters now enjoy. As an example of these worries, the GATT secretariat recently wrote of the "increased difficulty, not only in furthering trade liberalization, but also in safeguarding previously negotiated levels of market access." Gerard and Victoria Curzon, experts in world trade law, were even more outspoken in saying that the GATT "is now incapable of halting daily violations of its most innocuous rules, let alone defend its basic principles. Evidence of breakdown is everywhere. . . . An undeclared trade war is in progress." Such observers fear that Canada could protect itself from the current aggressive use of American countervail laws by using GATT appeal mechanisms.

Second, these GATT observers anticipate little further trade liberalization from the next round of negotiations. They argue that Canada should push as hard as possible for multilateral tariff reductions within the GATT but that tying Canada's prosperity as a trading nation exclusively to the success of the next round of GATT negotiations is a risky course.

The joint multilateral-bilateral approach. If the current round of GATT negotiations produces little or nothing by way of trade liberalization and if the Canadian-American initiative fails, Canada will be caught as a little actor on a big, fiercely competitive stage with no secure market to rely on. Pessimism about the success of the GATT leads to a search for an alternative route to preserve and enhance market access. The other main route is a bilateral one. Since 80 percent of Canadian trade is with the United States, there is no other significant bilateral possibility than a trade-liberalizing deal with the United States. Advocates of this joint approach supported the Canadian initiative to form a free trade area with the United States. The object was to gain secure access to the American market by forming what would be considered under the GATT a free trade area.

Advocates of the exclusively multilateral approach were mistrustful of any bilateral agreement with the United States. They feared it would turn the two countries into a "Fortress North America," making it easier for Canada and the United States to turn their backs on the rest of the world. Many Canadians who mistrusted both the inward-looking approach and closer ties with the United States supported putting all of Canada's effort into the multilateral GATT approach.

Among supporters of the bilateral approach, some embraced the Fortress North American concept. Others argued that the bilateral approach need not preclude the multilateral approach. They argued that Canada should push as hard as possible to make the GATT work. However, they agreed with the many GATT observers who are pessimistic about the future of the GATT and thus saw a bilateral agreement with the United States as the only way of securing Canada's existing market access and increasing future access. The object was to provide Canadian exporters with the same secure, barrier-free access to a market in the hundreds of millions as is now available to the industries of the United States, Japan, and Europe.

The Great Free Trade Debate

Among the options just discussed, the Conservative government focused on the proposal for the formation of a free trade area between Canada and the United States (also referred to as trade liberalization or trade enhancement). Under GATT rules, if any two countries negotiate a reduction in their tariffs, these reductions must be extended to all GATT members. Article 24 of the GATT allows, however, for an exception if the contracting parties remove tariffs on the major portion of their trade. The arrangement is then called a free trade area (FTA), and the tariff concessions need not be extended to other GATT members.

What Is a Free Trade Area?

The three main arrangements under which contracting countries agree to remove their tariffs on each other's goods are called a common market, a customs union, and a free trade area. The most comprehensive of these is a common market, which has three main characteristics:

1. No tariffs on goods produced in member countries

2. Common tariffs—and, where possible, nontariff barriers—on goods imported from non-member countries
3. Free movement of labor and capital among member countries

A customs union has the first two features but not the third. A free trade area, which is the least comprehensive of the three arrangements, has only the first feature.

Because each member is free to have its own restrictions on trade with the outside world, a characteristic problem of an FTA is to prevent goods from non-members coming into all member countries' markets through the member with the lowest restrictions on each particular good. To deal with this problem, an FTA has two features not found in either of the other two types of association. First, there must be customs points at borders between member countries to check that goods entering the country duty free actually were produced by another member country and not merely transshipped through it. Second, there must be rules of origin to determine how much domestic value must be added to define each good as one that has been manufactured in a member country and thus eligible to move duty free to other member countries. This is to prevent a good produced by a non-member entering the member country with the lowest tariff on that good and then being repackaged or slightly altered in order to qualify it as a good produced by that member and exported to a higher-tariff member.

The European Free Trade Area As a Model

The European Community, which we have already discussed, is a common market. A number of countries in Europe did not wish to join the EC because they feared the very tight form of association implied by such an arrangement. In particular, they wished to preserve their independence to follow their own trade policies with the rest of the world. They also feared pressures to harmonize many economic and social policies that would result from the tight form of economic association implied by the EC. However, they also feared losing their access to the large market of the EC countries. In response, they set up the European Free Trade Area (EFTA), which was designed to give them access to the EC market while avoiding the pressures to harmonize economic and social policies that they thought would accompany membership in a common market. These hopes have been fulfilled. Countries such as Sweden have full access to the EC market while remaining free to maintain their own distinctive economic and social policies, as well as their own independent commercial policies with the rest of the world.

This is the model that supporters of the Canadian-American free trade area sought to copy. They saw Canada's position vis-à-vis the United States under a Canadian-American free trade area as similar to Sweden's position vis-à-vis the EC under the EFTA. Opponents worried that the EFTA experience could not be transplanted to North America.

The Arguments for a FTA

The major advantages that supporters saw in a trade area are the following:

1. Eliminating tariffs on all trade between the two countries would complete, for at least 80 percent of Canada's trade, the process that began in 1935 when Canada first began to cut tariffs and let market forces shift emphasis to Canadian products that could stand up to international competition.
2. Enhanced access to the U.S. market would lead to further intra-industry specialization and further intra-industry trade of the sort that has accompanied all previous rounds of tariff reductions. This would have the effect of raising Canadian living standards by an estimated 5 to 10 percent of current GDP.
3. An agreement between the two countries would secure the access to the U.S. market that Canadian exporters now enjoy. The United States has been unilaterally inhibiting Canadian access to the U.S. market by reinterpreting its rules of fair trade to find new reasons for countervailing many Canadian goods exported to the United States.
4. Secure access to the American market would leave successful Canadian exporting firms able to serve the market in the two countries from locations in Canada without having to fear existing or new American trade restrictions. This would reduce the current outflow of Canadian direct investment in the United States.

5. The loose type of association implied by a free trade area would not involve any loss of Canadian sovereignty or policy independence. It is possible that Canadian independence could *increase* because securing access to the American market by mutual agreement would eliminate the American Congress's ability to make unilateral decisions to countervail Canadian exports to the United States because these exports were affected by some domestic Canadian policy of which Congress disapproved. This is an option that Congress was increasingly resorting to in ways that greatly worried Canadian policymakers.
6. Support of some Canadian cultural industries, where the Canadian market was too small to support them, should be an agreed exception to the principle of free trade. In any case, existing supports usually had only a marginal effect on Canadian culture, which, along with the distinctive Canadian identity, was too deep to be destroyed by a little more of what Canada had been doing for nearly half a century—trading a great deal, and on increasingly free terms, with the United States.

The Argument Against FTA

Various opponents saw major disadvantages in a free trade area. The following are some of the major arguments that were advanced by these opponents.

1. Canada would get small economic gains at best because, contrary to the experience of previous Canadian tariff cuts, American firms would outcompete Canadian manufacturing firms, and Canada would consequently become a less industrial society.
2. Canada would lose sovereignty in ways that the European countries who joined the EFTA arrangement with the EC had not. As a result, Canada might even be absorbed by the United States politically.
3. Canada would lose employment as U.S. branch plants and subsidiaries, which had located in Canada because of the Canadian tariff, returned to the United States when the tariff was eliminated.
4. Canada would be overwhelmed by U.S. investment as American capital flooded in to take advantage of the growing possibilities in Canada opened up by access to the United States. Indeed, the supporters of the arrangement were intending to sell out Canada economically to the United States. (This charge was made frequently by publisher Mel Hurtig, an outspoken opponent of the proposal.)
5. Canadian cultural industries would be overwhelmed by U.S. competition, and the distinctive Canadian culture would be weakened and might disappear altogether.

The Agreement

The preceding alleged pros and cons were the substance of the arguments in the two years leading up to the agreement. During the summer of 1987, the negotiations themselves reached a climax. After some cliff-hanging sequences, which included a walkout by the Canadian negotiating team, the two countries reached an agreement literally hours before the American negotiating authority ran out. The principles of the agreement were published on October 4, and a detailed text followed in the middle of December.

Two points stood out in the deal. First, a *comprehensive* free trade agreement was worked out. Second, Canada failed in its attempt to achieve *full* security of access to the U.S. market by eliminating the unilateral application of U.S. fair trade laws to imports from Canada.

Free trade. Judged as a simple free trade area, the agreement was a notable success. Tariffs were to be eliminated on all manufactured goods—some instantly, others over five years, and the rest over ten. Import quotas were also to be removed. Much to everyone's surprise, most of agriculture was covered, including grain and meat. However, exclusion was granted to those industries, such as poultry and eggs, where marketing boards have followed restrictive practices. Some minor tinkering was done to the Auto Pact, but it was not altered in major substance. Agreement was reached on a broad range of service industries to give national treatment—no discrimination on the basis of the nationality of a firm's owners—and right of establishment—each country's service firms could set themselves up in the other's country.

The energy part of the agreement effectively legalized the status quo, which is free trade in energy.

Contrary to many fears that had been expressed earlier, the cultural industries were largely untouched. This was a substantial victory for the Canadian negotiators, since a major American objective had been to restrict, or eliminate, some of Canada's major cultural support policies.

On investment, Canada agreed to raise the minimum size of a company whose acquisition by foreign owners could be reviewed. Only large companies would now be subject to review. Both sides also agreed to give national treatment to the other country's investment. Each country would still be free to pass any laws controlling investment in any part of its economy. What it could not do was apply such laws differently to foreign and domestically owned companies.

Security of access. The big disappointment on the Canadian side was the failure to get comprehensive relief from the NTB aspect of American fair trade laws. Antidumping and countervailing duties could still be used as unilaterally imposed trade barriers. The Canadian negotiators did, however, get two concessions in this area.

First, they got agreement to establish a tribunal to review disputes relating to the fair trade laws—a tribunal whose decisions were to be binding. Cases could only be referred after one of the countries had made its unilateral decision to apply an antidumping or a countervailing duty. The grounds for appeal appeared to be restricted to cases where the country's laws and procedures were incorrectly applied, or where the decision was "capricious." United States appeal procedure is, however, much less restrictive than Canadian procedure. It appears that, as long as objections get read into the transcript of the original hearings, the appeals will be very wide-ranging. As an experienced American trade lawyer put it at a seminar in Toronto in October 1987, "the Canadians have succeeded in turning a procedure that was subjectively biased in the United States' favour into one that is objective." The debate that followed the publication of the agreement made it clear, however, that most people wanted to praise or condemn the agreement's dispute settlement proposals without understanding what they really implied.

The second concession won by Canadians was an agreement to review all subsidy, dumping, and related practices with a view to establishing a mutually agreed code within five to seven years. Such agreement would be a substantial victory for Canada. Five years seems a long time to currently harassed exporters, but it is short in the lifetime of a nation. The main concern was how Canada could exert pressure on the United States to reach a reasonable agreement. The free trade pact allowed either country to cancel the entire pact if agreement on the issues of subsidies and dumping could not be reached in seven years. But in seven years, Canadian firms would have adjusted to the removal of 100 percent of some tariffs and 70 percent of the rest. Many people doubted that Canada could make a believable threat to withdraw at that time. After so much adjustment had occurred, turning back the clock might well prove impossible.

The Renewed Debate

The elements of the proposed pact were no sooner published than renewed debate broke out in Canada.

Critics argued that the Auto Pact had been emasculated. Supporters replied that the Pact was largely untouched, that auto firms still had major incentives to abide by its domestic content rules, and that the main losers were Japanese and European auto firms located in Canada, who were formally excluded from any future participation in the pact.

Critics argued that the energy agreement prevented Canada from keeping Canadian energy solely for Canadian use in any future energy crises and from charging Canadians lower prices for energy than was being charged to Americans. Supporters agreed, but argued that as a small actor on the world energy stage, it was not in Canada's own interests to charge domestic prices that differed from the world price. They also argued that another energy crisis was a long way into the future, while free access to the U.S. market for such commodities as natural gas was very valuable to the energy industry now.

Critics argued that Canada had given up the right to adopt restrictive policies directed at most foreign investment. Supporters agreed, but pointed out that the right was maintained for very large firms, and asserted that, in any case, the real problem was to attract, rather than discourage, foreign investment.

Others pointed out that Canada had become one of the three largest foreign investors in the United States. Agreement for national treatment would prevent the United States from attacking Canadian investment in the ways that, in the past, Canada had attacked U.S. investment. Those who feared a U.S. nationalist backlash against the growing foreign ownership of U.S. assets argued that getting the United States to agree to national treatment now would seem a substantial achievement by the early 1990s.

On broader issues, critics charged that Canada's social and environmental programs would be eroded. Although not included in the deal, it was alleged that their high cost would make it difficult for firms to compete in the fierce climate of free trade with the United States. Pressure to cut social expenditures would then come from struggling firms. Critics replied that, just as high and low productivity countries could trade to their mutual profit, so could countries with and without costly social programs. After all, they pointed out, Sweden manages to trade satisfactorily with the EC in spite of its costly social welfare programs.

Critics argued that Canadian sovereignty was seriously compromised, and that the argument could even mean an end to Canada's way of life and national identity. Supporters argued that a free trade agreement would have trivial effects on these broader aspects of society. They observed that many other countries had managed to trade freely with each other, while still maintaining their national identities. Why, they asked, should it be any different with Canada and the United States?

So the debate continued. Was it a good deal, judged as a traditional free trade pact? Was it sensible to get involved in a traditional agreement with no more than a commitment to look at the fair trade laws over the next seven years? Was Canada at risk as a separate national and cultural entity?

By the time this section is read, the decision to accept or reject the proposed pact will have been made. If the agreement is to go ahead, the allegations of gains and losses will be tested over the next couple of decades. If the agreement is rejected, all of the arguments reviewed here will be heard over and over again as Canadians and Americans debate the advisability of trying once again to reach a free trade agreement.

Summary

1. The case for free trade is that world output of all commodities can be higher under free trade than when protectionism restricts regional specialization.
2. Free trade among nations may be restricted intentionally by protectionist policies which seek to raise prices, lower quantities, or reduce the demand for imports.
3. Protection can be urged as a means to ends other than maximizing world living standards. Examples of such ends are to produce a diversified economy, to reduce fluctuations in national income, to retain distinctive national traditions, and to improve national defense.
4. Protection can also be urged on the grounds that it may lead to higher living standards for the protectionist country than would a policy of free trade. Such a result might come about through exploiting a monopoly position or by developing a dynamic comparative advantage by allowing inexperienced or uneconomically small industries to become efficient enough to compete with foreign industries.
5. Almost everyone would choose free trade if the only alternative

were *no* trade. Cutting existing tariff barriers offers gains that may seem small expressed as a percentage of GDP, but are large in terms of the total of goods and services involved.

6. Some fallacious free trade arguments are that (a) because free trade maximizes world income, it will maximize the income of every individual country and (b) because infant industries seldom admit to growing up and thus try to retain their protection indefinitely, the whole country necessarily loses by protecting its infant industries.

7. Some fallacious protectionist arguments are that (a) mutually advantageous trade is impossible because one trader's gain must always be the other's loss; (b) buying abroad sends our money abroad, while buying at home keeps our money at home; (c) our high-paid workers must be protected against the competition from low-paid foreign workers; (d) imports are to be discouraged because they lower national income and cause unemployment.

8. As tariff barriers have been reduced over the years, they have been at least partially replaced by nontariff barriers. Voluntary export agreements are straightforward restrictions on trade. Antidumping and countervailing duties can provide legitimate restraints on foreign unfair trading practices, but they can also be used as nontariff barriers to trade.

9. The General Agreement on Tariffs and Trade, whereby countries agree to extend to all members tariff reductions that they negotiate on a bilateral basis, has brought great reductions in world tariffs since its inception in 1947. The European Free Trade Area, and the European Community (formerly the European Economic Community), are regional arrangements for free trade in goods between their members.

10. International trade has always been important to the Canadian economy. Canadian trade policy supported relatively free trade until 1878 when the National Policy was introduced. This was a high-tariff policy that sought to encourage Canadian manufacturing industries to serve the Canadian market. Since 1935 Canadian trade policy has supported trade liberalization, first with reciprocal agreements with the United States and then through the GATT.

11. Reductions in tariffs on Canadian-American trade have led mainly to intra-industry specialization, with both countries' imports and exports tending to increase in each industry as firms specialized in particular product lines.

12. Most people believe that maintaining the status quo is not a viable policy for Canada over the next few years. Current policy options are the inward-looking option that seeks to raise the degree of protection of the Canadian market for Canadian producers, and the outward looking option that seeks to continue the long-standing policy of trade liberalization. The two major alternatives within the outward-looking option are the strict multilateral approach through the GATT and the two-pronged approach which, as well as GATT, includes a bilateral initiative for trade liberalization with the United States.

13. Negotiations in 1986–1987 sought to set up a Canadian-American free trade area that would allow for free trade in goods and some services, as well as some agreements on nontariff barriers, and procedures with respect to foreign investment.
14. Agreement was reached in October 1987 to set up a free trade area covering manufactured goods, some agricultural goods, and many services. Controversy centered on parts of the agreement relating to autos, energy, cultural industries, and investment. Although a dispute-settlement body was to be established, its powers were limited. Bilateral agreement on the use of fair trade laws as nontariff barriers to trade was to be negotiated over the next five years. Whether the agreement was accepted or rejected, the issues raised by it will be in the forefront of discussion over the next decade.

Topics for Review

Free trade and protectionism
Tariff and nontariff barriers to trade
Countervail and voluntary export agreements
Fallacious arguments for free trade
Fallacious arguments for protectionism
Countervailing duties
Dumping and antidumping duties
General Agreement on Tariffs and Trade (GATT)
Common markets, customs unions, and free trade associations

Discussion Questions

1. It has been calculated that the voluntary export agreement to reduce Japanese car imports into the North American market cost Canadians and Americans over $150,000 per job saved. Who gained and who lost from this arrangement?
2. The policy of "aggressive reciprocity" has recently been urged on the Canadian and the American governments. Under it, every time a foreign government introduced a new barrier to trade Canada and the United States would reciprocate aggressively by introducing a new barrier of their own. Discuss the likely outcome of such a policy. What are some alternative policies for enhancing world trade?
3. Discuss some of the major changes that might occur in the Canadian economy if the inward-looking option were seriously adopted.
4. Look at the Canadian tariffs shown in Table 21–1. What economic and political reasons can you see for duties on some commodities being above the average rate of duty charged and for others being below it? What other forms of protectionism could make some duties misleading?
5. Suppose Quebec formed a separate state, refusing to trade with the rest of Canada. What predictions would you make about the standard of living compared to what it is in Canada today? Does the

fact that Canada, the United States, and Mexico are separate countries lead to a lower standard of living in the three countries than if they were united into a new country called Northica?

6. Suppose each of the Canadian provinces was a separate country. If free trade were permitted among these "countries," would you expect a pattern of production to exist different from the one that does exist? If Manitoba prohibited all trade, what would be the effect on Manitoba and on the other nine countries? Suppose all ten countries prohibited all trade. What would be the result?
7. If the European Common Market caused such a rise in efficiency that the price of every good produced in Germany, France, and Italy fell below the prices of the same good manufactured in Canada, what would happen? Would Canadians gain or lose because of this?
8. Discuss the following statements made during the great Canadian free trade debate. All but one of the quotations can be refuted using points of economic theory.
   a. "Tariff reductions, which should help both countries, disproportionately benefit the United States because average Canadian tariffs are higher." Jeff Simpson, *Toronto Globe and Mail,* October 9, 1987.
   b. "The historical records show that the concerns expressed two decades ago about the Auto Pact were not entirely misplaced. In only 9 years of the Pact's 22 years of operation has Canada been in a surplus position in Auto Pact trade." Glen Williams, *Toronto Globe and Mail,* November 28, 1987.
   c. "We would like to think we are about to get the best of both worlds—Canadian stability and a more caring society, [combined with] U.S. markets—but what if instead, we get their crime rates, health programs, and gun laws and they get our markets, or what is left of them?" Margaret Atwood, testimony to parliamentary committee on free trade, November 4, 1987.
   d. "The complete removal of tariffs doesn't help Canadian exporters as much as the devaluation of our dollar, because the key to breaking into the U.S. market is to be able to flog it with cheaper goods than they have at home." Edgar Benson, former Liberal Minister of Finance, *Toronto Star,* October 10, 1987.
   e. "One cost of doing business is taxation. No Canadian would be so naive as to believe that Washington would amend its tax laws to conform with Canada. So Canadians would then urge Ottawa to make Canadian tax practices conform with those of the United States, even more than they already do. That a comparable tax system [and soon thereafter monetary union] should be seen as an essential element in a successful free trade area may sound reasonable, but it means in essence that taxation would be decided in Washington, not in Ottawa. That different levels and types of taxation are necessary in two different countries would be ignored.

   "If Canadian social programs such as medicare, pensions, regional incentives and environmental protection could not then be adequately financed, so much the worse. Those programs should then be changed to conform with United States practices." Roy MacLaren, *Toronto Globe and Mail,* November 10, 1987.

22

Growth in the Less-Developed Countries

It is only about 10,000 years since human beings became food *producers* rather than food *gatherers*. Only within the last few centuries could a significant proportion of the world's population look forward to anything but a hard struggle to wrest subsistence from a reluctant nature. The concept of leisure, combined with high consumption standards as a right to be enjoyed by all, is new in human history.

The Uneven Pattern of Development

More than 4.5 billion people are alive today, but the wealthy parts of the world—where people work no more than 40 or 50 hours per week, enjoy substantial leisure, and have a level of consumption at or above *half* that attained by North Americans—contain less than 15 percent of the world's population. Many of the rest struggle for subsistence. Many exist on a level at or below that enjoyed by peasants in ancient Egypt or Babylon.

Data on per capita income levels throughout the world (as in Table 22-1) cannot be accurate down to the last $100.[1] Nevertheless, such data do reflect enormous real differences in living standards that no statistical discrepancies can hide. The *development gap*—the discrepancy between the standards of living in countries at either end of the distribution—is real and large.

There are many ways to look at inequality of income distribution among the world's population. One is a Lorenz curve, as shown in Figure 22-1 (p. 442). The more the curve bends away from the straight, 45° line, the greater is the inequality in income distribution. The Lorenz curve of income distribution among people in Canada gives perspective on the disparity in income among countries. It is much closer to equality than the world distribution.

Another way of looking at inequality is to look at the geographic distribution of income per capita, as in Figure 22-2 (p. 443). Recent

[1] There are many problems in comparing national incomes across countries. For example, home-grown food is vitally important to living standards in underdeveloped countries, but it is excluded, or at best imperfectly included, in the national income statistics of most countries. So is the contribution of a warm climate.

TABLE 22-1 Income and Population Differences Among Groups of Countries, 1983

Classification (based on gross domestic product per capita in 1980 U.S. dollars)		(1)	(2)	(3)	(4)	(5)	(6)	(7)
Group	Average income level	Number of countries[a]	GDP (billions)	Population (millions)	GDP per capita	Percentage of world GDP	Percentage of world population	Growth rate[b]
I	$400 or less	15	$ 548	2,099	$ 241	4.6	49.8	1.3
II	$401–$1,000	18	274	421	690	2.3	10.0	0.1
III	$1,001–$5,000	31	1,619	635	2,420	13.4	15.1	1.7
IV	$5,001–$10,000	13	4,175	613	6,794	34.7	14.5	2.0
V	More than $10,000	16	5,417	448	13,251	45.0	10.6	1.4

Source: IMF International Financial Statistics Yearbook, 1985; *Handbook of Economic Statistics,* 1984.

[a] Countries for which data are not available, and therefore not represented in the table, account for about 9 percent of the world's population and mostly in the poorer categories.

[b] Average annual percentage rate of growth of real GDP per capita, 1975–1983.

Over half the world's population lives in poverty. Many of the very poorest are in countries that have the lowest growth rates and thus fall ever farther behind. The unequal distribution of the world's income is shown in columns 5 and 6. Groups I and II, which have about 60 percent of world population, earn less than 10 percent of world income. Groups IV and V, with 25 percent of world population, earn 80 percent of world income. Column 7 shows that the poorest countries are not closing the gap in income between rich and poor countries.

political discussions of income distribution have distinguished between richer and poorer nations as "North" versus "South." The map reveals why.

The Consequences of Underdevelopment

The consequences of low income levels can be severe. In a rich country such as Canada, variations in rainfall are reflected in farm output and farm income. In poor countries such as those of the Sahel area of Africa, variations in rainfall are reflected in the death rate. In these countries, many people live so close to subsistence that slight fluctuations in the food supply bring death by starvation to large numbers. Other less dramatic characteristics of poverty include inadequate diet, poor health, short life expectancy, illiteracy, and, importantly, an attitude of helpless resignation to the caprice of nature.

For these reasons, reformers in underdeveloped countries, now often called **less-developed countries (LDCs)**, feel a sense of urgency not felt by their counterparts in rich countries.[2] Yet, as the first two rows of Table 22-1 show:

The development gap for the very poorest countries has been widening.

As we will see, this is a problem of both output and population. It is also an international political problem.

Incentives for Development

Obviously underdevelopment is nothing new. Concern with it as a remediable condition, however, is recent; it has become a compelling policy issue only within the present century. One incentive behind this

[2] The terminology of development is often confusing. *Underdeveloped, less developed,* and *developing* do not mean the same thing in ordinary English, yet each has been used to describe the same phenomenon. For the most part we shall refer to the underdeveloped countries as the *less-developed countries,* or LDCs. Some of them are making progress, that is, developing; others are not.

FIGURE 22-1 Lorenz Curves Showing Inequalities Among the Nations of the World and Within Canada

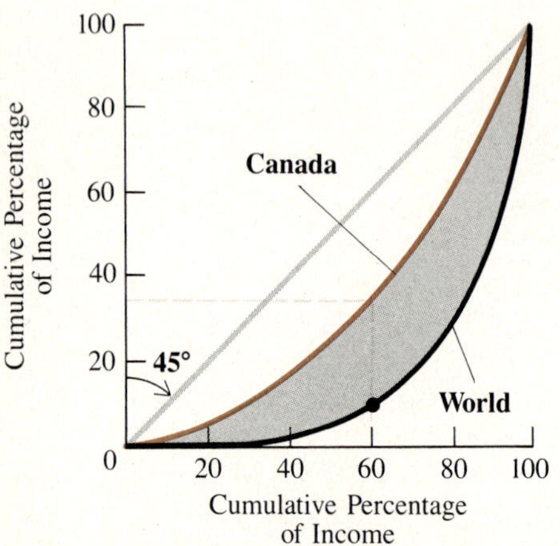

The inequality in the distribution of income is much less within Canada than it is among all the nations of the world. In a Lorenz curve, a wholly equal distribution of income would be represented by the 45° line; 20 percent of the population would have 20 percent of the income, 50 percent of the population would have 50 percent of the income, and so on. The very unequal distribution of world income is shown by the black curve. For example, 60 percent of the world's population lives in countries that earn only 10 percent of the world's income, as shown by the black dot.

Contrast this with the distribution of income within Canada: the poorest 60 percent of the Canadian population earns 33 percent of the nation's income. This is not equality, but it is much less unequal than the differences between rich and poor countries.

new attention to development has been the apparent success of planned programs of "crash" development, of which the Soviet experience is the most remarkable and the Chinese the most recent. Leaders in other countries ask, "If they can do it, why not us?"

Demonstration effects should not be underestimated. It has been said that the real secret of the atomic bomb was that it *could* be made, not how. Much the same is true of economic development. Observing other developing countries, people see that it is possible to achieve better lives for themselves and their children. It is bad enough to be poor, but it is doubly galling to be poor when others are escaping poverty.

A second incentive for development has come from the willingness of developed countries to aid less-developed countries. We shall discuss such programs and their motivation later.

A third incentive for development results from the emergence of a relatively cohesive bloc of LDCs within the United Nations. The bloc is attempting to use political power to achieve economic ends.

What are the causes of underdevelopment, and how may they be overcome?

Barriers to Economic Development

Income per capita grows when aggregate income grows faster than population. Many forces can impede such growth.

Population and Natural Resources

Rapid Population Growth

Population growth is a central problem of economic development. If population grows as quickly as national income, per capita income does not increase. Many less-developed countries have rates of population growth that are nearly as large as their rates of growth of gross domestic product (GDP). As a result, their standards of living are barely higher than they were a 100 or even a 1,000 years ago. They have made appreciable gains in aggregate income, but most of the gains have been literally eaten up by the increasing population. This is shown in Table 22-2 (p. 444).

The population problem has led economists to talk about the *critical minimum effort* that is required not merely to increase capital but to increase it fast enough so that the increase in output outpaces the increase in population. When population control is left to nature, it is often solved in a cruel way. Population increases until many people are forced to live

FIGURE 22-2 Countries of the World, Classified by Per Capita GDP, 1985

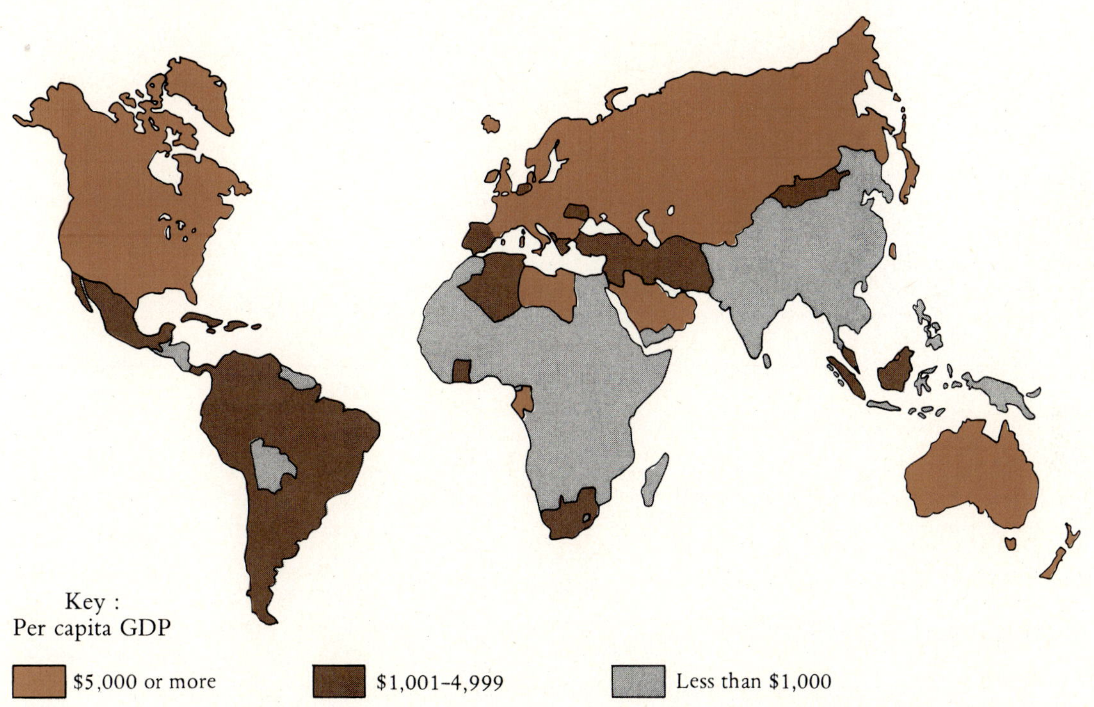

There is a sharp geographic division between "North" and "South" in the level of income per capita. The nations of the world are classified here according to three levels of measured per capita GDP. The poorest group, shown in gray, represents 31 percent of the world's population. The middle group, shown in dark color, represents about 41 percent of world population. The wealthiest group, shown in light color, includes all of North America, Europe, the Soviet Union, and Japan and represents only 25 percent of the world's population. Areas in white indicate no data available. See Table 22-1 for more detail.

at a subsistence level; further population growth is halted by famine, pestilence, and plague. This grim possibility was perceived early in the history of economics by Thomas Malthus.

In some ways the population problem is more severe today than it was even 50 years ago because advances in medicine and in public health have brought sharp and sudden decreases in death rates. It is ironic that much of the compassion shown by wealthier nations for the poor and underprivileged people of the world has traditionally taken the form of improving their health, thereby doing little to avert their poverty. We praise the medical missionaries who brought modern medicine to the tropics, but the elimination of malaria has doubled population growth in Sri Lanka. Cholera, once a killer, is now largely under control. No one argues against controlling disease, but other steps must also be taken if the child who survives the infectious illnesses of infancy is not to die of starvation in early adulthood.

Figure 22-3 illustrates actual and projected world population growth. The population problem is not limited to underdeveloped countries, but about

TABLE 22-2 The Relation of Population Growth to Per Capita Income, 1975–1983 ***(percentages)***

Classification of countries (based on GDP per capita in 1980 U.S. dollars)			Average annual growth rate of			Population growth as percentage of real GDP growth
Group	Average income level	Percentage of world population	Real GDP	Population	Real GDP per capita	
I–II	$1,000 or less	59.8	3.2	2.6	0.6	81
III–IV	$1,001–$10,000	29.6	3.6	1.8	1.8	50
V	More than $10,000	10.6	2.7	1.3	1.4	48

Source: Calculated from *IMF International Financial Statistics Yearbook*, 1985; *Handbook of Economic Statistics*, 1984.

Growth in per capita real income depends on the difference between growth rates of real national income and population. The very poorest countries spend much of their increase in income on a rising population. Thus their increase in income per capita is less than half that of the countries that are already richer.

seven-eighths of the expected growth in the world's population is in Africa, Asia, and Latin America, areas where underdevelopment is the rule rather than the exception.

Insufficient Natural Resources

A country with ample fertile land and a large supply of easily developed resources will find growth in income easier to achieve than one poorly endowed with such resources. Kuwait has an income per capita above that of both Canada and the United States because by accident it sits on top of the world's greatest known oil field. A lack of oil proved a devastating setback to many LDCs when the OPEC cartel increased oil prices tenfold during the 1970s. Without oil, their development efforts would be halted, but to buy oil took so much scarce foreign exchange that it threatened to cripple their attempts to import needed capital goods.

The amount of resources available for production is at least in part subject to control. Badly fragmented land holdings may result from a dowry or inheritance system. When farmland is divided into many small parcels, it may be much more difficult to achieve the advantages of modern agriculture than it is when the land is available in huge tracts for large-scale farming.

Lands left idle because of lack of irrigation or spoiled by lack of crop rotation are well-known examples of barriers to development. Ignorance is another. The nations of the Middle East sat through recorded history alongside the Dead Sea without realizing that it was a substantial source of potash. Not until after World War I were these resources utilized; now they provide Israel with raw materials for its fertilizer and chemical industries.

Inefficient Use of Resources

Low levels of income and slower than necessary growth rates may result from the inefficient use of resources as well as the lack of key resources.

It is useful to distinguish between two kinds of inefficiency. An hour of labor would be used inefficiently, for example, if a worker, even though working at top efficiency, were engaged in making a product that no one wanted. Using society's resources to make the wrong products is an example of *allocative inefficiency.*

In terms of the production possibility boundary encountered in Chapter 1, allocative inefficiency represents operation at the wrong place on the boundary. It will occur if the signals to which people respond are distorted (both monopoly and tariffs are commonly cited sources of distortions) or if market imperfections prevent resources from moving to their best uses.

FIGURE 22-3 World Population Growth, 1400–2000

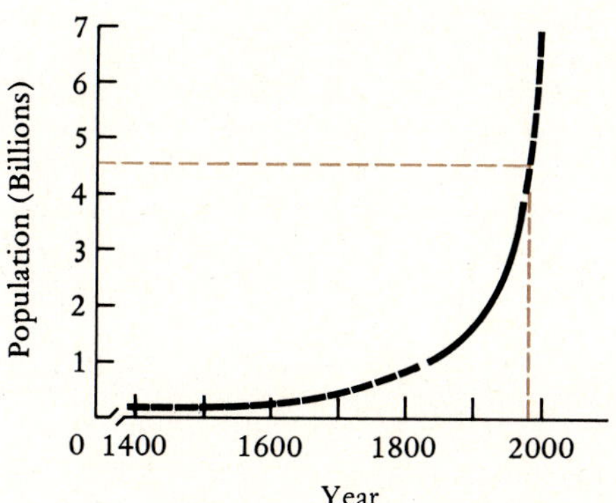

The trend of growth in the world's population is explosive. The solid line reflects present measurements. The dashed line involves projections from observed trends. It took about 50,000 years from the emergence of modern human beings for the world's population to reach 1 billion. It took 100 years to add a second billion, 30 years to add the third billion, and 15 years to add the fourth billion. If these trends continue, the population will reach 7 billion by the year 2000.

FIGURE 22-4 Allocative Inefficiency Versus X-Inefficiency

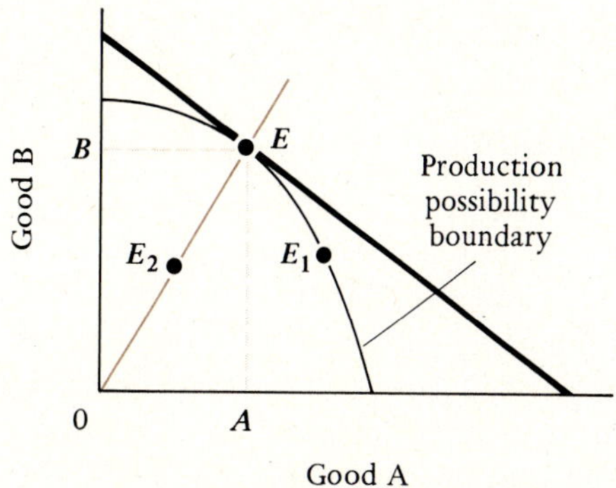

Allocative inefficiency places the society at an inappropriate point on its production possibility boundary, while X-inefficiency places the society inside this boundary. The thinner black curve represents a society's production possibilities between two goods, A and B. The slope of the thicker black line represents the opportunity cost of good B in terms of good A as given by prices set on world markets. The efficient output of A and B is represented at point *E*, and the country can trade to achieve any position on the thicker line. Point E_1 is inefficient in the allocative sense. The economy is operating on its production possibility boundary, but it is producing too much A and too little B for the given opportunity cost. In contrast, at point E_2 the proportions of B and A are the same as at *E*, but the economy is operating inside its boundary. This is X-inefficiency.

A second kind of inefficiency has come to be called **X-inefficiency,** following Professor Harvey Leibenstein. X-inefficiency arises whenever resources are used in such a way that even if workers are making the right product, they are doing so less productively than is possible. One example would be workers too hungry or too unmotivated to concentrate on their tasks. X-inefficiency may be the price societies pay when they give more weight to friendship, loyalty, and tradition than to productivity.

The distinction between allocative inefficiency and X-inefficiency is illustrated in Figure 22-4.

Inadequate Human Resources

A well-developed entrepreneurial class, motivated and trained to organize resources for efficient production, is often missing in less-developed countries. Its absence may be a heritage of a colonial system that gave the local population no opportunity to develop; it may occur because managerial positions are awarded on the basis of family status or political patronage; it may reflect the presence of economic or cultural attitudes that do not favor acquisition of wealth by organizing productive activities; or it may simply be due to the absence of the quantity or quality of education or training that is required.

Poor health is likewise a source of inadequate human resources. When the labor force is healthy, less time is lost and more effective effort is expended. The economic analysis of medical advances is a young field, however, and there is a great deal to be learned about the drag of poor health on the growth of an economy.

Institutional and Cultural Patterns

Inadequate Infrastructure

Key services called **infrastructure,** such as transportation and a communications network, are necessary to efficient commerce. Roads, bridges, railways, and harbors are needed to transport people, materials, and finished goods. The most dramatic confirmation of their importance comes in wartime, when belligerents always place high priority on destroying each other's transportation facilities.

Phone and postal services, water supply, and sanitation are essential to economic development. The absence, whatever the reason, of a dependable infrastructure can impose severe barriers to economic development.

Unstable Financial Institutions

The lack of an adequate and trusted system of financial institutions is often a barrier to development. Investment plays a key role in growth, and an important source of funds for investment is the savings of households and firms. When banks and other financial institutions do not function well and smoothly, the link between private saving and investment may be broken and the problem of finding funds for investment greatly intensified.

Many people in LDCs do not trust banks, sometimes with good reason, more often without. Either they do not maintain deposits or they panic periodically, drawing them out and seeking security for their money in mattresses, in gold, or in real estate. When banks cannot count on their deposits being left in the banking system, they cannot engage in the kind of long-term loans needed to finance investments. When this happens, increases in savings do not become available for investment in productive capacity.

Developing countries must not only create banking institutions, but must also develop enough stability and reliability that people will trust their savings to those who wish to invest.

Cultural Barriers

Traditions and habitual ways of doing business vary among societies, and not all are equally conducive to productivity. Max Weber argued that the "Protestant ethic" encouraged the acquisition of wealth and hence encouraged more growth than systems of belief that directed activity away from the economic sphere.

Often in LDCs, personal considerations of family, past favors, or traditional friendship or enmity are more important than market incentives in motivating behavior. One may find a too-small firm struggling to survive against a larger rival and learn that the owner prefers to remain small because expansion would require use of nonfamily capital or leadership. To avoid paying too harsh a competitive price for built-in inefficiency, the firms' owners may then spend much of their energies in an attempt to influence the government to prevent larger firms from being formed or to try to secure restrictions on the sale of output—and they may well succeed. Such behavior will inhibit economic growth.

In an environment where people believe that it is more important who your father is than what you do, it may take a generation to persuade employers to change their attitudes and another generation to persuade workers that times have changed. In a society in which children are expected to stay in their fathers' occupations, it is more difficult for the labor force to change its characteristics and to adapt to the requirements of growth than in a society where upward mobility is itself a goal.

Structuring incentives is a widely used form of policy action in market-oriented economies. But if people habitually bribe the tax collector rather than pay taxes, they will not be likely to respond to policies that are supposed to work by raising or lowering taxes. All that will change is the size of the bribe.

There is lively debate on how much to make of the significance of differing cultural attitudes. Some analysts believe that traditional considerations dominate peasant societies to the exclusion of economic responses; others suggest that any resulting inefficiency may be relatively small.

The fact that existing social, religious, or legal patterns may make growth more difficult does not in itself imply that they are undesirable. Instead it suggests that the benefits of these patterns must be weighed against the costs, of which the limitation on growth is one. When people derive satisfaction from a religion whose beliefs inhibit growth, when they value a society in which every household owns its own land and is more nearly self-sufficient than in another society, they may be quite willing to pay a price in terms of growth opportunities foregone.

Some Basic Choices

There are many barriers to economic development that, singly and in combination, can keep a country poor.

Economic development policy involves identifying the barriers to the level and kind of development desired and then devising ways to overcome them. Although the problems and strategies vary greatly from country to country, there are common basic choices that all developing countries must face.

How Much Government Control?

How much government control over the economy is necessary and desirable? Practically every shade of opinion from "The only way to grow is to get the government's dead hand out of everything" to "The only way to grow is to get a fully planned, centrally controlled economy" has been seriously advocated.

The extreme views are easily refuted by historical evidence. Many economies have grown with very little government assistance: Great Britain in the Industrial Revolution; the Netherlands during the heyday of its colonial period; Singapore, Hong Kong, and Taiwan during modern times. Others, such as the Soviet Union and Austria, have sustained growth with a high degree of centralized control. Other countries have successfully used almost every conceivable mix of state and private initiative.

The Case for Planning

The case for active government intervention in the management of a country's economy rests on the real or alleged failure of market forces to produce satisfactory results. The major appeal of such intervention is that it is expected to accelerate the pace of economic development.

Many barriers to development may be lowered by appropriate government actions.

For example, when living standards are low, people have urgent uses for their current incomes, so savings tend to be low. Governments can intervene in a variety of ways and force people to save more than they otherwise would in order to ease a shortage of investment funds.

Compulsory saving has been one of the main aims of most development plans of centralized governments, such as those of the USSR and China. The goal of such plans is to raise savings and thus lower current consumption below what it would be in an unplanned economy. A less authoritarian method is to increase the savings rate through tax incentives and monetary policies. The object is the same: to increase investment in order to increase growth and thus to make future generations better off.

Authoritarian central governments can be particularly effective in overcoming some of the sources of X-inefficiency. A dictatorship may suppress social and even religious institutions that are barriers to growth, and it may hold on to power until a new generation grows up that did not know and does not value the old institutions. It is much more difficult for a democratic government, which must command popular support at each election, to do currently unpopular things in the interest of long-term growth. Whether the gains in growth that an authoritarian government can achieve are worth the political and social costs is, of course, an important value judgment.

The Case for the Market

Most people would accept that government must play an important part in any development program, especially in programs concerning education, transportation, and communication. But what of the sectors usually left to private enterprise in advanced capitalist countries?

The advocates of relying on market forces in these sectors place great emphasis on human drive, initiative, and inventiveness. Once the infrastructure has been established, they argue, an army of entrepreneurs will do vastly more to develop the economy than will an army of civil servants. The market will provide the opportunities and direct their efforts. People who seem lethargic and unenterprising when held down by lack of incentives will show bursts of energy when given sufficient self-interest in economic activity.

Furthermore, the argument goes, individual capitalists are far less wasteful of the country's capital than civil servants. A bureaucrat investing capital that is not his own (raised perhaps from the peasants by a state marketing board that buys cheap and sells dear) may choose to enhance his own prestige at the public's expense by spending too much money on cars, offices, and secretaries and too little on truly productive activities. Even if the bureaucrat is genuinely interested in the country's well-being, the incentive structure of a bureaucracy does not encourage creative risk taking. If his ventures fail, his head will likely roll; if they succeed, he will receive no profits—and his superior may get the medal. Thus he will be cautious about taking risks.

What Sorts of Education?

Most studies of less-developed countries suggest that undereducation is a barrier to development and often urge increased expenditures on education. This poses a choice: whether to spend educational funds on erasing illiteracy and increasing the level of mass education or on training a small cadre of scientific and technical specialists.

To improve basic education requires a large investment in school building and in teacher training. This investment will result in a visible change in the level of education only after 10 or more years, and it will not do much for productivity even over that time span. The opportunity cost of basic education expenditures always seems high. Yet it is essential to make them because the gains will be critical to economic development a generation later.

Many developing countries have put a large fraction of their educational resources into training a small number of highly educated men and women, often by sending them abroad for advanced study, because the results of acquiring a few hundred doctors or engineers or Ph.D.s are relatively more visible than the results of raising the school-leaving age by a year or two, say, from age 10 to age 12. It is not yet clear whether the policy of "educating the few" pays off, but it is clear that it has some drawbacks.

Many of the educated elite are recruited from the privileged classes on the basis of family position, not merit; many regard their education as the passport to a new aristocracy rather than as a mandate to serve their fellow citizens; and an appreciable fraction emigrate to countries where their newly acquired skills bring higher pay than they do at home. Of those who return home, many seek the security of a government job, which they may use to advance their own status in what is sometimes a self-serving and unproductive bureaucracy.

What Population Policy?

The race between population and income has been a dominant feature of many less-developed countries.

Where population is growing rapidly, there are only two possible ways for a country to win this race. One is to make a massive effort to achieve an income growth rate well in excess of the population growth rate. The other is to control population growth.

The problem *can* be solved by restricting population growth. However, the issues of whether and how to restrict population growth are controversial, since considerations of religion, custom, and education are involved.

The consequences of different population policies are large. The birthrate in Sweden is 12 per 1,000, in Venezuela, it is 42 per 1,000, and the two countries have similar death rates. The variations in birthrates have economic consequences. In Venezuela the net increase of population per year is 33 per 1,000 (3.3 percent), but it is only 3 per 1,000 (0.3 percent) in Sweden. If each country were to achieve an overall rate of growth of output of 3 percent per year, Sweden's living standards would be increasing by 2.7 percent per year, while Venezuela's would be falling by 0.3 percent per year. In 1983 Sweden's income per capita ($8,400) was 2½ times as high as Venezuela's ($3,400)—and Venezuela is the wealthiest country south of the Rio Grande. The gap will widen rapidly if present population trends continue.

Population control can take forms as mild as public education programs designed to alter attitudes toward family size and to encourage the avoidance of involuntary pregnancies. At the other extreme are massive programs of compulsory sterilization, such as Prime Minister Indira Gandhi attempted in India in the mid 1970s. Between these extremes are many possibilities, most of which use various economic and legal incentives or penalties to encourage a lower birthrate.

Customs can be changed to raise the average marriage age and hence lower the birthrate. Prohibition of child labor and the establishment of compulsory education alters the costs and benefits of having children and reduces desired family size. Changing the role of women and providing career alternatives outside the home can also lower the birthrate.

University of Maine Professor Johannes Overbeck reported recently that a comprehensive family planning program—involving the provision of a broad selection of birth control techniques, a broad range of social services, and accelerated research to develop more effective and cheaper contraceptives—would have an annual cost of $1 per capita in a typical less-developed country. Excluding mainland China, this amounts to around $2 billion per year for all LDCs combined, a relatively modest sum compared to the more than $500 billion currently spent annually on armaments. If this estimate is roughly accurate, population policy offers an extremely high return on spending to promote per capita growth in LDCs.

Different countries have adopted very different positions with respect to population. Kenya, with a birthrate of 50 per 1,000, until recently rejected any serious national policy of population control. Mexico, with nearly as high a birthrate in the early 1970s, began to dispense free contraceptives and family planning information and saw its annual rate of population growth drop from 3.2 percent to 2.5 percent in less than five years.

The Chinese—today a quarter of the world's population—have reduced their rate of population increase from more than 3 percent to less than 1 percent in the past 25 years by promoting later marriages and exhorting parents to value daughters as well as sons and thus to be content with fewer children. In 1980 China began more aggressive steps in an announced attempt to achieve zero population growth by the year 2000. Families that have only one child receive bonuses and preferential treatment in housing and in education for their offspring. (Housing space is allocated to all families as though they had one child.) Families that do not comply with the policy have their salaries decreased and are promoted more slowly.

The political, religious, and cultural dimensions of population policy lead some governments to resist population control. Positive economics cannot decide whether population control is desirable, but it can describe the consequences of any choice. Economic development is much easier to achieve with population control than without it.

How to Acquire Capital?

A country can raise funds for investment in three distinct ways: from the savings (voluntary or forced) of its domestic households and firms, by loans or investment from abroad, and by contributions from foreigners.

Capital from Domestic Saving: The Vicious Circle of Poverty

If capital is to be created at home by a country's own efforts, resources must be diverted from the production of goods for current consumption. This means a cut in present living standards. If living standards are already at or near the subsistence level, such a diversion will be difficult. At best, it will be possible to reallocate only a small proportion of resources to the production of capital goods.

Such a situation is often described as the *vicious circle of poverty*: Because a country has little capital per head, it is poor; because it is poor, it can devote few resources to creating new capital rather than to producing goods for consumption; because little new capital can be produced, capital per head remains low, and the country remains poor.

The vicious circle can be made to seem an absolute constraint on growth rates. Of course it is not; if it were, we would all still be at the level of Neanderthal man. The grain of truth in the vicious circle argument is that some surplus must be available somewhere in the society to allow saving and investment. In a poor society with an even distribution of income, where nearly everyone is at the subsistence level, saving may be very difficult. But this is not the common experience. Usually there is at least a small middle class that can save and invest if opportunities for the profitable use of funds arise. Also in most poor societies today the average household is above the physical subsistence level. Even the poorest households will find that they can sacrifice some present living standards for a future gain. For example, presented with a profitable opportunity, villagers in Ghana planted cocoa plants at the turn of the century even though there was a seven-year growing period before any return could be expected.

An important consideration is that in less-developed countries one resource that is often *not* scarce is labor. Profitable home or village investment that requires mainly labor inputs may be made with relatively little sacrifice in current living standards. However, this is not the kind of investment that will appeal to planners mesmerized by large and symbolic investments such as dams, nuclear power stations, and steel mills.

Imported Capital

Another way of accumulating the capital needed for growth is to borrow it from abroad. When a poor country borrows from a rich country, it can use the borrowed funds to purchase capital goods produced in the rich country. The poor country thus accumulates capital and needs to cut its current output of consumption goods only to pay interest on its loans. As the new capital begins to add to current production, it is possible to pay the interest on the loan and also to repay the principal out of the increase in output. This method has the great advantage of giving a poor country an initial increase in capital goods far greater than it could possibly have created by diverting its own resources from consumption industries.

However, many countries, developed or undeveloped, are suspicious of foreign capital. They fear that foreign investors will gain control over their industries or their government. The extent of foreign control depends on the form foreign capital takes. When foreigners buy bonds in domestic companies, they do not own or control anything. When they buy common stocks, they own part or all of a company, but their control over management may be small. When foreign companies establish plants and import their own managers and technicians, they have much more control. Finally, when foreign firms subsidize an LDC government in return for permission to produce, they may feel justified in exacting political commitments.

Whether foreign ownership of one's industries carries political disadvantages sufficiently large to outweigh the economic gains is a subject of debate. In Canada, for example, there is serious political opposition to having a large part of Canadian industry owned by U.S. nationals. Many other countries actively seek increased foreign investment.

During the period 1974 to 1984 reliance on foreign borrowing exploded to the point where it became a serious international problem for both LDCs and their creditors. During the 1970s the rising cost of oil to many oil-importing less-developed countries, combined with overly optimistic income expectations, led to massive borrowing by the LDCs. High interest rates in the 1980s greatly raised the cost of servicing this debt. World recession and rising protectionism in the developed world made it more difficult to earn the money necessary to pay interest on, let alone repay, the principal. For oil-importing countries the collapse of oil prices in 1985 provided some relief, but for oil exporters such as Mexico the oil price decline made things much worse. This problem, which had reached the dimensions of a crisis by the mid 1980s, is discussed with reference to Mexico in Box 22-1.

Contributed Capital

Investment funds for development are being received today by LDCs from the governments of the developed countries. These governments sometimes act unilaterally (for example, the program of the U.S. Agency for International Development and a similar Soviet program) and sometimes act through international agencies such as the World Bank, the Export-Import Bank, and the OPEC Fund established in January 1980. These funds are not really outright gifts but are "soft" loans on which repayment is not demanded in the near future. It is common to label them *contributed capital* to distinguish them from hard loans, on which repayment is expected under normal commercial terms.

The heyday of contributed capital occurred during the late 1970s and early 1980s, when the United States, the Soviet Union, and others sought to win the allegiance of third world LDCs by making soft loans and outright gifts. (See Box 22-2 on p. 454 for further discussion.)

Development Strategies

In the search for development, individual LDCs have a number of policy options. The choice of options is in part a matter of what the planners believe will work and in part a question of the nature of the society that will be created once development has occurred.

The noneconomic aspects of the choice of a development strategy may be illustrated by the Greek government's explicit decision in the mid 1960s to change the direction of its growth. At that time Greece was achieving rapid growth largely because of a booming tourist trade and the emigration of many young Greeks to West Germany to work in factories there. The emigrants had been earning incomes in Greece that were substantially below the Greek average, and their remittances home to their families increased both domestic income and foreign exchange reserves. Although these events were helpful to the Greek growth rate, they threatened an image of life that visualized "Greece for the Greeks." Even at the prospect of some loss in growth, Greek planners recommended the restriction of emigration, the moderation of the size of the tourist role in the economy, and the development of new industry for the Greek economy.

There may also be economic reasons for choosing a different pattern of growth than the free market would provide. An important role of planning is to direct growth in a different direction, one that the planners guess will have the greatest chance of long-run success.

Unplanned growth will usually tend to exploit the country's present comparative advantages; planners may choose a pattern of growth that involves trying to change the country's future comparative advantages.

One reason planners seek to do so is their belief that they can evaluate the future more accurately than the countless individuals whose decisions determine market prices. As argued in Chapter 20, a country need not passively accept its current comparative advantages. Many skills can be acquired, and fostering an apparently uneconomic domestic industry may, by changing the characteristics of the labor force, develop a comparative advantage in that line of production. Critics point to the many notable failures where governments evaluated possibilities much less successfully than private markets did. They say that these failures must be studied as cautionary tales before planners are carried away by the spectacular successes of such newly industrializing countries as Singapore, South Korea, Taiwan, and Hong Kong.

The Japanese had no visible comparable advantage in any industrial skill when Commodore Matthew Perry opened that feudal country to Western influence in 1854, but they became a major industrial power by the end of the century. Their continuing gains relative to competitors in North America and Europe in fields such as steel, automobile production, and electronics do not need to be called to anyone's attention today. (Neither, however, were

BOX 22-1

Debt and the LDCs

The 1970s and early 1980s witnessed explosive growth of the external debt of many LDCs. Recently a number of these countries have experienced difficulties in making the payments required to service their debt. "Debt reschedulings"—putting off until tomorrow payments that cannot be made today—have been common, and many observers feel that major defaults are inevitable unless ways of forgiving the debt can be found. Recently several countries, most notably Brazil, have been unable even to meet their scaled-down interest payments, and under present circumstances repayment of any principal seems quite impossible.

The trend to increased debt started when OPEC quadrupled the world price of oil in 1973. Because many LDCs relied on imported oil, their balance of trade moved sharply into deficit. At the same time, the OPEC countries developed massive trade surpluses. Commercial banks helped *recycle* the deposits of their OPEC customers into loans to the deficit LDCs. These loans financed some necessary adjustments and worthwhile new investment projects in the LDCs. However, not all of the funds were used wisely; wasteful government spending and lavish consumption splurges occurred in a number of borrowing countries.

A doubling of energy prices in 1979 led to a further increase in LDC debt. The severe world recession that began in 1981 reduced demand for the exports of many of the LDCs. As a result, the LDCs were unable to achieve many benefits from the adjustments and investment expenditures they had made. Furthermore, sharp increases in real interest rates led to increased debt-service payments; as a result, many of the LDCs could not make their payments.

The lending banks had little choice but to reschedule the debt—essentially lending the LDCs the money to make interest payments while adding to the principal of the existing loans. The International Monetary Fund (IMF) played a central role in arranging these reschedulings, making further loans and concessions conditional on appropriate policies of adjustment and restraint. These conditions presumably were intended to limit wasteful government expenditure and consumption and thus increase the likelihood that the loans would eventually be repaid. Critics of the IMF's role, however, argued that much of the restraint resulted in reduced investment, and thus the IMF conditions were counterproductive.

In the mid 1980s the world economy recovered and interest rates fell. As a result, the LDC's export earnings grew, their debt-service obligations stabi-

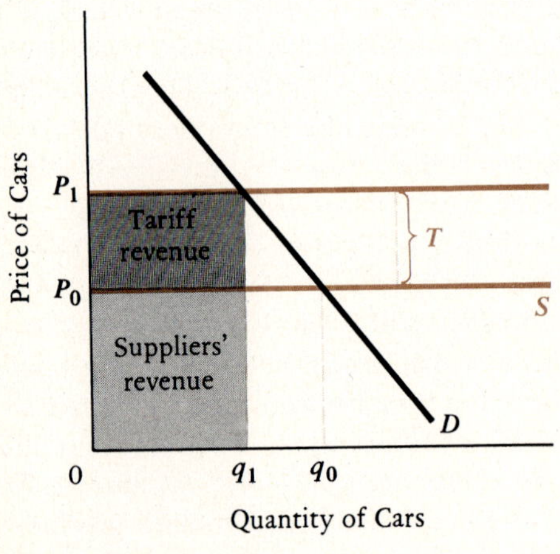

(i) Tariff of T Dollars Per Car

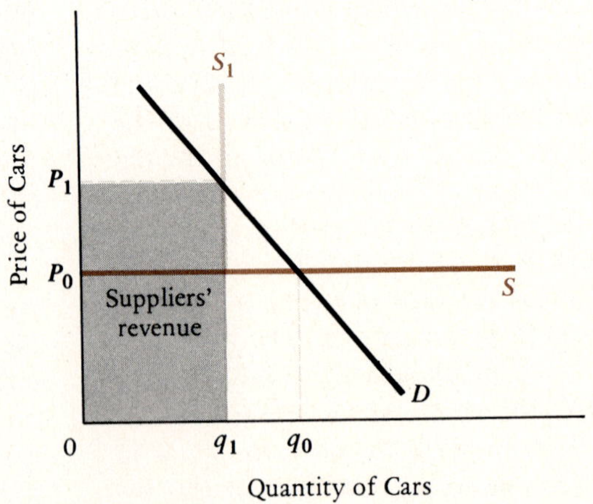

(ii) Quota of Q_1 Cars

lized, and the crisis appeared to subside. The sharp *fall* in the price of oil, which started in late 1985, further eased the problems of the oil-importing LDCs, but it also created a new debt problem.

Throughout the period of rising energy prices, a number of *oil-exporting* LDCs—including Mexico, Venezuela, and Indonesia—saw in those high prices new opportunities for investment and growth. Based on their high oil revenues, their ability to borrow improved. Their external debt grew, and they were able to avoid many of the adjustments that the oil-importing LDCs had been forced to undertake. When oil prices fell, these oil-exporters found themselves in a very difficult position.

Mexico provides an illustrative case study. Its oil revenues doubled from around $8 billion in 1978 to $16 billion by 1982. This increased earning capacity led to increased borrowing, and its external debt also doubled in the same period, from $40 billion in 1978 to $80 billion in 1982. Even with its high oil revenues, however, not all was well; in the words of the *The Economist,* "Mexico officially opened the international debt crisis in 1982."

For a number of reasons, including bad investment decisions and the world recession, Mexico's export earnings did not increase as fast as its debt. Soaring real interest rates meant that by 1982 Mexico was unable to service its debt. Only a major debt rescheduling, conditional on severe fiscal restraint and a devaluation to stimulate exports, prevented a probable default.

Continued borrowing, much of it necessary just to service its existing debt, meant that Mexico's debt continued to rise; by 1986 the debt had risen to $100 billion. For much of this period, the spending restraint in Mexico combined with the recovery in the world economy and the fall in world interest rates led to a gradual improvement in Mexico's prospects for growing out from under its debt burden. But in 1986 world oil prices fell, and Mexico's oil revenues plummeted to around $8 billion. A new crisis emerged.

The 1986 situation was different from the situation in 1982 in several important ways. The world economy and the international financial system were both healthier. Lower real interest rates and lower oil prices meant that other LDCs were able to repay their loans; hence there was less fear of a collapse of the international financial system.

But for Mexico the 1986 crisis was worse than the 1982 one. Domestic restraint had been pushed virtually to the limit; the government deficit had been cut by over 6 percent of GNP in just two years. Headlines in the international press proclaimed, "With Mexico Focusing on Debt Repayment, Ports and Roads Suffer" and "Mexican Children Scrounge for Food as Schools Drop Free Lunch."

Projections showed that Mexico would require major foreign borrowing if it were to continue to meet its interest obligations on existing debt. Commercial banks were not eager to lend any more on their own initiative. The IMF tried to negotiate a loan package based on further restraint, and U.S. Secretary of the Treasury James Baker proposed a plan with renewed lending conditional on major economic adjustment. But further restraint and rapid adjustment seemed politically impossible in a country already racked by massive restraint and plummeting export revenues; many economists argued that restraint would in any event retard growth and prove counterproductive.

A major impasse thus arose. Using the threat of default, Mexico demanded major concessions on the terms of its new borrowing. The "crisis" situation stimulated innovative proposals. One proposal was for the banks to forgive some debt in return for equity participation in Mexico's oil and other industries; this would reduce the burden of Mexico's debt-service payments while sharing some of the risks of the Mexican situation between Mexico and its creditors.

In mid 1986 an agreement was reached providing for major new borrowing; for the first time in IMF history, the terms not only included conditions that appropriate adjustment policies be undertaken but also a provision for repayment linked to the price of the borrowing country's exports, in this case oil. This provision is intended to forestall further crises by allowing the required payments to fluctuate with the country's ability to pay.

BOX 22-2

"Aid," "Trade," or "Restitution"

The motivations behind international giving are the subject of debate. Do developed nations give aid for humanitarian reasons, because it serves their political objectives, or because it is economically self-serving? Of course, all three motives can play a role, but which one dominates? Should LDCs demand aid, accept it gratefully, or reject it?

LDCs more or less chronically lack capital and lack wealth. Typically they have large foreign debts as a result of past borrowing. In these circumstances one might think that foreign aid, whether from a single country or from an international agency, would be eagerly sought and gratefully received. This is not always so; there is some significant resistance to accepting aid.

The slogan "Trade, not aid" reflected political opposition in certain recipient countries in the 1950s to economic aid coming from the developed countries. Yugoslavia turned down much aid proffered by the Soviets after 1948, and China accepted no foreign aid after 1960. In 1975 Colombia made the decision to forego further U.S. aid on the grounds that it bred an unhealthy economic dependency.

The primary explanation of this attitude lies in a country's noneconomic goals. It may suspect the motives of the givers and fear that hidden strings may be attached to the offer. Independent countries prize their independence and want to avoid either the fact or the appearance of being satellites. Pride—a desire to be beholden to no one—is also a factor.

One response was to do without aid, no matter how badly it was needed. Another, increasingly the pattern in the 1970s, was to reject "aid" but to demand "wealth transfers," not as a matter of charity but as a matter of "restitution" or redress for past sins by colonial powers against their former colonies. The obvious problem of asserting such claims against noncolonial powers such as the United States and the USSR has been no deterrent. There is a generalized sense that the inhabitants of the "North" exploited the nations of the "South" in past centuries and that present generations should redress the balance. The paradoxical aspect of this is that while "restitution, not charity" makes LDCs willing to accept aid, precisely that claim decreases the willingness of developed countries to offer it.

What *are* the motives of givers of aid? Nobel Laureat in Economics Gunnar Myrdal argued that humanitarian considerations have played a large role. The evidence for the existence of humanitarian motives is in part the success of voluntary appeals in developed countries for food, funds, and clothes for persons in stricken areas of the world. As per capita incomes have risen in the Western world, so have contributions, private as well as public. It is the policy of the governments of most of the so-called Western democracies to devote some resources to alleviating poverty throughout the world.

American Professor Edward S. Mason, among others, has argued that U.S. aid can best be understood by looking to political and security motives. He points to the substantial U.S. congressional preference for military assistance over economic assistance, the denial of aid to countries such as Sri Lanka that traded with communist countries, and the fostering of Yugoslavia *because* of its anti-Soviet stand—all of which reveal a strong political motive. Many critics of OPEC think that the large contributions made by member countries were designed to quiet opposition among LDCs to the oil price hikes that proved so profitable to the oil producers and so painful to oil users, LDCs and developed countries alike.

Canada has a record of less politically motivated aid, being willing to help governments representing a much wider coverage of the political spectrum than has the United States. Though accounting for less than 5 percent of Canadian GDP, its aid program has made a significant impact in a number of LDCs.

Should motives and attitudes, either of givers or of receivers, matter? After all, it is economically beneficial to receive aid when you are poor. Economists cannot say that fears, aspirations, pride, and "face" are either foolish or unworthy; they can only note that they do have their cost.

the gains primarily centrally planned, and the importance of support from the Japanese planning agency, MITI, remains a subject of debate.) Soviet planners in the 1920s and 1930s chose to create an industrial economy out of a predominantly agricultural one and succeeded in dramatically changing the mix between agriculture and industry in a single generation.

These illustrations suggest why the choice of development strategy is crucial. Governments must choose between agricultural and industrial emphases, between different kinds of industrial development, and between more or less reliance on foreign trade. Several possibilities have been widely advocated, and each has been tried. None is without difficulties.

Agricultural Development

Everyone needs food. An LDC may choose to devote a major portion of its resources to stimulating agricultural production, say, by mechanizing farms, irrigating land, and using new seeds and fertilizers. If successful, the country will stave off starvation for its current population, and it may even develop an excess over current needs and so have a crop available for export. A food surplus can earn foreign exchange to buy needed imports.

Among the attractions of the agricultural strategy are that it does not require a great deal of technical training or hard-to-acquire know-how, nor does it place the country in direct competition with highly industrial countries.

India, Pakistan, Taiwan, and other Asian countries have achieved dramatic increases in food production by the application of new technology and the use of new seed in agricultural production. Increases of up to 50 percent have been achieved in grain production, and it has been estimated that with adequate supplies of water, pesticides, fertilizers, and modern equipment, production could be doubled or tripled. This has been labeled the *green revolution*.

Big, rural, poor countries are usually well advised to start with policies designed to increase agricultural output in order to use the existing labor force and increase standards of living. But the gains from this strategy, while large at first, are subject to diminishing returns. Further gains in agricultural production have an ever higher opportunity cost, in the resources needed to irrigate land and to mechanize production. Critics of sole reliance on agricultural output argue that underdeveloped economies must start at once to develop other bases for economic growth.

One problem with heavy reliance on the agricultural strategy is that it frequently requires heavy initial subsidization of agricultural production and also some means of subsidizing consumption of increased quantities of food by a poor population. A common device is to provide artificially high prices to producers and artificially low prices to consumers. Once such a program is put in place, it creates a serious potential dilemma. Continuation of the artificially high prices for producers and low prices for consumers creates a substantial drain on the government's finances. Lowering the subsidy to producers risks a rural revolution; eliminating the subsidy to consumers risks an urban revolution. The government finds itself with an untenable policy and no room for maneuver.

Specialization in a Few Commodities

Many LDCs have unexploited resources such as copper, uranium, or opportunities for tourism. The principle of comparative advantage provides the traditional case for the desirability of relying on such resources. By specializing in producing products in which it has the greatest comparative advantage, the country can achieve the most rapid growth in the short run. To neglect these opportunities will result in a lower standard of living than would result from specialization accompanied by increased international trade.

These are cogent reasons in favor of *some* specialization. But specialization involves risks, and it may be worthwhile to reduce the risks by maintaining diversification even at the cost of loss of some income. Specialization in a few commodities makes the economy highly vulnerable to cyclic fluctuations in world demand and supply. For example, a recession in developed countries or fear of terrorism decreases overseas travel and creates problems for an LDC that has relied on tourism for foreign exchange.

The problem is not only short-run. When

changes in technology or taste render a product partially or wholly obsolete, a country can face a major calamity. Just as individual firms and regions may become overspecialized, so too may countries.

Import Substitution Industrialization

During the Great Depression the collapse in world agricultural prices caused the value of the exports of agricultural countries to decline drastically relative to the prices of goods those countries imported. During World War II many countries found that the manufactured goods they wished to import were unavailable. In each of those situations dependence on foreign trade for necessities was unattractive. During the 1970s the rising prices of fuel and other imports created enormous balance-of-payments problems for many LDCs. Such countries were forced to reduce imports, increase exports, or resort to foreign borrowing.

Much of the industrialization by LDCs in the 1950s and 1960s was directed toward **import substitution industry (ISI),** that is, industry to produce at home goods that were previously imported. It is often necessary both to subsidize the home industry and to restrict imports to allow the ISI time to develop.

LDCs sometimes pursue certain lines of production on a subsidized basis for prestige purposes or because of a confusion between cause and effect. Because most wealthy nations have a steel industry, the leaders of many underdeveloped nations regard their countries as primitive until they develop a domestic steel industry. Because several LDCs have succeeded in producing consumer durables, many others assume that they should try to do so. However, if a country has a serious comparative disadvantage in steel or in making consumer durables, fostering such industries will make that country even poorer.

The ISI strategy has many problems. It fosters *inefficient* industries, and in the long run countries do not get rich by being inefficient. It aggravates inequalities in income distribution by raising the prices of manufactured goods relative to agricultural goods and by favoring profits over wages.

Export Development

Most development economists believe that industrialization ought to be encouraged only in areas where the country can develop a reliable and efficient industry that can compete in world markets.

Obviously, if Tanzania or Peru could develop steel, shipbuilding, and manufacturing industries that operated as efficiently as those of Japan or West Germany, they might share in the rapid economic growth enjoyed by those industrial countries. Indeed, if a decade or two of protection and subsidization could give infant industries time to mature and become efficient, the price might be worth paying. After all, within living memory Japan and Russia were underdeveloped countries.

Industrialization for export can sometimes be done by employing inexperienced workers in simple, labor-intensive enterprises, such as sewing clothing. But it often means devoting resources for a long period to education, training, infrastructure development, and overcoming any cultural and social barriers to efficient production. This is difficult but not impossible. Indeed, there have been some spectacular success stories. Brazil, Korea, Hong Kong, and Taiwan are charter members in the category of **newly industrializing countries (NICs)** that are providing vigorous competition in manufactured goods in world markets.

Their success has led to a further (and bitterly resented) problem for the industrialization strategy. When an LDC succeeds, it is likely to find the developed countries trying to protect *their* home industries from the new competition.

Import substitution and export development do not need to be seen as alternative development strategies. Many now successful trading countries used import substitution in the first stages of their development strategy. The intention was to create the domestic industrial base, and the human capital, that were needed for industrial success. Once that base was in place, emphasis could be shifted to export encouragement.

Canada used import substitution to build its industries behind high tariff walls in the first half of the twentieth century. Throughout the second half of the century it has lowered tariffs to integrate its developing export industries into the world economy. Singapore and Korea used import substitution policies in their early stages of development. Japan also did so in selected industries. The most recent example was in semiconductors (which include the chips that drive computers): The domestic industry developed behind a prohibitive Japanese tariff and then went on to lead the world in exports of semiconductors.

The challenge is not, therefore, to choose at an early stage of growth between import substitution and export development policies for all time. The challenge, if import substitution policies are adopted first, is to be able to shift into export-encouraging policies at a later stage. Such a shift will not occur if the wrong industries are chosen for import substitution so that they remain sickly infants indefinitely or if strong vested interests in the sheltered industries are able to prevent the country's later transition to an export-oriented strategy.

Cartelization

When all or most producers of a commodity can agree on price and output levels, they can achieve monopoly profits not available in competitive markets. Many LDCs are heavily committed to the production and export of one or more basic commodities such as bananas, bauxite, cocoa, coffee, copper, cotton, iron ore, jute, manganese, meat, oil, phosphates, rubber, sugar, tea, tropical timber, and tin. Why do not all producers of, say, bananas get together and create an effective cartel that gives producers the enormous profits that are potentially available?

Cartelization has been tried many times in history. Until OPEC it has always failed, yet everyone knows that OPEC transformed a handful of formerly poor LDCs into the wealthiest of nations.[3] OPEC's success was substantial, but it proved difficult to sustain. The special reasons for its success for almost 10 years and its subsequent difficulties are discussed in Chapter 14.

Wheat, coffee, cocoa, tin, rubber, and copper have all been suggested as potential subjects for similar commodity price stabilization agreements, but they lack the small number of politically cohesive producers and inelastic short-run demand and supply conditions that gave the OPEC cartel its initial successes.

[3] This has added to the terminological confusion. It was once fashionable to speak of a nonaligned *third world* as another term for LDCs, the first two "worlds" being the developed capitalist countries and the developed socialist countries. Now some commentators divide the LDCs into a richer (oil-producing) *third world* and a still poor *fourth world*.

Some Controversial Unresolved Issues

There are some lively current controversies among development economists. Among them are the following.

A New International Economic Order (NIEO)

In May 1974 the General Assembly of the United Nations adopted (over the objections of the developed countries) the Declaration on the Establishment of a New International Economic Order. This represented an attempt on the part of LDCs to use collective *political* power to achieve a larger share of the world's goods.[4]

The NIEO proposals are aimed basically at wealth transfers instead of wealth creation; they are concerned with a more equal distribution of existing wealth rather than economic development.

The major proposals were threefold. First, marketing boards for primary products exported by the developing nations should be established. These, modeled along the lines of OPEC, would reduce output, raise prices, and thus create monopoly profits for producers. Second, exports of manufactured goods from developing countries should receive

[4] An excellent introduction to this development is Rachel McCulloch's *Economic and Political Issues in the NIEO* (International Institute for Economic Research, 1979).

preferential tariffs or quotas in the markets of developed countries. Third, the enormous debts of the developing countries, incurred partly to finance development projects and partly to finance the increased cost of oil imports during the 1970s, should be partly forgiven and partly rescheduled to provide for longer repayment periods and easier terms of finance.

Thus far, the NIEO demands have produced few results, although attention to the debt burdens of LDCs has occurred in response to other forces. The NIEO proposals have been discussed extensively, but little major redistribution of wealth has resulted. To most market-oriented economists, NIEO has two major flaws. First, it focuses too much on redistribution and too little on seeking real growth in world output. Second, it relies on bureaucratic allocations of wealth, trade, and natural resources rather than on market mechanisms. Nothing in the world's experience to date suggests that this will increase total world output; indeed, it will probably decrease it.

The Pace of Development

Reformers in less-developed countries often think in terms of transforming their economies within a generation or two. The sense of urgency is quite understandable, but unless it is tempered by some sense of historical perspective, totally unreasonable aspirations may develop, only to be dashed all too predictably.

Many underdeveloped countries are probably in a stage of economic development analogous to that of medieval England, having not yet achieved anything like the commercial sophistication of the Elizabethan era. It took 600 years for England to develop from the medieval economic stage to its present one. Such a change would be easier now, for much of the needed technology can be imported rather than invented. But what is the proper pace? To effect a similar growth within 50 or 100 years would require a tremendous achievement of the kind accomplished by the United States, Japan, and a handful of other countries; to aspire to do it in 20 or 30 years may be to court disaster—or to invite repressive political regimes.

The View of Population Policy

The view presented in this chapter of population growth as a formidable barrier to development is neo-Malthusian and constitutes much of current conventional wisdom on underdevelopment.

This view allows little place for the enjoyment value of children by their parents. Critics point out that the psychic value of children should be included as a part of the living standards of their parents. They also point out that in rural societies even young children are a productive resource, and in societies where state help for the aged is negligible, fully grown children provide old-age security for their parents.

The neo-Malthusian theory is also criticized for assuming that people breed blindly, as animals do. Critics point out that traditional methods of limiting family size have been known and practiced since the dawn of history. Thus they argue that large families in rural societies are a matter of choice.

The population explosion came not through any change in "breeding habits" but as a result of medical advances that greatly extended life expectancy (which surely must be counted as a direct welfare gain for those affected). Critics argue that once an urban society has developed, family size will be reduced voluntarily. This was certainly the experience of Western industrial countries; why, critics ask, should it not be the experience of the developing countries?

The Cost of Creating Capital

Is it true that LDCs must suffer by sacrificing current consumption if they wish to grow? A recent criticism of this conventional wisdom questions the alleged heavy opportunity cost of creating domestic capital. Production of consumption and capital goods are substitutes only when factor supplies are constant and fully employed. But, critics say, the development of a market economy will lead people to substitute work for leisure.

For example, the arrival of Europeans with new goods to trade led the North American Indians to collect furs and other commodities needed for exchange. Until they were decimated by later generations of land-hungry settlers, the Indians' standard of living rose steadily with no immediate sacrifice. They created the capital needed for their production—weapons and means of transport—in their abundant leisure time. Thus their consumption began to rise immediately.

This, the argument says, could happen in less-developed countries if market transactions were allowed to evolve naturally. The spread of a market economy would lead people to give up leisure in order to produce the goods needed to buy the goods that private traders are introducing from the outside world. In this view it is the pattern of development chosen, rather than development itself, that imposes the need for heavy sacrifices.

Is There a "Best" Strategy for Development?

Each of the five strategies discussed—agricultural development, specialization, import substitution, export development, and cartelization—has been tried, and each has problems. Because countries differ, there is no single best strategy, but a substantial consensus is being reached among experts that rapid economic development requires at least three simultaneous thrusts: (1) sufficient agricultural development to provide a healthier, better-fed population and work force, (2) sufficient restraint on population growth to permit rising per capita income, and (3) sufficient development of export commodities to allow the country to trade for essentials it must import. Whether the export commodities should be agricultural, natural resources, light manufactures, heavy manufactures, or services depends on comparative advantage.

Import substitution policies that do not lead eventually to industries that can compete in world markets and price stabilization agreements seem much less promising strategies than they did a decade ago, although there may be specific situations in which each may be helpful.

Finally, a word of warning is in order. The view presented in this chapter is perhaps the mainline view of economists in developed economies such as our own. Problems look different when viewed from the inside out, and they look different from the perspective of socialist nations than they do from market-oriented economies.

Summary

1. Sustained economic development is relatively recent in history and has been highly uneven. About one-fourth of the world's population still exists at a level of bare subsistence, and nearly three-fourths are poor by American standards. The gap between rich and poor is large, keenly felt, and not decreasing.
2. Incentives for economic development include the demonstration effect of other countries' successful transformation from peasant economy to industrial power and the opportunity to receive aid from developed countries.
3. Impediments to economic development include population growth, resource limitations, inefficient use of resources, and institutional and cultural patterns that make economic growth difficult.
4. A series of basic choices face LDCs as they contemplate development. How much should governments intervene in the economy, and how much should the economy be left to operate on the free market? History has demonstrated that growth is possible with almost any conceivable mixture of free-market and central control. Centralized planning can change both the pace and the direction of

economic development; it can also prove highly wasteful and destroy individual initiative.

5. Educational policy, while vitally important to the long-run rate of economic development, yields its benefits only in the future. Improvement of basic education for the general populace is sometimes bypassed for the more immediate visible results of educating a selected technical and political elite.
6. The race between output and population is a critical aspect of development efforts in many countries. Different countries have different attitudes toward limiting population growth and have chosen different population policies.
7. Capital for development is invariably a major concern in development. It can be acquired from domestic savings, but the vicious circle of poverty may arise: A country that is poor because it has little capital cannot readily forego consumption to accumulate capital because it is poor. Importing capital rather than using domestic savings permits heavy investment during the early years of development, but imported capital is available only when the LDC has opportunities that are attractive to foreign investors. Much foreign capital for LDCs since the 1950s has been in the form of soft loans or contributions by foreign governments and international institutions.
8. Development involves choices among different strategies: agricultural development, specialization based on natural resources, development of import substitution industries, development of new export industries, and cartelization. None of these strategies is without problems and risks.
9. Most experts in development believe that the most appropriate approach is a multipronged strategy that includes at least some agricultural development, some development of new export commodities, and some restraint on population growth.
10. Among controversial unresolved issues is the appropriateness of attempting to solve problems of underdevelopment by wealth transfers rather than wealth creation. This is the thrust of the NIEO proposals. Other controversies concern the pace of development, the neo-Malthusian view of population growth as a problem, and the cost of creating capital in terms of sacrifices of current consumption.

Topics for Review

Gap between LDCs and developed countries
Barriers to development
Infrastructure
Role of planning in development
Alternative development strategies
Wealth creation versus wealth transfers

Discussion Questions

1. Each of the following is a headline from the *New York Times*. Relate them to the problem of economic development.
   a. "Black Africa: Economies on the brink of collapse because of OPEC"
   b. "Hungary reforming economy to attract tourists"
   c. "Goodyear to build plant in Congo for $16 million"
   d. "Algeria's 4-year plan stresses industrial growth"
   e. "India: Giant hobbled by erratic rainfall"
   f. "Foreign banks to finance New Guinea copper mine"
   g. "Not all benefit by green revolution"
   h. "OPEC nations provide loans to underdeveloped nations to pay for oil imports"
2. If you were a member of a Canadian foreign aid team assigned to study needed development projects for a poor recipient country, to which of the following would you be likely to give relatively high priority, and why?
   a. Birth control clinics
   b. A national airline
   c. Taxes on imported luxuries
   d. Better roads
   e. Modernization of farming techniques
   f. Training in engineering and business management
   g. Primary education
   h. Scholarships to students to receive medical and legal training abroad
3. China requires 5 million tons more grain each year just to keep up with its annual population growth of 17 million people. This is about five times Canada's wheat supply at present. What policy choices do these facts pose for the Chinese government? How should it resolve those choices?
4. "This natural inequality of the two powers of population and of production in the earth . . . form the great difficulty that to me appears insurmountable in the way to perfectability of society. All other arguments are of slight and subordinate consideration in comparison of this. I see no way by which man can escape from the weight of this law which pervades all animated nature. No fancied equality, no agrarian revolutions in their utmost extent, could remove the pressure of it even for a single century" (T. R. Malthus, *Population: The First Essay,* page 6).

   Discuss Malthus' "insurmountable difficulty" in view of the history of the past 100 years.
5. To what extent does the vicious circle of poverty apply to poor families living in developed countries? Consider carefully, for example, the similarities and differences facing a poor family living in Cape Breton Island and one living in Ghana, where per capita income is less than $400 per year. Did it apply to immigrants who arrived on the Montreal docks with $10 in their pockets?
6. The president of an LDC said in 1980, "A decision by OPEC members to raise petroleum prices should be applauded by all third world countries. It represents the irrevocable decision to dignify the

terms of trade, to revalue raw materials and other basic products of the third world." Can you guess whether that country was an oil exporter or importer? Might an underdeveloped country that is an oil importer want to see OPEC succeed in raising oil prices?

7. "High coffee prices bring hope to impoverished Latin American peasants," reads the headline. Mexico, Kenya, and Burundi, among other LDCs, have the right combination of soil and climate to increase their coffee production greatly. Discuss the benefits and risks to them if they pursue coffee production as a major avenue of their development.

PART SEVEN

The Market Economy: Problems and Policies

23

Benefits and Costs of Government Intervention

There are two caricatures of the Canadian economy. One pictures Canada as one of the last strongholds of free enterprise, with millions of Canadians involved in a mad and brutal race for the almighty dollar. In the other, Canadian business people, workers, and farmers are seen strangling slowly in a web of red tape spun by the spider of government regulation. Neither is realistic.

Many aspects of economic life in Canada are determined by the operation of a free-market system. Private preferences, expressed through private markets and influencing private profit-seeking enterprises, determine much of what is produced, how it is produced, and the incomes of productive factors.

But even casual observation makes it clear that public policies and public decisions play a large role. Laws restrict what people and firms may do, and taxes and subsidies influence their choices. Much public expenditure is not market determined, and this influences the distribution of national product. Canada's is in fact a mixed economy.

The general case for some reliance on free markets is that allowing decentralized decision making is more efficient in a number of ways than having all economic decisions made by a centralized planning body. This is a lesson that the governments of the USSR and Eastern Europe have learned the hard way.

The general case for some public intervention is that almost no one wants to let the market decide everything about our economic affairs. Most people's moral and practical sense argues for some state intervention to mitigate the disastrous results that the market deals out to some. Most people believe that there are areas where the market does not function well and where state intervention can improve the general social good. For such reasons, there is no known economy where the people have opted for complete free market determination of all economic matters and against any kind of government intervention.

Although many nineteenth century economists advocated a policy of **laissez faire**, the absence of any government interference with the operation of markets, the operative choice today is not between an unhampered free-market economy and a fully centralized command economy. It is instead the choice of what mix of markets and government intervention best suits a people's hopes and needs. Although all economies are mixed, the mixture varies greatly among economies and over time. Whether the existing mixture is wrong—and if so, in which direction—is debated continually.

One reason there are mixed economies lies in what an unkind critic once called the economists' two great insights: *Markets can work, and markets can fail.* A second reason is what the critic might have called the political scientists' two great insights: *Government intervention can work, and government intervention can fail.*

In this chapter we discuss the role of the government in economic markets. Why is it there at all? What does it do well, and what does it do badly? Do we need more or less government intervention? Box 23-1 explores the relationship between economic analysis and the formation of economic policy.

How Markets Coordinate

Any economy consists of thousands upon thousands of individual markets. There are markets for agricultural goods, for manufactured goods, and for consumers' services; there are markets for intermediate goods such as steel and pig iron, which are outputs of some industries and inputs of others; there are markets for raw materials such as iron ore, trees, bauxite, and copper; there are markets for land and for thousands of different types of labor; there are markets in which money is borrowed and in which securities are sold. An economy is not a series of markets functioning in isolation but an interlocking system in which an occurrence in one market affects many others.

Any change, such as an increase in demand for a product, requires many further changes and adjustments. Should production of the product change? If so, by how much and in what manner? This in turn will require changes in other markets and will start a chain of adjustments. Someone or something must decide what is to be produced, how, and by whom and what is to be consumed and by whom.

The essential characteristic of the market system is that its coordination occurs in an unplanned, decentralized way. Millions of people make millions of independent decisions concerning production and consumption every day. Most of these decisions are not motivated by a desire to contribute to the social good or to make the whole economy work well but by fairly immediate considerations of self-interest. The price system coordinates these decentralized decisions, making the whole system fit together and respond to the wishes of the individuals who compose it.

The basic insight into how this system works is that decentralized, private decision makers, acting in their own interests, respond to such signals as the prices of what they buy and sell. Economists have long emphasized price as a signaling device. When a commodity becomes scarce, its free-market price rises. Firms and households that use the commodity are led to economize on it and to look for alternatives. Firms that produce it are led to produce more of it. How the price system guides these decisions has been examined at several places in this book (for example, with respect to carrots and brussels sprouts in Chapter 3, agriculture in Chapter 6, and ball-point pens in Chapter 17). When a shortage occurs in a market, price rises and profits develop; when a glut occurs, price falls and losses develop. These are *signals,* for all to see, that arise from the overall conditions of total supply and demand.

The Role of Windfall Profits and Losses

Although the free-market economy is often described as the *price system,* the basic engine of the economy is economic profits, often called windfall profits.[1] Windfall profits and losses are symptoms of *disequilibrium,* and they are the driving force in the adaptation of the economy to change.

A rise in demand or a fall in production costs creates profits for that commodity's producers, whereas a fall in demand or a rise in production costs creates losses. Profits make an industry attractive to new investment. They signal that there are too few

[1] The term *windfall* has the connotation of "undeserved" or "unearned," and this is often the case, as when a rise in demand confers profits on all producers in an industry. But whether such profits (or losses) arise this way or as a result of the firm's own efforts is immaterial. It is their existence, not their source, that matters. The key point is that windfall profits are *temporary* economic profits.

Windfall gains and losses were discussed in Chapter 17 in relation to all factors of production, where they were referred to by their more technical name, *dynamic differentials.*

BOX 23-1

Economic Analysis and Economic Policy

All governments have economic policies. Even the decision not to act but to let nature take its course is a policy choice. Whether to rely on marketplace decision making or to replace it by government controls is as much a policy choice as the decision to tax cigarettes.

Every year thousands of economic policy choices are made by federal, provincial, and municipal governments. Most of them are never seriously debated, nor is every facet of existing policy debated anew each year. Indeed, many current policies (such as giving unions the right to organize) were made decades ago. Only a few policy issues attract attention and become the subject of debate in a particular year.

Any policy action has two aspects: the goals that the decision makers are attempting to achieve and the means by which the goals are to be achieved. Economists do not establish goals, but they are often involved in resolving conflicts among competing goals, forging the links between goals, and evaluating policy proposals.

Governments have many goals. A particular policy that serves one goal may hinder another and have no effect on a third. Unemployment compensation, for example, may promote justice by protecting unemployed families from debilitating hardships; at the same time, it may hinder the quickness with which labor moves from labor-surplus to labor-scarce occupations, thereby causing inefficient use of resources. Moreover, it will have no effect one way or the other on air pollution.

Economics helps us to discover conflicts between competing goals of policy. For example, raising the minimum wage may seem desirable to people who believe that the lowest-paid workers are not earning enough income to maintain a decent standard of living. But if that policy results in some workers' being laid off and becoming unemployed, the advantages to those who get higher wages must be balanced against the disadvantages of the extra unemployment.

Economists are frequently called on to suggest policies. The Economic Council of Canada has contributed to policy formation through its Annual Reviews, published each year since 1964. Among academic economists who have influenced policy in Canada, the most outstanding figure was W. A. Mackintosh, whose influence spanned a period of 50 years. A frequent vehicle for extragovernmental influence on policy is the Royal Commission. The report of the Carter Commission of 1964 is well known within and outside Canada as a classic statement of the equity aspects of taxation. More recently, the Macdonald Commission provided a wide-ranging analysis of Canadian economic problems and past forward a large number of policy recommendations.

Forming and Evaluating Policies

Economists must frequently determine whether a particular policy proposal—which may or may not have originated with them—is the best way to meet a particular problem. Five main questions need to be asked in every case: (1) What are the policy goals? (2) Do the proposed means achieve those goals? (3) What costs are directly imposed? (4) Do the proposed means have adverse side effects? (5) Are there better alternative means?

Policy Formation: An Example

Suppose that in anticipation of a possible war in the Middle East and a sudden decrease in the availability of gasoline, a team of economists is asked to evaluate a proposal that the federal government institute rationing of gasoline by issuing coupons to every registered automobile owner. Each dated coupon per-

resources devoted to that industry. In search of these profits, more resources enter the industry, increasing output and driving down price, until windfall profits are driven to zero. Losses signal the reverse. Resources leave the industry until those left behind are no longer suffering losses.

mits the holder to purchase a specific number of gallons of gasoline during a particular week. The economists are told that the purpose is, first, to limit total purchases of gasoline to a specific number of gallons per week and, second, to do so in a way that shares the reduction in gasoline supply equitably among all drivers.

The economists may well conclude that the proposal can achieve its first objective but not the second. They may find that issuing coupons to *owners* does not achieve equal treatment of *drivers.* Some persons own two or more cars; others own no car and depend on borrowed or rented cars. Moreover, some people must drive long distances to and from work. The rationing plan tends to impose equal mileage, not equal sacrifice of mileage, on coupon receivers.

Therefore, the economists may point out that a revised plan, based on demonstrated needs plus a small free-driving allowance, would correct the deficiency. Suppose that a number of modifications in the plan have been made and that the economists have concluded it will fulfill its basic goals.

The economists will now ask how costly the plan would be to put into effect and enforce. They would estimate the direct costs of printing and distributing the coupons, establishing a means to hear the inevitable appeals from outraged citizens, and policing the use of coupons.

Next the economists might search for ways in which this policy relates to conflicts with other goals. Does it serve the public interest by encouraging production of more efficient cars? Does it work against the public interest by encouraging crime in the form of the counterfeiting or theft of coupons or the bribing of officials who allocate coupons?

Ideally, the existence and importance of each side effect must be estimated. When a policy action helps to achieve one goal but hinders the attainment of others, it is necessary to establish trade-offs among them. Usually there will be some rate at which people will be willing to trade a loss in one direction for a gain in another. Suppose that if this were the end of the matter, the economists and policymakers would conclude that, all things considered, the gasoline rationing plan is better than nothing and deserves further study.

The final step for the economists is to consider whether modifications of the plan, or alternatives to it, will achieve the goals equally well but at lower cost in terms of setbacks to other policy objectives. They may well consider, for example, whether allowing the coupons to be sold legally will lead to fairer, more efficient gasoline usage, less crime, and smaller enforcement costs. Another proposal they may consider is to discourage gas consumption by an extra $1 per gallon gasoline tax, combined with a series of money grants to poorer people who must drive as part of their work. This final step is important. It compares a particular proposal not only against a "do nothing" approach but also against other feasible proposals.

Do the views and prejudices of the investigators have much to do with the outcome of their investigation? A particular group of economists may have strong views on the specific measure it is attempting to assess. If the economists do not like the measure, they are likely to be relentless in identifying costs and searching out possible unwanted effects and somewhat less than thorough in discovering effects that help to achieve the desired goals. It is important, though difficult, to guard against an unconscious bias of this sort. Fortunately, there are likely to be other economists with different biases. One advantage of publishing evaluations and submitting them to review and discussion is that it provides opportunities for those with different biases to discover arguments and evidence originally overlooked.

The importance of windfall profits and losses is that they set in motion forces that tend to move the economy toward a new equilibrium.

Individual households and firms respond to common signals according to their own best interests. There is nothing planned or intentionally coordinated about their actions, yet when, say, a shortage causes price to rise, individual buyers begin to reduce the quantities they demand and individual firms begin to increase the quantities they supply. As a result the shortage begins to lessen. As it does, price begins to come back down, and windfall profits are reduced. These signals in turn are seen and responded to by firms and households. Eventually, when the shortage has been eliminated, there are no windfall profits to attract further increases in supply. The chain of adjustments to the original shortage is completed.

Even if profits or losses are wholly undeserved, in the sense that they result from changes over which the beneficiaries have no control, this does not mean they should be eliminated by government action. If the government taxed away *all* windfall profits and replaced by subsidy *all* windfall losses, it would effectively destroy the market economy by removing its driving force.

Because the economy is continuously adjusting to shocks, a snapshot of the economy at any given moment reveals substantial positive windfall profits in some industries and substantial windfall losses in others. A snapshot at another moment will also reveal windfall profits and losses, but their locations will be different.

The price system, like an *invisible hand* (Adam Smith's famous phrase), coordinates the responses of individual decision makers who seek only their own self-interests. Because they respond to signals that reflect market conditions, their responses are coordinated without any conscious planning.

Who Responds?

Notice that in the sequence of signal-response-signal-response no one had to foresee at the outset the final price and quantity. Nor did any government agency have to specify who would increase production and who would decrease consumption. Some firms responded to the signals for "more output" by increasing production, and they kept on increasing production until the signals got weaker and weaker and finally disappeared. Some buyers withdrew from the market when they thought prices were too high, and perhaps they re-entered gradually, when they wanted to, as prices became "more reasonable." Households and firms responding to market signals, not to the orders of government bureaucrats, "decided" who would increase production and who would limit consumption. No one was forced to do something against his or her best judgment. Voluntary responses collectively produced the end result.

Consider an example. Suppose that 10,000 families from neighboring areas decide that at existing prices they all want to move into single-family houses in the British Properties in West Vancouver. However, that beautiful residential area is already heavily populated. Suppose there are at most 1,000 vacant houses or building sites. Obviously, not all of the present and potential residents can live there. Which ones will be able to do so, and which ones will be disappointed?

The market system makes the allocation in the following way. The first impact of the great increase in demand would be a sharp rise in the asking prices of houses in the Properties. This would persuade some residents, who previously had not intended to move, to sell their houses and move to other areas. The same rises in price would discourage many who had hoped to move into the Properties. The rising prices will also lead some owners of vacant lots to sell or develop them.

One way or the other—by reducing quantity demanded and by encouraging an increase in quantity supplied—the market will make the allocation. Of the 10,000 families who originally wanted to move in, 3,000 may end up living there, while 2,500 old residents move away and 500 of the vacant houses or lots become occupied. Which 3,000 move in? Those who value it the most. Which 2,500 move out? Those who value the extra money more than the privilege of staying in the Properties. The market sorts them out without the need for anyone to issue orders on who stays or who goes or for a court or board to hear appeals from people who object to the orders.

Of course, it is not *necessary* to rely on the market system to achieve coordination. Had prices not been free to rise, some other system for allocating supply would be needed. Suppose prices had been frozen by law in order to "keep British Properties housing within the reach of the ordinary family." There would be dozens of applicants for any house that became available. The sellers would then have had great power to decide to whom to sell (and thus whom to turn down). They might exercise their prejudices, or they might find ways to get a secret payoff.

Alternatively, the city council might set up a British Properties Authorized Waiting List to determine the order in which people would be permitted to become residents. This would give some public official the duty (or perhaps the privilege) of making personal judgments about the relative worthiness of potential residents and ranking them accordingly. It would also provide opportunities for bribery of those with allocative authority.

The Limited Information Required in Market Coordination

Another important characteristic of the market economy is that it functions with very limited information. As Professor Thomas Schelling put it:

> The dairy farmer doesn't need to know how many people eat butter and how far away they are, how many other people raise cows, how many babies drink milk, or whether more money is spent on beer or milk. What he needs to know is the prices of different feeds, the characteristics of different cows, the different prices . . . for milk . . . , the relative cost of hired labor and electrical machinery, and what his net earnings might be if he sold his cows and raised pigs instead.

By responding to such limited information as the costs and prices of what he buys and sells, the dairy farmer helps to make the whole economy fit together, producing more or less what people want, where and when they want it.

It is, of course, an enormous advantage that all the producers and consumers of a country can collectively make the system operate without any one of them, much less all of them, having to understand how it works. Such a lack of knowledge becomes a disadvantage, however, when people have to vote on schemes for interfering with market allocation.

Coordination in the Absence of Perfect Competition

To say that the price system coordinates is not to imply that it leads to the results that perfect competition would produce. The price system coordinates responses even to prices "rigged" by monopolistic producers or altered by government controls. The signal-response process occurs in a price system even when the prices have not been determined in freely competitive markets.

When an international cartel of uranium producers decided to reduce production and raise price, they created a shortage (and a fear of worse future shortages) among electric utilities that depend on uranium to fuel nuclear power plants. The price of uranium shot up from under $10 per pound to over $40 in less than a year. This enormous price rise greatly increased efforts among producers outside the cartel to find more uranium and to increase their existing production by mining poorer-grade ores previously considered too costly to mine.

The increases in production from these actions slowly began to ease the shortage. On the demand side, high prices and short supplies led some utilities to cancel planned nuclear plants and to delay the construction of others. Such actions implied a long-run substitution of oil or coal for uranium. Only the fact that the OPEC cartel had also sharply raised the price of oil prevented an even more rapid reversal of the previous trend from oil to nuclear-powered generators. With the prices of both uranium and oil quadrupling, the demand for coal increased sharply, and its price and production rose. Thus the market mechanism generated adjustments to the relative prices of different fuels, even though some prices were set by cartels rather than by the free-market forces of supply and demand. It also set in motion reactions that placed limits on the power of the cartel.

The Case for the Market System

In presenting the case for free-market economies, economists have used two different approaches. One of these may be characterized as the formal defense. It is based on showing that a free-market economy consisting of nothing but perfectly competitive industries would lead to an optimal allocation of resources. The case was discussed in Chapter 14.

The other approach, which may be characterized as the informal or intuitive defense, is at least as old as Adam Smith. It is based on variations and implications of the theme that the market system is an effective coordinator of decentralized decision making. The case is intuitive in the sense that it is not laid out in equations leading to some mathematical optimality result. But it does follow from some hard reasoning, and it has been subjected to some searching intellectual probing. What is the nature of this defense of the free market?

Flexible and Automatic Coordination

Defenders of the market economy argue that compared with the alternatives, the decentralized market system is more flexible and leaves more scope for adaptation to change at any moment in time and for quicker adjustment over time.

If, for example, a scarcity raises the price of oil, one household can elect to leave its heating up high and economize on its driving, while another may wish to do the reverse, and a third may instead give up air conditioning. This flexibility is surely preferable to forcing the same pattern on everyone, say, by rationing heating oil and gasoline, regulating permitted temperatures, and limiting air conditioning to days when the temperature exceeds 26° C.

Furthermore, as conditions change over time, prices will change, and decentralized decision makers can react continually. In contrast, government quotas, allocations, and rationing schemes are much more difficult to adjust. The great value of the market is that it provides automatic signals *as a situation develops,* so that all of the consequences of some major economic change do not have to be anticipated and allowed for by a body of central planners. Millions of adaptations to millions of changes in tens of thousands of markets are required every year; it would be a Herculean task to anticipate and plan for them all.

Stimulus to Innovation and Growth

Major changes in resource availabilities will surely occur in all economies over the next decades. New products, new inputs, and new techniques will have to be devised in order to cope with those vast changes.

In a market economy individuals risk their time and money in the hope of earning profits. While many fail, some succeed. New products and processes appear and disappear. Some are passing fads or have little impact; others become items of major significance. The market system works by trial and error to sort them out and allocates resources to what prove to be successful innovations.

In contrast, more centralized systems have to guess which are going to be productive innovations or wanted products. Planned growth may achieve wonders by permitting a massive effort in a chosen direction, but central planners may also guess wrong about the direction and put far too many eggs in the wrong basket or reject as unpromising something that will turn out to be vital.

Relative Prices Reflect Relative Costs

A market system tends to drive prices toward the average total costs of production. When markets are close to perfectly competitive, this occurs quickly and completely; but even where there is substantial market power, it occurs as new products and new producers respond to the lure of profits and their output drives prices down toward the costs of production.

Whenever private costs to firms reflect social costs to society, there is an advantage in having relative prices reflect relative costs because market choices are then made in the light of social opportunity costs. Firms will not choose methods that use more valuable resources over methods that use less valuable resources. Households will choose commodities that use more valuable resources over commodities that use less valuable ones only when they value the chosen commodities correspondingly more at the margin.

Having relative prices reflect relative costs tends to be efficient in that it encourages both producers and consumers to use the nation's resources to achieve allocative efficiency.

Self-correction of Disequilibrium

The economic system is continually thrown out of equilibrium by change. If the economy does not "pursue" equilibrium, there will be little comfort in saying that if only it reached equilibrium, things would be bright indeed. (We all know someone who would have been a great surgeon if only he or she had gone to medical school.)

An important characteristic of the price system is its ability to set in motion forces that tend to correct disequilibrium.

To review the advantages of the price system in this respect, imagine operating without a market mechanism. Suppose that planning boards make all market decisions. The Board in Control of Women's Clothing hears that pantsuits are all the rage in neighboring countries. It orders a certain proportion of clothing factories to make pantsuits instead of the traditional women's skirt. Conceivably the quantities of pantsuits and skirts produced could be just right, given shoppers' preferences. But what if the board guessed wrong, producing too many skirts and not enough pantsuits? Long lines would appear at pantsuit counters while mountains of unsold skirts piled up. Once the board saw the lines for pantsuits, it could order a change in quantities produced. Meanwhile, it could store the extra skirts for another season or ship them to a country with different tastes.

Such a system can correct an initial mistake, but it may prove inefficient at doing so. It may use a lot of resources in planning and administration that could instead be used to produce commodities. Further, many consumers may be greatly inconvenienced if the board is slow to correct its error. In such a system the members of the board may have no incentive to admit and correct a mistake quickly. Indeed, if the authorities do not like pantsuits, the board may get credit for having stopped that craze before it went too far!

In contrast, suppose that in a market system a similar estimation of the demand for pantsuits and skirts was made by the women's clothing industry. Lineups would develop at pantsuit counters, and inventories of skirts would accumulate. Stores would raise pantsuit prices and run skirt sales. Pantsuit manufacturers could earn profits by raising prices and running extra shifts to increase production. Some skirt producers would be motivated to shift production quickly to pantsuits and to make skirts more attractive to buyers by cutting prices. Unlike the planning board, the producers in a market system would be motivated to correct their initial mistakes as quickly as possible. Those slowest to adjust would lose the most money and might even be forced out of business.

Decentralization of Power

Another important part of the case for a market economy is that it tends to decentralize power and thus requires less coercion of individuals than any other type of economy. Of course, even though markets tend to diffuse power, they do not do so completely; large firms and large unions clearly do have and do exercise substantial economic power.

Although the market power of large corporations and unions is not negligible, it tends to be constrained both by the competition of other large entities and by the emergence of new products and firms. This is the process of creative destruction described by Joseph Schumpeter (pages 296–297). In any case, say defenders of the free market, even such aggregations of private power are far less substantial than government power.

Government authority must be exercised if markets are not allowed to allocate people to jobs and commodities to consumers. Not only will such decisions be regarded as arbitrary by those who do not like the results, but the power surely creates major opportunities for bribery, corruption, and allocation according to the tastes of the central administrators. If at the going prices and wages there are not enough apartments or coveted jobs to go around, the bureaucrat can allocate some to the people who pay the largest bribe, some to those with religious beliefs, hairstyles, or political views that he or she likes, and only the rest to those whose names come up on the waiting list.

The Case for Intervention

Canada does not have a laissez faire economy. What has led a majority of Canadians to believe that a pure private enterprise system is not the best of all possible worlds? What led them over many decades to lessen their reliance on the unrestricted workings of the free market and, in many cases, to impose regulations on markets or to substitute collective for individual action? What leads many Canadians today to question whether we have gone far enough—or too far—away from free markets?

Whenever market performance is judged to be faulty, it is the practice to speak of **market failure.** The word *failure* in this context may convey the wrong impression.

Market failure does not mean that nothing good has happened but that the *best attainable outcome* has not been achieved.

There are two somewhat different senses in which the phrase is sometimes used. One is the failure of the market system to achieve efficiency in the allocation of society's resources; the other is the failure to serve social goals other than efficiency, such as a desired distribution of income or the preservation of value systems.

As a result of market failure, many people believe it desirable to modify, restructure, complement, or supplement the unrestricted workings of the market. There are several major sources of dissatisfaction with market allocation and distribution, and it is important to understand how they arise.

Failure to Achieve Efficiency

Externalities As a Source of Inefficiency

Cost, as economists define it, concerns the value of resources used in the process of production. According to the opportunity-cost principle, value is the benefit the resources would produce in their best alternative use. But who decides what resources are used and their opportunity cost? When a timber company buys a forest, it perhaps regards the alternative to cutting the trees this year as cutting them five years hence. But citizens in the area may value the forest as a nature sanctuary or a recreation area. The firm values the forest for the trees; the local residents may value the trees for the forest. The two values need not be the same.

Private and social costs. The difference in the viewpoint of the firm and the residents illustrates the important distinction between private cost and social cost. **Private cost** measures the best alternative uses of the resources available to *the producer.* Private cost is usually measured by the *market price of the resources* that the firm uses. **Social cost** measures the best alternative uses of resources that are available to the whole society.

For some resources social cost may be the same as private cost; the price set by the market may well reflect the value of the resources in their best alternative use. For other resources, as will soon be clear, social cost may differ sharply from private cost.

Discrepancies between private and social cost lead to market failure from society's point of view.

The reason is that efficiency requires that prices cover social cost, but private producers, adjusting to private costs, will neglect the elements of social cost that are not included in private costs. When an element of social cost is not part of a private firm's profit and loss calculation, it is *external* to its decision-making process.

Discrepancies between social and private cost lead to **externalities,** costs or benefits of a transaction incurred or received by members of the society but not taken into account by the parties to the transaction. They are also called **third-party effects** because parties other than the two primary participants in the transaction (the buyer and the seller) are affected. Externalities arise in many ways and may be beneficial or harmful.

Some externalities are beneficial. When I paint

my house, I enhance my neighbors' view and the value of their property. When an Einstein or a Rembrandt gives the world a discovery or a work of art whose worth is far in excess of what he is paid to produce it, he confers an external benefit. Private producers will tend to produce too little of commodities that generate beneficial externalities because they bear all of the costs while others reap part of the benefits.

Other externalities are harmful. Before we consider several examples, we can observe that private producers will tend to produce too much of commodities that generate harmful externalities because they bear none of the extra costs suffered by others.

Externalities, whether adverse or beneficial, cause market outcomes to be inefficient because they lead to the wrong allocation of resources from society's point of view.

Pollution. A major source of differences between private cost and social cost occurs when firms use resources they do not regard as scarce. This is a characteristic of most examples of pollution. When a paper mill produces pulp for the world's newspapers, more people are affected than its suppliers, employees, and customers. Its water-discharged effluent hurts the fishing boats that ply nearby waters, and its smog makes many resort areas less attractive, thereby reducing the tourist revenues that local motel operators and boat renters can expect. The firm neglects these external effects of its actions because its profits are not affected by them.

Dumping of hazardous wastes, air pollution, and water pollution may occur as a result of calculated decisions as to what and how to produce or consume and as a result of private producers' taking risks that prove to inflict injury on others. Even an apparent accident, such as an oil blowout or the breakup of a tanker, which is desired by no one, may be caused by a private firm's insufficient avoidance of the risk, since it bears only part of the costs.

Common-property resources. The world's oceans once teemed with fish, but today overfishing has caused a worldwide fish shortage. How could this happen?

Fish are an example of what is called a **common-property resource**, a resource that is owned by no one and may be used by anyone. No one owns the oceans' fish until they are caught. The world's international fishing grounds are common property for all fishermen. If by taking more fish one fisherman reduces the catch of other fishermen, he does not count this as a cost, but it is a cost to society.

It is socially optimal to add to a fishing fleet until the last boat increases the value of the fleet's total catch by as much as it costs to operate the boat. This is the size of fishing fleet that a social planner would choose.

The free market will not, however, produce that result. Potential new entrants will judge entry to be profitable if the value of their own catch is equal to the costs of operating their boats. But a new entrant's catch is *partly* an addition to total catch and *partly* a reduction of the catch of other fishermen—because of congestion, each new boat reduces the catch of all other boats. Thus under free entry there will be too many boats in the fleet. Indeed, boats will continue to enter until there are no longer any profits for the marginal boat. In other words, boats will enter until the *average* value of the catch of a typical boat is equal to the cost of running that boat. At this point, however, the net addition to the *total* catch brought about by the last boat will be substantially less than the cost of operating the boat.

With common-property resources the level of activity will be too high because each new entrant will gain revenue not only from the amount that it adds to total product but also from the amount that it takes away from the outputs of other producers.

This is not an untested theory. Fishing grounds and other common-property resources show a typical pattern of overexploitation. As a result, governments often use quotas and other restrictions in an attempt to reduce the size of the industry to what is socially optimal.

Congestion. Collisions between private planes and commercial airliners are headline news when they occur. They cannot occur unless *both* planes are in the air; this is what creates the externality. Suppose that the probability of a midair plane crash is roughly proportional to the number of planes in the air. Suppose, too, that I have the choice of flying from Kamloops to Vancouver in my own plane or on a commercial airliner that has 100 of its 150 seats filled. In choosing to fly by myself, I decide that the slight extra risk to me of a midair collision is more than balanced by the fun or convenience of my own plane.

What I have neglected is the social cost of my action: the increased risk for every other person in the air on my route of flight that results from one more plane in the air. Since I do not consider other travelers' increased risk, my private decision may have been the wrong social decision.

Neglect of future consequences of present actions. When private producers undervalue future effects on others, they neglect an externality. A business facing bankruptcy tomorrow may be motivated to cheat on safety standards to cut costs today, even if it hurts the firm's reputation in the long term and imposes heavy future costs on others.

A less callous example is taking an action without finding out whether there are as-yet-unknown adverse externalities. One dramatic example of the neglect of future effects was the use of DDT. In 1948 the Swiss chemist Paul Mueller won the Nobel Prize for his discovery of its extraordinary value as a pesticide. Gradually, however, it was confirmed that DDT did more than kill unwanted insects. Once sprayed, the chemical did not break down for years. It worked its way up the food chain from insects to birds and fish to small mammals and to larger and larger birds and mammals, including human beings. Arctic penguins, though thousands of miles from any sprayed areas, have measurable amounts of DDT in their bodies. DDT has thinned the egg shells of large birds to the point where breakage threatens many species, among them the peregrine falcon, the osprey, and the eagle. In 1962 Rachel Carson labeled DDT an "elixir of death," and by 1972 its use had been banned in the United States.

Unavoidable ignorance of the future can never be described as market failure, of course, but unwillingness to determine whether there will be future adverse effects may be a form of market failure.

Other Sources of Inefficiency

The efficiency of the price system depends on firms' and households' receiving and responding to the signals provided by prices, costs, and windfall profits. Forces that seriously distort these signals or distort the required response to them may cause a market to fail to perform efficiently. These forces are often referred to as *market imperfections* and *market impediments*. Consider a few examples.

Moral hazard, adverse selection, and other situations of unequal information. When an individual or firm can take advantage of special knowledge to make profits while engaging in socially uneconomic behavior, **moral hazard** arises. For example, suppose that a person who has ample fire insurance does not take reasonable precautions against fire, or suppose that because of the availability of unemployment insurance a person refuses to accept a job he or she would otherwise have taken. In each of these cases the individuals have special knowledge that they can afford to take certain actions that impose unexpected costs on those who provide the insurance, but the insurers cannot identify them as the persons taking unintended advantage of the system. The socially valid purpose of insurance is to permit people to share given risks, not to increase the size of the aggregate risk. But in these two examples the behavior described does increase the risk and thus the social cost.

Closely related to moral hazard is the problem of **adverse selection.** A person suffering a heart attack may immediately seek to increase his life insurance coverage by purchasing as much additional coverage as is available without medical examination. People taking out insurance almost always know more about themselves as individual insurance risks than their insurance companies do. The company can try to limit the variation in risk by setting up broad categories based on variables, such as age and occupation, over which actuarial risk is known to vary. The rate charged is then different across categories based on the average risk in the category. But there must always be much variability of risk *within* any one category. People who know they are well above average risk within their category are offered a bargain and will be led to take out more car, health, life, or fire insurance than they otherwise would. Someone who knows she is a low risk pays more than her own risk really warrants and is motivated to take out less insurance than she otherwise would.

More generally, any time either party to a transaction lacks information the other party has or is deceived by claims of the other party, market results will tend to be affected, and such changes may lead to inefficiency. Economically (but not legally) it is but a small step from such unequal knowledge to outright fraud. The arsonist who buys fire insurance before setting a fire or the business person with fire insurance who decides that a fire is preferable to bankruptcy are extreme examples of adverse selection and moral hazard.

Unequal information is involved in many other situations. For example, the apparent overdiscounting of the prices of used cars because of the buyer's risk of acquiring a "lemon" is a case of differences in information between buyer and seller affecting behavior. An adverse selection problem arises in that the stock of used cars offered for sale will not be representative of the entire population of used cars in existence. Any particular model year of automobiles will include a certain proportion of "lemons"—cars that have one or more serious defects. Purchasers of new cars of a certain year and model take a chance on their car's turning out to be a lemon. Those who are unlucky and get a lemon are more likely to resell their car then those who are lucky and get a quality car. Hence in the used-car market there will be a disproportionately large number of lemons for sale. Similarly, not all cars are driven in the same manner. Those that are driven long distances or under bad conditions are much more likely to be traded in or sold used than those that are driven on good roads and in moderate amounts.

Thus buyers of used cars are right to be suspicious of why the car is for sale, while salespeople are quick to invent reasons ("It was owned by a little old lady who only drove it on Sundays"). Because it is very difficult to identify a lemon, or a badly used car, before buying it, the purchaser will be prepared to buy a used car only at a price low enough to offset the increased probability that it is of poor quality.

Principal-agent issues. A firm's managers act for the firm as *agents* of the owners, who are legally called the *principals* of the firm. If profits are the spur to efficient performance, it is clear that when a firm's managers choose to pursue their own goals rather than the *firm's* profits, they impede the functioning of the market system. A manager or a salesperson may incur unnecessary costs because the activities entailing these costs provide him or her with enjoyment. On a small scale this occurs whenever a purchasing agent is swayed by the Christmas present from a salesperson or when a car renter is motivated to hire a more expensive car by the premium she will receive while her employer pays the bill. More serious are cases where managers regularly pursue their own goals at the expense of minimizing the costs of production. Most serious yet are outright sellouts of company interests or secrets to other firms in return for personal rewards.

Barriers to mobility. Another kind of impediment to efficiency that occurs in the market is factor immobility. If increases in a factor's pay do not lead to increases in supply (for any of the reasons discussed in Chapters 17 and 18), the market will fail to reallocate resources promptly in response to changing demands. Monopoly power creates market imperfections by preventing resources from moving in response to the market signals of high profits. In this case barriers to entry rather than factor immobility frustrate the flow of resources.

Collective consumption goods. Certain goods and services, if they provide benefits to anyone, necessarily provide them to many people. Such goods are called **collective consumption goods.** National defense is the prime example of a collective consumption good. An adequate defense establishment protects all people in the country whether they want it or not, and there is no market where one individual can buy more of it and another individual less. The quantity of national defense provided must be decided collectively. Other examples of collective consumption goods are the beautification of a city, a levee to protect a city from a flood, and a hurricane-warning system.

In general, market systems cannot compel payment for a collective consumption good since there is no way to prevent a person who refuses to pay for the good from receiving its services. Governments, by virtue of their power to tax, can provide the services and collect from everyone.

Excessive or prohibitive transactions costs. The costs incurred in negotiating and completing a transaction, such as the costs of billing or the bad-debt cost of buyers who never pay, are examples of **transactions costs**. They are always present to some degree, and they are a necessary cost of doing business. If buyers cannot be made to pay for the product, the producer will not be motivated to provide it. To stay in business, a private firm must be able to recover both production and transactions costs. If transactions costs are higher than they need to be because of imperfections in the private market, some products that are efficient to produce will not be produced, and the market will have failed. Consider an example.

Could a private firm provide a road system for Montreal, covering its costs by collecting tolls? The answer is surely no (at least with today's technology).[2] It would be prohibitively expensive, both in money and in delays, to erect and staff a tollbooth at every freeway exit. Requiring collection of revenues via tolls would impose a prohibitive transactions cost. The users of a road system may be more than willing to pay the full costs of its construction and maintenance, but without an inexpensive way to make them pay, no private firm can produce the road. The government, collecting revenue by means of a gasoline tax, can do what the private market fails to do. (Whether it can do so without making a different mistake—producing more of the product than users are willing to pay for—will be discussed shortly.)

Market imperfections may lead to market failure by preventing firms and households from completing transactions that are required for efficient resource allocation or by causing too much or too little production of particular goods.

[2] The warning about technology merits an additional comment. Technology changes rapidly. For example, the electronic metering of road use may make the tollbooth unnecessary, just as the postage meter has made licking stamps unnecessary. Thus what a private market cannot do today, it may be able to do efficiently tomorrow.

Failure to Achieve Other Social Goals

Income Distribution

An important characteristic of a market economy is the *distribution* of the income that it determines. People whose services are in heavy demand relative to supply, such as television anchors and superior football players, earn large incomes, while people whose services are not in heavy demand relative to supply, such as Ph.D.s in English and high school graduates without work experience, earn much less.

The distribution of income produced by the market can be looked at in equilibrium or in disequilibrium. In equilibrium, in an efficiently operating free-market economy, similar efforts of work or investment by similar people will tend to be similarly rewarded everywhere in the economy. Of course, dissimilar people will be dissimilarly rewarded.

In disequilibrium similar people making similar efforts are likely to be dissimilarly rewarded. People in declining industries, areas, and occupations suffer the punishment of low earnings through no fault of their own. Those in expanding sectors earn the reward of high earnings through no extra effort of their own.

These rewards and punishments serve the important function in decentralized decision making of motivating people to adapt. The "advantage" of such a system is that individuals can make their own decisions about how to alter their behavior when market conditions change; the "disadvantage" is that temporary rewards and punishments are dealt out as a result of changes in market conditions that are beyond the control of the individuals affected.

Moreover, even the equilibrium differences may seem unfair. A free-market system rewards certain groups and penalizes others. Because the workings of the market may be stern, even cruel, society often chooses to intervene. Should heads of households be forced to bear the full burden of their misfortune if, through no fault of their own, they lose their jobs? Even if they lose their jobs through their own fault, should they and their families have to bear the whole burden, which may include starvation? Should the ill and aged be thrown on the mercy of their families?

What if they have no families? Both private charities and a great many government policies are concerned with modifying the distribution of income that results from such things as where one starts, how able one is, how lucky one is, and how one fares in the free-market world.

Often the goal of a more equitable distribution conflicts with the goal of a more efficient economy. Some of the problems that this can create in policy debates are discussed further in Box 23-2.

Preferences for Public Goods

Police protection, even justice, might be provided by private market mechanisms. Watchmen, detectives, and bodyguards all provide policelike protection. Privately hired arbitrators, "hired guns," and vigilantes of the Old West represent private ways of obtaining "justice." Yet the members of society may believe that a public police force is *preferable* to a private one and that public justice is *preferable* to justice for hire.

For another example, public schools may be better or worse than private schools, but they are likely to be different, particularly because persons others than parents, teachers, and owners influence their policies. Much of the case for public education rests on the advantages to you of having other people's children educated in a particular kind of environment that is *different* from what a private school would provide. The market will be said to produce unsatisfactory results by those who believe the public product is preferable.

Protecting Individuals from Others

People can use and even abuse other people for economic gain in ways that the members of society find offensive. Child labor laws and minimum standards for working conditions are responses to such actions.

Yet direct abuse is not the only example of this kind of market failure. In an unhindered free market, the adults in a household would usually decide how much education to buy for their children. Selfish parents might buy no education, while egalitarian parents might buy the same quantity for all their children regardless of their abilities. The members of society may want to interfere in these choices, both to protect the child of the selfish parent and to ensure that some of the scarce educational resources are distributed according to intelligence rather than wealth. All households are forced to provide a minimum of education for their children, and strong inducements are offered—through public universities, scholarships, and other means—for gifted children to consume more education than they or their parents might choose if they had to pay the entire cost themselves.

Paternalism

Members of society acting through the state often seek to protect adult (and presumably responsible) individuals not from others but from themselves. Laws prohibiting heroin and other drugs and laws prescribing the installation and use of seat belts are intended primarily to protect individuals from their own ignorance or shortsightedness.

This kind of interference with the free choices of individuals is called **paternalism.** Whether such actions reflect the wishes of the majority of the society or whether they reflect overbearing governments, there is no doubt that the market will not provide this kind of protection. Buyers do not buy what they do not want, and sellers have no motive to provide it.

Social Obligations

In a market system, if you can pay another person to do things for you, you may do so. If you persuade someone else to clean your house in return for $35, presumably both parties to the transaction are better off: You prefer to part with $35 rather than clean the house yourself, and the person you hire prefers $35 to not cleaning your house. Normally society does not interfere with people's ability to negotiate mutually advantageous contracts.

Most people do not feel this way, however, about activities that are regarded as social obligations. For example, when military service is compulsory, contracts similar to one between you and a housekeeper could also be negotiated. Some persons faced with the obligation to do military service could no doubt

BOX 23-2

Distribution Versus Efficiency

Economists recognize that government actions can affect both the allocation of resources and the distribution of income. Because it is possible to talk about *efficient* and *inefficient* allocations, but not about *better* or *worse* distributions of income without introducing normative considerations, much of economics concerns efficiency and neglects effects on the distribution of income. Many disagreements can be understood in terms of a different emphasis on these things.

Consider the OPEC-induced rise in oil prices during the 1970s. From the point of view of efficiency alone, the correct policy was to let domestic oil prices in all oil-importing countries rise along with the world price. Instead many governments held the price down. They were concerned with, among other things, the effect of rising prices on the windfall profits earned by large oil companies and on the welfare of poorer citizens. "We just cannot let the poor find their heating bills rise so much and so fast while the profits of the oil companies soar" was a common reaction.

Here is a genuine conflict for which economics cannot provide a solution—because in the end the answer must rest on value judgments. However, economics can make the consequences of various choices apparent and can suggest policy alternatives. The consequences of holding down the price of oil (out of concern for the effect of higher prices on the poor) was an inefficient use of the countries' resources. Total national income was reduced, and some new investment was misdirected into high-cost (rather than low-cost) methods of production. Thus in the long run average standards of living were reduced. Whether the reduction in the average was a reasonable price to pay for shielding the poor is an open question; yet it is unlikely that the question was ever posed or the calculations made.

Can one have both efficiency and desired redistributions? One way is to let the price system do the job of signaling relative scarcities and costs, thereby ensuring some efficiency in the allocation of resources, but at the same time to use taxes or expenditures to transfer income to achieve redistributive goals. This method does not seek to help the poor (or other underprivileged groups) by subsidizing oil or any other price. Rather, it seeks to provide these groups with sufficient income by direct income transfers. Then it leaves producers and consumers free to respond to relative prices that approximately reflect relative opportunity costs.

Advocates of this method argue that it is surer, more direct, and less costly in its side effects than the method of subsidizing the prices of particular goods. Moreover, the price-subsidy method surely ends up subsidizing some who are rich and missing some who are very poor. Subsidizing gasoline prices, for example, benefits the Cadillac owner and does nothing for people too poor to own a car. Thus even in redistribution this method of subsidization is haphazard.

Supporters of redistribution through the price system usually counter with two arguments. First, it is well and good to say we *could* let oil prices rise and simultaneously subsidize the poor and tax the rich, but the political process makes it unlikely that we *will* do so. They point to U.S. policy in the early 1980s, which deregulated prices and simultaneously *decreased* aid to the poor. Thus, say supporters of redistribution, holding prices down may be the best or even the only practical way to get a fairer distributive result.

Second, certain commodities such as food, heat, medical care, and housing are claimed to be basic to a civilized life and therefore should be provided to households cheaply, whatever their real opportunity cost. The supporters of redistribution through the price system believe that the inefficiencies resulting from prices that do not reflect opportunity costs are a burden worth bearing to ensure that everyone can afford these basics.

pay enough to persuade others to do their tour of service for them.[3] By exactly the same argument as before, we can presume that both parties will be better off if they are allowed to negotiate such a trade. But such contracts are usually prohibited. Why? Because there are values other than those that can be expressed in a market. In times when it is necessary, military service by all healthy males is usually held to be a duty independent of an individual's tastes, wealth, influence, or social position. It is felt that everyone *ought* to do this service, and exchanges between willing traders are prohibited.

Nor is this the only example. Citizens cannot buy their way out of jury duty or legally sell their votes to another, even though in many cases they could find willing trading partners.

Even if the price system allocated goods and services with complete efficiency, members of a society may not wish to rely solely on the market if they have other goals they wish to achieve.

Government Intervention

Private collective action can sometimes remedy the failures of private individual action. (Private charities can help the poor; volunteer fire departments can fight fires; insurance companies can guard against adverse selection by more careful classification of clients.) However, by far the most common remedy for market failure is government intervention.

It is useful to ask several questions about possible government policies designed to correct market failure. First, what tools does the government have? Second, when and how vigorously should the tools be used? Third, under what circumstances is government intervention likely to fail?

The Tools of Microeconomic Policy

There are numerous ways in which one or another level of government can prevent, alter, complement, or replace the workings of the unrestricted market economy. It is convenient to group these methods into four broad categories:

1. *Public provision.* Goods and services may be provided publicly as well as or instead of privately.
2. *Redistribution.* Public expenditures and taxes may be used to provide a distribution of income and output different from what the private market provides.
3. *Rule making.* Rules and regulations may be adopted to compel, forbid, or specify within acceptable limits the behavior that private decision makers may engage in.
4. *Structuring incentives.* Government may alter market signals to persuade rather than force decision makers to adopt different behavior.

All four methods are used frequently, and all have great capacity to change the outcomes the unregulated market would provide. The first two will be discussed in detail in Chapter 24; the remainder of this section concerns rule making and structuring incentives.

Rule Making

Rules require, limit, or forbid certain activities and market actions. It is helpful to distinguish between *proscriptive* and *prescriptive* rules.

Proscriptive rules. Some regulations are like the Ten Commandments: They tell people and firms what they can and cannot do. Such rules require parents to send their children to school and to have them inoculated against measles and diphtheria. Laws that prohibit gambling and pornography attempt to enforce a particular moral code on the whole society. In Chapter 16 we discussed an important form of policy by prohibition—combines policy.

There are many other examples. Children cannot legally be served alcoholic drinks. Prostitution is prohibited in most places, even between a willing buyer and a willing seller. In most provinces you must buy automobile insurance. A person who offers goods for sale, including his or her own house, cannot refuse to sell because of a dislike for the customer's

[3] During the U.S. Civil War it was a common practice for a wealthy man to avoid the draft by hiring a substitute to serve in his place.

color or dress. There are rules against fraudulent advertising and the sale of substandard, adulterated, or poisonous foods.

Such rules set limits to the decisions that firms and households can make; they do not replace those decisions. But the allowed limits can be changed. An important means of government regulation is to change old rules or add new ones that redefine the boundary between forbidden and permitted behavior.

Prescriptive rules. Prescriptive rule making substitutes the rule maker's judgment for the firm's or the household's judgment about such things as prices charged, products produced, and methods of production. It tends to restrict private action more than proscriptive regulation because it replaces private decision making rather than limiting it to an acceptable set of decisions. Regulation of public utilities is an important example of prescriptive regulation (see Chapter 15), but prescriptive regulation goes far beyond the natural monopoly regulation we have discussed.

Federal regulatory commissions regularly decide such matters as who may broadcast and on what frequencies, which airlines may fly which routes, what rates bus lines and pipeline operators may charge for different kinds of services, what prices may be paid for gasoline, and how much foreign textiles may be imported into Canada. The trend toward deregulation in the 1980s has reduced but not eliminated prescriptive rule making.

Problems with rule making. Rule making often appears to be a cheap, easy, and direct way of compelling desirable behavior in the face of market failure. But this appearance is deceptive. Rules must be enforceable and enforced, and once enforced they must be effective in obtaining the hoped for results. These conditions are often difficult and expensive to achieve.

Consider the requirement for the installation of an antipollution device that will meet a certain standard in reducing automobile exhaust emissions. Such a law may be the outcome of parliamentary debate on pollution control—and having passed the bill, Parliament will turn to other things. Yet certain problems must be solved before the rule can achieve its purpose. Even with perfect compliance by the manufacturer, the device will not work well unless it is kept in working order by the owner. Yet it would be expensive to inspect every vehicle regularly and to force owners to keep the devices at the standard set by law.

Even a well-designed rule will work only until the people regulated figure out a way to evade its intent while obeying its letter. There will be substantial incentive to find such a loophole, and resources that could be used elsewhere will be devoted by the regulated to the search—and then, in turn, by the regulators to counteract such evasion.

Structuring Incentives

Government can change the incentives of households and firms in a variety of ways. It can fix minimum or maximum prices (as we saw in the discussion of agriculture and rent control in Chapter 6). It can adjust the tax system with exemptions and deductions. Making mortgage interest payments tax deductible, for example, can make owned housing relatively more attractive than rental housing. Such tax treatment sends the household different signals from those sent by the free market. Scholarships to students to become nurses or teachers may offset barriers to mobility into those occupations. Fines and criminal penalties for violating the rules imposed are another part of the incentive structure.

Internalizing Externalities

An important means of influencing incentives is to change the prices that firms and households pay in such a way as to eliminate externalities. Because externalities are a major source of market failure, much attention has been given to means of inducing decision makers to take them into account. Charging a producing firm for the pollution it causes can motivate the firm to alter its production in a socially desirable way. Procedures that make firms take account of the external effects (or extra social costs) of production are said to *internalize* them. How exactly does internalization work?

First we need to define terms. The **marginal net private benefit (*MNPB*)** of a unit of production is the difference between that unit's contribution to a firm's revenue and its contribution to the firm's cost. In other words, it is the contribution to profit of that unit. If we think of each unit of production as contributing to social welfare (and call that contribution **marginal social benefit**) and to social cost (defined on page 472), we can call the difference between marginal social benefit and marginal social cost **marginal net social benefit (*MNSB*).**

Marginal net social benefit is the key concept in judging efficiency. A unit of output should be produced if, but only if, its *MNSB* is greater than or equal to zero. To go from *MNPB* to *MNSB* we need to add beneficial externalities and subtract adverse externalities. In the following discussion, we consider an adverse externality (such as pollution) so that *MNSB* is less than *MNPB* at each level of production.

Consider, as an example, a private firm that responds only to private benefits and costs. Such a firm will produce up to the point at which marginal net private benefit (*MNPB*) becomes zero. But at that output marginal net social benefit (*MNSB*), being less than *MNPB*, is necessarily negative; too much has been produced from the social point of view. This market failure can be avoided by the procedure shown in Figure 23-1. Once the firm has been forced to pay for what were previously externalities, the new net private benefit is exactly the same as net social benefit; that is, *MNPB* = *MNSB*. Thus the firm will be motivated to produce only as long as *MNSB* is not negative.

Internalization avoids the market failure caused by externalities.

There are many ways to internalize external costs. Consider two. If the amount of the external cost imposed per unit of output is known, it is possible to impose an **effluent charge,** or pollution tax, that compels the producer to pay a tax on every unit of polluting production. Such a charge might lead the producer to find a way to produce without polluting.

Another way to internalize external costs is to give legal standing to private citizens to sue for damages against polluters or to seek court injunctions against polluting activities. The legal action makes it costly for polluters; there will be damage payments if they lose, and legal payments, win or lose.

FIGURE 23-1 Externalities

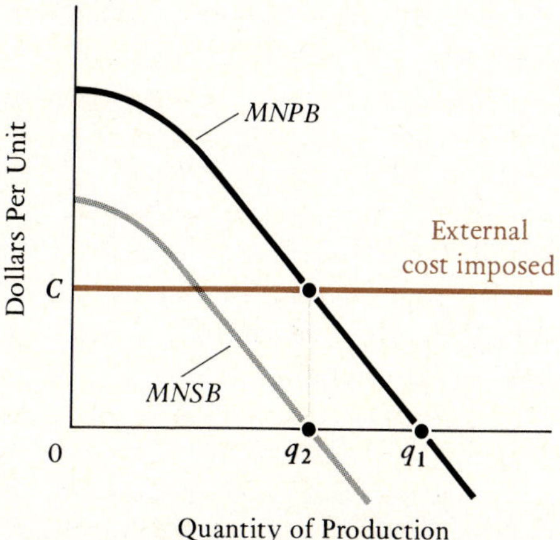

Internalizing an externality can correct market failure. The marginal net private benefit curve, *MNPB*, shows the benefit to the firm from producing each unit of output. The *MNPB* is the *difference between* the marginal revenue (*MR*) and the marginal cost (*MC*) associated with each unit of output. Since the firm is motivated to produce all units that make a positive contribution to its profits, its equilibrium output is q_1 where *MNPB* equals zero (i.e., $MR = MC$). However, this production imposes an external cost on others in society of \$C *per unit*, as shown by the colored line. Subtracting this marginal social cost from the *MNPB* yields the marginal net social benefit curve, *MNSB*. The socially optimal output is q_2, where *MNSB* just equals zero. At this output marginal private benefit is just equal to the marginal external cost imposed on others in society by each unit of production. At q_2 the outsiders still have costs inflicted on them by the firm's production, but these costs *plus* the firm's private costs are just equal to the marginal benefit from its last unit of production.

Suppose the firm is required to pay an effluent charge of \$C per unit. Its *MNPB* now becomes the *MNSB* curve. The externality has been *internalized,* and the profit-maximizing firm is motivated to reduce its output from q_1 to q_2. It does this because any units produced beyond q_2 would now subtract from total profits.

The Costs of Government Intervention

Consider the following argument: (1) The market system is working imperfectly, and (2) government has the legal means to improve the situation; (3)

therefore, the public interest will be served by government intervention.

This appealing argument is deficient because it neglects two important considerations. First, government intervention is costly. For that reason not every market failure is worth correcting. Second, government intervention may be imperfect. Just as markets sometimes succeed and sometimes fail, so government intervention sometimes succeeds and sometimes fails. In this section we consider costs of intervention, neglecting government failure. Later we consider the added problem imposed by imperfect governmental intervention.

The *benefits* of government intervention are the value of the market failures averted. To evaluate governmental intervention it is necessary to consider the costs of the intervention and compare costs with benefits.

Large potential benefits do not necessarily justify government intervention, nor do large potential costs necessarily make it unwise. What matters is the balance between benefits and costs.

There are several kinds of costs of government intervention. Consider three: internal costs, direct external costs, and indirect external costs.

Internal Costs

When government inspectors visit plants to see whether they are complying with federally imposed standards of health, industrial safety, or environmental protection, they are imposing costs on the public in the form of the salaries and expenses of the inspectors, among other ways. When regulatory bodies develop rules, hold hearings, write opinions, or have their staff prepare research reports, they are incurring costs. The costs of the judges and clerks and court reporters who hear and transcribe and review evidence are likewise costs imposed by regulation. All these activities use valuable resources, resources that could have provided very different goods and services.

Government expenditures on activities that regulate market behavior alone are large indeed. Such costs have grown greatly in the past several decades, and they represent one cause of growth in the size of government in the economy. However, they are only the most visible part of the total costs of government regulatory activities.

Direct External Costs

The nature and size of the extra costs borne by firms subject to government intervention vary with the type of regulation. A few examples are worth noting.

Changes in costs of production. Antipollution regulations force producers not to burn high-sulfur coal. As a result, extra fuel costs are imposed on many firms. Such cost increases are directly attributable to regulation.

For 50 years (until the mid 1970s), the price of automobiles relative to other consumer goods was falling because of continuing advances in automotive engineering. Federal safety and emission standards added so much to the cost of producing automobiles over the decade from 1976 to 1986 that Canadians had to adjust to a steadily rising trend in the relative price of North American autos, and automobile workers to the decreases in production that resulted.

Costs of compliance. Government regulation and supervision generate a flood of reporting and related activities that are often summarized in the phrase *red tape*. The number of hours of business time devoted to understanding, reporting, and contesting regulatory provisions is enormous. Affirmative action, occupational safety, and environmental control have greatly increased the size of nonproduction payrolls. The legal costs alone of a major corporation can run into tens or hundreds of millions of dollars per year. While all this provides lots of employment for lawyers and economic experts, it is costly because there are other tasks such professionals could do that would add more to the production of consumer goods and services.

Losses in productivity. Quite apart from the actual expenditures, the regulatory climate may reduce the incentive for experimentation, innovation, and the introduction of new products. Requiring advance government clearance before a new method or product may be introduced (on grounds of potential safety hazards or environmental impact) can eliminate the incentive to develop it. Requiring advance approval by a regulatory commission before entry is permitted into a regulated industry can discourage potential competitors.

Indirect External Costs

It has been estimated that regulatory activities substantially decrease the growth rate of output per person. This lost growth translates into a big loss in the real living standards that could have been achieved. (For example, an extra 0.4 percent growth for 100 years would lead to a 50 percent increase in purchasing power.) Such lost purchasing power is an externality of government intervention because the regulators do not take it into account. It is ironic that government intervention to offset adverse externalities can create new adverse externalities.

Consider an example. Government regulations designed to ensure the effectiveness and safety of new drugs have the incidental effect of delaying by an average of about nine months the introduction of drugs that are both effective and safe. The benefits of these regulations are related to the unsafe and ineffective drugs kept off the market. The cost includes the unavailability for about nine months of all those safe and effective drugs whose introduction was delayed.

Optimal Intervention

Economic principles are useful in making decisions concerning the optimal correction of market failure. To develop these principles, we shall look at the question of preventing pollution.

Pollution problems range from threats to our survival to minor nuisances. Nearly all activity leaves some waste product; to say that all pollution must be removed whatever the cost is to try for the impossible and to ensure a vast commitment of society's scarce resources to many projects that will yield a low social value. But somewhere in the middle ground between trying for the impossible and callous indifference to the problem is a point of optimal action.

We approach the problem by assuming that government intervention is free from error. Later we shall relax this artificial assumption.

Costless intervention. We start with the easiest case. Assume that government intervention is costless except for the direct costs imposed by changes in the nature of production. All the government must do is identify the best form of pollution control, determine the right amount of it, and institute the appropriate means of achieving it. How should it proceed?

The first step is to choose the best means of pollution control. Suppose in this case that a factory is emitting the noxious gas sulfur dioxide (SO_2), and it is determined that the best control method is to install filters on the smokestacks.[4]

The next step is to decide how much of the pollution should be eliminated. Suppose that simple recirculation of the gases would reduce the discharge of SO_2 by 50 percent; after that, the cost would double for each further 10 percent reduction in the remaining SO_2. At most it would be possible to eliminate 99.44 percent of all SO_2, but the cost would be vast. In economic terms the marginal costs of removal rise sharply as the amount of SO_2 eliminated rises from 50 percent to 99.44 percent.

What percentage of the gases should be eliminated? The answer depends on the marginal benefits relative to marginal costs. The marginal benefits of pollution control are the external effects avoided. The optimal amount of prevention is the amount at which the marginal costs of further prevention equal the marginal benefits. This is illustrated in Figure 23-2.

The optimal amount of pollution prevention will be less than the maximum possible when pollution is costly to prevent. Thus the optimal amount of pollution is not equal to zero.

[4] This choice of *means* is neither trivial nor always easy. Alternatives might include changing the method of production or moving people out of the path of the polluting gases. This first-step determination among alternative means is of prime importance in achieving the correct solution. A major source of "government failure" is choice of the wrong technique of control.

FIGURE 23-2 The Optimal Amount of Pollution Prevention

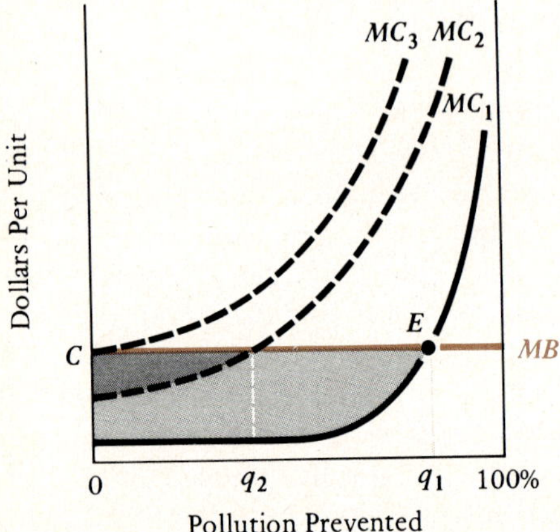

The amount of pollution prevention is optimal when the quantity of prevention is being produced at which marginal benefits from prevention equal marginal costs. MB represents the marginal benefit achieved by pollution prevention, assumed in this example to be constant at \$$C$ per percentage point. MC_1 represents the marginal costs of preventing pollution; it rises sharply as more and more pollution is eliminated. The optimal level of pollution control is q_1, where $MB = MC_1$. *Notice that not all pollution is eliminated.* For all units up to q_1, marginal benefits from pollution prevention exceed marginal costs. Net benefits are shown by the total shaded area. Any further pollution elimination would add more to costs than to benefits.

If the marginal cost curve shifts to MC_2, due, say, to the addition of enforcement costs, the quantity of optimal prevention will decrease to q_2 and the net benefits will be reduced to the darker shaded area. If costs increase to MC_3, the optimal amount of prevention becomes zero.

Costs of intervention. Next we add to our consideration the fact that government intervention brings with it enforcement costs—costs to the government, to the firm, and to third parties—of the kinds already discussed. These costs have to be added to the direct costs we have just considered.

Suppose for simplicity that enforcement costs are variable and rise as the level of pollution to be eliminated increases. The marginal costs of enforcement must be added to the marginal direct costs of prevention, thereby shifting upward the marginal costs of prevention. (This is shown by the marginal cost curves MC_2 and MC_3 in Figure 23-2.) The addition of such costs will surely decrease the amount of prevention that is optimal. If the costs are large enough, they may even make any prevention uneconomical.

The optimal amount of government intervention to avoid market failure will be lower, the greater are the costs of prevention and intervention.

Government Failure

All costs of intervention discussed in the preceding section would be present with a government that had perfect foresight in defining goals, an unerring ability to choose the least costly means of achieving them, and intelligent and dedicated officials whose concern was to do the things—and only those things—that achieved the greatest possible efficiency of the economy. Government intervention usually falls short of the high standard just described. This is not because bureaucrats are more stupid, more rigid, or more venal than other people. It is because they are like others, with the usual flaws and virtues.

Causes of Government Failure

Here are six reasons why government intervention can fail to achieve its potential.

Imperfect knowledge or foresight. Regulators may not know enough to set correct standards. For example, natural gas prices may, with the best of intentions, be set too low. The result will be too much quantity demanded and too little quantity supplied, with no automatic correction. Or the automobile emission standards prescribed for a particular year may be too demanding, thereby proving unexpectedly expensive to achieve, or too lax, thereby leading to unexpected excessive pollution.

Rigidities. Regulatory rules and allocations are hard to change, but technology and economic circumstances change continually. Regulations that at one time protected the public against a natural monopoly may unnecessarily perpetuate a monopoly long after technological changes have made competition possible. In the United States, giving AT&T a monopoly in long-distance communication and specifying its price structure made sense when the technology for transmitting messages (use of cable) led to natural monopoly. After a communications satellite had been placed in orbit, there was room for many competitors, but the regulatory commission was not free simply to open up the industry to anyone. Too many people had invested in the telephone industry and accepted limited profits on the expectation of continued regulation.

Inefficient means. Government may fail to choose the least costly means of solving a problem. It may decree a specific form of antipollution device that proves less effective and more expensive than another. It may pass a strict rule that proves all but impossible to enforce when a milder one would have achieved higher compliance at lower enforcement cost.

Myopic regulation. Regulation may become too restricted and too narrowly defined because the regulators are forced to specialize. Specialization may lead to expertise in a given area, but the regulators may lack the breadth to relate their area to wider concerns. Officials charged with the responsibility for a healthy railway industry (dating from the time when railways were the dominant means of transportation) may fail to see that the encouragement of trucking, even at the expense of the railways, may be necessary for a healthy transportation industry.

Political constraints. Political realities may prevent the "right" policy from being adopted, even when it has been clearly identified. This is particularly true in a government based on checks and balances. Suppose a technically perfect tax (or tariff or farm policy) is designed by the experts. It will surely hurt some groups and benefit others. Lobbyists will go to work. The policy is likely to be modified, mutilated, rebuilt, and finally passed in a form the experts know is inadequate. Although most members of Parliament may be aware of its flaws, it will be passed because it is "better than nothing."

This scenario occurs because the political process responds to political realities. "After all," the politician may reason as he yields to the demands of the widget lobby (against his best judgment about the public interest), "if I'm defeated for re-election, I won't be here to serve the public interest on even more important issues next year." (Next year he will probably support widgets out of a sense of consistency!)

FIGURE 23-3 Effects of Government Failure

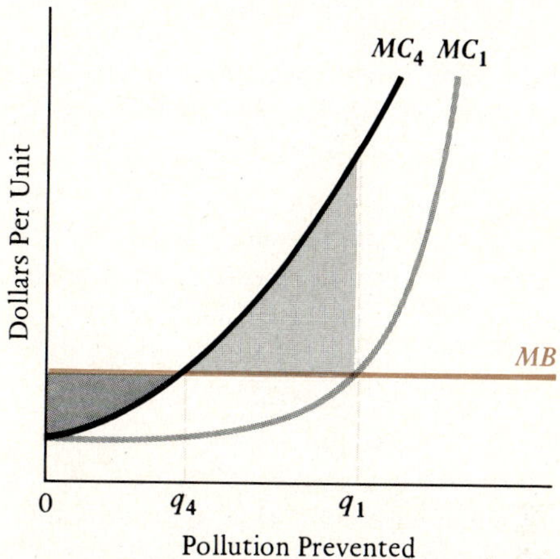

Choice of the wrong method of control will reduce the optimal amount of intervention and may convert the gains from intervention into losses. The MB and MC_1 curves are similar to those in Figure 23-2. One common form of government failure is to specify the wrong method of intervention. Suppose the government specifies a method of pollution control that leads to the costs shown by MC_4. This is inefficient because costs at every level of pollution prevention are higher than necessary. Under such a method, the optimal level of prevention falls to q_4, with net benefits shown by the dark shaded area. Government failure reduces the amount of prevention that is optimal. The government will compound its failure if it insists on the level of prevention q_1 while requiring use of the inefficient method. The cost of every unit of pollution prevented beyond q_4 is in excess of its benefits, as shown by the light shaded area. Indeed, the result is worse than no intervention at all (the light shaded area is larger than the dark shaded area). Whereas the best possible government intervention would have produced a net gain, government failure in this case produces a net loss.

Decision maker's objectives. Public officials almost always wish to serve the public interest. But they

BOX 23-3

New England and the Atlantic Provinces: A Tale of Two Regions

There are many similarities between the American New England states and the Canadian Atlantic provinces. Both have highly educated populations concentrated in relatively small areas. Both have access by waterway to foreign and domestic markets. The Atlantic provinces, however, have abundant supplies of hydroelectricity, iron, coal, and zinc that are not found in New England; thus they would seem to be more likely to be able to generate and sustain an economic boom.

Why then has just the reverse occurred? In the 1970s New England experienced a significant and sustained manufacturing investment boom; by the 1980s New England had a healthy manufacturing base and an unemployment rate lower than that of most other regions in the United States. In contrast, the Atlantic provinces experienced a sharp slump in the 1970s and has remained stagnant in the 1980s.

At the beginning of the 1970s cuts in defense spending and the aerospace program and the large oil price increases that occurred simultaneously had a severe negative impact on New England. By 1975 the region's per capita income had been falling steadily for five years, and its unemployment rate was the worst in the nation. Consequently, the region had available a pool of relatively cheap, highly educated workers. This labor supply attracted new firms, particularly in the fields of computer and scientific technology. The result was that from 1975 to 1979 nonagricultural employment grew at a rate faster than the average for the whole nation. Like a phoenix from the ashes, the boom of the late 1970s arose from the recession of the early 1970s.

Superficially, the manufacturing sector in the Atlantic provinces did well during the early and mid 1970s. Wages and salaries increased faster here than they did for Canada as a whole. Yet employment and output grew more slowly than in the rest of Canada. Why should a region with as many advantages as the Atlantic provinces have a performance in such an important sector that was so much worse than that of New England?

Although many reasons account for the different patterns of development in the two regions, one striking difference lies in government policies. The U.S. government essentially left the New England economy alone to adjust to its own problems. As a result, wages fell relative to those in the rest of the nation, and the region became an attractive place for new firms to locate.

At a recent conference, American economist Lester Thurow argued:

have their careers, their families, and their prejudices as well. This is not unlike the principal-agent problem mentioned as a source of market failure. Public officials' own needs are seldom wholly absent from their consideration of the actions they will take. Similarly, their definition of the public interest is likely to be influenced heavily by their personal views of what policies are best.

A close relationship often exists or develops between the regulators and the regulated. Many government regulators come from industry and plan to return to it. The broadcasting official who serves five years on the Canadian Radio and Television Commission and hopes to become a network vice-president after that term of office may view the networks' case in a not wholly disinterested way. Indeed, regulators may protect an industry in ways that would be quite illegal if done from within the industry.

The Effect of Government Failure

Suppose, for any of the reasons just discussed, that the government makes a mistake in regulation. Say the government mistakenly specifies a method of pollution control that is less effective than the best method. This will increase the cost of achieving any given level of prevention. If the government insists on the level of control appropriate to the correct method but requires the incorrect method, it can

New England is a prosperous region because it got out of its old dying industries and into new growth industries. If Washington had protected New England's old dying industries, New England would still be depressed.

In contrast, the Canadian government has used many policies to support the Atlantic provinces. And these policies have been disappointingly ineffective. Many of the policies failed to recognize that much of the disparity between regions reflects regional equilibrium (see Box 17-1 on pages 334–335). Many economists believe that the policy of propping up dying industries has inhibited growth by reducing the region's ability to develop new industries.

Much of the support to the region has come in the form of transfer payments. Since the 1970s the provinces of the Atlantic region have experienced current account deficits of up to *50 percent* of GDP, financed largely by intergovernmental transfers. Transfers serve the intended purpose of redistributing income to the region, but they have had the unintended side effect of impeding the process of regional adjustment. These policies may also have resulted in what has become known as "transfer dependency." Transfer dependency not only frustrates the market mechanism by propping up wages, thereby discouraging out-migration and new investment, but it also undermines the economy in other ways. In 1973 a report prepared for the Department of Regional Economic Expansion stated:

> The Atlantic Region . . . has been dependent on assistance and support for a long period; this has left its mark on the outlook of the region. It has tended to become a part of the conventional wisdom that only government subsidies or some form of special consideration point the way to achieving prosperity. The result has been to weaken the confidence of the region in its ability to take initiatives and operate independently.

In Newfoundland, where in 1985 over 10 percent of the population received unemployment insurance benefits amounting to about 8 percent of personal income, the provincial Royal Commission on Unemployment concluded that the UI system was "crippling the work ethic" and recommended major changes to eliminate "the disincentives to work and to improve one's education level" that exist in the current system.

Will the two regions continue to develop in such different ways? Many observers believe that as long as government transfers and support for declining industries remain a central part of Canadian regional policy, the Atlantic provinces will languish in transfer dependency.

convert a social gain from control into a social loss. This is illustrated in Figure 23-3 (p. 485).

To generalize from the specific example, it is clear that any form of government failure adds to the costs or decreases the benefits of government intervention. Thus the lower the public's confidence in government's ability to do the right thing, the lower will be its willingness to have government intervention.

Government Intervention in Canada

Each of the theoretical principles for determining the optimal amount of intervention is accepted by almost everyone. What they add up to, however, is more controversial. Some further issues involved in advocating or opposing government intervention are discussed in Box 23-3.

Does government intervene too little or too much in response to market failure? This question reflects one aspect of the argument about the role of government in the economy.

Much of the rhetoric of society's concern with ecology urges government intervention against heartless, profit-mad, giant corporations that destroy the environment for their own crass purposes. Such feelings lead to the demand for more—and more stringent—government regulation.

At the same time, others see the heavy hand of

government regulation as burdening private companies with regulations that add to costs, impede innovation, and thus keep prices and wages artificially high. Even perfect intervention would be costly, but imperfect intervention makes it much too costly. In this view, the deregulation movement that started in the 1980s was long overdue.

Evaluating the costs and the probable effectiveness of government intervention requires a comparison of the unregulated economic system as it is working (not as it might work ideally) with the pattern of government intervention as it is likely to perform (not as it might perform ideally).

The Role of Analysis

Economic analysis and measurement can help to eliminate certain misconceptions that cloud and confuse the debate. We have noted one such misconception: The optimal level of a negative externality, such as pollution, is not, as some urge, zero.

Another mistake is to equate market failure with the greed of profit-motivated corporations. Externalities do not require callous, thoughtless, or deliberately deceptive practices of private, profit-seeking firms; they occur whenever the signals to which decision makers respond do not include social as well as private benefits and costs. Such situations are not limited to private firms in a capitalist system. Cities and nationalized industries pollute just as much as privately owned industries when they neglect externalities in their operations, as they often do.

A third mistake is to think that the profits of a corporation tell something about neglected externalities. It is possible for a profitable firm (such as General Motors of Canada) or an unprofitable one (such as Massey-Ferguson) to spend too little on pollution control or on safety, but it is also possible for it to spend too much. The existence of profits provides no clue as to which is the case.

The Role of Ideology

Although analysis has a role to play, there are several reasons why ideology plays a bigger role in evaluating government intervention than in other areas.

First, measuring the costs of government intervention is difficult, particularly with respect to indirect costs, because some of the trade-offs are inherently uncertain. How important and how unsafe is nuclear power? Does the ban on some pesticides cause so much malnutrition that it offsets the ecological gains it brings? What cannot be readily measured can be alleged to be extremely high (or low) by opponents (or supporters) of intervention. The numerous findings by scholars on both sides of each of these subjects has led one economist to the cynical conclusion that "believing is seeing."

Second, classifying the actual pattern of government intervention as successful or not is in part subjective. Has government safety regulation been (choose one) useful if imperfect, virtually ineffective, or positively adverse? All three views have been expressed and "documented."

Third, specifying what constitutes market failure is difficult. Does product differentiation represent market success (by giving consumers the variety they want) or failure (by foisting expensive and useless variations on them)?

In Canada in the 1980s it seems safe to conclude that confidence in the existing mix of free market and government regulation is at a relatively low ebb. Not only are specific policy suggestions hotly argued, but so is the whole philosophy of intervention. There is no consensus yet as to what is wrong; the pressures for changes are strong in *both* directions.

Summary

1. The various markets in the economy are coordinated in an unplanned, decentralized way by the price system. Profits and losses play a key role in achieving a coordinated market response. Changes in prices and profits, resulting from emerging scarcities and surpluses, lead decision makers to adapt to a change in any one market

of the economy. Such responses tend to correct the shortages and surpluses as well as to change the market signals of prices and profits.

2. Important features of market coordination include voluntary responses to market signals, the limited information required by any individual, and the fact that coordination will occur under any market structure.
3. A widely held argument in favor of the free market goes beyond its ability to provide automatic coordination. Many analysts believe that its flexibility and adaptability make it the best coordinator and also encourage innovation and growth. The tendency of the market to push relative prices toward the costs of production fosters efficient allocation of resources and self-correction of disequilibrium. Furthermore, the market economy tends to be impersonal, to decentralize power, and to rely heavily on voluntary behavior of individuals.
4. Markets do not always work perfectly. Dissatisfaction with market results often leads to government intervention. Three main kinds of market failure are (a) externalities arising from differences between private and social costs and benefits, (b) market imperfections and impediments, and (c) failure to achieve social goals other than efficiency.
5. Pollution is an example of an externality. An important source of pollution is producers' use of water and air that they do not regard as scarce. Since they do not pay all the costs of using these resources, they are not motivated to avoid the costs. Individual use of common-property resources, congestion, and neglect of future consequences are other sources of externalities.
6. Market imperfections and impediments are anything that prevents the prompt movement of resources in response to market signals. They include unequal information, barriers to mobility, excessive transactions costs, and the existence of collective consumption goods.
7. Changing the distribution of income is one of the roles for government intervention that members of a society desire. Others include values placed on public provision for its own sake, protection of individuals from themselves or from others, and recognition of social obligations.
8. Microeconomic policy concerns activities of the government that alter the unrestricted workings of the free-market system in order to affect either the allocation of resources or the distribution of income. Major tools of microeconomic policy include (a) public provision, (b) redistribution, (c) rule making, and (d) structuring incentives. (The first two are the subject of Chapter 24.) Both prescriptive and proscriptive rule making occurs in a variety of forms. Incentives can be structured in a number of ways including the use of fines, subsidies, taxes, and effluent charges. Each of these

is a means of internalizing the externality and thus avoiding market failure.

9. The costs and benefits of government intervention must be considered in deciding whether, when, and how much intervention is appropriate. Among the costs are the direct costs incurred by the government; the costs imposed on those regulated, direct and indirect; and the costs imposed on third parties. These costs are seldom negligible and are often large.
10. If government intervention fails, the costs of intervention are incurred without realizing the benefits of avoiding market failure. The possibility of government failure must be balanced against the potential benefits of removing market failure. It is neither possible nor efficient to correct all market failure; neither is it always efficient to do nothing.

Topics for Review

Market coordination
Market failure
Externalities and their internalization
Net social benefit and net private benefit
MNPB and *MNSB*
Benefits and costs of government intervention
Government failure
Optimal amount of intervention

Discussion Questions

1. Should the free market be allowed to determine the price for the following, or should government intervene? Defend your choice for each.
   a. Transit fares
   b. Plastic surgery for victims of fires
   c. Garbage collection
   d. Postal delivery of newspapers and magazines
   e. Fire protection for churches
   f. Ice cream
2. The following activities have known harmful effects. In each case identify any divergence between social and private costs.
   a. Cigarette smoking
   b. Driving a car at 120 kph
   c. Private ownership of guns
   d. Drilling for offshore oil
3. Suppose that the facts asserted below are true. Should they trigger government intervention? If so, what policy alternatives are available?
   a. Hospital costs have been rising at about four times the rate of increase of personal income, and proper treatment of a serious illness has become extraordinarily expensive.
   b. The cost of the average one-family house in Ottawa is now over

$140,000, an amount beyond the reach of many government employees.

c. Cigarette smoking tends to reduce life expectancy of the smoker by eight years.

d. Saccharin in large doses has been found to cause cancer in Canadian mice.

4. Consider the possible beneficial and adverse effects of each of the following forms of government interference.

a. Charging motorists a tax for driving in the downtown areas of large cities and using the revenues to provide peripheral parking and shuttle buses

b. Prohibiting doctors from purchasing malpractice insurance

c. Mandating no-fault auto insurance, in which the car owner's insurance company is responsible for damage to the insured vehicle no matter who causes the accident

d. Requiring automobile manufacturers to warrant the tires on cars they sell instead of (as at present) having the tire manufacturer be the warrantor

5. Consider the following (alleged) facts about pollution control and indicate what, if any, influence they might have on policy determination.

a. In the mid 1980s the cost of meeting federal pollution requirements in the United States was about $100 per person per year.

b. More than a third of the world's known oil supplies lie under the ocean floor, and there is no known blowout-proof method of recovery.

c. Sulfur removal requirements and strip mining regulations have led to the tripling of the cost of a ton of coal used in generating electricity.

d. Every million dollars spent on pollution control creates 67 new jobs in the economy.

6. The president of Goodyear Tire and Rubber Company complained that government regulation had imposed $30 million per year in "unproductive costs" on his company, as listed below. How would one determine whether these costs were "productive" or "unproductive"?

a. Environmental regulation, $17 million

b. Occupational safety and health, $7 million

c. Motor vehicle safety, $3 million

d. Personnel and administration, $3 million

7. During a Pittsburgh air pollution alert, a 69-year-old retired steelworker was interviewed. He said, "I've got a heart condition myself, and I know that when I look out the window and see the air like it was this morning, I've got to stay inside. Yesterday, I tried to drive to the store, and I couldn't see 50 feet ahead of me, it was so thick, so I just came home. I remember that when I was young, we never thought about pollution. Everybody was working, and everybody had money, and the smokestacks were smoking, and the air was dirty, and we were all happy. I think the best air we ever had in Pittsburgh was during the Depression. That's when nobody was working." Comment on this statement in terms of the issues discussed in this chapter.

8. The Aswan Dam has been called Egypt's "wall against hunger," by virtue of its provision of both irrigation water and electric power to the Nile Valley. Among its less salutary side effects are these:
   a. The reduced flow of water and silt in the river have allowed the Nile Delta to be overrun by sea water, leaving harmful salts.
   b. Laker Nasser, in back of the dam, has become a breeding place for malaria mosquitoes.
   c. Homes of 122,000 Nubian villagers have been inundated, along with countless antiquities for 310 miles upstream from the dam.

   Should the dam have been built? Discuss the issues involved, using the concepts of private and social cost and externalities.

24

Taxation and Public Expenditure

All governments spend money, and they must raise revenue to do so. Governments in Canada are no exception. But government spending and government taxation today go far beyond the minimum required to provide such essentials as a system of justice and protection against foreign enemies. Spending and taxing are also key tools of both macroeconomic and microeconomic policy.

In this chapter we look at spending and taxing as tools of microeconomic policy. Public expenditure and public finance (raising revenue through taxation) inescapably affect both the allocation of resources and the distribution of income—sometimes intentionally, sometimes not.

There is no simple and sharp distinction between the uses of expenditure and tax policies. One way to deal with polluted rivers, for example, is by public expenditure to clean them up. An alternative is to use taxes to penalize polluters or to give tax concessions to firms that install pollution-abating devices. Tax concessions that seek to induce market responses are now called **tax expenditures**—that is, sacrifices of revenue by the taxing authorities that are designed to achieve purposes that the government believes are desirable.

In this chapter we are concerned with public expenditure and taxation. We ask how these activities of government affect the allocation of resources and the distribution of income. We also ask about the extent to which they are effective tools of public policy.

Taxation As a Tool of Microeconomic Policy

There is a bewildering array of taxes, some highly visible (such as sales taxes and income taxes) and others all but invisible to the consumer because they are imposed on producers of raw materials and intermediate products. People are taxed on what they earn, on what they spend, and on what they own. Firms are taxed as well as households. Taxes are not only numerous, but they take a big bite. Aggregate taxes amount to roughly one-third of the total value of goods and services produced in Canada each year. The diversity and yield of various taxes are shown in Table 24-1.

TABLE 24-1 Government Tax Revenues by Source, 1986

	Revenue		Percentage division		
Kind of tax	Billions of dollars	Percentage	Federal	Provincial	Municipal
Income tax, persons	85.0	41	63	37	—
Income and other taxes, corporations	13.4	7	73	26	—
General sales taxes	43.3	21	46	54	—
Customs duties	4.2	2	100	—	—
Property tax	16.6	8	—	—	100
All other taxes	43.5	21	—	—	—
Total	206.0	100	44	39	17

Source: National Income and Expenditure Accounts, Statistics Canada, 13-001.

Income taxes are the major source of revenue for the federal and provincial governments. Substantial yields are also obtained from the federal manufacturer's sales tax and the provincial retail levies that make up the sales tax category. Municipal governments rely almost entirely on property taxes.

The Tax System and the Distribution of Income

A government that taxes the rich and gives tax concessions to the poor is changing the distribution of income. How much redistribution is achieved by Canadian taxes today?

Progressivity of Taxation

Rhetoric about income distribution and tax policy often invokes the important but hard-to-define concepts of equity and equality.

Equity. Equity—fairness—is a normative concept; what one group thinks is fair may seem outrageous to another. In considering equity, two concepts need to be distinguished.

Vertical equity concerns equity across income classes; it focuses on comparisons between individuals or families with different levels of income. This concept is central to our discussion of the progressivity of taxes.

Horizontal equity concerns equity within a given income class; it recognizes certain types of costs or expenditures as "required" and thus focuses on differences that may arise among individuals or families with the same income levels but different circumstances. For example, two families with the same income but different numbers of children might be taxed differently on grounds of horizontal equity. We consider the issue of horizontal equity in more detail in Chapter 25, "Social Policy," where the issue is often of central importance.

Equality. Equality is a straightforward concept—or is it? To tax everyone equally can mean several things. It might mean that everyone should pay the same amount—which would be hard on the unemployed worker and easy on Wayne Gretzky. It might mean that everyone should pay the same proportion of income, say, a flat 20 percent, whether rich or poor, living alone or supporting eight children, healthy or suffering from a disease that requires heavy use of expensive drugs. It might mean that each should pay an amount of tax such that everyone's income after taxes is the same—which would remove any incentive to earn above average income. Or it might mean none of these things.

Progressivity. People may not agree on what redistributions are fair, but they can agree on what redistributions actually occur. To get precise measurements of what happens, the distributional effects of taxes are usually discussed using the concept of **progressivity of taxation,** the ratio of taxes to income at different levels of income.

1. A **proportional tax** takes amounts of money from people in direct proportion to their income.
2. A **regressive tax** takes a larger percentage of income from people, the lower their income.
3. A **progressive tax** takes a larger percentage of income from people, the larger their income.

A tax system is said to be progressive if it decreases the inequality of income distribution and to be regressive if it increases the inequality.

Excise and sales taxes. An excise tax is levied on a particular commodity (such as liquor); a sales tax is levied on all or most sales.

If two families spend the same proportion of their income on a certain commodity that is subject to a sales or an excise tax, the tax is proportional in its effects on them. If the tax is on a commodity, such as food, that takes a larger proportion of the income of lower-income families, it is regressive. If it is on a commodity, such as jewelry, on which the rich spend a larger proportion of their income than the poor, it is progressive. But a general sales tax is regressive because poorer families tend to spend a larger proportion of their incomes than do richer families.

Commodities with inelastic demands provide attractive sources of revenue. In many countries commodities such as tobacco, alcohol, and gasoline are singled out for high rates of excise taxation. Because these commodities usually account for a much greater proportion of the expenditure of lower-income than higher-income groups, the taxes on them are regressive.

Sales and excise taxes in Canada today are generally regressive.

One type of sales tax that has been widely discussed recently is the **value-added tax (VAT).** Widely used in Western Europe, it is nothing more than a generalized sales tax that is applied not at a single stage like the provincial retail sales tax but as a multistage tax that is collected on the value added to goods as they move through the production and distribution systems. It shares the regressivity of the retail sales tax, although recent proposals to introduce a VAT in Canada have included changes to other elements of the tax system to offset this regressivity.

Property taxes. The progressivity of the property tax has been studied extensively. It is well known that the rich live in more expensive houses than the poor, but all that this establishes is that the rich tend to pay more dollars in property tax than the poor. Because the rich tend to live in different communities from the poor and thus pay taxes at different rates, and because they tend to spend a different proportion of their income for housing, the question of the progressivity of the property tax is difficult. Most studies have shown that the proportion of income spent for housing tends to decrease with income. Many, but not all, public finance experts believe that the property tax tends to be regressive in its overall effect.

Personal income taxes. The personal tax rate is itself a function of taxable income, and it is useful to distinguish between two different rates. The **average tax rate** paid by a taxpayer is their income tax payment divided by total income. The **marginal tax rate** is the amount of tax the taxpayer would pay on an additional dollar of income.

Prior to the tax reform of 1987, the federal personal income tax appeared to be quite progressive.[1] There were 11 tax brackets with the marginal rate rising from 16 percent to 43 percent; typically provinces top-up federal taxes by a further one-half so the total marginal rate ranged from 24 percent to over 54 percent. However, because of how the taxable income was defined, the overall effect of the

[1] The provinces also collect income taxes; Quebec runs its own income tax system while the other nine provinces simply use the federal tax base (and federally distributed tax forms) and essentially "top-up" federal taxes. The Quebec system is discussed in Chapter 25. For present purposes we can understand the total system by looking at the federal system.

income tax system was less progressive than suggested by the rising marginal tax rates. To arrive at taxable income, total income was reduced by a number of eligible exemptions and deductions, and some forms of income were taxed differently than others.[2] Because the value in terms of reduced taxes of these exemptions and deductions is higher the higher is one's marginal tax rate, they tended to lessen the progressivity in the tax table.

In June 1987 Finance Minister Michael Wilson introduced a major reform of the personal income tax system. The new federal tax structure is shown in Table 24-2; as can be seen, the system is considerably simpler. There are now just three tax brackets. The conversion of the basic personal exemption to a personal tax credit—worth the same to each taxpayer regardless of their income level—contributes to, rather than detracts from, the progressivity of the system. Further, marginal rates have been reduced for most Canadians, and many other low-income Canadians now not only pay no taxes but do not have to file. (This reform is discussed later in Box 24-2 on pages 506–507.)

Corporate income taxes. The federal corporate income tax is, for practical purposes, a flat-rate tax on profits as defined by the taxing authorities. In 1986 the rate was reduced from 50 to 36 percent, and in 1988 it will fall to 28 percent. Other changes in the tax laws raised the overall taxes paid by corporations. It is difficult to determine the effect of corporate taxation on income distribution, for there is great controversy over the extent to which it is "shifted" to consumers. (The question of tax shifting is called the problem of *incidence,* that is, who really pays a tax imposed on any one group. It is discussed later in this chapter.) So far as the tax is paid by stockholders, there is a tendency toward progressivity because stockholders as a group tend to be wealthier than individuals who do not own stock. But within the stockholder group, the results are uneven. If a dollar were paid out in dividends instead of taxes, rich stockholders would keep a much smaller share than poorer stockholders because of their high marginal personal tax rates.

The Overall Redistributive Effect of the Tax System

It is more difficult to assess the overall impact of a tax system than the impact of any particular tax, but economists often ask whether the whole array of taxes tends to increase or decrease the degree of inequality of the income distribution. One aspect of this question depends on the mix of taxes of different kinds. Federal taxes (chiefly income taxes) tend to be somewhat progressive. Provincial and municipal governments rely heavily on property and sales taxes and thus have tax systems that are regressive.

The matter of assessing progressivity is complicated by other factors. Is progressivity defined for the individual or for the family? When a couple with two children pays the same tax as a childless couple with the same income, is this proportional or regressive taxation? If the *family* is the relevant unit, it is proportional taxation. If the *person* is the relevant unit, equal tax rates on families of different sizes having the same income would be regressive. As it is, a household with children pays less *income* tax than a household with the same income without children. (This does not mean, as childless people often assume, that the household with children pays less total taxes. Other taxes, such as sales taxes, tend to fall more heavily on large families than on small ones.)

The difficulty of determining progressivity is increased by the fact that income from different sources is taxed at different rates. For example, in the federal individual tax, income from royalties on oil wells is taxed more lightly than income from royalties on books, and profits from sales of assets (capital gains) are taxed more lightly than wages and salaries. To evaluate progressivity one needs to know the way in which different levels of income correlate with different sources of income.

The offsetting effects of the various elements of the tax system have led many writers to conclude that, overall, the tax system has very little net effect

[2] Until 1972 most capital gains were not taxable in Canada, but beginning in 1972 taxpayers were required to include one-half of gains received in their taxable income. In his May 1985 budget, Federal Minister of Finance Michael Wilson introduced a $500,000 personal lifetime exemption for capital gains. In the June 1987 tax reform, the lifetime exemption was reduced to $100,000.

TABLE 24-2 The Rate Structure of the Personal Income Tax, 1988

	Federal income tax		Provincial income tax[a]		Combined tax rates	
Assessed income (dollars)	Tax (dollars)	Marginal rate (percent)	Tax (dollars)	Marginal rate (percent)	Average (percent)	Marginal (percent)
$ 9,295	0	17	0	9	0	26
27,500	3,655	17	1,915	9	20	26
40,000	6,905	26	3,665	14	26	40
55,000	10,805	26	5,765	14	30	40
70,000	15,155	29	8,165	16	33	45
100,000	23,855	29	12,965	16	37	45

Source: Department of Finance, *Tax Reform 1987—Income Tax Reform.*

[a] The typical provincial tax equals 55 percent of the federal tax.

Both marginal and average tax rates rise with income; thus the tax is progressive in structure. The combined marginal tax rate rises from 26 percent to a maximum of 45 percent while the combined average rate also climbs steadily with assessed income. Under the income tax structure introduced in the 1987 reform of the tax system, a single taxpayer receives a federal tax credit of $1020 and (typically) a provincial credit of $560, so that he or she can earn up to $9,295 before incurring any tax liability.

on the distribution of income, except for very low-income persons. Thus:

The tax system tends to be roughly proportional for most income classes, and mildly progressive for low-income persons.

Can Progressivity Be Increased?

Taxes can be levied on any of three different monetary magnitudes: assets, incomes, and expenditures. Inheritance taxes and gift taxes are taxes on assets; such taxes do not now play a large role in the overall revenue picture. Taxes on incomes are important and can be quite progressive. Taxes on expenditures—especially sales and excise taxes—are related to the dollar value of expenditures, not the incomes of the people spending the money; they are known to be regressive.

Substantial progressivity in income taxes is required to achieve proportionality in the overall tax pattern.

Many observers have argued that to achieve overall proportionality in the tax structure is in itself a significant accomplishment. Some argue that, given the large fraction of national income that is taxed away, more progressivity cannot be achieved, since we are already forced to levy heavy taxes on average and below average incomes simply to meet revenue requirements.

It may seem obvious that since income taxes are progressive, raising income tax rates would increase progressivity. Surprisingly, some conservative economists have argued that this is not the case. A shift to higher tax rates would raise both the average and marginal *rate* of tax on incomes, but it might not raise the total *amount* of revenue actually collected. The change in the amount would depend on the incentive effects of tax rates.

A curve that attempts to relate the government's income tax revenue yield to the level of tax rates is the **Laffer curve**, named for economist Arthur Laffer, whose views were influential during the early years of the Reagan administration in the United States, which came to power in 1981. Its essential feature is that tax revenues reach a maximum at some rate of taxation well below 100 percent (see Figure 24-1).

The general shape of the Laffer curve is argued as a matter of simple logic. At a zero tax rate no

FIGURE 24-1 A Laffer Curve

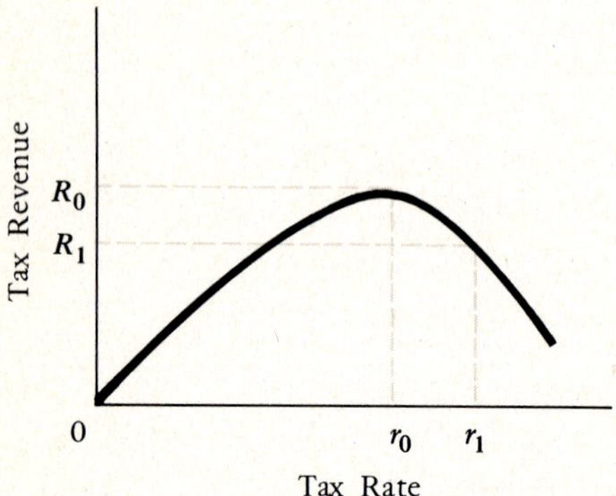

Increases in tax rates beyond some level will decrease rather than increase tax revenue. The curve relates the government's tax revenue to the tax rate. As drawn, revenue reaches a maximum level of R_0 at average tax rate r_0. If tax rates were r_1, *reducing* them to r_0 would increase revenue to the government.

revenue will be collected. Similarly, at a 100 percent tax rate revenues will again be zero because no one would bother to earn taxable income just to support the government. At intermediate rates people will both earn income and pay taxes. Government tax revenues will reach an upper limit at some rate of taxation below 100 percent. For rates higher than the rate that produces this maximum, every increase in tax rates will lead to a decrease in tax revenues.

Just where this maximum occurs—whether at average tax rates of 40 percent or 80 percent or 95 percent—is an important empirical matter. Laffer believed that by the 1970s the United States had already increased taxes past the point where higher tax rates yielded more revenue. As a result, he argued, any attempt to increase progressivity by raising income tax rates would be self-defeating.

Many other economists disagreed. They might concede that some countries may have reached such a point, but they argued that this had not happened in the United States. A number of careful studies showed that the then top U.S. marginal tax rate of 50 percent was still short of being self-defeating in terms of tax revenue. These studies suggest that Professor Laffer identified a potential rather than an actual problem. Box 24-1 describes an early precursor of the Laffer curve.

Increasing Progressivity by Changing the Income Tax Structure

If the government raises income taxes for one group and lowers them for another in a way that leaves the total tax yield constant, the *structure* of the income tax will have been changed. Much repeated demand for tax reform relates to proposed changes in the structure of income taxes. Most economists believe that such changes can be made (whether or not they consider them desirable) and that if they were made, they could change the progressivity of the total tax system. Here are four important proposals, widely discussed by economists in the decades preceding the tax reform of 1987.

Negative income tax (NIT). A tax is negative when the government pays the "taxpayer" instead of the other way around. The so-called **negative income tax (NIT)** is a policy tool designed to increase progressivity and combat poverty by making taxes *negative* at very low incomes. Such a tax would extend progressivity to the very lowest incomes.

Many versions of the NIT have been proposed; the one described here illustrates the basic idea. The underlying belief is that a family of a given size should be allowed a minimum annual income. The aim is to guarantee this income without eliminating the incentive to become self-supporting. This is done by combining a grant with a tax. At a break-even income level, well above the minimum income guaranteed, the family neither receives money from the government nor pays any tax. Below this break-even level the family is paid by the government, that is, the family pays a negative tax. Above this level it pays a positive tax. An example based on a minimum annual income of \$6,000, a break-even level of \$12,000, and a marginal tax rate of 50 percent is given in Figure 24-2 (see page 500).[3] Of course, the grant

[3] The example is unrealistic in assigning a 50 percent marginal tax at such low levels of income as \$12,000. But the cost to the government in lost revenue of an NIT would be much higher if it were combined with a sharply graduated rate structure.

BOX 24-1

The Laffer Curve 600 Years Before Laffer

In the fourteenth century the Arabic philosopher Ibn Khaldun wrote:

It should be known that at the beginning of the dynasty, taxation yields a large revenue from small assessments. At the end of the dynasty, taxation yields a small revenue from large assessments. . . .

When the dynasty follows the ways of group feeling and [political] superiority, it necessarily has at first a desert attitude. The desert attitude requires kindness, reverence, humility, respect for the property of other people, and disinclination to appropriate it, except in rare instances. Therefore, the individual imposts and assessments, which together constitute the tax revenue, are low. When tax assessments and imposts upon the subjects are low, the latter have the energy and desire to do things. Cultural enterprises grow and increase, because the low taxes bring satisfaction. When cultural enterprises grow, the number of individual imposts and assessments mounts. In consequence, the tax revenue, which is the sum total of [the individual assessments], increases.

When the dynasty continues in power and their rulers follow each other in succession, they become sophisticated. The Bedouin attitude and simplicity lose their significance, and the Bedouin qualities of moderation and restraint disappear.

As a result, the individual imposts and assessments upon the subjects, agricultural laborers, farmers, and all the other taxpayers, increase. Every individual impost and assessment is greatly increased, in order to obtain a higher tax revenue. Customs duties are placed upon articles of commerce. Gradual increases in the amount of assessments succeed each other regularly, in correspondence with the gradual increase in the luxury customs and many needs of the dynasty, and the spending required in connection with them. Eventually, the taxes will weigh heavily upon the subjects and overburden them. Heavy taxes become an obligation and tradition, because the increases took place gradually, and no one knows specifically who increased them or levied them. They lie upon the subjects like an obligation and tradition.

The assessments increase beyond the limits of equity. The result is that the interest of the subjects in cultural enterprises disappears, since when they compare expenditures and taxes with their income and gain and see the little profit they make, they lose all hope. Therefore, many of them refrain from all the activity. The result is that the total tax revenue goes down.

Finally, civilization is destroyed, because the incentive for cultural activity is gone. It is the dynasty that suffers from the situation, because it [is the dynasty that] profits from cultural activity.*

* *From the Muqaddimah: An Introduction to History,* translated from the Arabic by Franz Rosenthal. Bollingen Series XLIII. Copyright © 1958 and 1967 by Princeton University Press. Reprinted by permission of Princeton University Press.

---

is not actually given and then taxed away; thus it is spoken of as a "notional" grant.

Supporters of the negative income tax believe that it would be a particularly effective tool for reducing poverty. It provides a minimum level of income as a matter of right, not of charity, and it does so without removing the incentive to work of people who are eligible for payments. Every dollar earned adds to the after-tax income of the family.

As a potential replacement for many other relief programs, it promises to avoid the most pressing cases of poverty with much less administrative cost and without the myriad exceptions that are involved in most programs. An incidental advantage is that it removes whatever incentive people might have to migrate to provinces with better welfare programs, but it does not discourage migration to places where work may be available.

One step toward an NIT would be to replace many or all of existing personal exemptions with personal tax credits. Exemptions serve to reduce taxable income and thus to reduce taxes due for any given level of pre-tax income. Exemptions tend to be regressive since a given exemption is worth more to someone with a high pre-tax income and hence a high marginal tax rate than it is to someone with a low income. A tax credit reduces taxes due by the amount of the credit and hence is worth the same to all taxpayers. If the credit is refundable, someone who has no taxable income would receive the credit

FIGURE 24-2 The Negative Income Tax

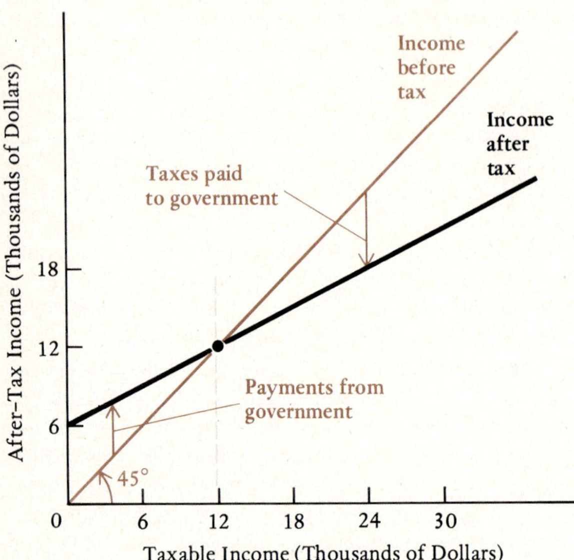

Instead of a zero income tax up to some level and a positive tax above that level, there could be a negative tax up to a break-even income and a positive tax above it. The scheme illustrated here works as if every family is given an untaxed grant of $6,000 and then taxed at a rate of 50 percent on all other income. (Of course, only the *difference* between the notional grant and the tax payable is actually paid or collected.)

The heavy black line shows the after-tax income for different levels of taxable income under this particular scheme. The 45° line shows the income before tax. Therefore, the vertical distance between it and the heavy black curve shows the payments by or to the government at any level of income under this scheme. A family with $12,000 taxable income breaks even. A family with income below $12,000 taxable income is paid by the government. A family with taxable income above $12,000 pays taxes.

from the government; that is, the person would pay negative income taxes.

Comprehensive income taxation. Joseph Pechman of the Brookings Institution took the lead in arguing that it is possible to raise more revenue from the income tax, increase its progressivity, and at the same time *reduce* both average and marginal tax rates. This sounds like magic, but it is a matter of simple arithmetic. The **tax base** is total *taxable* income. Taxable income is much less than total income because of deductions and exemptions. If all income were taxed, regardless of source, it would be possible to raise more revenue by applying lower rates to this larger tax base. The idea of **comprehensive income taxation (CIT)** is to eliminate nearly all the loopholes, deductions, and exemptions that make taxable income less than total income. By eliminating some or all personal deductions, homeowner preferences, special treatment of capital gains, and exemptions for dependents, old age, and blindness, the tax base could be increased substantially. It would then be possible to reduce tax *rates* in all income brackets.

Comprehensive income taxation could achieve substantially more progressivity without increasing anyone's marginal tax rate at all. For example, imagine a definition of the CIT where comprehensive income is 150 percent of previous taxable income. Rates could be slightly reduced for high-income taxpayers and greatly reduced for middle- and low-income taxpayers in such amounts as to maintain the same total tax revenue but increase progressivity.

Needless to say, even if everyone's tax *rates* went down under the CIT, not everyone's tax *payments* would do so because the elimination of exclusions, deductions, and exemptions would raise the tax liability of those taxpayers who had utilized them.

Flat-rate tax. An extreme form of the CIT is the *flat-rate plan,* which would tax all income, from any source, above some minimum per family at a fixed rate, such as 17 percent. This single tax bracket would make the personal income tax virtually a proportional tax and without modifications to other elements of the tax system would surely make the overall system regressive.

Consumption taxation. An alternative approach to personal tax reform is to change the direct personal tax base from income to current consumption plus bequests and gifts. The household is taxed on its income minus saving. People are not taxed at all on what they earn, only on what they spend on consumption.[4]

To make sure that any income that is saved is ultimately subject to tax, there is full taxation of gifts and bequests. By not allowing intergenerational transfers of income to go untaxed, a good deal of income redistribution would occur over the long period. The authors of one such proposal, Professors Robin Broadway, Neil Bruce, and Jack Mintz of Queen's University, argue that such a scheme could achieve current levels of revenue with graduated rates rising to a maximum below the current top marginal income tax rate and at the same time encourage working, saving, and investment.

Political Barriers to Tax Reform

While almost everyone agrees that our present tax structure is much too complex and in many ways illogical, the calls for fundamental and sweeping tax reform are unlikely to be answered. The purely political barriers to tax reform are formidable. Any single reform is likely to impose large costs on a relatively well-identified group, while the benefits it gives would be more widely diffused.

The 10 people who would each lose a million dollars from a particular tax reform are much more interested in the issue than the 10 million people who would each gain a dollar. The 10, not the 10 million, hire lobbyists and make campaign contributions. Legislators usually respond to these pressures if they want long public careers.

Political considerations tend to make redistribution by expenditures more attractive than redistribution by tax reform.

How Much Progressivity Is Desirable?

Suppose that increased progressivity could be achieved; would we want it? Many say no.

Some simply oppose progressivity as a goal. A second group is motivated not by distributive considerations but by opposition to government spending. They oppose changes that would make it easier for the government to raise more money. Such people fear schemes such as CIT precisely because such schemes do not generate tax revolts even if they increase progressivity. Rates that are lowered today can be raised tomorrow.

A third source of opposition to increasing progressivity by means of tax reform is that every aspect of present tax policy was introduced to benefit some group whose members believe they have valid claims to special treatment. Consider almost any deduction that CIT could reduce—say, charitable contributions. The tax deductibility of contributions provides incentive for gifts to churches, universities, and private charities and foundations.

Fourth, tax reform may conflict with what is seen as fair. Adjustments made in the name of equity have eroded the tax base. Special tax treatment of the aged seems fair in view of their probable need for extensive medical treatment. More favorable tax treatment of families with children than of childless couples seems fair to some on horizontal equity grounds, but not to people who think population is already too high.

Finally, the case against tax policy as a means of achieving redistributive goals has some support even among those who favor more redistribution of income from rich to poor. They argue that it is misleading, unnecessary, and poor tactics politically to pay so much attention to *tax* progressivity. After all, how the money is spent is just as important, and often less controversial, than how it is collected. A regressive tax, say, a sales tax, may provide funds for increasing welfare payments and thus redistribute income to the poor. It is the combined overall effect of the two that is important. It may be easier for those who want to redistribute income to the poor to get the government to adopt progressive expenditure programs than to enact more progressive taxes.

The Tax System and Allocation of Resources

The tax system influences the allocation of resources by changing the *relative* prices of various goods and

[4] Consumption taxation is not without problems of interpretation. Expenditures on higher education are one example. If viewed as investment, education expenditures would be treated as saving and would not be taxed. If viewed as consumption, such expenditures would be included in the tax base.

factors and the *relative* profitability of various industries and various uses of factors of production.

Though it is theoretically possible to design a neutral tax system—one that leaves all relative prices unchanged—actual tax policy, both intentionally and unintentionally, is never neutral. It leads to a different allocation of resources than would occur without it.

Intended Effects

The tax structure is often used deliberately to change incentives and thus to affect resource allocation. Taxing gasoline to discourage energy consumption is one example; an effluent charge on polluters is another.

Tax provisions may be used as a carrot as well as a stick. One way is to allow the deduction of some expenditures from income before computing the amount of taxes payable or to give tax credits for some kinds of expenditures. Every $100 spent by a wealthy family in the 40 percent marginal tax bracket on an item that is tax deductible costs it just $60 in after-tax income. Every $100 it spends on items that are not tax deductible costs the full $100 in after-tax income. This encourages the family to contribute to charitable and educational institutions, for example.

Interest payments for a mortgage are tax deductible under the U.S. tax code, and a similar proposal was included in the budget on which the Progressive Conservative government of Joe Clark was defeated in 1979. Since payments for rental housing are not deductible, such a provision would encourage home ownership by lowering the cost of buying a house relative to the cost of renting one.

Allowing corporations "accelerated depreciation" or "investment credits" on certain investments encourages them to make such investments in larger amounts. Governments use changes in these provisions in corporation taxes to try to regulate investment demand, both in the aggregate and in its allocation among various sectors and industries.

Unintended Effects

Not all the allocative effects of the tax system are intended. Unintended and undesirable by-products of a tax system occur, for example, when high income taxes discourage work or induce people to spend money on tax avoidance.

Consider the transferability of personal exemptions between spouses, which means that a married couple qualifies for the same total exemption whether one or both spouses work. This creates a disincentive for any nonworking spouse to seek employment. The value of his or her exemption that can be transferred is reduced, dollar for dollar, by any new income they might earn, and hence the family is effectively taxed at the marginal tax rate of the person already employed. This disincentive is surely an unintended effect.

Tax Incidence

The major unresolved question about taxes and resource allocation is empirical: Just how different is the allocation because of tax policy? Perhaps surprisingly, there is no consensus on this question. The reason is that we are not sure who really pays the taxes that are levied. This is called the problem of **tax incidence,** or the identification of who ultimately bears the burden of a tax.

When a tax is imposed on a firm, does the firm bear the burden of the tax, or does it pass it on to the consumer in the form of higher prices? To see why this is a difficult question to answer, consider two examples.

Do Landlords or Tenants Pay the Property Tax?

Landlords characteristically protest that the crushing burden of property taxes makes it impossible for them to earn a reasonable living from renting buildings to tenants, who as often as not abuse the property. Tenants are likely to reply that landlords typically shirk their responsibilities for building maintenance and that the whole burden of the tax is passed on to the tenants in the form of higher rents. Both sides cannot be right in alleging that each bears the entire burden of the tax!

To examine the incidence, suppose that a city inposes a property tax. The thousands of landlords in the city decide to raise rents by the full amount of

FIGURE 24-3 Incidence of a Tax on Rental Housing

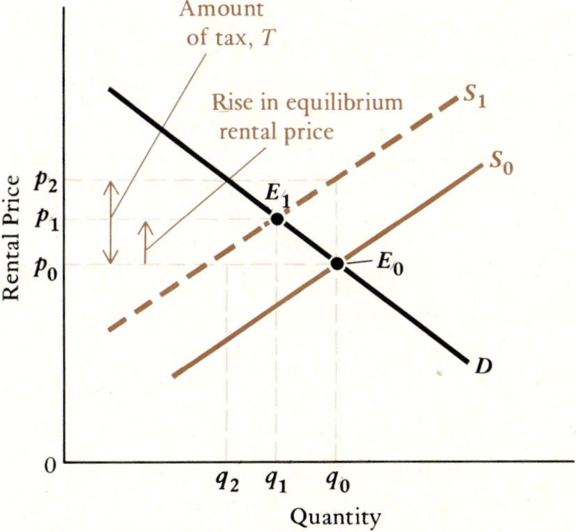

Since the equilibrium rent rises by less than the amount of the tax, landlords and tenants share the burden. The supply schedule S_0 reflects landlords' willingness to supply rental housing at different levels of rents received. Before the tax, equilibrium is at E_0. When a tax of T is imposed on landlords, the supply curve shifts up by the full amount of the tax to S_1. Suppose that landlords attempt to raise rents by the full amount of the tax, from p_0 to p_2. There will be an excess supply of housing of q_2q_0 at p_2, and rents will fall. At the new equilibrium E_1, with rental price p_1, landlords have succeeded in raising the rental price by p_0p_1, less than p_0p_2, the full amount of the tax. Thus landlords are paying p_1p_2 of the total tax on each unit rented.

the tax. This scenario is shown graphically in Figure 24-3. There will be a decline in the quantity of rental accommodation demanded as a result of the price increase.

The decline in the quantity demanded without any change in the quantity supplied will cause a surplus of rental accommodations at the higher prices. Landlords will find it difficult to replace tenants who move out, and the typical unit will remain empty longer between tenancies. Prospective tenants will find alternative sites from which to choose and will become very particular in what they expect from landlords.

Some prospective tenants, seeing vacant apartments, will offer to pay rents below the asking rent. Some landlords will accept such offers rather than earn nothing from vacant premises. Once some landlords cut rents, others will have to follow suit or find their properties staying unrented for longer periods of time.

Eventually rentals will reach a new equilibrium at which the quantity demanded equals the quantity supplied. The equilibrium rental price will be higher than the original before-tax rent but lower than the rent that passes the entire tax on to the tenants.

The incidence of the property tax is shared by landlords and tenants.

Just how it is shared by the two groups will depend on the elasticity of the demand and supply curves.[5] These elasticities, in turn, will depend on how quickly landlords and tenants can react to changes.

Notice that the question of incidence does not depend on who writes the check to pay the tax bill. In many European countries, the tenant rather than the landlord is sent the tax bill and pays the tax directly to the city; even in this case, however, the landlord bears part of the burden. As long as the existence of the tax reduces the quantity of rental accommodations demanded below what it otherwise would be, the tax will depress the amount received by landlords. In this way landlords will bear part of its burden.

Notice also that this result emerges even though neither landlords nor tenants realize it. Because rents are changing for all sorts of other reasons, no one will have much idea of what equilibrium rentals would be in the absence of the tax. It does not do much good just to look at what happens immediately after tax rates are changed because, as we have al-

[5] We suggest that you draw a series of diagrams with demand and supply curves of different slopes to see how this works. In each case shift the supply curve up by the same vertical amount—to represent the property tax—and see what proportion of the increase is reflected in the new equilibrium price.

ready seen, landlords may begin by raising rents by the full amount of the tax. Although they think they have passed the tax on, this creates a disequilibrium. In equilibrium prices will have risen by less than the full amount of the tax.

Do Profits Taxes Affect Prices?

Economic theory predicts that a general percentage tax on economic profits will have no effect on price or output, and thus the full incidence of such a tax will fall on producers. To see this, suppose that one price-quantity combination gives the firm higher pre-tax profits than any other. If the government imposes a 20 percent profits tax, the firm will have only 80 percent as much profits after tax as it had before; *this will be true for each possible level of output.* The firm may grumble, but it will not be profitable for it to alter its price or output.

Notice that this argument is independent of the tax rate. [32] It applies equally whether the tax rate is 10 percent or 75 percent.

A tax on corporation income. Corporate income taxes are taxes on profits as defined by the tax laws. The definitions make them a tax on a combination of economic profits plus some of the return to the factors of production, capital, and risk taking.

Because such a profits tax will reduce the returns to these important factors of production, it can have significant effects on the allocation of resources and on the prices and output of goods. Suppose that a risky industry requires a 24 percent return on its capital to make prospective owners willing to take the risk of investing in the industry. Suppose that every firm is earning 30 percent on its investment before taxes. A 28 percent corporate income tax will reduce the after-tax return to 21.6 percent, below the point that makes investment attractive, and resources will leave the industry. Obviously, price and output changes will occur. As firms leave the industry and supply decreases, prices will rise until the remaining firms can earn a sufficient level of after-tax profits so that they are once again compensated for the risks involved. Thus customers must bear part of the burden of the tax through a price increase.

A corporate income tax will have an effect on prices and outputs and thus will be shared by the consumer.

Because industries differ in degree of risk, the impact of a corporate income tax will be different in different industries—greater in more risky industries, smaller in less risky ones. It will thus affect the allocation of resources among industries. The federal government's June 1987 proposals for tax reform are discussed further in Box 24-2 (see pages 506–507).

Public Expenditure As a Tool of Microeconomic Policy

Public expenditure is large and growing. It affects both the distribution of income and the allocation of resources. In recent years spending by the public sector in Canada has amounted to about 40 percent of national income. Health care, education, and social welfare are the largest items; collectively they make up more than half the total. Defense, transportation and communication, and interest on the public debt add up to another 30 percent of the total. The remainder covers everything else, from police protection and sanitation to general administration of government and scientific research. In Canada about 40 percent of public expenditure is made by the federal government, the rest by provincial and municipal governments.

Types of Government Expenditures

In addition to classifying budget expenditures by function, as in Table 24-3, we may classify them by type of expenditure. This is done for the federal and provincial governments in Table 24-4 (see page 508). Figure 24-4 (see page 509) shows the changing importance of different types of federal government expenditures.

Provision of goods and services. As Table 24-4 indicates, the largest type of federal expenditure until 1971, and still the dominant type for provincial and municipal governments, was the provisions of goods and services. Roughly half of total expenditures at

TABLE 24-3 Expenditure of All Governments by Function, 1986

Category	Billions of dollars	Percentage distribution	Average annual rate of growth 1976–1986
Health	29.8	13	9
Social welfare	57.0	24	11
Education	28.2	12	8
Defense	9.4	4	6
Transportation and communication	13.0	6	6
Interest on the public debt	42.4	18	15
All other	54.1	23	12
Total	233.9	100	10

Source: Statistics Canada, 68–202.

Health, social services, and debt service charges were the fastest-growing categories of government expenditure in the 1960s and 1970s. The table shows combined expenditures for federal, provincial, and municipal governments. The category "All other" includes sanitation and waste removal, natural resources, general government, police and fire protection, recreation, and cultural activities.

all levels of government are made for the provision of goods and services that it is assumed are desired and desirable but that the market itself would fail to provide. Among these goods and services are defense, transportation facilities, education, and municipal services. In these activities the government acts in much the same way as a firm acts, using factors of production to produce outputs. By and large these are outputs of collective consumption goods, goods with strong third-party effects, or services whose benefits are not marketable.

Public opinion polls show that the majority of Canadians support public provision of such services as basic education, hospital care, and medical care. Nonetheless, rising costs of such services are becoming a serious problem.

Transfer payments. Transfer payments are defined generally as payments that do not arise out of current productive activity. (They include intergovernment transfers, that is, transfers from one level of government to another, but they do not include interest on the national debt.) Some federal transfers are made to foreigners as part of foreign aid programs. Some transfer payments are private, such as private pensions and charitable contributions by individuals and corporations. Many are made by provincial and municipal governments, often using funds they have received as transfers from the federal government.

Although government purchases of goods and services are large (about $24 billion in 1986), they have remained roughly constant in real terms since the early 1960s. They have been overtaken by transfer payments as the largest form of federal government expenditure. Transfer payments have been steadily increasing in importance, and this has led to significant changes in both the distribution of income and the allocation of resources.

Public Expenditure and Distribution of Income

The federal government, as Table 24-1 indicates, raises most of its revenues by income-related taxes. When these federal receipts are transferred back to individuals or to provincial and municipal governments, they have a substantial redistributive effect.

Federal Transfer Payments to Individuals

In 1970 a federal government white paper on income security classified transfers to individuals according to four types: demogrants, guaranteed income, social

BOX 24-2

Comprehensive Tax Reform in Canada, 1987

On June 18, 1987, Finance Minister Michael Wilson introduced a White Paper entitled "Tax Reform 1987." In it he proposed major changes to the personal and corporate income taxes; this so-called Phase I involved specific changes that were to become effective during the coming year. Mr. Wilson also tabled a discussion paper outlining options for sales tax reform; this Phase II of the reform was to be introduced only after a period of consultation and refinement of the proposals.

Over a long period of time, the Canadian tax system had gradually given favored treatment to certain types of income and certain classes of taxpayers. These provisions often had unintended side effects on income distribution and work disincentives, sometimes as a result of interactions with social policies. (These interactions are discussed in detail in Chapter 25; see especially Box 25-1.) The previous two decades also saw a gradual increase in the share of government revenues coming from personal taxes relative to corporate taxes.

In 1986, tax reform in the United States lowered tax rates for both individuals and corporations. In the absence of any change in the Canadian tax system, this created incentives for the relocation of economic activity to the United States that, of course, would have led to a fall in Canadian jobs and incomes, and to a fall in Canadian government tax revenues.

These circumstances were seen by many to call for a comprehensive reform of the tax system. In the White Paper, Mr. Wilson identified five broad objectives for the tax-reform proposals: fairness, competitiveness, simplicity, consistency, and reliability. Many of the changes that were introduced were in fact elaborations of smaller specific changes the government had made in 1985 and 1986.

The comprehensive nature of the proposed reforms was widely welcomed, given the general dissatisfaction with the piecemeal approach to change that had been the order of the day prior to Mr. Wilson's announcement. However, many commentators and interested parties took issue with some of the specific measures that were proposed.

Personal income tax reforms. The proposed personal income tax reforms combined, to some extent, a number of the reforms discussed in the text.

Base broadening measures, including the elimination of the $1,000 investment income deduction and the tightening of restrictions applicable to allowable deductions for use of automobiles and for meals and entertainment, made the income tax base much more *comprehensive*. Marginal tax rates could then be lowered without lowering tax revenues. Further, the elimination of special preferences made the tax system easier to understand and reduced the perception of an unfair tax system full of "loopholes that only benefit the rich."

The reduction in the number of tax brackets and the narrowing of the spread between the low and high marginal tax rates, while not going all the way to a *flat tax,* served the interests of tax simplicity.

The conversion of a number of exemptions and deductions to credits increased progressivity. Further, the conversion of the spousal exemption also improved economic efficiency by eliminating the disincentive facing a nonworking spouse from joining the labor force—discussed in detail in Chapter 25.

Not all of the proposed changes were popular. Groups who had benefited from the special provisions that were being eliminated voiced their objections. A number of economists objected to the lack of provisions for inflation indexing and to the proposed tightening of restrictions on RRSP contributions. The latter meant that the alleged advantages that were noted in the text of taxing expenditure rather than income were lost.

Corporate income taxation. The changes to the corporate income tax system combined *broadening the base* and *lowering marginal tax rates.* Base broadening was accomplished primarily by eliminating tax concessions—called investment tax credits—that had been used to encourage investment. Some other changes were also introduced in order to curb tax avoidance and hence to encourage investment decisions made on the basis of sound economic prospects rather than merely "on the advice of tax lawyers and accountants."

The elimination of tax incentives for investment meant that the tax rate on newly acquired capital was increased while the reductions in corporate tax rates meant that the tax rate on existing capital was reduced. Many people questioned the wisdom of this combination on the grounds that the rate cuts on old capital merely created windfall gains for owners of capital but created no incentives for the economy, while the increase in effective tax rates on new investment tended to discourage economic activity.

Nevertheless, the changes were probably inevitable given that similar changes had just been introduced in the United States. If Canada had not lowered corporate tax rates, many international companies would have found ways of shifting their profits from their Canadian operations to their American ones, with disastrous effects for Canadian government revenues and, perhaps, for the Canadian economy.

While the changes may have been inevitable, many observers feel that a reversal of the policy—toward increased investment incentives and increased corporate tax rates—is also inevitable in the United States, and hence ultimately in Canada.

Sales tax reform. The third leg of the tax reform was a proposed overhauling of the nation's sales tax system. At present there is a federal sales tax (the FST) and nine out of ten provinces impose a retail sales tax.

The FST is not a tax that is very visible to the general public; unlike the provincial sales taxes, the FST is applied before the retail transaction and hence its effect is hidden in retail selling prices. Nevertheless, most economists agree that the FST is a source of considerable inefficiency; the tax base has been severely eroded as many industries and sectors have succeeded in obtaining exemptions, and there exists a variety of rates that apply differentially to different goods. As a result, the FST creates large distortions and reform of the sales tax system is a high priority.

The White Paper proposes that the FST be reformed in such a way that the economic costs of the sales tax system are reduced while the total tax revenue obtained from it is increased. Because sales taxes are generally agreed to be regressive, the proposal also involves increasing the refundable tax credit now in place so as to compensate lower- and middle-income people for the increased tax burden they would bear as a result of the increased government reliance on sales tax revenues.

The White Paper proposes a national sales tax that would integrate the federal and provincial sales taxes into one unified tax with a common base and rate structure. The efficiency gains both in terms of administration and elimination of distortions would be substantial. Because provincial government agreement would be required to make such a system work, the White Paper also identified two options for reform of the FST in case agreement with the provinces could not be obtained.

All three options for sales tax reform involved the introduction of a *multi-stage* tax. Rather than simply applying the tax at one stage, as in the retail sales taxes that apply only at the time of the final retail sale, a multi-stage tax would be levied on and collected from businesses in stages as goods move from primary producers and processors to wholesalers, retailers, and consumers. Debate focusses on alternative means of collecting the tax, and on whether the alleged benefits outweigh the burden for recordkeeping and paperwork that such an apparently complicated system entails.

TABLE 24-4 Federal and Provincial Expenditures by Type, 1986

	Federal		Provincial	
	Billions of dollars	Percentage of total	Billions of dollars	Percentage of total
Purchases of goods and services	24.1	21	33.0	32
Transfers to persons	33.2	29	20.4	20
Interest on the public debt	26.4	23	12.5	12
Transfers to other levels of government	21.1	19	33.0	32
Other transfers	9.0	8	4.8	4
Total	113.8	100	103.7	100

Source: Statistics Canada, 11-003E.

Purchases of goods and services constitute less than a quarter of federal government expenditure and less than a third of provincial government expenditure. The table shows total expenditure by type for each of the federal and provincial governments. Transfer payments constitute the majority of expenditures. For the federal government, transfers to persons plus interest on the debt account for almost 60 percent of its total expenditure, while transfers to governments (mostly the provinces) account for another 21 percent. For the provinces, transfers to municipalities account for 32 percent of total expenditure.

insurance, and social assistance. Old age security and family allowance payments are in the first group, guaranteed income supplements and child tax credits are examples of the second, the Canada Pension Plan and unemployment insurance are examples of the third, and the fourth includes special programs for widows, single parents, and others who have no recourse to other support programs.

Transfers to individuals by the federal government have grown as a proportion of expenditures from about 15 percent in 1930 to about 33 percent by the mid 1980s.[6] These transfers are often intended as a form of insurance or as an incentive for individuals to redirect expenditure toward specific items such as housing or health. Many of them are part of income maintenance programs. The net effect of the transfers is to reduce inequality in the distribution of income.

There are several reasons for the growth of transfer payments. First, both the number of people eligible for them and the amounts they receive have increased. For example, there has been a general liberalization of the eligibility requirements for unemployment insurance benefits. Second, persistent unemployment during the 1970s and early 1980s greatly increased unemployment compensation payments.

While some transfer payments go to people with above average incomes, most do not. Transfer payments have thus tended to redistribute income to the poor.

The percentage of all personal income received in the form of government transfer payments has increased sharply, from about 9 percent in 1965 to more than 15 percent in 1986.

Intergovernmental Transfers As a Form of Redistribution

In addition to the federal government, there are 10 provincial governments, 2 territories, more than 4,000 municipalities, and thousands of townships in Canada. Moreover, a large number of overlapping counties or districts are responsible for such local authorities as school boards. Each of these governmental units spends public money, and each must get the money in order to spend it. Not all units

[6] The relative importance of the federal government in making transfers to individuals has been declining since the early 1960s while that of the provinces has been increasing. We shall discuss the related issue of growth in intergovernmental transfers.

FIGURE 24-4 The Changing Form of Major Federal Expenditures

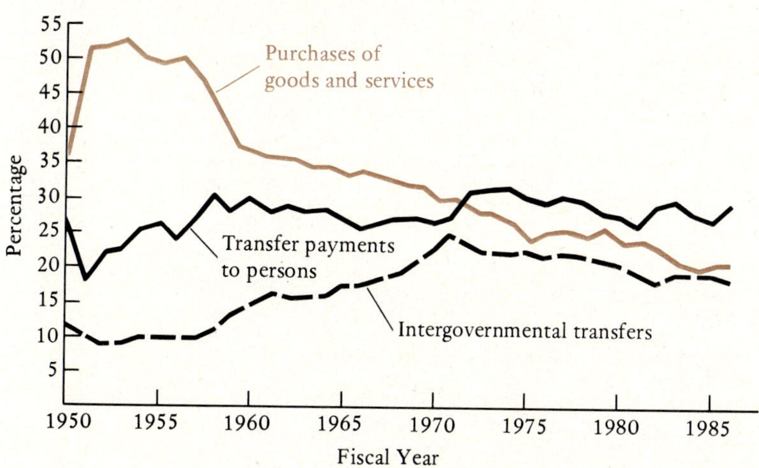

Transfer payments to persons and to provincial and municipal governments have been growing steadily in importance. In 1951 half of all federal expenditures were for purchases of goods and services. By 1980 the fraction was less than one-fourth. Transfer payments to persons in Canada and to provincial and municipal governments have increased from less than 30 percent to more than half the total. The three categories of expenditure graphed account for almost 75 percent of total federal expenditures. The largest item not shown on the graph is net interest paid by the government.

have equal access to revenue, and this necessitates both the division of responsibility and intergovernmental financial flows.

The transfer of funds from higher to lower levels of government has been an important aspect of the Canadian federal system since confederation. Transfers are also the focus of much of the controversy over federal-provincial relations.

The scope and nature of intergovernmental grants has changed dramatically in the postwar period. Federal transfers to provincial governments expanded from $200 million in 1950 to almost $21 *billion* in 1986, a more than hundred-fold increase. This represented an increase from 6.8 percent to 19 percent of federal revenues; for the provincial governments federal transfers as a share of their revenues increased, on average, from 20 percent to over 35 percent. For some provinces federal transfers now represent more than half their total revenues. The transfers occur under four basic programs: revenue sharing, equalization payments, conditional grants, and established programs financing.

Revenue sharing. Under the terms of the Constitution, the federal government may levy any tax it likes, but the provinces are restricted to *direct* taxes. This has been interpreted by the courts to mean that the provinces may levy personal and corporate income taxes, property taxes, and taxes on retail sales.

Historically, most provinces have made **tax-rental arrangements** whereby the federal government collected income taxes and made a per capita payment to the provinces for that right. Today, with the exception of the Quebec personal income tax and the Alberta, Ontario, and Quebec corporate levies, all income taxes in Canada are collected by the federal government.

Federal income tax rates are set at levels that allow substantial "tax room" to the provinces. Outside Quebec, the provincial income tax is calculated as a percentage of the federal tax payable at rates determined by the individual provinces. A similar arrangement applies to the corporate income tax.

Equalization payments. To ensure that citizens in all regions of the country have access to a reasonable level of public services, the federal government makes **equalization payments** to provinces with below average tax capacity. It is important to note that this is not a revenue-sharing program (provinces with above average tax capacity do not pay in), nor is it a conditional grants program. These grants are calculated by a complicated formula that in 1986 involved 29 revenue sources.

Equalization payments are a relatively new phenomenon in Canada, but they have exhibited rapid growth. From their inception with the 1957 Tax-sharing Act to the time of the 1977 Fiscal Arrangements Act, they expanded from $130 million to $2.2 billion. Equalization payments for 1986 are over $5.4 billion, as shown in Table 24-5.

Conditional grants. Conditional grants are transfers made to the provinces to enable them to provide services in a specified area at some minimum national standard. Historically, these shared-cost programs have been a central part of federal-provincial fiscal arrangements. Their increasing number and extent was a source of considerable friction between the provinces and the federal government during the early 1970s. Participation was optional, but a province that declined to participate in a particular scheme forfeited the revenues that would otherwise have been transferred to it. This led to considerable dispute over constitutional issues and to the development of complicated schemes for compensating provinces that opt out. These programs thus became a focal point in the protracted debate over the constitutional division of powers in Canada.

A major concern to the federal government was the open-ended nature of its commitments to shared-cost programs that were controlled by the provincial government. The provinces complained that they had initiated projects on the basis of federal sharing of the costs—often referred to disparingly as "50-cent federal dollars"—and then faced the threat of withdrawal of federal support.

Under the Fiscal Arrangement Act of 1977, the system of relating federal contributions to provincial expenditures was discontinued in favor of a system under which federal contributions rise each year in accordance with the overall growth in the economy. The contributions are administered under a program to be discussed shortly. The major remaining conditional grants relate to regional development programs; the projected breakdown of conditional grants for fiscal year 1985–1986 is given in Table 24-5.

TABLE 24-5 Estimated Federal Payments to Provinces and Municipalities, Fiscal 1986–1987

Category	Millions of dollars
Unconditional payments	
Subsidies under the constitution	36
Revenue equalization	5,434
Public utilities income tax transfers	290
Other	932
Total	6,692
Conditional grants (established programs)	
Hospital insurance	5,513
Medicare	1,140
Post-secondary education	2,320
Total	8,981
Conditional grants (other)	
Canada Assistance Plan	4,059
Municipal grants in lieu of taxes	781
Other health and welfare	151
Total	4,991
Total payments	20,664

Source: The National Finances.

Unconditional grants compose the largest and fastest-growing category of federal payments to provinces and municipalities. The table shows the transfers of revenue from the federal government other than those arising from income tax abatements. Equilization payments make up the bulk of the unconditional grants and are made to the lower-income provinces.

Established programs financing (EPF). The 1977 Fiscal Arrangements Act placed federal financing of three major programs previously treated as conditional grants on a new basis. These are hospital insurance, medicare, and post-secondary education; they are referred to as established programs to indicate that their existence is not conditional on federal involvement. That federal contributions are independent of the costs of the programs re-establishes federal control over its own contribution. The provinces have gained, for they need not now be confined by narrowly defined federal program conditions.

Meech Lake Accord. In 1987 the federal and provincial governments signed the Meech Lake Accord, which gave the provinces the right to "opt out with compensation" from federal government shared-cost programs provided the province itself "carries on a program or initiative that is compatible with the national objective."

The Overall Redistributive Effects of Public Expenditures

Since the tax system tends to be roughly proportional in its effect, the overall progressivity of government policies depends on the progressivity of government expenditures. The large and growing role of transfer payments to the poor and federal-provincial transfers probably assured that from the mid-1950s until 1980 there was some net redistribution of income from high- and middle-income groups to the poor. But such redistribution was never large.

Changes in the degree of income inequality from decade to decade have been small.

Why does government expenditure not have a bigger effect on income distribution? One view is that government programs overall are less progressive than observers once thought because progressive programs are offset by regressive ones. Another view is that market forces exert steady pressure toward more inequality, which government programs merely offset.

To understand the second view—that one must run hard just to stay even with inequality—imagine that the government today created complete equality in wealth and income. Inevitably, market forces would produce inequality by next year, as some people and firms did well because they worked hard and long, were lucky, and invested wisely, while others did poorly or failed because they took it easy, were unlucky, or squandered their resources on a binge.

Most economists agree that there is a limit to how much inequality can be eliminated. There is controversy as to how close we are to that limit. And beyond that there is controversy as to how close it is desirable to get to "as much equality as possible," both on ethical grounds of justice and economic grounds of incentives.

Public Expenditure and Allocation of Resources

Governments in Canada spent over $57 billion in 1986 to provide goods and services. In these activities government units act like firms, using factors of production to produce outputs. Governments produce some commodities rather than leave production to the free market because the people, acting through their municipal councils, provincial legislatures, and Parliament have so chosen in response to the sources of dissatisfaction with market outcomes discussed in Chapter 23.

Whether the government should be attempting to influence further the allocation of resources directly is usually a subject of intense debate when a major new or expanded program is proposed. A central debate of the 1970s concerned the role of government in providing medical care to the population. This is discussed briefly in Box 24-3.

By and large these outputs are the collective consumption goods, of goods with strong externalities, or of services whose benefits are not marketable. Governments make both current consumption and investment expenditures, and thus they directly influence the economy's accumulation of capital.[7] In so doing governments are plainly changing the allocation of resources.

Under the British North American Act, Canada was established as a federal state with governing powers divided between the central authority and the provinces. Municipalities provide a third level of government whose powers are determined by the provincial legislatures. A number of economic considerations bear on the distribution of functions among governments. As we have seen, since revenue

[7] Tax expenditures are an important force in this regard. One major tax expenditure is the program of Registered Retirement Savings Plans, which allow some personal savings as a tax-deductible expense, thereby encouraging saving in the private sector.

BOX 24-3

The Rising Cost of Health Care

Health care is an emotional and provocative issue. Almost everyone would agree that in a wealthy society, such as Canada in the 1980s, some minimum level of health care should be available to all citizens by right. At the same time, the public remains concerned about the high cost of medical care. Economic analysis shows that these two elements—the belief in the right to free medical care and the concern over its high social cost—are not unrelated.

Explaining the High Cost

Without some kind of health insurance, a single major operation can be an enormous financial burden and a prolonged illness will impoverish even the most prudent middle-income household. Why has health care become so costly?

One reason is that health care is highly labor intensive. The wages of nurses, laboratory technicians, and other medical service personnel have risen substantially relative to their productivity (the number of temperatures taken, beds made, and meals served per employee do not increase much over time).

A second reason is the steadily rising quality of medical care. Available knowledge, techniques, equipment, and the training of new physicians all have improved over time. Thus it becomes possible not only to provide quicker, surer cures for common and recurring ailments but also to prevent and treat other less common ailments and complications. Moreover, the demand for medical care tends to rise with rising real income. As per capita income rises, people are prepared to pay for more and better health. The demand for health care has proven to be income-elastic.

A third reason for rising medical costs is that the way medical care is provided and paid for has tended to weaken incentives to economize on its use or to keep costs down. Doctors (in their role as experts) often prescribe expensive medical care, which they or other doctors provide. Will the patient contradict the doctor?

Most insurance and publicly provided medical programs have eliminated significant *marginal* charges to the patient for the incremental medical or hospital care consumed. An individual has no incentive to economize on the quantity or quality of his or her own elective care. As a result, every patient wants the very best care to which he or she is entitled.

Free public provision of health care is virtually sure to lead to higher costs. This is an example of moral hazard, discussed in Chapter 23. In the market system individual patients would choose medical care (as they choose housing) from a wide variety of price-quality alternative forms of health care.

If patients had to pay their own bills, and if they could make fully informed choices, many might prefer to pay less and not have the best available equipment and doctors in all circumstances. But at zero marginal cost patients will naturally prefer to have the extra benefits of the best possible care, no matter what the extra cost to the government. They will consume hospital and medical services that are free at the margin until the marginal utility from these services is zero.

Nor do doctors and hospitals have strong incentives to hold costs down. They can pass along the higher costs of advanced modern techniques to the government. They may well reason, "Our job is to give the best treatment; let others worry about the costs." Indeed, unscrupulous doctors can prescribe unnecessary surgery or other medical care to increase the demand for their services.

What Is the Right Quantity and Quality of Medical Care?

Though everyone agrees that some minimum level of health care should be provided to all who need it, the definition of that minimum is controversial. No doubt the acceptable minimum level of health care to be provided by public support if necessary has risen over time; accordingly we have had increasing public intervention in the health sector.

The issue provokes more emotion than a discussion of housing or clothing, however. After all, human lives are at stake. True enough, but that does not end the matter. A first response is that much (although, of course, not all) medical and hospital care is elective and has almost nothing to do with life or death. By way of analogy, to say that no one should starve is not to say that all people should receive all the free food they want to eat. Nonvital attention accounts for a large part of our demand for health care. If it is offered at little or no marginal cost to users, it will be consumed beyond the point where marginal utility is equal to the cost of providing it.

But even where life is at stake, do we really always want the very best? Suppose that the extra cost of the very best at all times does pay off in a small increased probability of survival. How much would we pay to have, say, 9 instead of 10 people in 10,000 die from a particular disease? Surely few would want to spend a billion dollars per life saved; most would say that the opportunity cost was too high. Yet doctors in hospitals often make a different decision implicitly by ordering the best of everything. This then passes the costs on to society as a whole through increased resource allocation to the health sector. The issue is not whether to save lives but the opportunity cost of doing so. Money spent to save lives here is money not available to save lives (or improve the quality of life) elsewhere.

Because the issues are difficult to face, the political process has tended to avoid them. Instead of asking *how much* care we should provide, we have asked *to whom* it should be provided at substantially less than its average or marginal cost.

Controlling the Cost

Neither providers nor patients have sufficient incentive under many of the current schemes to keep down the costs of medical care. The most obvious solution is to place enough of a marginal charge on users that they will ask themselves whether this doctor's visit, this extra day in the hospital, or this use of the most expensive health monitoring system is worth the cost to them.

The spread of health maintenance organizations (HMOs) that agree to provide specified levels of care for a fixed fee have created institutions with some incentives to bargain hard with doctors and hospitals to keep their costs down. These are discussed in more detail in Chapter 25.

In health care, as elsewhere, if the price paid by users is kept below the marginal cost of providing the services, the private market will have excess demand. The government must either provide the services demanded directly or subsidize others to do so, or some way must be found to limit the demand to the quantity available. In countries with national health services, rationing is accomplished in part by long lines at doctors' offices and long waits for hospital admissions and in part by a lower average quality of medical services, which then reduces demand.

In adopting a policy toward health care there are at least three separable decisions: how much care to provide, how to allocate the costs of that care, and how to ration the supply. In the market system prices do all three. When we elect to have the government intervene in health care because we do not like the free-market results, someone has to make these decisions.

sources do not always match revenue needs at each level, a large volume of intergovernmental transfers is required. Whereas the revenue-sharing and equalization payments transfers are largely directed at income distribution, the conditional grants and EPF have perhaps their main impact on resource allocation. They allow the various functions to be distributed among governments in a manner not dictated by revenue sources.

Factors Influencing the Intergovernmental Division of Activities

Our discussion in Chapter 23 of reasons for government intervention suggested a number of principles that ideally should determine the distribution of activities among levels of government.

Geographic extent of externalities. Because the government of a province or municipality is unlikely to be responsive to the needs of citizens outside its jurisdiction, public services that involve geographic spillovers may not be provided adequately unless responsibility for them is delegated to a higher level of government. The prime example of the collective consumption good, national defense, is a function normally delegated to the central government for this reason. Control of pollution is another obvious case, since contamination of air and water often quite literally spills over provincial and municipal boundaries. In Canada the third-party effects involved in both examples are not even confined within national boundaries.

Regional differences in preferences. The delegation of some functions to lower levels of government may provide a political process that is more responsive to regional differences in preferences for public versus private goods. Some people may prefer to live in communities with higher-quality schools and police protection, and they may be prepared to pay the higher taxes required. Another important issue at the local level is the extent to which industry should be attracted in order to broaden the property tax base. Individual valuations of the social costs in terms of aesthetic or environmental effects are bound to differ.

At the provincial level, the distinct aspirations of French Canada are a primary consideration in the distribution of functions between Ottawa and the provinces. Indeed, dissatisfaction with the present arrangements, not only in Quebec but also in other provinces, continues to be a major political problem.

Redistribution of income. An important activity of government is the redistribution of income through taxing the relatively well off and channeling the funds to those in need by means of transfer payments. Clearly this function must be carried out by the central government unless per capita income happens to be the same in all regions. This is of course not the case in Canada and hence provincial governments actively pursue redistributive policies. At the same time, alleviating regional disparities is a major concern of the federal government.

Administrative efficiency. At a minimum, administrative efficiency demands that there be no duplication of the services provided at different levels of government and that related programs be coordinated. On the revenue side, it is desirable that a particular tax be collected by only one level of government. This consideration has led to the negotiation of federal-provincial tax agreements that provide for efficient collection and revenue sharing.

Changes in the Relative Shares of Government Expenditure

Total government expenditures increased 25-fold over the period 1950–1980, indicating an increase in the ratio of government expenditure to total goods and services produced in the economy from 22 to about 40 percent. In the period since 1960 increases in expenditure have been largest in such areas of provincial and municipal responsibility as health and education. As a result, the federal share of total government expenditures has been falling while that of provincial and municipal governments has been rising.

These developments are documented in Table 24-6. Since personal and corporate income tax yields tend to rise more rapidly than income, while property and sales taxes respond less rapidly, these developments made necessary a reduction in the federal share of income tax revenues—from 70 percent in 1950 to 65 percent in 1986—that resulted in the

TABLE 24-6 Expenditures by Level of Government, Selected Years, 1950–1986

	Total expenditure, all levels of government		Expenditure of government level (as a percentage of total government expenditures)[a]		
Year	Percentage of GDP	Millions of dollars	Federal	Provincial	Municipal
1950	22.1	4,080	51.9	26.0	22.1
1960	29.7	11,380	50.5	24.8	24.7
1970	36.4	31,148	38.3	35.6	26.0
1980	39.0	116,084	42.4	39.4	18.2
1986	44[b]	233,855	45.2	36.2	18.6

Source: Department of Finance, *Economic Review,* and Statistics Canada, 13-001.

[a] Excluding transfers to other levels of government.

[b] Percentage of GDP.

Total government expenditure has grown from 22 percent of national income in 1950 to 44 percent in 1986. Federal government spending, excluding transfers to the provinces and municipalities, has declined slightly as a share of national income over the period, while provincial spending has risen; in part this reflects a shift in administration of some programs to the provinces financed by transfers from the federal government.

increase in intergovernmental transfers discussed earlier. Several reasons for the changing distribution of government size can be mentioned.

Rising demand for government services. One of the reasons provincial and municipal government expenditures have been rising more rapidly than their residents' incomes is the high income elasticity of demand for city services. As societies become wealthier, their residents want more parks, more police protection, more and better schools and universities, and more generous treatment of their less fortunate neighbors. This alone, combined with the limited tax sources available, would create budgetary problems for provincial and municipal governments in a period of rising incomes and rising expectations. Taxpayers increasingly want the social services governments provide, but they do not always want to pay the taxes required to meet their cost. Elected officials arouse the people's wrath when they fail to provide wanted programs, but they sometimes do the same when they provide the services and then raise taxes.

Rising relative cost of municipal government services. Government services tend to use much labor of a kind whose productivity (output per hour of work) has increased much less rapidly than its cost. Thus cost per unit of output has risen. While the national average output per hour of work in manufacturing has risen about 50 percent in a decade, the size of the beat covered by a police officer, the number of students taught by each schoolteacher, the number of families that can be effectively handled by a social worker, or the number of temperatures that can be taken by one hospital nurse have not risen in proportion. Because wage levels tend to rise with national average productivity, the costs of services in the low-productivity sectors have soared. Although a rise in relative prices tends to lead to a decline in the quantity demanded in the market sector of the economy, these forces are not nearly so strong in the government sector.

Evaluating the Role of Government

Almost everyone would agree that the government has some role to play in the economy because of the many sources of possible market failure. Yet there is no consensus that the present level and role of government intervention is about right.

One aspect of the contemporary debate about the

efficient level of government intervention was discussed at the end of Chapter 23. There we asked when and to what degree government is justified in attempting to modify private market behavior—say, by affecting the way a paper mill discharges its wastes. Other issues arise when government provides goods and services that the private sector does not and will not provide.

Do Benefits of Public Programs Exceed Costs?

The federal government has utilized techniques of evaluation designed to provide estimates of benefits and costs in order to determine whether the former exceed the latter. If they do, the program is said to be *cost effective.* For some government programs, such as flood control, there are well-defined benefits and costs, and it is relatively easy to decide whether the project is beneficial.

But consider the evaluation of a program such as the great American space adventure of the 1960s—placing a man on the moon before the end of the decade.

The budgetary costs were easily defined. At its peak in 1966, the program absorbed (in 1985 U.S. dollars) about $21 billion per year. Unmistakably, the project succeeded; it met its stated objective. But was the "giant step for mankind" worth the billions it cost? The benefits certainly included the psychological lift the moon walks gave the American people and the substantial advances in technology and knowledge that the space program spawned. The real costs are the things that the expenditure replaced.

But what was the alternative? More arms to Vietnam? Massive urban redevelopment? A return of funds to private spenders to use as they saw fit? Most of us will evaluate the worth of the space program very differently, depending on what we see as the alternative uses of the resources involved.

Such questions can never be answered unambiguously. As a result, the evaluation of government programs is inherently political and controversial. Economic analysis of benefits and costs is involved, but it does not play the sole or even the dominant role in answering some big questions.

What Is the Correct Balance Between Private and Public Sectors?

When the government raises money by taxation and spends it on an activity, it increases the spending of the public sector and decreases that of the private sector. Since the public sector and the private sector spend on different things, the government is changing the allocation of resources. Is that good or bad? How do we know if the country has the right balance between the public and private sectors? Should there be more schools and fewer houses or more houses and fewer schools?

Because automobiles and houses are sold on the market, consumer demand has a significant influence on the relative prices and quantities produced of these commodities and thus on the allocation of the nation's resources. This is true for all goods produced and sold on the market. But there is no market that provides relative prices for private houses versus public schools; thus the choice between allowing money to be spent in the private sector and spending it for public goods is a matter to be decided by Parliament and other legislative bodies.

John Kenneth Galbraith's best seller *The Affluent Society* proclaimed the "liberal" message that a correct assignment of marginal utilities would show them to be higher for an extra dollar's worth of expenditure on parks, clean water, and education than for an extra dollar's worth of expenditure on television sets and deodorants. In this view the political process often fails to translate preferences for public goods into effective action; thus more resources are devoted to the private sector and fewer to the public sector than would be the case if the political mechanism were as effective as the market.

The "conservative" view has a growing number of supporters who agree with 1986 Nobel Laureate James Buchanan that society has already gone beyond the point where the value of the marginal dollar spent by the government is greater than the value of that dollar left in the hands of households or firms that would have spent it had it not been taxed away. Because bureaucrats, the conservatives argue, are spending other people's money, they regard a few million (or billion) dollars here or there as a mere nothing. They have lost all sense of the opportunity cost of public expenditure and thus tend to spend far beyond the point where marginal benefits equal marginal costs.

What Is the Role of Government Today?

One of the most difficult problems for the student of the Canadian economic system is to maintain perspective about the scope of government activity in the market economy. There are literally tens of thousands of laws, regulations, and policies that affect firms and households. Many people believe that significant additional deregulation would be possible and beneficial.

But private decision makers still have an enormous amount of discretion about what they do and how they do it. One pitfall is to become so impressed (or obsessed) with the many ways in which government activity impinges on the individual that one fails to see that these only make changes—sometimes large, but often small—in market signals in a system that basically leaves individuals free to make their own decisions. In the private sector most individuals choose their occupations, earn their livings, spend their incomes, and live their lives. In this sector too, firms are formed, choose products, live, grow, and sometimes die.

A different pitfall is to fail to see that some, perhaps most, of the highly significant amounts paid by the private sector to the government as taxes also buy goods and services that add to the welfare of individuals. By and large, the public sector complements the private sector, doing things the private sector would leave undone or do very differently. To recognize this is not to deny that there is often waste, and sometimes worse, in public expenditure policy. Nor does it imply that whatever is, is just what people want. Social policies and social judgments evolve and change.

Yet another pitfall is failing to recognize that the public and private sectors compete in the sense that both make claims on the resources of the economy. Government activities are not without opportunity costs, except in those rare circumstances in which they use resources that have no alternative use.

Public policies in operation at any time are not the result of a single master plan that specifies precisely where and how the public sector shall seek to complement or interfere with the workings of the market mechanism. Rather, as individual problems arise, governments attempt to meet them by passing ameliorative legislation. These laws stay on the books, and some become obsolete and unenforceable. This is true of systems of law in general.

Many anomalies exist in our economic policies; for example, laws designed to support the incomes of small farmers have created some agricultural millionaires, and commissions created to assure competition often end up creating and protecting monopolies. Neither individual policies nor whole programs are above criticism.

In a society that elects its policymakers at regular intervals, however, the majority view on the amount and type of government interference that is desirable will have some considerable influence on the interference that actually occurs. This has become one of the major political issues of the 1980s. Fundamentally, a free-market system is retained because it is valued for its lack of coercion and its ability to do much of the allocating of society's resources. But we are not mesmerized by it; we feel free to intervene in pursuit of a better world in which to live. We also recognize, however, that some intervention has proven excessive or ineffective.

Summary

1. Two of the most powerful tools of microeconomic policy are taxation and public expenditure.
2. While the main purpose of the tax system is to raise revenue, tax policy is potentially a powerful device for income redistribution because the progressivity of different kinds of taxes varies greatly. Personal income tax rates have traditionally been highly progressive,

but their effect on progressivity is reduced by other provisions of the tax law. Sales and excise taxes are likely to be regressive.

3. Evaluating the effects of taxes on resource allocation requires first determining tax incidence, that is, determining who really pays the taxes. For most taxes, the incidence is shared. Excise taxes, for example, affect prices and are thus partially passed on and partially absorbed by producers. The actual incidence depends on such considerations as demand and supply elasticities.
4. A large part of public expenditure is for the provision of goods and services that private markets fail to provide. Direct and indirect subsidies, transfer payments to individuals, and intergovernmental transfers are all rising sharply. The four major types of federal-provincial transfers are revenue sharing, equalization payments, conditional grants, and established programs financing.
5. The major redistributive activities of the federal government take the form of direct transfer payments to individuals and to provincial and municipal governments for economic welfare payments and regional adjustments. While the public sector has a tendency to redistribute some income from high- and middle-income groups to the poor, the change in income inequality from decade to decade has been relatively small.
6. Government expenditure of all kinds has a major effect on the allocation of resources. The government determines how much of our total output is devoted to national defense, education, and highways. It is also influential in areas where private provision of goods and services is common; health care is a notable example.
7. Intergovernmental transfers are a key form of public expenditure policy; they lead to a different allocation of resources than would occur without them. The need for such transfers is dramatically revealed by regional imbalances in Canada.
8. Evaluating public expenditures involves reaching decisions about absolute merit (do benefits exceed costs?) and about the relative merit of public and private expenditures.
9. The Canadian economy is a mixed economy, and a changing one. Each generation faces anew the choice of which activities to leave to the unfettered market and which to encourage or repress through public policy.

Topics for Review

Tax expenditures
Horizontal and vertical equity
Progressive, proportional, and regressive taxes
Tax incidence
Transfer payments to individuals
Intergovernmental transfers
Choosing between private and public expenditures

Discussion Questions

1. The Canadian taxpayer is assaulted by dozens of different taxes with different incidence, different progressivity, and different methods of collection. Discuss the case for and against using at most two different kinds of taxes. Discuss the case for and against a single taxing authority that would share the revenue with all levels of government.
2. Consider a change in the tax law that lowers every taxpayer's marginal tax rate, with the maximum rate dropping from 50 percent to 33 percent, but with an increase in the tax base that leaves total tax revenue unchanged.
   a. Is it possible that everyone's average tax *rate* will fall?
   b. Is it possible that everyone's tax *bill* will fall?
   c. Suppose contributions to universities and colleges are tax deductible under the original tax law but not under the revised one. Would you predict that such contributions would increase, decrease, or remain the same?
   d. If such contributions are fully deductible under both the original and revised tax law, would the amount of such contributions be expected to increase, decrease, or remain the same?
   e. Consider now taxpayers whose marginal tax rate falls from 50 percent to 33 percent *and* whose tax bills are less after the revision. Repeat question *d*.
3. How might each of the following affect the incidence of a real estate property tax imposed on central-city rental property?
   a. The residents of the community are largely immigrants who face racial discrimination in neighboring areas.
   b. The city installs a good, cheap rapid transit system that makes commuting to the suburbs less expensive and more comfortable.
   c. Rent control is imposed; no existing building may raise the rents presently being charged.
4. In reaction to Finance Minister Michael Wilson's proposal to convert the basic personal exemption and some deductions to tax credits, the *Toronto Star* ran a column, under the sensational headline "Sneaking Some Socialism Through the Back Door," that argued that the proposed changes would "replace measures which allow the rich to shield their income with provisions that raise the income level of the poor." How might the measures proposed accomplish this?
5. In Canada each individual has a lifetime \$100,000 exemption for capital gains income, and subsequent capital gains are taxed at one-half the rates applicable to other income. Who benefits from this provision? What are its effects on the distribution of income and the allocation of resources?
6. "Taxes on tobacco and alcohol are nearly perfect taxes. They raise lots of revenue and discourage smoking and drinking." In this statement, to what extent are the two effects inconsistent? How is the incidence of an excise tax related to the extent to which it discourages use of the product?
7. The benefit principle is often used to justify excise taxes on particular commodities when their use depends on the availability of govern-

ment-provided services or facilities. In such cases the tax provides a means of placing the burden of financing expenditures on those who benefit from them. Can you think of any examples where this principle applies? Can it be used to justify the use of property taxes as a major source of revenue by municipal governments?

8. *a.* Suppose it is agreed to spend $1 billion in programs to provide the poor with housing, better clothing, more food, and better health services. Argue the case for and against assistance of this kind rather than giving the money to the poor to spend as they think best.
   b. Should federal transfers to the provinces be conditional grants or grants with no strings attached? Is this the same issue raised in the previous question or a different one?
9. Develop the case for and against having the federal government (rather than provincial and municipal governments) provide each of the following:
   a. Police protection
   b. Teachers' salaries
   c. Highways
   d. Welfare payments to the poor
10. Classify each of the following programs as transfer payment, purchase of goods and services, or neither. Which ones clearly tend to decrease the inequality of income distribution?
   a. Unemployment insurance payments to unemployed workers
   b. Payments to provinces for support of universities
   c. A negative income tax
   d. Pensions of retired Supreme Court justices
   e. An excess-profits tax on oil companies
11. Medical and health costs were 4.5 percent of GDP in 1950 and over 10 percent in 1985. Is 10 percent too much? Is it necessarily a sign that we are providing better health care? How might an economist think about what is the right percentage of GDP to devote to medical care?

25

Social Policy

Controversies over Canada's social programs have been major news items in recent years. Canadian governments have been urged to re-examine and redesign these programs with the twin objectives of improving their ability to deliver benefits to the intended beneficiaries and reducing costs. Of course, the relevant concept of cost that applies here is broader than just the direct cost of financing the programs; it is the concept of social cost encountered in Chapter 23.

The serious recession in the early 1980s put many Canadian families in financial need and strained the "social safety net" to its limits. In response, many Canadians argued that the system of social programs had to be expanded to deliver more benefits to less advantaged citizens.

At the same time, concern was expressed that existing social programs were already too expensive. These programs had flourished during the boom years of the 1950s and the 1960s; in the period of slower economic growth and higher unemployment of the 1970s and 1980s many Canadians asked if the country could afford such generous social programs—programs that absorbed almost 60 percent of government program (that is, non-interest) expenditures. Given the concern over the $30 billion federal budget deficit, it was natural that such an important category of spending should come under scrutiny.

In this chapter we review the debate over Canada's social programs. The first half of the chapter looks at these programs in general and raises many issues that relate to social policies considered as a whole. The second half goes into much more detail on individual programs. This detailed discussion should persuade the reader that assessing program effectiveness and evaluating proposals for reform of Canada's social policies are not simple matters. One-line evaluations, such as "Nothing needs to be changed" or "The whole system needs to be swept away," ignore the complexity of the system and the need for a careful approach to reforming it.

Canada's Social Programs in Perspective

Figure 25-1 documents the importance and growth of social spending in Canada. The data show the gradual growth in aggregate social spending by all levels of governments as well as the gradual increase in the relative importance of spending by the provincial governments.

FIGURE 25-1 **Social Spending by Canadian Governments, 1950–1985**

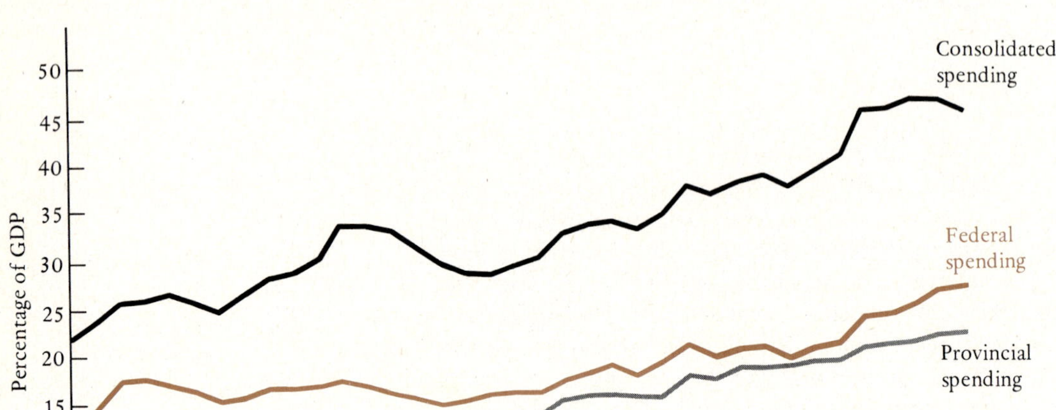

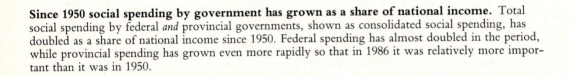

Since 1950 social spending by government has grown as a share of national income. Total social spending by federal *and* provincial governments, shown as consolidated social spending, has doubled as a share of national income since 1950. Federal spending has almost doubled in the period, while provincial spending has grown even more rapidly so that in 1986 it was relatively more important than it was in 1950.

The Variety of Social Programs

Some social programs are universal, in the sense that they pay benefits to anyone meeting only such minimal requirements as age or residence. These are called **demogrants.** Other programs are selective, in the sense that they pay benefits only to people who meet more stringent, specific conditions. These conditions are usually related to income, in which case the term **income-tested** or **income-related benefits** is used. Some of these benefits are taxable and so confer after-tax benefits that decline as income rises; others are not taxable and therefore confer after-tax benefits that are independent of income. Some are expenditure programs (including direct transfers to persons), while others are delivered through the tax system in the form of special tax concessions called *tax expenditures*. Some programs are administered by the federal government, some by the provincial governments, and still others by the municipalities.

Table 25-1 gives a breakdown of the $54 billion spent by the federal government on all social programs.

Fiscal, Economic, and Demographic Setting

Figure 25-2 (see page 524) shows projections of social spending under alternative assumptions about future economic and demographic trends. After falling in the short term, social spending starts to climb as a proportion of GDP after 2010 and according to the pessimistic scenario takes a larger proportion of GDP than in 1980.

Three major challenges must be met by any Canadian social spending policy that is to succeed in

TABLE 25-1 Details of Federal Spending on Social Programs, 1986 *(in billions of dollars)*

	Direct spending	Tax expenditures[a]	Total
Child benefits			
Family allowance (FA)	2.5	−.5	2.0
Child tax exemption (CTE)		.7	.7
Child tax credit (CTC)		1.8	1.8
Subtotal	2.5	2.1	4.6
Elderly benefits			
Old age security (OAS)	9.3	−.7	8.6
Age exemption		.7	.7
Guaranteed income supplement (GIS) and spouses allowance (SPA)	3.6		3.6
Pension income exemption		.1	.1
Subtotal	13.0	.1	13.1
Income security and other transfers			
Unemployment insurance (UI)	9.9	−1.5	8.4
Canada Assistance Plan (CAP)	4.1		4.1
Registered savings plans (RRSP/RP)[b]		4.9	4.9
Subtotal	14.0	3.4	17.3
Human resources			
Skill development	1.3		1.3
Colleges and universities	2.4	2.4	4.8
Job creation	.6		.6
Subtotal	4.3	2.4	6.7
Health care	6.8	5.1	12.0
Totals	40.4	13.1	53.6

Source: "Information on Selected Federal Social Tax-Transfer Programmes" and "Account of the Cost of Selective Tax Measures" (Finance, 1986) and "1986–1987 Estimates" (Treasury Board, 1986).

[a] Includes federal component only. The provinces also collect tax revenues on FA and OAS (approximately $195 million and $435 million, respectively) and contribute tax revenues forgone for the CTE ($290 million), the age exemption ($305 million), and the pension income exemption ($50 million), for a net fiscal position of $15 million.

[b] Registered retirement savings plan and registered pension plan.

Of the over $53 billion spent on social programs by the federal government in 1986, nearly 80 percent came from direct spending, and 20 percent was delivered through the tax system. Child and elderly benefits, each of which include both demogrant and income-tested components, accounted for over $18 billion of the total. Three key programs—unemployment insurance, the Canada Assistance Plan (provincially administered welfare programs), and registered savings plans—accounted for over $17 billion. Human resource development—including contributions to post-secondary education and to labor market schemes—amounted to over $6 billion, while transfers to the provinces for health care accounted for almost $12 billion.

FIGURE 25-2 Two Projections for Social Spending

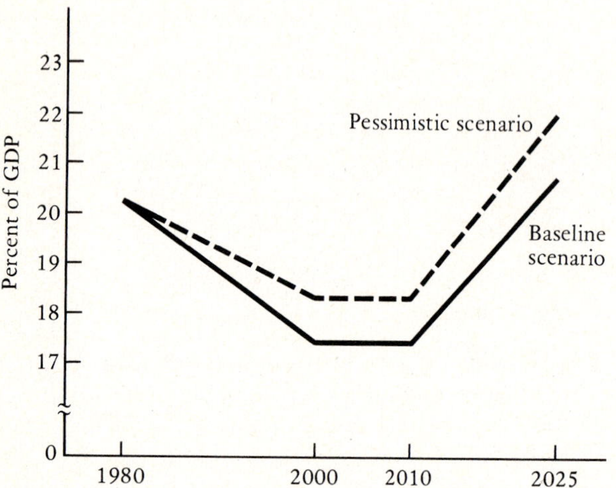

Social spending is expected to fall, stay stable, and then rise as a percentage of GDP over the next 40 years. The pessimistic scenario assumes a slower rate of economic growth and a more rapidly aging population. In both cases the percentage of GDP devoted to social spending falls until 2000, remains steady until 2010, then rises until the end of the projection period in 2025. According to the pessimistic scenario the proportion of GDP absorbed by social spending is higher at the end of the projection period than it is today; according to the baseline scenario the proportion is about the same. *Source: Long-term Trends in Social Expenditures in the Group of Seven Major Industrialized Countries* (Washington, D.C.: International Monetary Fund, 1985).

these future decades. These are the challenges posed by government deficits, technological changes, and demographic trends.[1]

The fiscal challenge. The fiscal challenge to social programs is a serious one. With the federal deficit running at about $30 billion annually and with $40 billion, or 40 percent of total federal expenditures, being spent each year on social programs and another $16 billion annually in tax expenditures, it is inevitable that social programs be reviewed carefully.

Anyone who would leave social spending untouched while still seeking to reduce the deficit substantially must look to tax increases. In view of the significant tax cuts in the United States in the mid 1980s, however, it is hard for Canada to increase its tax rates significantly without setting up pressures on the part of firms and higher-income individuals to move to the United States. Serious inroads in the deficit can be made only through spending cuts, in which case it will be hard to leave untouched the enormous part of total spending accounted for by social programs.

Fiscal constraints are also severe at the provincial level. Health care expenditures alone account for over 30 percent of total provincial expenditures and are rising. In 1987 all 10 provinces, whether economically depressed or booming, were running budget deficits. In the mid 1980s many provinces were already scrambling to find ways to curtail spending, and if provincial debt is not to become an intolerable burden, these spending restraints will become even more severe over the next few years.

Of course, a return to a period of sustained low unemployment and high economic growth would ease the fiscal pressures by automatically generating higher tax revenues and curtailing expenditures on unemployment benefits and welfare schemes.

In the absence of sustained economic growth or new revenue sources, the relevant policy question is not *whether* social programs should be rationalized to reduce their total spending requirements but *how* this should be done.

The adjustment challenge. Many recent studies of the Canadian economy, including the one by the Macdonald Royal Commission, have stressed the fierce competition and the rapid change that characterizes the international trading world of the 1980s.

To improve, or even maintain, living standards in a competitive and changing world, countries need to adjust continuously.

[1] We have adopted this trilogy, and much of the discussion, from T. J. Courchene, *Social Policy in the 1990s: Agenda for Reform* (Toronto: C. D. Howe Institute, 1987).

This is especially true for small countries such as Canada that are heavily dependent on international trade. As Courchene puts it:

> The challenge to social policy is twofold: first, to ensure that the incentives within the social policy network will encourage, rather than inhibit, the required adjustment on the economic front; second, to ensure that the social safety net evolves in a manner that reflects the changing needs of citizens as they adapt to the new economic order.

For example, if the economic system requires that people change jobs more frequently than in the past, it is important that pensions be fully portable (that is, that workers be able to take their pension rights with them when they change jobs).

The demographic challenge. Important demographic developments that are already under way imply that social policies designed for the 1960s are unlikely to be well suited to the needs of the 1990s and subsequent decades. This is one reason why economists criticize those who oppose any change to the present system.

Consider just a few of these developments:

An increasingly aging population is putting stresses on the health system. As we have already seen, expenditure on health care is large and growing; demographic trends suggest that this growth will continue, and possibly even accelerate, unless changes are made in the current system.

The increasingly aging population will also put stress on the pension system. Although the federal government is currently taking in more in pension contributions than it is paying out as benefits, the situation will be reversed before the end of the century, after which time the gap between benefits and contributions will grow steadily. The federal government's liability to pay these pensions is unfunded; that is, the excess of current contributions over current benefits is being spent on current activities rather than being set aside to meet the excess of benefits over contributions when it occurs sometime in the 1990s.

A rise in single-parent families, particularly those with women as head of household, is causing an increase in the number of working poor whose needs are different from the unemployed or the unemployable poor.

The rise in two-worker households brings a demand for expanded day-care facilities.

Many workers are finding that after 20 or 30 years of working in the same job, their skills become obsolete. They must then retrain or face a decade or more of unemployment before they reach normal retirement age. Retraining facilities and organized assistance in finding new jobs are needed if such workers are to remain gainfully employed.

Nearly a decade of unacceptably high youth unemployment means that many people now in the 30–40 age group have had no continuous work experience. As these people move up through the age distribution, their needs will not diminish.

The Federal-Provincial Perspective

Canada's constitution originally granted all authority in social policy to the provinces. As social policy became increasingly important, agreements between the two levels of government gave the federal government responsibility for a large amount of social spending. In some cases this involves direct federal spending, as with the old-age security and the family allowance programs, and in other cases it involves transferring funds to the provincial governments. Some federal payments to provinces are then distributed directly to persons; this is the case with the federal government's Canada Assistance Plan, which is used by the provinces to finance their own welfare programs. Other payments, such as those related to health and post-secondary education, are used by the provinces to finance various expenditures. (The latter were discussed in Chapter 24.)

Although we focus on federal programs in most of this chapter, the role of the provinces cannot be ignored. A number of factors make the provinces important players in determining the cost and effectiveness of Canadian social policy.

First, as we have already observed, a large amount of federal spending is for transfers to the provinces. While some transfers are nominally earmarked for specific purposes (in particular, post-secondary education and health), the provinces are not required to match changes in their spending in these areas to changes in federal transfers received. In recent years growth in provincial spending in these areas has often been less than the growth in transfers from the federal government. Hence to analyze the efficacy of these programs in terms of the delivery of services, it is not sufficient to focus only on federal transfers. Further, since every province allocates over 60 percent of its spending to social policy, any dramatic change in provincial spending would also represent a significant change in national spending.

Second, Canada's regional pressures play a major role in shaping federal-provincial fiscal relations—especially in social policy, where regional disparities are so important. Equalization grants, discussed in Chapter 24, are relevant here. Although they are not considered part of federal social spending, they are a transfer to the provinces (similar to the health and education transfers) whose explicit purpose is to compensate for any shortfall in the fiscal capacity of the relatively poorer provinces to provide a minimum level of government services—primarily social services.

Finally, since the multitude of federal and provincial social programs overlap in their effects, any program change made by one level of government will have one effect if it is offset by the other level and another effect if it is not offset. In fact, a single change made by the federal government is sometimes totally offset in one province, left intact in another, and partially offset in a third. For example, when in its May 1985 budget the federal government enriched the child tax credit to increase the after-tax income of very poor families with children, a number of provinces reacted by cutting back on their welfare programs. In those provinces benefits delivered to the poor were not changed in aggregate, but the burden of financing those benefits was shifted to the federal government, and the distribution of benefits was shifted from families without children to those with children.

Experiences such as this illustrate an important point:

Effective reform of Canadian social policy requires changes that are coordinated and sweeping, not piecemeal. The inherent difficulties of such coordination are aggravated by the never easy, and often stormy, nature of federal-provincial relations in Canada.

At this time it is not clear what the implications of the Meech Lake Accord (discussed in Chapter 24, page 511) will be.

The International Perspective

Recently two major international organizations, the International Monetary Fund in Washington and the Organization for Economic Cooperation and Development in Paris, have each published studies comparing spending on social programs for a number of countries. Figure 25-3 presents data from the IMF study. Although the data are for 1980, the latest year available on an internationally consistent basis, they are still useful because changes in these percentages occur quite slowly over the years. Both studies show that Canada is below the average of industrialized nations in terms of the share of national income devoted to social spending.

The international perspective offered by these comparisons would seem to counter the most extreme calls for drastic cuts in Canada's social policies. However, differences in circumstances among the countries studied make comparisons based on numbers such as those in the table difficult and potentially misleading.

First, social programs delivered via tax expenditures play an important role in the overall package of Canadian social programs. Hence an accurate international comparison should include information—excluded from the data in the table—on tax expenditures.

Second, Canada's national income is high relative to many of the other nations in the study. As a result, delivering a given level of social services requires a smaller share of GDP than in poorer countries. Further, the need for some types of social spending such as welfare does not rise in proportion to growth in living standards. Thus even when they respond more generously to basic social needs, the relatively rich countries may spend a smaller fraction of their national incomes on social services than the relatively

FIGURE 25-3 Social Spending As a Share of GDP for Seven Countries

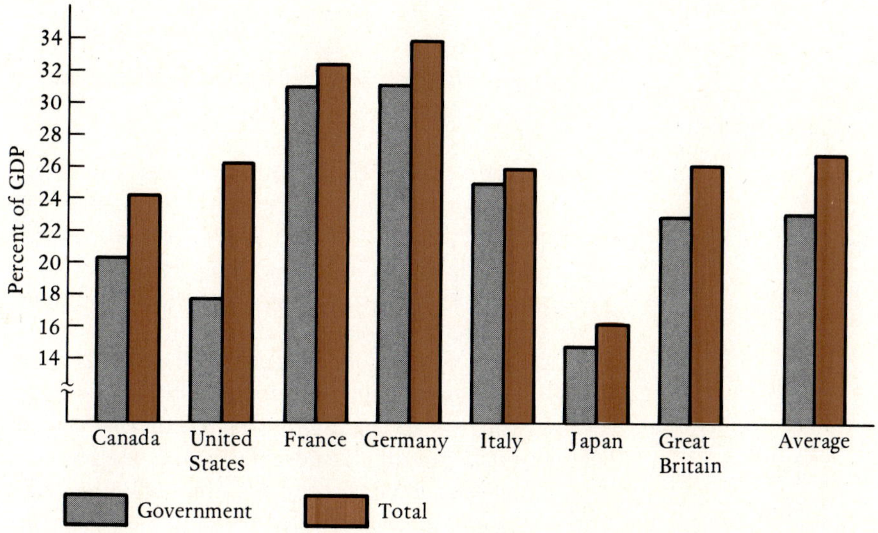

Canada devotes a comparatively low proportion of its GDP to social spending. The figure shows the percentage of GDP accounted for by both government and total (government plus private) social spending for the seven largest industrial countries. Included are spending on medical care, education, welfare payments, public pension plans, and unemployment insurance; excluded are direct housing expenditures and tax expenditures. In government expenditures Canada is lower than all countries except the United States and Japan; in total expenditure Canada is lower than all except Japan. (Note that in the United States, a great deal of expenditure on health care occurs in the private sector.) *Source: Long-term Trends in Social Expenditures in the Group of Seven Major Industrialized Countries* (Washington, D.C.: International Monetary Fund, 1985).

poor countries. In other cases such as health and education, however, expenditure may behave like luxuries, rising as a share of income as total income rises.

Third, because a relatively large fraction of the Canadian population is in the work force, retirees, who tend to require high expenditures on pensions and health care, represent a relatively small fraction of the Canadian population. Further, the Canadian pension plan (the CPP) is still relatively new, so many currently retired Canadians are receiving only partial benefits. When the plan matures, the proportion of Canadians covered will rise to the fraction currently found in the European countries, whose plans have been in place for a much longer time. It is interesting to note that for pension plans, Canadian governments spend 3.5 percent of GDP while France spends 8.0 percent and Germany 8.7 percent. The figures based on total (government and private) spending present an even sharper contrast: 4.8 percent for Canada, 10 percent for France, and 13.3 percent for Germany.

Issues in Assessing Social Programs

The complex array of Canadian social programs raises a number of issues that must be addressed before their impact can be analyzed or proposals for their reform assessed.

Policy Interactions

The various programs interact to such an extent that the effects of any one cannot be judged in isolation.

For a meaningful analysis of the current state of any social program and proposed changes in it, the program must be viewed in the context of the overall system.

Interactions between schemes are important not only at the federal provincial level, but also within one level of government. For example, the unemployment insurance plan clearly interacts with federal job creation and job training programs as well as with other social programs designed to direct resources to needy families and regions. (This is why the Forget commission, discussed in some detail later, which had such an apparently narrow mandate to study the unemployment insurance system, thought it appropriate to bring in a wide range of recommendations involving the restructuring of virtually all existing social programs.)

Policy Objectives

Given the wide array of programs, each directed at a narrow goal but each interacting with other programs, policy objectives must be clearly stated if policies are to be evaluated intelligently.

Policy evaluation often involves trade-offs among objectives.

The need for normative judgments. A primary objective of most social policies is to redistribute income away from people least in need toward those most in need. Evaluating need requires making value judgments, which are expressed in the political rather than the economic arena. Economists can, of course, play a role in measuring the distribution of income (as discussed in Chapter 24) and in measuring need once criteria of need are established.

Vertical and horizontal equity. The concepts of vertical and horizontal equity need to be distinguished when studying the distribution of income. As explained in Chapter 24, *vertical equity* concerns equity across income classes while *horizontal equity* concerns equity within a given income class. One obvious social policy example concerns the appropriate treatment of children in the tax system. Two families with the same income but different numbers of children are usually treated differently on grounds of horizontal equity.

Distribution versus efficiency. A major issue in the design of social policy is the potential conflict between achieving the desired distribution of income and ensuring that the economy operates efficiently so as to produce the maximum possible total income. Let us see how this conflict arises.

When a person who receives income-tested benefits earns enough income to have the benefits reduced, there is an *implicit tax-back rate* on that income because the person's disposable income increases by less than the newly earned income. (The tax-back rate is sometimes also referred to as the *claw-back* rate.) For example, consider a person earning no income and receiving income-tested benefits of $8,000 who takes a part-time job paying $2,000. If her income-tested benefits are reduced by $1,000, her implicit tax rate is 50 percent. If a second person in the same situation has his income-tested benefits reduced by $2,000, he faces an implicit tax rate of 100 percent.

When people pay income taxes and also receive income-tested social benefits, the explicit income tax rate on their income and the implicit tax-back rate on their benefits are said to be *stacked,* and the total effect is called the **effective marginal tax rate.** For example, if one person earns an extra dollar and pays $0.25 in income tax while having her benefits reduced by $0.30, her effective marginal tax rate is 55 percent.

Because of the high tax-back rates which apply to many income-tested benefits, very high effective marginal tax rates are faced by many beneficiaries—the rates sometimes reach, or even exceed, 100 percent! It should not surprise anyone if beneficiaries reject the opportunity to work when their net income after work would be no more, or even *less,* than their net income when they choose not to work but receive full benefits. Box 25-1 (see pages 530–531) discusses further the stacking and disincentive problems associated with a number of Canada's existing social programs.

Some of the most serious efficiency effects of the tax-transfer system follow from its creation of high effective marginal tax rates that discourage beneficiaries from actions that would improve the performance of the economy and increase their own self-reliance.

In a background study for the Quebec White Paper of 1984, Bernard Fortin and Henri-Paul Rousseau of Laval University estimated that the average efficiency cost of Quebec's existing tax transfer system is $0.27 per dollar. This means that, on average, for $1.00 of tax revenue raised by the government, $0.27 is lost due to efficiency costs associated with the distortion of incentives by the tax system. More important, they estimate that the marginal social cost of the tax-transfer system is $0.56. This means that for each additional dollar raised from a weighted-average increase in Quebec taxes, the private sector loses $1.56 in income.

There are other costs not included in their study. First, there is the direct costs of raising tax revenues and enforcing tax laws and, second, the costs of distributing social benefits. Taking these into account, it is clear that delivering a dollar's worth of benefits to some needy Quebecois is a very costly procedure. While the generosity of Quebec's social programs means that these costs probably overestimate those for Canada as a whole, they nevertheless make it clear that the social costs of Canada's social programs are far from trivial.

The social costs arising from disincentives in the tax-transfer system hurt everyone in the economy, including the people that the social programs are designed to help.

Open-economy considerations. In a small open economy such as Canada's a further efficiency issue relates to the international mobility of labor and capital. The issue can be seen by considering a more extreme case that applied for many years in the U.K. In the 1960s and 1970s marginal rates of income tax, running over 80 percent, encouraged a brain drain of successful people leaving the United Kingdom for lower-tax countries such as the United States. (Many rock groups, including the Beatles, were among the emigrants.)

Considerations of equity meant that many people in the U.K. accepted this emigration as the price of eliminating very high after-tax incomes for U.K. residents. Some people wondered, however, if it was really better to have high-income people living abroad avoiding all U.K. taxes. If these high-income earners lived in the U. K. under a regime of, say, 40 to 45 percent maximum income tax rates, then for any given level of tax-financed spending, lower-income persons would have to pay less taxes than if the high-income earners had emigrated.

Similar considerations apply to capital. Is it better to have capital in one's own country paying 40 or 50 percent income tax or abroad in order to avoid an 80 percent domestic tax rate and thus paying no domestic taxes? Egalitarianism may argue for the high rate, but the loss of revenue and other benefits from the location of industry at home must be set against this perceived gain in equity.

Everyone will have personal value judgments on these matters. One pragmatic egalitarian view is that the tax rate should be as high as possible without encouraging significant emigration of labor and capital. This would give maximum equity consistent with keeping high-income-earning labor and capital at home to contribute both to reducing the tax load on lower-income groups and to developing the economy.

The relative ease with which many Canadians find that they can move into the United States because of similarities of language and culture makes labor and capital highly mobile between the two countries. Thus:

If Canada lets its rates of taxes and benefits get seriously out of line with those in the United States, it risks suffering a significant brain and capital drain to that country. Thus there are always substantial "harmonization pressures" between Canadian and American policies.

Of course, Canadian policies need not be identical to those in the United States, but if they get out of line

BOX 25-1

Stacking and Disincentives

A study prepared for the Quebec government in 1984 presented some explicit calculations of the effective marginal tax rate facing beneficiaries of major Quebec social programs. These provide striking evidence of the extent of the stacking problem and the disincentives that it creates.

Consider the case of a single man between 30 and 64 years of age with no employment income during the course of the year. (All calculations are based on the tax and transfer programs as they existed in 1983.) He would have received $4,932 in social assistance (including a refundable property tax credit). Suppose that he had the opportunity to work full time at the then prevailing minimum wage rate of $4 per hour, thus earning $8,000 in employment income (a full working year is about 2,000 hours). Although this $8,000 is by no means a princely sum, it would appear to represent a significant increase in income.

Of course, his employment income would be taxable, but only at the relatively low tax rate that applies at the low end of the income scale. As a result of working and earning this modest income, however, he would no longer qualify for some of the social assistance that he had been receiving. On some forms of social assistance that he would be receiving, benefits are reduced by a dollar for every dollar of income earned, making the implicit tax rate 100 percent. Other benefits, including the refundable tax credit, would be substantially reduced even if not eliminated altogether. Under the provisions of the Quebec tax and transfer systems, the individual's disposable income would have risen by only $2,560 as a result of working for the whole year. Because of the stacking of the implicit tax rates on the social benefits with the explicit income tax rate, this individual had an effective marginal tax rate of 68 percent, higher than the highest marginal income tax rate faced by the country's wealthiest people.

Now consider the situation of an unemployed couple with two young children. They receive more total assistance, because each parent qualifies for some of the programs, and the family receives additional assistance for the children. However, if either parent were to return to work, there are more benefits to be taxed back, and hence the effective marginal tax rate facing them is even higher than that facing the single person. The Quebec study calculated the effective marginal tax rate in this case to be 79 percent: Of every dollar earned from work, 79 cents will go in taxes or benefit reductions!

These are realistic cases that represent the situation facing many thousands of Canadians. It is not difficult to think of situations—perhaps less common but certainly not rare—where the effective tax rate is even higher, much higher. A single mother of two on welfare, living in subsidized housing and sending her children to subsidized day care, could, if she wanted to improve her lot in life, go to a technical school for 18 months and retrain as a word processor. She could then earn considerably more than the minimum wage. She would, however, then face an effective mar-

in a way that labor and capital regard as undesirable, they risk inducing an emigration of factors that will do harm to the Canadian economy. It is also worth noting that insofar as income is related to productivity, the people driven abroad by high marginal income taxes tend to be the most productive members of the society.

Security versus adjustment. In addition to redistributing income, social policies usually have as a goal the provision of economic security, a kind of safety net in the form of social "insurance" to cushion economic shocks. Indeed, some commentators argue that this motivation has been more important than income distribution in the historical development of Canadian social policies and that this explains the importance of universality in the Canadian debate.

We have already discussed the importance of adjustment to the Canadian economy. It is possible to ginal income tax rate of over 150 percent! No wonder when people fall into poverty they find it hard to escape. In our efforts to help such people, we have designed a system that severely penalizes them if they try to become more self-reliant by substituting work income for social assistance payments.

Nor is it just people of working age who are affected by these disincentives. The elderly poor who receive the guaranteed income supplement (GIS) also face a marginal tax rate that is higher than that faced by the very rich. In their case benefits are reduced by 50 cents for every dollar of income earned. When combined with a positive rate of income tax, the overall effective rate of tax is well over 50 percent. This means, for example, that elderly single persons who earned $7,000 of private pension income could face a marginal effective tax rate of over 70 cents on the dollar. Furthermore, this figure does not take account of provincial top-ups that are usually reduced when income rises and could combine with the factors already discussed to make the effective tax rate over 100 percent.

One might think that this is not much of a problem because work disincentives are not likely to have much effect on the nonworking elderly. However, since income from capital is included in taxable income, there are strong disincentives to work and save in the pre-retirement years, because any accumulated savings will just reduce post-retirement social benefits.

The tax-transfer system has been built up over the years in a piecemeal fashion; the resulting lack of integration is the major source of the stacking problem. Each program has its own threshold level at which benefits start to get taxed back; benefits from other programs are often included in that threshold level, and each has its own tax-back rate, which is then stacked on the other tax-back rates and on the explicit income tax rate. Effective reform of the system means more than reform of the individual programs; they must be integrated and rationalized so as to eliminate many of the undesirable and avoidable interactions.

The Quebec white paper of 1984 proposed the principle that anyone who receives transfers should not pay any income tax and that anyone who paid income tax should not receive any transfers. This dramatic change from the system now in force would amount to a negative income tax system as discussed in Chapter 24. The Newfoundland Royal Commission on unemployment reported in 1986 that in spite of the huge income transfers that the social security system was generating—particularly in the form of UI payments—the disincentive effects of the system were destroying the economic viability (one could almost hear them saying the moral fiber) of the province. In saying so in spite of the enormous financial advantage to Newfoundland of the existing system, it must go down as one of the most remarkably honest documents of the decade.

cushion people against shocks without inhibiting adjustment; retraining and relocation grants are examples. It is also possible to cushion them in ways that inhibit adjustment; shoring up declining industries and providing government jobs for declining occupations are examples.

Most people accept that in today's fiercely competitive world, assistance should be provided to those most hurt by economic shocks, and that it should encourage rather than inhibit adaptation.

When particular cases arise, it is not always easy to stick to this general principle. Many specific, politically motivated interventions that were designed to increase security have had the effect of reducing adaptability. It is important, therefore, that such anti-adjustment assistance mechanisms not be built into the statutory part of the social system.

Intergenerational issues. Many aspects of social policy are targeted at retired persons. Many of today's retired started their working life during the Great Depression, a time when there were few pensions and when saving was difficult, given the low incomes then prevailing. Thus today's elderly tend on average to be low-income persons, and transfers from younger to older citizens seem appropriate.

With the high incomes that were earned in the 1950s, 1960s, and 1970s and the generous pension plans that were established during those years, the outlook is that many of tomorrow's elderly will be well off. Of course, many of those who were poor when young will remain poor when they are old, but many of tomorrow's elderly will not be in this category. Thus there will be large income variations among the elderly, and the assumption that on average they are low-income persons will no longer be valid. Furthermore, the population is slowly aging, and in the early part of the twenty-first century the proportion of the population who are elderly will be much higher than it is today.

These considerations suggest the following conclusion:

On grounds of equity and fiscal capacity, help for the elderly and the retired should be more focused on lower-income groups than it is at present.

We return to this issue later in the chapter.

The Universality Issue

Controversy has raged over the universality of Canada's social policies. Supporters feel that many of the programs should be available to all Canadians regardless of their incomes or other circumstances. This is the concept of universality. Critics argue that programs should be made more selective, targeted toward people in real need, as the only way of preserving the high standard of the Canadian system at an affordable cost.

The universality principle arouses great passions. Indeed, preserving this characteristic of the Canadian social policy system has been described by Prime Minister Brian Mulroney as a "sacred trust." However, the issue of universality is not so clear cut as the Prime Minister's comments may have suggested.

Because the benefits paid by most universal programs are taxable, their net after-tax yield depends on the income of the recipient, and hence while their gross payments may be universal, their net benefits are not.

In the words of Queen's University political scientist Keith Banting:

> There really are no universal programs in Canada. So the debate over universality, as conducted in this country, has all the marks of a red herring which, of course, is the best possible subject for political controversy.[2]

As Banting points out, the whole history of the development of the welfare state in Canada, as in most advanced industrialized countries, can be seen as a flight from selectivity. The early Canadian system was modeled on the British system of local relief, which was a means-tested system of delivering relief to those in real, often desperate need. The 1930s showed this system to be inadequate in dealing with a major economic disaster such as the Great Depression. Benefits were provided, when they were provided at all, on a grudging and demeaning basis.

In the 1940s the flight from selectivity was confirmed. At first this involved more humane but still means-tested forms of relief. Later, however, the system involved the establishment of universal programs for selected groups, such as the elderly or the unemployed, or for specific purposes, such as health insurance.

As well as dealing with the inadequacies of the system of delivering relief to the needy in the 1930s, the idea of universality came to be accepted as the best way of providing security. The development of the social insurance system in the 1940s was part of a search for security in a fundamentally insecure and

[2] "Universality and the Development of the Welfare State," in A. Green and N. Olewiler, *Report of the Policy Forum on Universality and Social Policies in the 1980s* (Kingston: John Deutsch Institute for Public Policy, 1985). This section relies heavily on Banting's excellent treatment of the universality issue.

changing world. In the 1940s the Marsh report put it this way:

> The general sense of security which would result from such programs would provide a better life for the great mass of people and a potent antidote to the fears and worries and uncertainties of the times. The post-war world would not have to be anticipated with fear and apprehension.

Generalizing from the experience of the 1930s, these risks were assumed to be felt by everyone. The need was for mass and guaranteed protection, rather than for conditional systems that produced benefits at the whim of the granting body. What was required was a *right* to social security for every citizen.

Demogrants, sometimes met out of general tax revenue and sometimes out of contributions of the potential recipients, would mean that no individual had to feel demeaned by receiving social benefits when his or her turn came. Universality was also thought to provide better protection from tampering than selective systems. It was thought that if everyone benefited, there would be a powerful constituency to protect the system should any future politician try to dismantle it. A selective system targeted at the poor would be much more vulnerable to such an attack since the poor have a weaker political voice than the middle class. As the designer of much of the original American social security system, President Franklin Roosevelt, put it:

> We put those payroll contributions there so as to give the contributors a legal, moral, and political right to collect their pensions and unemployment benefits. With those taxes in there, no damn politician can ever scrap my social security program.

The importance of this consideration can be seen in the ease with which President Ronald Reagan dismantled much of the American anti-poverty program in the 1980s. Little complaint was heard at the curtailment of food stamps and other income-tested measures, a change that allowed the number of people living in poverty to double in the United States in less than a decade. The contrast with the outcry when Reagan tried to tamper even slightly with the universal old age pension scheme (called Old Age and Survivor's Insurance, OASI) is striking.

These reasons for universality suggest that this aspect is not likely to be dropped from many of Canada's social welfare schemes. Greater targeting and cost effectiveness are likely to be obtained, however, by ensuring that more of the benefits are taxable and by making greater use of tax credits instead of tax deductions.

An Assessment of Some Specific Social Programs

Now we shall look in some detail at the various elements of Canada's existing social programs and at some suggestions for reform of those that seem inadequate at present.

Human Resource Development Programs

One of the earliest types of social expenditure in Canada was public education. This remains one of the most important even today, although it has been supplemented by numerous other programs aimed at developing human resources.

Basic Education

Basic instruction, directed in the main at youth, is available in primary and secondary schools, which teach literacy and numeracy, the skills that are needed before further marketable skills can be acquired. Studies show that there are many functional illiterates in Canada—people who cannot comprehend simple written instructions well enough to carry them out. One important educational target should be to reduce illiteracy and innumeracy, deficiencies that are lifetime handicaps for their sufferers.

Basic primary and secondary education is supplemented by further education and training. This occurs in post-secondary institutions as well as in the workplace, in technical schools, and in universities. In 1987 the federal government operated about a dozen non-university job creation and training schemes, enrolling nearly half a million people and costing nearly $2 billion. Although few doubt that these schemes are of great value, the Neilson task force noted many deficiencies in the programs and recommended major changes.

Post-secondary Education

Post-secondary education is a provincial responsibility in Canada. As a result of tax-sharing arrangements discussed in Chapter 24, the federal government makes large grants to the provinces—amounting to nearly $5 billion in 1987—which are nominally geared to financing the necessary expenditures. The provinces are free, however, to spend this money as they wish, and in 1986 five provinces were spending less money on their universities than the federal higher-education grants that they received. In these cases the provincial contribution to university education is actually negative.

In Canada all universities are public institutions, and university education is heavily subsidized by government, with student fees accounting for only about 15 percent of total costs. Two arguments can be advanced for subsidizing higher education. First, there are externalities for the whole country from higher education. In many cases these externalities cannot be internalized by the students receiving the education, so, left to their own maximizing decisions, students who had to pay the whole cost of their education would choose less than is socially optimal. Second, charging anything like the full cost would make education prohibitively expensive to low- and even middle-income families.

Arguments to reduce the subsidy to higher education, and thus to finance a larger fraction of the costs of running universities from tuition fees, start with the observation that the value of many kinds of education can be internalized and recaptured in higher incomes earned by the recipients in their later life. This is particularly true of professional training in such fields as law, medicine, dentistry, higher education, and computer science. Yet students in these fields typically pay a smaller part of their real education costs than students in the arts, where the argument for externalities is greatest. Also, the subsidized education does represent a significant income transfer from taxpayers to students. Since the bulk of tax revenue comes from people with modest incomes and since the average university student earns a lifetime income that is well above the national average, there is some reason for concern on grounds of equity.

A major question about the subsidization of higher education is, "Does the transfer from lower-income, non-university-trained taxpayers to potentially higher-income-earning university students satisfy our ideas of equity?"

People who worry about the equity issue in this context often argue for a system of student loans, where more of the cost of education is recouped from the students themselves later in their lifetimes. People opposed to loans argue, among other things, that even loans will discourage children in lower-income families from continuing on to higher education because, from the vantage point of their family's current low income, the liability to be taken on by the student will seem enormous.

Job Creation Programs

People with few skills and little job experience often find themselves in a catch-22 situation:

Employers are reluctant to hire inexperienced persons, but the only way to gain experience is to be employed.

To help with this problem, the federal government operates a number of job creation programs that attempt to provide the long-term unemployed and new labor-market entrants with job experience and basic labor market skills. Job training plus mobility assistance can also encourage the regional movement of labor out of areas of heavy unemployment into areas with better employment opportunities.

People receiving unemployment insurance anywhere in Canada can enroll in job training programs, completing apprenticeship or journeyman requirements while still receiving UI benefits. The federal government has recently announced that funds will be set aside for job creation for people on social assistance. The Quebec government is experimenting with a program that gives supplementary benefits to welfare recipients who voluntarily accept on-the-job training. These examples illustrate a major point on which many experts agree:

To reduce unemployment and raise the earning power of the labor force, job creation programs need to be coordinated with both the unemployment insurance program and provincial welfare programs to produce a unified scheme that overcomes disincentive effects in existing programs.

Income Transfer and Security Programs

Income transfer and security programs provide assistance for people in financial need due to unemployment, injury, or inadequate wages. (The last group constitute the working poor.) These programs—which comprise the so-called social safety net—include welfare, unemployment insurance, and family benefits. They make payments to approximately 9 million adult Canadians each year and cost the federal government about $18 billion.

As can be seen from the variety of schemes, the income transfer and security system has many goals. One of the most important is to prevent the occurrence of poverty wherever possible and to alleviate poverty where it occurs. Though nothing like the serious problem it was in Canada's past and still is in many other countries, poverty remains a matter of real concern to Canadian policymakers. Not the least cause for concern is that the majority of the poverty that can be eliminated by economic growth may have already been eliminated, while much of the remaining poverty may represent the "hard core" that will persist no matter how wealthy the society becomes. This type of poverty can only be alleviated by active public policy. The problem of poverty is discussed in more detail in Box 25-2.

Unemployment Insurance (UI)

Unemployment insurance is the most costly single program administered by the federal government, accounting for over $10 billion of payments in 1987. Originally instituted in 1940 as an insurance scheme against temporary bouts of unemployment, it has been extended in scope and generosity several times since then. The last major revision was in 1971, and many of the changes instituted at that time have been the object of recent criticism.

Recently criticized changes to UI. Here are some of the ways that changes to the UI system have caused it to depart from its original purpose of insuring against temporary bouts of involuntary unemployment, changes that have been the subject of recent criticism and suggestions for change.

Benefits are now paid to people who leave employment voluntarily. Canada is one of the few countries that provide benefits to those who quit jobs voluntarily and the incentive for abuse is obvious.

By providing benefits after as little as 10 weeks of work each year, the scheme has effectively become a subsidy for seasonal employment. The short qualification period has also encouraged several provinces to provide make-work schemes whereby local labor is employed just long enough to qualify for UI.

In an effort to help regions with high unemployment rates, *extended regional benefits* were introduced in 1974. Although their purpose is to compensate individuals living in areas providing below average employment prospects, the scheme also effectively rewards those who do not find steady employment with benefits that may extend up to 40 weeks after only 10 weeks of employment. The researchers of the Macdonald Royal Commission showed that labor mobility, both toward occupations and toward places offering more stable employment prospects, is actually discouraged and that high regional unemployment rates are encouraged by this scheme.

Proposals for reform of UI. The Macdonald commission severely criticized current UI policies and suggested many reforms. Subsequently the federal government set up a commission of inquiry under Quebec economist Claude Forget to investigate these criticisms further and to make recommendations.

The main thrust of the reports by both Macdonald and Forget was that the system had become overburdened by being used for too many, often conflicting objectives. It should, they argued, be returned to its prime objective of providing insurance

BOX 25-2

Poverty in Canada

What is poverty, and whom does it affect? One definition says one lives in poverty if one is poorer than most of one's fellow citizens. Since there will always be a bottom 10 percent of any income distribution who are poorer than the remaining 90 percent, poverty in this sense will always be with us. If a completely relative definition is not very revealing, neither is an unchanging absolute definition. The living standards of Canadians regarded as poor would have looked more than adequate to Canadians of 200 years ago and would look princely to citizens of many countries even today.

To meet both of these concerns economists define poverty as some given level of income, rather than just in relative terms, but they also recognize that as average living standards rise over time, so will our ideas of what constitutes poverty.

In 1985 Statistics Canada defined the **poverty level** (or *low-income cut-off*) as the level of income at which a household spends on average more than 58.5 percent of its income on the three basic necessities of food, shelter, and clothing. For a family of four, the Canadian poverty level in 1986 ranged from $15,310 in rural to $20,812 in the largest cities.

The levels of income just mentioned, low though they seem by our standards, are above the average level of income of all Canadians in 1890 and also above the income of three-quarters of the families in the world today. Neither of these comparisons, however, should lead you to underestimate the hardship of being poor in Canada today. While $15,310 will buy enough food, shelter, and clothing for a family of four to get by, it does not provide enough money for the full range of commodities that most of us take for granted, such as having a refrigerator, a TV set that works, constant hot water, and an occasional night out at a movie. Many of the poor are understandably bitter and resentful that they and their children are outsiders looking in on the comfortable way of life shown in ads and on television. "I'd like, just once," one of the poor said to a magazine interviewer, "to buy Christmas presents the children want instead of presents they need."

Who Are the Poor?

According to the criterion just outlined, 13.3 percent of Canadian families and 36.8 percent of unattached individuals were living in poverty in 1985.

There are poor among all ages, races, and educational levels, employed as well as unemployed. Yet some groups have much higher incidences of poverty than others. For example, the table shows that you are more likely to be poor if you live in a rural area, if you live in the Atlantic provinces, if you are a member of a large family, or if you are over 65 years of age.

Poverty is, however, by no means restricted to these groups. More than half the poor families live in urban areas, live in Ontario and the western provinces, have no more than one child, and are headed by persons of working age. Furthermore, about one-fourth of those in poverty work full time (the so-called working poor), and over half work at least part time. These facts help to dispose of two superficial caricatures: the slothful father who feigns a disability because he is too lazy to do an honest day's work and the family with so many children that an ordinary decent wage is spread so thin that the entire household is reduced to poverty. Individual households that come close to these extremes can be found, but most poor households do not.

The Historical Experience

Between 1969 and 1986 the proportion of Canadians living in poverty fell to a little more than half its former level. In part this reflected a variety of government initiatives of the sort discussed in this chapter. But in large measure it reflected the growth in average income. Historically, the greatest source of relief from poverty has come through economic growth.

Incidence of Poverty Among Canadian Families by Selected Characteristics, 1985

Characteristics	Percentage of families falling below the poverty line
All families	13.3
Place of residence	
Metropolitan	13.5
Other urban	13.2
Rural	12.9
Region	
Atlantic	15.9
Quebec	15.8
Ontario	10.2
Prairies	13.4
British Columbia	12.6
Number of children under 16 years	
0	11.1
1 or 2	20.3
3 or more	30.3
Age of head of family	
Under 25	32.0
25–54	12.7
55–64	11.8
65 and over	10.0
Sex of head of family	
Male	9.5
Female	42.3
Employment status of head of family	
In labor force	9.6
Not in labor force	25.5

Source: Statistics Canada, 13–207.

Today's Poverty: Causes and Cures

It would be a mistake, however, to expect growth to eliminate all poverty. Much of today's poverty problem is no longer rooted in low *average* income but in the fact that particular groups are left behind in the general rise in living standards caused by economic growth. It is little consolation—indeed, it must add to the gall—that they are poor in an increasingly affluent society.

The causes of this "hard core" of poverty are various. The fact that many of the poor are over age 65 shows that age and illness force people out of the labor market. Other important groups suffering poverty include the rural poor, who strive in vain to earn a decent living from the land under worsening market conditions; the urban poor, who simply lack the skill to command a wage high enough to support themselves and their families above the poverty level; the immobile poor who are trapped by age and outdated skills in areas and occupations where the demand for their services is declining faster than their number; people with mental or physical handicaps severe enough to restrict their ability to earn an adequate income but not severe enough to cause them to be confined to an institution; and a host of dropouts such as alcoholics and drug addicts.

There is no single answer to the question of what causes poverty in the midst of plenty. It is partly a result of mental and physical handicaps, partly of low motivation, partly of the raw deal that fate gives to some, partly the result of changing market conditions when industries and occupations no longer can prosper, partly a result of unwillingness or inability to invest in the kind of human capital that does pay off in the long run, partly the result of the market's valuing the particular abilities an individual does have at such a low price that even in good health and with full-time employment the income that can be earned leaves that person below the poverty line.

Just as there is no single reason for poverty, there is no single cure. Many of the social programs outlined in this chapter attempt to get at various of the causes. If poverty has fallen steadily in Canada, the two main groups of causes are economic growth and social programs that seek to provide assistance for those who cannot help themselves and to assist those who can to learn to do so.

against temporary bouts of involuntary unemployment, while other schemes should be used to achieve other objectives. It is important to note that both reports did not advocate reform of UI in isolation. They saw UI reform as part of a larger package of reform, with any hardship introduced by making UI more effective strictly as an insurance program being alleviated by other measures to help people with very low incomes.

The suggestion that has aroused perhaps the most controversy was the Forget commission's recommendation for the *annualization* of UI benefits. According to this scheme, each claimant would be eligible for a full year's benefits after a uniform qualifying period of, say, 10 weeks of work. The benefits would be based on weekly earnings averaged over the last 52 weeks, rather than over the last 10 to 20 weeks as is now the case. The gainers would be people who had worked continuously over the past year, while the losers would be those who had worked for only the minimum qualifying period.

Other reforms that have been suggested, some by the Forget commission and some by other groups, include the following:

Raise the number of weeks of work required to qualify for UI, thus making it *work-related* while leaving those who cannot obtain sufficient work to be supported by other programs.

Make the payments of UI premiums *experience-related.* Currently the premiums are unrelated to the unemployment experience of each industry, so premiums are the same in an industry with highly variable employment and one where employment is stable. This violates the insurance principle, whereby premiums usually vary with risk category, and it subsidizes employers and employees in variable-employment industries at the expense of both groups in stable-employment industries.

Remove the extended regional benefits. Under the present system a worker earning $495 per week for 10 weeks in a high-unemployment area is eligible for 42 weeks of benefits worth $12,474. An identical worker in another part of Canada is eligible for only 10 weeks of benefits worth $4,950. Furthermore, the second worker will probably pay more in UI premiums than the first. Critics say not only that this is inequitable but also that it provides a strong incentive for workers to remain in the area of high unemployment rather than to migrate to an area where the chance of gaining employment is higher.

When the Forget report was published, the commissioners could not agree among themselves, and the main report was accompanied by two minority reports—one signed by the two labor representatives, who disagreed with most of the report, and one signed by an industry representative, who disagreed only with the recommendation of annualization. In the storm of debate and rhetoric that followed, the earlier consensus that the UI system was in need of reform and could be made to do its job better than it now does was lost from sight by many. Since any move would be highly controversial, the government chose to do nothing, and it seems likely to follow the same course in the near future.

In the debate that followed the publication of the Forget report, many participants did not distinguish the positive observation that people respond rationally to incentives from the normative judgment that various responses might be deemed morally good or bad. What the Macdonald commission's research showed, and the Forget report confirmed, is that people do respond to price signals—a fact well known to economists. In this particular case UI gives incentives to remain in seasonal jobs and in areas with poor employment prospects, and to take UI-financed holidays. Rational people respond by doing so, thus increasing the national unemployment rate.

Saying that the UI system encourages behavior that increases unemployment and reduces regional mobility does *not* say that the unemployed themselves are responsible for the "abuses" of the system that lead to these results.

The responsibility lies with the people who designed the incentives and those who strive to preserve them. It is they who can alter the system to make it deliver the intended benefits with fewer incentives for undesired behavior. Some of the political problems facing potential reform of the UI system are discussed in Box 25-3.

Public Assistance Programs

Social assistance for individuals below retirement age, usually called welfare, is mainly a provincial and

BOX 25-3

Social Policy Reform: A Case Study of Unemployment Insurance

Many economic policies, particularly those directed at redistributing income, concentrate significant benefits on a relatively small fraction of the population while spreading the costs across the entire population. As a result, the costs borne by any particular individual for any particular policy are trivial—though neither the total costs borne by all members of society of any given policy nor the total costs for all policies borne by each member of society are trivial. Economists and political scientists have long recognized the problems for reform posed by those policies by the fact that each individual bears a small cost for any single program.

Because the beneficiaries have a significant *vested interest* in maintaining the policies, they will protest strongly when any proposed change threatens to reduce their benefits. At the same time, each general taxpayer will be relatively indifferent, since the personal implications of reform of any one program will be trivial. Hence, although the majority of the population has a preference for reform, the vocal minority who opposes change will tend to dominate the political debate. Not surprisingly, politicians and public administrators are reluctant to change any program (other than occasionally to enrich it).

This problem applies particularly to social policies, since such policies have as their *raison d'être* the redistribution of income. In Canada these issues are further complicated by regional economic disparities—the benefits from given programs are often highly concentrated in particular regions or provinces. Political sensitivities are particularly strong when the cries of protest are concentrated in particular regions. Those who would lose directly are often joined by other residents of the region who feel a particular personal interest in the program because of the benefits it brings to the regional economy. Also, provincial politicians clearly have an interest in speaking out on behalf of the province's interest when threatened by federal policies. Federal politicians will naturally be reluctant to reform policies in a manner that costs them support in entire regions or provinces.

These issues are vividly illustrated by recent Canadian attempts to reform unemployment insurance. No policy has been studied more frequently or more thoroughly. While there is disagreement over the details of beneficial reforms, there is a broad consensus on the general thrust of the necessary reform. Yet UI has survived virtually untouched; indeed, if anything, the disincentives and inefficiencies in the system have gotten worse.

UI is now clearly much more than a labor market policy. It is a social program that involves hugh transfers that are regionally focused. But even though UI does target benefits toward the poorest regions, it does not target benefits at all well toward the neediest within the region. It does nothing, for example, to help the poverty-stricken, destitute individuals and families who are unemployable and who have left the labor force. It is a generous subsidy to the "working poor," particularly those with seasonal jobs.

Because UI as currently constituted is a substantial regional transfer or subsidy program, politically acceptable reform must, in the first instance, maintain those transfers. Any attempt to cut the transfers would cause such a political storm that all hope of political acceptance would be lost. The solution is to maintain the transfers but to alter the incentives attached to them. Instead of creating anti-adjustment incentives to stay in the region or industry or skill group (causing what is called "transfer dependency"), incentives should be created that will reduce the need for the transfer. These include retraining and relocation allowance and other forms of adjustment assistance.

Not the least of the problems facing such policy changes is that the incentives might, in many cases, greatly reduce the population of some region or even depopulate it altogether. This would pose obvious political difficulties, since it cuts at the very heart of Canadian political and economic issues.

municipal responsibility in Canada. Under the Canada Assistance Plan (CAP), however, the federal government contributes half of the costs of eligible provincial social assistance programs. In 1987 the federal government's contribution under the CAP was about $4 billion, and the amount has been rising steadily over recent years.

Although the existing welfare system is accepted as necessary by most Canadians, many observers believe that it could be substantially improved by a series of reforms. Suggested reforms take two main forms. First, remove the disincentives to work implied by the present stacking of reductions in income-tested benefits and income taxes on earning that have already been discussed. Second, provide positive incentives to self-help by increasing benefits for recipients who accept work or training for work.

Child Benefits System

Benefits related to children cost the federal government about $4.5 billion in 1987. Prior to tax reform proposals of 1987, the Canadian tax system included three elements in its child benefits system. The first is the family allowance scheme, which is a universal, or demogrant, scheme paid directly to beneficiaries. The other two child benefits—the child tax exemption and the child tax credit—are both delivered via the tax system. The child benefits system not only influences vertical equity, but elements of it are also intended to improve horizontal equity in the tax system—that is, they recognize that a family with children has a lesser ability to pay taxes than a family with the same income but no children. Table 25-2 shows the value of these benefits to a typical, two-parent, two-child family.

Family allowance (FA). Under the family allowance plan, a cheque is mailed monthly to mothers according to the number of children they have (and in Alberta and Quebec according to the age structure of their children). The family allowance is taxable in the hands of the spouse with the higher income. The net cost of the system is about $2 billion, which is the total value of the cheques distributed less the income taxes collected by the federal government as a result of the increased disposable income of the recipients.

Some supporters of the scheme see as an advantage the fact that the cheque goes directly to the wife. In many households, nonworking wives have no discretionary income of their own other than the monthly family allowance cheque.

The gross family allowance received is independent of income—it depends only on the number of children in the family. Thus the family allowance scheme is a universal program. Because families with the same levels of income receive more benefits the more children they have, the FA provides a large measure of horizontal equity. Further, because the family allowance is taxable, after-tax benefits decline with income—with a progressive tax structure, the higher the income, the higher the average and marginal tax rate, and hence the lower the after-tax benefits of the transfer. The after-tax benefits of the FA payments are shown in the second column of Table 25-2.

The family allowance contributes to both the horizontal and the vertical equity of the tax-transfer system.

Child tax exemption (CTE). The child tax exemption, which was a major part of the child benefits system prior to tax reform, allowed a reduction in taxable income for each child; the exemption applied to the spouse claiming the family allowance. Thus the value of the CTE benefit depended on both the number of children, each providing an exemption, and the family's income. The higher the spouse's income, the higher was the value of the exemptions; thus the operation of the CTE was regressive. This is illustrated for a two-child family by the third column of Table 25-2.

The child tax exemption serves the purpose of horizontal equity but clearly operates against vertical equity.

Net effects of FA and CTE. In the best of all technically precise worlds, one might argue that a family allowance and a child tax exemption can be used together to ensure both horizontal and vertical equity. However, in our imperfect world it is hard to discern the net effect of the two systems operating together.

TABLE 25-2 Net Child Benefits Received by a Typical Two-Parent, Two-Child Family ***(1989 structure of federal child benefits in 1986 dollars; pre-tax-reform benefit and rate structure)***

Income[a]	Net family allowance	Child tax exemption	Child tax credit	Total net benefits
0	760	0	1,030	1,790
10,000	580	180	1,030	1,790
20,000	540	220	1,030	1,790
30,000	490	270	740	1,500
40,000	460	300	240	1,000
50,000	400	360	0	760

Source: Department of Finance, "Information on Selected Social Tax/Transfer Programs," 1986.

[a] Includes income from all sources received by the parents, excluding family allowance and the child tax credit.

The net effect of all three schemes working together is progressive: The higher the income, the lower the benefit. Family allowance payments are taxable, so the net benefit falls as income rises. The child tax credit is income-tested and so falls as income rises. The child tax exemption is a deduction from taxable income, so its value rises with income. The net benefit from all three schemes falls as income rises.

In its May 1985 budget, however, the federal government introduced a gradual reduction of the exemption and partially de-indexed the FA so that by 1989 the two would be exactly equal. The net effect would be that each family receives the FA tax free; the increase in family income would be exactly matched by the increase in deductions, so taxable income, and hence taxes paid, would be unaffected. Thus the family's after-tax income would by the amount of the FA received, and the net effect of the two programs would be that benefits are independent of income. Though one can dispute the desirability of this change—it satisfied the horizontal equity issue but contributes little to vertical equity—it did have the distinct advantage of "rationalizing" the two programs so that their net effect could be determined.

Child tax credit (CTC). The third element of the child benefits package is the child tax credit. Recall from Chapter 24 that a tax credit reduces one's tax bill by the amount of the credit; a given credit is thus of equal value to all people who qualify, regardless of their income. (This is in contrast to an exemption, which is a deduction from taxable income and is therefore more valuable the higher is income.) The CTC is refundable—if taxes are negative as a result of the credit, a refund is due.

The child tax credit is, however, an income-tested program designed to reduce the tax liabilities only of lower-income groups. The entire credit is received by low-income families; when family income reaches $24,000 the CTC starts to be phased out at a rate such that when family income reaches $45,000, the value of the CTC is zero. The CTC does not accrue automatically; it must be applied for. Since it is a credit, its financial value to the family is independent of which spouse claims it. The value of the CTC to a two-child family is shown in the fourth column of Table 25-2.

The implications of tax reform. As we have seen, prior to the tax reform proposed in 1987, the progressivity of the FA system was offset by the regressivity of the CTE, so that the main progressivity of the child benefits system was due to the operation of the CTC.

Tax reform included a proposal to convert the CTE into a nonrefundable tax credit for dependents that would operate in addition to the existing refundable CTC. As a result, the new system will exhibit more progressivity since it will combine the progressive elements of the FA and the two tax credits, while eliminating the regressive CTE. Nevertheless, the reformed system has been criticized on a number of grounds.

Criticism of this type of reform is often based on the increased emphasis it puts on the mechanism of tax credits, a mechanism that suffers from several faults. The main fault is that the credit, being related to one's income tax return and hence based on last year's income, is delivered only once a year and then only with a considerable lag after filing a return. This lag means that the credit is insensitive to current economic conditions and hence provides no safety net against current exigencies. As a source of help for the newly poor, it will often come too late, even if it is not too little.

To gain needed funds immediately, some beneficiaries often sell their expected tax refunds to tax discount firms. (What these firms do, in effect, is loan the refund money now—accepting some risk that they have not been given full and correct data to justify the refund. The difference between the discounted price that they pay now and the refund they eventually get is their interest payment, which is usually quite high.)

Day care. The great rise of two-income families in which both husband and wife work has led to a growth of day-care facilities. Working couples with preschool-age children who cannot afford to pay someone to come to their own home must rely on day-care facilities. Currently there is a great demand for a universal program to provide such facilities either free or at a heavily subsidized price.

Advocates argue that the state ought to provide such care just as it provides free medical and hospital care. Women's groups also argue that affordable day care is a necessary part of women's liberation. Without it, they say, many women will not be allowed to fulfill themselves by taking on meaningful work outside the home. There is also an externality argument that goes like this: If people are determined to put their children into day-care facilities, it is in society's interest to see that these facilities are fully adequate to the job of caring for children at a very formative stage in their lives. Regulations will not be able to do the job since high-quality care implies high costs. If many parents are unable or unwilling to pay that cost, their children may end up in inadequate facilities, and society at large will be the long-run loser.

Opponents argue on efficiency grounds that if the second income earner cannot earn enough to pay for day care, it is inefficient for that person to work. Total income would be higher if he or she stayed home, freeing the resources that would have been used to keep the family's children in day care. Opponents also argue on equity grounds that there is no reason why two-income parents with children in day care should be subsidized by funds collected from single persons, married couples who elect to have a parent stay at home to look after the children, and two-income families without children of day-care age. On present evidence, it is not clear whether the average income of the group that pays the subsidy will be higher or lower than the average income of the group that receives the subsidy. It is clear, however, that many individuals who pay the subsidy will have incomes below those of many individuals who receive it. Day care is not, therefore, a simple system for transferring income from richer to poorer households.

Benefits for the Elderly

The biggest concern with retirement schemes of all sorts is that the Canadian population is aging. Over the next decades, a larger and larger fraction of Canadians will be retired, and thus the working people who will be directly or indirectly supporting the retired will constitute a smaller and smaller fraction of the population.

The danger with the present youthful age structure of the country is that we may think we as a nation are richer than we actually are. When only a small proportion of the population is retired, it is easy to be generous to them because the burden is spread over so many working persons. However, if overly generous schemes are established, they may become difficult to honor when a large proportion of the population is at retirement age. This crunch is projected to come for Canada somewhere early in the twenty-first century.

The next decade carries the danger that Canadians may accept obligations toward the retired that become hard to honor a decade or two down the line.

Registered retirement savings plans (RRSP). RRSPs provide an incentive for individuals to provide for their own retirement, either because they are not covered by a company plan or because they wish to supplement their company plan. Funds contributed are deductible from taxable income but become fully taxable when they are withdrawn. It is thus a tax deferral plan, and as such it is more valuable the higher one's current taxable income and the lower one's expected future income. Approximately 2.3 million people, or about 29 percent of the labor force, contributed $5 billion to RRSP plans in 1986, of which about 25 percent of the funds came from persons with incomes below $20,000.

Proposals for reform include making some or all of the contributions a tax credit rather than an income deduction. However, the government rejected this option in its 1987 tax reform proposals. Another suggestion is to lock the funds in until retirement age to prevent them from being used to average income, and thus reduce one's tax liabilities, by purchasing a plan in a year when income is high and collapsing it in a year when income is low.

The Canada Pension Plan (CPP). The CPP provides a basic level of retirement income for all Canadians who have contributed to it over their working lives. (A separate but similar scheme exists in Quebec.) Unlike some private programs, the pension provided by the CPP is "portable"—changing jobs does not cause any loss of eligibility.

The most important concern about the plan is that it subsidizes people who are currently receiving pensions. Rates were very low when these people were young, and as a result they will receive pensions more than five times as large as what their contributions would actually have bought. This makes the plan a very good deal for those presently retired, but it means that any extension of the plan will be at much greater cost to those who are currently young—any increase in future benefits will have to be paid for on top of the existing subsidy to those already retired. To make the scheme self-supporting, the government currently plans for contributions nearly to double between 1985 and 2011.

Private-sector pensions. Problems with private-sector pensions include *portability,* since often some or all eligibility is lost when a worker changes employers; the *minimum period* of employment needed to qualify, which is often quite long; and *vestibility,* how soon the pension contributions made by employer and employee belong to the employee.

Recent changes to the Federal Pension Benefits Standards Act have significantly changed the requirements on these matters. This legislation covers approximately 1 million employees under federal labor jurisdiction, and it is also expected to serve as a model for provincial pension reforms. These amendments will permit individuals to accumulate pension credits after only two years of employment and to tranfer these benefits easily as they move among jobs. In addition, there is some significant extension of eligibility to part-time workers—an important matter since part-time work is increasing in many sectors of the economy.

Retirement income security programs. The existing public benefits system for the elderly is in many ways analogous to the child benefits system. There are three programs, each similar to a corresponding program in the child benefits system.

First, there is a universal benefit, or demogrant, called the *old age security (OAS)* program, that acts much like the family allowance. Under the OAS program, the government sends out about 2.5 million monthly benefit cheques of about $300 each, one to each Canadian over the qualifying age of 65. After UI, the OAS is the single most expensive program administered by the federal government, accounting for almost $10 billion in 1986.

Second, there are tax breaks available to the elderly that serve to reduce their tax liabilities. Prior to the 1987 tax reform these included an age exemption available to anyone 65 or older and a pension income deduction that serves to make the first $1,000 of pension income tax free. These two deductions served approximately to offset the tax liability of the OAS, thus essentially rendering the OAS tax free.

In the 1987 tax reform these deductions were both converted to tax credits.

Third, there is an income-tested program, called the guaranteed income supplement (GIS), which provides benefits targeted to the low-income elderly. (In some provinces this is supplemented by further target assistance.) The GIS provides for most of the progressivity that arises in the elderly benefits system.

As with the child benefits system, and indeed with most social programs, the elderly benefits system started out as a pure income-tested benefit scheme and then evolved into its current mixture of universal and income-tested elements. Many currently debated proposals for reform focus on the mix of universal and tested elements. The increased emphasis on universality took place during a period when most elderly people were in lower income categories. Recently, more and more people who receive these payments are in income brackets that are higher than that of the average taxpayer who finances them. For example, in 1983 approximately 35 percent of married OAS recipients had family incomes of more than $22,000, and approximately 20 percent had family incomes of more than $30,000. This situation will become even more anomalous in future years as the proportion of retired persons who are better off than the typical taxpayer increases, so that the typical income transfer under the OAS will be increasingly from poorer to richer Canadians.

Although the structure of the system appears similar to that of the child benefits system, one important difference is that the prospects are poor for short-term, expenditure-neutral reform (redistribution of elderly benefits among those currently receiving them while keeping the total benefits unchanged). Although the average income of the elderly has improved, and will continue to do so in the future, the elderly population is still currently concentrated at the relatively low end of the income scale. Hence very little revenue can be transferred from the high- to the low-income elderly because there is too little total income at the top to be redistributed to the many people at the bottom.

There is very little scope for expenditure-neutral redistribution within the current elderly benefits system while pressures on the system are mounting over time.

Thus suggestions for reform focus more on longer-term structural changes in the system.

One option is to apply a surtax to OAS funds received by persons with incomes over a threshold level (say, around $25,000). This would increase equity and would save up to $1 billion of net federal expenditures, but it has the inefficient aspect of paying out the funds with one hand and recovering them with the other, resulting in a deadweight loss equal to the costs of disbursement and collection.

A second suggestion is to index the GIS fully while de-indexing the OAS. Inflation would then slowly phase out the OAS by reducing its real value, while the fully indexed GIS would protect the elderly poor from genuine poverty. This might be politically more practicable than removing the program from the statute books—although economists tend to oppose letting inflation bring in implicitly policies that people are unwilling to let in explicitly.

Another proposal is to follow the United States in gradually raising the eligibility age for full OAS benefits. In the United States the age is to rise from 65 to 66 between the years 2000 and 2009 and then to 67 between 2017 and 2027.

A fourth proposal is to reduce (or even eliminate) the pension income tax credit and the old age tax credit. Both of these can be argued to be anachronisms. While they may have served useful functions when they were introduced, given the low incomes of the elderly and the sparsity of other programs, they are anomalies in a world of enriched pensions, health benefits, and OAS and GIS programs.

Health Care

Taking federal and provincial payments into account, Canada's public health care system is the country's single most expensive social policy expenditure. In 1985 health expenditures accounted for 8.5 percent of Canadian GDP. The annual cost of the part of health care that is paid for by government amounted in that year to about $1,100 for every man, woman, and child in the country—or about $2,200 for every person who pays income taxes. It has also been rising rapidly in recent years.

One major possibility of cost containment is to move from the present system of *fee for service* to a system of *capitation* payments. In the system used in most of Canada, the physician and the hospital charge a prescribed fee for each service that is performed. Since under any provincial health scheme the doctor's and hospital's collection rate is 100 percent, there is no reason for the provider of health services to economize on those services. Indeed, much research shows that the rate of elective surgery—operations that are not necessary for survival but may be useful—rises with the ratio of physicians to the population. In areas where there are many physicians, the typical physician has time on his hands, and the rate of elective surgery goes up. In areas where doctors are in short supply, much less elective surgery is performed.

This illustrates a quite general point. The case for the free market is strongest when consumers are the best judges of their own needs. The case for market efficiency is greatly weakened when suppliers can determine the demand for the product they supply. But most people do not have the knowledge to second-guess their medical adviser. Thus in the many cases where judgment is needed to decide among several courses of action, all of which have something to recommend them, the evidence is that doctors create their own demand. This does not imply dishonesty on the part of doctors, merely that where judgment calls must be made, the amount of spare time available to doctors will influence their decisions, possibly unconsciously.

Health maintenance organizations (HMOs) or, as they are sometimes called, health service organizations (HSOs) provide a possible way around this problem. Large hospitals and large groups of doctors work on what is called a capitation basis. This means that the health maintenance organization is paid an annual fee for each person registered with it. Since payment is on a per capita basis rather than on a service-rendered basis, there is no incentive to prescribe more care than is needed. The HMO at Sault Ste. Marie, pioneered by the steelworkers' union and their employers, is an early and successful Canadian example of such an organization. In 1987 the city of Toronto agreed to start an HMO.

As with all social institutions, there are pros and cons to HMOs. They have their strong supporters and their strong detractors. No doubt their value in holding costs down while maintaining the quality of health services will be debated for a long time to come.

Conclusion

We have seen that Canada's social policy is made up of a complex system of transfers and tax expenditures. There is no doubt that it achieves many of its goals. There is also no doubt that the system could be improved by an integrated set of reforms. Some critics also assert that it is run by an often impersonal bureaucracy that is frequently overrun with red tape. They would like to see decentralization and more funds provided for private-sector experimentation. We say little about such complaints here, not because we believe them to be unfounded but because they are not easy to assess. A more detailed treatment would, however, have to pay them considerable attention.

Reforming the system is unpopular because people who run the risk of losing some net benefits tend to be very vocal and to find ready political champions. It remains to be seen whether any Canadian government will have the political courage to attempt a major overhaul of the system—an overhaul that most observers feel could make the system fairer, less costly, yet more effective but would cause a short-term political outcry.

Summary

1. Canadian governments have been urged to re-examine and redesign social programs with the twin objectives of improving their ability to deliver benefits to the intended beneficiaries and reducing costs wherever possible.
2. Some social programs, called demogrants, are universal, paying ben-

efits to anyone meeting such minimal requirements as residence or age. Other programs are selective, which usually means that they are income-tested. Some are taxable and so confer after-tax benefits that decline as income rises; others are not taxable and so confer after-tax benefits that are independent of income. Some are expenditure programs (including direct transfers to persons), and others are delivered through the tax system in the form of special tax concessions (called tax expenditures). Some programs are administered by the federal government, some by the provincial governments, and still others by the municipalities.

3. Three major challenges must be met by a successful Canadian social spending policy for the 1990s. These are the challenges posed by government deficits, technological changes, and demographic trends. In the absence of renewed economic growth and major new revenue sources, it is not a question of whether social programs should be rationalized but of how this should be done.
4. Social programs, and proposed changes to them, must be understood in the context of the overall tax-transfer system.
5. Social policies cannot be evaluated without value judgments about desirable goals and trade-offs among objectives. In evaluating social policies, attention must be paid to vertical and horizontal equity and to the effective marginal tax rate implied by the terms of any program. When a person simultaneously pays income taxes and receives income-tested social benefits, the explicit income tax rate and the implicit tax-back rate applied to the social benefits are said to be *stacked*. Because of the high rate at which many income-tested benefits are reduced as income rises, the effective marginal tax rate—equal to the sum of the tax-back rates on social benefits received and the marginal income tax rate—faced by many beneficiaries can become very high. These high effective tax rates create disincentives, such as encouraging people to withhold labor services from the market.
6. In open economies it is also necessary to consider the effect of the tax-transfer system on the movement of mobile labor and capital.
7. In changing economies it is also necessary to ensure that measures designed to increase economic security do not seriously inhibit adjustment to change.
8. Although there has been much rhetoric about preserving the universality of Canada's social welfare system, the facts that many schemes are income-tested and that many benefits are taxable mean that the whole system is progressive, with net benefits tending to fall as income rises.
9. The two major categories of programs are human resource development programs, which include post-secondary education, job creation, and unemployment insurance, and the income transfer and security programs. This second category includes unemployment insurance, public assistance programs (welfare), child benefits schemes (family allowances, the child tax exemption, and the child tax credit), benefits for the elderly (RRSPs, the CPP, private-sector

pensions, and retirement income security programs), and health care, which, when provincial and federal expenditures are counted, is the single most expensive social program in the country, accounting for over 8 percent of total national income.

Topics for Review

Types of social programs
Fiscal, economic, and demographic pressures
Vertical and horizontal equity
Universal versus selective programs
Demogrants
Tax exemptions and tax credits
Adjustment versus security
Disincentives and social costs

Discussion Questions

1. Discuss the concept of universality as it applies to the family allowance system.
2. Writing in a recent conference volume, Queen's University professor Keith Banting wrote the following:

   > The issue is not whether we want a universal or selective welfare state. Rather the questions are what is the basic structure of the universal programs which we must maintain, and what is the appropriate supplement of selective programs which can be woven in and around that basic universal structure or framework.

   Discuss this quotation.
3. Discuss the implications for social policy objectives of basing social programs on family rather than individual income.
4. Is the deduction allowed for contributions to RRSP plans regressive?
5. In a 1985 book about Britain, Hermione Parker listed 10 reasons why the British tax and benefit system must be changed:

   > It is incomprehensible.
   > It is uncoordinated.
   > It is unnecessarily expensive to administer.
   > It is a system of pauperization, not a welfare state.
   > It is a major cause of unemployment.
   > It is deteriorating, not improving.
   > It is discriminatory, arbitrary, and unfair.
   > It penalizes marriage and subsidizes family breakup.
   > It destabilizes and divides society.
   > It undermines the rule of law.

   Assess several of these in the context of the Canadian system.

6. In the February 1986 federal budget, Finance Minister Michael Wilson identified four objectives for reform of social policy:

   Maintaining universal access
   Directing more resources to the people most in need

Improving opportunities for individuals to become self-reliant
Reducing the after-tax value of benefits to higher-income Canadians who do not need assistance

Examine a couple of existing programs (or recent reforms) in terms of these criteria.

7. How would converting the basic personal income exemption to a tax credit affect the disincentives faced by the low-income spouse entering the labor market?
8. "As currently constituted, the unemployment insurance program has very little to do with either unemployment or insurance." Discuss.

PART EIGHT

National Income and Fiscal Policy

26

An Introduction to Macroeconomics

Inflation, unemployment, recession, and economic growth are everyday words. Governments worry about how to prevent recessions and how to increase growth. After having reduced the inflation rate in the early 1980s, governments now worry about how to keep inflation under control while continuing to fight unemployment. Firms are concerned about how inflation affects their costs and how recessions affect their sales. Households are anxious to avoid the unemployment that comes with recessions and to protect themselves against the hazards of inflation.

What Is Macroeconomics?

Each of the concerns mentioned above plays a major role in macroeconomics. As we saw in Chapter 3 (see pages 49–54), economics is customarily divided into two main branches, microeconomics and macroeconomics. Now we look further at the difference between the two approaches to the economy and in more detail at what constitutes macroeconomics.

Macroeconomics studies in broad outline the flow of income in the economy (illustrated in Figure 3-1) without dwelling on much of its interesting but sometimes confusing detail. In contrast, microeconomics deals with the behavior of individual markets, such as the market for wheat, coal, or strawberries.

The following example illustrates the difference between the two branches of economics.

A microeconomic issue. For decades automobile prices fell in relation to the prices of most other commodities. Beginning in the 1970s this trend was reversed, and automobiles became increasingly expensive relative to many other goods and services. In microeconomics we seek to understand the causes and effects of such changes in relative prices.

A macroeconomic issue. Over the decades, as well as changing relative to other prices, automobile prices have tended to follow the general trend of all prices to rise. The average of all prices is called the *price level*. Why does the price level stay relatively stable in some periods and rise rapidly in others? In macroeconomics we seek to understand the causes and effects of changes in the general price level.

Major Macroeconomic Issues

The economy proceeds in fits and starts rather than in a smooth pattern. Why did the 1930s see the greatest economic depression in recorded history, with up to a fifth of the Canadian labor force unemployed and with massive unemployment in all other major industrial countries? Why were the 25 years following World War II a period of sustained boom with only minor interruptions from modest recessions? Why did the early 1980s see the onset of the worst worldwide recession since the 1930s? What fueled the recovery of the mid-1980s?

Why did the pace of inflation during the 1970s and early 1980s reach levels never before seen in peacetime in most advanced Western nations? Has our attitude toward inflation permanently changed? In the early 1970s when inflation crept up to 4 percent, concern was so great that emergency measures were considered. By the mid-1980s the government was claiming credit for having reduced inflation to 4 percent.

Alternating bouts of inflationary boom and deflationary slump have caused many policy headaches in the past. Why were the recessions of the 1970s and early 1980s accompanied not only by their familiar companion, high unemployment, but also by an unexpected fellow traveler, rapid inflation? Will stagflation—simultaneous high unemployment and rapid inflation—return?

Both total output and output per person have risen for several decades in many countries. These long-term trends have meant rising average living standards. Does the slowdown in worldwide growth rates over the 1970s and early 1980s represent a basic change in underlying trends, or is it just a reflection of a prolonged downturn? Can governments do anything to affect growth rates?

Key Macroeconomic Variables

The price level, employment, and total output are key variables in macroeconomics. We hear about them on television; politicians give campaign speeches about them; economists theorize about them. Why are we concerned about them? How have they behaved over the past half century?

Index Numbers

Many key macro variables are expressed as index numbers, so our first task is to understand them.

Macroeconomists frequently ask such questions as "How much have prices risen this year?" or "Has the nation's output increased this year and, if so, by how much?" There is no perfectly satisfactory way to answer these questions because all prices do not move together and because one cannot add tons of steel, pieces of furniture, and gallons of gasoline to get a meaningful total. Yet these are not foolish questions. There *are* trends in prices and production, and thus there are real phenomena to describe. It is of little direct help to someone who wants to know about how prices have changed over some period of time to be given a list of changes in 4,682 individual prices.

Index numbers are statistical measures that are used to give summary answers to the inherently complex questions of the kind just suggested. Note that price indexes provide a measure of the *average* of all prices included, while quantity indexes provide a measure of the *total* of all quantities included. We refer to both the average of prices and the total of quantities as an *aggregate* measure. **Index numbers** measure the percentage change that has occurred in some aggregate over some particular time span. They point to overall tendencies or general drifts, not to detailed facts.

Calculating index numbers. To calculate any index number, we must have a procedure to add up the individual items that are to be included. Such a procedure involves assigning "weights" to the individual items.

Why do we bother with weights? Why not simply take the average of all prices or the sum of all units of output?

A moment's reflection suggests the answer. Changes in the price of bread, for example, are much more important to the average consumer than changes in the price of, say, caviar. Similarly, producing 1,000 additional automobiles is more important for the economy than producing 1,000 additional can openers. Weights are chosen to reflect the importance of each price. Usually the weights are the quantities from some particular period, called the *base period for weighting purposes.*

Once the weights are chosen, the aggregate can be calculated for each period, usually a year. For example, it might be $600 million in 1982, $720 million in 1985, and $900 million in 1988. Next, some **base period** for comparison purposes (or **base year**) is chosen.[1] The value of the aggregate for each period can then be prorated by dividing it by the value for the base period and multiplying by 100. The resulting series is called an *index number series*; by construction the base period value in this series equals 100. In the example, if 1982 is chosen as the base year for comparison purposes, the index would be 100 in 1982, 120 in 1985, and 150 in 1988.

Index numbers are constructed by assigning weights to reflect the importance of the individual items being combined. The value of the index is set equal to 100 in the base period.

An index number always compares two or more time periods. If a particular index number for 1985 is equal to 130 with 1982 as the base year (i.e., 1982 equals 100), the index shows an increase between 1982 and 1985 of 30 percent in whatever is being measured.

Interpreting index numbers. People often treat these numbers as though they had an accuracy and significance their compilers do not claim for them, but being aware of their limitations should not lead one to neglect index numbers for the useful information they can show: average changes over time. We shall learn more about index numbers in Chapter 27.

The Price Level and Inflation

The **price level** refers to an index number computed from the prices of a broad group of goods and services. It is usually denoted by the symbol P. One common index number of prices is the *Consumer Price Index, or CPI,* computed by Statistics Canada. We will learn more about the details of how the CPI and other price indexes are constructed in the next chapter.

The **inflation rate** is the percentage rate of increase in some price index from one period to another. In the rare event of a drop in the price level, we speak of a *deflation*. The formula for measuring the inflation rate is as follows:

$$\textbf{Inflation rate} = \frac{P_2 - P_1}{P_1} \times 100\%$$

where P_1 is the price level in the first period and P_2 is the price level in the second period.

If the periods being compared are not a year apart, it is common to convert the result to an *annual rate*. For example, if the CPI was 150 last month and rose by 1 percent during the month to 151.5, we might say that over the last month the price level rose at an *annual* rate of approximately 12 percent. This means that *if* the rate of increase persisted for a year, the price level would rise by 12 percent over the year. Box 26-1 (p. 554) identifies a source of confusion that sometimes arises from failing to distinguish other ways of calculating the annual inflation rate.

Inflation: The Historical Experience

Figure 26-1 shows the behavior of the price level and the inflation rate for the period 1930 to 1986. In this figure, the price level is measured by the Consumer Price Index and the inflation rate by the annual rate of change of the CPI. Several facts stand out.

First, the price level is constantly changing, although by a rate that varies considerably from year to year, as reflected by the fluctuations in the inflation rate.

Second, and more important, in only 2 out of the 57 observations did the price level fall; in all 55 other years the inflation rate was positive. The cumulative effect of this sequence of steady price increases is quite dramatic; in 1986 the price level was more than six times higher than that in 1930.

The price level has displayed a distinct upward trend in recent decades.

[1] Usually, but not always, the base period *for weighting purposes* and the base period *for comparison purposes* are the same. For simplicity we use the term *base period* to refer to both concepts.

FIGURE 26-1 The Canadian Price Level and Inflation Rate, 1930–1986

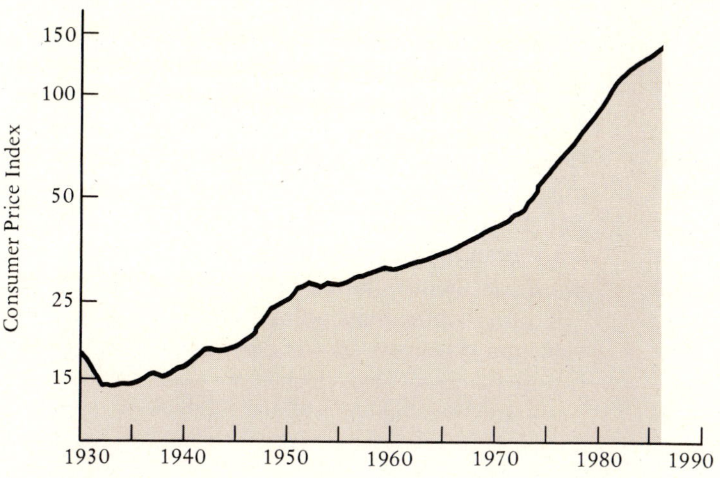

(i) Price level

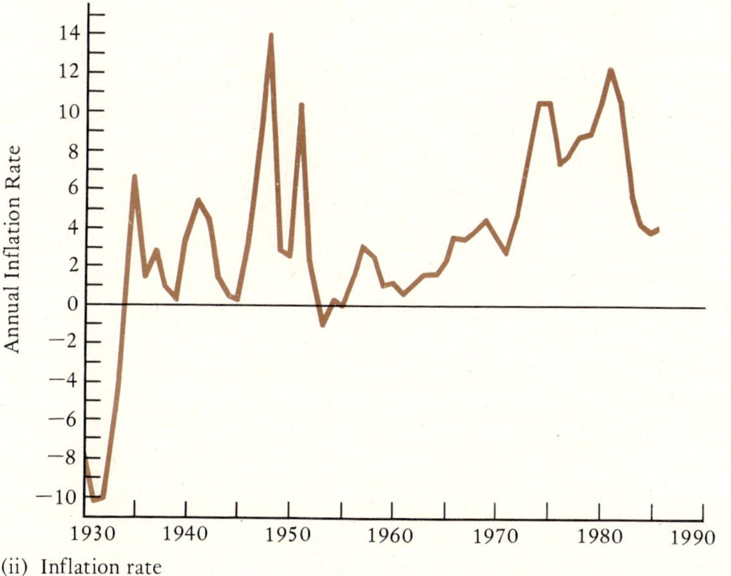

(ii) Inflation rate

(i) The overwhelming trend movement in the price level has been upward over the past 50 years. The data are for the consumer's price index from 1930 to 1986 with 1981 equal to 100. They are plotted on a semi-log scale where equal vertical distances represent equal percentage changes. Any acceleration in the rate of increase in the price level shows up as increasing steepness of the curve.

(ii) The rate of inflation has varied from −10 percent to +14 percent over the period since 1930. Prices fell dramatically during the onset of the Great Depression. They rose sharply during and after World War II and during the Korean War. Although variable, there was no discernible trend in the inflation rate from the end of the Korean War to the mid 1960s. The period starting in the mid 1960s, however, experienced a strong upward trend in the inflation rate, interrupted by short-term fluctuations. In 1983, however, the inflation rate fell to the lowest figure since the early 1970s, and it has remained in the four percent range ever since. (*Source:* M.C. Urquhart, ed., *Historical Statistics of Canada;* Department of Finance, *Economic Review.*)

Third, whereas the long-term trend stands out when one looks at the price level, the short-term fluctuations stand out when one looks at the inflation rate. The general rise in inflation from the mid-1960s through the mid-1980s is quite marked—from 1965 to 1974 inflation averaged 4.7 percent, while from 1975 to 1984 it averaged 9.1 percent! The sharp swings in the inflation rate in the late 1970s and early 1980s are even more dramatic. The increase in the inflation rate to double-digit levels in 1974 and again in 1979 are associated with major shocks to the world price of oil and foodstuffs, while the declines in inflation that followed were delayed responses to major recessions. Note that even when the *inflation rate* falls (as it did in 1982, for example), *as long as inflation remains positive, the price level rises.*

BOX 26-1

Understanding Annual Rates

New values of the index numbers for many key macroeconomic variables are announced each month. But the announcements often lead to a confusing array of interpretations of what the numbers mean for the annual rate of change of the variable in question.

Consider a hypothetical example. The release of the latest monthly figure for a particular price index (PI) for some country, by that country's Bureau of Statistics, elicits the following three responses: "Inflation receding," reads a newspaper headline; "Inflation continues to rise," reports a TV newscaster; "Inflation unchanged," says the official releasing the statistic.

How can this be when all three commentators are talking about the same announcement? The different interpretations arise from different ways of converting monthly statistics into an annual rate of change. (The problem can arise with any index number.)

To understand what is involved, consider the hypothetical values for the PI set out in the table. According to the table, at the end of 1984 the PI (100.0) exceeded its average for the year (95.2). At the end of 1985 it was the same (100.0) as at the start of the year and equal to its average for the year; assume that it was in fact constant and equal to 100 for *each* month of 1985. In 1986 prices started to rise again.

Date	PI	Date	PI
December 1984	100.0	October 1986	106.8
1984 average	95.2	November 1986	108.9
		December 1986	110.0
December 1985	100.0	1986 average	105.0
1985 average	100.0		

Annual averages are the sum of the 12 monthly figures for the calendar year divided by 12.

Comparing annual averages. In stating that the inflation rate was unchanged, the official was comparing annual averages. Comparing the 1984 average PI (95.2) and the 1985 average (100.0) gave a change of approximately 5 percent, as did comparing the 1985 average (100.0) with the 1986 average (105.0). Thus, concludes the official, the annual inflation rate had stayed constant at 5 percent over the two years.

Comparing this month with the same month last year. Using this procedure, the annual inflation rate in December 1986 is 10 percent; in December 1986 the PI is 10 percent higher than it was in December 1985. In November 1986 the annual inflation rate was only 9 percent, since the PI was 9 percent higher than in November 1985. Using this measure the annual inflation rate increased from 9 percent to 10 percent during the month. This procedure could lie behind the television news report that inflation is rising.

Comparing this month with last month. Using this method, the annual inflation rate in December 1986 was 12 percent; the PI had risen by 1 percent over the month, and the annual rate is approximately 12 times the monthly percentage change. In November 1986 the annual inflation rate had been 24 percent, since the November PI was 2 percent higher than the October figure. This calculation would provide the basis for the headline that inflation is receding.

Which Measure Is Best?

Properly understood, all three measures give useful and complementary information.

Comparing annual averages is the least erratic. But because it focuses almost entirely on underlying trends, it is not sensitive to current changes. In our example it misses the stability in prices that prevailed throughout 1985 and the fairly sharp upturn in prices that was apparent in 1986.

Comparing this month with the same month last year is more sensitive to current events. However, it gives a lot of weight to particular events in the most recent month, events that often have little to do with the underlying trend of prices.

Comparing this month with last month is the most erratic measure. The timing of major price changes at or near the end of the month will have a substantial accidental effect on the measure. For some purposes this sensitivity may be desirable, but for understanding the underlying trend in inflation, it is misleading.

The three measures can be used selectively to support almost any position. But people who understand the meaning of each measure need not be fooled by such selective presentation of the data. Figures lie only to those uninformed about what a measure does and does not say.

Why Inflation Is a Matter of Concern

Changes in the price level are associated with changes in the **purchasing power of money** or **value of money**. Both terms refer to the amount of goods and services that can be purchased with a given amount of money. The purchasing power of money is negatively related to the price level. (For example, if the price level doubles, a dollar will buy only half as much.) Thus inflation, which is a rise in the general level of all prices, reduces the purchasing power of money. Conversely, the purchasing power of money rises whenever the price level falls.

Unanticipated inflation. Any given rate of inflation tends to cause more harm when it is unforeseen than when it is foreseen. Contracts freely entered into when the inflation rate is expected to remain constant will mean hardships for some and windfall gains for others if the inflation rate changes unexpectedly.

For example, consider a wage contract that specifies wage increases of 3 percent. If both employers and workers expect the price level to remain constant, then they expect that the purchasing power of wages paid will rise by 3 percent as a result of the new contract. But if the price level unexpectedly rises by 10 percent over the course of the wage contract, the workers' wages will be able to buy less than they would have before the wage increase was negotiated. A 3 percent increase in money wages combined with a 10 percent increase in prices means a reduction in the purchasing power of wages of about 7 percent.

Inflation also has different effects on borrowers and lenders. Suppose that when the price level is expected to be constant, a bank lends a customer $100 in return for a promise to repay $105 a year hence. If the price level rises during the year, the purchasing power of the $105 repaid will be less than it was expected to be; hence the borrower benefits and the lender suffers relative to their expectations.

One of the most serious effects of inflation is what it does to anyone living on a fixed money income. If a retirement pension specifies an income as so many dollars per year, a rise in the price level lowers the purchasing power of that income. For example, anyone who retired on a fixed money income in 1970 found the purchasing power of that income reduced to about one fourth of its original value by 1985. This means that the retiree could buy in 1985 only one fourth what could be bought in 1970. For such people, rapid inflation causes a great loss of purchasing power.

Some effects of inflation can be avoided by indexing. **Indexing** links the payments made under the terms of a contract to changes in the price level. For example, a retirement pension might specify that it will pay the beneficiary $15,000 per year starting in 1990 and that the amount paid will increase each year in proportion to the increase in some specified index of the price level. Thus if the price index rises by 10 percent between 1990 and 1991, the pension payable in 1991 would rise by 10 percent, to $16,500.

Anticipated inflation. Indexing provides an automatic correction that does not require anticipating future changes in the price level. However, even without formal indexing, it is possible to allow for the effects of inflation if the rise in the price level is anticipated and contracts take account of the expected rise.

Wage and price contracts are major examples. If, say, inflation of 10 percent is expected over the next year, a money wage that rises by 10 percent over that period will keep the expected purchasing power of wages at a constant level. A money wage that increases by 13 percent will provide a 3 percent increase in the expected purchasing power of wages—10 percent to preserve purchasing power in the face of the expected rise in prices and 3 percent to increase the real purchasing power of the wages.

Labor Force Variables

Employment denotes the number of adult workers (defined in Canada as workers aged 15 and older, including those in the military) who hold jobs. **Unemployment** denotes the number of adult workers who are not employed and are actively searching for a job. The **labor force** is the total number of employed and unemployed. The **unemployment rate**, usually represented by the symbol U, is unemployment expressed as a percentage of the labor force:

$$U = \frac{\textbf{unemployed}}{\textbf{labor force}} \times 100\%$$

Unemployment: The Historical Experience

Figure 26-2(i) shows the trends in the labor force, employment, and unemployment since 1930. Despite booms and slumps in the economy, the main trend has clearly been growth in employment that roughly matches growth in the labor force. The growth in both reflects growth in the total population, although the labor force and employment have recently grown faster than the total population. This fact reflects the steadily increasing participation of youths and women in the labor force.

Although the long-term growth trend dominates the employment figures, some unemployment is always present. Figure 26-2(ii) shows that the short-term fluctuations in the unemployment rate have been quite marked. The unemployment rate has been as low as 1.4 percent in 1944 and as high as 19.3 percent in 1933; in the period since 1955 the unemployment rate fell as low as 3.4 percent in 1956 and rose as high as 12.6 percent in 1983.

The high unemployment rate of the Great Depression in the early 1930s tends to dwarf the fluctuations in unemployment that have occurred since then. This is misleading since, as we shall see, the fluctuations in unemployment in recent decades have been neither minor nor unimportant.

Unemployment can rise not only when employment falls but also when the labor force rises. In recent decades the number of people entering the labor force has exceeded the number leaving it. The resulting rise in the labor force has meant that unemployment has sometimes grown even in periods when employment was also growing.

Consideration of employment and unemployment suggests another concept, that of *full employment*. Full employment does not mean zero unemployment. There is a constant turnover of individuals in given jobs and a constant change in job opportunities. New members enter the work force, some people quit their jobs, and others are fired. It may take some time for these people to find jobs. So at any time there is unemployment due to the normal turnover of labor that exists in any economy. Such unemployment is called **frictional unemployment**.

Full employment is said to occur when all existing unemployment is frictional. When the economy is at less than full employment, other types of unemployment, including cyclical (or deficient-demand) unemployment and real-wage unemployment, are present in addition to frictional unemployment. We shall study these in more detail in Chapter 37.[2]

The unemployment rate that occurs when the economy is at full employment is often called the **natural rate of unemployment**. Estimates of the natural rate of unemployment are difficult to obtain and are often a source of disagreement among economists. Nevertheless, such estimates are a useful benchmark against which to gauge the current performance of the economy, as measured by the actual unemployment rate. Estimates indicate that the natural rate rose throughout the 1970s from around 5.5 percent to a high of around 7.5 percent in the late 1970s and has now stabilized or may even be declining. (We shall discuss the reasons for these changes in Chapter 37.)

Why Unemployment Is a Matter of Concern

The social and political significance of the unemployment rate is enormous. The government is blamed when it is high and takes credit when it is low. Few macroeconomic policies are planned without some consideration of how they affect the unemployment rate. No other summary statistic, with the possible exception of the inflation rate, carries as much weight in setting macroeconomic policy as does the unemployment rate.

Unemployment causes economic waste and human suffering. The economic waste is obvious. Human effort is the least durable of economic commodities. If a fully employed economy with a constant labor force has 20 million people willing to work in 1988, their services must either be used in 1988 or wasted. When the services of only 18 million are used because 10 percent of the labor force is unemployed, the potential output of 2 million workers is lost forever. In an economy where there is not enough output to meet everyone's needs, any waste of potential output seems undesirable, and large wastes seem tragic.

The human cost of unemployment is also obvious. Severe hardship and misery can be caused by

[2] In that chapter we shall also distinguish a particular type of frictional unemployment called structural unemployment.

FIGURE 26-2 Canadian Labor Force, Employment and Unemployment, 1930–1986

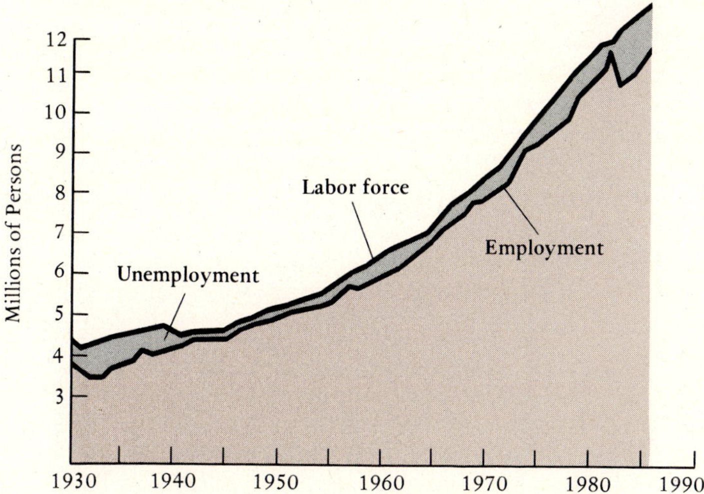

(i) Labor force, employment, and unemployment

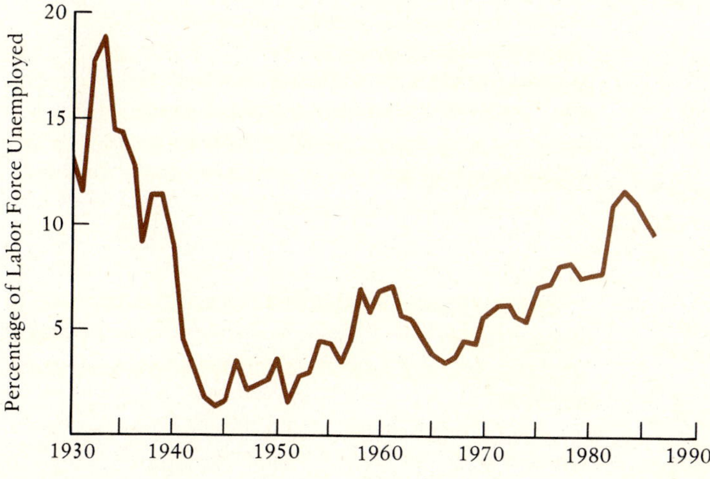

(ii) Unemployment rate

(i) The labor force and employment have grown since the 1930s with only a few interruptions. The size of the Canadian labor force has more than doubled since 1930, and so has the number of the employed. The fall in the labor force in the early 1940s was in the civilian labor force. The missing workers were in the military. Unemployment, the gap between the labor force and employment, has fluctuated. It reached a peak of 800,000 in 1933 and did not reach that level again until 1977. In 1983 it reached 1½ million, although as we see in (ii), as a fraction of the labor force this is smaller than the 1933 figure.

(ii) The unemployment rate responds to the cyclical behavior of the economy. Booms are associated with low unemployment, slumps with high unemployment. The Great Depression of the 1930s produced record unemployment rates for an entire decade. During World War II unemployment rates fell to very low levels. Since 1945, however, the unemployment rate has demonstrated a gradual upward trend. The recession of the early 1980s produced unemployment rates second only to those of the 1930s; these rates were extremely high by the standards of the post-World War II behavior of the Canadian economy. Over the period 1983–1986 the rate fell slowly but steadily, reaching 9.4 percent at the end of 1986. (*Source:* M.C. Urquhart, ed., *Historical Statistics of Canada*; Department of Finance, *Economic Review.*)

prolonged periods of unemployment. A person's spirit can be broken by a long period of wanting work but being unable to find it. Crime, divorce, and general social unrest usually rise with unemployment.

In the not so distant past, only private charity or help from friends and relatives stood between the unemployed and starvation. Today welfare and unemployment insurance have softened those effects. However, when an economic slump is deep and prolonged, as in the mid-1970s and again in the early 1980s, people begin to exhaust their unemployment insurance and must fall back on savings, welfare, or charity. In the early 1980s many people sank below the poverty level for the first time in their lives. They did so because they had used up their unemployment insurance, but were unable to find jobs because of a persistently high unemployment level.

Output and Income Variables

The value of a nation's total production of goods and services is called its *national product.* Since all the value that is produced must ultimately belong to someone in the form of a claim on that value, the national product is equal to the total income claims generated by the production of goods and services. Hence when we study *national product,* we are also studying *national income.*

There are several related measures of the nation's total output and total income. Their various definitions and calculations, and the relationships among them, are discussed in detail in the next chapter. In this chapter we use the generic term **national income** to refer to both the value of total output and the value of the income generated by the production of that output.

Aggregating Total Output

To measure total output, quantities of a variety of goods must somehow be added up, or *aggregated.* Just as there is a problem in obtaining an "average" of the variety of prices in the economy, so is there a problem in obtaining a measure of the total output of the wide variety of goods and services produced in the economy.

Consider this problem in terms of a single firm. If that firm produces only a single, well-defined commodity, say, loaves of French bread, then to measure its total output all we need do is sum the number of loaves baked during the period under consideration. But if it also produces muffins, fancy pastries, cakes, and doughnuts, we have to find a way of adding its output of these different products.

The same problem arises when we try to add the outputs of literally hundreds of thousands of different goods and services to measure the nation's total output.

We do this by summing *values* of the different products. We cannot add tons of steel to loaves of bread, but we can add the money value of steel production to the money value of bread production. By multiplying the physical output of a good by its price per unit and then summing this value for all goods produced in the nation, we can find the quantity of total output *measured in dollars.*

Real and Nominal Values

The total just described gives the *money value* of national output, often called **nominal national income**. When nominal national income changes, it is important to know to what extent the change is due to a change in prices and to what extent it is due to a change in quantities produced. To answer this question we calculate **real national income**, a measure of total output in which the value of individual outputs is measured not at current prices but at the prices that prevailed in some base period chosen for this purpose.[3] Real national income is denoted by the symbol *Y.*

Real national income tells us the value of current output measured at base period prices, that is, the sum of the quantities valued at prices prevailing in the base period. Comparing the real national income for different years provides a measure of the change in real output that has occurred during the interval between the years.

Since prices are held constant in calculating it, real national income changes only when output quantities change.

[3] Nominal national income is often referred to as *money* national income or *current dollar* national income. Real national income is often called *constant dollar* national income.

Since our interest is almost exclusively with the real output of goods and services, we shall take the term *national income* (and output) to refer to *real national income* unless otherwise specified. (For an example of this important distinction, see Box 27-3 on page 572.)

National Income: The Historical Experience

In order to look at the actual experience of national income, in this section we look at one of the most commonly used measures, called *gross domestic product*, or GDP.[4] The details of its calculation are discussed in Chapter 27. GDP can be measured in either real or nominal terms; in this section we focus on real GDP.

Part (i) of Figure 26-3 shows real GDP produced by the Canadian economy since 1930; part (ii) shows the annual percentage rate of growth of real GDP for the same period. The series in part (i) shows two kinds of movement. The major one is a trend increase that resulted in a sevenfold increase of real output in the half century from 1932 to 1982. Since the trend has generally been upward in the modern era, it is referred to as *economic growth*.

Long-term growth in real national income is reflected in the trend increase in real GDP.

A second feature of the real GDP series is the short-term fluctuations around the trend, often described as the cyclical behavior of the economy. Overall growth so dominates the real GDP series that this cyclical behavior is hardly visible in part (i) of Figure 26-3. However, as can be seen in part (ii), cyclical fluctuations in real GDP have not been insignificant.

The cyclical behavior of real national income is reflected in the annual fluctuations in the growth rate of real GDP.

Why National Income Is a Matter of Concern

Short-run fluctuations in national income reflect the ebbs and flows of economic activity referred to as the *business cycle*. In periods of high activity, often called *booms* or *expansions*, real GDP and employment are high and unemployment is low. In periods of low activity, called *slumps* or *contractions*, real GDP and employment are low and unemployment is correspondingly high. Policymakers care about short-term fluctuations in national income because slumps bring unwanted unemployment and output foregone, and booms may create strong inflationary pressures.

The long-run trend in real national income is also important. Not only has national income grown, but real income per person (also called real income per capita) has also grown. Indeed, it has more than tripled in the last 60 years. When income per person grows, each generation can expect, on average, to be substantially better off than preceding ones. For example, if real income per capita grows at the relatively modest rate of 1.5 percent per year, the average person's lifetime income expectancy will be *twice* that of his or her grandparents. (Of course, although on average people are better off, it does not follow that every individual will in fact be better off.)

Potential Income and the Output Gap

Actual national income is what the economy does in fact produce. We now introduce the important additional concept of **potential national income**, or just **potential income**, also called *full-employment national income*.[5]

[4] Until very recently, national income in Canada was typically discussed in terms of another measure, gross *national* product (GNP). In 1986, in order to follow international convention more closely and thus facilitate international comparisions, Statistics Canada began reporting national income in terms of gross *domestic* product (GDP). As we will see in the next chapter, the two measures are closely related, and for most purposes it does not really matter which measure is used.

[5] The words *real* and *actual* have similar meanings in everyday usage, but they are used quite differently in this context of describing national income. *Real* national income is distinguished from *nominal* national income, while *actual* national income is distinguished from *potential* national income. The latter both refer to real measures, so the full descriptions are actual real national income and potential real national income.

FIGURE 26-3 Canadian Real National Income and Growth Rate, 1930–1986

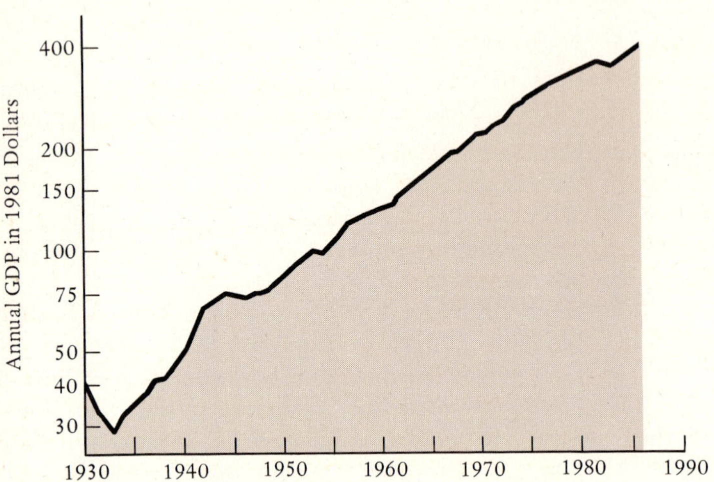

(i) Annual GNP/GDP in constant (1981) dollars

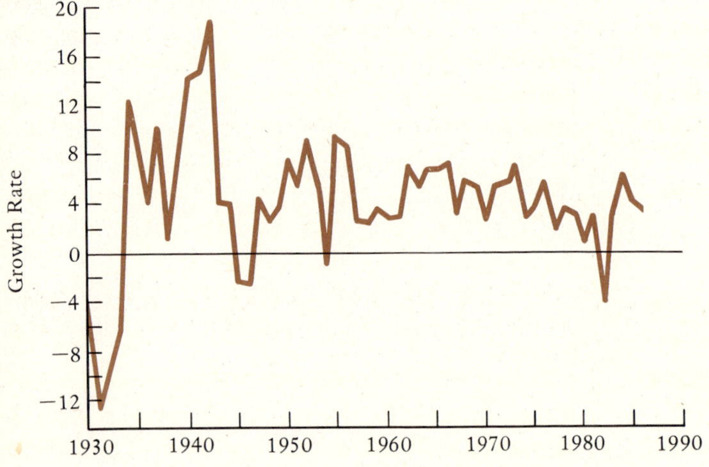

(ii) Annual rate of growth of GNP/GDP in constant (1981) dollars

(i) Real national income, which measures the total production of goods and services produced in the economy over the period of a year, has grown steadily since 1930, with only a few interruptions. In (i) we see the long-term growth of the economy reflected in the upward trend of real national income. Shorter-term fluctuations are obscured by this trend in (i) but are highlighted in (ii).

(ii) Real growth in the economy, as measured by the annual rate of change of real national income, has fluctuated considerably but has been mostly positive. In (ii) the short-term fluctuations are readily apparent, but the long-term upward trend still shows up because the majority of observations are positive.

(Data prior to 1947 are based on GNP; data for 1947–1986 are based on GDP, which is now the standard measure of real national income; see footnote 4 on page 559.) *Source:* M.C. Urquhart, ed., *Historical Statistics of Canada;* Department of Finance, *Economic Review*.

Potential national income is what the economy would produce if its productive resources were fully employed at their normal intensity of use.

This would mean, in terms of labor force variables, that any unemployment of labor is frictional and thus that the unemployment rate is equal to the natural rate of unemployment. It would also mean that the nation's factories and other productive equipment are being used at their normal capacity levels.

Potential national income is represented by the symbol Y^*; it refers to potential *real* income.

The Output Gap

If we subtract actual national income from potential income ($Y^* - Y$), we obtain a measure called the **output gap**.[6] It is the difference between what could have been produced at the potential or full-employment level and what is actually produced, as measured by GDP.

When the gap is positive, that is, when potential income is greater than actual real national income, the output gap is the market value of goods and services that *could have been* produced if the economy's resources had been fully employed but that *actually* went unproduced. This is sometimes referred to as the *deadweight loss of unemployment*.

Slumps in business activity are associated with large positive output gaps, booms with small ones. In a major boom the gap may even become negative, indicating that actual national income exceeds the economy's potential national income. A negative output gap can arise because potential income is defined for a normal rate of utilization of factors of production, and there are many ways in which these normal rates can be exceeded temporarily. Labor may work longer hours than normal; factories may operate an extra shift or not close for routine repairs and maintenance. Although these expedients are only temporary, they are effective in the short run.

Measuring potential national income is not straightforward since it cannot be observed directly. The problem is not only one of observation and measurement but also one of establishing acceptable definitions for such concepts as "normal level of utilization" and "full-employment capacity." Because Y^* is hard to measure, the output gap is correspondingly hard to measure.[7]

Potential Income and the Output Gap: The Historical Experience

Figure 26-4 shows the output gap for the Canadian economy for the years 1954–1986. Growth in the economy's productive capacity means that potential income has risen steadily. Actual real national income has roughly kept pace with potential, but has fluctuated around it. The difference between the two, the output gap, thus reflects fluctuations of real national income around a rising trend.

Fluctuations in economic activity are apparent from fluctuations in the size of the output gap. The deadweight loss from unemployment over any time span is indicated by the overall size of the gap over that span. It is shown in the figure by the shaded area between the curve and the horizontal line, which represents the level at which actual equals potential output.

Why Potential Income and the Output Gap Are Matters of Concern

Potential national income measures the economy's capacity to produce goods and services and hence its capacity to generate income for its people. Because potential income is measured at normal utilization rates of the economy's factors of production, changes in it do not reflect short-term cyclical fluctuations but rather the long-term trend in potential level of output and income. It is this long-term trend that is important for changes in living standards from generation to generation. The low living standards at

[6] Unfortunately economics, in common with most living and changing subjects, has no agreed, standard set of terms. In countries where the GNP is the standard measure of output, this gap is often called the GNP gap. Where GDP is the standard measure, it could be called the GDP gap. *Output gap* is more general and is a common international term, so we adopt it here.

[7] Just as the unemployment rate is not zero when the economy is at full employment, measured capacity utilization is not 100 percent. In fact, manufacturing capacity utilization has exceeded 90 percent only once since 1956, and its normal value is in the 80 to 85 percent range.

FIGURE 26-4 The Output Gap, 1954–1986

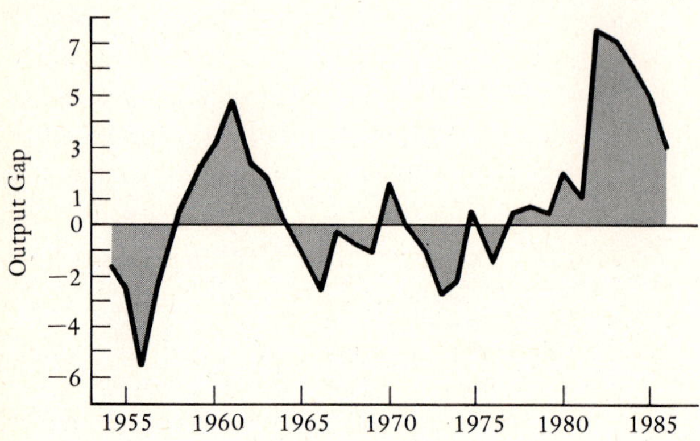

The output gap measures the difference between the economy's potential output and its actual output; it is expressed here as a percentage of potential output. The cyclical behavior of the economy is clearly apparent from the behavior of the output gap from 1954 to 1983. Slumps in economic activity cause large gaps, booms reduce the gap. The recession of 1982–1983 and the sustained recovery over the period 1983–1986 are both evident in the figure. The shaded area above the zero line represents the deadweight loss from unemployment. (*Source*: Pre 1983, from the Department of Finance, *Economic Review*; post 1983, from authors' calculations.)

the start of the Industrial Revolution are no longer with us, primarily because economic growth has resulted in more and more output for less and less work over the past century.

The output gap is important because it reflects the actual performance of the economy relative to its potential. A large output gap means that actual national income falls short of potential, and hence the unemployment rate will be high. It is therefore indicative of economic waste and human suffering as 540 of failure to use the economy's resources (including its human resources) at their normal intensity of use.

A negative output gap, indicating that actual national income exceeds potential, also imposes serious costs. Short-run policies that involve utilizing resources at above normal levels, in order to raise actual output temporarily, create inflationary pressures in the economy. As we saw earlier, inflation can impose severe costs on the economy.

The Relation Between Output and Employment

Output and employment (and therefore unemployment) are closely related. If more is to be produced, either more workers must be used in production or existing workers must produce more. The first change means a rise in employment; the second means a rise in output per person employed, which is called a rise in **productivity**. Increases in productivity are a major source of economic growth. (Productivity was discussed in Chapter 11 and will be discussed again in Chapter 38.)

Changes in productivity and in the labor force dominate the long-term trend of output and employment. But productivity and the labor force usually change slowly. As we study the main elements of macroeconomic theory over the next few chapters, we will treat both the labor force and productivity as constant. This not only greatly simplifies our discussion, but it is also a reasonable approximation of reality for purposes of analyzing the short-term behavior of the Canadian economy. In later chapters we study productivity changes.

A Preview

Why are the price level, national income, and employment what they are today? What causes them to change? These are some of the questions that we seek to answer in macroeconomics.

To answer them, it is useful to make a number of assumptions that serve to simplify the analysis and can be dropped later once we have mastered the simple case. We have just encountered one such assumption: that productivity and the labor force are constant in the short run, meaning that any increase in national income will be accompanied by an increase in employment and a decrease in unemployment. Hence we do not need separate theories to explain employment and unemployment—the theory of national income that we develop over the next few chapters will also serve to explain these variables. Hence we focus on explaining national income and the price level.[8]

As we have already seen in this chapter, the time series describing national income and the price level have two important properties. Both series exhibit long-term trends and short-term fluctuations around those trends. The analysis of the next few chapters is to be understood as establishing how the price level, and national income, will behave *relative to trend*. A fluctuation that takes the price level, or national income, above its long-term trend will be indicated by an increase in its value, while a fluctuation that takes the price level, or national income, below its trend will be indicated by a decrease in its value.

For simplicity, in the next few chapters we take these trend values to be constant.[9] When the trend is not constant, the results must be interpreted accordingly. For example, a force that causes national income to fall by 2 percent in the short term when its long-term trend is constant will cause it to increase by 1 percent when its long-term trend is growth at 3 percent per year. Similarly, a force that causes the price level to fall by 3 percent in the short term when the long-term trend is constant will cause the price level to rise by 2 percent when its long-term trend is inflation at 5 percent per year.

[8] In fact, we proceed sequentially by first treating the price level as given and only explaining national income, then explaining both.

[9] Later in the book we study long-term trends in inflation and growth in some detail.

Summary

1. Macroeconomics examines the behavior of such broad aggregates and averages as the price level, national income, potential national income, the output gap, employment, and unemployment.
2. Index numbers are summary measures that give the average percentage change in a set of related items between a base year and another given year.
3. The price level has displayed a continual upward trend since 1930. The inflation rate measures the rate of change of the price level. Although it fluctuates considerably, the inflation rate has been consistently positive. Inflation imposes serious costs on the economy.
4. The unemployment rate is the number of adult workers who are not employed and are actively searching for a job, expressed as a percentage of the labor force. The labor force and employment have both grown steadily for the past half century. The unemployment rate fluctuates considerably from year to year. Unemployment imposes serious costs in the form of economic waste and human suffering.
5. The value of total production of goods and services is called national product. Since production of output generates income in the form of claims on that output, it is also common to talk of national income. The most commonly used measure of Canadian national income is gross domestic product (GDP). Nominal national income

evaluates output in current prices. Real national income evaluates output in base period prices. Changes in real national income reflect changes in quantities of output produced.

6. Potential real national income measures the capacity of the economy to produce goods and services when factors of production are employed at their normal intensity of use. The output gap is the difference between potential and actual real national income.
7. The dominant theme of the economy is the growth of real output and employment. A secondary theme involves cyclical factors represented by fluctuations in output and unemployment around their trend values. To study these fluctuations, we focus on the unemployment rate and the output gap.

Topics for Review

The price level and rate of inflation
Employment, unemployment, and labor force
The unemployment rate
Real and nominal national income
Real national income and economic growth
Potential and actual national income and the output gap

Discussion Questions

1. Classify as microeconomic or macroeconomic (or both) the issues raised in the following newspaper headlines.
   a. "Lettuce crop spoils as strike hits B.C. lettuce producers."
   b. "Analysts fear rekindling of inflation as economy recovers toward full employment."
   c. "Index of industrial production falls by 4 points."
   d. "Price of bus rides soars in Centerville as city council withdraws transport subsidy."
   e. "A fall in the unemployment rate signals the beginning of the end of the recession in the Edmonton area."
   f. "Silicon chip technology brings falling prices and growing sales of microcomputers."
   g. "Rising costs of imported raw materials cause most Canadian manufacturers to raise prices."
2. When GDP figures for the fourth quarter of 1986 were released, one headline read "Growth Falls to 0.2%" while another read "Economy Continues to Grow at Steady 3.1%." How could both be right? Which do you think is the most accurate description of what really happened?
3. Between 1979 and 1986, employment in Canada grew by over 10 percent, from 10.4 million to 11.6 million. However, over that same period unemployment grew from 836 thousand to 1.2 million, and the unemployment rate rose from 7.4 percent to 9.6 percent. How do you reconcile these apparently conflicting statistics? Which do you think gives the most accurate description of developments in the economy?

4. During the economic recovery from 1983 through 1986, GDP at current prices grew at an average rate of 8.3 percent per year. To what extent does this imply an improvement in the economic circumstances of the average Canadian? What would we need to know in order to distinguish the effects on (a) a bank president, (b) an autoworker in Oshawa who was unemployed in 1982, (c) a pensioner living in retirement in Victoria, B.C., and (d) an oil-field rigger living in Alberta?
5. Why is unemployment not as serious a matter now as it was at the beginning of this century?
6. If you thought the inflation rate was going to be 10 percent next year, why would most people be unwilling to lend money at 5 percent interest? Say 5 percent was all they could get and they had money they didn't want to spend for a year. Would they do better just to hold the money? What could they do that would be better than lending your money at 5 percent?

27

Measuring Macroeconomic Variables

In Chapter 26 a number of key macroeconomic variables were introduced. Before we delve into the analysis of macroeconomic events, it will be helpful to look in some detail at the measurement and interpretation of these variables. This will give a clearer notion of the concepts. It will also provide some warning about how to avoid misusing or misinterpreting measures that play a prominent role in everyday discussion of the economy.

We focus on two key variables, the price level and real national income.[1] In the first section we study the construction of price indexes and measures of real and nominal national income. In the second section we study the system of National Income Accounts, which provides the framework for gathering and organizing data on the production of output and the generation of income in the economy.

Calculating Price Indexes and Measures of Aggregate Output

We saw in Chapter 26 that in order to measure aggregate variables, we must assign weights to the individual components. We now examine how this is done when calculating price indexes and measures of total output.

The Price Level

The price level refers to an index number computed using some broad group of prices in the economy. A **price index** measures the price level at a *given period* relative to the *base period.* Several issues are involved in the construction of price indexes.

First, what group of prices should be used? This depends on the index. The **Consumer Price Index (CPI)** covers prices of commodities commonly bought by households. Changes in the value of the CPI are meant to measure changes in the typical household's "cost of living." Other price indexes, some of which we will encounter later in this chapter, incorporate prices of different groups of commodities.

[1] The measurement of labor force variables is relatively straightforward, and further details are deferred until our treatment of unemployment in Chapter 37. For present purposes it is sufficient to recall from Chapter 26 that real national income and employment tend to be positively related, while real national income and unemployment tend to be negatively related.

Second, what kind of average should be used? If all prices always changed in the same proportion, this would not matter. A 10 percent rise in each and every price would mean a 10 percent rise in the price level no matter how the index was constructed. But what if, as is always the case, different prices change in different proportions? Now it matters how much importance we give to each price change.

In calculating any price index, statisticians weight each price according to its importance. Let us see how this is done for the CPI. Statistics Canada periodically surveys a group of households to discover how they spend their incomes. The average bundle of goods bought is determined and the quantities of the particular goods in this bundle become the weights attached to the respective prices when calculating the CPI. As a result, the CPI weights rather heavily the prices of commodities on which consumers spend a lot of their income and weights rather lightly the prices of commodities on which consumers spend only a little.

The average *change* in the price level is then calculated by comparing the cost of purchasing the typical bundle of commodities at the prices that prevailed in the base year with the cost of purchasing the same bundle of commodities at the prices prevailing in the given year. The procedure is illustrated in Table 27-1.

A price index for a given year gives the ratio of the cost of purchasing a bundle of commodities in that year to the cost of purchasing the *same* bundle in the base year, multiplied by 100. [33]

At the beginning of 1987 the CPI was approximately 136 (1981 = 100). This means that in 1987 it cost 1.36 times as much to buy the representative bundle of goods as it did in the base year of 1981.

A price index is meant to reflect the broad trend in prices rather than the details. This means that although the information it gives may be extremely valuable, it must be interpreted with care. Some of the potential difficulties are discussed in Box 27-1.

Measuring Aggregate Output

We noted in Chapter 26 that there are several related measures of the nation's total output and total income. We now examine a measure obtained by aggregating the contributions to total output made by all producers in the economy. This is called the *output approach*, and the measure arrived at using it, **gross**

TABLE 27-1 The Calculation of a Consumer Price Index Covering Three Commodities

		Base year 1982		Given year 1987	
Commodity	Quantity in fixed bundle	Price in 1982	Value in 1982	Price in 1987	Value in 1987
A	500 units	$1.00	$ 500	$2.00	$1,000
B	200 units	5.00	1,000	7.00	1,400
C	50 units	2.00	100	9.60	480
			1,600		2,880

$$\text{Index value 1982} = \frac{1{,}600}{1{,}600} \times 100 = 100$$

$$\text{Index value 1987} = \frac{2{,}880}{1{,}600} \times 100 = 180$$

A price index shows the ratio of the costs of purchasing a fixed bundle of goods between two years (multiplied by 100). The cost of purchasing the fixed bundle is calculated at the prices prevailing in each year. The index for year 1987 is the cost of purchasing that bundle in 1987 expressed as a percentage of the cost of purchasing the same bundle in the base year (1982 in this example). The price index is thus always 100 in the base year. The index of 180 means that prices have risen on average by 80 percent between the base year and the year in question. This index weights price changes by their *importance* in the average household's budget in the base year.

BOX 27-1

Problems in Interpreting the Consumer Price Index

First, the weights in the index refer to an average bundle of goods. This average, though typical of what is consumed in the nation, will not be typical of what each household consumes. The rich, the poor, the young, the old, the single, the married, the urban, and the rural household will typically consume different bundles. An increase in air fares, for example, will raise the cost of living of a middle income traveler, while leaving that of a poor stay-at-home unaffected. In the example in Table 27-1, the cost of living would have risen by 100 percent, 40 percent, and 380 percent, respectively, for three different families, one of whom consumed only commodity A, one only commodity B, and one only commodity C. The index in the table shows, however, that the cost of living went up by 80 percent for a family that consumed all three goods in the relative quantities indicated.

The more an individual household's consumption pattern conforms to that of the typical pattern used to weight prices in the price index, the better the price index will reflect the average change in prices relevant to that household.

To assess the importance of this problem, separate indexes are calculated to reflect the different consumption patterns of different groups. For example, separate price indexes are calculated for a number of major Canadian cities.

Second, households usually alter their consumption patterns in response to price changes. A price index that shows changes in the cost of purchasing a *fixed* bundle of goods does not allow for this. For example, a typical cost of living index for middle income families at the turn of the century would have given heavy weight to the cost of maids and laundresses. A doubling of servants' wages in 1900 would have significantly increased the middle-class cost of living. Today it would have little effect, for the rising cost of labor has long since caused middle income families to cease to employ full-time servants. A household that has dispensed with a commodity altogether finds its cost of living unaffected by any increase in the price of that commodity, no matter how large.

A fixed-weight price index tends to overstate cost of living changes because it does not allow for changes in consumption patterns that shift expenditure away from commodities whose prices rise most and toward those whose prices rise least.

Third, as time passes, new commodities enter the typical consumption bundle and old ones leave. A cost of living index in 1890 would have had a large item for horse-drawn carriages but no allowance at all for automobiles and gasoline.

A fixed-weight index makes no allowance for the increased importance of new products or the declining importance of old in the typical household's consumption bundle.

The longer the period of time that passes, the less some fixed consumption bundle will be typical of current consumption patterns. For this reason Statistics Canada makes a new survey of household expenditure patterns every 15 or 20 years and revises the weights. The base period is then usually changed to be near the year in which the new set of commodity weights was calculated. At the end of 1983, using 1971 weights, the CPI stood at 283.4 (1971 = 100). This meant that the cost of purchasing the bundle of goods bought by a typical household in 1971 had risen 183 percent in the intervening 13 years. (The percentage change in the cost of purchasing the bundle since the base year is the level of the index minus 100.) Thirteen years is a long time for fixed weights to be used, and in 1986 Statistics Canada completed estimating a new set of weights in order to shift the base year for the CPI to 1981.

domestic product (GDP), is the one we used in our historical discussion in Chapter 26.

When we set out to measure GDP, we wish to measure the total output of all producers in the economy. It might appear at first that this could be done simply by adding up the market value of the outputs of every producer. A problem arises, however, because production occurs in stages: One firm may produce output that is used as inputs by other firms, and these other firms in turn may produce output that is used as inputs by yet other firms.

Stages of production, and the consequent interfirm sales of intermediate products, make it difficult to measure national income from production data. If we merely added up the market values of all outputs of all firms, we would obtain a total greatly in excess of the value of output actually available. Consider as an example the production of bread. If we added the total value of the sales of the wheat farmer, the flour mill, and the baker, we would be counting the value of the wheat three times, the value of the milled flour twice, and the value of the bread once. The error that arises in estimating final output by adding all sales of all firms is called **double counting.** (*Multiple counting* would be a better term, since if we add up the values of all sales, the same output is counted every time it is sold from one firm to another.)

The problem of double counting makes important the distinction between intermediate and final goods. **Intermediate goods** are outputs of some producers that are in turn inputs for other producers in the chain of production. **Final goods** are goods that are not, in the period of time under consideration, used as inputs by other firms. They are goods that are produced for final demand, to be sold—that is, for consumption, for investment (including inventory accumulation), for government, or for export.

Value added. If the sales of firms could be readily disaggregated into sales for final use and sales for further processing by other firms, measuring GDP would still be straightforward. GDP would equal the value of all *final goods* produced by firms, and all intermediate goods would be excluded. However, when the Steel Company of Canada sells steel to the Ford Motor Company, it does not necessarily know whether the steel is for final use (say, construction of a new warehouse) or whether it is to be used as an intermediate good in the production of automobiles.[2] The problem of double counting must therefore be resolved in some other manner.

To avoid double counting, statisticians use the important concept of **value added.** Each firm's value added is the value of its output minus the value of the inputs that it purchases from other firms (and which in turn were the outputs of those other firms). Thus a steel mill's value added is the value of its output minus the value of the ore it buys from the mining company, the value of the electricity and fuel oil it uses, and the values of all other inputs that it buys from other firms. A bakery's value added is the value of the baking products it produces minus the value of the flour and other inputs that it buys from other firms.

The concept of value added is further illustrated in Box 27-2, where it is shown that calculating the value of total output of final goods can be achieved by summing all values added.

Gross Domestic Product

Table 27-2 (p. 571) shows the composition of Canadian GDP by industry for 1986. The table also introduces a distinction between GDP valued at factor cost and GDP valued at market prices. The two differ because of indirect taxes—taxes on the production and sale of goods and services—and subsidies.

Suppose that a firm's value added as measured by the market value of its sales less the market value of its purchases of intermediate goods is $10, and that $1 of this represents excise taxes. Then only $9 of the value added is attributable to the costs of factors used producing the output. Thus while the market value of its value added is $10, in terms of factor costs its value added is only $9. The other dollar representing the government's claim on the market value of the firm's value added.

Government subsidies on goods and services also cause the two measures of value added to differ. For example, consider a firm that produces a product

[2] Even with our earlier example of bread, a bakery cannot be sure that its sales are for final use since the bread may be further "processed" by a restaurant prior to its final sale to a customer for eating.

BOX 27-2

Value Added Through Stages of Production

Because the output of one firm often becomes the input of other firms, the total value of goods sold by all firms greatly exceeds the value of the output of final products. This general principle is illustrated by a simple example in which firm R starts from scratch and produces goods (raw materials) valued at $100; the firm's value added is $100. Firm I purchases raw materials valued at $100 and produces semi-manufactured goods that it sells for $130. Its value added is $30 because the value of the goods is increased by $30 as a result of the firm's activities. Firm F purchases the semi-manufactured goods for $130, works them into a finished state, and sells the final products for $180. Firm F's value added is $50. The value of the final goods, $180, is found either by counting only the sales of firm F or by taking the sum of the values added by each firm. This value is much smaller than the $410 that we would obtain if we merely added up the market value of the commodities sold by each firm.

	Transactions at three different stages of production			
	Firm R	Firm I	Firm F	All firms
A. Purchases from other firms	$ 0	$100	$130	$230 Total interfirm sales
B. Purchases of factors of production (wages, rent, interest, profits)	100	30	50	180 Total value added
A + *B* = value of product	$100	$130	$180	$410 Total value of all sales

with a market value of $25,000, which, after subtracting $15,000 worth of inputs purchased from other firms, has a value added of $10,000. This is the firm's value added at market prices. But also assume that the firm's wages and other production costs (excluding inputs for other firms) amounted to $14,000, with the extra $4,000 being covered by a government subsidy. The firm's value added measured at factor cost is therefore $14,000.

Real and Nominal National Income

We saw in Chapter 26 that prices of individual outputs are used as weights when constructing an aggregate measure of total output. Although we cannot add tons of steel and loaves of bread, we can add the money value of steel produced to the money value of bread produced. When we add up money values of individual outputs, we end up with a measure of what we have called *nominal national income*.[3] Suppose that we found that our measure of nominal national income had risen by 140 percent between 1980 and 1987. If we wanted to compare *real national income* (i.e., real output) in 1987 to that in 1980, we would need to determine how much of that 140 percent increase in nominal national income was due to increases in prices and how much was due to increases in quantities produced.

There are many possible approaches to distinguishing real from nominal income and many details in the procedures. But the basic principle in calculating real income is to compute the value of output in each period using a common set of (base period) prices. The common set of prices thus provides the weights used in the index of real income. We speak of real income as being measured in *constant (base period) dollars*.

Total output calculated by summing values using current prices is a measure of nominal national income. Total output calculated by summing values using base period prices is a measure of real national income, computed in terms of constant dollars.

[3] To simplify the discussion, in this section we proceed as if all outputs are final products; for the present purpose of distinguishing between real and nominal income, the complications introduced by the presence of intermediate goods are not important.

TABLE 27-2 Real Gross Domestic Product, 1986

	Billions of 1981 dollars	Percent of GDP
Value added by sector		
Agriculture, fishing, and forestry	$ 14.9	4.2
Mines, quarries, and oil wells	19.0	5.3
Manufacturing	66.2	18.4
Construction	24.6	6.9
Electric power, gas, and water utilities	11.0	3.1
Transportation, storage, and communication	26.5	7.4
Real and wholesale trade	40.9	11.4
Financial, insurance, and real estate	53.2	14.8
Community, business, and personal services	39.1	10.9
Nonbusiness sector	64.1	17.8
GDP (at factor cost)	$358.7	100
Add: Indirect taxes less subsidies	48.3	
GDP (at market prices)	$407.0	

Source: Statistics Canada 11-003E; 15–001.

GDP, a measure of total output produced in Canada, can be decomposed into the contribution to that total by each of a number of sectors. GDP at factor cost equals the sum of values added of each sector. As can be seen, manufacturing is the largest sector, contributing over 18 percent. To convert *GDP at factor cost* to *GDP at market prices,* we have to add indirect taxes net of subsidies to the former.

Any changes in nominal income are due to the combined effects of changes in prices and changes in outputs. But any changes in real income are due solely to changes in output.

The Implicit Deflator

Any differences between nominal and real national income for a given year must be due to changes in prices between that year and the base year used in calculating real income. Such a comparison thus implies a price index relating the two years. This *implicit price index* or *implicit deflator* is defined as follows:

$$\textbf{Implicit deflator} = \frac{\textbf{nominal national income}}{\textbf{real national income}} \times 100\%$$

The implicit deflator is the most comprehensive index of the price level because it covers all the goods and services produced by the entire economy. While the CPI is a fixed-weight index, the implicit deflator is a variable-weight index. It uses the current year's bundle of production to compare the current year's prices with those prevailing in the base period. Thus the 1986 deflator uses 1986 weights and the 1987 deflator will use 1987 weights. Box 27-3 illustrates the calculation of real national income, nominal national income, and the implicit deflator for a simple hypothetical economy that produces only wheat and steel.

Any change in nominal income can be split into a change due to prices and a change due to quantities. For example, in 1986 Canadian nominal income was 147 percent higher than in 1970. This increase was due to a 212 percent increase in prices and an 85 percent increase in real income. Table 27-3 (p. 573) gives nominal and real income and the implicit deflator for selected years since 1935.

National Income Accounting

In Chapter 26 we used the generic term *national income* to describe both the value of output produced and purchased, and the value of income generated

BOX 27-3

Calculation of Nominal and Real National Income

To see what is involved in calculating nominal national income, real national income, and the implicit deflator, an example may be helpful. Consider a simple hypothetical economy that produces only two commodities, wheat and steel.

Table 1 gives the basic data for outputs and prices in the economy for two years.

Table 1 Data for a Hypothetical Economy

	Quantity produced		*Prices*	
	Wheat (bushels)	**Steel (tons)**	**Wheat (dollars per bushel)**	**Steel (dollars per ton)**
Year 1	110	20	10	50
Year 2	110	16	12	55

Table 2 shows nominal national income, calculated by adding the money values of wheat output and of steel output for each year. In year 1 the value of both wheat and steel production was $1,000, so nominal income was $2,000. In year 2 wheat output rose and steel output fell; the value of wheat output rose to $1,320 and that of steel fell to $880. Since the rise in value of wheat was bigger than the fall in value of steel, nominal income rose by $200.

Table 2 Calculation of Nominal National Income

Year 1 (100 × 10) + (20 × 50) = $2,000
Year 2 (110 × 12) + (16 × 55) = $2,200

Table 3 shows real national income, calculated by valuing output in each year by year 2 prices; that is, year 2 becomes the base year for weighting purposes. In year 2 wheat output rose but steel output fell. Using year 2 prices, the value of the fall in steel output exceeded the value of the rise in wheat output, and real national income fell.

Table 3 Calculation of Real National Income Using Year 2 Prices

Year 1 (100 × 12) + (20 × 55) = $2,300
Year 2 (110 × 12) + (16 × 55) = $2,200

In Table 4 the ratio of nominal to real national income is calculated for each year and multiplied by 100. This ratio implicitly measures the change in prices over the period in question and is called the *implicit deflator* or *implicit price index.*

Table 4 Calculation of the Implicit Deflator

Year 1 (2,000 ÷ 2,300) × 100 = 86.96
Year 2 (2,200 ÷ 2,200) × 100 = 100.00

The implicit deflator shows that the price level increased by 15 percent between year 1 and year 2.

In Table 4 we used year 2 as the base year for comparison purposes, but we could have used year 1. The implicit deflator would then have been 100 in year 1 and 115 in year 2, and the increase in price level would still have been 15 percent.

by that production. Earlier in this chapter we studied how output could be measured by summing values added; we called this aggregate measure GDP. In this part we examine two other methods of calculating GDP and then relate GDP to other aggregate measures that are sometimes encountered.

It is useful to look again at Figure 3-1, on page 53, which shows the circular flow of expenditure and income. The bottom half of the circular flow focuses on expenditure to purchase the nation's output in product markets, and the top half focuses on factor markets where the receipts of firms are distributed to those factors used in producing the nation's output.

Corresponding to these two halves of the circular flow are two ways of measuring national income: the value of what is produced *and* the value of incomes generated by production. We can add up the total expenditure on each of the main components of final output; this is called *the expenditure approach*.

TABLE 27-3 GDP in Current and Constant Dollars

Year	(1) GDP in billions of current dollars	(2) GDP in billions of 1981 dollars	(3) Implicit national income deflator (1981 = 100)
1935	4,301	34,685	12.4
1945	11,863	66,585	16.8
1955	29,250	109,104	26.8
1965	57,523	175,359	32.8
1975	171,540	283,187	60.5
1980	309,891	343,384	90.2
1985	479,446	393,817	121.7

Source: M. C. Urquhart, ed., *Historical Statistics of Canada;* Department of Finance, *Economic Review.*

Current dollar GDP tells us about the money value of output; constant dollar GDP tells us about changes in physical output. GDP in current dollars gives the total value of all final output in any year, valued in the selling prices of that year. GDP in constant dollars gives the total value of all final output in any year, valued at the prices prevailing in one particular year, in this case, 1981.

The ratio of *GDP in current dollars* to *GDP in constant dollars* times 100 is the implicit GDP deflator. (It is in effect a price index with current year quantity weights.)

We can also measure the incomes generated by the act of production; this is called the *income approach.*

The expenditure approach and the income approach are two different ways of looking at one magnitude: the market value of the nation's output.

The two approaches are conceptually identical, and result in measures of GDP that differ in practice only because of errors of measurement. Each approach is of interest, however, because each gives a different and useful breakdown of national income. Also, having two independent ways of measuring the same thing also gives a useful check on the statistical procedures and unavoidable measurement errors.

National income accounting is the set of rules and techniques for measuring the total flow of output produced and the total flow of incomes generated by this production.

The conventions of double-entry bookkeeping require that all value produced must be accounted for by a claim someone has to that value.

Thus it is merely a matter of accounting convention that the two measures of GDP should be equal. (Measured values differ only to the extent that measurement errors arise. Any discrepancy arising from such errors is then reconciled so that one common total is given as *the* measure of GDP; that common total is also reconciled with the measure of GDP obtained using the output approach studied earlier in this chapter.)

The Expenditure Approach

The expenditure approach calculates GDP as the market value of final output by adding up the expenditures made to purchase final output. Total expenditure on final output is the sum of four broad categories of expenditure: consumption, investment, government, and net exports.

Consumption Expenditure

Consumption expenditure includes expenditure on all goods and services produced and sold to households during the year (with the exception of residential housing, which is counted as investment). It includes services such as haircuts, medical care, and legal advice; nondurable goods such as fresh meat, cut flowers, and fresh vegetables; and durables such as cars, television sets, and air conditioners. We denote actual (i.e., measured) consumption expenditure by the symbol C^a.

Investment Expenditure

Investment expenditure is expenditure on the production of goods not for present consumption, including inventories, capital goods such as plant and equipment, and residential housing. Such goods are called **investment goods**.

Inventories. Almost all firms hold stocks of their inputs and their own outputs. These stocks are called **inventories**. Inventories of inputs and unfinished materials allow production to continue at the desired pace in spite of short-term fluctuations in the deliveries of inputs bought from other firms. Inventories of outputs allow firms to meet orders in spite of temporary fluctuations in the rate of outputs or sales.

Inventories are an important part of the production process. They require an investment of the firm's money, since the firm has paid for but not yet sold the goods. An accumulation of inventories counts as current investment because it represents goods produced but not used for current consumption. A drawing down, often called a *decumulation,* counts as disinvestment because it represents a reduction in the stock of finished goods available to be sold.

Additions to inventories are a part of the economy's final production of investment goods. These are valued in the national income accounts at market value, which includes the wages and other costs the firm incurred in producing the goods and the profit the firm will make when the inventories are sold. Thus, in the case of inventories of a firm's own output, the expenditure approach measures what will have to be spent to purchase them when they are sold rather than what has actually been spent to produce them.

Plant and equipment. All production uses capital goods: manufactured aids to production such as tools, machines, and factory buildings. The economy's total quantity of capital goods is called the **capital stock.** Creating new capital goods is an act of investment and is called fixed business investment, or **fixed investment** for short.

Residential housing. A house is a durable asset that yields its utility over a long life. For this reason housing construction is counted as investment expenditure rather than as consumption expenditure. This is done by assuming that the investment is made by the firm that builds the house and that the sale to a user is a mere transfer of ownership that is not a part of national income.

Gross versus net investment. The total investment that occurs in the economy is called **gross investment.** Gross investment is divided into two parts, replacement investment and net investment. **Replacement investment** is the amount of investment that just maintains the existing capital stock intact; it is called the **capital consumption allowance** or simply **depreciation.** Gross investment minus replacement investment is **net investment.** Positive net investment increases the economy's total stock of capital, while replacement investment keeps the existing stock intact by replacing what has been used up.

All of gross investment is included in the calculation of national income. This is because all investment goods are part of the nation's total output and their production creates income (and employment) whether the goods produced are a part of net investment or are merely replacement investment. Actual (i.e., measured) total investment expenditure is denoted by the symbol I^a.

Government Expenditure on Goods and Services

When governments provide goods and services that households want, such as roads and air traffic control, it is obvious that they are adding to the sum total of valuable output in the same way as do private firms that produce the trucks and airplanes that use the roads and air lanes. With other government activities, the case may not seem so clear. Should expenditures by the federal government to send a scientific probe into space or to pay a civil servant to refile papers from a now defunct department be regarded as contributions to national income? Some people believe that many (or even most) activities "up in Ottawa" or "down at City Hall" are wasteful, if not downright harmful. Others believe that it is governments, not private firms, that produce many of the important things of life, such as education and pollution control.

National income statisticians do not speculate about which government expenditures are or are not worthwhile. Instead, they include all government expenditures on goods and services as part of national income. (Government expenditure on investment goods is included as government rather than investment expenditure.) Just as the national product includes, without distinction, the output of both gin and Bibles, it also includes bombers and the upkeep of parks, along with the services of RCMP officers, members of Parliament, and even Revenue Canada investigators. Actual government expenditure on goods and services is denoted by the symbol G^a.

Government output is typically valued at cost rather than market value. In many cases there is really no choice. What, for example, is the market value of the services of a court of law? No one knows. But we do know what it costs the government to provide these services, so we value them at their cost of production.

Although valuing at cost is the only possible thing to do with many government activities, it does have one curious consequence. If, due to a productivity increase, one civil servant now does what two used to do and the displaced worker shifts to the private sector, the government's contribution to national income will register a decline. In contrast, if two now do what one used to do, the government's contribution will rise. Both changes could occur even though what the government actually does is unchanged. This is an inevitable consequence of measuring the value of the government's output by the cost of the factors, mainly labor, used to produce it.

There is an important exception to the rule that all government expenditure is included in national income. **Transfer payments,** or government payments that are not made in return for factor services, do not lead directly to any increase in output, and they are not included in national income. For example, when a government agency makes welfare payments to a retired person, the government does not receive, nor does it expect to receive, any marketable services from the retiree in return for the welfare payments. The payment itself adds neither to employment of factors nor to total output. The major transfer payments are unemployment insurance, welfare payments, and interest on the national debt (which transfers income from taxpayers to holders of government bonds).

Thus when we refer to government expenditure as part of national income or use the symbol G^a, we include all government expenditure on currently produced goods and services and we *exclude* all government transfer payments. (The term government *outlays* might be used to describe all government spending, including transfer payments.)

Net Exports

The fourth category of aggregate expenditure, and one that is extremely important to the Canadian economy, arises from foreign trade. How do imports and exports influence the national income?

Imports. One country's national income is the total value of final commodities produced in that country. If your cousin spends $12,000 on a car made in Japan, only a small part of that value will represent expenditure on Canadian production. Some of it goes for the services of the Canadian dealers and transportation; the rest is the output of Japanese firms and expenditure on Japanese products. If you take your next vacation in Italy, much of your expenditure will be on goods and services produced by Italians and thus will contribute to Italian GDP.

Similarly, when a Canadian firm makes an investment expenditure on a Canadian-produced machine tool made partly with imported raw materials, only part of the expenditure is on Canadian production. The rest is expenditure on the production of the countries supplying the raw materials. The same is also true for government expenditure on such things as roads and dams; some of the expenditure is for imported materials and only part of it for domestically produced goods and services.

Consumption, investment, and government expenditures all have an import content. To arrive at total expenditure on Canadian products, we need to subtract from total Canadian expenditure any expenditure on imports. Actual expenditure on imports is given the symbol M^a.

Exports. If Canadian firms sell goods to German households, the goods are a part of German consumption expenditure but also constitute expenditure on Canadian output. Indeed, all goods and services produced in Canada and sold to foreigners must be counted as part of Canadian production and income; they create incomes for the Canadians who produce them. To arrive at the total value of expenditure on Canadian national product, it is necessary to add in the value of Canadian exports. Actual exports are denoted by the symbol X^a.

It is customary to group actual imports and actual exports together as **net exports.** Net exports are defined as exports minus imports ($X^a - M^a$). The value of net exports is usually small in relation to the total value of either X^a or M^a.

GDP As Measured by the Expenditure Approach

The expenditure approach to measuring national income yields GDP as the sum of consumption, investment, government, and net export expenditures.

Table 27-4(i) shows Canadian GDP for 1986 calculated according to the expenditure approach.

The Income Approach

The income approach calculates the value of GDP as the total of all incomes generated in the process of production.

The production of the nation's output generates income. Labor must be employed, land rented, and capital used. The income approach to measuring GDP involves adding up factor payments and other claims on the value of output until all of it is accounted for. As we have already seen, because all value produced must be owned by someone, the value of production must equal the value of income claims generated by that production.

Factor Payments

National income accountants distinguish four main components of factor incomes: wages, rent, interest, and profits.[4]

Wages. Wages and salaries (which national income accountants call *compensation to employees* but are usually just called *wages*) are the payment for the services of labor. Wages include take-home pay, taxes withheld, social insurance, and pension fund contributions and other fringe benefits. In total, wages represent the part of the value of production attributable to labor.

Rent. Rent is the payment for the services of land and other factors that are rented. It includes payments for rented housing and imputed rent for the use of owner-occupied housing. For the purposes of national income accounting, homeowners are viewed as renting accommodation from themselves. This allows national income measures to reflect the value of all housing services used, whether or not the housing is owned by its user.

Interest. Interest includes interest earned on bank deposits, interest earned on loans to firms, and miscellaneous other investment income. Hence it is one of the payments for the services of capital.

Profits. Some profits are paid out as **dividends** to owners of firms; the rest are retained for use by firms. The former are called **distributed profits**, the latter **undistributed profits** or **retained earnings.** Both distributed and undistributed profits are included in the calculation of GNP. For accounting purposes, total profits are reported in two separate

[4] The concepts of wages, rent, interest, and profits used in macroeconomics do not correspond exactly to the concepts of the same names used in microeconomics, but the details of the differences need not detain us.

TABLE 27-4 Components of GDP, 1986

(i) Expenditure approach

Expenditure category	Billions of dollars	Percentage of GDP
Consumption	299	58.5
Government	101	19.8
Investment	106	21.0
Net exports	6	1.1
Statistical discrepancy	−2	−0.4
GDP at market prices	510	100.0

(ii) Income approach

Income component	Billions of dollars	Percentage of GDP
Compensation to employees	274	53.7
Corporate profits (before taxes)	45	8.8
Net interest	41	8.0
Rental income	36	7.1
Net indirect taxes	54	10.6
Capital consumption allowance	58	11.4
Statistical discrepancy	2	0.4
GDP at market prices	510	100.0

Source: Quarterly Economic Review (Department of Finance, June 1987).

Canada's 1986 nominal gross domestic product (GDP) of $510 billion can be classified according to the expenditure or income approaches. In (i) the expenditure approach shows that consumption is the biggest component of GDP, accounting for almost 60 percent, while net exports account for less than 1 percent. Investment and government expenditure together account for about 40 percent.

In (ii) the income approach shows that compensation to employees accounts for almost 60 percent of GDP. The other 40 percent is accounted for by corporate profits before taxes, capital consumption allowance, indirect taxes less subsidies, interest, and rental income.

categories—corporation profits and incomes of unincorporated businesses (mainly small businesses, farms, partnerships, and professionals).

Net domestic income at factor cost. The sum of the four components of factor incomes—wages, rent, interest, and profits—is called **net domestic income at factor cost.**

Indirect Taxes Net of Subsidies

When using the income approach, we must distinguish between national income valued *at factor cost* and national income valued *at market prices.* The difference between the two results from the effects of indirect taxes and subsidies. An important claim on the market value of output arises out of indirect taxes—taxes on the production and sale of goods and services.

As we saw on page 569, when adding up income claims to determine GDP, it is necessary to add in the part of the total market value of output that is the government's claim arising out of its taxes on goods and services. Recall that we also saw on page 570 that it is also necessary to subtract government subsidies on goods and services, since these allow incomes to *exceed* the market value of output.

Depreciation

Another component in the income approach arises from the distinction between net and gross investment. One claim on the value of final output is depreciation, or capital consumption allowance. This is the value of final output that embodies capital used up in the process of its production. It is part of gross profits, but being the part needed to compensate for capital used up in the process of production, it is not part of net profits. Hence it is not income earned by any factor of production. Instead it is value that must be reinvested just to maintain the existing stock of capital equipment.

GDP As Measured by the Income Approach

Adding depreciation and indirect taxes net of subsidies to net domestic income at factor cost gives gross domestic product at market prices, or GDP.

The income approach measures GDP as the sum of the factor incomes generated in the process of producing final output, plus indirect taxes net of subsidies, plus depreciation.

GDP in the Canadian economy in 1986 as calculated by the income approach is shown in Table 27-4(ii).

Income Produced and Income Received: An Important Distinction

GDP provides a measure of total output *produced in Canada,* and of the total income generated as a result of that production. However, the total income received by Canadians can differ from GDP for two reasons. Some Canadian production creates factor earnings for foreigners who have previously invested in Canada or who sell services to producers in Canada; on this account income received by Canadians will be less than Canadian GDP. Second, many Canadians earn income as a result of foreign investments and of factor services sold abroad; on this account income received by Canadians will be greater than Canadian GDP.

As with total output produced, total income received by Canadians can be measured using either the income or the expenditure approach. The term **Gross National Product (GNP)** is used to describe total income received by Canadians as measured by the income approach. The term **Gross National Expenditure (GNE)** describes the same total measured using the expenditure approach. Hence GNE and GNP give conceptually identical measures of national income.[5]

Total output produced in the economy, measured by GDP, differs from total income received by Canadians, measured by GNP and GNE, due to net foreign factor payments.

Reconciling GDP with GNP and GNE. Table 27-5 shows the reconciliation of GDP with GNP, and hence with GNE. Recall that GNP and GNE both measure income received by Canadians while GDP measures output produced in Canada. Since Canada has had a long history of importing capital from abroad, factor payments to foreigners exceed factor payments received from foreigners, and hence GDP exceeds GNP. (This does not mean that the net effects of Canada's foreign borrowing has been to reduce incomes of Canadians; most estimates show that foreign investment has contributed more to GDP than it has to the repatriation of factor payments, and hence has increased GNP. We return to this important issue in Chapter 41.)

TABLE 27-5 Reconciling GDP with GNP and GNE

	Billions of dollars
GDP at market prices (from Table 27-4)	510
Plus: investment income received from foreigners	7
Less: investment income paid to foreigners	−24
GNP (and GNE) at market prices	493

Source: Quarterly Economic Review (Department of Finance, June 1987).

GNP, income owned or received by Canadians, is equal to GDP, income produced in Canada, plus factor income received from foreigners, less factor income paid to foreigners. Since Canada has traditionally experienced significant net foreign investment, investment income paid to foreigners is large, and hence net international factor payments for Canada are negative. As a result GNP (and GNE, since GNE equals GNP) is less than GDP.

Other Income Concepts

We have seen how the most comprehensive measures of national income—GDP, GNP, and GNE—are reconciled. We now turn to a discussion of some related but less-comprehensive measures.

Gross national income, however measured, is the most comprehensive income concept. The next most comprehensive measure is net national product (NNP). As we saw in building up the income approach, this is GNP minus the capital consumption allowance. NNP is thus a measure of the net output of the economy after deducting from gross output an amount sufficient to maintain intact the existing stock of capital. It is the maximum amount that could be consumed without actually running down the economy's capital stock.

Personal income is income earned by or paid to individuals before allowance for personal income taxes. Some personal income goes for taxes, some for saving, and the rest for consumption. A number of adjustments to NNP are required to arrive at

[5] In the United States, the term GNP is used to describe *both* measures, and the term GNE is not used in official statistics.

personal income. The most important are (1) subtracting from NNP indirect taxes (net of subsidies), which are the part of the market value of output that goes directly to governments (this, as we have seen, gives net national income at factor cost), (2) subtracting from NNP business earnings retained by corporations, (3) subtracting from NNP income taxes paid by business, and (4) adding to NNP transfer payments to households. The first three are parts of the value of output not paid to households; the fourth is paid to households and thus is income that households have available to spend or to save, even though the payments are not part of GNP.

Disposable income is the amount of current income that households have to spend and to save; it is personal income minus personal income taxes.

Disposable income is GNP *minus* any part of it that is not actually paid to households *minus* personal income taxes paid by households *plus* transfer payments received by households.

The relations among GNP, NNP, personal income, and disposable income are shown in Table 27-6.

TABLE 27-6 Various National Income Measures, 1986

	Billions of dollars[a]
A. GDP at market prices	510
Less: net foreign investment income	−17
B. GNP at market prices	493
Less: capital consumption allowance	−58
C. NNP at market prices	435
Less: indirect taxes of net subsidies	−54
D. NDI at factor cost	380
Less: retained earnings and business taxes	−9
Plus: government transfer payments to households	62
E. Personal income	433
Less: personal income taxes	−88
F. Disposable income	343

[a] Figures may not match because of rounding.

Each of the six related national income measures focuses on a different aspect of the national output. GDP measures total output produced in Canada. GNP measures the market value of total income received by Canadians. NNP measures the net value of national income after an allowance for maintaining the capital stock. NNI at factor cost converts market price values to factor costs by adjusting for government indirect taxes net of subsidies. Personal income measures income earned or received by persons before personal income taxes. Disposable income measures after-tax income of persons; it is the amount they have available to spend or to save.

Interpreting National Income Measures

The information provided by measures of national income is useful, but unless carefully interpreted it can also be misleading. Furthermore, each of the specialized measures gives different information. Thus each may be the best statistic for studying a particular range of problems.

Money values and real values. We have seen that national income can be valued in current dollars to yield nominal income or constant dollars to yield real income. When studying the effect of inflation on national income, we need to look at nominal income. When studying changes in the economy's quantity of output, we need to look at real income.

Total values and per capita values. The rise in real GDP during this century has had two main causes: an increase in the amounts of land, labor, and capital used in production and an increase in output per unit of input. In other words, more inputs have been used, and each input has become more productive. For some purposes, such as assessing a country's potential military strength or the total size of its market, we want to measure total output. For other purposes, such as studying changes in living standards, we require per capita measures, which are obtained by dividing a total measure such as GDP by the population.

There are many useful per capita measures. GDP divided by the total population gives a measure of how much GDP there is on average for each person in the country; this is called **per capita GDP.** GDP

FIGURE 27-1 Disposable Income Per Capita in Canada, in Constant (1981) Dollars

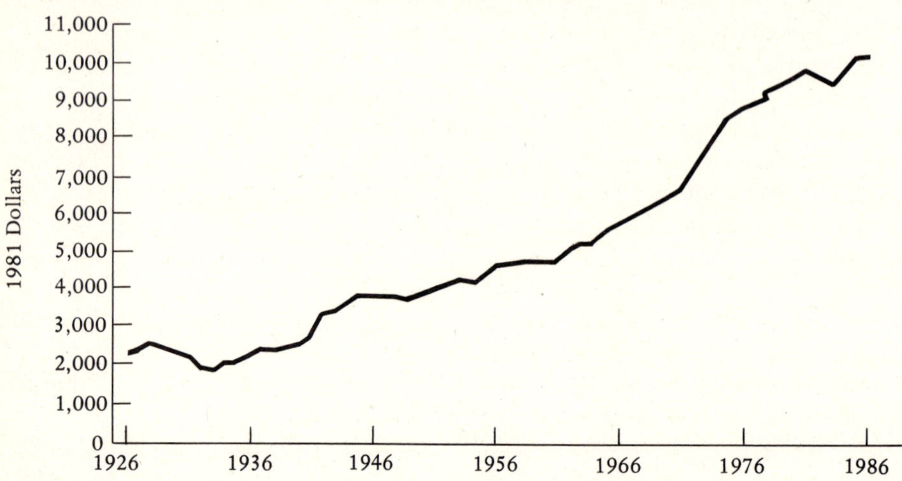

Disposable income per capita in constant dollars provides a measure of the real purchasing power available to the average Canadian household. Disposable income per capita fell during the early 1930s and late 1940s but it has risen in every decade since the thirties, including the 1970s. It underestimates the average living standard because it leaves ou the contribution of government expenditure to such items as police, fire, justice, defense, and recreation. (*Source*: M.C. Urquhart, ed., *Historical Statistics of Canada; Bank of Canada Review*.)

divided by the number of persons employed tells us the average output per employed worker. GDP divided by the total number of hours worked measures output per hour of labor input. A widely used measure of the purchasing power of the average person is disposable income per capita in constant dollars. This measure is shown in Figure 27-1.

Omissions from Measured National Income

Several types of economic activity are not included in GDP and therefore are excluded from other measures based on GDP. The importance of these omissions depends on the purpose for which the data are to be used. Box 27-4 takes up some other aspects of national income accounting.

Illegal activities. GDP does not measure illegal activities, even though many of them are ordinary business activities that produce goods and services sold on the market and generate factor incomes. The liquor industry during American Prohibition (1919–1933) is an important example because it accounted for a significant part of total economic activity in the U.S. Today the same is true of many forms of illegal gambling, prostitution, and the drug trade. To gain an accurate measure of the *total* demand for factors of production in the economy or of *total* marketable output, we should include these activities, regardless of whether we as individuals approve of the products.[6]

The omissions of illegal activities is no trivial matter. The drug trade alone is a multibillion dollar business. No one knows the exact value of its output,

[6] Some of them do get included because people sometimes report their earnings from illicit activities as part of their earnings from legal activities in order to avoid the fate of Al Capone, a famous Chicago gangster in the 1930s. Having avoided conviction on many counts, he was finally prosecuted and jailed for tax evasion.

BOX 27-4

The Significance of Arbitrary Decisions

National income accounting uses many arbitrary decisions. Goods that are finished and held in inventories are valued at market value, thereby anticipating their sale even though the actual sales price may not be known. In the case of a Ford in a dealer's showroom, this practice may be justified because the *value* of this Ford is perhaps virtually the same as that of an identical Ford that has just been sold to a customer. But what is the correct market value of a half-finished house or an unfinished novel? Accountants arbitrarily treat goods in process at cost (rather than at market value) if the goods are being made by business firms. They ignore completely the value of the novel in progress. These decisions are arbitrary—but so would any others be. Clearly, practical people must arrive at some compromise between consistent definitions and measurable magnitudes.

The definition of final goods provides further examples. Business investment expenditures are treated as final products, as are all government purchases. Intermediate goods purchased by business for further processing are not treated as final products. Thus when a firm buys a machine or a truck, the purchase is treated as a final good; when it buys a ton of steel, the steel is treated as a raw material that will be used as an input into the firm's production process. But if the steel sits in inventory, it is regarded as a business investment and thus *is* a final good.

Such arbitrary decisions surely affect the size of measured GDP. Does it matter? The surprising answer, for many purposes, is no. In any case, it is wrong to believe that a statistical measure is useless if it falls short of perfection; in fact, all statistical measures do. Crude measures often give estimates to the right order of magnitude, and substantial improvements in sophistication may make only second-order improvements in these estimates.

In the third century B.C., for example, the Alexandrian astronomer Eratosthenes measured the angle of the sun at Alexandria at the moment it was directly overhead 500 miles south at Aswan, and he used this angle to calculate the circumference of the earth to within 15 percent of the distance as measured today by the most advanced measuring devices. For the knowledge he wanted—the approximate size of the earth—his measurement was satisfactory. To launch a modern earth satellite, it would have been disastrously inadequate.

Absolute figures mean something in general terms, although they cannot be taken seriously to the last dollar. In 1985 GDP was measured as \$389 billion. It is certain that the market value of all production in Canada in that year was not \$100 billion, or \$1 trillion, but it might well have been \$350 billion or \$420 billion had different measures been defined with different arbitrary decisions built in.

International and intertemporal comparisons, though tricky, may be meaningful when they are based on measures all of which contain roughly the same arbitrary decisions. Canadian per capita GDP is a little less than three times the Spanish per capita GDP and is 20 percent higher than the Japanese per capita GDP. Other measures might differ, but it is unlikely that any measure would reveal that either Spanish or the Japanese per capita production was higher than per capita production in Canada. But the statistics also show that per capita GDP was about 2 percent higher in the United States than in Canada, a difference too small to have much meaning. Canadian output grew at a rate of 4.9 percent per year for the 30 years following World War II; it is unlikely that another measure of output would have indicated a 7.5 percent increase. Further, Japanese output grew at about 9 percent per year over the same period. It is inconceivable that another measure would change the conclusion that Japanese national output rose faster than Canadian national output in recent decades.

but even if it were only 1 percent of GDP, that would amount to $5 billion in 1987.

Unreported activities. An important omission from the measured GDP is the so-called underground economy. The transactions in the underground economy are perfectly legal in themselves. The only illegal thing about them is that they are not reported for tax purposes. For example, a carpenter repairs a leak in your roof and takes payment in cash or in kind in order to avoid tax. Because such transactions go unreported, they are omitted from GDP.

There are many reasons for the growth of the underground economy. Taxes, safety regulations, minimum-wage laws, anti-discrimination regulations, and social insurance payments may all be avoided. Its growth is also facilitated by the rising importance of services in the nation's total output. It is much easier for a carpenter to pass unnoticed by government authorities than it is for a manufacturing establishment.

Estimates of the value of income earned in the Canadian underground economy run from 2 to 15 percent of GDP. In other countries the figures are much higher. The Italian underground economy, for example, was recently estimated at close to 25 percent of that country's total GDP!

Clearly, the omission of unreported activities matters. This causes the actual amount of legal income and employment-creating market transactions to be underestimated. Changes in the proportion of GDP that go unreported can affect measures of growth in output and hence living standards. If, for example, *actual* GDP grows by 2 percent but an additional 1 percent goes unrecorded, *measured* GDP will grow by only 1 percent. (In 1985 and 1986 Italy was one of the fastest-growing countries in Europe, according to official statistics. A number of commentators have argued that this is in part due to a decrease in the proportion of economic activity that was unreported.)

Nonmarketed activities. If a homeowner hires a firm to do some landscaping, the value of the landscaping enters into GDP; if the homeowner does the landscaping herself, the value of the landscaping is omitted from GDP. Such omissions also include, for example, the services of homemakers, any do-it-yourself activity, and voluntary work such as canvassing for a political party, helping to run a volunteer day-care center, or leading a Boy Scout troop.

In most advanced industrial economies the nonmarket sector is relatively small. The omissions become serious, however, when GDP or disposable income figures are used to compare living standards in very different economies. Generally, the nonmarket sector of the economy is larger in rural than in urban settings and in less developed than in more developed economies. Be a little cautious, then, in interpreting data from a country with a very different climate and culture. When you hear that the per capita GDP of Nigeria is about $900 per year, you should not imagine living in Hamilton Ontario on that income.

Other omitted factors. Many factors that contribute to human welfare are not included in GDP. Leisure is one. In fact, although a shorter work week may make people happier, it will tend to reduce measured GDP.

Nor does GDP allow for the capacity of different goods to provide different satisfactions. A million dollars spent on a bomber or a missile makes the same addition to GDP as a million dollars spent on a school or on candy bars—expenditures that may produce very different amounts of consumer satisfaction.

Do the Omissions Matter?

If we wish to measure the flow of goods and services through the market sector of the economy or to account for changes in the opportunities for employment for households that sell their labor services in the market, most of these omissions will have negligible effects on our results. If, however, we wish to measure the overall flow of goods and services available to satisfy people's wants, whatever the source of the goods and services, the omissions are undesirable and potentially serious.

Is There a "Best" Measure?

To ask which is *the* best income measure is something like asking which is *the* best carpenter's tool. The answer is that it all depends on the job to be done. Which measure is used will depend on the problem at hand, and solving some problems may require information provided by several different measures or information not provided by any conventional measures. If we wish to predict households' consumption behavior, disposable income may be what we need. If we wish to account for changes in employment, constant dollar GDP is wanted. For an overall measure of economic welfare, we may need to supplement or modify conventional measures of national income, none of which measures the *quality of life.* To the extent that material output is purchased at the expense of overcrowded cities and highways, polluted environments, defaced countrysides, maimed accident victims, longer waits for public services, and a more complex life that entails a frenetic struggle to be happy, conventional measures of national income include only part of the things that contribute to human well-being.[7]

Even if we do use some new or modified measures for some purposes, we are unlikely to discard GDP (and its relatives) entirely. Economists and politicians who are interested in changes in market activity and in employment opportunities for factors of production will continue to use GDP and GNP as the measures that come closest to telling them what they need to know.

[7] Concepts that come closer to measuring economic welfare have been developed. One was worked out by Professors William Nordhaus and James Tobin. It tries to measure consumption of things that provide utility to households rather than total production; it gives value to such nonmarketed activities as leisure and makes subtractions for such "disutilities" as pollution and congestion.

Summary

1. The Consumer Price Index (CPI) is a price index constructed to reflect changes in the prices of the bundle of goods consumed by a "representative" household. Changes in it are taken as a measure of changes in the "cost of living."
2. Gross Domestic Product (GDP) is the total value of final goods and services produced in the economy during a year. It can be measured by the output approach which sums the values added of all producers in the economy; this avoids the problem of double counting by excluding all intermediate goods produced.
3. Real income is a measure of total output calculated using base period prices as weights; changes in it reflect changes in quantity produced. Nominal income is a measure of total output calculated to reflect changes in both prices and quantities. Any change in nominal income can be split into a change in real income and a change due to prices. Comparing nominal and real income yields the implicit deflator.
4. GDP can also be measured using the expenditure and income approaches. Using the expenditure approach, GDP $= C^a + I^a + G^a + (X^a - M^a)$. C^a is consumption expenditures of households. I^a is investment in plant and equipment, residential construction, and inventory accumulation. Gross investment can be split into replacement investment (necessary to keep the stock of capital intact) and net investment (net additions to the stock of capital). G^a is government expenditures except transfer payments. $(X^a - M^a)$ is the excess of exports over imports; it will be negative if imports exceed exports.
5. The income approach measures GDP according to who has a claim to the value arising from the production and sale of commodities. Wages, interest, rents, profits, depreciation (called capital consumption allowance), and indirect taxes are the major categories. By virtue

of standard accounting conventions, gross domestic product measured by each of the two approaches will be the same.

6. GDP measures total production located in Canada. A distinct concept is total income received by Canadians. The difference is due to income from net foreign investment. Total income received by Canadians can also be measured using either the expenditure or the income approach. When measured by the income approach, it is called gross national product (GNP). When measured by the expenditure approach, it is called gross national expenditure (GNE).
7. Several related but different income measures are used in addition to GDP, GNP, and GNE. Net national product (NNP) measures total income after deducting the capital consumption allowance. Personal income is income actually earned by Canadian households before any allowance for personal taxes. Disposable income gives the amount that is actually available to households to spend or to save.
8. GDP and related measures of national income must be interpreted with care, given their limitations. GDP excludes production resulting from activities that are illegal, take place in the underground economy, or do not pass through markets (such as what is produced by do-it-yourself activities). Moreover, GDP does not measure everything that contributes to human welfare.
9. Notwithstanding their limitations, GDP and GNP remain the best measures available for estimating the total economic activity that passes through the markets of our economy and for accounting for changes in the employment opportunities that face households who sell their labor services on the open market.

Topics for Review

Index numbers and the Consumer Price Index (CPI)
Final goods, intermediate goods, and value added
Gross domestic product (GDP)
Real and nominal national income
Implicit deflator
Output, expenditure, and income approaches to measuring national income
Gross national product (GNP) and gross national expenditure (GNE)
National income measured at factor cost and at market prices
Net domestic income (NDI), net national product (NNP), personal income, and disposable income
Omissions from measured income

Discussion Questions

1. If Canada and the United States were to join together as a single country, what would be the effect on their total GDP (assuming that output in each country is unaffected)? Would any of the components in their GDPs change significantly?
2. "Every time you rent a U-Haul, brick in a patio, grow a vegetable, fix your own car, photocopy an article, join a food co-op, develop

your own film, sew a dress, avoid purchasing a convenience food, stew fruit, or raise a child, you are committing a productive act, even though these activities are not reflected in the gross domestic product." To what extent are each of these things "productive acts"? Are any of them included in GDP? Where they are excluded, does the exclusion matter?

3. What would be the effect of the following events on the measured value of real GDP? Speculate on the effects of each event on the true well-being of Canadians.
   a. Destruction of a thousand homes by flood water
   b. Passage of a constitutional amendment making abortion illegal
   c. Complete cessation of all imports from South Africa

4. In measuring GNE, which of the following expenditures are included? Why?
   a. Expenditures on automobiles by consumers and by firms
   b. Expenditures on food and lodging by tourists and by business people on expense accounts
   c. Expenditures on new machinery and equipment by Canadian firms
   d. The purchase of one corporation by another corporation
   e. Increases or decreases in business inventories

5. In the United States a Social Security Administration study, using 1972 data, found the "average American housewife's value" to be $4,705 a year. (In 1982 dollars this amount to over 12,000 a year.) It arrived at this total by adding up the hours she spent cooking multiplied by a cook's wage, the hours spent with her children multiplied by a babysitter's wage, and so on. Should the time a parent spends taking children to a concert be included? Are dollar amounts assigned to such activities a satisfactory proxy for market value of production? For what, if any, purposes would such values be excluded from or included in national income?

6. Use the table on the endpaper at the back of this book to calculate the percentage increase over the most recent two decades of each of the following measures. Can you account for the relative size of these changes?
   a. GDP in current dollars
   b. GDP per capita in constant dollars

7. Consider the effect on measured GDP and on economic well-being of each of the following.
   a. Reduction in the standard work week from 40 hours to 30 hours
   b. Hiring of all welfare recipients as government employees
   c. Increase in the salaries of priests and ministers as a result of increased contributions of churchgoers

8. A recent newspaper article reported that Switzerland was considered to be the "best" place in the world to live. In view of the fact that Switzerland does not have the highest per capita income in the world, how can it be ranked the "best"?

9. In 1986 Statistics Canada switched from reporting national income in terms of GNP to reporting it in terms of GDP. How do these two measures differ? Do you think GDP is a better or worse measure of national income than GNP is? Does your answer to the last question depend on the purpose the measure is being used for?

28

National Income and Aggregate Expenditure

In Chapters 26 and 27 we encountered a number of important macroeconomic variables. We described how they are measured and how they had behaved over the past half century or so. We now turn to a more detailed study of what *caused* these variables to behave as they did. In particular we wish to study the factors that determine national income, and hence employment and unemployment, and the price level.

Because it is easier to deal with things one at a time, we look first at the forces that determine national income *when the price level is treated as being constant.* In later chapters we will see what happens when the price level also varies. In this chapter, therefore, two questions are key:

1. **Why is national income what it is?**
2. **Why does it change?**

Our answers to these two questions depend on our understanding of why households and firms spend what they do and why they change their spending. Thus our analysis begins with an examination of the expenditure decisions of households and firms. As a first step we distinguish between *desired* expenditure and *actual* expenditure.

Desired Expenditure

In Chapter 27 we discussed how national income statisticians measure gross national expenditure and its components: consumption, C^a; investment, I^a; government, G^a; and net exports, $(X^a - M^a)$.

In this chapter we are concerned with a different concept. It is variously called *desired, planned,* or *intended expenditure.* Of course, all people would like to spend virtually unlimited amounts if only they had the resources. Desired expenditure does not refer, however, to what people would like to do under imaginary circumstances. It refers instead to what people want to spend out of the resources at their command. The *actual* values of the various categories of expenditure are indicated by C^a, I^a, G^a, and $(X^a - M^a)$. We use the same letters without the superscript *a* to indicate the *desired* expenditure in the same categories: C, I, G, and $(X - M)$.

Everyone with income to spend makes expenditure decisions. Fortunately, it is unnecessary for our purpose to look at each of the millions of such individual decisions. Instead it is sufficient to place decision makers in four main groups: domestic households, firms, governments, and foreign purchasers of domestically produced products. Their actual purchases account for the four main categories of expenditure studied in the preceding chapter: consumption, investment, government, and net exports.

Their desired purchases can also be divided in the same fashion: desired consumption, desired investment, desired government expenditure, and desired exports. Allowing for the fact that some commodities desired by each group will have an import content, we subtract import expenditure to obtain total desired expenditure on domestically produced goods and services, called **aggregate expenditure,** *AE:*

$$AE = C + I + G + (X - M)$$

Desired expenditure need not equal actual expenditure, either in total or in each individual category. For example, firms may not plan to invest in inventory accumulation this year but may do so unintentionally. If they produce goods to meet estimated sales, but demand is unexpectedly low, the unsold goods that pile up on their shelves are undesired, and unintended, inventory accumulation. In this case actual investment expenditure, I^a, will exceed desired investment expenditure, I.

National income accounts measure *actual expenditures* in each of the four categories: consumption, investment, government, and net exports. National income theory deals with *desired expenditures* in each of these four categories.

To develop a theory of national income determination, we need to know what determines desired aggregate expenditure. First, however, we recall the important distinction between *autonomous* and *induced* expenditure. (The distinction between autonomous and induced variables was first introduced in Chapter 2 on page 21.)

Autonomous and Induced Expenditure

Components of aggregate expenditure that do *not* depend on national income are called autonomous expenditures. Autonomous expenditures can and do change, but such changes do not occur systematically in response to changes in national income. Components of aggregate expenditure that *do* change in response to changes in national income are called induced expenditures. As we will see, the induced response of aggregate expenditure to a change in national income plays a key role in the determination of equilibrium national income.

We need to examine the determinants of each of the components of desired aggregate expenditure. In this chapter we focus on desired consumption expenditures. Consumption is the largest single component of actual aggregate expenditure, and as we will see, desired consumption expenditure provides the single most important link between desired aggregate expenditure and national income.

In an open economy such as Canada's, net exports are also an important link between desired aggregate expenditure and national income. Hence we also examine the factors that influence net exports. The two other components of *AE* are desired investment and government expenditures. We treat each briefly here; we look at both in more detail later in the book.

Desired Consumption Expenditure

Households can do one of two things with their disposable income: spend it on consumption or save it. **Saving** is defined as all disposable income that is not consumed. In effect a household has only one decision to make about disposable income.

Since by definition there are only two possible uses of disposable income, spending or saving, when the household decides how much to put to one use, it has automatically decided how much will go to the other.

What determines the amount that households decide to spend on goods and services for consumption and the amount they decide to save? The factors that influence this decision are summarized in the consumption function and the saving function.

The Consumption Function

The **consumption function** relates the total desired consumption expenditure of all households in the economy to the factors that determine it. It is, as we shall see, one of the central relations in macroeconomics.

While we are ultimately interested in the relationship between consumption and national income, the underlying behavior of households depends on the income they actually have to spend—their disposable income. Therefore, we shall start with the relationship between consumption and disposable income and then go on to relate consumption to national income.

Consumption and Disposable Income

One important influence on desired consumption expenditure is household disposable income, represented by Y_d. As disposable income rises, households have more money to spend on consumption—and the evidence is that they do just that. We therefore treat desired consumption expenditure as varying positively with disposable income.

Other factors such as interest rates and inflationary expectations also exert an influence, but we shall neglect them for the moment. The simple theory of consumption focuses on changes in disposable income to explain changes in consumption.

The term *consumption function* describes the relationship between consumption and disposable income.

In Chapter 27 we examined the calculation of disposable income; for the purposes of this discussion all we need to know is that disposable income tends to be a relatively constant fraction of national income.

Some consumption expenditure is autonomous, but most is induced; that is, most varies with disposable income and hence with national income. A schedule relating disposable income to desired consumption expenditure for a hypothetical economy appears in the first two columns of Table 28-1. In this example autonomous consumption expenditure is $100 billion, whereas induced consumption expen-

Table 28-1 The Calculation of Average Propensity to Consume (*APC*) and Marginal Propensity to Consume (*MPC*) (*billions of dollars*)

Disposable income (Y_d)	Desired consumption (C)	$APC = C/Y_d$	ΔY_d (Change in Y_d)	ΔC (Change in C)	$MPC = \Delta C/\Delta Y_d$
$ 0	$ 100	—			
			$ 100	$ 80	0.80
100	180	1.800			
			300	240	0.80
400	420	1.050			
			100	80	0.80
500	500	1.000			
			500	400	0.80
1,000	900	0.900			
			1,000	800	0.80
2,000	1,700	0.850			
			1,000	800	0.80
3,000	2,500	0.833			
			1,000	800	0.80
4,000	3,300	0.825			

***APC* measures the proportion of disposable income that households desire to spend on consumption; *MPC* measures the proportion of any *increment* to disposable income that households desire to spend on consumption.** The data are hypothetical. We call the level of income at which desired consumption equals disposable income the break-even level; in this example it is $500 billion. *APC*, calculated in the third column, declines steadily as income rises. APC exceeds unity—that is, consumption exceeds income— below the break-even level of income. Above the break-even level, *APC* is less than unity.

The last three columns are set between the lines of the first three columns to indicate that they refer to changes in the levels of income and consumption. *MPC*, calculated in the last column, is constant at 0.80 at all levels of Y_d. This indicates that in this example $0.80 of *every* additional $1.00 of disposable income is spent on consumption and $0.20 is allocated to saving.

diture is 80 percent of disposable income. In what follows we use this hypothetical example to illustrate the various properties of the consumption function.

Average and marginal propensities to consume. To discuss the consumption function concisely, economists use two technical expressions.

The **average propensity to consume (*APC*)** is total consumption expenditure divided by total disposable income. The third column of Table 28-1 shows the *APC*s calculated from the data in the table.

The **marginal propensity to consume (*MPC*)** relates the *change* in consumption to the *change* in disposable income that brought it about. *MPC* is the change in disposable income divided into the resulting consumption change, $MPC = \Delta C/\Delta Y_d$ (where the Greek letter Δ, delta, means "a change in"). The last column of Table 28-1 shows the *MPC*s calculated from the data in the table. [34]

The slope of the consumption function. Part (i) of Figure 28-1 shows a graph of the consumption function plotted from the first two columns of Table 28-1. The consumption function has a slope of $\Delta C/\Delta Y_d$, which is, by definition, the marginal propensity to consume. The upward slope of the consumption function shows that *MPC* is positive; increases in income lead to increases in expenditure.

Using the concepts of the average and marginal propensities to consume, we can summarize the properties of the short-term consumption function:

1. There is a break-even level of income at which *APC* equals unity. Below this level *APC* is greater than unity; above it *APC* is less than unity.
2. *MPC* is greater than zero but less than unity for all levels of income.

The 45° line. Figure 28-1(i) contains a line that is constructed by connecting all points where desired consumption (measured on the vertical axis) equals disposable income (measured on the horizontal axis). Since both axes are given in the same units, this line has an upward slope of unity, or (what is the same thing) it forms an angle of 45° with the axes. The line is therefore called the **45° line.**

The 45° line makes a handy reference line. In Figure 28-1(i) it helps locate the break-even level of income at which consumption expenditure equals disposable income. The consumption function cuts the 45° line at the break-even level of income, in this instance \$500. (The 45° line is steeper than the consumption function because *MPC* is less than unity.)

The saving function. Households decide how much to consume and how much to save. As we have said, this is a single decision: how to divide disposable income between consumption and saving. It follows that once we know the dependence of consumption on disposable income, we also automatically know the dependence of saving on disposable income. (This is illustrated in Table 28-2.)

Two saving concepts are exactly parallel to the consumption concepts of *APC* and *MPC*. The **average propensity to save (*APS*)** is the proportion of disposable income that households want to save, derived by dividing total desired saving by total disposable income, $APS = S/Y_d$. The **marginal propensity to save (*MPS*)** relates the *change* in total desired saving to the *change* in disposable income that brought it about, $MPS = \Delta S/\Delta Y_d$.

There is a simple relation between the saving and the consumption propensities. *APC* and *APS* must sum to unity and so must *MPC* and *MPS*. Since

Table 28-2 Consumption and Saving Schedules (*billions of dollars*)

Disposable income	Desired consumption	Desired saving
0	100	−100
100	180	− 80
400	420	− 20
500	500	0
1,000	900	+100
2,000	1,700	+300
3,000	2,500	+500
4,000	3,300	+700

Saving and consumption account for all household disposable income. The first two columns repeat the data from Table 28-1. The third column, desired saving, is disposable income minus desired consumption. Consumption and saving both increase steadily as disposable income rises. In this example the break-even level of disposable income is \$500 billion.

FIGURE 28-1 The Consumption and Saving Functions

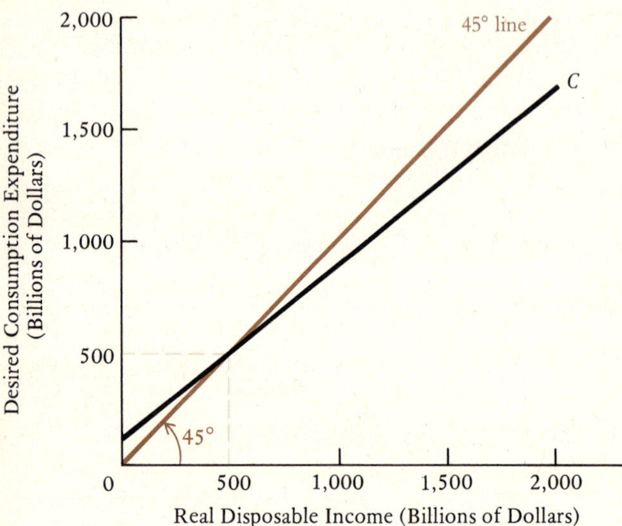

(i) Consumption function

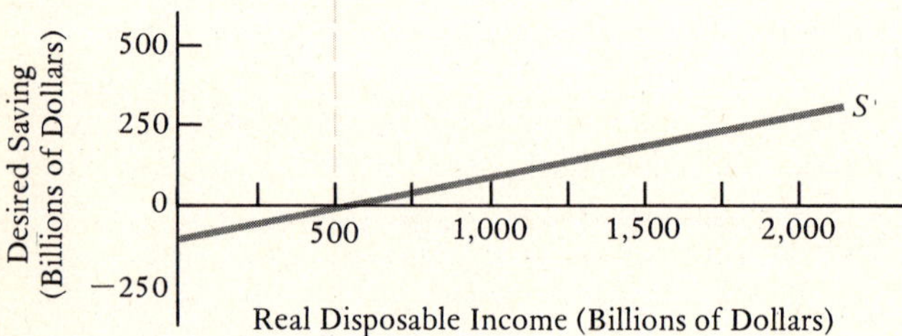

(ii) Saving function

Both consumption and saving rise as disposable income rises. Line C in part (i) relates desired consumption expenditure to disposable income using the hypothetical data from Table 28-1. Its slope, $\Delta C/\Delta Y_d$, is the marginal propensity to consume (MPC). The consumption line cuts the 45° line at the break-even level of disposable income, $500 in this case.

Saving is all disposable income not spent on consumption ($S = Y_d - C$). The relationship between desired saving and disposable income is derived in Table 28-2, and the resulting relationship is shown in part (ii) by line S. Its slope, $\Delta S/\Delta Y_d$, is the marginal propensity to save (MPS). The saving line cuts the horizontal axis at the break-even level of income. The vertical distance between C and the 45° line in part (i) is by definition the height of S in part (ii). That is, any given level of disposable income must be accounted for by the amount consumed plus the amount saved.

income is either spent or saved, it follows that the fractions of incomes consumed and saved must account for all income ($APC + APS = 1$). It also follows that the fraction of any increment to income consumed and saved must account for all of that increment ($MPC + MPS = 1$). [35]

Calculations from Table 28-2 will allow you to confirm these relations in the case of the example given. MPC is 0.80 and MPS is 0.20 at all levels of income, while, for example, at income of $2,000 billion APC is 0.85 and APS is 0.15.

Part (ii) of Figure 28-1 shows the saving schedule given in Table 28-2. At the break-even level of income, where desired consumption equals disposable income, desired saving is zero. The slope of the saving line $\Delta S/\Delta Y_d$ is MPS.

Consumption and Wealth

We have seen that disposable income is an important factor in the consumption-saving decision. A second important factor is the real value of each household's wealth. By a household's **wealth** we mean the sum of all the valuable assets it owns. This includes its car, its house and contents, the value of its money in the bank, pension fund, and any stocks, bonds, or other investments that it holds.

Households save in order to add to their wealth. Other things being equal, a rise in wealth tends to reduce the incentive to add further to wealth; that is, it reduces the incentive to save. Obviously, it is the real value of wealth that matters. Should the money value of wealth and the price level change in the same proportion, leaving real wealth unchanged, the household's incentive to save will be unchanged.

A rise in wealth tends to cause a larger fraction of disposable income to be spent on consumption and a smaller fraction to be saved. This shifts the consumption function upward and the saving function downward, as shown in Figure 28-2. A fall in wealth increases the incentive to save in order to restore wealth. This shifts the consumption function downward and the saving function upward.

Individual households experience both expected and unexpected changes in wealth. For example, either planned saving or unplanned bequests will in-

FIGURE 28-2 Wealth and the Consumption Function

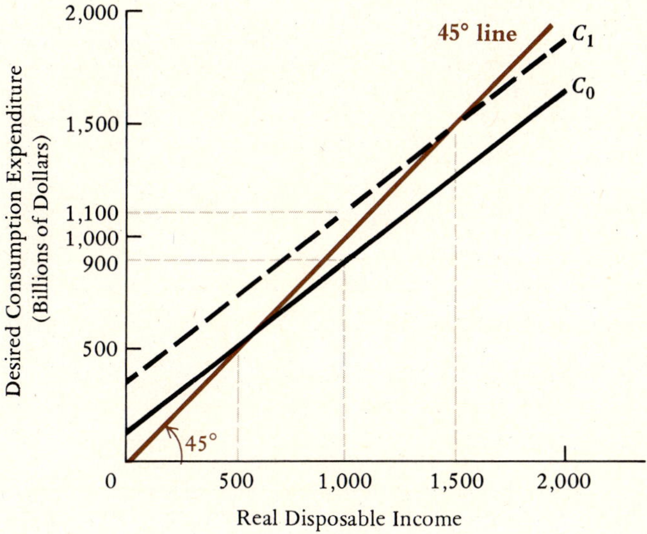

(i) The consumption function shifts up with an increase in wealth

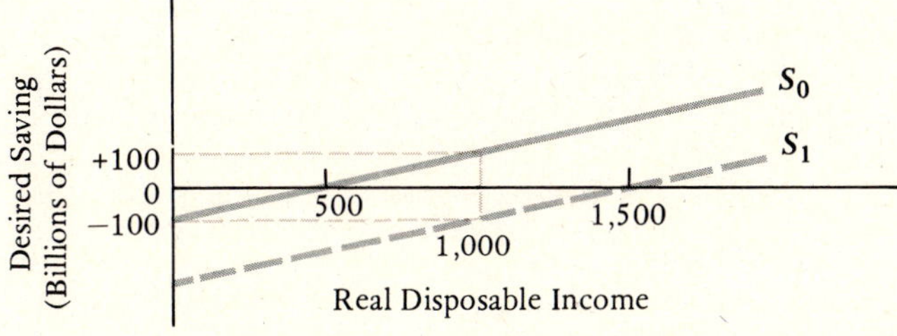

(ii) The saving function shifts down with an increase in wealth

Changes in wealth shift consumption as a function of disposable income. In part (i) line C_0 reproduces the consumption function from Figure 28-1(i). An increase in the level of wealth raises desired consumption at each level of disposable income, thus shifting the consumption line up to C_1. In the figure the consumption function shifts up by \$200, so with disposable income of \$1,000, for example, desired consumption *rises* from \$900 to \$1,100. As a result of the rise in wealth, the break-even level of income rises to \$1,500.

The saving function in part (ii) shifts down by \$200, from S_0 to S_1. Thus, for example, at a disposable income of \$1,000, saving *falls* from plus \$100 to minus \$100.

crease wealth. Similarly, either planned dissaving or unplanned losses reduce wealth.

Many unexpected changes in wealth cancel out across households and so are unimportant for the macroeconomic consumption function. We will see, however, that inflation can be an important source of unexpected changes in wealth in most households.

Planned increases in wealth as a result of past accumulation of wealth can be important for the whole society and can lead to upward shifts in the macro consumption function as wealth accumulates. This effect operates only slowly since wealth accumulates only slowly.

Because for the moment we are focusing on short-term issues, the consumption function used in the text does not include the effects of changes in wealth.

Consumption and National Income

We have related desired consumption to *disposable* income. For a theory of the determination of national income, however, we need to know how consumption is related to national income.

The transition from a relation between consumption and disposable income to one between consumption and national income is readily accomplished since disposable income and national income are themselves related to each other.

The relation between disposable income and national income. On pages 578 and 579 we saw the adjustments required to derive disposable income from national income. Since transfer payments (the major addition) are smaller than total income taxes (the major subtraction), the net effect is for disposable income to be substantially less than national income. (It was about 68 percent of GDP in 1986.)

Relating desired consumption to national income. If we know how consumption relates to disposable income and how disposable income relates to national income, we can derive the relation between consumption and national income.

As an example, assume that disposable income is always 90 percent of national income. Then, whatever the relation between C and Y, we can always substitute $0.9Y$ for Y_d. Thus if changes in consumption were always 80 percent of changes in Y_d, changes in consumption would always be 72 percent (80 percent of 90 percent) of Y. [36]

Table 28-3 shows that we can write desired consumption as a function of Y as well as of Y_d. We can then derive the marginal response of consumption to changes in Y by determining the proportion of any change in *national income* that goes to a change in desired consumption.

The marginal response of consumption to changes in *national income* ($\Delta C/\Delta Y$) is equal to the marginal propensity to consume out of *disposable income* ($\Delta C/\Delta Y_d$) multiplied by the fraction of national income that becomes disposable income ($\Delta Y_d/\Delta Y$).

Table 28-3 Consumption as a Function of Disposable Income and National Income (*billions of dollars*)

(1) National income (Y)	(2) Disposable income ($Y_d = 0.9Y$)	(3) Desired consumption ($C = 100 + 0.8Y_d$)
100	90	172
1,000	900	820
2,000	1,800	1,540
3,000	2,700	2,260
4,000	3,600	2,980

If desired consumption depends on disposable income, which in turn depends on national income, desired consumption can be written as a function of either income concept. The data are hypothetical. They show deductions of 10 percent of any level of national income to arrive at disposable income. Deductions of 10 percent of Y imply that the remaining 90 percent of Y becomes disposable income. The numbers also show consumption as \$100 billion plus 80 percent of disposable income.

By relating columns 2 and 3, one sees consumption as a function of disposable income. By relating columns 1 and 3, one sees the derived relationship between consumption and national income. In this example the change in consumption in response to a change in disposable income (i.e., the *MPC*) is 0.8, while the change in consumption in response to a change in national income is 0.72.

We now have a function showing how desired consumption expenditure varies as national income varies. The relation is defined for real income and real expenditure (i.e., income and expenditure measured in constant dollars). For every given level of real income, measured in terms of purchasing power, households desire to spend some fraction of that purchasing power and to save the rest.

Desired Net Exports

Canada is rich in natural resources and raw materials, which it exports to many other countries that are less favorably endowed. Also, Canada's manufacturing sector is both specialized and export-oriented. As we will see, fluctuations in exports play a key role in explaining fluctuations in the level of economic activity in the Canadian economy.

Similarly, imports play an important role in the Canadian economy; Canadian households typically consume a wide range of imported goods, and Canadian industry uses imported parts and components. A large segment of the Canadian economy is involved in foreign trade—primarily, but not exclusively, with the United States.

The Net Export Function

Exports depend on spending decisions made by foreign households that purchase Canadian goods and services. Therefore, exports will not necessarily change as a result of changes in Canadian national income.

Imports, however, depend on the spending decisions of Canadian households. All categories of expenditure have an import content—even domestic cars, for example, use some imported components in their manufacture. Thus imports rise when the other categories of expenditure rise. Because consumption rises with income, imports of foreign-produced consumption goods and materials that go into the production of domestically produced consumption goods also rise with income.

Desired net exports are negatively related to national income because of the positive relationship between desired expenditure on imports and national income.

This negative relationship between net exports and national income is called the *net export function*. Data for a hypothetical economy with constant exports and with imports that are 10 percent of national income are given in Table 28-4 and illustrated in Figure 28-3. In this example exports form the autonomous component and imports the induced component of the desired net export function.

Shifts in the Net Export Function

We have seen that the net export function relates net exports ($X - M$) to national income. It is drawn on the assumption that everything that affects net exports except domestic national income remains constant. The major factors that must be held constant are foreign national income, domestic and foreign prices, and the exchange rate. A change in any of these will affect the amount of net exports that will occur at each level of Canadian national income and hence will shift the net export function.

Notice that anything that affects Canadian exports will change the values in the export column in Table 28-4 and so will shift the net export function parallel to itself, upward if exports increase and downward if exports decrease. Also notice that any-

Table 28-4 A Net Export Schedule (*billions of dollars*)

National income (Y)	Exports (X)	Imports ($M = 0.1Y$)	Net exports
1,000	240	100	140
2,000	240	200	40
2,400	240	240	0
3,000	240	300	−60
4,000	240	400	−160
5,000	240	500	−260

Net exports fall as national income rises. The data are hypothetical. They assume that exports are constant and that imports are 10 percent of national income. Net exports are then positive at low levels of national income and negative at high levels.

FIGURE 28-3 The Net Export Function

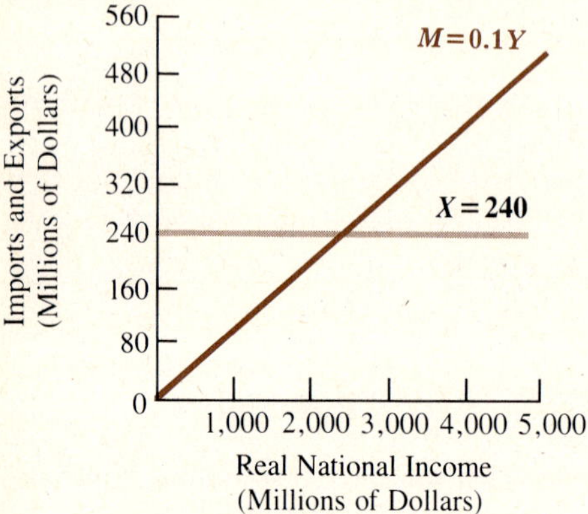

(i) Export and import functions

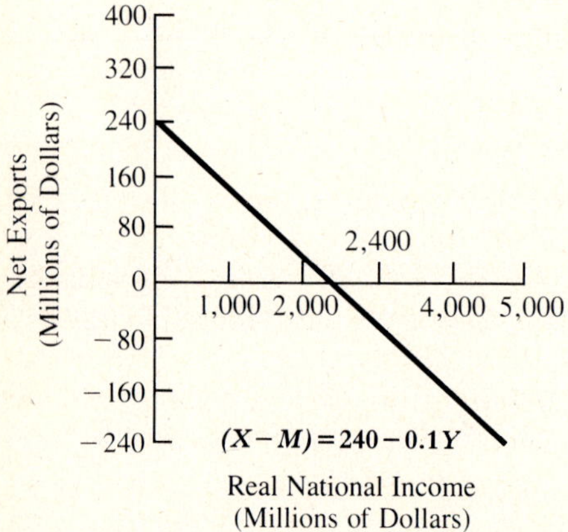

(ii) Net export function

Net exports, defined as the difference between exports and imports, are inversely related to the level of national income. In part (i) exports are constant at $240 million while imports rise with the national income. Therefore net exports, shown in part (ii), decline with national income. The figure is based on the hypothetical data in Table 28-4. With national income equal to $2,400 million, imports are equal to exports at $240 million and net exports are zero. For levels of national income below $2,400 million, imports are less than exports and hence net exports are positive. For levels of national income above $2,400 million, imports are greater than exports and hence net exports are negative.

thing that affects the proportion of income Canadians wish to spend on imports will change the values in the import column in Table 28-4 and thus will change the slope of the net export function by making imports more or less responsive to changes in domestic income.

Foreign income. An increase in foreign income, other things being equal, will lead to an increase in the quantity of Canadian goods demanded by foreign countries, that is, to an increase in Canadian exports. The increase is in the constant X of the net export function, which shifts upward as a result. A fall in foreign income leads to a downward shift in the net export function.

Foreign prices. An increase in foreign prices will cause both foreign and domestic agents to substitute cheaper Canadian goods for the now more expensive foreign goods. This will cause changes in both exports and imports. Exports will rise, and the amount of imports associated with any given level of Canadian national income will fall. As a result the net export function will shift upward. A fall in foreign prices has the reverse effect, with substitution away from Canadian goods in favor of foreign goods and a downward shift in the net export curve.

Domestic prices. An increase in domestic prices leads both foreign and domestic agents to substitute foreign goods for the now more expensive Canadian goods. The export part of net exports falls, and more imports will be associated with each level of domestic income. As a result the net export function shifts downward. A fall in domestic prices leads to substitution in favor of Canadian goods and an upward shift in the net export function.

The exchange rate. A depreciation of the Canadian dollar has the effect of raising the Canadian price of imports while lowering the prices paid by foreigners for Canadian exports. It thus shifts expenditure away from foreign goods and toward Canadian goods. Canadians will import less at each level of Canadian national income, and foreigners will buy more of our export goods. The net export function thus shifts upward. An appreciation of the Canadian dollar has the opposite effect, causing substitution of foreign for Canadian goods, thus shifting the net export function downward.

Other Expenditure Categories

We have seen that desired consumption expenditure and desired net export expenditure each have an autonomous and an induced component. The induced components mean that desired aggregate expenditure depends on national income.

The relationship between desired aggregate expenditure and national income depends not only on desired consumption and net exports but also on the behavior of the other major expenditure categories, I and G. As we shall see in later chapters, changes in each of these play an important role in understanding changes in national income. For our present purposes of understanding how the equilibrium level of national income is determined, it is useful to keep things as simple as possible. Where we can, we treat these components as constant and include them in autonomous expenditure.

Desired investment expenditure. For the present it is convenient to study how the level of national income adjusts to a fixed level of planned real investment. So we assume that firms plan to make a constant amount of business fixed investment in plant each year and that they plan to hold their inventories constant. In Chapter 31 we shall drop these assumptions and study the important effects on national income caused by changes in the level of desired investment.

Desired government expenditure. Governments intend to spend, and succeed in spending, many billions of dollars on currently produced goods and services. In this chapter we take desired and actual real government expenditure as a constant. We assume that the real value of government expenditure does not change as the circumstances of the economy change. This assumption allows us to see how national income adjusts to a constant level of real government expenditure. In Chapter 32 we shall drop this assumption and study how national income responds to changes in desired and actual government expenditure.

The Aggregate Expenditure Function

The aggregate expenditure function relates the level of desired real expenditure to the level of real income. Total desired expenditure on the nation's output is the sum of desired consumption, investment, government, and net export expenditures, or

$$AE = C + I + G + (X - M)$$

Table 28-5 illustrates how such a function can be calculated, given the consumption function and the levels of desired investment, government, and net exports expenditures at each level of income. The resulting aggregate expenditure function is illustrated in Figure 28-4 (p. 597).

The Propensity to Spend out of National Income

Earlier we defined propensities to consume and to save that together account for all household disposable income. We now define propensities to spend and not to spend that together account for all national income.

The fraction of any increment to national income that will be spent on domestic production is measured by the change in aggregate expenditure divided by the change in income, symbolized by $\Delta AE/\Delta Y$. It is called the economy's **marginal propensity to spend.** The value of the marginal propensity to spend, which is something greater than zero but less than one, may be indicated by the letter z. The amount $1 - \Delta AE/\Delta Y$ is the fraction of any increment to national income that is not spent. This is the **marginal propensity not to spend.**[1] This makes the value of the marginal propensity not to spend $1 - z$.

[1] More fully, these terms would be called the marginal propensity to spend *on national income* and the marginal propensity to not spend *on national income*. Expenditures on imports are included in the latter. The marginal propensity not to spend ($1 - z$) is often referred to as the *marginal propensity to withdraw*. Not spending a part of one's income amounts to a *withdrawal* from the circular flow of income as described in Figure 3-1.

Table 28-5 The Aggregate Expenditure Function (*billions of dollars*)

National income (Y)	Desired consumption expenditure ($C=100+0.72Y$)	Desired investment expenditure ($I=250$)	Desired government expenditure ($G=170$)	Desired net exports expenditure ($X-M=240-0.10Y$)	Desired aggregate expenditure ($AE=C+I+G+[X-M]$)
100	172	250	170	230	952
400	388	250	170	200	1,008
500	460	250	170	190	1,070
1,000	820	250	170	140	1,380
2,000	1,540	250	170	40	2,000
3,000	2,260	250	170	−60	2,620
4,000	2,980	250	170	−160	3,240
5,000	3,700	250	170	−260	3,860

The aggregate expenditure function is the sum of desired consumption, investment, government, and net export expenditures. The table is based on the hypothetical data given in Tables 28-3 and 28-4. The autonomous components of desired aggregate expenditure are desired investment, desired government, desired export expenditures, and the constant term in desired consumption expenditure. The induced components are the second term in desired consumption expenditure ($0.72Y$) and desired imports ($0.1Y$).

The marginal response of consumption to a change in national income is 0.72, calculated as the product of the marginal propensity to consume (0.8) times the fraction of national income that becomes disposable income (0.9). Because this exceeds the marginal propensity to import out of national income (0.1), desired aggregate expenditure is positively related to national income, as shown in the column at the far right. The marginal response of desired aggregate expenditure to a change in national income, $\Delta AE/\Delta Y$, is 0.62.

To illustrate, suppose that the economy produces \$1.00 of extra income and that the response to this is governed by the relationships in Tables 28-3 and 28-4. Since \$0.10 is collected by the government as taxes, \$0.90 is converted into disposable income, and 80 percent of this amount (\$0.72) becomes consumption expenditure. But import expenditure also rises by \$0.10, so expenditure on domestic goods, that is, aggregate expenditure, rises by \$0.62. Thus z, the marginal propensity to spend, is 0.62 (0.62/1.00). What is not spent on domestic output includes the \$0.10 in taxes, the \$0.18 of disposable income that is saved, and the \$0.10 of import expenditure, for a total of \$0.38. Hence the marginal propensity not to spend, $1 - z$, is $0.38 = (1 - 0.62)$.

Determining Equilibrium National Income

Now we can see how equilibrium national income is determined, *given a constant price level*. To do this we study the *equilibrium conditions,* the conditions that must be fulfilled if national income is to be in equilibrium.

Table 28-6 illustrates the determination of equilibrium national income for our simple hypothetical economy. Suppose that firms are producing a final output of \$1,000 and thus national income is \$1,000. According to the table, aggregate desired expenditure is \$1,380 at this level of income. If firms persist in producing a current output of only \$1,000 in the face of an aggregate desired expenditure of \$1,380, one of two things must happen.[2]

One possibility is that households, firms, and governments will be unable to spend the extra \$380 that they would like to spend, so lines or waiting lists of unsatisfied customers will appear. These queues will send a signal to firms that sales can be increased if production is increased. When the firms increase production, national income rises. Of course, the individual firms are interested only in

[2] A third possibility, that prices would rise, has been excluded by assumption in this chapter.

FIGURE 28-4 An Aggregate Expenditure Function

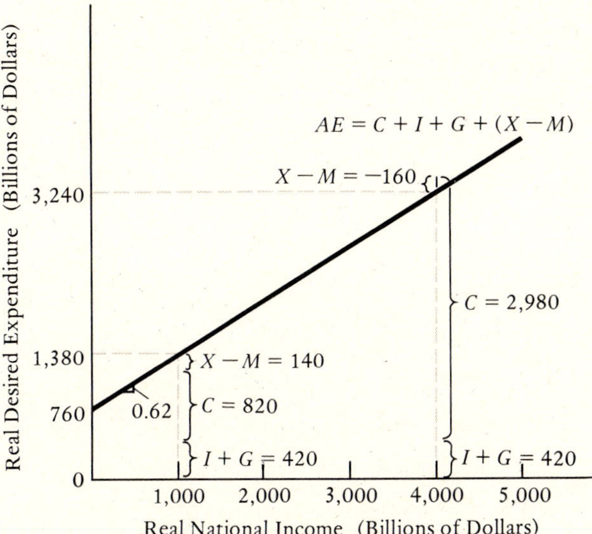

The aggregate expenditure function is derived by adding the four components of expenditure: consumption (*C*), investment (*I*), government (*G*), and net exports (*X* − *M*). The figure is drawn using the hypothetical data from Table 26-5. Substituting in the expressions from the table for each of the four components of *AE* gives

$$AE = (100 + 0.72Y) + 250 + 170 + (240 - 0.1Y)$$

Combining these terms we get

$$AE = 760 + 0.62Y$$

Hence in the figure the *AE* function is drawn as a straight line with an intercept of 760 and a slope of 0.62. The intercept is the sum of the two constant components ($I + G = 420$) plus the constant terms from the other two components (100 from *C* and 240 from $X - M$). The slope, 0.62, is the marginal propensity to spend. It represents the marginal response of consumption to a change in national income, 0.72, net of the marginal propensity to import, 0.10.

Two examples are illustrated. When income equals $1,000,

$$AE = 760 + (0.62 \times 1,000) = 1,380$$

If income rises by $3,000 to equal $4,000, investment and government expenditures remain at 420, consumption expenditure rises by 2,160 (0.72 × 3,000) to 2,980, and net exports fall by 300 (0.10 × 3,000) to −160. Thus *AE* rises by 1,860 to 3,240.

TABLE 28-6 The Determination of Equilibrium National Income (*billions of dollars*)

National income (Y)	Desired aggregate expenditure ($AE = C + I + G + [X - M]$)	
100	952	Pressure on
400	1,008	income to
500	1,070	rise
1,000	1,380	↓
2,000	2,000	Equilibrium income
3,000	2,620	↑
4,000	3,240	Pressure on
5,000	3,860	income to
		fall

National income is in equilibrium where aggregate desired expenditure equals national income. The date are taken from Table 28-5. When national income is below its equilibrium level, aggregate desired expenditure exceeds the value of current output. This creates an incentive for firms to increase output and hence for national income to rise. When national income is above its equilibrium level, desired expenditure is less than the value of current output. This creates an incentive for firms to reduce output and hence for national income to fall. Only at the equilibrium level of national income is aggregate desired expenditure exactly equal to the value of the current output.

their own sales and profits, but their individual actions cause an increase in GDP.

The second possibility is that all spenders will spend everything they wanted to spend. But then expenditure will exceed current output, which can happen only when some expenditure plans are fulfilled by purchasing inventories of goods that were produced in the past. In this example the fulfillment of plans to purchase $1,380 worth of commodities in the face of a current output of only $1,000 will reduce inventories by $380. As long as inventories last, more goods can be sold than are currently being produced.

Eventually inventories will run out, but before this happens, firms will increase their output as they see their inventories being drawn down. Extra sales can then be made without a further pulling down of inventories. Once again the consequence of each individual firm's behavior, in search of its own individual profits, is an increase in national income. Thus the final response to an excess of aggregate desired expenditure over current output is a rise in national income toward its equilibrium value.

At any level of national income at which aggregate desired expenditure exceeds total output, there will be pressure for national income to rise.

Next consider national income equal to \$4,000 in Table 28-6. At this level desired expenditure on domestically produced goods is only \$3,240. If firms persist in producing \$4,000 worth of goods, \$760 worth must remain unsold. Therefore, inventories must rise. But firms will not allow inventories of unsold goods to rise indefinitely; sooner or later they will reduce the level of output to the level of sales. When they do, national income will fall.

At any level of income for which aggregate desired expenditure falls short of total output, there will be a pressure for national income to fall.

Finally, consider national income equal to \$2,000 in the table. At this level, and only at this level, aggregate desired expenditure is exactly equal to national income. Purchasers fulfill their spending plans without causing inventories to change. There is no incentive for firms to alter output. Since total output is the same as national income, national income will remain steady; it is in equilibrium.

The equilibrium level of national income occurs where aggregate desired expenditure equals total output.

This conclusion is quite general and does not depend on the numbers used in the specific example. **[37]**

Equilibrium Illustrated

Figure 28-5 shows the determination of the equilibrium level of national income. The line labeled *AE* graphs the aggregate expenditure function. Its slope is the marginal propensity to spend. The line labeled $AE = Y$ shows the equilibrium condition that desired aggregate expenditure, *AE*, equals national income, *Y*. Since the $AE = Y$ line plots points where the vertical distance equals the horizontal distance, it forms an angle of 45° with the axes. Any point on this line is a possible equilibrium.

FIGURE 28-5 Equilibrium National Income

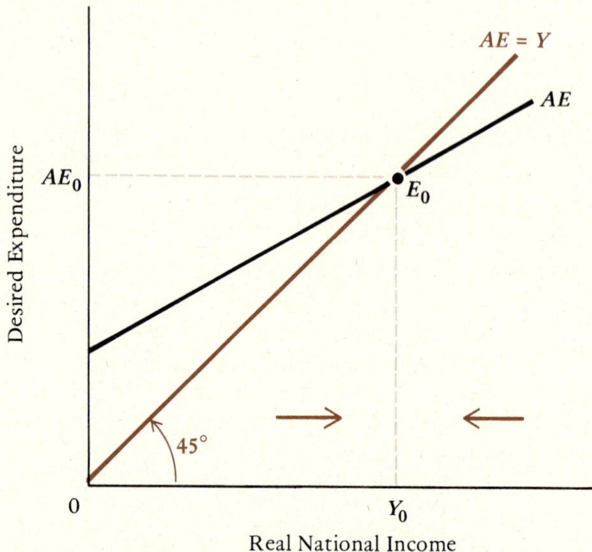

The equilibrium level of national income occurs at E_0, where the desired aggregate expenditure line intersects the 45° line. If real national income is below Y_0, desired aggregate expenditure will exceed national income, and production will rise. This is shown by the arrow to the left of Y_0. If national income is above Y_0, desired aggregate expenditure will be less than national income, and production will fall. This is shown by the arrow to the right of Y_0. Only when real national income is Y_0 will desired aggregate expenditure equal real national income ($AE_0 = Y_0$).

Graphically, equilibrium occurs at the level of income at which the aggregate desired expenditure line intersects the 45° line. This is the level of income where desired expenditure is just equal to total national income and therefore is just sufficient to purchase total final output.

We have now explained the equilibrium level of national income that arises at a *given price level*. In the rest of this chapter we study the forces that cause equilibrium income to change; we continue with our simplifying assumption that the price level remains constant.

Changes in National Income

Since the *AE* curve plays a central role in our explanation of the equilibrium value of national income, you should not be surprised to hear that the behavior of the *AE* curve also plays a central role in explaining why national income changes. To understand this influence we must recall an important distinction first encountered in Chapter 4.

Suppose desired aggregate expenditure rises. This may be either a response to a change in national income or the result of an increased desire to spend at each level of national income. A change in national income causes a *movement along* the aggregate expenditure function. An increased desire to spend at each level of national income causes a *shift in* the aggregate expenditure function. Figure 28-6 illustrates this important distinction.

Shifts in the Aggregate Expenditure Function

For any specific aggregate expenditure function there is a unique level of equilibrium national income. If the aggregate expenditure function shifts, the equilibrium will be disturbed and national income will change. Thus if we wish to find causes of changes in national income, we must look for causes of shifts in the *AE* function.

The aggregate expenditure function shifts when one of its components shifts, that is, when there is a shift in the consumption function, in desired investment expenditure, in desired government expenditure, or in desired net exports. Such shifts were defined earlier as changes in *autonomous* aggregate expenditure.

Increases in Autonomous Expenditure

What will happen if households permanently increase their levels of consumption spending at each level of disposable income? If the Ford Motor Company increases its rate of annual investment by $25 million

FIGURE 28-6 Movements Along and Shifts of the *AE* Curve

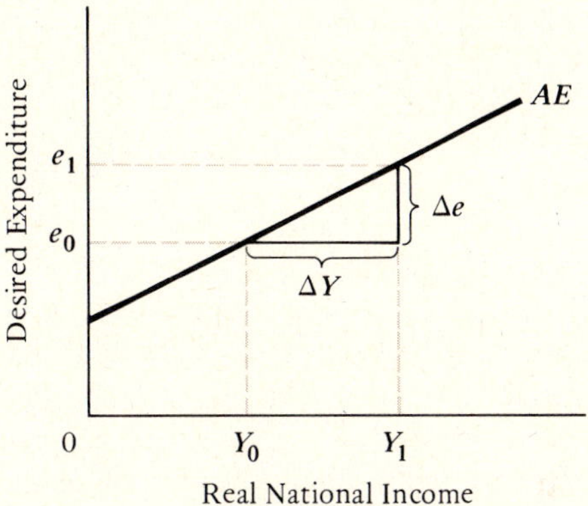

(i) A movement along the *AE* function

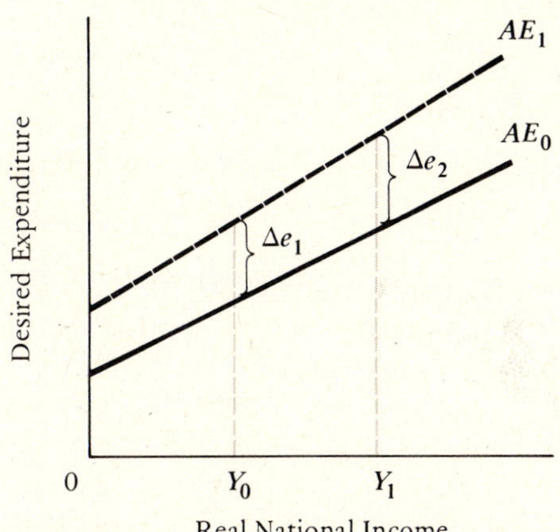

(ii) A shift of the *AE* function

A movement along the aggregate expenditure function occurs in response to a change in income; a shift of the *AE* function indicates a different level of desired expenditure at each level of income. In part (i) a change in income of ΔY, from Y_0 to Y_1, changes expenditure by Δe, from e_0 to e_1. In part (ii) a shift in the expenditure function from AE_0 to AE_1 raises the amount of expenditure associated with *each* level of income. At Y_0, for example, desired aggregate expenditure is increased by Δe_1; at Y_1, it is increased by Δe_2. (If the shift is a parallel one, $\Delta e_1 = \Delta e_2$.)

in order to meet the threat from imported cars? If the government increases its defense spending? Or if grain exports soar? (In considering these questions, remember that we are dealing with continuous flows measured as so much per period of time. An upward shift in the expenditure function means that expenditure rises to and stays at a higher amount.)

Because any such increase shifts the entire aggregate expenditure function upward, the same analysis applies to all of the changes mentioned. Two types of shift in *AE* occur. First, if the same addition to expenditure occurs at all levels of income, the *AE* curve shifts parallel to itself, as shown in Figure 28-7(i). Second, if there is a change in the propensity to spend out of national income, the slope of the *AE* curve changes, as shown in Figure 28-7(ii). (Recall

FIGURE 28-7 Shifts in the *AE* Function

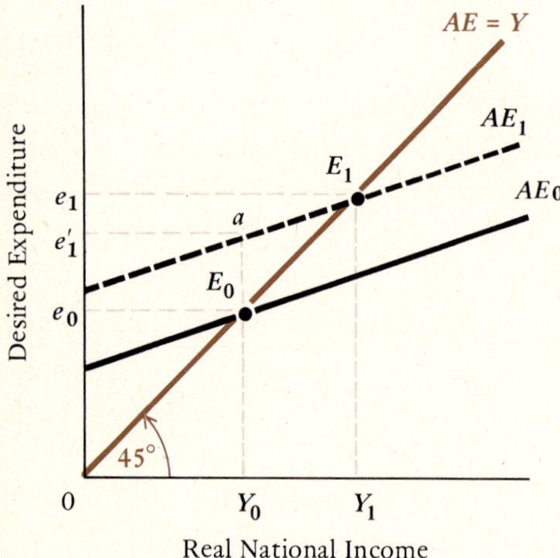

(i) A parallel shift in *AE*

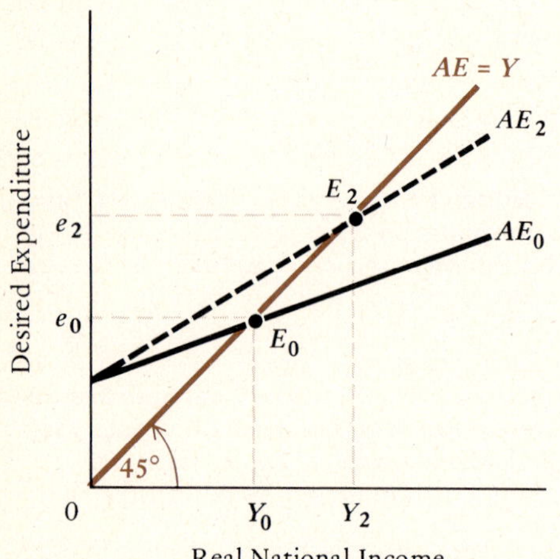

(ii) A change in the slope of *AE*

Upward shifts in the *AE* function increase equilibrium income; downward shifts decrease equilibrium income. In both part (i) and part (ii) the aggregate expenditure function is initially AE_0, with national income Y_0.

In part (i) a parallel upward *shift* in the *AE* curve from AE_0 to AE_1 means that desired expenditure has increased by the same amount at each level of national income. For example, at Y_0 desired expenditure rises from e_0 to e_1' and therefore exceeds national income. Equilibrium is reached at E_1, where income is Y_1 and expenditure e_1. The increase in desired expenditure from e_1' to e_1, represented by a *movement along* AE_1, is an induced response to the increase in income from Y_0 to Y_1.

In part (ii) a nonparallel upward shift in the *AE* curve, say, from AE_0 to AE_2, means that the marginal propensity to spend at each level of national income has increased. This leads to an increase in equilibrium national income. Equilibrium is reached at E_2, where the new level of expenditure e_2 is equal to income Y_2. Again, the initial *shift* in the *AE* curve induces a *movement along* the new *AE* curve.

Downward shifts in the *AE* function, from AE_1 to AE_0 or from AE_2 to AE_0, would lead to a fall in equilibrium income to Y_0.

that the slope of the *AE* curve is z, the marginal propensity to spend.)

Figure 28-7 shows that upward shifts in the aggregate expenditure function increase equilibrium national income. There we see that an upward *shift* of the *AE* curve will induce a *movement along* the new *AE* curve. This will not stop until a new equilibrium occurs. At the new, higher equilibrium level of national income, the flow of desired aggregate expenditure again equals national income. (We continue to assume that the price level is constant.)

Decreases in Autonomous Expenditure

What will happen to national income if consumption, investment, government spending, or exports decrease? All these changes shift the aggregate expenditure function downward. A constant reduction in expenditure at all levels of income shifts *AE* parallel to itself. A fall in the propensity to spend out of national income reduces the slope of the *AE* function.

Changes in Tax Rates

If tax rates change, the relationship between disposable income and national income changes.[3] For the same level of national income there will be a different level of disposable income and thus a different level of consumption. This is illustrated in Table 28-7. Consequently, z, the marginal propensity to spend out of national income, will have changed.

Consider a decrease in tax rates. If the government decreases its rate of income tax so that it collects 10 cents less out of every dollar of national income, disposable income rises in relation to national income. Thus consumption also rises at every level of national income. This results in a (nonparallel) upward shift of the *AE* curve, that is, a change in the slope of the curve, as shown in Figure 28-7(ii). The result of this shift will be a rise in equilibrium national income, as is also shown in Figure 28-7(ii).

A rise in tax rates has the opposite effect. It reduces disposable income and hence less consumption expenditure at each level of national income. This results in a (nonparallel) downward shift of the *AE* curve and thus decreases the level of equilibrium national income. This, too, is illustrated in Figure 28-7(ii).

[3] Effective tax rates can be changed either by changes in the percent of taxable income that is taken in taxes or by changes in the percent of national income that is taxable. For simplicity, in the text we have assumed that all national income is taxable.

The results restated. We have now derived two important general predictions of the elementary theory of national income.

1. **A rise in the amount of desired consumption, investment, government, or export expenditure associated with each level of national income will increase equilibrium national income.**
2. **A fall in the amount of desired consumption, investment, government, or export expenditure associated with each level of national income will lower equilibrium national income.**

A change in desired consumption in relation to national income can arise, as we have seen, either because the consumption function shifts or because the relation between disposable income and national income is altered.

The Multiplier

We now know the *direction* of the changes in national income that occur in response to various shifts in the aggregate expenditure function. But what about the *magnitude* of these changes?

Economists need an answer to this question to determine the effects of changes in expenditures in both the private and public sectors. During a recession the government often takes measures to stimulate the economy. If these measures have a larger effect than estimated, demand may rise too much and full employment may be reached with demand still rising. This outcome will have an inflationary impact on the economy. If the government greatly overestimates the effect of its measures, the recession will persist longer than is necessary. In this case there is a danger that the policy will be discredited as ineffective, even though the correct diagnosis is that too little of the right thing was done.

TABLE 28-7 Tax Changes Shift the Function Relating Consumption to National Income (*billions of dollars*)

	Disposable income equal to 80 percent of national income		Disposable income equal to 90 percent of national income	
(1) National income (Y)	(2) Disposable income ($Y_d = 0.8Y$)	(3) Consumption ($C = 100 + 0.8Y_d$)	(4) Disposable income ($Y_d = 0.9Y$)	(5) Consumption ($C = 100 + 0.8Y_d$)
100	80	164	90	172
500	400	420	450	460
1,000	800	740	900	820

The consumption function shifts if the relation between disposable and national income changes. The table is based on the simplified hypothetical consumption function from Table 28-1 combined with the assumption that Y_d is a constant fraction of Y. Initially, $Y_d = 0.8Y$. This yields a schedule relating consumption to national income that is given in columns 1 and 3 and is described by the equation $C = 100 + 0.64Y$. Income tax rates are then decreased so that now 90 percent of national income becomes disposable income. Column 4 indicates the Y_d that corresponds at the decreased tax rate to each level of Y shown in column 1. With an unchanged consumption function, consumption at the new tax rate is given by column 5. Columns 1 and 5 give the new schedule relating consumption to national income, described by the equation $C = 100 + 0.72Y$.

Definition. A measure of the magnitude of changes in income is provided by the multiplier. We have just seen that a shift in the aggregate expenditure curve will cause a change in equilibrium national income. Such a shift will be caused by a change in any autonomous component of aggregate expenditure, for example, an increase or decrease in investment or government spending. An increase in desired aggregate expenditure increases equilibrium national income by a multiple of the initial increase in autonomous expenditure. The **multiplier** is the ratio of changed income to changed expenditure, that is, the change in national income divided by the change in autonomous expenditure that brings it about.

Why the multiplier is greater than unity. What will happen to national income if, with unchanged tax rates, the government increases its spending on road construction by $1 billion per year?

Initially the road program will create $1 billion worth of new national income and a corresponding amount of employment for households and firms on which the initial billion dollars is spent. But this is not the end of the story. The increase in national income of $1 billion will cause an increase in disposable income, which will cause an induced rise in consumption expenditure. Road crews and road contractors, who gain new income directly from the government's road program, will spend some of it on food, clothing, entertainment, cars, television sets, and other consumption commodities. When output expands to meet this demand, employment will increase in all the affected industries. New incomes will then be created for workers and firms in these industries. When they in turn spend their newly earned incomes, output and employment will rise further. More income will be created and more expenditure induced. Indeed, at this stage you could wonder whether the increases in income will ever come to an end. To deal with this concern, we need to consider the multiplier in more precise terms.

The simple multiplier. Consider an increase in autonomous expenditure of ΔA, which might be, say, $1 billion per year. Remember that ΔA stands for *any* increase in autonomous expenditure; this could be an increase in investment, in government purchases, in exports, or in the autonomous component of consumption. The new autonomous expenditure shifts the aggregate expenditure function upward by that amount. National income is no longer in equilibrium at its original level since desired aggregate

FIGURE 28-8 The Simple Multiplier

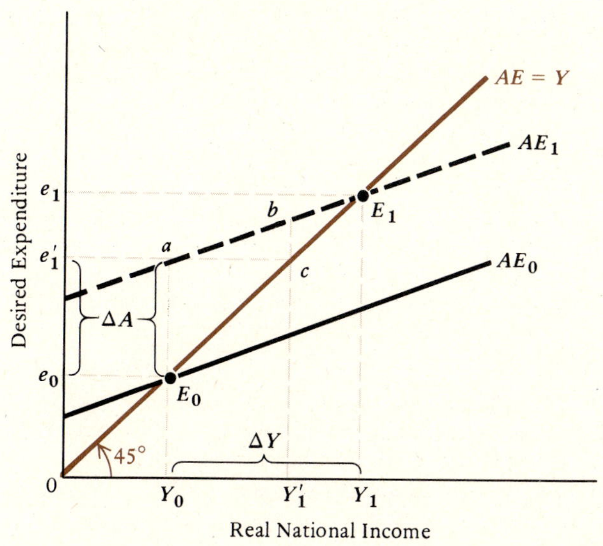

An increase in desired aggregate expenditure increases equilibrium national income by a multiple of the initial increase in autonomous expenditure. The initial equilibrium occurs at E_0 where AE_0 intersects the 45° line. At this point, desired expenditure e_0 is equal to national income Y_0. An increase in autonomous expenditure of ΔA then shifts the desired expenditure function upward to AE_1. If national income stays at Y_0, desired expenditure at point a is e_1'. Since this level of desired expenditure is greater than income, national income will rise. If income rises only by ΔA, it rises to Y_1' (point c, where $e_1' = Y_1'$). But at Y_1' desired expenditure still exceeds income by the amount bc.

Equilibrium occurs when income rises to Y_1. Here desired expenditure e_1 equals income Y_1. The extra expenditure of $e_1'e_1$ represents the induced increases in expenditure. It is the amount by which the final increase in income, ΔY, exceeds the initial increase in autonomous expenditure, ΔA. Since ΔY is greater than ΔA, the multiplier is greater than unity.

expenditure now exceeds income. Equilibrium is restored by a *movement along* the new AE curve.

The **simple multiplier** measures the change in equilibrium national income that occurs in response to a change in autonomous expenditure *at a constant price level*. We refer to it as simple because we have simplified the situation by assuming that the price level is constant. Figure 28-8 illustrates the simple multiplier and makes clear that it is greater than unity. Box 28-1 (p. 605) provides a numerical example.

The Size of the Simple Multiplier

The size of the multiplier depends on the slope of the AE function, that is, on the marginal propensity to spend, z. This is illustrated in Figure 28-9.

A high marginal propensity to spend means a steep AE curve. The expenditure induced by any initial increase in income is large, with the result that the final rise in income is correspondingly large. By contrast, a low marginal propensity to spend means a relatively flat AE curve. The expenditure induced by the initial increase in income is small, and the final rise in income is not much larger than the initial rise in autonomous expenditure that brought it about.

The larger the marginal propensity to spend, the steeper the aggregate expenditure function and the larger the multiplier.

The precise value of the simple multiplier can be derived by using elementary algebra. The derivation is given in Box 28-2 (p. 606). The result is that the simple multiplier, which we call K, is

$$K = \Delta Y/\Delta A = 1/(1 - z)$$

where z is the marginal propensity to spend out of national income. (As we have seen, z is the slope of the aggregate expenditure function.)

As we saw earlier, the term $1 - z$ stands for the marginal propensity not to spend out of national income. For example, if \$0.80 of every \$1.00 of new national income is spent ($z = 0.80$), then \$0.20 is the amount not spent. The value of the multiplier is then calculated as $K = 1/0.20 = 5$.

The simple multiplier can be written as the reciprocal of the marginal propensity not to spend.

FIGURE 28-9 The Size of the Simple Multiplier

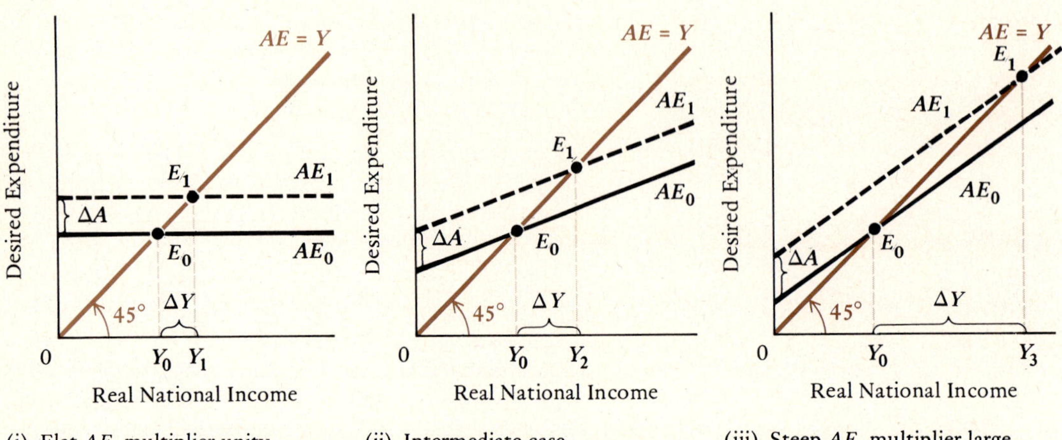

(i) Flat AE, multiplier unity

(ii) Intermediate case

(iii) Steep AE, multiplier large

The larger the marginal propensity to spend out of national income (z), the steeper the AE curve and the larger the multiplier. In each part of the figure the aggregate expenditure function is AE_0, equilibrium is at E_0, with income Y_0. The AE curve then shifts upward to AE_1 as a result of an increase in autonomous expenditure of ΔA. ΔA is the same in each part. The new equilibrium is at E_1.

In part (i) the AE function is horizontal, indicating a marginal propensity to spend of zero ($z = 0$). The change in income ΔY is only the increase in autonomous expenditure since there is no induced expenditure by those who receive the initial increase in income. The simple multiplier is then unity, its minimum possible value.

In part (ii) the AE curve slopes upward but is still relatively flat (z is low). The increase in national income to Y_2 is only slightly greater than the increase in autonomous expenditure that brought it about.

In part (iii) the AE function is quite steep (z is high). Now the increase in income to Y_3 is much larger than the increase in autonomous expenditure that brought it about. The simple multiplier is quite large.

From this we see that if $1 - z$ is very small, the multiplier will be very large (because extra income induces much extra spending). The largest possible value of $1 - z$ is unity, when z equals zero, indicating that all extra national income is not spent. In this case the multiplier itself has a value of unity, indicating that the increase in equilibrium national income is confined to the initial increase in autonomous expenditure. This is illustrated in Figure 28-9.

To estimate the size of the multiplier in an actual economy, we need to estimate the value of the marginal propensity not to spend out of national income in that economy. Evidence suggests that the Canadian value is larger than the 0.2 we used in our example.

The various elements of national income that are "not spent," that is, that are in $1 - z$, include income taxes, savings, and import expenditures. For the Canadian economy in the 1980s this leads to a realistic estimate of about 0.5 for z and thus also about 0.5 for $1 - z$. Thus the simple multiplier is approximately equal to 2, not 5 as in the example.

The simple multiplier is a useful starting point for understanding the effects of expenditure shifts on national income; however, many complications will arise in subsequent chapters.

BOX 28-1

The Multiplier: A Numerical Example

Consider an economy that has a marginal propensity to spend out of national income of 0.80. Suppose that autonomous expenditure increases by $1 billion per year because the government spends an extra $1 billion per year on new roads. National income initially rises by $1 billion. But that is not the end of it. The factors of production involved in road building that received the first $1 billion spend $800 million. This second round of spending generates $800 million of new income. This new income in turn induces $640 million of third-round spending. And so it continues, with each successive round of new income generating 80 percent as much in new expenditure. Each additional round of expenditure creates new income and yet another round of expenditure.

The table carries the process through 10 rounds. Students with sufficient patience (and no faith in mathematics) may compute as many rounds in the process as they wish; they will find that the sum of the rounds of expenditures approaches a limit of $5 billion, which is five times the initial increase in expenditure. [38] The graph of the cumulative expenditure increases shows how quickly this limit is approached. The multiplier is thus 5, given the assumption about the marginal propensity to spend. Had the marginal propensity to spend been lower, say, 0.667, the process would have been similar, but it would have approached a limit of three instead of five times the initial increase in expenditure.

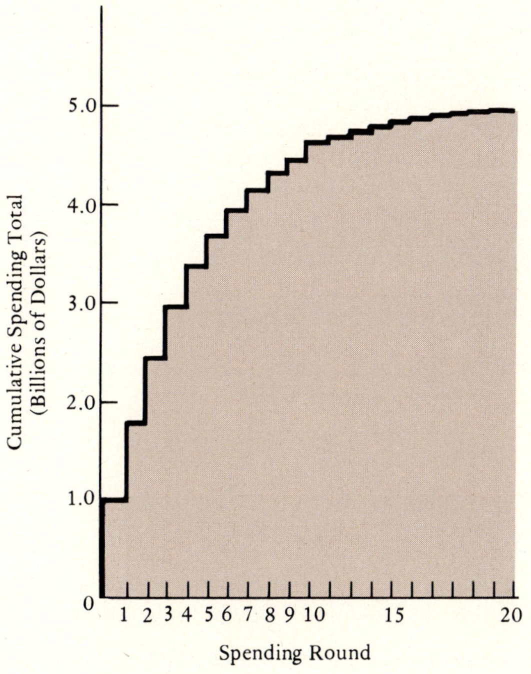

Round of spending	Increase in expenditure (millions of dollars)	Cumulative total (millions of dollars)
Initial increase	1,000.0	1,000.0
2	800.0	1,800.0
3	640.0	2,440.0
4	512.0	2,952.0
5	409.6	3,361.6
6	327.7	3,689.3
7	262.1	3,951.4
8	209.7	4,161.1
9	167.8	4,328.9
10	134.2	4,463.1
11 to 20 combined	479.3	4,942.4
All others	57.6	5,000.0

BOX 28-2

The Multiplier: An Algebraic Approach

High school algebra is all that is needed to derive the exact expression for the multiplier. Readers who feel at home with algebra may want to follow this derivation. Others can skip it and rely on the graphical and numerical arguments given in the text.

First we derive the equation for the *AE* curve. Aggregate expenditure is divided into autonomous expenditure, *A*, and induced expenditure, *N*.* So we write

$$AE = N + A \qquad [1]$$

Since *N* is expenditure that varies with income, we can write

$$N = zY \qquad [2]$$

where *z* is the marginal propensity to spend out of national income. (It is a positive number between zero and unity.) Substituting Equation 2 in Equation 1 yields the equation of the *AE* curve.

$$AE = zY + A \qquad [3]$$

Now we write the equation of the 45° line,

$$AE = Y \qquad [4]$$

which states the equilibrium condition that aggregate desired expenditure must equal national income. Equations 3 and 4 are two equations with two unknowns, *AE* and *Y*. To solve we substitute Equation 3 in Equation 4 to obtain

$$Y = zY + A$$

Subtracting *zY* from both sides yields

$$Y - zY = A$$

Factoring out *Y* yields

$$Y(1 - z) = A$$

Dividing through by $1 - z$ yields

$$Y = A/(1 - z)$$

This tells us the equilibrium value of *Y* in terms of autonomous expenditures *A* and the propensity not to spend out of national income $(1 - z)$. The expression $Y = A/(1 - z)$ tells us that if *A* changes by ΔA, the change in *Y*, which we call ΔY, will be

$$\Delta Y = \Delta A/(1 - z)$$

Dividing through by ΔA gives the value of the multiplier, which we designate by *K*:

$$K = \Delta Y/\Delta A = 1/(1 - z)$$

* In simple models *N* is mainly consumption expenditure, but in other models it may include other types of expenditure. All that matters is that there is one class of expenditure, *N*, that varies with income and another class, *A*, that does not.

Summary

1. When the price level is fixed, national income depends on desired aggregate expenditure.
2. Desired aggregate expenditure includes desired consumption, desired investment, and desired government expenditures plus desired net exports. It is the amount that decision makers want to spend on purchasing the national product.
3. A change in disposable income leads to a change in consumption and saving. The responsiveness of these changes is measured by the marginal propensity to consume (*MPC*) and the marginal propensity to save (*MPS*), which are both positive and sum to one.
4. A change in wealth tends to cause a change in the allocation of

disposable income between consumption and saving. The change in consumption is positively related to the change in wealth, while the change in saving is negatively related to this change.

5. Since desired imports increase as national income increases, desired net exports decrease as national income increases, other things being equal. This gives rise to a negatively sloped net export function.
6. At the equilibrium level of national income, purchasers wish to buy neither more nor less than what is being produced. At incomes above equilibrium, desired expenditure falls short of national income, and output will sooner or later be curtailed. At incomes below equilibrium, desired expenditure exceeds national income, and output will sooner or later be increased.
7. Equilibrium national income is represented graphically by the point at which the aggregate expenditure curve cuts the 45° line, that is, where total desired expenditure equals total output.
8. Equilibrium national income is increased by a rise in the desired consumption, investment, government, or export expenditure associated with each level of the national income. Equilibrium national income is decreased by a fall in desired expenditures.
9. Equilibrium national income is decreased by a rise in the taxes associated with each level of national income, and increased by a fall in taxes.
10. The magnitude of the effect on national income of shifts in autonomous expenditure is given by the multiplier. It is defined as $K = \Delta Y/\Delta A$, where ΔA is the change in autonomous expenditure.
11. The simple multiplier is the multiplier when the price level is constant. It is equal to $1/(1 - z)$, where z is the marginal propensity to spend out of national income. Thus the larger z is, the larger is the multiplier. It is a basic prediction of national income theory that the simple multiplier is greater than unity.

Topics for Review

Desired expenditure
Consumption function
Average and marginal propensities to consume and to save
Aggregate expenditure function
Marginal propensities to spend and not to spend
Equilibrium national income at a given price level
Shifts of and movements along expenditure curves
Effect on national income of changes in desired expenditures
Effect on national income of a change in tax rates
The simple multiplier and the slope of the *AE* curve

Discussion Questions

1. "The concept of an equilibrium level of national income is useless because the economy is never in equilibrium. If it ever got there, no economist would recognize it anyway." Discuss.

2. Interpret each of the following statements either in terms of the shape of a consumption function or the values of *MPC* and *APC*.
   a. "Tom Green has lost his job, and his family is existing on its past savings."
   b. "The Grimsby household is so rich that they used all the extra income they earned this year to invest in a wildcat oil-drilling venture."
   c. "The widow Hammerstein can barely make ends meet by clipping coupons on the bonds left to her by dear Henry, but she would never dip into her capital."
   d. "We always thought Harris was a miser, but when his wife left him he took to wine, women, and song."
   e. "When the Schultzes' rich aunt died and left them some money, they stopped putting $10 a week to their account with the trust company."
3. Why might an individual's marginal propensity to consume be higher in the long run than in the short run? Why might it be lower? Is it possible for an individual's average propensity to consume to be greater than unity in the short run? In the long run? Can a country's average propensity to consume be greater than unity in the short run? In the long run?
4. Explain carefully why national income changes when aggregate desired expenditure does not equal national income. Sketch scenarios that fit the cases of too much and too little desired expenditure.
5. Predict whether each of the following events will, other things being equal, increase, decrease, or leave unchanged the size of the multiplier.
   a. Shift from foreign travel to holidays at home
   b. Increase in expenditures on highways
   c. Decisions by corporations to decrease the percentage of earnings they pay out in dividends and to increase their bank balances whenever national income falls
   d. Widespread adoption by cities of a city income tax
   e. Large increase in the percentage of disposable income saved by households
6. Explain how a sudden unexpected fall in consumer expenditure would initially cause an increase in investment expenditure by firms.
7. State the implied impact on the *AE* curve, and hence on equilibrium national income, relating to each of the following headlines.
   a. "Ottawa's planned spending up 10.5%."
   b. "Soviet Union agrees to buy more Canadian wheat."
   c. "Major Canadian companies expected to cut capital outlays."
   d. "Tax Reform Promises Lower Personal Tax Rates."
   e. "Ottawa Considers Major Cut in Old Age Security Payments."
   f. "Decrease in Spending on Foreign Travel Reflected in Increase in Saving."
   g. "Import cars boom spell trouble for Canadian Auto Industry."
8. Homer Hardcrust, chairman of the Economic Council of Canada, proposes that because of the current heavy unemployment, government should prepare an austerity program and cut down government expenditures to set an example for private households. What do you think the effects of his policy would be?

29

National Income and the Price Level in the Short Run

In Chapter 28 we treated the price level as constant. This was a reasonable simplification, on the principle that it is easier to study things one at a time than all at once. It allowed us to focus on the questions of how equilibrium national income is determined and why it changes. However, the assumption that the price level is constant is obviously unrealistic, and the time has now come to drop it.

We make the transition to a variable price level in two steps. First, we study the consequences for national income of exogenous changes in the price level—changes that happen for reasons that are not explained by our theory. Then we elaborate our theory to make the price level endogenous so that we can use our theory to study and explain movements in *both* national income and the price level.

Exogenous Changes in the Price Level

What happens to equilibrium national income when the price level changes for some exogenous reason, such as a rise in the prices of imported raw materials? To find out we need to understand how a change in the price level affects the desired aggregate expenditure curve.

Desired Aggregate Expenditure

The important result that we now wish to establish is that the price level and desired aggregate expenditure are negatively related to each other. In other words, a rise in the price level shifts the aggregate expenditure curve downward, while a fall in the price level shifts it upward. The explanation lies in two effects: what the change in the price level does to imports and exports, and what it does to the real value of wealth and hence to desired consumption expenditure. It is sufficient to look only at the implications of an increase in the price level in detail, since a decrease merely reverses everything.

Changes in international relative prices. When the domestic price level rises, Canadian goods become more expensive relative to foreign goods. As we saw in Chapter 28, this change in relative prices causes Canadians to reduce their purchases of Canadian goods, which have now become relatively more expensive, and to increase their purchases of foreign goods, which have now become relatively less expensive. At the same time consumers in other countries reduce their purchases of the now relatively expensive Canadian goods. We saw in Chapter 28 that these changes can be summarized as a downward shift in the net export function.

A rise in the domestic price level shifts the net export function downward, which in turn implies a downward shift in the desired aggregate expenditure curve. A fall in the domestic price level shifts the net export and desired aggregate expenditure curves upward.

Changes in the real value of wealth. Much of the private sector's total wealth is held in the form of assets with a fixed nominal money value. One obvious example is money itself—cash and bank deposits. Other examples are provided by many kinds of debt, including treasury bills and bonds. When a bill or a bond matures, the owner is repaid a stated sum of money. What that money can buy—its real value—depends on the price level. For this reason, a rise in the domestic price level lowers the real value of all assets denominated in money units and hence lowers the wealth of their owners.

How does a fall in the real value of the private sector's wealth affect the aggregate expenditure curve?[1] As we saw in Chapter 28 (see Figure 28-2 on page 591), there is a direct link between wealth and consumption. Because households have less wealth, they increase their saving so as to restore their wealth to the level they desire for such purposes as retirement. An increase in saving of course implies a reduction in consumption.

A rise in the domestic price level lowers the real value of total wealth, which leads to a fall in desired consumption; this in turn implies a downward shift in the desired aggregate expenditure curve. A fall in the domestic price level leads to a rise in wealth and desired consumption and thus to an upward shift in the desired aggregate expenditure curve.

We have concentrated here on the direct effect of the change in wealth on desired consumption expenditure. There is also an indirect effect that operates through the interest rate. Although this effect is potentially very powerful, we cannot study it until we have studied the macroeconomic role of money and interest rates. Further discussion of this point must therefore be postponed until Chapter 34.[2]

Effects on Equilibrium National Income

Both because of a fall in the net export function and because of a fall in desired consumption, a rise in the price level causes the aggregate desired expenditure curve to shift downward. This is shown in Figure 29-1. The figure also allows us to reconfirm what we already know from Chapter 28: when the *AE* curve shifts downward, the equilibrium level of national income falls.

A rise in the price level causes the *AE* curve to shift down and thus leads to a fall in equilibrium national income.

Now suppose that there is a fall in the price level. Since this is the opposite of the case just studied, we can summarize the two key effects briefly. First, Canadian goods become relatively cheaper internationally, so net exports rise. Second, the purchasing power of some existing assets that are denominated in money terms is increased, so households spend more. The resulting increase in desired expenditure on Canadian goods causes the *AE* curve to shift up

[1] It is worth noting that all changes in the real value of a person's wealth do not change the total wealth of the private sector. In many cases the change in wealth of a creditor is exactly offset by the change in wealth of a debtor. For example, a rise in the price level lowers the real wealth of a bond holder but raises the real wealth of the bond issuer, who will have to part with less purchasing power when the bond is redeemed. However, many assets held by individuals are government debt, and hence any change in the price level causes a net change in the wealth of the private sector.

[2] Here is a brief summary of what is involved. When the price level rises, firms and households need to cover their increased money expenses between one payday and the next. This means they need to hold more money on average. The increased demand for money bids up the price that must be paid to borrow money (the interest rate). Firms that borrow money to build plants and to purchase equipment, and households that borrow money to buy durable goods and housing, respond to rising interest rates by choosing to spend less. This means a decrease in the aggregate demand for the nation's output.

FIGURE 29-1 Aggregate Expenditure and the Price Level

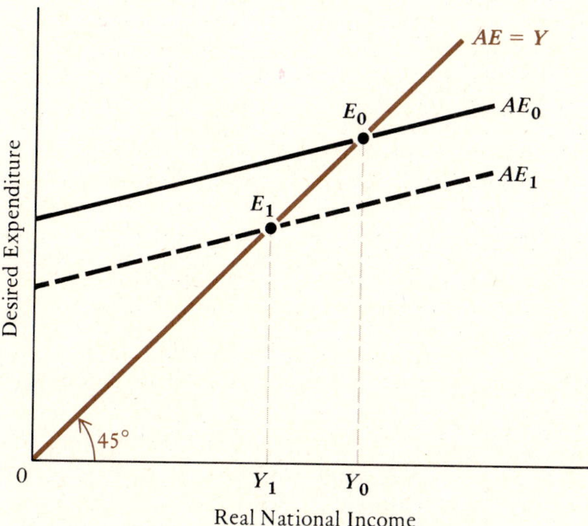

Changes in the price level cause the *AE* curve to shift and thus cause equilibrium national income to change. At the initial price level, the *AE* curve is given by the solid line AE_0 and hence equilibrium national income is Y_0. An increase in the price level reduces desired aggregate expenditure and thus causes the *AE* curve to shift down to the dashed line AE_1. As a result equilibrium national income falls to Y_1.

Starting with the dashed line AE_1, a fall in the price level would increase desired aggregate expenditure, shifting the *AE* curve up to AE_0 and raising equilibrium national income to Y_1.

and hence raises equilibrium national income. This is also shown in Figure 29-1.

A fall in the domestic price level leads to a rise in net exports and desired consumption expenditure; this causes the aggregate expenditure curve to shift up and equilibrium national income to rise.

The Aggregate Demand Curve

We now know from the behavior underlying the aggregate expenditure curve that the price level and real national income are negatively related to each other; that is, a change in the price level changes equilibrium national income in the opposite direction. This negative relationship can be shown in an important new concept called the *aggregate demand curve.*

Recall that the *AE* curve relates equilibrium national income to desired expenditure for a given price level, plotting national income on the horizontal axis. The **aggregate demand (*AD*) curve** relates equilibrium national income to the price level, again plotting national income on the horizontal axis. Because the horizontal axes of both the *AE* and the *AD* curves measure real national income, the two curves can be placed one above the other so that the level of national income on each can be compared directly. This is shown in Figure 29-2.

Now let us see how the *AD* curve is derived. Given a value of the price level, equilibrium national income is determined in part (i) of the figure by the now familiar condition that the *AE* curve crosses the 45° line. In part (ii) of the figure, the combination of the equilibrium level of national income and the corresponding value of the price level is plotted, giving one point on the *AD* curve.

When the price level changes, the *AE* curve shifts, for the reasons just seen. The new position of the *AE* curve gives rise to a new equilibrium level of national income that is associated with the new price level. This determines a second point on the *AD* curve in Figure 29-2(ii).

Any change in the price level leads to a new *AE* curve and hence to a new level of equilibrium income. Each combination of equilibrium income and its associated price level becomes a particular point on the *AD* curve.

Note that since the *AD* curve relates equilibrium national income to the price level, changes in the price level that cause shifts in the *AE* curve cause movements along the *AD* curve. A movement along the *AD* curve thus traces out the response of equilibrium income to a change in the price level.

The Slope of the AD Curve

We already know enough to establish that the *AD* curve is negatively sloped.

FIGURE 29-2 The *AD* Curve and the *AE* Curve

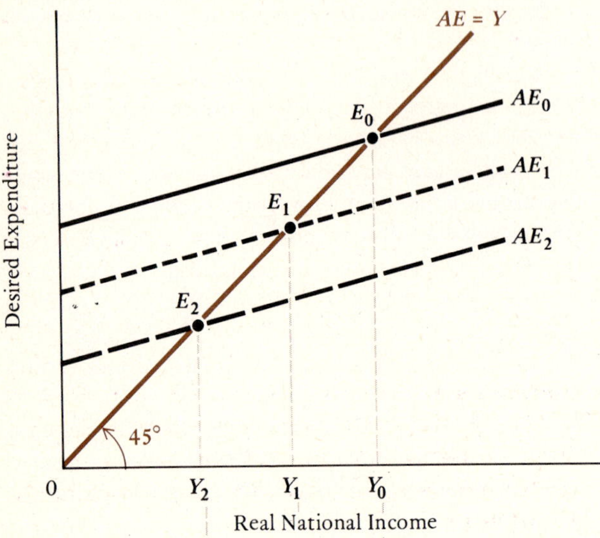

(i) Aggregate expenditure

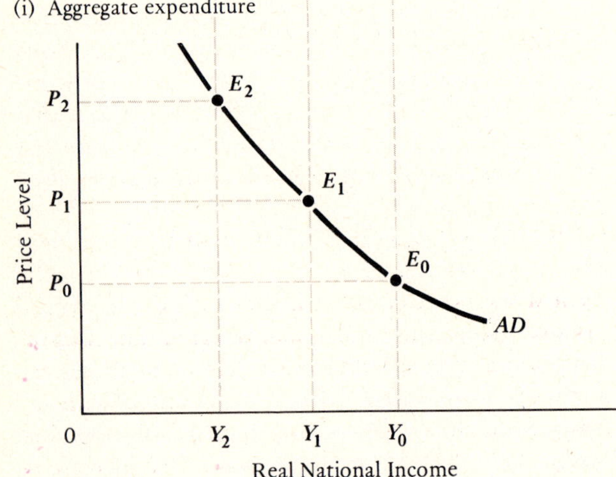

(ii) Aggregate demand

Equilibrium income is determined by the *AE* curve for each given price level; the level of income and its associated price level are then plotted to yield the *AD* curve. When the price level is P_0, the *AE* curve is AE_0 and hence equilibrium national income is Y_0, as shown in part (i). (This reproduces the initial equilibrium from Figure 29-1.) Plotting Y_0 against P_0 yields the point E_0 on the *AD* curve in part (ii).

An increase in the price level to P_1 causes AE_0 in part (i) to shift down to AE_1 and thus causes equilibrium national income to fall to Y_1. Plotting this new lower level of national income Y_1 against the higher price level P_1 yields a second point, E_1, on the *AD* curve in part (ii). A further increase in the price level to P_2 causes the *AE* curve in part (i) to shift down further, to AE_2, and thus causes equilibrium national income to fall further, to Y_2. Plotting Y_2 against P_2 yields a third point, E_2, on the *AD* curve in part (ii).

Thus a change in the price level causes a shift in the *AE* curve in part (i) and a movement along the *AD* curve in part (ii).

1. **A rise in the price level causes the aggregate expenditure curve to shift down and hence leads to a movement up and to the left along the *AD* curve, reflecting a fall in the equilibrium level of national income.**
2. **A fall in the price level causes the aggregate expenditure curve to shift up and hence leads to a movement down and to the right along the *AD* curve, reflecting an increase in the equilibrium level of national income.**

Early in our study (Chapter 4) we saw that demand curves for individual goods such as carrots or automobiles are also negatively sloped. However, the reasons for the negative slope of the *AD* curve are very different from the reasons for the negative slope of individual demand curves used in microeconomics; this important point is discussed further in Box 29-1.

Equilibrium National Income and Price Level

So far we have explained the equilibrium level of national income that arises *when the price level is taken as given.* We have also seen how that equilibrium level of national income would change if the price level were to change. What we have not yet done is explain what would cause the price level to change. We are now ready to take the important step of adding to our story an *explanation* of the behavior of the price level.

The equilibrium condition we have used so far is that desired aggregate expenditure be the same as national income, and thus our focus has been on spending decisions. To see how we might add an explanation of the price level to the model, let us briefly re-examine the aggregate demand curve.

Another Look at the Aggregate Demand Curve

The *AD* curve shows, for any given price level, the level of national income at which desired aggregate expenditure will equal national income. If that level of output were produced, purchasers would just be prepared to buy it. If a lower level were produced, desired purchases would exceed output. If a larger level were produced, desired purchases would be less than output.

Thus the *AD* curve only describes a demand equilibrium:

Any point on the *AD* curve is such that *if* the level of national income given by that point is produced, *then* at the corresponding price level desired aggregate expenditure will equal national income.

This is illustrated in Figure 29-3 (p. 615). A point on the *AD* curve thus indicates the equilibrium level of national income as long as we can take the price level as given and as long as we can assume that the associated level of national income will in fact be produced.

By treating the price level as given and by assuming that the quantity of output produced will equal whatever is demanded, we have been able to ignore supply decisions. Now, in order to *explain* the price level, we need to incorporate the supply decisions of firms into our analysis.

Aggregate Supply

Aggregate supply refers to the total output of goods that firms wish to produce.[3] Aggregate supply thus reflects decisions of firms to hire workers in order to produce goods and services to sell to households, governments, and other firms.

Suppose that firms wish to increase output above current production levels. For the moment, suppose further that the prices of all the inputs that firms use—labor, capital, and so forth—remain constant. Constant factor prices do not, however, mean that either the per unit costs that firms incur or the output prices they charge will remain unchanged as they expand output.

Increasing output may require that less efficient standby machines and plants are used, that less efficient workers are employed, and that existing workers are given overtime hours at premium wages. Thus even with the restriction that input prices remain constant, higher output is associated with increased costs because it requires the use of more and more costly methods of production. This increase in cost per unit of output is referred to as rising **unit costs.**

Since expanding output often means incurring higher unit costs, firms will generally expand output only if the higher output can be sold at higher prices.

Now consider what happens when firms wish to reduce their output. The forces just mentioned work

[3] Recall from Chapter 27 that total output equals national income.

BOX 29-1

The Shape of the Aggregate Demand Curve

In Chapter 4 we studied the demand curves for individual products. It is tempting to think that the properties of the aggregate demand curve arise from the same behavior that gives rise to those individual demand curves. Unfortunately, life is not so simple. Let us see why we cannot take such an approach.

If we assume that we can obtain a downward-sloping aggregate demand curve in the same manner that we derived downward-sloping individual market demand curves, we would be committing the *fallacy of composition*. This is to assume that what is correct for the parts must be correct for the whole.

Consider a simple example of the fallacy. Any art collector can go into the market and add to her private collection of nineteenth century French paintings provided only that she has enough money. But to assume that because any one person can do this, everyone could do so simultaneously is plainly wrong. The world's stock of nineteenth century French paintings is totally fixed. All of us cannot do what any one of us with enough money can do.

How does the fallacy of composition relate to demand curves? An individual demand curve describes a situation in which the price of one commodity changes while the prices of all other commodities and consumers' money incomes are constant. Such an individual demand curve is negatively sloped for two reasons. First, as the price of the commodity rises, each consumer's given money income will buy a smaller *total* amount of goods, so a smaller quantity of the commodity will be bought. Second, as the price of the commodity rises, consumers buy less of it and more of the now relatively cheaper substitutes.

The first reason has no application to the aggregate demand curve, which relates the total demand for all output to the price level. All prices and total output are changing as we move along the *AD* curve. Since the value of output determines income, there is no reason to expect consumers' money incomes to be constant along this curve.

The second reason does have some, but very limited, application to the aggregate demand curve. A rise in the price level entails a rise in all domestic commodity prices. Thus there is no incentive to substitute among domestic commodities. But it does give rise, as we saw in Chapter 28, to some substitution between domestic and foreign goods.

---

in reverse. There will be cost savings as overtime hours are reduced, the least efficient labor is laid off, and the least efficient capital is put on standby. For these reasons the lower output will be associated with somewhat lower unit costs and hence with lower output prices.

Since reducing output means reducing unit costs, firms will contract output when the price at which their output can be sold falls.

The Short-Run Aggregate Supply Curve

We can summarize the supply decisions of firms in terms of the implied relation between desired output and the price level, which we call the **aggregate supply (*AS*) curve.** For the moment we maintain the assumption that *input prices are constant,* and refer to the *AS* curve as a *short-run aggregate supply curve.* The **short-run aggregate supply (*SRAS*) curve** shows the relation between the price level and the total output that firms wish to produce and sell, with input prices given.

Slope of the *SRAS* curve. For the reasons just given, the *SRAS* curve will usually be positively sloped, indicating that the higher the price level, the more output will be produced. This is illustrated in Figure 29-4 (p. 616).

The positive slope of the *SRAS* curve shows that with input prices constant, higher output is associated with higher prices because unit costs of

FIGURE 29-3 The Relation Between the *AE* and *AD* Curves

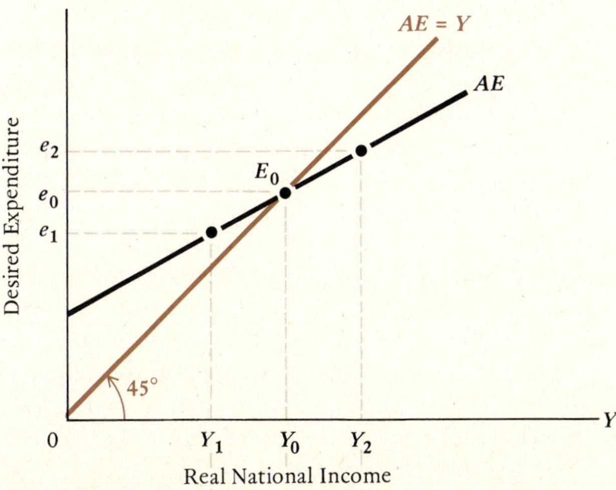

(i) Aggregate expenditure

(ii) Aggregate demand

The *AD* curve plots the price level against the level of national income consistent with expenditure decisions at that price level. In the figure the price level is constant at P_0. The *AE* curve in part (i) is drawn for that price level. The equilibrium level of national income is Y_0, as shown in part (i) by the intersection of the *AE* curve with the 45° line at E_0. At Y_0 national income is equal to desired aggregate expenditure, given by e_0. Y_0 is then plotted against P_0 in part (ii) to yield point E_0 on the *AD* curve.

Consider a level of national income of Y_1, less than Y_0. As can be seen in part (i), if national income were equal to Y_1, desired aggregate expenditure would be e_1, which is greater than Y_1. Hence Y_1 is not an equilibrium level of national income when the price level is P_0, and the combination (P_0, Y_1) is not a point on the *AD* curve in part (ii)—as shown by point *X*.

Now consider a level of national income of Y_2, greater than Y_0. As can be seen in part (i), if national income were equal to Y_2, desired aggregate expenditure would be e_2, less than Y_2. Hence Y_2 is not an equilibrium level of national income when the price level is P_0, and the combination (P_0, Y_2) is not a point on the *AD* curve in part (ii)—as shown by point *Z*.

production increase as the level of output increases.

The possibility of a horizontal *SRAS* curve, which gives rise to the level of national income being demand determined as in Figure 29-3, is discussed in Box 29-2 (p. 617).

The relation described by the *SRAS* curve holds only in the short run. This is because it is based on the assumption that input prices are constant, and changes in economic conditions will eventually cause input prices to change. Later we will examine the effects of changing input prices. For the moment let us see how the *SRAS* curve helps us explain the equilibrium values of national income *and* the price level.

FIGURE 29-4 **A Short-Run Aggregate Supply Curve**

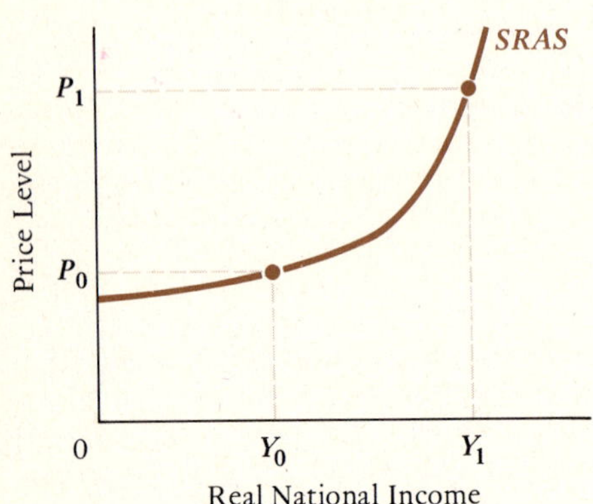

The *SRAS* curve is positively sloped. The positive slope of the *SRAS* curve shows that with the prices of labor and other inputs given, total desired output and the price level will be positively associated. Thus a rise in the price level from P_0 to P_1 will be associated with a rise in the supply of total output from Y_0 to Y_1.

FIGURE 29-5 **Macroeconomic Equilibrium**

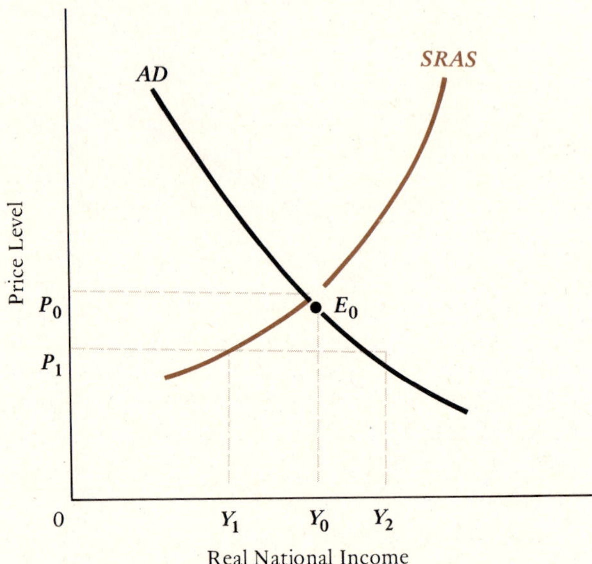

Macroeconomic equilibrium occurs at the intersection of the *AD* and *SRAS* curves and determines the equilibrium values for national income and the price level. Given the *AD* and *SRAS* curves in the figure, macroeconomic equilibrium occurs at E_0, with national income equal to Y_0 and the price level equal to P_0. At P_0 the desired output of firms, as given by the *SRAS* curve, is equal to the level of national income consistent with expenditure decisions, as given by the *AD* curve.

If the price level were equal to P_1, less than P_0, the desired output of firms, given by the *SRAS* curve, would be Y_2. But at P_1 the level of output consistent with expenditure decisions, given by the *AD* curve, would be Y_1, greater than Y_2. Hence when the price level is P_1, or at any other level less than P_0, the desired output of firms will be less than the level of national income consistent with expenditure decisions.

Similarly, for any price level above P_0, the desired output of firms given by the *SRAS* curve would exceed the level of output consistent with expenditure decisions given by the *AD* curve. Hence the only price level where the supply decisions of firms are consistent with desired expenditure is at macroeconomic equilibrium.

Macroeconomic Equilibrium

The equilibrium values of national output and the price level occur at the intersection of the *AD* and *SRAS* curves, as shown by the pair Y_0 and P_0 that arise at point E_0 in Figure 29-5. We describe the combination of national income and price level that is on both the *AD* and the *SRAS* curves as a *macroeconomic equilibrium*.

To see why this pair is the only macroeconomic equilibrium, consider what would happen if the price level were below P_0. At that lower price level, the desired output of firms, as given by the *SRAS* curve, is less than the level of output consistent with expenditure decisions, as given by the *AD* curve. If firms were to produce their desired level of output, desired expenditure would exceed the amount of goods supplied. Hence there can be no macroeconomic equilibrium when the price level is below P_0.

Similarly, when the price level is above P_0, the behavior underlying the *SRAS* and *AD* curves are not consistent. In this case producers will wish to supply more than the level of income that is consis-

BOX 29-2

The Keynesian SRAS Curve

In this box we consider an extreme version of the *SRAS* curve that is horizontal over some range of national income. This curve is called the **Keynesian short-run aggregate supply curve,** after the English economist John Maynard Keynes, who in his famous book *The General Theory of Employment, Interest and Money* (1936) pioneered the study of the behavior of economies under conditions of high unemployment.

The behavior that gives rise to the Keynesian *SRAS* curve can be described as follows. When real national income is below potential national income, individual firms are operating at less than normal capacity output. Firms respond to cyclical declines in demand by holding their prices constant at the level that would maximize profits if production were at normal capacity. They then respond to demand variations below that capacity by altering output. In other words, they will supply whatever they can sell at their existing prices as long as they are producing below their normal capacity. This means that the firms have horizontal supply curves and that their output is *demand determined.**

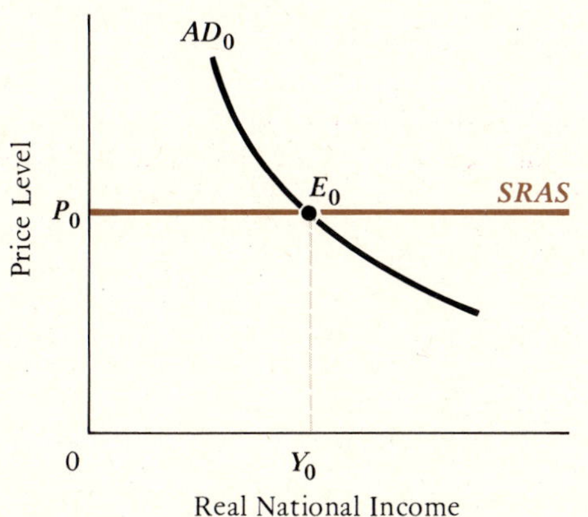

Under these circumstances, the economy has a horizontal aggregate supply curve, indicating that any output up to some level below or equal to potential output will be supplied at the going price level. The amount that is actually produced is then determined by the position of the aggregate demand curve, as shown in the figure. Thus we say that real national income is demand-determined.

If demand rises enough so that firms are trying to squeeze more than normal output out of their plants, their costs will rise, and so will their prices. Thus the horizontal Keynesian *SRAS* curve applies only to national incomes below potential income.

* The evidence is strong that firms, particularly in the manufacturing sector, do behave like this in the short run. One possible explanation is that changing prices frequently is too costly, so firms set the best possible (profit-maximizing) prices when output is at normal capacity and then do not change prices in the face of normal cyclical fluctuations in demand. This is discussed further in Chapter 15.

---

tent with demand at that price level. If firms were to produce their desired level of output, desired expenditure would not be large enough to purchase all output produced.

Only at the combination of national income and price level given by the intersection of the *SRAS* and *AD* curves are spending behavior and supply behavior consistent.

When the price level is less than its equilibrium value, expenditure behavior is consistent with a level of national income greater than the desired output of firms. When the price level is greater than its equilibrium value, expenditure behavior is consistent with a level of national income less than the desired output of firms.

Macroeconomic equilibrium thus requires that two conditions be satisfied. The first is familiar from Chapter 28: At the prevailing price level, desired aggregate expenditure must be equal to national income. The second is introduced by consideration of aggregate supply: At the prevailing price level, firms must wish to produce the prevailing level of national income.

Changes in National Income and the Price Level

The aggregate demand and aggregate supply curves can now be used to show why national income and the price level change.

Shifts in the Aggregate Curves

A shift in the *AD* curve is called an **aggregate demand shock.** A *rightward* shift in the *AD* curve is an *increase* in aggregate demand; it means that at any given price level, expenditure decisions will now be consistent with a *higher* level of real national income. Similarly, a *leftward* shift in the *AD* curve is a *decrease* in aggregate demand; it means that at any given price level, expenditure decisions will now be consistent with a *lower* level of real national income.

A shift in the *SRAS* curve is called an **aggregate supply shock.** A *rightward* shift in the *SRAS* curve is an *increase* in aggregate supply; at any given price level, *more* real national income will be supplied. A *leftward* shift in the *SRAS* curve is a *decrease* in aggregate supply; at any given price level, *less* real national income will be supplied.[4]

What happens to real national income and to the price level when one of the aggregate curves shifts?

A shift in either the *AD* or the *SRAS* curve leads to changes in the equilibrium values of the price level and real national income.

Aggregate Demand Shocks

Figure 29-6 shows the effects of an increase in aggregate demand. This increase could have occurred because of, say, increased investment or government spending; it means that more national output would be demanded at any given price level. For now we are not concerned with the source of the shock; we are interested in its implications for the price level and real national income.[5]

As is shown in the figure, following an increase in aggregate demand both the price level and real national income rise. Figure 29-6 also shows that both the price level and real national income fall as the result of a decrease in aggregate demand.

Aggregate demand shocks cause the price level and real national income to change in the same direction; both rise with an increase in aggregate demand, and both fall with a decrease.

FIGURE 29-6 Aggregate Demand Shocks

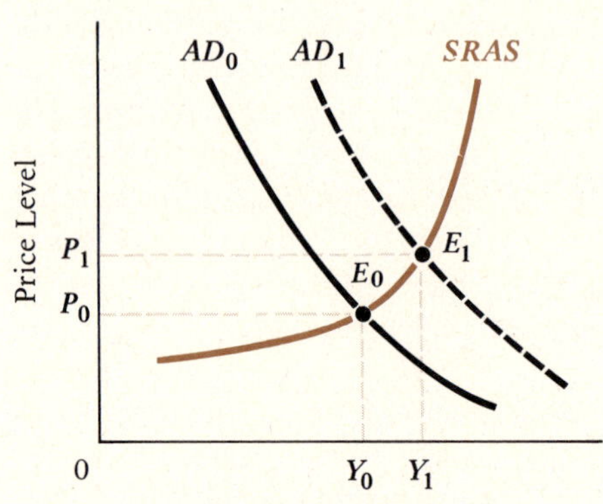

Shifts in aggregate demand cause the price level and real national income to move in the same direction. An increase in aggregate demand shifts the *AD* curve to the right, say, from AD_0 to AD_1. Macroeconomic equilibrium moves from E_0 to E_1. The price level rises from P_0 to P_1, and real national income rises from Y_0 to Y_1, reflecting a movement along the *SRAS* curve.

A decrease in aggregate demand shifts the *AD* curve to the left, say, from AD_1 to AD_0. Equilibrium moves from E_1 to E_0. Prices fall from P_1 to P_0, and real national income falls from Y_1 to Y_0, again reflecting a movement along the *SRAS* curve.

[4] The distinction between movements along and shifts of curves encountered in Chapter 4 and again in Chapter 28 is also relevant here. Recall that the phrase "a change in quantity demanded" refers to a *movement along* a demand curve, whereas "a change in demand" refers to a *shift of* the demand curve. A similar distinction applies to the supply curve.

Note that for either the *AD* or the *SRAS* curve, a shift to the right means an increase and a shift to the left a decrease. If we speak of upward and downward shifts, however, the meaning differs for the two curves. An upward shift of the *AD* curve reflects an increase in aggregate demand, but an upward shift in the *SRAS* curve reflects a decrease in aggregate supply.

[5] Later (starting in Chapter 32) we will study how government policy can influence these variables.

An aggregate demand shock means a shift in the *AD* curve (for example, from AD_0 to AD_1 in the figure). Adjustment to the new equilibrium following an aggregate demand shock involves a movement along the *SRAS* curve (for example, from point E_0 to point E_1).

Causes of Aggregate Demand Shocks

We have seen that the *AD* curve plots equilibrium national income as a function of the price level. Thus anything that alters equilibrium national income at a given price level must shift the *AD* curve; that is, any change other than a change in the price level that causes the *AE* curve to shift will also cause the *AD* curve to shift. (Recall that a change in the price level causes a *movement along* the *AD* curve.) This allows us to restate the conclusions on page 601 as follows:

A rise in the amount of desired consumption, investment, government, or net export expenditure associated with each level of national income shifts the *AD* curve to the right. A fall in any of these expenditures shifts the *AD* curve to the left.

Another Look at the Simple Multiplier

We have seen that the simple multiplier measures the magnitude of the change in equilibrium national income when the price level is constant. It follows that the simple multiplier gives the magnitude of the *horizontal* shift in the *AD* curve in response to a change in autonomous expenditure. This is shown in Figure 29-7.

The simple multiplier measures the horizontal shift in the *AD* curve in response to a change in autonomous expenditure.

If the *SRAS* curve were horizontal, indicating that firms will supply everything that is demanded at the going price level, the simple multiplier also tells us the change in equilibrium income that will occur in response to a change in autonomous expenditure. The case of a horizontal *SRAS* curve is discussed in Box 29-2 on page 617.

What happens in the more usual case where the aggregate supply curve slopes upward? In this case a rise in national income caused by an increase in autonomous expenditure will be associated with a rise in the price level. But we have seen that a rise in the price level (by reducing net exports and by lowering the real value of household wealth) shifts the *AE* curve downward, which tends to lower national income. The outcome of these conflicting forces is easily seen using aggregate demand and aggregate supply curves.

The Multiplier When the Price Level Varies

As can be seen in Figure 29-6, when the *SRAS* curve is positively sloped, the change in national income caused by a change in autonomous expenditure is no longer equal to the size of the horizontal shift in the *AD* curve. A shift to the right of the *AD* curve causes the price level to rise, which in turn causes the rise in national income to be less than the horizontal shift of the *AD* curve. Part of the expansionary impact of an increase in demand is dissipated by a rise in the price level, and only part is transmitted to a rise in real output. Of course, there still is an increase in output, so a multiplier may still be calculated—but its value is less than the simple multiplier.

When the *SRAS* curve is positively sloped, the multiplier is smaller than the simple multiplier.

Why is the multiplier smaller when the *SRAS* curve is positively sloped? The answer lies in the behavior that is summarized by the *AE* curve. To understand this, it is useful to think of the final change in national income as occurring in two stages, as shown in Figure 29-8 (p. 621).

First, with prices constant, an increase in autonomous expenditure shifts the *AE* curve up and therefore shifts the *AD* curve to the right. This is shown by a shift up of the *AE* curve in part (i) of the figure and a shift to the right of the *AD* curve in part (ii). The horizontal shift in the *AD* curve is measured by the simple multiplier. But this cannot be the final equilibrium position because firms are unwilling to produce enough to satisfy the extra demand at the existing price level.

Second, we take account of the rise in the price level that occurs due to the positive slope of the *SRAS* curve. As we have seen, a rise in the price

FIGURE 29-7 The Simple Multiplier and Shifts in the *AD* Curve

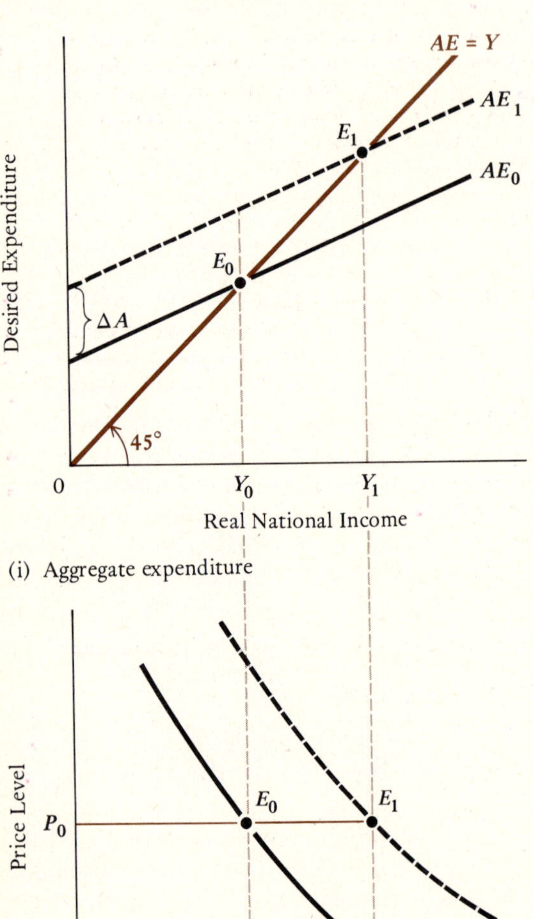

A change in autonomous expenditure changes equilibrium national income for any given price level, and the simple multiplier measures the resulting horizontal shift in the aggregate demand curve. The original desired expenditure function is AE_0 in part (i). Equilibrium is at E_0, with national income Y_0 at price level P_0. This yields point E_0 on the curve AD_0 in part (ii).

The *AE* curve in part (i) then shifts upward from AE_0 to AE_1 due to an increase in autonomous expenditure of ΔA. Equilibrium income now rises to Y_1, with the price level still constant at P_0. Thus the *AD* curve in part (ii) shifts to the right to point E_1, indicating the higher equilibrium income Y_1, associated with the same price level P_0. The magnitude of the shift, ΔY, is given by the simple multiplier.

A fall in autonomous expenditure can be analyzed by shifting the *AE* curve from AE_1 to AE_0, which shifts the *AD* curve from AD_1 to AD_0 at the price level of P_0. The equilibrium value of national income falls from Y_1 to Y_0.

level, via its effect on net exports and on wealth, leads to a downward shift in the *AE* curve. This second shift of the *AE* curve partially counteracts the initial rise in national income and so reduces the size of the multiplier. The second stage shows up as a shift down of the *AE* curve in part (i) of Figure 29-8 and a movement up and to the left along the *AD* curve in part (ii).

The Importance of the Shape of the SRAS Curve

We have now seen that the shape of the *SRAS* curve has important implications for how the effects of an aggregate demand shock are divided between changes in real national output and the price level. Figure 29-9 (p. 622) highlights this by considering

FIGURE 29-8 The *AE* Curve and the Multiplier When the Price Level Varies

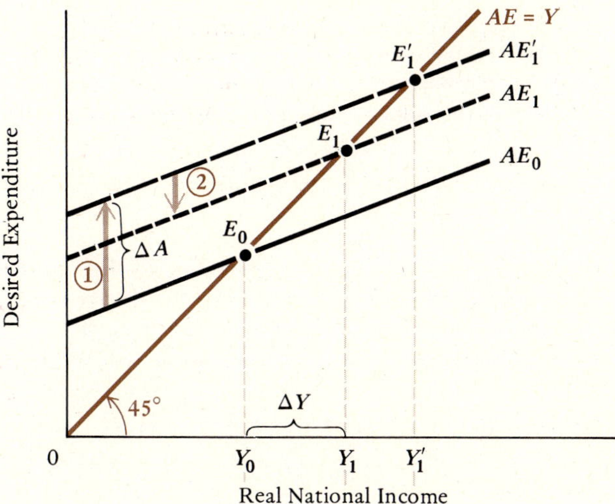

(i) Aggregate expenditure

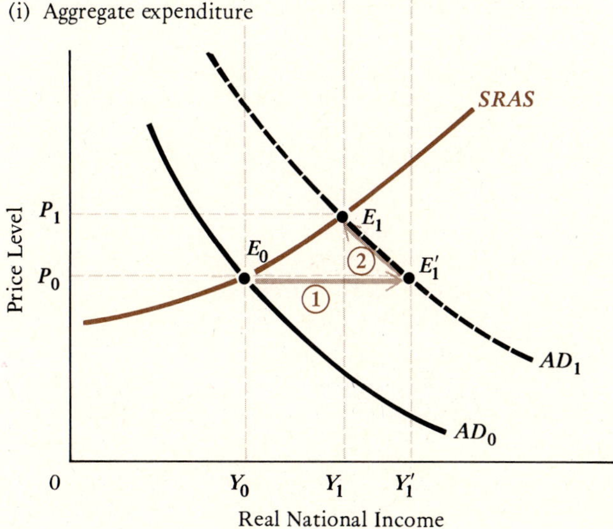

(ii) Aggregate demand

An increase in autonomous expenditures causes the *AE* curve to shift up, but the rise in the price level causes it to shift part of the way down again. Hence the multiplier effect on income is smaller than when the price level is constant. Originally, equilibrium is at point E_0 in both part (i) and part (ii), with real national income Y_0 and price level P_0. Desired aggregate expenditure then shifts by ΔA to AE_1', taking the aggregate demand curve to AD_1, as shown by arrow 1 in both parts. If the price level had remained constant at P_0, the new equilibrium would have been E_1' and real income would have risen to Y_1'. The amount Y_0Y_1' is the change called for by the simple multiplier.

Instead, however, the shift in the *AD* curve raises the price level to P_1 because the *SRAS* curve is positively sloped. The rise in the price level shifts the aggregate expenditure curve down to AE_1, as shown by arrow 2 in part (i). This is shown as a movement along the *AD* curve, as shown by arrow 2 in part (ii). The new equilibrium is thus at E_1. The amount Y_0Y_1 is ΔY, the actual increase in real income, whereas the amount Y_1Y_1' is the shortfall relative to the simple multiplier due to the rise in the price level.

The multiplier adjusted for the effect of the price increase is the ratio of $\Delta Y/\Delta A$ in part (i).

AD shocks in the presence of an *SRAS* curve that exhibits three distinct ranges.

Over the *flat* range, from 0 to Y_0, any change in aggregate demand leads to little change in prices and, as seen earlier, a response of output nearly equal to that predicted by the simple multiplier.

Over the *intermediate* range along which the *SRAS* curve is positively sloped, from Y_1 to Y_4, a shift in the *AD* curve gives rise to appreciable changes in both real income and the price level. As we saw earlier in this chapter, the change in the price level means that real income will change by less in response to a change in autonomous expenditure than it would if the price level were constant.

Over the *steep* range, for output above Y_4, virtually nothing more can be produced, however large

FIGURE 29-9 The Effects of Increases in Aggregate Demand

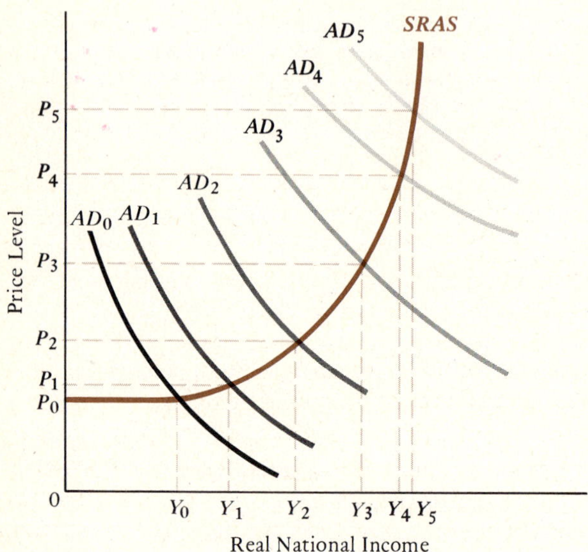

Increases in aggregate demand will have their major impact on increases in real income, increases in prices, or increases in both income and prices, depending on the shape of the *SRAS* curve. Because of the increasing slope of the *SRAS* curve, increases in aggregate demand up to AD_0 have virtually no impact on price. When aggregate demand increases from AD_0 to AD_1, there is a relatively small increase in price, from P_0 to P_1, and a relatively large increase in output, from Y_0 to Y_1. Successive further increases bring larger price increases and relatively smaller output increases. By the time aggregate demand is at AD_4 or AD_5, virtually all of the effect is on the price level.

the demand. This range depicts an economy near its capacity constraints. Any change in aggregate demand leads to a sharp change in the price level and to virtually no change in real national income. The multiplier in this case is nearly zero. Box 29-3 explores the reasons for such an increasing slope of the *SRAS*.

Let us consider the nearly vertical range in more detail using Figure 29-10 (p. 624) and in so doing look again at the *AE* curve. An increase in autonomous expenditure shifts the *AE* curve upward, thus raising the amount demanded. But a nearly vertical *SRAS* curve means that output cannot be expanded to satisfy the increased demand. Instead, the extra demand merely forces prices up, and as prices rise, the *AE* curve is shifted down once again. The rise in prices continues until the *AE* curve is nearly back to where it started. Thus the rise in prices offsets the expansionary effect of the original shift and, as a result, leaves both real aggregate expenditure and equilibrium real income virtually unchanged.

The discussion of Figures 29-9 and 29-10 illustrates a general proposition:

The effect of any given shift in aggregate demand will be divided between a change in real output and a change in the price level, depending on the conditions of aggregate supply. The steeper the *SRAS* curve, the greater the price effect and the smaller the output effect.

For reasons discussed in Boxes 29-2 and 29-3, many economists think that the *SRAS* curve is shaped like that in Figure 29-9, relatively flat for low levels of income and becoming steeper as the level of national income increases. This shape of the *SRAS* curve implies that at low levels of national income (below potential), shifts in aggregate demand affect mainly output, and at high levels of national income (above potential), shifts in aggregate demand affect mainly prices.

Of course, as we have already noted, treating wages and other factor prices as constant is appropriate only when the time period under consideration is short. Hence the *SRAS* curve is used only to analyze short-run, or *impact,* effects. In the next chapter we see what happens in the *long run* when factor prices respond to changes in national income and the price level. But first, to conclude this chapter and set the stage for that long-run analysis, we consider the short-run effects of aggregate supply shocks.

Aggregate Supply Shocks

A decrease in aggregate supply is reflected in a shift to the left in the *SRAS* curve and means that less national output will be supplied at any given price level. An increase in aggregate supply is reflected in a shift to the right in the *SRAS* curve and means that more national output will be produced at any given price level. As with the discussion of aggregate

BOX 29-3

Another Look at the Shape of the SRAS Curve

The *SRAS* curve relates the price level to the quantity of output that producers are willing to sell. Such an *SRAS* curve is reproduced in Figure 29-3. Notice two things about its shape: In general it has a positive slope, and the slope increases as output rises.

Positive slope. The positive slope of the *SRAS* curve indicates that a higher price level is associated with a higher volume of real output, other things being equal. Since the prices of all of the factors of production are being held constant along the *SRAS* curve, why is the curve not horizontal, indicating that firms would be willing to supply as much output as might be demanded with no increase in the price level?

You have already encountered an answer to this question. Even though *input prices* are constant, *unit costs of production* rise as output increases because of the bottlenecks that are likely to arise as firms in the economy approach full use of their capacity. Thus a higher price level for increasing output—rising short-run aggregate supply—is generally necessary to compensate firms for rising costs. (Recall the particular circumstances noted in Box 29-2 where this might not occur, and hence the *SRAS* curve might be flat.)

The preceding paragraph addresses the question "What has to happen to the price level if national output increases, with input prices held constant?" One may ask a different question: "What will happen to firms' willingness to supply output if product prices rise with no increase in input prices?" If there is an increase in the prices of products that firms sell, while the prices of everything that firms use to make their products remain constant, production becomes more profitable. Since firms are interested in making profits, when production becomes more profitable, they will usually produce more.* Thus when the price level of final output rises while input prices are held constant, firms are motivated to increase their outputs. This is true for the individual firm and also for firms in the aggregate. This increase in the amount that will be produced leads to an upward slope of the *SRAS* curve.

Thus whether we look at how the price level will respond in the short run to increases in output or how the level of output will respond to an increase in the price level with input prices held constant, we find that the *SRAS* curve has a positive slope.

Increasing slope. A somewhat less obvious but nevertheless important property of a typical *SRAS* curve is that its slope *increases* as output rises. It is rather flat to the left of potential output and rather steep to the right. Why? Below potential output, firms typically have unused capacity—some plant and equipment are idle. When firms are faced with unused capacity, only a small increase in the price of their output may be needed to induce them to expand production, at least up to normal capacity.

Once output is pushed far beyond normal capacity, however, unit costs tend to rise quite rapidly. Many higher cost expedients may have to be adopted. Standby capacity, overtime, and extra shifts may have to be used. Such expedients raise the cost of producing a unit of output. These higher-cost methods will not be used unless the selling price of the output has risen enough to cover them. The further output is expanded beyond normal capacity, the more rapidly unit costs rise and hence the larger the rise in price needed to induce firms to increase output even further.

This increasing slope is sometimes called the *first important asymmetry* in the behavior of aggregate supply. (The second important asymmetry, "sticky wages," is discussed in the next chapter.)

* Those who have already studied microeconomics can understand this in terms of price-taking firms being faced with higher prices and thus expanding output *along* their marginal cost curves until marginal cost is once again equal to price.

FIGURE 29-10 Demand Shocks When the *SRAS* Curve Is Nearly Vertical

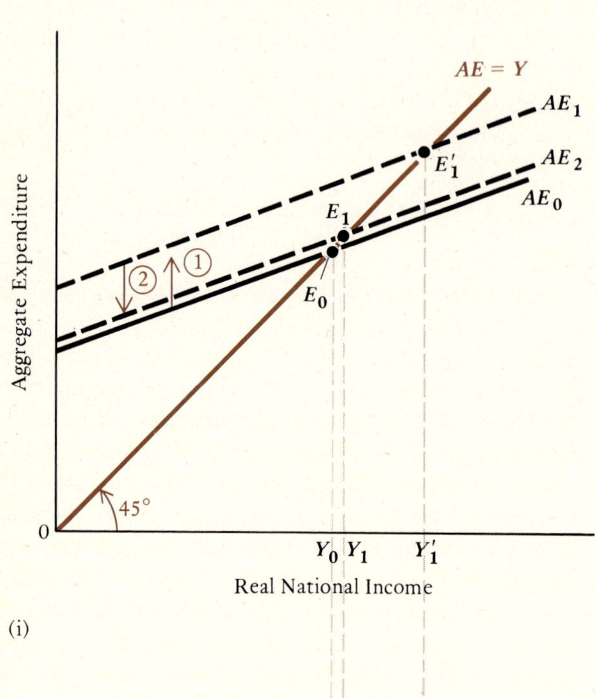

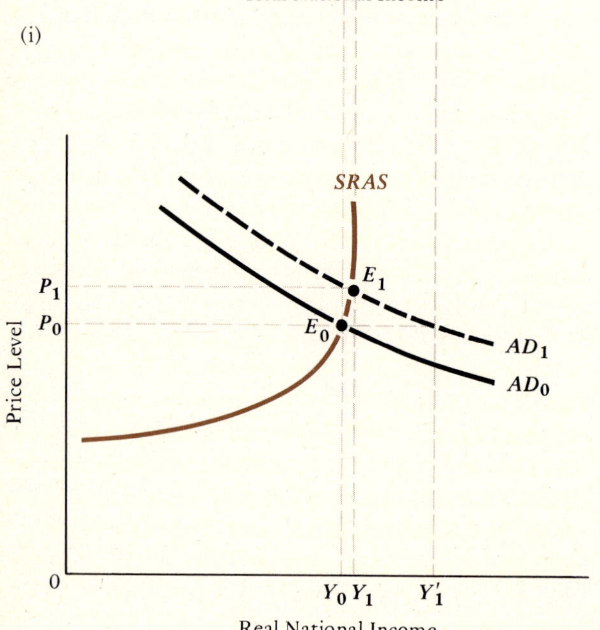

When the *SRAS* curve is nearly vertical, the effect of an increase in autonomous expenditure is mainly a rise in the price level. An increase in autonomous expenditure shifts the *AE* curve up from AE_0 to AE_1, as shown by arrow 1 in part (i). Given the initial price level P_0, equilibrium would shift from E_0 to E_1', and real national income would rise from Y_0 to Y_1'. (We use primes on these variables because these results cannot persist, since real national income cannot rise to Y_1'.) But the price level does not remain constant. This is shown by the *SRAS* curve in part (ii). Instead, the price level rises to P_1. This causes the *AE* curve to shift back down to AE_2, as shown by arrow 2 in part (i), and equilibrium income increases only to Y_1. If the *SRAS* curve were completely vertical, equilibrium income would return all the way to Y_0.

FIGURE 29-11 Aggregate Supply Shocks

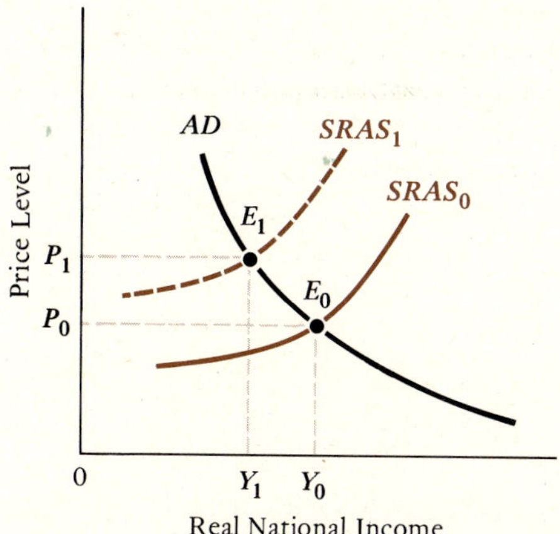

Shifts in aggregate supply cause the price level and real national income to move in opposite directions. A decrease in aggregate supply shifts the *SRAS* curve to the left, say, from $SRAS_0$ to $SRAS_1$. Equilibrium moves from E_0 to E_1. The price level rises from P_0 to P_1, but real national income falls from Y_0 to Y_1, reflecting a movement along the *AD* curve.

An increase in aggregate supply shifts the *SRAS* curve to the right, say, from $SRAS_1$ to $SRAS_0$. Equilibrium moves from E_1 to E_0. The price level falls from P_1 to P_0, but real national income rises from Y_1 to Y_0, again reflecting a movement along the *AD* curve.

demand shocks, we are not now concerned with the source of the aggregate supply shock.

Figure 29-11 illustrates the effects on the price level and real national income of aggregate supply shocks. As can be seen from the figure, following the decrease in aggregate supply, the price level rises and real national income falls. This combination of events is called **stagflation,** a rather inelegant word derived by combining *stagnation* (a term sometimes used to mean less than full employment) and *inflation.*

Figure 29-11 also shows that an increase in aggregate supply leads to an increase in real national income and a decrease in the price level.

Aggregate supply shocks cause the price level and real national income to change in opposite directions; with an increase in supply, the price level falls and income rises; with a decrease in supply, the price level rises and income falls.

An aggregate supply shock means a shift in the *SRAS* curve (for example, from $SRAS_0$ to $SRAS_1$ in the figure). Adjustment to the new equilibrium following the shock involves a movement along the *AD* curve (for example, from E_0 to E_1).

Causes of Aggregate Supply Shocks

The *SRAS* curve can shift for many reasons. Two sources of shift are of particular importance.

Changes in input prices. The fact that input prices are held constant along the *SRAS* curve suggests an important reason for the *SRAS* curve to shift. If input prices rise, firms will find that the profitability of their current production has been reduced. For any given level of output to be produced, an increase in the price level will be required. If prices did not rise, firms would react by decreasing production.[6] For the economy as a whole this would mean less output at each price level than before the input price increases. Thus if input prices rise, the *SRAS* curve shifts upward. This is what we have called a decrease in supply, as illustrated in Figure 29-11.

Similarly, a fall in input prices will cause the *SRAS* curve to shift downward (or, what is the same thing, to the right), reflecting what we have called an increase in supply.

Increases in productivity. If labor productivity rises, meaning that each worker can produce more, the unit costs of production will fall as long as wage rates remain constant. Lower costs generally lead to lower prices. Competing firms cut prices in attempts to raise their market shares, and the net result of such competition is that the fall in production costs is accompanied by a fall in prices.

Since the same output is sold at a lower price, this causes a shift to the right in the *SRAS* curve. This shift is an increase in supply, as illustrated in Figure 29-11.

[6] Students who have already studied microeconomics will recognize that such an upward shift in a firm's marginal cost curve leads to a decrease in the output that is profitable for the firm to produce. This is discussed in Chapter 12.

A change in either input prices or productivity will shift the *SRAS* curve because any given output will be supplied at a different price level than previously. An increase in input prices shifts the *SRAS* curve to the left; an increase in productivity or a decrease in input prices shifts it to the right.

A leftward shift in the *SRAS* curve, brought about, for example, by an increase in the price of basic raw materials and imported oil as occurred during the 1970s, lowers real national income and raises the price level. Stagflation, the unhappy combination of rising prices and falling real national income, can result from such supply shocks, as it did during the 1970s.

A rightward shift in the *SRAS* curve, brought about, for example, by an increase in productivity with no increase in factor prices, raises real national income and lowers the price level. This happier combination is the object of government policies seeking to encourage productivity increases. As we shall see in the next chapter, it has proved hard to achieve in practice.

Summary

1. The *AE* curve shows desired aggregate expenditure for each level of income, at a particular price level. Its intersection with the 45° line determines equilibrium national income for that price level. A change in the price level shifts the *AE* curve and leads to a new equilibrium level of national income.
2. The *AD* curve plots the equilibrium level of income against the corresponding price level. A change in the equilibrium level of income following a change in the price level is shown by a movement along the *AD* curve.
3. The short-run aggregate supply *(SRAS)* curve, drawn for given factor prices, is positively sloped because unit costs rise with increasing output and because rising product prices make it profitable to increase output.
4. A macroeconomic equilibrium refers to equilibrium values of national income and the price level, as determined by the intersection of the *AD* and *SRAS* curves.
5. Shifts in the *AD* and *SRAS* curves, called aggregate demand shocks and aggregate supply shocks, respectively, cause the equilibrium values of national income and the price level to change.
6. An aggregate demand shock can be caused by a change in autonomous expenditure. The simple multiplier measures the size of the resulting horizontal shift in the *AD* curve. It measures the actual size of the change in equilibrium real national income only if the price level is constant.
7. When the *SRAS* curve is positively sloped, part of the effect of an aggregate demand shock is dissipated in a change in the price level, and only part goes to change real income. Thus an aggregate demand shock causes the price level and national income to move in the same direction. The division of the effects between a change in national income and a change in the price level are easily discovered from *AD* and *AS* curves.
8. The steepness of the *SRAS* curve determines how the impact of a

shift in the *AD* curve is divided between a change in output and a change in the price level. When the *SRAS* curve is flat, shifts in the *AD* curve affect mainly real national income. When the *SRAS* curve is steep, shifts in the *AD* curve affect mainly the price level.

9. An aggregate supply shock can be caused by a change in factor costs or a change in productivity. The resulting shift in the *SRAS* curve will lead to a movement along the *AD* curve. Thus an aggregate supply shock causes the price level and national income to move in opposite directions.
10. A decrease in aggregate supply—a shock that shifts the *SRAS* curve to the left—can lead to stagflation—rising prices and falling national income. An increase in aggregate supply—a shift to the right of the *SRAS* curve—leads to an increase in real national income and a fall in the price level.

Topics for Review

Effects of a change in the price level
Relation between the *AE* and *AD* curves
Negative slope of the *AD* curve
Positive slope of the *SRAS* curve
Macroeconomic equilibrium
Aggregate demand shocks
The multiplier when the price level varies
Aggregate supply shocks
Stagflation

Discussion Questions

1. Explain the following by shifts in either or both the aggregate demand and aggregate supply curves. Pay attention to the initial position before the shift(s) occurs.
   a. Output and unemployment rise, while prices hold steady.
   b. Prices soar, but employment and output hold steady.
   c. Inflation accelerates even as the recession in business actively deepens.
2. A survey of private economic forecasters in mid 1986 showed that the consensus economic outlook for 1987 was cautiously optimistic—most thought that inflation and real growth would both remain roughly constant at their then 4.0 percent levels while unemployment would fall slightly. Explain what predictions about factors underlying the *AD* and *SRAS* curves would give rise to such a forecast. In retrospect, how accurate were these forecasts? What happened to the underlying determinants to cause actual events to differ from the forecasts?
3. In 1979–1980 the British government greatly reduced income taxes, but restored the lost government revenue by raising excise and sales taxes. This led to a short burst of extra inflation and a fall in employment. Explain this in terms of shifts in the aggregate demand and/or supply curves.
4. Indicate whether each of the following events is the cause or the

consequence of a shift in aggregate demand or supply. If it is a cause, what do you predict will be the effect on the price level and on real national income?

a. Unemployment decreases in 1984.
b. OPEC raises oil prices in 1979.
c. OPEC is forced to accept lower oil prices in 1982–1983.
d. In the late 1960s and early 1970s Canada experiences a rapid inflation under conditions of approximately full employment.
e. In country X income and employment continue to fall while the price level is quite stable.
f. Defense Minister Perrin Beatty promises a large increase in defense spending in 1988–1991.

5. A number of economists argued that as a result of the major tax reform introduced in 1987 by the Canadian government, a number of "disincentives to work" were being removed, and hence there would be an improvement in productivity and an increase in labor-force participation. If this proves true, what would you expect to be the effects on national income and the price level?
6. What would happen to American employment and income if, in an attempt to lower American unemployment, the American Congress enacted large increases in American tariff rates? What would happen if, in the face of a worldwide recession, all countries did the same?
7. Using your understanding of the chapter, analyze the following recent statements made by business people.
   a. "We must be successful; our sales have increased every year for the past ten years."
   b. "I can see why prices may rise in boom times, but rising prices and falling output just don't make sense."
   c. "I can't understand why there is so much unemployment; our business is booming."
8. Interpret each of the following news items in terms of *AD* and *SRAS* curves.
   a. "Management representative says union wage demands are irresponsible in the face of current high unemployment rates."
   b. "Government spokesman says that although the recovery is expected to be vigorous, it will witness only modest reductions in the unemployment rate."
   c. "Inflation in the U.S. fell quickly in 1982 due to the 'lucky break' of reduced union strength in the automobile and steel sectors."
   d. "Wage increases have failed to keep up with inflation during the current boom."
   e. "Innovations in microelectronic technology will lead to an increase in both national output and unemployment."
   f. "Reagan's tough stance with public sector unions has vastly improved the inflation outlook for the U.S. over the next few years."

30

National Income and the Price Level in the Long Run

In Chapter 29 we studied how national income and the price level are determined in the short run, where the short run was taken to mean a period of time short enough that wages and other factor costs could be taken as given. We also examined the impact effects on national income and the price level of an aggregate demand shock or an aggregate supply shock.

We now need to see what happens in a longer-term setting when changes in national income and the price level in turn *induce* changes in factor prices.

Induced Changes in Factor Prices

We start by briefly reconsidering two concepts that we first encountered in Chapter 26—potential income and the output gap.

Another Look at Potential Income and the Output Gap

We saw in Chapter 26 that actual national income often diverges from potential national income, the difference being called the output gap (see Figure 26-3 on page 560 and Figure 26-4 on page 562).

Since potential income can be viewed as the level of total output that would be produced if factors of production were being efficiently used at their normal rates of utilization, potential income can be assumed constant for the purposes of this chapter.[1]

Determination of the output gap is illustrated in Figure 30-1. The actual level of national income is determined by the intersection of the *AD* and *SRAS* curves. Since potential national income is a constant, it is shown by the vertical line at Y^*. In part (i), potential income Y^* exceeds actual income Y_0, so there is a positive output gap of Y^*Y_0. In part (ii), Y^* is less than actual income Y_1, thus giving rise to a negative output gap of Y_1Y^*.

[1] In Chapter 38 we shall see that economic growth gives rise to a steady increase in potential national income over time. In this chapter we ignore the effects of growth on potential income. (Recall our discussion on page 563.)

FIGURE 30-1 Actual Income, Potential Income, and the Output Gap

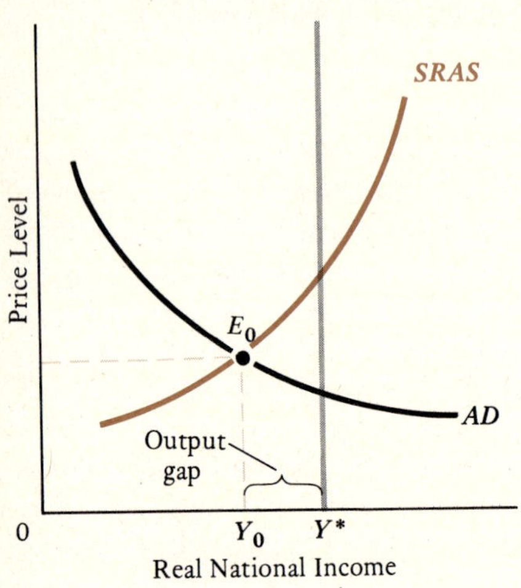

(i) A positive output gap

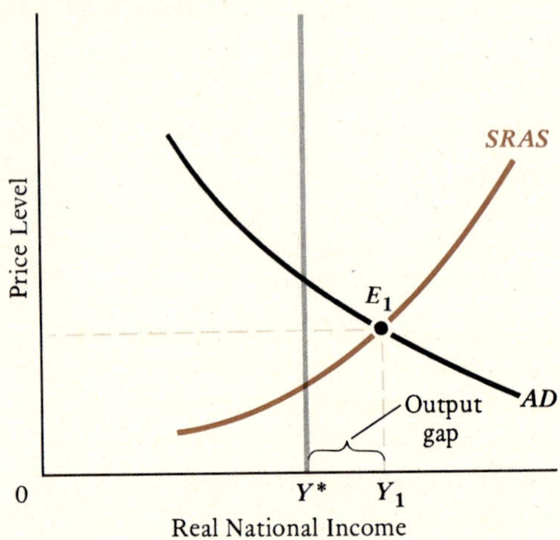

(ii) A negative output gap

The output gap is the difference between potential national income, Y^*, and actual national income, Y. Potential income is shown by a vertical line because it refers to a given, constant level of national income. Actual national income is determined by the intersection of the aggregate demand (*AD*) and short-run aggregate supply (*SRAS*) curves.

In part (i) the *AD* and *SRAS* curves are such that there is a positive output gap. This is because equilibrium is at E_0, so actual national income is given by Y_0, less than potential income. The output gap is thus $Y^* - Y_0$.

In part (ii) the *AD* and *SRAS* curves are such that there is a negative output gap. Although potential income is unchanged at Y^*, equilibrium is now at E_1, so actual national income is given by Y_1, greater than potential income. The output gap is thus $Y^* - Y_1$.

Wage Adjustments and the Output Gap

The output gap is a measure of the actual level of national income relative to potential. As such, it provides a convenient measure of the actual state of demand in markets for factor services relative to "normal rates of utilization." Although this applies to all factor services, for simplicity and ease of exposition in what follows, we focus on labor as the key factor of production and hence on its price, the wage rate, as the key factor price.

When there is a negative output gap—that is, when actual national income exceeds potential—the demand for labor services will be relatively high. When there is a positive output gap—that is, when actual national income is less than potential—the demand for labor services will be relatively low. Each of these situations will have implications for wages. Before turning to a detailed analysis of each, we first consider a benchmark for the behavior of wages.

Upward and downward wage pressures. In what follows we consider *upward* and *downward* pressure on wages caused by the output gap. Upward or downward in relation to what? One answer would be in relation to zero—upward pressure would be for wages to rise and downward pressure would be for wages to fall. However, most wage bargaining starts from the assumption that, other things being equal, workers should get the benefit of increases in their own productivity by receiving higher wages. Because of this, when there is neither upward nor downward pressure on wages emanating from the labor market, we would expect wages to be rising at the same rate as productivity is rising.[2] When wages and productivity change proportionately, labors cost per unit of output, which we have earlier called *unit labor costs,* remain unchanged. For example, if each worker produces 4 percent more and earns 4 percent more, unit labor costs will remain constant.

This, then, is our benchmark:

When there is neither excess demand nor excess supply in the labor market, wages will tend to be rising as fast as labor productivity; in this case unit labor costs will remain constant.

Note that with unit labor costs constant, there is no pressure coming from the labor market for the *SRAS* curve to shift, and hence no pressure for the price level to rise or fall.

In comparison with this benchmark, upward pressure on wages means pressure for wages to rise faster than productivity is rising. When this occurs, unit labor costs will also be rising. For example, if money wages rise by 8 percent while productivity rises by only 4 percent, labor cost per unit of output will be rising by about 4 percent. In this case the *SRAS* curve will be shifting leftward, and hence there will be upward pressure—emanating from the labor market on the price level.

Downward pressure on wages means pressure for wages to rise less fast than productivity. When this occurs, unit labor costs will be falling. For example, if productivity rises by 4 percent while money wages rise by only 2 percent, labor costs per unit of output will be falling by about 2 percent. In this case the *SRAS* curve will be shifting rightward, and hence there will be downward pressure—emanating from the labor market—on the price level.

[2] Ongoing inflation would also influence the normal pattern of wage changes. Wage contracts often allow for changes in prices that are expected to occur during the life of the contract. For now we maintain the simplifying assumption that the price level is expected to be constant; hence changes in money wages are also expected to be changes in real wages. The distinction between changes in money wages and real wages and the important role that expectations of price level changes play are discussed in Chapters 36 and 39.

A negative output gap. Consider a situation in which the *AD* and *SRAS* curves are such that actual output exceeds potential, as illustrated in part (ii) of Figure 30-1. Firms are producing beyond their normal capacity output, so there is an unusually large demand for all factor inputs, including labor. Labor shortages will emerge in some industries and among many groups of workers, particularly the skilled. Firms will try to bid workers away from other firms in order to maintain the high levels of output and sales made possible by the boom conditions.

As a result of tight labor market conditions, workers will find that they have considerable bargaining power with their employers, and they will put upward pressure on wages.[3] Firms, recognizing that demand for their goods is strong, will be anxious to maintain a high level of output. Thus to prevent their workers from either striking or quitting and moving to other employers, firms will be willing to accede to some of these upward pressures.

The boom associated with a negative output gap generates a set of conditions—high profits for firms and unusually large demand for labor—that puts sharp upward pressure on wages.

A positive output gap. Now consider a situation where the *AD* and *SRAS* curves are such that actual output is less than potential, as illustrated in part (i) of Figure 30-1. In this situation firms will be producing below their normal capacity output, so there is an unusually low demand for all factor inputs, including labor. The general conditions in the market for labor will be the opposite of those when actual output exceeds potential. There will now be labor surpluses in some industries and among some groups of workers. Firms will have below normal sales and will not only resist upward pressures on wages but will also tend to offer wage increases below productivity increases and may even seek reductions in wages.

[3] Additional upward pressures on the level of wages may be created by the fact that the price level, P_1, will be higher than P^*, the price level that would have prevailed had output attained its potential level.

The slump associated with a positive output gap generates a set of conditions—low profits for firms, unusually low demand for labor, and a desire on the part of firms to resist wage demands and even to push for wage concessions—that puts downward pressure on wages.

Adjustment asymmetry. At this stage we encounter an important asymmetry in the economy's aggregate supply behavior. Boom conditions with severe labor shortages do cause wages to rise rapidly. In conditions of strong excess demand for labor, wage increases will bear little relation to productivity increases. Money wages may be rising 10 or 15 percent while productivity is rising at only 2 or 3 percent. This means that unit labor costs will be rising rapidly.

The experience of many economies suggests, however, that downward pressures on wages during slump conditions are not nearly so effective as are upward pressures during booms. Even in quite severe slumps, wages may continue to rise although their rate of increase falls below that of productivity. For example, productivity might be rising at, say, 3 percent while money wages were rising at 2 percent. In this case unit labor costs would be falling at only about 1 percent per year, and the leftward shift in the *SRAS* and downward pressure on the price level would be correspondingly slight.[4]

The inflationary and recessionary gaps. We have seen that a negative output gap puts upward pressure on wages and prices while a positive output gap puts downward pressure on wages and prices. Box 30-1 (p. 634) discusses the same wage adjustment process in terms of the famous *Phillips curve*.

As we saw in Chapter 29 (see especially Figure 29-11), the increases in unit costs that occur when upward pressure on wages cause them to rise faster than productivity cause the *SRAS* curve to shift leftward. A leftward shift in the *SRAS* curve—a decrease in supply—causes the equilibrium price level to rise. Thus because a negative output gap induces large shifts in the *SRAS* curve that drive up the price level, any excess of actual output Y above potential Y^* is often called an **inflationary gap**.

We also know that when wages rise less fast than productivity, unit costs fall, and this shifts the *SRAS* curve to the right. As a result of this increase in supply, the equilibrium price level will fall. However, to stress the asymmetry just discussed—which means that the potential for wage-induced reductions in the price level is quite weak—any shortfall of actual output relative to potential is called a **recessionary gap** (rather than a deflationary gap).

The induced effects on unit labor costs and consequent shifts in the *SRAS* curve play an important role in our analysis of the long-run consequences of aggregate demand shocks, to which we now turn.

The Long-Run Consequences of Aggregate Demand Shocks

We can now add to the preceding chapter's study of impact effects. We do this by considering the longer-run consequence of an aggregate demand shock. Shifts in the *AD* curve cannot be expected to leave input prices unchanged in the long run. However, we need to examine the effect of aggregate demand shocks on input prices separately for expansionary and for contractionary shocks, since the behavior of the economy is not symmetrical for the two. In what follows we make the simplifying assumption that labor productivity is constant, so that all changes in wages are also changes in unit labor costs and hence cause the *SRAS* to shift.

Expansionary AD Shocks

Suppose that the economy starts off in a position of full employment, so that actual national income equals potential. Further suppose that the price level is stable at the level consistent with income being at its potential level. This is shown by the initial equilibrium at E_0 in Figure 30-2(i).

Now suppose that this happy situation is disturbed by an increase in autonomous expenditure,

[4] This is the second asymmetry in aggregate supply that we have encountered. The first refers to the changing slope of the *SRAS* curve, as discussed in Box 29-3.

FIGURE 30-2 Demand-Shock Inflation

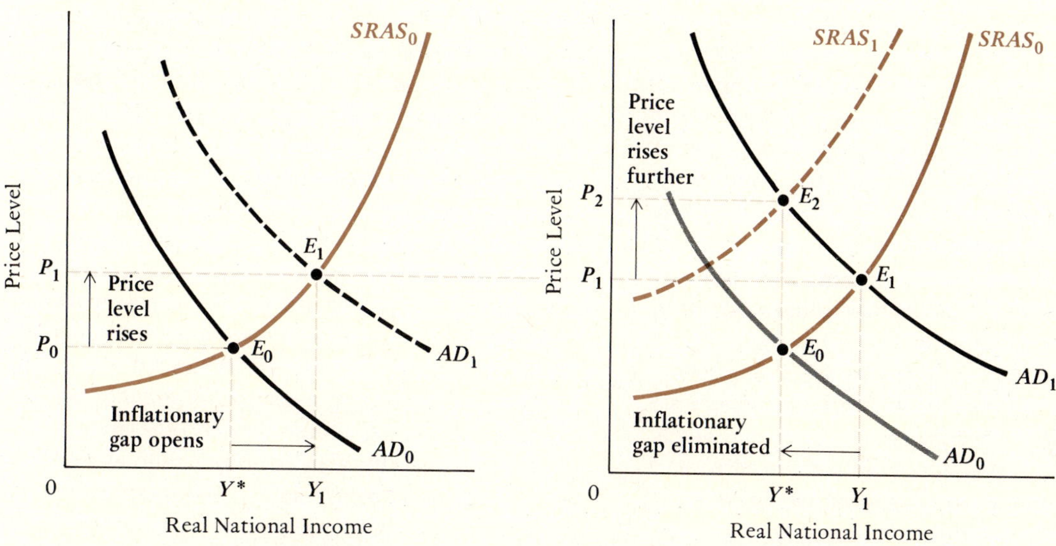

(i) Autonomous increase in aggregate demand

(ii) Induced shift in aggregate supply

A rightward shift of the *AD* curve first raises price and output along the *SRAS* curve. It then induces a shift of the *SRAS* curve that further raises prices but lowers output along the *AD* curve. In part (i) the economy is in equilibrium at E_0, at its level of potential output Y^* and price level P_0. The *AD* curve then shifts to AD_1. This moves equilibrium to E_1, with income Y_1 and price level P_1, and opens up an inflationary gap of Y^*Y_1.

In part (ii) the inflationary gap results in an increase in wages and other input costs, shifting the *SRAS* curve leftward. As this happens, income falls and the price level rises along AD_1. Eventually, when the *SRAS* curve has shifted to $SRAS_1$, income is back to Y^* and the inflationary gap has been eliminated. However, the price level has risen to P_2.

perhaps caused by a sudden boom in consumption spending. As also shown in part (i) of Figure 30-2, the impact effects of this aggregate demand shock are that the price level and national income both rise. Thus following the shock actual national income exceeds potential, creating an inflationary gap.

As we have just seen, an inflationary gap leads to an increase in wages. Sharp rises in wages mean sharp rises in costs. These lead to leftward shifts of the *SRAS* curve as firms seek to pass on their increases in input costs by increasing their output prices. For this reason the initial increases in the price level and in real national income shown in Figure 30-2(i) are *not* the final effects of the demand shock. As seen in part (ii) of the figure, the leftward shift of the *SRAS* curve causes a further rise in the price level, but this time the price rise is associated with a fall in output.

The cost increases (and the consequent leftward shifts of the *SRAS* curve) go on until the inflationary gap has been removed, that is, until income returns to Y^*, its potential level. Only then is there no abnormal demand for labor, and only then do wages and costs, and hence the *SRAS* curve, stabilize.

This important expansionary demand-shock sequence can be summarized as follows:

1. Starting from full employment, a rise in aggregate demand raises the price level and raises income

BOX 30-1

The Phillips Curve and the Shifting SRAS Curve

In the early 1950s Professor A. W. Phillips of the London School of Economics was doing pathbreaking research on macroeconomic policy. He included in his early models an equation relating the rate of inflation to the difference between actual and potential income, $Y - Y^*$. Later he investigated the empirical underpinnings of this equation by studying the relation between the rate of increase of wage costs and the level of unemployment. In 1958 he reported that a stable relation had existed between these two variables for 100 years in the United Kingdom.

The relation, which came to be called the *Phillips curve,* is illustrated in the figure on the left. The curve shows money wages rising when unemployment is below the natural rate of unemployment, U_N, and falling when unemployment is above that critical level. It illustrates the effect that an output gap has on wages.

Recall that the rate of unemployment is related negatively to national income: The higher is national income, the lower is unemployment. Thus the Phillips curve can also be drawn with national income on the horizontal axis, as in the figure on the right.

Both figures show the same information. Inflationary gaps (which correspond to low unemployment rates) are associated with *increases* in wages, while recessionary gaps (which correspond to high unemployment rates) are associated with slow *decreases* in wages.

The Phillips curve must be clearly distinguished from the *SRAS* curve. The *SRAS* curve has the *price level* on the vertical axis while the Phillips curve has the *rate of wage inflation.* Therefore the Phillips curve tells us how fast the *SRAS* curve is shifting when actual income does not equal potential income.

Only when $Y = Y^*$ is the *SRAS* curve not shifting on account of demand pressures. When income is at its potential level, aggregate demand for labor equals aggregate supply; the only unemployment would thus be frictional unemployment. There would be neither upward nor downward pressure of demand on wages. Thus the Phillips curve cuts the axis at potential income Y^* and at the corresponding level of unemployment U_N.

The Phillips curve soon became famous. It provided a link between national income models and labor markets. This link allowed macroeconomists to drop the uncomfortable assumption, which they had

above its potential level as the economy expands along a given *SRAS* curve.

2. The expansion of income beyond its normal capacity level puts heavy pressure on factor markets; factor prices begin to rise, shifting the *SRAS* curve to the left.
3. The shift of the *SRAS* curve causes income to fall along the *AD* curve. This process continues *as long as* actual income exceeds potential income. Therefore, actual income eventually falls back to its potential level. The price level is, however, now higher than it was after the initial impact of the increased aggregate demand, but inflation will have come to a halt.

The ability to wring more output and income from the economy than its underlying potential output (as in point 2) is only a short-term possibility. National income greater than Y^* sets up inflationary pressures that tend to push national income back to Y^*.

There is a self-adjustment mechanism that brings any inflation caused by a one-time demand shock to an eventual halt by returning output to its potential level and thus removing the inflationary gap.

Contractionary AD Shocks

Let us return to that fortunate economy with full employment and stable prices. It appears again in part (i) of Figure 30-3 (p. 636), which is similar to Figure 30-2(i). Now assume a *decline* in aggregate demand, perhaps due to a major reduction in consumption expenditure.

The impact of the decline is a fall in output and

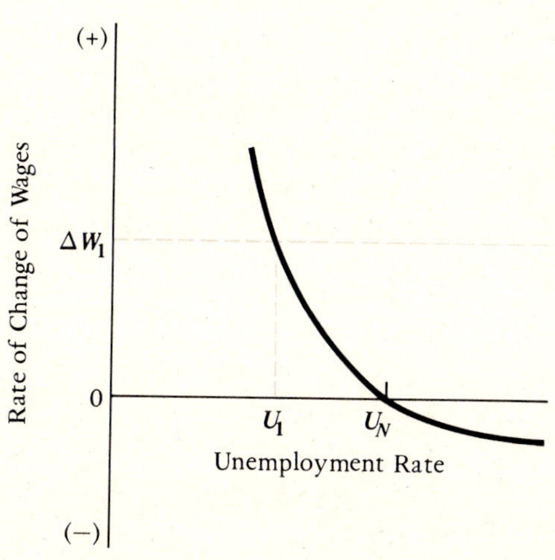

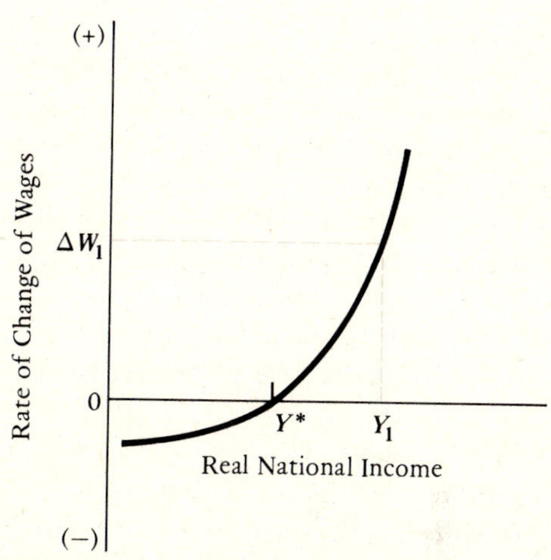

often been forced to use in many of their earlier formal models, that money wages were rigidly fixed and neither rose nor fell as national income varied. The Phillips curve relation between money wages and national income determines (in conjunction with productivity changes) the speed at which the *SRAS* curve shifts.

Consider, for example, the situation shown in part (ii) of Figure 30-1, where the level of income determined by the *AD* and *SRAS* curves is Y_1. Plotting Y_1 on the Phillips curve in the figure on the right tells us that wage costs will be rising at ΔW_1. Then the *SRAS* curve in Figure 30-1(ii) will be shifting upward by that amount. The same information can be seen in the figure on the left, where national income of Y_1 corresponds to unemployment of U_1.

some downward adjustment of prices, as shown in part (i) of the figure. As output falls, unemployment rises. The difference between potential output and actual output is, as we have seen, the output gap. When the output gap is positive, as in Figure 30-3, it is a recessionary gap.

Flexible wages. Consider what would happen if severe unemployment caused wage rates to fall sharply. Falling wage rates would lower costs for firms and cause a rightward shift of the *SRAS* curve. As shown in Figure 30-3(ii), the economy would move along its fixed *AD* curve with falling prices and rising output until full employment was restored at potential national income Y^*. We conclude that *if* wages were to fall whenever there was a recessionary gap, the resulting fall in the *SRAS* curve would restore full employment.

Flexible wages that fell when there was a recessionary gap would provide an automatic adjustment mechanism that would push the economy back toward full employment whenever output fell below potential.

Sticky wages. Boom conditions with severe labor shortages do cause wages to rise rapidly, shifting the *SRAS* curve upward. But as we noted earlier (see page 632, where we encountered the second asymmetry of aggregate supply behavior), the experience of many economies suggests that wages are sticky—that is, they are not very flexible—in a downward direction. If wages are sticky, unemployment has a weak and slow-acting downward effect on wages. The adjustment mechanism that depends on rightward shifts of *SRAS* is, therefore, weak and sluggish.

FIGURE 30-3 **Demand-Shock Deflation with Flexible Wages**

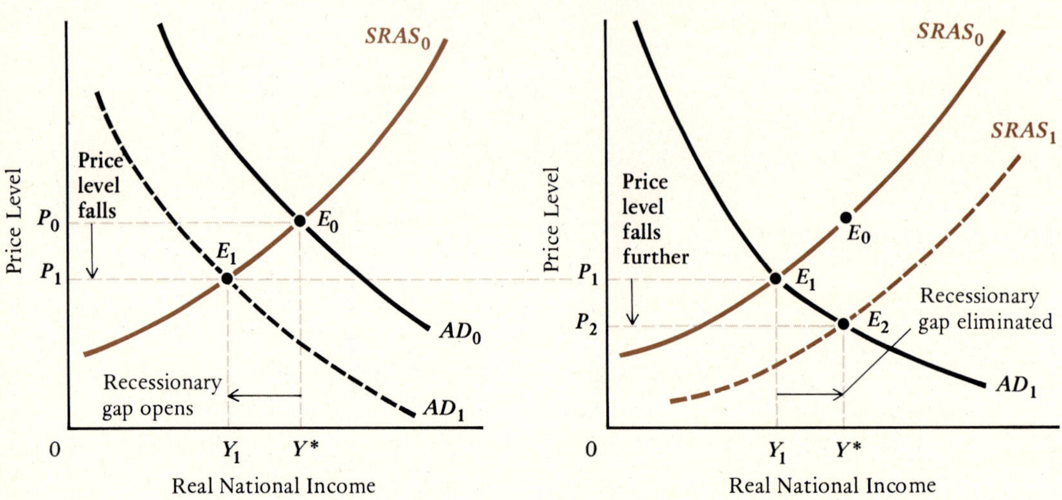

(i) Autonomous fall in aggregate demand

(ii) Induced shift in aggregate supply

A leftward shift of the *AD* curve first lowers price and output along the *SRAS* curve and then induces a (slow) shift of the *SRAS* curve that further lowers prices but raises output along the *AD* curve. In part (i) the economy is in equilibrium at E_0, at its level of potential output Y^* and price level P_0. The *AD* curve then shifts to AD_1, moving equilibrium to E_1, with income Y_1 and price level P_1, and opens up an output (or recessionary) gap of Y_1Y^*.

Part (ii) shows the adjustment back to full employment that would occur from the supply side of the economy if wages were sufficiently flexible downward. The fall in wages would shift the *SRAS* curve to the right. Real national income would rise, and the price level would fall further along the *AD* curve. Eventually, the *SRAS* curve would reach $SRAS_1$, with equilibrium at E_2. The price level would stabilize at P_2 when income had returned to Y^*, eliminating the recessionary gap.

The weakness of the automatic adjustment mechanism does not mean that slumps will last indefinitely. What it means is that speedy recovery back to full employment must be generated mainly from the demand side. If the economy is to avoid a lengthy stagnation, the force leading to recovery must be a rightward shift of the *AD* curve rather than a rightward drift of the *SRAS* curve.

The *SRAS* curve shifts to the left fairly rapidly when national income exceeds Y^*, but it shifts to the right only slowly when national income falls short of Y^*.

The asymmetry. This difference in speed of adjustment is a consequence of the important asymmetry in the behavior of aggregate supply noted earlier in this chapter. This asymmetry helps explain two key facts about our economy. First, unemployment *can* persist for quite long periods without causing large decreases in wages and prices (which, if they did occur, would help to remove the unemployment). Second, booms, with labor shortages and production beyond normal capacity, cannot persist for long periods without causing large increases in wages and prices.

The Long-Run Aggregate Supply (*LRAS*) Curve

The possibility of automatic adjustments gives rise to an important concept: the **long-run aggregate**

supply (*LRAS*) curve. This curve relates the price level to real national income *after wage rates and all other input costs have been fully adjusted to eliminate any difference between actual and purely frictional unemployment.*[5]

Shape of the *LRAS* curve. Once all the adjustments required have occurred, the economy will have eliminated any excess demand or excess supply of labor. In other words, full employment will prevail, and output will necessarily be at its potential level Y^*. It follows that the aggregate supply curve becomes a vertical line at Y^* as shown in Figure 30-4.[6]

Notice that the vertical *LRAS* curve does not represent the same thing as the vertical portion of the *SRAS* curve (see Figure 29-9). Over the vertical range of the *SRAS* curve, the economy is at its utmost limit of productive capacity, when no more can be squeezed out, as might occur in an all-out war effort. The vertical shape of the *LRAS* curve is due to the workings of an adjustment mechanism that is assumed always to bring the economy back to its level of potential output, even though it may stray away in the short run. It is called the *long-run* aggregate supply curve because it refers to adjustments that take a substantial amount of time.

Along the *LRAS* curve all the prices of *all outputs* and *all inputs* have been fully adjusted to eliminate any excess demands or supplies. Proportionate changes in money wages and the price level (which, by definition, will leave real wages unaltered) will also leave equilibrium employment and output unchanged. The key concept is this: If the price of absolutely everything (including labor) doubles, nothing real changes. When the price of everything bought *and* sold doubles, neither workers nor firms gain any advantage and hence neither has any incentive to alter their behavior. Output, therefore, is unchanged. The level of output will be what can be produced in the economy when all factors of production, including labor, are utilized at "normal" levels of their capacity.

FIGURE 30-4 The Long-Run Aggregate Supply (*LRAS*) Curve

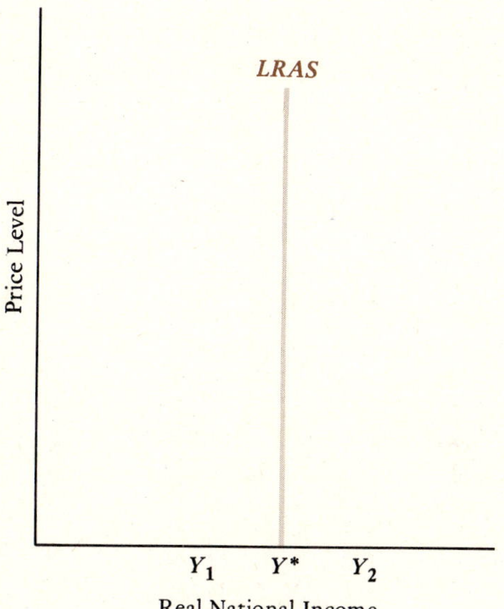

The long-run aggregate supply curve is a vertical line drawn at the level of national income equal to potential income, Y^*. It is a vertical line because the total amount of goods that the economy produces when all factors are efficiently used at their normal rate of utilization does not vary with the price level. If the price level were to rise from P_1 to P_2 *and* wages and all other factor prices were to rise by the same proportion, the desired output of firms would remain at Y^*.

If income were Y_1, less then Y^*, wages would be falling and the *SRAS* curve would be shifting right; hence the economy would not be on its *LRAS* curve. If income were Y_2, greater than Y^*, wages would be rising and the *SRAS* curve would be shifting left; hence the economy would not be on its *LRAS* curve.

The vertical *LRAS* curve shows that given full adjustment of input prices, potential income, Y^*, is compatible with *any* price level.

Long-Run Equilibrium

Figure 30-5 shows the equilibrium output and the price level determined by the intersection of the *AD*

[5] Students who have studied microeconomics will notice that this use of the term *long run* appears different from its meaning in microeconomics. Note, however, the key similarity that the long run has more flexibility for adjustment than does the short run.

[6] The *LRAS* curve is sometimes called the classical aggregate supply curve because the classical economists were mainly concerned with the behavior of the economy in long-run equilibrium.

FIGURE 30-5 Long-Run Equilibrium and Aggregate Supply

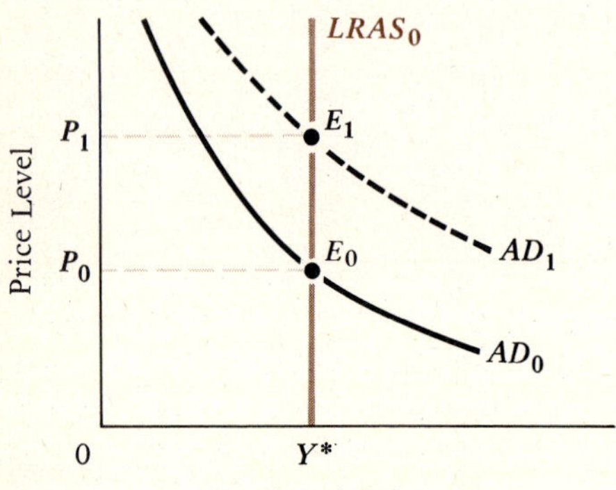

(i) A rise in aggregate demand

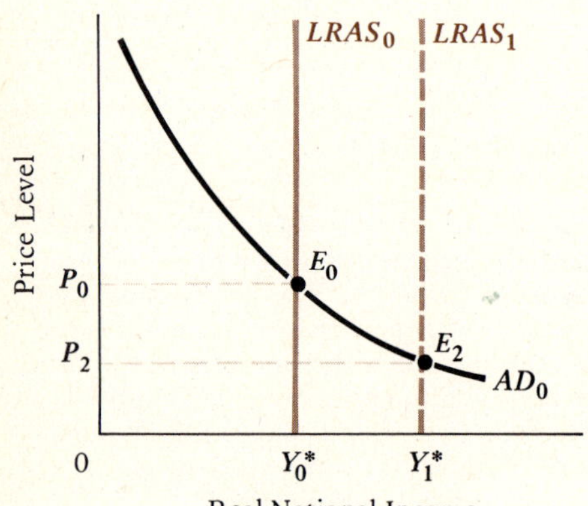

(ii) A rise in long-run aggregate supply

When the *LRAS* curve is vertical, aggregate supply determines the long-run equilibrium value of national income at *Y. Given *Y**, aggregate demand determines the long-run equilibrium value of the price level.** In both parts of the figure the initial long-run equilibrium is at E_0, so the price level is P_0 and national income is Y_0^*.

In part (i) a shift in the *AD* curve from AD_0 to AD_1 with the *LRAS* curve unchanged moves the long-run equilibrium from E_0 to E_1. This raises the price level from P_0 to P_1 but leaves national income unchanged at Y_0^* in the long run.

In part (ii) a shift in the *LRAS* curve from $LRAS_0$ to $LRAS_1$ with the aggregate demand curve constant at AD_0 moves the long-run equilibrium from E_0 to E_2. This raises national income from Y_0^* to Y_1^* but lowers the price level from P_0 to P_2.

curve and the vertical *LRAS* curve. Because the *LRAS* curve is vertical, shifts in aggregate demand change the price level but not the level of equilibrium output, as shown in part (i). In contrast, a shift in aggregate supply changes both output and the price level, as shown in part (ii). For example, a rightward shift of the *LRAS* curve increases national income and leads (eventually) to a fall in the price level.

With a vertical *LRAS* curve, output is determined solely by conditions of supply, and the role of aggregate demand is simply to determine the price level.

Of course, these are only long-term tendencies. To see the short-term impact of demand and supply shocks, we need to use the short-run aggregate supply curve. Because of wage stickiness, downward adjustments of wages and prices may take a long time, and so there may be long periods when the economy is not at, or even near, long-run equilibrium.[7]

Supply-Side Economics

Both of Ronald Reagan's U.S. presidential campaigns featured a theory of economic policy that came to be known as *supply-side economics.* To some the policy promised a quick cure for both high inflation and low growth in real national income. To others it seemed an exercise in wishful thinking.

The theoretical tools developed in this chapter can be used to explore both the theory and the doubts. Although supply-side economics has many aspects, we are here concerned specifically with the effects of supply-side policies on the price level and on real national income, starting from a situation with a large inflationary gap. When Ronald Reagan became president in January 1981, the inflation rate was about 10 percent and unemployment about 7 percent; any policy that would decrease them both would have been welcomed.

[7] The rest of this chapter may be omitted without loss of continuity.

How It Was Supposed to Work

The theory of supply-side economics called for adopting measures that would shift the *LRAS* curve to the right far enough and fast enough to eliminate the inflationary gap. In the most favorable case there would be no offsetting demand-side effects. This case is illustrated in Figure 30-6.

A major part of supply-side economics was the provision of tax incentives that were to increase potential national income by increasing the nation's supplies of labor and capital. Incentives were to be given to firms to increase their investment, thus increasing national productive capacity. Personal taxes were to be cut across the board to give everyone an incentive to work more. It was argued that people already employed would be more inclined to work longer and harder when they were able to keep a larger fraction of their pre-tax earnings, and people outside of the labor force would be drawn in as a result of the higher after-tax wages. Extra tax incentives were to be given to persons at high income levels so as to increase the incentives for work and risk taking on the part of the most productive people. It was anticipated that the resulting increases in productive capacity and increases in productivity would shift the *LRAS* curve to the right.

It was also assumed that no budget deficits would result from the cuts in tax rates and increases in tax exemptions. The increase in national income, it was argued, would create a larger tax base so that even at the lower tax *rates*, total tax *revenues* (which would fall initially) would be restored. For example, if a 10 percent cut in tax rates were followed by a 10 percent

FIGURE 30-6 The Theory of Anti-inflationary Supply-Side Economics

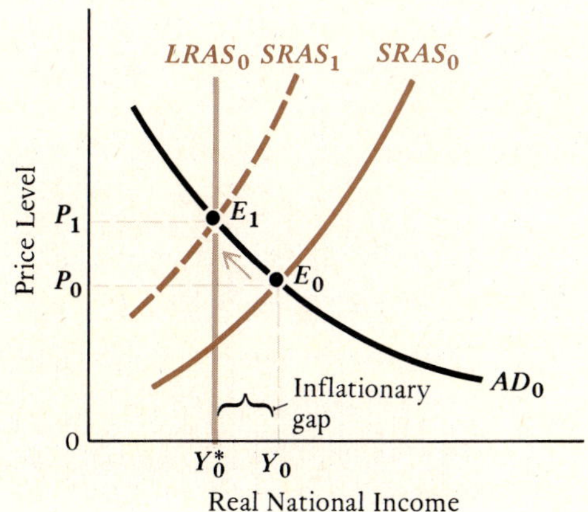

(i) An inflationary situation

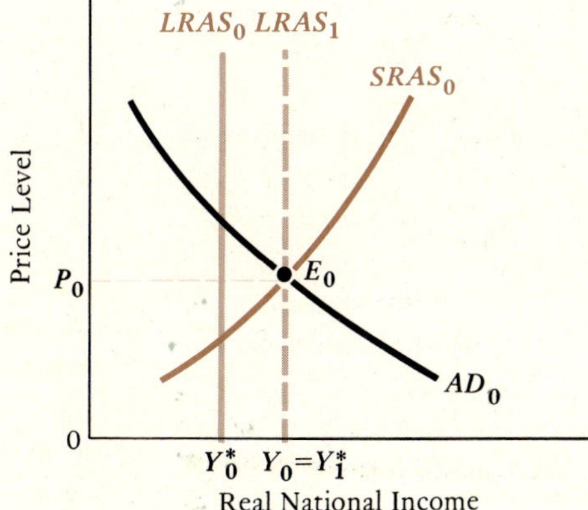

(ii) Supply-side success

Supply-side economics seeks to eliminate an inflationary gap by shifting the *LRAS* curve to the right without changing aggregate demand. Part (i) shows an economy in short-run equilibrium at E_0 on AD_0 and $SRAS_0$, with income Y_0 and price level P_0. As a result of the inflationary gap of $Y_0{}^*Y_0$, the *SRAS* curve will shift upward, taking the equilibrium along AD_0 (as shown by the arrow), with falling national income and rising price level. Other things being equal, the inflation will come to a halt once the curve has reached $SRAS_1$ and equilibrium is established at E_1, with price level P_1, and national income at its potential level $Y_0{}^*$.

Part (ii) shows the same economy after supply-side measures shift the *LRAS* curve to $LRAS_1$. This makes $Y_1{}^*$ the new level of potential income and removes the inflationary gap. The fall of income and rise in the price level shown in part (i) are both prevented.

increase in real national income, it would leave tax revenues approximately the same.[8]

Doubts About the Theory

One major worry of critics of the theory was that demand-side effects would swamp any supply-side effects for at least the first several years. Whatever the long-term effects on the supply side, economic theory is clear about the short-term effects of these measures on the demand side. Cuts in personal tax rates that are intended to be permanent leave households with an increase in their current and expected future disposable income. As a result they spend more, causing a rightward shift in the aggregate demand curve. Also we know that an increase in investment increases aggregate demand. In the short run the extra expenditure on capital goods creates new incomes for the factors of production that produce these goods and, through the multiplier process, new incomes for others as well.

Thus the short-run effect of supply-side measures would surely be to shift the aggregate *demand* curve to the right. In the least favorable situation, if all the demand-increasing effects were to occur and none of the favorable aggregate supply effects, the result would surely be an increase in the inflationary gap. This possibility is illustrated in Figure 30-7.

Neither of the extreme cases illustrated in Figures 30-6 or 30-7 is likely to occur. Supply-side measures will lead to shifts to the right of both the *LRAS* and *AD* curves, and the effects of the policies will depend on the magnitude and timing of the two shifts. For example, if the effects on demand occur first but are followed by large increases in long-run aggregate supply, the initial effect would be to increase inflation, but the long-run effect would be for prices to come back down and for output to rise.

FIGURE 30-7 Demand Effects of Supply-Side Measures

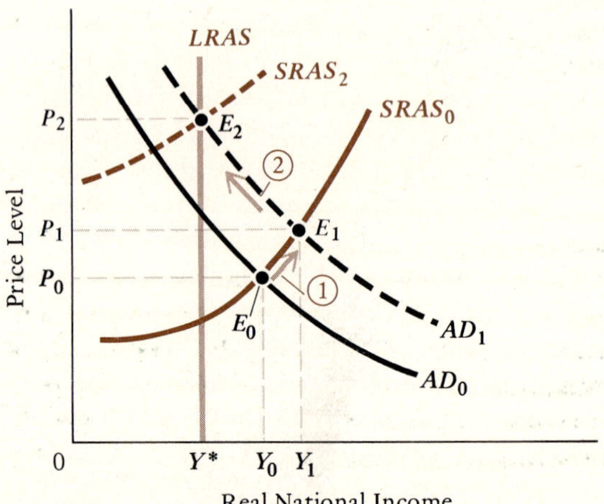

The effect of supply-side measures on aggregate demand is inflationary. The figure shows the economy in the same short-run initial equilibrium at E_0 as in Figure 30-6(i). However, it assumes that demand-side effects of the policy measures occur and are fully felt before any supply-side effects come into play. The *AD* curve shifts to the right to AD_1, and the economy moves toward equilibrium at E_1, as shown by arrow 1. This gives a temporary increase in output to Y_1 at the cost of an immediate rise in the price level to P_1. But the inflationary gap is also increased, to Y^*Y_1. Now the *SRAS* curve starts to shift upward, taking the equilibrium along AD_1 in the direction shown by arrow 2, with falling output and rising prices. If nothing else happens, the inflation will finally come to an end at price level P_2 and output Y^*. As a result of the supply-side measures, the rise in the price level, from P_0 to P_2, is *greater* than it would have been without the measures, that is, from P_0 to P_1.

Supply-siders with training in economics surely knew that the short-term effects via aggregate demand would occur. But they believed that the supply-side shifts of long-run aggregate supply would be large enough, and quick enough, to dominate them. Critics not only doubted this view as to timing, but they also questioned whether the tax changes proposed would have the desired effects even in the long run. Economic theory makes no definite prediction about the effects of tax cuts on how much people will work. It might make them work more, because they earn more for each additional hour that they work. But it might make them work less, because the tax cut means that they can, if they wish, have both more disposable income and more leisure. For example, if in response to a 10 percent tax cut they worked 5 percent less, they would have ap-

[8] Students who have read Chapter 24 and encountered the Laffer curve (see page 498) will be familiar with this argument.

proximately 5 percent more disposable income and 5 percent more leisure. (This is discussed in greater detail in Box 18-2 on page 350.)

Evaluating the Theory

It is difficult to resolve all the factual matters at issue in the supply-side debate on the basis of the Reagan administration's experiences. First, the proposed measures were never fully implemented. Second, the inflationary conditions postulated in the theory were changed by other policies, especially monetary policies, which will be examined in Chapter 34. It is clear, however, that aggregate *demand* effects did dominate in the short run.

Beyond this, most economists would agree on at least two aspects of the experience. First, policymakers and economists are much more alert to the supply-side effects of economic policies than many of them used to be. This is an important achievement.

Second, the timing of effects is such that measures that do succeed in shifting both aggregate demand and long-run aggregate supply will likely have their initial effects through a rapid shift in the *AD* curve. Their effects through a shift in the *LRAS* curve will occur only gradually. Thus the view of a number of Reagan supporters that supply-side measures would provide a *quick* fix to inflationary pressures is, simply, discredited. Such measures may, however, have contributed to the sustained recovery of 1983–1987.

Summary

1. Potential income is treated as given and thus can be represented by a vertical line at Y^*. The output gap is equal to the horizontal distance between Y^* and the actual level of income as determined by the intersection of the *AD* and *SRAS* curves.
2. A negative output gap means that demand in the labor market is relatively high. As a result, wages rise, the *SRAS* curve shifts leftward, and the price level rises. Thus any excess of actual national income over potential national income is called an inflationary gap.
3. A positive output gap means that demand in the labor market is relatively low. While there is some resulting tendency for wages to fall, asymmetrical behavior means that the strength of this force will be much weaker than that indicated in summary point 2. There will be very little deflation while the output gap will persist; thus any shortfall of actual national income relative to potential is called a recessionary gap.
4. An expansionary demand shock will create an inflationary gap that will induce factor price increases. These will shift the *SRAS* curve to the left, resulting in a higher level of prices, with output eventually decreasing to its potential level.
5. A contractionary demand shock will work in the opposite direction. If, however, factor prices are sticky, the automatic adjustment process may be slow, and a recessionary gap may not be quickly eliminated.
6. The long-run aggregate supply (*LRAS*) curve relates the price level and national income after all wages and other costs have been fully adjusted to long-run equilibrium. The *LRAS* curve is vertical at the level of potential income, Y^*.
7. Because the *LRAS* curve is vertical, output in the long run is determined by the position of the *LRAS* curve, and the only long-run role of the *AD* curve is to determine the price level.
8. Supply-side economics in an inflationary situation seeks to reduce an

inflationary gap and increase output by tax cuts and other incentive measures designed to shift the *LRAS* curve to the right and thus increase potential output. Whether or not this will work in the long run is a matter of current debate. In the short run such measures increase aggregate demand, thus adding to inflationary pressures.

Topics for Review

The output gap and the labor market
Asymmetry of wage adjustment
Inflationary gap
Recessionary gap
Aggregate demand shocks and induced wage changes
Long-run aggregate supply (*LRAS*) curve
Supply-side economics

Discussion Questions

1. Discuss the following in terms of the *AD*, *SRAS*, and *LRAS* curves:
   "The best way to combat inflation is to promote economic growth."
2. "Starting from a full-employment equilibrium, an increase in government spending can produce more output and employment at the cost of a once-and-for-all rise in the price level."
   "Increased spending can never lead to a permanent increase in output above its full employment level."
   Discuss these two statements in terms of short- and long-run aggregate supply curves.
3. Identify the effects of each of the following events on the *SRAS* and *LRAS* curves.
   a. Increase in the price of imported raw materials used in key manufacturing industries
   b. Increase in the price of imported consumption goods such as coffee or bananas
   c. An attempt to combat acid rain by tightening restrictions on pollution emissions
   d. Projections of increased federal government deficits over the next five years
   e. An improved economic outlook leading to an investment boom
   f. Increased labor force participation rate of key sectors of the population
4. Discuss the following 1986 quotation:
   "Wages are surely sticky since unemployment during the recovery has remained above 9 percent, but wages have continued to grow at more than 4 percent."
5. Show the effects on the price level and output of income tax cuts that induce people to work more in an economy currently experiencing an inflationary gap.
6. Discuss the reasoning behind the statement of the government critic who argued that:
   "There is no sense in the government trying to stimulate demand since all that will do is cause inflation; it won't help reduce unemployment."

31

Business Cycles: The Ebb and Flow of Economic Activity

Changing, always changing; this is the dominant characteristic of the GDP for as far back as we have records. Long-term growth (which is studied in Chapter 38) appears in the upward trend in potential GDP. Short-term fluctuations are seen in oscillations of actual GDP around potential GDP. Such oscillations are caused by changes in aggregate demand and aggregate supply. They lead to changes in total real output and hence in the amount of employment and unemployment. They also affect living standards since the total amount of goods and services available varies as total output varies.

Cyclical Fluctuations

As we saw in Chapter 26, most economic series exhibit two types of change. The first is the long-term trend. In the case of GDP, there is an upward trend throughout the twentieth century associated with economic growth. In the case of unemployment, the series for the twentieth century is trend-free, exhibiting no long-term tendency for the unemployment rate to rise or fall.

The second type of change is fluctuation around the long-term trend. These fluctuations are far from random; they exhibit a systematic pattern. A year of relatively high output is likely to occur in conjunction with other years of high output, and such groups are likely to be separated by groups of years of relatively low output. This pattern of a sequence of highs followed by a sequence of lows followed again by another sequence of highs is the source of the term *cyclical* used to describe such economic fluctuations.

The Concept of the Business Cycle

The **business cycle** refers to the continual ebb and flow of business activity that occurs around any long-term trend after seasonal adjustments have been made.[1] Such cyclical fluctuations can be seen in many economic series. For example, continual oscillations in GDP are apparent in Figure 26-3 on page 560.

[1] When economists wish to analyze monthly or quarterly data, they often try to remove fluctuations that can be accounted for by a regular seasonal pattern. This *seasonal adjustment* is made because many economic series show a marked seasonal pattern over the year. For example, logging activity tends to be low in the winter months and high in the summer, while fuel oil sales tend to have the reverse seasonal pattern.

FIGURE 31-1 Three Indicators of Economic Activity in Canada, 1950–1986

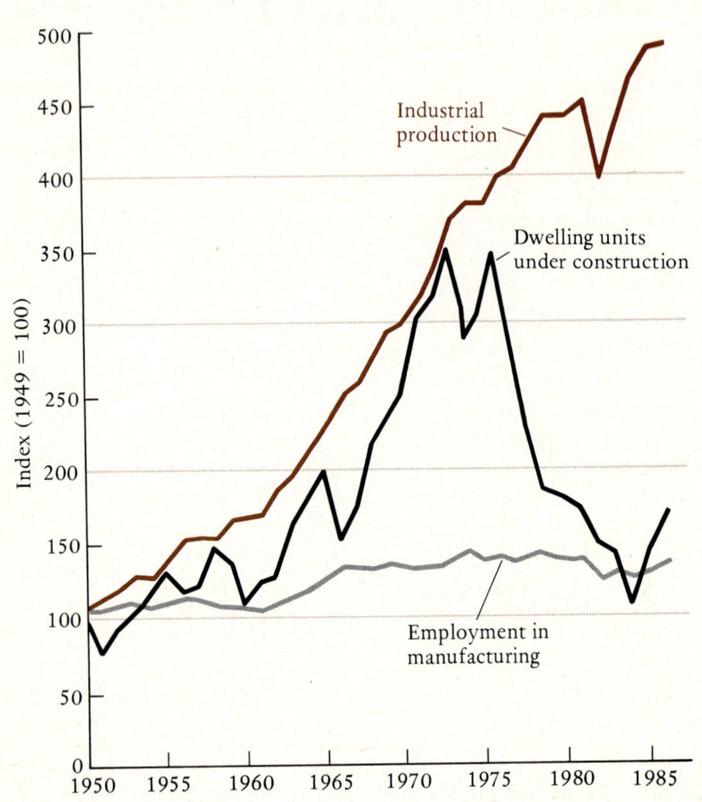

Short-term variability and a long-term upward trend characterize many indexes of Canadian economic activity. All three series are index numbers with 1949 = 100, so all pass through 100 at 1949. All series exhibit differing degrees of short-term variability and differing trend rates of growth. Dwelling starts under construction vary greatly from year to year. Employment in manufacturing does not fluctuate greatly because even a large change in unemployment, say from 4 percent to 8 percent of the labor force, makes a relatively small percentage change in employment. The serious recession of 1981–82 and the sustained recovery of 1983–86 are apparent in all three series. (*Source:* Statistics Canada, 11-003E.)

But the concept of the business cycle refers to fluctuations in the general pace of economic activity. This cannot be fully caught by a single statistic, even one as important as GDP. Figure 31-1 shows three other economic series. Each of these, as well as a dozen others that might be studied, tells us something about the general variability of the economy. It is clear that some series vary more than others and that they do not all move exactly together.

The picture suggested by Figures 26-3 and 31-1 is not one of occasional sharp shifts in the aggregate demand and supply curves. If it were, we would expect national income to show occasional sharp changes followed by long periods of little or no change. Instead the short-term situation is one of continual change at varying rates.

Evidently there are factors at work causing economic activity to display continual short-term fluctuations around the economy's long-term growth trend.

While all cycles are not alike in duration or intensity, each appears to have tendencies toward cumulative movements that eventually reverse themselves. This was true long before governments attempted to intervene to stabilize their economies, and it is true still.

The late Alvin Hansen, a distinguished American authority on business cycles, once reported that there were 17 cycles in the U.S. economy between 1795 and 1937, with an average duration of 8.35 years. A shorter "inventory cycle" of 40 months' duration was also found, as well as longer cycles associated with building booms (15 to 20 years). The Russian economist Kondratieff thought he could identify long waves of 40 to 50 years associated with the introduction of major innovations. Some economists have argued that in many Western democracies there exists a political business cycle associated with the pattern of elections.

Though the evidence is diverse, it is nevertheless possible to identify some basic characteristics of the pattern of business cycles:

1. **A common pattern of variation more or less pervades all economic series.**
2. **Economic series differ in their particular patterns of fluctuations.**
3. **Cycles differ substantially in the length and the size of the swings involved.**

The Terminology of Business Fluctuations

Although recurrent fluctuations in economic activity are neither smooth nor regular, a vocabulary has developed to denote their different stages. Figure 31-2 shows stylized cycles that illustrate some terms.

Trough. A trough is, simply, the bottom. A trough is characterized by high unemployment of labor and a level of consumer demand that is low in relation to the capacity of industry to produce goods for consumption. There is thus a substantial amount of unused industrial capacity. Business profits are low; for some individual companies they are negative. Confidence in the future is lacking, and firms are consequently unwilling to risk making new investments. If a trough is deep enough, it may be called a *slump* or a **depression.**

Recovery. When something sets off a recovery, the lower turning point of the cycle has been reached. The symptoms of a recovery (or expansion) are many: Worn-out machinery is replaced; employment, income, and consumer spending all begin to rise; expectations become more favorable as a result of increases in production, sales, and profits. Investments that once seemed risky may now be undertaken as the climate of business opinion starts to change from pessimism to optimism. As demand expands, production can be expanded with relative ease merely by re-employing the existing unused capacity and unemployed labor.

Peak. A peak is the top of the cycle. At the peak there is a high degree of utilization of existing capacity; labor shortages may be severe, particularly in key skill categories; and shortages of essential key

FIGURE 31-2 A Stylized Business Cycle

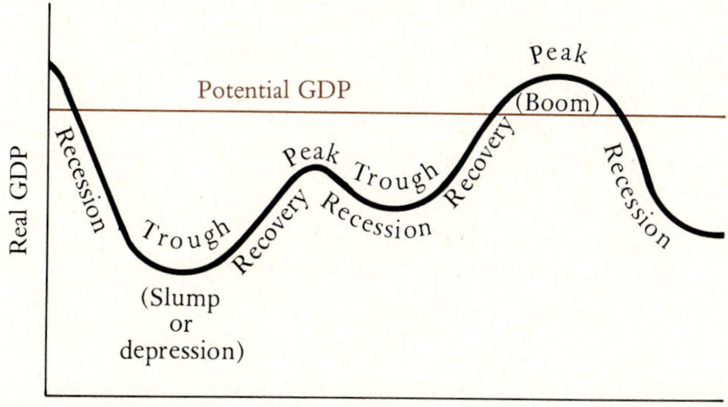

Although the phases of business fluctuations are described by a series of commonly used terms, no two cycles are the same. Starting from a lower turning point, a cycle goes through a phase of recovery, or expansion, reaches an upper turning point, and then enters a period of recession. Cycles differ from one another in the severity of their troughs and peaks and in the speed with which one phase follows another. Severe troughs are called *depressions*; extreme peaks are called *booms*.

raw materials may develop. Output can be raised further only by investment that increases capacity. Because such investment takes time, further rises in demand are now met more by increases in prices than by increases in production. As shortages develop in more and more markets, a situation of general excess demand for factors develops. Costs rise, but prices rise also, and business remains generally very profitable. A peak that exceeds the level of potential output may be referred to as a **boom.**

Recession. A **recession,** which often follows a peak, is a sustained fall in the level of economic activity. Demand falls off, and as a result production and employment fall. As employment falls, so do households' incomes; falling income causes demand to fall further. Profits drop and more and more firms get into difficulties. Investments that looked profitable on the expectation of continual rising demand suddenly appear unprofitable, and investment is reduced to a low level. It may not even be worth replacing capital goods as they wear out because unused capacity is increasing steadily.

Turning points. The point at which a recession begins is often called the **upper turning point.** The point at which a recovery begins is referred to as the **lower turning point**.

Explaining Business Cycles

An explanation of the business cycle must answer two questions: (1) What are the factors that cause GDP and other key macro variables to fluctuate? (2) What are the factors that cause those fluctuations to form a cyclical pattern? These two questions are taken up in the two main sections that follow.

FIGURE 31-3 A Demand-driven Business Cycle

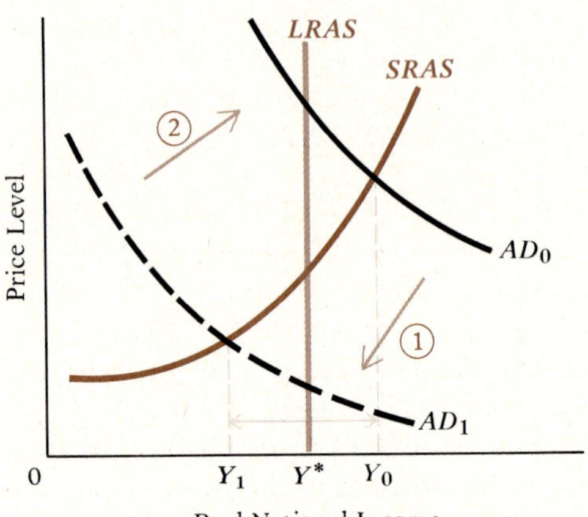

Fluctuations in aggregate demand can cause fluctuations in income and employment. Assume that over the course of the business cycle aggregate demand oscillates regularly. The economy starts with a high level of aggregate demand, AD_0, and income at its peak, Y_0. The AD curve then falls continuously, as shown by arrow 1, until it reaches AD_1. Income falls through Y^* and reaches its trough at Y_1.

The AD curve then rises continuously, as shown by arrow 2. Income is taken back through Y^* and reaches Y_0 at the next peak.

Why Do Income and Employment Fluctuate?

Figure 31-3 presents an explanation of the fluctuations of GDP in terms of a fluctuating AD curve and a stable $SRAS$ curve.

There is general agreement that over the course of Canadian economic history, the business cycle has been driven mainly by fluctuations in aggregate demand. Nevertheless, particular cycles can sometimes be explained in part by aggregate supply shocks. Indeed, events of the mid 1970s made the citizens of advanced industrial countries acutely aware of supply-side causes.

Aggregate demand shocks are a major historical source of fluctuations in GDP; aggregate supply shocks are another source.

Sources of Aggregate Demand Shocks

To say that cycles are caused mainly by fluctuations in aggregate demand only pushes the need for explanation one stage back. What are the sources of the continual disturbances to aggregate demand? The theory of income determination suggests four main candidates: shifts in each of the four main components of aggregate expenditure. Some key facts are illustrated in Figure 31-4.

Changes in Consumption

Consumption is the largest single component of aggregate expenditure, about two-thirds of the total. When searching for the causes of income changes, we are not concerned with changes in consumption *in response* to changes in income but instead with *shifts* in the function relating consumption to income. Such shifts can have many causes.

Changes in tastes. In the mid 1980s there was a significant increase in the demand for North American cars. If enough of the money that was spent on automobiles would have been saved instead, there would be a significant rightward shift in the aggregate demand curve. Jobs and incomes would first be gained in the auto industry. The induced increase in spending by workers in that industry would then set up a multiplier effect as increases in output, income, and spending spread throughout the economy.

Changes in expectations and interest rates. Expectations of future inflation may lead to a burst of spending to buy now while goods are cheap. By contrast, a wave of uncertainty about the future may lead to a rise in saving and hence a cut in spending. High interest rates can be a powerful incentive to postpone buying durable goods. For example, in 1981 rates of over 20 percent helped to depress the markets for automobiles and other consumer durables, and subsequent declines in interest rates led to a boom in those markets.

In an inflationary world it is important to distinguish between the real and the nominal rate of interest. The *nominal* rate of interest is the ratio of the *amount of money* repaid to the amount of money borrowed. The *real* rate of interest is the ratio of the *purchasing power of the money* repaid to the purchasing power of the money borrowed. The real rate of interest is the difference between the nominal rate of interest and the rate of inflation. It is this real interest rate that matters for most expenditure decisions. This distinction is further elaborated in Box 31-1 (page 649).

Changes in taxes. As we saw in Chapter 28, tax changes can also shift the aggregate consumption function. Income tax cuts mean that more *total* income becomes *disposable* income, leading to an increase in consumer spending. Tax increases have the opposite effect.

Changes in transfer payments. Government transfer payments amount to roughly one-eighth of personal income. Sharp changes in transfer payments could influence aggregate expenditure through their effects on personal consumption and investment.

Changes in Government Expenditures

As Figure 31-4 shows, World War II brought a rapid expansion of economic activity. Government spending was a major contributing factor. Wars generally result in an enormous increase in federal governmental expenditures as men and materials are shifted from civilian to military purposes, a shift that is then reversed in the postwar period. For example, federal government purchases of goods and services rose from \$683 million in 1939 to \$4,978 million in 1944 and fell back to \$1,541 million by 1947. Changes in government purchases of goods and services from 1940 to 1946 were the dominant influence on GDP, and they had a substantial effect during the Korean War at the beginning of the 1950s.

Aside from periods of major wars, government expenditures have not often been destabilizing. For peacetime periods before 1940, government expenditures were both small and relatively stable. Since 1955 they have been large and stable and growing rather steadily. Thus whatever their potential for being a major source of cyclical instability, they have not proven to be such except during wars.

As Figure 31-4 shows, the shocks caused by changing government expenditure have been much smaller on average than the shocks caused by either changing net exports or changing private investment expenditure.

FIGURE 31-4 Changes in GDP and Selected Components, 1927–1986

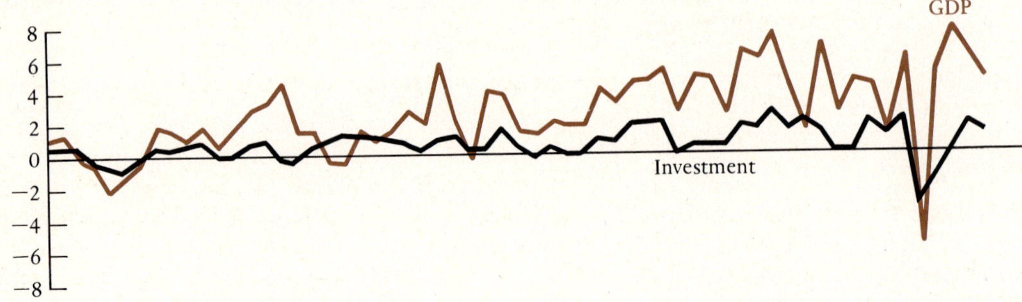

(i) Changes in GDP and investment

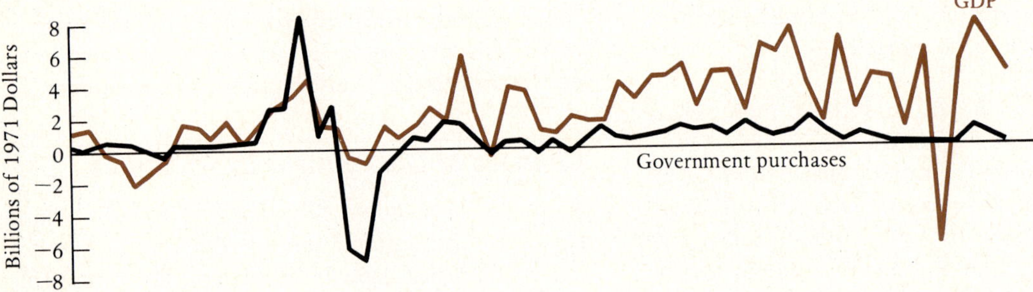

(ii) Changes in GDP and government purchases

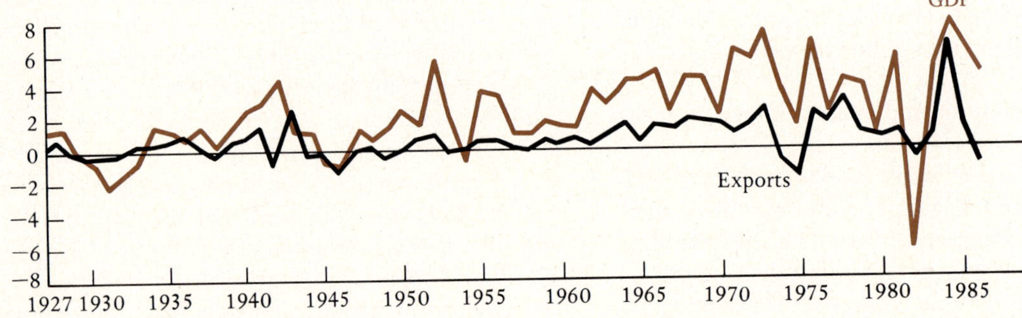

(iii) Changes in GDP and exports

Changes in GNP have been closely related to changes in investment expenditure. The year-to-year fluctuations in GNP correlate closely to changes in investment except during World War II and its aftermath, when changes in government expenditures were the dominant influence. Changes in merchandise exports have reinforced the destabilizing influence of the other two expenditure categories. (*Source*: Statistics Canada, 13–531, 13–201, 11–003 E.)

BOX 31-1

Real and Nominal Interest Rates: An Important Distinction

If you pay me $8 interest for a $100 loan for one year, the nominal rate is 8 percent. The real rate that I earn, however, depends on what happens to the overall level of prices in the economy.

If the price level remains constant over the year, the real rate that I earn would also be 8 percent, because I can buy 8 percent more goods and services with the $108 that you repay me than with $100 that I lent you. However, if the price level rises by 8 percent, the real rate would be *zero*, because the $108 you repay me buys the same quantity of goods as the $100 that I gave up. If I am unlucky enough to lend money at 8 percent in a year in which prices rise by 10 percent, the real rate I earn would be −2 percent.

If lenders and borrowers are concerned with real costs measured in terms of purchasing power, the nominal rate of interest will be set at the rate they want as return on their money plus an amount to cover any expected rate of inflation. Consider a one-year loan that is meant to earn a real return to the lender of 5 percent. If the expected rate of inflation is zero, the nominal rate set for the loan will be 5 percent. If a 10 percent inflation is expected, the nominal interest rate will be 15 percent.

To provide a given expected real rate of interest, the nominal rate will be set at the desired real rate of interest plus the expected annual rate of inflation.

Because they overlook this point, people are often surprised at the high nominal rates of interest that exist during periods of rapid inflation. For example, when the nominal interest rates rose drastically in 1979, many commentators expressed shock at the "unbearably" high rates. Most of them failed to notice that with inflation running at about 12 percent, an interest rate of 15 percent represented a real rate of only 3 percent. Had the government given in to the pressure to hold interest rates to the more "reasonable" level of 10 percent, it would have been imposing a negative real rate of interest. Lenders would then have been "rewarded" for lending their money by receiving less purchasing power in interest plus principal than the purchasing power of the principal they parted with initially.

Concern about the burden of borrowing should be directed at the real, not the nominal, rate of interest.

For example, a nominal rate of 8 percent combined with a 2 percent rate of inflation is a much greater real burden on borrowers than a nominal rate of 16 percent combined with a 14 percent rate of inflation.

Cash Flow Problems

Some of the effects of inflation can be compensated for by changes in the nominal interest rate, but not all. The inflation premium on interest rates represents an early repayment of capital and hence causes cash flow problems for borrowers. Consider a simple example. A firm borrows $1,000 for 10 years at 4 percent when the price level is constant. The firm will pay $40 of interest per year, and at the end of 10 years it must repay in one lump sum the capital of $1,000.

Now assume that the same bargain is struck except that a 5 percent rate of inflation will occur *and is fully expected* over the period of the loan. In this case the nominal rate of interest is set at 9 percent, and annual interest payments will be $90.

In one sense the real situation is unchanged, but in another important sense it is different. The firm is now paying an annual inflation premium of $50. This compensates the lenders for the loss of purchasing power on the principal of their loans. But for the borrowers it constitutes an early repayment of capital. Note that the $1,000 repaid at the end of the 10-year period has a much smaller real value in the second (inflationary) situation.

So the stream of real payments is very different when a 4 percent interest rate is combined with a zero inflation rate and when a 9 percent interest rate is combined with a 5 percent inflation rate.

BOX 31-2

Fluctuations in National Income and the Balance of Trade

Exports are an important source of demand for domestically produced goods. A key determinant of a country's exports is the level of activity in its major trading partners. When the United States experiences a boom, as it did in the period 1983–1986, there is a large American demand for Canadian exports. In turn, via the multiplier process, the increase in exports will cause an expansion in Canadian national income. Similarly, when the United States experiences a recession, as it did in 1981–1982, American demand for Canadian goods will be low. Again the change in exports causes a multiplier effect, this time leading to a reduction in Canadian national income.

As a result of this *export multiplier*, the business cycles of major trading partners tend to be closely correlated.

Imports and the Size of the Multiplier

As we saw in Chapter 28, expenditure on imports will grow as domestic national income grows. Since imports represent spending on other countries' outputs, they raise the economy's marginal propensity not to spend, and hence, as we saw in Chapter 28, they reduce the size of the multiplier. [39] Of course this has both desirable and undesirable consequences. It is undesirable because it reduces the effectiveness of domestic policies that attempt to change the level of domestic income. It is desirable because it reduces the impact on national income of fluctuations in such autonomous expenditure items as investment and exports.*

Net Exports and Domestic Absorption

The model of national income determination outlined in Chapter 28 provides an important perspective on the determination of net exports. Recall the basic condition for equilibrium national income:

$$Y = C + I + G + (X - M)$$

The sum of $C + I + G$ corresponds to total expenditure on all goods and services (domestic and foreign) for use *within* the economy; this total is often referred to as **domestic absorption (A).** The equilibrium relationship can therefore be rewritten as

$$Y = A + (X - M)$$

The right-hand side of this equation is desired aggregate expenditure on Canadian goods and services, represented as the sum of expenditure for *internal* use (domestic absorption) plus expenditure due to net *external* demand (net exports). Subtracting A from both sides, we get

$$Y - A = X - M$$

* The consequence of the latter effect is that imports act as a *built-in stabilizer.* We encounter built-in stabilizers again in Chapter 32 in our analysis of fiscal policy.

Changes in Net Exports

A country such as Canada, in which foreign trade plays a large role, is subject to destabilizing influences from foreign demand. Since about one-half of all goods produced in Canada are exported, fluctuations in the national income of other countries can be transmitted to our economy through fluctuations in their demand for our exports. As Figure 31-4 shows, changes in merchandise exports played an important role during the Great Depression. The fall in export demand triggered by the depression in the economies of our major trading partners led to a fall in our exports, thereby reinforcing the early stages of the recession in Canada. Similarly, during World War II exports boomed at the same time that the domestic economy was expanding.

Similar influences of exports on the domestic economy can be seen throughout the period. One notable episode was the boom in the economy during the early 1970s followed by the decline in the mid 1970s. Exports rose sharply from 1971 to 1973 and

This makes it clear that net exports can be positive only if national income exceeds domestic absorption—that is, only if total demand for goods and services to be used in Canada is less than total output of goods and services in Canada. And if net exports are positive, it must be the case that national income exceeds the absorption of goods and services within Canada.†

Absorption Versus Component Approaches to the Trade Balance

Organizing the theory of income determination in this way has led economists to view the trade balance as an aggregate phenomenon: It must equal the difference between the two aggregates, *national income* and *domestic absorption*.

The trade balance, by definition, is also equal to the sum of all exports minus the sum of all imports. This makes it tempting to try to explain changes or trends in the trade account by "counting" the changes in particular exports and imports. Since both this "component" definition and the absorption definition are correct as *definitions* of the trade balance, either is valid as a framework that can be used to organize information in order to *analyze* the trade account.

† Note that foreigners can influence the demand for Canadian goods and services in two ways: by demanding exports and by investing in Canada.

The danger with the component approach is that the analyst may ignore the interaction between the items included in the trade balance and other variables such as national income. The absorption approach tends to draw attention to such interactions.

In order to compare the approaches, consider the effect on the trade balance of an exogenous increase in the foreign demand for one particular Canadian export. An increase in a particular export, *other things being equal*, will lead to an increase in national income. This increase in national income will lead in turn to increased expenditure on some imports. If one takes the component approach to analyzing the trade account, one may miss this induced effect. For example, if exports of wheat rose by $20 million in a given year, one might conclude that the trade balance would improve by $20 million. But the increased wheat exports would be reflected in higher incomes for farmers and the producers of transportation services who ship the wheat. These groups will spend some of their increased incomes on imports and some on domestic goods. The latter will lead to a multiplier effect on national income and result in further increases in spending on imports.

Clearly the net effect on the trade balance of the increased wheat exports must include the induced increases in imports. By relating the trade balance to the difference between total income and total spending in the domestic economy, this is exactly what the absorption approach does. [40]

then fell sharply in the years 1973 to 1975. More recently, the strength of the U.S. recovery over the 1982–1987 period stimulated Canadian exports and contributed to the recovery of the Canadian economy.

Factors other than foreign incomes also affect Canadian exports. One of the most important is the ability of Canadian firms to compete in international markets, as influenced in the short run by changes in the exchange rate and more directly by changes in domestic costs relative to foreign costs. Labor costs as reflected in wages are important, as are the costs of material inputs and energy.

In an open economy, fluctuations in exports exert an important influence on cyclical fluctuations.

Some further aspects of the relationship of net exports to cyclical movements in income are discussed in Box 31-2.

Changes in Investment

An important source of disturbance is investment expenditure. Consider the period 1929–1932. In 1929 total investment expenditure of firms and households in the Canadian economy was $1.2 billion, almost double the amount of expenditure needed to replace the capital goods that we used up that year in the process of producing a GDP of $6.1 billion. The Canadian economy in 1929, then, was adding rapidly to its stock of capital equipment. Four years later, in 1933, total investment expenditure was $145 million. This was less than one-third of the amount needed merely to keep the stock of capital intact. The Canadian economy in 1933, with its GDP reduced to $3.5 billion, was rapidly reducing its stock of capital equipment.

As Figure 31-4 shows, investment expenditure is quite volatile. Quite large shocks due to changes in investment expenditure hit the economy frequently. On average the change in investment from one year to the next has been about three times the average change in government expenditure.

Changes in investment are also quite closely correlated with changes in national income, as also shown in Figure 31-4. Rising investment tends to be associated with rapidly rising GDP, while falling investment tends to be associated with slowly rising or falling GDP. This is consistent with the view that investment shocks are a major cause of changes in national income.

Investment expenditures play a key role in most theories of cyclical fluctuations.

Why Does Investment Change?

The three major components of total investment expenditure are inventories, business fixed investment, and residential housing. Changes in investment are one of the prime causes of short-term fluctuations, but we do not have the whole story unless we know why investment fluctuates. In discussing the theory of income determination in Chapters 28 and 29 we talked simply of shifts in investment, not of the underlying causes of such shifts.

The Interest Rate and Investment

Empirical evidence shows that investment responds to many influencing factors. One of the most important is the rate of interest. Other things being equal, the higher the interest rate, the higher the cost of borrowing money for investment purposes and the less the amount of investment expenditure. Although in basic theory we talk of "the" interest rate, reality is not so simple; a few of these complications are discussed in Box 31-3 (see pages 654–655).

While each dollar of investment has the same consequences for aggregate demand, different types of investment respond to different sets of causes. Thus it is useful to discuss separately the determinants of the three major types of investment expenditures, both to see why the interest rate is such an important influence on investment and to determine what other factors are important.

Inventories. Inventory changes represent only a small fraction of private investment in a typical year, but their average size is not an adequate measure of their importance. They are one of the more volatile elements of total investment and therefore have a major influence on shifts in investment expenditure.

Studies show that the stock of inventories held tends to rise as production and sales rise. Because the size of inventories is related to the level of sales, the *change* in inventories (which is current investment) is related to the *change* in the level of sales.

A firm may decide, for example, to hold inventories of 10 percent of its sales. If sales are $100,000, it will wish to hold inventories of $10,000. If sales increase to $110,000, it will want to hold inventories of $11,000. Over the period during which its stock of inventories is being increased, there will be a total of $1,000 new inventory investment.

The higher the level of production and sales, the larger the desired stock of inventories. Changes in the rate of production and sales cause temporary bouts of investment (or disinvestment) in inventories.

When a firm ties up funds in inventories, those same funds cannot be used elsewhere to earn income. At the very least the money could be lent out at the going rate of interest. Thus the higher the real rate of interest, the higher will be the cost of holding an inventory of a given size. And the higher that rate of interest, the more firms will try to lower their inventories. By causing firms to change the inventory levels that they desire to hold, a change in the rate of interest can lead to a flurry of investment or disinvestment in inventories.

The higher the real rate of interest, the lower the desired stock of inventories. Changes in the rate of interest cause temporary bouts of investment (or disinvestment) in inventories.

Residential housing construction. Since 1970 spending on residential construction has varied between one-fifth and one-third of all gross private investment and between 3.5 percent and 6.5 percent of GDP. Because expenditures for housing construction are both large and variable, they have a major impact on the economy.

Many influences on residential construction are noneconomic and depend on demographic or cultural considerations such as new family formation. But households must not only want to buy houses; they must also be able to do so. Periods of high employment and high average family earnings tend to lead to increases in house building and those of unemployment and falling earnings to decreases in such building.

Almost all houses are purchased with money borrowed on mortgages. Interest on the borrowed money typically accounts for over one-half of the purchaser's annual mortgage payments; the remainder is repayment of principal. It is for this reason that sharp variations in interest rates exert a substantial effect on the demand for housing.

Box 31-4 (see page 656) provides an illustration of the importance of interest rates for housing expenditures. This importance was borne out by experiences from 1979 to 1982. During this period mortgage rates rose from less than 11 percent to just over 15 percent and housing starts fell from 197,000 units to a mere 126,000 in 1982. (Since inflation fell from 1980, the increased nominal interest rates also meant increased real rates.) The construction industry itself and its major suppliers, such as the cement and the lumber industries, felt the blow of a dramatic fall in demand. Conversely, in the mid 1980s interest rates fell sharply and there was a boom in the demand for new housing.

Expenditures for residential construction tend to vary positively with changes in average income and negatively with interest rates.

Business fixed investment. Investment in plant and equipment is the largest component of domestic investment. Much of it is financed by firms' retained profits (profits *not* paid out to its shareholders). This means that current profits are an important determinant of investment.

A second major determinant is the rate of interest. Much investment is financed by borrowed money. As became abundantly clear in the early 1980s, very high interest rates greatly reduce the volume of investment as more and more firms find their expected profits from investment do not cover the interest on borrowed investment funds.

A third major determinant is changes in national income. If there is a rise in aggregate demand that is expected to persist and cannot be met by existing capacity, investment in new plant and equipment will be needed. Once the new plants have been built and put into operation, however, the rate of new investment will fall.

This further illustrates an important characteristic of investment already encountered in the case of inventories: *If the desired stock of capital goods increases, there will be an investment boom while the new capital is being produced.* But if nothing else changes, even though business conditions continue to look rosy enough to justify the increased stock of capital, investment in new plant and equipment will cease once the larger capital stock is achieved. This aspect of investment leads to the *accelerator* theory of investment, which requires a closer look.

The Accelerator Theory of Investment

According to the accelerator theory, usually called the **accelerator,** investment is related to the rate of change of national income. When income is increasing, investment is needed to increase the capacity to

BOX 31-3

Many Rates of Interest

In the real world there are many different rates of interest. Speaking in terms of a single interest rate can be a valid simplification for many purposes because the whole set of rates *tends* to move upward or downward together. For some purposes, however, it is important to take into account the different rates that prevail at any one time.

At the same time that you receive an interest rate of 6 or 7 percent on deposits at a trust company you may have to pay 11 or 12 percent to borrow from that same trust company to finance your purchase of a house. Interest rates on consumer installment credit of 16 percent and 20 percent are common. A small firm pays a higher rate on funds it borrows from banks than does a giant corporation. Different government bonds pay different rates of interest, depending on the length of the period for which the bond runs. Corporation bonds tend to pay higher interest than treasury bills, and there is much variation among bonds of different companies.

Considering the extreme mobility of money, why do such differences exist? Why do funds not flow between different uses to eliminate these differences? The answer is that money *does* flow quite rapidly between alternative assets in response to interest differentials, but differences nevertheless prevail because quoted interest rates reflect many factors.

Differences in risk. Corporation bonds generally have higher interest rates than government bonds because they have a greater degree of risk. For example, in mid 1986 many corporate issues were yielding more than 10 percent, while federal government bonds were paying less than 9 percent. Why? Investors were sure of the ability of the government to pay both the interest and the principal on their bonds, but they were less sure about the financial condition of private corporations.

Secured loans, where the borrower pledges an asset as collateral, tend to have lower interest rates than unsecured loans, other things being equal. Loans secured by houses (mortgages) tend to have lower interest rates than loans secured by automobiles, in part because it is harder to run away with a house than with a car and in part because a car can depreciate much more rapidly and unpredictably than a house.

Differences in duration. The *term*, or duration, of a loan also affects its price. The same bank will usually pay a higher rate of interest on a certificate of deposit

---

produce consumption goods; when income is falling, it may not even be necessary to replace old capital as it wears out, let alone to invest in new capital.

The main insight the accelerator theory provides is the emphasis on net investment as *disequilibrium* behavior—the situation in which the actual stock of capital goods differs from what firms and households would like it to be. Anything that changes the desired size of the capital stock can generate investment. The accelerator focuses on one such source of change, changing national income. This gives the accelerator its particular importance in connection with *fluctuations* in national income. As we shall see, it can itself contribute to those fluctuations.

How the accelerator works. To see how the theory works, suppose that there is a particular capital stock needed to produce each given level of an industry's output. The ratio of the value of capital to the annual value of output is called the **capital-output ratio.** Suppose that the industry is producing at capacity and the demand for its product increases. If the industry is to produce the higher level of output, its capital stock must increase. This necessitates new investment.

Table 31-1 (see page 657) provides a simple numerical example of the accelerator. Working through the data step by step leads to three conclusions:

1. **Rising rather than high levels of sales are needed to call forth net investment.**
2. **For net investment to remain constant, sales must rise by a constant amount per year.**
3. **The amount of net investment will be a mul-**

that cannot be redeemed at the bank (without penalty) for at least one year than on a straight savings account from which funds can be withdrawn in a matter of minutes. Yet many savers prefer savings accounts because they want to be able to withdraw their money on short notice. Except when interest rates are thought to be temporarily abnormally high, borrowers are usually willing to pay more for long-term loans than for short-term loans because they are certain of having use of the money for a longer period. Lenders usually require a higher rate of interest the longer is the time before the borrower must repay. Other things being equal, the shorter the term of a loan, the lower the interest rates.

Differences in costs of administering credit. There is great variation in the cost of different kinds of credit transactions. It is almost as cheap (in actual dollars) for a bank to lend an airline $1 billion that the airline agrees to pay back with interest after one year as it is for the same bank to lend you $14,000 to buy a new car that you agree to pay back over two years in 24 equal installments.

The installment loan to you requires many more bookkeeping entries than the loan to the airline. In addition, it is easier, and therefore less costly, to check the airline's credit rating than it is to check yours. The difference in the cost *per dollar* of each loan is considerable. The bank may very well make less profit per dollar on a $14,000 loan at 20 percent per year than on a $1 billion loan at 10 percent per year. In general, the bigger the loan and the fewer the payments, the less the cost per dollar of servicing the loan. Why, then, do banks and finance companies usually insist that you repay a loan in frequent installments? They worry that if you do not pay regularly, you will not have the money when the loan comes due.

In the market for borrowed funds there is a structure of various interest rates for credit transactions of different kinds.

Individual rates will be set that take into account such factors as risk premiums, duration of loan, and costs of administration. Nevertheless, it is useful and usual to talk about movements of interest rate structures up and down as changes in "the" interest rate. This simplification is appropriate when the entire structure of rates moves up or down together such that changes in a single rate can capture changes in all rates.

tiple of the increase in sales because the capital-output ratio is greater than one.[2]

The data in Table 31-1 are for a single industry, but if many industries behave in this way, one would expect aggregate net investment to bear a similar relation to changes in national income. This is what the accelerator theory predicts. **[41]**

The accelerator theory says nothing directly about replacement investment, but it does have implications for such investment. When sales are constant (no net investment required), replacement investment will be required to maintain the capital stock at the desired level. When sales are increasing from a position of full capacity, both net investment and replacement investment will be required. When sales are falling, not only will net investment be zero, but there will be a tendency to forgo replacement investment as well.

Limitations of the accelerator. Taken literally, the accelerator posits a rigid response of investment to changes in sales (and thus, aggregatively, to changes in national income). In fact, the relation is more subtle.

Changes in sales that are thought to be temporary will not necessarily lead to new investment. It is

[2] In the example in the table the capital-output ratio is 5:1. Why should anyone spend $5 on capital stock to get $1 of output? It is not unreasonable to spend $5 to purchase a machine that produces only $1 of output *per year,* provided that the machine will last enough years to repay the $5 plus a reasonable return on this investment.

BOX 31-4

The Cost of Buying a House on Time

Few people who buy a house can pay cash. Most purchases are financed by borrowing money on a *mortgage.* A mortgage is a loan to the house purchaser (sometimes of as much as 85 or 90 percent of the purchase price, but 60 to 75 percent is common). In return, the borrower promises to make fixed monthly payments that cover interest on the money borrowed and repay the amount borrowed (the principal) over some agreed period, commonly 20 or 30 years. (The monthly payments often include an amount to cover insurance and taxes, but this is ignored in what follows.) The house itself acts as security for the loan. Loans of this type are said to be *amortized,* which means that fixed payments over a stated period gradually repay the principal and cover the interest on the principal outstanding.

Because the loan stretches over a long period, a great deal of the total amount paid by the borrower is interest on the outstanding loan. For example, on a 20-year mortgage for $50,000 at a nominal annual interest rate of 8 percent per year (a monthly rate of 8/12 of 1 percent), a total of $100,375 would be paid in 240 monthly installments of $418.23 each. This is $50,000 to repay the principal of the loan and $50,375 in interest. At a 12 percent nominal annual rate (a monthly rate of 1 percent), the total payments would be $132,130, making $82,130 total interest on top of the $50,000 to repay the principal.

The interest on a mortgage is calculated on the amount of the loan still outstanding. After each payment the amount outstanding is reduced so that, with fixed annual payments, most of the total amount paid goes to paying interest in the early years and to repaying principal in later years. It follows that the purchaser's equity in the house (the down payment plus the total amount of the loan that has been repaid over the years) builds up slowly at first, then more and more rapidly as the terminal date approaches.

Note in the table that when half the life of the mortgage has passed, only about a quarter of the principal has been repaid. In the first year of the mortgage, $4,965 goes as interest and only $825 to reduce the principal on the loan. In the last year, only $300 is interest and $5,490 goes to repay the principal.

Breakdown of Payments in Selected Years on a 20-Year Mortgage for $50,000 at 10 Percent (*all figures to the nearest dollar*)

Year	Payments made over the year	Interest paid over the year	Principal repaid over the year	Equity (cumulative total over all the years)*
1	5,790	4,965	825	825
2	5,790	4,875	915	1,745
5	5,790	4,560	1,230	5,100
10	5,790	3,765	2,025	13,490
15	5,790	2,455	3,335	27,290
19	5,790	820	4,970	44,510
20	5,790	300	5,490	50,000

* In addition to equity due to down payment.

usually possible to increase the level of output for a given capital stock by working overtime or extra shifts. While this solution would be more expensive per unit of output in the long run, it is usually preferable to making investments in new plant and equipment that would lie idle after a temporary spurt of demand had subsided. Thus expectations about what the required capital stock will be may lead to

TABLE 31-1 An Illustration of the Accelerator Theory of Investment

(1) Year	(2) Annual sales	(3) Change in sales	(4) Required stock of capital[a]	(5) Net investment: increase in required capital stock
1	$10	$0	$ 50	$ 0
2	10	0	50	0
3	11	1	55	5
4	13	2	65	10
5	16	3	80	15
6	19	3	95	15
7	22	3	110	15
8	24	2	120	10
9	25	1	125	5
10	25	0	125	0

[a] Assuming a capital-output ratio of 5:1.

With a fixed capital-output ratio, net investment occurs only when it is necessary to increase the stock of capital in order to change output. Assume that it takes $5 of capital to produce $1 of output per year. In years 1 and 2 there is no need for investment. In year 3 a rise in sales of $1 requires investment of $5 to provide the needed capital stock. In year 4 a further rise of $2 in sales requires an additional investment of $10 to provide the needed capital stock. As columns 3 and 5 show, the amount of net investment is proportional to the *change* in sales. When the increase in sales tapers off in years 7–9, investment declines. When sales no longer increase in year 10, net investment falls to zero because the capital stock of year 9 is adequate to provide output for year 10's sales.

a much less rigid response of investment to income than the accelerator suggests.

Another limitation of the accelerator theory is that it takes a limited view of what constitutes investment. The fixed capital-output ratio emphasizes investment in what economists call **capital widening,** the investment in additional capacity that uses the same ratio of capital to labor as existing capacity. It does not explain **capital deepening,** which is the increase in the amount of capital per unit of labor that occurs, say, in response to a fall in the rate of interest. Neither does the theory say anything about investments brought about as a result of new processes or new products. Furthermore, it does not allow for the fact that investment in any period is likely to be limited by the capacity of the capital-goods industry.

For these and other reasons, the accelerator does not by itself give anything like a complete explanation of variations in business fixed investment. It should not be surprising that a simple accelerator theory provides a relatively poor overall explanation of changes in investment. Yet accelerator-like influences do exist, and empirical evidence continues to suggest that they play a role in the cyclical variability of investment.

Theories of the Cycle

There are several main theories about the cycle. They do not have to be regarded as competing. Indeed, each one captures some of the forces that contribute to the cycle.

Systematic Spending Fluctuations

The most commonly accepted theory looks to systematic fluctuations in aggregate expenditure brought about by systematic alterations in spending behavior as the cause of the cycle. Several influences can cause such alterations.

The Multiplier-Accelerator Mechanism

The combination of the multiplier and the accelerator can make upward or downward movements in the economy cumulative. Imagine that the economy is settled into a depression with heavy unemployment. Then a revival of investment demand occurs. Orders are placed for new plant and equipment, which creates new employment in the capital-goods industries. The newly employed workers spend most of their earnings. This creates new demand for consumer goods. A multiplier process is now set up, with new employment and incomes created in the consumer-goods industries.

The spending of the newly created incomes in turn means further increases in demand. At some stage the increased demand for consumer goods creates, through the accelerator process, an increased demand for capital goods. Once existing equipment is fully employed in any industry, extra output requires new capital equipment, and the accelerator theory takes over as the major determinant of investment expenditure. Such investment increases or at least maintains demand in the capital-goods sector of the economy. So the process goes on, the multiplier-accelerator mechanism continuing to produce a rapid rate of expansion in the economy.

The upper turning point. A rapid expansion can continue for some time, but it cannot go on forever. Eventually the economy will run into bottlenecks in terms of certain resources. For example, investment funds may become scarce, and as a result interest rates rise. Firms now find new investments more expensive than anticipated, and thus some become unprofitable. Or suppose that what limits the expansion is exhaustion of the reservoir of unemployed labor. The full-employment ceiling guarantees that any sustained rapid growth rate of real income and employment will eventually be slowed.

At this point the accelerator again comes into play. A slowing in the rate of increase of production leads to a decrease in business fixed investment. This decrease causes a drop in employment in the capital-goods industries and, through the multiplier, a fall in consumer demand. As consumer demand falls, investment in plant and equipment is reduced to a low level because firms already have more productive capacity than they can use. Unemployment rises, and the upper turning point has been passed.

The lower turning point. A contraction, too, is eventually brought to an end. Consider the worst depression imaginable, one in which every postponable expenditure of households, firms, or governments is postponed. Even then aggregate demand does not fall to zero. Figure 28-1 on page 590 shows that as aggregate disposable income falls, households spend a larger and larger fraction of that falling income. Finally, should income fall to the break-even level, all disposable income is spent (and none is saved).

Neither does government spending fall in proportion to the fall in government tax revenues. Government expenditures on most programs continue even if tax revenues sag to low levels.

Finally, even investment expenditures, in many ways the most easily postponed component of aggregate expenditure, does not fall to zero. Industries providing basics still have substantial sales and need replacement investment. Even in the worst depression some new processes and new products appear, and these require new investment.

Taken together, the minimum levels of consumption, investment, and government expenditure will assure a minimum equilibrium level of national income that, although well below the full-employment level, will not be zero. There is a floor below which income will not fall.

Sooner or later, an upturn begins. If nothing else causes an expansion of business activity, there will eventually be a revival of replacement investment because as existing capital wears out, the capital stock eventually falls below the level required to produce current output. At this stage new machines are bought to replace those that are worn out.

The rise in the level of activity in the capital-goods industries causes, by way of the multiplier, a further rise in income. The economy turns the corner. An expansion, once started, triggers the sort of cumulative upward movement that has already been discussed.

Other Endogenous Forces

The multiplier-accelerator is one endogenous force contributing to cyclical fluctuations. Two others are inventories and construction.

Inventory cycles. As we have seen, there are good reasons to suppose that the required size of inventories is related to the level of firms' sales and that sales are related to the level of national income. If firms maintain anything like a rigid inventory-to-sales ratio, this will cause an accelerator-like linkage between investment in inventories and *changes* in national income.

Many observers believe that these sharp and somewhat periodic fluctuations lead to an "inventory cycle" of roughly 40 months' average duration.

Construction cycles. Economists have noted some long-run, wave-like movements of roughly 20 years' duration in the statistics for expenditures on residential construction. These are sometimes referred to as "building cycles." Some economists suggest an accelerator-like explanation that runs from external events to demographic changes, to changes in the demand for housing and other buildings, and thence to changes in construction activity.

A major war, by taking males away from home, tends to retard family formation and thereby tends to depress the demand for private housing. When the war ends, there is typically an increase in marriages and household formation, an increase in the demand for housing, and a boom in the construction industry.

Depending on the capacity of the building industry, the boom may last many years before the desired increases in the stock of buildings of various kinds are achieved, but eventually it ends. Then, approximately 20 years after the end of the war that triggered the boom, there is likely to be a further boom in the number of marriages and births as the new generation starts its process of family formation. Wars are not the only source of such population-induced cycles; a severe depression will lead to a similar postponement of family formation.

The evidence concerning construction spending over the past century is thought by many economists to support the theory just outlined, a theory very much like the accelerator, though with changes in demographic factors, rather than changes in income, providing the impetus.

Random Shocks and Long Lags

One other model of the cycle does not assume cyclical behavior from firms and households. It suggests instead that random shifts in expenditure are transformed into systematic cycles of output and employment.

This theory begins with lags. For example, if a fall in the rate of interest makes an investment in a new project profitable, it may take 6 months to plan it, 3 months to let contracts, 6 months before spending builds up to its top rate, and another 24 to complete the project. These lags mean that changes in the rate of interest will cause reactions in investment expenditure that are distributed over quite a long period of time.

These lags have important implications for key macro variables. Although the disturbances might be random or erratic, income and employment both follow a cyclical path.

Each major component of aggregate expenditure has sometimes undergone shifts large enough to disturb the economy significantly. Long lags can convert such shifts into cyclical oscillations in national income.

A recent controversy in economics has emerged in response to research that shows that most of the cyclical patterns in the American economy can be explained by the effects of unpredictable technological disturbances that buffet the economy. These models argue that uncertainty about those shocks mean that when they do occur, households and firms react to them in a manner that spreads their effects out over several time periods. Thus, these *real business cycle* models predict that sporadic random shocks will give rise to smooth cyclical behavior of key macroeconomic variables.

While these models are able to explain many business cycle facts, many economists remain skeptical about them. In particular, they are doubtful about the nature and source of the shocks that play such a central role in the models, and in the limited role they assign to economic policies in either causing business cycles or in offsetting the effects of other disturbances.

Policy-induced Cycles

Yet another theory of the cycle is based on the allegation that government-induced demand shocks have sometimes caused cyclical fluctuations. Government expenditure has not often been the cause of major shocks due to sudden large changes. But government tax policy and monetary policy have both been shifted enough to cause significant demand shocks. Why should the government administer such potentially disturbing demand shocks? Several reasons have been suggested.

A political business cycle. As early as 1944 Polish-born Keynesian economist Michael Kalecki warned of a political business cycle. He argued that once governments had learned to manipulate the economy, they would engineer an election-geared business cycle. In pre-election periods they would raise spending and cut taxes. The resulting expansionary demand shock would create high employment and good business conditions, which would bring voters' support for the government. But the resulting inflationary gap would lead to a rising price level. So after the election was won, the government would depress demand to remove the inflationary gap and provide some slack for expansion before the next election.

This theory invokes the image of a cynical government manipulating employment and national income solely because it wants to stay in office. Few people believe that governments deliberately do this all the time, but the temptation to do it some of the time, particularly before elections, may prove irresistible.

Alternating policy goals. A variant of the policy-induced cycle does not require a cynical government and an easily duped electorate. Instead both sides need only be rather shortsighted and have rather narrow vision.

In this theory, when there is a recession and relatively stable prices, the public and the government identify unemployment as the number one economic problem. The government then engineers an expansionary policy shock through some combination of tax cuts and spending increases. This, plus such natural cumulative forces as the multiplier-accelerator, expands economic activity. Unemployment falls and income rises, but as income rises above potential national income, the price level begins to rise. It first rises along the stable *SRAS* curve and then rises further as boom conditions raise factor prices and shift the *SRAS* curve upward (see Figure 30-2 on page 633).

At this point the unemployment problem is declared cured. Now inflation is seen as the nation's number one economic problem. A contractionary demand shock is engineered. The natural cumulative forces again take over, causing a recession. The inflation subsides but unemployment rises, setting the stage once again for an expansionary shock to cure the unemployment problem.

Many economists have criticized government policy over the past few decades as sometimes causing fluctuations by alternately pushing expansion to cure unemployment and then contraction to cure inflation. We shall see in Chapter 39 that this charge is particularly strong against monetary policy. But whatever the policy, the charge is that policymakers have sometimes been too shortsighted in alternating their concern between unemployment and inflation.

Misguided stabilization policy. In a variant of the theory just expounded, the government tries to hold the economy at potential national income by countering fluctuations in private-sector expenditure with offsetting changes of its own spending and taxes. The government can in principle dampen such cyclical fluctuations by its stabilization policies. But unless it is very sophisticated, bad timing may accentuate rather than dampen fluctuations. We return to this possibility in subsequent chapters.

Securities Markets (Stock Markets)

It is commonplace to observe that stock market values have sometimes displayed cumulative upward movements and at other times cumulative downward movements. The first are called *bull markets* and the second *bear markets*. Most people also know that the Great Depression of the 1930s was preceded by the great stock market crash of 1929.

The association between fluctuations in the stock market and in the economy is there, but is there a causal connection? Do stock market booms help to cause business cycle booms, and do stock market slumps help to cause business cycle slumps? Before we can answer this question, we need to learn a bit about such markets.

The Function of Securities Markets

When a household buys shares newly issued by a company, it becomes one of the firm's owners. The company will not return the household's money, except in the rare event that the firm is liquidated. If the household wishes to get its money back, it can only persuade someone else to buy its shares in the company.

Similarly, when a household buys a bond from a company, it cannot get its money back from the company before a specified date. If I bought a 2007 bond in 1987, the bond will be redeemed by the company (i.e., the loan will be paid back) only in 2007. If I wish to get my money back sooner, all I can do is sell the bond to someone who is willing to become one of the company's creditors.

An organized market where stocks and bonds are bought and sold is called a **securities market,** or a **stock market.** Two of the best known are the New York Stock Exchange and the Toronto Stock Exchange. The trading of existing shares on the stock market indicates that ownership is being transferred; it does not indicate that companies are raising new money from the public.

Securities markets are important because by providing for the ready transfer of corporate securities, they make it possible for individuals to save without having to commit themselves for long periods.

Securities markets allow people to put their savings into stocks and bonds that are not themselves directly or quickly redeemable. For example, if I want to invest in a particular stock that pays an attractive yield, I may do so even though I know that I will want my money back after only a year. Given a securities market, I can be confident of my ability to sell the security a year from now. But while securities markets provide for the quick sale of stocks and bonds, they do not guarantee that securities can be sold at the same price at which they were bought. The price at any time is the one that equates the demand and supply for a particular security, and rapid fluctuations in stock prices are common.

Prices on the Stock Market

Figure 31-5 shows the wide swings in a well-known index of stock market prices, the Toronto Stock Exchange (TSE) Industrial Composite Index. The most recent swing in the period covered in the figure began from a trough in September 1982 when the index was about 1500. The index then rose, almost without interruption, until in mid 1987 it passed through 3800, a rise of 150 percent in just 50 months. Then in October 1987 it suffered a dramatic fall, tumbling 25 percent in less than two weeks to below 2900. It will probably have again changed significantly since then.

This was only one in a series of "booms" and "busts" that have periodically interrupted the long-term trend for stock market prices to rise slowly but steadily over the years. There had also been two large swings in the mid 1970s. Between 1979 and May 1981 the average stock price rose by 80 percent, yielding large gains for people who were wise or lucky enough to have bought at the beginning and sold at the end of this upswing. But then a downward movement occurred, with stock prices losing more than 30 percent of their value within a little over a year. Just a little earlier, in 1973, stocks lost 20 percent of their value and then recovered quite rapidly.

FIGURE 31-5 Fluctuations in an Index of Stock Prices, 1960–1986

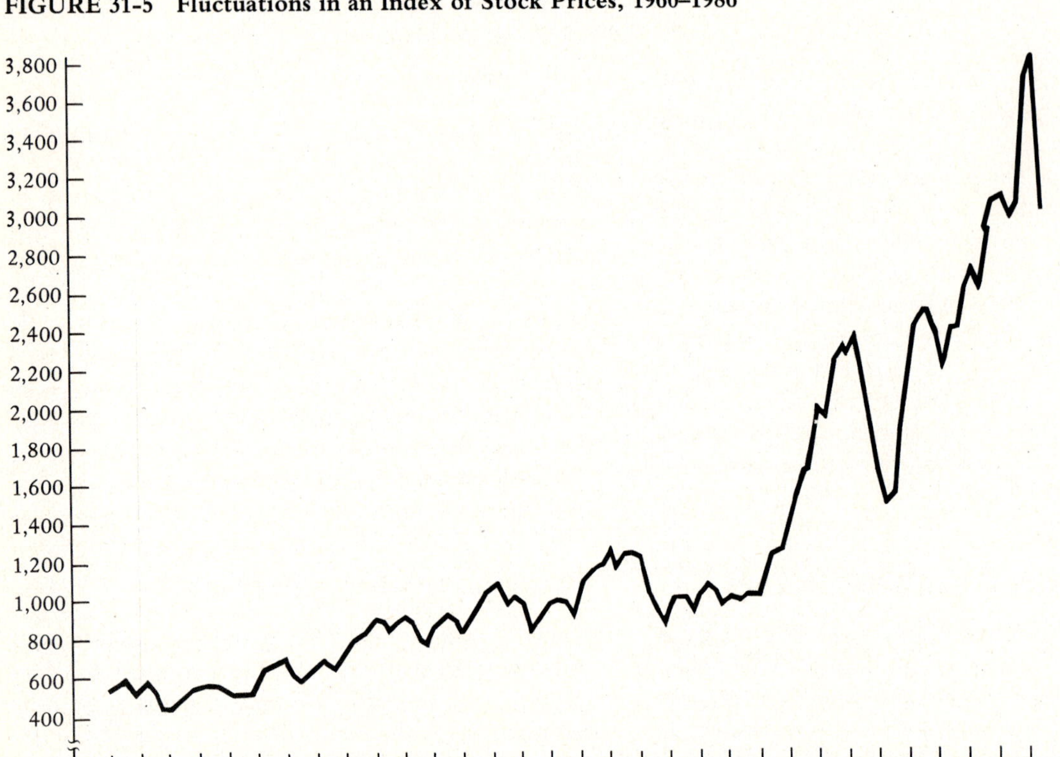

Stock market fluctuations are very sharp and irregular, and have witnessed a sharp increase. The chart shows quarterly variations in the Toronto Stock Exchange Industrial Composite Index. The index grew steadily from 1962 to 1972 and then displayed very little trend over the next 16 years. Over that period the index did, however, fluctuate sharply; it is these fluctuations that make large speculative gains and losses possible. Two notable falls in the index occurred during the economic downturns in 1970.

The market fell during the 1981–1982 recession, but the economic recovery of 1982 to 1986 was accompanied by a dramatic sustained increase in the TSE index; the index rose from about 1800 at the end of 1982 to over 3700 at the beginning of 1987, and then fell dramatically in late October to under 3000.

Measuring Stock Market Swings

Commentators are often careless about making the key distinction between the *number of points* by which the index changes over some period and the *percentage change* in that index over the same period. For example, when the TSE Industrial Composite fell by just over 500 points from a value of over 3800 in one week in October 1987, newspaper reporters were quick to point out that this was one of the largest one-week falls ever, measured by the number of points. But was it the greatest loss of stock values in any meaningful sense?

The answer is no. To see the significance for wealth holders of changes in stock market prices, we need to deal not in index points but in percentages. When we do this, the dramatic collapse of 1987 is put into perspective. Serious though it was, the loss of 25 percent in stock values was by no means unprecedented. As noted, in 1973–1974 stocks lost 20 percent of their value and then recovered; in 1975–1976 they lost 15 percent of their values before recovering. These losses, as well as those of September 1986, remain dwarfed by the loss everyone hopes will never be repeated: Over 80 percent of the value of stocks was lost over the three-year period from 1929 to 1933!

Causes of Stock Market Swings

What causes such rapid gains and losses, and what do they have to do with business cycles?

When investors buy a company's stocks, they are buying rights to share in the stream of dividends to be paid out by that company. They are also buying an asset that they can sell in the future at a gain or loss.

The value of that stock depends on two things: first, what people expect the stream of future dividend payments to be, and second, what capital gain or loss people expect to realize when the stock is sold.

Both things make dealing in stocks an inherently risky operation. Will the company in which you are investing pay more or less in dividends in future years? Will the company's value rise or fall so that you can sell your share in it for more or less than what you bought it for? While dividend policies of most established companies tend to be fairly stable, stock prices are subject to wide swings.

The Influence of Present and Future Business Conditions

We have observed that many influences act on stock market prices; these include the state of the business cycle and the stance of government policies.

Cyclical forces. If investors expect a firm's earnings to increase, the firm will become more valuable, and the price of its stock will rise. Such influences cause stock prices to move with the business cycle, being high when current profits are high and low when current profits are low. It also causes stock prices to vary with a host of factors that influence expectations of future profits. A poor crop, destruction of trees by acid rain, announcement of new defense spending, a change in the foreign-exchange value of the dollar, or a change in the political complexion of the administration can all affect profit expectations and hence stock prices.

Policy factors. We shall see later in this book that major alterations in monetary policy can cause major changes in interest rates. Such changes, or just the expectations of them, will have major effects on stock prices. Say, for example, that interest rates rise rapidly. Investors will see that they can now earn an increased amount by purchasing government bonds. As a result, they will wish to alter their investment portfolios to hold more bonds and fewer stocks. But everyone cannot do this, since only so many stocks and so many bonds are available to be held at any given time. As all investors try to sell their stocks, prices fall. The fall will only stop when the expected rate of return to investment in stocks, based on their lower purchase price, makes stocks equally attractive as bonds. Then investors will no longer try to shift out of bonds *en masse.*

Speculative Booms

In addition to responding to a host of factors that can reasonably be expected to influence the absolute and relative earnings of companies, stock prices often develop an upward or downward movement of their own, propelled by little more than speculation that feeds on itself.

In major stock market booms, people begin to expect rising stock prices and hurry to buy while stocks are cheap. This action bids up the prices of shares and creates the capital gains that justify the original expectations. This is an example of the phenomenon of *self-realizing expectations.* Investors get rich on paper in the sense that the market value of their holdings rises. Money-making now looks easy to others, who also rush in to buy, and new purchases push up prices still further. At this stage attention to current earnings all but ceases. If a stock can yield, say, a 50 percent capital gain in one year, it does not matter much if the current earnings represent only a small percentage yield on the purchase price of the stocks. Everyone is "making money," so more people become attracted by the get-rich-quick opportunities. Their attempts to buy bid up prices still further. In such speculative booms, current earnings represent an ever-diminishing percentage yield on the current price of the stocks.

Capital gains can be so attractive that investors may buy stocks on margin—that is, borrow money to buy them, using the stocks themselves as security for the loans. In doing this, many investors may be borrowing money at a rate of interest considerably in excess of the yield from current dividends. Even if $50,000 is borrowed at 10 percent (interest payments are $5,000 per year) to buy stocks yielding a current dividend return of only 4 percent (dividend receipts are $2,000 per year), never mind, says the investor's logic; the stocks can be sold in a year or so for a handsome capital gain that will more than repay the $3,000 of interest not covered by dividends. Some people have the luck or good judgment to sell out near the top of the market, and they actually make money. Others wait eagerly for ever-greater capital gains, and in the meantime they get richer and richer—on paper.

Eventually something breaks the period of unrestrained optimism. Some investors may begin to worry about the very high prices of stocks in relation not only to current yields but also to possible future yields, even when generous allowances for growth are made. Or it may be that the prices of stocks become depressed slightly when a sufficiently large number of persons try to sell out in order to realize their capital gains. As they offer their securities on the market, they cannot find purchasers without some fall in prices. Even a modest price fall may be sufficient to persuade others that it is time to sell. But every share that is sold must be bought by someone. A wave of sellers may not find new buyers at existing prices, causing prices to fall. Panic selling may now occur.

A household that borrowed $50,000 to buy stocks near the top of the market may find the paper value of its holdings sliding below $50,000. How will it repay its loan? Even if it does not worry about the loan, its broker will. The household may sell now before it loses too much, or its broker may "sell the customer out" to liquidate the loan. All this causes prices to fall even further and provides another example of self-realizing expectations. If enough people think prices are going to come down, their attempt to sell out at the present high prices will create the fall in prices the expectations of which caused the selling.

This is a very simple and stylized description of a typical speculative cycle, yet it describes the basic elements of market booms and busts that have recurred throughout stock market history. The biggest boom of all began in the mid 1920s and ended on Black Tuesday, October 29, 1929. The collapse was dramatic, with stocks losing about half of their value in about two months. Nor did it stop there. For three long years stock prices continued to decline until the average value of stock sold on the New York Stock Exchange had fallen from its 1929 high of $89.10 a share to $17.35 a share by late 1933. It also happened, although less dramatically, in the booms and busts of the 1970s and 1980s discussed earlier in this section.

Stock Market Swings: Cause or Effect of Business Cycles?

Stock markets tend often to lead, and sometimes to follow, booms and slumps in business activity. In both cases the causes usually run from real business conditions, whether actual or anticipated, to stock market prices. This is the dominant theme, the stock market as reflector.

It is also possible for the stock market to be a causal factor in the business cycle. For example, some people held that the wild boom of the late 1920s tied up funds in speculative uses that would otherwise have gone to the real investment spending needed to sustain the boom into the 1930s. Such circumstances are possible, but they are only a minor theme.

Stock market fluctuations are more typically a consequence than a cause of the business cycle.

In many cases the stock market and the business cycle both reflect the common influence of other factors. For example, stock markets often react to changes in interest rates that may be caused by government policy; as we have seen, such interest-rate changes can also play a causal role in cyclical fluctuations in the economy. Typically the stock market responds quicker than does the economy to such influences, and for this reason many observers look to it as a "leading indicator" of likely future economic developments.

The relationship between the stock market and the economy is further complicated by the existence of occasional speculative booms and busts. There are often real economic forces influencing expectations of stock prices, but at least for a while the prices may become dominated by speculative psychology. Unfortunately, speculative behavior causes the stock market to react to many events that turn out to have little or no enduring implications for the economy. As one wag put it, the stock market has predicted seven out of the last two recessions!

As an example, consider the long upswing that took stock prices up by about 85 percent in less than three years between early 1984 and early 1987. At the time Canada enjoyed a very strong recovery, and the rising stock prices no doubt reflected the resulting favorable profit outlook of Canadian companies. Added onto all that may have been a speculative component. Certainly many doubted that the full increase in stock values of over 85 percent in less than four years was justified by underlying business opportunities. Only time can tell how much, if any, of the rise in values was due to transitory speculative behavior. Certainly the fall of over 25 percent in October 1987 indicated that much of the run-up in values was a result of a speculative form.

Stock Markets: Investment Marketplaces or Gambling Casinos?

Stock markets fulfill many important functions. It is doubtful that the great aggregations of capital needed to finance modern firms could be raised under a private ownership system without them. There is no doubt, however, that they also provide an unfortunate attraction for many naive investors whose get-rich-quick dreams are more often than not destroyed by the fall in prices that follows the occasional speculative booms they help to create.

To some extent public policy has sought to curb the excesses of stock market speculation through supervision of security issues. This is an area of complex overlap between federal and provincial jurisdiction. Policy seeks, among other things, to prevent both fraudulent or misleading information and trading by "insiders" (those in a company with confidential information). Moreover, the regulators can limit the ability of speculators to trade on margin.

All in all, the stock market is both a real marketplace and a place to gamble. As in all gambling situations, players who are less well informed and less clever than the average tend to be losers in the long term.

Causes of Business Cycles: A Consensus View?

Economists once argued long and bitterly about which was the best explanation of the recurrent cyclical behavior of the economy.

Today most economists agree that there is not a single cause or class of causes governing business cycles.

In an economy that has tendencies for both cumulative and self-reversing behavior, any large shock, whether from without or within, can initiate a cyclical swing. Wars are important; so are major technical inventions. A rapid increase in interest rates and a general tightening of credit can cause a sharp decrease in investment. Expectations can be changed by a political campaign or a development in another part of the world. The list of possible initial impulses, autonomous or induced, is long. It is probably true that the characteristic cyclical pattern involves many outside shocks that sometimes initiate, sometimes reinforce, and sometimes dampen the cumulative tendencies that exist within the economy.

Cycles differ also in terms of their internal structure. There are variations in timing, duration, and amplitude. In some cycles full employment of labor may be the bottleneck that determines the peak. In others high interest rates and shortages of investment funds may nip an expansion and turn it into a recession at the same time that the unemployment of labor is still an acute problem. In some cycles the recession phase is short; in others a full-scale period of stagnation sets in. In some cycles the peak develops into a severe inflation; in others the pressure of excess demand is hardly felt, and a new recession sets in before the economy has fully recovered from the last trough. Some cycles last long; others are short.

In this chapter we have suggested reasons why an economy that is subjected to periodic external shocks will tend to generate a continually changing pattern of fluctuations, as cumulative and then self-reversing forces alternatively come into play. In the next chapter we study how governments seek to influence the cycle and remove some of its extremes through the use of fiscal policy.

Summary

1. The economy experiences continual fluctuations. A self-reinforcing cumulative process leads to a cyclical pattern of fluctuations.
2. Economists break a stylized cycle into four phases: trough, recovery, peak, and recession. These phases have certain characteristic features, although no two real-world cycles are exactly the same.
3. Short-term fluctuations in GDP are usually, though not always, the result of variations in aggregate demand. Overall, these fluctuations show a fairly clear pattern that is described as cyclical. Despite the overall pattern, the evidence is that the cycles are irregular in amplitude, in timing, in duration, and in the way they affect particular industries and sectors of the economy.
4. Any explanation of the business cycle must explain both *why* income fluctuates and *how* those fluctuations get transformed into cycles.
5. Shifts in consumption, government, and export expenditures can cause major fluctuations in Canadian national income and employment.
6. Investment expenditure causes fluctuations in aggregate demand. The three principal components of private investment are changes in business inventories, residential construction, and business fixed investment. The interest rate is an important determinant of investment spending.
7. Changes in business inventories, the smallest of the three major components of investment expenditure, often account for an important fraction of the year-to-year changes in the level of investment. They respond both to changes in the level of production and sales and to the rate of interest.
8. Residential construction shows a cyclical pattern of its own. House building responds to economic (as well as noneconomic) influences, varying directly with the level of national income and inversely with the rate of interest. The rate of interest is important because interest payments are a large fraction of the mortgage payments that greatly affect a household's ability to purchase a house.
9. Business fixed investment depends on a number of variables. These include innovation, expectations about the future, level of profits, rate of interest, and changes in national income.
10. The accelerator theory relates net investment to changes in national

income on the assumption of a fixed capital-output ratio. Its central prediction is that rising income is required to maintain a given level of investment. Its central insight is that net investment is a disequilibrium phenomenon that occurs when the actual capital stock is different from the desired capital stock.

11. There are several explanations of the cyclical pattern of economic fluctuations. Among these are (1) that expenditure shifts themselves are systematic; (2) that lags in the system transform random expenditure shifts into systematic cyclical changes in income; and (3) that in part the cycle is either the conscious or the accidental result of government policy.
12. Securities (stock) markets allow firms to raise new capital from the sale of newly issued securities and allow the holders of existing securities to sell their securities to other investors. Prices on the stock market tend to reflect the public's expectations both of firms' future earnings and of future changes in prices (for whatever reason). This necessarily puts a strong speculative dimension into security prices, and large speculative swings do occur. Such swings are accentuated by the phenomenon of self-realizing expectations.

Topics for Review

Business cycles and economic fluctuations
Phases of the cycle
Causes of cyclical fluctuations
Components of investment
The accelerator
Interactions of the multiplier and the accelerator
Political business cycle
The stock market

Discussion Questions

1. How and in what direction might each of the following shift the function relating consumption expenditure to disposable income?
   a. Introduction of user-fee charges for medical care
   b. A change in attitudes so that we become a nation of conspicuous conservers rather than conspicuous consumers, taking pride in how little we eat or spend for housing, clothing, and so on
   c. Increases in income taxes
   d. News that due to medical advances everyone can count on more years of retirement than ever before
   e. A spreading belief that all-out nuclear war is likely within the next 10 years
   f. Sharp increases in the down payments required on durable goods
2. Suppose the government wished to reduce private investment in order to reduce an inflationary gap. What policies might it adopt? If it wished to do so in such a way as to have a major effect on residential housing and a minor effect on business fixed investment expenditures, which measures might it use?

3. What effect on total investment—and on which categories of investment—would you predict as a result of each of the following?
  a. Widespread endorsement of zero population growth by young couples
  b. A sharp increase in the frequency and duration of strikes in the transportation industries
  c. Forecasts of very low growth rates of real national income over the next five years
  d. Tax reform that eliminates deductions for property taxes in computing taxable personal income

4. When interest rates rose sharply in the early 1980s, home construction fell dramatically, but sales of mobile homes increased. How does the rise in the sale of mobile homes relate to the notion that investment responds to the rate of interest?

5. Empirical studies show that as the volume of a firm's sales increases, the size of its inventories of raw materials tends to increase in proportion. It is common for business firms to speak of such inventories in terms of "a 20-day supply of coal" rather than "52,000 tons of coal" or "$280,000 worth of coal." Why should relative size be more important than absolute quantity or dollar value?

6. Which "cause" of business investment is being relied on in each of the following quotes?
  a. An aluminum industry spokesman, justifying a $0.50 a pound increase in aluminum prices: "We must have it to build the new capacity we need."
  b. A major steel company, in a newspaper ad: "We need lower taxes, not cheaper money or government deficits, to help lower barriers to capital formation."
  c. "The government used a credit crunch to bring on a recession and reduce inflation."

7. Since different series behave differently, does it make sense to talk about a business cycle? Predict the comparative behavior of the following pairs of series in relation to fluctuations in the GDP.
  a. Purchases of food, purchases of consumer durables
  b. Tax receipts, bankruptcies
  c. Unemployment, birth rates
  d. Employment in Montreal, employment in Oshawa

  Check your predictions against the facts for the past decade.

8. The highest interest rates in Canadian history occurred in 1981–1982. The deepest recession since the 1930s occurred in 1982. How might these facts be related? What has happened to interest rates and economic activity since?

32

Fiscal Policy

As we have seen, national income fluctuates continually due to shifts in aggregate demand and short-run aggregate supply. **Fiscal policy** involves the use of government spending and tax policies to influence the *AD* curve and, to a lesser degree, the *SRAS* curve in order to damp fluctuations in the economy.

Since government expenditure increases aggregate demand and taxation decreases it, the *direction* of the required changes in spending and taxation is generally easy to determine once we know the direction of the desired change in national income. But the *timing, magnitude,* and *mixture* of the changes pose more difficult issues.

Any policy that attempts to stabilize national income at or near a desired level (usually potential national income) is called **stabilization policy.** This chapter deals first with the theory of fiscal policy as a tool of stabilization policy and then with the experience of using it.

There is no doubt that the government can exert a major influence on national income. Prime examples are the massive military spending during major wars. During World War II the Canadian government's defense expenditures rose from 1.2 percent of national income in 1939 to 36 percent in 1944. At the same time the unemployment rate fell from 11.4 percent to 1.4 percent. Economists agree that the increase in government spending helped bring about the fall in unemployment and the associated rise in GDP. Similar experiences occurred in the United States and most European countries before or immediately following the outbreak of the war in 1939.

When used appropriately, fiscal policy can be an important tool for stabilizing the economy. In the heyday of fiscal policy, from 1945 to late 1965, many economists were convinced that the economy could be adequately stabilized just by varying the size of the government's taxes and expenditures. That day is past. Today most economists are aware of the limitations of fiscal policy.

The Theory of Fiscal Policy

Fiscal policy is often referred to as the government's budgetary policy or simply as the budget.

The Budget Balance

The **budget balance** is the difference between all government revenue and all government expenditures. In this definition *government expenditure* includes both transfer payments and purchases of currently produced goods and services. Thus the budget balance is the difference between all the money the government takes in as revenue and all the money it pays out. These are called its *budget receipts* and *outlays,* respectively.

Changes in either government spending or tax policies influence the budget balance. If receipts are exactly equal to outlays, the government has a **balanced budget.** If receipts exceed outlays, there is a **budget surplus;** if receipts fall short of outlays, there is a **budget deficit.** If the government raises its outlays without raising taxes, the extra expenditure is said to be *deficit-financed.* If the extra outlays are accompanied by an equal increase in tax rates that yields an equal increase in receipts, we speak of a *balanced budget change in spending.*

Financial Implications of Deficits and Surpluses

When the government spends more than it raises, where does the money come from? If the government raises more than it spends, where does the money go? The difference between expenditure and current revenue shows up as changes in the government's debt.

A deficit requires an increase in borrowing, for which there are two main sources: the central bank and the private sector. The government borrows money from these sources by selling treasury bills and bonds. A **treasury bill,** or note, is a promise to repay a stated amount at some specified date between 90 days and one year from the date of issue. A government *bond* is also a promise to pay a stated sum of money in the future, but in the more distant future than a bill—as much as 25 years from the date of issue.[1]

When the government borrows from the private sector, this action merely shifts funds between the two sectors. When the government "borrows" from the central bank, however, the central bank creates new money. Since the central bank can create as much money as it likes, there is no limit to what the government can "borrow" from it.

A surplus allows the government to reduce its outstanding debt. Treasury bills and bonds may be redeemed from the excess tax revenue.

The Paradox of Thrift

When a government follows a balanced budget policy, as most governments tried to do during the Great Depression of the 1930s, its spending becomes procyclical. It must restrict its spending during a recession because its tax revenue will necessarily be falling at that time. During a recovery, when its revenue is rising, it must increase its spending. In other words, it rolls with the economy, raising and lowering its spending in step with everyone else.

Not long ago people generally accepted, and indeed many still fervently believe, that a prudent government should always balance its budget. This belief is based on an analogy with what seems prudent behavior for the individual household. It is a foolish household whose current expenditure consistently exceeds its current revenue so that it goes steadily further into debt. From this commonsense observation some people argue that if avoiding an ever-rising debt is good for the individual, it must also be good for the nation. But the *paradox of thrift* suggests that the analogy between the government and the household may be misleading.

The theory of national income developed in Chapters 26 through 30 predicts that if all spending units in the economy simultaneously try to increase the amount that they save, the combined increase in thriftiness will *reduce* the equilibrium level of income. The contrary case, a general decrease in thriftiness and increase in expenditure, increases national income. This prediction has come to be known as the paradox of thrift.[2]

[1] Bills carry a promise to return a fixed amount at maturity. Interest arises because they are initially sold at a discount; the difference between their current price and their redemption value represents interest. Bonds carry a fixed "coupon rate of interest" on their redemption value. They guarantee not only the repayment of a fixed sum on the redemption date but also the periodic payment of fixed sums between sale and redemption.

[2] The prediction is not actually a paradox. It is a straightforward implication of the theory of the determination of income. The expectations that lead to the "paradox" are based on the fallacy of composition, the belief that what is true for the parts is necessarily true for the whole.

The policy implication of this prediction is that substantial unemployment is correctly combated by encouraging governments, firms, and households to spend more, *not* to save more. In times of unemployment and depression, frugality will only make things worse. This prediction goes directly against the idea that we should tighten our belts when times are tough. The concept that it is not just possible but acceptable to spend one's way out of a depression touches a sensitive nerve in people raised on the belief that success is based on hard work and frugality and not on prodigality; as a result, the idea often arouses great emotional hostility.

Applications. As discussed in Box 32-1, the implications of the paradox of thrift were not generally understood during the Great Depression. However, by the middle of the 1930s, many economists had concluded that the government was not making the most of its potential to control the economy in a beneficial manner. Why, they asked, should not the government try to stabilize the economy by doing just the opposite of what everyone else was doing—by increasing its demand when private demand was falling and lowering its demand when private demand was rising? At best this policy could hold aggregate demand constant even though its individual components were fluctuating.

When Milton Friedman said, "We are all Keynesians now," he was referring to (among other things) the general acceptance of the view that the government's budget is much more than just the revenue and expenditure statement of a very large organization. Whether we like it or not, the sheer size of the government's budget inevitably makes it a powerful tool for influencing the economy.

Limitations. The paradox of thrift concentrates on shifts in aggregate demand caused by changes in saving (and hence spending) behavior. Thus it applies only in the short run, when the *AD* curve plays an important role in the determination of national income.

In the long run, when the economy is on its *LRAS* curve and hence aggregate demand is not important for the determination of national income (see Figure 30-5), the paradox of thrift ceases to apply. The more people save, the larger the supply of funds available for investment. The more people invest, the greater the growth of potential income. Increased potential income causes the *LRAS* curve to shift to the right.

These longer-term effects are taken up in Chapter 38 in the discussion of economic growth. In the meantime we concentrate on the short-run demand effects of saving and spending.

The paradox of thrift is based on the short-run effects of changes in saving and investment on aggregate demand.

Fiscal Policy with Stable Private Expenditure Functions

A relatively easy problem faces fiscal policymakers when private-sector expenditure functions for consumption, investment, and net exports are given and unchanging. What is needed then is a once-and-for-all fiscal change that will remove any existing inflationary or recessionary gap.

Changes in tax rates or expenditure. The necessary policies were explained in Chapter 29. A reduction in tax rates or an increase in government expenditure shifts the *AD* curve to the right, leading to an increase in national income. An increase in tax rates or a cut in government expenditure shifts the *AD* curve to the left, leading to a decrease in national income.

The key proposition in the theory of fiscal policy follows these results.

Government taxes and expenditure, by shifting the *AD* curve, can be used to remove output gaps.

Balanced budget changes. Another policy available to the government is to make a balanced budget change by changing spending and taxes equally. Say the government increases tax rates enough to raise an extra $1 billion that it then uses to purchase goods and services. Aggregate expenditure would remain unchanged if, and only if, the $1 billion that the government takes from the private sector would otherwise have been spent by the private sector. If

BOX 32-1

Fiscal Policy and the Great Depression

Failure to understand the implication of the paradox of thrift led many countries to adopt policies during the Great Depression that were disastrous. Failure to understand the role of built-in stabilizers has also led many observers to conclude, erroneously, that fiscal expansion had been tried in the Great Depression but had failed. Let us see how these two misperceptions are related.

The Paradox of Thrift in Action

In Canada, Prime Minister R. B. Bennett said in 1932, in the worst recession in recorded history, "We are now faced with the real crisis in the history of Canada. To maintain our credit we must practice the most rigid economy and not spend a single cent." His government that year brought down a budget based on the principle of trying to balance revenues and expenditures, and it included *increases* in tax rates.

U.S. President Franklin D. Roosevelt, in his first inaugural address (1933), urged: "Our great primary task is to put people to work. . . . [This task] can be helped by insistence that the Federal, State and local governments act forthwith on the demand that their costs be drastically reduced. . . . There must be a strict supervision of all banking and credits and investments."

Across the Atlantic, King George V told the British House of Commons in 1931, "The present condition of the national finances, in the opinion of His Majesty's Ministers, calls for the imposition of additional taxation and for the effecting of economies in public expenditure."

As the paradox of thrift predicts, these policies reduced aggregate demand and hence tended to worsen, not cure, the depression.

Interpreting the Deficit in the 1930s

Government deficits did increase in the 1930s, but they were not the result of a program of deficit-financed public expenditure. They were the result of the fall in tax yields brought about by the fall in national income as the economy sank into depression. The various governments did not advocate a program of massive deficit-financed spending to shift the *AD* curve to the right. Instead, they hoped that a small amount of government spending plus numerous policies designed to stabilize prices and to restore confidence would lead to a recovery of private investment expenditure that would substantially shift the aggregate demand curve. To have expected a massive revival of private investment expenditure as a result of the puny increase in aggregate demand instituted by government now seems hopelessly naive.

When we judge these policies from the viewpoint of modern multiplier theory, their failure is no mystery. Indeed, Professor E. Cary Brown of MIT, after a careful study, concluded, "Fiscal policy seems to have been an unsuccessful recovery device in the 'thirties—not because it did not work, but because it was not tried."

The performance of the North American economies from 1930 to 1945 is quite well explained by modern national income theory. It is clear that the governments did not effectively use fiscal measures to stabilize their economies. War cured the depression because war demands made acceptable a level of government expenditure sufficient to remove the recessionary gap. Had the Canadian and American administrations been able to do the same, they might have ended the waste of the Depression many years sooner.

that is the case, the government's policy would reduce private expenditure by $1 billion and raise its own spending by $1 billion. Aggregate demand, and hence national income and employment, would remain unchanged.

But this is not the usual case. When an extra $1 billion in taxes is taken away from households, they usually reduce their spending on domestically produced goods by less than $1 billion. If the marginal propensity to consume out of disposable income is, say, 0.75, consumption expenditure will fall by only $750 million. If the government spends the entire $1 billion on domestically produced goods, aggregate expenditure will increase by $250 million. In this case the balanced budget increase in government expenditure has an expansionary effect because it shifts the aggregate expenditure function upward and hence shifts the *AD* curve to the right.

A balanced budget increase in government expenditure will have an expansionary effect on national income, and a balanced budget decrease will have a contractionary effect.

The **balanced budget multiplier** measures these effects. It is the change in income divided by the balanced budget change in government expenditure that brought it about. Thus if the extra $1 billion of government spending financed by the extra $1 billion of taxes causes national income to rise by $500 million, the balanced budget multiplier is 0.5; if income rises by $1 billion, it is 1.0.

Now compare the sizes of the multipliers for a balanced budget and a deficit-financed increase in government spending. With a deficit-financed increase in expenditure, there is no increase in tax rates and hence no consequent decrease in consumption expenditure to offset the increase in government expenditure. With a balanced budget increase in expenditure, however, the offsetting increase in tax rates and decrease in consumption does occur. Thus the balanced budget multiplier is much lower than the multiplier that relates the change in income to a deficit-financed increase in government expenditure with tax rates constant.

Fiscal Policy with Shifting Private Expenditure Functions

As we saw in Chapter 31, private expenditure functions are constantly changing. Investment expenditure shifts a great deal with business conditions, and consumption functions sometimes shift upward as the public goes on a spending spree or downward as people become cautious and increase their saving. This makes stabilization policy much more difficult than it would be if it were possible simply to identify a stable inflationary or recessionary gap and then take steps to eliminate it once and for all.

What can the government reasonably expect to achieve by using fiscal policy when private expenditure functions are shifting continually? Fiscal policy might be altered often in an effort to stabilize the economy completely, or it might be altered less frequently, responding only to gaps that appear to be large and persistent while ignoring small, transitory fluctuations.

Fine Tuning

In the heyday of Keynesian fiscal policy in the 1950s and 1960s, many economists advocated the use of fiscal policy to remove even minor fluctuations in national income around its full-employment level. Fiscal policy was to be altered frequently and by relatively small amounts to hold national income almost precisely at its full-employment level. This is called **fine tuning** the economy.

A necessary condition for fine tuning is a relatively short **decison lag,** the period of time between perceiving a problem and making the desired reaction to it. Many things contribute to the length of this lag. Experts must study the economy and agree among themselves on what fiscal changes are most desirable; they must then persuade the government to initiate the action they endorse.

In countries where political institutions keep the decision lag short, fine tuning has been attempted. Careful assessment of the results shows that their successes, if any, have fallen far short of what was hoped. One basic reason lies in the complexity of any economy. Although economists and policymakers can identify broad and persistent trends, they do not have detailed knowledge of what is going on at any particular moment, of all the forces that are operating to cause changes in the immediate future, or of all the short-term effects of small changes in the various government expenditures and tax rates.

Further difficulties for fine tuning also arise because of an **execution lag,** the time it takes to put policies in place after the decision is made, and because of lags between the introduction of a given policy measure and its effects being felt in the economy. Often by the time the effects of a given policy decision are felt, circumstances in the economy have changed and the policy is no longer appropriate.

Fine tuning often has done as much to encourage fluctuations in the economy as to remove them.

As a result of these experiences, fine tuning is currently out of favor.

Removal of Persistent Gaps

In addition to more or less continual fluctuations, the economy occasionally develops severe and persistent output gaps. For example, an inflationary gap developed in the United States in the late 1960s as Vietnam War expenditures accelerated, while a recessionary gap developed between 1981 and 1983 when Canada, along with many Western countries, experienced the deepest and longest-lasting recession since the 1930s. Gaps such as these may persist long enough for their major causes to be studied and understood and for fiscal remedies to be carefully planned and executed.

A persistent recessionary gap. The removal of a recessionary gap is illustrated in Figure 32-1. There are three possible ways in which the gap may be removed.

First, wages and other factor prices may eventually be forced down enough to shift the *SRAS* curve to the right by enough to reinstate full employment and potential income (at a lower price level). The evidence is, however, that this process takes a long time.

Second, the natural cyclical forces of the economy could induce a demand-side recovery for the reasons spelled out in Chapter 31. This would cause a shift to the right of the *AD* curve, moving the economy back to full employment and potential income. The evidence is that such recoveries do occur. Sometimes they happen quickly; often, however, a recession can be both deep and prolonged.

Third, government expenditure can be increased or taxes cut in an effort to shift the *AD* curve to the right. The advantage of using fiscal policy is that it may substantially shorten the length of what would otherwise be a long recession. The disadvantage is that it may stimulate the economy just before private-sector spending recovers due to natural causes. If it does, the economy may overshoot its potential output, and a serious inflationary gap may open up.

A persistent inflationary gap. Figure 32-2 (see page 676) shows the three ways in which an inflationary gap can be removed.

First, wages and other factor prices may be forced upward by the excess demand. This will shift the *SRAS* curve to the left, eventually eliminating the gap, reducing income to its potential level, and raising the price level.

Second, a cyclical reduction in aggregate demand may occur for the reasons outlined in Chapter 31. This might reduce income to its potential level without the rise in the price level associated with a shift of the *SRAS* curve. But unless aggregate demand declines quickly, rising wages and other input prices will lead to a shift to the left of the *SRAS* curve and hence to rising prices.

Third, the government, by raising taxes or cutting spending, may force aggregate demand down sufficiently to remove the inflationary gap. The advantage of this approach is that it avoids the inflationary increase in prices that accompanies the first method. The disadvantage is that if private-sector expenditures fall off to their more normal level, national income may be pushed below potential, thus opening up a recessionary gap.

Policy. Many economists who do not believe in the value of fine tuning do feel that fiscal policy can aid in removing persistent output gaps. Others believe that even with persistent gaps, the risks that fiscal policy will destabilize the economy are still too large. They would have the government abandon any attempt at stabilization policy, instead setting its budget solely in relation to such long-term considerations as the desirable size of the public sector and the need to obtain a satisfactory long-term balance between revenues and expenditures.

Tools of Fiscal Policy

The major fiscal tools can be classified in many ways; one important classification is the division between automatic and discretionary tools.

FIGURE 32-1 **Removal of a Recessionary Gap**

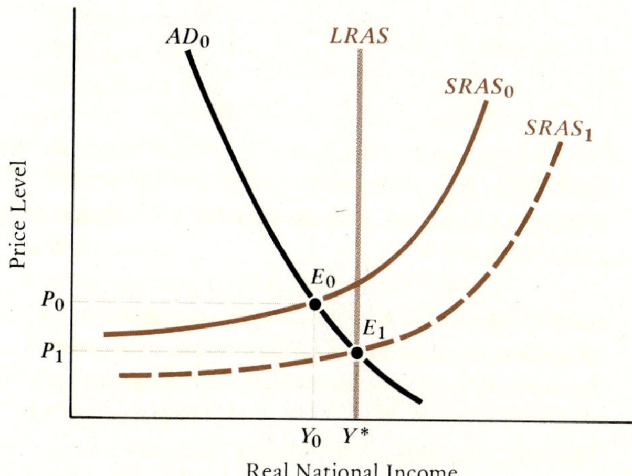

(i) A recessionary gap removed by a rightward shift in *SRAS*

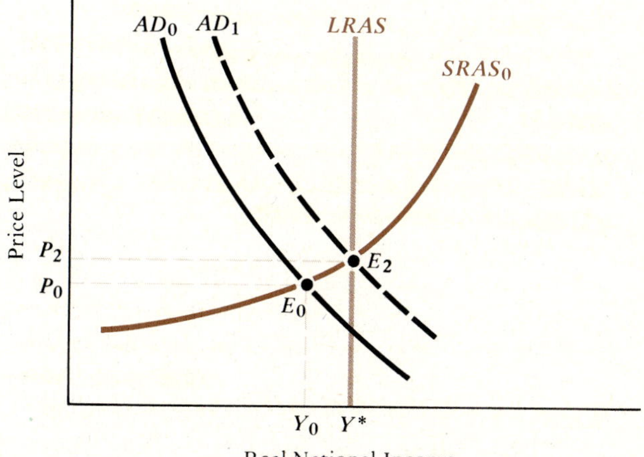

(ii) A recessionary gap removed by a rightward shift in *AD*

A recessionary gap may be removed by a (slow) rightward shift of the *SRAS* curve, a natural revival of private-sector demand, or a fiscal policy-induced increase in aggregate demand. Initially equilibrium is at E_0, with national income at Y_0 and the price level at P_0. The recessionary gap is Y_0Y^*.

As shown in part (i), the gap might be removed by a shift in the *SRAS* curve to $SRAS_1$. This increase in aggregate supply could occur as a result of reductions in wage rates and other input prices. The shift in the *SRAS* curve causes a movement down and to the right along AD_0. This establishes a new equilibrium at E_1, achieving potential income, Y^*, and lowering the price level to P_1.

As shown in part (ii), the gap might also be removed by a shift of the *AD* curve to AD_1. This increase in aggregate demand could occur either because of a natural revival of private-sector expenditure or because of a fiscal policy-induced increase in expenditure. The shift in the *AD* curve causes a movement up and to the right along $SRAS_0$. This shifts the equilibrium to E_2, taking income to Y^* and the price level to P_2.

Automatic Fiscal Tools: Built-In Stabilizers

For reasons discussed in Chapter 31, the *AD* curve is continually fluctuating. A stabilization policy for fine tuning the economy would thus require a policy that was itself ever changing. If such a conscious fine tuning policy is impossible, must we say that nothing can be done through fiscal policy except to reduce major, long-lived output gaps?

Fortunately, this is not so. Much of the adjustment of fiscal policy to an ever-changing economic environment is done automatically by what are called built-in stabilizers. A **built-in stabilizer** is anything

FIGURE 32-2 Removal of an Inflationary Gap

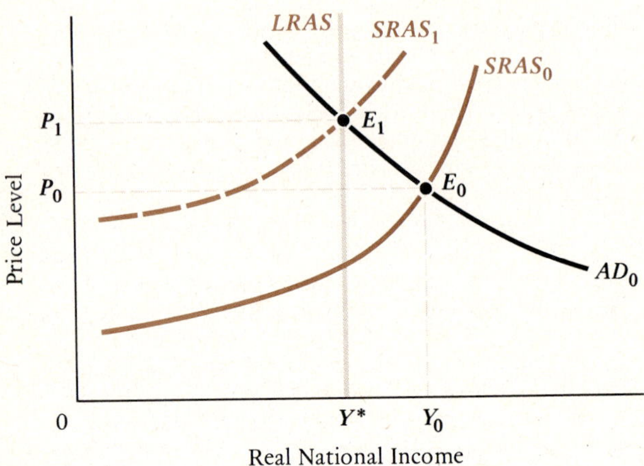

(i) An inflationary gap removed by a leftward shift in *SRAS*

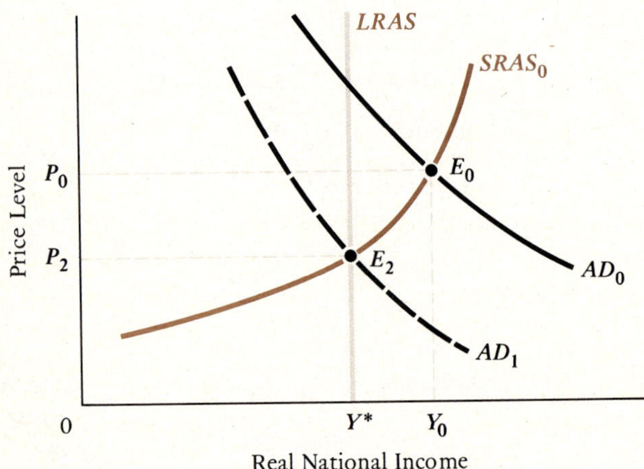

(ii) An inflationary gap removed by a leftward shift in *AD*

An inflationary gap may be removed by a leftward shift of the *SRAS* curve, a natural reduction in private-sector demand, or a policy-induced reduction in aggregate demand. Initially equilibrium is at E_0, with national income at Y_0 and the price level at P_0. The inflationary gap is Y^*Y_0.

As shown in part (i), the gap might be removed by a shift in the *SRAS* curve to $SRAS_1$. This decrease in aggregate supply could occur as a result of increases in wage rates and other input prices. The shift in the *SRAS* curve causes a movement up and to the left along AD_0. This establishes a new equilibrium at E_1, reducing income to its potential level, Y^*, and raising the price level to P_1.

As shown in part (ii), the gap might also be removed by a shift in the *AD* curve to AD_1. This decrease in aggregate demand could occur either because of a natural fall in private spending or because of contractionary fiscal policy. The shift in the *AD* curve causes a movement down and to the left along $SRAS_0$. This shifts the equilibrium to E_2, taking income to Y^* and the price level to P_2.

that reduces the marginal propensity to spend out of national income and hence, as we saw on page 606, reduces the multiplier. Built-in stabilizers lessen the magnitude of the fluctuations in national income caused by autonomous changes in such expenditures as investment. Furthermore, they do so without the government's having to react consciously to each change in national income as it occurs.

The three principal built-in stabilizers are taxes, government expenditure on goods and services, and government transfer payments.

Taxes

Direct taxes act as a built-in stabilizer. If there were no taxes, every change in national income of $1.00

would cause a change in disposable income of nearly a dollar.[3] With a marginal propensity to consume out of disposable income (*MPC*) of, say, 0.8, consumption would change by $0.80. With taxes, however, disposable income changes by less than $1.00; hence consumption expenditure will change by less than $0.80 when national income changes by $1.00 (even though the *MPC* is still 0.8).

Consider, for example, the extreme case in which the marginal personal income-tax rate is 100 percent. If there is an autonomous rise of $1 billion in investment expenditure, none of the $1 billion that accrues to households will be disposable income. There are no induced rounds of secondary expenditure; the rise in national income is limited to the initial $1 billion in new investment, and the multiplier is unity.

Similarly, a drop in investment expenditure of $1 billion reduces incomes earned in the investment industry by $1 billion and hence reduces government tax revenue by $1 billion. But it does not affect disposable income. Thus there are no secondary rounds of induced contractions in consumption experience to magnify the initial drop in national income caused by the investment decline.

Table 32-1 illustrates the principle by comparing the effects of two different marginal tax rates on the marginal propensity to spend out of national income in otherwise identical situations. The general proposition can be stated as follows.

Direct taxes reduce the magnitude of fluctuations in disposable income associated with any given fluctuation in national income. Hence, for a given marginal propensity to consume out of disposable income, they reduce the marginal propensity to spend out of national income.

Tax rates have increased greatly over this century. Although citizens complain about the burden of high taxes—perhaps with good reason—few are aware that high taxes have helped to reduce the large swings in national income and employment that would have otherwise plagued all industrial economies.

Government Purchases

Government purchases of goods and services tend to be relatively stable in the face of cyclical variations in national income. Much spending is already committed by earlier legislation, so only a small proportion can be varied at the government's discretion from one year to the next. And even this small part is slow to change. In contrast, private consumption and investment expenditure tend to vary with national income.

Thus the higher the share of government spending in the economy, the lower the cyclical instability of total expenditure. The twentieth century rise in the importance of the government's role in the economy may be a mixed blessing. One benefit, however, has been to put a large built-in stabilizer into the economy.

Social insurance and welfare services. Welfare payments rise with the unemployment that accompanies falling national income. Many welfare schemes are financed by taxes based on payrolls or earnings, and these taxes yield less when income is low. Thus welfare schemes act to make net additions to disposable income in times of slumps. They also make net subtractions in times of boom, when payments are low and revenues high.

The Canada Pension Plan is financed by taxes (called *contributions*) paid jointly by employers and employees. Unemployment insurance is financed by a payroll tax on employers and employees. During recessions these tax collections decrease while payments to the unemployed rise.[4]

Agricultural support policies. When there is a slump in the economy, there is a general decline in the demand for all goods, including agricultural prod-

[3] Undistributed profits and other minor items would still hold disposable income below national income. We ignore these in the text because taxes are the major source of the discrepancy between national income and disposable income.

[4] The Unemployment Insurance Act requires the federal government to adjust the payroll tax (referred to as the unemployment insurance premiums) annually so as to finance some of the changes in benefits paid out. This greatly reduces the automatic stabilizing influence of the unemployment insurance scheme.

TABLE 32-1 The Effect of Tax Rates on the Marginal Propensity to Spend out of National Income

Marginal rate of tax	Change in national income (millions) ΔY	Change in tax revenue (millions) ΔT	Change in disposable income (millions) ΔY_d	Change in consumption (millions) ΔC	Marginal propensity to spend out of national income $\Delta C/\Delta Y$
0.2	$1,000	$200	$800	$640	0.65
0.4	1,000	400	600	480	0.48

The higher the marginal rate of tax, the lower the marginal propensity to spend out of national income. When national income changes by $1,000, disposable income changes by $800 when the tax rate is 20 percent and by $600 when the tax rate is 40 percent. Although the *MPC* out of disposable income is 0.8 in both examples, consumption changes by $640 in the first case and by only $480 in the second. Although that households' *MPC* out of their disposable income is unchanged, an increase in tax rates lowers the marginal propensity to spend out of national income on which the size of the multiplier depends.

ucts. The free-market prices of agricultural goods fall, and government agricultural supports come into play. This means that government transfers, which support agricultural disposable income, rise as national income falls.

Transfer payments, which act as built-in stabilizers, tend to stabilize disposable income, and hence consumption expenditure, in the face of fluctuations in national income.

To illustrate this important proposition suppose that investment expenditure falls by $10 billion. In the absence of transfer payments, this would reduce disposable income by $6 billion. With an *MPC* out of disposable income of 0.8, this $6 billion reduction would cause an initial induced fall in consumption expenditure of $4.8 billion. Now assume instead that the fall in national income is accompanied by an increase in transfer payments of $4 billion. Instead of falling by $6 billion, disposable income now falls by only $2 billion. With the *MPC* out of disposable income still at 0.8, the initial induced fall in consumption expenditure is only $1.6 billion instead of $4.8 billion.

The Role of Built-In Stabilizers

Most built-in stabilizers are fairly new phenomena. Sixty years ago high marginal tax rates, high and stable government expenditures, farm stabilization policies, and large unemployment and other transfer payments were unknown in Canada. Each of these built-in stabilizers was the unforeseen by-product of policies originally adopted for other reasons. The progressive income tax arose out of a concern to make the distribution of income less unequal. Social insurance and agricultural support programs were adopted more because of a concern with the welfare of the individuals and groups involved than with preserving the health of the economy. But unforeseen or not, they work. (Even governments can be lucky.)

No matter how lucky governments have been in finding built-in stabilizers, these cannot reduce fluctuations to zero. Stabilizers work by producing stabilizing reactions to changes in income. But until income changes, the stabilizer is not even brought into play.

Discretionary Fiscal Policy

Short-term, minor fluctuations that are not removed automatically by built-in stabilizers cannot, given present knowledge and techniques, be removed by consciously fine tuning the economy. We have already seen, however, that larger and more persistent gaps sometimes appear. In these cases there may be time for the government to operate a discretionary fiscal policy, that is, to institute changes in taxes and spending that are designed to offset gaps. To do this effectively an administration must periodically make conscious decisions to alter fiscal policy. The Department of Finance must study current economic trends and predict the probable course of the economy. If the predicted course is unsatisfactory, the cabinet must be persuaded to adopt the appropriate fiscal stance.

In considering discretionary fiscal policy, we shall deal with two related questions. First, is it important that the fiscal change be easily reversible? Second, does it matter whether households and firms regard the government's fiscal changes as temporary or as long-lived?

The Need for Reversibility

To see what is involved in the issue of reversibility, assume that national income is normally at or near potential. A *temporary* slump in private investment then opens up a large recessionary gap. If the gap persists, eventually the government decides to adopt some combination of tax cuts and spending increases to push the economy back toward full employment. If private investment recovers to its pre-slump level and the government does not quickly reverse this policy, an inflationary gap will open up as the combination of rising investment expenditure and continuing fiscal stimulus takes national income into the inflationary range. The process is illustrated in Figure 32-3.

Alternatively, assume that starting from the same situation of approximately full employment, a temporary investment boom opens up an inflationary gap. Rather than let the inflation persist, the government reduces expenditure and raises taxes to remove the gap. If, when the investment boom is over and investment expenditure returns to its original level, the government does nothing, a recessionary gap will open up and a slump may ensue. This, too, is analyzed in Figure 32-3.

Fiscal policies designed to remove persistent output gaps resulting from abnormal levels of private expenditure will destabilize the economy unless the policies can be rapidly reversed once private expenditure returns to its more normal level.

FIGURE 32-3 Effects of Fiscal Policies That Are Not Reversed

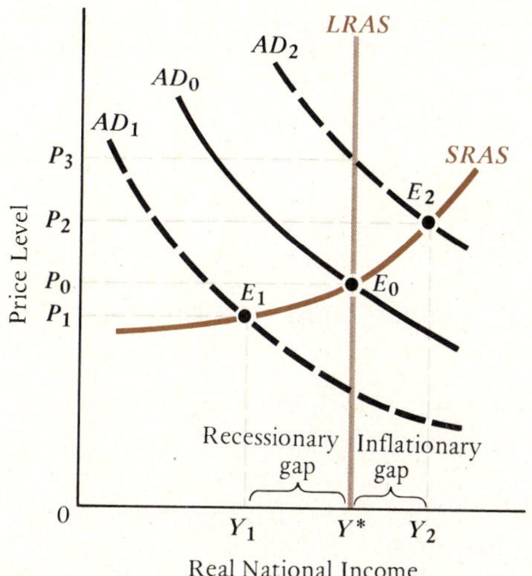

Fiscal policies that are initially appropriate may become inappropriate when private expenditure shifts. The normal level of the aggregate demand function is assumed to be AD_0, leaving income normally at Y^* and the price level at P_0. Suppose a slump in private investment shifts aggregate demand to AD_1, lowering national income to Y_1 and causing a recessionary gap of Y^*Y_1.

The government now introduces fiscal expansion to restore aggregate demand to AD_0 and national income to Y^*. Suppose that private investment recovers, raising aggregate demand to AD_2. If fiscal policy can be quickly reversed, aggregate demand can be returned to AD_0 and income stabilized at Y^*. If the policy is not quickly reversed, equilibrium will be at E_2 and an inflationary gap Y^*Y_2 will open up. This will cause wages to rise and thus shift the *SRAS* curve leftward and eventually restore Y^* at a price level P_3.

Now suppose that starting from equilibrium E_0 a persistent investment boom takes AD_0 to AD_2. To stop the price level from rising in the face of the newly opened inflationary gap, the government introduces fiscal restraint, thereby shifting aggregate demand back to AD_0. Further assume, however, that the investment boom soon comes to a halt so that the aggregate demand curve shifts down to AD_1. Unless the fiscal policy can be rapidly reversed, a recessionary gap will open up and equilibrium income will fall to Y_1.

Even if the output gaps persist long enough for fiscal changes to be agreed on and to be made, subsequent rapid changes in private expenditure may require a quick reversal of the fiscal stance—a reversal that cannot always be made easily. As a result, many economists argue that caution dictates responding only to large output gaps that are expected to persist and even then attempting to close only part of the gap in anticipation of some stabilizing change in private expenditure.

"Temporary" Versus "Long Lasting" Changes

Consider the attempt to remove a persistent output gap through changes in tax rates. Such a gap, though persistent, is unlikely to be a permanent feature of the economy. The relevant tax changes should therefore be advocated only "for the duration," that is, for as long as the government thinks the gaps would persist without the tax changes. A discretionary fiscal policy designed to remove such a gap might take the form, say, of a surcharge on income taxes for a two-year period. Similarly, a recession might be fought by temporary tax rebates.

Such tax changes cause changes in household disposable income and, according to the theory of the consumption function encountered in Chapter 28, would cause changes in consumption expenditure. Consumption expenditure would increase as tax rebates rose in times of recessionary gaps and would decrease as tax surcharges rose in times of inflationary gaps. This theory of the effects of short-term tax changes relies on the assumption that household consumption depends on current disposable income.

Permanent-income theories. Many recent theories of the consumption function have emphasized what is called a household's expected **permanent income** or **lifetime income** as the major determinant of consumption. According to such theories, households have expectations about their lifetime incomes and adjust their consumption to those expectations. When temporary fluctuations in income occur, households maintain their long-term consumption plans and use their stocks of wealth as buffers to absorb income fluctuations. Thus when there is a purely temporary rise in income, households will save all the extra income; when there is a purely temporary fall in income, households will maintain their long-term consumption plans by using up part of their wealth accumulated through past saving.

To the extent that such behavior occurs, it will have serious consequences for short-lived tax changes. A temporary tax rebate raises households' disposable income, but households, recognizing it as temporary, would not revise their expenditure plans and instead save the extra money. Thus the hoped-for increase in aggregate expenditure would not occur. Similarly, a temporary rise in tax rates reduces disposable income, but that might merely cause a drop in saving. Thus total expenditure is again unchanged, and a temporary surcharge fails to reduce the inflationary gap.

If households' consumption expenditure is more closely related to lifetime income than to current income, tax changes that are known to be of short duration will have relatively small effects on current consumption.[5]

The advantage of having households perceive tax rate changes as long lasting conflicts with the need for the reversibility of cuts and surcharges if they are not to destabilize the economy at a later date. This conflict reduces the usefulness of changes in tax rates as a stabilizing tool.

Judging the Stance of Fiscal Policy

Governments seek to shift aggregate demand by consciously changing their fiscal policy stance. The *stance* of fiscal policy refers to its expansionary or contractionary effects on the economy. An expansionary fiscal policy increases aggregate demand and thus tends to increase national income; a contractionary fiscal policy reduces aggregate demand and tends to lower national income.

In Chapter 31 and earlier in this one, we looked separately at taxes, purchases of goods and services, and transfer payments as means of influencing ag-

[5] The permanent-income theory is not as devastating for fiscal policy as it may seem. This important matter is discussed further in the appendix to this chapter.

gregate demand. But people want a summary measure, one number to express the government's effect on the economy.

The Inadequacy of the Deficit As a Measure

Not surprisingly, people tend to focus on the government's budget deficit to judge the stance of fiscal policy. A rising government deficit is often taken to indicate an expansionary fiscal policy, and a falling deficit is often taken to indicate a contractionary policy. But a number of problems make the deficit an unreliable guide to judging the fiscal stance.

The deficit is the difference between the government's outlays and receipts, its receipts being largely tax revenue. But tax revenue is the result of the interaction of tax rates, which the government sets, and the level of national income, which is influenced by many forces beyond the government's control.

The major tools of fiscal policy are government expenditure and tax *rates*. The budget deficit or surplus is the relation between government expenditure and tax *revenues*.

Assume, for example, that government expenditure is constant at $100 billion and that at current tax rates the government takes 20 percent of national income in taxes. Suppose that national income is $500 billion, so tax revenues are also $100 billion. Now assume that tax revenues sink to $75 billion, opening up a $25 billion budget deficit. This could be the result of a discretionary cut in tax rates so that they now yield only 15 percent of an unchanged national income. It could also be the result of a fall in national income itself to $375 billion, with tax rates constant. In the first case a conscious change in the government's fiscal policy causes the fall in tax revenues. In the second case a fall in national income that is not the result of fiscal policy causes tax revenue to fall; the increase in the deficit simply reflects the operation of the automatic stabilizers discussed earlier in this chapter.

This example illustrates why judging changes in the stance of fiscal policy from changes in the government's budget balance can be misleading. Doing so confuses changes in the deficit due to fluctuations in national income, which may not be the result of shifts in fiscal policy, with changes in the deficit that are the result of shifts in fiscal policy.

Cyclically Adjusted Deficit

When measuring changes in the stance of fiscal policy, it is common to calculate changes in the estimated budget balance on the assumption that national income is constant at some base level. Holding income constant ensures that measured changes in the budget balance are due to changes in policy. The base most commonly used is potential national income. Because estimating the budget balance for a given level of national income controls for cyclically induced fluctuations in expenditures and tax revenues, it is referred to as making the *cyclical adjustment;* the resulting measure is referred to as the *cyclically adjusted budget balance,* or **cyclically adjusted deficit (CAD).**[6] It is an estimate of government expenditure minus government tax revenues, not as they actually are but as they would be if national income had been at its potential level. Table 32-2 shows the actual and cyclically adjusted deficit on an annual basis since 1970.

Changes in the cyclically adjusted deficit are an indicator of changes in the stance of fiscal policy.

Box 32-2 (see page 683) introduces the concept of the *budget deficit function* and discusses how it, along with the cyclically adjusted deficit, can avoid the errors that arise from using the current budget balance as an indicator of the stance of fiscal policy.[7]

[6] This concept used to be called the full-employment surplus. The change from *full-employment* to *cyclically adjusted* came when the amount of unemployment associated with potential income rose rapidly in the 1970s, and referring to so much unemployment as full employment became embarrassing. The change from *surplus* to *deficit* occurred because in the 1960s people were trying to stress the depressing effects of surpluses whereas in the 1980s people wanted to stress the alleged harmful effects of deficits.

[7] The cyclically adjusted deficit is vastly superior to the actual budget deficit for estimating year-to-year changes in the stance of fiscal policy. But the balanced budget multiplier indicates one reason why even the cyclically adjusted deficit is not a completely reliable measure of the fiscal stance. The balanced budget multiplier suggests that a dollar of spending will increase aggregate demand by more than a dollar of tax revenue will decrease it. Therefore, to measure the effect of fiscal actions on aggregate demand properly a more sophisticated measure that takes account of these differential effects is required. Such a measure, called the *weighted cyclically adjusted deficit,* is often used by economists in detailed empirical work assessing fiscal policy.

TABLE 32-2 Measured, Cyclically Adjusted, and Structural Budget Balances for the Federal Government, 1970–1986 *(billions of dollars)*

Year	Measured budget deficit[a]	Cyclically adjusted budget deficit[a]	Structural budget deficit (cyclically and inflation adjusted)
1970	−0.3	−0.5	−0.9
1971	0.1	0.0	−0.3
1972	0.6	0.7	0.2
1973	−0.4	0.6	−0.5
1974	−1.1	0.5	−0.9
1975	3.8	3.9	3.0
1976	3.4	4.1	3.0
1977	7.3	6.8	5.8
1978	10.7	9.9	8.3
1979	9.3	8.9	4.8
1980	10.1	8.2	3.6
1981	8.0	6.2	0.0
1982	21.1	11.8	5.0
1983	24.0	13.3	8.2
1984	30.5	21.3	18.4
1985	32.3	24.3	19.2
1986	24.9	18.3	13.2

Source: Department of Finance, *Economic Review*.

[a] A minus sign indicates a surplus.

Changes in the measured budget balance reflect both changes in output and inflation. The cyclically adjusted deficit controls for the influences of the level of output, while the last column adds to this an adjustment for the effect of the inflation rate. Changes in the last column thus give a measure of changes in fiscal policy. Several things can be noted about the adjustments. First, the inflation adjustment is always negative, so column 3 is always smaller than column 2 (if column 2 shows a deficit, column 3 will show a smaller deficit or even a surplus). Second, because the economy has operated at less than full employment since 1975, the cyclical adjustment has also been negative, so column 2 has been smaller than column 1. Actual budget deficits have been growing rather dramatically. Part of this is due to persistent slack in the economy and to high inflation, but column 3 indicates that fiscal policy was expansionary in the early 1980s before turning contractionary in 1986.

The cyclical adjustment just discussed distinguishes between changes in the budget balance that arise due to the operation of *automatic* stabilizers and those that arise due to *discretionary* policy. To judge the stance of fiscal policy, it is necessary to make a second adjustment to the measured budget balance—one that focuses on a component of the budget that has (virtually) no impact on aggregate demand. This component is the inflation premium included in the nominal interest payments made by the government to service the national debt.

As we saw in Box 31-1, nominal interest rates can be divided into a real component and an inflation premium. Debt-service payments made by the government thus also have a real and an inflation premium component. Whereas the real component constitutes a transfer from the government to holders of the government debt as payment for use of the principal, the inflation premium does not. This is because the inflation premium is exactly offset by a reduction in the real value of the principal.

Suppose that the current value of the government's debt is $200 billion. Suppose also that in the current year the government runs a deficit of $20 billion and that the current inflation rate is 10 percent. On crude measures the government has a deficit of $20 billion; this corresponds to the increase in the nominal value of the government's indebtedness. On an inflation-adjusted basis, the deficit is zero. This is because the real value—or purchasing power—of the debt is unchanged, even though the nominal stock of debt has risen by $20 billion (10 percent) from $200 billion to $220 billion. Because the real value of the government's indebtedness is unchanged, the "effective," or inflation-adjusted, deficit is zero. The *inflation adjustment* is equal to the inflation premium component of government debt-service payments.

This makes it clear why the inflation premium component of the deficit contributes little or nothing to aggregate demand. The private sector receives the payment but suffers an equivalent reduction in the real value of its holdings of government bonds. To maintain their asset position, recipients of the government interest payments must save the entire inflation premium component. Hence the net effect of this component on aggregate demand will be approximately zero—the government's demand will be

BOX 32-2

The Budget Deficit Function

The distinction between changes in the budget balance due to changes in the fiscal stance and those due to cyclical changes in the economy is easily seen in what is called the government's *budget deficit function.*

The budget deficit function (curve B in the figure) expresses the difference between the government's expenditures and its tax revenues at each level of national income for given levels of government expenditure and tax rates. The curve in part (i) shows that deficits are associated with low levels of income and surpluses with high levels of income; this is because at a given tax *rate,* tax *revenue* rises with national income.

Changes in the government's budget balance induced by changes in national income are shown by *movements along* a given budget deficit function. Changes in the budget balance due to policy-induced changes in the level of government expenditure or tax rates are shown by *shifts* in the budget function. Such shifts indicate a different budget balance at each level of national income.

In part (ii), a fall in national income from Y_0 to Y_1 causes the actual budget to go from a surplus of D_0 to a deficit of D_1. Government expenditure and tax rates are unchanged; that is, the fiscal policy stance is unchanged. The unchanged fiscal stance is correctly captured by the constant cyclically adjusted deficit, *CAD*, measured at the (constant) potential level of national income, Y^*.

Part (iii) illustrates a contractionary change in the stance of fiscal policy. A government expenditure cut or a tax rate increase shifts the budget deficit function from B_0 to B_1. Now there is a smaller budget deficit *at each level of national income.* This change is correctly captured by the fall in the cyclically adjusted deficit from *CAD* to *CAD'*.

To see the misleading effects of judging changes in the policy stance from changes in the measured deficit, suppose that national income had fallen from Y_0 to Y_1 at the same time that the budget deficit function shifted from B_0 to B_1. In that case the measured balance would have gone from surplus (D) to deficit (D') despite the fall in the cyclically adjusted deficit from *CAD* to *CAD'*. Thus the measured balance would have indicated an expansionary fiscal policy when the fiscal stance was in fact contractionary.

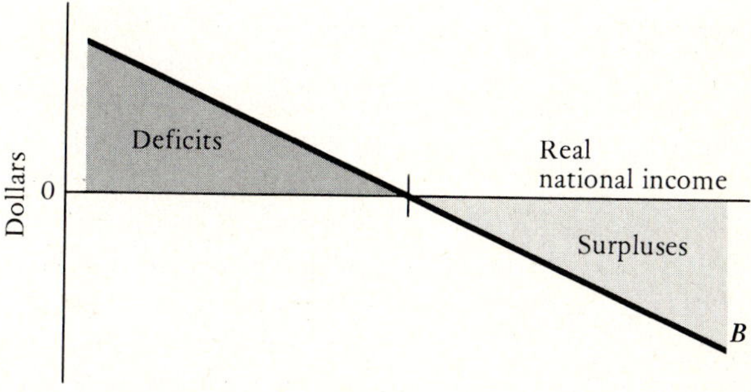

(i) The budget deficit function

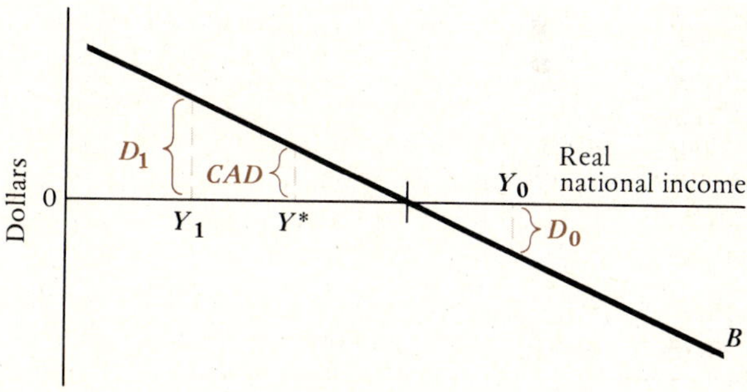

(ii) Changes in the measured deficit

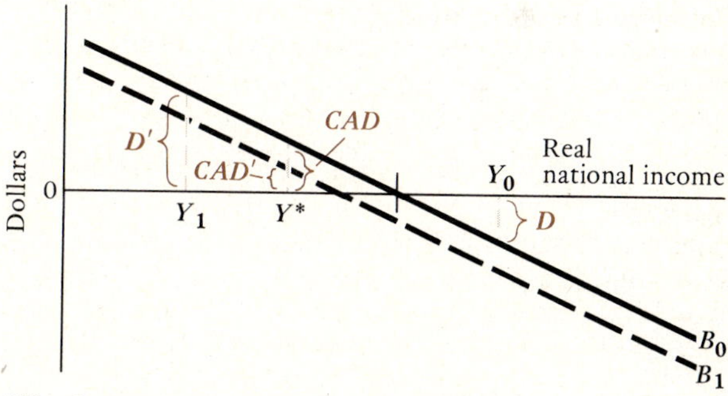

(iii) Changes in the cyclically adjusted deficit

offset by a fall in private-sector demand as households raise their saving in order to recoup some of the inflation-induced fall in their real wealth.

Hence to measure the net influence of the government on aggregate demand, it is necessary to subtract the inflation premium component of nominal interest payments from the measured budget balance.

The structural balance. When the cyclical and inflation adjustments are made to the government's budget balance, a useful measure of discretionary fiscal policy is obtained. This is called the *structural balance,* or, more commonly, the structural deficit. This is shown in the third column in Table 32-2.

The Experience of Fiscal Policy

The 1930s saw massive unemployment that persisted through nearly a decade. This experience left many people with the misconception that discretionary fiscal policy cannot solve an unemployment problem. The facts, as reviewed in Box 32-1, show that fiscal policy contributed little to recovery from the depression not because it failed to work but because it was not used. Most of the increase in the deficit that occurred was due to the decline in national income rather than to any shift in the high-employment deficit that would have signaled the adoption of a more expansive policy stance. When Keynesian fiscal policy was finally tried under the impetus of the wartime emergency, it proved spectacularly successful.

An important legacy of World War II was a radically altered view of the role of government expenditures and taxes as instruments of government policy. The 1945 White Paper on Employment and Income established the principle that the federal government had a responsibility to maintain high and stable levels of employment and income.

The implementation of this policy was greatly complicated by the unsettled state of federal-provincial relations. As early as 1940 a proposal to widen federal jurisdiction had been made by the Rowell-Sirois Commission, but the division of powers has continued to be a contentious issue to the present day. Through a succession of temporary agreements (see Chapter 24), the federal government has retained sufficient power to operate a flexible fiscal policy, and consideration of the desired degree of fiscal stimulus or restraint has become an important element in the budgets presented to Parliament.

The 1960s and 1970s

In comparison with earlier and later periods, the quarter century following World War II was one of prosperity and steady growth. One prolonged slump occurred in 1958–1963. By 1965 the recessionary gap had been virtually eliminated, but in retrospect it appears that policymakers misjudged the situation and allowed the economy to develop an inflationary gap. Tax increases and some expenditure cuts were imposed in the years 1966–1968, but the effects of the fiscal restraint came too late to prevent the buildup of inflationary forces. At the end of the 1960s tight monetary policy reinforced the fiscal restraint, and unemployment rose in 1969 and 1970.

The 1970s began with a substantial recessionary gap. Expansionary policies were put into place. But the situation was misread because of a leftward shift in the long-run aggregate supply curve. (The reasons for this are discussed in Chapter 37.) Looking back we now see that the shift in the *LRAS* curve created an inflationary gap, which the government's expansionary policy inadvertently served to widen.

In late 1974 a series of shocks caused a downturn in the world economy. In response, an expansionary budget was brought down late in the year. As Table 32-2 shows, the federal budget moved to a deficit position in 1975, and the deficit grew steadily through the rest of the decade. In part this reflects discretionary fiscal policy, because the structural balance also moved into substantial deficit. However, the actual deficit also reflects the influence of other factors, including more generous unemployment insurance provisions and a relatively high rate of inflation. The latter caused outlays to grow rapidly because many federal transfer payments such as old-age pensions were indexed to inflation. Tax revenues also rose due to inflation, although not as quickly as they would have had the income tax system not been indexed. Since both expenditures and revenues grew, the difference between them also grew. (See Box 32-3 on page 686 for further discussion of indexation of the tax system.)

Tax cuts were introduced in 1977 and 1978 when, despite steady but gradual growth, the economy was thought to be operating below capacity. In December 1979 the minority Conservative government introduced a budget that aimed to reduce the size of the deficit. But the government fell on the issue of the budget, and the Liberals were returned to power in the election of February 1980. Just two months later a Liberal minibudget reintroduced two of the tax measures proposed in the defeated Conservative budget.

The 1960s and 1970s were thus years of fiscal activism, if not fiscal fine tuning. Discretionary tax and expenditure changes were constantly used in an attempt to stabilize the economy. Much of the reason active fiscal policy was so much in vogue was the dramatic success of tax cuts introduced in the United States in 1964. This episode, still cited by proponents of fiscal activism, is discussed in Box 32-4 (see page 688).

The overall evidence from the period, however, suggests that the record of fiscal activism was quite mixed: Sometimes fiscal policy moderated cyclical swings, and sometimes it accentuated them. As a result, fiscal activism fell from favor in most circles.[8]

The 1980s

In the early 1980s fiscal policy was complicated by two major problems. First, as already noted (see Table 32-2), the federal budget deficit had become so large that worries were emerging about its implications. Second, the rate of inflation was unacceptably high despite an (also unacceptable) high rate of unemployment. (Inflation was about 10 percent and unemployment was over 8 percent at the beginning of 1980.) For the first time since the government has accepted responsibility for stabilizing the economy, the direction—not simply the extent—of desirable changes in the stance of fiscal policy was at issue. Reducing the recessionary gap called for an expansionary fiscal stance; reducing inflation and concern about the deficit called for a contractionary fiscal stance. Successive budgets in the 1980s introduced small changes in the overall fiscal stance, being pulled one way and the other by the two competing objectives.[9]

In late 1981 a major worldwide downturn set in, turning 1982 into the worst recession since the Great Depression. Still caught on the horns of the dilemma, the budget of 1982 made little change in the fiscal stance.

In 1983 the budget tried to resolve the dilemma with short-term measures aimed at unemployment and longer-term measures aimed at the deficit. The budget introduced moderate stimulus—about $6 billion phased in over two years—combined with a series of measures, including tax increases, to offset this stimulus later. This *tilt*—stimulus now, restraint later—was widely viewed as an appropriate way to stimulate the economy without increasing the future cyclically adjusted deficit.

In 1983 there was a strong recovery. Real output grew by over 6 percent and inflation slowed dramatically. The budget introduced in February 1984 maintained a steady course, giving rise to very little change in the stance of fiscal policy. It also did very little to address the persistent budget deficit.

A Conservative government was elected in fall 1984. The new government had strong support in the business and financial communities and appeared committed to reversing the trend of rising government deficits. In November 1984 it published an Agenda Paper that laid out a number of "fundamental principles" to guide fiscal policy, including these:

1. To achieve sizable year-over-year reductions in the deficit
2. To ensure that the majority of the reduction in

[8] The fall from favor of fiscal policy activism was given a further push with the election of U.S. President Ronald Reagan, an avowed fiscal conservative, in 1980. Ironically, despite the Reagan administration's disavowal of fiscal *policy,* its actions had significant fiscal *effects.* Many economists believe that the dramatic increase in the deficit under him played a major role in stimulating the economy and ending the 1982 recession. It also stimulated an extensive public debate about the consequences of persistent budget deficits, and Congress debated and passed legislation (the Gramm-Rudman-Hollings Bill) to try to reduce the deficit.

[9] One important feature of the October 1980 budget was the introduction of the National Energy Program, designed to increase the federal government's share of the revenues from petroleum production mainly at the expense of the industry. Also, to help increase Canadian participation in the industry, a series of grants for exploration and development that would increase with the Canadian ownership of a firm were introduced. The NEP was dismantled by the Conservative government in 1984.

BOX 32-3

Inflation Indexing of Income Taxes

In Canada, marginal tax rates rise with income, as Table 24-2 on page 497 shows. Many economists believe that beyond some point high marginal tax rates provide strong disincentives to the supply of effort. A steelworker with a high marginal tax rate is less inclined to work overtime in periods of boom, and a lawyer or a highly trained technical consultant is less likely to accept one more case, the higher his or her marginal tax rate.

In inflationary situations, when an individual's money income rises, the purchasing power of this income does not necessarily rise. For example, a secretary who gets a 10 percent raise is no better off when the prices of everything she purchases also rise by 10 percent *and* the fraction of income she pays in taxes does not change. However, with marginal tax rates that rise with money income, the fraction of income she pays in taxes will rise; as a result, her *after-tax money income* will rise by less than 10 percent. Even though her *before-tax real income* remains unchanged (prices and before-tax money income both rise by 10 percent), her *after-tax real income* will fall because she now pays in taxes a larger fraction of her income.

This is because inflation, by increasing the dollar value of the taxpayer's money income, moves the taxpayer into a tax bracket with a higher marginal tax rate. Unless the growth of before-tax nominal (money) income exceeds the rate of inflation, the increase in taxes will necessarily reduce after-tax real income.

Indexation of income tax prevents this automatic increase in tax rates in response to inflation. When a tax system is indexed, the rate of taxation at any given level of *real* income remains constant. The tax schedule—that is, the tax bracket at which a particular marginal rate applies—is adjusted each year to allow for the effects of inflation on nominal incomes. If inflation has averaged 10 percent in the economy but average real income is unchanged, the average person's nominal income will go up by 10 percent. If before the inflation there was a $30,000 cutoff for a 40 percent marginal tax rate, the cutoff would now move up by 10 percent, to $33,000. People whose initial incomes were under $30,000 and whose real income remained unchanged would now have money income under $33,000 and would not move to a higher tax bracket. People whose income before the inflation was $30,000 and whose *real* income grew would, by definition, have nominal incomes that grew in excess of the 10 percent inflation rate; they would move to a

---

the deficit is achieved through better management and expenditure restraint

3. To reduce the growth rate of the national debt to less than that of national income by the end of the decade[10]

Finance Minister Michael Wilson brought down three budgets over the following 2½ years. How did they stack up against the fundamental principles?

The first fiscal principle was clearly honored—as shown in Figure 32-4 (see page 690), the trend of rising deficits was reversed. Each of the Wilson budgets received some vote of confidence from financial markets, although the vote was in most cases reserved rather than enthusiastic; the deficit cuts were in fact smaller than many market participants had hoped for. Further, as we shall discuss shortly, his third budget, delivered in February 1987, caused concern that the deficit was not firmly on a downward track.

There was also progress on the commitment to achieve some expenditure restraint; approximately 70 percent of the deficit reductions came on the expenditure side of the budget. Total program spending (all spending exclusive of interest payments on the national debt) declined not only as a share of GDP but also in absolute terms in fiscal 1985–1986, the first such decline in 25 years. Nevertheless, these budgets involved substantial tax increases. Personal

[10] The paper also included a commitment to reduce the government's financial requirements, the amount the government actually borrows on financial markets, equal to the deficit less the government's net revenues on "off-budget" items, the major component of which is the money it collects from its employees' contributions to the public service pension plan.

higher tax bracket. Similarly, people whose real income fell would move to a lower tax bracket.

In an indexed tax system, average and marginal tax rates depend only on real income.

In his 1973 budget John Turner, then minister of finance, indexed the Canadian income tax system. In the very high inflation of the 1970s indexation held Canadian tax burdens below what they would have been had the tax schedule of 1972 remained in force in terms of money income. By the same token it has reduced the tax revenues of the federal government over the same period.

There are arguments against indexing the tax system. For example, some people think that indexation is inflationary because it reduces the public's resistance to inflation. With an unindexed tax system, inflation leads to higher taxes and people will therefore resist inflation. Indexation of the tax system, it is argued, reduces public opposition to inflation and thus makes it easier for governments to justify inflationary policies. Others argue that indexation will reduce inflation because it reduces the payoff to governments from pursuing inflationary policies. The increased tax bite that arises from an unindexed tax system in the presence of inflation provides a great incentive for governments to follow inflationary policies; real resources can be transferred from the private sector to the public purse simply by inflating people into higher tax brackets. Thus it is not clear whether indexation leads to more or less inflationary policies.

Politicians do not necessarily like inflation-indexed tax systems. In the United States the tax system has not been indexed. However, since 1975 the U.S. Congress has passed a series of tax cuts that can be understood as an attempt to undo the automatic increases in taxes that would have resulted from inflation. Politicians were in reality indexing the tax system each year, and they were doing it in a manner that gave them political credit for passing tax cuts. This option has not been available to Canadian politicians until the last few years as a number of the indexation provisions in the Canadian tax system have been eliminated or restricted. (Ironically, in 1981 the Reagan administration committed itself to eventual indexation of the U.S. tax system, while the Canadian tax reform of 1987 did nothing to restore indexation to the Canadian tax system.)

---

income taxes and the federal sales tax—both highly visible—were increased. Less widely known was that less visible corporate and energy tax revenues fell as a share of GDP. (Some of these tax measures, in particular changes in the corporate tax system and the broadening of the federal sales tax base, could be interpreted as the first stages of the comprehensive tax reform package introduced in June 1987. See the discussion in Box 24-2 on page 506.)

Mr. Wilson's third principle—reducing the rate of growth of debt to below that of GDP—appeared also to be within grasp in his first two budgets. But events subsequent to the February 1986 budget suggested that the goal would not be achieved before the end of the decade.

In the summer of 1986 the Canadian economy suffered from two major international shocks—a dramatic fall in the world price of oil and a collapse in the international markets for Canadian agricultural exports. Automatic stabilizers in the form of increased payments under the terms of various agricultural support programs and reduced tax revenue from the energy sector were thus triggered, and in addition the government decided to provide farmers with an additional $1 billion in discretionary funds. As a result the deficit and debt projections made in the February 1986 budget had to be revised; the 1986–1987 deficit was no longer expected to fall below $30 billion, and the rate of growth of the debt was no longer expected to be below that of GDP by the end of the decade.

Thus while progress in controlling the federal deficit was certainly visible, the reductions were judged quite modest. After four years of sustained

BOX 32-4

Fiscal Drag and the 1964 U.S. Tax Cuts: A Fiscal Policy Success

Fiscal drag, first diagnosed in the early 1960s, is the problem produced by economic growth acting on stable government expenditure and fixed tax rates. In normal circumstances, growth leads to a falling cyclically adjusted budget deficit. (In terms of the figure in Box 32-2, the drag is due to a movement along the budget deficit function as potential income grows.)

Throughout the 1950s potential output rose 2 to 3 percent per year because of economic growth. With tax rates constant, rising national income causes rising tax revenues. But because in the 1950s government expenditure was relatively stable, rising tax revenues exerted a drag on the growth of aggregate demand by taking income away from households, who would have spent it, and transferring it to governments, who did not. There was thus a falling cyclically adjusted deficit.

This is illustrated in the figure, where we start with the curves AD_0, $LRAS_0$, and $SRAS_0$. These yield equilibrium at E_0 and potential income Y_0^*. Economic growth now shifts the supply curves to $LRAS_1$ and $SRAS_1$. As a result of fiscal drag, however, the aggregate demand curve shifts only to AD_1 rather than to AD_2, which would have been required to sustain full employment. An output gap of $Y_1Y_2^*$ is thus created.

To prevent the exertion of an ever-stronger depressing effect on national income by a falling *CAD*, it is necessary periodically either to increase government spending or to reduce tax rates. This problem

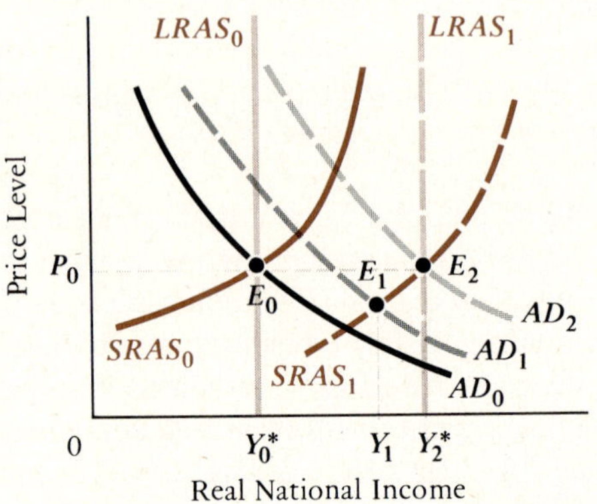

arose in the American economy during the 1950s. Economic growth was producing a declining *CAD*. As a result each cyclical upswing was weaker than the one before it, and the average level of unemployment over the cycle was creeping upward. By the beginning of the 1960s many economists were calling for a tax cut to remove the drag and restore full employment. Their concern was not with cyclical stabilization of the economy but with solving a problem associated with long-term economic growth.

When the 1964 tax cut was enacted, the predicted effects occurred. The tax cuts were perceived to be permanent and the increased (current and expected future) disposable income caused an increase in consumption expenditure that in turn caused an increase in national income and employment.

economic growth, and after three federal budgets that focused on deficit reduction, government deficits remained historically very large. Many commentators felt that deficits would soon start to grow again, given that a federal election was on the horizon. The various parties were gearing up to articulate expenditure programs and tax reductions that they felt would help their popularity with the electorate but could only serve to maintain or enlarge the deficit and thus continue to add to the growing stock of public debt.

In the mid 1980s a new phenomenon began to emerge as a source of concern—provincial government deficits. We take this up below when we discuss the implications of persistent large government deficits and consequent growth of the national debt.

The Economics of Budget Deficits

The average Canadian has some idea of the size of the federal budget deficit (or at least a sense that it is too big). The average West German is not likely to have any idea of the size of the government's budget deficit or a strong opinion on whether it is too large. Why is our budget deficit so large? Why do we worry so much about it? Is it really such a big problem?

Facts About the Deficit

The recent emergence of record federal budget deficits is shown in Figure 32-4. Part (i) shows total federal spending (on goods and services and transfers) and total federal revenues since 1970 as a share of GDP. Over the period 1975–1980 expenditures were a relatively constant fraction of GDP, while tax revenues fell sharply. This is the basis for the Department of Finance view that discretionary tax cuts introduced in the 1970s were responsible for the growing deficit. Other analysts, however, argue that it was the failure to constrain expenditure in the face of the tax cuts that is responsible and that there was also a switch toward delivering some transfers through tax concessions rather than direct expenditure.

If the source of the growth in the deficit in the 1970s was unclear, it was less so in the 1980s. The increase in the deficit that occurred in the 1981–1983 period reflect the combined effects of the severe recession in 1982, some mild discretionary fiscal expansion, and increased interest payments on the government's debt. The latter was due to both the sharp rise in interest rates that occurred and the cumulative effect of the persistent deficits on the size of the government debt.

Part (ii) shows the deficit, again measured as a share of GDP—this is the shaded area between the two lines in part (i). The government budget had been in deficit prior to 1982, although as a percentage of GDP the deficit had not been unusually large by historical standards. After 1982, however, the deficit increased dramatically as a share of GDP. As can be seen from Table 32-2, the cyclically adjusted deficit grew even more than the actual deficit over the period 1982–1985.

So far we have focused on the federal government budget balance. We could also consider the deficit on a total government basis; the difference between that and the federal deficit is due to the net deficit position of the provincial and municipal governments. For most of the past two decades, provincial and municipal governments combined have experienced only relatively small budget imbalances, and hence most of the concern about budget deficits in Canada has been focused on the federal government. In fact, for most of the last two decades, the total government deficit was smaller than the federal government deficit, reflecting the combined surpluses of the other two levels of government. But in 1986 the total government deficit was larger.

The reduction in the deficit of the federal government has been offset by the increase in the deficits of provincial and municipal governments.

In 1986 *all* 10 provincial governments were running deficits. Although deficits had been the order of the day in certain provinces, they had traditionally been offset by surpluses in other provinces. In 1986 a deficit emerged in Alberta, which had typically been a surplus province due to large oil revenues. It began running a deficit in response to depressed economic conditions brought about by adverse shocks to the agricultural and energy sectors. Most worrisome, perhaps, was the deficit in Ontario, a province that had been experiencing a sustained economic boom since 1983.

Why Worry About Deficits?

It is possible to identify a set of conditions whereby neither government deficits nor the public debt would matter in the economy. However, the required conditions (discussed in more detail in Appendix B to Chapter 39) are so stringent that most economists believe that the deficit does exert important influences on the economy.

One such influence is the short-run stabilizing or destabilizing role in the economy emphasized earlier in this chapter. A second is a potential adverse long-run effect on income and welfare, to which we now turn. People worry about the long-run effects of persistent deficits for many reasons. We will look at four.

FIGURE 32-4 Federal Revenues, Expenditures, and Budget Balances, 1967–1986 ***(percentage of GDP, national accounts basis)***

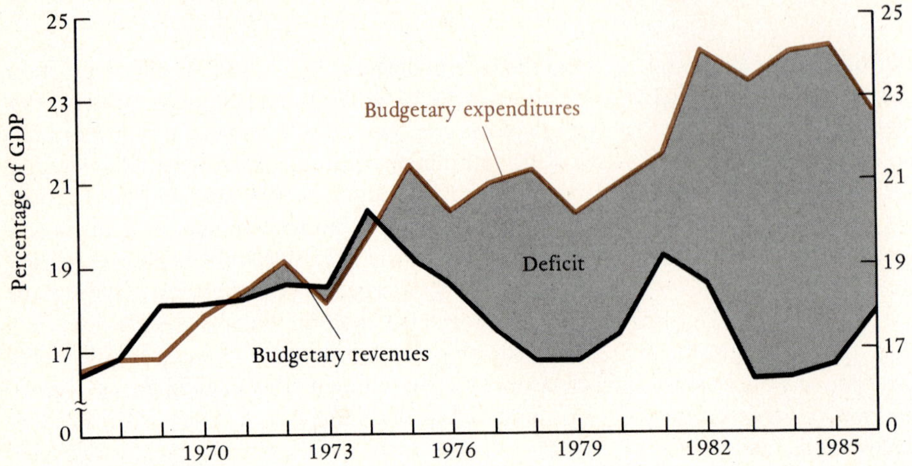

(i) Revenues and expenditures

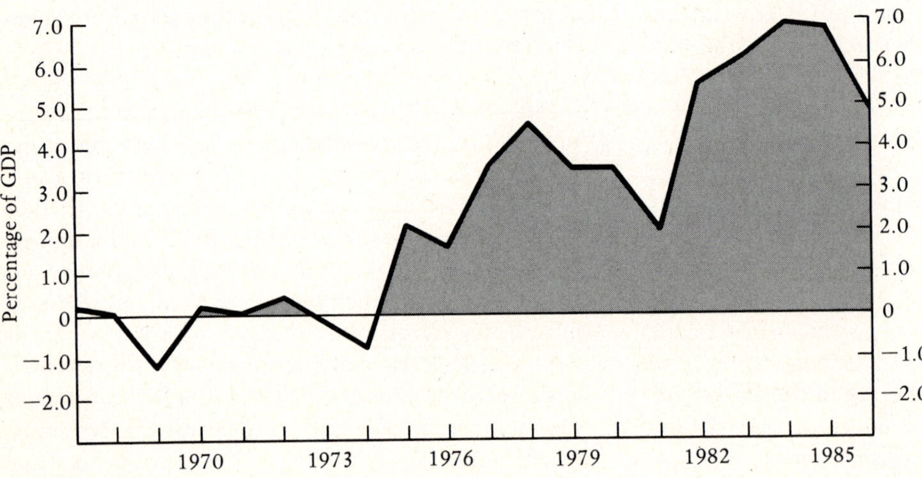

(ii) The budgetary deficit

The deficit has grown sharply in recent years, reflecting rapid increases in expenditures relative to revenues. Part (i) shows expenditures and revenues of the federal government, both as a percentage of national income. The difference is the federal deficit, shown in part (ii).

From 1967 though 1973 expenditures grew steadily while revenue fluctuated around a rising trend; as a result the budget balance fluctuated between deficit and surplus positions but showed no significant trend. Persistent deficits emerged in the next five years as expenditures remained roughly constant while revenues fell.

In the 1980s the deficit increased dramatically. In the early part of this decade the growth in the deficit reflected the effects of the recession; as can be seen in Table 32-2, the cyclical adjustment grew sharply in this period. Revenues fell sharply and have recovered only slowly since. Expenditures rose rapidly, in part reflecting the operation of automatic stabilizers. More recently, government restraint curtailed growth in program spending, but this was more than offset by the rapid growth in interest payments on the national debt, so that, as shown, total expenditure continued to rise. In 1986 the deficit fell both in absolute terms and as a percentage of GDP. (*Source:* Department of Finance, *Budget Papers*, February 1987.)

Will a deficit cause inflation? Neither economic theory nor the available evidence suggests that deficits by themselves are sufficient to cause inflation.

The worry that persistent deficits may cause inflation arises out of the fear that a continuous deficit will lead to a continuous expansion in the money supply, that is, that it would eventually lead to pressure in the Bank of Canada to expand the money supply and thus cause inflation. This case cannot be studied in detail until Chapter 36. For now we merely observe that if a deficit is financed by "borrowing" from the Bank, the money supply will be increased every year. (In effect the Bank *creates* the money to finance the deficit.) If this increase is too rapid, it will cause inflation.

Deficits financed by the continual creation of new money may cause inflation.

No one believes that this is desirable.

Will the deficit crowd out private investment? People fear that deficit spending may lead to a more or less equivalent reduction in private-sector investment spending. Government borrowing to finance its deficit can absorb a significant proportion of private savings. In 1986, for example, the federal deficit was equal to about 52 percent of household savings and fully 24 percent of total private-sector savings by households and firms. The fear is that heavy government borrowing drives up the interest rate and that the higher interest rate reduces private investment expenditure. This "crowding out" process is illustrated in Figure 32-5.

If government borrowing to finance the deficit drives up the interest rate, some private investment expenditure will be crowded out.

However, interest rates in an open economy such as Canada are closely tied to those prevailing in international markets. Hence the scope for increases in the interest rate and crowding out of investment is quite limited. By and large, the budget deficit will result in increased foreign borrowing (not necessarily by the government, but by other borrowers in the economy who are forced to borrow abroad since the government deficit has absorbed most of the available domestic saving). Domestic interest rates and investment will remain relatively unchanged.[11]

Will the debt harm future generations? To the extent that government borrowing to finance current expenditures crowds out private investment, there will be a smaller stock of capital to pass on to future generations. Less capital means less output; this is the long-term burden of the debt.

However, we have seen that investment in an open economy will not be reduced much by a government deficit. Does this mean there is no burden of the debt in an open economy? Unfortunately, the answer is no. While private investment can be maintained, foreign lenders will supply much of the funds. Future generations may well inherit a capital stock that is not significantly reduced as a result of the deficit, but they will also inherit an increased stock of foreign liabilities. Future payments of interest and dividends to foreigners will lower GNP (income owned by Canadians) in relation to GDP (output produced in Canada) since some income generated by the output will accrue to foreigners. These will also lower GNP relative to what it would have been in the absence of the deficits.

Attracting funds from abroad entails a transfer of purchasing power to domestic residents when the funds enter the country and a transfer back to foreigners when interest and dividend payments and repayments of principal occur.

The alternative view, that the debt does not matter because we largely owe it to ourselves, is taken up in Box 32-5 (see pages 694–695).

This argument is dramatically illustrated by recent experience in the United States. The United States slowly built up a net creditor position over the six decades before 1980. That position was completely dissipated as a result of massive foreign borrowing during Ronald Reagan's presidency. Most econo-

[11] The crowding-out debate is closely related to debates about the effectiveness of fiscal policy, a debate we take up in Chapter 39. In an open economy a government deficit does not always crowd out investment because interest rates don't rise. Instead, the increased foreign borrowing may cause the currency to appreciate and thus crowd out net exports. We discuss this possibility in Chapter 42.

FIGURE 32-5 Crowding Out Private Investment by Government Borrowing

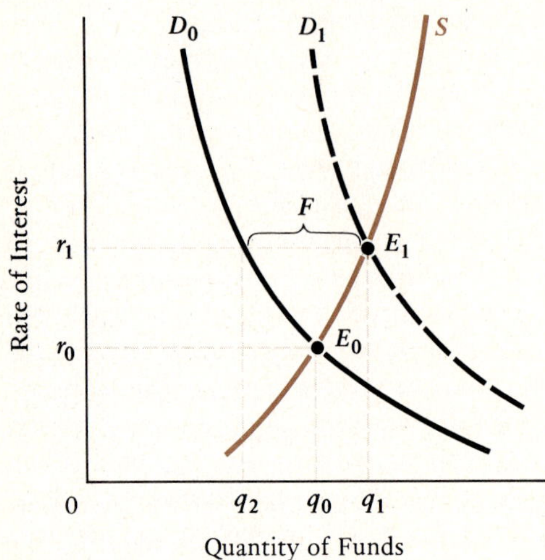

(i) Effects of government borrowing with constant national income

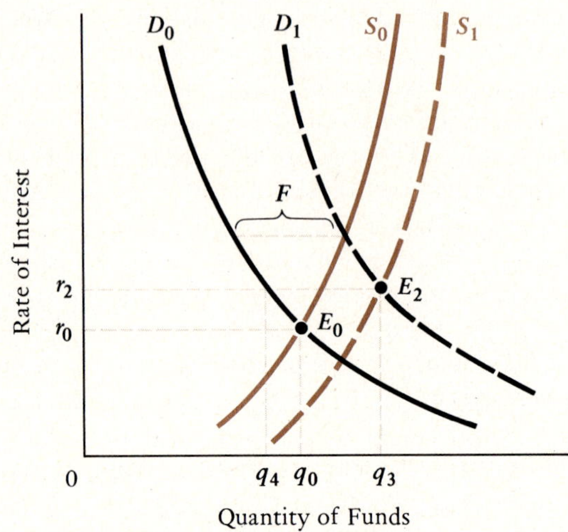

(ii) Effects of government borrowing with increased national income

Government borrowing may crowd out private-sector borrowing and investing. Part (i) of the figure shows a supply of funds available to be lent, S, that is fairly insensitive to the interest rate. Initially the demand to borrow funds is D_0, giving an equilibrium interest rate of r_0 and a quantity of funds borrowed for all purposes of q_0.

Government spending now increases by F, all of which is borrowed. This shifts the demand for funds to the right, from D_0 to D_1, taking equilibrium to E_1. The interest rate rises to r_1, and the quantity of funds borrowed rises to q_1. But q_2q_1 of these go to the government, so the private sector borrows only q_2, which is q_2q_0 less than it was able to borrow, and hence invest, before the deficit forced the government into the market.

If, however, the extra government expenditure increases national income, it will boost saving. The savings function will then shift to the right, say, from S_0 to S_1 in part (ii) of the figure. Crowding out will then be lessened. At equilibrium E_2 the interest rate rises to r_2, and private borrowing is only q_4q_0 less than before the government entered the market.

mists attribute this foreign borrowing to the enormous government budget deficits that occurred. As a result of these large deficits, the United States has become one of the world's largest debtor nations.

Does the size of the debt hamper the operation of policy? The large interest bill on the national debt puts a strain on the budget process. For example, in 1986 a full 28 percent of all tax revenues went to pay interest on the national debt! The government's freedom of fiscal maneuver is obviously hampered by such a large and rising claim on the national tax revenues. When the government's interest obligations grow, it can, of course, incur an even larger deficit, at least for a while, but eventually interest on the stock of debt must be paid from new revenues.[12] Eventually the government must either reduce its expenditure on other programs or raise taxes.

[12] Of course for a while interest on current debt can be paid by incurring new debt, but this is an explosive process. The interest demands on old and new debt would soon absorb the whole of government tax revenue and eventually all of national income.

Although interest payments on the national debt have not yet reached crisis proportions, the large claim on existing government revenues is a cause for concern.

Deficits and the National Debt

The foregoing indicates that much of the concern about government budget deficits arises from their *cumulative* effect on the national debt and therefore on the government's interest obligations.

Facts About the Debt

The national debt in December 1986 was over $200 billion, about $8,000 for every man, woman, and child in the country. About 10 percent of the debt was held by the government itself and by the Bank of Canada; interest payments on this part of the debt are only bookkeeping transactions.[13]

The national debt of over $200 billion represents money that the federal government has borrowed by selling bonds to Canadian and foreign households, firms, and financial institutions.

In this sense the national debt is owed by all of us to some of us and to foreigners.

The debt in relation to GDP. The figures for debt per person, which are often quoted in an attempt to shock the reader, require interpretation. For a government, as for a household, the significance of debt depends on what it represents and on whether the income is available to pay the interest. No one would be shocked, for example, to find that a Canadian family of four earning $60,000 a year had a mortgage of $50,000 on a $100,000 home.

It is useful in evaluating the national debt and the government's interest payments on it to consider them *relative* to the size of the economy. Worries about the debt arise primarily when the debt grows faster than the economy; it is really the debt-to-GDP ratio that matters. A national debt of $200 billion clearly has different implications when GDP is $50 billion and when it is $500 billion.

Figure 32-6 (see page 696) shows historical data for the debt and interest payments on it as a proportion of GDP.

Part (i) shows that national debt as a proportion of GDP started to fall at the end of World War II and continued to fall until 1976. The debt rose relative to GDP after 1977, and by 1986 the debt had reached almost 50 percent of GDP. That figure is still much less than the more than 100 percent at the postwar peak. Nevertheless, the trend is worrisome, and medium-term projections suggest that the debt-to-GDP ratio will continue to rise.

Consider next the interest payments on the debt, often called the *debt-service payments,* shown in part (ii) of the figure. Clearly, there is genuine cause for worry here. If the trend continues, interest payments could eventually put an intolerable burden on the government's taxing capacity. Ever-bigger deficits would occur, and with them even more borrowing.

In view of the costs imposed by a rising debt-to-GDP ratio, many economists and others have argued that the government's fiscal policies are imprudent and have called for a commitment to control the deficit.

Proposals to Control the Deficit

As we have seen, government deficits contribute to aggregate demand and hence can play a useful role in damping cyclical fluctuations in the economy. As we have also seen, government deficits contribute to increases in the national debt and hence in the long term might lead to a reduction in living standards. This conflict between the short-term stabilization role of deficits and the long-term adverse effects of a large public debt has long been a subject of debate among economists and others.

Views range from those who dismiss the long-run costs of the national debt and hence are not concerned about the deficit to those who wish to eschew the short-term stabilization role for the deficit entirely and impose a virtual straitjacket on the government, requiring it always to balance its budget.

[13] The Bank of Canada buys government bonds in the course of operating monetary policy (see Chapter 35). Government departments sometimes acquire government bonds when they have funds that they do not need for short, or even long, periods of time.

BOX 32-5

Does the National Debt Matter? The Owe-It-to-Ourselves View

A few economists have argued that since the national debt simply involves a debt of some Canadians payable to other Canadians, it imposes no net burden on the country. Of course these economists recognize that the debt is a burden to taxpayers in general who must ultimately provide the funds for the government to make interest payments on the debt. But, the "owe-it-to-ourselves" argument holds, that burden is exactly offset by the interest payments that are made to those Canadians who own government bonds.

The owe-it-to-ourselves view thus argues that the major effect of the national debt is that interest payments on it merely redistribute income from the general taxpayer towards bond-holders. Since the ownership of government bonds is widely held, being a major component of most public and private pension funds, the argument holds that even this redistribution of income is not a serious matter.

This contention raises several issues.

Crowding Out. First, suppose that the basic facts alleged in the owe-it-to-ourselves view are true—that is, that virtually all Canadian government debt is in fact held by Canadians. Even in this case, it does not follow that there is no net burden to the Canadian economy arising from the government debt.

A good deal of economic theory and evidence suggests that government bonds are held in place of claims on income streams produced by real capital. That is, if the debt did not exist, people would still wish to hold assets to provide for future consumption; in the absence of the government debt they would have invested in corporations engaged in producing goods and services. Thus the bonds, which on net contribute nothing to the economy but merely redistribute income from one group to another, crowd out investment in real capital that would have created wealth and income for Canadians.

On this argument, it is the very fact that the government debt only redistributes income between Canadians that means that it gives rise to a net burden to the economy. By crowding out investment in physical capital, it leads to a lower capital stock and hence to reduced levels of income and wealth for Canadians.

International Capital Mobility. The basic contention that the debt is merely owed-to-ourselves is not completely true. While the vast majority of Canadian government bonds (90 percent) is held by Canadian citizens, government bonds are also sold on international markets so that the remaining 10 percent is held by foreigners. Accordingly, the interest

We now look at some of the specific proposals that have been put forward; some of the general options are illustrated in Figure 32-7 (see page 697).

An annually balanced budget? Much current rhetoric of fiscal restraint calls for a balanced budget. In the United States, the Gramm-Rudman-Hollings bill, passed in late 1985, was an attempt to eliminate the federal deficit by 1991 by mandating expenditure cuts.

The discussion earlier in this chapter suggests that an annually balanced budget would be extremely difficult, perhaps impossible, to achieve. With fixed tax rates, tax revenues fluctuate as national income fluctuates. Much government expenditure is fixed by past commitments, and most of the rest is hard to change quickly.

But suppose that an annually balanced budget, or something approaching it, were feasible. What would its effects be? Would they be desirable?

We saw earlier that a larger government sector whose expenditures on goods and services are not very sensitive to the cyclical variations in national income is a major built-in stabilizer. To insist that annual government expenditure be tied to annual tax receipts would be to abandon the present built-in stability provided by government. Government expenditure would then become a major *destabilizing* payments on these bonds, which must be financed by Canadian taxpayers, accrue to foreign nationals.

The fact that some Canadian government debt is held abroad is enough to refute the owe-it-to-ourselves myth. But in fact the situation is even more complicated—and more damaging to the owe-it-to-ourselves view.

Suppose a large Canadian corporation wishes to float a new debt issue in order to finance an expansion in its existing capacity. While it might expect to sell a large fraction of the new bonds on the Canadian market, the fact that the Canadian government is flooding that market with debt of its own in order to finance its budget deficit means that the Canadian corporation will have to sell its debt abroad. (Ontario Hydro and Quebec Hydro are examples of two organizations that have found themselves in exactly this position in recent years.)

Again there will be a burden to the national debt, not in the form of a reduced capital stock in Canada, but nevertheless in the form of reduced income and wealth for Canadians. Foreign nationals will now own claims to the income from the new Canadian investment projects, and some of the income from these Canadian projects will accrue to those foreign nationals who acquired these financial claims.

In this case the burden to the national debt arises *indirectly* because of the need that it creates for Canadian firms to finance their investment by selling bonds and equities abroad. Once this indirect effect is recognized, simply looking at the share of foreign ownership of the national debt does not give a good indication of how much is owed-to-ourselves and how much is actually owed-to-foreign-nationals.

What Limits the Acceptable Size of the Deficit? The arguments given in the text provide a basis for balancing the need for short-run fiscal stabilization with the longer-run concerns for fiscal prudence. But the owe-it-to-ourselves view is not helpful in this regard.

If the owe-it-to-ourselves view were correct, why would we not want a $200 billion deficit, or even a $500 billion one, rather than the controversial $30-plus billion one we have now? Surely the politicians would like that, as it would allow them to avoid many of the hard decisions involved in restraining expenditures and raising taxes. Of course, no one would seriously advocate such a deficit. But if the owe-it-to-ourselves view were correct, there would be no reason for objecting to such a deficit.

force. Tax revenues necessarily rise in booms and fall in slumps; an annually balanced budget would force government expenditure to do the same. Changes in national income would then cause induced changes not only in household consumption expenditure but also in government expenditure. This would greatly increase the economy's marginal propensity to spend and hence increase the value of the multiplier.

An annually balanced budget would accentuate the swings in national income that accompany changes in such autonomous expenditure flows as investment and exports.

A further problem is that the goal of budget *balance* is in fact stricter than is required to avoid a rising debt-to-GDP ratio. Growth in GDP means that some growth in the debit, and hence a (small) deficit, is consistent with a stable debt-to-GDP ratio. In the rest of this chapter, we shall assume that the term *budget balance* allows for this possibility.

A zero structural balance? The concept of the structural balance was designed to assess changes in the stance of fiscal stabilization policy. It was not intended to help assess the long-term viability of fiscal policy. Yet it has often been used in this way by people who have argued that the national debt is

FIGURE 32-6 Relative Significance of the National Debt

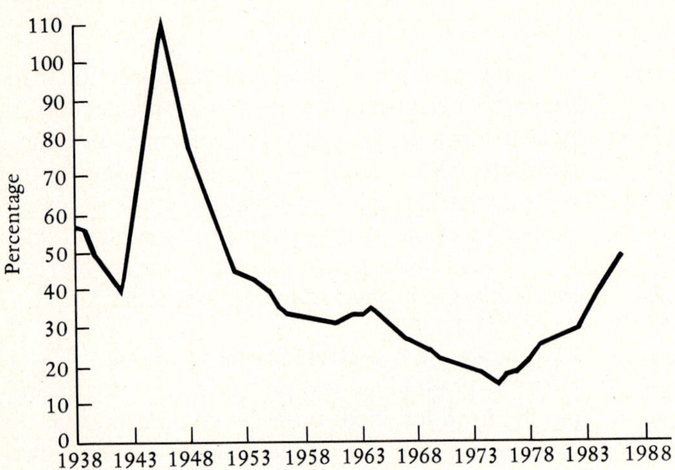

(i) Net government debt as a percentage of GDP

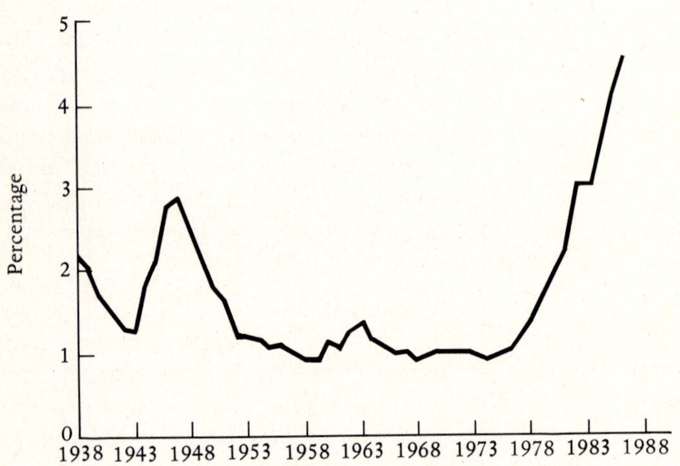

(ii) Net interest on government debt as a percentage of GDP

After falling for 30 years, the national debt and interest payments on it have both started to rise as a share of national income. Part (i) plots net federal government debt while part (ii) plots net interest payments made by the federal government, both as a percentage of GDP.

The national debt, after rising sharply through World War II, was a declining fraction of GDP until 1975. Since 1975 there has been a continuing rise, with the rise being quite sharp in the last few years shown. In 1986 the ratio reached 48.7 percent.

Interest payments on the national debt have followed a similar pattern; since interest rates rose in the late 1970s and early 1980s, the upturn in interest payments was sharper and occurred sooner than with the debt. Interest payments on the debt reached 2.9 percent of national income in 1948 and remained under three percent for the next 33 years. In 1983 they rose to 3.3 percent, and in 1986 they reached 4.6 percent. (*Source: Public Accounts,* Department of Finance.)

not a long-term problem as long as the structural balance is not in deficit.

A zero structural balance is not, however, a good target for long-run fiscal prudence because the economy usually is expected to operate at or below potential income. Thus a budget that is balanced at potential income will produce deficits whenever output is below potential, a balance at potential income, and a surplus only in the rare event that output exceeds potential.

A second problem with the structural deficit as an indicator of fiscal imprudence arises from the inflation adjustment. In arriving at a measure of the structural deficit, the inflation adjustment is typically made using the *actual* stock of government debt. Thus the larger the stock of debt, the larger the

FIGURE 32-7 Balanced and Unbalanced Budgets

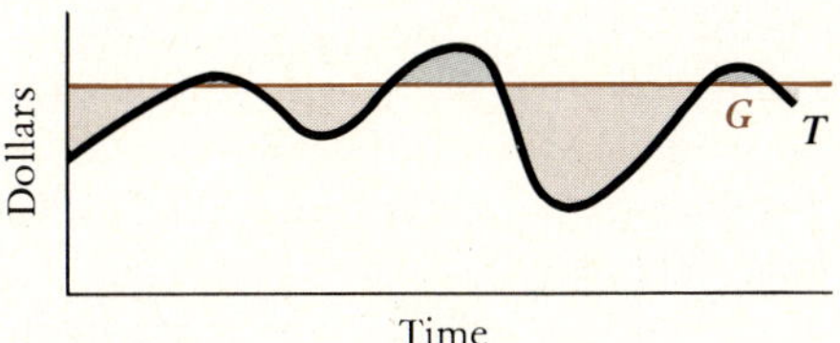

(i) A cyclically unbalanced budget

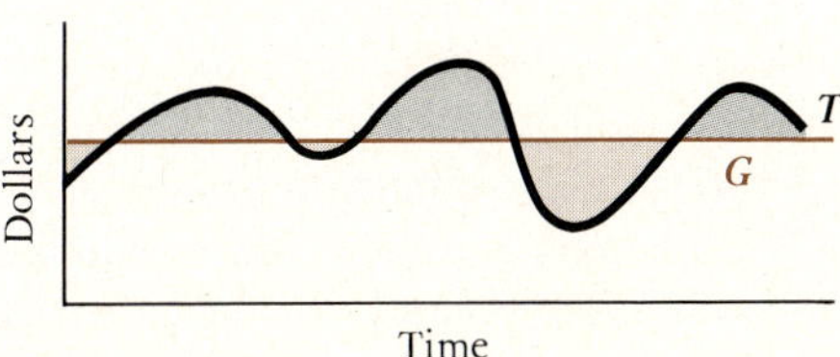

(ii) A cyclically balanced budget

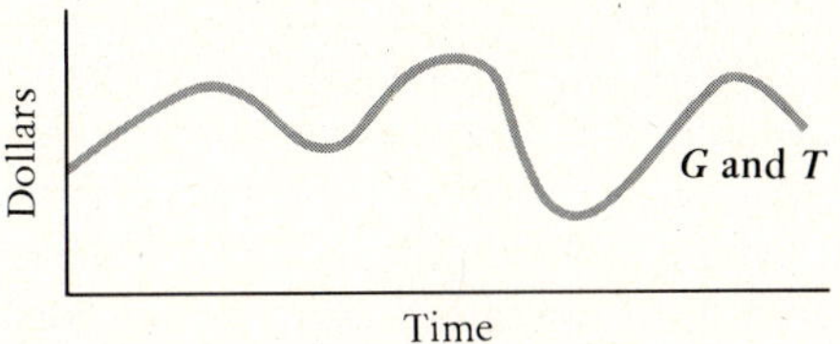

(iii) A constantly balanced budget

An annually (constantly) balanced budget is a destabilizer; a cyclically balanced budget is a stabilizer. The flow of tax receipts, *T*, is shown varying over the business cycle, while in parts (i) and (ii) government expenditure, *G*, is shown at a constant rate.

In part (i) deficits (dark areas) are common and surpluses (light areas) are rare because the average level of expenditure exceeds the average level of taxes. Such a policy will tend to stabilize the economy against cyclical fluctuations, but the average fiscal stance of the government is expansionary.

In part (ii) government expenditure has been reduced until it is approximately equal to the average level of tax receipts. The budget is now balanced cyclically. The policy still tends to stabilize the economy against cyclical fluctuations because of deficits in slumps and surpluses in booms. But the average fiscal stance is neither strongly expansionary nor strongly contractionary.

In part (iii) a balanced budget has been imposed. Deficits have been prevented, but government expenditure now varies over the business cycle, tending to destabilize the economy by accentuating the cyclical swings in aggregate expenditure.

inflation adjustment will be, and the smaller will be the structural component of any given measured deficits. Thus small structural deficits can hide the very problem fiscal imprudence is concerned with: a too rapidly rising stock of debt.

A cyclically balanced budget? An alternative policy, one that would prevent continual deficits (and could also inhibit the growth in the size of the government sector), would be to balance the budget over the business cycle. This would be more feasible than the annually balanced budget, and it would not make government expenditure a destabilizing force.

Although more attractive in principal than the annually balanced budget, a cyclically balanced budget would carry problems of its own. Government might well spend in excess of revenue in one year, leaving an obligation to spend less than current revenue in following years. Could such an obligation to balance over a period of years be made binding? What a government commits itself to in one year does not necessarily restrict what it (or its successor) does the next year.

Perhaps even more of a problem is that there is always room for some disagreement about the current state of the business cycle. Critics of the cyclically balanced budget proposal argue that many governments have often misinterpreted long-term factors such as demographic changes that lead to an increase in the measured unemployment rate or structural change that leads to a fall in the measured rate of income growth as short-term cyclical factors that call for fiscal stimulus. Thus the critics argue that while governments can appear to accept the need for balance over the cycle, this has not in fact stopped them from running persistently large deficits and hence imprudently running up the national debt.

Although a budget balanced over the course of the business cycle is in principle an acceptable way of reconciling short-term stabilization and long-term prudence, the business cycle may not be well enough defined in practice to make the proposal operational.

The medium-term fiscal plan. In a study published in 1984, Professors Neil Bruce and Douglas Purvis of Queen's University addressed the issue of fiscal prudence by evaluating the government's medium-term fiscal plan. That plan gives projections for the key economic variables such as output, inflation, interest rates, and unemployment as well as for government revenues and expenditures.

Bruce and Purvis defined the *imprudent deficit* as the part of projected deficits that contributes to growth in the debt-to-GDP ratio above some target level. Thus they allow for trend growth in the economy and for projected inflation. The imprudent deficit nets out cyclical and inflation adjustments in much the same manner as calculations of the structural deficit do. The crucial difference is that the inflation adjustment is applied only to the level of debt consistent with the target debt-to-GDP ratio rather than to the actual stock of debt. This means that current deficits, which contribute to the actual debt, do not also automatically lead to an increase in the inflation adjustment applied to future deficits.

Their calculation showed the imprudent deficit to be significant. They concluded that there was cause for concern about the long-term implications of projected deficits and that some concerted but systematic phasing-in of budget cuts was in order. Further, they argued that even though the actual cuts could be implemented gradually, the process had to be started quickly so that the program for re-establishing fiscal prudence be flexible enough that the short-term objectives of fiscal stabilization need not be abandoned.

Summary. The need for fiscal prudence is accepted by virtually everyone. How to evaluate it and enforce it, however, is still subject to controversy. Indeed, there is serious doubt that the idea of a balanced budget over any time period is operational.

Many economists believe that a superior alternative to insisting on a precise balance is to pay attention to the balance without making a fetish of never adding to the national debt.

The Political Economy of the Debt

Almost all economists accept that if the debt got so large that it could not be serviced without either putting a crushing burden on taxpayers or forcing the government to create new money to service it, there would be serious problems. But many think we are still a long way from that point. To them the overriding principle is that the debt should be changed according to the needs of stabilization policy.

An alternative view is what has come to be called *fiscal conservatism*. The conservative view takes a broad historical perspective. It says that in the eighteenth century spendthrift European rulers habitually spent more than their tax revenues and so created harmful inflation. By the end of the nineteenth century the doctrine was well established that a balanced budget was the citizen's only protection against profligate government spending and consequent wild inflation. Thus the conservatives hold that the balanced budget doctrine was not silly and irrational, as Keynes made it out to be. Instead it was the symbol of the people's victory in a long struggle to control the spendthrift proclivities of their nations' rulers.

The Keynesian revolution swept away that view. Budget deficits became, according to Keynesians, the tool by which benign and enlightened governments sought to ensure full employment. But, say the conservatives, deficit spending let the tiger out of the cage. Inflationary gaps, recessionary gaps, or full employment notwithstanding, governments spent and spent and spent. Deficits accumulated, national debt rose, and inflation became the rule.

The main premise of the conservative view is that governments are not passive agents who do what is necessary to create full employment and maximize social welfare. Governments are composed of individuals—elected officials, legislators, and civil servants—who, like everyone else, seek mainly to maximize their own well-being. Their welfare is best served by a big government role and a satisfied electorate. Thus they tend to favor spending and to resist tax increases. This creates a persistent tendency toward deficits that is quite independent of any consideration of a sound fiscal policy.

The debate reflects deeply held views about the role of government, the nature and motivation of public officials, and the desirability of stabilization. Keynesians tend to regard government officials as well meaning, and substantial government intervention as essential to an effective and humane society.

Fiscal conservatives regard public officials as self-serving and of limited competence. They see public intervention, however well motivated, as probably inept and ultimately destabilizing. Both recognize that an interventionist government will play a large role in economic affairs. Conservatives regard that prospect with concern, Keynesians with relative equanimity.

Summary

1. Fiscal policy uses government expenditure and tax policies to influence the economy by shifting the aggregate demand curve. Changes in either government spending or tax policies also influence the budget balance.
2. The so-called paradox of thrift is not a paradox at all. It applies to the short-run effects of saving and investment on aggregate demand. It predicts that severe recessions can be combated by encouraging an increase in spending.
3. When private expenditure functions are fixed, it is a relatively simple matter to increase expenditure, to cut tax rates, or to make a balanced budget increase in expenditure in order to remove a recessionary gap (and to make the opposite changes to remove an inflationary gap).
4. Fiscal policy is more difficult when, as is almost always the case, private expenditure functions are continually shifting. Fine tuning, the attempt to hold the aggregate expenditure function virtually constant by offsetting even small fluctuations in private expenditure, has been largely discredited. Many economists still believe, however, that large and persistent gaps can be offset by fiscal policy.
5. Short-term stabilization by fiscal policy operates largely through such automatic stabilizers as tax revenues, which vary directly with national income; expenditures on goods and services, which do not vary with national income; and transfer payments, which vary negatively with national income.
6. Discretionary fiscal policy is also used sometimes to attack large and persistent gaps. It must be reversible; otherwise the economy may overshoot its target once private investment recovers from a temporary slump or falls back from a temporary boom. However, tax changes need to be perceived as relatively long-lived if they are to induce major changes in household spending patterns. (Temporary changes may merely affect the current saving rate and not expenditure.) The need to have tax changes perceived as long-lived, however, conflicts with the need to have fiscal policy easily reversible.
7. Changes in the stance of fiscal policy may be reasonably judged by changes in the structural deficit. This is the balance between revenues and expenditures as they would be if full employment prevailed and with the inflation premium component of interest payments on the national debt netted out.
8. Canadian national debt and debt-service payments have risen and

fallen as a percentage of national income, but they have not shown a long-term trend to grow inexorably. Recent increases in these ratios reflect the cumulative effect of recent large deficits. Persistent deficits are a cause for concern for several reasons, including inflation, crowding out of investment, and reducing national income in the long run.

9. An annually balanced budget would be unfeasible; even if it were possible, it would destabilize the economy. A cyclically balanced budget would act as a stabilizer while also curbing the growth of the government sector. Growth of GDP and some minimal acceptable inflation rate both create room for the average budget balance over the course of the business cycle to show some deficit; a deficit persistently in excess of this can be viewed as imprudent.
10. Keynesians take a relatively sanguine view of the national debt. As long as it does not grow wildly as a proportion of national income, they view its short-term fluctuations and its long-term upward trend in absolute terms as a stabilizing device. Fiscal conservatives mistrust government and view insistence on a balanced budget as the only effective means of curtailing reckless government spending, which wastes scarce resources and feeds the fires of inflation. In an open economy, deficits can cause foreign borrowing and therefore lead to a reduction in living standards in the long run when interest payments are made to foreigners.

Topics for Review

Fiscal policy
Budget balance, balanced budget, budget surplus, and budget deficit
Fine tuning
Built-in stabilizers
Discretionary fiscal policy
The stance of fiscal policy
Actual, cyclically adjusted, and structural budget balances
National debt and debt service
Keynesian and fiscal conservative views of debt

Discussion Questions

1. In 1986, falling world energy prices and collapsing world agricultural markets caused a slowdown in the Canadian economy. The operation of automatic stabilizers in the face of these adverse shocks meant that the deficit would be larger than anticipated, and in addition the government announced an additional one billion dollar discretionary expenditure program to assist farmers. Write a brief critique of the government's decision to let the deficit rise relative to its target path in these circumstances.
2. The Gramm-Rudman-Hollings bill, called the Balanced Budget Act of 1985, passed in the United States Congress, stipulates annual reductions in the federal deficit through 1991, when the budget

must balance. If the targets are not met, the bill mandates specific spending cuts that must be made. It was criticized as arbitrary, unbalanced, mechanical, inflexible, and not credible. On the basis of the analysis in this chapter, write a brief defense of or attack on the bill.

3. As the recovery from the 1982 recession entered its fifth year in 1987, government deficits remained historically large, and concern over them was widespread. Another concern, however, was that in the event of a downturn, emphasis on the deficit might lead to procyclical fiscal policy. Explain how this might happen. Focus on what measure might allow it to be avoided. Should it be avoided?
4. "Fiscal policy has been a relatively weak instrument in Canada because of our heavy dependence on foreign trade and because of the wide regional disparities in employment opportunities." Discuss.
5. Arrange the following in order in terms of the expected size of their effect on aggregate demand and employment.
   a. Government subsidies to farmers of $100 million, financed by an increase in income taxes of $100 million
   b. Government deficit expenditure of $100 million during a recession
   c. Government deficit expenditure of $100 million near the end of a recovery
   d. A general tax cut, costing $100 million in lost revenue to the government
6. Which of the following would be built-in stabilizers?
   a. Food stamps for the needy
   b. Cost of living escalators in government contracts and pensions
   c. Income taxes
   d. Free college tuition for unemployed workers after six months of unemployment, provided that they are under 30 years old and have had five or more years of full-time experience since high school
7. The U.S. Employment Act of 1946 made no explicit mention of price stability as an objective of macroeconomic policy. Why do you suppose this was so? What is the relationship between fiscal policy and the price level?
8. Consider the typical annual expenditures and revenues of the organizations listed below. Comment on the appropriate debt policy for each, taking into account their respective goals, life span, and resources.
   a. Family household
   b. Two private corporations, one growing rapidly and the other a mature firm
   c. A village of 5,000 inhabitants
   d. The Canadian government
   e. The United Nations
9. President Reagan said in 1982, "I don't place very much faith in those various deficit forecasts." Why would the president of the United States be skeptical about deficit forecasts? Does the evidence suggest that this skepticism was misplaced?

10. In his first inaugural address President Franklin D. Roosevelt expounded the doctrine of "sound finance"—that the government's budget should always be balanced. During his term, however, government spending rose faster than taxes, and deficits resulted. How would the effectiveness of the New Deal on employment have been changed if Roosevelt had been successful in keeping the budget balanced throughout his first term?

The Permanent-Income and Life-Cycle Hypotheses of Household Consumption

In the Keynesian theory of the consumption function, current consumption expenditure is related to current income—either current disposable income or current national income. Recent research has produced hypotheses that relate consumption to some longer-term concept of income than the income that the household is currently earning.

The two most influential theories of this type are the **permanent-income hypothesis (PIH)**, developed by 1976 Nobel Laureate Milton Friedman, and the **life-cycle hypothesis (LCH)**, developed by 1985 Nobel Laureate Franco Modigliani and his collaborators. Although there are differences between these hypotheses, it is their similarities that are important. In particular, we note that in both the PIH and the LCH household behavior tends to smooth the time pattern of consumption relative to that of disposable income.

In discussing this "consumption smoothing" issue, it is important to ask: What variables do these theories seek to explain? What assumptions do they make? What are the major implications of these assumptions?

Variables

Three variables need to be considered: consumption, saving, and income. Keynesian-type theories seek to explain the amounts that households spend to purchase goods and services for consumption. This concept is called *consumption expenditure*. Permanent-income theories seek to explain the actual flows of consumption of the *services* that are provided by the commodities that households buy. This concept is called *actual consumption*.[1]

With services and nondurable goods, expenditure and actual consumption occur more or less at the same time, and the distinction between the two concepts is not important. Consumption of a haircut, for example, occurs at the time it is purchased, and an orange or a package of corn flakes is consumed very soon after it is purchased. Thus if we knew purchases of such goods and services at some time, say, last year, we would also know last year's consumption of those goods and services.

But this is not the case with durable consumer goods. A house is purchased at one point in time, but it yields its services over a long time, possibly as long as the purchaser's lifetime. The same is true of a personal computer and a watch and, over a shorter period of time, a car and a dress. For such products, if we know purchases last year, we do not necessarily know last year's consumption of the services that the products yielded.

Thus one important characteristic of durable goods is that *expenditure* to purchase them is not necessarily synchronized with *consumption* of the stream of services that the goods provide. If in 1988 Alice Smith buys a car for $12,000, runs it for six years, and then discards it as worn out, her expen-

[1] Because Keynes' followers did not always distinguish carefully between the concepts of consumption expenditure and actual consumption, the word *consumption* is often used in both contexts. We follow this normal practice, but where there is any possible ambiguity in the term, we will refer to *consumption expenditure* or *actual consumption*.

diture on automobiles is $12,000 in 1988 and zero for the next five years. Her consumption of the services of automobiles, however, is spread out at an average annual rate of $2,000 for six years. If everyone followed Alice Smith's example by buying a new car in 1988 and replacing in in 1993, the automobile industry would undergo wild booms in 1988 and 1993 with five intervening years of slump, even though the actual consumption of automobiles would be spread more or less evenly over time. This example is extreme, but it illustrates the possibilities, where consumers' durables are concerned, of quite different time paths of *consumption expenditure*, which is the subject of Keynesian theories of consumption, and *actual consumption*, which is the subject of permanent-income theories.

Now consider saving. The change in emphasis from consumption expenditure to actual consumption implies a change in the definition of saving. Saving is no longer income minus consumption expenditure; it is now income minus the value of actual consumption. When Alice Smith spent $12,000 on her car in 1988 but used only $2,000 worth of its services in that year, she was actually consuming $2,000 and saving $10,000. The purchase of a consumers' durable is thus counted as saving, and only the value of its services actually consumed is counted as consumption.

The third important variable is income. Instead of using current income, the theories use a concept of long-term income. The precise definition varies from one theory to another, but basically it is related to the household's expected income stream over a fairly long planning period. In the LCH it is the income that the household expects to earn over its lifetime, called its *lifetime income*.

Every household is assumed to have a view of its lifetime income. This is not as unreasonable as it might seem. Students training to be doctors have a very different view of expected lifetime income than those training to become schoolteachers. Both expected income streams will be different from that expected by an assembly line worker or a professional athlete. One possible lifetime income stream is shown in Figure 32A-1.

The household's expected lifetime income is then converted into a single figure for *annual* **permanent income**. In the LCH this permanent income is the maximum amount the household could spend on consumption each year without accumulating debts that are passed on to future generations. If a household were to consume a constant amount equal to its permanent income each year, it would add to its debts in years when current income was less than permanent income and reduce its debts or increase its assets in years when its current income exceeded its permanent income. Over its lifetime, however, it would just break even, leaving neither accumulated assets nor debts to its heirs. If the interest rate were zero, permanent income would be just the sum of all expected incomes divided by the number of expected years of life.[2] With a positive interest rate,

FIGURE 32A-1 Current Income and Permanent Income

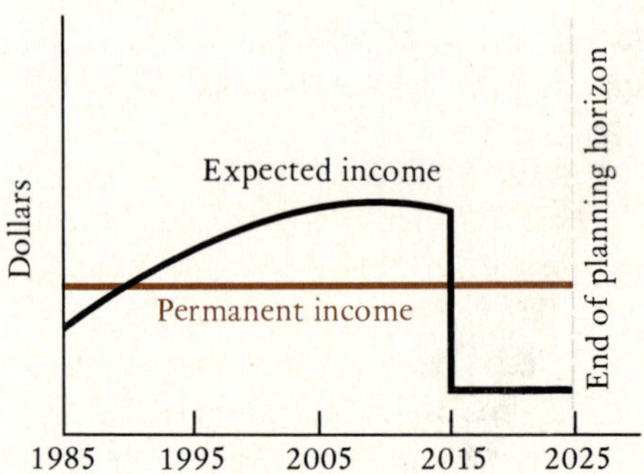

Expected current income may vary greatly over a lifetime, but expected permanent income is defined to be the constant annual equivalent. The graph shows a hypothetical expected income stream from work for a household whose planning horizon was 40 years from 1985. The current income rises to a peak, then falls showly for a while, and finally falls sharply on retirement. The corresponding permanent income is the amount the household could consume at a steady rate over its lifetime by borrowing early against future earnings (as do most newly married couples), then repaying past debts, and finally saving for retirement when income is at its peak without either incurring debt or accumulating new wealth to be passed on to future generations.

[2] In the PIH the household has an infinite time horizon and the relevant permanent-income concept is the amount the household could consume forever without increasing or decreasing its present stock of wealth.

permanent income will diverge from this amount because of the costs of borrowing and the extra income that can be earned by investing savings.

Assumption

The basic assumption of this type of theory, whether PIH or LCH, is that the household's actual consumption is related to its permanent rather than its current income. Two households that have the same permanent income (and are similar in other relevant characteristics) will have similar consumption patterns even though their current incomes may behave differently.

Implications

The major implication of these theories is that changes in a household's current income will affect its actual consumption only so far as they affect its permanent income. Consider two income changes that could occur in a household with a permanent income of $20,000 per year and an expected lifetime of 30 or more years. In the first case suppose that the household receives an unexpected extra income of $2,000 *this year only.* The increase in the household's permanent income is small. If the rate of interest were zero, the household could consume an extra $66.66 per year for the rest of its expected life span; with a positive rate of interest, the extra annual consumption would be more because money not spent this year could be invested and would earn interest.[3] In the second case the household gets a toally unforeseen increase of $2,000 a year *for the rest of its life.* In this event the household's permanent income has risen by $2,000 because the household can actually consume $2,000 more every year without accumulating new debts. Although in both cases current income rises by $2,000, the effect on permanent income is very different.

Keynesian theory assumes that *consumption expenditure* is related to current income and therefore predicts the same change in this year's consumption expenditure in each of the cases just discussed. Permanent-income theories relate *actual consumption* to permanent income and therefore predict different changes in actual consumption in each case. In the first case there would be only a small increase in actual annual consumption; in the second there would be a large increase.

In the LCH and the PIH any change in current income that is thought to be temporary will have only a small effect on permanent income and hence on actual consumption.

Implications for the Behavior of the Economy

According to the PIH and the LCH, actual consumption is not much affected by temporary changes in income. Does this mean that aggregate expenditure, $C + I + G + (X - M)$, is not much affected? *Not necessarily.* Consider what happens when households get a temporary increase in their incomes. If actual consumption is not greatly affected by this, households must be saving most of this increase. But from the point of view of these theories, households save when they buy a durable good just as much as when they buy a financial asset such as a stock or a bond. In both cases actual current consumption is not changed.

Thus spending a temporary increase in income on bonds or on new cars is consistent with both the PIH and the LCH. But it makes a great deal of difference to the short-run behavior of the economy which is done. If households buy stocks and bonds, aggregate expenditure on currently produced final goods will not rise when income rises temporarily.[4] If households buy automobiles or any other durable consumer good, aggregate expenditure on currently produced final goods will rise when income rises temporarily. Thus the PIH and the LCH leave unsettled the question that is critical in determining the size of the multiplier: What is the reaction of household *expenditures* on currently produced goods and services, particularly durables, to short-term, temporary changes in income?

[3] If the rate of interest were 7 percent, the household could invest the $2,000, consume an extra $161 a year, and have nothing left at the end of 30 years.

[4] Except for such indirect effects as changes in interest rates, or in a dozen other ways.

The PIH and LCH leave unanswered the critical question of the ability of short-term changes in fiscal policy to remove inflationary and recessionary gaps.

Assume, for example, that a serious recessionary gap emerges and that the government attempts to stimulate a recovery by giving tax rebates and by cutting tax rates—both on an announced temporary basis. This will raise households' current disposable incomes by the amount of the tax cuts, but it will raise their permanent incomes by only a small amount. According to the PIH, the flow of actual current consumption should not rise much. Yet it is quite consistent with the PIH that households should spend their tax savings on durable consumer goods, the consumption of which can be spread over many years.

In this case, even though actual consumption this year would not respond much to the tax cuts, expenditure would respond a great deal. Since current output and employment depend on expenditure rather than on actual consumption, the tax cut would be effective in stimulating the economy. However, it is also consistent with both the LCH and the PIH that households spend only a small part of their tax savings on consumption goods and seek to invest the rest in bonds and other financial assets. In this case the tax cuts may have only a small stimulating effect on the economy. It is important to note that the PIH and the LCH do *not* predict unambiguously that changes in taxes that are announced to be only short-lived will be ineffective in removing inflationary or deflationary gaps.

PART NINE

Money, Banking, and Monetary Policy

33

The Nature of Money and Monetary Institutions

What is the significance of money to the economy, and why are economists concerned about it? Indeed, what is money, and how did it come to play its present role?

Many people believe that money is one of the more important things in life and that there is never enough of it. Yet economists argue that increasing the world's money supply would not make the average person better off. The reason is that although money allows its owners to buy someone else's output, the total amount of goods and services available for everyone to buy depends on the total output that is produced, not on the total amount of money that people possess. Increasing the world's money supply would not change the total quantity of goods produced and hence available for consumption, although it would likely cause an inflation.

The Real and Monetary Sectors of the Economy: The Classical Dichotomy

Early in the history of economics, changes in the quantity of money were seen to be associated with changes in the price level. Eighteenth century economists developed the first comprehensive theories in which the economy was conceived of as being divisible into a "real" part and a "monetary" part.

The real sector. In such theories the allocation of resources is determined in the real sector of the economy by demand and supply. This allocation depends on *relative* prices. For example, whether a lot of beef is produced relative to pork depends on the relative prices of beef and pork, not on the money price of either. If the price of beef is higher than the price of pork and both commodities cost about the same to produce, there is an incentive to produce beef rather than pork. At prices of $1 a pound for pork and $3 for beef, the *relative* incentive is the same as it would be at $2 for pork and $6 for beef. As with beef and pork, so it is with all other commodities:

The allocation of resources among different production activities depends on relative prices.

The monetary sector. According to the early economists the price *level* is determined in the monetary sector of the economy. An increase in the money supply leads to an increase in all money prices. In the beef and pork example, an increase in the total money available might raise the price of pork from $1 to $2 a pound and the price of beef from $3 to $6, but in equilibrium it would leave their relative prices unchanged. Hence it would have no effect on the real part of the economy, that is, on the amount of resources allocated to beef and to pork production (or to anything else). If the quantity of money were doubled, the prices of all commodities would double, and money income would also double, so everyone earning an income would be made no better or worse off by the change.

Thus, in equilibrium, the real and the monetary parts of the economy were believed to have no effect on each other. The doctrine that the quantity of money influences the level of money prices but has no effect on the real part of the economy is called the doctrine of the **neutrality of money.**

Because early economists believed that the most important questions—How much does the economy produce? What share of it does each group in the society get?—were answered in the real sector, they spoke of money as a "veil" behind which occurred the real events that affected material well-being.

The modern view. Modern economists still accept the insights of the early economists that relative prices are a major determinant of the allocation of resources and that the quantity of money has a lot to do with determining the absolute level of prices. They accept the neutrality of money in long-run equilibrium when all forces causing change have fully worked themselves out. We shall see in Chapter 34, however, that most do not accept the neutrality of money when the economy is undergoing change from day to day, that is, when the economy is not in a state of long-run equilibrium.

In this chapter we look first at the experience of price level changes—one aspect of the importance of money—and then at the nature of money itself and the operation of the modern institutions that comprise the monetary system of our economy.

Historical Experience

In Chapter 26 (on pages 552–553) we discussed some important introductory material related to the price level and changes in it (inflations and deflations). That material should be reviewed at this stage. In the figures in this chapter we present some further details of the behavior of the price levels over very long periods of time. Figure 33-1 shows the course of producer (or wholesale) prices in Canada from 1867 through 1986. Considerable year-to-year fluctuations are apparent. Despite large fluctuations in the nineteenth century, the price trend during that period was neither upward nor downward. In contrast, so far the twentieth century has seen both large fluctuations *and* a distinct rising trend in the price level.

Although admittedly a long time, even two centuries may still not be enough to give a clear perspective of very long term price fluctuations. The experience of the period since 1946 looks much more dramatic and unusual when compared only with the nineteenth century than when considered in longer perspective. For an indication of the longer-term course of price levels, we can look across the Atlantic. Figure 33-2 (page 711) shows the course of the price level in England over seven centuries. It shows that there was an overall inflationary trend but that it was by no means evenly spread over the centuries.

The Nature of Money

Inflation is a monetary phenomenon in the sense that a rise in the general level of prices is the same thing as a decrease in the purchasing power of money. But what exactly is money? Probably more folklore and general nonsense are believed about money than about any other aspect of the economy. In this section we describe the functions of money and briefly outline its history. One purpose of this account is to remove some of these misconceptions. In addition, the recent revival of interest in the gold standard makes some discussion of early monetary systems relevant.

What Is Money?

Traditionally in economics **money** has been defined as any generally accepted medium of exchange. A **medium of exchange** is anything that will be accepted by virtually everyone in a society in exchange for goods and services. But money is more than that.

FIGURE 33-1 Index of Canadian Wholesale Prices, 1867–1986

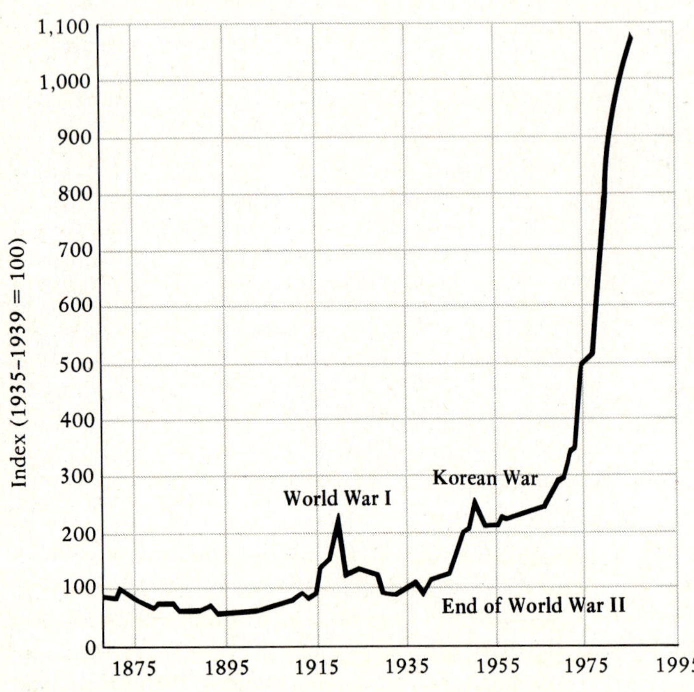

Persistent peacetime inflation is only a recent problem in Canada. Although the price level has fluctuated throughout Canadian history, no long-term trend was visible during the period from confederation to 1940. From the time of World War II to the present, the price level has shown a consistent upward trend. (*Source:* Statistics Canada, Industrial Price Index, 62–0112.)

Money has several functions. It acts as a medium of exchange, as a store of value, and as a unit of account.

Different kinds of money vary in the degree of efficiency with which they fulfill these functions, and different definitions of money may be required for different purposes.

A Medium of Exchange

If there were no money, goods would have to be exchanged by barter, one good being swapped directly for another. We discussed this cumbersome system in Chapter 3. The major difficulty with barter is that each transaction requires a *double coincidence of wants*. For an exchange to occur between A and B, not only must A have what B wants, but B must have what A wants. If all exchange were restricted to barter, anyone who specialized in producing one commodity would have to spend a great deal of time searching for satisfactory transactions.

The use of money as a medium of exchange removes these problems. People can sell their output for money and subsequently use the money to buy what they wish from others. The double coincidence of wants is unnecessary when a medium of exchange is used.

Without money the economic system, which is based on specialization and the division of labor, could not function, and we would have to return to primitive forms of production and exchange. It is not without justification that money has been called one of the great inventions contributing to human freedom.

To serve as an efficient medium of exchange, money must have a number of characteristics. It must be readily acceptable. It must have a high value relative to its weight (otherwise it would be a nuisance to carry around). It must be divisible, because

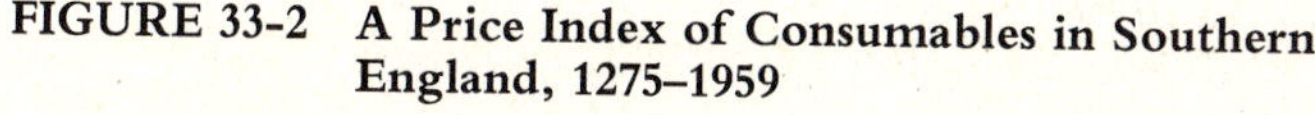

FIGURE 33-2 A Price Index of Consumables in Southern England, 1275–1959

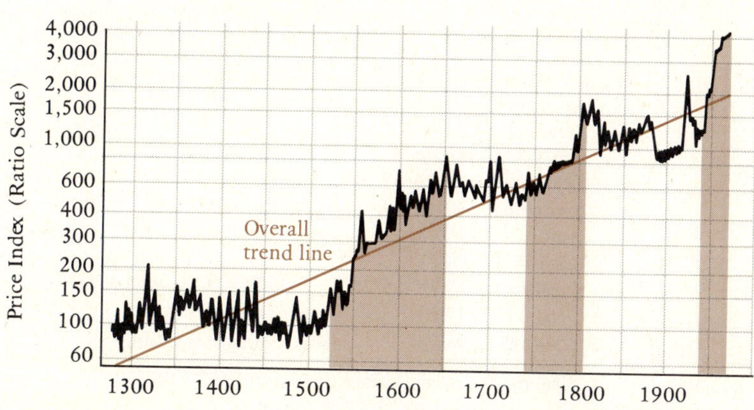

Over the past seven centuries long periods of stable prices have alternated with long periods of rising prices. This remarkable price series shows an index of the prices of food, clothing, and fuel in southern England from 1275 through 1959. The trend line shows that the average change in prices over the whole period was 0.5 percent per year. The shaded areas indicate periods of unreversed inflation. The series also shows that even the perspective of a century can be misleading because long periods of stable or gently falling prices tended to alternate with long periods of rising prices. (*Source: Lloyds Bank Review*, No. 58, October 1960.)

money that comes only in large denominations is useless for transactions having only a small value. It must not be readily counterfeitable, because if money can be easily duplicated by individuals, it will lose its value.

A Store of Value

Money is a convenient way to store purchasing power; goods may be sold today and money stored until it is needed. The money provides a claim on someone else's goods that can be exercised at a future date. The two sides of the transaction can be separated in time with the obvious increase in freedom that this confers.

To be a satisfactory store of value, however, money must have a relatively stable value. When the price level is stable, the purchasing power of a given sum of money is also stable. When the price level changes, this is not so. Such changes undermine the usefulness of money as a store of value. An extreme example is discussed in Box 33-1.

Although money can serve as a satisfactory store of accumulated purchasing power for a single individual, it cannot do so for the society as a whole. If a single individual accumulates a pile of dollars, he or she will, when the time comes to spend it, be able to command the current output of some other individual. The whole society cannot do this. If all individuals were to save their money and then retire simultaneously to live on their savings, there would be no current production to purchase and consume. The society's ability to satisfy wants depends on goods and services being available; if some of this want-satisfying capacity is to be stored up for the whole society, goods that are currently producible must be left unconsumed and carried over to future periods.

A Unit of Account

Money may also be used purely for accounting purposes without having a physical existence of its own. For instance, a government store in a truly communist society might say that everyone had so many "dollars" to use each month. Goods could then be assigned prices and each consumer's purchases recorded, the consumer being allowed to buy until the allocated supply of dollars was exhausted. These dollars need have no existence other than as entries in the store's books, yet they would serve as a perfectly satisfactory unit of account.

Whether they could also serve as a medium of exchange between individuals depends on whether

BOX 33-1

Hyperinflation

Can the price level ever rise so rapidly that money loses its usefulness either as a medium of exchange or as a store of value? The answer appears to be that very occasionally this has happened. Inflation rates of 50, 100, and even 200 percent or more a year have occurred year after year and proven manageable as people adjust their contracts to real terms. While there are strains and side effects, the evidence shows such situations to be possible without causing money to become useless.

Does this mean that there is no reason to fear that rapid inflation will turn into hyperinflation that will destroy the value of money completely? The historical record is not entirely reassuring. There have been a number of instances where prices began to rise at an ever-accelerating rate until the nation's money ceased to be a satisfactory store of value even for the short period between receipt and expenditure and hence ceased also to be useful as a medium of exchange.

Consider the index of wholesale prices in Germany during and after World War I given in the table. The index shows that a good purchased with one 100-mark note in July 1923 would have required *10 million* 100-mark notes for its purchase only four months later! While Germany had experienced substantial inflation during World War I, averaging more than 30 percent per year, the immediate postwar years of 1920 and 1921 gave no sign of an explosive inflation. Indeed, during 1920 price stability was experienced. But in 1922 and 1923, the price level exploded. On November 15, 1923, the mark was officially repudiated, its value wholly destroyed. How could this happen?

When an inflation becomes so rapid that people lose confidence in the purchasing power of their currency, they rush to spend it. But people who have goods become increasingly reluctant to accept the rapidly depreciating money in exchange. The rush to spend money accelerates the increase in prices until people finally become unwilling to accept money on any terms. What was once money ceases to be money.

Date		German wholesale price index (1913 = 1)
January	1913	1
January	1920	13
January	1921	14
January	1922	37
July	1922	101
January	1923	2,785
July	1923	74,800
August	1923	944,000
September	1923	23,900,000
October	1923	7,096,000,000
November	1923*	750,000,000,000

* The mark was repudiated on November 15, 1923.

The price system can then be restored only by repudiation of the old monetary unit and its replacement by a new unit. This destroys the value of monetary savings and of all contracts specified in terms of the old monetary units. It wipes out many people's savings by destroying the value of assets denominated in money terms.

There are about a dozen documented hyperinflations in world history, among them the collapse of the continental during the American Revolution, the ruble during the Russian Revolution, the drachma during and after the German occupation of Greece in World War II, the pengö in Hungary during 1945 and 1946, and the Chinese national currency during 1946–1948. Every one of these hyperinflations was accompanied by great increases in the money supply; new money was printed to give governments purchasing power they could not or would not obtain by taxation. And every one occurred in the midst of a major political upheaval in which grave doubts existed about the stability and future of the government itself.

Is hyperinflation likely in the absence of civil war, revolution, or collapse of the government? Most economists think not. And it is clear that high inflation rates over a period of time do not mean the inevitable or even likely onset of a hyperinflation, however serious the distributive and social effects of such rates may be.

the store would agree to transfer dollar credits from one customer to another at the customer's request. Banks will transfer dollars credited to demand deposits in this way, and thus a bank deposit can serve as both a unit of account and a medium of exchange. Notice that the use of *dollars* in this context suggests a further sense in which money is a unit of account. People think about values in terms of the monetary unit with which they are familiar.

Another related function of money is sometimes distinguished. It can be used as a standard of deferred payments. Payments that are to be made in the future, on account of debts and so on, are reckoned in money. Money is used as a unit of account with the added dimension of time because the account will not be settled until later.

The Origins of Money

The origins of money are lost in antiquity; most primitive tribes known today make some use of it. The ability of money to free people from the cumbersome necessity of barter must have led to its early use as soon as some generally acceptable commodity appeared.

Metallic Money

All sorts of commodities have been used as money at one time or another, but gold and silver proved to have great advantages. They were precious because their supply was relatively limited, and they were in constant demand by the rich for ornament and decoration. Also, they do not easily wear out. Thus they tended to have a high and stable price. They were easily recognized and generally known to be commodities that, because of their stable price, would be readily accepted. They were also divisible into extremely small units.

Precious metals thus came to circulate as money and to be used in many transactions. Before the invention of coins it was necessary to carry the metals in bulk. When a purchase was made, the requisite quantity of the metal was carefully weighed on a scale. A sack of gold and a highly accurate set of scales were the common equipment of the merchant and trader.

The invention of coinage eliminated the need to weigh the metal at each transaction. The prince or ruler weighed the metal and made a coin out of it to which he affixed his own seal to guarantee the amount of precious metal it contained. If a coin was certified to contain exactly 1/16 of an ounce of gold and a commodity was priced at 1/8 of an ounce of gold, two coins could be given over without weighing the gold. This was clearly a great convenience as long as traders knew they could accept the coin at its "face value." The face value was nothing more than a statement that a certain weight of metal was contained therein.

Abuses of metallic money. The ruler's subjects, however, could not let a good opportunity pass. Someone soon had the idea of clipping a thin slice off the edge of the coin. If he collected a coin stamped as containing half an ounce of gold, he could clip a slice off the edge and pass the coin off as still containing half an ounce of gold. ("Doesn't the stamp prove it?" he would argue.) If he got away with this, he would have made a profit equal to the market value of the clipped metal.

Whenever this practice became common, even the most myopic traders noticed that things were not what they seemed in the coinage world. It became necessary to weigh each coin before accepting it at its face value; out came the scales again, and most of the usefulness of coins was lost. To get around this problem, the idea arose of minting the coins with a rough edge. The absence of the rough edge would immediately be apparent and would indicate that the coin had been clipped. The practice, called milling, survives on some coins as an interesting anachronism to remind us that there were days when the market value of the metal in the coin (if it were melted down) was equal to the face value of the coin.

Debasement of metallic money. Not to be outdone by the cunning of their subjects, the rulers were quick to seize the chance of getting something for nothing. The power to mint placed rulers in a good position to work a *really* profitable fraud. When faced with debts that could not be paid or repudiated, rulers merely used some suitable occasion—a marriage, an anniversary, an alliance—to remint the coinage. Subjects would be ordered to bring their gold coins into the mint to be melted down and coined afresh with a new stamp. The subjects could then go away with one new coin for every old coin they had brought in. Between the melting down and the recoining, however, the rulers had only to toss some inexpensive base metal in with the molten gold to earn a handsome profit. If the coinage were debased by adding, say, 1 pound of new base metal to every 4 pounds of old coins, five coins would be made for every four turned in. For every four coins brought in, the rulers could return four and have one left as profit with which to pay off debts.

Since gold and silver are softer and more malleable than most base metals, an experienced trader could usually tell if a coin had been seriously debased by testing its hardness. This is why, in films depicting ancient markets, you will often see a merchant biting a coin to see how easily it could be bent.

The result of debasement was inflation. The subjects had the same number of coins as before and hence could demand the same quantity of goods. When rulers paid their bills, however, the recipients of the extra coins could be expected to spend some or all of them, and this caused a net increase in demand. The extra demand would bid up prices. Debasing the coinage thus led to a rise in prices.

It was the experience of such inflations that led early economists to propound the *quantity theory of money and prices*. They argued that there was a relation between the average level of prices and the quantity of money in circulation, such that an increase in the quantity of money would lead to a proportionate increase in the price level. (We shall have more to say about this theory in Chapter 34.)

Gresham's law. The early experience of currency debasement led to the observation known as **Gresham's law** after the Elizabethan financial expert Sir Thomas Gresham. Gresham's hypothesis that "bad money drives out good" has stood the test of time.

When Queen Elizabeth I of England first came to the throne in the middle of the sixteenth century, the coinage had been severely debased. Seeking to help trade, Elizabeth minted new coins containing their full face value in gold. But as fast as she fed these new coins into circulation, they disappeared. Why? Gresham reasoned as follows to the young queen.

Suppose that you possessed one new and one old coin, each with the same face value, and had a bill to pay. What would you do? Clearly, you would pay the bill with the debased coin and keep the undebased one. You part with less gold that way. Suppose that you wanted to obtain a certain amount of gold bullion by melting down the gold coins (as was frequently done). Which coins would you use? Clearly, you would use new, undebased coins because you would part with less "face value" that way. The debased coins would thus remain in circulation and the undebased coins would disappear. Whenever people got hold of an undebased coin, they would hold on to it; whenever they got a debased coin, they would pass it on. The example in Box 33-2 shows that Gresham's law is as applicable in the twentieth century as it was in the sixteenth century.

Paper Money

The next important step in the history of money was the evolution of paper currency. Artisans who worked with gold required secure safes, and the public began to deposit their gold with such goldsmiths for safekeeping. Goldsmiths would give their depositors receipts promising to hand over the gold on demand. When any depositor wished to make a large purchase, she could go to her goldsmith, reclaim some of her gold, and hand it over to the seller of the goods. If the seller had no immediate need for the gold, he would carry it back to the goldsmith for safekeeping.

If people knew the goldsmith to be reliable, there was no need to go through the cumbersome and risky business of physically transferring the gold. The buyer need only transfer the goldsmith's receipt to the seller, who would accept it, secure in the knowledge that the goldsmith would pay over the gold whenever it was needed. If the seller wished to buy a good from a third party, who also knew the goldsmith to be reliable, this transaction, too, could be effected by passing the goldsmith's receipt from the buyer to the seller. The convenience of using pieces of paper instead of gold is obvious.

Thus, when it first came into being, paper money

BOX 33-2

Where Has All the Coinage Gone?

Tourists traveling in Chile in the 1970s (and in other countries with rapid inflation) often wondered aloud why paper currency was used even for transactions as small as the purchase of a newspaper or a pack of matches. Metallic currency in such places was scarce and sometimes nonexistent. Similarly, the silver dollar, silver half-dollar, silver quarter, and silver dime have disappeared from circulation in North America. The reason for these things is an example of Gresham's law.

Consider a country that has three different "tokens," each of them legal tender in the amount of $0.25. One is a silver quarter with $0.10 worth of recoverable silver in it; a second is made of cheaper metals with $0.05 worth of recoverable metal in it; the third is a $0.25 bill, a brightly colored piece of paper money that says plainly on its face "legal tender for all debts public and private."

If prices are stable and the government produces all three forms of money, there is no reason why they should not all circulate freely and interchangeably. Each is legal tender, and each is worth more as money than as anything else.

However, suppose an inflation starts and prices—including, proportionally, the prices of silver and other metals—begin to rise sharply. By the time prices have tripled, the silver quarters will have disappeared because the silver in each one is now worth $0.30, and people will hoard them or melt them down rather than spend them to buy goods priced at only $0.25. While not everyone will do this, coins passing from hand to hand will eventually reach someone who withdraws them from circulation.

What about the coins made of cheaper metal? Since prices have tripled, they now contain metal worth $0.15, still less than their face value. Will they too disappear? They will if there is further inflation of, say, 100 percent. This raises the market value of the metal in the coin above its face value. The coins will disappear as they are melted down. By that time, only the paper money will be in circulation. The "bad" paper money will have driven out the "good" metal money.

Thus inflation may make some money "good" and some "bad" in Gresham's sense. If it does, the bad will displace the good.

---

was a promise to pay on demand so much gold, the promise being made first by goldsmiths and later by banks. Banks, too, became known for their vaults ("safes") where the precious gold was stored and protected. As long as the institutions were known to be reliable, their pieces of paper would be "as good as gold." Such paper money was *backed* by precious metal and was *convertible* on demand into this metal. When a country's money is convertible into gold, the country is said to be on a *gold standard.*

In nineteenth century Canada private banks operating initially under provincial charters commonly issued paper money nominally convertible into gold. **Bank notes** represented banks' promises to pay. They remained an important part of the money supply well into the current century, and they were not completely supplanted by government-issued paper money until 1950.

Fractionally backed paper money. For most transactions individuals were content to use paper currency. It was soon discovered that it was not necessary to keep an ounce of gold in the vaults for every claim to an ounce circulating as paper money. It was necessary to keep some gold on hand because paper would not do for some transactions. If someone wished to make a purchase from a distant place where her local bank was not known, she might have to convert her paper into gold and ship the gold. Further, she might not have perfect confidence in the bank's ability to honor its pledge to redeem the notes in gold at a future time. Her alternative was to exchange her notes for gold and store the gold until she needed it.

For these and other reasons, some holders of notes demanded gold in return for their notes. However, some of the bank's customers received gold in various transactions and stored it in the bank for safekeeping. They accepted promises to pay (i.e., bank notes) in return. At any one time, then, some of the bank's customers would be withdrawing gold, others would be depositing it, and most would be trading in the bank's paper notes without any need or desire to convert them into gold. Thus the bank was able to issue more money redeemable in gold than the amount of gold held in its vaults. This was good business, because the money could be profitably invested in interest-earning loans to households and firms.

This discovery was made by the early goldsmiths. From that time to the present, banks have had many more claims outstanding against them than they actually had in reserves available to pay those claims. We say that the currency issued in such a situation is *fractionally backed* by the reserves.

In the past the major problem of a fractionally backed, convertible currency was maintaining its convertibility into the precious metal backing it. The imprudent bank that issued too much paper money found itself unable to redeem its currency in gold when the demand for gold was even slightly higher than usual. It would then have to suspend payments, and all holders of its notes would suddenly find the notes worthless. The prudent bank, which kept a reasonable relation between its note issue and its gold reserve, found that it could meet a normal range of demand for gold without any trouble.

If the public lost confidence and en masse demanded redemption of their currency, the banks would be unable to honor their pledges. The history of nineteenth and early twentieth century banking on both sides of the Atlantic is full of examples of banks ruined by "panics," sudden runs on their gold reserves. When this happened the banks' depositors and the holders of their notes would find themselves with worthless pieces of paper.

Central banks were a natural outcome of this sort of banking system. Where were the commercial banks to turn when they had good investments but were in temporary need of cash? If they provided loans for the public against reasonable security, why should not some other institution provide loans to them against the same sort of security? Central banks evolved in response to such needs.

Fiat currencies. As time went on, note issue by private banks became less common and central banks took control of the currency. Central banks in turn became governmental institutions. In time *only* central banks were permitted to issue notes.

Originally the central banks issued currency that was fully convertible into gold. In those days gold would be brought to the central bank, which would issue currency in the form of "gold certificates" that asserted the gold was available on demand. The gold supply thus set some upper limit on the amount of currency. But central banks could issue more currency than they had gold because not all of the currency was presented for payment at any one time. Thus even under a gold standard, central banks had substantial discretionary control over the quantity of currency outstanding.

During the period between World Wars I and II, almost all the countries of the world abandoned the gold standard; their currencies were no longer convertible into gold. Money that is not convertible by law into anything valuable depends on its acceptability for its value. Money that is declared by government order, or fiat, to be legal tender for settlement of all debts is called a **fiat money.** Some issues raised by the abandoning of the gold standard are discussed in Box 33-3.

Today almost all currency is fiat money.

Some countries (including the United States until 1968) preserve the fiction that their currency is backed by gold, but no country allows its currency to be converted into gold on demand. Gold backing for Canadian currency was eliminated in 1940, although note issues continued to carry the traditional statement "will pay to the bearer on demand" until 1954. The holder of a $20 bill who took this seriously and demanded $20 could hand over the $20 bill and receive in return a different but identical $20 bill! Today's Bank of Canada notes simply say, "This note is legal tender." It is, in other words, fiat money pure and simple.

Legal tender is anything that by law must be accepted when offered either for the purchase of goods or services or to discharge a debt. If you are offered something that is legal tender in payment for

BOX 33-3

Should Currency Be Backed by Gold?

The gold standard imposed an upper limit on the quantity of convertible currency that could be issued. Now that the system has been abandoned, does it matter that the central bank is not limited to its ability to issue currency?

Gold derives its value because it is scarce relative to the demand for it (the demand being derived from its monetary and its nonmonetary uses). Tying a currency to gold meant that the quantity of money in a country was determined by such chance occurrences as the discovery of new gold supplies. This was not without advantages, the most important being that it provided a check on governments' ability to cause inflation. Gold cannot be manufactured at will; paper currency can.

There is little doubt that in the past, if the money supply had been purely paper, many governments would have attempted to pay their bills by printing new money rather than by raising taxes. Such increases in the money supply, in periods of full employment, would lead to inflation in the same way that the debasement of metallic currency did.

Thus the gold standard provided some check on inflation by making it difficult for the government to change the money supply. Periods of major gold discoveries, however, brought about inflations of their own. In the 1500s, for example, Spanish gold and silver flowed into Europe from the New World, bringing inflation in their wake.

A major problem caused by a reliance on gold is that although it is usually desirable to increase the money supply when real national income is increasing, this cannot be done on a gold standard unless, by pure chance, gold is discovered at the same time. The gold standard took discretionary powers over the money supply out of the hands of government. Whether or not one thinks this is a good thing depends on how one thinks governments would use this discretion.

In general, a gold standard is probably better than having the currency managed by an ignorant or irresponsible government, but it is worse than having the currency supply adjusted by a well-informed and intelligent one. *Better* and *worse* in this context are judged by the criterion of having a money supply that varies adequately with the needs of the economy but does not vary so as to cause violent inflations or deflations.

---

a debt and you refuse to accept it, the debt is no longer legally collectible.

Not only is our modern currency fiat money, so is our coinage. Modern coins, unlike their historical ancestors, contain a value of metal that is characteristically a minute fraction of the value of the coin. Modern coins, like modern paper money, are merely tokens.

Why Is Fiat Money Valuable?

Today paper money and coinage are valuable because they are generally accepted. Because everyone accepts them as valuable, they *are* valuable; the fact that they can no longer be converted into anything has no effect on their functioning as a medium of exchange.

In the early days of the gold standard, paper money was valuable because everyone believed it was convertible into gold on demand. Experience during periods of crisis, when there was often a temporary suspension of convertibility into gold, and of panic, when there were bank failures, served to demonstrate that the mere *promise* of convertibility was not sufficient to make money valuable. Gradually the realization grew that neither was convertibility necessary.

Fiat money is valuable when it will be accepted in payment for goods and for debts.

Many people are disturbed to learn that present-day paper money is neither backed by nor convertible into anything more valuable—that it consists of nothing but pieces of paper whose value derives from common acceptance and from confidence that it will continue to be accepted in the future. Most people believe their money should be more substantial than that; after all, what of "dollar diplomacy" and the "bedrock solidity" of the Swiss franc? But money is in fact made of nothing more than pieces of paper. There is no point in pretending otherwise.

If paper money is acceptable, it is a medium of exchange; if its purchasing power remains stable, it is a satisfactory store of value; and if both of these things are true, it will also serve as a satisfactory unit of account.

Modern Money

By the twentieth century private banks had lost the authority to issue bank notes. Yet they did not lose the power to create deposit money.

Deposit Money

Banks' customers frequently deposit coins and paper money with the banks for safekeeping, just as in former times they deposited gold. Such a deposit is recorded as an entry on the customer's account. A customer who wishes to pay a debt may come to the bank and claim the money in dollars, then pay the money to another person. This person may then redeposit the money in a bank.

Like the gold transfers, this is a tedious procedure, particularly for large payments. It is more convenient to have the bank transfer claims to this money on deposit. The common cheque is an instruction to the bank to make the transfer. Such transfers soon became easy and inexpensive, and cheques soon became widely accepted in payment for commodities and debts. The deposits became a form of money called **deposit money,** defined as money held by the public in the form of deposits in banks that can be withdrawn on demand.

When individual A deposits $100 in a bank, the bank credits A's account with $100. This is the bank's promise to pay $100 cash on demand. If A pays B $100 by writing a cheque that B then deposits in the same bank, the bank merely reduces A's account by $100 and increases B's by the same amount. Thus the bank still promises to pay on demand the $100 originally deposited, but it now promises to pay it to B rather than to A. What makes all this so convenient is that B can actually deposit A's cheque in any bank, and the banks will arrange the transfer of credits.

Cheques are in some ways the modern equivalent of old-time bank notes issued by commercial banks. The passing of a bank note from hand to hand transferred ownership of a claim against the bank. A cheque on a deposit account is similarly an order to the bank to pay the designated recipient, rather than oneself, money credited to the account. Cheques, unlike bank notes, do not circulate freely from hand to hand; thus cheques themselves are not currency. The balance in the demand deposit *is* money; the cheque transfers money from one person to another. Because cheques are easily drawn and deposited and because they are relatively safe from theft, they are widely used. Over 6 billion cheques a year are now drawn in Canada. During the past decade the number of cheques drawn increased at about 7 percent per year.

Thus, when chartered banks lost the right to issue notes of their own, the form of bank money changed but the substance did not. Today banks have money in their vaults (or on deposit with the central banks) just as they always did. Once it was gold; today it is the legal tender of the times—fiat money. It is true today, just as in the past, that most of the bank's customers are content to pay their bills by passing among themselves the bank's promises to pay money on demand. Only a small proportion of the transactions made by the bank's customers is made in cash.

Bank deposits are money. Today, just as in the past, banks can create money by issuing more promises to pay (deposits) than they have cash reserves available to pay out.

The Banking System

Many types of institutions make up a modern banking system such as exists in Canada today. The **central bank** is the government-owned and -operated institution that serves to control the banking system. Through it, the government's monetary policy is conducted. In Canada the central bank is the Bank of Canada; we study it in detail in Chapter 35. *Financial intermediaries* are privately owned institutions that serve the general public. They are called intermediaries because they stand between savers, from whom they accept deposits, and investors, to whom they make loans. In this chapter we focus on an important class of financial intermediaries, the *chartered banks*.

Modern commercial banking systems are of two main types. One type has a small number of banks, each with a large number of branch offices; the other consists of many independent banks. The banking systems of Britain and Canada are of the first type, with only a few banks accounting for the overwhelming bulk of the business. The American system is of the second type. The functioning of the banking system is, however, essentially the same in both systems.

The Canadian System

The Canadian banking system is controlled by the provisions of the Bank Act, first passed in 1935 and revised several times since. Under the Bank Act charters can be granted to financial institutions to operate as banks, and up until 1980 there were only a few chartered banks, most of which were very large and each of which operated under identical regulatory provisions. (In 1980 there were only 11 chartered banks, and the five largest together held more than 90 percent of total chartered bank assets.)

The 1980 revisions to the Bank Act allowed for foreign banks to commence operations in Canada, although it limited severely the scale and scope of their activity. Subsequent revisions have altered some of these restrictions and made it easier to obtain new banking charters, but the revisions have maintained the distinction between these newer institutions and banks operating under what are essentially the pre-1980 provisions of the Bank Act. The original provisions, in slightly modified form, are now known as Schedule A of the Bank Act; the foreign banks and the new, smaller domestic banks operate under Schedules B and C. The term **chartered banks** is used to refer to the Schedule A banks.

The chartered banks have common attributes: They hold deposits for their customers; they permit certain deposits to be transferred by cheque from an individual account to other accounts held in any bank branch in the country; they make loans to households and firms; and they invest in government securities.

Banks are not the only financial institutions in the country. Many other privately owned, profit-seeking institutions, such as trust companies, mortgage loan companies, and credit unions, accept savings deposits and grant loans for specific purposes. Finance companies make loans to households for practically any purpose—sometimes at very high effective interest rates. The post office and the telegraph system will transfer money, and credit card companies will extend credit so that purchases can be made on a buy-now, pay-later basis.

The chartered banks (including Schedule B and C banks) are subject only to federal regulations and are required to hold reserves with the Bank of Canada against their deposit liabilities. Other institutions do not face reserve requirements, but most are subject to various federal and provincial regulations concerning ownership and control and the types of financial activities they are allowed to engage in. Thus there are differences among all types of financial institutions, not just between banks and others.

The chartered banks have historically been such a stable and dominant group that the terms *chartered banks* and *banking system* have been considered virtually synonymous. However, recent events may serve to break this identification. First, there have been dramatic changes in the makeup of the chartered banks—in 1985 two relatively new, regionally based chartered banks failed, and in 1986 two other chartered banks merged and yet two others were taken over by foreign banks. Second, the federal government and several provincial governments have recently proposed extensive changes in regulations, including the abolition of reserve requirements for the chartered banks, that would further blur the distinction between the chartered banks and other financial institutions.

Interbank Activities

Chartered banks have a number of interbank cooperative relationships. For example, banks often share loans. Even the biggest bank cannot meet all the credit needs of a giant corporation, and often a group of banks will offer a "pool loan," agreeing on common terms and dividing the loan up into manageable segments.

Another form of interbank cooperation is the bank credit card. Visa and MasterCard are the two most widely used credit cards, and each is operated by a group of banks.

Probably the most important form of interbank cooperation is cheque clearing and collection. Bank deposits are an effective medium of exchange only because banks accept each other's cheques. If a depositor in bank X writes a cheque to someone who deposits it in bank Y, bank X now owes money to bank Y. This creates a need for the banks to present cheques to each other for payment.

There are millions of such transactions in the course of a day, and they result in an enormous sorting and bookkeeping job. Multibank systems make use of a **clearing house** where interbank debts are settled. At the end of the day, all the cheques drawn by bank X's customers and deposited in bank Y are totaled and set against the total of all the cheques drawn by bank Y's customers and deposited in bank X. It is necessary only to settle the difference between the two sums. The actual cheques are passed through the clearing house back to the bank on which they were drawn. Both banks are then able to adjust the individual accounts by a set of book entries. A flow of cash between banks is necessary only when there is a net transfer of cash from the customers of one bank to those of another. This flow of cash is accomplished by a transfer of deposits held by the chartered banks with the Bank of Canada.

Profit Seeking

Banks are private firms that start with invested capital and seek to "earn money" in the same sense as firms making neckties or bicycles. A chartered bank provides a variety of services to its customers: a safe place to store money; the convenience of demand deposits that can be transferred by personal cheque; a safe and convenient place to earn a modest but guaranteed return on savings; and often financial advice and estate management services. The bank earns some revenue by charging for these services, but such fees are a small part of the bank's total earnings. The largest part (typically about five-sixths) of a bank's earnings is derived from the bank's ability to invest profitably the funds placed with it.

Principal Assets and Liabilities

Table 33-1 is the combined balance sheet of the chartered banks in Canada. The bulk of a bank's liabilities are deposits owed to its depositors. The principal assets of a bank are the *securities* it buys (including government bonds), which pay interest or dividends, and the *loans* it makes to individuals and to businesses. A bank loan is a liability to the borrower (who must pay it back) but an asset to the bank. The bank expects not only to have the loan repaid but also to receive interest that more than compensates for the paperwork involved and the risk of nonpayment.

Most money deposited with banks is "at work," having been invested in loans or securities. Deposits are the lifeblood of a chartered bank. Without them the bank has nothing to lend or invest except the small amount of its initial capital. Banks attract deposits by paying interest to depositors and by providing them, for a fee that does not cover the banks' full cost, with services such as clearing cheques and providing regular monthly statements. Banks earn profits by lending and investing money deposited with them for more than they pay their depositors in terms of interest and other services provided.

Reserves

The Need for Reserves

All bankers would as a matter of convenience and prudence keep sufficient cash on hand to be able to meet depositors' day-to-day requirements for cash. But just as the goldsmiths of old discovered that only a fraction of the gold they held was ever withdrawn at any given time, and just as banks of old discovered that only a fraction of convertible bank notes were actually converted, so, too, have modern banks discovered that only a fraction of their deposits will be

TABLE 33-1 Consolidated Balance Sheet of Canadian Chartered Banks, December 31, 1986 *(billions of dollars)*

Assets		Liabilities	
Reserves (including deposits with Bank of Canada)	8	Deposits: Demand	19
Loans (determined in Canadian dollars)	182	Savings	129
Government of Canada securities	20	Time	46
Foreign-currency assets	207	Foreign-currency liabilities	207
Other assets	51	Other liabilities	46
	468	Capital account	21
			468

Source: Bank of Canada Review.

Reserves are only a small fraction of deposit liabilities. If all the bank's customers who held demand deposits tried to withdraw them in cash, the banks could not meet this demand without liquidating $11 billion of other assets. This would be impossible without assistance from the Bank of Canada.

withdrawn in cash at any one time. Most deposits of any individual bank remain on deposit with it; thus an individual bank need keep only fractional reserves against its deposits.

The reserves needed to assure that depositors can withdraw their deposits on demand is quite small in normal times.

In abnormal times, however, nothing short of 100 percent might do the job if the commercial banking system had to stand alone. When a few bank failures cause a general loss of confidence in banks' ability to redeem their deposits, the results can be devastating. Until relatively recent times, such an event—or even the rumor of it—could lead to a "run" on banks as depositors rushed to withdraw their money. Faced with such a panic, banks would have to close until they had borrowed funds or liquidated enough assets to meet the demand or until the demand subsided. But banks could not instantly turn their loans into cash since the borrowers had the money tied up in such things as real estate or business enterprises. Neither could the banks obtain cash by selling their securities to the public since payments would be made by cheques, which would not provide cash with which to pay off depositors.

To avoid panics reserves must be large enough to meet extraordinary demands for cash.

The need of the banking system for reserves against depositors' panics has been diminished by government policies. First, the central bank can provide chartered banks with needed cash either by lending them money or by buying the securities they want to sell. Second, the government provides insurance that guarantees that depositors will get their money back even if a bank fails completely. Such insurance decreases the likelihood of a widespread panic because one bank's failure is much less likely to lead to a run on other banks. Most depositors will not withdraw their money as long as they are *sure* they can get it when they need it.

Actual and Required Reserves

As Table 33-1 shows, in 1986 only a fraction of the total major assets of the chartered banks consisted of cash and interest-earning assets that could quickly be converted into cash. Cash reserves are held in the form of deposits in the Bank of Canada and notes. All banks need to keep some reserves of cash to satisfy their depositors' day-to-day requirements. The Canadian banking system is a **fractional reserve system,** with banks holding reserves of only a fraction of their deposits. The size of the reserve reflects not only the judgment of bankers but also the legal requirements imposed by the Bank Act.

A bank's **reserve ratio** is the fraction of its deposits that it holds as reserves either as currency in its vaults or as deposits with the central bank. Reserves that the banks are required to hold under the Bank Act are called **required reserves.** Any reserves that a bank holds over and above required reserves are called **excess reserves.** Since 1980 the required reserve ratios have been 10 percent for demand deposits and 4 percent for term deposits.

Most liquid assets are held in the form of bonds and treasury bills (government securities with usual terms to maturity of three or six months) issued by the government of Canada. These assets generally yield a lower rate of return than loans, but they act as **secondary reserves** that can be used to replenish cash holdings should they be run down.

Central Banks

All advanced free-market economies have a central bank. Many of the world's early central banks were private, profit-making institutions that provided services to ordinary banks. Their importance, however, led them to develop close ties with the government. Central banks soon became instruments of the government, though not all of them were publicly owned. The Bank of England (the "Old Lady of Threadneedle Street"), one of the world's oldest and most famous central banks, began to operate as the central bank of England in the seventeenth century but was not "nationalized" until 1947. In the United States the central bank is called the Federal Reserve System (popularly known as the Fed), and in this country it is the Bank of Canada.

The similarities of central banks in the functions they perform and the tools they use are much more important than their differences in organization. Although our attention is focused on the operations of the Bank of Canada, the basic situation is not different for the Bank of England, the Bank of Greece, or the Federal Reserve System.

Organization of the Bank of Canada

The Bank of Canada is a publicly owned corporation; all profits accruing from its operations are remitted to the government of Canada. The responsibility for the bank's affairs rests with a board of directors composed of the governor, the senior deputy governor, the deputy minister of finance, and 12 directors. The governor is appointed by the directors, with the approval of the cabinet, for a seven-year term. In January 1987, John Crow was appointed governor, replacing Gerald Bouey, who retired after serving two seven-year terms.

The organization of the Bank of Canada is designed to keep the operation of monetary policy free from day-to-day political influence. Thus the Bank is not responsible to Parliament for its day-to-day behavior in the way that the Department of Finance is for the operation of fiscal policy. Nonetheless, the governor of the Bank and the minister of finance consult regularly. Furthermore, in the case of fundamental disagreement over policy, the governor must resign or acquiesce to the cabinet's desired policy as enunciated by the minister.[1]

Basic Functions of the Bank of Canada

A central bank serves four main functions: as a banker for private banks, as a bank for the government, as the controller of the nation's supply of money, and as a supporter of financial markets. The first three functions are revealed by a study of Table 33-2, which shows the balance sheet of a central bank.

Banker to the chartered banks. The central bank accepts deposits from the chartered banks and will, on order, transfer them to the account of another bank. In this way the central bank provides the chartered banks with the equivalent of a chequing account and with a means of settling debts to other banks. The deposits of the chartered banks with the central bank appear in Table 33-2. Notice that the cash reserves of the chartered banks deposited with the central bank are *liabilities* of the central bank (because it promises to pay them on demand), just as the money reserves of an individual or corporation deposited with a chartered bank are the liabilities of the chartered bank.

Historically, one of the earliest services provided by central banks was that of "lender of last resort"

[1] In 1962, when James Coyne was governor, such a fundamental disagreement arose and Coyne was eventually forced to resign. This incident is discussed further in Box 42-3.

TABLE 33-2 Assets and Liabilities of the Bank of Canada, December 1986 *(millions of dollars)*

Assets		Liabilities	
Government of Canada securities	$18,211	Notes in circulation	$17,911
Advances to banks	868	Government of Canada deposits	49
Foreign-currency assets	323	Deposits of chartered banks	2,446
Other assets	1,543	Foreign-currency liabilities	87
	$20,945	Other liabilities and capital	1,452
			$20,945

Source: Bank of Canada Review, April 1987.

The balance sheet of the Bank of Canada shows that it serves as banker to the chartered banks and the government and as issuer of our currency; it also suggests the bank's role as regulator of money markets and the money supply. The principal liabilities of the Bank are the basis of the money supply. Bank of Canada notes are currency, and the deposits of the chartered banks give them the reserves they use to create deposit money. The bank's holdings of Government of Canada securities arise from its operations designed to regulate the money supply and financial markets.

to the banking system. Central banks would lend money to private banks that had sound investments (such as government securities and safe loans to individuals) but were in urgent need of cash. If such banks could not obtain ready cash, they might be forced into involvency because they could not meet the demands of their depositors, in spite of their being basically sound. Today's central banks continue to be the lender of last resort.

U.S. banks borrow extensively from the Federal Reserve System in order to maintain their reserves, but the corresponding institutional arrangement that Canadian banks use is somewhat more complicated. Some Bank of Canada holdings of government securities, shown in Table 32-2, are held under **purchase and resale agreements (PRA).** Rather than rely on loans from the Bank of Canada, the chartered banks meet their immediate cash requirements by varying the amount of **day-to-day loans** they make available to a group of investment dealers who carry inventories of Government of Canada securities. When necessary, these dealers can obtain financing from the Bank of Canada under PRA; that is, they can sell securities to the Bank of Canada and agree to buy them back at a later date. Thus when the chartered banks reduce their day-to-day loans, they induce an increase in PRA. The result is the same as if the banks had borrowed from the Bank of Canada directly.

Banker to the government. Governments, too, need to hold their funds in an account into which they can make deposits and on which they can write cheques. The government of Canada keeps its chequing deposits at the Bank of Canada, replenishing them from much larger accounts kept at the chartered banks. When the government requires more money, it too needs to borrow, and it does so by printing bonds. Most are sold directly to the public, but occasionally the government raises funds by selling securities (mostly short-term) to the central bank, which "buys" them by crediting the government's account with a deposit for the amount of the purchase. In December 1986 the Bank of Canada held over $18 billion in Government of Canada securities. These securities play an important role in the monetary system.

Controller and regulator of the money supply. One of the most important functions of a central bank is to control the money supply. From Table 33-2 it is clear that the overwhelming proportion of a central bank's liabilities (its promises to pay) are either notes (money) or the reserves of the chartered banks, which underlie the deposits (money) of households and firms.

The central bank can change the levels of its assets and liabilities in many ways, and as its liabilities rise and fall, so does the money supply. Consider a single example. Suppose the central bank buys $100 million worth of newly printed bonds from the government of Canada. The bank's assets (government bonds) rise by $100 million, and so do its liabilities (Government of Canada deposits). The government has an extra $100 million of purchasing power to spend. As easy as printing money, you say. Indeed, it is the same thing.

Regulator and supporter of money markets. Central banks usually assume a major responsibility to support the country's financial system and to prevent serious disruption by wide-scale panic and resulting bank failures. Various institutions are in the business of borrowing on a short-term and lending on a long-term basis. To some extent the chartered banks do this when they take in demand (or savings) deposits and lend money for various terms. But trust and mortgage loan companies are the major institution for this kind of transaction. They receive deposits from the public and lend the money on long-term mortgages.

Large, unanticipated increases in interest rates tend to squeeze these institutions. The average rate they earn on their investments rises only slowly as old contracts mature and new ones are made, but they must either pay higher rates to hold on to their deposits or accept wide-scale withdrawals that could easily bring about insolvency. To prevent such financial disasters, central banks often buy and sell government bonds either to slow the rate of change in interest rates or to narrow the range over which the rates are allowed to fluctuate.

Money Creation by the Banking System

The fractional reserve system provides the leverage that permits chartered banks and other financial institutions to create new money. The process is important, so it is worth examining in some detail.

Some Simplifying Assumptions

To focus on the essential aspects of how banks create money, assume that banks can invest in only one kind of asset, loans, and that there is only one kind of deposit, a demand deposit.

Three other assumptions are provisional. When we have developed the basic ideas concerning the bank's creation of money, these assumptions will be relaxed.

1. *Fixed required reserve ratio.* It is assumed that all banks have the same required reserve ratio, which does not change. In our numerical illustration we shall assume that the required reserve ratio is 20 percent (i.e., 0.20), that is, at least $1 of reserves for every $5 of deposits.
2. *No excess reserves.* It is assumed that all banks want to invest any reserves they have in excess of the legally required amount. This implies that they always believe there are safe investments to be made when they have excess reserves.
3. *No cash drain from the banking system.* It is assumed that the public holds a fixed amount of currency in circulation. Thus changes in the money supply will take the form of changes in deposit money.

The Creation of Deposit Money

A typical bank's balance sheet is shown in Table 33-3. The Canadian Immigrants Bank of Commerce (CIBC) has assets of $200 of reserves (all figures are in thousands of dollars), held partly as cash on hand and partly as deposits with the central bank, and $900 of loans outstanding to its customers. Its liabilities are $100 to those who initially contributed capital to start the bank, and $1,000 to current depositors. The bank's ratio of reserves to deposits is 200/1,000 = 0.20, exactly equal to its minimum requirement.

TABLE 33-3 Initial Balance Sheet of the Canadian Immigrants Bank of Commerce *(thousands of dollars)*

Assets		Liabilities	
Cash and other reserves	$ 200	Deposits	$1,000
Loans	900	Capital	100
	$1,100		$1,100

The CIBC has a reserve of 20 percent of its deposit liabilities. The chartered bank earns money by finding profitable investments for much of the money deposited with it. In this balance sheet loans are its earning assets.

TABLE 33-4 Balance Sheet of CIBC After an Immigrant Deposits $100 ***(thousands of dollars)***

Assets		Liabilities	
Cash and other reserves	$ 300	Deposits	$1,100
Loans	900	Capital	100
	$1,200		$1,200

The immigrant's deposit raises deposit liabilities and cash assets by the same amount. Since both cash and deposits rise by $100, the cash reserve ratio, formerly 0.20, increases to 0.27. The bank has more cash than it needs to provide a 20 percent reserve against its deposit liabilities.

TABLE 33-5 Monopoly Bank Balance Sheet After Making a $400 Loan ***(thousands of dollars)***

Assets		Liabilities	
Cash and other reserves	$ 300	Deposits	$1,500
Loans	1,300	Capital	100
	$1,600		$1,600

The loan restores the reserve ratio of 0.20. By increasing its loans by a multiple of its new cash deposit, the bank restores its reserve ratio of 0.20.

An immigrant arrives in the country and opens an account by depositing $100 with the CIBC. This is a wholly new deposit for the bank, and it results in a revised balance sheet (Table 33-4). As a result of the immigrant's new deposit, both cash assets and deposit liabilities have risen by $100. More important, the reserve ratio has increased from 0.20 to 0.27 (300/1,100). The bank now has excess reserves; with $300 in reserves it could support $1,500 in deposits.

A Single Monopoly Bank

If the CIBC were the only bank in the system, it would know that any loans that it made would eventually give rise to new deposits of an equal amount. It would then be in a position to say to the next business executive who comes in for a loan, "We will lend your firm $400 at the going rate of interest." The bank would do so by adding that amount to the firm's deposit account. Table 33-5 shows what would happen in this case. The new immigrant's deposit initially raised cash assets and deposit liabilities by $100. The new loans created an additional $400 of deposit liabilities. This restored the reserve ratio to its legal minimum (300/1,500 = 0.20), and no further expansion of deposit money is possible. As the bank's customers do business with one another, settling their accounts by cheques, the ownership of the deposits will be continually changing. But what matters to the bank is that its total deposits will remain constant.

The extent to which a monopoly bank could increase its loans *and thus its deposits* depends on the reserve ratio. Because in this case the ratio is 1/5 (= 0.20), the bank would be able to expand deposits to five times the original acquisition of money. In general, if the reserve ratio is r, a monopoly bank can increase its deposits by $1/r$ times any new reserves. As we shall see, this relation holds for *any* banking system, not just for one with a single bank. **[42]**

Many Banks

Deposit creation is more complicated in a multibank system than in a single-bank system, but *the end result is exactly the same.* It is more complicated because when a bank makes a loan, the recipient of the loan may pay the money to someone who deposits it in another bank.

To follow the sequence by which a multibank system creates deposits, we first return to Tables 33-3 and 33-4. The CIBC is shown in equilibrium in Table 33-3. After it has received a new cash deposit as shown in Table 33-4, it is no longer in equilibrium. Whereas the monopoly bank could immediately create $400 of new deposits, one of many banks in a multibank system cannot do this because many of the new deposits that it creates will end up in other banks, causing a cash drain to these other banks. What now happens is most easily seen under an extreme assumption. We assume that every new borrower immediately uses the borrowed funds to pay people who deal with a different bank.

With its present level of deposits at $1,100, the bank needs only $220 of reserves (0.20 × $1,100 = $220), so it can lend the $80 excess that it has on

TABLE 33-6 CIBC Balance Sheet After a New Loan and Cash Drain of $80
(thousands of dollars)

Assets		Liabilities	
Cash and other reserves	$ 220	Deposits	$1,100
Loans	980	Capital	100
	$1,200		$1,200

The bank lends its surplus cash and suffers a cash drain. The bank keeps $20 as a reserve against the immigrant's new deposit of $100. It lends $80 to a customer who writes a check to someone who deals with another bank. When the check is cleared, the CIBC suffers an $80 cash drain. Comparing Tables 33-3 and 33-6 shows that the bank has increased its deposit liabilities by the $100 deposited by the new immigrant and increased its assets by $20 of cash reserves and $80 of new loans. It has also restored its reserve ratio of 0.20.

TABLE 33-7 Changes in the Balance Sheets of Second-Generation Banks
(thousands of dollars)

Assets		Liabilities	
Cash and other reserves	+$16	Deposits	+$80
Loans	+ 64		
	+$80		+$80

Second-generation banks receive cash deposits and expand loans. The second-generation banks gain new deposits of $80 as a result of the loan granted by the CIBC, which is used to make payments to customers of the second-generation banks. These banks keep 20 percent of the cash they acquire as their reserve against the new deposit, and they can make new loans using the other 80 percent. When the customers who borrowed the money make payments to the customers of third-generation banks, a cash drain occurs.

hand. Table 33-6 shows the position after this has been done and after the proceeds of the loan have been withdrawn to be deposited to the account of a customer of another bank. The CIBC once again has a 20 percent reserve ratio.

So far deposits in the CIBC have increased by only the initial $100 of the new immigrant's money with which we started, as shown in Table 33-4. (Of this, $20 is held as a cash reserve against the deposit and $80 has been lent out in the system.) But other banks have received new deposits of $80 as the persons receiving payment from those who borrowed the $80 from the CIBC deposited those payments in their own banks. The receiving banks are sometimes called *next-generation banks* or, more specifically according to the situation, *second-generation, third-generation,* and so on. In this case the second-generation banks receive new deposits of $80, and when the checks clear, they have new reserves of $80. Because they require an addition to their reserves of only $16 to support the new deposit, they have $64 of excess reserves. They now increase their loans by $64. After this money is spent by the borrowers and has been deposited in other, third-generation banks, the balance sheets of the second-generation banks will have changed, as in Table 33-7.

The third-generation banks now find themselves with $64 of new deposits. Against these they need hold only $12.80 in cash, so they have excess reserves of $51.20 that they can immediately lend out. Thus there begins a long sequence of new deposits, new loans, new deposits, and new loans. The stages are shown in Table 33-8. The series in the table should look familiar, for it is the same convergent process underlying the multiplier encountered in Chapter 28.

The banking system has created new deposits and thus new money, although each banker can honestly say, "All I did was invest my excess reserves. I can do no more than manage wisely the money I receive."

If r is the reserve ratio, the ultimate effect on the deposits of the banking system of a new deposit will be $1/r$ times the new deposit. [43] This is exactly the same result in the monopoly bank case.[2]

Many Deposits

The two cases just discussed, the monopoly bank and a single new deposit in a multibank situation, show that under either set of opposite extreme assumptions, the result is the same. So it is, too, in intermediate situations. A far more realistic picture of deposit creation is one in which new deposits accrue simultaneously to all banks, perhaps because

[2] The "multiple expansion of deposits" that has just been worked through applies in reverse to a withdrawal of funds. Deposits of the banking system will fall by $1/r$ times any amount withdrawn from the bank and not redeposited at another.

TABLE 33-8 Many Banks, a Single New Deposit ***(thousands of dollars)***

Bank	New deposits	New loans	Addition to reserves
CIBC	$100.00	$ 80.00	$ 20.00
Second-generation bank	80.00	64.00	16.00
Third-generation bank	64.00	51.20	12.80
Fourth-generation bank	51.20	40.96	10.24
Fifth-generation bank	40.96	32.77	8.19
Sixth-generation bank	32.77	26.22	6.55
Seventh-generation bank	26.22	20.98	5.24
Eighth-generation bank	20.98	16.78	4.20
Ninth-generation bank	16.78	13.42	3.36
Tenth-generation bank	13.42	10.74	2.68
Total first 10 generations	446.33	357.07	89.26
All remaining generations	53.67	42.93	10.74
Total for banking systems	$500.00	$400.00	$100.00

The banking system as a whole can create deposit money whenever it receives new reserves. The table shows the process of the creation of deposit money on the assumptions that all the loans made by one set of banks end up as deposits in another set of banks (the next-generation banks), that the required reserve ratio (r) is 0.20, and that there are no excess reserves. Although each bank suffers a cash drain whenever it grants a new loan, the system as a whole does not, and the system ends up doing in a series of steps what a monopoly bank would do all at once; that is, it increases deposit money by $1/r$, which in this example is five times the amount of any increase in reserves that it obtains.

of changes in the monetary policy of the government.

Say, for example, that the community contains 10 banks of equal size and that each received new deposits of $100 in cash. Now each bank is in the position shown in Table 33-4, and each can begin to expand deposits based on the $100 of excess reserves. (Each bank does this by granting loans to customers.)

Because each bank does one-tenth of the total banking business, an average of 90 percent of any newly created deposit will find its way into other banks as the customer pays other people in the community by cheque. This will represent a cash drain from the lending bank to the other banks. However, 10 percent of each new deposit created by every other bank should find its way into this bank. All banks receive new cash, and all begin creating deposits simultaneously; no bank should suffer a significant cash drain to any other bank.

Thus all banks can go on expanding deposits without losing cash to each other; they need only worry about keeping enough cash to satisfy those depositors who will occasionally withdraw cash. The expansion can go on with each bank watching its own ratio of cash reserves to deposits, expanding deposits as long as the ratio exceeds 1/5 and ceasing when it reaches that figure. The process will come to a halt when each bank has created $400 in additional deposits, so that for each initial $100 cash deposit, there is now $500 in deposits backed by $100 in cash. Now *each* of the banks will have entries in its books similar to those shown in Table 33-5.

The general rule, if there is no cash drain, is that a banking system with a reserve ratio of r can change its deposits by $1/r$ times any change in reserves.

Excess Reserves and Cash Drains

Two of the simplifying assumptions made earlier can now be relaxed.

Excess reserves. If banks do not choose to invest excess reserves, the multiple expansion discussed will not occur. Turn back to Table 33-4. If the CIBC had been content to hold 27 percent reserves, it might well have done nothing more. Other things being equal, banks will choose to invest excess reserves because of the profit motive. But there may be times when they believe the risk is too great. It is one thing to be offered a good rate of interest on a loan, but if the borrower defaults on the payment of interest and principal, the bank will be the loser. Similarly, if the bank expects interest rates to rise in the future, it may hold off making loans now so that it will have reserves available to make more profitable loans after the interest rate has risen.

There is nothing automatic about deposit creation; it rests on the decisions of bankers. If banks do not choose to use excess reserves to expand their investments, there will not be an expansion of deposits.

The money supply is thus at least partially determined by the chartered banks in response to such forces as changes in national income and interest rates. However, the upper limit of deposits is determined by the required reserve ratio and by the reserves available to the banks, both of which are under the influence of the central bank.

Cash drain. Suppose that firms and households find it convenient to keep a fixed *fraction* of their money holding in cash (say, 5 percent) instead of a fixed *amount* of dollars. In that case an extra $100 in money supply will not all stay in the banking system; only $95 will remain on deposit, while the rest will be added to money in circulation. In such a situation any multiple expansion of bank deposits will be accompanied by a cash drain to the public that will reduce the maximum expansion below what it was when the public was content to hold all its new money as bank deposits. Table 33-9 shows the position of a typical bank after a credit expansion of $400 and a cash drain of $20.

The story of deposit creation when all banks receive new deposits and there is a cash drain to the public goes like this. Each bank starts creating deposits and suffers no significant cash drain to other banks. But because approximately 5 percent of newly created deposits is withdrawn to be held as cash, each bank suffers a cash drain to the public. The expansion continues, each bank watching its own ratio of cash reserves to deposits, expanding deposits as long as the ratio exceeds 1/5 and ceasing when it reaches that figure. Because the expansion is accompanied by a cash drain, it will come to a halt with a smaller deposit expansion than in the case of no cash drain.[3]

TABLE 33-9 Monopoly Bank Balance Sheet After a Credit Expansion and an Accompanying Cash Drain (*thousands of dollars*)

Assets		Liabilities	
Cash and reserves	$ 280	Deposits	$1,480
Loans	1,300	Capital	100
	$1,580		$1,580

The limit to the amount of deposit expansion is reduced by a cash drain. This example differs from that shown in Table 33-5 because, after a new deposit of $100 and a new loan of $400, 5 percent of the newly created money is withdrawn as cash to be held by the public. Cash and deposits each fall by $20 and the reserve ratio falls below 20 percent.

The Money Supply

The total stock of money in the economy at any moment is called the **money supply.** Economists and financial analysts use several different definitions for the money supply, most of which are regularly reported in the *Bank of Canada Review.* Typically the definitions involve the sum of currency in circulation plus some types of deposit liabilities of financial institutions. Definitions vary in terms of what deposits are included. Different definitions come into or go out of favor as the importance of different types of deposits changes.

[3] It can be shown algebraically that the percentage of cash drain must be added to the reserve ratio to determine the maximum possible expansion of deposits. [44]

Kinds of Deposits

Most of the deposits held by the average person are either demand deposits or savings deposits.

Demand Deposits

A **demand deposit** means that the customer can withdraw the money on demand (i.e., without giving any notice of intention to withdraw). Demand deposits are transferable by cheque. A cheque instructs the bank to pay without a delay a stated sum of money to the person to whom the cheque is made payable.

Savings Deposits

Prior to recent changes in the Bank Act, a **savings deposit** was an interest-bearing deposit legally withdrawable only after a certain notice period. (Hence another word for savings deposit used to be *time* deposit.) In practice, although it was impossible to pay a bill by writing a cheque on a savings deposit, such deposits were always quickly convertible into a medium of exchange. A depositor wishing to use a savings deposit to pay a bill had to withdraw money from a savings account and then either pay the bill in cash or deposit the funds in a demand account and write a cheque on the demand account.

The Disappearing Distinction

For decades interest rates on savings deposits amounted to only a few percent, and people were content to keep most of their money in savings deposits and their reserves of cash for ordinary transactions in demand deposits. Then, interest rates available on savings deposits and other safe liquid investments grew, and it became more and more expensive (in terms of lost interest) to keep cash in demand deposits, even for a week or two. Starting in the early 1970s, several devices were invented that tended to make it easier to convert interest-bearing deposits into demand deposits transferable by cheque.

Chequable savings accounts are now common, and some banks even offer a service whereby fixed sums are automatically transferred from a customer's savings account to his or her demand account when funds in the demand account become insufficient to meet newly presented cheques. The effective distinction is no longer between demand and savings accounts but rather between a multitude of types of accounts, each offering different combinations of interest payments, service provided, and service charges levied. The deposit that is genuinely tied up for a period of time now takes the form of a **term deposit (TD),** which is purchased with a statement of a particular withdrawal date, a minimum of 30 days into the future, and which pays a much reduced interest rate in the event of early withdrawal.

Demand deposits offer other services to compensate for the lack of interest earnings. These include free traveler's cheques, detailed monthly statements, and return of canceled cheques.

Definitions of the Money Supply

The definition of the money supply varies with the type of deposits considered. The narrowly defined money supply, called **M1,** includes currency and demand deposits. Broader definitions such as **M2** and **M3** add in savings accounts and term deposits, which serve the temporary store-of-value function and are in practice quickly convertible into a medium of exchange at a known price ($1 on deposit in a savings account is always convertible into a $1 demand deposit or $1 in cash). Table 33-10 shows the principal elements in the money supply.

Near Money and Money Substitutes

Over the past two centuries what has been accepted by the public as money has expanded from gold and silver coins to include first bank notes and then bank deposits subject to transfer by cheque. Until recently, most economists would have agreed that money stopped at that point. No such agreement exists today, and an important debate centers on the definition of money appropriate to present circumstances.

If we concentrate only on the medium-of-exchange function of money, there is little doubt about what is money in Canada today. Money consists of notes, coins, and deposits subject to transfer by

TABLE 33-10 Canadian Money Supply, January 1987 ***(billions of dollars)***

Currency	$ 14.8
Plus: Demand deposits	17.8
Equals M1	32.6
Plus: Daily interest chequable savings deposits and nonpersonal notice deposits	40.2
Equals M1A	72.8
Plus: Other personal savings deposits and personal fixed-term deposits at the chartered banks	103.0
Equals M2	175.8
Plus: Nonpersonal fixed-term deposits and foreign-currency deposits	40.5
Equals M3	216.3

Source: Bank of Canada Review, April 1987.

The money supply can be defined in a variety of ways: M1, M1A, M2, and M3 figures are all published regularly by the Bank of Canada. M1 is the narrowly defined money supply that includes items that serve directly as a medium of exchange. M1A also includes nonpersonal notice and chequable savings deposits. M2 includes additional categories of bank deposits that serve the store-of-value function and can be readily converted into demand deposits or currency. M3 adds in bank term deposits that cannot be converted easily because the funds must remain on deposit for a fixed term and foreign-currency deposits whose value in terms of Canadian dollars varies with the exchange rate. (Series called M2+ and M3+ add to M2 and M3, respectively, related deposits with trust companies, credit unions, and Quebec savings institutions called *caisses populaires*.)

TABLE 33-11 The Dollar As a Store of Value Since 1962

$1 put aside in	Had the purchasing power 5 years later of	Its average annual loss of value over the 5-year period was
1962	$.86	2.8%
1967	.79	4.2%
1972	.47	10.7%
1977	.37	12.6%
1982	.76	4.3%

The dollar has become an increasingly less satisfactory store of value since the 1960s. The second column shows the purchasing power, measured by the Consumer Price Index, of $1 five years after it was saved (assuming it earned no interest). In order for it to have maintained its real purchasing power, it would have had to earn the annual percentage return shown in the last column. The increase in the required return explains the growing use of near money and money substitutes that (unlike currency and demand deposits) earn interest.

cheque or cheque-like instruments. No other asset constitutes a generally accepted medium of exchange; indeed, even notes and cheques are not universally accepted—as you will discover if you try to buy a pack of cigarettes with a $1,000 bill (or even a $100 bill in a corner grocery store). But such exceptions are unimportant.

The problem of deciding what is money arises because some media of exchange—currency, which carries no interest yield, and demand deposits, whose interest yield tends to be quite low—may provide relatively poor ways to meet the store-of-value function (see Table 33-11). Assets that earn a higher-interest return will do a better job of meeting this function of money than will currency or demand deposits. At the same time, however, these other assets are less capable of filling the medium-of-exchange function.

Near Money

Assets that fulfill adequately the store-of-value function and are readily converted into a medium of exchange but are not themselves a medium of exchange are sometimes called **near money.** Deposits at a trust company are a characteristic form of near money. When you have such a deposit, you know exactly how much purchasing power you hold (at current prices), and, given modern banking practices, you can turn your deposit into a medium of exchange—cash or a chequing deposit—at a moment's notice. Additionally, your deposit will earn some interest during the period that you hold it.

Why then does not everybody keep their money in such deposits instead of in demand deposits or currency? The answer is that the inconvenience of continually shifting money back and forth may outweigh the interest that can be earned. One week's interest on $100 (at 5 percent per year) is only about $.10, not enough to cover carfare to the bank or the cost of mailing a letter. For money that will be needed soon, it would hardly pay to shift it to a time deposit.

In general, whether it pays to convert cash or demand deposits into interest-earning savings deposits for a given period will depend on the inconvenience and other transaction costs of shifting funds and on the amount of interest that can be earned.

There is a wide spectrum of assets in the economy that pay interest and also serve as reasonably satisfactory temporary stores of value. The difference between these assets and savings deposits is that their capital values are not quite as certain as those of savings deposits. If I elect to store my purchasing power in the form of a treasury bill that matures in 30 days, its price on the market may change between the time I buy it and the time I want to sell it, say, 10 days later. If the price changes, the purchasing power available to me changes. But because of the short horizon to maturity, the price will not change very much. (After all, the government will pay the face value in a few weeks.) Such a security is thus a reasonably satisfactory short-run store of purchasing power. Indeed, any readily salable capital asset whose value does not fluctuate significantly with the rate of interest will satisfactorily fulfill this short-term store-of-value function.

Money Substitutes

Things that serve as a temporary medium of exchange but are not a store of value are sometimes called **money substitutes.** Credit cards are a prime example. With a credit card, many transactions can be made without either cash or a cheque. The evidence of credit, the credit slip you sign and hand over to the store, is not money because it cannot be used to make other transactions. Furthermore, when your credit card company takes advantage of an arrangement to have your bank pay each bill as it is presented or when it sends you a bill, you have to use money to pay for the original transaction. The credit card serves the short-run function of a medium of exchange by allowing you to make purchases even though you have no cash or bank deposit currently in your possession. But this is only temporary; money remains the final medium of exchange for these transactions when the credit account is settled.

Conclusion

Since the eighteenth century, economists have known that the amount of money in circulation is an important economic variable. As theories became more carefully specified in the nineteenth and early twentieth centuries, they included a variable called "the money supply." But for theories to be useful, we must be able to identify real-world counterparts of these theoretical magnitudes.

What is an acceptable enough medium of exchange to count as money has changed and will continue to change over time. New monetary assets are continually being developed to serve some, if not all, the functions of money, and they are more or less readily convertible into money. There is no single, timeless definition of what is money and what is only near money or a money substitute. Indeed, as we have seen, our monetary authorities use several definitions of money, and these definitions change from year to year.

Summary

1. Early economic theorists regarded the economy as divided into a real part and a money part. The real sector is concerned with production, allocation of resources, and distribution of income—determined by relative prices. The level of prices at which all transactions take place is determined by the monetary sector, that is, by the demand for and supply of money. With the demand for money constant, an increase in the money supply would cause all equilibrium money prices to increase, but relative prices, and hence everything in the real sector, would be left unaffected.

2. Traditionally in economics, money has referred to any generally accepted medium of exchange. A number of functions of money may be distinguished. The major ones are serving as a medium of exchange, a store of value, and a unit of account.
3. Money arose because of the inconvenience of barter, and it developed in stages from precious metal, to metal coinage, to paper money convertible to precious metal, to token coinage and paper money fractionally backed by precious metals, to fiat money, and to deposit money. Societies have shown great sophistication in developing monetary instruments to meet their needs.
4. The banking system in Canada consists of two main elements: chartered banks and the central bank, the Bank of Canada. Each has an important effect on the money supply.
5. Chartered banks are profit-seeking institutions that allow their customers to transfer demand deposits from one bank to another by means of cheques. They create and destroy money as a by-product of their commercial operations—by making or liquidating loans and various other investments.
6. Because most customers are content to pay their accounts by cheque rather than by cash, banks need only small reserves to back their deposit liabilities. Consequently, banks are able to create deposit money. When the banking system receives a new cash deposit, it can create new deposits to some multiple of this amount. The amount of new deposits created depends on the legal minimum reserves the Bank of Canada enforces on the banks, the amount of cash drain to the public, and whether the banks choose to hold excess reserves.
7. All advanced free-market economies have a central bank that serves as banker for private banks, banker for the government, controller and regulator of the money supply, and regulator and supporter of money markets.
8. The money supply—the stock of money in the country at a specific moment—can be defined in various ways. M1 is currency plus demand deposits plus chequable substitutes, the narrowest definition now in use. (M1 was about $32 billion in 1986.) M3, the widest commonly used definition, adds in all time and savings deposits. (M3 was about $216 billion in 1986.)
9. Near money includes interest-earning assets that are convertible into money on a dollar-for-dollar basis but are not currently included in the definition of money. Money substitutes such as credit cards temporarily serve as a medium of exchange but are not money.

Topics for Review

Real and monetary sectors of the economy
Functions of money
Gresham's law
Fully backed, fractionally backed, and fiat money

The banking system and the central bank
Creation and destruction of deposit money
Reserve ratio, required reserves, and excess reserves
Demand and savings deposits
The money supply
Near money and money substitutes

Discussion Questions

1. " For the love of money is the root of all evil" (I Timothy 6:10). If a nation were to become a theocracy in which money was illegal, would you expect the level of national income to be affected? How about the productivity of labor?
2. Consider each of the following with respect to its potential use as a medium of exchange, a store of value, and a unit of account. Which would you think might be regarded as money?
   a. A $100 Bank of Canada note
   b. An American Express credit card
   c. A painting by Picasso
   d. A treasury bill payable in three months
   e. A savings account with a trust company in London, Ontario
   f. One share of General Motors stock
   g. A lifetime pass to the Art Gallery of Ontario
3. When the Austrian government minted a new 1,000-shilling gold coin—worth $78 face value—the 1-inch-diameter coin came into great demand among jewelers and coin collectors. By law, the number of such coins to be minted each year is limited. Lines of people eager to get the coins formed outside the government mint and local banks. "There is exceptional interest in the new coin," said a Viennese banker. "It's a numismatic hit and a financial success." It has disappeared from circulation, however. Explain why.
4. A Canadian who receives a U.S. coin has the option of spending it at face value or taking it to the bank and converting it to Canadian money at the going rate of exchange. When the rate of exchange was near par, so that $1 Canadian was within $0.03 of $1 U.S., American and Canadian coins circulated side by side, exchanging at their face values. Use Gresham's law to predict which coinage disappeared from circulation in Canada when the Canadian dollar fell to $0.75 U.S. Why did a $0.03 differential not produce this result?
5. Some years ago a strike closed all banks in Ireland for several months. What do you think happened during the period?
6. During hyperinflations in several foreign countries after World War II, American cigarettes were sometimes used in place of money. What made them suitable?
7. Assume that on January 1, 1986, a couple had $25,000 that they wished to hold for use one year later. Calculate, using library sources, which of the following would have been the best store of value over that period. Will the best store of value over that period necessarily be the best over the next 24 months?
   a. The dollar
   b. Stocks whose prices moved with the Toronto Stock Exchange Industrial 300 average

   c. A Labatts 11¾ percent 2005 bond
   d. Gold
   e. Silver
8. If all depositors tried to turn their deposits into cash at once, they would find that there are not sufficient reserves in the system to allow all of them to do this at the same time. Why then do we not still have panicky runs on the banks? Would a 100 percent reserve requirement be safer? What effect would such a reserve requirement have on the banking system's ability to create money? Would it preclude any possibility of a panic?
9. What would be the effect on the money supply of each of the following?
   a. Declining public confidence in the banks
   b. A desire on the part of banks to increase their levels of excess reserves
   c. Monopolizing of the banking system into a single superbank
   d. Increased use of credit cards
   e. Transfer of deposits from banks to new nonbank institutions

34

The Role of Money in Macroeconomics

At one time or another most of us have known the surprise of opening our wallet to discover that we had either more or less money than we thought. There can be pleasure in deciding how to spend an unexpected windfall in the first case, just as there can be pain in deciding what expenditure to eliminate in the second.

What determines how much money people hold in their wallets and how much they keep in the bank? What happens when people discover that they are holding more, or less, money than they believe they need to hold? These turn out to be key questions for our study of the influence of money on output and prices.

Financial Assets

At any one moment households have a given stock of wealth. This wealth is held in many forms. Some of it is money in the bank or in the wallet; some is in short-term securities such as term deposits or treasury bills; some is in long-term bonds; and some is in real capital, which may be held directly (in the form of family businesses) or indirectly (in the form of shares of stock that indicate ownership of a corporation's assets).

Kinds of Assets

These ways of holding wealth may be grouped into three main categories: (1) assets that serve as a medium of exchange, that is, paper money, coins, and bank deposits on which cheques may be drawn, (2) financial assets, such as bonds earning a fixed rate of interest, that will yield a fixed money value at some future date (called the *maturity date*) and can usually be sold before maturity for a price that fluctuates on the open market, and (3) claims on real capital (physical objects such as factories and machines).

To simplify our discussion, we will regroup wealth into just two categories: money and bonds. By money we mean M1 as defined in Chapter 33, and by bonds we mean all other forms of wealth. Money therefore includes currency, demand deposits, and chequable savings deposits. Bonds include all other interest-earning financial assets *plus* claims in real capital.[1]

The Rate of Interest and the Price of Bonds

A bond is a promise by the issuer to pay a stated sum of money as interest each year and to repay the face value of the bond at some future maturity date, often many years distant. The time until the date is called the **term to maturity,** often simply the **term,** of the bond. Some bonds, called perpetuities, pay interest forever and never repay the principal.

The **present value (*PV*)** of a bond, or of any asset, refers to the value now of the future payment, or payments, to which the asset represents a claim. The present value is thus the amount someone would be willing to pay now to secure the right to the future stream of payments conferred by ownership of the asset.

This amount depends critically on the rate of interest as is most easily seen in the case of a perpetuity. Assume that such a bond will pay $100 per year to its holder. The *present value* of this bond depends on how much $100 per year is worth, and this in turn depends on the rate of interest.

A bond that will produce a stream of income of $100 a year forever is worth $1,000 at 10 percent interest because $1,000 invested at 10 percent per year will yield $100 interest per year forever. But the same bond is worth $2,000 when the interest rate is 5 percent per year because it takes $2,000 invested at 5 percent per year to yield $100 interest per year. The lower the rate of interest obtainable on the market, the more valuable is a bond paying a fixed amount of interest.

Similar relations apply to bonds that are not perpetuities, though the calculation of present value must allow for the lump-sum repayment of principal at maturity.[2]

The present value of any asset that yields a stream of money over time is negatively related to the interest rate.

This proposition has two important implications: (1) If the rate of interest falls, the value of an asset producing a given income stream will rise, and (2) a rise in the market price of an asset producing a given income is equivalent to a decrease in the rate of interest earned by the asset. Thus a promise to pay $100 one year from now is worth $92.59 when the interest rate is 8 percent and only $89.29 when the interest rate is 12 percent: $92.59 at 8 percent interest ($92.59 × 1.08) and $89.29 at 12 percent interest ($89.29 × 1.12) are both worth $100 in one year's time.

The present value of bonds that are not perpetuities becomes increasingly dominated by the fixed redemption value as the maturity date approaches. Take an extreme case. The present value of a bond that is redeemable for $1,000 in a week's time will be very close to $1,000 no matter what the interest rate. Thus its value will not change much even if the rate of interest leaps from 5 percent to 10 percent during that week.

The sooner the maturity date of a bond, the less the bond's value will change with a change in one the rate of interest.

For example, a rise in the interest rate from 8 to 12 percent will lower the value of $100 payable in one year's time by 3.6 percent, but it will lower the value of $100 payable in 10 years' time by 37.9 percent.[3] (Although some assets that we included in our definition of money do earn interest, they are so short-term that their values remain unchanged when the interest rate changes.)

The discussion should make it clear that the pres-

[1] This simplification can take us quite a long way. However, for some problems it is necessary to treat debt and equity as distinct assets so that three categories—money, debt (bonds), and equity stocks—are used.

[2] Further details on the calculation of present value are given in Chapter 18, pages 356–357.

[3] The example assumes annual compounding. The first case can be calculated from the numbers of the previous example: (92.59 − 89.29)/92.59. The 10-year case uses the formula

$$\text{Present value} = \frac{\text{Principal}}{(1 + r)^n}$$

which gives $46.30 with 8 percent and $28.75 with 12 percent. The percentage fall in value is thus (46.30 − 28.75)/46.30 = 0.379.

ent value of an asset determines its market price. If the market price of any asset is greater than the present value of the income stream it produces, no one will want to buy it; if the market value is below its present value, there will be a rush to buy it. These facts lead to the following conclusions:

In a free market the equilibrium price of any asset will be the present value of the income stream it produces.

Supply of Money and Demand for Money

The Supply of Money

The money supply is a stock. (It is so many billions of dollars, *not* a flow of so much per unit of time.) In January 1987 M1 was approximately $33 billion.

We saw in Chapter 33 that deposit money is created by the commercial banking system, but only within limits set by their reserves. We also saw in Chapter 33 that the reserves of the commercial banking system are under the control of the Bank of Canada, ultimate control of the money supply is also in the hands of the Bank. In this chapter we shall assume that the money supply can be precisely controlled by the Bank of Canada.

The Demand for Money

The amount of wealth everyone in the economy wishes to hold in the form of money balances is called the **demand for money.** Because households have only one decision to make on how to divide their given stock of wealth between money and bonds, it follows that if we know the demand for money, we also know the demand for bonds. With *a given level of wealth* a rise in the demand for money necessarily implies a fall in the demand for bonds; if people wish to hold $1 billion more money, they must wish to hold $1 billion less of bonds. It also follows that if households are in equilibrium with respect to their money holdings, they are in equilibrium with respect to their bond holdings.

When we say that on January 1, 1987, the demand for money was $33 billion, we mean that on that date the public wished to hold money balances that totaled $33 billion. But why do firms and households wish to hold money balances at all? There is a cost to holding any money balance. The money could instead be used to purchase bonds; it would then earn more interest.[4]

The opportunity cost of holding any money balance is the extra interest that could have been earned if the money had instead been used to purchase interest earning assets.

Clearly, money will be held only when it provides services that are valued at least as highly as the opportunity cost of holding it. The services provided by money balances are, first, to finance purchases and sales; second, to provide a cushion against uncertainty about the timing of cash flows; and third, to provide a hedge against uncertainty over the prices of other financial assets.

The desire to hold money to obtain each of these services is summarized by the transactions, precautionary, and speculative motives for holding money. We now examine each of these motives in detail.

The Transactions Motive

Most transactions require money. Money passes from households to firms to pay for the goods and services produced by firms; money passes from firms to households to pay for the factor services supplied by households to firms. Money balances that are held to finance such flows are called **transactions balances.**

In an imaginary world, where the receipts and

[4] As we saw in Chapter 33 (see especially Table 33-10), some definitions of the money supply (even narrow definitions like M1A) include some interest-bearing chequable deposits. This complicates but does not fundamentally alter the analysis of the demand for money. In particular, it means that the opportunity cost of holding those interest-bearing components of M1A is not the *level* of interest rates paid on bonds but the *differential* between that rate and the rate paid on M1A assets. For simplicity, we treat the interest rate on all M1A assets as being zero so that we can identify the *level* of the interest rate on bonds as the opportunity cost of money.

disbursements of households and firms were perfectly synchronized, it would be unnecessary to hold transactions balances. If every time a household spent $10 it received $10 as part payment of its income, no transactions balances would be needed. In the real world, however, receipts and disbursements are not perfectly synchronized.

Consider, for example, the balances held because of wage payments. Assume, for purposes of illustration, that firms pay wages every Friday and that households spend all their wages on the purchase of goods and services, with the expenditure spread out evenly over the week. Thus on Friday morning firms must hold balances equal to the weekly wage bill; on Friday afternoon households will hold these balances.

Over the week, households' balances will be drawn down as a result of purchasing goods and services. Over the same period, the balances held by firms will build up as a result of selling goods and services until, on the following Friday morning, firms will again have amassed balances equal to the wage bill that must be met on that day.

On the average over the week firms will hold balances equal to half the wage bill and so will households. Thus, in this example total money balances held will be equal to the total weekly wage bill. Notice that while the money circulates so that each group holds a varying balance over the week, the combined demand for balances summed over the two groups remains constant.

Our argument has been conducted in terms of the wage bill, but a similar analysis holds for all receipts and payments of households and firms. Because their receipts and payments are not perfectly synchronized, they must hold money balances to bridge the gap.

The transactions demand for money arises because of the nonsynchronization of payments and receipts.

What determines the size of the transactions balances to be held? It is clear that in our example total transactions balances vary with the value of the wage bill. If the wage bill doubles for any reason (e.g., because twice as much labor is hired at the same wage rate or because the same amount of labor is hired at twice the wage rate), the transactions balances held by firms and households on this account will also double. As it is with wages so it is with all other transactions: The size of the balances held is positively related to the value of the transactions.

Next we ask how the total value of transactions is related to national income. Because of the "double counting" problem first discussed in Chapter 27, the value of all transactions exceeds the value of the economy's final output. When the flour mill buys wheat from the farmer and when the baker buys flour from the mill, both are transactions against which money balances must be held, although only the value added at each stage is part of national income. Typically, the total value of transactions is many times as large as the total value of final output, which is national income.

We now make an added assumption that there is a stable, positive relation between transactions and national income. If a rise in aggregate expenditure leads to a rise in national income, it also leads to a rise in the total value of all transactions and hence to an associated rise in the demand for transactions balances. This allows us to relate transactions balances to national income. [45]

The larger the value of national income, the larger the value of transactions balances that will be held.

The Precautionary Motive

Many goods and services are sold on credit. The seller can never be certain when payment will be made, and the buyer can never be certain of the day of delivery and thus when payment will fall due. As a precaution against cash crises when receipts are abnormally low or disbursements are abnormally high, firms and households carry money balances. These are called **precautionary balances.** The larger such balances, the greater the protection against running out of money because of temporary fluctuations in cash flows.

How serious this risk is depends on the penalties for being caught without sufficient money balances.

A firm is unlikely to be pushed into insolvency, but it may incur considerable costs if it is forced to borrow money at high interest rates in order to meet a temporary cash crisis.

The precautionary motive arises because households and firms are uncertain about the degree to which payments and receipts will be synchronized.

The protection provided by a given quantity of precautionary balances depends on the volume of payments and receipts. A $100 precautionary balance provides a large cushion for a household whose volume of payments per month is $800 and a small cushion for a firm whose monthly volume is $10,000. Fluctuations of the sort that create the need for precautionary balances tend to vary directly with the size of the firm's cash flow. To provide the same degree of protection as the value of transactions rises, more money is necessary.[5]

The precautionary motive also causes the demand for money to vary positively with the money value of national income.

The Speculative Motive

Firms and households hold some money in order to avoid the risks inherent in fluctuating prices of bonds. Money balances held for this purpose are called **speculative balances.** This motive was first analyzed by Keynes, and modern analysis is the work of Professor James Tobin of Yale University.[6]

When a household or firm holds money balances, it foregoes the extra interest income that it could earn if it held bonds instead. But market interest rates fluctuate, and so do the market prices of existing bonds (since their present values depend on the interest rate). Because their prices fluctuate, bonds are a risky asset. Many households and firms do not like risk; they are said to be *risk-averse.*

In choosing between holding money or holding bonds, wealth holders must balance the extra interest income that they could earn by holding bonds against the risk that bonds carry. At one extreme, if a household or a firm holds all its wealth in the form of bonds, it earns extra interest on its entire wealth, but it also exposes its entire wealth to the risk of changes in the price of bonds. At the other extreme, if the household or firm holds all its wealth in the form of money, it earns less interest income, but it does not face the risk of unexpected changes in the price of bonds. Wealth holders usually do not take either extreme position. They hold part of their wealth as money and part as bonds; that is, they *diversify* their holdings.

Influence of wealth. The motivation to hold money in order to diversify wealth holdings means that the demand for money varies positively with wealth. For example, Ms. B. O'Reiley might elect to hold 5 percent of her wealth in money and the other 95 percent in bonds. If her wealth is $50,000, her demand for money will be $2,500. If her wealth increases to $60,000, her demand for money will rise to $3,000.

Although an individual's wealth may rise or fall rapidly, the total wealth of a society changes only slowly. For the analysis of short-term fluctuations in national income, the effects of changes in wealth are fairly small, and we shall ignore them for the present. (Over the long term, however, variations in wealth can have a major effect on the demand for money.)

Influence of interest rates. Wealth held in cash earns no interest; hence the reduction in risk involved in holding more money carries a cost in terms of interest earnings forgone.

The speculative motive leads households and firms to add to their money holdings until the reduction in risk obtained by the last dollar added is just balanced (in each wealth holder's

[5] Institutional arrangements affect precautionary demands. In the past, for example, a traveler would have carried a substantial precautionary balance in cash, but today a credit card covers most unforeseen expenses that may arise while traveling.

[6] Professor Tobin was awarded the Nobel Prize in economics in 1981 for his research in monetary economics and the analysis of financial markets.

view) by the cost in terms of the interest forgone on that dollar.

When the rate of interest falls, the opportunity cost of holding money falls. This leads to more money being held both for the precautionary motive (to reduce risks caused by uncertainty about the flows of payments and receipts) and for the speculative motive (to reduce risks associated with fluctuations in the market price of bonds). When the rate of interest rises, the cost of holding money rises. This leads to less money being held for speculative and precautionary motives.

The demand for money is negatively related to the rate of interest.[7]

Real and Nominal Money Balances

In referring to the demand for money, it is important to distinguish real from nominal values. Real values are measured in purchasing power units, nominal values in money units.

First, consider the demand for money in real terms. This means the number of units of purchasing power the public wishes to hold in the form of money balances. In an imaginary one-product wheat economy, this would be measured by the number of bushels of wheat that could be purchased with the money balances held. In a more complex economy it could be measured in terms of the number of weeks of national income; for example, the real value of the amount of money demanded might be equal to one month's national income.

When we come to measure the real demand for money, we measure the amount demanded in constant dollars. This means that the real demand is the nominal quantity demanded divided by an index of price level (where the base year is given a value of 1 rather than 100).

The real demand for money is the nominal quantity demanded divided by the price level.

For example, in the decade from 1976 to 1986 the nominal quantity of M1 balances held in Canada rose by 175 percent from $18.6 billion to $32.6 billion. Over the same period, however, the price level, as measured by the CPI, roughly doubled—if we let the price level be 1 in 1976, it was 2.1 in 1986. This tells us that the real quantity of M1 held actually fell slightly, from $18.6 billion to $15.5 billion measured in constant 1976 dollars.

From real demand to nominal demand. Our discussion has identified the determinants of the demand for real money balances as real national income, real wealth, and the interest rate. Notice that the real demand for money depends, among other things, on real national income; it is not influenced by the price level. Now suppose that, with the interest rate, real wealth, and real national income constant, the price level doubles. The demand for real money balances will be unchanged. For this to be true, however, the demand for nominal balances must double. If the public used to demand $30 billion worth of nominal money balances, they must now demand $60 billion worth. This keeps the real demand unchanged at $60/2 = $30. The constancy of the level of demand for real balances is shown in this example by the fact that $60 billion at the new, higher price level represents exactly the same purchasing power as did $30 billion at the old price level.

Other things being equal, the nominal demand for money balances varies in proportion to the price level; doubling the price level doubles desired nominal money balances.

This is a central proposition of the quantity theory of money, discussed further in Box 34-1.

Total Demand for Money: Recapitulation

Figure 34-1 (see page 742) summarizes the influences of national income, the rate of interest, and the price level, the three variables that account for most of the

[7] When the price level is changing continually, it is necessary to distinguish the real from the nominal rate of interest. This was discussed in Box 31-1 on page 649. For now, there is no need to distinguish these two concepts of the interest rate since they are the same when the price level is constant, and they are measured by the market rate of interest.

BOX 34-1

The Quantity Theory of Money and the Velocity of Circulation

The basic quantity theory of money can be set out formally in terms of the following four equations. Equation 1 states that the demand for money balances depends on the value of transactions as measured by nominal income, which is real income multiplied by the price level, *PY.*

$$M^D = kPY \quad [1]$$

Equation 2 states that the supply of money, *M,* is set by the central bank.

$$M_S = M \quad [2]$$

Equation 3 states the equilibrium condition that the demand for money must equal its supply.

$$M^D = M_S \quad [3]$$

Substitution produces the basic relation among *P, M,* and *Y*, as shown in Equation 4.

$$M = kPY \quad [4]$$

The original form of the classical quantity theory assumes that *k* is a constant given by the transactions demand for money and that *Y* is constant because full employment is maintained. Thus *M* and *P* move proportionally. Increases or decreases in the money supply lead to proportional increases or decreases in prices.

Often the quantity theory is presented using the concept of the velocity of circulation, *V*, instead of the proportion of the money income that people wish to hold in cash, *k*. The **velocity of circulation** is defined as national income divided by the quantity of money.

$$V = PY/M \quad [5]$$

Rearranging gives what is called the *equation of exchange.*

$$MV = PY \quad [6]$$

Velocity may be interpreted as showing the average amount of "work" done by a unit of money. Thus, if the annual national income is $400 billion and the stock of money is $100 billion, on average each dollar's worth of money is used four times to create the values added that compose the national income.

There is a simple relation between *k* and *V*. One is the reciprocal of the other, as may be seen immediately by comparing Equations 4 and 6. Thus it makes no difference whether we choose to work with *k* or *V*. Further, if *k* is assumed to be constant, this implies that *V* must also be treated as being constant. An example may help to illustrate the interpretation of each.

Assume that the stock of money people wish to hold is equal to one-fifth of the value of total transactions. Thus *k* is 0.2 and *V*, the reciprocal of *k*, is 5. This indicates that if the money supply is to be one-fifth of the value of annual transactions, the average unit of money must account for $5 worth of transactions; that is, each dollar must be used on average five times.

Modern versions of the quantity theory do not assume that *k* is exogenously fixed but nevertheless argue that it will not change in response to a change in the quantity of money.

---

short-term variations in the nominal quantity of money demanded. The function relating money demand to the rate of interest is often called the **liquidity preference (LP) function.** Whatever name is used, the relation describes how the quantity of money people wish to hold varies as the rate of interest varies.

Monetary Forces and National Income

We are now in a position to examine the relationship between monetary forces and the equilibrium values of national income and the price level. The first step

FIGURE 34-1 Demand for Money As a Function of Interest Rates, Income, and Price Level

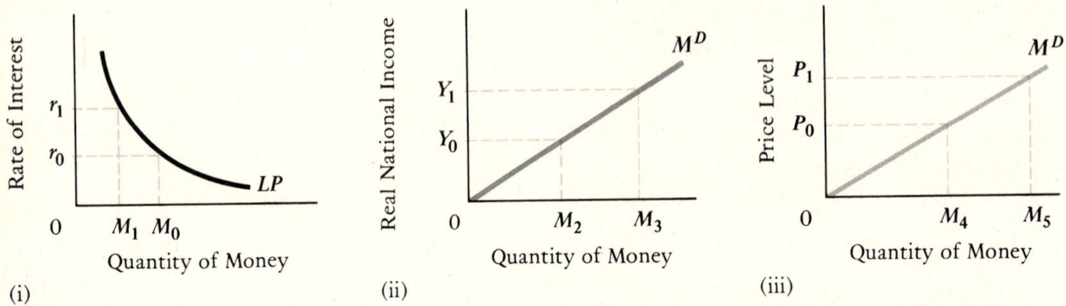

The quantity of money demanded varies negatively with the rate of interest and positively with both national income and the price level. In part (i) the demand for money is shown varying negatively with the interest rate along the liquidity preference function. When the interest rate rises from r_0 to r_1, households and firms reduce the quantity of money demanded from M_0 to M_1.

In part (ii) the demand for money is shown varying positively with national income. When national income rises from Y_0 to Y_1, households and firms increase the quantity of money demanded from M_2 to M_3.

In part (iii) the demand for money is shown varying positively with the price level. When the price level rises from P_0 to P_1, households and firms increase the quantity of money demanded from M_4 to M_5.

in explaining this relationship is a new one: the link between monetary equilibrium and aggregate demand. The second is familiar from earlier chapters: the effects of shifts in aggregate demand on equilibrium values of national income and the price level.

Monetary Equilibrium and Aggregate Demand

Monetary equilibrium occurs when the demand for money equals the supply of money. In Chapter 4 we saw that in a competitive market for some commodity such as carrots, the price will adjust so as to ensure equilibrium. The rate of interest does the same job with respect to money demand and money supply.

The Liquidity Preference Theory of Interest

Figure 34-2 shows how the interest rate will change in order to equate the demand for money with its supply. When a single household or firm finds that it has less money than it wishes to hold, it can sell some bonds and add the proceeds to its money holdings. This transaction simply redistributes given supplies of bonds and money among individuals; it does not change the total supply of either money or bonds.

Now assume that all the firms and households in the economy have an excess demand for money balances. They all try to sell bonds to add to their money balances. But what one person can do, all persons cannot do. At any moment the economy's total supplies of money and bonds are fixed; there are just so much money and so many bonds in existence. If everyone tries to sell bonds, there will be no one to buy them. Instead the price of bonds will fall.

We saw that a fall in the price of bonds means a rise in the rate of interest. As the interest rate rises, people economize on money balances because the opportunity cost of holding such balances is rising. This is what we saw in Figure 34-1(i), where the quantity of money demanded falls along the liquidity

FIGURE 34-2 The Liquidity Preference Theory of Interest

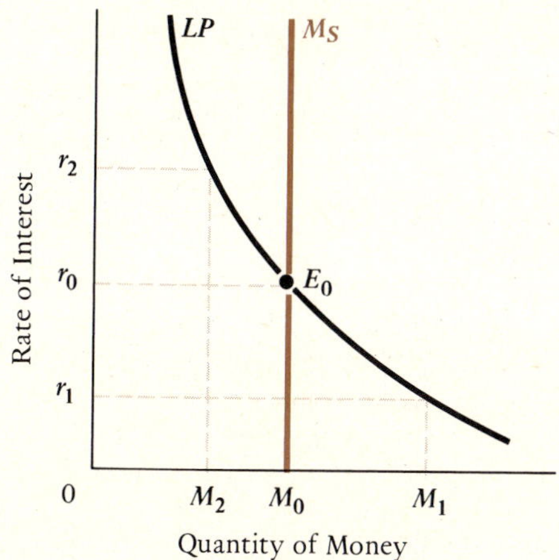

The interest rate rises when there is an excess demand for money and falls when there is an excess supply of money. The fixed quantity of money, M_0, is shown by the completely inelastic supply curve M_S. The demand for money is *LP*; its negative slope indicates that a fall in the rate of interest causes the quantity of money demanded to increase. Equilibrium is at E_0, with a rate of interest of r_0.

If the interest rate is r_1, there will be an excess demand for money of M_0M_1. Bonds will be offered for sale in an attempt to increase money holdings. This will force the rate of interest up to r_0 (the price of bonds falls), at which point the quantity of money demanded is equal to the fixed available quantity of M_0. If the interest rate is r_2, there will be an excess supply of money M_2M_0. Bonds will be demanded in return for excess money balances. This will force the rate of interest down to r_0 (the price of bonds rises), at which point the quantity of money demanded has risen to equal the fixed supply of M_0.

preference curve in response to a rise in the rate of interest. Eventually the interest rate will rise enough that people will no longer be trying to add to their money balances by selling bonds. At that point there is no longer an excess supply of bonds, and the interest rate will stop rising. The demand for money again equals the supply.

Assume next that firms and households hold larger money balances than they would like. A single household or firm would purchase bonds with its excess balances, achieving monetary equilibrium by reducing its money holdings and increasing its bond holdings. But just as in the example, what one household or firm can do, all cannot do. At any moment the total quantity of bonds is fixed, so everyone cannot simultaneously add to personal bond holdings. When all households enter the bond market and try to purchase bonds with unwanted money balances, they bid up the price of existing bonds, and the interest rate falls. Hence households and firms become willing to hold larger quantities of money; that is, the quantity of money demanded increases along the liquidity preference curve in response to a fall in the rate of interest. The rise in the price of bonds continues until firms and households stop trying to convert bonds into money. In other words, it continues until everyone is content to hold the existing supply of money and bonds.

Monetary equilibrium occurs when the rate of interest is such that the existing supply of money is willingly held, that is, when the demand for money equals its supply.

The determination of the interest rate depicted in Figure 34-2 is often described as the *liquidity preference theory of interest* and sometimes as the *portfolio balance theory*.

As we shall see, a shift either in the demand for money or in the supply will lead to a change in the interest rate. But, as we saw in Chapter 31, desired investment expenditure is sensitive to changes in the interest rate. Here, then, is a link between monetary factors and real expenditure flows.

The Transmission Mechanism

The mechanism by which changes in the demand for and the supply of money affect aggregate demand is called the **transmission mechanism.** The transmission mechanism operates in three stages: first, the link between monetary equilibrium and the interest rate; second, the link between the interest rate and investment expenditure; and third, the link between investment expenditure and aggregate demand.

From monetary disturbances to changes in the interest rate. The interest rate will change if the supply of money changes or if there is a shift in the demand for money. For example, as shown in Figure 34-3(i), an increase in the supply of money, with an unchanged liquidity preference function, will give rise to an excess supply of money at the original interest rate. As we have seen, an excess supply of money will cause the interest rate to fall. As also shown in part (i) of the figure, a decrease in the supply of money will cause the interest rate to rise.

As shown in Figure 34-3(ii), an increase in the demand for money, with an unchanged supply of money, will give rise to an excess demand for money at the original interest rate and cause the interest rate to rise. As also shown in part (ii) of the figure, a decrease in the demand for money will cause the interest rate to fall.

Monetary disturbances, which can arise due to either changes in the demand for or the supply of money, cause changes in the interest rate.

From changes in the interest rate to shifts in aggregate expenditure. The second link in the transmission mechanism relates interest rates to expenditure.

FIGURE 34-3 Monetary Disturbances and Interest-Rate Changes

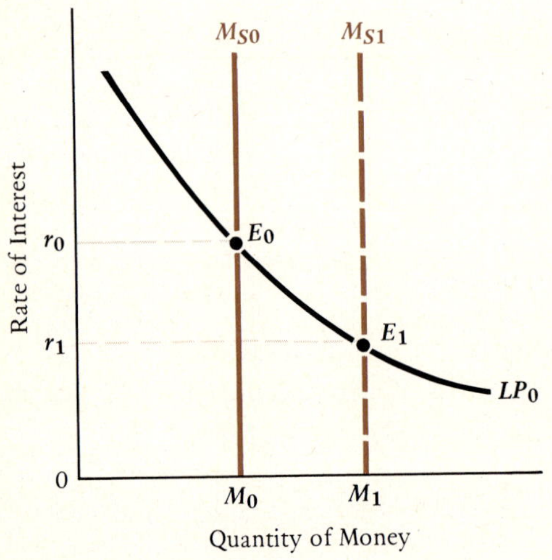

(i) A change in the supply of money

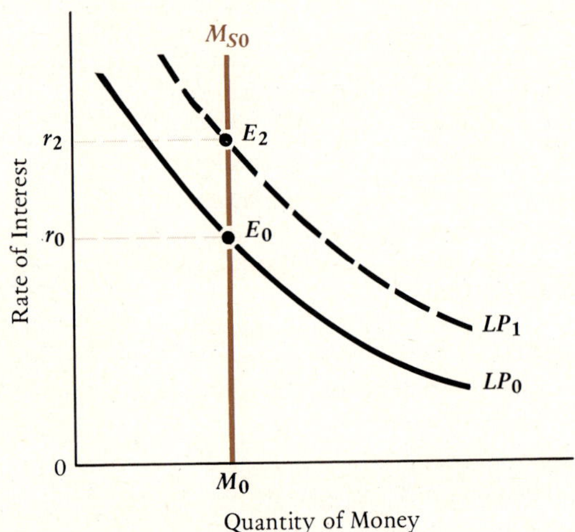

(ii) A change in the demand for money

Shifts in the supply of money or in the demand for money cause the equilibrium interest rate to change. In both parts of the figure the money supply is shown by the vertical curve M_{S0} and the demand for money is shown by the negatively shaped curve LP_0 The initial equilibrium is at E_0 with corresponding interest rate r_0.

In part (i) an increase in the money supply causes the money supply curve to shift to the right from M_{S0} to M_{S1}. The new equilibrium is at E_1, where the interest rate is r_1, less than r_0. Starting at E_1 with M_{S1} and r_1, it can be seen that a decrease in the money supply to M_{S0} leads to an increase in the interest rate from r_1 to r_0.

In part (ii) an increase in the demand for money causes the LP curve to shift to the right from LP_0 to LP_1. The new equilibrium occurs at E_2, and the new equilibrium interest rate is r_2, greater than r_0. Starting at E_2, we see that a decrease in the demand for money from LP_1 to LP_0 leads to a decrease in the interest rate from r_2 to r_0.

FIGURE 34-4 Effects of Changes in the Money Supply on Investment Expenditure

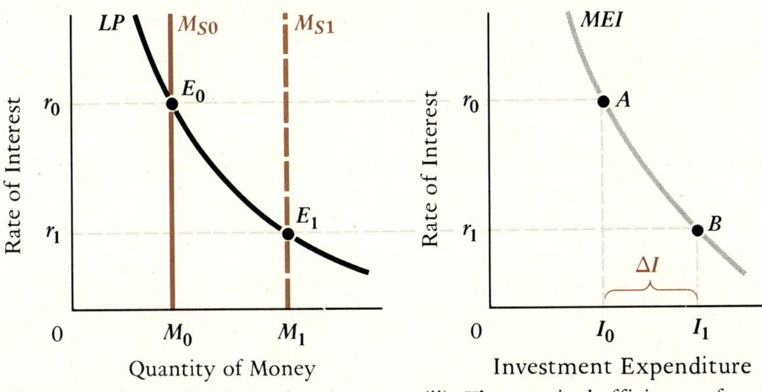

(i) Money demand and supply

(ii) The marginal efficiency of investment

Increases in the money supply reduce the rate of interest and increase desired investment expenditure. Equilibrium is at E_0, with a quantity of money of M_0 (shown by the inelastic money supply curve M_{S0}), an interest rate of r_0, and an investment expenditure of I_0 (point A). The Bank of Canada then increases the money supply to M_1 (shown by the money supply curve M_{S1}). This lowers the rate of interest to r_1 and increases investment expenditure by ΔI to I_1 (point B). A reduction in the money supply from M_1 to M_0 raises interest rates from r_1 to r_0 and lowers investment expenditure by ΔI, from I_1 to I_0.

We saw in Chapter 31 that investment, which includes expenditure on inventory accumulation, residential construction, and business fixed investment, responds to changes in the rate of interest. Other things being equal, a decrease in the rate of interest makes borrowing cheaper and generates new investment expenditure.[8] This negative relation between investment and the rate of interest is called the **marginal efficiency of investment (*MEI*)** function.

The first two links in the transmission mechanism are shown in Figure 34-4. We concentrate for the moment on changes in the money supply, although, as we have already seen, the process can also be set in motion by changes in the demand for money. In part (i) we see that a change in the money supply causes the rate of interest to change in the opposite direction. In part (ii) we see that a change in the interest rate causes the level of investment expenditure to change in the opposite direction. Therefore, changes in the money supply cause investment expenditure to change in the same direction.

[8] In Chapter 31 we saw that purchases of durable consumer goods also respond to changes in interest rates. In this chapter we concentrate on investment expenditure, which may be taken to stand for *all interest-sensitive expenditure.*

An increase in the money supply leads to a fall in the interest rate and an increase in investment expenditure. A decrease in the money supply leads to a rise in the interest rate and a decrease in investment expenditure.

From shifts in aggregate expenditure to shifts in aggregate demand. Now we are back on familiar ground. In Chapter 29 we saw that a shift in the aggregate expenditure curve can lead to a shift in the *AD* curve. This is shown again in Figure 34-5.

A change in the money supply, by causing a change in investment expenditure and hence a shift in the *AE* curve, causes the *AD* curve to shift.

An increase in the money supply causes an increase in investment expenditure and therefore an increase in aggregate demand. A decrease in the money supply causes a decrease in investment expenditure and therefore a decrease in aggregate demand.

The transmission mechanism connects monetary forces and real expenditure flows. It works from a change in the demand for or the supply

FIGURE 34-5 Effects of Changes in the Money Supply on Aggregate Demand

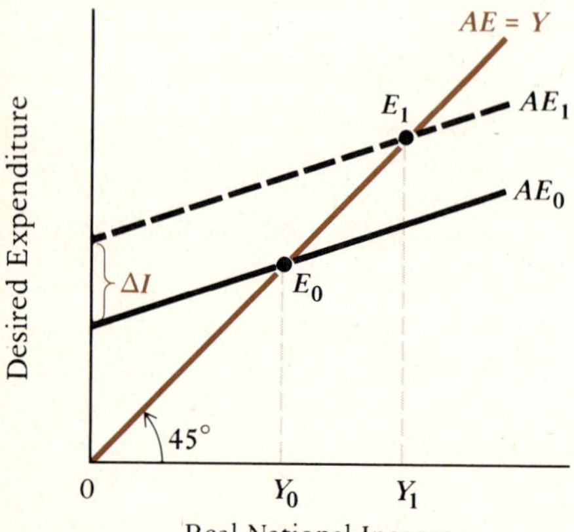

(i) Shift in aggregate expenditure

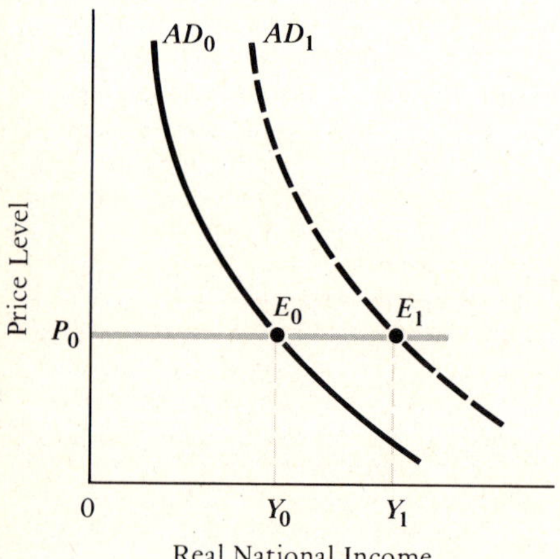

(ii) Shift in aggregate demand

Changes in the money supply cause shifts in the aggregate expenditure and aggregate demand functions. In Figure 34-4 an increase in the money supply increased desired investment expenditure by ΔI. In part (i) of the present figure the aggregate expenditure function shifts up by ΔI (which is the same as ΔI in Figure 34-4), from AE_0 to AE_1. At the fixed price level P_0, equilibrium income rises from Y_0 to Y_1, as shown by the horizontal shift in the aggregate demand curve from AD_0 to AD_1 in part (ii).

When the supply of money falls (from M_{S1} to M_{S0} in Figure 34-4), investment falls by ΔI, thereby shifting aggregate expenditure in the above figure from AE_1 to AE_0. At the fixed price level P_0, this reduces equilibrium income from Y_1 to Y_0.

of money to a change in bond prices and interest rates, to changes in investment expenditure, to a shift in the aggregate demand curve.

This is illustrated in Figure 34-6 for the case of an expansionary monetary shock, that is, a shift in money demand or money supply that tends to increase aggregate demand.

The Strength of Monetary Forces

How much will a given change in the money supply cause the *AD* curve to shift? The size of the shift in

FIGURE 34-6 Transmission Mechanism for an Expansionary Monetary Shock

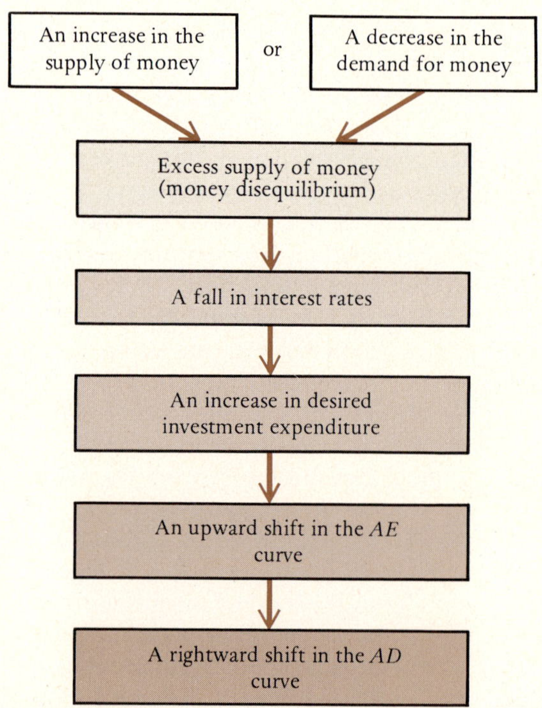

An increase in the supply of money or a decrease in the demand for money leads to an increase in aggregate demand. The excess supply of money following an expansionary monetary disturbance leads to a fall in the interest rate and an increase in investment. This causes an upward shift in the *AE* curve, and thus a rightward shift in the *AD* curve.

aggregate demand in response to an increase in the money supply depends on the size of the increase in investment expenditure. This in turn depends on two factors that play a key role in the transmission mechanism.

The first factor is how much interest rates fall in response to the increase in the money supply. The more interest-sensitive the demand for money, the less interest rates will have to fall to induce firms and households willingly to hold the increase in the money supply.

The second is how much investment expenditure increases in response to the fall in interest rates. The more interest-sensitive investment expenditure, the more it will increase in response to any given fall in the interest rate.

It follows that the size of the shift in aggregate demand in response to a change in the money supply depends on the shapes of the liquidity preference and marginal efficiency of investment curves. The influence of the shapes of the two curves is shown in Figure 34-7 below and may be summarized as follows:

FIGURE 34-7 Two Views on the Strength of Monetary Changes

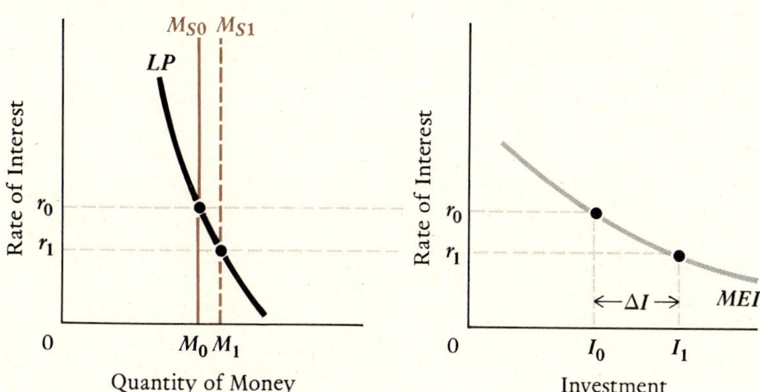

(i) Changes in the money supply effective

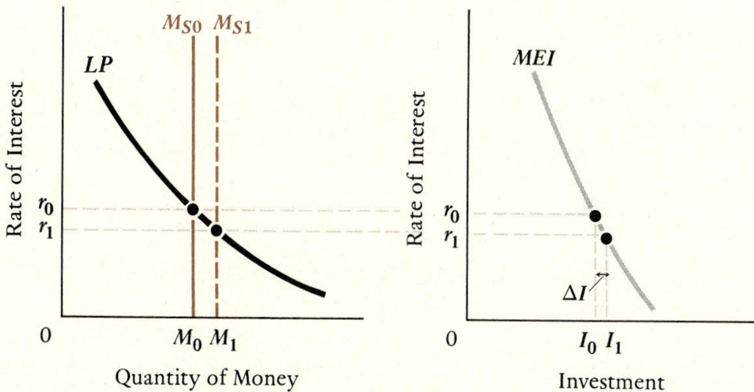

(ii) Changes in the money supply ineffective

The strength of the effect of a change in the money supply on investment and hence on aggregate demand depends on the interest elasticity of both the demand for money and desired investment expenditure. Initially the money supply is M_{S0}, and the economy is in equilibrium with an interest rate of r_0 and investment expenditure of I_0.

In both parts of the figure the central bank expands the money supply from M_{S0} to M_{S1}. The rate of interest thus falls from r_0 to r_1, as shown in each of the left panels. This causes an increase in investment expenditure of ΔI, from I_0 to I_1 as shown in each of the right panels.

In part (i) the demand for money is highly interest-inelastic, so the increase in the money supply leads to a large fall in the interest rate. Further, desired investment expenditure is highly interest-elastic, so the large fall in interest rates also leads to a large increase in investment expenditure. Hence in this case the change in the money supply will be effective in stimulating aggregate demand.

In part (ii) the demand for money is interest-elastic, so the increase in the money supply leads only to a small fall in the interest rate. Further, desired investment expenditure is highly interest-inelastic, so the small fall in interest rates also leads only to a small increase in investment expenditure. Hence in this case the change in the money supply will not be effective in stimulating aggregate demand.

1. **The steeper (the less interest-sensitive) the *LP* function, the greater the effect a change in the money supply will have on interest rates.**
2. **The flatter (the more interest-sensitive) the *MEI* function, the greater the effect a change in the interest rate will have on investment expenditure and hence on aggregate demand.**

The combination that produces the largest effect on aggregate demand for a given change in the money supply is a steep *LP* function and a flat *MEI* function. This combination is illustrated in Figure 34-7(i). It accords with the view, which we shall see later is often associated with so-called monetarists, that monetary policy is relatively effective as a means of influencing the economy. The combination that produces the smallest effect is a flat *LP* function and a steep *MEI* function. This combination is illustrated in Figure 34-7(ii). It accords with the view, which we shall see later is often associated with some so-called Keynesians, that monetary policy is relatively ineffective.

FIGURE 34-8 Effects of Changes in the Money Supply

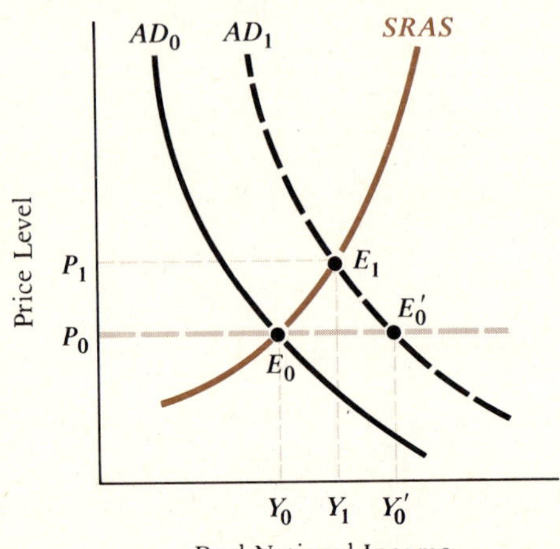

A change in the money supply leads to a change in national income that is smaller than the horizontal shift in the *AD* curve. An increase in the money supply causes the *AD* curve to shift to the right, from AD_0 to AD_1. With the price level constant, national income would rise from Y_0 to Y_0'. With the upward-sloping *SRAS* curve, income rises only to Y_1, and the price level rises to P_1.

Aggregate Demand, the Price Level, and National Income

Effect of a change in the money supply. We have just seen that a change in the money supply shifts the aggregate demand curve. If we want to know what it does to real national income and to the price level, we need to know the slope of the aggregate supply curve. This step, which is familiar from earlier chapters, is recalled in Figure 34-8.[9]

The key result is that the increase in equilibrium real income is less than the horizontal shift in the *AD* curve. This is because part of this shift is dissipated by a rise in the price level. If the aggregate demand curve were vertical, the rise in the price level would not diminish the effect on real output; real output would rise by an amount equal to the horizontal shift of the *AD* curve. But because the *AD* curve is negatively sloped, the rise in real output is smaller.

Effect of a change in the price level. We can now use the transmission mechanism to explain the negative slope of the *AD* curve, that is, to explain why equilibrium national income is negatively related to the price level.

In Chapter 29 when we explained the negative slope of the *AD* curve, we mentioned three reasons but relied on the wealth effect (real balance effect) because it was simple and direct. Now that we have

[9] Since the demand for money in general will depend on the level of national income, as shown in Figure 34-1(ii), our analysis at this stage is incomplete. The induced change in equilibrium national income will lead to a shift in the liquidity preference function in Figure 34-2. For simplicity we have assumed in the text that the liquidity preference function does not shift in response to a change in national income. The Appendix to Chapter 39 presents a formal analysis in which this effect is allowed for and in which equilibrium levels of the interest rate and national income are determined simultaneously.

developed a theory of money and interest rates, we are able to understand the indirect effect that works through the transmission mechanism.

The essential feature of this indirect effect is that a rise in the price level raises the money value of transactions. This leads to an increased demand for money, which brings the transmission mechanism into play. People try to sell bonds to add to their money balances, but collectively all they succeed in doing is forcing up the interest rate. The rise in the interest rate reduces investment expenditure and so reduces equilibrium national income.

This effect is important because, empirically, the interest rate is the most important link between monetary factors and real expenditure flows. Box 34-2 is for readers who wish to study the reasons for the negative slope of the *AD* curve in more detail.

The Monetary Adjustment Mechanism

Suppose that an economy in equilibrium with real national income equal to its potential level were disturbed by an increase in the money supply. Since real national income would increase, there would be an inflationary gap, as shown in Figure 34-9(i). Let us now examine the mechanism by which such an inflationary gap is eliminated. This involves an important but subtle implication of the theory.

A sufficiently large rise in the price level will eliminate any inflationary gap, *provided the nominal money supply remains constant.*

Operation of the monetary adjustment mechanism. Because it causes excess demand in factor markets,

FIGURE 34-9 The Monetary Adjustment Mechanism

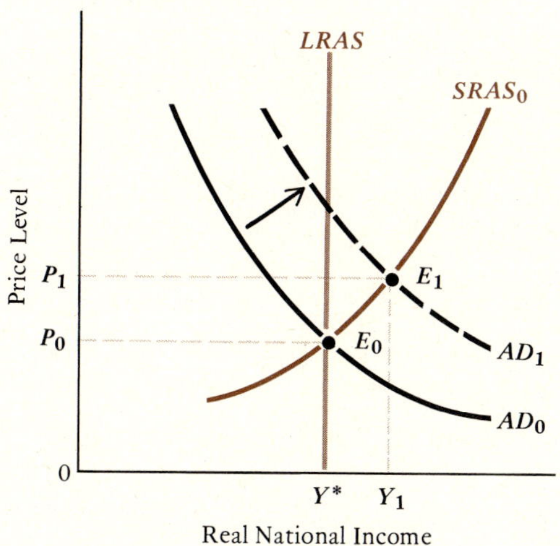

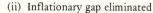

(i) Inflationary gap created

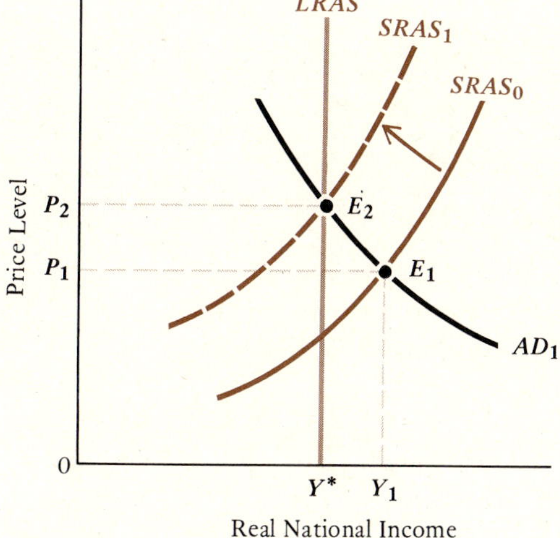

(ii) Inflationary gap eliminated

A rise in the price level will eliminate an inflationary gap. The economy is initially in long-run equilibrium at E_0 with price level P_0 and real income Y^*. In part (i) some disturbance shifts the *AD* curve to the right, leading to equilibrium E_1 with a higher price level P_1 and an inflationary gap of Y^*Y_1.

E_1 is also shown in part (ii). The inflationary gap causes wages to rise, shifting the *SRAS* curve to the left so that the price level starts to rise. The monetary adjustment mechanism (working through a rising interest rate and falling investment) lowers aggregate expenditure so that the economy moves upward along the *AD* curve. Eventually, the inflationary gap is eliminated and equilibrium reached at E_2 with income at Y^* and price level P_2.

BOX 34-2

The Slope of the Aggregate Demand Curve

The *AD* curve relates the price level to the equilibrium level of real national income. It is negatively sloped because the higher the price level, the lower the equilibrium national income. The main reason for this negative slope is found in the transmission mechanism.

Let us look at this process in detail. Although the argument contains nothing new, it does require that you follow carefully through several steps.

We start with an initial position depicted in part (i) of the figure. The liquidity preference schedule is LP_0, and the money supply is M_S. Equilibrium is at E_0 with the interest rate at r_0. The *MEI* schedule given in part (ii) shows that at the rate of interest r_0, desired investment expenditure is I_0. In part (iii) the aggregate expenditure curve AE_0 is drawn for that level of investment (I_0). Equilibrium is at E_0 with a real national income of Y_0. Plotting Y_0 against the initial price level (P_0) yields point *A* on the aggregate demand curve in part (iv).

An increase in the price level to P_1 raises the money value of transactions and increases the quantity of money demanded at each possible value of the interest rate. As a result, the liquidity preference function shifts from LP_0 to LP_1. This raises interest rates to r_1 and lowers investment expenditure by ΔI_1 to I_1.

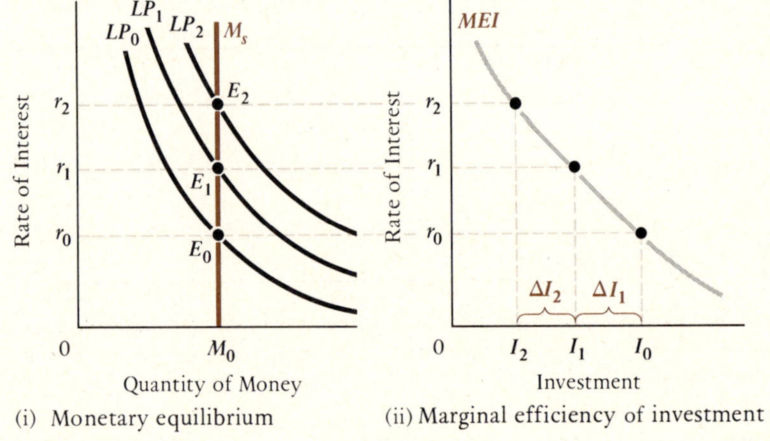

(i) Monetary equilibrium

(ii) Marginal efficiency of investment

the inflationary gap will cause factor prices to rise. This will shift the *SRAS* curve up and take the price level with it. This raises the money value of transactions, and the resulting increase in the demand for money raises interest rates. Hence at any level of real income, desired real expenditure falls. The fall in real expenditure as the price level rises is shown by a movement upward to the left *along* the *AD* curve. This reduces the inflationary gap. When the price level has risen enough, the inflationary gap disappears and the price level stops rising.

This mechanism, illustrated in Figure 34-9(ii), may be called the *monetary adjustment mechanism*. It works through the transmission mechanism.

The monetary adjustment mechanism will eliminate any inflationary gap, provided that the nominal money supply is held constant.

Thus inflationary gaps tend to be self-correcting as long as the money supply does not increase. They will cause the price level to increase, but those increases set in motion a chain of events in the markets for financial assets that will eventually remove the inflationary gap.

The self-correcting mechanism is one reason why price levels and the money supply have been linked for so long in economics. Many things can cause the price level to rise for some time. Yet whatever the

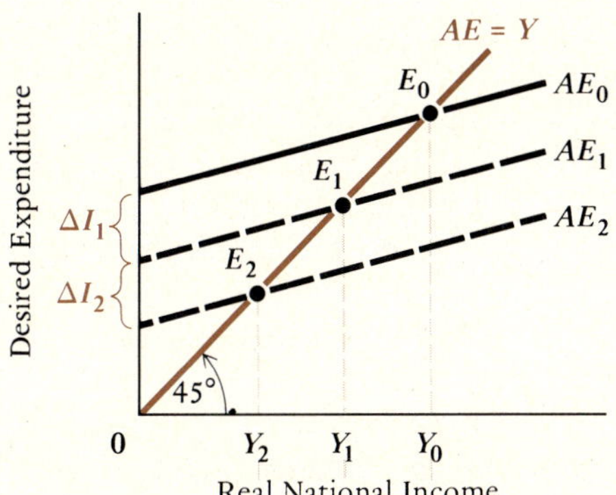

(iii) Equilibrium national income

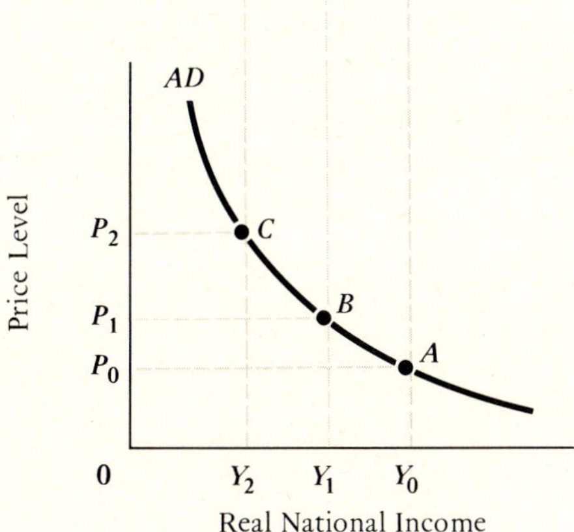

(iv) The aggregate demand curve

The fall in investment causes the *AE* curve in part (iii) to shift down by an equal amount to AE_1. Equilibrium income falls to Y_1. Plotting Y_1 against P_1 produces point *B* on the *AD* curve in part (iv).

A further increase in the price level to P_2 shifts the liquidity preference function to LP_2, raises the interest rate to r_2, and lowers investment expenditure to I_2. The fall in investment shifts the *AE* curve in part (iii) to AE_2, and equilibrium income falls to Y_2. Plotting Y_2 against P_2 produces point *C* on the *AD* curve in part (iv).

The negative relation between the price level and equilibrium real income shown by the *AD* curve occurs because, other things being equal, a rise in the price level raises the *demand* for money. Notice the qualification "other things being equal." It is important for this process that the nominal money *supply* remain constant. The transmission mechanism operates because the demand for money increases when the price level rises, while the money supply remains constant. The attempt to add to money balances by selling bonds is what drives the interest rate up and reduces desired expenditure, thereby reducing equilibrium national income. (This argument is conducted in terms of the nominal supply and demand for money. Arguing in terms of the real demand and supply of money leads to identical results.) [46]

reason for the rise, unless the money supply is expanded, the price level increase itself sets up forces that will remove the initial inflationary gap and so bring demand inflation to a halt.

Frustration of the monetary adjustment mechanism. The self-correcting mechanism for removing an inflationary gap can be frustrated indefinitely if the money supply is increased at the same rate that prices are rising. Say the price level is rising 10 percent a year under the pressure of a large inflationary gap. Demand for nominal money balances will also be rising at about 10 percent per year. Now suppose that the Bank of Canada increases the money supply at 10 percent per year. No excess demand for money will develop, since the extra money needed to meet the rising demand will be forthcoming. The real interest rate will not rise, and the inflationary gap will not be reduced. This process is analyzed in Figure 34-10.

If the money supply increases at the same rate as the price level rises, the real money supply and hence the real interest rate will remain constant, and the monetary adjustment mechanism will be frustrated.

An inflation is said to be *validated* when the money supply is increased as fast as the price level

FIGURE 34-10 Frustration of the Monetary Adjustment

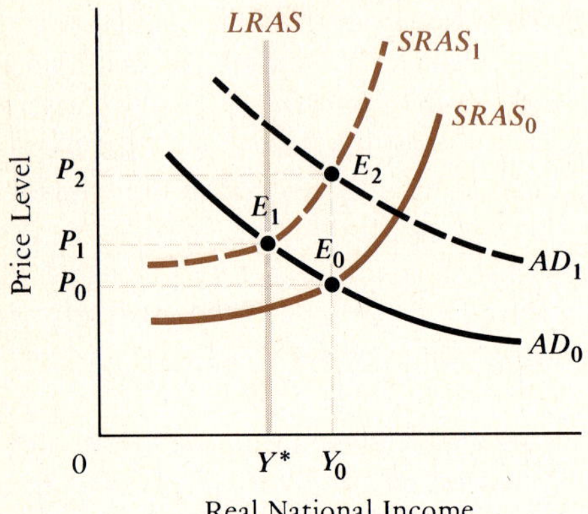

An inflationary gap can persist indefinitely if the money supply increases as fast as the price level. Suppose the economy is at E_0, with income Y_0 and price level P_0. Since potential income is Y^*, there is an inflationary gap of Y^*Y_0. The price level now rises; this tends to shift the economy upward along the *AD* curve, thereby tending to reduce the excess aggregate demand. But the Bank of Canada increases the money supply so that the *AD* curve shifts outward, thereby tending to increase excess aggregate demand. If the two forces just balance each other, by the time the price level has risen to P_2 the curve will have shifted to AD_1, leaving the inflationary gap unchanged, with equilibrium at E_2.

so that the monetary adjustment mechanism is frustrated. A validated inflation can go on indefinitely, although, as we shall see in Chapter 37, possibly not at a constant rate.

A recessionary gap. In principle, the monetary adjustment mechanism will operate to eliminate a recessionary gap. If the recessionary gap led to a fall in factor prices, the *SRAS* curve would shift to the right, causing the price level to fall and national income to rise. However, as we saw in Chapter 30, many economists argue that wages and other factor costs are quite rigid in the face of a recessionary gap. (This was referred to as the second asymmetry of aggregate supply—see page 632.) In this circumstance the monetary adjustment mechanism will not be very effective in causing national income to return quickly to its potential level. Thus many economists argue that aggregate demand should be stimulated in the face of a recessionary gap, either through fiscal policy, which we studied in Chapter 32, or through monetary policy, which we study in the next chapter.

Summary

1. For simplicity we divide all forms in which wealth is held into money, which is a medium of exchange, and bonds, which earn a higher interest return than money and can be turned into money by selling them at a price that is determined on the open market.
2. The price of bonds varies negatively with the rate of interest. A rise in the interest rate lowers the prices of all bonds. The longer its term to maturity, the greater the change in the price of a bond for a given change in the interest rate.
3. The value of money balances that the public wishes to hold is called the *demand for money*. It is a stock (not a flow), measured as so many billions of dollars.
4. Money balances are held, despite the opportunity cost of bond interest forgone, because of the transactions, precautionary, and speculative motives. They have the effect of making the demand

for money vary positively with real national income, the price level, and wealth and vary negatively with the rate of interest. The nominal demand for money varies proportionally with the price level.

5. When there is an excess demand for money balances, people try to sell bonds. This pushes the price of bonds down and the interest rate up. When there is an excess supply of money balances, people try to buy bonds. This pushes the price of bonds up and the rate of interest down. Monetary equilibrium is established when people are willing to hold the fixed stocks of money and bonds at the current rate of interest. The liquidity preference (*LP*) function is the relation between money demand and the interest rate.
6. A change in the interest rate causes desired investment to change along the marginal efficiency of investment (*MEI*) function. This shifts the aggregate desired expenditure function and causes equilibrium national income to change. This means that the aggregate demand curve shifts.
7. Points 5 and 6 together describe the transmission mechanism that links money to national income. A decrease in the supply of money tends to reduce aggregate demand. An increase in the supply of money tends to increase it.
8. The steeper the *LP* curve and the flatter the investment curve, the greater the effect of a given change in the money supply on aggregate demand.
9. The negatively sloped aggregate demand curve indicates that the higher the price level, the lower equilibrium national income. The explanation lies with the monetary adjustment mechanism: The higher the price level, the higher the demand for money, the higher the rate of interest, the lower the aggregate expenditure function, and thus the lower equilibrium income.
10. The monetary adjustment mechanism that causes the aggregate demand curve to have a negative slope means that a sufficiently large rise in the price level will eliminate any inflationary gap. However, this mechanism can be frustrated if the Bank of Canada validates the price rise by increasing the money supply as fast as the price level is rising.

Topics for Review

Interest rates and bond prices
Transactions, precautionary, and speculative motives for holding money
Demand for money
Liquidity preference (*LP*) function
Monetary equilibrium
Transmission mechanism
Marginal efficiency of investment (*MEI*) function
The strength of monetary forces
Monetary adjustment mechanism

Discussion Questions

1. "Central banker says using monetary policy to lower interest rates now would only cause inflation to rise and lead to higher interest rates in the future." Explain how this might be so.
2. "Bond prices pressed downward by news of M1's sharp rise, economy's rebound." Does this *Wall Street Journal* headline necessarily contradict our theory about the direct link between money supply and bond prices?
3. The Governor of the Bank of Canada recently expressed concern about the record government deficit and the growing level of public debt in the economy. Why should these things concern him?
4. Describing a possible future "cashless society," a public report recently said, "In the cashless society of the future, a customer could insert a plastic card into a machine at a store and the amount of the purchase would be deducted from his 'bank account' in the computer automatically and transferred to the store's account. No cash or cheques would ever change hands." What would such an institutional change do to the various motives for holding money balances? What functions would remain for commercial banks and for the central bank if money as we now know it disappeared in this fashion? What benefits and disadvantages can you see in such a scheme?
5. What motives do you think explain the following holdings?
   a. Currency and coins in the cash register of the local supermarket at the start of each working day
   b. The payroll account of the Ford Motor Company in the local bank
   c. Certificates of deposit that mature after one's retirement
   d. Government bonds held by private individuals
6. What would be the effects on the economy if Parliament were to vote a once-and-for-all universal social dividend of $5,000 paid to every Canadian over the age of 17, to be financed by the creation of new money?
7. Suppose that you alone know that the Bank of Canada is going to engage in policies that will decrease the money supply sharply, starting next month. How might you make speculative profits by purchases or sales of bonds now?
8. What would happen if, starting from a situation of 10 percent rates of inflation and of monetary expansion, the Bank of Canada cut the rate of monetary expansion to 5 percent?
9. Trace the full sequence of events by which the monetary adjustment mechanism would work if, in the face of a constant money supply, workers and firms insisted on actions that raised prices continually at a rate of 10 percent per year. "Sooner or later in this situation something would have to give." What possible things could "give"? What would be the consequence of each "giving"?

35

Monetary Policy

The Bank of Canada conducts monetary policy in order to influence such key macroeconomic variables as real national income, employment and unemployment, inflation, interest rates, and the exchange rate. The primary way in which it seeks to influence these variables is through control of the money supply.

Later in this chapter we study in detail how the Bank chooses to conduct monetary policy . . . and what is involved in choosing between different operating procedures and deciding how much emphasis to place on each of the potential policy targets.

Control of the Money Supply

The Bank Act requires each chartered bank to maintain reserves in the form of Bank of Canada notes and deposits at the Bank of Canada, and it permits the central bank to buy and sell various financial assets. The provisions enable the central bank to vary the amount of cash reserves available to the banking system and thus to regulate the money supply.

Open-Market Operations

The most important tool the central bank has for influencing the supply of money is the purchase or sale of government securities on the open market. In a typical year the Bank of Canada buys and sells over $7 billion worth of government securities. What is the effect of these purchases and sales?

Central-bank purchases and sales of government securities in financial markets are known as **open-market operations.** Just as there are stock markets, there are active and well-organized markets for government securities. You or I, General Motors, the Bank of Montreal, or the Bank of Canada can enter this market and buy or sell negotiable government securities at whatever price supply and demand establishes.

Purchases on the Open Market

When the Bank of Canada buys a security from someone in the nonbank private sector, it pays for it with a cheque drawn on the central bank and payable to the seller. The seller deposits this cheque in a chartered bank, which then presents the cheque to the Bank of Canada for payment. The central bank makes a book entry increasing the deposit of the chartered bank at the central bank.

At the end of these transactions, the central bank has acquired a new asset in the form of a security and a new liability in the form of a deposit by the chartered bank. The seller has reduced its security holdings and increased its deposits. The chartered bank has a new deposit equal to the amount paid for the security by the central bank. The chartered bank's reserves and its deposit liabilities have increased by an equal amount.

When the central bank buys securities on the open market, the reserves of the chartered banks are increased. These banks in turn can expand deposits, thereby increasing the money supply.

Table 35-1 shows the changes in the balance sheets of the several parties in response to a central-bank purchase of $100 in government securities from the nonbank private sector. After these transactions, the chartered banks have excess reserves and are in a position to expand their loans and deposits. Indeed, the chartered banks are in precisely the position studied on page 725 (see Table 33-4). The new deposit made by the immigrant might just as well have been made by someone who had sold a security to the Bank of Canada.

If the central bank buys many securities in the open market, the entire banking system will gain new reserves. Whether the seller is a household, a firm, or a bank, the Bank of Canada's purchase of securities on the open market sets in motion a series of book transactions that increase the banking system's reserves and thus make possible a multiple expansion of credit.[1]

TABLE 35-1 Balance Sheet Changes Caused by an Open-Market Purchase from a Household

Assets		Liabilities	
Private household			
Bonds	−$100	No change	
Deposits	+ 100		
Chartered banks			
Reserves (deposits with central bank)	+$100	Demand deposits	+$100
Central bank			
Bonds	+$100	Deposits of chartered banks	+$100

The money supply is increased when the Bank of Canada makes an open-market purchase from the nonbank private sector. When the Bank of Canada buys a $100 bond from a household, the household gains money and gives up a bond. The chartered banks gain a new deposit of $100 and thus new reserves of $100. Chartered banks can now engage in a multiple expansion of deposit money of the sort analyzed in Chapter 33.

Sales on the Open Market

When the central bank sells a $100 security to a household or firm, it receives in return the buyer's cheque drawn against its own deposit in a chartered bank. The central bank presents the cheque to the chartered bank for payment. Payment is made by a book entry that reduces the chartered bank's deposit at the central bank.

The changes in this case are the opposite of those shown in Table 35-1. The central bank has reduced its assets by the value of the security it sold and reduced its liabilities in the form of the deposits of chartered banks. The household or firm has increased its holdings of securities and reduced its cash on deposit with a chartered bank. The chartered bank has reduced its deposit liability to the household or firm and reduced its reserves (on deposit with the central bank) by the same amount. Each of the asset changes is balanced by a liability change. Indeed, everything balances.

But the chartered bank finds that the equal change in its reserves and deposit liabilities causes its ratio of reserves to deposits to fall. Consider, for example,

[1] In Chapter 33 we studied a case in which the Bank sold a bond to a household or a non-bank firm. If instead the purchaser was a chartered bank, the end result would have been the same. In this case the chartered bank gives up one asset (a bond) and gains another (cash or a deposit with the central bank). But now the chartered bank has excess reserves (liabilities unchanged, cash reserves increased) on the basis of which it can engage in the expansion of deposits.

a bank with $10 million in deposits backed by $1 million reserves in fulfillment of a 10 percent reserve ratio. As a result of the Bank's open-market sales of $100,000 worth of bonds, the bank loses $100,000 of deposits and reserves. Reserves are now $900,000 while deposits are $9.9 million, a reserve ratio of only 9.09 percent.

Banks whose reserve ratios are driven below the minimum requirement must take immediate steps to restore their reserve ratios. The necessary reduction in deposits can be accomplished by not making new investments when old ones are redeemed (e.g., by not granting new loans when old ones are repaid) or by selling (liquidating) existing investments.

When the central bank sells securities on the open market, the reserves of the chartered banks are decreased. These banks in turn are forced to contract deposits, thereby decreasing the money supply.

But what if the public does not wish to buy the securities the Bank of Canada wishes to sell? Can it force the public to do so? The answer is that there is always a price at which the public will buy. In its open-market operations, the Bank must be prepared to have the price of the securities fall if it insists on suddenly selling a large volume of them. As we have seen, a fall in the price of securities is the same thing as a rise in interest rates, so if the Bank wishes to curtail the money supply by selling bonds, it may well drive up interest rates. This process was illustrated in Figure 34-4 on page 745.

Notice in Table 33-2 on page 723 that the Bank's holdings of government securities are large relative to the reserves of chartered banks. By selling securities it can contract those reserves very sharply if it chooses. Similarly, by buying securities it can expand reserves. Open-market operations are a potent weapon for affecting the size of bank reserves—and thus for affecting the money supply.

Tools Other Than Open-Market Operations

The major tool the Bank of Canada uses in conducting monetary policy is its open-market operations. But other tools are available and have on occasion been used extensively.

Reserve Requirements

One way that a central bank can control the money supply is by altering the required minimum reserve ratios. Suppose the banking system is loaned up; that is, it has no excess reserves. If the Bank increases the required reserve ratio (say from 20 percent to 25 percent), the reserves held by the chartered banks will no longer be adequate to support their outstanding deposits. Chartered banks will then be forced to reduce their deposits until they achieve the new, higher required reserve ratio.[2] This decrease in deposits is a decrease in the money supply. This process is illustrated in Table 35-2.

A reduction in reserve requirements immediately provides banks with excess reserves. Of course, if banks choose not to increase their loans, they will not need to respond to a decrease in required reserves, since those are only minimum requirements. In normal times the profit motive will lead most banks to respond by increasing loans and deposits—and thus lead to an increase in the money supply.

Increases in required reserve ratios force banks with no excess reserves to decrease deposits and thus reduce the money supply. Decreases in required reserve ratios permit banks to expand deposits, which increases the money supply.

This method of controlling the money supply has been used in the United States but not in Canada. Given the small margin of excess reserves held by the chartered banks, increases in the required reserve ratios would force abrupt adjustments in bank assets. An equivalent contraction in the money supply can be brought about by using the more flexible tool of open-market operations, which can be spread out over time to induce a more orderly adjustment. Changes in reserve requirements are occasionally made, but this is usually done for purposes other

[2] They will do this by gradually decreasing their loans and/or selling some of their securities. In the short term they may undertake purchase and resale agreements to give themselves time to meet the increased reserve requirements without disrupting financial markets.

TABLE 35-2 Balance Sheet for a Loaned-Up Banking System

(a) Before: 20 percent reserve ratio				(b) After: 25 percent reserve ratio			
Assets		Liabilities		Assets		Liabilities	
Reserves	$1,000	Deposits	$5,000	Reserves	$1,000	Deposits	$4,000
Loans	4,100	Capital	100	Loans	3,100	Capital	100
	$5,100		$5,100		$4,100		$4,100

Increasing the required reserve ratio forces a loaned-up bank to reduce its deposits and thus decreases the supply of deposit money. The banking system in part (a) has a ratio of reserves to deposits of 0.20. If the Bank of Canada raises the required reserve ratio to 0.25, the reserves of $1,000 will support deposits of only $4,000. As shown in part (b), the banking system can reduce its deposits by reducing its loans. A reduction in reserve requirements from 0.25 to 0.20 would permit a banking system in the position of (b) to expand its loans and deposits to those of (a) with no increases in its dollar reserves.

than stabilizing the economy. For example, reforms of the Bank Act in 1980 reduced the reserve requirement on demand deposits from 12 to 10 percent.

Changes in the Bank Rate

The rate of interest at which the Bank of Canada makes loans to the chartered banks is called the **bank rate.** In some countries, commercial banks that find themselves short of reserves borrow from the central bank. A rise in the bank rate in such countries will cause the commercial banks to be more prudent in their lending activities. If they lend so much out that they have insufficient reserves, they will have to pay a higher rate to borrow from the central bank. However, this mechanism is not very important in Canada because the chartered banks rarely borrow from the Bank of Canada.

Prior to March 1980 the bank rate was simply set by the Bank of Canada. Changes in the rate had an "announcement effect"—such changes were widely interpreted as a signal of changes in the stance of monetary policy, which would cause market interest rates quickly to move in the same direction. Since March 1980 the bank rate itself has become a "market rate." It is now set at a premium of one-quarter of a percentage point over the average rate determined in the weekly Thursday auction of three-month treasury bills.

Most observers believed that a market-determined bank rate would lessen the role played by the bank rate by eliminating the announcement effect; however, the financial press now gives more attention to changes in the bank rate, and it is not at all clear that it is less important as a signal about monetary policy. The Bank of Canada is a major participant in the market for treasury bills, and its purchases or sales clearly influence the bank rate by influencing the treasury bill rate. But its purchases and sales also influence the money supply. Hence the bank rate now signals actual rather than intended monetary policy.

Secondary Reserve Requirements

When the central bank attempts to restrain inflationary forces, it may wish to dampen expenditures not only through higher interest rates but also through some form of direct control over the expansion of bank loans. Restricting the supply of cash reserves will not restrain the banks from extending credit if they have substantial quantities of liquid assets that can be sold off to finance new loans. The Bank of Canada is empowered to restrict the ability of the chartered banks to expand their loans through the imposition of a required minimum secondary reserve ratio within the range of 0 to 12 percent of deposits. Secondary reserves are defined as holdings of treasury bills, day-to-day loans, and excess cash reserves. A required minimum ratio of 8 percent was in effect from the end of 1971 until the end of 1974, when it was lowered to 7 percent. Further reductions were made during 1975 and 1977; at the beginning of 1978, the required ratio was 5 percent. It has not changed since.

Moral Suasion

The term *moral suasion* is generally used to describe attempts by the central bank to enlist the cooperation of private financial institutions in the pursuit of some objective of monetary policy. In a country such as Canada, where there are only a few banks, the central bank can easily communicate its view to the chartered banks. In some cases moral suasion involves general discussions aimed at improving understanding of the current financial situation and the objectives of policy. In other cases specific requests have been issued to the banks. For example, on a number of occasions in recent years the Bank of Canada has attempted to restrain the growth of term deposits by requesting the observance of ceilings either on the interest rates offered or on the volume of deposits.

Effects of Changes in the Money Supply: A Review

We have now seen how the Bank of Canada can alter the money supply. Before turning to a more detailed discussion of the Bank's operating procedure and the policy choices it faces, we review the analysis in Chapter 34 of the effects of changes in the money supply.

Suppose that initially the economy is in equilibrium at less than potential income. The Bank then increases the money supply. Firms and households now hold excess money balances, and they try to buy bonds. This action forces up the price of bonds, which implies a fall in the rate of interest.

The resulting increase in desired investment expenditure shifts the aggregate demand curve rightward, thus raising equilibrium national income. This process is shown in Figures 34-4 and 34-5 on pages 745 and 746.

When the Bank decreases the money supply, this creates an excess demand for money because firms and households no longer have the money balances they wish to hold at the existing level of interest rates. In an effort to replenish their inadequate holdings of money, firms and households seek to sell bonds, causing an increase in the interest rate. The increased interest rate causes a reduction in investment expenditure. This in turn shifts the aggregate demand curve leftward and lowers equilibrium income.

Monetary policy works through the transmission mechanism to shift the aggregate demand curve and so to change equilibrium national income. An increase in the money supply is expansionary, a decrease contractionary.

As a result, changes in the money supply will cause real national income and the price level to change in the same direction, as shown in Figure 34-8 on page 748.

Instruments and Objectives of Monetary Policy

The Bank of Canada conducts monetary policy in order to influence real national income and the price level. These ultimate objectives of the Bank's policy are called **policy variables.** The variables that it controls *directly* in order to achieve these objectives are called its **policy instruments.** Variables that are neither policy variables nor policy instruments but nevertheless can play a key role in the execution of monetary policy are called **intermediate targets;** their importance lies in the influence they exert on the policy variables.

Policy Variables

The Bank's twin policy variables are real national income and the price level. In practice the two are often lumped into a single variable, nominal national income.

Nominal national income as a policy variable. Changes in nominal national income arise from changes in both real national income and the price level. In principle the central bank will be concerned about how a given change in nominal national income is divided between these two components.

We saw in Chapter 34 that monetary policy operates by influencing aggregate demand. In the short run the effects of a monetary policy that shifts the *AD* curve will be divided between the price level and real output in a manner determined by the slope of the *SRAS* curve. Thus, while the central bank cares about the price level and real output, there is little it can do in the short run to achieve separate goals with respect to each. For any price-level response that is achieved, the real output consequence must be accepted. Alternatively, for any real output response that is achieved, the price-level consequence must be accepted. Monetary policy is not capable of pursuing two objectives of pushing the price level (*P*) and national income (*Y*) toward independently determined targets. For this reason we choose to focus on nominal national income (*PY*) as the target for monetary policy in the short run.

Price level as the policy variable in the long run. We have seen that in the long run, when the level of wages is fully adjusted to the price level, the *LRAS* curve is vertical and hence the major impact of monetary policy will be on the price level.

Although monetary policy influences both real output and the price level in the short run, its main effects in the long run are only on the price level.

Policy Instruments

Having selected its policy variables and formulated targets for their behavior, the Bank must decide how to achieve these targets. How can the policy variables be made to perform in the way that the Bank wishes? Since the Bank can control neither income nor the price level directly, it must employ its policy instruments, which it does control directly, to influence aggregate demand in the desired manner.

The primary instrument used by the Bank of Canada to conduct monetary policy is open-market operations.

Open-market operations change the size of the Bank's monetary liabilities, which are the currency in circulation plus reserves of the chartered banks. Chartered bank reserves are held on deposit with the Bank and are the Bank's liability because it must redeem them on demand. The Bank of Canada's monetary liabilities, as we saw in Chapter 33, form the *base* on which chartered banks can expand and create deposits. For this reason their liabilities are often referred to as the **monetary base.**

The central bank cannot expect to be able to use its open-market operations to control both the interest rate and the monetary base independently. This is because of the liquidity preference function, which relates the quantity of money to the rate of interest.

The Bank must therefore choose between two alternative procedures in conducting its open-market operations. It may set the *price* (and hence the interest rate) at which it sells or buys bonds on the open market. In this case the quantity of bonds sold or purchased is determined by market demand. If the Bank wishes to change its policy, it must change the price at which it is willing to buy and sell bonds. This approach is called **interest-rate control**, and here the interest rate is properly viewed as a policy instrument.

Alternatively, the Bank may choose to set the *quantity* of open-market sales or purchases. It does this in order to set the reserves of the chartered banks. In this case it is the price of bonds, and hence the interest rate, that is determined by market demand. If the Bank wishes to change its policy, it changes the amount of its open-market purchases or sales. (Of course, this means that the interest rate at which these transactions are made may also change.) In this case, where the Bank chooses to set the quantity of its open-market operations, it is directly deciding how much the monetary base will change. For this reason it is said to be using **base control**, and the monetary base is properly viewed as the policy instrument.

Intermediate Targets

Major changes in the direction or method of monetary policy are usually made only infrequently. Decisions regarding the implementation of policy must, however, be made almost daily. Given the values that the Bank wishes its policy variables to take on, and given the current state of the economy, is a purchase or a sale in the open market called for? How big a purchase or sale? At what interest rate? Such questions must be answered continually by the Bank in its day-to-day operations.

Daily information about the policy variables, however, is rarely available. Inflation and unemployment rates are available only on a monthly basis and with a considerable lag. National income figures are available even less frequently; they appear on a quarterly basis. Thus the policymakers do not know exactly what is happening to the policy variables when they make decisions about their policy instruments.

How, then, does the Bank of Canada make decisions? Central banks have typically used *intermediate targets* to guide them when implementing monetary policy in the very short run. To serve as an intermediate target, a variable must satisfy two criteria. First, information about it must be available on a frequent basis, daily if possible. Second, its movements must be closely correlated with those of the policy variable so that changes in it can reasonably be expected to indicate that the policy variable is also changing.

The two most commonly used intermediate targets have been the money supply and the interest rate. Since the two are not independent, it is important that the central bank not choose a target for one that is inconsistent with the other. By the same token, since the two are closely related, it might appear not to matter much which one is used.

For example, if the Bank wishes to remove an inflationary gap by forcing interest rates up, it will sell securities and thus drive their prices down. These open market sales will also contract the money supply. It is largely immaterial whether the Bank seeks to force interest rates up or to contract the money supply; doing one accomplishes the other. Similarly, driving interest rates down by open-market purchases of government securities will tend to expand the money supply as the public gains money in return for the securities it sells to the Bank.

Nevertheless, there are differences between a monetary regime where interest rates are taken as the intermediate target and a regime that uses the money supply as target.

Choice of intermediate targets. Over the years there has been controversy over which intermediate target the Bank should rely on most. In the earlier part of the postwar period, many central banks relied mainly on interest rates.

A majority of economists, including most monetarists, have long been critical of the practice of using the interest rate as an intermediate target. These economists pointed out that since interest rates tended to vary directly with the business cycle, rising on the upswing and falling on the downswing, it was difficult for the central bank to determine the impact of its monetary policy by observing the interest rate alone. Historical examples were pointed to where central banks, trying to restrain a boom, thought their restrictive policies were working because interest rates were rising sharply. In retrospect it was concluded, however, that interest rates were rising because of rapidly expanding national income and, hence, increasing demand for money.

As a result of such criticisms, many central banks, including the Bank of Canada, turned to rely almost exclusively on the narrow monetary aggregate M1 as their intermediate target. When M1 turned out to be a less than completely reliable guide, broader monetary aggregates were used.

Today, however, after more than a decade's experience with such aggregates, similar criticisms can be levied at exclusive concentration on them. The reason is that changes in the money supply are reliable indicators of the direction of monetary policy *only* if the demand for money is relatively stable. Recent experience suggests that the demand for money can change quite substantially and that a central bank can discover what is happening to this demand only after much time-consuming research. Critics of the use of monetary aggregates as intermediate variables can point to historical circumstances in which a central bank incorrectly thought it was exerting a restraining force on the economy through a restrictive monetary policy because monetary aggregates were growing slowly. In retrospect, however, it turned out that monetary policy had been expansionary. There was an excess supply rather than an excess demand for money, the reason being that the demand for money had fallen more than had been appreciated at the time.

TABLE 35-3 Assignment of Variables Under Alternative Operating Regimes of Monetary Policy

Regime	Policy instrument	Intermediate target	Policy variable
1. Monetary targeting—base control	Open-market operations: regulate volume of open-market sales and purchases	Quantity of money (M1) via money supply process	
2. Monetary targeting—interest-rate control	Open-market operations: regulate price at which open-market sales and purchases are made (i.e., regulate interest rate)	Quantity of money (M1) via liquidity preference	1. Real national income and the price level *or* 2. Nominal national income
3. Interest-rate targeting	Open-market operations: regulate intermediate target directly	Interest rates	

Even with a given set of policy variables, central banks might adopt a variety of operating regimes. The central bank could use either the quantity of money or the interest rate as its intermediate target.

When the central bank opts for monetary targeting, it can influence its target only indirectly. Through its open-market operations it can control directly either the size of the monetary base or the level of interest rates. If it controls the monetary base (regime 1), the quantity of money is influenced via the money supply process, while the interest rate is determined via monetary equilibrium as in Figure 34-2. If the central bank controls the interest rate (regime 2), the influence on the quantity of money operates via the liquidity preference function.

Should the central bank choose to use the interest rate as an intermediate target (regime 3), it can achieve its target directly by using open-market operations to control the interest rate. Although this appears to be a simpler process (and in terms of operation, it is simpler), many economists favor monetary targeting.

Other variables, such as the interest rate and the exchange rate, might also appear as policy variables. The interest rate could then appear as a policy instrument, an intermediate target, or a policy variable, depending on the policy regime.

Today some central banks still try to target on a money supply figure while others, including the Bank of Canada, use no single target but try to assess their monetary stance by looking at interest rates, various money supply measures, and other targets.

Operating Regime

A central bank's **operating regime** refers to the combination of intermediate targets and the policy instruments it selects to achieve those targets.

Table 35-3 illustrates some possible operating regimes for the central bank. If the Bank chooses the interest rate as its intermediate target, it can achieve that target directly by using interest rate control as its instrument. In this case the distinction between intermediate target and policy instrument is superfluous. If the Bank chooses the money supply as its intermediate target, it can achieve its target indirectly by means of either base control or interest-rate control. The somewhat confusing multiple roles that can be played by the various economic variables are clarified in the table and summarized as follows.

Nominal national income is a policy variable. The money supply can be an intermediate target or a policy instrument. The interest rate can be a policy variable, an intermediate target, or a policy instrument.

Whichever operating regime is adopted, attempts to use monetary policy to fine-tune the economy remain fraught with dangers. The problems come mainly from the lags between a change in the policy instruments and the reaction of the policy variables that the Bank wishes to control. The way in which long lags can make stabilization policy become destabilizing has already been discussed in Chapter 32 in the context of fiscal policy, and it is further discussed in Box 35-1 in the context of monetary policy.

Monetary Policy in Action

Having studied its objectives and instruments, we now consider how monetary policy has actually operated since World War II.

Throughout the 1950s and 1960s, the Bank of Canada used interest rates as its main intermediate target. In spite of difficulties in judging the stance of monetary policy by observing interest rates in some periods, in others the stance was clear. For example, there is little doubt that monetary policy was contractionary in 1968 and 1969 when the Bank tried to stop Canada from importing the U.S. inflation.[3]

There is also little doubt that monetary policy was quite expansionary in the early 1970s. By 1974 inflation was close to the double-digit level. Then the first OPEC supply-side shock sent oil prices, and then the general price level, soaring. Inflation accelerated, output fell, and unemployment grew.

Monetary Gradualism: 1975–1980

In 1975 the Bank of Canada announced a policy of "monetary gradualism." The rate of increase in the money supply (narrowly defined as M1) was to be reduced gradually in an effort to reduce the inflation rate gradually. To accomplish this, a target range for money supply growth was to be stated publicly and periodically revised downward.

The first target range was set at 10 to 15 percent growth per year. The first reduction, to a range of 8 to 12 percent, came in August 1976. Successive steps further reduced the range; in mid February 1981 the target range was 4 to 8 percent. The Bank was quite successful at keeping actual money growth inside the target range, although there was considerable movement within that range. But after some reduction during the early periods of gradualism, the inflation rate again accelerated, and by the end of the decade it was not far below the rate prevailing when the policy was introduced in 1975. This was because the restraint sought through money supply control was offset by shifts in the demand for money, many of which were caused by the very inflation the policy was attempting to curb.

Inflation raises the cost of holding non-interest-bearing M1 balances, since one consequence of rapid inflation is a high nominal rate of interest. This provides an incentive to economize on M1 balances and invest the funds instead in interest-earning assets.

A series of spectacular institutional changes showed just how adaptive the financial system can be to changes in the needs of its users; many of these changes were noted in Chapter 33. Firms learned how to reduce their M1 balances by careful cash management. In some countries funds were even moved to banks in remote areas where cheques were cleared once rather than twice a day, so that once cheques were cleared, cash managers knew they had the use of their remaining balances for a whole 24 hours! Banks introduced automatic transfer systems where money could be held in interest-earning accounts and transferred to chequing accounts only when needed. As a result of such changes, the demand for M1 balances often fell faster than the supply was being restricted. Thus M1 control did not always create the desired conditions of tight money.

In 1982 the Bank of Canada formally abandoned monetary targeting, although many commentators felt that it had really abandoned the policy in mid 1981 when it allowed the money supply to fall well below the target range and focused considerable attention on propping up the exchange rate. The Bank remained committed to trying to control the economy through aggregate demand. It stated, however, that no observed relation between M1 or any other monetary magnitude on the one hand and national income on the other hand was stable enough to make complete reliance on monetary targets useful.

[3] The attempt was frustrated by the Bank's commitment to a fixed rate of exchange between the Canadian dollar and the U.S. dollar. As we shall see in Chapter 42, monetary policy cannot simultaneously control the money supply and the exchange rate.

BOX 35-1

How Monetary Policy Can Be Destabilizing

In the real world the full effects of monetary policy occur only after quite long time lags. *Execution lags,* lags that occur after the decision is made to implement the policy, can have important implications for the conduct of monetary policy.

Sources of Execution Lags

1. Open-market operations affect the reserves of the chartered banks. The full increase in the money supply occurs only when the banks have granted enough new loans and made enough investments to expand the money supply by the full amount permitted by existing reserve ratios. This process can take quite a long time.
2. The division of all assets into just two categories, money and bonds, is useful for showing the underlying forces at work in determining the demand for money. In fact, however, there is a whole series of assets—from currency and demand deposits to term deposits, to treasury bills and short-term bonds, to long-term bonds and equities. When households find themselves with larger money balances than they require, a chain of substitution occurs, with short-term and long-term interest rates falling as households try to hold less money and more interest-earning assets. The change in longer-term interest rates in turn affects interest-sensitive expenditures. These adjustments along a chain of interest rates can take considerable time to work out.
3. It takes time for new investment plans to be drawn up, approved, and put into effect. It may easily take up to a year before the full increase in investment expenditure builds up in response to a fall in interest rates.
4. The increased investment expenditures set off a multiplier process that increases national income by some multiple of the initiating increase in investment expenditure. This, too, takes some time to work out.

Similar considerations apply to contractionary monetary policies that seek to shift the aggregate expenditure function downward.

Furthermore, although the end result is fairly predictable, the speed with which the entire expansionary or contractionary process works itself out can vary from time to time in ways that are hard to predict.

Monetary policy is capable of exerting expansionary and contractionary forces on the economy, but it operates with a time lag that is long and unpredictably variable.

Implications of Execution Lags

To see the significance of execution lags for the conduct of monetary policy, assume that the execution lag is 18 months. If on December 1 the Bank of Canada decides that the economy needs stimulus, it can be increasing the money supply within days, and by the end of the year a significant increase may be registered.

But because the full effects of this policy take time to work out, the policy may prove to be destabilizing. By the fall of next year a substantial inflationary gap may have developed due to cyclical forces unrelated to the Bank's monetary policy. The Bank

Monetary Stringency: 1981–1983

The early 1980s saw an extremely restrictive monetary policy, one that reduced inflation to low levels, but at the cost of a very severe recession. Since during this period the Bank of Canada was mainly following the lead of the U.S. Federal Reserve System (the Fed), the period is best studied by observing the forces operating in the United States.

The United States Experience

In 1980 the Fed embarked on a policy of monetary restraint aimed at fighting inflation. As a result, interest rates rose sharply, as shown in Figure 35-1[4]

[4] In 1980 the Fed switched from a regime of interest-rate control to a regime of base control. Although this policy requires that interest rates be free to find their own level, many economists did not expect the degree of interest rate volatility shown in Figure 35-1.

may then call for a contractionary policy, but the full effects of the monetary expansion initiated nine months earlier are just being felt, so an expansionary monetary stimulus is adding to the existing inflationary gap. If the Bank now applies the monetary brakes by contracting the money supply, the full effects of this move will not be felt for another 18 months. By that time a contraction may have already set in because of the natural cyclical forces of the economy. If so, the delayed effects of the monetary policy may turn a minor downturn into a major recession.

The long execution lag of monetary policy makes monetary fine tuning difficult, and it may make it destabilizing.

If the execution lag were known with certainty, it could be built into the Bank's calculations. But the fact that the lag is highly variable makes this nearly impossible. Of course, when a persistent output gap has existed and is predicted to continue for a long time, monetary policy may be stabilizing even when its effects occur after a long time lag.

A Monetary Rule?

The poor record of monetary policy as a short-run stabilizer has lent force to the monetarists' persistent criticisms of monetary fine tuning. Monetarists argue that (1) monetary policy is a potent force of expansionary and contractionary pressures; (2) monetary policy works with lags that are both long and variable; and (3) central banks are often given to sudden and sharp reversals of policy stance. Consequently, monetary policy has a destabilizing effect on the economy, the policy itself accentuating rather than dampening the economy's natural cyclical swings.

Monetarists argue from this position that the stability of the economy would be much improved if the central bank stopped trying to stabilize it. What then should the central bank do? Since growth of population and of productivity lead to a rising level of output, the central bank ought to provide the extra money needed to allow the holding of additional desired money balances as real income and wealth rise over time.

According to the monetarists, the central bank should expand the money supply year in and year out at a constant rate equal to the rate of growth of real income. When the growth rate shows signs of long-term change, the central bank can adjust its rate of monetary expansion. It should not, however, alter this rate with a view to stabilizing the economy against short-term fluctuations.

This reasoning led a number of central banks, including the Bank of Canada, to focus on the growth of the money supply in formulating their policies. As we shall see, the results have been mixed. Experience has shown that the demand for money can sometimes shift quite substantially. A stable money supply rule in the face of demand instability guarantees monetary shocks rather than monetary stability.

(see page 766). The sharp rise in interest rates in late 1980 helped choke off the recovery that had just started. A further rise in rates in early 1982 fed the downturn and helped make it the most serious recession since the 1930s.

These interest rates, and the recession they wrought, were more severe than might have been expected from the monetary policy that was intended. What happened to cause the high interest rates and the severe recession in the face of this moderate showdown in the rate of growth of the money supply? Once again, the key to the puzzle lay in the relation between the demand for money and national income.

As a result of an unanticipated surge in the demand for money, there was a severe money shortage—that is, monetary policy was much tighter than the Fed had expected. This was not because money

FIGURE 35-1 **Short-Term Interest Rates, Canada and the United States, 1979–1986**

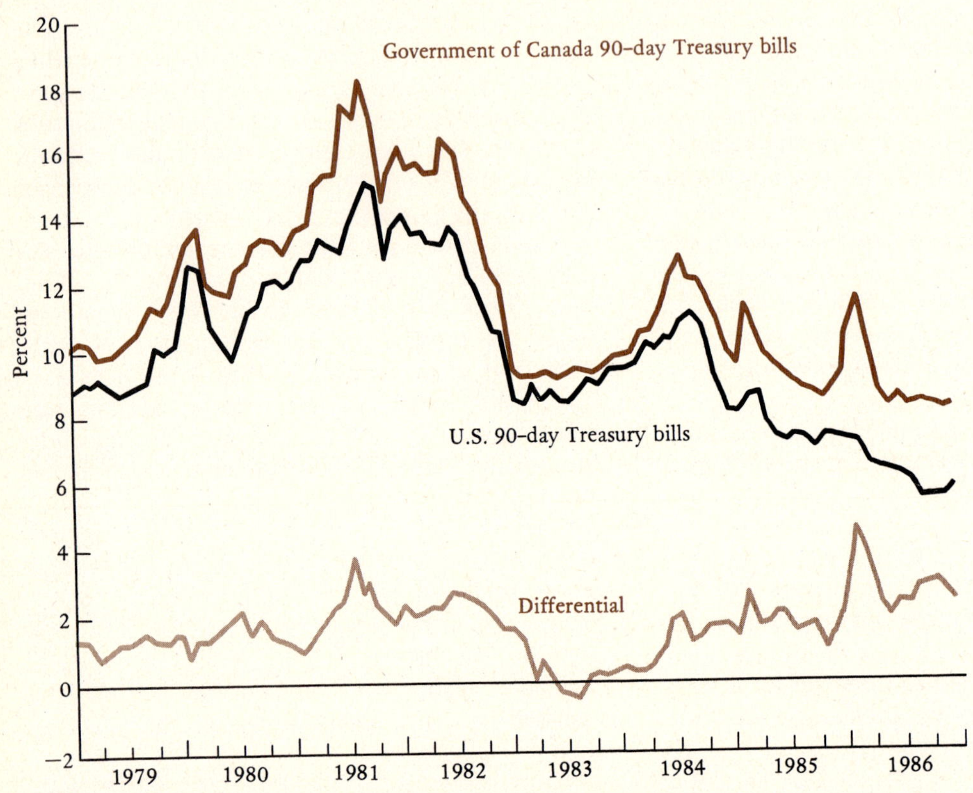

Short-term interest rates have moved together in Canada and the United States, both rising until mid 1982 and both falling since. During 1979 and 1980 interest rates displayed an upward trend, reflecting increases in inflation. Tight monetary policy then led to sharp increases in interest rates in 1981. Subsequent declines in inflation then led to declines in nominal interest rates.

The interest differential shows that Canadian interest rates were typically a little higher than American interest rates. The differential was especially large in 1981 and 1982 when sharp increases in U.S. rates were more than matched by increases in Canadian rates, and in late 1985 and early 1986 when sharp decreases in U.S. rates were not matched by decreases in Canadian rates. (*Source: Bank of Canada Review*, several issues.)

supply targets were missed—in fact, M1 rose above its target range in this period. Rather, monetary policy was tight because money demand was again misestimated—this time it was underestimated.[5]

[5] Note that this was the opposite of the shift that disrupted Canadian monetary policy in the 1970s.

In part the Fed's reaction was to raise the rate of monetary growth. But basically the Fed stuck to its monetary targets, and as a result it pursued very restrictive monetary policy. This created a heated controversy in the financial press and caused many critics to attack the Fed's policies.

By June 1982 M1 was back in its target range.

But the serious weakness in the economy and the "room for monetary ease" created by the return of M1 to its target range led to a loosening of monetary policy in the second half of 1982.

Why did the Fed allow this severely contractionary policy to persist so long? One possibility is that the Fed was actually quite happy to have a very contractionary policy. Many observers had come to the view that only a sharp monetary contraction would lower inflationary expectations and so allow the actual inflation rate to fall. Another possibility is that having announced its targets for monetary growth, the Fed had to adhere to them in order to maintain its own credibility. Failure to meet the targets, this argument runs, would undermine belief in the Fed's commitment to reducing inflation. Such a loss of confidence would in turn work to make interest rates and the actual inflation rate respond sluggishly to the Fed's policies.

The Canadian Reaction

The very tight monetary policy in the United States led to similar monetary restraint in Canada. As in the United States, there is a question about why this was done. Two reasons are probably important. One is that the high degree of integration of capital markets means there is not very much scope for Canadian interest rates to be held far below U.S. rates. (This matter is discussed further in Chapter 39.) Insofar as the Bank of Canada had some freedom to hold rates below those in the United States, it did not exercise its freedom (see Figure 35-1). The second reason suggested is that, discouraged by the failure of gradualism to control inflation, the Bank of Canada welcomed the opportunity to follow the United States in a more severe bout of monetary restraint. By the early 1980s many commentators had begun to wonder if the problem of inflation was intractable. If it could be solved, the failure of gradualism suggested that a severe jolt of very restrictive policy might be needed to do the job.

The severe monetary restraint did have powerful effects on the Canadian economy—in fact, the effects were more powerful than many economists predicted at the time. As we have already noted (see Figure 35-1), interest rates soared and a severe recession occurred. Real output growth was *negative* throughout 1982, and by the end of that year the unemployment rate reached 12.8 percent, its highest level since the Great Depression of the 1930s. The monetary restraint also had a strong restraining effect on inflation—the rate of change of the CPI fell from its peak of 12.7 percent in the third quarter of 1981 to 4.6 percent at the end of 1983. The fall in inflation brought with it a fall in nominal interest rates; for example, the 90-day commercial paper rate fell from a peak of just over 17 percent in mid 1982 to 9.3 percent by the end of 1983.[6]

Low Inflation and Economic Recovery: 1983–1987

In early 1983 a sustained recovery began, and by mid 1987 national income had moved back toward potential. Much of the growth was centered in the export-oriented manufacturing industries in Ontario and Quebec. Although painfully slow for those who remained unemployed, the first four years of the recovery saw a record 990,000 jobs created and cumulative output growth of 15.7 percent.

The main challenge for monetary policy in this period was to create a sufficient increase in the money supply to accommodate the recovery without triggering a return to the high inflation rates that prevailed at the start of the decade.

This task was not as simple as it may appear. The transition from high inflation to low inflation led to what has become known as the *re-entry problem* for monetary policy. The combination of falling nominal interest rates and rising national income led to a sharp increase in the demand for real money balances. Since an increase in real balances can be achieved by either relatively slow growth in the price level or a rapid increase in the nominal money supply, the Bank of Canada basically had two alternatives.

It could continue its policy of maintaining a low growth rate of the nominal money supply. This

[6] Real interest rates did not fall as much, if indeed they fell at all, as inflation fell to an equal or greater extent than nominal interest rates.

would restrain aggregate demand and thus guard against the risk of a resurgence of inflation, but at the cost of slowing the pace of the recovery. With this policy real balances would begin to increase only when the rate of price increase fell below the rate of monetary growth. For that to occur, national income would have to be kept below potential for a prolonged period.

Alternatively, the Bank could allow a short but rapid burst of growth in the nominal money supply, thus generating the desired increase in real money balances. Once the new level of real balances was achieved, money growth could again be cut back to a rate consistent with low inflation, allowing for the underlying rate of growth in real income. But the trick with this policy was to avoid triggering expectations of renewed inflation—essentially the Bank had to generate a one-shot increase in the level of the money supply without creating the impression that it was raising the rate of growth of the money supply.

Most economists agreed that the second policy was preferable *in principle*. But there was wide disagreement over the size and duration of the required monetary expansion and hence whether the Bank's actual policy was appropriate. In late 1983 and early 1984, when growth in monetary aggregates first started to surge, many voiced the fear that the Bank was being overly expansionary and was risking a return to higher inflation. As the re-entry problem came to be more widely understood and as inflation pressures failed to re-emerge, these criticisms subsided and the consensus appeared to be that the Bank had done a commendable job of handling the re-entry problem.

Recently some critics have suggested that perhaps the Bank was too cautious in expanding liquidity during the re-entry problem. Professor Peter Howitt of the University of Western Ontario has argued that excessive caution by the Bank caused the recovery to be slower than necessary.[7] Howitt argues that the Bank erred in focusing almost exclusively on the narrowly defined money supply. The declines in interest rates that occurred as inflation fell caused a substitution out of interest-bearing deposits into demand deposits. Hence the demand for M1 grew rapidly. The demand for broader money aggregates did not grow nearly as fast since the broader aggregates include both demand deposits (which were growing) and interest-bearing deposits (which were falling). If the Bank had focused more on a broader aggregate, the argument goes, it would have seen that the relevant rate of monetary expansion was not excessive.

It is true that Canadian monetary expansion was slower during this period than American monetary expansion. But it is also true that inflation fell more slowly in Canada than in the United States. If the Bank did err in following a monetary policy that was too tight, it was probably because of a commitment not to relax monetary restraint before inflation had unquestionably fallen to the lower, more acceptable range that the Bank was striving for.

Whatever the judgment of monetary policy in that period, many observers now worry that Canadian policymakers have been too complacent in accepting the current 4 percent range Canadian inflation seems to have settled into.[8] In 1987 the question of whether monetary policy should be tightened in an attempt to lower inflation even further was widely debated. Some economists argued that if that were not done, Canada would experience gradually increasing inflation until once again a severe monetary restriction would be necessary. We return to this debate in Chapter 36.

Some Tentative Conclusions

The search for a single monetary aggregate to be *the* correct intermediate target was slowly abandoned. Gradually, it became accepted that the economy was too complicated for a single magnitude to provide all the information that the Bank needed in developing an effective monetary policy. The high degree of substitutability among M1, M2, and M3 meant that all three magnitudes needed to be surveyed for the information that they could provide. Furthermore, institutional developments meant that the de-

[7] *Monetary Policy in Transition* (Toronto: C. D. Howe Institute, 1986).

[8] In 1974, when inflation rose to the "unprecedented peak" of 4 percent, it was considered a national emergency that led to the introduction of wage and price controls in the United States and their serious consideration in Canada!

gree of substitutability was subject to continual change so that no one magnitude could be taken as an appropriate intermediate target in all circumstances.

The behavior of interest rates conveyed information that might not be available from monetary aggregates alone. For example, in the mid 1980s real interest rates were high by historical standards. A goal of monetary policy, therefore, became to create the stable conditions that would allow interest rates to return to more normal levels, but to do this without rekindling inflationary expectations. The important lesson was also drawn from the earlier period of the 1970s that even if all the monetary aggregates are only increasing slowly, real interest rates that are low or negative, as they often were, cannot be the symptom of a tight monetary policy. Thus the combination of low rates of growth of monetary aggregates and unusually low interest rates probably indicates major reductions in the demand for money and, hence, that monetary policy is more expansionary than the behavior of any monetary aggregate would reveal.

New goals of monetary policy in addition to the traditional ones of income and price level have emerged. The two new goals of greatest importance are the health of the financial system and the behavior of exchange rates.

1. The enormous debt that third world countries, particularly oil exporters, piled up in the 1970s became unsustainable in the 1980s. Much of this debt was owed to banks in the developed countries, the United States and Canada being important creditors. As oil revenues fell, the oil-exporting countries found it impossible to pay the interest on their debt without further loans, let alone trying to repay any of the principal. Central banks became acutely aware that a sudden default of these debtor countries could cause a financial crisis in the banking system. It also became aware that every time the interest rate rose 1 percent, the burden on these debtor countries was measured in billions of dollars of extra payments. There is little hope that these countries can ever generate the revenues necessary to repay the principal of these loans. What the banking community of the developed world could at most try to do was to delay the final day of reckoning by rescheduling some of the loans and lending some of the money needed to repay the remaining interest until the major banks could adjust their portfolios sufficiently to write off enormous amounts of loans without going into insolvency.
2. The exchange rate has always been important in Canada, and it became an important variable for the United States in the mid 1980s. Central banks in the developed countries can no longer worry only about domestic variables. The behavior of the exchange rate influences the health of domestic industries that either export or compete with imports and therefore has an important influence on domestic economic performance.

The Bank of Canada seems to have come more and more to take nominal national income as its target variable. In the past the Bank has often concentrated on real national income as its goal of stabilization policy (remove recessionary or inflationary gaps) and the price level as its traditional goal of preserving the purchasing power of the nation's currency. Recently, however, the understanding has spread that the Bank can, at best, influence the *AD* curve, and how this influence divides itself between income and the price level depends on the shape of the *SRAS* curve, which is beyond the Bank's control. The Bank is still concerned with the long-term trend in the price level as its most important goal, but in the shorter term it seems to accept that it can influence nominal national income and adjust its policies to the behavior of that variable, which is a composite of changes in real income and the price level.

As the enormous federal budget deficit is reduced, there may be a need for the Bank to adopt a compensating monetary policy. The reduction in the deficit means some combination of tax increases and expenditure decreases on the part of the government. As we saw in Chapter 32, both of these changes reduce aggregate demand and tend to contract economic activity. To offset these forces, the Bank could engage in a once-and-for-all monetary expansion. As we saw in Chapter 34, this increases aggregate demand. There is no reason in theory why a change in the *mix* of macroeconomic policy to a more restrictive fiscal policy and a more expansionary monetary policy cannot leave the level of aggregate demand unchanged. This would mean that the policy changes did not significantly affect either national income or the price level. This shift in policy mix requires that the Bank be willing to play a more sophisticated role than merely following blind rules for the growth of monetary aggregates. This is a role that some would say is fraught with dangers of trying to do things that are beneficial in theory but that, given the imperfections of practical policy, may turn out to be harmful in practice—harmful in the specific way of increasing inflationary pressures. Whether or not this is a serious worry should become apparent by the end of the decade.

Summary

1. The major tool the Bank of Canada uses to control the supply of money is open-market operations. Purchases of bonds on the open market expand the money supply because they create new deposits that permit (but do not force) a multiple expansion of bank credit. Sales on the open market reduce bank reserves and force a multiple contraction of bank credit on the part of all banks that do not have excess reserves.
2. Other policies at the Bank of Canada's disposal include changing the reserve requirements of the chartered banks, changing the bank rate, and using moral suasion.
3. The ultimate objectives of monetary policy are called policy variables. In principle these include real national income and the rate of change of the price level. However, in practice nominal income is often taken to be the policy variable in the short term since the Bank of Canada cannot expect to be able to influence the composition of changes in nominal income between real growth and inflation.
4. Where the Bank of Canada cannot influence its policy variables directly, it must work through policy instruments that it can control and that will in turn influence its policy variables. Intermediate targets are used to guide decisions about policy instruments. The money supply and the interest rate may both be either intermediate targets or policy instruments.
5. National income can be influenced by open-market operations. Since it cannot control both independently, the Bank must choose between the interest rate and the money supply as the intermediate target of such operations. To reduce national income the Bank sells bonds on the open market, thereby reducing bank reserves, driving up the rate of interest, and shifting the *AD* curve to the left. To increase national income the Bank buys bonds on the open market, thereby increasing reserves, driving down the rate of interest, and shifting the *AD* curve to the right.
6. In the period up to 1975, the Bank of Canada used interest rates as its main intermediate target. In 1975 the Bank converted to monetarism and based its monetary policy on targets for the rate of increase of the money supply (defined as M1).
7. In the period of monetary gradualism from 1975 to 1980, the stance

of monetary policy was meant to be restrictive by gradually reducing the rate of increase of the money supply. However, due to innovations in banking practices, the demand for M1 often fell faster than the supply, making monetary policy expansive rather than restrictive.

8. In the period of stringency (1981–1983) the Fed, followed by the Bank of Canada, adopted a policy of severe monetary restraint. Interest rates soared to unprecedented heights, and the aggregate demand curves of both countries were driven sharply to the left. This led to a severe recession and a sharp fall in inflation.
9. During the long recovery from the recession that broke the inflation, the Bank largely accommodated the increase in the demand for real balances that resulted from the fall in the inflation rate and the rise in national income.
10. It is generally agreed that rapid changes in the money supply and interest rates can have large effects on the economy. There is disagreement, however, on how much monetary policy can and should be used as a device for stabilizing national income at its potential level or coping with temporary bouts of rising prices.

Topics for Review

Open-market operations
The Bank rate
Policy variables, policy instruments, and intermediate targets
Variability of monetary policy and monetary rules
Appropriateness of monetary targets when money demand is shifting

Discussion Questions

1. Professor Peter Howitt has recently argued that the Bank of Canada pursued an overly restrictive monetary policy during the recovery of 1983–1985. Describe the basic policy problem facing the Bank in this period and evaluate the basis for Howitt's view. On the basis of evidence available to it at the time, was it unreasonable for the Bank to be concerned about a resurgence of inflation? What has been the experience of inflation since that time?
2. During the recovery of the Canadian economy from 1983 to 1985, two different views were often expressed. Some analysts said that adherence to a long-run constant growth rate was particularly important for monetary growth lest inflationary expectations be rekindled by an overly fast rate of monetary expansion. Others said that encouraging the recovery required a temporary burst of monetary expansion. Discuss these two views.
3. The Federal Reserve Board runs a facility in Culpeper, Virginia, that costs \$1.8 million per year to maintain and to guard against robbery, according to Senator William Proxmire of Wisconsin. Inside this "Culpeper switch," a dugout in the side of a mountain, the government has hidden \$4 billion in new currency for the purpose, it says,

of "providing a hedge against any nuclear attack that would wipe out the nation's money supply." Comment on the sense of this policy.

4. Describe the chief instruments of monetary policy available to the Bank of Canada, and indicate whether they might be used for each of the following purposes and, if so, how.
   a. To create a mild tightening of bank credit
   b. To signal that the Bank favors a sharp curtailment of bank lending
   c. To permit an expansion of bank credit with existing reserves
   d. To supply banks and the public with a temporary increase of currency for Christmas shopping
5. It is often said that an expansionary monetary policy is like "pushing on a string." What is meant by such a statement? How does this contrast with a contractionary monetary policy?
6. In what situations might the following pairs of objectives come into conflict?
   a. Lowering the cost of government finance and using monetary policy to change aggregate demand
   b. Ending a deep recession and maintaining a currently achieved target for monetary growth
   c. Maintaining stable interest rates and controlling inflation
7. Writing in 1979, Nobel Laureate Milton Friedman accused the Fed of following "an unstable monetary policy," arguing that while the Fed "has given lip service to controlling the quantity of money . . . it has given its heart to controlling interest rates." Why might the desire to stabilize interest rates create an "unstable" monetary policy?
8. In 1982 the Bank of Canada stopped formally announcing and trying to attain precise target rates of growth for some monetary aggregate. Discuss the reasons behind this, and indicate whether you agree with the Bank's decision.

PART TEN

Issues and Controversies in Macroeconomics

36

Inflation

If you look again at Figure 26-1 on page 553 you will see that for 20 years following World War II inflation remained low. The only exceptions were the "bubbles" immediately following World War II and the Korean War. During the second half of the 1960s, the inflation rate slowly inched upward. It reached the double-digit range in the mid 1970s. By then inflation had been declared public enemy number one. Even more worrisome, it fell only slightly in the face of a concerted anti-inflationary attack during the late 1970s, rose again to the double-digit level in 1980, then remained quite stubborn during the recession of 1981–1982. At last, in 1983 inflation fell dramatically, then drifted down slowly to around 4 percent, where it remained through 1987. Although this was an improvement over the double-digit inflation rates experienced earlier, 4 percent is historically a very high inflation rate with which to emerge from a serious recession.

What are the causes of inflation? How was the great anti-inflationary battle of the early 1980s fought? Can inflation be prevented from skyrocketing into the double-digit range again? Can inflation ever be eliminated altogether?

Inflationary Shocks

We start by noting a key distinction.

It is important to distinguish between the forces that cause a once-and-for-all increase in the price level and the forces that can cause a continuing (or sustained) increase.

Some terms that are sometimes used to stress this distinction are further discussed in Box 36-1.

Any event that tends to drive the price level upward is called an *inflationary shock.* To examine the causes and consequences of such shocks, we begin with an economy in long-run equilibrium: The price level is stable, and national income is at its potential level. We then study the economy as it is buffeted by different types of inflationary shocks.

Supply Shocks

Suppose there is a decrease in short-run aggregate supply, that is, that the *SRAS* curve shifts up and to the left. This might be caused, for example, by a rise in the costs of imported raw materials or a rise in domestic wage costs per unit of output. The price level rises and output

BOX 36-1

Inflation Semantics

The distinction between *once-and-for-all* and *continuing* rises in the price level is important. Some economists have sought to emphasize it by reserving the term *inflation* for a continuing or sustained rise in the price level and using other expressions such as *a rise in the price level* for a once-and-for-all increase.

One difficulty with this is that it is counter to ordinary usage, where inflation refers to any rise in the price level. Indeed, using the restricted definition causes difficulty when communicating with the public. If we were to use it, we would have to keep saying such things as "only some of the current rise in prices is an inflation, while the rest is merely a rise in the price level" and "we won't know whether or not the current rise in the price level is an inflation or not until we see if it is sustained."

In this book we use the term *inflation* as it is commonly used to mean any rise in the price level. We then make the distinction by referring to *temporary* or *once-and-for-all* inflations on the one hand and to *continuing* or *sustained* inflations on the other.

No matter of substance turns on the terms that we use to refer to clearly defined concepts. We use the expressions *temporary inflation* and *once-and-for-all rise in the price level* interchangeably. We use *sustained inflation* where some other economists, using the more restricted meaning, might merely talk of an inflation.

This discussion is important because students need to guard against being confused by different usages. Our selection of terms reflects only a desire to keep our language as close as possible to everyday usage.

---

falls. The rise in the price level shows up as a temporary burst of inflation.

What happens next depends on whether the shock to the *SRAS* curve is an isolated event or one of a series of recurring shocks. We choose import price increases as an example of an isolated supply shock because such shocks have occurred during the past two decades. We choose continued wage-cost push as an example of a repeated supply shock because, as we shall see later in this chapter and again in Chapter 39, this possibility has worried many economists ever since governments accepted responsibility for maintaining full employment.

What happens also depends on how the Bank of Canada reacts. If the Bank responds by increasing the money supply, we say that the supply shock has been *accommodated*. If the Bank holds the money supply constant, the shock is not accommodated. (Notice that our terminology distinguishes between the Bank's response to a supply shock, which we describe as accommodating the shock, and its response to a demand shock, which we describe in Chapter 34 and again later in this chapter, as validating the shock.)

Isolated Supply Shocks

Suppose that the leftward shift in the *SRAS* curve is an isolated event; say it is caused by a once-and-for-all increase in the cost of imported raw materials. How does monetary policy affect the economy's response to such an isolated supply shock?

No monetary accommodation. The leftward shift in the *SRAS* curve causes the price level to rise and pushes income below its full-employment level, opening up a recessionary gap. Pressure now mounts for wages and other factor costs to fall. When they do, the *SRAS* curve shifts downward, causing a return of income to full employment and a fall in the price level. In this case the period of inflation accompanying the original supply shock is eventually followed by a period of deflation, that is, a fall in the average level of all prices. The deflation continues until the original long-run equilibrium is re-established. This is discussed in the second paragraph of the caption to Figure 30-3. Given that wages and prices fall slowly, the recovery to full employment takes a long time.

Monetary accommodation. Now let us see what happens if the money supply is changed in response to the isolated supply shock. Suppose the Bank reacts to the fall in national income by increasing the money supply. This shifts the *AD* curve to the right and causes both the price level and output to *rise*. When the recessionary gap is eliminated, the price level, rather than falling back to its original value, has risen further. The effects are illustrated in Figure 36-1.

Monetary accommodation of a supply shock causes the initial rise in the price level to be followed by a further rise, resulting in a higher price level than if the recessionary gap were relied on to reduce costs and prices.

FIGURE 36-1 Monetary Accommodation of a Single Supply Shock

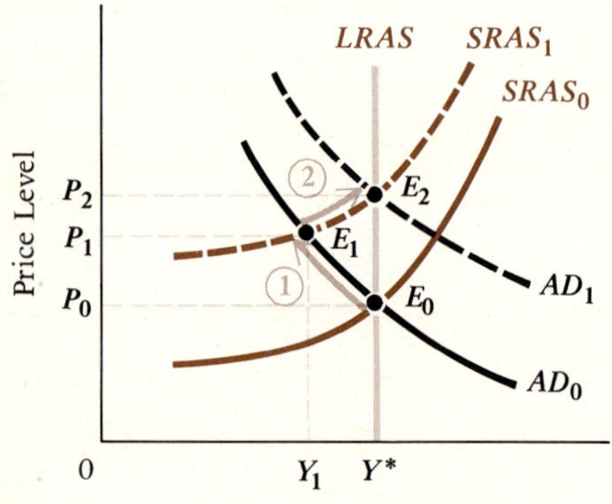

Monetary accommodation of a single supply shock causes costs, the price level, and money supply all to move in the same direction. A supply shock causes the *SRAS* curve to shift leftward from $SRAS_0$ to $SRAS_1$, as shown by arrow 1. Equilibrium is established at E_1.

If there is no monetary accommodation, the unemployment would put downward pressure on wages and other costs, causing the *SRAS* curve to shift slowly back to the right to $SRAS_0$. Prices would fall and output would rise until the original equilibrium was restored.

If there is monetary accommodation, the *AD* curve shifts from AD_0 to AD_1, as shown by arrow 2. This reestablishes full employment equilibrium at E_2 but with a higher price level, P_2.

The monetary authorities might decide to accommodate the supply shock because relying on cost deflation to restore full employment forces the economy to suffer through an extended slump. Monetary accommodation can return the economy to full employment quickly, but at the cost of a once-and-for-all increase in the price level.

Repeated Supply Shocks

We have been assuming that a recessionary gap would be associated with downward pressure on wages. This implies that labor markets behave much like commodity markets, so that wages fall when there is excess supply and rise only when there is excess demand.

As an example of a repeated supply shock, assume that powerful unions are able to raise wages in the absence of excess demand for labor and even in the face of significant excess supply. Large manufacturing firms pass these higher wages on in the form of higher prices. This type of supply shock causes what is called **wage-cost push inflation:** an increase in the price level due to increases in money wages that are not associated with excess demand for labor.

No monetary accommodation. Suppose the Bank does not accommodate these supply shocks. The initial effect of the leftward shift in the *SRAS* curve is to open up a recessionary gap, as shown in Figure 36-1. If unions continue to negotiate increases in wages, subjecting the economy to further supply shocks, prices continue to rise and output continues to fall. Eventually the trade-off between higher wages and unemployment will become obvious to everyone.

Might not really powerful unions continue to force wages up despite this realization? As long as they did so, the recessionary gap would go on growing until, finally, unemployment reached 100 percent. Of course, this would not happen because long before everyone is unemployed, unions would cease forcing up wages in order to maintain jobs for those who are still employed.

Once the wage-cost push ceases, there are two possible scenarios. First, the unions may succeed in holding on to their high wages but not push for further increases. The economy then comes to rest with a stable price level and a large recessionary gap. Second, the persistent unemployment may eventually erode the power of the unions so that wages begin to fall. In this case the supply shock is reversed, and the *SRAS* curve shifts downward until full employment is eventually restored.

Non-accommodated wage-cost push tends to be self-limiting because the rising unemployment that it causes tends to restrain further wage increases.

Monetary accommodation. Now suppose that the Bank accommodates the shock with an increase in the money supply, thus shifting the *AD* curve to the right, as shown in Figure 36-1. In the new full-employment equilibrium both money wages and prices have risen. The rise in wages has been offset by a rise in prices. Workers are no better off than they were originally, although those who remained in jobs were temporarily better off in the transition after wages had risen (taking equilibrium to E_1 in Figure 36-1) but before the price level had risen (taking equilibrium to E_2).

The stage is now set for the unions to try again. If they succeed in negotiating further increases in money wages, they hit the economy with another supply shock. If the Bank again accommodates the shock, full employment is maintained, but at the cost of a further round of inflation. If this process goes on repeatedly, it can give rise to a continual wage-cost push inflation. The wage-cost push tends to cause a stagflation, with rising prices and falling output. Monetary accommodation tends to reinforce the rise in prices but to offset the fall in output. This case is illustrated in Figure 36-2.

Two things are required for wage-cost push inflation to continue. First, powerful groups, such as industrial unions or government employees, must press for and employers must grant increases in money wages, even in the absence of excess demand for labor and goods. Second, governments must accommodate the resulting inflation by increasing the money supply and so prevent the unemployment that would otherwise occur. The process set up by this sequence of wage-cost push and monetary accommodation is often called a *wage-price spiral*.

FIGURE 36-2 Monetary Accommodation of a Repeated Supply Shock

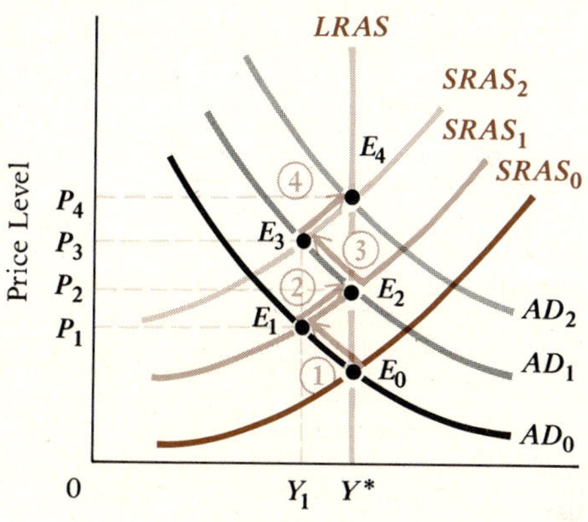

Monetary accommodation of a repeated supply shock causes a continuous inflation in the absence of excess demand. The initial equilibrium is at E_0. A supply shock then takes equilibrium to E_1, just as in Figure 36-1. This is the stagflation phase of rising prices and falling output; it is indicated by arrow 1.

The Bank of Canada then accommodates the supply shock by increasing the money supply, taking the *AD* curve to AD_1 and equilibrium to E_2. This is the expansionary phase of rising prices and output (arrow 2).

A second supply shock followed by monetary accommodation takes equilibrium to E_3 (arrow 3) and then to E_4 (arrow 4). As long as the supply shocks and the monetary accommodation continue, the inflation continues.

Is monetary accommodation desirable? Once started, a wage-price spiral can be halted only if the Bank stops accommodating the supply shocks that are causing the inflation. The longer the Bank waits to do so, the more entrenched will be the expectations that it will continue its policy of accommodating the shocks. These entrenched expectations may cause wages to continue to rise after accommodation has ceased. Because employers expect prices to rise, they go on granting wage increases. If expectations are firmly enough entrenched, the wage push can continue for quite some time in spite of the downward pressure caused by the rising unemployment associated with the growing recessionary gap.

Because of this possibility, some economists argue that the process should not be allowed to begin. One way to ensure this is to refuse to accommodate any supply shock whatsoever.

To some people, caution dictates that no supply shocks be accommodated lest a wage-price spiral be set up. Others are willing to risk accommodating isolated shocks in order to avoid the severe, though transitory, recessions that otherwise accompany them.

This key issue is discussed further in Chapter 39.

Demand Shocks

Now suppose that an initial equilibrium is disturbed by a rightward shift in the aggregate demand curve. This causes the price level and output to rise, as shown in Figures 36-3 and 36-4. The shift in the *AD* curve could have been caused by either an increase in autonomous expenditure or an increase in the money supply.[1] As with a supply shock, it is important to distinguish between the case in which the Bank reacts and that in which it does not. As we have seen, when the Bank reacts to the demand shock by increasing the money supply, it is said to be validating the shock.

No monetary validation. This case is shown in Figure 36-3. Because the initial *AD* shock takes output above the full-employment level, an inflationary gap opens up. The pressure of excess demand soon causes wages and other costs to rise, shifting the *SRAS* curve up and to the left. As long as the Bank holds the money supply constant, the rise in the price level brings into play the monetary adjustment mechanism (discussed in detail in Chapter 34): The economy moves up and to the left along the fixed *AD* curve, and the rise in the price level acts to reduce the inflationary gap. Eventually the gap is eliminated as equilibrium is established at a higher but stable price level and with income at its potential level. In this case the initial period of inflation is followed by further inflation that lasts only until the new equilibrium is reached.

FIGURE 36-3 An Unvalidated Demand-Shock Inflation

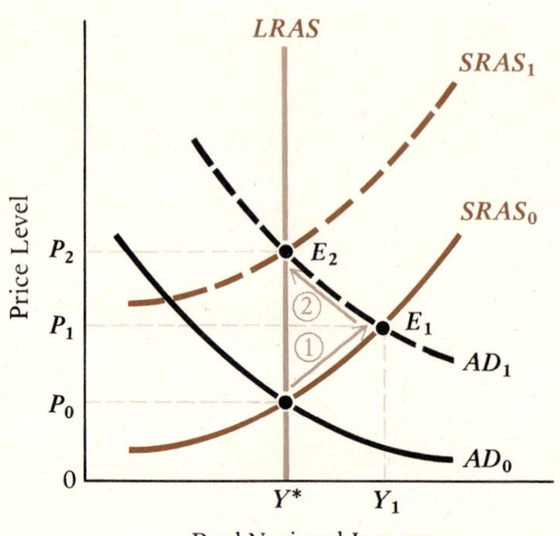

An unvalidated demand shock raises the equilibrium price level but leaves equilibrium income unchanged. The initial equilibrium is at E_0, with full-employment income Y^* and the price level P_0. A demand shock shifts the *AD* curve from AD_0 to AD_1, shifting equilibrium from E_0 to E_1, as shown by arrow 1. At E_1 income is Y_1 and the price level is P_1. The inflationary gap of Y^*Y_1 causes wages to rise, shifting the *SRAS* curve to the left. Equilibrium moves along AD_1 to E_2, as shown by arrow 2. At E_2, income has returned to Y^*, removing the inflationary gap, while the price level has risen to P_2.

Monetary validation. Next, suppose that after the demand shock has created an inflationary gap, the Bank frustrates the monetary adjustment mechanism by increasing the money supply when output starts to fall. This is the case illustrated in Figure 36-4.[2] Two forces are now brought into play. Spurred by

[1] As we saw in Chapter 34, an increase in the money supply works through the transmission mechanism—excess supply of money, higher price of bonds, lower interest rates, increased investment expenditure—to shift the *AD* curve to the right.

[2] Although we distinguish between a single supply shock and a continuing one, we do not make a similar distinction with a demand shock. This is because the accommodation of a single supply shock restores full-employment equilibrium, whereas the validation of a demand shock perpetuates the disequilibrium.

FIGURE 36-4 A Validated Demand-Shock Inflation

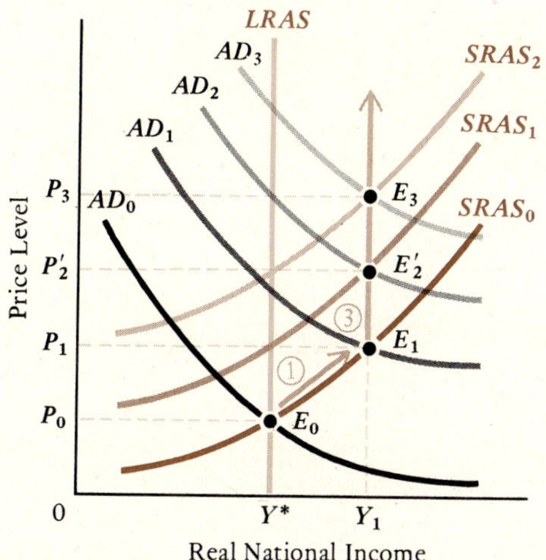

Monetary validation will cause the *AD* curve to shift rightward, offsetting the leftward shift in the *SRAS* curve and so leaving an inflationary gap in spite of the ever-rising price level. As in Figure 36-3, an initial demand shock shifts equilibrium from E_0 to E_1, taking income to Y_1 and the price level to P_1. The resulting inflationary gap then causes the *SRAS* curve to shift to the left. This time, however, the money supply is increased, shifting the *AD* curve to the right. By the time the aggregate supply curve has reached $SRAS_1$, the aggregate demand curve has reached AD_2. Now instead of being at E_2 in Figure 36-3, equilibrium is at E_2'. Income remains constant at Y_1, leaving the inflationary gap constant at Y^*Y_1, while the price level rises to P_2'.

The persistent inflationary gap continues to push the *SRAS* curve to the left, while the continued monetary validation continues to push the *AD* curve to the right. By the time the aggregate supply reaches $SRAS_2$, the aggregate demand has reached AD_3. The price level has risen still further to P_3, but because of the frustration of the monetary adjustment mechanism, the inflationary gap remains unchanged at Y_1Y^*. As long as this monetary validation continues, the economy moves along the vertical path of arrow 3.

the inflationary gap, the wage increases cause the *SRAS* curve to shift to the left. Fueled by the expansionary monetary policy, the *AD* curve shifts to the right. As a result of both of these shifts, the price level rises, but output need not fall. Indeed, if the shift in the *AD* curve exactly offsets the shift in the *SRAS* curve, the inflationary gap will remain constant.

Validation of a demand shock turns what would have been a transitory inflation into a sustained inflation fueled by monetary expansion.

Because of the validation process, all subsequent shifts in the *AD* curve that perpetuate the inflation are caused by monetary forces.

Inflation As a Monetary Phenomenon

There has been heated debate among economists about the extent to which inflation is a monetary phenomenon. Does it have purely monetary causes—changes in the demand for or the supply of money? Does it have purely monetary consequences—only the price level is affected? One slogan stating an extreme position on this issue was made popular by Milton Friedman: "Inflation is *everywhere* and *always* a monetary phenomenon."

To consider these issues, let us summarize what we have already learned. First, look at causes.

1. Many forces can cause the price level to rise. On the demand side, anything that shifts the *AD* curve to the right will cause the price level to rise. This includes such expenditure changes as an autonomous increase in investment or government expenditure and such monetary changes as an increase in the money supply or a decrease in money demand. On the supply side, anything that increases costs of production will shift the *SRAS* curve to the left and cause the price level to rise.
2. Such inflations can continue for some time without any increases in the money supply.
3. The rise in prices must eventually come to a halt, unless monetary expansion occurs.

Points 1 and 2 provide the sense in which, looking at causes, a temporary burst of inflation need not be a monetary phenomenon. It need not have monetary causes, and it need not be accompanied by monetary expansion. Point 3 is the sense in which, looking at causes, a sustained inflation must be a monetary phenomenon. If a rise in prices is to continue, it must be accompanied by continuing increases in the money supply (or decreases in money demand). This is true regardless of the cause that set the rise in motion.[3]

Second, let us summarize the consequences of an inflation on the assumption that we begin from a situation where actual national income is at its potential level ($Y = Y^*$).

1. In the short run a demand-shock inflation tends to be accompanied by an increase in national income.
2. In the short run a supply-shock inflation tends to be accompanied by a decrease in national income.
3. When all adjustments have been fully made (so that the relevant supply-side curve is the *LRAS* curve), shifts in either the *AD* or *SRAS* curve leave national income unchanged and affect only the price level.

Points 1 and 2 provide the sense in which, looking at consequences, inflation is not, in the short run, a purely monetary phenomenon. Point 3 provides the sense in which, looking at consequences, inflation is a purely monetary phenomenon from the point of view of long-run equilibrium.

We have now established three important conclusions.

1. Without monetary accommodation, supply shocks cause temporary bursts of inflation accompanied by recessionary gaps. The gaps are removed if and when wages fall, restoring equilibrium at potential income and at the initial price level.
2. Without monetary validation, demand shocks cause temporary bursts of inflation accompanied by inflationary gaps. The gaps are removed as wages rise, returning income to its potential level, but at a higher price level.
3. With an appropriate response from the Bank, an inflation, initiated by either supply or demand shocks, can continue indefinitely; an ever-increasing money supply is necessary for an ever-continuing inflation.

[3] The statement that inflation is everywhere and always a monetary phenomenon depends on a restricted and specific definition of the term *inflation*. To justify the statement, a temporary burst of inflation with nonmonetary causes must be called a rise in the price level, and the term *inflation* must be reserved for increases in the price level that are sustained for long enough that they must be accompanied by monetary expansion. Variations in the use of these terms are discussed in Box 36-1.

Sustained Inflation

The price level has risen in almost all years since the end of the Second World War. The decade from 1972 to 1982 was one of sustained inflation, often at rates of over 10 percent per year. In the mid 1980s the inflation rate was around 4 percent. Although this was lower than had been achieved in the previous 20 years, the rate would have been judged unsatisfactory at any time in the twentieth century before 1975. Four percent is a rate of inflation that will halve the purchasing power of money in about 18 years, less than the life expectancy of most people who retire in their sixties.

Why do we have sustained inflations of either the rapid sort, as in the 1970s, or the more gradual sort, as in the 1980s? What are the costs and benefits of reducing or eliminating such inflations?

Before we can deal with these questions, we must look in greater detail at what is involved in a sustained inflation. We have already stressed the role of monetary validation in allowing the *AD* curve to shift up continually. We now focus on the forces that cause the *SRAS* curve to shift upward.

Upward Shifts in the *SRAS* Curve

A rise in the cost of producing each unit of output, which is called unit cost, will cause the *SRAS* curve to shift upward. What is it then that causes unit costs to rise?

Influence of wage rates and productivity. Does every rise in wage rates force up unit costs? The answer is no, because what happens to unit costs depends on what happens to the cost of labor in relation to what happens to the productivity of labor (output per unit of labor input).

Although wages are usually the largest single element of production costs, a rise in wages is not by itself enough to raise unit costs. This is because productivity—output per unit of labor input—is usually rising as well. For example, if wages and productivity both rise by 3 percent, each unit of labor earns 3 percent more, but it also produces 3 percent more. Thus costs per unit of output remain unchanged.

If wage increases are to cause a rise in unit costs, money wage rates must rise by more than productivity has risen.

In what follows, it is simplest to assume that productivity does not change so that a rise in money wages causes a rise in unit costs. To apply the analysis to cases where productivity is changing, the statement "wages rise" needs only to be replaced by the statement "wages rise by more than productivity rises."

Why Wages Change

Let us now ask what we know about the behavior of money wages and hence of the *SRAS* curve. Up to now it has been enough to say that an inflationary gap implies excess demand for labor, low unemployment, upward pressure on wages, and, hence, an upward-shifting *SRAS* curve.

But now we need to look in more detail at three forces that can cause wage costs to change and thus shift the *SRAS* curve upward. These are demand for labor, expectations, and random forces. Much of what we say in the case of demand forces is a recapitulation, but the points are important enough to bear repeating.

Demand Forces

The excess demand for labor associated with an inflationary gap puts upward pressure on wages. Wages rise more rapidly than they otherwise would.

The excess supply of labor associated with a recessionary gap puts downward pressure on wages. Wages rise less rapidly (or fall more rapidly) than they otherwise would.

The absence of either an inflationary or a recessionary gap means that there is no demand pressure on wages. Demand forces do not exert any pressure on wages either to rise or to fall.

Natural rate of unemployment. We saw in Chapter 26 that when current national income is at its potential level ($Y = Y^*$), unemployment is not zero. Instead there may be a substantial amount of frictional unemployment caused by the movement of people between jobs. The amount of unemployment (all of it frictional) that exists when national income is at its potential level is called the **natural rate of unemployment (U_N)**. It follows from this definition that when current national income exceeds full-employment income ($Y > Y^*$), current unemployment will be less than the natural rate ($U < U_N$). When current national income is less than full-employment income ($Y < Y^*$), current unemployment will exceed the natural rate ($U > U_N$).

We can now use the natural rate terminology to restate the three results about the pressure that is put on wage rates, and through them on the *SRAS* curve, by inflationary and recessionary gaps.

When the unemployment rate is below the natural rate, demand forces put upward pressure on wages.

When the unemployment rate is above the natural rate, demand forces put downward pressure on wages.

When unemployment is at its natural rate, demand forces exert neither upward nor downward pressure on wages.

The influence of demand forces on wages is shown by the *Phillips curve,* discussed in Box 30-1 on pages 634–635.

Expectational Forces

A second force that can influence wages is *expectations.* Suppose, for example, that both employers and employees expect a 4 percent inflation next year. Unions will start negotiations from a base of a 4 percent increase in money wages, which would hold their real wages constant. Firms may also be inclined to begin bargaining by conceding at least a 4 percent increase in money wages, since they expect that the prices at which they sell their products will rise by 4 percent. *Starting from that base,* unions will attempt to obtain some desired increase in their real wages.

At this point such factors as profits, productivity, and bargaining power become important.

The general expectation of an *x* percent inflation creates pressures for wages to rise by *x* percent and hence for the *SRAS* curve to shift by *x* percent.

Other Random Forces

Wage changes are also affected by forces that are associated with neither excess demand nor expected inflation. These forces can be positive, pushing wages higher than they otherwise would go, or negative, pushing wages lower than they otherwise would go. Furthermore, they are assumed to be many in number and independent of one another, so that they exert an overall random influence on wages—sometimes speeding wage increases up a bit, sometimes slowing them down a bit, but having a net effect that more or less cancels out when taken over several years. Over the long term they may be regarded as random events and are referred to as *random shocks*.

One example of such forces occurs when an exceptionally strong union or an exceptionally weak management comes to the bargaining table and produces a wage increase that is a percentage point or two *above* what would have occurred under more typical bargaining conditions. Another example is when a new government policy that is favorable to management causes this year's negotiated wage rates to be a percentage point or two *below* what they would have been.

Random shocks may be important causes of temporary bursts of inflation, but they are less important for sustained inflations. Although they may have a large positive or negative effect in any one year, over the period of a sustained inflation positive shocks in some years will tend to be offset by negative shocks in other years so that, in total, they contribute little to the long-term trend of the price level.

Overall Effect

The overall change in wage costs is a result of the three basic forces just studied. We express this as:

$$\text{percentage increase in money wages} = \text{demand effect} + \text{expectational effect} + \text{random shock effect}$$

It is important to realize that what happens to wage costs is the net effect of all three of these forces. Consider two examples. Assume that both labor and management expect a 3 percent inflation next year and are willing on this account to allow wages to increase by 3 percent. This would leave the relation between wages and other prices unaltered. Next assume that there is a significant inflationary gap with an associated labor shortage. The demand pressure causes wages to rise by 2 percentage points more than they otherwise would have risen. Finally, assume a shock, in the form of a temporary concern on the part of labor unions with foreign competition, that moderates wage claims by 1 percentage point this year. The final outcome is that wages rise by 4 percent, which is the net effect of +3 from expectations, +2 from demand forces, and −1 from the random shock.

For the second illustration, assume that there is once again a 3 percent expected inflation but that this time there is a recessionary gap. The associated heavy unemployment puts downward pressure on wage bargains, and hence the demand effect now works to moderate wage increases, say, to the extent of 2 percentage points. Finally assume that some unusual cost-plus government contracts reduce employer resistance to wage rises to the extent of contributing an upward pressure on wage bargains of 1 percentage point. The net effect is for wages to rise by 2 percent, which is the net effect of +3 from expectations, −2 from demand forces, and +1 from shock effects.

The overall effect of the three forces acting on wage costs—demand, expectations, and random shocks—determines what happens to the *SRAS* curve.

Inflationary gaps, expectations of inflation, and positive random shocks put pressure on wage rates to rise and hence on the *SRAS* curve to shift upward. Recessionary gaps, expectations of deflation, and negative random shocks put pressure on wage rates to fall and hence on the *SRAS* curve to shift down. What happens to the *SRAS* curve in any one year is the overall effect of all of these forces.

Accelerating Inflation

One of the reasons that policymakers worry so much about inflation is their concern that even a moderate inflation may be hard to keep under control. They worry that inflation often has a tendency to accelerate. They fear that if the Bank of Canada relaxes and is willing to accept, say, 4 percent inflation, 4 percent may soon become 5 percent, and once 5 percent becomes accepted, 5 percent may become 6 percent, and so on.

In this section we first consider the reasons for worrying that the inflation rate will tend to drift upward unless it is held rigidly in check.

Look again at Figure 36-4, which represents a continuing inflation. The *SRAS* curve is shifting up due to the inflationary gap, and the *AD* curve is shifting up because the inflation is being validated by increases in the money supply. What this analysis shows is that if income is held above potential, the price level will be rising. We know that inflation is positive, but we do not know whether the rate of inflation is rising, falling, or constant.

One of the most important results in the theory of inflation concerns what happens to the rate of inflation when a central bank takes steps to perpetuate an inflationary gap. This is the *acceleration hypothesis* to which we now turn. The argument is in several steps.

Initial pure demand inflation. Suppose that initially prices are rising in the presence of neither random shocks nor expectations of inflation. This means that the inflation is due solely to the existence of excess demand. Suppose also that the level of output is held constant. For this to happen, the upward shift in the *SRAS* curve has to be accompanied by an increase in the money supply such that the *AD* curve shifts up by the same amount. When the *SRAS* and the *AD* curves are shifting up at the same speed, the inflationary gap remains unchanged.

Expectational effects. Eventually people will begin to expect that monetary validation, and hence inflation, will continue. As these inflationary expectations emerge, additional upward pressure will be put on wages as the inflationary effect comes into play. Now that the demand effect on wages has been augmented by an expectational effect, the *SRAS* curve will begin to shift upward more rapidly.

More rapid monetary validation required. If the Bank still wishes to hold the level of output constant, it must increase the rate at which the money supply is growing. This is because, to hold *Y* constant, the *AD* curve must be shifted more rapidly to compensate for the more rapid shifts in the *SRAS* curve.

An increasing rate of inflation. As a result of the increasingly rapid upward shifts in both the *AD* and *SRAS* curves, the rate of inflation must now be increasing. The rise in the actual inflation rate will in turn cause an increase in the expected inflation rate. This will then cause the actual inflation rate to increase, which will in turn increase the expected inflation rate, and so on. The net result is a *continually increasing rate of inflation*.

Conclusion. The foregoing analysis of the response of inflationary expectations to a persistent inflationary gap leads to what is called the **acceleration hypothesis.**

According to the acceleration hypothesis, as long as an inflationary gap persists, expectations of inflation will be rising, and this will lead to increases in the actual rate of inflation.

The tendency for inflation to increase is discussed further in Box 36-2.

Constant Inflation

Must a sustained inflation always accelerate? Or is it possible for an inflation to go on at a constant rate indefinitely?

The answer is that not all sustained inflations must accelerate. When the demand effect is absent and all inflation is thus expectational, inflation can persist indefinitely at a constant rate. Let us see why this is so.

BOX 36-2

The Phillips Curve and Accelerating Inflation

Professor Phillips was interested in studying the short-run behavior of an economy subjected to cyclical fluctuations (see Box 30-1 on pages 634–635). Others, however, treated the curve as establishing a long-term trade-off between inflation and unemployment.

Let the government fix income at Y_1 (and thus unemployment at U_1) in the figures and validate the ensuing wage inflation of ΔW_1 per year. By doing this the government is apparently able to choose a particular combination of inflation and unemployment, with lower levels of unemployment being attained at the cost of higher rates of inflation.

In the 1960s Phillips curves were fitted to the data for many countries, and governments made decisions about where they wished to be on the trade-off between inflation and unemployment. Then, in the late 1960s, in country after country, the rate of wage and

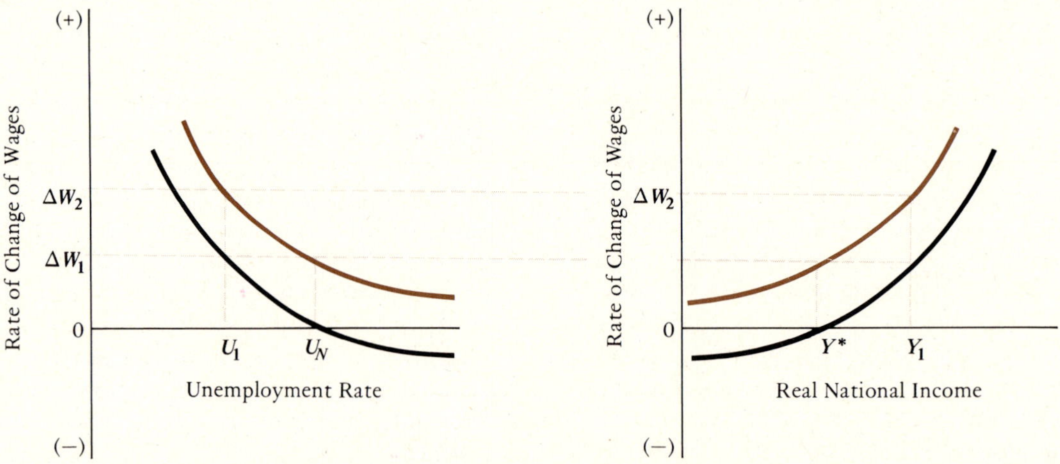

When national income is at its potential level, there is neither an inflationary nor a recessionary gap. In this case there is no demand effect operating on wage bargains. Leaving random shocks aside, the only force operating on wages is expectations. Say, for example, that both workers and employers expect a 4 percent inflation and employers are prepared to raise wages by 4 percent per year to keep wages in line with everything else. Wages will rise by 4 percent per year, and the *SRAS* curve will shift upward by that amount each year. If the Bank accommodates the resulting inflation by increasing the money supply by 4 percent each year, the *AD* curve will also be shifting up by that amount.

This case is illustrated in Figure 36-5 (see page 786). Here wage costs are rising due to expectations of inflation, and these expectations are being fulfilled.

Steady inflation with full employment results when the rate of monetary growth, the rate of wage increase, and the expected rate of inflation are all consistent with the actual inflation rate.

The key point about a pure expectational inflation at a constant rate is that there is no demand effect operating on wage bargains. Wages rise at the expected rate of inflation and that is just enough to preserve the existing relation between wages and all other prices. If there were a labor shortage, there would be pressure for wages to rise relative to other prices, and this would push the rate of wage increase above the expected rate of inflation. If there were more unemployment than the normal frictional amount, there would be a tendency for wages to fall price inflation associated with any given level of unemployment began to rise. Instead of being stable, the Phillips curves were shifting upward. The explanation lay primarily in a shifting relation between the pressure of demand and wage increases due to expectations, as discussed in the text.

In the text we noted that two important influences on wages are demand and expectations. It was gradually understood that the original Phillips curve concerned only the influence of demand and left out inflationary expectations. This proved to be an important and unfortunate omission. An increase in expected inflation shows up as an upward shift in the original Phillips curve drawn in Box 30-1.

The importance of expectations can be shown by drawing what is called an **expectations-augmented Phillips curve,** as in the figures. The heights of the Phillips curves above the axis at Y^* and at U_N show the expected inflation rate. This is the amount that wages will rise when there is neither excess demand nor excess supply pressure in labor markets. The actual wage increase is shown by the augmented curve, with the increase in wages exceeding expected inflation when $Y > Y^*$ ($U < U_N$) and falling short of expected inflation when $Y < Y^*$ ($U > U_N$). *The demand component shown by the simple Phillips curve tells us by how much wage changes will deviate from the expected inflation rate.*

Now we can see what was wrong with the idea of a stable inflation-unemployment trade-off. Targeting on income Y_1 or unemployment U_1 in the figure is fine as long as no inflation is *expected.* But once some particular rate of inflation comes to be expected, people will demand that much just to hold their own. The Phillips curve will shift upward to the position shown in the figure. Now there is inflation ΔW_2 because of the combined effects of expectations and excess demand.

But this higher rate is above the expected rate. Once that higher rate comes to be expected, the Phillips curve will shift upward once again. *The expectations-augmented Phillips curve shows that the actual rate of inflation exceeds the expected rate whenever there is an inflationary gap.* Sooner or later this will cause inflationary expectations to be shifted upward. The inflation rate associated with any given level of Y or U rises over time. This is the theory of accelerating inflation that is further studied in the appendix to this chapter.

relative to other prices, and this would hold wage increases below the expected rate of inflation.

The negative demand effect of a recessionary gap is rather weak. Thus when the recessionary gap is relatively small, the demand effect may be swamped by the expectational and random shock effects so that an approximately stable inflation rate is the net result. This is what seems to have occurred in the mid 1980s, when a fairly stable inflation rate persisted for several years in spite of a modest recessionary gap.

Breaking an Entrenched Inflation

When an inflation has been going on for a long time, can it be reduced without inflicting major hardships in terms of unemployment and lost output?

This question greatly worried policymakers in the early 1980s when they set out to break the existing two-digit inflation. It also worried those who, later in the 1980s, were unsatisfied with the 4 percent inflation rate that had persisted for several years. The issue was then, and still is, how to reduce inflation when people have come to accept the existing rate as normal and have adapted their behavior to the belief that the rate will continue.

Our analysis begins with a situation of a continuing, fully validated inflation, with actual income at its potential level ($Y = Y^*$). The inflation has been going on for some time, and people expect it to continue. Firmly held expectations of a continuation of the current inflation rate are what leads to the concept of an *entrenched inflation.*

Now suppose that the Bank decides to reduce the

FIGURE 36-5 Steady Inflation at the Natural Rate of Unemployment

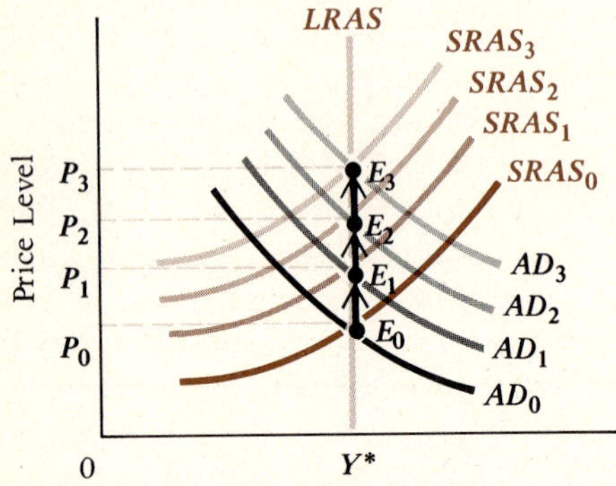

When income equals Y^* (and hence unemployment equals U_N) there is no demand effect on wages, and steady inflation can proceed at a rate consistent with inflationary expectations. With no demand effect the *SRAS* curve shifts upward at the expected rate of inflation. If the Bank raises the money supply at the same rate, the upward shift in the *AD* curve will match that of the *SRAS* curve. Output will stay at Y^*, unemployment will be at the natural rate, and inflation will be steady. The steady inflation is shown by the rising price level as equilibrium moves along the arrows from E_0 to E_1 to E_2 to E_3 in the figure.

inflation rate by reducing its rate of monetary validation. The events that follow generally fall into three phases.

Phase 1: Removing the inflationary gap. The first phase, shown in Figure 36-6(i), consists of slowing the rate of monetary expansion below the current rate of inflation. This slows the rate at which the *AD* curve is shifting upward. To illustrate, we take an extreme case: the "cold turkey approach," where the rate of monetary expansion is cut to zero so that the upward shift in the *AD* curve is halted abruptly.

Under the combined influence of an inflationary gap and expectations of continued inflation, wages continue to rise, and the *SRAS* curve thus continues to shift upward. Eventually the gap is removed. If the only influence on wages were demand, that would be the end of the story. At Y^* there is no upward demand pressure on wages. Wages would stop rising, the *SRAS* curve would be stabilized, and the economy would remain at full employment with a stable price level.

Phase 2: Stagflation. Governments around the world have many times wished that things were really that simple. However, wages depend not only on excess demand but also on inflationary expectations. Once inflationary expectations have been established, it is not always easy to get people to revise them downward, even in the face of changed monetary policies. Thus the *SRAS* curve continues to shift upward, causing the price level to continue to rise and income to fall further.

Expectations may cause inflation to persist after its original causes have been removed. What was initially a demand inflation due to an inflationary gap becomes an expectational inflation.

This is phase 2, shown in Figure 36-6(ii).

The emerging recessionary gap has two effects. First, there is rising unemployment. Thus the demand influence on wages becomes negative. Second, as the recession deepens and monetary restraint continues, people revise their expectations of inflation downward. When they have no further expectations of inflation, there are no further increases in wage costs, and the *SRAS* curve stops shifting. The stagflationary phase is over. The inflation has come to a halt, but a large recessionary gap now exists.

Keynesians tend to be pessimistic and to expect a severe and long lasting slump in phase 2. Monetarists tend to be optimistic and to expect a relatively mild and short-lived recession in phase 2. These opposing views are investigated in Box 36-3 (pages 788–789).

Phase 3: Recovery. The final phase is the return to full employment. When the economy comes to rest at the end of the stagflation, the situation is exactly the same as when the economy is hit by an isolated supply shock (see Figure 36-1). The move back to full employment can be accomplished in either of two ways. First, the recessionary gap can be relied on to reduce wages, thus shifting the *SRAS* curve down. Second, the money supply can be increased to shift the *AD* curve to a level consistent with full

FIGURE 36-6 Eliminating an Entrenched Inflation

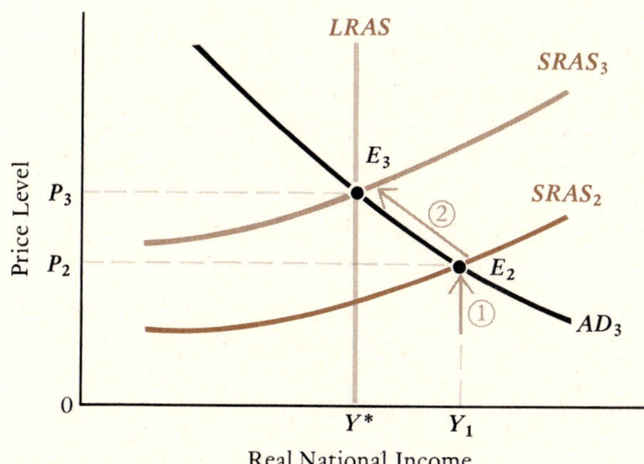

(i) Phase 1: removing the inflationary gap

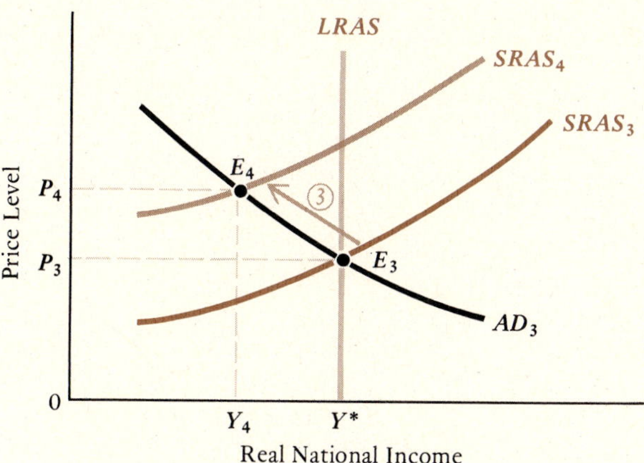

(ii) Phase 2: stagflation

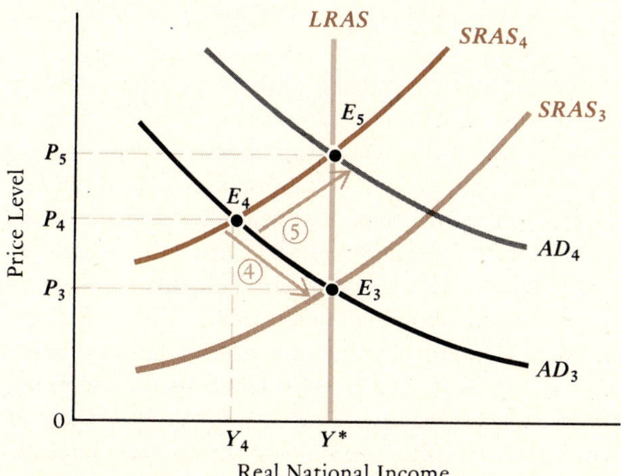

(iii) Phase 3: recovery

(i) Phase 1: The elimination of an entrenched inflation begins with a demand contraction to remove the inflationary gap. A fully validated inflation of the type shown in Figure 36-4 is taking the economy along the path shown by arrow 1 here. When the curves reach $SRAS_2$ and AD_3, the Bank stops expanding the money supply, thus stabilizing aggregate demand at AD_3. Wages continue to rise, taking the *SRAS* curve leftward. The economy moves along arrow 2 with income falling and the price level rising. When aggregate supply reaches $SRAS_3$, the inflationary gap is removed and equilibrium is established at income Y^* and price level P_3.

(ii) Phase 2: Expectations and wage momentum lead to a stagflation, with falling output and continuing inflation. The economy moves along the path shown by arrow 3. The driving force is now the *SRAS* curve, which continues to shift because inflationary expectations cause wages to continue to rise. The recessionary gap grows as income falls. The inflation continues, but at a diminishing rate. If wages stop rising when income has reached Y_4 and the price level P_4, the stagflation phase is over, with equilibrium at E_4.

(iii) Phase 3: After expectations are reversed, recovery takes income to Y^* and the price level is stabilized. There are two possible scenarios for recovery. In the first the recessionary gap causes wages to fall (slowly), taking the *SRAS* curve back to $SRAS_3$ (slowly) as shown by arrow 4. The economy retraces the path originally followed in part (ii) back to E_3. In the second scenario, the Bank increases the money supply sufficiently to shift the *AD* curve to AD_4. The economy then moves along the path shown by arrow 5. This restores potential income at the cost of a further temporary inflation that takes the price level to P_5. Full employment and a stable price level are now achieved.

BOX 36-3

Controversies over the Length of the Stagflation Phase Needed to Break an Entrenched Inflation

Keynesian View

Keynesians cite two reasons for believing that the phase 2 stagflation in the process of breaking a sustained inflation will often tend to be long and painful. The first has to do with wage momentum and the second with expectations.

Keynesians allege the existence of a self-perpetuating momentum to wage increases. According to this view, workers are concerned about their own wage rates *relative* to rates in closely related occupations and industries. Because wage contracts fix wage rates for periods of one to three years, any particular wage will be negotiated in a situation where many related wage rates are already fixed for some time into the future (until existing contracts expire). Assume, for example, that excess demand caused many existing wages to be raised by, say, 10 percent in contracts negotiated in the recent past. As a result, people currently negotiating new wage contracts will tend to hold out for something close to 10 percent, even if the pressure of excess demand has weakened greatly.

This concern over wage comparability tends to give momentum to rounds of wage increases. The process is sometimes called a *wage-wage spiral*: Once started, wages tend to chase each other in a rising spiral as bargainers seek to avoid falling behind increases that have already been agreed on for other workers.

The second main reason concerns expectations. In its simplest version, this reason is based on the so-called extrapolative theory, according to which people tend to believe that recent trends will continue. They require much new evidence before they conclude that an established inflationary trend has changed. The argument is that unless a deviation from the trend persists, people tend to dismiss a deviation—say, a fall in the inflation rate—as a transitory change and do not let it influence their long-term wage- and price-setting behavior.

The combination of the momentum of wage increases, even in the face of large recessionary gaps, and slowly adjusting expectations means that phase 2 will be long.

Monetarist View

Monetarists expect phase 2 to be over rapidly. Some say that under ideal circumstances it may never occur at all. They offer two reasons.

First, monetarists deny that significant wage-wage

employment. These two possibilities are illustrated in Figure 36-6(iii).

Economists who worry about waiting for wages and prices to fall fear that the process will take a very long time. The worry about a temporary burst of monetary expansion is that expectations of inflation may be rekindled when the Bank increases the money supply. If inflationary expectations are revived, the Bank will then have an unenviable choice. Either it must let another severe recession develop to break these new inflationary expectations, or it must validate the inflation in order to reduce unemployment. In the latter case it is back where it started, with a validated inflation on its hands.

Inflation in the 1970s

In the late 1960s Canadian inflation began to creep up toward the 4 to 5 percent range. This caused great concern and led to the adoption of tight monetary and fiscal policies. These in turn led to a downturn in the economy in late 1969, and inflation started to fall by mid 1970. However, the early 1970s witnessed quite expansionary policies, and inflation again began to rise. Expansion continued until early 1974, and inflation rose throughout that period. Then a recession set in. As a recessionary gap began to open up, the normal expectation was for a moderation of inflation. Just then, the first OPEC shock hit, and momentum exists. They believe that new wage bargains respond to current market conditions. Thus a large recessionary gap with unemployment above the natural rate will lead quickly to new wage settlements well below the expected rate of inflation. The only lag in the adjustment of wage costs to current demand conditions is caused by the length of wage contracts. Thus it will take time for *all* wages to adjust to depressed market conditions.

Second, many monetarists argue that expected inflation falls rapidly during phase 2. They accept one version of the theory of **rational expectations**, according to which people look to the government's *current* macroeconomic policy when forming their expectations of future inflation. People are assumed to understand how the economy works and to form their expectations about future inflation rates by predicting the outcome of the monetary policies currently being followed. Their expectations need not always be correct, but the rational expectations hypothesis assumes that people do not continue to make systematic errors in forming their expectations.

Rational expectations have the effect of shortening the deflationary period. Instead of being strongly influenced by past inflation rates, people act in anticipation of the outcome of current government policies. Once they realize that the Bank has stopped validating the inflation, they will quickly revise their inflationary expectations downward, and their consequent wage- and price-setting behavior will produce a rapid slowdown in the actual inflation rate. Expected inflation falls quickly to zero, and there is no further upward push to wages arising from expectations.

This happy result occurs only if people believe the Bank is going to stick to its restrictive policies. If they are skeptical about the Bank's resolve, they may expect the inflation to continue. They will then increase wages and prices in anticipation of the inflation, and their actions will generate the very inflation that they expected. Thus monetarists lay heavy stress on the credibility of the Bank's monetary policy.

Keynesians argue in response that sophisticated financial market operators may understand the underlying monetary causes of inflation, but the general public and most labor leaders and business managers hold different, sometimes crude, theories of inflation. They will tend, so the Keynesians argue, to extrapolate from past experiences and will not even know what the Bank is doing to the money supply, let alone base their expectations on it.

The experience of the early 1980s, and its relation to this debate, is discussed later in this chapter.

inflation jumped into the double-digit range. The result was stagflation.

1975–1980: Wage and Price Controls and Monetary Gradualism

By the summer of 1975 Canadian policymakers were concerned about the accelerating rate of inflation. They thought they perceived an accelerating wage-push inflation in a time of world recession. Having failed in an attempt to secure agreement of labor in a voluntary incomes policy, the Canadian cabinet decided in the autumn of 1975 to impose wage and price controls. The Anti-Inflation Board (AIB) was set up and given power to control wages and prices for three years. At roughly the same time, the Bank of Canada adopted a policy of "monetary gradualism" by announcing its intention to reduce gradually the rate at which the money supply was growing.

Whether by accident or design, the two policies made a coherent package. The monetary policy was meant to reduce the speed with which the *AD* curve was shifting upward. Wage-price controls were meant to reduce the speed with which the *SRAS* curve was shifting upward. If the upward rush of the two curves could be slowed at the same rate, the inflation rate could be reduced without having to endure the stagflation phase (phase 2 in Figure 36-6), which occurs when the upward rush of the *AD* curve is checked faster than that of the *SRAS* curve.

The AIB's targets for wage increases were 10 percent in 1976, 8 percent in 1977, and 6 percent in 1978. The very modest targets for reduction in wage inflation given by the AIB in its first year were probably at or above the rates the market would have produced in any case. In 1977–1978, however, the targets were reduced on schedule, and there seems little doubt that some restraint on wages was exercised. The AIB had perhaps its clearest and strongest impact on the rate of increase of wages in the public sector. The government had found it increasingly difficult to restrain public-sector wages since the growth of unionization in that sector in the late 1960s. In the private sector, some wage restraint was also clearly achieved, although less than in the public sector and perhaps in part in response to the public-sector slowdown.

The AIB attempted to influence inflation by acting through the cost side, acting on the aggregate supply curve. Monetary gradualism, which we discussed in Chapter 35, attempted to influence inflation primarily by acting on the *AD* curve. At first all seemed to go well. The inflation rate fell in successive years starting in 1975. Then in 1979 and in 1980 it rose, taking it back to where it had been at the peak of the 1975 "crisis." Developments in early 1981 were no more encouraging; inflation was over 10 percent in mid 1981. Had five years of gradualism accomplished nothing?

The problem was that the demand-for-money function had become a major source of economic disturbances. As we saw in Chapter 35, major innovations in monetary institutions led to sharp reductions in the demand for M1 balances over that period. Instead of a gradually tightening money supply, money was becoming more plentiful *relative to demand.*

As we noted in Chapter 35 and earlier in this chapter, the proposition that a loose monetary policy stimulates the economy and leads to inflation and that a tight monetary policy does the opposite remains valid. The problem is that it is not always possible to identify a tight or loose policy by the rate of growth of the money supply.

The failure of gradualism did not upset any basic economic theory. What it did upset was the proposition that aggregate demand could be precisely controlled by merely controlling the supply of money.

Indeed, if central banks had paid more attention to the interest rate—which had been discredited as an intermediate target—they might have realized that monetary policy was not restrictive. Several times during this period the real interest rate (the money rate corrected for the rate for inflation) was negative.

In retrospect, although a case can be made that the AIB should never have been created, it is a shame that once it was created, a more severe attack on inflation was not attempted. If over three years the rate of monetary expansion had been reduced to amounts consistent with inflation in the range of 0–2 percent and wage inflation forced to that range by the AIB, the inflation might have been halted.

Inflation in the 1980s

We have seen that the 1970s was a period of a rising inflationary trend. By the turn of the decade inflation was firmly entrenched, and a major controversy arose over how to reduce it. Everyone agreed on the goal of returning to a much lower inflation rate, but there was disagreement as to the means of achieving the goal.

Monetarists advocated breaking the inflation with monetary restraint in the manner analyzed earlier in this chapter. Since they felt that there would be a short phase 2, they were willing to rely exclusively on monetary policy to bring about the transition from a high to a low inflationary environment.

Keynesians agreed that a low rate of monetary growth was a necessary condition for returning to a low rate of inflation. However, because they felt that phase 2 would be long—some talked in terms of five to ten years—they were reluctant to use monetary policy alone during the transition. As a result, many Keynesians advocated using **incomes policies,** a term that covers any direct government intervention used to affect wage and price setting. They hoped that such intervention would shorten phase 2 by helping to break inflationary expectations. This and other possible uses of incomes policies are discussed in Box 36-4.

The Reduction of Inflation

After some minor policy vacillations, a severe anti-inflationary monetary policy was initiated in the United States in 1981. For a variety of reasons, the Bank of Canada chose to follow the U.S. lead and also adopted a more restrictive policy. In the budget of June 1982, the Canadian government felt that fiscal restraint was not appropriate in the face of the recession, but it tried to contribute to the disinflation process by introducing a package of controls on civil service compensation—the so-called *6&5 Program*.

There is still debate over the effects of the program. Some feel it stiffened the resistance of private-sector firms to continued inflationary wage increases. Be that as it may, serious recession, falling sales, and falling profits eventually had to have an effect in moderating wage increases. When it came, the fall in inflation was dramatic: from a peak of 13 percent in mid 1981 to around 5 percent by early 1984.

By 1984 the restrictive policies had succeeded in reducing inflation to a level not seen since the early 1960s, but it had also produced a major recession with all its attendant costs, including unemployment, lost output, business bankruptcies, and foreclosed mortgages.

The results came out somewhere between the extremes that had been predicted. Keynesians were right in predicting that the anti-inflationary policies would induce a severe recession. But the inflation rate came down much faster than Keynesians had predicted. Jobs rather than wages quickly became the focus of many contract settlements. Not only were new wage agreements moderated in response to the excess supply of labor, but also some existing contracts were reopened and lower wages agreed on.

Thus, as so often happens with great debates, neither the extreme pessimists nor the extreme optimists were right. The truth lay somewhere in between. Whatever the reasons, during the early 1980s inflation fell faster than many Keynesians had expected, and the slump was deeper and more prolonged than many monetarists had expected.

A Stable Inflation Rate

For several years following 1984, the Canadian inflation rate stabilized at a figure around 4 percent, and it was a time of low inflation in the world as a whole. How is it that a relatively steady inflation rate persisted for several years with no clear tendency toward acceleration? The answer is that there was no inflationary gap in the economy. Thus the inflation was purely expectational and so fulfilled the conditions for a stable, rather than an accelerating, rate.

But since there clearly was a recessionary gap, why did inflation not decelerate further? The answer here seems to be that the weak demand forces that work toward deceleration when there is excess supply were swamped by the forces of expectational inflation and random shocks. (Recall from Chapter 30 the second asymmetry of the *SRAS* curve: It shifts rapidly upward when there is excess demand but only slowly downward when there is excess supply.)

As the recovery proceeded through the late 1980s, concern grew that inflation could accelerate if the economy moved into the range of an inflationary gap. This concern was mitigated to some extent, however, by the collapse in oil prices in 1986, which, by reducing costs of production, helped to shift the *SRAS* curve downward.

The unfortunate inflationary experience of the 1970s and early 1980s is still fresh in the memories of policymakers, and there is a clear resolution to prevent a high rate of inflation from returning, let alone becoming entrenched in people's expectations. So it is likely that any outbreak of demand inflation in the near future would be met by contractionary fiscal and monetary policies designed to remove the inflationary gap. However, as time passes and the memory of inflation dims, the risk of inflation's being rekindled increases.

BOX 36-4

Incomes Policies

In the past Keynesian economists have often recommended the use of incomes policies as an anti-inflationary device. There is a wide range of such policy measures. Voluntary guidelines for wage and price increases can be set, as they were in the United States under the Kennedy administration in the 1960s. The government may consult labor and business leaders with a view to moderating their wage demands and price hikes, as has often been done in European countries. More drastically, compulsory controls may be imposed on wage, price, and profit increases. A proposal commonly made in the 1970s and early 1980s was for a **tax-related incomes policy (TIP),** which would operate through the tax system to provide penalties for "excessive" wage and price hikes and rewards for moderate ones.

Incomes policies might be used for three quite distinct purposes: (1) to suppress a demand inflation, (2) to break an expectational inflation, and (3) to control a permanent wage-cost push inflation. We discuss the first two purposes in this box and the third in Chapter 39.

Demand Inflation

One reason incomes policies have such a bad reputation throughout the world is that they have often been used, as they were in the United States during Richard Nixon's presidency, in a futile attempt to stop a demand inflation. To see why such an attempt is futile, consider the situation shown at E_1 in Figure 36-3 on page 778. If nothing else is done, the inflationary gap will cause the price level to rise to P_2. Wage and price controls could be used to hold the price level at P_1, but once the controls are removed, the excess demand will cause prices to rise.

The conclusion that using incomes policy in an attempt to control a demand inflation will be ineffective (while the cost in terms of social stress and economic disruption can be enormous) is borne out not only by the U.S. experience of the early 1970s but by the experience of Britain and a number of other European countries as well.

Expectational Inflation

When an entrenched inflation exists, incomes policies may help to break expectations. If successful, incomes policies will greatly reduce the stagflation phase. This could happen if, once phase 1 is over and the inflationary gap has been eliminated, incomes policies were used to stop wages and prices from rising because of the expectational effect. The *SRAS*

Are Full Employment and Stable Prices Compatible?

A debate has raged on both sides of the Atlantic for many decades: Are full employment and a low, stable inflation rate compatible in the long term? As long as the *SRAS* curve shifts only because of demand, expectational, and random shock effects, as we assumed earlier in this chapter, the answer is yes. But what worries some observers is the possibility of a cost push that pushes wages up faster than productivity once the fear of unemployment is reduced by the continued achievement of potential income. As far back as the 1940s many Keynesians were worried that once the government was committed to maintaining full employment, much of the discipline of the market would be removed from wage bargains. The scramble of every group trying to get ahead of every other group would lead to a wage-cost push inflation. The commitment to full employment would then lead to accommodating increases in the money supply.

There is evidence that something like this has happened periodically over the last 40 years in Britain and in many of the countries of continental Europe. Most economists are more skeptical that it has been a serious force in North America. Nonetheless, some observers still worry that full employment and a low, stable inflation rate may in the end prove incompatible. They argue for some permanent form of incomes policy. (See Box 36-4.)

curve would not continue to shift upward and thereby open up a recessionary gap. Once expectations have adjusted to the new anti-inflationary monetary policy and to the existing stable price level, the controls could be removed. The economy would then be at a position of stable prices and full employment.

The sequence of events seems almost too good to be true. The stagflation phase is eliminated, and the economy goes directly from phase 1, with an inflationary gap, to the final situation of an equilibrium at Y^*. If such a policy had been tried as many advocated during the early 1980s, *and if it had worked*, the recession of the early 1980s, with all of its consequent unemployment and lost output, would have been avoided.

Controls were used when the AIB formed part of a package to counter the explosive double-digit inflation of the 1974–1975 period. It seems probable, however, that the rapid rates of inflation of around 10 percent did not persist long enough to build up strongly felt or uniformly held expectations of continued inflation at those rates. The underlying or *core* rate of inflation was still widely perceived to be in the 6 to 7 percent range that had persisted throughout most of the decade. The rise in inflation above this core rate was fairly easily reversed.

What Can We Conclude?

Opponents of incomes policies believe that the costs of using incomes policies will exceed the alleged benefits. First, they argue that the benefits, in terms of shortening the stagflation phase, would be small because the policies would not be wholly successful in restraining wage and price increases. Second, they argue that the costs, in terms of direct administrative burdens and indirect frustration of the workings of the price system, would be large.

Although most experience internationally is with incomes policies used in a futile attempt to control a demand inflation, the evidence about the costs of using such policies may be relevant, even where the objective is not futile. The evidence suggests that when prices are set by government administrators rather than market forces, the allocation of resources becomes increasingly arbitrary, with serious consequences for the efficient working of the economic system.

An interesting argument presented by some economists is that the best way to ensure that the two objectives can be obtained most of the time is for governments to make clear that a stable price level, rather than full employment, is their overriding commitment and that whenever the two come into short-run conflict, price stability will be given priority over full employment! They argue that once this message has been accepted by the public, there will be two benefits. First, wage-cost push inflations may not occur, even at full employment. Second, incipient inflations of the supply or the demand-shock variety will be easy to quell with only minor recessions because inflationary expectations and inertias will never have a chance to become strongly entrenched. In this environment major policy-induced recessions would not be required to control an outbreak of inflation. Paradoxically, by abandoning its full-employment commitment, the government might make the maintenance of something close to full employment much more likely—at least, that is how the argument goes.

Throughout the history of economics, inflation has been recognized as a harmful phenomenon. This view was given renewed strength as a result of the worldwide experiences of high inflation rates since the 1960s. The resolve is there, at least in advanced industrial countries, to prevent another outbreak of rapid inflation and, should one occur for reasons of unavoidable supply-side shocks, to prevent the inflation from continuing long enough to become firmly entrenched in people's expectations. The resolve is a matter settled in the past decade; the success in fulfilling this resolve is a matter to be tested in the coming decade.

Summary

1. Either supply shocks or demand shocks can cause a temporary inflation. For either to lead to sustained inflation, it must be accompanied by a continuing expansion of the money supply so that the *AD* curve is shifting upward.
2. A sustained price inflation will also be accompanied by a closely related growth in wages and other factor costs, so that the *SRAS* curve is shifting up.
3. Factors that influence shifts in the *SRAS* curve can be divided into three main categories: demand, expectations, and random shocks.
4. The influence of demand can be expressed in terms of the inflationary and recessionary gaps, which relate national income to potential income, or in terms of the difference between the actual and natural rates of unemployment.
5. Expectations of inflation tend to cause wage settlements that preserve the expected real wage and hence lead to nominal wage increases.
6. It is impossible to have a sustained, steady inflation when income exceeds its potential level. As expectations constantly catch up to the existing inflation rate, that rate, which is the sum of the expectations and demand effects, must accelerate.
7. It is possible to have a sustained inflation at potential national income (and hence at the natural rate of unemployment). There is then no demand pressure on prices, but expectations can cause wages and hence prices to grow at the same rate as the money supply.
8. Stopping an inflation through restrictive monetary policy will lead to a recession that lasts while inflation only gradually falls to a rate consistent with the new lower rate of money growth. The length and depth of the recession will depend on the strength of the downward pressure on wages and on the speed with which inflationary expectations adjust.
9. In the early 1980s the rate of monetary expansion was reduced dramatically in an attempt to bring inflation down rapidly. This resulted in a larger recession than most monetarists had predicted, but also in a faster reduction in inflation than most Keynesians had predicted.
10. Some economists believe zero inflation is an achievable goal of the policy of price stability; others believe a gradual upward drift of the price level on the order of 1 to 2 percent per year must be accepted.
11. Some observers doubt that continued full employment is compatible with stable prices. They advocate permanent incomes policies to

control wage inflation and so make the two objectives compatible. Many economists are skeptical that such policies are needed and see no compelling evidence why full employment and stable prices cannot coexist in a flexible market economy.

Topics for Review

Temporary and sustained inflations
Monetary accommodation of supply shocks
Monetary validation of demand shocks
Demand inflation
Expectational inflation
Natural rate of unemployment
Accelerating inflation
Entrenched inflation
Incomes policies

Discussion Questions

1. In the period 1984–1986, Canada's underlying inflation rate appeared to stabilize in the 4 percent range. What has happened to inflation since? Why? How does the 4 percent rate compare to (i) the average since World War II, (ii) the average over the past decade, (iii) inflation in other periods when unemployment was 9 percent, and (iv) inflation when monetary growth was over 15 percent? Do you think that the Bank of Canada should allow inflation to rise in order to reduce unemployment, or maintain the inflation rate at or below 4 percent.
2. On what source or sources of inflation do the following statements focus attention?
   a. "The one basic cause of inflation is the government's spending more than it takes in. The cure is a balanced budget."
   b. "Wage bargains currently being negotiated in autos and several other basic industries will soon cause inflation to accelerate."
   c. "Canadians have become so accustomed to 4 percent inflation that it would be difficult for the Bank of Canada to induce the transition to 1 or 2 percent inflation."
   d. Newspaper editorial in Manchester, England: "If American unions were as strong as those in Britain, American inflationary experience would have been as disastrous as has Britain's."
   e. Study issued in 1980 by the Worldwatch Institute: "The nation's spiraling inflation reflects a global depletion of physical resources and therefore cannot be cured by traditional fiscal and monetary tools."
   f. Article in the London *Economist*: "Oil price collapse will reduce 1986 inflation rate."
3. When OPEC radically increased the price of oil in 1974, the world was hit with a severe supply shock. The Bank of Canada decided to accommodate this with a rapid burst of monetary expansion, while the U.S. Central Bank decided on a policy of non-accommodation.

What do you think happened to the inflation rate and the national incomes of the two countries over the following two years?

4. When the entrenched inflation of the early 1980s was broken, the economies of many industrial countries came to rest with a relatively stable price level and high unemployment. People who feared the outbreak of inflation opposed even a temporary increase in the rate of monetary expansion. Use aggregate demand and aggregate supply analysis to show why some people felt that a *temporary* burst of monetary expansion might bring increases in employment without increases in inflation.
5. Discuss the following views expressed in 1986.
   a. "Now that inflation has been beaten to the ground, we can get on with reducing unemployment."
   b. "Eternal vigilance is the price of a low inflation rate."
6. Inflations cannot long persist, whatever their initiating causes, unless they are validated by increases in the money supply. Why is this so? Does it not imply that control of inflation is merely a matter of not allowing the money supply to rise faster than the rate of increase of real national income?
7. Discuss the following views on the effects of inflation.
   a. "The beast [of inflation] is a luminescent specter, a killer, a threat to society, public enemy No. 1."
   b. "In the early 1980s inflation became the national obsession, . . . the catchall scapegoat for individual and societal economic difficulties, the symptom that diverts attention from the basic maladies."
8. In an article on the harmful effects of inflation written early in the 1980s, a reporter wrote: "With the rise in mortgage interest rates to 11 percent, heaven only knows the price of what was once idealized as 'the $100,000 house.' " At the time the inflation rate was 8 percent. Did the 11 percent interest rate represent a heavy burden of inflation on the new homeowner? What do you think the mortgage interest rate would have been if the inflation rate had been zero? Which situation would have meant a heavier real burden on the purchaser of a new house?
9. Discuss the apparent conflict between the following views. Can you suggest how they might be reconciled using aggregate demand and aggregate supply analysis?
   a. "A rise in interest rates is deflationary, since business investment and household demand for durables both fall when interest rates rise."
   b. "A rise in interest rates is inflationary, since interest is a major business cost, and as with other costs, a rise in interest will be passed on by firms in terms of higher prices."

Appendix to Chapter 36

Sustained Inflation and the Phillips Curve

In this appendix we use the Phillips curve, introduced in Chapter 30, to analyze sustained inflations.

The Price Phillips Curve

The Phillips curve shown in Box 30-1 on pages 634–635 described a relationship between the rate of change of *wages* and the state of demand, as measured by the level of national income. As we saw, changes in wages cause the *SRAS* curve to shift, giving rise to changes in the price level. These two steps are commonly combined to produce a new curve relating the rate of change of the *price level* and the level of national income. Such a curve, often referred to as a *price Phillips curve*, is shown in Figure 36A-1.

The conditions under which it is possible to derive a price Phillips curve from the original relation between wages and national income are fairly complicated.[1] But the curve is commonly used, and we shall focus on it in this appendix. (We shall henceforth refer to the price Phillips curve simply as the Phillips curve.) The key simplification is that once the level of income has been determined—by the intersection of the *SRAS* and *AD* curves, as before—the rate of inflation can be read *directly* from the Phillips curve.

Notice that the Phillips curve in Figure 36A-1 has the *rate of change of prices* on the vertical axis. The *SRAS* curve that appears so frequently in the text has the *level of prices* on the vertical axis. Since both curves have real national income on the horizontal axis, they might be easily confused. They must therefore be carefully distinguished.

[1] For example, at any given level of income the relationship between the rate of change of wages given by the figure in Box 30-1 and the rate of change of prices given by Figure 36A-1 depends on what is assumed about how fast the central bank is causing the *AD* curve to shift.

Components of Inflation

Recall the three influences that cause the *SRAS* curve to shift upward and hence the price level to rise: demand, expectations, and random shocks. In this appendix we continue to use the terms *demand* and *shock*, but we introduce the term *core inflation* as a generalization of the term *expectations* used in the text. The rate of increase of prices can now be written as the sum of the three components:

$$\Delta p = C + DE + SE$$

where Δp is the annual percentage rate of changes of prices (i.e., the rate of inflation), C refers to core inflation, DE to demand effect, and SE to shock effect. We now look at these components one at a time.

Demand Inflation

Demand inflation refers to the influence on the price level of inflationary and recessionary gaps. We have seen that an inflationary gap involves upward pressure on wages and hence on the price level, while a recessionary gap involves downward pressure. This is shown in Figure 36A-1 by the vertical distance between the Phillips curve and the horizontal axis.

The Phillips curve in Figure 36A-1 is merely a novel way of expressing relations we have used many times before. (It is important to remember, however, that Figure 36A-1 does not tell the whole story of inflation; it describes only the effects of *demand*.) These relations include the following.

1. There is neither upward nor downward pressure of demand on the price level when national income is at its potential level. Graphically, the Phillips curve cuts the axis at Y^*.
2. When there is an inflationary gap, wages and

FIGURE 36A-1 Price Phillips Curve

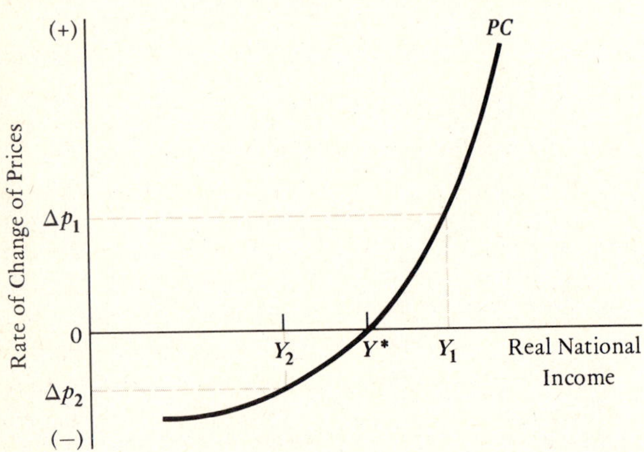

The price Phillips curve shows the positive relationship between the level of national income and rate of increase in the *price level*. An increase in national income leads to an increase in the rate of change of wages and, other things being equal, to an increase in the rate of change of prices. A fall in income leads to a decrease in the rate of change of wages and, other things being equal, to a decrease in the rate of change of prices.

With zero core inflation and output at its capacity level Y^*, inflation is zero as shown. When output is above Y^* at, say, Y_1, inflation is positive at Δp_1. When output is below Y^* at, say, Y_2, inflation is negative at Δp_2.

other costs will rise. As we have seen, this shifts the *SRAS* curve and causes the price level to rise. The inflation continues as long as the gap persists. Graphically, the Phillips curve lies above the axis where Y exceeds Y^*.

3. When there is a recessionary gap, wages and other costs will fall. This shifts the *SRAS* curve downward and causes the price level to fall. The deflation continues as long as the gap persists. Graphically, the Phillips curve lies below the axis when Y is less than Y^*.
4. The speed of the upward adjustment of the price level in the face of an inflationary gap exceeds the speed of the downward adjustment in the face of a recessionary gap. Graphically, the Phillips curve gets steeper the further to the right one moves along it. [47]

Core Inflation

The demand component cannot be the whole explanation of inflation since, if it were, inflation would only occur if national income exceeded Y^* and inflation could be quickly removed by forcing income back to Y^*. This behavior is emphatically rejected by the recent experiences of Canada and other Western economies. To explain what we observe about inflation we add the concept of core inflation. Core inflation refers to the underlying trend of inflation, and it is referred to by several different names: *core* inflation, *expectational* inflation, *inertial* inflation, and the *underlying rate* of inflation.

In the text we singled out expectations as a main influence on the price level in addition to demand. But we also saw that how expectations are formed is a major source of controversy among economists. The controversy actually runs deeper than that; some analysts question whether it is explicit expectations about the future or inertia based on past experience that really dominates wage settlements. For example, past experience may matter if recent wage increases have failed to keep up with price increases; in such circumstances current wage settlements may have a "catch-up" component.

For these and other reasons, we use the general term *core inflation* to describe persistent effects that do not depend on current demand conditions. These include expectations and other elements that stem from both forward- and backward-looking behavior. Some elements may change quickly, others only slowly. Their total influence at any point in time is summarized in the term *core inflation.*

Core inflation operates on the *SRAS* curve through the effects of wages and other costs.[2] Core

[2] Some variations in net profit margins can and do occur. These cause price inflation to diverge temporarily from cost inflation and are included in shock inflation.

inflation may also be related to *expected future changes* in wage and capital costs, since firms who plan to change prices only infrequently must set prices on the basis of their expected costs over their planning period. If that is the case, to make our concept of core inflation operative, we need a theory of how firms form their expectations of the future movement of costs. Some of the theories on how the expectations that determine the core inflation rate are formed are discussed in Chapter 39.

Graphically, the core inflation rate is added to the demand effect by shifting the Phillips curve upward by the amount of the core rate. This gives rise to a *core-augmented Phillips curve,* or more commonly an *expectations-augmented Phillips curve,* as shown in Figure 36A-2. At any given level of income, the height of the core-augmented Phillips curve is given by the sum of the demand effect and the core rate of inflation. For example, at $Y = Y^*$, when demand inflation is zero, the height of the Phillips curve is given by the core rate. At any other level of income the rate of inflation differs from the demand effect by an amount equal to the core rate.

Short-run Phillips curve. Because the Phillips curve shifts upward or downward as the core rate of inflation rises or falls, it is called a **short-run Phillips curve (*SRPC*)** when it is drawn at any particular height above Y^* (that is, for any given level of core inflation).

The short-run Phillips curve is drawn for a given rate of core inflation.

Shock Inflation

Shock inflation refers to once-and-for-all changes that give a temporary upward or downward jolt to the price level. These included changes in indirect taxes, changes in profit margins, changes in import prices, and all kinds of other factors often referred to as *supply shocks.* Shock inflation includes everything that is not included in demand and core inflation.

Summary

Putting all of this together, the current inflation rate depends on the influence of (1) demand as indicated by the inflationary or recessionary gap, demand inflation; (2) expected increase in costs, core inflation; and (3) a series of exogenous forces coming mainly from the supply side, shock inflation. These three components of inflation may be illustrated both numerically and graphically.

For a numerical example, assume that in the absence of any demand pressure, prices would rise by 10 percent because firms expect underlying costs to rise by 10 percent; that this price rise is moderated by 1 percentage point because costs only rise by 9 percent due to heavy unemployment; and that the price rise is augmented by 3 percentage points because large increases in indirect taxes force prices up. The final inflation is 12 percent, made up of 10 percent core inflation minus 1 percent demand inflation plus 3 percent shock inflation.

Graphically, the components of inflation are illustrated in Figure 36A-3 (see page 801) for two cases with a common positive core inflation component. The curve labeled *SRPC* is the expectations-augmented Phillips curve, that is, the Phillips curve shifted up by the core inflation rate. Its height above the axis at Y^* thus indicates core inflation. Points along *SRPC* where Y does not equal Y^* indicate how much the pressures of excess or deficient demand cause inflation to deviate from the core rate. The amount by which actual inflation lies above or below the *SRPC* shows the amount by which shocks cause the actual inflation rate to deviate from the sum of the core and the demand effects.

Expectations and Changes in Inflation

Originally the Phillips curve of Figure 36A-1 was thought to provide the whole explanation of inflation. When it was realized that the short-run Phillips curve shifted upward or downward, the concept of core inflation was added to explain this. Changes in the core rate cause shifts in the short-run Phillips curve. As a result we have the following conclusion.

There is a family of short-run Phillips curves, one for each core rate of inflation.

This is illustrated in Figure 36A-4 (see page 802). Let us now see what governs changes in the core rate and hence shifts in the *SRPC*.

FIGURE 36A-2 Core Inflation and the Short-Run Phillips Curve

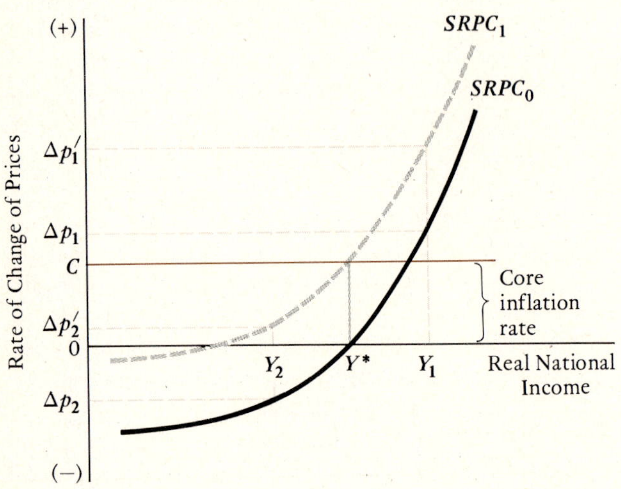

Core inflation shifts the price Phillips curve and so changes the rate of inflation that corresponds to any given level of national income. The curve $SRPC_0$, which reproduces the Phillips curve from Figure 36A-1, corresponds to a zero core inflation rate. When core inflation rises to, say, C, the Phillips curve shifts up to $SRPC_1$. The rate of inflation at Y^* rises from 0 to C. At Y_1, which is greater than Y^*, inflation rises from Δp_1 to $\Delta p_1'$. At Y_2, which is less than Y^*, inflation was initially negative at Δp_2 but now becomes positive at $\Delta p_2'$.

Look at point Z on $SRPC_1$ in Figure 36A-5 (see page 803), which is $SRPC_1$ reproduced from Figure 36A-4 and corresponds to a core inflation rate of C_1. At the point Z shock inflation is zero and demand inflation is positive (since $Y_1 > Y^*$), so the actual inflation rate is above the core rate of C_1. Sooner or later this excess will come to be expected, the core rate will then rise, and the $SRPC$ will shift upward. As long as national income is held above Y^*, the actual inflation rate will exceed the core rate, and as a result sooner or later the core rate will rise. This means that the short-run Phillips curve will sooner or later shift upward, as indicated by the arrow above point Z.

Now look at point W in Figure 36A-5 where again core inflation is C_1 and shock inflation is zero. At W demand inflation is negative (since $Y_2 < Y^*$), so the actual inflation rate is below the core rate of C_1. Sooner or later this difference will influence expectations, and the core rate will fall. As long as national income is held below Y^*, the actual inflation rate will be less than the core rate, and sooner or later the core rate will fall. This means that sooner or later the short-run Phillips curve will begin to shift downward, as indicated by the arrow below W.

So we have a basic prediction of the theory:

A persistent inflationary gap will sooner or later cause the inflation rate to accelerate, whereas a persistent recessionary gap will sooner or later cause the inflation rate to decelerate.

This, of course, is the acceleration hypothesis that we encountered in the text. Let us now examine it in more detail.

Accelerating Inflation

Consider an economy with a core inflation of C_1 that has just experienced an increase in aggregate demand so that output is above Y^* as at point Z in Figure 36A-5. There is an inflationary gap with a positive inflation rate; the $SRAS$ curve will be shifting upward, while monetary validation by the central bank is shifting the AD curve upward. (It may be worth

FIGURE 36A-3 The Components of Inflation Illustrated

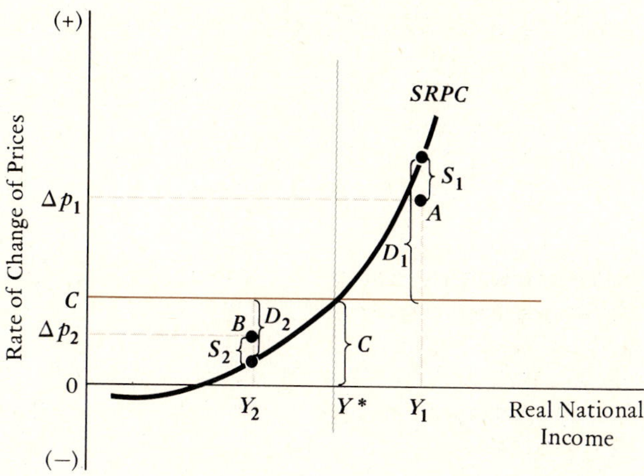

The inflation rate can be separated into three components: core inflation, demand inflation, and shock inflation. The Phillips curve is drawn for a given core rate of inflation and hence is labeled as a short-run Phillips curve. The given core rate, C, is shown by the height of the horizontal colored line.

Point A indicates a national income of Y_1 combined with an inflation rate of Δp_1. This rate is composed of the following: a core rate, C; a positive demand component, D_1 (determined by the shape of *SRPC*); and a negative shock component, S_1.

Point B indicates a national income of Y_2 combined with an inflation rate of Δp_2. This rate is composed of the following: core inflation, once again given by C; the demand component, D_2, which is now negative (since income Y_2 is less than Y^*); and a positive shock component, S_2.

reiterating what is happening here: Core inflation produces the rise in prices that results from firms' expectations about the long-run trend in costs; the demand component produces the addition to inflation due to what are thought to be transitory demand factors; shock inflation is still treated as zero.)

Is this situation sustainable? Only if the Phillips curve remains stable. If the short-run Phillips curve stayed put, policymakers could conclude that they had achieved a pretty good trade-off. They would have gained a permanent increase in output of Y^*Y_1 at the cost of a permanent increase in inflation from C_1 to Δp_1.

But as we have seen, this is not all that is happening. The persistence of a demand inflation will eventually cause the core inflation rate to rise and hence cause the *SRPC* to shift upward. In turn, this increases the rate at which the *SRAS* curve is shifting upward. Let us trace this process in detail.

At point Z prices and costs are rising at Δp_1 per year, and sooner or later firms and workers will stop believing that this increase from the old rate C_1 is a transitory phenomenon. They will come to expect some of this increase to persist and incorporate it into core inflation. Let us say that after a passage of time firms come to expect wages and other costs to rise at the rate C_2 each period. This will produce a core inflation at a rate of C_2 per annum in Figure 36A-5. The short-run Phillips curve now shifts up to $SRPC_2$ in the figure. The rise in the core rate of inflation increases the actual inflation rate corresponding to each possible level of national income. If national income is maintained at Y_1 so that demand inflation remains positive, the actual inflation rate rises above Δp_1.

Now the *SRAS* curve will be shifting upward more rapidly. If output is to be maintained at Y_1, the central bank will have to increase the rate of monetary expansion. This will cause the *AD* to shift up more rapidly to match the more rapid upward shift in *SRAS*. This is illustrated in terms of the *SRAS* and *AD* curves in Figure 36-3.

The actual inflation rate, Δp_2, is well above the core rate, C_2. Sooner or later this will cause the core rate to rise again, and the short-run Phillips curve will again shift upward. As long as output is main-

FIGURE 36A-4 A Family of Short-Run Phillips Curves

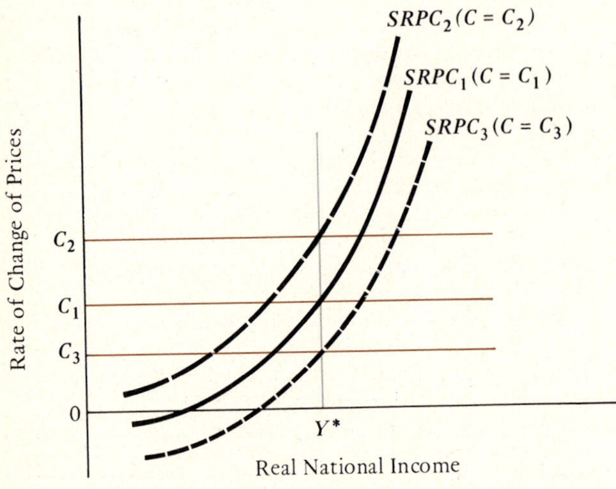

There is a separate short-run Phillips curve for each core rate of inflation. The Phillips curve of Figure 36A-3, shown here as $SRPC_1$, relates national income to inflation on the assumption that core inflation is C_1. The actual rate of inflation depends on both the core rate and the level of national income (as well as on shock inflation, assumed here to be zero).

For each positive core rate of inflation there is a short-run Phillips curve that lies above the axis at $Y = Y^*$ by the particular core rate to which it relates. If the core rate were C_2, greater than C_1, the Phillips curve would lie above $SRPC_1$, as shown by $SRPC_2$. If the core rate were C_3, less than C_1, the curve would lie below $SRPC_1$, as shown by $SRPC_3$.

tained at Y_1 so that demand inflation is positive, this process of growing core inflation will continue.

From this an important conclusion follows.

If the central bank validates any rate of inflation that results from *Y* being held above *Y, the inflation rate itself will accelerate continuously *and* the rate of monetary expansion required to frustrate the monetary adjustment mechanism will also accelerate.**

The Long-Run Phillips Curve

Is there any level of income in this model that is compatible with a constant actual rate of inflation? The answer is yes, potential income. When income is at Y^*, the demand component of inflation is *zero*, as shown in Figure 36A-1. This means that, still letting shock inflation be zero, actual inflation equals core inflation. Since the core rate is determined by what people expect the inflation rate to be when actual inflation equals core inflation, the actual inflation rate is equal to the expected rate. There are no surprises. No one's plans are upset, so no one has any incentive to alter plans as a result of what actually happens to inflation.

Providing that the inflation rate is fully validated and shock inflation is zero, any rate of inflation can persist indefinitely as long as income is held at its potential level.

We now define the **long-run Phillips curve (LRPC)** as the relation between *national income* and *stable rates of inflation* that neither accelerate nor decelerate. This occurs when the core and actual inflation rates are equal. According to the theory just described, the long-run Phillips curve is vertical. This is illustrated in Figure 36A-6 on the facing page.

Maintaining a point on the *LRPC* leads to steady inflation at the core rate. This is illustrated in Figure 36A-7 (see page 804), where we show a situation with a positive core inflation rate and where there is full accommodation by the central bank. In part (i) the intersection of the *SRAS* and *AD* curves determines *Y* at Y^*. In part (ii) the Phillips curve shows the rate of inflation. There is no demand effect on inflation, so the actual and core inflation rates are equal. As a result the situation is sustainable (as long as the central bank continues to validate the core inflation). The increasing price level in part (i) reflects the positive inflation rate indicated in part (ii). Note

FIGURE 36A-5 Shifts in the Short-Run Phillips Curve

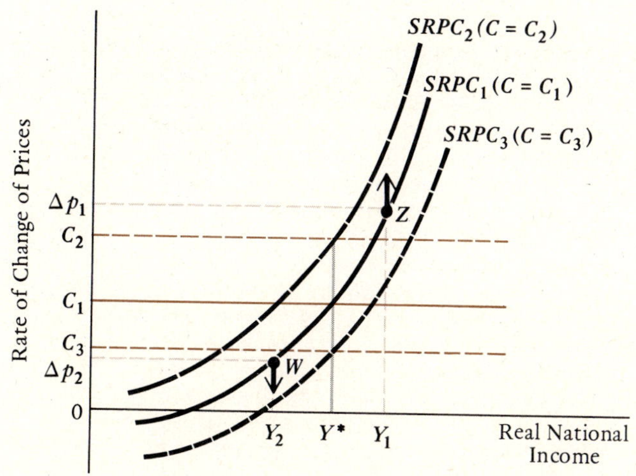

Changes in the core rate of inflation, which arise when actual inflation differs from the core rate, cause the short-run Phillips curve to shift. With a core inflation rate of C_1, the short-run Phillips curve is $SRPC_1$, reproduced from Figure 36A-4.

If income is maintained at Y_1, greater than Y^*, actual inflation will be Δp_1, greater than the core rate, as indicated by point Z. Eventually, this excess of the actual inflation rate over the core rate will cause the core rate to rise, from C_1, say, to C_2, shifting the short-run Phillips curve to $SRPC_2$, as indicated by the arrow above point Z.

If income is maintained at Y_2, less than Y^*, actual inflation will be Δp_2, less than the core rate, as indicated by point W. Eventually, the shortfall of actual inflation below the core rate will cause the core rate to fall below C_1, say, to C_3, causing the short-run Phillips curve to shift down to $SRPC_3$, as indicated by the arrow below W.

that in part (ii), since the core rate is not changing, the *SRPC* will be stable, which means we are also on the *LRPC*.

We can now state a general conclusion.

The long-run Phillips curve is vertical at Y^*; only Y^* is compatible with a stable rate of inflation, and any stable rate is, if fully validated, compatible with Y^*.

The Natural Rate of Unemployment

We have talked about variations of Y from Y^*, but for every level of national income there is an associated level of unemployment. Recasting these conclusions in terms of unemployment we have the following: As before, call the unemployment associated with Y^* the natural rate of unemployment. Note that unemployment can be pushed below the natural rate, but only at the cost of opening up an inflationary gap. If the government seeks to maintain this lower rate of unemployment, the inflation rate will accelerate and will have to be validated by ever-increasing rates of monetary expansion.

FIGURE 36A-6 Vertical Long-Run Phillips Curve

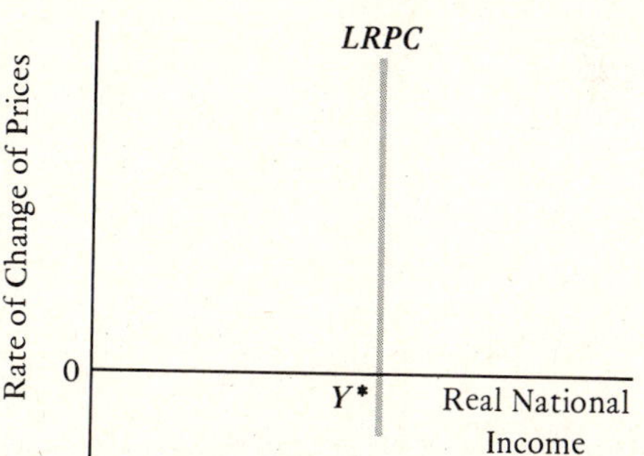

When actual inflation equals expected inflation, there is no trade-off between inflation and unemployment. In long-term equilibrium the actual rate of inflation must remain equal to the expected rate (otherwise expectations would be revised). This can only occur at potential income Y^*, that is, along the *LRPC*.

At Y^* there is no demand pressure on the price level; hence the only influence on actual inflation is expected inflation. Any stable rate of inflation (provided it is validated by the appropriate rate of monetary expansion) is compatible with Y^* and its associated natural rate of unemployment.

FIGURE 36A-7 Monetary Accommodation and Steady Inflation

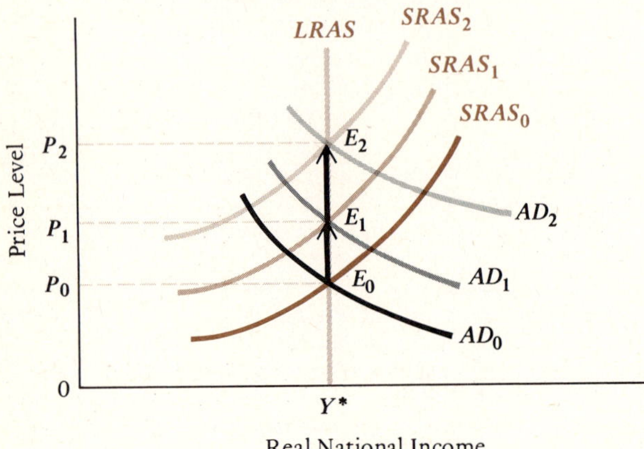

(i) Upward shifting AD and $SRAS$ curves

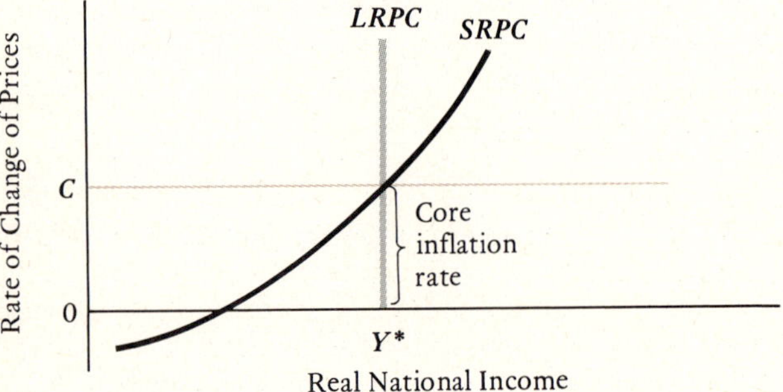

(ii) Steady inflation

Positive core inflation means that wage costs will be rising even when output is just at its capacity level; monetary accommodation can keep output constant and sustain the inflation rate. Core inflation is shown in part (ii) by C, the height of the short-run Phillips curve above the axis at Y^*. This translates into an upward-shifting $SRAS$ curve from $SRAS_0$ to $SRAS_1$ to $SRAS_2$ in part (i). Monetary accommodation means that the AD curve in part (i) also shifts upward, from AD_0 to AD_1 to AD_2. As drawn, the monetary accommodation just keeps output constant at Y^*, so inflation persists at the core rate C.

The positive wage inflation in part (ii) is reflected in an equal rate of price increase from P_0 to P_1 to P_2 in part (i). Since we are on the $LRPC$, core inflation is constant and the $SRPC$ is stable.

The lowest rate of unemployment that can be maintained without a tendency for the rate of inflation to accelerate is the natural rate.

Implications for Monetary Policy

The foregoing analysis has three major implications for the understanding and conduct of monetary policy.

First, the interaction among money, inflation, and output is complex. In particular, it depends on how expectations are formulated. Monetary policies may affect expectations differently at different times. Therefore, it would be wrong to expect a simple, mechanical relationship between the money supply and the behavior of output and the price level.

Second, differences between the expected rate of inflation and the rate that is being validated by monetary policy lead to changes in the level of output and in the actual rate of inflation. Hence changes in the rate of monetary expansion can have powerful though not entirely predictable effects on the economy.

Third, in the long run GDP will move to the level indicated by the long-run aggregate supply curve and the long-run Phillips curve. This means that changes in the rate of monetary expansion will cause only temporary changes in the level of output. In the long run changes in the rate of monetary expansion have their only influence on the rate of inflation.

Some Extensions

Shock inflation. All of the foregoing analysis has been done on the assumption that shock inflation is zero. In today's world many shocks hit the price level. What we see is a much less regular experience than the simple combination of core plus demand inflation. The inflation rate varies quite substantially from period to period due to the action of the many shocks that impinge on it. When such shocks occur, the economy's output-inflation combination will lie off the current expectations-augmented Phillips curve—above it for a positive shock and below it for a negative shock.

Asymmetrical speeds of reaction. The shape of the Phillips curve means that it is easier to raise the core rate than to lower it. The change in the core rate from period to period depends on the discrepancy between the actual rate and the core rate. The steepness of the short-run Phillips curve above Y^* means that it is easy to create a substantial gap between the actual rate and the core rate by increasing the inflationary gap. This will tend to drag up the core rate fairly quickly. The flatness of the short-run Phillips curve below Y^* means that only a small discrepancy between the actual and the core rates can be created by even a large recessionary gap. Therefore, the core rate can be depressed only slowly by creating recessionary gaps.

It is an important prediction of this theory that the core rate of inflation can accelerate fairly quickly but will decelerate only slowly.

Summary

We now summarize the key points of the theory of the expectations-augmented Phillips curve and indicate where there is substantial agreement and where there is controversy with competing theories.

1. *The rate of price inflation must follow the trend rate of cost inflation quite closely.* There is little disagreement over this relation, which defines the core rate of inflation. Notice, however, that it is just a matter of simple arithmetic that the major determinant of price inflation is cost inflation. This says nothing about causes. Costs could be rising because of the pressure of excess demand in factor markets or because of the exercise of arbitrary power on the part of unions.
2. *The influence of demand on inflation is asymmetrical.* Inflationary gaps cause inflation to rise well above the core rate, whereas recessionary gaps force the actual rate only slightly below the core rate. The evidence for this asymmetry is strong, although some economists deny it.
3. *The core inflation rate falls slowly even in the face of large recessionary gaps.* There is a substantial disagreement over this point, for some economists believe that the core rate can fall quite rapidly. This key controversy underlies many differences in policy recommendations.
4. *Shocks caused by such influences as changes in indirect taxes, agricultural crop failures, or increases in import prices temporarily affect the inflation rate.* Economists do not always agree on this point; at the time of the first OPEC oil-price shocks in 1974, some said that if oil-related prices rose, other prices would fall, keeping the price level constant. As a result of the evidence of the OPEC shocks, most economists now agree that supply shocks affect the price level, causing temporary deviations in the rate of inflation from what it would otherwise be. Another example of a clear supply-shock inflation was the rise in the price level that occurred in Britain in 1979 and 1980 after income taxes were cut and value-added taxes raised by the new Conservative government.
5. *Demand-induced rises in the inflation rate yield only temporary increases in national income.* Any departure of national income from Y^* sets in motion forces that cause a return to Y^*. Output in excess of Y^* causes an inflation that sets in motion the monetary adjustment mechanism. Frustration of the monetary adjustment mechanism by monetary expansion can sustain output above Y^*, but only if the rate of increase of wages, prices, and money is continually accelerating.

37

Employment and Unemployment

In the early 1980s worldwide unemployment rose to high levels. It remained high in many advanced industrial countries and only began to come down, and then very slowly, during the latter half of the decade. Canada's experience reflects rather closely these international developments. From a high of 12.8 percent in late 1982, Canada's unemployment rate fell to 9.4 percent at the start of 1987.

As we shall see later in this chapter, those overall figures hide large variations in rates for specific groups. For example, in 1986 the unemployment rate was 8 percent for males over 25 years of age and 16.5 percent for males between the ages of 15 and 24.

Many social policies designed to alleviate the short-term economic consequences of unemployment have been instituted since the 1930s, and their success may be counted as a real triumph of economic policy. Being unemployed, even for some substantial period of time, is no longer the economic disaster that it once was. But the longer-term effects of high unemployment rates in terms of the disillusioned who have given up trying to make it within the system and who contribute to social unrest should be a matter of serious concern to the haves as well as the have-nots.

Many Canadians believe that unemployment is the most serious macroeconomic problem facing the nation. Is this so? What policies might be effective in reducing the problem?

Kinds of Unemployment

The unemployed can be classified in various ways. They can be grouped by personal characteristics, such as age, sex, degree of skill or education, and ethnic group. They can also be classified by geographic location, occupation, duration of unemployment, or reasons for their unemployment.

In this chapter we are concerned mainly with the reasons for unemployment. Although it is not always possible to say why a particular unemployed person has no job, it is often possible to gain some idea of the total numbers of people unemployed for each major cause.

In Chapter 26, we distinguished two types of unemployment: *deficient-demand* unemployment, which is unemployment due to a recessionary gap, and *frictional* unemployment, which was used to account for the unemployment that exists when national income is at its potential level and hence there is neither a recessionary nor an inflationary gap.

For our more detailed study we will now distinguish a second reason why there is unemployment at potential income. We call this second reason *structural* unemployment. We also discuss an additional type, *real-wage* unemployment.

Frictional Unemployment

Frictional unemployment results from the normal turnover of labor. Young people enter the labor force and look for jobs. People leave jobs for many reasons. Some quit because they are dissatisfied with the working conditions; others are fired. Whatever the reason, they must search for new jobs, which takes time. Persons who are unemployed while searching for jobs are said to be frictionally unemployed.

Frictional unemployment would persist even if the structure of jobs in terms of skills, industries, occupations, and location was unchanging.

Normal turnover of labor will always produce a pool of persons who are frictionally unemployed. The search aspect of frictional unemployment is emphasized in a branch of modern theory that studies the rational behavior of people searching for jobs.

In looking at causes of unemployment, Keynes made a basic distinction between voluntary and involuntary unemployment. *Voluntary* unemployment occurs when there is a job available, but the unemployed person is not willing to accept it at the going wage rate. *Involuntary* unemployment occurs when a person is willing to accept a job at the going wage rate but cannot find one. In Box 37-1, where we discuss search unemployment in more detail, we see that the distinction between voluntary and involuntary unemployment is not as clear as Keynes suggested.

Structural Unemployment

Structural adjustments can cause unemployment. When the pattern of demand for goods changes, the pattern of demand for labor also changes. Until labor adjusts fully, structural unemployment develops.

Structural unemployment may be defined as unemployment caused by a mismatch between the structure of the labor force—in terms of skills, occupations, industries, or geographic location—and the structure of the demand for labor. In Canada today, structural unemployment exists, for example, in the oil and gas industry in Alberta and in many of the older foundry and mill towns in Ontario.

Natural causes. Economic growth can cause structural unemployment. As growth proceeds, the mix of required inputs changes, as do the proportions in which final goods are demanded. These changes require considerable economic adjustment. Structural unemployment occurs when such adjustments are slow enough that severe pockets of unemployment develop in areas, industries, and occupations in which the demand for factors of production is falling faster than the supply.

Changes that accompany economic growth shift the structure of the demand for labor. Demand rises in such expanding areas as Ontario and industrial Quebec and falls in such contracting areas as the western resource-based provinces. Demand rises for workers with certain skills, such as computer programming and electronics engineering, and falls for workers with other skills, such as stenography and bookkeeping. Demand rises, say, for airline pilots and short-order cooks and falls for lumberjacks and riggers and for crew members on transatlantic passenger liners. To meet changing demands, the structure of the labor force must change. Some existing workers can retrain, and some new entrants can acquire fresh skills.

Structural unemployment will increase if there is either an increase in the speed at which the structure of the demand for labor is changing or a decrease in the speed at which labor is adapting to these changes.

Policy causes. Government policies can influence the economy's ability to adapt.

Policies that discourage movement of labor among regions, industries, and occupations also raise structural unemployment.

BOX 37-1

Search Unemployment

Some frictional unemployment is involuntary: No acceptable job in the person's occupational and skill category has yet been located. Often, however, it is voluntary. The unemployed person is aware of available jobs but is searching for better options. Voluntary frictional unemployment is often called **search unemployment.**

The existence of search unemployment shows that the distinction between voluntary and involuntary unemployment is not as clear as it might seem at first sight. How, for example, should we classify an unemployed woman who refuses to accept a job at a lower skill level than the one for which she feels she is qualified? What if she turns down a job for which she is trained because she hopes to get a higher wage offer for a similar job from another employer?

In one sense people in search unemployment are voluntarily unemployed because they could find some job; in another sense they are involuntarily unemployed because they have not yet succeeded in finding the job for which they feel they are suited at a rate of pay that they believe exists.

Workers do not have perfect knowledge of all available jobs and rates of pay, and they may be able to gain information only by searching the market. Faced with this uncertainty, it may be sensible to refuse a first job offer, for the offer may prove to be a poor one in light of further market information. Too much search—for example, holding off while being supported by others in the hope of finding a job better than that for which one is really suited—is an economic waste. Thus search unemployment is a gray area: Some is useful, some wasteful.

It is socially desirable for there to be sufficient search unemployment to give unemployed people time to find an available job that makes the best use of their skills.

How long it will pay to remain in search unemployment depends on the economic costs of being unemployed. By lowering the costs of being unemployed, unemployment insurance tends to increase the amount of search unemployment. This is not necessarily undesirable. If the amount of search unemployment would otherwise be too little, the insurance scheme can increase economic efficiency. If, however, the amount of search unemployment is already too much, unemployment insurance will lower economic efficiency.

Policies that discourage firms from replacing human labor with machines may protect employment in the short term. If, however, such policies lead to the decline of an industry because it cannot compete effectively with innovative foreign competitors, structural unemployment can result in the long run.

One further cause of structural unemployment is the persistence of a disequilibrium structure of relative wages. Typical causes of such a structure are minimum wages, union agreements that narrow wage differentials, nationally negotiated wage structures that take no account of local market conditions, and equal pay laws that apply in situations where the groups concerned do not in fact all contribute equally to the profitability of the enterprise. Such policies cause particular groups to lose employment because their relative wages are above their equilibrium value.

For example, an elderly person may be prepared to work for $100 a week as a caretaker of an apartment. Further, the owner may believe that this person is capable of doing what is needed. But suppose the minimum wage is $150 a week. If there were no minimum wage, the elderly person would get the job. But because of the minimum wage, the owner either goes without a caretaker or hires someone else who can provide her with more services than she needs. She reasons that since she has to pay more, she might as well get something for it.

The same considerations apply to an inexperienced worker just out of school who would accept $100 a week for a first job. A potential employer is willing to pay this wage, but the minimum wage is $150. Once again the employer hires someone else who is overqualified for the job. A further unfortunate effect is that such young workers do not get the on-the-job training and experience that would equip them to hold down a stable, higher-paying job a year or two later.

Much empirical research supports the conclusion that imposed wage structures such as minimum wages tend to transfer employment from those whose relative wages are raised by the intervention to those whose relative wages are lowered. But do imposed wages affect overall employment? That is a difficult question, but, as we discussed in Chapter 19, the evidence suggests that overall employment falls as a result of minimum wages. If such policies lead to an increase in the average wage paid, they may contribute to what we will call real-wage unemployment.

The Distinction Between Frictional and Structural Unemployment

As with many distinctions, the one between structural and frictional unemployment becomes blurred at the margin. In a sense structural unemployment is really long-term frictional unemployment. For illustration, consider a change that requires labor to reallocate from one sector to another. If the reallocation occurs quickly, we call the unemployment frictional; if the reallocation occurs slowly, we call the unemployment structural.

The major characteristic of both frictional and structural unemployment is that there is a job available—that is, an unfilled vacancy—for each unemployed person.

In the case of pure frictional unemployment, the job vacancy and the searcher are matched. The only problem is that the searcher has not yet located the vacancy. In the case of structural unemployment, the job vacancy and the searcher are mismatched in one or more relevant characteristics such as occupation, industry, location, or skill requirements.

The sum of frictional plus structural unemployment is what we have earlier called the *natural rate of unemployment*.

Deficient-Demand Unemployment

We have called unemployment that occurs because total demand is insufficient to purchase all the output that could be produced by a fully employed labor force *deficient-demand unemployment*. It is the unemployment that exists because there is a recessionary gap. As a result there are fewer available jobs than there are unemployed persons. Deficient-demand unemployment can be measured as the number of persons currently employed minus the number of persons who would be employed at potential income. (It is thus the employment counterpart of the output gap.) When deficient-demand unemployment is zero, there is some job available for every person unemployed. In this situation unemployment persists either for structural or frictional reasons. This is the natural rate of unemployment.

National income theory seeks to explain the causes of and cures for unemployment in excess of frictional and structural unemployment. *Full employment* does not mean zero unemployment; it means that all unemployment is frictional or structural.

National income theory thus seeks to explain the deficient-demand unemployment associated with variations in the nation's total national income around its potential income.

Real-Wage Unemployment

Unemployment due to too high a real wage is called **real-wage unemployment** or sometimes **Classical unemployment.** This latter term is used because many economists, whom Keynes dubbed the Classical economists, believed that unemployment in the 1930s was caused by high real wages. The remedy they suggested for unemployment was to reduce wages. Keynes argued that the unemployment was due to too little aggregate demand, and his remedy was to raise demand; not cut wages. Keynesians won that debate, and there is now general agreement that the unemployment of the 1930s was caused by deficient aggregate demand rather than excessive real wages.

Because the debates of the 1930s aroused strong emotions, many modern Keynesians have refused to believe that *any* unemployment could be caused by high real wages. There is concern, however, that some current unemployment in Western Europe and elsewhere (including Canada) may be traced to excessive real wage levels.

So far in this book we have used the term *real wages* to mean the purchasing power of money wages. This is measured by deflating the money wage by the Consumer Price Index. In this section we are concerned with the real cost to the employer of hiring a worker. We call this the **real product wage.** The nominal cost to the employer includes the pre-tax wage rate, any extra benefits such as pension plan contributions, and any government payroll taxes such as employers' contributions to social insurance. The real product wage is the nominal cost for a specific time period, say, per hour of labor employed, divided by the value of the output produced by labor during the same time period. Thus, for example, if it costs $20 to employ labor that produces output valued at $30, the real product wage is 0.666, which says that labor costs absorb two-thirds of the value of output.

Too high a real product wage can affect employment through forces operating both in the short run and in the long run. Consider the short run first. At any moment in time many industries have an array of plants, ranging from those that embody the oldest technologies in use and can do little more than cover their variable costs to those that embody the latest technology and can make a handsome return over variable costs. A rise in the real product wage of 10 percent will mean that some plants can no longer cover their variable costs and so will close down. If, for example, a plant had wages of $0.70 and other variable costs of $0.25 for every $1 of sales, production would be worthwhile, since $0.05 of every $1 of sales would be available as a return on already invested capital. If the product wage rose so that $0.77 for every $1 of sales was paid in wages, the plant would be shut down, since it would not even be covering its variable costs. The plant's employees would then lose their jobs. This also applies to the economy as a whole.

An economy-wide rise in real product wages, other things being equal, means that some plants and firms will no longer be able to cover their variable costs and will shut down. When they do, the unemployment rate will rise.

Now consider a period of time long enough for the demand for labor to be adjusted to the real product wage by replacing old plant and equipment with new capital that requires different capital-labor ratios. In the long run firms will adopt technologies that replace expensive labor with less expensive capital, and this will increase the amount of real-wage unemployment. Thus when the real wage is too high across the whole economy, a structural mismatch will develop between the labor force and the capital stock. This mismatch will show up as unemployment; when the capital stock is working at full capacity, there is still unemployed labor. The unemployment will continue until one of two things happens. Unemployment may force down the real wage until it pays firms to employ all of the existing labor. Alternatively, new technologies may be invented that make profitable use of the unemployed labor in spite of its high real product wage.

One approach to distinguishing between the various types of unemployment empirically is discussed in Box 37-2.

Experience of Unemployment

Measured and Nonmeasured Unemployment

The number of unemployed persons is estimated from a sample survey conducted each month by Statistics Canada. Persons who are currently without a job but say they have actively searched for one during the sample period are recorded as unemployed. The total number of estimated unemployed is then expressed as a percentage of the labor force (employed plus unemployed) to obtain the figure for percentage unemployment.

BOX 37-2

Distinguishing Types of Unemployment

One useful measure of the natural rate of unemployment is the percentage of the labor force unemployed when the number of unfilled job vacancies is equal to the number of persons seeking jobs. When these two are equal, there is a job opening for every person seeking a job. Any unemployment that remains must be either frictional or structural.

This measure is illustrated in the figure, which plots the number of unfilled vacancies (v) against the number of unemployed (u). The 45° line is the locus of points where $u = v$. On that line there is some job available to match every unemployed person, so there is no deficient-demand unemployment. The uv curve shows the actual relationship between unemployment and vacancies that is suggested by empirical evidence. In an economy with the relation uv_1, zero deficient-demand unemployment occurs at the point x, with frictional plus structural unemployment given by the amount a measured on either axis.

When a boom occurs, employers seek to hire more workers, so more vacancies open up. Since there are more jobs available, the unemployed spend less time searching before finding an acceptable job. Thus the pool of unemployed falls. A boom therefore takes the economy to some point such as y, where there are more vacancies than unemployed. A slump takes the economy to some point such as z, where there are fewer vacancies than unemployed.

A change in structural plus frictional unemployment shifts the uv curve. For example, if people lose their jobs in Alberta while more jobs are created in Toronto, there may be a rise in the number of unemployed (in Alberta) and a rise in the number of unfilled job vacancies (in Toronto). Hence both u and v increase. In the diagram a shift to uv_2 indicates a rise in frictional plus structural unemployment from a to b.

In most countries where reliable vacancy data are available the uv relation shifted outward in the late 1960s and early 1970s. This indicated a rise in the natural rate of unemployment.

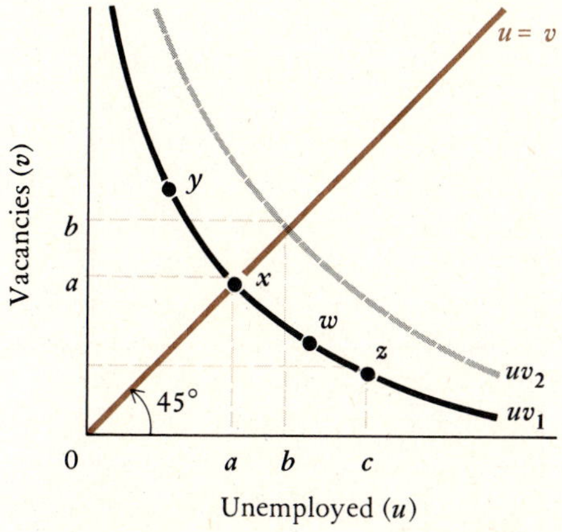

Deficient-Demand Unemployment

We can measure deficient-demand unemployment as total unemployment minus estimated frictional plus structural unemployment. Graphically it is actual unemployment minus the unemployment where the uv relation cuts the 45° line. If the economy is at point z, this measure is ac in the figure.*

Real-Wage Unemployment

Unemployment due to excessive increases in the real wage will show up in the figure approximately as a movement along the existing uv curve, say from point x to w, rather than as a shift of that curve. There will be a large rise in unemployment and a small fall in vacancies (which would otherwise have resulted from the normal turnover of labor in the now-closed plants). A general rise in the real product wage can lead to a general rise in unemployment that looks like deficient-demand unemployment because there is a rise in unemployment with no corresponding rise in unfilled vacancies.

* Notice that the measure is not current unemployment minus current vacancies but current unemployment minus the vacancies that would exist were there no output gap.

The measured figure for unemployment may overstate or understate the number of people who are involuntarily unemployed.

On the one hand, the measured figure overstates unemployment by including people who are not involuntarily unemployed. For example, unemployment insurance benefits provide protection against genuine hardship, but they also induce some people to stay out of work and collect benefits for as long as they last. Such people have in fact voluntarily withdrawn from the labor force, but they are usually included in the ranks of the unemployed because, for fear of losing their benefits, they report to the survey that they are actively looking for a job.

On the other hand, the measured figure understates involuntary unemployment by omitting some people who would accept a job if one were available but who did not actively look for one in the sample week. For example, people who have not found jobs by the time their unemployment benefits are exhausted may become discouraged and stop seeking work. Such people have withdrawn from the labor force and will not be recorded as unemployed. They are, however, truly unemployed in the sense that they would willingly accept a job if one were available.

People in this category are referred to as **discouraged workers.** They have voluntarily withdrawn from the labor market because they believe they cannot find a job under current conditions.

In addition there is part-time unemployment. If some workers are working six hours a day instead of eight hours because there is insufficient demand for the product they manufacture, that group is suffering 25 percent unemployment even though no individual is reported as unemployed. Twenty-five percent of the potential manpower is going unused. Involuntary part-time work is a major source of unemployment of labor resources not reflected in the overall unemployment figures reported in the press.

For example, in mid 1983 some 425,000 workers were in part-time unemployment, accounting for 23 million hours per month of unrecorded unemployment—equivalent to 138,000 full-time unemployed persons. Between 1981 and 1984 the number of part-time jobs rose by 16 percent, while the number of full-time jobs *fell* by 3 percent.

The Overall Unemployment Rate

Figure 26-2 (see page 557) shows the behavior of the unemployment rate since the end of World War II. Until 1970 the rate fluctuated cyclically but showed no clear rising or falling trend. During the 1950s the average rate was 4.4 percent, and during the 1960s it was 5.0 percent—not a significant difference.[1] From 1970, however, the cyclical fluctuations appear to be superimposed on a rising trend. The *low* figure of 5.3 percent unemployment for the post-1970 period was above the *average* of 4.7 percent for the previous two decades, and the high figure of 12.8 percent was the highest since the Great Depression of the 1930s. The low figure was achieved during the boom of 1972–1973; the high occurred in 1982. The average rate of unemployment was 6.6 percent during the 1970s and 10.1 percent during the first six years of the 1980s. The sustained recovery that Canada experienced in the mid 1980s still left unemployment at 9.4 percent at the beginning of 1987.

Figure 37-1 presents one estimate of the natural rate of unemployment, prepared by Professor Pierre Fortin of Laval University.[2] This estimate takes into account the effects of variables measuring demographic, policy, institutional, and sectoral changes. His estimate shows the natural rate of unemployment rising steadily in the early 1960s to a peak in 1978. After 1978 it declines steadily through to 1985. Below we discuss some of the reasons for these movements in the natural rate.

The excess of actual unemployment over the natural rate, called *cyclical unemployment,* is equal to deficient demand unemployment plus real-wage unemployment. Fortin's estimate thus indicates that at the start of 1987 cyclical unemployment was around 3 percent. Other researchers, including those whose

[1] Yearly figures in this section are based on annual averages for unemployment.

[2] "How Natural Is Canada's High Unemployment Rate?" *Eastern Economic Journal,* 1987.

FIGURE 37-1 Actual and Natural Unemployment Rates, 1966–1985

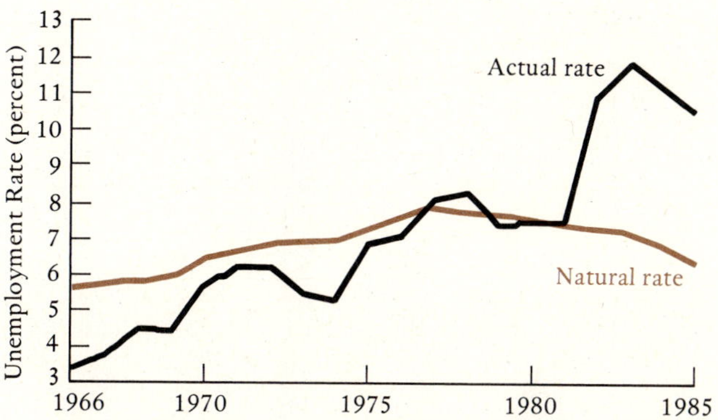

Fluctuations in aggregate unemployment reflect cyclical movements around a slowly changing natural rate of unemployment. The natural unemployment rate rose gradually from 5.3 percent in 1966 to 7.8 percent in 1978. It then fell gradually to 6.2 percent in 1985.

The actual unemployment rate fluctuated much more but also reflected some of the trend movements in the natural rate. The actual rate showed a distinct upward trend over the early part of the period, starting out at 3.4 percent, below the natural rate, in 1966 and reaching 8.1 percent, above the natural rate, in 1978. The actual rate then rose sharply in the early 1980s, reaching 11.9 percent in 1983, showing that the effects of the recession far outweighed the gradual decline in the natural rate. Since 1983 the actual rate has fallen steadily, reflecting the combined effects of the recovery and the fall in the natural rate.

research was reflected in the final report of the Macdonald Royal Commission in 1985, have estimated the natural rate to be somewhat higher, and hence would argue that cyclical unemployment was perhaps as low as 1.0 percent at the start of 1987. Nevertheless, most researchers agree that:

The rise in the actual unemployment rate over the late 1960s and most of the 1970s was accompanied by a rise in the natural unemployment rate; since then the natural rate has probably fallen somewhat.

Expressed as percentage points, the difference between 1.5 percent and 3.5 percent cyclical unemployment may not seem very big, but a reduction of two percentage points in the unemployment rate means that over a quarter of a million more people have jobs.

It is important to know how much deficient-demand unemployment exists. Raising aggregate demand when national income is already at its potential level, and hence when there is no deficient-demand unemployment, would open up an inflationary gap. This would accelerate inflation while achieving only a transitory fall in unemployment. We return to this below.

The Relative Importance of the Various Kinds of Unemployment

At the beginning of 1987 there were about 1.3 million unemployed in Canada, about 9.4 percent of the labor force. According to the most widely accepted estimates, most of this unemployment was frictional and structural, with deficient-demand accounting for something between 200,000 and 500,000.

Most of the deficient-demand unemployment that existed at the end of the recession in 1982 was eliminated by the subsequent recovery, and the remainder will be eliminated *if* the recovery takes the economy all the way to its potential income. But what of the more than a half million unemployed who will remain after deficient-demand unemployment is eliminated? To study them further we look at some of the characteristics of the unemployed.

Figure 37-2 gives some idea of the current duration of the spells of unemployment.[3] Data are given for 1982, a year of severe recession, and for 1986, when the economy was much closer to its potential income. The differences between the two sets of figures are due mainly to the reduction in deficient-demand unemployment over the period.

[3] The figures are based on the Labor Force Survey, which asks currently unemployed individuals how long they have been out of work. Notice that this gives us the duration of *currently uncompleted* bouts of unemployment. It gives different and shorter figures than the duration of *completed bouts* of unemployment, which is obtained by asking people who have just found a job how long they were out of work.

In 1986 some 28 percent of the unemployed had been out of work for 13 weeks or less. Long-term unemployment accounted for only 41 percent of the unemployed in that year. These figures represent some improvement over the recession year 1982, when only 18 percent of the unemployed had been without jobs for 4 weeks or less and 52 percent for more than 13 weeks. But the 1986 figures were not yet back to the more favorable ones for 1979, probably the last year when national income was at its potential level. In that year just less than one-third of the unemployed had been out of work for more than 13 weeks.

Three facts stand out about the unemployed. First, there is a group of marginal workers who move in and out of jobs, sometimes several times a year, and who account for a significant fraction of the total spells of unemployment. Second, most spells of unemployment are of short duration. Third, the bulk of total unemployment is accounted for by those in long-term unemployment. The consistency of the second and third points can be seen by a simple example. Consider four people, each unemployed for a week, and a fifth who is unemployed for nine months. For this group of five people, 80 percent of the spells of unemployment are short-term, but the long-term bout counts for 90 percent of the total weeks of unemployment.

It seems that the potentially soul-destroying bouts of prolonged periods without a job are confined to a relatively small part of the labor force, but a part that rises significantly in recessions.

Figures 37-3 and 37-4 document some of the inequalities in unemployment rates. Males and females, the young and the experienced have very different unemployment experiences, as Figure 37-3 shows. Equally dramatic are the differences between sectors, as shown in Figure 37-4.

FIGURE 37-2 Duration of Unemployment

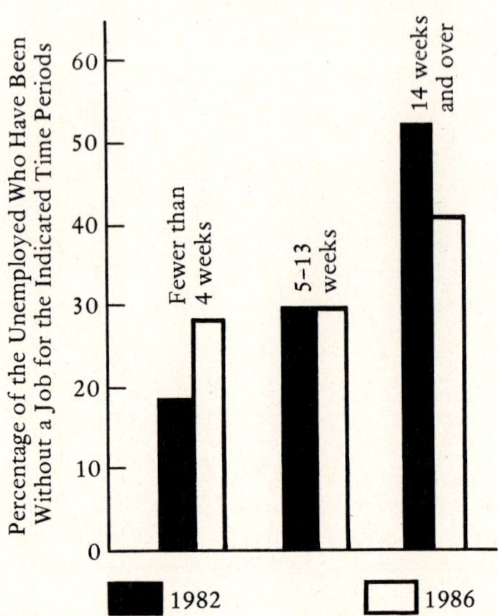

In recession years, the average duration of unemployment rises. In 1982, which was a year of severe recession and high overall unemployment, over half of the unemployed were without jobs for more than 13 weeks, while less than one-fifth were without jobs for less than 5 weeks. In 1986, a year of relative prosperity, only 41 percent of the unemployed were without jobs for more than 13 weeks, while over a quarter were without jobs for less than 5 weeks. (*Source:* Statistics Canada, *The Labour Force.*)

Why Does the Natural Rate of Unemployment Change?

Structural unemployment can increase because the pace of change accelerates or the pace of adjustment to change slows down. An increase in the rate of growth, for example, usually speeds up the rate at which the structure of the demand for labor is changing. The adaptation of labor to the changing structure of demand may be slowed by such diverse factors as a decline in education and new regulations that make it harder for workers in a given occupation to take new jobs in other states. Any of these changes will cause the natural rate of unemployment to rise. Changes in the opposite direction will cause the natural rate to fall.

Demographic changes. Because people usually try several jobs before settling into one for a longer period of time, young or inexperienced workers have higher unemployment rates than experienced workers. The proportion of inexperienced workers in the

FIGURE 37-3 Variations in Experience of Unemployment, 1982 and 1986

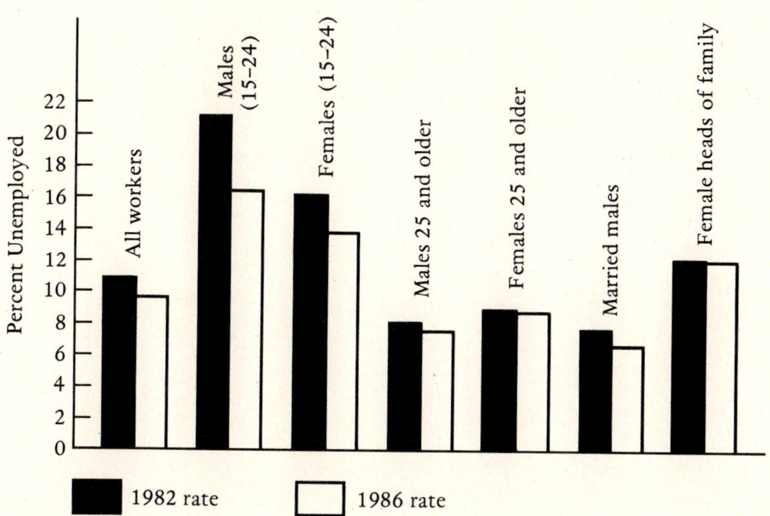

Unemployment is very unevenly divided among sex and skill groups. The overall unemployment rates of 11.0 and 9.6 percent in 1982 and 1986, respectively, concealed large variations in the unemployment rates of different groups. The recession of 1982 led to higher unemployment rates for most groups, but the difference between the 1982 rate and the 1986 rate varied considerably from group to group, with the largest decline being experienced by males between 15 and 24. The unemployment rate for this group fell from 21.2 percent in 1982 to the still high rate of 16.5 percent in 1986. (*Source: Canadian Statistical Review.*)

labor force rose significantly as the baby boom generation of the 1950s entered the labor force along with an unprecedented number of women who elected to work outside the home. It is estimated that these demographic changes added nearly a percentage point to the natural rate of unemployment. Since

FIGURE 37-4 Unemployment Rates by Sector, 1982 and 1986

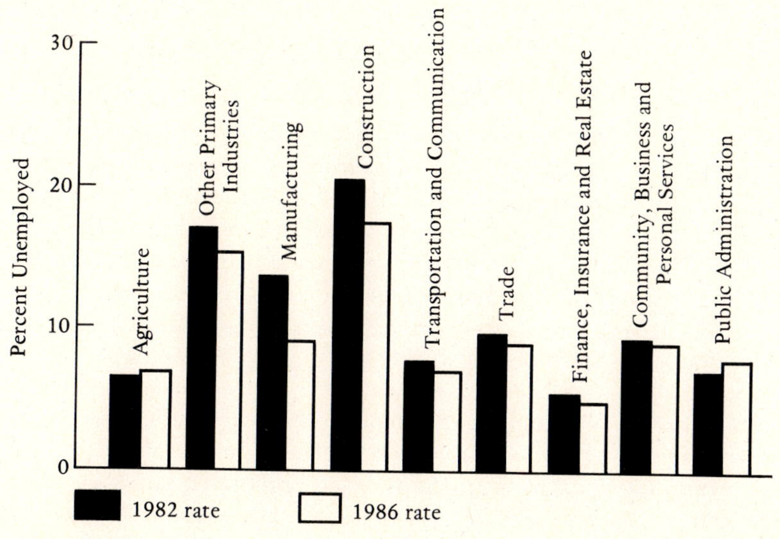

Unemployment rates vary greatly across sectors in both recessions and booms. Unemployment was highest in construction and lowest in finance, insurance, and real estate in both the recession year 1982 and the relatively prosperous year 1986. The ranking of unemployment rates by sector was unchanged between the two years, but there were considerable changes in the differences between sectors. (*Source:* Statistics Canada, *The Labour Force.*)

birthrates were low in the 1960s and a further increase in the percentage of females entering the labor force is unlikely, some demographically induced fall in this type of unemployment has been occurring recently and will continue over the next decade.

Although the natural rate of unemployment, and youth unemployment in particular, should fall as the baby boom generation passes on to middle age, many worry that although the brighter, the more energetic, and the luckier of that generation will do well, many others will not. Learning by on-the-job experience is a critical part of developing marketable labor skills. Many who are in the ranks of youth unemployment have been denied that experience early in their working careers. They may be condemned to remain at best marginal workers taking temporary jobs with low current pay and little future job security.

Other significant changes include the large increase in female participation rates and the related increase in the number of households with more than one income earner. In 1960 only 30 percent of females 20 years and older were in the labor force; in 1972 the figure was 38 percent; by 1986 it had jumped to almost 50 percent. When both husband and wife work, it is possible for one to support both while the other looks for "a really good job" rather than accepting the first job offer that comes along.

Wage and price rigidity. Recent research suggests that the speed with which wages and prices adjust to changing market conditions may have slowed over the years. Anything that slows the speed of adjustment to the economy's ever-changing conditions will create a larger pool of structural unemployment.

Social insurance programs. Minimum-wage laws are of real help to those who keep their jobs when their wages are forced up. They hurt those who lose their jobs as a result of the higher wage rates. They may also have a longer-term harmful effect. Employers are discouraged from hiring young people at low wages while providing on-the-job training. During a period of training, employees acquire marketable skills that allow them subsequently to command a higher wage. By discouraging such practices, minimum-wage laws create a pool of people without skills who alternate between low-paid jobs and bouts of unemployment, thus raising the number of people who are in structural or frictional unemployment at any one time.

Enriched unemployment insurance benefits will, as discussed in Box 37-1, make it easier for the unemployed to maintain living standards while searching for a new job. As a result they can afford to turn down job offers in anticipation of potential better offers. This serves to increase the amount of search unemployment and probably played a role in the increase in the natural rate in the 1970s.

Increasing structural change. The amount of resource reallocation across industries and areas appears to have increased in the 1970s. In part this is the result of the increasing integration of the Canadian economy with that of the rest of the world. Most observers feel that on balance this integration has been beneficial. But one less fortunate consequence is that changes in demand or supply conditions anywhere in the world requiring adjustments throughout the world's trading sectors increasingly affect Canada.

Internationally, one of the most significant demand changes for North America in the 1970s was the emergence of the Eastern bloc countries as major food importers. The failure of their system of collective agriculture to meet domestic demand led them to become large importers of grain. To pay for these imports, they had to become major exporters of other commodities such as natural gas.

A further demand change was the input price shocks that buffeted the world in the 1970s and early 1980s: two enormous oil price increases in the 1970s and an increase of over 200 percent in average basic materials prices in the early 1970s. Such changes have shifted competitive advantages in industrial production, leading to growth in some areas and countries and decline in others.

Changing prices have also caused changes in quantities demanded. The high cost of gas and oil led to a shift to small cars, an enormous investment program to retool North American industry, and major car imports from Japan and Germany that cut heavily into the demand for North American cars and for their major inputs such as steel. The results were all too evident in the unemployment figures. At the beginning of 1983, when the overall unemployment rate was just below 12 percent, unemployment was estimated to be more than double that rate in the auto industry and in primary metals. Some of these workers were recalled as output recovered, but many had to find jobs in other industries and areas where new skills were required. Rising oil prices also led to a shift to natural gas for home heating, a large demand for insulation, and alterations in typical designs of new houses.

In the mid 1980s another set of changes more or less reversed the ones just discussed. These entailed a new and equally dramatic set of adjustments. More than a decade of high oil prices had led to a reduction in demand for oil and a great increase in its supply. Finally the OPEC countries were no longer able to control the price of oil, which tumbled in a few months during 1985–1986 to about one-third of its earlier value. The immediate effects were felt by the world's oil producers, Canada among them. A rash of business bankruptcies and bank difficulties (including two bank failures) were brought on by the sudden loss of prosperity among both oil producers and organizations that sold to them or had lent to them. Oil users benefited greatly. Just as the high price of oil set in motion a series of adjustments that economized on oil, the low price set in train the opposite series of adjustments. Once again the pattern of advantage of different technologies, products, and geographic areas changed, and major adaptations occurred.

The world food shortages in the 1970s and the accompanying high prices of foodstuffs caused a number of supply reactions to occur throughout that decade. Many countries, including a number of less-developed countries, expanded their food production enormously. They were aided by technological developments that greatly increased crop yields per acre. By the mid 1980s food shortages were threatening to turn into surpluses for many products. Difficult times for Canadian farmers were already evident by the mid 1980s—although these were to some extent due to overborrowing during the earlier period of expansion. Serious slumps in world agricultural markets could have serious consequences for Canadian agriculture and would entail further major readjustments in the Canadian economy, among both farmers and all who depend on farm income for their own sales.

A further factor on the cost side has been the increased use of robots in factories and computer-based processes in offices. These changes have eliminated many assembly line and clerical jobs and forced their former holders to look elsewhere for new jobs.

Another major set of forces leading to structural change arises from the shifting pattern of demand. As a result of rising income and changing social patterns, people spend a higher proportion of their income on services than they used to and a correspondingly smaller proportion on manufactured goods. Restaurant meals and day-care facilities for children are two services with rising demands. This shift is dramatically illustrated by the fact that the *increase* in employment in the North American fast food industry during the past two decades exceeded the total combined employment in the automobile and steel industries!

The pace of technological change since the start of the 1970s has contributed greatly to an increase in the level of structural unemployment.

Future outlook. Certain factors may work to reduce the natural rate of unemployment in the future. First, the proportion of youths and females newly entering the labor force will diminish as the baby boom generation ages and the female participation rate stabilizes. Second, educational systems in some or all provinces may be revamped to give students better job-related training. Third, governments may become more aware of the importance of structural changes in the economy and of the need for policies to encourage rather than inhibit adaptability and flexibility in the economy.

Unemployment Policies

All kinds of unemployment have costs in terms of the output that could have been produced by the unemployed workers. Yet reducing unemployment is also costly. For example, retraining and reallocation schemes designed to reduce structural unemployment use scarce resources.

BOX 37-3

Difficulties in Using Demand Management to Reduce Unemployment

Deficient demand unemployment represents an unnecessary waste of human resources and causes serious economic and social costs. Macroeconomics explains how monetary and fiscal policies can be used to reduce such unemployment. But the issues encountered in this chapter suggest that it may be difficult to identify the extent of deficient demand unemployment, and hence to identify the appropriate policy stance.

Changes in the Natural Unemployment Rate

Policy errors can result from a failure to distinguish between changes in the natural rate of unemployment and cyclical fluctuations around the natural rate.

If the actual unemployment rate rises because the natural rate has risen, stimulating aggregate demand would not be an appropriate response. Increased demand will have little effect on unemployment but will lead to increased inflation. Most observers agree that this is what happened in Canada in the early 1970s.

Similarly, pursuing contractionary policies because the actual unemployment rate is falling may cause a recessionary gap to open up if the natural rate is also falling. Many observers warn that this may be a problem for the late 1980s and early 1990s when the natural rate is expected to fall.

Real-Wage Unemployment

Even if the natural rate of unemployment, and hence the cyclical component of actual unemployment, are correctly measured, the correct policy stance may be difficult to determine. As we also saw in the text, cyclical unemployment includes both deficient demand and real-wage unemployment. Stimulating aggregate demand in the face of real-wage unemployment may cause inflation without reducing unemployment.

We saw in Chapter 36 (see especially Figure 36-1 on page 776) that a real-wage shock opens up a recessionary gap, and hence increases unemployment. If the real-wage shock is temporary, monetary accommodation reduces the recessionary gap at the cost of a once-and-for-all rise in the price level. If, however, the real-wage shock was permanent, so that nominal wages increase in response to the rise in the price level, monetary accommodation would trigger a wage-price spiral with little or no effect on the unemployment rate.

The Natural Rate Revisited

Recently some economists have argued that the natural rate of unemployment itself may have a cyclical component.

The argument is that business cycles are often accompanied by large swings in key relative prices. The international terms of trade, the price of raw materials and resources relative to manufactures, and the relative price of services are examples of relative prices that change substantially in the face of cyclical fluctuations. As a result, the relative profitabilities of different firms, sectors, and regions change, and workers laid off in declining sectors seek employment in other sectors. For all the reasons discussed in the text, this "mismatch" of workers with job opportunities, which occur as a result of aggregate cyclical fluctuations, will temporarily increase the level of structural unemployment in the economy.

A related reason for structural unemployment to respond to cyclical fluctuations lies in the operation

It would be neither possible nor desirable to reduce unemployment to zero. The causes of unemployment could never be removed completely, and reducing the amount of unemployment stemming from those causes is costly.

Unemployment insurance is one method of helping people cope with unemployment. Certainly, it has reduced significantly the human costs of the bouts of unemployment that are inevitable in a changing society. Nothing, however, is without cost.

of Canada's Unemployment Insurance Act. The regional extended benefits provisions of the Unemployment Insurance Act allow for extended benefits to accrue to workers in regions with unusually high unemployment rates. During the 1982–1983 recession many Canadian regions suffered high enough unemployment to qualify for these extended benefits. The increased generosity of benefits not only provided for more support for the unemployment during the deep recession, it also allowed for increased search and hence increased structural unemployment during the recovery. As a result, the actual unemployment rate in these regions fell only slowly during the recovery. But this slow decline was because of the persistent structural unemployment, not because of continued deficient demand unemployment.

Economists who stress the importance of these cyclical movements in structural unemployment argue that estimates of the natural rate of unemployment, such as those reported in Figure 37-1, *understate* the extent of structural unemployment following a major recession such as occurred in Canada in the early 1980s.

Implications for Policy

The estimates presented in Figure 37-1 suggest that cyclical unemployment in 1986 stood at about 3 percent. Many economists—including the author of those estimates, Professor Pierre Fortin of Laval University—argue that there is little real wage unemployment, so that the entire 3 percent represents deficient demand unemployment. Not surprisingly, these economists call for substantial demand stimulus to eliminate what they perceive to be an enormous recessionary gap.

At the other extreme, some economists argue that the natural rate is currently much larger than the 6.2 percent of Figure 37-1, and hence that cyclical unemployment is smaller than indicated by the figure. They also argue that there is considerable real wage unemployment in Canada, so that the remaining deficient demand unemployment is negligible. As a result these economists oppose the introduction of any demand stimulus on the grounds that such stimulus will only create an inflationary gap.

A third group of economists believe that deficient demand unemployment in 1986 was somewhere between the two extremes identified above but were nevertheless opposed to the use of demand stimulus. Their argument was that the deficient demand unemployment was the necessary price of combatting inflation—indeed, creating deficient demand was an explicit goal of policy. These economists argue that in order to maintain the credibility of the government's commitment to fighting inflation, it was necessary to wait for the automatic adjustment mechanism to reduce the recessionary gap, rather than to reverse the stance of aggregate demand policies.

A further lesson arises from the inherent uncertainty attached to identifying the amount of deficient demand unemployment. One view is that because of the uncertainty, demand management should be used cautiously. While fine tuning may be ruled out, periods with persistent deficient demand unemployment can be identified and expansionary demand policy can then be safely used. Other economists argue, however, that the extent of the uncertainty makes any targeting of demand policy on unemployment ill-advised—they would argue that demand policies should focus only on controlling inflation.

While unemployment insurance alleviates the suffering caused by some kinds of unemployment, it can itself contribute to unemployment for, as we have observed, it encourages search unemployment.

Supporters of unemployment insurance emphasize its benefits. Critics emphasize its costs. As with any policy, a rational assessment of the value of unemployment insurance requires a balancing of its undoubted benefits against its undoubted costs. Most Canadians seem convinced that when this calculation

BOX 37-4

Industrial Change: An Economist's Cautionary Tale

The audience hushed as the royal commissioners filed into the room. The chief forecasting wizard—behind his back some called him the economic soothsayer—began his report. "I have identified beyond reasonable doubt the underlying trends now operating," he declared to an expectant audience. "The nation's leading industry, industry X, is in a state of decline. From its current position of employing 50 percent of our work force it will, within the duration of one human lifetime, employ only 5 percent."

"Forty-five percent of the nation's jobs destroyed within one lifetime!" proclaimed the newspaper headlines.

"Where can new jobs possibly come from at so rapid a pace?" asked a labor leader.

"We must protect industry X; we just cannot let all these jobs go down the tubes," argued an employer.

"Perhaps we should identify and promote new 'sunrise industries,' " said a mandarin. Indeed, it was widely believed that a new high-tech product, product Y, would be the wave of a future new transportation revolution, and a call went out for subsidies and tax expenditures to back its development.

"Is there any hope that the private sector might provide the new jobs?" someone asked.

"Possibly," said a junior economist, more out of desperation than hope, "the new product Z that is being produced by a few people in backyard sheds might grow to be a significant employer."

He was immediately pounced on by a chorus of more realistic thinkers. "Product Z! It's noisy, it's smelly, and it's a plaything for the rich. Surely *it* will never provide significant employment."

All of the economic facts in the above tale are true; only the royal commission and the policy initiatives are fictitious.

The country was Canada.

The time was 1900.

Industry X, the employer of 50 percent of the work force, was agriculture.

Product Y, the sunrise industry, was zeppelins.

Product Z, the scorned plaything of the rich, was automobiles.

The decline of some traditional industries is a cause for concern. Some are suffering a temporary decline, and some are declining permanently. In either event, the hardships on those losing their jobs are severe. The tale does, however, have a serious message. Here are a few of the lessons that can be gleaned from a look at the Canadian economy of 1900:

1. The economy is constantly changing. Indeed, the motto of any market economy could be "nothing is permanent." New products appear continually, while others disappear.

At the early stage of a new product, total demand is low, costs of production are high, and many small firms are each trying to get ahead of their competitors by finding the twist that appeals to consumers or the

---

is made, the benefits greatly exceed the costs, although many also recognize the scope for reform of certain aspects of the program, as discussed in Chapter 25 (pages 535–538).

Deficient-Demand Unemployment

We do not need to say much more about this type of unemployment since its control is the subject of stabilization policy, which we have studied in several earlier chapters. A major recession that occurs due to natural causes can be countered by monetary and fiscal policy to reduce deficient-demand unemployment. Some potential pitfalls in using aggregate demand management to reduce perceived deficient demand unemployment are identified in Box 37-3 (see pages 818–819).

The 1970s and 1980s saw the emergence of *policy-induced* deficient-demand unemployment. This occurred when, in an attempt to combat inflation, the government adopted drastic contractionary policies that opened up large recessionary gaps. As we saw in Chapter 36, a temporary bout of deficient-demand unemployment was the price of reducing inflation.

technique that slashes costs. Sometimes new products never get beyond that phase—they prove to be passing fads. Others, however, do become items of mass consumption.

Successful firms in growing industries buy up, merge with, or otherwise eliminate their less successful rivals. Simultaneously, their costs fall, owing to scale economies. Competition drives prices down along with costs.

Eventually, at the mature stage, a few giant firms often control the industry. They become large, conspicuous, and important parts of the nation's economy. Sooner or later, new products arise to erode the position of the established giants. Demand falls off, and unemployment occurs as the few firms run into financial difficulties.

A large, sick, declining industry may appear to many as a national failure and a disgrace. At any moment, however, firms can be found in all phases—from small firms in new industries to giant firms in declining industries. Large declining industries are as much a natural part of a healthy changing economy as large stable industries and small growing ones.

2. The policy of shoring up the declining industries of the 1980s could be just as destructive of our living standards as the policy of protecting the agricultural sector from decline in 1900 would have been. (Policies that ease the human cost of the adjustment are, however, to be recommended.)

3. To tell where the new employment will come from requires the kind of crystal ball our young economist would have needed in 1900 to stick by his wild guess of identifying the new plaything of the rich as the massive automobile industry 30 years later.

Economists are continually asked, "Where will the new employment come from?" The answer "we don't know" is *wrongly* taken to mean "it won't come." In the past, the new jobs have come, and we see no new identifiable forces to prevent their coming in the future. For example, in the course of the current recovery, many people gaining employment are starting in *new* jobs—jobs with firms and in locations that did not exist or would not have been predicted even five years ago.

4. Picking winners and backing them by government policy is a sure way to waste public funds and inhibit the development of the real winners. People risking their own money and diversifying risks over many ventures are a surer route to employment creation than governments risking taxpayers' money and mesmerized by a few current fads and fashion.

5. The industrial policy we do need is one that encourages private initiatives and risk taking. Small businesses are often, if not always, the route to the creation of new employment. Risk taking and the growth of small firms should not be discouraged by such things as complicated regulatory rules and tax laws.

Real-Wage Unemployment

If this type of unemployment is a major problem, its cure is not an easy matter. Basically what is required is a fall in the real product wage combined with measures to increase aggregate demand so as to create enough total employment. But, as many European countries have discovered, the cure is slow and requires enough time to install new labor-using capital.

The steps might be as follows. First, the real product wage would have to fall substantially. Then, since wages enter into disposable income and disposable income determines consumer demand, the cut in wages would tend to reduce aggregate demand and hence reduce equilibrium national income. This deflationary force could then be countered by expansionary fiscal and monetary policy that would create sufficient aggregate demand to restore full employment.

Frictional Unemployment

The turnover that causes frictional unemployment is an inevitable part of the functioning of the economy.

Insofar as it is caused by ignorance, increasing the knowledge of workers about market opportunities may help. But such measures have a cost, and that cost has to be balanced against the benefits.

Some frictional unemployment is an inevitable part of the learning process. One reason that there is a high turnover rate, and hence high frictional unemployment, is that new entrants have to try jobs to see if they are suitable. They will typically try more than one job before settling into one that most satisfies, or least dissatisfies, them.

Structural Unemployment

The reallocation of labor among occupations, industries, skill categories, and regions that gives rise to structural unemployment is an inevitable part of growth. There are two basic approaches to reducing structural unemployment: First, try to arrest the changes that accompany growth, and, second, accept the changes and try to speed up the adjustments. Throughout history labor and management have advocated, and governments have tried, both approaches. Box 37-4 (see pages 820–821) gives a cautionary tale concerning the choice between the two.

Resisting change. Since the beginning of the Industrial Revolution workers have often resisted the introduction of new techniques to replace the older techniques at which they were skilled. This is understandable. New techniques often destroy the value of the knowledge and experience of workers skilled in the displaced techniques. Older workers may not even get a chance to start over with the new technique. Employers may prefer to hire younger persons who will learn the new skills faster than older workers who are set in their ways of thinking. From society's point of view, new techniques are beneficial because they are a major source of economic growth. From the point of view of the workers they displace, new techniques can be an unmitigated disaster.

Here are two characteristic ways in which economic change has been resisted. First, a declining industry may be supported with public funds. If the market would support an output of X, but subsidies are used to support an output of $2X$, jobs are provided for, say, half the industry's labor force who would otherwise become unemployed and have to find jobs elsewhere. Second, change may be accepted but agreement reached to continue to employ workers who would otherwise be made redundant by the new technology. Both these policies are attractive to the people who would otherwise become unemployed. It may be a long time before they can find another job, and when they do, their skills may not turn out to be highly valued in their new occupations.

In the long term, however, such policies are not beneficial. Agreements to hire unneeded workers raise costs and can hasten the decline of an industry threatened by competitive products. An industry that is declining due to economic change becomes an increasingly large burden on the public purse as economic forces become less and less favorable to its success. Sooner or later, public support is withdrawn, and an often precipitous decline then ensues.

In assessing these remedies for structural unemployment, it is important to realize that although they are not viable in the long run for the economy, they may be the best alternatives for the affected workers during their lifetimes.

There is often a genuine conflict between the workers threatened by structural unemployment, whose interests lie in preserving their jobs, and the general public, whose interest is served by economic growth, which is the engine of rising living standards.

Aiding adjustments to change. Another policy to deal with structural change is to accept the decline of industries and the destruction of specific jobs that go with it and to try to reduce the cost of adjustment for those affected. Retraining and relocation grants make movement easier and reduce structural unemployment without inhibiting economic change and growth. Retraining programs exist in a number of countries but have met with mixed success at best. Relocation grants are used successfully in countries such as Sweden but have not played a role in Canada.

A number of policies have been introduced in Canada. These have focused on two sources of adjustment problems. One is imperfections in capital markets that make it difficult for workers to borrow funds in order to retrain or relocate. The other is the lack of good information about current and future job prospects.

A major aspect of labor market policies is education. Between 1960 and 1986, university enrollment rose from 107,000 to 467,000 and community college enrollment increased from 50,000 to 322,000. Over the same period, the number of persons undertaking technical training increased from fewer than 5,000 to over 350,000, partly under the stimulus of the Adult Occupational Training Act of 1967.

Policies to improve the flow of information include the creation of job banks and information centers and initial steps toward a nationwide computerized information system called Jobscan. Job creation programs such as the Local Employment Assistance Programme, Canada Community Services Projects, New Technology Employment Programme, and Summer Canada are also major labor market policies aimed at structural unemployment.

A number of programs that aid adjustment in a variety of ways exist under the National Training Act and the Labour Adjustment Benefits Act. The Canadian Mobility Programme, which finances relocation and travel assistance, spends about $8 million annually, and each year helps about 5,000 workers relocate permanently and another 20,000 temporarily. Women's employment counseling centers serve 5,000 women entering or re-entering the work force each year. Other services meet the special needs of such groups as the physically disabled, criminal offenders, and youths.

In 1985 the Conservative government introduced a Canadian Job Strategy. This strategy involved federal expenditures of about $1.4 billion annually toward six programs, the biggest of which were Job Development, Job Entry, and Skill Shortages. These programs were directed to groups such as women, aboriginal peoples, and disabled persons who were perceived as being "disadvantaged" in labor markets. The funds are allocated on a regional basis. The $1.4 billion does not, however, all represent new expenditures, as a number of existing labor market adjustment programs—including the Industry and Labour Adjustment Program and the Canadian Industrial Renewal Program—were discontinued.

Some of the changes appear to be merely window-dressing, but some real changes were effected. The government defended the changes on the grounds that the old programs provided only "short-term responses to labour market fluctuations," while the new programs concentrated on directing help to individuals who need it most. Critics of the changes argued that short-term assistance is all that is needed to promote adjustment, and that the changes in some cases replace pro-adjustment policies with disguised welfare payments, often distributed in a manner more geared to the political interests of the government than to the adjustment needs of the economy.

Summary

1. Unemployment may be voluntary or involuntary. Involuntary unemployment is a serious social concern both because it causes economic waste due to lost output and because it is a source of human suffering.
2. Looking at causes, it is useful to distinguish several kinds of unemployment: (a) frictional unemployment, which is due to the time it takes to find a first job and to move from job to job as a result of normal labor turnover; (b) structural unemployment, which is caused by the need to reallocate resources among occupations, regions, and industries as the structure of demands and supplies changes; (c) deficient-demand unemployment, which is caused by too low a level of aggregate demand; and (d) real-wage unemployment, which is caused by too high a real product wage. Together the amounts of

frictional unemployment and structural unemployment make up what is now called the natural rate of unemployment.

3. Measured unemployment figures may overestimate or underestimate the actual number of unemployed, for they may include some people who are voluntarily unemployed and omit discouraged workers who have left the labor force.
4. The natural rate of unemployment has risen in recent years. This is due in part at least to demographic changes in the work force, increasing wage and price rigidity in the economy, increasing generosity of unemployment compensation and other social insurance programs, and increasing structural change in the economy.
5. Unemployment insurance helps to alleviate the human suffering associated with inevitable unemployment. It also increases unemployment by encouraging voluntary unemployment.
6. Unemployment can be reduced by raising aggregate demand, by making it easier to move between jobs, by slowing down the rate of change in the economy, and by raising the cost of staying unemployed. However, it is neither possible nor desirable to reduce unemployment to zero.

Topics for Review

Voluntary and involuntary unemployment
Deficient-demand unemployment
Frictional unemployment
Structural unemployment
Real-wage unemployment
Effects of demographic and structural changes on unemployment

Discussion Questions

1. Interpret the following statements from newspapers in terms of types of unemployment
   a. Recession hits local factory, 2,000 laid off.
   b. "A job? I've given up trying," says mother of three.
   c. "We closed down because we could not stand the competition from Taiwan," says local manager.
   d. "When they raised the minimum wage, I just could not afford to keep all of these retired policemen on my payroll as security guards," says local shopping center owner.
   e. Slack demand puts local foundry on short time.
   f. "Of course, I could take a job as a dishwasher, but I'm trying to find something that makes use of my high school training," says local teenager in our survey of the unemployed.
   g. "Thank God for the minimum wage. Without it, I couldn't earn enough to feed the kids," says single father of four.
   h. Retraining main challenge in increased use of robots.
   i. Modernization may cut textile employment.
   j. Uneven upturn: signs of recovery hit Ontario, but B.C. and Alberta still in recession.

2. What differences in approach to unemployment are suggested by the following facts?
   a. Britain has spent billions on subsidizing firms that would otherwise have gone out of business in order to protect the jobs of the employees.
   b. Sweden has pioneered in spending large sums to retrain and relocate displaced workers.
3. Discuss the following views:
   a. "Canadian workers should resist automation, which is destroying their jobs," says a labor leader.
   b. "Given the fierce foreign competition, it's a case of automate or die," says an industrialist.
4. Discuss the following quotation: "There is nothing natural about the natural rate of unemployment; we should not let the inappropriate name 'natural' mislead us into believing that this amount of unemployment should be accepted as normal."
5. Use the latest *Bank of Canada Review* to compare the percentage of total long-term unemployment in the most recent year available with the figures for earlier years given in the text of this chapter. Can you think of any reasons why the figures have changed?
6. What theories can you suggest to explain why unemployment rates stay persistently above average for youths and below average for males over 25?
7. It is often argued that the true unemployment figure for Canada is much higher than the officially reported figure. What are possible sources of "hidden unemployment"? On the other side, are there reasons for expecting some exaggeration of the number of people reported as unemployed? Would the relative strength of these opposing forces change over the course of the business cycle? What would you expect if a short recession turned into a long and deep depression?
8. At a time when the Canadian unemployment rate stood at close to 10 percent, the press reported, "Skilled labor shortage plagues many firms—newspaper ads often draw few qualified workers; wages over time are up." What type of unemployment does this suggest to be important?

38

Economic Growth

Popular debate is bedeviled by confusion about the various causes of change in national income. Some commentators argue that governments can spend their way into a rising national income. Others argue that while expansionary government policies may stimulate the economy in the short run, they often have adverse effects on growth in the economy in the long run.

Causes of Increases in Real National Income

Figure 38-1 illustrates some of the most important possibilities. If there is a recessionary gap, raising aggregate demand will yield a once-and-for-all increase in national income. But once potential income is achieved, further increases in aggregate demand yield only transitory increases in real income but lasting increases in the price level.

Measures that reduce structural unemployment can also increase the employed labor force and thus increase potential income. The increase in income resulting from this change might not be very large. There would, however, be social gain resulting from the reduction in unemployment, especially the long-term unemployment that occurs when people are trapped in declining areas, industries, or occupations.

Over the long haul, however, what really raises national income is *economic growth*, that is, the increase in potential income due to changes in factor supplies (labor and capital) or in the productivity of factors (output per unit of factor input). The removal of a serious recessionary gap might raise national income by 10 percent, while the elimination of all structural unemployment might raise it by somewhat less. But a modest growth rate of 3 percent per year raises national income by 10 percent in 3 years and *doubles* it in about 24 years.

Over any long period of time, economic growth rather than variations in aggregate demand or in structural unemployment exerts the major effect on real national income.

Effects of Investment and Saving on National Income

Short-Run and Long-Run Effects of Investment

The theory of income determination that we studied in Part Eight is a short-run theory. It takes potential income as constant and concentrates

FIGURE 38-1 Ways of Increasing National Income

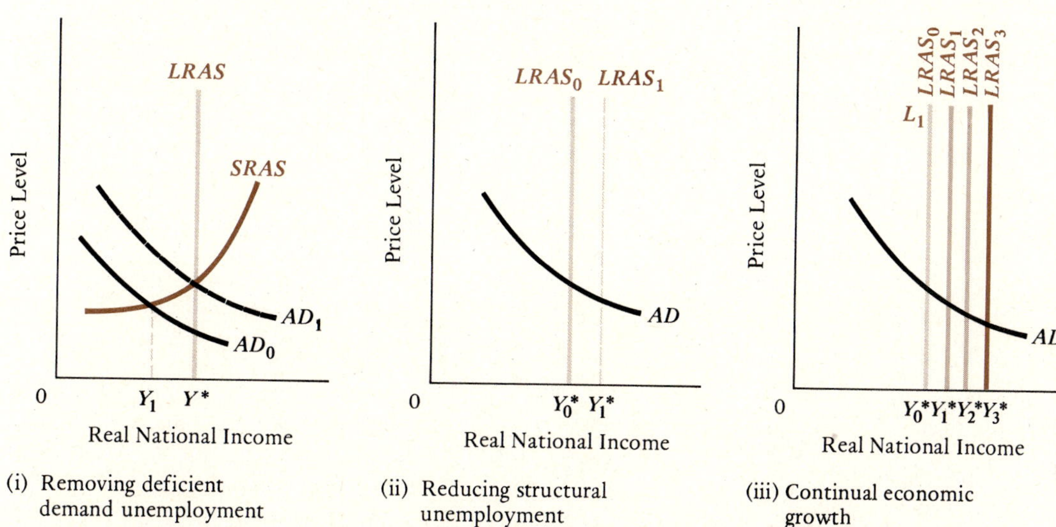

(i) Removing deficient demand unemployment

(ii) Reducing structural unemployment

(iii) Continual economic growth

A once-and-for-all increase in national income can be obtained by raising aggregate demand to remove a recessionary gap or by shifting the *LRAS* curve by cutting structural unemployment. Continued increases in national income are possible by shifting the *LRAS* curve through continued economic growth. In part (i), with the aggregate demand curve at AD_0, there is a recessionary gap of Y_1Y^*. An increase in aggregate demand from AD_0 to AD_1 takes equilibrium to E_1, achieving a once-and-for-all change in national income from Y_1 to Y^*.

In part (ii) potential output rises from Y_0^* to Y_1^* due to measures that reduce structural unemployment. The *LRAS* curve shifts from $LRAS_0$ to $LRAS_1$ because people who were formerly unemployed due to having the wrong skills or being in the wrong place are now available for employment.

In part (iii) increases in factor supplies and productivity lead to increases in potential income. This *continually* shifts the long-run aggregate supply curve outward. In successive periods it moves from $LRAS_0$ to $LRAS_3$, taking potential income from Y_0^* to Y_1^* to Y_2^* to Y_3^* *and so on, as long as growth continues.*

on the effect of investment expenditure on aggregate demand. Short-run national income theory concentrates on variations of actual national income around a given potential income. This short-term viewpoint is the focus of Figure 38-1(i).

In the long run, by adding to the nation's capital stock, investment raises potential income. This effect is shown by the continuing outward shift of the *LRAS* curve in Figure 38-1(iii).

The theory of economic growth is a long-run theory. It ignores short-run fluctuations of actual national income around potential income and concentrates on the effects of investment in raising potential income.

The contrast between the short- and long-run aspects of investment is worth emphasizing. In the short run, any activity that puts income into people's hands will raise aggregate demand. Thus the short-run effect on national income is the same whether a firm invests in digging holes and refilling them or in building a new factory. The long-run growth of potential income, however, is affected only by the part of investment that adds to a nation's productive capacity, that is, by the factory but not by the refilled hole.

This point is important because some of what is classified as investment in the national income accounts is really consumption expenditure. Assume, for example, that a firm discards an adequate but dingy office building and "invests" in a lavish new head office building with superior facilities for its staff. This will count as investment in the national income data, and the expenditure will add to aggregate demand. In terms of growth, however, it is (at least in part) really disguised consumption for the firm's staff, not investment that will increase the productivity of its labor force.

Similar observations are true of public-sector expenditure. Any expenditure will add to aggregate demand and raise national income if there are unemployed resources. But only some expenditure adds to the growth of full-employment income. Indeed, public investment expenditure that shores up a declining industry in order to create employment may have an adverse effect on growth. Such expenditure may prevent the reallocation of resources in response to shifts both in the pattern of world demand and in the country's comparative advantage. Thus in the long run the country's capacity to produce commodities that are demanded on open markets may be diminished.

Short-Run and Long-Run Effects of Saving

The short-run effects of an increase in saving are to reduce aggregate demand. If, for example, households elect to save more, this means they spend less. The resulting downward shift in the consumption function lowers aggregate demand and thus lowers equilibrium national income.

In the longer term, however, higher savings are necessary for higher investment. Firms usually reinvest their own savings, while the savings of households pass to firms, either directly through the purchase of stocks and bonds or indirectly through financial intermediaries. If full employment is more or less maintained in the long run, the volume of investment will be strongly influenced by the volume of savings. The higher the savings, the higher the investment—and the higher the investment, the greater the rate of growth due to the accumulation of more and better capital equipment.

In the long run there is no paradox of thrift; societies with high savings rates have high investment rates and, other things being equal, high growth rates.

The Cumulative Nature of Growth

Growth is a much more powerful method of raising living standards than removing either recessionary gaps or structural unemployment *because it can go on indefinitely*. For example, a growth rate of 2 percent per year may seem insignificant, but if it continues for a century, it will lead to a more than sevenfold increase in real national income!

The cumulative effect of small annual growth rates is large.

To appreciate the cumulative effect of what seems like very small differences in growth rates, examine Table 38-1. Notice that when one country grows faster than another, the gap in their respective standards widens progressively. If countries A and B start from the same level of income, and if country A grows at 3 percent per year while country B grows at 2 percent per year, A's income per capita will be twice B's in 72 years. You may not think it matters much whether the economy grows at 2 percent or 3 percent per year, but your children and grandchildren will! (A helpful approximation device is the "rule of 72." Divide 72 by the growth rate, and the result is approximately the number of years it will take for income to double.) [48]

To dramatize the powerful long-run effects of differences in growth rates, we included in early editions of this text a table showing students of the 1960s that if the then current growth trends continued, the United States would not long remain the world's richest nation, for Sweden, Canada, Japan, and others were growing at a much faster rate. Many readers of that era rejected the notion as a textbook gimmick; deep down they knew that the material

TABLE 38-1 The Cumulative Effect of Growth

Year	Rate of growth per year 1%	2%	3%	5%	7%
0	100	100	100	100	100
10	111	122	135	165	201
30	135	182	246	448	817
50	165	272	448	1,218	3,312
70	201	406	817	3,312	13,429
100	272	739	2,009	14,841	109,660

Small differences in growth rates make enormous differences in levels of potential national income over a few decades. Assume that potential national income is 100 in year zero. At a rate of growth of 3 percent, it will be 135 in 10 years, 448 after 50 years, and over 2,000 in a century. Compound interest is a powerful force!

standard of living of the United States was and would remain the highest the world had ever known. Such a table is no longer even interesting, for by 1980 several industrial countries had indeed passed the United States in terms of per capita national income, and several more were within 10 percent of the U.S. level. Japan's experience is discussed in Box 38-1.

Growth, Efficiency, and Redistribution

Without any doubt, the most important single force leading to long-run increases in living standards is economic growth. To see this, let us compare the effects of growth with policies that increase economic efficiency or redistribute income. For the moment, we will consider a country with a constant population.

Making the economy more efficient can increase national income. But a once-and-for-all increase of between 5 and 10 percent would be an extremely optimistic estimate of what could be obtained by removing all economic inefficiencies.

Redistributing income can make lower-income people better off at the expense of higher-income people, but increasing the incomes of the bottom 20 percent of the people by, say, 10 percent above what they now are would be a very optimistic prediction of what could be done with further redistribution policies. In any case, without growth the magnitude of the income gains that can be achieved for lower-income groups through redistribution is limited by the size of national income.

Economic growth, however, can go on raising national income for as long as growth continues, which can be for centuries. Even the modest rate of growth of 2 percent per year takes less than five years to make it possible to raise everyone's income by the 10 percent that was suggested as the maximum that could be achieved by policies that raise efficiency once and for all. It takes just over nine years for the 2 percent growth rate to raise the living standards of the poor (and everyone else) by 20 percent—which is a very high estimate of what might be obtained through redistribution policies. Furthermore, the gain continues beyond those time horizons as long as the growth persists. The 2 percent growth rate doubles average living standards about every 35 years, so average living standards will quadruple over one biblically allotted lifetime of three score years and ten.

The continued importance of efficiency and redistribution. When we say that over the long term by far the most potent force for raising living standards is economic growth rather than reducing inefficiencies or redistributing income, we are *not* asserting the unimportance of policies designed to increase economic efficiency or to redistribute income.

Consider efficiency first. If at any moment we could increase national income by removing certain inefficiencies, the gains would be valuable. After all, any increase in national income is welcome in a world where there is not enough to satisfy everyone's wants. Furthermore, inefficiencies may themselves serve to reduce the growth rate. For example, rent control, which we saw in Chapter 7 can be criticized for reducing the efficiency of the housing market, may also be criticized for reducing the geographic mobility of labor that is necessary for economic growth.

Now consider redistribution. It may be some consolation for the poor to know they are vastly better off, thanks to economic growth, than they

BOX 38-1

A Case Study of Rapid Growth: Japan, 1953–1973

The real national income of Japan was 5.4 times as large in 1973 as it was in 1953. Japan's economic growth rate was more than double the average rate in 10 North American and European countries and greatly exceeded the rate in any of them. What accounted for the extraordinarily rapid growth of Japan's economy?

To answer that question, two economists, Edward F. Denison and William K. Chung, analyzed and measured the sources of economic growth in Japan over two decades and compared the results with those for 10 Western countries. They also measured the difference between levels of output per worker in the United States and Japan in 1970 and identified its sources and magnitude. The results were published in 1976.*

They found that no single factor was responsible for Japan's high postwar growth rate. Rather, the Japanese economy benefited from several major sources of growth: an increase in quantity of labor, an increase in quantity of capital, improved technology in production, and economies of scale. Japan gained more in each of these respects than any of the 10 other countries studied. In addition, Japan had the greatest reallocation of labor from agriculture to industry of all the countries studied except Italy. Since productivity is generally higher in industry than in agriculture, a shift of this kind raises average productivity and thereby contributes to growth even without an increase in output per person in either sector.

The overall growth record of Japan was high partly because of a low initial *level* of productivity. It is easier to improve from a low base than a high one. At the end of the period productivity was still more than 40 percent lower in Japan than in the United States, even after eliminating the effects of differences between the countries in working hours, in composition and allocation of the labor force, in amounts of capital and land, in size of markets, and in the cyclical positions of the two economies. There was thus an obvious potential for still further Japanese growth relative to the United States.

A question was, could Japan's growth rate be sustained? The authors stressed the probability of a decline in the growth rate as the various ways of securing fast growth by "catching up" are successively exhausted. Nevertheless, they considered a fairly high rate of long-term growth in Japan—between 5 and 8 percent per year—likely for the rest of this century. (This prediction proved accurate for the decade following the period covered by their study.) By the year 2000 Japan may well be enjoying the highest standard of living of any industrialized country in the world.

* Edward F. Denison and William K. Chung, *How Japan's Economy Grew So Fast: The Sources of Postwar Expansion* (Washington, D.C.: Brookings Institution, 1976).

would have been if they had lived 100 years ago. But this does not make it less upsetting if they cannot afford the basic medical treatment for themselves or schooling for their children that is available to higher-income citizens.

Interrelations among the policies. One important implication of the foregoing discussion is that policies to reduce inefficiencies or redistribute income need to be examined carefully for any effects they may have on economic growth. Any policy that reduces the growth rate may be a bad bargain, even if it increases the immediate efficiency of the economy or creates a more equitable distribution of income. Consider, for example, a hypothetical redistributive policy that raises the incomes of lower-income people by 5 percent but lowers the rate of economic growth from 2 to 1 percent. In 10 years, those who gained from the policy would be no better off than if they had not received the redistribution of income while the growth rate had remained at 2 percent (and, of course, everyone who did not gain from the redistribution would be worse off from the beginning). After 20 years' time, those who had gained from the redistribution would have 5 percent more of a national income that was 12 percent smaller than it would have been if the growth rate had remained at 2 percent.

Of course, not all redistribution policies have unfavorable effects on the growth rate. Some may have no effect, and others—by raising health and educational standards of ordinary workers—may raise the growth rate.

Theories of Economic Growth

In theoretical discussions of growth it is useful to have a measure of the ability of an economy to convert its resources into goods and services. One widely used measure is output per hour of labor, or *productivity*. Obviously, productivity depends not only on labor input but also on the amount and kind of machinery used, the raw materials available, and so on. The focus of this measure is explained by the special emphasis human beings place on labor.[1]

Economists today recognize that many different factors may contribute to or impede economic growth. Although our present knowledge of the relative importance of these factors is far from complete, modern economists look at the problems of growth more optimistically than did the classical economists of a century or more ago. Of particular importance is the nature and source of the investment opportunities that can lead to growth. The differences between the classical and contemporary points of view can best be understood by considering a revealing though extreme case.

Growth in a World with No Learning

Suppose that there is a known and fixed stock of projects that might be undertaken. Suppose also that nothing ever happens to increase either the supply of such projects or knowledge about them. Whenever the moment is right, some of the investment opportunities are utilized, thereby increasing the stock of capital goods and depleting the reservoir of unutilized investment opportunities. Of course, the most productive opportunities will be used first.

Such a view of investment opportunities can be represented by a fixed marginal efficiency of capital (*MEC*) schedule of the kind presented in Chapter 18. Such a schedule is graphed in Figure 38-2. It relates the stock of capital to the productivity of an additional unit of capital. The productivity of a unit of capital is calculated by dividing the annual value of the additional output resulting from an extra unit of capital by the value of that unit of capital. Thus, for example, a marginal efficiency of capital of 0.2 means that $1 of new capital adds $0.20 per year to the stream of output.

The downward slope of the *MEC* schedule indicates that, with knowledge constant, increases in the stock of capital bring smaller and smaller increases in output per unit of capital. That is, the rate of return on successive units of capital declines. This shape is a consequence of the law of diminishing returns discussed on pages 194–195.

If, with land, labor, and knowledge constant, more and more capital is used, the net amount added by successive increments will diminish and may eventually reach zero. As capital is accumulated in a state of constant knowledge, the society will move down its *MEC* schedule.

In such a "nonlearning" world, where new investment opportunities do not appear, growth occurs only so long as there are unutilized opportunities to use capital effectively to increase output. Growth in a nonlearning world is a transitory phenomenon that occurs as long as the society has a backlog of unutilized investment opportunities.

So far we have discussed the *marginal* efficiency of capital. The *average* efficiency of capital refers to the average amount produced in the whole economy per unit of capital employed. It is common in discussions of the theory of growth to talk in terms of the *capital-output ratio,* which is the reciprocal of output per unit of capital. In a world without learning the capital-output ratio is increasing.

[1] The discussion of productivity on pages 208–210 of Chapter 11 is relevant here. It should be read now and treated as part of this chapter. (Indeed, the whole section on the very long run, pages 207–211, could be usefully read now.)

FIGURE 38-2 The Marginal Efficiency of Capital Schedule

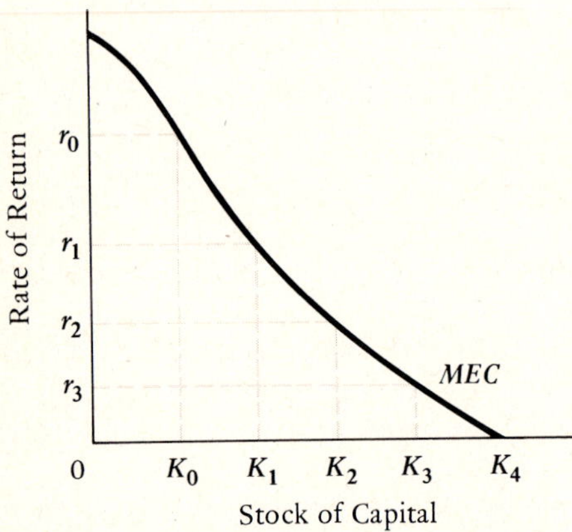

A declining *MEC* schedule shows that successive increases to the capital stock bring smaller and smaller increases in output and thus a declining rate of return. A fixed *MEC* schedule can represent the theory of growth in an economy with some unutilized investment opportunities but no learning. Increases in investment that increase the capital stock from K_0 to K_1 to . . . K_4 lower the rate of return from r_0 to r_1 to . . . zero. Because the productivity of successive units of capital decreases, the capital-output ratio rises.

In a world without learning the growth in the capital stock will have two important consequences:

1. **Successive increases in capital accumulation will be less and less productive, and the capital-output ratio will be increasing.**
2. **The marginal efficiency of new capital will be decreasing and will eventually be pushed to zero as the backlog of investment opportunities is used up.**

Consequences of Learning

The steady depletion of growth opportunities with constant knowledge results from the fact that new investment opportunities are never discovered or created. However, if investment opportunities are created as well as used up with the passage of time, the *MEC* schedule will shift outward over time, and the effects of increasing the capital stock may be different. This is illustrated in Figure 38-3.

Such outward shifts can be regarded as the consequences of "learning" either about investment opportunities or about the techniques that create such opportunities. As shown in the figure, when learning occurs, what matters is how rapidly the *MEC* schedule shifts relative to the amount of capital investment being undertaken.

Gradual reduction in investment opportunities: The classical view. If, as in Figure 38-3(i), investment opportunities are created, but at a slower rate than they are used up, there will be a tendency toward a falling rate of return and an increasing ratio of capital to output. The predictions in this case are the same as those given for the world without learning.

This figure illustrates the theory of growth held by most early economists. They saw the economic problem as one of fixed land, a rising population, and a gradual exhaustion of investment opportunities. These conditions, they believed, would ultimately force the economy into a static condition with no growth, high capital-output ratios, and the marginal return on additional units of capital forced down toward zero.

Constant or rising investment opportunities: The contemporary view. The pessimism of the classical economists came from their failure to anticipate the possibility of really rapid innovation—of technological progress that could push investment opportunities outward as shown in parts (ii) and (iii) of Figure 38-3.

In a world with rapid innovation:

1. **Successive increases in capital accumulation may prove highly productive, and the capital-output ratio may be constant or decreasing.**
2. **Despite large amounts of capital accumulation, the marginal efficiency of new capital may remain constant or even increase as new investment opportunities are created.**

FIGURE 38-3 Shifting Investment Opportunities: Three Cases

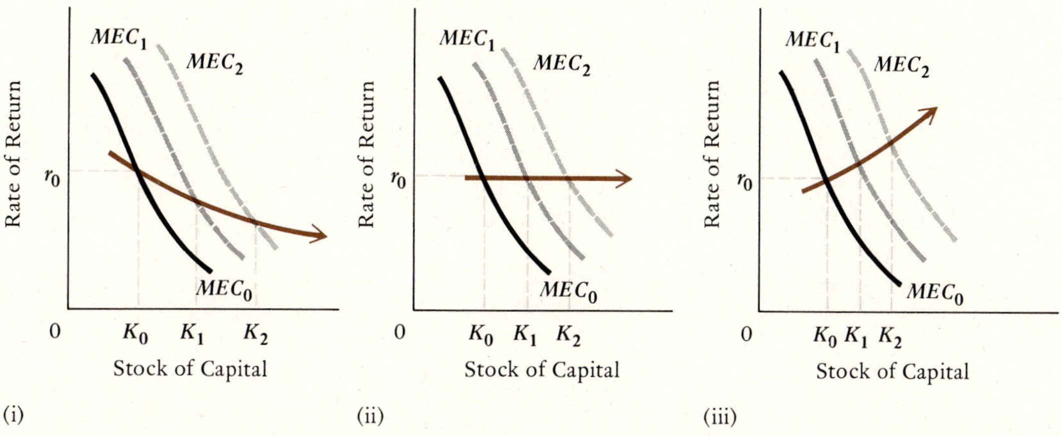

When both knowledge and the capital stock grow, the actual marginal efficiency of capital depends on their relative rates of growth. In each case the economy at period 0 has the MEC_0 curve, a capital stock of K_0, and a rate of return of r_0. In period 1 the curve shifts to MEC_1 and there is investment to increase the stock of capital to K_1. In period 2 the curve shifts to MEC_2 and there is new investment that increases the capital stock to K_2. It is the relative size of the shift of the *MEC* curve and the additions of the capital stock that are important.

In part (i) investment occurs more rapidly than increases in investment opportunities, and the rate of return falls along the black arrow. In part (ii) investment occurs at exactly the same rate as investment opportunities, and the rate of return is constant. In part (iii) investment occurs less rapidly than increases in investment opportunities, and the rate of return rises.

The historical record suggests that outward shifts in investment opportunities over time have led to the reality of sustained growth. Evidently modern economies have been successful in generating new investment opportunities at least as rapidly as old ones were used up. Modern economists devote more attention to understanding the *shifts* in the *MEC* schedule over time and less to its shape in a nonlearning situation.

Box 38-2 takes up some of the controversies surrounding government policies to promote learning and innovation.

A Contemporary View of Growth

The classical economists had a relatively simple theory of growth because they viewed a single mechanism—capital accumulation—as decisively important. Contemporary theorists begin by recognizing a number of factors that influence growth, no one of which is necessarily dominant.

Quantity of Capital Per Worker

Human beings have always been tool users. It is still true that more and more tools tend to lead to more and more output. As long as a society has unexploited investment opportunities, productive capacity can be increased by increasing the stock of capital. The effect on output per worker of "mere" capital accumulation is so noticeable that it was once regarded as virtually the sole source of growth.

But if capital accumulation were the only source of growth, it would lead to movement down the *MEC* schedule and to a rising capital-output ratio and a falling rate of return on capital. The evidence

BOX 38-2

Should Canada Adopt Policies to Promote R&D Expenditure?

Various groups have regularly argued that Canada's expenditure on research and development is too low and that the government should adopt policies to promote R&D spending. However, many economists are skeptical.

First, they insist that the actual level of R&D spending is difficult to measure. Professor Kristian Palda of Queen's University argues that current estimates of Canadian R&D expenditure are in fact serious underestimates. He writes:

> The leading edge of innovative industrial activity is widely found in small enterprises launched by engineers or scientists. . . . Their fairly high salaries are not carried on the R&D line of their corporate financial statements. In Canada, due to the heavy representation of the small-scale manufacturing firm, this undoubtedly leads to a substantial underestimate of industrial R&D effort and personnel.

In addition, "high technology" itself is difficult to define; it could mean "capital intensive," "value added per employee," or perhaps "skill level requirements per employee," depending on the circumstances. The blanket application of any one definition leads to absurd results. Professor Palda notes that if, for example, high technology were defined as an industry where research expenditures make a large contribution to the productivity of that industry, then agriculture would be the most technology-intensive industry in North America. Yet most blanket statements about the state of R&D expenditure in Canada do not even consider agriculture.

There is the related question, given the presence of foreign-owned subsidiaries in the Canadian economy, of whether the percentage of R&D expenditure within Canada is a relevant measure of technical performance. One study conducted by the federal Ministry of State for Science and Technology estimated that in one year in the mid 1970s the cost of "invisible" R&D performed for Canadian subsidiaries by their parent firms was $688 million. Canada may or may not be backward in its research *performance,* but that it suffers in terms of *access* to R&D results seems implausible.

Nevertheless, some groups have lobbied actively for policies to encourage R&D expenditure in Canada. What strategies are involved?

---

does not support these predictions. The facts suggest that investment opportunities have expanded as rapidly as investments in capital goods, roughly along the pattern of Figure 38-3(ii). While capital accumulation has taken place and has accounted for much observed growth, it cannot have been the only source of growth.

Quality of Capital

New knowledge and inventions can contribute markedly to the growth of potential national income, even without capital accumulation. To see this, assume that the proportion of the society's resources devoted to the production of capital goods is just sufficient to replace capital as it wears out. Thus if the old capital were merely replaced in the same form, the capital stock would be constant and there would be no increase in the capacity to produce. But if there is a growth of knowledge, so that as old equipment wears out it is replaced by different, more productive equipment, national income will be growing.

Increases in productive capacity that are intrinsic to the form of capital goods in use are called **embodied technical change.** The historical importance of embodied technical change is clear: The assembly line and automation transformed much of manufacturing, the airplane revolutionized transportation, and electronic devices now dominate the information technology industries. These innovations plus less well known but no less profound ones—for

One often quoted strategy is to "pick winners" and subsidize them. This approach raises two questions: Is the political will strong enough to let the losers sink, and is the political intellect bright enough to identify the potential winners? The evidence is that the answer to the first is often negative, and the answer to the second is that private investors making decisions about where to invest their own funds usually make better decisions.

Another proposal is to subsidize R&D directly. But it is possible that if governments actively promoted R&D, the private sector would reduce its R&D expenditure correspondingly. And giving R&D subsidies to firms that do not have a sufficient market may well be a waste of money: Technological improvements are of no advantage when they do not contribute to a marketable product; hence access to a large market is necessary.

A related proposal is to screen the import of foreign technology. Presumably this would stimulate R&D expenditure by keeping foreign technology out. Some would prefer to try to direct the import of technology into Canadian firms rather than to foreign subsidiaries. This would tend to reduce the role of foreign ownership in the Canadian economy, but it would result in a slower transmission of new technology and a higher price for what is transmitted.

Common to all these proposals is the advocacy of increased government involvement to promote "high technology" industries. But what are the costs of such intervention? Foreign experience tells us that the costs could be enormous. In examining the French experience with nuclear energy, aerospace computers, and electronics, Professor Palda shows that technology was ultimately imported from abroad only after expensive domestic programs had failed to be technically or economically successful.

Most economists remain rather skeptical about the need and the effectiveness of R&D policies. Professor Donald McFetteridge of Carleton University has argued that researchers have yet to produce any statistical evidence that the rate of return to industrial and R&D development in Canada is positive—let alone so high that it should be favored over alternative uses of scarce investment money.

example, improvements in the strength of metals, the productivity of seeds, and the techniques for recovering basic raw materials from the ground—create new investment opportunities.

Less obvious but nonetheless important changes occur through **disembodied technical change,** that is, changes in the organization of production that are not embodied in the form of the capital goods or raw materials used. One example is improved techniques of managerial control.

Most innovations involve both embodied and disembodied changes. But whatever the form of innovation, the nature of the goods and services consumed and the way they are made change continually as innovations occur. Major innovations of the past century have resulted from the development of the telephone, the linotype, the automobile, the airplane, plastics, the assembly line, coaxial cable, xerography, computers, transistors, and silicon chips. It would be hard for us to imagine life without them.

Quality of Labor

The "quality" of labor—or what is often called *human capital*—has several aspects. One involves improvements in the health and longevity of the population. Of course, these are desired as ends in themselves, yet they have consequences for both the size of the labor force and its productivity. There is no doubt that they have increased productivity per worker-hour by cutting down on illness, accidents, and absenteeism. At the same time the extension of the normal life span with no comparable increase in the working life span has created a larger group of nonworking aged that exercises a claim on total output. Whether health improvements alone have increased output per capita in the United States is not clear.

A second aspect of the quality of human capital concerns technical training, from learning to operate a machine to learning how to be a scientist. Training is clearly required to invent, operate, manage, and repair complex machines. More subtly, there are often believed to be general social advantages to an educated population. It has been shown that productivity improves with literacy and that, in general, the longer a person has been educated, the more adaptable he or she is to new and changing challenges and thus, in the long run, the more productive. But education may also increase feelings of alienation in a society that is thought to be arbitrary or unjust.

Quantity of Labor

The size of a country's population and the extent of its participation in the labor force are important in and of themselves, not merely because they affect the quantity of a factor of production. For this reason it is less common to speak of the quantity of people available for work as a source of or detriment to growth than it is to speak of the quantity of capital or iron ore in the same way. But clearly, for any given state of knowledge and supplies of other factors of production, the size of the population can affect the level of output per capita. Every child born has both a mouth and a pair of hands; over a lifetime each person will be both a consumer and a producer. Thus, on average, it is meaningful to speak of overpopulated or underpopulated economies, depending on whether the contribution to production of additional people would raise or lower the level of per capita income.

Because population size is related to income per capita, we can define a theoretical concept, *optimal population,* that maximizes income per capita.

Many countries have or have had conscious population policies. America in the nineteenth century sought immigrants, as did Australia until recently. Greece in the 1950s and 1960s tried to stem emigration to Western Europe. All are examples of countries that believed they had insufficient population, though the motives were not in every case purely economic. In contrast, many underdeveloped countries of South America, Africa, and Asia desire to limit population growth.

Structural Change

Changes in the economy's structure can cause large fluctuations in its growth rate. For example, an expansion in such low-productivity sectors as agriculture and a decline in such high-productivity sectors as manufacturing will temporarily lower the measured aggregate growth rate.

When one type of energy (say, solar) supplants another type (say, oil), much existing capital stock specifically geared to the original energy source may become too costly to operate and will be scrapped. New capital geared to the new energy source will be built. During the transition, investment expenditure is high, thus stimulating aggregate demand. But there is little if any expansion in the economy's output capacity because the old capital goods have been scrapped. Gross investment is high, but net investment is low since the capital expenditure *transforms* the capital stock, but does not *increase* it. Similarly, new pollution control laws will affect investment expenditure but will not lead to growth in capacity. (The reduction in pollution may nonetheless be socially desirable.)

A rise in the international price of *imported* energy will also lower productivity. Although the same volume of goods can be produced with a given input of labor, a smaller portion of the output's value now accrues as income to domestic workers and firms because more must be used to pay for the energy imports. The higher-priced imported energy input means that domestic *value added* falls, and with it GDP per worker. This shows up in the statistics as a decline in productivity and a temporary fall in growth rates.

These are some of the many factors that were operative in the 1970s and early 1980s. They worked to depress growth rates for some considerable period of time. But they are not permanent factors. When the structural adjustments are complete, their depressing effects will pass. Further, many of the effects were reversed when oil prices fell in early 1986, giving a boost to the productivity of many domestic factors of production.

Institutional Considerations

Almost all aspects of a country's institutions can foster or deter the efficient use of a society's natural and human resources. Social and religious habits, legal institutions, and traditional patterns of national and international trade are all important. So, too, is the political climate. In Chapter 22 many of these institutions were discussed as potential influences on development.

Is There a Most Important Source of Growth?

The modern theory of growth tends to reject a dominant source of growth and to recognize that several influences singly and in interaction affect the growth rate.

Among the major contributors to rapid economic growth are a capital stock that is steadily growing and improving in quality, a healthy and well-educated labor force, and a rate of population growth that is small enough to permit per capita growth in capital.

These factors are more likely to be used effectively in some institutional settings than in others.

A complete theory of growth would do more than list a series of influences that affect the growth rate. It would include assessments of their relative importance, the trade-offs involved in having more of one beneficial influence and less of another, and the interactions among the various influences. This poses a formidable program for further empirical research.

While much remains to be learned, an important tentative conclusion of initial research on growth is that improvements in *quality* of capital, human as well as physical, have played a larger role than increases in the *quantity* of capital in the economic growth of Canada since 1900. (This conclusion was first reached by Professor Robert Solow of MIT, who received the 1987 Nobel Prize in Economics.) Whether quality rather than quantity of capital is also the more important source of growth for countries with different cultural patterns, more acute population problems, or more limited natural resources is a matter of continuing research.

Benefits and Costs of Growth

In the remainder of this chapter, we shall outline some more general considerations concerning economic growth. We start by looking at the benefits and then the costs of growth. Boxes 38-3 and 38-4 outline the popular arguments on both sides of the growth debate.

Benefits of Growth

Growth in Living Standards

A country whose per capita output grows at 3 percent per year doubles its living standards about every 24 years.

A primary reason for desiring growth is to raise general living standards.

The extreme importance of economic growth in raising income can be illustrated by comparing the real income of a father with the real income of the son who follows in his father's footsteps. If the son neither rises nor falls in the relative income scale compared with his father, his share of the country's national income will be the same as his father's. If the son is 30 years younger than his father, he can expect to have a real income nearly twice as large as the one his father enjoyed when his father was the same age. These figures assume that the father and son live in a country such as Canada where the growth rate has been 2 or 3 percent per year. If they live in Japan, where growth has been going on at a rate of about 8 percent per year, the son's income will be about 10 times as large as his father's.

For those who share in it, growth is a powerful

BOX 38-3

An Open Letter to the Ordinary Citizen from a Supporter of the Growth-Is-Bad School

Dear Ordinary Citizen:

You live in a world that is being despoiled by a mindless search for ever higher levels of material consumption at the cost of all other values. Once upon a time, men and women knew how to enjoy creative work and to derive satisfaction from simple activities undertaken in scarce, and hence highly valued, leisure time. Today the ordinary worker is a mindless cog in an assembly line that turns out ever more goods that the advertisers must work overtime to persuade the worker to consume.

Statisticians and politicians count the increasing flow of material output as a triumph of modern civilization. Consider not the flow of output in general but the individual products that it contains. You arise from your electric-blanketed bed, clean your teeth with an electric toothbrush, open with an electric can opener a can of the sad remnants of a once-proud orange, and eat your bread baked from super-refined and chemically refortified flour; you climb into your car to sit in vast traffic jams on exhaust-polluted highways. And so it goes, with endless consumption of high-technology products that give you no more real satisfaction than the simple, cheaply produced equivalent products used by your great-grandfathers: soft woolly blankets, natural-bristle toothbrushes, real oranges, coarse but healthful bread, and public transport that moved on uncongested roads and gave its passengers time to chat with their neighbors, to read, or just to daydream.

Television commercials tell you that by consuming more you are happier. But happiness lies not in increasing consumption but in increasing the ratio of *satisfaction of wants* to *total wants*. Since the more you consume, the more the advertisers persuade you that you want to consume, you are almost certainly less happy than the average citizen in a small town in 1900 whom we can visualize sitting on the family porch, sipping a cool beer or a lemonade, and enjoying the antics of the children as they play with scooters made out of old crates and jump rope with pieces of old clothesline.

Today the landscape is dotted with endless factories producing the plastic trivia of the modern industrial society. They drown you in a cloud of noise, air, and water pollution. The countryside is despoiled by strip mines, petroleum refineries, acid rain, and dangerous nuclear power stations producing energy that is devoured insatiably by modern factories and motor vehicles.

Worse, our precious heritage of natural resources is being fast used up. Spaceship earth flies, captainless, in its senseless orgy of self-consuming consumption.

Now is the time to stop this madness. We must stabilize production, reduce pollution, conserve our natural resources, and seek justice through a more equitable distribution of existing total income.

A long time ago Malthus taught us that if we do not limit population voluntarily, nature will do it for us in a cruel and savage manner. Today the same is true of output: If we do not halt its growth voluntarily, the halt will be imposed on us by a disastrous increase in pollution and a rapid exhaustion of natural resources.

Citizens, awake! Shake off the worship of growth, learn to enjoy the bounty that is yours already, and reject the endless, self-defeating search for increased happiness through ever-increasing consumption.

Upward!

A. Nongrowthman

---

weapon against poverty. A family earning $9,500 today can expect an income of $14,000 within 10 years (in constant dollars) if it just shares in a 4 percent growth rate. The transformation of the life-style of blue-collar workers in North America (as well as in Europe and Japan) in a generation provides a notable example of the escape from poverty that growth makes possible.

BOX 38-4

An Open Letter to the Ordinary Citizen from a Supporter of the Growth-Is-Good School

Dear Ordinary Citizen:

You live in the world's first civilization that is devoted principally to satisfying *your* needs rather than those of a privileged minority. Past civilizations have always been based on leisure and high consumption for a tiny upper class, a reasonable living standard for a small middle class, and hard work with little more than subsistence consumption for the great mass of people. In the past the average person saw little of the civilized and civilizing products of the economy, except when toiling to produce them.

The continuing Industrial Revolution is based on mass-produced goods for you, the ordinary citizen. It ushered in a period of sustained economic growth that has raised consumption standards of ordinary citizens to levels previously reserved throughout history for a tiny privileged minority. Reflect on a few examples: travel, live and recorded music, art, good food, inexpensive books, universal literacy, and a genuine chance to be educated. Most important, there is leisure to provide time and energy to enjoy these and thousands of other products of the modern industrial economy.

Would any ordinary family seriously doubt the benefits of growth and prefer to go back to the world of 150 or 500 years ago in its same relative social and economic position? Surely, the answer is no. But we cannot say the same for those with incomes in the top 1 or 2 percent of the income distribution. Economic growth has destroyed much of their privileged consumption position. They must now vie with the masses when visiting the world's beauty spots and be annoyed, while lounging on the terrace of a palatial mansion, by the sound of charter flights carrying ordinary people to inexpensive holidays. Many of the rich resent the loss of exclusive rights to luxury consumption. Some complain bitterly, and it is not surprising that they find their intellectual apologists.

Whether they know it or not, the anti-growth economists are not the social revolutionaries they think they are. They are counterrevolutionaries who would set back the clock of material progress for the ordinary person. They say that growth has produced pollution and wasteful consumption of all kinds of frivolous products that add nothing to human happiness. But the democratic solution to pollution is not to go back to where so few people consume luxuries that pollution is trivial; it is to accept pollution as part of a transitional phase connected with the ushering in of mass consumption, and to learn to control the pollution it tends to create.

It is only through further growth that the average citizen can enjoy consumption standards (of travel, culture, medical and health care, etc.) now available to people in the top 25 percent of the income distribution—which includes the intellectuals who earn large royalties from the books they write denouncing growth. If you think that extra income confers little real benefit, just ask those in that top 25 percent to trade incomes with the average citizen. Or see how hard *they* struggle to reduce their income taxes.

Ordinary citizens, do not be deceived by disguised elitist doctrines. Remember that the very rich and the elite have much to gain by stopping growth and even more by rolling it back, but you have everything to gain by letting it go forward.

Onward!

A. Growthman

Growth and Income Redistribution

Not everyone benefits equally from growth. Many of the poorest are not even in the labor force and thus are least likely to share in the higher wages that, along with profits, are the primary means by which the gains from growth are distributed. For this reason, even in a growing economy redistribution policies will be needed if poverty is to be averted.

Economic growth makes many kinds of redistributions easier to achieve. For example, a rapid growth rate makes it more feasible politically to alleviate poverty. If existing income is to be redistributed, someone's standard of living will actually have to be lowered. However, when there is economic growth, and when the increment in income is redistributed (through government intervention), it is possible to reduce income inequalities without actually having to lower anyone's income. It is much easier for a rapidly growing economy to be generous toward its less fortunate citizens—or neighbors—than it is for a static economy.

Growth and Life-style

A family often finds that a big increase in its income can lead to a major change in the pattern of its consumption—that extra money buys important amenities of life. In the same way the members of society as a whole may change their consumption patterns as their average income rises. Not only do markets in a country that is growing rapidly make it profitable to produce more cars, but the government is led also to produce more highways and to provide more recreational areas for its newly affluent (and mobile) citizens. At yet a later stage, a concern about litter, pollution, and ugliness may become important, and their correction may then begin to account for a significant fraction of GDP. Such "amenities" usually become matters of social concern only when growth has assured the provision of the basic requirements for food, clothing, and housing of a substantial majority of the population.

National Defense and Prestige

When one country is competing with another for power or prestige, rates of growth are important. If our national income is growing at 2 percent, while another country's is growing at 5 percent, the other country will only have to wait for our relative strength to dwindle. Moreover, the faster its productivity is growing, the easier a country will find it to bear the expenses of an arms race or a program of foreign aid.

More subtly, growth has become part of the currency of international prestige. Countries that are engaged in persuading other countries of the might or right of their economic and political systems point to their rapid rates of growth as evidence of their achievements.

Costs of Growth

The benefits of growth suggest that it is a great blessing. It is surely true that, other things being equal, most people would regard a fast rate of growth as preferable to a slow one, but other things are seldom equal.

Social and Personal Costs of Growth

Industrialization can cause deterioration of the environment. Unspoiled landscapes give way to highways, factories, and billboards; air and water become polluted; and unique and priceless relics of earlier ages—from flora and fauna to ancient art and ruins—often disappear. Urbanization tends to move people away from the simpler life of farms and small towns and into the crowded, slum-ridden, and often darkly evil life of the urban ghetto. Those remaining behind in the rural areas find that rural life, too, has changed. Larger-scale farming, the decline of population, and the migration of children from the farm to the city all have their costs. The stepped-up tempo of life brings joys to some but tragedy to others. Accidents, ulcers, crime rates, suicides, divorces, and murders all tend to be higher in periods of rapid change and in more developed societies.

When an economy is growing, it is also changing. Innovation renders some machines obsolete and also leaves some people partially obsolete. No matter how well trained workers are at age 25, in another 25 years most will find that their skills are at least partially obsolete. A rapid growth rate requires rapid adjustments, which can cause much upset and misery to the individuals affected.

It is often argued that costs of this kind are a small price to pay for the great benefits that growth can bring. Even if that is true in the aggregate (which is a matter of debate), these personal costs are very unevenly borne. Indeed, many of those for whom growth is most costly (in terms of jobs) share least in the fruits of growth. Yet it is also a mistake to see only the costs—to yearn for the good old days while enjoying higher living standards that growth alone has made possible.

The Opportunity Cost of Growth

In a world of scarcity almost nothing is free. Growth requires heavy investments of resources in capital goods as well as in activities such as education. Often these investments yield no immediate return in terms of goods and services for consumption; thus they imply sacrifices by the current generation of consumers.

Growth, which promises more goods tomorrow, is achieved by consuming fewer goods today. For the economy as a whole this is the primary cost of growth.

An example will suggest the magnitude of this cost. Suppose the fictitious economy of USSA has full employment and is experiencing growth at the rate of 2 percent per year. Its citizens consume 85 percent of the GDP and invest 15 percent. The people of USSA know that if they are willing to decrease immediately their consumption to 77 percent, they will produce more capital and thus shift at once to a 3 percent growth rate. The new rate can be maintained as long as they keep saving and investing 23 percent of the national income. Should they do it?

Table 38-2 illustrates the choice in terms of time paths of consumption. How expensive is the "invest now, consume later" strategy? On the assumed figures, it take 10 years for the actual amount of consumption to catch up to what it would have been had no reallocation been made. In the intervening 10 years a good deal of consumption is lost, and the cumulative losses in consumption must be made up before society can really be said to have broken even. It takes an additional nine years before total consumption over the whole period is as large as it would have been if the economy had remained on the 2 percent path. **[49]**

A policy of sacrificing present living standards for a gain that does not begin to be reaped for a generation is hardly likely to appeal to any but the altruistic or the very young. The question of how much of its living standards one generation is prepared to sacrifice for its heirs (who are in any case likely to be richer) is troublesome. As one critic put it: Why should we sacrifice for them? What have they ever done for us?

TABLE 38–2 The Opportunity Cost of Growth

Year	(1) Level of consumption at 2% growth rate	(2) Level of consumption at 3% growth rate	(3) Cumulative gain (loss) in consumption
0	85.0	77.0	(8.0)
1	86.7	79.3	(15.4)
2	88.5	81.8	(22.1)
3	90.3	84.2	(28.2)
4	92.1	86.8	(33.5)
5	93.9	89.5	(37.9)
6	95.8	92.9	(40.8)
7	97.8	95.0	(43.6)
8	99.7	97.9	(45.4)
9	101.8	100.9	(46.3)
10	103.8	103.9	(46.2)
15	114.7	120.8	(28.6)
20	126.8	140.3	19.6
30	154.9	189.4	251.0
40	189.2	255.6	745.9

Transferring resources from consumption to investment goods lowers current income but raises future income. The example assumes that income in year zero is 100 and that consumption of 85 percent of national income is possible with a 2 percent growth rate. It is further assumed that to achieve a 3 percent growth rate, consumption must fall to 77 percent of income. A shift from (1) to (2) decreases consumption for 10 years but increases it thereafter. The cumulative effect on consumption is shown in (3); the gains eventually become large.

Many governments, particularly those seeking a larger role in world affairs, have chosen to force the diversion of resources from consumption to investment. The Germans under Hitler, the Russians under Stalin, and the Chinese under Mao Tse-tung adopted four-year and five-year plans that did just this. Many less-developed countries are using such plans today. Such resource shifts are particularly important when actual growth rates are small (say, less than 1 percent), for without some current sacrifice there is little or no prospect of real growth in the lifetimes of today's citizens. The very lowest growth rates are frequently encountered in the very poorest countries. This creates a cruel dilemma, often called the vicious circle of poverty.

Are There Limits to Growth?

Opponents of growth argue that sustained growth is undesirable; some even argue that it is impossible. Of course, all terrestrial things have an ultimate limit. Astronomers predict that the solar system itself will die as the sun burns out in another 6 billion or so years. To be of practical concern, a limit must be within some reasonable planning horizon. Best-selling books of the 1970s by Jay Forrester (*World Dynamics,* 1973) and D. H. Meadows et al. (*The Limits to Growth,* 1974) predicted an imminent growth-induced doomsday. Living standards were predicted to reach a peak about the year 2000 and then, in the words of Yale Professor William Nordhaus, a leading critic of these models, to "descend inexorably to the level of Neanderthal man." What lessons are there to be learned from this debate?

The Uncontroversial Fact of Increasing Pressure on Natural Resources

The years since World War II have seen a rapid acceleration in the consumption of the world's resources, particularly fossil fuels and basic minerals. World population has increased from under 2.5 billion to over 4 billion in that period, and this alone has increased the demand for all the world's resources. But the single fact of population growth greatly understates the pressure on resources.

Calculations by Professor Nathan Keyfitz of Harvard and others focus on the resources used by those who can claim a life-style of the level enjoyed by 90 percent of American families. This so-called middle class, which today includes about one-sixth of the world's population, consumes 15 to 30 times as much oil per capita and, overall, at least 5 times as much of the earth's scarce resources per capita as do the other "poor" five-sixths of the population.

The world's poor are not, however, content to remain forever poor. Whether they live in the USSR, Argentina, Korea, or Kenya, they have let their governments understand that they expect policies that generate enough growth to give *them* the higher consumption levels that all of *us* take for granted. This upward aspiration is being fulfilled to some degree in many countries. The growth of the middle class has been nearly 4 percent per year—twice the rate of population growth—over the postwar period. The number of persons realizing middle-class living standards is estimated to have increased from 200 million to 700 million between 1950 and 1980 and is predicted almost to double again by the turn of the century.

Growth is a major factor in the recently recognized or projected shortages of natural resources. Yet the 4 percent growth rate of the middle class, which is too fast for present resources, is too slow for the aspirations of the billions who live in underdeveloped countries and see the fruits of development all around them. Thus the pressure on world resources of energy, minerals, and food is likely to accelerate, even if population growth is reduced.

A Tentative Verdict

Most economists agree that conjuring up absolute limits to growth based on the assumptions of constant technology and fixed resources is not warranted. Most agree that any barrier can be overcome by technological advances—but not in an instant, and not automatically. Clearly there is a problem of timing: How soon can we discover and put into practice the knowledge required to solve the problems that are made ever more imminent by growth in the population, the affluence, and the aspirations of the billions who now live in poverty? There is no guarantee that a whole generation may not be caught in transition, with social and political consequences that promise to be enormous even if they are not cataclysmic. The nightmare conjured up by the doomsday models served its purpose by helping focus our attention on these problems.

Summary

1. National income can increase as a result of reduction in the recessionary gap, reduction in structural unemployment, or growth in the level of potential national income.
2. Investment has short-term effects on national income through aggregate demand and long-term effects through growth in potential national income. Such growth is frequently measured using rates of change of potential real national income per person or per hour of labor employed.
3. Savings reduce aggregate demand and therefore reduce national income in the short run, but in the long run savings finance the investment that leads to growth in potential income.
4. The cumulative effects of even small differences in growth rates become large over periods of a decade or more.
5. Understanding growth involves understanding both the utilization of existing investment opportunities and the process of creating new investment opportunities. The source of economic growth was once thought to be almost entirely capital accumulation and the utilization of a backlog of unexploited investment opportunities. Today most economists recognize that many investment opportunities can be created, and much attention is given to the sources of outward shifts in the *MEC* schedule through both embodied and disembodied technical change.
6. The most important benefit of growth lies in its contribution to the long-run struggle to raise living standards and escape poverty. It also makes more manageable the policies that would redistribute income among people. Growth also plays an important role in a country's national defense and its struggle for international prestige.
7. Growth, while often beneficial, is never costless. The opportunity cost of growth is the diversion of resources from current consumption to capital formation. For individuals who are left behind in a rapidly changing world the costs are higher and more personal. The optimal rate of growth involves balancing benefits and costs. Most people do not wish to forgo the benefits growth can bring, but neither do they wish to maximize growth at any cost.
8. In addition to mere increases in quantity of capital per person, any list of factors affecting growth includes the extent of innovation, the quality of human capital, the size of the working population, and the whole institutional setting.
9. The critical importance of increasing knowledge and new technology in sustaining growth is highlighted by the great drain on existing natural resources resulting from the explosive growth of the past two or three decades. Without continuing new knowledge, the present needs and aspirations of the world's population cannot come anywhere close to being met.

Topics for Review

Short-run and long-run effects of investment and saving
Cumulative nature of growth
Factors affecting growth
Effects of capital accumulation with and without new knowledge
Embodied and disembodied technical change
Benefits and costs of growth

Discussion Questions

1. We usually study and measure economic growth in macroeconomic terms. But in a market economy, who makes the decisions that lead to growth? What kind of decisions and what kind of actions cause growth to occur? How might a detailed study of individual markets be relevant to understanding economic growth?
2. Dr. David Suzuki has recently argued that despite the fact that "in the 20th century the list of scientific and technological achievements has been absolutely dazzling, the costs of such progress are so large that negative economic growth may be right for the future." Policies to achieve this include "rigorous reduction of waste, a questioning and distrustful attitude towards technological progress, and braking demands on the globe's resources." Identify some of the benefits and costs of economic growth, and evaluate Dr. Suzuki's position.
3. Why is rising productivity a more significant contributing factor for economic growth than simply increasing the quantity of productive resources? Define *productivity*. List all the factors that increase the productivity of labor and the productivity of capital. Comment on the differences and similarities of the two lists.
4. *Family Weekly* recently listed among "inventions that have changed our lives" microwave ovens, digital clocks, bank credit cards, freeze-dried coffee, tape cassettes, climate-controlled shopping malls, automatic toll collectors, soft contact lenses, tubeless tires, and electronic word processors.

   Which of them would you hate to do without? Which, if any, will have a major impact on life in the twenty-first century? If there are any that you believe will not, does that mean they are frivolous and unimportant?
5. The Overseas Development Council recently introduced "a new measure of economic development based on the physical quality of life." Its index, called PQLI, gives one-third weight to each of the following indicators: literacy, life expectancy, and infant mortality. While countries such as the United States and Canada rank high on either the PQLI or on an index of per capita real national income, some relatively poor countries, such as Sri Lanka, rank much higher on the PQLI index than much richer countries such as Algeria and Kuwait. Discuss the merits or deficiencies of this measure.
6. "The case for economic growth is that it gives man greater control over his environment, and consequently increases his freedom." Explain why you agree or disagree with this statement by Nobel Laureate W. Arthur Lewis.
7. Consider a developed economy that decides to achieve a zero rate

of growth for the future. What implications would such a "stationary state" have for the processes of production and consumption?

8. Suppose solar energy becomes the dominant form of energy in the twenty-first century. What changes will this make in the growth rates of Africa and Northern Europe?
9. Discuss the following newspaper headlines in terms of the sources, costs, and benefits of growth.
   a. "Stress addiction: 'Life in the fast lanes' may have its benefits"
   b. "Education: An expert urges multiple reforms"
   c. "Industrial radiation risk higher than thought"
   d. "Developments in the field of management design are looking ahead"
   e. "Ford urged by federal safety officials to recall several hundred thousand of its 1981–1982 front-drive vehicles because of alleged fire hazards"
10. In the late 1970s and early 1980s productivity growth was historically low, but it rebounded after 1983. How might you explain this?

39

Macroeconomic Controversies

How well do markets work? Can government improve market performance? In various guises these two questions are the basis of most disagreements over economic policy. We shall see that different answers to these questions imply big differences in macroeconomic policy prescriptions.

Alternative Views: Conservative and Interventionist

Macroeconomics is mainly concerned with the behavior of three important variables: employment (and unemployment), the price level, and the rate of economic growth. Macroeconomic policy suggests goals for each: full employment, stable prices, and a satisfactory growth rate. The advantages of full employment and a positive growth rate are obvious and not subject to serious dispute. Although most people agree that inflation is harmful, there is much debate about what can really be blamed on it.

Broadly speaking, we can identify a non-interventionist and an interventionist view with respect to each of the policy goals just specified. The non-interventionist view says that the unaided market economy can best achieve the goal. The interventionist view says that government policy can improve the economy's performance in terms of that goal. Since one can take a non-interventionist or an interventionist position with respect to each of these three goals, there are eight different possible policy combinations.[1]

Consider two extreme policy stances: *conservatives* are non-interventionist on all issues, while *interventionists* support government intervention at all times. A few people may actually be conservative or interventionist in this sense. Most, however, would favor intervention on some issues and oppose it on others. They might still identify themselves as conservative or interventionist because they were more often on one side than the other.

It is popular to equate monetarist with conservative and Keynesian with interventionist. It is true that many monetarists are on the conservative side and many Keynesians on the interventionist side. But it is not always so. For example, it is quite possible to be Keynesian in accepting the Keynesian macro model as a reasonable description of the economy's macroeconomic behavior but conservative in believing that the unaided market usually does the best job of allocating resources.

[1] Since each of the three issues breaks up into hundreds of different subissues, thousands of different policy stances are available on one side or the other of each issue.

The Conservative View

Conservatives believe that the free-market economy performs quite well on balance. Although shocks do hit the system, they lead rather quickly, and often painlessly, to the adjustments dictated by the market system. For example, relative prices in booming sectors rise, drawing in resources from declining sectors or regions. As a result, resources (and particularly labor) usually remain fully employed, so there is no need for full-employment policies.

Conservatives hold that macroeconomic performance will be most satisfactory if determined solely by the workings of the free market.

Of course, few believe that the market system functions perfectly, thereby ensuring *continuous* full employment. But the view is that the market system works well enough to preclude any constructive role for policy.

In addition, many conservatives believe that policy instruments are so crude that their use is often counterproductive. A policy's effects may be so uncertain, with regard to both strength and timing, that it may often impair rather than improve the economy's performance.

In a modern economy some government presence is inevitable. Thus a stance of no intervention is impossible; rather, what is advocated by conservatives is minimal direct intervention in the market system. This involves the government's bearing responsibility for providing a *stable environment* in which the private sector can function.

The Interventionist View

Interventionists believe that the functioning of the free-market economy is often far from satisfactory. Sometimes markets show weak self-regulatory forces, and the economy settles into prolonged periods of heavy unemployment. At other times markets tend to "overcorrect," causing the economy to lurch between the extremes of large recessionary and inflationary gaps.

This behavior can be improved, argue the interventionists. Even though interventionist policies may be imperfect, they may be good enough to improve the functioning of the economy with respect to all three main goals of macro policy.

Macroeconomic Issues

Everyone agrees that the economy's performance is often less than perfectly satisfactory. Serious unemployment has been a recurring problem. Inflation was a serious problem throughout the 1970s and early 1980s. For most of that period growth rates were unsatisfactorily low. Conservatives and interventionists differ in diagnosing the causes of these economic ills.

The Business Cycle

We saw in Chapter 26 that cyclical ups and downs can be observed for as far back as records exist. Monetarists and Keynesians have long argued about the causes. As was noted in Chapter 34, monetarists often are identified with conservative views, and Keynesians with intervention.[2]

Monetarist views. Monetarists believe that the economy is inherently stable because private-sector expenditure functions are relatively stable. In addition, they believe that shifts in the aggregate demand curve are mainly due to policy-induced changes in the money supply.[3]

The view that business cycles have mainly monetary causes relies heavily on the evidence advanced by Milton Friedman and Anna Schwartz in their monumental study *A Monetary History of the United States, 1867–1960*. They establish a strong correlation between changes in the money supply and changes

[2] Appendix A to this chapter presents the widely used *IS/LM* model of the influence of monetary and fiscal policy. The *IS/LM* model expands on the theory developed in Chapter 34.

[3] The view that fluctuations often have monetary causes is not new. The English economist R. G. Hawtrey, the Austrian Nobel Laureate F. A. von Hayek, and the Swedish economist Knut Wicksell are prominent among those who have given monetary factors an important role in explaining the turning points in cycles and/or the tendency for expansions and contractions, once begun, to become cumulative and self-reinforcing. Modern monetarists carry on this tradition.

in the level of business activity. Major recessions have been associated with absolute declines in the money supply and minor recessions with the slowing of the rate of increase in the money supply below its long-term trend.

The correlation between changes in the money supply and changes in the level of business activity is now accepted by almost all economists. But there is controversy over how this correlation is to be interpreted. Do changes in money supply cause changes in the level of aggregate demand and hence of business activity, or vice versa?

Friedman and Schwartz maintain that changes in the money supply cause changes in business activity. They argue, for example, that the severity of the Great Depression was due to a major contraction in the money supply that shifted the aggregate demand curve far to the left. The Great Depression is discussed in Box 39-1.

According to monetarists, fluctuations in the money supply cause fluctuations in national income.

This leads the monetarists to advocate a policy of stabilizing the growth of the money supply. In their view this would avoid policy-induced instability of the aggregate demand curve.

Keynesian views. The Keynesian view on cyclical fluctuations in the economy has two parts. First, it emphasizes variations in investment as a cause of business cycles and stresses the nonmonetary causes of such variations.[4]

Keynesians reject what they regard as the extreme monetarist view that only money matters in explaining cyclical fluctuations. Many Keynesians believe that both monetary and nonmonetary forces are important in explaining the cyclical behavior of the economy. Although they accept serious monetary mismanagement as one potential source of economic fluctuations, they do not believe that it is the only or even the major source of such fluctuations. Thus they deny the monetary interpretation of business cycle history given by Friedman and Schwartz. They believe that most fluctuations in the aggregate demand curve are due to variations in the desire to spend on the part of the private sector and are not induced by government policy.

Keynesians also believe that the economy lacks strong natural corrective mechanisms that will always force it easily and quickly back to full employment. They believe that while the price level rises fairly quickly to eliminate *inflationary* gaps, the price level does not fall quickly to eliminate *recessionary* gaps. Keynesians stress the asymmetries noted in earlier chapters that imply that prices and wages fall only slowly in response to a recessionary gap. As a result, Keynesians believe that recessionary gaps can persist for long periods of time unless they are eliminated by an active stabilization policy.

The second part of the Keynesian view on cyclical fluctuations is that they accept the correlation between changes in the money supply and changes in the level of economic activity, but their explanation questions the causality suggested by the monetarists. Many Keynesians accept that changes in the money supply can be an important source of fluctuations in economic activity, but they argue that much of the evidence adduced by monetarists actually reflects causality in the other direction. These Keynesians argue that changes in the level of economic activity tend to cause changes in the money supply. They offer several reasons for this, but only the most important need be mentioned.

Keynesians point out that from 1945 to the early 1970s most central banks tended to stabilize interest rates as the target variable of monetary policy. To do this they had to increase the money supply during upswings in the business cycle and decrease it during downswings. When an expansion got under way, the demand for money tended to increase, and if there was no increase in the money supply, interest rates would rise. The central bank might prevent this rise in interest rates by buying bonds offered for sale at

[4] Like the monetarists, the Keynesians are modern advocates of views that have a long history. The great Austrian (and later American) economist Joseph Schumpeter stressed such explanations early in the present century. The Swedish economist Wicksell and the German Speithoff both stressed this aspect of economic fluctuations before the emergence of the Keynesian school of thought.

BOX 39-1

Two Views on the Great Depression in the United States

The stock market crash of 1929, and other factors associated with a moderate downswing in American business activity during the late 1920s, caused the public to wish to hold more in cash and less in demand deposits. The banking system could not, however, meet this increased demand for liquidity without help from the Federal Reserve System. (As we saw in Chapter 33, banks are never able to meet from their own reserves a sudden demand to withdraw currency on the part of a large fraction of their depositors. Their reserves are always inadequate to meet such a demand.) The Fed had been set up to provide just such emergency assistance to banks that were basically sound but were unable to meet sudden demands by depositors to withdraw cash. However, the Fed refused to extend the necessary help, and successive waves of bank failures followed as a direct result. During each wave hundreds of banks failed, ruining many depositors and thereby worsening an already severe depression. In the last half of 1931 almost 2,000 American banks were forced to suspend operations! One consequence of this was a sharp drop in the money supply; by 1932 the money supply was 35 percent below the level of 1929. To monetarists these facts seem decisive.

While Keynesians accept the argument that the Fed's behavior was perverse, they argue that the cyclical behavior of investment and consumption expenditure was the major cause of the Great Depression. In support of this view they point out that in Canada and the United Kingdom, where the central bank came to the aid of the banking system, bank failures were few during the Great Depression, and as a consequence the money supply did *not* shrink drastically as it did in the United States. Despite these markedly different monetary histories, the behavior of the recessionary gap, investment expenditure, and unemployment was very similar in the three countries.

current prices, but in so doing it would increase banks' reserves and thereby inject new money into the economy. Similarly, in a cyclical contraction interest rates would tend to fall unless the central bank stepped in and sold bonds to keep interest rates up. Generally it did so, thereby decreasing the money supply. This behavior created the positive correlation on which the monetarists rely.

According to Keynesians, fluctuations in national income are often caused by fluctuations in expenditure decisions. Further, they believe that fluctuations in national income cause fluctuations in the money supply.

Nevertheless, most Keynesians also agree that policy-induced changes in the money supply can cause national income to change.

The Price Level

As we saw in Chapter 36, sustained inflation requires a sustained expansion of the money supply.

Motives for such excessive monetary expansions have varied from time to time and place to place. Sometimes central banks have rapidly increased the money supply in an effort to end a recession. Then when the economy expanded due to its own natural recuperative forces, the increased money supply allowed a significant inflation during the boom phase of the cycle. At other times central banks have tried to hold interest rates well below their free-market levels. To do this they buy bonds to hold bond prices up. We have seen that these open-market operations increase the money supply and so fuel an inflation. At still other times central banks have helped governments finance large budget deficits by buying up the new public debt. These open-market operations provide what is popularly known as *printing press finance*. The steady increase in the money supply fuels a continuous inflation.

Monetarist views. As we have said, many monetarists hold that inflation is everywhere and always a monetary phenomenon. They thus focus on changes in the money supply as the key source of shifts in the *AD* curve.

According to monetarists, all inflations are caused by excessive monetary expansion and would not occur without it.

Keynesian views. Keynesians agree that a sustained rise in prices cannot occur unless it is accompanied by continued increases in the money supply. Keynesians also emphasize, however, that temporary bursts of inflation can be caused by shifts in the *AD* curve brought about by increases in private- or public-sector expenditure. If such inflations are not validated by monetary expansion, they are brought to a halt by the monetary adjustment mechanism.

Keynesians also accept the importance of supply-shock inflations. Again, they accept that such inflations cannot go on indefinitely unless accommodated by monetary expansion. But Keynesians argue that "temporary" inflation due to either *AD* or *SRAS* shifts can go on long enough to be a matter of serious policy concern.

Many Keynesians also take seriously the possibility of wage-cost push inflation that we studied in Chapter 36. This type of inflation, if it exists, makes full employment incompatible with a stable price level. Again, the central bank is faced with the agonizing choice of whether or not to accommodate.

Growth

Conservative views. Conservatives, and indeed most monetarists, feel that in a stable environment free from government interference growth will take care of itself. Large firms will spend much on research and development. Where they fail, or where they suppress inventions to protect monopoly positions, the genius of backyard inventors will come up with new ideas and will develop new companies to challenge the positions of the established giants. Left to itself, the economy will prosper as it has in the past, provided only that inquiring scientific spirit and the profit motive are not suppressed.

Interventionist views. Interventionists, and indeed most Keynesians, are less certain than conservatives about the ability of market forces to produce growth. While recognizing the importance of invention and innovation, they fear the dead hand of monopoly and cautious business practices that choose security over risk taking. Therefore, the state needs at the very least to give a nudge here or there to help the growth process along.

The Role of Policy

The conservative and the interventionist diagnoses of the economy's ills lead, not surprisingly, to very different prescriptions about the appropriate role of economic policy.

Conservative Prescriptions

It is not necessary to distinguish conservative policies with respect to full employment and with respect to stable prices. This is because conservatives believe that both goals will be achieved by the same basic policy: provision of a stable environment in which the free-market system may operate.

Full Employment and Stable Prices: Providing a Stable Environment

Creating a stable environment, as the conservatives advocate, may be easier said than done. Let us focus on the prescriptions for establishing stable fiscal and monetary policies.

One major problem to keep in mind is that macro variables are interrelated. The stability of one may imply the instability of another. In such cases, a choice must often be made. How much instability of one aggregate can we tolerate to secure stability in another related aggregate?

Assume, for example, that the government decides to adopt the goal of stability in the budget balance as part of the stable environment. This "stability" would require great *instability* in tax and expenditure policy. Tax revenues depend on the interaction between tax rates and the level of national income. With given tax rates, tax revenues change with the ebb and flow of the business cycle. A stable budget balance would require that the government raise tax rates and cut expenditure in slumps and lower tax rates and raise expenditures in booms.

Not only does this squander the budget's potential to act as a stabilizer, but great instability of the fiscal environment is also caused by continual changes in tax rates and expenditure levels. A stable fiscal environment requires substantial stability in government expenditures and tax rates. Stability is needed so that the private sector can make plans for the future in a climate of known patterns of tax liabilities and government demand.

Any target budget balance must be some average over a period long enough to cover a typical cycle. Stability from year to year should be found in tax rates and expenditure programs, *not* in the size of the budget balance.

This in turn requires that the budget deficit vary cyclically, showing its largest deficits in slumps and its largest surpluses in booms.[5]

Advocates of a stable monetary environment are actually advocating stable inflation. Whether a *zero* rate is feasible or not is discussed in Box 39-2. The central bank is urged to set a target rate of increase in the money supply and hold it. To establish the target, the central bank estimates the rate at which the demand for money would be growing if actual income equaled potential income and the price level were stable. As a first approximation this can be taken to be the rate at which potential income itself is growing. This then becomes the target rate of growth of the money supply. The key proposition is that the money supply should be changing gradually along a stable path that is independent of short-term variations in the demand for money caused by cyclical changes in national income. This is referred to as a ***k* percent rule.**

Will the *k* percent rule really provide monetary stability? The answer is not necessarily.

Assuring a stable rate of monetary growth does not assure a stable monetary environment. Monetary shortages and surpluses depend on the relation between the supply and the demand for money.

The *k* percent rule looks after supply, but what about demand?

Problems for the *k* percent rule arise when the demand for money shifts. For example, payment of interest on checking deposits increases the demand for M1. In this event, if the central bank adheres to a *k* percent rule, there will be an excess demand for money, and interest rates will rise. Thus contractionary pressure will be put on the economy.

Should the central bank commit itself to a specific *k* percent rule or merely work toward unannounced and possibly variable targets? The announced rule makes it easier to evaluate how well the central bank is doing its job. It also helps to prevent the central bank from succumbing to the temptation to fine tune the economy.

One disadvantage of the announced rule is that it sets up speculative behavior. Assume, for example, that when weekly money supply figures are announced there is too much money. Speculators then know that the central bank will sell more bonds in the future to reduce the excess. This will depress the price of bonds. Speculators are thus induced to sell bonds, hoping to rebuy them at bargain prices once the central bank acts.

Stable pre-announced M1 targets can introduce instability into interest-rate behavior.

A second disadvantage of such a rule is that the central bank, to preserve its credibility, may fail to take discretionary action that would otherwise be appropriate. For example, after an entrenched inflation is broken, the economy may come to rest with substantial unemployment and a stable price level (see Figure 36-6). There is then a case for a once-and-for-all discretionary expansion in the money supply to get the economy back to full employment. The *k* percent rule precludes this, condemning the economy to a slump.

Despite these problems, conservatives believe the *k* percent rule is superior to any known alternative. Some would agree that in principle the central bank

[5] Appendix B to this chapter takes up the recent debate that has emerged among economists over whether the deficit matters.

BOX 39-2

Is a Zero Inflation Rate a Feasible Policy Goal?

The 1950s were characterized by what would be regarded today as satisfactory price stability. But prices were not exactly steady. The inflation rate varied between 0.5 percent and 3 percent. Despite what appeared to most observers to be a slowly growing average recessionary gap throughout this period, the inflation rate never reached zero in any year. Between 1955 and 1961 there were only two years when the rate was below 1 percent: 1955 (0.2 percent) and 1961 (0.7 percent).

This creeping inflation worried observers at the time. An inflation, even a gradual one in the face of an obvious recessionary gap, seemed hard to understand.

The explanation in modern theory would likely come from the supply side. The combination of rising prices and recessionary gaps usually suggests a supply-shock inflation. The explanation that satisfied many observers at the time was the **structural rigidity theory** of inflation, which was indeed a supply-shock explanation.

The structural rigidity theory assumes that resources do not move quickly from one use to another and that it is easy to increase money wages and prices but hard to decrease them. Given these conditions, when patterns of demand and costs change due to such forces as economic growth, real adjustments occur slowly. Shortages appear in potentially expanding sectors, and prices rise because the slow movement of resources prevents these sectors from expanding rapidly enough. Factors of production remain in contracting sectors on part-time employment or become unemployed because mobility in the economy is low. Wages and prices are slow to move downward, so there are few significant wage and price reductions in these contracting sectors.

Thus the mere process of adjustment in an economy with structural rigidities causes inflation to occur. Prices in the expanding sectors rise; prices in the contracting sectors stay about the same; on average, therefore, the price level rises.

The inflation of the late 1950s and early 1960s was mild, and the debate on its causes was inconclusive. However, this was the first suggestion of a force that later became a plaguing policy problem: inflations originating in shifts in the aggregate supply curve.

Although the structural rigidity theory cannot be a major part of the explanation of the high inflation rates of the 1970s and early 1980s, it suggests that a zero inflation rate may not be an achievable target. Of course, good luck—such as the fall in the world price of oil that occurred in early 1986, when the inflation rate was already low and perhaps still declining—can temporarily drive the inflation rate to zero or even below zero. But if there is anything in the structural rigidity theory, the minimum inflation rate compatible with a changing economy may be 1 percent to 2 percent rather than zero. A test of this theory might occur by the end of the 1980s; if inflation continues to fall, will it reach zero, or get stuck in the 1–2 percent range?

could improve the economy's performance by occasional bouts of discretionary monetary policy to offset such things as major shifts in the demand for money. But they also believe that once given any discretion, the central bank would abuse it in an attempt to fine tune the economy. The resulting instability would, they believe, be much more than any instability resulting from the application of a *k* percent rule in an environment subject to some change.

Long-Term Growth

Conservatives want to let growth take care of itself. They argue that governments cannot improve the workings of free markets and that their interventions can interfere with market efficiency. Thus they push for reducing the current level of government intervention.

Given the large web of government rules, regulations, and perverse tax incentives that has grown up over many years, the conservatives' agenda for reducing government intervention is usually a long one. Such an agenda was adopted by so-called supply siders during the later 1970s and early 1980s. The supply-side, conservative view that growth is best encouraged by reducing the present degree of government intervention has already caused some significant policy changes and will no doubt always find numerous supporters.

The agenda includes *eliminating* the following policies:

Supporting declining industries. This policy causes resources that could be more productively employed elsewhere to leave the industry more slowly. Most economists agree that such policies are costly, harmful to growth, and in the end self-defeating.

Encouraging monopolies and discouraging competition. Most economists tend to oppose such policies, although there is disagreement over how much competition is desirable in certain industries. For example, conservatives tend to support complete deregulation of fare and route setting by airlines, while interventionists tend to worry that cutthroat competition may reduce airline quality and safety.

Taxing income rather than consumption. Consider a woman in the 25 percent tax bracket who earns an extra $1,000 and pays $250 income tax. If she spends her after-tax income, she will be able to buy $750 worth of goods. If she saves the money, she will be able to buy a $750 bond. If the bond pays a 4 percent real return, she will earn $30 interest per year. But a 25 percent tax must then be paid on the interest earnings, leaving only a $22.50 annual income. This is a 3.0 percent after-tax return on the bond and *a 2.25 percent after-tax return on the original $100 income.* Conservatives allege that this "double taxing" of saving is a serious disincentive to saving. They argue for taxes on consumption, not on income, so that any income that is saved would be untaxed. A tax would be levied only when the interest earned on the savings was actually spent on consumption.

High rates of income tax. Conservatives allege that high taxes discourage work. But the effect of high taxes may actually be to make people work either more or less hard. Theory is silent on which is more likely, and no hard evidence has yet shown that lowering current tax rates makes people work harder. Many elements of tax reform, introduced in the United States in 1986 and proposed in Canada in June 1987, which saw tax bases broadened and tax rates reduced, were well received by conservatives.

"Double taxation" of business profits. Business profits are taxed first as income of firms and second as income of households when paid out as dividends. This and other policies that reduce business profits and hence discourage the return to investing in equities are alleged to discourage households from saving and investing in businesses that are the mainspring of economic growth.

All these policies are alleged to reduce the rate of growth below what it would otherwise be. Problems arise in assessing the existence and importance of the alleged harmful effects of each policy and also, since the government needs revenue, in finding alternative revenue sources that will have less harmful effects than the ones being criticized.

Interventionist Prescriptions

Interventionists call for different policies for the three policy goals of full employment, price stability, and growth. As we consider their prescriptions, we give their reasons for rejecting the conservative case.

Full Employment

Interventionists call for discretionary fiscal and monetary policies to offset significant inflationary and recessionary gaps. Some of the major problems associated with discretionary stabilization policy have been discussed in earlier chapters. The issues in the debate that is popularly known as "rules versus discretion" are discussed further in Box 39-3.

A Stable Price Level

Some interventionists, particularly a group called *post-Keynesians,* believe that the *k* percent rule may not be enough to achieve full employment and stable

BOX 39-3

Rules Versus Discretion

Three of the main issues involved in the rules versus discretion debate are problems created by lags, type of stabilization needed, and adequacy of information.

Lags. Economists hostile to discretionary policy emphasize the long and variable lags of both fiscal and monetary policy. Monetary policy can be put into effect quickly, but it takes 6 to 18 months for the full effects of a change in interest rates to be felt in terms of altered private-sector expenditures. It often takes a long time to put fiscal policy into effect since federal budgets are usually several months in the making. Once the changes are made, however, their effects spread quickly through the economy.

Conservatives feel that these lags destroy the presumption that discretionary full-employment policy will usually be stabilizing. Interventionists feel that although the lags are serious, discretionary policies can be effective in reducing persistent recessionary gaps. Few interventionists, however, now call for fine tuning.

A stable climate for planning. Supporters of rules emphasize the need for a stable climate for firms and households to plan for the future. They argue that continual changes in tax rates and the money supply designed to stabilize the economy are destabilizing because they create a climate of uncertainty that makes long-term planning difficult.

Supporters of discretionary policy argue that they want discretion exercised only when the occasional serious recession develops and that large fluctuations in income and employment can be as upsetting to long-term planning as the occasional changes in tax rates and expenditures required by stabilization policy.

Do we know enough? Discretionary stabilization policy requires that we forecast what the state of the economy will be in the absence of that policy. Generally, actual information is available only with a lag. Policymakers know approximately what GDP was last quarter and what unemployment was last month. (The first preliminary figures for many economic variables can be subject to substantial errors. Often these estimates are revised several times over subsequent months and even years.) On the basis of these data, projections of future behavior of the economy must be made and policy set.

Supporters of discretionary policy accept that errors in projections may be large in relation to the recessionary gaps created by minor recessions but believe that the errors are small in relation to major recessions. They argue that for major recessions policymakers will be in no doubt about the existence of a large recessionary gap or the need for some significant stimulus, even though its exact amount cannot be precisely determined.

---

prices simultaneously. This is because they accept the wage-cost push theory of inflation discussed in Chapter 36.

Some Keynesians call for incomes policies to restrain the wage-cost push and so make full employment compatible with stable prices. They believe that such policies should become permanent features of the economic landscape.

Wage-price controls might work as *temporary* measures to break inflationary inertias (see Chapter 36, pages 788–789), but as permanent features they would introduce inefficiencies and rigidities.

More permanent incomes policies might be of two types. The first type, commonly used in Europe in past decades but now out of favor, is often called a *social contract.* Labor, management, and the government consult annually and agree on target wage changes. These are calculated to be non-inflationary, given the government's projections for the future and its planned economic policies. Such a scheme is most easily initiated in a centralized economy such as West Germany's, where a few giant firms and unions exert enormous power, or in a country such as Britain, where the party in power during much of the period in which social contracts were used had strong official links with the labor unions.

The other main type of incomes policy is **tax-related incomes policy (TIP),** which we first encountered in Chapter 36. TIPs provide tax incentives for management and labor to conform to government-established wage and price guidelines. For example, increases in wages and prices in excess of the guidelines would be taxed heavily. TIPs have not yet been tried, although they have been strongly advocated by some economists.

TIPs rely on tax incentives to secure voluntary conformity with wage and price guidelines, whereas wage and price controls try to impose conformity by law.

Advocates of TIPs argue that their great advantage is leaving decisions on wages and prices in the hands of labor and management while influencing behavior by altering the incentive system. Critics, however, argue that they would prove to be an administrative nightmare.

Growth

Policies for intervention to increase growth rates are of two sorts. Some policies seek to alter the general economic climate in a way favorable to growth. They typically include subsidization or favorable tax treatment for research and development, for purchase of plant and equipment, and for other profit-earning activities. Measures to lower interest rates temporarily or permanently are urged by some as favorable to investment and growth. Most interventionists support these general measures.

Some also support more specific intervention, usually in the form of what is called *picking and backing winners* in one way or another. Advocates of this view, such as Professor Lester Thurow of MIT, want governments to pick the industries, usually new ones, that have potential for future success and then back them with subsidies, government contracts, research funds, and all the other encouragements at the government's command.

Opponents argue that picking winners requires foresight and that there is no reason to expect the government to have better foresight than private investors. Indeed, since political considerations inevitably get in the way, the government may be less successful than the market in picking winners. If so, channeling funds through the government rather than through the private sector may hurt rather than help growth rates. (This debate is continued in Box 38-2 on page 834.)

Rational Expectations and the Micro Foundations of Macroeconomics[6]

For many years Keynesian economics seemed successful both in explaining the overall behavior of the economy and in suggesting policies for controlling inflation and unemployment. As long as it appeared to work, few were interested in *how*. During the late 1960s and the 1970s, however, control of the economy by means of traditional fiscal and monetary policies seemed to become more difficult. This raised concerns about the foundations of Keynesian theory. The main question was, What behavior in the individual markets for goods and factors of production is implied by the Keynesian aggregate relationships? This question concerns what are called the *micro foundations,* or *micro underpinnings*, of macro models.

While these concerns about the Keynesian model were surfacing, the monetarist model seemed to provide an alternative for understanding the macro behavior of the economy and for prescribing appropriate policies. This elicited a debate about the merits of the two models, a debate that still rages today. Micro foundations are at the heart of the debate between monetarism and Keynesianism. The issues are important; because they are at the frontier of modern research, they are also difficult. The analysis depends on material that is treated in detail in more advanced courses. At this stage, therefore, we can discuss the issues only in broad outline.

Monetarist Micro Foundations

There is no single set of accepted monetarist micro foundations. Most monetarists, however,

[6] The rest of this chapter may be omitted without loss of continuity.

view markets as competitive.[7] One important characteristic of competitive markets is that prices and wages are flexible; they adjust to establish equilibrium at all times. When a competitive market is in equilibrium (see Chapter 4), the market is said to have *cleared.* This means that every purchaser has been able to buy all he or she wishes to buy at the going price and every seller has been able to sell all he or she wishes to sell at that price.[8] When each and every market is in equilibrium, there is full employment of all resources. The prices that clear markets are called **market-clearing prices**.

According to the monetarists, strong forces ensure that departures from full-employment equilibrium are quickly rectified. That is, monetarists believe that the *automatic adjustment mechanism* works quite efficiently.

We now consider two particular monetarist views.

Traditional Monetarism

The monetarist school of thought that evolved in the 1960s was led by Professor Milton Friedman of the University of Chicago. Economists of that school, often called *traditional monetarists,* hold that the economy, when left to its own, tends to stabilize at the full-employment level. They also hold that, historically, monetary policies have been erratic. We saw in Chapter 34 that monetarists believe that monetary policy exerts a powerful influence on the economy, so they reach the following conclusion:

Traditional monetarists believe that fluctuations in the money supply are a major source of fluctuations in output and the price level.

Although monetary policy has strong effects, it operates with a long and variable lag. According to Friedman and his followers, these long and variable lags not only doom monetary policy to failure but make it counterproductive as well. In their view monetary policy has actually served to destabilize the economy in the past. The best course for monetary policy is held to be to follow the *k* percent rule, that is, to set the rate of increase of the money supply at some given value and hold it there.

New Classical Monetarism

The *new Classical monetarists* follow Professors Robert Lucas and Thomas Sargeant in holding that temporary departures from full employment occur mainly because people make mistakes. This viewpoint can be best understood in terms of the proposition derived from microeconomics that individual supply and demand behavior depends only on the structure of relative prices.

To follow their argument, let us start by assuming that each of the economy's markets is in equilibrium; there is full employment, prices are stable, and the actual and expected rates of inflation are zero. Now suppose the government increases the money supply by 5 percent. People find themselves with unwanted money balances, which they seek to spend.[9] For simplicity, assume that this leads to an increase in desired expenditure on all commodities; the demand for each commodity shifts to the right, and all prices, being competitively determined, rise. Individual decision makers see their selling prices go up and mistakenly interpret this increase as a rise in their own relative price. This is because they expect the overall rate of inflation to be zero. Firms will produce more and workers will work more; both groups think they are getting an increased *relative* price for what they sell. Thus total output and employment rise.

When both groups eventually realize that their own relative prices are in fact unchanged, output and employment fall back to their initial levels. The extra

[7] They realize, of course, that perfect competition does not exist everywhere in the economy, but they believe that the forces of competition are strong—strong enough that analysis based on the theory of perfect competition will be close to the real behavior of the economy.

[8] Competitive markets clear only at the equilibrium price. At any other price there are either unsatisfied purchasers (excess demand) or unsatisfied sellers (excess supply).

[9] Most monetarists accept the theory of the transmission mechanism (discussed in Chapter 34) according to which the excess money balances are used to buy financial assets, thus driving down interest rates and stimulating expenditure *indirectly*. However, most monetarists tend to stress the relative importance of the *direct* expenditure effects created by excess money balances.

output and employment occur only while people are being fooled. When they realize that *all* prices have risen by 5 percent, they revert to their initial behavior. The only difference is that now the price level has risen by 5 percent, leaving relative prices unchanged.

According to the new Classical theory, deviations from full employment occur only because people make mistakes that cause markets to clear at more or less than full-employment output. People are not prevented from selling as many commodities or as much labor as they wish; the contraction or expansion in output is voluntary.

New Classical monetarists focus on the role of changes in relative prices in signaling appropriate information in a world where tastes and technology are constantly changing. They hold that fluctuations in the money supply will lead to increased fluctuations in all prices. This makes it hard for households and firms to distinguish changes in relative prices, to which they do wish to respond, from changes in the price level, to which they do not wish to respond. Such confusion, created by fluctuations in the money supply, thus leads to mistakes in supply and demand decisions.

This discussion highlights the importance for firms and households of distinguishing the causes of any price changes. Consider, for example, what happens if there is an unexpected and unperceived increase in the money supply. This will lead to an increase in most, if not all, prices above what most agents had expected. Most firms perceive this as an increase in the relative price of their own output and hence increase their level of production above what it normally would have been. Consequently, national income rises above the full-employment level. A similar argument shows that an unanticipated and unperceived decrease in the money supply would cause output to fall below its full-employment level.

The Lucas aggregate supply curve. The behavior just described gives rise to the **Lucas aggregate supply curve.**

The Lucas aggregate supply curve posits that national output will vary positively with the ratio of the actual to the expected price level.

This is often also referred to as the *surprises only* supply curve since it implies that only changes in the price level that are unexpected (surprises) will give rise to fluctuations in aggregate supply.

To see this, consider what happens if there is again an increase in the money supply, but this time suppose that it has been widely expected in advance by firms and households. Again prices will rise. Most firms will now take this to mean only that the *observed* change in the price of their own output has roughly matched the *expected* change in the average of all other prices. Hence they will not interpret it as a rise in the relative price of their own output and will maintain their production level at its normal level. National income will not rise above potential despite the rise in the general price level.

According to the new Classical theory, expected changes in the price level do not lead to fluctuations in aggregate supply.

New Classical policy views. New Classical monetarists support the *k* percent rule, just like the traditional monetarists. They believe that firms and households make better decisions when monetary and fiscal policies are stable than when they are highly variable. They believe that active interventionist policies designed to stabilize the economy make it harder for people to interpret the signals generated by the price system and so lead them to make more errors in forming their expectations. This then increases rather than reduces the fluctuations of output around its full-employment level and increases rather than reduces the fluctuations of unemployment around the natural rate.

According to the new Classical theory, active use of monetary policy in an attempt to stabilize the economy will lead to confusion about relative and absolute prices. This will cause people to make mistakes in their output and purchasing decisions and therefore increase aggregate output fluctuations.

This conclusion depends on the particular view adopted by the new Classical monetarists about how people form predictions or expectations, a subject that has recently become an important part of macroeconomic debates.

The Theory of Rational Expectations

The new Classical model is augmented by the theory of *rational expectations*. People look to the government's current macroeconomic policy to form their expectations of future inflation. They understand how the economy works, and they form their expectations rationally by predicting the outcome of the policies being pursued. People learn fairly quickly from their mistakes; though random errors occur, systematic and persistent errors do not. In an obvious sense, such expectations are *forward-looking*.

According to the theory of rational expectations, people do not make persistent, systematic errors in predicting the overall inflation rate; they may, however, make unsystematic errors.

Policy invariance. Rational expectations, combined with the Lucas aggregate supply curve, give rise to the new Classical *policy invariance*, or policy neutrality, with this result:

Systematic attempts to use monetary policy to stabilize the economy will lead to systematic changes in the price level but will not influence the behavior of output.

Thus, according to the new Classicists, monetary policy can do harm—by creating confusion about the source of price changes—but cannot do good, except by random chance. Thus even in the face of major recessions, laissez faire is the best conceivable stabilization policy.

Let us review how this follows from combining the monetarist micro foundations with the theory of rational expectations.

1. According to the new Classical theory's micro foundations, deviations from full employment occur only because of errors in predicting the price level (which cause workers and firms to mistake changes in the price level for changes in relative prices).
2. According to the theory of rational expectations, errors in predicting the price level are only random.
3. It follows from the first two points that there is no room for active government policy to stabilize the economy. The causes of fluctuations are random.[10] It is in the nature of random fluctuations that they cannot be foreseen and offset. Thus there is no room for stabilization policy to reduce the fluctuations in the economy by offsetting the disturbances that emanate from the private sector.

Not all monetarists accept the theory of rational expectations. For those who do, however, the contrast with the Keynesians is extreme.

The most extreme monetarist attack on stabilization policy has two parts. The first is a model of an economy where deviations from full employment occur only because of errors. The second is a theory of people's expectations that predicts that persistent, systematic errors—and hence systematic deviations from full employment—will not occur.

Monetarist Conclusions

The two monetarist schools obviously do not agree on everything. Both agree, however, that monetary policy should not be used actively to stabilize the economy. This is for two reasons: (1) Fluctuations in the money supply are the major source of fluctuations in output and inflation, and (2) there is no long-term trade-off between inflation and national income.[11]

Most economists accept the view that monetary forces are important in influencing inflation and unemployment, but many do not agree that monetary forces are the *most* important force. Most economists

[10] However, long lags may cause macro variables to display cyclical fluctuations, as discussed in Chapter 31.

[11] Recall that any attempt to hold income above its full-employment level will lead not to a constant rate of inflation but to a continuously accelerating inflation. This is just a restatement of the acceleration hypothesis and the natural rate hypothesis developed in detail in Chapter 36 and its appendix.

also agree that inflation will tend to accelerate if income is held permanently above its full-employment level.

One aspect of the monetarist model that is particularly controversial is the belief in downward flexibility of prices, which leads to the prediction that as long as national income is below its full-employment level, the price level would *fall* at an ever-accelerating rate. Keynesians say that the observed downward inflexibility of the price level refutes this view. They reject the prediction that the main cause of recessionary gaps is *voluntary* reductions in employment and output due to errors in reading the signals provided by the price system. Most Keynesians do not believe that output deviates from its potential level *only* because workers and firms make mistakes.

Keynesian Micro Foundations

The Keynesian micro foundations emphasize the noncompetitive nature of the economy. Most firms are seen as setting their own prices rather than accepting those set on competitive markets. Their per unit output costs tend to be fairly constant, and they set prices by adding a relatively inflexible markup to their costs.[12] They then sell what they can at the going price. Cyclical fluctuations in aggregate demand cause cyclical fluctuations in the demand for each firm's products, which in turn cause individual firms to make cyclical variations in output and employment rather than in price.

While in the monetarist model the main impact of fluctuations in aggregate demand is on prices, in the Keynesian model their main impact is on output and employment.

A similar argument holds for labor markets in the Keynesian model. Wages respond to the price level and productivity, but are relatively insensitive to short-term cyclical fluctuations in demand. (This is discussed in detail in Chapter 20.) A recent proposal to change wage-setting arrangements is discussed in Box 39-4.

[12] Complete cyclical inflexibility of markup is not necessary. What matters is that firms do not adjust prices continually and as a result are willing to sell further units at the same price. This much price inflexibility need not imply an absence of profit maximization. Instead it may follow from profit maximization when it is costly to alter prices. This is discussed further in Chapter 15.

This short-term wage inflexibility can stem from rational behavior on the part of workers. If wage rates adjust to clear labor markets, wages will vary over the cycle. *All* workers will then bear the uncertainty associated with the cyclical movements in wages. However, if wages are set in response to long-term considerations but do not vary cyclically so as to clear labor markets, cyclical fluctuations in demand will cause employment to fluctuate. Since most layoffs and rehires are based on seniority, employment fluctuations are all borne by the 10 or 20 percent of workers who are the least senior. The majority of workers will then have little uncertainty in the face of cyclical fluctuations in demand, all the uncertainty having been placed on the minority with low seniority. Thus contracts that fix wages over the cycle and allow employment to vary may be preferable to the majority of workers compared to contracts that allow wages to vary in order to clear the labor market continually and thus prevent unemployment.

In Keynesian macroeconomics, the economy does not have a unique short-term equilibrium. Because firms would like to sell more and some workers would be willing to work more at current prices, fluctuations in aggregate demand cause output and employment to fluctuate in the short term.

The Keynesian macro model allows for systematic disturbances that can cause prolonged deflationary or recessionary gaps.

According to the Keynesians, stabilization policy can then be used to offset at least the gaps that are large and persistent.

Such policies seek to alter aggregate demand using both fiscal and monetary tools.

Differences Between the Two Models

There are many differences in the micro behavior that underlies the models. Probably the most impor-

BOX 39-4

The Share Economy

Several times in this text we have noted that wage rigidity is widely perceived to be a major impediment to the efficient functioning of the economy. In his important book *The Share Economy,* Professor Martin Weitzman of the Massachusetts Institute of Technology proposed a dramatic policy designed to restore flexibility of wages and thus enhance economic performance.

How the Share Economy Works

The basic idea is quite simple. Under Weitzman's proposal, part of the payment that any firm makes to labor would be tied directly to that firm's net revenues. This payment, which is like an annual bonus, is called the *share wage.* In addition, workers would also receive a *base wage,* which is fixed for the duration of the labor contract and is much lower than their wage under existing, traditional labor contracts.

When the firm is prosperous and net revenues are high, the share wage paid to workers would be correspondingly high. In these circumstances the total wage, equal to the base wage plus the share age, would exceed the initial wage that prevailed prior to the scheme's introduction. But when the firm's sales are down and thus net revenues are low, the share wage would also be low. In these circumstances the total wage would be below the initial wage.

Consider, for example, a firm that is currently paying its workers a fixed wage of $20 an hour. Now suppose that under the share contract it pays them a base wage of only $10 an hour and that it also promises to pay workers a fixed percentage of its net revenues. Finally, suppose that this percentage is such that if net revenues are at their average or normal level, each worker will receive a combined base plus share wage of $20 an hour, just equal to the wage in the absence of the share contract.

If the firm's net revenues turn out to be above their normal level, the share wage will rise to reflect this; thus the total payment to workers will exceed $20 an hour, and the workers will share in the prosperity of the firm. If the firm's net revenues turn out to be below their normal level, the share wage will fall; in this case the total wage will be below $20 an hour, and the workers will "share" in the ill fortunes of the firm.

Implications of the Share Economy

Under traditional wage-setting arrangements, rigid wages mean that a firm will lay off workers in the face of a fall in demand for its output. Under a share

tant relates to the distinction between voluntary and involuntary unemployment.

In the monetarist model all unemployment and output below capacity are voluntary. Workers decide to be unemployed, and firms decide to produce less than capacity output as a result of errors they make in predicting the general price level (and therefore the relative price of what they sell). So if surveyed, the millions of unemployed around the world in the early 1980s would have said that they could have had a job at the going wage, but they refused to accept it because, given their expectations about inflation, the expected real wage was too low.

In the Keynesian model, prices and wages do not fluctuate to clear markets. Unemployment and production below capacity are involuntary in the sense that unemployed workers would like jobs at the going wage rate but cannot find them, and firms would like to sell more at going prices, but customers are not forthcoming.[13] So if surveyed, the millions of unemployed around the world in the early 1980s would have said that they would have accepted a job at the going wage rate, but none was available.

Major current debate centers around these two prototype models and some of their subtler offshoots. Issues such as what determines the degree of wage and price flexibility in the economy, the conditions under which it can be expected that people can form accurate expectations and act on them, and

[13] Of course, one could still argue that this unemployment is voluntary because the workers had earlier voluntarily agreed to the contracts.

contract, firms will have a much smaller incentive to lay off workers during a downturn, since the total wage paid to each worker falls. Thus workers will face a more stable employment pattern with the share contract. However, workers will have to accept the risk of a fluctuating total wage compared to the initial situation in which they received a fixed wage of $20 *if they remained employed.*

Many observers feel that the situation under a share contract, where each worker bears a small part of the burden of the downturn, is more equitable than the situation under a fixed total wage, where those workers who keep their jobs bear none of the burden while the minority who get paid off bear the total burden. Further, many observers feel that the economy would operate more efficiently in the presence of the enhanced wage flexibility that the share contracts would generate.

Weitzman proposes that tax incentives be introduced to encourage firms to enter into such contracts. For example, share income could be subject to a special low tax rate, with regular tax rates still applying to any income from a fixed wage rate. Firms and workers would thus have an incentive to arrange for a large fraction of the total payment to labor to be share income.

This proposal is controversial. Some unions have criticized it, arguing that if the contract specifies a given fraction of net revenues is to be paid to all workers, firms will have an incentive to add to their work force and thus reduce each worker's share. This practice, the argument continues, will drive wages down to very low levels. Other unions reply that the expansion in employment is precisely one of the desirable features of the system, and there is no reason to expect *total* wages to fall. Some observers fear the impact on the deficit of the special tax incentives that might be required; others reply, using reasoning reminiscent of the Laffer curve (see page 498), that the improvement in the performance of the economy will be so great that total tax revenues will rise, not fall. Perhaps the highest praise of all came in a *New York Times* editorial in which *The Share Economy* was referred to as "the best idea since Keynes."

the potential for destabilizing the economy by pursuing an active stabilization policy are at the forefront of modern research. Views on how the economy behaves at both the micro and macro levels will be influenced by the progress of the debate. So will views on the place of fiscal and monetary policy as possible ways to eliminate inflationary or recessionary gaps.

The Progress of Economics

In this chapter we have discussed a number of current controversies about the behavior of the economy and the evidence that relates to them. General acceptance of the view that the validity of economic theories should be tested by confronting their predictions with the mass of all available evidence is fairly new in economics.

Since 1936 when Keynes's *The General Theory of Employment, Interest, and Money* was published, great progress has been made in economics in relating theory to evidence. This progress has been reflected in the superior ability of governments to achieve their policy objectives. The financial aspects of World War II were handled far better than those of World War I. When President Roosevelt tried to reduce unemployment in the 1930s, his efforts were greatly hampered by the failure even of economists to realize the critical importance of budget deficits in raising aggregate demand and in injecting newly created money into the economy. When the Vietnam War forced the government to adopt expansive fiscal and monetary policies, economists had no trouble in predicting the outcome. More involvement abroad was obtained at the cost of heavy inflationary pressure at home.

The general propositions of theories are tested in such important policy areas as running wars, curing major depressions, and coping with inflations, even if all their specific predictions are not. In some sense, then, economic theories have always been subjected to empirical tests. When they were wildly at variance with the facts, the ensuing disaster could not but be noticed, and the theories were discarded or amended in the light of what was learned.

The advances of economics in the past 50 years reflect economists' changed attitudes toward empirical observations. Today economists are much less likely to dismiss theories just because they do not like them and to refuse to abandon theories just because they do like them. Economists are more likely to try to base their theories as much as possible on empirical observation and to accept empirical relevance as the ultimate arbiter of the value of theories. As human beings, we may be anguished at the upsetting of a pet theory; as scientists, we should try to train ourselves to take pleasure in it because of the new knowledge gained thereby. It has been said that one of the great tragedies of science is the continual slaying of beautiful theories by ugly facts. It must always be remembered that when theory and fact come into conflict, theory, not fact, must give way.

Summary

1. Macroeconomic performance is judged in terms of the behavior of many variables. The key variables are (a) output, employment, and unemployment, (b) the rate of change of the price level, and (c) long-term growth.
2. Views about the role of policy in improving macroeconomic performance range between two extremes. The conservative view is that there is only a minimum role for policy; macroeconomic performance will be most satisfactory when the market system is allowed to function as freely as possible. The interventionist view is that active use of policy will improve macroeconomic performance. It is common to identify monetarists with conservatives and Keynesians with interventionists.
3. Monetarists believe that because the economy is inherently stable, the goal of damping the business cycle is best achieved by avoiding fluctuations in policy, especially monetary policy. Hence they advocate a *k* percent rule. Keynesians believe that the economy is inherently unstable in that expenditure functions shift regularly and the economy's self-corrective mechanisms are weak. Hence they believe in an active role for both monetary and fiscal policy to stabilize the business cycle.
4. Monetarists believe that inflation is everywhere and always a monetary phenomenon and so advocate the same conservative policies to avoid price instability as they advocate to minimize policy-induced cycles in output. They also argue that to control inflation, the long-term growth rate of the money supply must not be too high. Keynesians accept the view that monetary expansion is necessary for inflation to persist in the long term, but they take seriously the role of other factors in causing short-term but substantial infla-

tion. Hence they believe in an active role for policy to offset these factors in the short term.

5. Conservatives believe that long-term growth will be maximized when the incentives provided by the profit motive are strongest. Interventionists see a need for special government programs to channel resources into research and development and other investment expenditures designed to raise potential output.
6. Conservatives see a role for policy in terms of providing a stable environment for individual decision makers. This involves maintaining a consistent set of "fiscal rules of the game" in terms of expenditure and tax rates and providing a steady but gradual growth in the money supply.
7. Interventionists have specific prescriptions for each policy variable. They advocate active use of discretionary monetary and fiscal policy to stabilize output and employment. Despite imperfections caused by lags and incomplete knowledge, they believe such policies are helpful. Similar policies can be combined with incomes policies to stabilize the fluctuations in the price level that arise from various sources and are subject to an upward bias. They also support policies to promote growth through subsidization, tax favors, and more specific intervention.
8. Monetarists view markets as competitive and hence believe that departures from full-employment equilibrium are quickly rectified. As a result, they believe that fluctuations in aggregate demand lead primarily to fluctuations in the price level rather than in the level of output. They believe that the best course for monetary policy is to follow a *k* percent rule. For traditional monetarists, this is because they believe that long and variable lags in the effect of monetary policy mean that an interventionist monetary policy would destabilize output.
9. New Classical monetarists believe that departures from full-employment output occur only when people make mistakes in predicting the price level. When combined with the theory of rational expectations, this leads to the policy invariance proposition. New Classical monetarists support the *k* percent rule because they believe an interventionist monetary policy will not be effective in stabilizing output.
10. Keynesians emphasize the noncompetitive nature of the economy. As a result they believe that fluctuations in aggregate demand lead primarily to fluctuations in output rather than in the price level. In this view, an interventionist stabilization policy can be effective in stabilizing fluctuations in output.

Topics for Review

Conservatives and interventionists
Micro foundations
k percent rule

Traditional and new Classical monetarists
Lucas aggregate supply curve
Theory of rational expectations
Policy invariance proposition

Discussion Questions

1. To what extent is today's unemployment a serious social problem? If people could vote to choose between 10 percent unemployment combined with zero inflation and 2 percent unemployment combined with 10 percent inflation, which alternative do you think would win? Which groups might prefer the first alternative and which groups the second?
2. Some economists urge the government to fight inflation and combat unemployment by encouraging private-sector saving and investment. How might expanded saving and investment help to reduce inflation and combat unemployment?
3. Nobel Laureate Paul Samuelson quoted a "conservative economist friend" as saying in mid 1980, "If you're contriving a teensy-weensy recession for us, please don't bother. It won't do the job. What's needed is a believable declaration that Washington will countenance *whatever* degree of unemployment is needed to bring us back on the path to price stability, and a demonstrated willingness to *stick* to that resolution no matter how politically unpopular the short-run joblessness, production cutbacks, and dips in profit might be." Discuss the "conservative friend's" view of inflation. Does experience since 1980 suggest that his advice was followed? If so, what was the consequence?
4. An ad that appeared in the *New York Times* in the early 1980s had this to say about inflation. "First [our politicians] blamed wage increases and price hikes for inflation. Then when 'voluntary guidelines' were established, the blame shifted to OPEC oil prices. Both explanations were wrong. Government policy is responsible for inflation—paying for deficit spending by 'creating money out of thin air.' " What theories of inflation are rejected and accepted by the writers of this ad?
5. In the mid 1980s a fervent national debate developed concerning the need to protect U.S. industries from foreign competition. How do the pro and con views of protectionism relate to the conservative and interventionist policies for promoting long-term growth?
6. A number of key microeconomic policy issues that were discussed earlier in this book are listed below. Go back and review the relevant discussion of some of them, and then present both the conservative case for "letting the market work" and the interventionist case in favor of a particular policy prescription. (Although the issues listed are "microeconomic" issues, their impact on the macroeconomic issues—in particular economic growth—can be important.)
   a. Rent controls (Chapter 6)
   b. De-industrialization (Chapter 17)
   c. Minimum-wage laws (Chapter 19)
   d. Increasing tariffs and other restrictions on imports (Chapter 21)
   e. Paying for social benefits (Chapter 25)
   f. Financing health care (Chapter 25)

Appendix A to Chapter 39

Money in the National Income Model

We have studied the interaction of money, interest rates, and national income in terms of the apparatus in Figures 34-3 through 34-6. A loose end in that model can best be seen by considering the impact of an increase in the money supply. This leads to a fall in interest rates as shown in Figure 34-4(i), to increases in expenditure as shown in Figure 34-4(ii), and to increased national income as shown in Figure 34-5. But increased national income in turn leads to an increased need for transactions balances. This increased demand for money must then be added to the liquidity preference schedule in Figure 34-4. How is the increase in demand satisfied? Does accounting for it radically alter the conclusions of the analysis of Chapter 34?

The answer to the last question is no. This appendix provides a model that integrates monetary and expenditure factors and shows how they jointly determine the interest rate and the level of national income. The British economist Sir John Hicks (awarded the Nobel Prize in economics in 1972) suggested the approach in his famous review of Keynes' *General Theory,* "Mr. Keynes and the Classics: A Suggested Interpretation." It involves identifying the relationship between income and interest rates that is imposed first by goods market equilibrium and then by money market equilibrium. We then bring the two together to determine the one combination of real national income and interest rate that satisfies both equilibrium conditions simultaneously. Finally, we use the model to examine the effects of monetary and fiscal policy.

The Interest Rate and Aggregate Expenditure: The *IS* Curve

As we saw in going from Figure 34-4(ii) to Figure 34-5(i), a fall in the rate of interest is associated with a rise in the level of real national income, due to increased investment expenditures. Figure 34A-1 depicts this relationship between interest rate and national income as the negatively sloped *IS* curve.[1] The *IS* curve shows the combinations of national income and the rate of interest for which aggregate desired expenditure just equals total production in the economy. The negative relationship is derived for *given* values of the other variables influencing the aggregate expenditure function of Figure 34-5(i).

For given settings of the relationships underlying the aggregate expenditure function, the condition of goods market equilibrium—national income equals aggregate expenditure—means that the level of national income will vary negatively with the interest rate.

Fiscal Policy

Increases in the level of government expenditure raise the total level of aggregate expenditure *for any given interest rate.* As Figure 32-1 shows, this in turn leads to a multiplier effect on national income. In terms of the present model, an increase in government expenditure causes the *IS* curve to shift upward and to the right, as shown in Figure 39A-1. Combinations of national income and the interest rate that were on the original *IS* curve and hence were initially positions of equilibrium in the goods market are now positions of excess demand due to the increase in autonomous government demand. Hence output must rise to satisfy the increased demand (in the process leading to the now familiar multiplier effect), interest rates must rise to reduce investment demand, or, as IS_1 shows, some combination of both must occur.[2]

[1] *IS* stands for investment and saving, since the equilibrium condition is often expressed in terms of the equality between these two aggregates.

[2] A reduction in taxes, by altering the relationship between national income and disposable income, would also lead to a rightward shift in the *IS* curve.

FIGURE 39A-1 Goods Market Equilibrium: The *IS* Curve

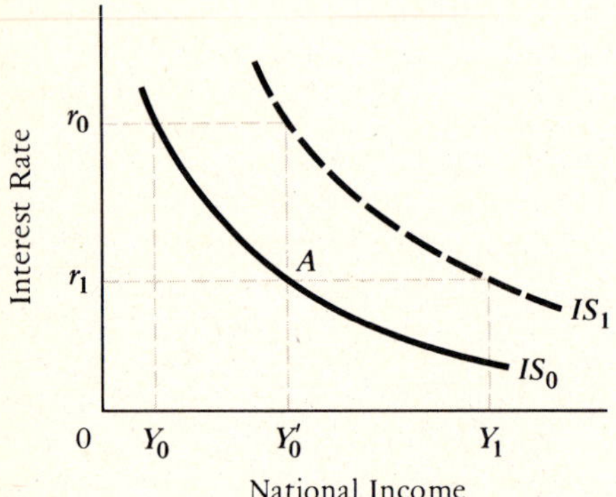

The locus of combinations of national income and the interest rate for which aggregate expenditure equals output is called the *IS* curve. The *IS* curve slopes downward and to the right, indicating that a fall in the interest rate from r_0 to r_1 leads, via increased investment, to an increase in the level of national income from Y_0 to Y_0'. Expansionary fiscal policy creates excess demand for output and causes the *IS* curve to shift to the right to IS_1; from an initial position at *A*, the interest rate must rise to r_0, national income must rise to Y_2, or some combination of both along IS_1 must occur.

Expansionary fiscal policy causes the *IS* curve to shift upward and to the right, creating a new locus of points at which aggregate expenditure equals national income.

By similar reasoning, cuts in government spending or tax increases shift the *IS* curve down to the left. [50]

Liquidity Preference and National Income: The *LM* Curve

When the money supply is held constant, if the demand for and the supply of money are to be equal the *total* demand for money arising from the transactions, speculative and precautionary motives must also be constant. As we have seen, the demand for money can be expected to vary positively with the level of national income and negatively with the rate of interest. If there is to be monetary equilibrium with a given money supply, any increase in national income must therefore be accompanied by an increase in the interest rate to keep total money demand constant. This is depicted by the positively sloped *LM* curve in Figure 39A-2. The *LM* curve shows the combinations of national income and interest rate for which total money demand is constant at the level of a given money supply.[3]

For a given money supply, the condition of monetary market equilibrium means that the

[3] The *L* stands for liquidity preference (or demand for money) and the *M* for money supply.

FIGURE 39A-2 Monetary Market Equilibrium: The *LM* Curve

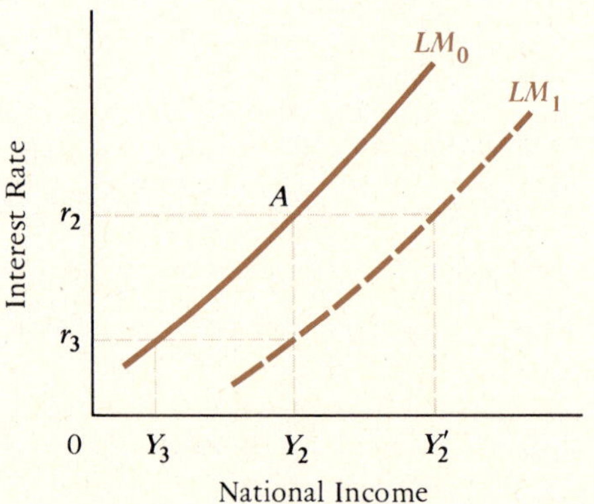

The locus of combinations of national income and the interest rate of which total money demand equals a given money supply is called the *LM* curve. The *LM* curve slopes upward and to the right, indicating that a fall in the rate of interest from r_2 to r_3, which causes the demand for money to rise, must be accompanied by a fall in the level of national income, say, from Y_2 to Y_3, in order to keep money demand equal to the constant money supply. An open-market purchase creates an excess supply of money and causes the *LM* curve to shift to the right to LM_1; from an initial position at *A*, the interest rate must fall to r_3, national income must rise to Y_2', or some combination of both along *LM* must occur.

level of national income will vary directly with the interest rate.

Monetary Policy

An increase in the supply of money resulting from an open-market purchase by the central bank causes the *LM* curve to shift downward and to the right, as in Figure 39A-2. The combinations of national income and interest rate that were on the original curve LM_0 and hence were initially positions of monetary equilibrium now correspond to excess supply due to the increase in the supply of money. To reestablish equilibrium, the demand for money must increase to match the larger money supply; hence national income must rise, the interest rate must fall, or, as LM_1 shows, some combination of both must occur.

An increase in the money supply causes the *LM* curve to shift downward and to the right, creating a new locus of points at which total money demand equals the money supply.

By similar reasoning, a decrease in the money supply causes the *LM* curve to shift upward to the left. [51]

Macroeconomic Equilibrium: Determination of National Income and the Interest Rate

The model is shown in Figure 39A-3. The intersection of the *LM* and *IS* curves indicates the only combination of national income and interest rate for which aggregate expenditure equals national income *and* the demand for money is equal to the supply.

The intersection of the *IS* and *LM* curves gives the equilibrium levels of national income and the rate of interest in a model that combines both expenditure and monetary influences.

Figure 39A-3 shows the effects of particular shifts in the *IS* and *LM* curves. This analysis leads to four general predictions.

1. A rightward shift in the *IS* curve raises national income and the rate of interest.
2. A leftward shift in the *IS* curve lowers national income and the rate of interest.
3. A rightward shift in the *LM* curve raises national income and lowers the rate of interest.
4. A leftward shift in the *LM* curve lowers national income and raises the rate of interest.

The Effects of Fiscal and Monetary Policy

Given our analysis of the effects of government expenditure on the *IS* curve and the effects of the money supply on the *LM* curve, we can summarize the analysis in our four basic predictions about the effects of monetary and fiscal policy.

1. An increase in government expenditure raises national income and raises the rate of interest.
2. An increase in the money supply raises national income and lowers the rate of interest.
3. A decrease in government expenditure lowers national income and lowers the rate of interest.
4. A decrease in the money supply lowers national income and raises the rate of interest.

These results represent what may be called the *Keynesian synthesis*, in which both monetary and fiscal policies have an effect on national income and interest rates.[4] [52]

At one time, debate in macroeconomics centered on the relative strengths of monetary and fiscal policy. *Monetarists* argued that monetary policy was powerful and fiscal policy was weak; *Keynesians* tended to argue that the opposite was the case. These views, and how they are related to the underlying behavioral relations, can be understood in terms of the *IS/LM* model.[5]

Consider first the strength of an increase in government spending. This increases expenditure directly and, as we have seen, shifts the *IS* curve rightward. The effect on national income is smaller than

[4] As we saw in Chapters 32 and 34, a cut in tax rates has effects similar to an increase in *G*, and a fall in the demand for money has effects similar to an increase in the money supply.

[5] This discussion expands on the analysis illustrated in Figure 34-7 on page 747.

FIGURE 39A-3 **Effects of Shifts in the *IS* and *LM* Curves**

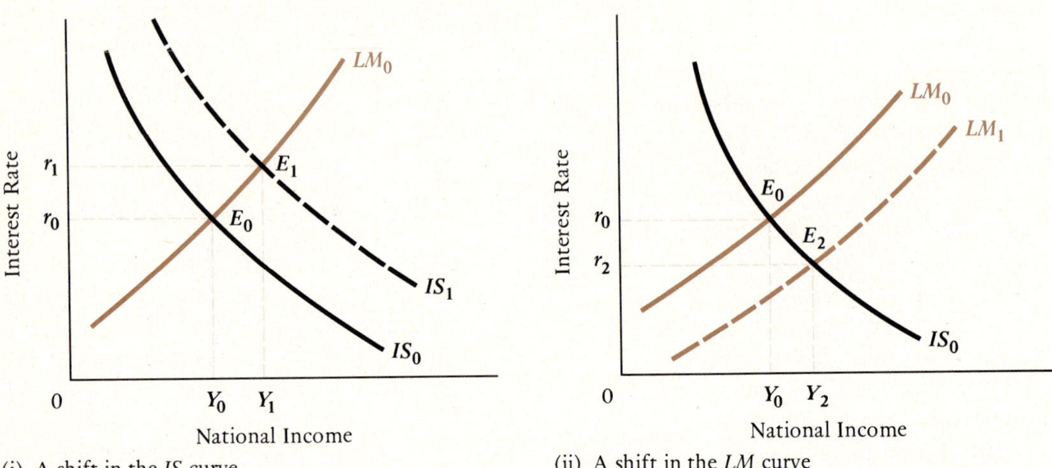

(i) A shift in the *IS* curve

(ii) A shift in the *LM* curve

Similar shifts in the *IS* and *LM* curves have similar effects on national income and opposite effects on the rate of interest. The initial levels of income and interest rate are Y_0 and r_0 in both parts of the figure. In part (i) a rightward shift in the *IS* curve from IS_0 to IS_1 raises national income from Y_0 to Y_1 and raises the rate of interest from r_0 to r_1. In part (ii) a rightward shift in the *LM* curve from LM_0 to LM_1 raises national income from Y_0 to Y_2 and lowers the rate of interest from r_0 to r_2. Part (i) shows the effect of an increase in government expenditure; part (ii) shows the effect of an increase in the money supply.

this rightward shift because (1) the conditions for monetary equilibrium summarized in the *LM* curve mean that an increase in national income must be accompanied by an increase in the interest rate, and (2) an increase in the interest rate gives rise to a fall in the level of interest-sensitive spending in the economy. The weaker either of these two effects is, the stronger the effects of the increase in government spending will be. The more interest-elastic the demand for money, the flatter will be the *LM* curve, and hence the less the interest rate will rise in response to the fiscal stimulus. The less interest-elastic desired expenditure is, the steeper will be the *IS* curve and the smaller the "crowding out" of private investment following a fiscal expansion.

Now consider monetary policy. An increase in the money supply causes the *LM* curve to shift to the right; this leads to a fall in the interest rate and an increase in interest-sensitive expenditure. As a result there is a movement down and to the right along the *IS* curve, and national income rises. The rise in national income will be larger (1) the larger the fall in the interest rate and (2) the larger the induced increase in interest-sensitive expenditure. The less interest-elastic the demand for money is, the steeper will be the *LM* curve and the larger the fall in the interest rate following a monetary expansion. The more interest-elastic desired expenditure is, the flatter will be the *IS* curve and the larger the induced increase in interest-sensitive expenditure.

Monetarists, then, in this debate tended to think of the demand for money as relatively interest-insensitive and desired expenditure as relatively interest-sensitive; this gives rise to the combination of a steep *LM* curve and a flat *IS* curve with the implication of effective monetary policy and ineffective fiscal policy. Keynesians, by contrast, tended to think of the opposite combination of interest-sensitive money demand and interest-insensitive desired expenditure; this gives rise to a steep *IS* curve and a flat *LM* curve with the implication of effective fiscal policy and ineffective monetary policy.

The Price Level and Aggregate Demand

So far we have treated the price level as given and presumed that all changes in national income were changes in *real* output. Consider now what would happen to the analysis if the price level were allowed to vary.

Changes in the Price Level

As we saw in Box 34-2 on pages 750–751, an increase in the price level leads to an increase in liquidity preference. For money market equilibrium to be preserved, the interest rate must rise, the level of income must fall, or, since either leads to a reduction in money demand, some combination of both must occur. That is, the *LM* curve must shift upward and to the left.

A fall in the price level reduces liquidity preference, and the *LM* curve shifts down and to the right.

Increases in the price level cause the *LM* curve to shift upward to the left; decreases in the price level cause the *LM* curve to shift downward to the right.

FIGURE 39A-4 Derivation of Aggregate Demand

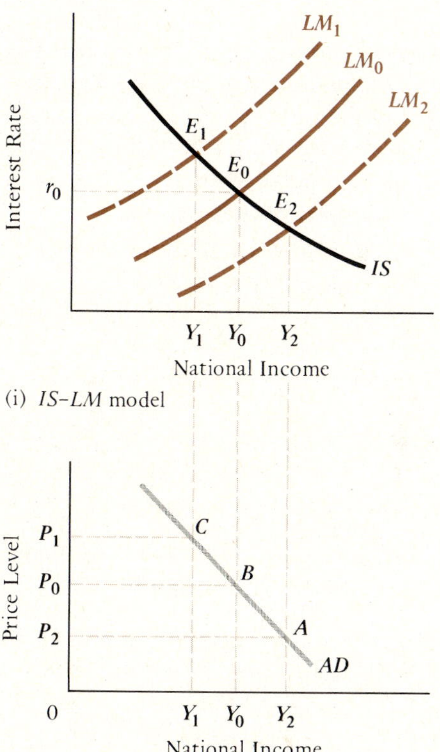

Changes in the price level shift the *LM* curve and thus change the equilibrium level of income. An increase in the price level increases the demand for money. Alternatively, it can be seen as reducing the real value of the existing money stock. The excess demand for money leads to a leftward shift in the LM_0 curve to LM_1 and a fall in national income. A fall in the price level creates an excess supply of money and a rightward shift in the LM_0 curve to LM_2. The price level and national income are inversely related, as shown by the *AD* curve in part (ii).

But we know that the effect in the first case is to reduce national income, while the effect in the second case is to increase national income. This is illustrated in Figure 39A-4.

Equilibrium in the money and goods markets combined implies that the price level and national income are negatively related, as summarized in the downward-sloping aggregate demand curve.

The negative relationship between the price level and national income summarized in the aggregate demand curve is a straightforward extension of the transmission mechanism running from liquidity preference to the rate of interest to aggregate expenditure.

Shifts in the Aggregate Demand Curve

The *AD* curve was derived on the basis of a given money supply and given relationships underlying the

IS curve; it is a straightforward exercise to demonstrate that fiscal and monetary policies, by influencing the *IS* and *LM* curves, cause the *AD* curve to shift. **[53]**

An increase in the money supply means that the *LM* curve corresponding to any particular price level shifts downward to the right. Hence that price level now corresponds to a higher level of real national income; that is, the *AD* curve shifts to the right as a result of an increase in the money supply.

An increase in government expenditure causes the *IS* curve to shift upward to the right as before; it now intersects any given *LM* curve at a higher level of national income. Again, any given price level now corresponds to a larger real national income; that is, the *AD* curve shifts to the right as a result of an increase in government expenditure.

Does the Deficit Matter?

Analysts who focus on the deficit as a summary description of the government's influence on the economy presuppose that tax-financed government expenditure contributes less to aggregate demand than bond-financed government expenditure, since the latter leads to a larger deficit. Note that deficit financing of government expenditure can be viewed as a deferral of taxes, increasing current disposable income and reducing future disposable income. This rearrangement of the timing of taxes may leave expected permanent income basically unchanged compared to the case where taxes were levied at the same time as the government expenditure occurred. While the Keynesian consumption function predicts that consumption would increase with the increase in current disposable income, the permanent-income hypothesis (PIH), discussed in the appendix to Chapter 32, predicts that households' consumption is related to their lifetime or permanent income, not their current disposable income. If the PIH is an accurate description of behavior, deficit finance will have little effect on consumption behavior.

Thus it is possible to identify a set of conditions that would mean that government expenditure have the same effect on the economy whether it is financed by raising current taxes or by issuing government bonds. That imaginary world, first considered by David Ricardo in 1817 and recently revived by Professor Robert Barro, is populated by far-sighted individuals whose consumption decisions depend on their "permanent" income only. Thus changes in the time pattern of income receipts that leave their permanent income unchanged would have no effect on private-sector expenditure decisions.

In this world government bonds would not be net wealth because the financial value of a bond would be matched exactly by a corresponding liability for future tax payments needed to service the debt. Specifically, households would be indifferent between paying \$1 of current taxes and paying a stream of future taxes that has a present value of \$1 when discounted at the market interest rate. In this case the government deficit would not matter; bond rather than tax finance would merely represent a rearrangement in the timing of income receipts that the private sector could (and would) offset in capital markets. Issuing bonds now and raising taxes later would be viewed as equivalent to raising taxes now.

The theory underlying this analysis requires that households have an infinite planning horizon, as in the PIH discussed in the Appendix to Chapter 32. Otherwise taxes accruing after the household's lifetime would not offset interest payments received during the household's lifetime, and government bonds would be viewed as net wealth by the household. Hence deficits would increase households' perceived net wealth, households would increase their consumption, and deficit-financed government expenditure would be more expansionary than tax-financed expenditure.

Barro's contribution was to show that debt neutrality could arise even in the context of the life-cycle hypothesis if the household's concern for its heirs caused its planning horizon to extend beyond its own lifetime. Suppose that the typical household, when making its own lifetime consumption plans, also plans for a positive bequest that it intends to leave to its heirs. Now consider the effects of a government decision to sell bonds rather than increase taxes in order to finance previously announced government expenditure; this of course increases the government budget deficit. (Thus we are focusing on the effects of the method of financing the expenditure, not on the effects of the expenditure itself.) If the households wished, they could simply spend the increased disposable income that results from not having to pay current taxes to finance the government expenditure, thus leaving the next generation with a liability to pay the taxes that will have to be levied when the government redeems the bonds. If the recipients behave in this manner, the fiscal authority's decision to rely on deficit financing will have stimulated the economy by inducing an increase in spending.

However, this behavior would reduce the net value of the bequest that the typical household would be leaving to its heirs, since the heirs now face an increased tax liability. This violates the notion that the members of a typical household make a rational plan that includes targets for their own consumption and for the bequest that they wish to leave to their heirs, since the government action does not change the options open to current households. The current households could have achieved this redistribution away from future generations toward themselves without the government action simply by increasing their own consumption and reducing the value of the estate they leave to their heirs.

If they wish to preserve their initial plan, all that current households need to do is maintain their spending plans and increase saving by the full amount of the increase in their disposable income, that is, by the increase in the government budget deficit. The resulting increase in the value of the next generation's inheritance will exactly offset the increase in tax liabilities that they face. Thus a government deficit that issues bonds now and "promises" taxes in the future would have no effect even if the taxes were expected only after the current generation were dead.

Note that the level of government expenditure is still important in this model—only the method of financing is irrelevant. But there are a number of reasons to believe that future taxes that have a present value of $1 are not equivalent to present taxes of $1 and thus that this debt-neutral Ricardian model does not provide an accurate description of the working of a modern economy. (Ricardo himself rejected it.) Let us cite but three reasons.

The private sector borrows on different terms than the government sector. This is perhaps the most important reason why deficit financing is not neutral in practice. In many circumstances households, and to some extent firms, face constraints that prevent them from borrowing all that they would like to at the prevailing market interest rate. Alternatively, they may be able to borrow but at a much higher interest rate than that facing the government. Consequently, when the government substitutes future taxes for present taxes by running a deficit, these "constrained" private-sector agents will feel wealthier and, consequently, will spend more.

Myopic perception. If some households imperfectly perceive the future tax liabilities implied by the government deficit, they will not offset government dissaving with private saving.

Finite lifetimes. Another reason why households might view future taxes as not equivalent to current taxes is that future taxes may extend beyond the expected lifetime of the household. Thus the household may anticipate escaping taxes by dying! As Barro points out, this would make no difference if households "care about their heirs"; in this case living households would simply alter any bequests they had planned to leave to their heirs by an amount equal to the expected increase in future taxes borne by their heirs. However, if currently alive households do not care or are unable to alter their bequests (perhaps because such bequests cannot be reduced below their current zero level), living households will in fact react to a change in the deficit in a manner that does not completely offset it.

Conclusions

The basic feature of the economy that makes government deficits and the public debt matter is that to a significant extent, current private-sector expenditure is tied to current private-sector income. The government deficit influences the current income of the private sector, since for a given level of government expenditure a larger deficit means lower current taxes and hence larger current private disposable income. In the first instance this debt finance simply causes an intertemporal rearrangement of private-sector income. But for the reasons noted, the private sector is not indifferent to this rearrangement of its income receipts. In particular, current private-sector expenditure rises in response to the increase in current income. This influence of government deficits on private spending not only creates the potential for a stabilization role for deficits over the business cycle, but it also creates the mechanism by which persistent deficits become costly and undesirable in the longer run.

PART ELEVEN

International Macroeconomics

40

Exchange Rates and the Balance of Payments

The value of the Canadian dollar is of great concern to many people. It affects the decisions of a Japanese firm wanting to sell cars in Canada, a Canadian wanting to buy a German government bond, a French exporter selling kitchen appliances to Canada, a Canadian firm hoping to sell commuter airplanes to American feeder airlines, and exporters of Canadian wood and mineral products in markets where prices are quoted in U.S. dollars. It also matters to Canadian tourists cashing their traveler's cheques in London, Athens, or Bangkok.

In this chapter we are concerned with what it means to speak of the "price of the dollar" and what causes that price to change. The discussion will bring together material on three topics studied elsewhere in this book: the theory of supply and demand (Chapter 4), the nature of money (Chapter 33), and international trade (Chapter 20).

We shall examine the simple case of a **small open economy (SOE),** which is an economy that can exert no influence on the world prices of traded goods. The quantities it exports and imports are small in relation to the total volume of world trade in these commodities. Thus the country must accept prices that are established in world markets. For many countries such as Canada, and for many commodities such as wheat, forest products, and minerals, this is a reasonable assumption.

The small open economy faces terms of trade that are fixed by forces beyond its control.

The Nature of Foreign Exchange Transactions

We have seen that money, which consists of any accepted medium of exchange, is vital in any sophisticated economy that relies on specialization and exchange. Yet money as we know it is a *national* matter, one closely controlled by national governments. If you live in Sweden, you will earn kronor and spend kronor; if you run a business in Austria, you borrow schillings and meet your payroll with schillings. The currency of a country is acceptable within the bounds of that country, but it will not usually be accepted by households and firms in another country. The Stockholm bus company will accept kronor for a fare but not Austrian schillings. The Austrian worker will not take Swedish kronor for wages but will accept schillings.

The situation is similar in Canada except that our proximity to the United States leads many Canadian sellers to accept U.S. dollars over the counter. Because U.S. dollars are so well known and so common, Canadian merchants are willing to accept them and then do what the customer would otherwise have had to do: take the money to the bank and exchange it for Canadian money.

When Canadian producers sell their products, they require payment in Canadian dollars. They must meet their wage bills, pay for their raw materials, and reinvest or distribute their profits. There is no problem when they sell to Canadian purchasers. However, if they sell their goods to Indian importers, either the Indians must exchange their rupees to acquire dollars to pay for the goods, or the Canadian producers must accept rupees. They will accept rupees only if they know that they can exchange the rupees for the dollars that they require. The same holds true for producers in all countries: They must eventually receive payment for the goods that they sell in terms of the currency of their own country.

In general, trade between nations can occur only if it is possible to exchange the currency of one nation for that of another.

The exchange rate. International payments that require the exchange of one national currency for another can be made in a bewildering variety of ways, but in essence they involve the exchange of currencies between people who have one currency and require another. Suppose that a Canadian firm wishes to acquire £3,000 for some purpose (£ is the symbol for the British pound sterling). The firm can go to its bank or to some other seller of foreign currency and buy a check that will be accepted in the United Kingdom as £3,000. How many *dollars* the firm must pay to purchase this check will depend on the price of pounds in terms of dollars.

The exchange of one currency for another is part of the process of foreign exchange. The term **foreign exchange** refers to the actual foreign currency or various claims on it, such as bank deposits or promises to pay, that are traded for each other. The **exchange rate** is the price at which purchases and sales of foreign currency or claims on it take place; it is the amount of home currency that must be paid in order to obtain one unit of the foreign currency. For example, if one must give up $2.00 to get £1.00, the exchange rate is 2.[1]

A rise in the price of foreign exchange (i.e., a rise in the exchange rate) is a **depreciation** of the home currency. *Foreign currencies have become more expensive; therefore, the relative value of the home currency has fallen.* A fall in the price of foreign exchange (i.e., a fall in the exchange rate) is an **appreciation** of the home currency. *Foreign currencies have become cheaper; therefore, the relative value of home currency has risen.* For example, when the dollar price of sterling rises from $2.00 to $2.50 (in other words, the sterling price of the dollar falls from £.50 to £.40), the dollar has *depreciated* and the pound has *appreciated*.

The mechanism of foreign exchange transactions. Let us see how foreign exchange transactions are carried out. Suppose that a Canadian firm wishes to purchase a British sports car to sell in Canada. The British firm that made the car requires payment in pounds sterling. If the car is priced at £15,000, the Canadian firm will go to its bank, purchase a cheque for £15,000, and send the cheque to the British seller. Let us suppose this requires that the firm pay $15,000.[2] (The exchange rate in this transaction is £1.00 = $1.67, or $1.00 = £.60.) The British firm deposits the cheque in its bank.

Now assume that in the same period of time a British wholesale firm purchases 25 Canadian refrigerators to sell in Britain. If the refrigerators are priced at $1,000 each, the Canadian seller will have to be paid $25,000. To make this payment the British importing firm goes to its bank, writes a cheque on its account for £15,000, and receives a cheque drawn on a Canadian bank for $25,000. The cheque is sent to

[1] This expresses the relative values of the two currencies in terms of the dollar price of one pound sterling. Alternatively, one could consider the pound sterling price of $1.00 which in this example is £.50.

[2] Banks charge a small commission for making currency exchanges, but we shall ignore this and assume that parties can exchange moneys back and forth at the going exchange rate.

Canada and deposited in a Canadian bank. The effects of these transactions are shown in Table 40-1.

The two transactions cancel each other out, and there is no net change in international liabilities. No money need pass between British and Canadian banks; each bank merely increases the deposit of one domestic customer and lowers the deposit of another. Indeed, as long as the flow of payments between the two countries is equal (Canadians pay as much to British residents as British residents pay to Canadians), all payments can be managed as in the example, and there will be no need for a net payment from British banks to Canadian banks.

All these calculations involve comparing magnitudes measured in different currencies. These comparisons are done using the exchange rate. We now turn to an analysis of how such exchange rates are determined.

Determination of Exchange Rates

As a first step we must look at the link between exchange rates and the prices of a country's imports and exports.

Exchange Rates and the Domestic Prices of Traded Goods

A small open economy faces prices of internationally traded goods that are fixed in foreign currency. The exchange rate translates these into domestic prices. If, for example, the price of wheat is £2 a bushel on international wheat markets, its dollar price in Canada depends on the exchange rate. When the rate is $2 to the pound, the Canadian domestic price of wheat is $4. This is because $4 must be earned from domestic sales in order to match in value the amount that could be earned by selling the wheat internationally for £2 a bushel and by selling the pounds for $2 each.

In Figures 4A-1 and 4A-2 (pages 78 and 79) we showed how imports and exports were determined in an economy facing given world prices for traded goods. We drew the domestic demand and supply curves plotted against domestic prices. We then used the world price, *stated in units of domestic currency,* to determine the quantity of imports and exports of a product. To do this we needed, although we did not say so at the time, an exchange rate so that we could convert world prices into local currency. Recall that we express the exchange rate, *e,* as the number of units of domestic currency needed to buy one unit of foreign currency. The *domestic* price of traded goods, p_d, is then the *world* price of traded goods expressed in foreign currency, p_f, multiplied by the exchange rate:

$$p_d = (e)\ (p_f)$$

For example, when the international price of wheat is £2 per bushel and the exchange rate is $2 to the pound, the Canadian dollar price of wheat is £2 per bushel times $2 per pound, which is $4 per bushel.

It is now a simple matter to see the effect of a change in the exchange rate on the domestic prices of traded goods. Say, for example, that the Canadian dollar appreciates so that it takes only $1.50 to buy £1.00. The domestic price of a bushel of wheat that costs £2.00 is now only $3.00, since $3.00 is now sufficient to buy £2.00. For a second example, say that the Canadian dollar depreciates so that it now takes $2.50 to buy £1.00. Now the dollar price of wheat rises to $5.00 since it takes $5.00 to buy £2.00. (The formula $p_d = (e)\ (p_f)$ gives the right answer, since $2.50 per pound times £2 per bushel equals $5 per bushel.)

An appreciation of the domestic currency lowers the domestic prices of traded goods, whereas a depreciation raises these prices.

To see the effects of changes in the exchange rate, let us return to the example of the Appendix to Chapter 4, a country that is exporting wheat and importing cloth. A 10 percent depreciation of the country's currency would mean that the domestic currency prices of the two goods must rise by 10 percent. First consider the export good, wheat. Since the sale of a unit of wheat abroad still yields the same amount of foreign exchange, it now yields 10 percent more in terms of domestic currency. Domestic purchasers too

TABLE 40-1 Changes in the Balance Sheets of Two Banks As a Result of International Payments

U.K. bank			Canadian bank		
Assets	Liabilities		Assets	Liabilities	
No change	(1) Deposits of car exporter	+£15,000	No change	(1) Deposits of car importer	−$25,000
	(2) Deposits of refrigerator importer	−£15,000		(2) Deposits of refrigerator exporter	+$25,000
	Net change	0		Net change	0

International transactions involve a transfer of deposit liabilities among banks. The table records two separate international transactions at an exchange rate of $1.00 = £.60: (1) a Canadian purchase of a British car for £15,000 (= $25,000) and (2) a British purchase of Canadian refrigerators for $25,000 (= £15,000). The Canadian's import of a car reduces deposit liabilities to Canadian residents and increases deposit liabilities to British residents. The Britisher's import of refrigerators does the opposite. When a series of transactions are equal in value, there is only a transfer of deposit liabilities among individuals within a country. The Canadian refrigerator manufacturer received (in effect) the dollars the Canadian car purchaser gave up to get a British-made car.

will have to pay 10 percent more, for if the domestic price did not rise, producers would sell only in the export market. Similarly, the purchase of cloth still requires the same amount of foreign currency, but 10 percent more of the domestic currency must be paid to obtain the required amount of foreign currency. Thus the domestic currency price of imported cloth also rises by 10 percent.

The effects of these price changes are illustrated in Figures 40-1 and 40-2. In the markets for wheat and cloth, the increase in the domestic price causes the quantity supplied domestically to rise and the quantity demanded domestically to fall. As a result, the quantity of wheat exported, which is equal to the excess of the quantity supplied domestically over the quantity demanded domestically, *rises* (see Figure 40-1). In the market for cloth, the domestic price rise also causes quantity supplied to increase and quantity demanded to fall. However, since the initial situation was one where domestic supply exceeded domestic demand, this response reduces that excess. As a result, the quantity of cloth imported *decreases* (see Figure 40-2).

For a small country, a depreciation of the domestic currency causes the domestic prices of traded goods to rise, thereby increasing the quantity supplied and reducing the quantity demanded domestically. Therefore, the volume of exports increases while the volume of imports falls.

As a result of these changes, actual net exports, $X - M$, rises. Since $X - M$ is a component of aggregate demand, the depreciation increases the country's aggregate demand. This in turn tends to increase equilibrium national income.

Similarly, an *appreciation* of the domestic currency *lowers* the domestic prices of traded goods. This leads to a reduction in the quantity supplied and an increase in the quantity demanded domestically for both; the quantity of cloth imports now rises while the quantity of wheat exports falls. This is also shown in Figures 40-1 and 40-2.

The Exchange Rate Between Two Currencies

For simplicity we shall consider an example involving trade between Canada and the United Kingdom and the determination of the exchange rate between their two currencies, dollars and sterling. The two-country example simplifies things, but the principles apply to all foreign transactions. Thus sterling stands for foreign exchange in general, and the dollar price of sterling stands for the foreign exchange rate in general.

We can relate our example to the demand and

FIGURE 40-1 Effects of an Increase in the Domestic Currency Price of an Exported Good (Wheat)

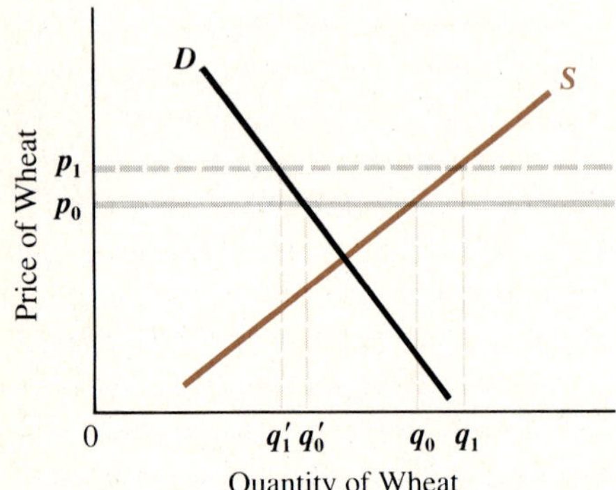

An increase in the domestic currency price of export goods leads to an increase in the volume of exports. Exports of wheat are determined by the domestic excess supply of the tradable good at the domestic price. (The domestic price is the world price adjusted by the exchange rate.) D and S are the domestic demand and supply schedules. If the world price expressed in domestic currency is p_0, quantity q_0 will be produced, of which q_0' will be consumed domestically and $q_0'q_0$ will be exported. A depreciation of the domestic currency or an increase in the world price causes the domestic currency price to rise to p_1. As a result, domestic consumption falls to q_1', quantity supplied rises to q_1, and exports rise to $q_1'q_1$.

FIGURE 40-2 Effects of an Increase in the Domestic Currency Price of an Imported Good (Cloth)

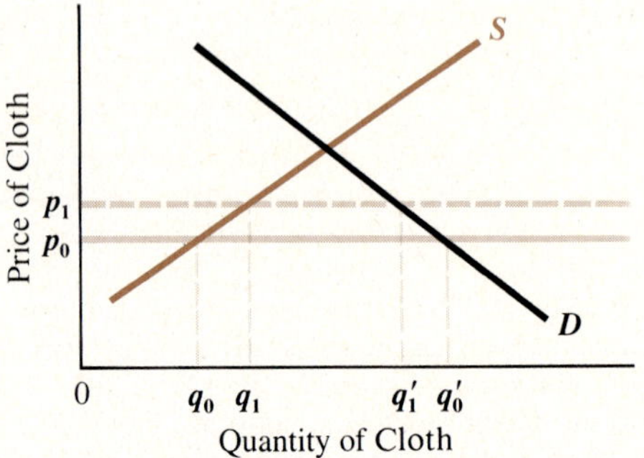

An increase in the domestic currency price of import goods leads to a decrease in the volume of imports. Imports of cloth are determined by the domestic excess demand for cloth at the domestic price. (The domestic price is the world price adjusted by the exchange rate.) D and S are the domestic demand and supply schedules. If the world price expressed in domestic currency is p_0, quantity q_0' will be consumed, of which q_0 will be produced domestically and $q_0'q_0$ will be imported. A depreciation of the domestic currency or an increase in the world price causes the domestic currency price to rise to p_1. As a result, quantity supplied rises to q_1, domestic consumption falls to q_1', and imports fall to $q_1'q_1$.

supply analysis of Chapter 4. To do so we need only to recognize that *in the market for pounds sterling,* the Canadian firm that wants pounds is a demander of pounds and the British firm that is selling pounds to buy dollars is a supplier of pounds. We can also look at the same transaction in the market for dollars: The Canadian firm is a supplier of dollars, and the British firm is a demander of dollars.

Because one currency is traded for another on the foreign exchange market, it follows that to demand dollars implies a willingness to supply foreign exchange, while to supply dollars implies a demand for foreign exchange.

When £1.00 equals $2.00, a British importer who offers to buy $6.00 with pounds must be offering to sell £3.00. Similarly, a Canadian importer who offers to sell $6.00 for pounds must be offering to buy £3.00. For this reason a theory of the exchange rate between dollars and pounds can deal either with the demand for and the supply of dollars or the demand for and the supply of pounds sterling; both need not be considered. We shall concentrate on the demand, supply, and price of pounds sterling (which may be taken to stand for all foreign exchange).

Figure 40-3 plots the exchange rate, the price of sterling measured in Canadian dollars, on the vertical axis, and the quantity of sterling on the horizontal axis. Moving down the vertical scale, the foreign currency (sterling) becomes *cheaper;* it is depreciating on the foreign market while the domestic currency

FIGURE 40-3 The Market for Foreign Exchange

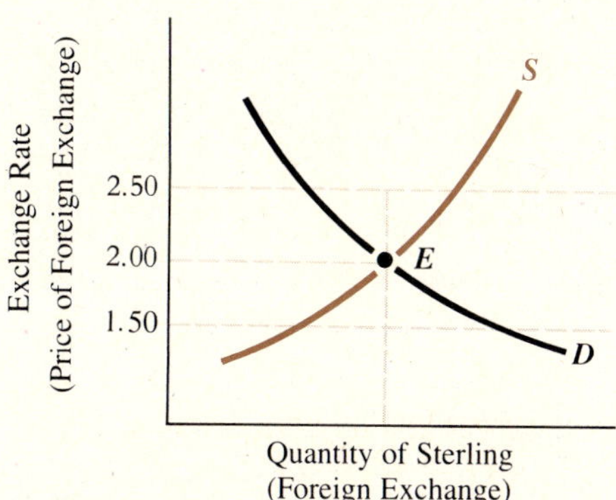

The equilibrium exchange rate equates the demand and supply of foreign exchange. The *S* curve is the supply of sterling to the foreign exchange market to be used to make purchases in Canada. The *D* curve is the demand for sterling in the foreign exchange market to be used to make purchases in the United Kingdom. The quantity of sterling demanded is equal to the quantity supplied at an exchange rate of $2.00 to the pound. If the price of sterling were low, say, $1.50, there would be an excess demand for sterling, which would bid its price up. If the price of sterling were high, say, $2.50, there would be an excess supply of sterling, which would bid its price down.

(the dollar) is appreciating. Moving up the scale, sterling becomes *more expensive;* it is appreciating while the dollar is depreciating.

In more general terms, Figure 40-3 represents the foreign exchange market. It plots the quantity of foreign exchange against the Canadian dollar price of foreign exchange, that is, the Canadian exchange rate. Although we continue to speak of sterling to make the argument easier to follow, everything said about sterling applies to any other foreign currency and to foreign exchange in general.

Supply of Sterling

The supply of sterling to the foreign exchange market arises to finance purchases by foreigners from Canadians. In addition to the purchase of exports studied before, there are purchases of assets previously owned or newly issued by Canadians (and Canadian governments). Such purchases are called **capital flows.** They play an important role in exchange markets, and we study them in detail later in this chapter; for the present, we continue to focus on international trade in goods and services.

Consider again a representative Canadian export good, wheat. What are the implications for the foreign exchange market of transactions in wheat? We saw in Figure 40-1 that a rise in the exchange rate (a depreciation of the dollar) led to an increase in the *quantity* of wheat exports. Since the pound sterling *price* of wheat is constant (being set on international wheat markets), the supply of pounds to the foreign exchange market must increase. People must be spending more pounds on Canadian wheat, and these pounds go to purchase the Canadian dollars needed to pay for this wheat.

What, then, is the shape of the supply curve of sterling? As we have just seen, if the exchange rate rises, the British will buy more Canadian wheat and will offer more sterling for this purpose. The quantity of pounds supplied will rise. In the opposite case, if the exchange rate falls, the British will buy less Canadian wheat and will thus spend fewer pounds sterling on it.

The supply curve of sterling on the foreign exchange market is upward-sloping when plotted against the dollar price of sterling—that is, against the exchange rate.

Demand for Sterling

In our two-country example, the demand for sterling on the foreign exchange market is merely the opposite side of the supply of dollars. Who wants to sell dollars for foreign exchange? In our example, Canadians seeking to purchase British cloth will require foreign exchange to make those transactions, and hence they will wish to supply dollars in exchange for pounds.[3]

[3] A demand for sterling may also result from capital flows if Canadians seek to buy pound sterling assets. As with the supply of sterling, we neglect this for now.

When the exchange rate rises (the Canadian dollar depreciates), the Canadian price of British cloth rises. As we saw in Figure 40-2, Canadians will import less of the now more expensive British cloth. Since the sterling price of cloth is unchanged, buying less cloth means needing less sterling to pay for it. Thus the Canadian demand for sterling falls.

When the exchange rate falls, British cloth exports to Canada become cheaper, and more will be sold. Since the sterling price of cloth is unchanged, buying more still means spending more sterling. Thus there is an increase in the amount of sterling demanded on the foreign exchange market. Together these two changes tell us the shape of the demand curve for sterling:

The demand curve for sterling on the foreign exchange market is downward-sloping when plotted against the dollar price of sterling—that is, against the exchange rate.

Equilibrium Exchange Rates in a Competitive Market

Consider a rate of exchange that is set on a freely competitive market. Like any competitive price, this rate fluctuates according to the conditions of demand and supply.

Assume that the current exchange rate is so low (say, $1.50 in Figure 40-3) that the quantity of sterling demanded exceeds the quantity supplied. Sterling will be in scarce supply; some people who require sterling to make payments to the U.K. will be unable to obtain it, and the price of sterling will be bid up. The dollar will depreciate against the pound, which is the same thing as the pound appreciating against the dollar.

As the dollar price of sterling rises, the dollar price of Canadian imports rise; hence the quantity of imports falls, as does the quantity of sterling demanded on the foreign exchange market to pay for these imports. This is a movement along the demand curve *D* in Figure 40-3. However, the depreciation of the dollar also leads to a rise in the dollar price of Canadian exports and a resulting increase in the quantity sold abroad. Thus the amount of sterling offered to buy more Canadian exports at an unchanged sterling price must rise. This is a movement along the supply curve *S* in Figure 40-3.

Thus a rise in the dollar price of the sterling reduces the quantity of sterling demanded and increases the quantity of sterling supplied. Where the two curves intersect, quantity demanded equals quantity supplied, and the foreign exchange market is in equilibrium.

What happens if the price of foreign exchange is too high? The quantity of sterling demanded will be less than the quantity of sterling supplied. With sterling in excess supply, some people who wish to convert sterling into dollars will be unable to do so. The price of sterling will fall, less sterling will be supplied, more will be demanded, and an equilibrium will be re-established.

A foreign exchange market is like other competitive markets in that the forces of demand and supply tend to lead to an equilibrium price in which quantity demanded equals quantity supplied.

Changes in Exchange Rates

What causes exchange rates to vary? The simplest answer to this question is changes in demand or supply in the foreign exchange market. Anything that shifts the demand curve for sterling to the right or the supply curve for sterling to the left leads to a depreciation of the dollar. Anything that shifts the demand curve for sterling to the left or the supply curve for sterling to the right leads to an appreciation of the dollar. This is nothing more than a restatement of the laws of supply and demand, applied now to the market for foreign currencies.

But what causes the shifts in demand and supply that lead to changes in exchange rates? There are many causes, some of them transitory and some persistent; we shall mention several of the most important ones.

Foreign Inflation

First consider the case where the rest of the world inflates while the local country does not, so that its domestic costs and the prices of domestic (nontraded) goods remain unchanged. But the world price of all traded goods rises, so that at the initial exchange rate the prices of traded goods also rise in the domestic country.

We saw in Figures 40-1 and 40-2 that the rise in the prices of exported and imported goods leads our country to increase the quantity of its exports while decreasing the quantity of its imports. These changes will cause shifts in the demand and supply curves in the foreign exchange market. More Canadian exports sold at a higher world price mean more foreign exchange offered in return for Canadian dollars. The supply curve of foreign exchange shifts right, as shown in Figure 40-4. Fewer imports purchased at higher foreign prices means less spent on imports, as long as the percentage fall in the quantity demanded exceeds the percentage rise in the price.[4] The demand curve for foreign exchange shifts left, as shown in Figure 40-4.

Now at the original exchange rate there is an excess supply of foreign exchange, and the market exchange rate falls to its new equilibrium level. The exchange rate falls, which is the same thing as an appreciation of the Canadian dollar.

A foreign inflation, other things equal, will lead to an appreciation of the Canadian dollar.

FIGURE 40-4 Foreign Inflation and the Exchange Rate

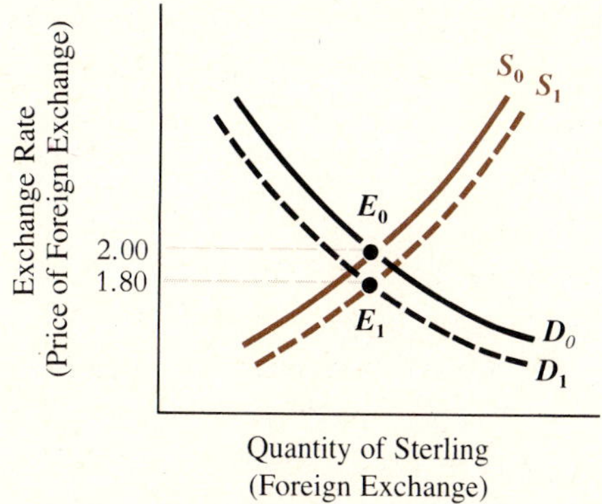

Foreign inflation will increase the supply of foreign exchange and decrease the demand, thus causing an appreciation of the dollar. The initial supply and demand curves are shown by the solid curves (labeled D_0 and S_0), and the initial equilibrium is at E_0. Now suppose that a foreign inflation occurs. This raises the foreign price of all tradable goods. At any given exchange rate, this will cause an increase in the dollar price of traded goods and, as we saw in Figures 40-1 and 40-2, the quantity of exports will increase and the quantity of imports will fall as a result. The increase in exports gives rise to an increase in the supply of sterling, as shown by the shift from S_0 to S_1. The decrease in imports gives rise to a fall in the demand for foreign exchange, as shown by the shift in the demand curve from D_0 to D_1. As a result, the dollar appreciates as the price of sterling falls from $2.00 to $1.80.

Domestic Inflation

Suppose now that foreign prices are constant but there is an increase in domestic wages and other costs of production and in the price of local goods and services—things such as haircuts and restaurant meals that are not traded internationally. As a result of the rise in costs, the supply curves for imports and exports will shift upward. As a result of the rise in prices of nontraded goods, the demand curves for traded goods will shift upward. This is because at any given exchange rate, traded goods are now cheaper relative to domestic or nontraded goods, so more will be demanded and less will be supplied. As a result, the quantity of imports will rise and the quantity of exports will fall. This situation is shown in Figure 40-5.

At any given exchange rate, these changes in the quantities of imports and exports will cause the supply and demand of foreign exchange to change. The decrease in exports will cause the quantity of sterling supplied to the foreign exchange market to decrease—in terms of Figure 40-4, the supply curve of sterling shifts left from S_1 to S_0. The increase in

[4] This is true as long as the elasticity of demand for imports is greater than one—the fall in the volume of imports will then swamp the rise in price, and hence fewer dollars will be spent on them. This elasticity condition is related to a famous, long-standing issue in international economics. In what follows, we adopt the standard case of the condition's being met. In a more general form, it is called the *Marshall-Lerner condition* after two famous economists who first studied the problem.

imports will cause the quantity of sterling demanded in the foreign exchange market to increase—in terms of Figure 40-4, the demand curve shifts right from D_1 to D_0. As a result, the equilibrium moves from E_1 to E_0 and the exchange rate rises; that is, the dollar depreciates.

A local Canadian inflation will lead to a depreciation of the Canadian dollar (a rise in the exchange rate).

Inflation in Both Countries

Now consider a case where the domestic country suffers exactly the same rate of inflation as the rest of the world. Now the demand and supply curves for traded goods in Figure 40-5 shift upward as before, but so does the world price of imports and exports. (The rise in the world price is not shown in the figure.) The two shifts offset each other. The upward shifts in the curves tend to reduce exports and increase imports, while the upward shift in world prices tends to increase exports and reduce imports. With equal rates of inflation in Canada and the rest of the world, relative prices of Canadian and the other country's goods remain unchanged at the old exchange rate. There is no reason to expect any change in either country's demand for imports at the original exchange rate and hence in the demands for and supplies of foreign exchange. The inflations in the two countries leave the equilibrium exchange rate unchanged.

Offsetting inflation in two countries will leave the incentive to import and to export unchanged and thus will cause no change in the exchange rate.

Unequal Inflation

The foregoing analysis suggests that the *relative rates of inflation* between two trading countries is an important determinant of exchange rate changes. Differences in the inflation rates will cause changes in imports and exports and hence changes in quantities demanded and supplied on the foreign exchange market. Thus the exchange rate between the two currencies will change. The general conclusion that follows from a simple extension of the cases just studied is this:

If the price level of one country is rising relative to that of another country, the equilibrium value of its currency will be falling relative to that of the second country.

Capital Movements

Major capital flows can exert strong influences on exchange rates. For example, an increased desire to invest in British assets will shift the demand curve for sterling to the right and cause the dollar to depreciate.

A movement of investment funds has the effect of appreciating the currency of the capital-importing country and depreciating the currency of the capital-exporting country.

This statement is true for all capital movements, short term or long term. Since the motives that lead to large capital movements are likely to be different in the short and long terms, however, it is worth considering each.

Short-term capital movements. A major motive for short-term capital flows is a change in interest rates. International traders hold transactions balances just as domestic traders do. These balances are often lent out on short-term loan rather than being left idle. Naturally, the holders of these balances will tend to lend them, other things being equal, in the markets where interest rates are highest. Thus if one major country's short-term rate of interest rises above the rates in most other countries, there will tend to be a large inflow of short-term capital into that country to take advantage of the high rate, and this will tend to appreciate the currency. If these short-term interest rates should fall, there will likely be a sudden shift away from that country as a source of transactions balances, and its currency will tend to depreciate.

A second motive for short-term capital movements is speculation about a country's exchange rate. If foreigners expect the dollar to appreciate, they will

FIGURE 40-5 Domestic Inflation and International Trade

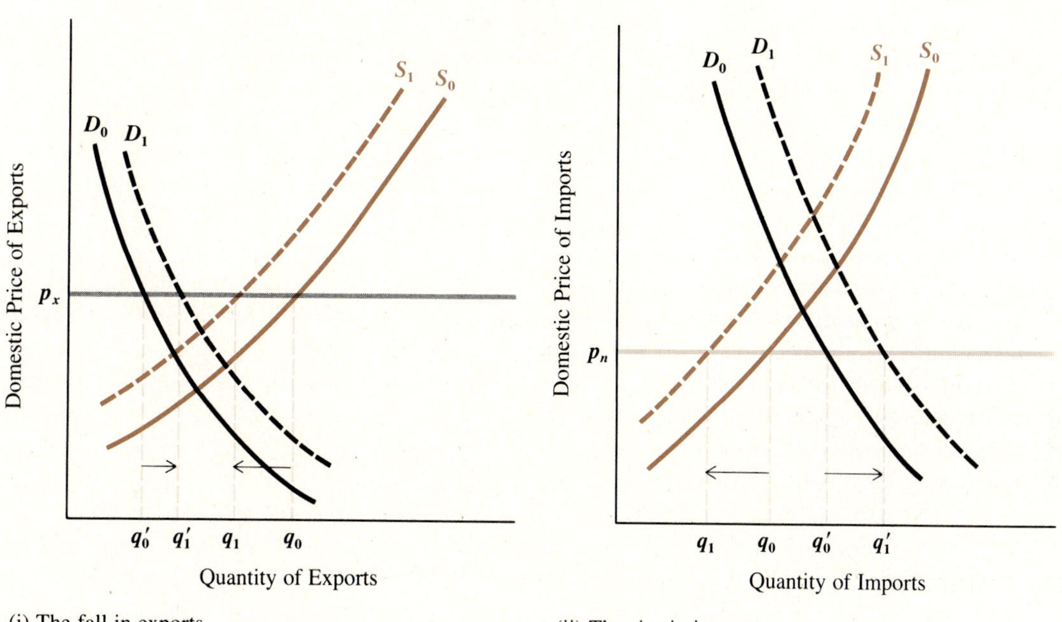

(i) The fall in exports

(ii) The rise in imports

Domestic inflation unmatched in the rest of the world increases the domestic demand for traded goods and reduces the domestic supply; as a result, the quantity of exports falls and the quantity of imports rises. The initial supply and demand curves are shown by the solid lines D_0 and S_0 in both parts of the figure. In each market the initial quantity supplied is given by q_0 and the initial quantity demanded by q_0'. Initial exports are given in part (i) by $q_0'q_0$ and initial imports in part (ii) by q_0q_0'.

A domestic inflation causes the demand curves for each traded good to shift rightward from D_0 to D_1 and the supply curve for each to shift leftward from S_0 to S_1. As a result, quantity demanded rises from q_0' to q_1' and quantity supplied falls from q_0 to q_1.

In the market for exports, where domestic supply initially exceeded demand, the inflation thus causes exports to fall, from $q_0'q_0$ to $q_1'q_1$. (In turn, this means that the demand for dollars in the foreign exchange market falls, as shown by a shift from D_1 to D_0 in Figure 40-4.)

In the market for imports, where domestic demand initially exceeded supply, the inflation thus causes imports to rise, from q_0q_0' to q_1q_1'. (In turn, this means that the supply of dollars to the foreign exchange market rises, as shown by a shift from S_1 to S_0 in Figure 40-4.)

rush to buy assets that pay off in dollars; if they expect the dollar to depreciate, they will be reluctant to buy or hold Canadian securities.

Long-term capital movements. Long-term movements are largely influenced by long-term expectations about another country's profit opportunities and the long-run value of its currency. A British firm would be more willing to purchase a Canadian factory if it expected that the dollar profits would buy more sterling in future years than the profits from investment in a British factory. This could happen if the Canadian firm earned greater profits than the British firm, with exchange rates unchanged. It could also happen if the profits were the same but the British firm expected the dollar to appreciate relative to the pound.

Structural Changes

An economy can undergo structural changes that alter the equilibrium exchange rate. *Structural change* is an omnibus term for a change in cost structures, the invention of new products, or anything else that affects the pattern of comparative advantage. For example, when a country's products do not improve as rapidly as those of some other country, consumer demand (at fixed prices) shifts slowly away from the first country's products and toward those of its foreign competitors. This causes a slow depreciation in the first country's currency because the demand for its currency is shifting slowly leftward.

TABLE 40-2 Canadian Balance of International Payments, 1986 ***(billions of dollars)***

Current Account	
Merchandise exports	+ 120.6
Merchandise imports	− 110.2
Balance of merchandise trade	+ 10.4
Exports of services	+ 17.7
Imports of services	− 20.9
Balance of trade	+ 7.2
Net investment income	− 16.9
Transfers	+ 1.5
Balance on current account	− 8.2
Capital Account	
New direct investment	+ 1.6
Other long-term capital flows	+ 15.9
Total long-term capital flows	+ 17.5
Short-term capital flows	− 3.2
Balance on capital account	+ 14.3
Current Plus Capital Account	+ 6.1
Statistical discrepancy[a]	− 5.0
Use of official reserves (increase −, decrease +)	− 1.1
Overall balance of payments	(Always zero)[a]

[a] In balance-of-payments accounts there is a "statistical discrepancy" item that results from the inability to measure some industrial items accurately. For example, many capital transactions are not recorded.

The overall balance of payments always balances, but the individual components do not have to. In 1986 Canada shows a positive (surplus) merchandise trade balance (exports exceed imports) and a negative (deficit) balance on current account. There is a positive (surplus) balance on capital account because capital exports exceeded capital imports. The capital *plus* current account balance is what is commonly referred to as the *balance of payments*. It is exactly matched by the balance in the official account, i.e., the use of official reserves.

The Balance of Payments

Balance-of-Payments Accounts

To know what is happening to the course of international trade, governments keep track of the transactions among countries. The record of such transactions is made in the **balance-of-payments accounts.** Each transaction, such as a shipment of exports or the arrival of imported goods, is classified according to the payments or receipts that would typically arise from it. Table 40-2 shows the major items in the Canadian balance-of-payments accounts for 1986.

Current Account

The **current account** records payments arising from trade in goods and services and from income in the form of interest, profits, and dividends arising from capital owned in one country and invested in another. The current account is divided into two main sections.

The first is variously called the **balance of trade,** the **trade account,** the **visible account,** and the **merchandise account.** It records payments and receipts arising from the import and export of tangible goods such as computers, cars, wheat, and shoes. Canadian imports require the use of foreign exchange and hence are entered as debit items on the visible account. Canadian exports earn foreign exchange and hence are recorded as credit items.

The second section of the current account is called the **invisible account** or the **service account.** It records payments arising out of trade in services and payments for the use of capital. Trade in such services as insurance, shipping, and tourism is entered in the invisible account, as are payments of interest, dividends, and profits made for capital used in one country but owned by residents of another country.

Items that use foreign exchange, such as purchases by Canadian residents of foreign insurance and shipping services, travel abroad by Canadians, and payments to foreign residents of interest earned in Canada, are entered as debit items. Items that earn foreign exchange, such as foreign purchases of Canadian insurance and shipping services, travel by foreigners in Canada, and payments to Canadian residents of interest earned abroad, are entered as credit items.

Given Canada's long history of being a net international borrower, the payment of interest and dividends on foreign loans and investments is a substantial item in the Canadian balance-of-payments accounts. When an American corporation owns a subsidiary in Canada, it receives dividend payments in Canadian dollars. If the American owners wish to spend these dividends at home, they will need to exchange Canadian for American dollars. Interest and dividends paid to foreigners thus use up foreign exchange and are entered as debit items on the balance of payments. Usually the debt-servicing entry is sufficiently large to cause the current account to be in deficit even when the trade account shows a substantial surplus. Some concerns about this tendency to run current account deficits are taken up in Box 40-1.

Capital Account

The second main division in the balance of payments is the **capital account,** which records transactions related to international movements of financial capital. The export of funds from Canada, called a *capital export,* uses foreign exchange and so is entered as a debit item in the Canadian payments accounts. The import of funds into Canada, called a *capital import,* earns foreign exchange and so is entered as a credit item in the payments statistics.

It may seem odd that a merchandise export is a credit item on current account but the export of capital is a debit item. To see that there is no contradiction between the treatments of goods and capital, consider the export of Canadian funds for investment in a British bond. The capital transaction involves the purchase, and hence the *import,* of a British bond, and this has the same effect on the balance of payments as the purchase, and hence the import, of a British good. Both items involve payments to foreigners, and both use foreign exchange. Both are thus debit items in Canadian balance-of-payments accounts.

The capital account often distinguishes between movements of short-term and long-term capital. Short-term capital is money held in the form of highly liquid assets, such as bank accounts and short-term treasury bills. If a nonresident merchant buys dollars and places them in a deposit account in Toronto, this represents an inflow of short-term capital into Canada, and it will be recorded as a credit item on short-term capital account. Long-term capital represents funds coming into Canada (a credit item) or leaving Canada (a debit item) to be invested in less liquid assets such as long-term bonds or physical capital such as a new car assembly plant.

The two major subdivisions of the long-term part of the capital accounts are direct investment and portfolio investment. **Direct investment** relates to changes in nonresident ownership of domestic firms and resident ownership of foreign firms. Thus one form of direct investment in Canada is capital investment in a branch plant or subsidiary corporation in Canada in which the investor has voting control. Another form is a takeover in which a controlling interest in a firm previously controlled by residents is acquired by foreigners. **Portfolio investment,** by contrast, is investment in bonds or a minority holding of shares that does not involve legal control.

Use of Official Reserves

The final section in the balance-of-payments account represents transactions in the *official reserves* held by a country's central bank. These transactions reflect the financing of the balance on the remainder of the accounts. The central banks of most countries hold reserves of funds to use to buy and sell in the foreign exchange market. Some of these reserves are held in

BOX 40-1

Is Canada's Current Account a Cause for Alarm?

Some observers have expressed alarm at the long-term trend in Canada's balance of payments, which shows a large current account deficit matched by a large capital account surplus. Here we address two sources of this alarm.

Is Canada Headed for Financial Ruin?

Concern often arises from the belief that Canada is borrowing abroad to finance a current account deficit that reflects excessive spending. Tourist expenditures of Canadians traveling abroad and interest payments to service past debts are commonly singled out as "causes" of Canada's heavy foreign borrowing. Two contentions are involved: first, that the country is borrowing abroad to help cover a current account deficit, and second, that the policy of financing investment by foreign borrowing is in some way unsound.

The first contention mixes up cause and effect. The various items in the balance of payments represents unrelated decisions by many individuals, firms, and governments, each seeking the best possible economic position. The coordination and reconciliation of these independent actions is accomplished by the foreign exchange market. No one *decides* to borrow in the United States in order to finance an excess of current account payments over receipts. If Canada is to have capital imports, there must be a deficit on current account. The currency will appreciate until the necessary deficit occurs.

If there had been less foreign borrowing during the period, the Canadian dollar would have depreciated, with the result that the foreign exchange required to finance Canadian travel abroad and the payment of interest and dividends to foreign investors would have been acquired in some other way. There would have been higher exports or lower imports or less travel abroad or more foreigners visiting Canada or some combination of these and other changes in individual balance-of-payments items.

The second contention is more easily dealt with. The relevant question to ask when assessing the economic implications of rapidly rising debt, whether foreign or domestic, is whether the funds raised are being used to finance new investment that will generate sufficient returns in the future to compensate for the burden of interest payments. If Canada's capacity to produce and export is being adequately enhanced by the investment, there is not reason to suppose the country is headed for financial ruin.

The current account deficit reflects the excess of current domestic spending over current income. If spending is high in part because investment is high, the deficit does not mean that Canada is "living beyond its means." If spending is high because current consumption expenditure is high, this may be justified

gold, some in foreign exchange, some as claims on various major foreign currencies, and some in an international currency called special drawing rights (which we study in Chapter 41).

The Bank of Canada, operating on behalf of the government, can intervene in the market for foreign exchange to influence the dollar's exchange rate. For example, to prevent the price of dollars from falling, the Bank must buy dollars. This means it must sell gold or foreign exchange. It can do so only if it holds reserves of these media. When the Bank wishes to stop the dollar from rising in value, it enters the market and sells dollars. In this case, the Bank buys foreign exchange, which it then adds to its reserves.

The Meaning of Payments Balances and Imbalances

We have seen that the payments accounts show the total of receipts of foreign exchange (credit items) and payments of foreign exchange (debit items) on account of each category of payment. It is also common to calculate the *balance* on separate items or groups of items. The concept of the balance of pay-by the high expected *future* income arising from the current investment. When that income is being earned, the debts accruing due to current borrowing can be repaid, and there will be a current account surplus.

Only to the extent that the foreign borrowing is not accompanied by productive domestic investment is a current account deficit a cause for concern. Recent deterioration of the current account has been linked to the borrowing requirements due to the federal government deficit and has been cited as a potential problem in the future.

Structural Problems and the Balance of Trade

It is commonly alleged that the chronic current account deficit reflects serious structural problems in the Canadian economy. This means essentially that Canada produces the wrong combination of goods so that exports are too low and imports are too high.* In this view, one of the problems arising from the deficit is that the high propensity to import frustrates expansionary policy from having its desired impact on domestic output and employment. The implied policy remedies include the encouragement of domestic production of import substitutes through the use of tariffs and other forms of protection.

If it is true that Canada is not allocating resources properly to exploit its comparative advantage—and hence is producing the "wrong" mix of output—this will be reflected in a reduced value of total output produced. But this reduction in real income will carry with it a reduction in expenditure. A balance-of-trade deficit will arise only if the reduction in real income is greater than the reduction in domestic spending. To put it another way, correction of the structural problem will lead to higher real domestic income *and* therefore higher real domestic spending. The current account deficit will be improved only if income rises by more than spending. (See Box 31–2 on pages 650–651.)

Professor Neil Bruce of Queen's University has challenged the view that structural changes have led to the increased deficit. His research showed fairly constant long-term shares of raw materials and manufactures in Canada's trade. The facts of the Canadian case are that its raw materials base is so broad and varied that *at the aggregate level* there are only relatively moderate changes in the division of total output between the raw materials and manufacturing sectors.

* A related contention is that our exports are concentrated on raw materials rather than manufacturing goods. For 1986 the merchandise trade balance was a surplus of $10.4 billion, composed of a $16.9 billion surplus in raw materials and a $6.5 billion deficit in manufactured goods.

ments is used in a number of ways. These can be confusing, so we must approach this issue in a series of steps.

The Balance of Payments Must Balance Overall

Notice two things about the payments accounts. First, they record *actual* payments, not *desired* payments. Second, they record *all* payments, whatever the reason for which they were made.

It is quite possible that at the existing exchange rate between dollars and yen, holders of yen want to purchase more dollars than holders of dollars want to sell in exchange for yen. In this situation the quantity of dollars demanded exceeds the quantity supplied. But holders of yen cannot actually buy more dollars than holders of dollars actually sell; every yen that is bought must have been sold by someone, and every dollar that is sold must have been bought by someone.

It follows that if we add up all the receipts arising from (1) payments received by Canadian residents on account of Canadian exports of goods and ser-

BOX 40-2

Why the Balance of Payments Always Balances: An Illustration

Trade Between Two Countries

Suppose that the sole international transaction made this year by a small country called Myopia was an export to Canada of Myopian coconuts worth \$1,000. Further suppose that the Myopian central bank issues a local currency, the stigma, but does not operate in the foreign exchange market, so there is no official financing. Finally, suppose that Myopia's self-sufficient inhabitants want no imports. Surely, then, you might think Myopia has an overall favorable balance of \$1,000, which is a current account receipt (C_R) with no balancing item on the payments side.

To see why this is wrong, we must ask what the exporter of coconuts did with the dollars he received for his coconuts. If he deposited them in a Toronto bank, this transaction represents a capital export from Myopia. Myopians have accumulated claims on foreign exchange, which they hold in the form of a deposit with a foreign bank. Thus there are two entries in the Myopian accounts—one a credit item for the export of coconuts (C_R = \$1,000) and the other a debit item for the export of capital (K_P = \$1,000). The fact that the same firm made both transactions is irrelevant. Although the current account shows a credit balance, the capital account exactly balances this with a debit item. Hence, looking at the *balance of payments* as a whole, the two sides of the account are equal. The balance of payments has balanced—as always it must.

Consider now a slightly more realistic case. If the coconut exporter wants to turn his \$1,000 into Myopian stigmas so that he can pay his coconut pickers in local currency, he must find someone who wishes to buy his dollars in return for Myopian currency. But we have assumed that no one in Myopia wants to import, so no one wants to sell Myopian currency for current account reasons. Assume, however, that a wealthy Myopian landowner would like to invest \$1,000 in Toronto by buying shares in a Canadian firm. To do so he needs \$1,000. The coconut exporter can sell his \$1,000 to the landowner in return for stigmas. Now he can pay his local bills. The landowner sells his stigmas to the exporter in return for dollars. Now he can buy the Canadian shares.

---

vices, (2) capital imports, and (3) purchase of foreign exchange or gold by the Bank of Canada, these must be exactly equal to all payments made by holders of dollars arising from (1) Canadian imports of goods and services, (2) exports of capital, and (3) sale of foreign exchange or gold by the Bank.

This relation is so important that it pays us to write it out in symbols. We let C, K, and F stand for current account, capital account, and use of official reserves, respectively, and use P for payments (debit items) and R for receipts (credit items). Now we can write

$$C_R + K_R + F_R = C_P + K_P + F_P \qquad [1]$$

All this tells us is that if we add up across all transactions, they must balance in total.

Although the relation given in the equation is necessarily true, it often worries students who feel that it need not be true. To help clarify the issue, some apparent exceptions are considered in Box 40-2.

Payments on Specific Parts of the Accounts Do Not Need to Balance

Although the overall total of payments must equal the overall total of receipts, the same zero balance does not have to hold on subsections of the overall accounts. We now look at the balances on parts of the accounts, balances that may be positive or negative. We do this first in relation to particular countries and then in relation to particular subsectors of the account.

Once again the Myopian balance of payments will show two entries, equal in size but opposite in sign. There is a credit item for the export of coconuts (the sale of coconuts earned foreign exchange) and a debit item for the export of capital (the purchase of the Canadian shares used foreign exchange).

Trade Involving Many Countries

In the example, Myopia had what is called a bilateral payments balance with Canada. The *bilateral balance of payments* between any two countries is the balance between the payments and receipts flowing between them. If there were only two countries in the world, their overall payments would have to be in bilateral balance; that is, one country's payments to the other would be equal to its receipts from the other. But this is not true when there are more than two countries.

Suppose that one year later Myopia again sells $1,000 worth of coconuts to Canada and that the landowner does not wish to invest further in Canada, but that the Myopian people wish to buy 200,000 yen's worth of parasols from Japan. (Assume also that on the foreign exchange market $1 trades for 200 yen.) Finally, assume that a Japanese importer wishes to buy $1,000 worth of skateboards from a Canadian company.

Now what in effect happens is that the Myopian coconut exporter sells his $1,000 to the Japanese skateboard importer for 200,000 yen, which the coconut dealer then sells to the Myopian parasol importer in return for Myopian stigmas. (In the real world the exchanges are all done through banks, but this is what happens in effect.) Now the Myopian payments statistics will show a $1,000 bilateral payments surplus with Canada—receipts of $1,000 from Canada on account of coconut exports and no payments to Canada—and a bilateral deficit with Japan of 200,000 yen (equal to $1,000)—$1,000 of payments to Japan on account of parasol imports and no receipts from Japan. But when both countries are considered, Myopia's multilateral payments are in balance.

Country balances. When all foreign countries are taken together, a country's balance of payments must balance, but a country can have bilateral surpluses or deficits with individual foreign countries or groups of countries. In general, the **multilateral balance of payments** refers to the balance between one country's payments to and receipts from the rest of the world. When all items are considered, every country must have a zero multilateral payments balance with the rest of the world, although it can have bilateral surpluses or deficits with individual countries. This important principle is illustrated in the second part of Box 40-2.

Subsection balances. The balance on visible account refers to the difference between the value of Canadian exports of goods and the value of imports of goods. A surplus occurs when exports of goods exceed imports of goods, while a deficit occurs when imports exceed exports. The balance on invisibles refers to the difference between the value of receipts on invisibles and the value of payments for invisibles. The **current account balance** is the sum of the balances on the visible and invisible accounts. It gives the balance between payments and receipts on all income-related items.

As a carryover from a long-discredited eighteenth century economic doctrine called mercantilism, a credit balance on current account (receipts exceed payments) is called a **favorable balance**, while a debit balance (payments exceed receipts) is called an **unfavorable balance**.

BOX 40-3

The Volume of Trade, the Balance of Trade, and the New Mercantilism

Media commentators, political figures, and much of the general public often judge the national balance of payments as they would the accounts of a single firm. Just as a firm is supposed to show a profit, the nation is supposed to secure a balance-of-payments surplus, with the benefits derived from international trade measured by the size of that surplus.

This view is related to the exploitation doctrine of international trade. Since one country's surplus is another country's deficit, one country's gain, judged by its surplus, must be another country's loss, judged by its deficit.

People who hold such views today are echoing an ancient economic doctrine called *mercantilism.* The mercantilists were a group of economists who preceded Adam Smith. They judged the success of trade by the size of the trade balance. In many cases this doctrine made sense in terms of their objective, which was to use international trade as a means of building up the political and military power of the state rather than raising the living standards of its citizens. A balance-of-payments surplus allowed the nation (then and now) to acquire foreign-exchange reserves. (In those days the reserves took the form of gold. Today they are a mixture of gold and claims on the currencies of other countries.) These reserves could then be used to pay armies, composed partly of foreign mercenaries; to purchase weapons from abroad; and generally to finance colonial adventures.

People who advocate this view in modern times are called *neo-mercantilists.* Insofar as their object is to increase the power of the state, they are choosing means that could achieve their ends. Insofar as they are drawing an analogy between what is a sensible objective for a business interested in its own material welfare and what is a sensible objective for a society interested in the material welfare of its citizens, their views are erroneous, for the analogy is false.

If we take the view that the object of economic activity is to promote the welfare and living standards of ordinary citizens, rather than the power of governments, the mercantilist focus on the balance of trade makes no sense. The law of comparative advantage shows that average living standards are maximized by having individuals, regions, and countries specialize in the things they can produce comparatively best and trading to obtain the things they can produce comparatively worst. The more specialization, the more trade.

In this view the gains from trade are to be judged by the volume of trade. A situation in which there is a *large volume* of trade but where each country has a *zero balance* of trade can thus be regarded as quite satisfactory. Furthermore, a change in commercial policy that results in a balanced increase in trade between two countries will bring gain, because it allows for specialization according to comparative advantage even though it causes no change in either country's trade balance.

To the business interested in private profit and to the government interested in the power of the state, it is the balance of trade that matters. To the person interested in the welfare of ordinary citizens, it is the volume of trade that matters.

Mercantilists, both ancient and modern, hold that the gains from trade arise from having a favorable balance of trade. This misses the whole point of the doctrine of comparative advantage, which states that countries can gain from a balanced increase in trade between themselves because of the opportunity it provides for each country to specialize according to its comparative advantage. The modern resurgence of mercantilist views is discussed in Box 40-3.

The balance on capital account gives the difference between receipts of foreign exchange and payments of foreign exchange arising out of capital movements. A surplus, or "favorable" balance, on capital account means that a country is a *net* importer of capital; while a deficit, or "unfavorable" balance, means that the country is a *net* exporter of capital.

Notice that a deficit on capital account, which is referred to as an unfavorable balance, merely indicates that a country is investing abroad. For a country to invest abroad and accumulate assets that will earn income in the future may be a desirable situation. So once again we observe that there is nothing necessarily unfavorable about having an "unfavorable" balance on any of the payments accounts.

A credit balance on official settlements account means that the Bank of Canada has bought more gold and foreign exchange than it has sold. This adds to its reserves of foreign exchange. A deficit balance means that the Bank has sold more gold and foreign exchange than it has bought. This reduces its foreign exchange reserves.

The Relation Between Various Balances

Two important points should be noted at this time. First, since overall payments must balance, the terms *balance-of-payments deficit* and *balance-of-payments surplus* refer to the balance on some part of the payments accounts. Second, because of the necessity for the balance of payments to balance overall, a deficit on any one part of the accounts implies an offsetting surplus on the rest of the accounts. We now consider two important applications of this second statement. The first concerns the balances on current and capital accounts, and the second concerns the use of official reserves and the balances on the remainder of the total accounts.

The current and capital account balances. To make the relation between current and capital balances clear, let us assume that the Bank of Canada does not engage in any foreign exchange transactions. This means that the use of official reserves is zero because both F_R and F_P in Equation 1 are zero.

Now any deficit or surplus on current account must be matched by an equal and opposite surplus or deficit on capital account. For example, if a country has a credit balance on current account, the foreign exchange earned must appear as a debit item in the capital account. The foreign exchange may be used to buy foreign assets or merely stashed away in foreign bank accounts. In either case there is an outflow of capital from Canada. It is recorded as a debit item because it uses foreign exchange.

We can see this clearly if we return to Equation 1 and set F_R and F_P equal to zero to indicate no transactions by the Bank of Canada. This gives

$$C_R + K_R = C_P + K_P \quad [2]$$

Now subtract C_P and K_R from both sides of the equation to get

$$C_R - C_P = K_P - K_R \quad [3]$$

This expresses in equation form what we have just stated in words: A surplus on current account must be balanced by a deficit on capital account (i.e., an outflow of capital), and a deficit on current account must be matched by a surplus on capital account (i.e., an inflow of capital).

One important implication relates to capital transfers. A country that is importing capital has a surplus on capital account and so it *must* have a deficit on current account. This is the position that the United States was in during the mid 1980s. Because of the borrowing requirements of a massive government budget deficit and because the boom made the United States an attractive place in which to invest, there was a massive capital inflow into the United States. This inflow made a current account deficit inevitable. As long as the capital inflow persisted, no policy measure could remove the current account deficit. This issue is considered in more detail in Chapter 41.

Use of official reserves and the rest of the accounts. When people speak of a country as having an overall balance-of-payments deficit or surplus, they are usually referring to the *balance of all accounts excluding use of official reserves.* A balance-of-payments surplus means that the central bank is adding foreign exchange reserves to its holdings; a balance-of-payments deficit means that the central bank is reducing its reserves.

If the central bank does not operate in the foreign exchange market, there can be no overall balance-of-payments deficit or surplus on current plus capital account. Suppose that holders of dollars are trying to buy more foreign exchange than holders of foreign currencies wish to sell in return for dollars. There will be an excess supply of dollars and an excess demand for foreign exchange. The dollar will depreciate on the foreign exchange market until demand equals supply. At this point both desired and actual international payments are in balance.

If exchange rates are completely free to vary, balance-of-payments deficits and surpluses will be eliminated though exchange rate adjustments.

In today's world, though no country need have a balance-of-payments problem, many do have them. As long as governments intervene in foreign exchange markets, there will be balance-of-payments deficits and surpluses. Surpluses will occur whenever the currency is held below its equilibrium level. Persistent deficits will cause persistent losses of reserves; they are evidence that the government is trying to resist longer-term trends for changes in the exchange rate.

Summary

1. International trade can occur only when it is possible to exchange the currency of one country for that of another. The exchange rate between two currencies is the amount of one currency that must be paid to obtain one unit of another currency. Where more than two currencies are involved, there will be an exchange rate between each pair of currencies.
2. The determination of exchange rates in the free market is simply an application of the laws of supply and demand studied in Chapter 4; the item being bought and sold is a nation's money.
3. The supply of foreign exchange arises from Canadian exports of goods and services and from long-term and short-term capital flows into Canada. The demand for foreign exchange arises from Canadian imports of goods and services and from capital flows out of Canada.
4. A depreciation of the dollar (a rise in the exchange rate) raises the domestic price of traded goods. This increases the quantities of such goods supplied domestically and reduces the quantity demanded. As a result, the volume of exports rises and, with it, the supply of foreign exchange. But the volume of imports falls, and with it the demand for foreign exchange. Thus the supply curve for foreign exchange is upward-sloping and the demand curve for foreign exchange is downward-sloping when the quantities demanded and supplied are plotted against the price of foreign exchange measured in terms of Canadian dollars—that is, against the exchange rate.
5. A currency will tend to depreciate if there is a shift to the right of the demand curve for foreign exchange or a shift to the left of the supply curve. Shifts in the opposite directions will tend to appreciate the currency. Shifts are caused by such things as changes in the prices of imports and exports, the rates of inflation in different countries, capital movements, structural changes, expectations about future trends in earnings and exchange rates, and the level of confidence in the currency as a source of reserves.
6. Actual transactions among the firms, households, and governments

of various countries are kept track of and reported in the balance-of-payments accounts. In these accounts any transaction that uses foreign exchange is recorded as a debit item and any transaction that produces foreign exchange is recorded as a credit item. If all transactions are recorded, the sum of all credit items necessarily equals the sum of all debit items since the foreign exchange that is bought must also have been sold.

7. Major categories in the balance-of-payments account are the balance of trade (exports minus imports), current account, capital account, and official financing. The so-called balance of payments is the balance of the current plus capital accounts; that is, it excludes the transactions on official account. Ignoring official settlements, a balance on current account must be matched by a balance on capital account of equal magnitude but opposite sign.
8. There is nothing inherently good or bad about deficits or surpluses. Persistent deficits or surpluses cannot be sustained because the former will eventually exhaust a country's foreign exchange reserves and the latter will do the same to a trading partner's reserves.

Topics for Review

Foreign exchange and exchange rates
Appreciation and depreciation
Sources of the demand for and supply of foreign exchange
Effects on exchange rates of capital flows, inflation, interest rates, and expectations about exchange rates
Balance of trade and balance of payments
Current and capital account
Official financing items
Mercantilist views on the balance and volume of trade

Discussion Questions

1. What is the probable effect of each of the following on the exchange rate of a country, other things being equal?
   a. The quantity of oil imports is greatly increased, but the value of imported oil is lower due to price decreases.
   b. The country's inflation rate falls well below that of its trading partners.
   c. Rising labor costs of the country's manufacturers lead to a worsening ability to compete in world markets.
   d. The government greatly expands its gifts of food and machinery to underdeveloped countries.
   e. A major boom occurs with rising employment.
   f. The central bank raises interest rates sharply.
   g. More domestic oil is discovered and developed.
2. In the mid 1980s the United States became a major importer of capital, partly to finance the large internal budget deficit and partly because the American boom and the European slump made the

United States a highly attractive place in which to invest foreign funds. Predict the effects of this large capital inflow on the U.S. dollar exchange rate and on the balance of payments on current account. Would these developments have anything to do with the upsurge of protectionist sentiment in the Congress during the latter part of the 1980s?

3. In recent years money wages have risen substantially faster in Canada than in the United States. Many Canadians have expressed the fear that their rapidly rising costs will price them out of U.S. markets. Did this fear make sense when the Canadian exchange rate was fixed relative to the American dollar? Does it make sense today when exchange rates are free to vary on the open market?
4. Indicate whether each of the following transactions increases the demand for dollars, the supply of dollars, or neither on foreign exchange markets.
   a. IBM moves $10 million from bank accounts in Canada to banks in Paris to expand operations in France.
   b. The Canadian government extends a grant of $3 million to the government of Peru, which Peru uses to buy farm machinery from a Winnipeg firm.
   c. Canadian investors, responding to higher profits of American rather than Canadian corporations, buy stocks through the New York Stock Exchange.
   d. Several countries stop interest payments on their large debts to Canadian and American banks.
   e. Lower interest rates in Montreal than in London encourage British firms to borrow in the Montreal money market, converting the proceeds into pounds sterling for use at home.
5. "The necessity of the government to stabilize the balance of payments through the settlement account is a relic of the past. It was a by-product of the adherence to a policy of fixed exchange rates." Do you agree?
6. "If a country solves its balance-of-payments problems, it will have solved its foreign trade problems." Discuss.
7. Outline the reasoning behind the following summer 1983 newspaper headline: "U.S. dollar tumbles as American interest rates weaken."

41

Alternative Exchange Rate Systems

The nations of the world have tried many different international monetary systems. No system has been fully satisfactory, and periods of crisis have alternated with periods of stability.

The twentieth century began with a system of fixed exchange rates under the gold standard. This system suffered periodic crises in the post–World War I years but did not collapse until the onset of the Great Depression. The 1930s was a period of experimentation with flexible, market-determined exchange rates. This ended with World War II, when governments fixed exchange rates.

In 1944 the fixed exchange rate regime was formalized by international agreement at a conference in Bretton Woods, New Hampshire. The Bretton Woods system lasted for over a quarter of a century, but its shortcomings and the periods of crisis it induced finally prevailed over its advantages and the periods of stability it afforded. After several attempts to patch it up in the 1970s, the system finally broke down and was gradually abandoned as countries turned one by one to market-determined, flexible exchange rates.

Fixed and Flexible Exchange Rates

Among the principal international monetary systems two extremes can be distinguished. The first is a system in which exchange rates are fixed at announced par values. The gold standard was such a system, and so was Bretton Woods. (The operation and decline of both systems are discussed in the appendix to this chapter.)

The second is a system of freely fluctuating rates determined by market demand and supply in the absence of government intervention. Some countries have come close to this system, first in the 1930s and then since 1971.

Between these two "pure" systems are a variety of possible intermediate cases. The two that we will encounter are known as the *adjustable peg* and the *managed float*. In the adjustable peg system, governments set and attempt to maintain par values for their exchange rates, but they explicitly recognize that circumstances may arise in which they will change the par value. In a managed float, the central bank seeks to have some stabilizing influence on the exchange rate but does not try to fix it at some publicly announced par value.

The International Monetary Fund (also called the IMF and the Fund) was created as part of the Bretton Woods system. Under its original charter the Fund had several tasks. It tried to ensure that countries kept their exchange rates fixed in the short run. It was supposed to ensure that any exchange rate change was really needed to remove a persistent payments disequilibrium and that a single devaluation did not set off a self-canceling round of devaluations. It also made loans—out of funds subscribed by member nations—to governments to support their exchange rates in the face of temporary payments deficits.

The Bretton Woods system has been abandoned, but the Fund survives, although its tasks have changed. For example, the Jamaica Agreement of 1976 amended the IMF charter to ratify the adoption of floating exchange rates and deemphasize gold as a basis for the international payments system.

A Fixed Exchange Rate System

In a system of **fixed exchange rates,** each country's central bank intervenes in the foreign exchange market to prevent that country's exchange rate from going outside a narrow band on either side of its par value.

This system presents one immediate difficulty in that one country must take a passive role with respect to its exchange rate. This is because there is one less exchange rate to be determined than there are countries. In a two-country world containing only Japan and the United States, for example, if the Bank of Japan fixes the exchange rate at 150 yen to the dollar, the U.S. Federal Reserve cannot fix a different rate making the dollar worth, say, 200 yen. Under the Bretton Woods system, all foreign countries fixed their exchange rate against the U.S. dollar. The Fed adopted the passive role; it was the only central bank in the world that did not have to intervene to support a particular value of its currency.

Having picked a fixed exchange rate for its currency against, say, the U.S. dollar, each foreign central bank then had to manage matters so that the chosen rate could actually be maintained. The bank had to be prepared to offset imbalances in demand and supply by government sales or purchases of foreign exchange. In the face of short-term fluctuations in market demand and supply, each central bank could maintain its fixed exchange rate by entering the market and buying and selling as required.

To do this the central bank has to hold reserves of acceptable foreign exchange. When there is an abnormally low demand for its country's currency on the market, the bank keeps the currency from depreciating by selling foreign exchange and buying up domestic currency. This depletes its reserves of foreign exchange. When there is an abnormally high demand for its country's currency on the foreign exchange market, the bank prevents the currency's appreciating by selling domestic currency in return for foreign exchange. This augments its stocks of foreign exchange.

As long as the central bank is trying to maintain an exchange rate that equates demand and supply for its currency on average, the policy can be successful. Sometimes the bank will be buying and other times selling, but its reserves will fluctuate around a constant average level.

If, however, there is a permanent shift in demand for or supply of a nation's currency on the foreign exchange market, the long-term equilibrium rate will move away from the **pegged rate**, that is, its par value. It will then be difficult to maintain the pegged rate. For example, if there is a major inflation in France while prices are stable in the United States, the equilibrium value of the franc will fall. In a free market the franc would depreciate and the U.S. dollar would appreciate. But a fixed exchange rate is not a free-market rate. If the Bank of France persists in trying to maintain the original exchange rate, it will have to meet the excess demand for U.S. dollars by selling from its reserves. This policy can persist only as long as the Bank has reserves that it is willing to spend to maintain an artificially high price of francs. But the Bank cannot do this indefinitely. Sooner or later the reserves that it has, and those that it can borrow, will be exhausted.

The management of a fixed rate is illustrated in Figure 41-1. The example used is the maintenance by the Bank of England of a fixed exchange rate between sterling and the U.S. dollar.

When the fixed rate is not near the free-market equilibrium rate, controls of various sorts may be introduced in an attempt to shift the demand curve for foreign exchange so that it intersects the supply curve at a rate close to the fixed rate. This is usually done by restricting imports of goods and services or by restricting the export of capital. If the central bank

FIGURE 41-1 A Fixed Exchange Rate

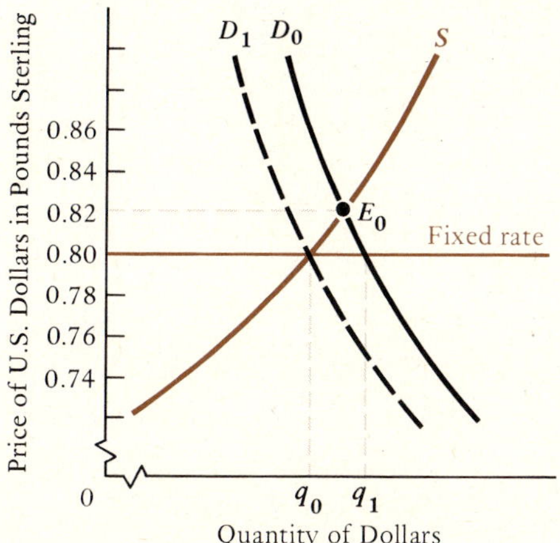

When an exchange rate is fixed at other than the equilibrium rate, either excess demand or excess supply will persist. Suppose demand and supply curves of dollars in the absence of government controls are D_0 and S; equilibrium is at E_0, with a price of £.82 per dollar. The equilibrium price of the pound is $1.22. Now the British authorities peg the price of the pound at $1.25; that is, they fix the price of the dollar at £.80. They have overvalued the pound and undervalued the dollar. As a result there is an excess of dollars demanded over dollars supplied of q_0q_1. To maintain the fixed rate it is necessary to shift either the demand curve or the supply curve (or both) so that the two intersect at the fixed rate. For example, demand might be shifted to D_1 by the British government's limiting imports. If the curves are not shifted, the fixed rate will have to be supported by the British government's supplying dollars in the amount of q_0q_1 per period out of its reserves.

cannot shift demand and supply in order to keep the equilibrium rate approximately as high as the fixed rate, it will have no alternative but to devalue its currency.

Problems with Fixed Exchange Rates

Three problems typically arise in a system of fixed exchange rates: (1) providing sufficient reserves, (2) adjusting to long-term trends, and (3) dealing with speculative crises.

Reserves. Reserves are needed to accommodate short-term balance-of-payments fluctuations arising from the current and the capital accounts. On current account, trade is subject to many short-term variations, some systematic and some random. This means that even if the value of imports does equal the value of exports on average over several years, there may be considerable imbalances over shorter periods.

With a market-determined exchange rate, fluctuations in current and capital account payments would cause the exchange rate to fluctuate. To prevent such fluctuations when rates are fixed, the monetary authorities buy and sell foreign exchange as required. These operations require the authorities to hold reserves of foreign exchange. If they run out of reserves, they cannot maintain the pegged rate.

As discussed in the appendix, the Bretton Woods system had difficulty providing sufficient reserves. This was because the ultimate reserve was gold, and there was not enough of it. As a result, the world's central banks held much of their reserves in U.S. dollars and British pounds sterling. Currencies that are widely held for this purpose are called **reserve currencies**.

This system worked well enough as long as these reserve currencies had a stable value. However, in the mid 1960s fear of an impending devaluation of sterling arose, and in the early 1970s a similar fear arose regarding the U.S. dollar. In both cases the fears were well founded: Sterling was devalued in late 1967, and the dollar was devalued in 1971 and again in 1973.

The devaluation of a reserve currency reduces the value of the reserves of that currency held by the world's central banks. Fear that a devaluation will occur reduces the acceptability of a currency as a means of holding reserves. This is discussed further in Box 41-1.

The problem of providing reserves, although serious, need not be insurmountable in any future system of fixed rates. After all, a balanced portfolio composed of some holdings of a number of currencies could be held as reserves. This would reduce the risks from holding reserves, since whenever one currency falls in value against a second currency, the second currency rises in value against the first.

BOX 41-1

Problems for Nations Whose Currency Is Held As a Reserve

Under the Bretton Woods system, the supply of gold was augmented by reserves of the key currencies, the U.S. dollar and the British pound sterling. While it is prestigious to have one's currency held as a reserve currency—and even advantageous as long as other countries are willing to increase their holdings of one's paper money without making claims on current output—there are both disadvantages and hazards for the country whose currency is involved.

Such a country is placed under great pressure not to devalue its currency. If it does devalue, all countries holding that currency will find the value of their reserves diminished. If it tries to avoid devaluation, the fear that it may be unable to do so will in any case impair the usefulness of the currency as a reserve because other countries will become reluctant to hold it. The result may well be that the domestic policy of the country whose currency is the reserve becomes unduly subservient to the overriding need to maintain its exchange rate.

The Loss of Confidence in the U.S. Dollar As a Reserve Currency

In the 1950s and 1960s America ran frequent deficits on its overall balance of payments. This resulted largely from American loans, investments, and contributions to other nations who were rebuilding their economies after World War II. As long as other nations were willing to accumulate dollar holdings, this caused no problem; indeed, the buildup of dollars provided the growth in foreign exchange reserves that was needed to finance the growing volume of world trade.

The effect of the dollar devaluations of the early 1970s. Had everyone believed that the devaluations of 1971 (7.9 percent) and 1973 (11 percent) were just isolated adjustments, they might well have licked their wounds and gone on as before. But no fundamental changes arose either in American policy or in international financial arrangements. Thus many believed that these devaluations were but preludes to inevitable future ones.

Fear of further devaluations not only made holders of U.S. dollars reluctant to increase their holdings but actually led many prudent holders to want to decrease reliance on such a shaky reserve. As people tried to get rid of U.S. dollars, the exchange rate began to slide. Between 1970 and 1973 the U.S. dollar declined 22 percent against the Japanese yen and 30 percent against the German mark. The lower value of the U.S. dollar reduced the adequacy of most countries' dollar reserves and threatened their financial stability.

Attempts to flee from the dollar. While one country (or one bank) can readily reduce its holdings of U.S. dollars by buying gold or other currencies, for everyone to do so requires major changes in the value of the dollar and its alternatives. In the late 1970s the dollar fell sharply relative to the yen and the mark, and one cause of the startling rise in the price of gold in 1979–1980 from $250 to over $900 an ounce was the attempt of many holders of U.S. dollars to flee to gold.

The return to stable prices in the United States restored some faith in the dollar; indeed, in the period 1981–1984 most observers felt that the dollar was overvalued, so its sharp decline in 1984 was welcomed. While the use of SDRs and other currencies has increased, the dollar still remains the key currency, and the problems discussed in this box remain.

Long-term disequilibria. With fixed exchange rates, long-term disequilibria can be expected to develop because of lasting shifts in the demands for and supplies of foreign exchange. There are three important reasons for these shifts. First, different trading countries have different rates of inflation. Chapter 40 explained how these varying rates produce changes in the equilibrium rates of exchange; if the rate is fixed, these would produce excess supply or excess demand in each country's foreign exchange market. Second, changes in the demands for and supplies of imports and exports are associated with long-term economic growth. Because the economies of different countries grow at different rates, their demands for imports and their supplies of exports can be expected to shift at different rates. Third, structural changes, such as major new innovations or a change in the price of oil, cause major changes in imports and exports.

The associated shifts in demand and supply on the foreign exchange market imply that there is no reason to believe that the exchange rate consistent with equilibrium in the market for foreign exchange will be unchanged.

The exchange rate consistent with balance-of-payments equilibrium will change over time; over a decade the change can be substantial.

Government may react to long-term disequilibria in at least three ways.

1. The exchange rate can be changed whenever it is clear that a balance-of-payments deficit or surplus is the result of a long-term shift in demands and supplies in the foreign exchange market and not the result of some transient factor.

2. Domestic price levels can be allowed to change in an attempt to make the present fixed exchange rates become the equilibrium rate. To restore equilibrium, countries with overvalued currencies need to have deflations and countries with undervalued currencies need to have inflations. But changes in domestic price levels have all sorts of domestic repercussions. Deflations are difficult and costly to accomplish (e.g., reductions in aggregate demand intended to lower the price level are likely to raise unemployment), and often the explicit goal of government policy is to avoid inflation. One might expect governments to be more willing to change exchange rates than to try to change their price levels.

3. Restrictions can be imposed on trade and foreign payments. Imports and foreign spending by tourists and governments can be restricted, and the export of capital can be slowed or even stopped. Surplus countries are often quick to criticize such restrictions on international trade and payments. But as long as exchange rates are fixed and price levels prove difficult to manipulate, deficit countries have little option but to restrict the quantity of foreign exchange their residents are permitted to obtain.

Since restrictions on trade and foreign payments are undesirable in a world economy characterized by large-scale international trade and foreign investment, and since deflations of the price level are difficult and costly to bring about, most countries will want to preserve the possibility of making occasional changes in their exchange rates even if fixed rates are the main rule of the day.

Under the Bretton Woods system, although most countries defended their exchange rates in the face of crises, there were still major rounds of exchange rate adjustments. Because exchange rates did have to be changed from time to time, the system of fixed rates under the Bretton Woods agreement was called an **adjustable peg system.**

Handling speculative crises. When enough people begin to doubt the government's ability to maintain the current exchange rate, speculative crises develop. The most important reason for such crises is that over time, equilibrium exchange rates get further and further away from any given set of fixed rates. When the disequilibrium becomes obvious to everyone, traders and speculators come to believe that a realignment of rates is due. There is a rush to buy currencies expected to be revalued and a rush to sell currencies expected to be devalued. Even if the authorities take drastic steps to remove the payments deficit, there may be doubt that these measures will work before the exchange reserves are exhausted. Speculative flows of funds can reach large proportions, and it may be impossible to avoid changing the exchange rate under such pressure.

Under an adjustable peg system, opportunities often arise for speculators to make large profits; this occurs when everyone knows the direction in which an exchange rate will be changed if it is to be changed at all.

As the equilibrium value of a country's currency changes, possibly under the impact of high inflation, it becomes obvious that the central bank is having more and more difficulty holding the pegged rate. So when a crisis arises, speculators sell the country's currency. If it is devalued, they can buy it back at a lower price and earn a profit. If it is not devalued, they can buy it back at the price at which they sold it and lose only the commission costs on the deal. This asymmetry, with speculators having a chance to make large profits by risking only a small loss, eventually destroyed the Bretton Woods system.

During the Bretton Woods period, governments tended to resist changing their exchange rates until they had no alternative. This made the situation so obvious that speculators could hardly lose, and their actions set off the final crises that forced exchange rate readjustments. If changes could be made more frequently and before they became inevitable, the number of speculative crises might diminish, and the system of fixed exchange rates might appear more viable. Such changes, however, would remove the day-to-day certainty that was one of the chief advantages of this system. Moreover, a surprise change might lead to suspicion that a devaluation was made to gain a competitive advantage for a country's exports rather than to remove a fundamental disequilibrium. After all, governments are not supposed to devalue under an adjustable peg system until it is *clear* that they are faced with a fundamental disequilibrium. If this is clear to them, it is also clear to ordinary traders and speculators.

Flexible Exchange Rates

Under a system of flexible exchange rates, demand and supply determine the rates without any government intervention. (This was illustrated in Figure 40-1 on page 878.) Such rates are called free, **flexible,** or **floating exchange rates**. Since the foreign exchange market always clears, the government can turn its attention to domestic problems of inflation and unemployment, leaving the balance of payments to take care of itself—at least so went the theory before flexible rates were introduced.

For reasons that we shall analyze later in this chapter, this optimistic picture did not materialize when the world went over to flexible exchange rates. Free-market fluctuations in rates were far greater, and hence potentially more upsetting to the performance of national economies and to the flow of international trade, than many economists had anticipated. As a result, central banks have felt the need to intervene quite frequently and extensively to stabilize exchange rates.

Managed Floats

A major difference between the present system and Bretton Woods is that central banks no longer publicly announce values for exchange rates that they are committed in advance to defend even at heavy cost. Central banks are thus free to adjust their exchange rate targets as circumstances change. Sometimes they leave the rate completely free to fluctuate, and at other times they interfere actively to alter the exchange rate from its free-market value. Such a system is called a **managed float** or a **dirty float**.

Some countries have opted for what is called a *currency block* by pegging their exchange rates against each other and then indulging in a joint float against the outside world. The best-known currency block is the European **snake**. Under this arrangement the countries of the EEC, with the exception of the United Kingdom, maintain fixed rates among their own currencies but allow them to float as a block against the dollar.

What Determines the Exchange Rate in a Floating System?

One surprise to supporters of floating exchange rates has been the degree of exchange rate volatility. Why have rates been so volatile?

The average value of exchange rates over the long term depends on their **purchasing power parity (PPP)** values. The PPP exchange rate is the one that holds constant the relative price levels in two countries *when measured in a common currency*. For example, assume that the U.S. price level rises by 20 percent, while the German price level rises by only 5 percent over the same period. The PPP value of the German mark then appreciates by approximately 15 percent. This would mean that in Germany the prices of all goods (both German-produced and imported American goods) would rise by 5 percent measured in

German marks, while in the United States the prices of all goods (both American-produced and imported German goods) would rise by 20 percent measured in U.S. dollars.

The PPP exchange rate adjusts so that the relative price of the two nations' goods (measured in the same currency) is unchanged because the change in the relative values of two currencies compensates exactly for differences in national inflation rates.

If the actual exchange rate equals the PPP rate, the competitive positions of producers in the two countries will be unchanged. Firms located in countries with high inflation rates will still be able to sell their outputs on international markets, since the exchange rate adjusts to offset the effect of the higher domestic prices.

Figure 41-2 shows that the exchange rate between U.S. dollars and sterling has followed the PPP rate over the long run. But notice also the large fluctuations around the PPP rate.

During the Bretton Woods period of fixed exchange rates, the advocates of floating rates argued that speculators would stabilize the actual rates within a narrow band around the PPP rates. The argument was that since everyone knew the normal value was the PPP rate, speculators seeking a profit when the rate deviated from its PPP level would quickly force the rate back to that level. To illustrate, suppose the PPP rate is U.S. $1.25 = £1.00 and that the actual rate falls to U.S. $1.15 = £1.00. Speculators would rush to buy pounds at U.S. $1.15 each, expecting to sell them for U.S. $1.25 when the rate returns to its PPP level. This very action would raise the demand for sterling and help push its value back toward U.S. $1.25.

FIGURE 41-2 Actual and PPP Exchange Rate, U.S. Dollar and Pound Sterling, 1972–1987

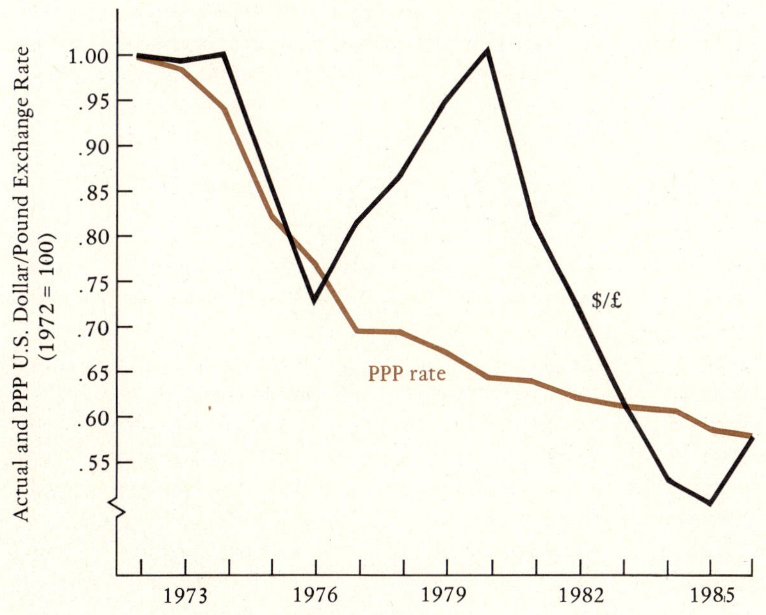

The actual exchange rate follows the trend value of the PPP exchange rate but fluctuates substantially around it. The black line shows the dollar/pound exchange rate; the colored line shows the ratio of the U.S. CPI to the British CPI. (Both series are set to 1.00 in 1972. The figures for 1987 are for the exchange rate at the end of April.)

The continual decline of the PPP exchange rate reflects the United Kingdom's higher inflation rate relative to that of the United States. Until 1976 the relative value of the pound fell in accordance with the PPP rate, but after 1976 the pound appreciated sharply through 1980. (Many observers associate this appreciation with the onset of production from large oil deposits in the North Sea and with high interest rates in 1979–1980.) In 1980 the relative value of the pound began to fall, bringing it back toward its PPP value. In 1983 the pound fell below its PPP value, and in 1985 it started to rise again toward its PPP value, and reached it by late 1986. *(Source: International Financial Statistics)*

Such speculative behavior would stabilize the exchange rate near its PPP value if speculators could be sure that the deviations would be small and short-lived. But in practice the swings around the PPP rate have been wide and have lasted for long periods. Thus if sterling fell to U.S. $1.15, speculators would know that it could go as low as U.S. $1.05 and stay there for quite a while before returning to U.S. $1.25. In that case it might be worth speculating on a price of U.S. $1.10 next week rather than a price of U.S. $1.25 in some indefinite future.

The wide swings in exchange rates that have occurred show that speculative buying and selling cannot be relied on to hold exchange rates close to their PPP values.

Why have these wide fluctuations occurred? One of the most important reasons is associated with international differences in interest rates.

Exchange Rate Overshooting

Suppose that American interest rates rise above those ruling in other major financial centers. A rush to lend money at the profitable rates found in the United States will lead to an appreciation of the U.S. dollar.

This process will stop only when the rise in value of the U.S. dollar on foreign exchange markets is large enough that investors expect the dollar subsequently to fall in value. This expected future depreciation then just offsets the interest premium from lending funds in U.S. dollars.

To illustrate, assume that interest rates are 4 percentage points higher in New York than in London due to a restrictive monetary policy in the United States. Investors believe the PPP rate is U.S. $1.60 = £1.00, but as they rush to buy dollars to take advantage of the higher U.S. interest rates, they drive the rate to, say, U.S. $1.40 = £1.00. (Since £1.00 now buys fewer U.S. dollars, sterling has depreciated, and since it takes fewer U.S. dollars to buy £1.00, the dollar has appreciated.) They do not believe this rate will be sustained and instead expect the U.S. dollar to lose value. If foreign investors expect it to depreciate at 4 percent per year, they will be indifferent between lending money in New York and doing so in London. The extra 4 percent of interest they earn in New York per year is exactly offset by the 4 percent they expect to lose when they turn their money back into their own currency.

Any policy that raises domestic interest rates above world levels will cause the external value of the domestic currency to appreciate enough to create an expected future depreciation sufficient to offset the interest differential.

A central bank that is seeking to meet a monetary target may have to put up with large fluctuations in the exchange rate. If, in the example, the high U.S. interest rates were the result of a restrictive monetary policy, the overshooting of the U.S. dollar beyond its PPP rate may put export- and import-competing industries under temporary but severe pressure from foreign competition.

The other side of this coin is that the high value of the U.S. dollar creates inflationary pressure in other countries. U.S. goods become much more expensive abroad, thus putting upward pressure on foreign prices and wages. Authorities in those countries are faced with the uncomfortable choice of accepting this increased inflation or raising their own interest rates and thus maintaining their exchange rates in terms of the U.S. dollar. In the early 1980s many foreign central banks chose this latter option, and the tight U.S. monetary policies were quickly imitated in other countries. This combined monetary contraction contributed to the severity of the world recession, as discussed further in Box 41-2 (pages 904–905).

Current Problems[1]

The Lack of an Alternative to the Dollar As a Reserve Currency

Governments operating dirty floats need reserves, just like governments operating adjustable pegs. The search for an adequate supply of reserves has continued unabated since the demise of the Bretton Woods system.

[1] The rest of this chapter can be omitted without loss of continuity.

One major form in which reserves are held is U.S. dollars; another, one that is growing in size, is the **special drawing rights (SDRs)** held with the IMF. First introduced in 1969, SDRs were designed to provide a supplement to existing reserve assets. The Special Drawing Account of the IMF was set up and kept separate from all other operations of the Fund. Each member country was assigned an SDR quota that was guaranteed in terms of a fixed gold value. Each country could use its quota to acquire an equivalent amount of convertible currencies from other participants. SDRs could be used without prior consultation with the Fund, but only to cope with balance-of-payments difficulties. SDR allocations grew from about $10 billion in 1970 to over $50 billion in 1986.

The commitment to lower inflation initiated by the Reagan administration in 1981 has restored some confidence in the U.S. dollar as a reserve asset. But overall these developments have not been seen as long-term solutions to the reserve problem. Other national currencies could take over the reserve role played by the U.S. dollar, but this is not likely.

Why does the world not turn to an international paper reserve system based on SDRs or some similar creation? Such a solution has much support from academic economists, who see an appropriate international institution managing the supply of international currency to accommodate growth and to avoid inflation.

Critics of such a system—among them most of the world's central bankers—distrust the concept of an international paper currency, pointing out that few countries have managed their own money supplies effectively. However difficult the task of the U.S. Federal Reserve may be, the task of a World Reserve Bank would be more difficult. Further, private acceptance and use of the SDR has been virtually nonexistent, indicating the enormous difficulties inherent in creating a new currency.

Some who are skeptical of an international paper monetary standard have urged a return to the gold standard. This approach has critical disadvantages. In fact, the IMF and the U.S. government have at various times taken the lead in the attempt to "demonetarize" gold completely.

For the moment at least, the world cannot agree on an international monetary reserve. Until it does, there will be crises whenever there is a desire to shift from one to another of the multiple sources of reserves: dollars, gold, SDRs, marks, francs, and yen. The speculative opportunities inherent in such a system remain large, as evidenced by the recent behavior of the price of gold shown in Figure 41-3 (see page 906).

The Impact of OPEC

One issue affecting the future payments system—and indeed the whole of international economic relations—is the variability of the price of oil.

Oil Price Increases

The OPEC cartel raised the price of oil dramatically in 1974 and again in 1979. In total these events led to a tenfold increase, which generated an unprecedented imbalance in the international economic system in the form of a massive payments surplus for the oil producers and a corresponding deficit for the oil-importing countries. The excess purchasing power in the hands of oil producers came to be called **petrodollars**. The cumulative stock of petrodollars may well have exceeded $500 billion. Petrodollars caused several different kinds of problems, some of them short term, others long term in nature.

Short-term problems of industrialized countries. Most petrodollars were eventually used for the purchase of consumption goods and services or investment goods from industrialized countries. But the oil-producing countries could not spend their oil revenues on goods and services as fast as they were earned in the late 1970s.[2] Nor could the industrialized oil-consuming countries produce the goods and services at the rate necessary for all the oil revenues to be spent without creating enormous inflationary pressures.

Thus in the short term the OPEC countries had excess dollars. They also had an understandable desire to earn a return on those funds. One way was

[2] There is a limit to the speed with which any country can absorb foreign goods, and many oil-producing countries were at that limit. Ships sometimes wait months to unload for want of dock capacity, unloaded goods sometimes sit in wharfside stockpiles for months, even years, for want of transportation capacity, and so on.

BOX 41-2

Beggar-My-Neighbor Policies, Past and Present

The Great Depression of the 1930s brought an end to the long-standing stability of the gold standard and ushered in a period of experimentation in exchange regimes. Experiments were tried with both fixed and fluctuating rates.

But the overriding feature of the decade was that considerations of massive unemployment came to dominate economic policies in almost every country, and all devices, including exchange rate manipulations, seemed fair game for dealing with them. Many of the policies adopted at this time were acts of desperation that would have made long-term sense only if other countries had not also been in crisis. Governments tended not to consider the long-term effects on trade or on their trading partners of the policies they adopted, hoping to gain short-term advantages before their policies provoked the inevitable reaction from others.

The use of devaluations to ease domestic unemployment rested on a simple and superficially plausible line of analysis: If a country has unemployed workers at home, why not substitute home production for imports and thus give jobs to one's citizens instead of to foreigners? One way to do this is to urge, say, Americans to "buy American." Another, probably more effective, way is to lower the prices of domestic goods relative to those of imports. The devaluation of one's currency does this by making foreign goods that much more expensive. (A 10 percent devaluation, means that it will take 10 percent more domestic money to buy the same imports; this is equivalent to a 10 percent rise in the prices of all foreign goods.)

Of course, if this policy works, other countries will find *their* exports falling and unemployment rising as a consequence. Because such policies attempt to solve one country's problems by inflicting them on others, they are called **beggar-my-neighbor policies** and are described as attempts to "export one's unemployment."

In a situation of inadequate world demand, a beggar-my-neighbor policy on the part of one country can work only in the unlikely event that other countries do not try to protect themselves. A situation in which all countries devalue their currencies in an attempt to gain a competitive advantage over one another is called a situation of **competitive devaluations**.

This is what happened during the 1930s. One country would devalue its currency in an attempt to reduce its imports and stimulate exports. But because other countries were suffering from the same kinds of problems of unemployment, they did not sit idly by. Retaliation was swift, and devaluation followed devaluation. But the simultaneous attempt of all countries to cut imports without suffering a comparable cut in exports is bound to be self-defeating.

When unemployment is due to insufficient world aggregate demand, it cannot be cured by measures designed to redistribute among nations the fixed and inadequate total of demand.

---

to invest their surplus revenues in the advanced industrialized nations, thereby returning on capital account the purchasing power extracted from the current accounts of the oil-importing nations. This creates many serious problems.

One of the most important concerns the havoc brought to foreign exchange markets when surplus oil funds are invested in liquid assets and switched between currencies in response to changes in interest rates and expected capital gains arising from possible exchange rate alterations. Surplus petrodollars can also be used speculatively, and many observers believe that a good part of the wild rise and sudden fall in gold prices in 1979–1980 was due to just such a use of petrodollars.

Short-term problems of underdeveloped countries. Consider an oil-importing country such as Kenya, for which the OPEC price increase turned a small trade surplus into a massive deficit overnight. The country was unable to generate revenues quickly enough to pay its oil bill, yet it could sharply decrease its use of oil only at the cost of a great slowdown in its domestic economy.

The IMF stepped in with loan arrangements to help countries most severely affected by the rising

These policies, along with other restrictive trade policies such as import duties, export subsidies, quotas, and prohibitions, led to a declining volume of world trade and brought no relief from the world-wide depression. Moreover, they contributed to a loss of faith in the economic system and in the ability of either economists or politicians to cope with economic crises.

To avoid a recurrence of the beggar-my-neighbor policies of the 1930s, trading nations designed some important institutions. The International Monetary Fund (IMF) was supposed to reduce the chances of competitive devaluations, and the General Agreement on Tariffs and Trade (GATT) was to reduce the chances of competitive increases in tariffs and other trade restrictions. These institutions worked well for over 30 years.

In 1980 the United States embarked on tight monetary policy, driving up U.S. interest rates and the external value of the U.S. dollar. Just as expansionary monetary policy in the face of world recession tends to "export unemployment" by leading to a depreciation of the home currency and reducing the demand for foreign goods, tight monetary policy in the face of the world inflation tends to "export inflation" by leading to an appreciation of the home currency and raising the demand for foreign goods.

Most other governments, notably Germany and Japan, were worried about the implications of this for their own inflation rates and reacted by also adopting tight monetary policies. This monetary tightness helped lead the world into the serious recession of 1981–1983.

Under the extreme pressures of this difficult economic situation, beggar-my-neighbor pressures surfaced, and many governments found them hard to resist politically. Throughout the 1980s American voters have shown strong support for advocates of increased tariffs. Many countries negotiated unofficial quotas restricting the importation of Japanese cars. European agricultural protectionism nearly wrecked the GATT negotiations in December 1982 and has been the focus of considerable debate in the United States for the past few years. Less-developed countries sought covert ways of protecting their own infant industries and complained, with some justice, that the developed nations paid lip service to, rather than really acting on, the slogan of "trade, not aid." It was clear that great pressure was being put on the whole postwar fabric designed to encourage trade and discourage beggar-my-neighbor policies. As the world recovered in the period from 1983 to 1986, some but not all of the pressures abated. But in the rest of the world in mid 1987 most observers were still worried about the threat of beggar-my-neighbor policies and the protectionist mood in the United States.

oil prices, the repayments of maturing loans were deferred, and the OPEC nations established a fund for short-term loans to such countries. Thus the purely short-term problems can be, and have been, solved through international cooperation and recognition of the need for accommodation on the part of creditor nations.

Oil Price Decreases

Many oil-exporting countries also borrowed heavily on the expectation of rising oil prices. In early 1983, however, OPEC had lost control of the market, and the price of oil started to fall. In early 1986 the price of crude oil fell sharply from over $30 a barrel to around $12.[3] Many international loans were threatened, including those made by large private banks to less-developed countries such as Mexico, which is heavily dependent on oil exports for repayment. The risk of a major default hangs over the system, and the IMF again finds itself facing the problem of rescheduling repayments of large international loans.

[3] Oil prices, like the prices of many other international commodities, are expressed in U.S. dollars.

FIGURE 41-3 Price of Gold, 1971–1987

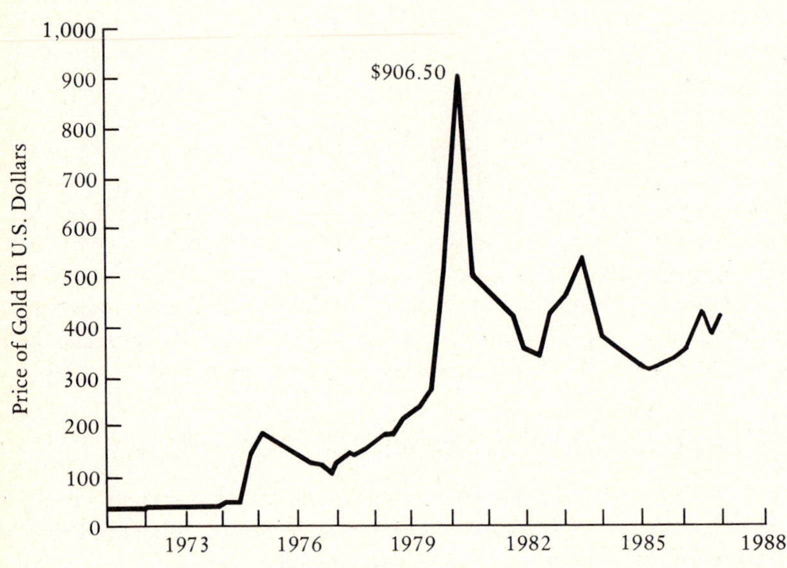

Gold soared in value and proved highly volatile after convertibility of the dollar was suspended in 1973. The two devaluations of the U.S. dollar in terms of gold that occurred under the adjustable peg system are barely visible. (These devaluations are discussed in the appendix to this chapter.) The effects of speculation on the price of gold is seen in subsequent experience. The price of gold more than quadrupled from 1977 to 1979, reaching a peak of over $900 per ounce. It subsequently fell to around $300 by 1981, then rose through 1984 before falling again.

Nevertheless, lower oil prices generally contributed to a reduction of interest rates and an increase in economic growth among the industrialized countries. Both of these contribute to the long-run health of the less-developed countries, whether oil exporting or not.

The U.S. Dollar and Protectionism

The dollar became overvalued during the period of tight monetary policy that began in 1980. If a temporary overshooting of the exchange rate was all that was involved in that overvaluation, the dollar would have come down shortly thereafter. Many economists expected it to do so, but in fact it remained high throughout 1981–1985.

Most observers believe that the dollar remained high because this period witnessed enormous capital inflows into the United States. These capital inflows were partly a result of the record U.S. government budget deficit. That deficit exceeded $200 billion in 1986 (over 5 percent of GNP); some of this was financed by domestic savings, but much also had to be financed by foreign borrowing, resulting in capital inflows. The large capital inflows that occurred were also responding to the combination of low inflation and relative prosperity in the United States, which made the country a safe and profitable place in which to invest.

As we saw in Chapter 40, equilibrium in the foreign exchange market means that the capital inflow is *necessarily* matched by a current account deficit (see page 891). Only when these two are equal will the demand for dollars by foreign investors wishing to buy American capital assets be matched by the supply of dollars by those Americans wishing to import foreign goods and services. The large capital inflows thus meant that there also had to be a current account deficit; from this perspective the high value of the dollar was simply the mechanism by which the required current account deficit was brought about.

The high value of the dollar placed American firms that produce traded goods (i.e., goods for export and goods that face competition from imports) at a cost disadvantage relative to foreign producers. Falling production, rising unemployment, and many business failures resulted. These events, combined with the increase in the demand for imports resulting from the fall in their relative price, contributed to the growth of the current account deficit.

In spite of the vigorous expansion of the macro economy from 1984 through 1986, these traded goods sectors remained depressed; the recovery was focused in the nontraded sectors. Not surprisingly, the plight of the import-competing and export sectors led to a call for protection. The United States put pressure on Japan, Germany, and Canada to reduce their current account surpluses and itself took many steps to curb imports. Some steps were specific, such as the tariff imposed in May 1986 on Canadian cedar shakes and shingles. Further, in 1987 protectionist trade bills were being considered in both the Congress and the Senate.

While the motivation for these protectionist measures was easy enough to understand, most economists felt that the measures were seriously misguided. First, they threatened to upset the fabric of international trading relations and cooperation carefully built up through multilateral negotiation during the post–World War II period. The growing protectionist sentiment in Congress led to a serious split between that body and the administration; in late 1985 President Reagan, an avowed "free trader," warned of a "mindless stampede to protectionism."

Second, the measures were likely to be largely ineffective in terms of their goal of reducing the current account deficit. As we have seen, the current account deficit was a necessary counterpart to the capital inflows that the U.S. economy was experiencing. Unless the root causes of the capital inflows were dealt with, the current account deficit would persist with or without protectionist measures. If the government deficit remained large, and if the United States remained attractive to foreign investors, the current account would have to remain in deficit in order to match the capital inflows.

To see this very important point, assume that import tariffs, surcharges, and quotas succeeded in bringing the current account into balance but that people still wished to bring capital into the United States. With a balanced current account, there would not be anyone willing to supply the dollars to the would-be capital importers, and consequently the dollar would start to appreciate. This would lead to a reduction in exports and an increase in imports until the original current account deficit was re-established.[4]

The Challenge for the Rest of the Century

The 1970s witnessed the replacement of a system of managed fixed exchange rates by a system of managed flexible exchange rates. The problems of the latter may have been revealed by the events of the last decade, but they cannot be said to have been solved. Officials understand the need to devise workable guidelines for managing flexible rates and to enhance cooperation more generally.

The Management of Exchange Rates

Managing floating rates poses several potential problems for the international monetary system. Let us discuss three key problems.

Inconsistent exchange rate policies. Different governments may try to fix their exchange rates at levels that are inconsistent with each other. For example, if the Fed's target is that the U.S. dollar should be worth 150 yen while the Bank of Japan's target is that the yen should be worth U.S. $0.005, both policies cannot succeed. If both banks persist in trying to meet such inconsistent targets, they can destabilize exchange markets.

Competitive devaluations. Countries may get involved in bouts of competitive devaluations similar to those that destabilized exchange markets in the 1920s and 1930s. For example, if one country devalues its currency in order to get a competitive advantage for its exports and other countries respond by devaluing their currencies, the rounds of successive devaluations will destabilize the exchange market without giving any country's exports a permanent advantage.

[4] Of course, to the extent that the tariffs create revenue and therefore reduce the government deficit, more domestic private saving would be available to finance domestic investment, and capital inflows and the current account both could be reduced correspondingly.

Destabilizing speculation. Speculative behavior can destabilize exchange markets. Before the system of floating exchange rates was adopted, many economists felt that rates would stay fairly close to their equilibrium values. Economists expected that speculators would then stabilize rates even further by buying currencies that seemed temporarily low in price and selling those that seemed temporarily high. In that event, however, very large and persistent deviations of exchange rates from the long-run equilibrium values occurred. This left speculators less clear on which way a particular rate was likely to go in the near future. When a particular currency started to fall in value, speculators might conclude that a large and persistent fall was just beginning. In this case their rush to sell the currency before its expected further fall would bring the fall about.

To help avoid these problems, the IMF has issued guidelines for exchange rate management. The guidelines emphasize that exchange rate policy is a matter for international consultation and surveillance by the IMF and that intervention practices by individual central banks should be based on three principles: (1) Exchange authorities should prevent sudden and disproportionate short-term movements in exchange rates and ensure an orderly adjustment to longer-term pressures. (2) In consultation with the IMF, countries should establish a target zone for the medium-term values of their exchange rates and keep the actual rate within that target zone. (3) Countries should recognize that exchange rate management involves joint responsibilities and is not just the responsibility of the individual country in question.

The experiences of the last decade have underlined one of the most important unsolved problems of managed floating rates: coping with the massive volume of short-term funds that can be switched rapidly between financial centers. Short-term capital flows forced the abandonment of exchange rates that had been agreed on in 1971 and have often caused violent fluctuations in floating rates since then. Severe "currency misalignments" have arisen and persisted, rendering uncompetitive on world markets the export- and import-competing sectors in countries with overvalued currencies, while creating enormous profit opportunities in countries with undervalued currencies.

Capital flows often prevent the quick return of exchange rates to their PPP values. Various attempts have been made to limit such capital flows. Italy has adopted a two-tier foreign exchange market, with one price for foreign exchange to finance current account transactions and another price (and another set of controls) for foreign exchange to finance capital movements. Germany has used direct controls on overseas borrowing. There has also been a considerable extension of arrangements under which central banks in surplus countries lend the funds they are accumulating back to central banks in deficit countries. Through such arrangements, the ability of banks to maintain stable exchange rates in the face of short-term speculative flights of capital is enhanced.

The major problem in managing speculative flows is to identify them accurately. Experience suggests that exchange rate management can smooth out temporary fluctuations but cannot resist underlying trends in equilibrium rates caused by relative inflation rates, structural changes, and persistent nonspeculative capital flows. In day-to-day management it is not always easy to distinguish among them.

Nevertheless, the excessive variability and persistent misalignment of exchange rates that continued to plague the flexible exchange rate system led to a number of proposals for reform. These are discussed further in Box 41-3.

The Need for Cooperation

One of the most impressive aspects of the international payments history of the past 30 years has been the steady rise of effective international cooperation. When the gold standard collapsed and the Great Depression overwhelmed the countries of the world, "every nation for itself" was the rule of the day. Rising tariffs, competitive exchange rate devaluations, and all forms of beggar-my-neighbor policies abounded.

After World War II the countries of the world cooperated in bringing the Bretton Woods system and the IMF into being. The system itself was far from perfect, and it finally broke down as a result of its own internal contradictions. But the international cooperation that was necessary to set up the system

BOX 41-3

Proposals for International Monetary Reform

The high degree of variability and persistent misalignment of exchange rates that plagued the flexible exchange rate system for over the first decade of its operation led in the mid 1980s to a number of proposals for reform.

Fixed Exchange Rates

Some observers advocated a return to fixed exchange rates. In fact, some even wanted the new system to be based on gold or some other group of commodities. This proposal was apparently motivated by the belief that *ruling out* exchange rate changes would allow some of the problems noted in the text to be avoided.

This proposal has not received wide support among economists since most believe that the flaws that led to the demise of the Bretton Woods system were indeed fatal and that a system of fixed exchange rates would have performed worse, not better, than flexible exchange rates did in the face of the shocks that have disturbed the world economy since Bretton Woods was abandoned. Proponents of fixed exchange rates counter that many of those shocks were in fact the result of bad policies that were made possible only by the freedom for independent domestic policy that exists under flexible exchange rates. They argue that the discipline imposed by fixed exchange rates would have improved the performance of policy over the period.

Target Exchange Rate Zones

Another proposal was for establishing *target zones* for exchange rates. Some advocates proposed "hard" zones, that is, narrowly defined zones with automatic intervention required whenever exchange rates moved outside the defined limits. This amounts to a fixed exchange rate system, and, not surprisingly, debate on this type of proposal paralleled that on fixed exchange rates.

Alternatively, some advocates proposed "soft" zones, defined more loosely and departures from which simply served as a signal to authorities that some policy reaction might be appropriate. Although these soft zones were more acceptable to some observers, many expressed a good deal of skepticism about what such weak arrangements might accomplish.

Objective Indicators

Other participants in the debate promoted the idea that "objective indicators" be calculated to provide a signal to authorities when policies become mutually inconsistent. Such indicators, which might involve measures of performance such as real growth and inflation as well as policy measures such as money growth rates and fiscal deficits, are an extension of the soft zone for exchange rate targets in that they serve merely as an indicator and do not themselves trigger automatic policy responses.

Though many commentators were sympathetic to this idea, there was little consensus as to how to calculate such indicators and how exactly they might work to avoid the problems in the system. Indeed, proponents of all these reforms concede that the high variability and persistent misalignment of exchange rates are really just symptoms of the real problems in the international economy and that any real reform must address the root causes of such problems. Many of those root causes are beyond the control of policymakers, but some of the problems result from undesirable economic policies in the industrialized countries. Recognizing this, Western leaders attending the economic summit held in Tokyo in May 1986 reached an agreement to establish objective indicators in an effort to improve international cooperation in formulating economic policies.

survived. The joint cooperative actions of central banks allowed them to weather speculative crises in the 1970s that would have forced them to devalue their currencies in the 1950s.

Thus the collapse of Bretton Woods did not plunge the world into the same chaos that followed the breakdown of the gold standard. The world was also better able to cope with the terrible strains caused by the sharp rise in oil prices in the 1970s. Of course, enormous oil-related problems remain, and they are matters for continuing international dialogue. Further, it is not yet clear how well the world economy will weather the upsurge of American protectionism of the mid 1980s. Prior to this upsurge, the United States provided essential leadership in working for lower restrictions on international trade. It is a serious question, then, whether other nations will now follow the American lead to *increased* protectionism and thus join in a mutually destructive round of competitive tariff increases and other restrictions.

Whatever the problems of the future, the world has a better chance of solving them—or even just learning to live with them—when countries cooperate through the IMF and other international organizations than when each country seeks its own solution without concern for the interests of others.

Summary

1. Various systems of international monetary arrangements have been tried. All involve aspects of the two extremes of fixed exchange rates and flexible exchange rates.
2. Under fixed exchange rates the central bank intervenes in the foreign exchange market to maintain the exchange rate at or near an announced par value. To do this the central bank must hold sufficient stocks of foreign exchange reserves. Reserves have historically been held in the form of gold or reserve currencies, particularly the U.S. dollar. The SDR is a relatively new international paper money meant to provide additional international reserves linked neither to gold nor to the U.S. dollar.
3. Any fixed exchange rate system will face three major problems: (1) providing sufficient international reserves, (2) adjusting to long-term trends in receipts and payments, and (3) handling periodic speculative crises.
4. Under a system of flexible, or floating, exchange rates, the exchange rate is market-determined by supply and demand for the currency.
5. Since their adoption in the mid 1970s, flexible exchange rates have fluctuated substantially. As a result, central banks have often intervened to stabilize the fluctuations. Thus the present system is called a managed, or dirty, float.
6. Fluctuations in exchange rates can be understood as fluctuations around a trend value that is determined by the purchasing power parity (PPP) rate. The PPP rate adjusts in response to differences in national inflation rates.
7. Current problems include the need to find an adequate reserve not tied to a national currency, to accommodate both the short-term and the longer-term impact of OPEC, and to develop rules for managing flexible exchange rates. A continuing commitment to international cooperation will help the world cope with these problems.

Topics for Review

Fixed and flexible exchange rates
Managed floats
Adjustable peg
Bretton Woods system
International Monetary Fund
Exchange rate overshooting
Petrodollars

Discussion Questions

1. From mid 1985 through the end of 1986 the U.S. dollar fell sharply in terms of the Japanese yen and the major European currencies. However, the U.S. current account deficit did not fall. Can you think of any reasons why? What happened to the Canadian dollar over this period? What were the implications for Canada?
2. The U.S. dollar is no longer convertible into gold because of a change in U.S. policy. Does this lack of convertibility make the dollar any less useful as an international medium of exchange?
3. Are Americans benefited or hurt when the U.S. dollar is the standard form of international reserves?
4. "Under a flexible exchange rate system no country need suffer unemployment, for if its prices are low enough there will be more than enough demand to keep its factories and farms fully occupied." The evidence suggests that flexible rates have not generally eliminated unemployment. Can you explain why? Can changing exchange rates ever cure unemployment?
5. The OPEC oil price increases during the 1970s caused grave problems in international payments and increased the need for IMF loans. Why did market adjustment of exchange rates not solve the problem?
6. In November 1985 the five major industrialized countries met and agreed that a major realignment of the world's currencies was appropriate. Why? What did they do about it? What was the result?
7. What role in international payments does or did gold play under (a) the gold standard, (b) the adjustable peg Bretton Woods system, and (c) the present system?
8. Might a person who regards inflation as the number one economic danger favor a return to the pre-1914 gold standard? Would you predict non-inflationary results if in order to restore the gold standard, the price of gold had to be set at U.S. $1,600 per ounce, either all at once or gradually?

Appendix to Chapter 41

The Gold Standard and the Bretton Woods System

Two episodes with fixed exchange rates were experienced in the twentieth century. Each ultimately failed. The gold standard, whose origins are as old as currency itself, was used until the late 1920s and early 1930s. The Bretton Woods system, which was the only payments system ever to be designed and established by conscious action, was born out of World War II and collapsed a little less than 30 years later. Their histories are instructive, not least because many people continue to propose returning to one or the other of these systems.

The Gold Standard

The gold standard was not *designed;* it just happened. It arose out of the general acceptance of gold as the commodity to be used as money. In most countries paper currency was freely convertible into gold at a fixed rate. In 1914 the U.S. dollar was worth 0.053 standard ounces of gold, while the British pound sterling was worth 0.257 standard ounces. This meant that the pound was worth 4.86 times as much as the dollar in terms of gold, thus making £1 worth U.S. $4.86. (In practice the exchange rate fluctuated within narrow limits set by the cost of shipping gold.) As long as all countries were on the gold standard, a person in one country could be sure of being able to make payments to a person in another.

The Gold-Flow, Price-Level Mechanism

The gold standard was supposed to maintain a balance of international payments by causing adjustments in price levels within individual countries. Consider a country that had a balance-of-payments deficit because the value of its imports (i.e., purchases) from other countries exceeded the value of its exports (i.e., sales) to other countries. The demand for foreign exchange would exceed the supply on this country's foreign exchange market. Some people who wished to make foreign payments would need to convert their domestic currency into gold and ship the gold. Therefore, some people in a surplus country would receive gold in payment for exports. They would deposit this to their credit and accept claims on gold—in terms of convertible paper money or bank deposits—in return. Thus deficit countries would be losing gold, while surplus countries would be gaining it.

Under the gold standard, the whole money supply was linked to the supply of gold. The international movements of gold would therefore lead to a fall in the money supply in the deficit country and a rise in the surplus country.[1] If full employment prevails, changes in the domestic money supply will cause changes in domestic price levels. Deficit countries would thus have falling price levels, while surplus countries would have rising price levels. The exports of deficit countries would become relatively cheaper, while those of surplus countries would become relatively more expensive. The resulting changes in quantities bought and sold would move the balance of payments toward an equilibrium position.

Actual Experience of the Gold Standard

The half century before World War I was the heyday of the gold standard. During this relatively trouble-free period, the adjustment mechanism just described seemed to work well.

Subsequent research has suggested, however, that the gold standard succeeded during the period mainly because it was not called on to do much work. No major trading country found itself with a serious and

[1] When the person who received gold deposited it in a bank, the bank would be in the position of the bank in Table 33-4 on page 725, and a multiple expansion of deposit money would ensue.

persistent balance-of-payments deficit, so no major country was called on to restore equilibrium through a large change in its domestic price level. Short-run fluctuations were ironed out either by movements of short-run capital in response to changes in interest rates or by changes in national income and employment.

In the 1920s the gold standard was called on to do a major job. It failed utterly, and it was abandoned. How did this happen? During World War I most belligerent countries had suspended convertibility of currency (i.e., they went off the gold standard). Most countries suffered major inflations, but the degree of inflation differed from country to country. As we have seen, this will lead to changes in the equilibrium exchange rates.

After the war countries returned to the gold standard (i.e., they restored convertibility of their currencies into gold). For reasons of prestige, many insisted on returning at the prewar rates. This meant that some countries' goods were overpriced and other countries' goods were underpriced. Large deficits and surpluses in the balance of payments inevitably appeared, and the adjustment mechanism required that price levels should change in each of the countries in order to restore equilibrium. Exchange rates were not adjusted, and price levels changed very slowly. By the onset of the Great Depression, equilibrium price levels had not yet been attained. The financial chaos brought on by the depression destroyed the existing payments system.

Major Disabilities of a Gold Standard

One may ask whether an altered gold standard, based on more realistic exchange rates, might not have succeeded. Some modern economists, notably Robert Mundell of Columbia University, think it would; most others believe that the gold standard suffered from key weaknesses.

Like any other exchange rate system, it required a mechanism for orderly adjustment to changes in the supply and demand for a nation's currency. The price adjustment process worked too slowly and too imperfectly to cope with large and persistent disequilibrium.

Furthermore, gold as the basis for an international money supply suffered several special disadvantages. These included a limited supply that could not be expanded as rapidly as increases in the volume of world trade required, an uneven distribution of existing and potential new gold supplies among the nations of the world, and a large and frequently volatile speculative demand for gold during periods of crisis. These factors could cause large, disruptive variations in the supply of gold available for international monetary purposes.

The Bretton Woods System

The one lesson that everyone thought had been learned from the 1930s was that a system of either freely fluctuating exchange rates or fixed rates with easily accomplished devaluations was a sure route to disaster. In order to achieve a system of orderly exchange rates that would facilitate the free flow of trade following World War II, representatives of most of the countries that had participated in the alliance against Germany, Italy, and Japan met at Bretton Woods, New Hampshire, in 1944. In the words of Charles Kindleberger of MIT, the Bretton Woods meeting was "the biggest constitution-writing exercise ever to occur in international monetary relations."

The Bretton Woods system had three objectives: (1) to create a set of rules that would maintain fixed exchange rates in the face of short-term fluctuations, (2) to guarantee that changes in exchange rates would occur only in the face of "fundamental" deficits or surpluses in the balance of payments, and (3) to ensure that when such changes did occur, they would not spark a series of competitive devaluations. The basic characteristic of the system was that U.S. dollars held by foreign monetary authorities were made directly convertible into gold at a price fixed by the U.S. government, while foreign governments fixed the prices at which their currencies were convertible into U.S. dollars. It was this characteristic that made the system a **gold exchange standard.** Gold was the ultimate reserve, but other currencies were held as reserves because directly or indirectly they could be exchanged for gold.

As we saw in the text, a system with a rate that is pegged against short-term fluctuations but can be adjusted from time to time is called an adjustable peg system. To maintain the convertibility of their currencies at fixed exchange rates, the monetary authorities of each country had to be ready to buy and sell their currency in foreign exchange markets to offset imbalances at the pegged rates.[2]

To be able to support the exchange market, the monetary authorities had to have reserves of acceptable foreign exchange. In the Bretton Woods system the authorities held reserves of gold and claims on key currencies, mainly the U.S. dollar and the British pound sterling. When a country's currency was in excess supply, its authorities would sell dollars, sterling, or gold. When a country's currency was in excess demand, its authorities would buy dollars or sterling. If they then wished to increase their gold reserves, they would use the dollars to purchase gold from the Fed, thus depleting the U.S. gold stock.

The problem for the United States was to have enough gold to maintain fixed-price convertibility of the dollar into gold as demanded by foreign monetary authorities. The problem for all other countries was to maintain convertibility (on either a restricted or unrestricted basis) between their currency and the U.S. dollar at a fixed rate of exchange.

Problems of the Adjustable Peg System

Here we see how the three problems of the Bretton Woods system discussed in the text actually worked out in the period after World War II.

Reserves to accommodate short-term fluctuations. It is generally believed that the average size and frequency of the gaps between demand and supply on the foreign exchange market created when central banks peg their exchange rates will increase as the volume of international payments increases. Since there was a strong upward trend in the volume of overall international payments, there was also a strong upward trend in the demand for foreign exchange reserves.

The ultimate reserve in the Bretton Woods system was gold. The use of gold as a reserve caused two serious problems during the 1960s and early 1970s. First, the world's supply of monetary gold did not grow fast enough to provide adequate reserves for the expanding volume of trade. As a result of the fixed price of gold, rising costs of production, and rising commercial uses, the world's stock of monetary gold during the 1960s was rising at less than 2 percent per year, while trade was growing at nearly 10 percent per year. Gold, which had been 66 percent of the total monetary reserves in 1959, was only 40 percent in 1970, and had fallen to 30 percent by 1972. Over this period reserve holdings of dollars and sterling rose sharply. Clearly, the gold backing needed to maintain convertibility of these currencies was becoming increasingly inadequate.

Second, the country whose currency is convertible into gold must maintain sufficient reserves to ensure convertibility. During the 1960s the United States lost substantial gold reserves to other countries that had acquired dollar claims through their balance-of-payments surpluses with the United States. By the late 1960s the reduction in U.S. reserves had been sufficiently large to undermine confidence in America's continued ability to maintain dollar convertibility.

Adjusting to long-term disequilibria. The second characteristic problem of a fixed-rate system is the adjustment to long-term disequilibria that develops because of secular shifts in the demands for and supplies of foreign exchange.

These disequilibria developed slowly. At first they led to a series of speculative crises as people expected a realignment of exchange rates to occur. Finally they led to a series of realignments that started in 1967. Each occurred amid quite spectacular flows of speculative funds that thoroughly disorganized normal trade and payments.

Speculative crises. The adjustable peg system often leads to situations in which speculators are presented with one-way bets. In these disequilibria situations, there is an increasing chance of an exchange rate adjustment in one direction with little or no chance of a movement in the other direction. Speculators then have an opportunity to secure a large potential gain with no corresponding potential for loss. Speculative crises associated with the need to adjust to

[2] The exchange rates were not quite fixed; they were permitted to vary by 1 percent on either side of their par values. Later the bands of permitted fluctuation were widened to 2.25 percent on either side of par.

fundamental disequilibria were the downfall of the system.

Collapse of the Bretton Woods System

The Bretton Woods system worked reasonably well for nearly 20 years. Then it was beset by a series of crises of ever-increasing severity that reflected the system's underlying weaknesses.

Speculation against the British pound. Throughout the 1950s and 1960s, the British economy was more inflation prone than the U.S. economy, and the British balance of payments was generally in deficit. Holders of sterling thus had reason to worry that the British government might not be able to keep sterling convertible into dollars at a fixed rate. When these fears grew strong, there would be speculative rushes to sell sterling before it was devalued.

The crises in the 1960s were of this kind. By the mid 1960s it was clear to everyone that the pound was seriously overvalued. Finally, in 1967 it was devalued in the midst of a serious speculative crisis. Many other countries with balance-of-payments deficits followed, bringing about the first major round of adjustments in the pegged rates since 1949.

Speculation against the American dollar. The U.S. dollar was not devalued in 1967. The lower prices of the currencies that were devalued in 1967 plus the increasing Vietnam War expenditures combined to produce a growing deficit in the American balance of payments. This deficit led to the belief that the dollar itself was becoming seriously overvalued. People rushed to buy gold because a devaluation of the U.S. dollar would take the form of raising its gold price. (Under the Bretton Woods system, the dollar was devalued by raising the official price at which the Fed would convert dollars into gold.)

The first break in the Bretton Woods system came in 1968 when the major trading countries were forced to stop pegging the free-market price of gold. Speculative pressure to buy gold could not be resisted, and from that point there were two prices of gold: the official price at which monetary authorities could settle their debts with each other by transferring gold and the free-market price, determined by the forces of private demand and supply independent of any intervention by central banks. The free-market price quickly rose far above the official U.S. price of $35 an ounce (see Figure 41-3).

Once the free-market price of gold was allowed to be determined independently of the official price, speculation against the dollar shifted to those currencies that were clearly undervalued relative to the dollar.[3] The German mark and the Japanese yen were particularly popular targets, and during periods of crisis billions and billions of dollars flowed into speculative holdings of these currencies. The ability of central banks to maintain pegged exchange rates in the face of such vast flights of funds was in question; on several occasions all exchange markets had to be closed for periods of up to a week.

Devaluation of the dollar. By 1971 the American authorities had concluded that the dollar would have to be devalued. This uncovered a problem, inherent in the Bretton Woods system, that had so far gone virtually unnoted. Because the system required each foreign country to fix its exchange rate against the dollar, the American authorities could not independently fix their exchange rate against other currencies.[4]

But when the U.S. economy began to inflate rapidly, it became necessary to devalue the U.S. dollar relative to most other currencies. Any other country in this situation would merely unilaterally devalue its currency. But the only way that the required U.S. devaluation could be brought about was for all other countries to agree to revalue their currencies relative to the dollar.

Prompted by continuing speculation against the

[3] When the free-market price of gold was held the same as the official price, a devaluation of the dollar entailed a rise in the free-market price—and hence profit for all holders of gold. Once the free-market price was left to be determined by the forces of private demand and supply independent of any central bank intervention, there was no reason to believe that a rise in the official price of gold would affect the (much higher) free-market price. Speculators against the dollar then had to hold other currencies whose price was sure to rise against the dollar in the event of the dollar's being devalued.

[4] If, for example, the British authorities pegged the pound sterling at $2.40, as they did in 1967, the dollar was pegged at £.417, and the Fed could not independently decide on another rate. Similar considerations applied to all other currencies.

dollar, President Nixon suspended gold convertibility of the dollar in August 1971. He also announced the intention of the United States to achieve a de facto devaluation of the dollar by persuading those nations whose balance of payments were in surplus to allow their rates to float upward against the dollar.

By ending the gold convertibility of the dollar, the U.S. government brought the gold exchange standard aspect of the Bretton Woods system officially to an end. The fixed-exchange-rate aspect of the system lasted a little longer.

The immediate response to the announced intention of devaluing the dollar was a speculative run against that currency. The crisis was so severe that for the second time that year foreign exchange markets were closed throughout Europe. When the markets reopened after a week, several countries allowed their rates to float. The Japanese, however, announced their intention of retaining their existing rate. Despite severe Japanese controls, $4 billion in speculative funds managed to find its way into yen in the last two weeks of August, and the Japanese were forced to abandon their fixed-rate policy by allowing the yen to float upward.

After some hard bargaining, an agreement among the major trading nations was signed at the Smithsonian Institution in Washington, D.C. in December 1971. The main element of the agreement was that all countries consented to a 7.9 percent devaluation of the dollar against their currencies.

De facto dollar standard. Following the Smithsonian agreements, the world was on a de facto **dollar standard**. Foreign monetary authorities held their reserves in the form of dollars and settled their international debts with dollars. But the dollar was not convertible into gold or anything else. The ultimate value of the dollar was given not by gold but by the American goods, services, and assets that dollars could be used to purchase.

One major problem with such a system is that the kind of American inflation that upset the Bretton Woods system is no less upsetting to a dollar standard because the real purchasing-power value of the world's dollar reserves is eroded by such an inflation.

Final breakdown of fixed exchange rates. The Smithsonian agreements did not lead to a new period of international payments stability. This doomed the hope that a de facto dollar standard could provide the basis for an international payments system free of crises and devaluations.

The U.S. inflation continued unchecked, and the U.S. balance of payments never returned to the relatively satisfactory position that had been maintained throughout the 1960s. Within a year of the agreements speculators began to believe that a further realignment of rates was necessary. In January 1973 speculative movements of capital once again occurred. In February the United States proposed a further 11 percent devaluation of the dollar. This was to be accomplished by raising the official price of gold to $42.22 an ounce and by not keeping other currencies tied to the dollar at the old rates. Intense speculative activity followed the announcement.

Five member countries of the European Economic Community then decided to stabilize their currencies against each other but to let them float together against the dollar. This joint float was called the *snake*. Norway and Sweden later joined the snake arrangement. The other EEC countries (Ireland, Italy, and the United Kingdom) and Japan announced their intention to allow their currencies to float in value. In June 1972 the Bank of England had abandoned the de facto dollar standard with the announcement that it had "temporarily" abandoned its commitment to support sterling at a fixed par value against the U.S. dollar. The events of 1973 led "temporarily" to become "indefinitely."

Fluctuations in exchange rates were severe. By early July 1973 the snake currencies had appreciated about 30 percent against the dollar, but by the end of the year they had nearly returned to their February values.

The dollar devaluation formally took effect in October. Most industrialized countries maintained the nominal values of their currencies in terms of gold and SDRs, thereby appreciating them in terms of the U.S. dollar by 11 percent. The devaluation quickly became redundant, for despite attempts to restore fixed rates, the drift to flexible rates had become irresistible by the end of 1973.

42

Macroeconomic Policy in an Open Economy

When we shift our attention to an *open* economy, we encounter a number of features that are of particular interest to the study of macroeconomic policy. New complications arise. These include the behavior of the terms of trade and their influence on net exports and national income, the nature and extent of foreign borrowing, and changes in foreign interest and inflation rates. The response of the economy to various policies is altered. For example, as we saw in Chapter 40, the size of the simple multiplier is smaller than that in a closed economy. Also, as we shall see in this chapter, since Canadian interest rates are closely tied to those prevailing in foreign markets, the mechanism by which macroeconomic policies influence the economy can differ sharply from the closed-economy mechanisms studied so far in this book.

Consideration of the openness of the economy also introduces some new policy targets that may be in conflict with policy targets arising solely from domestic considerations. In the next section we introduce the study of macroeconomic policy in an open economy by considering these possibly conflicting targets.

Internal and External Balance

In this chapter we summarize the domestic policy objectives in terms of a target level of real national income. Restricting our attention to one domestic policy target is done primarily for simplicity. However, it is perhaps more general than would first appear. For example, if one objective is to reduce the domestic rate of inflation, we know from our analysis in Chapter 36 that this can be accomplished by choosing a target level of real national income below the capacity level. When real national income is at its target level, we say the economy has achieved **internal balance.**

In this section we focus on the trade account as the external policy target. As we saw in Chapter 40, the trade account is related to the current and capital accounts. Hence such things as the level of interest payments that must be paid to foreigners, the need to accumulate or decumulate foreign exchange reserves, or the need for capital flows to finance new investment may influence the target level of the trade balance.[1] When the trade account is equal to its target level, we say the economy has achieved **external balance.**

In this section we also treat the exchange rate as fixed. Later in the chapter we study the complications that arise when the capital account and a flexible exchange rate are considered.

The conditions for internal and external balance are illustrated in Figure 42-1.

FIGURE 42-1 **Internal and External Balance**

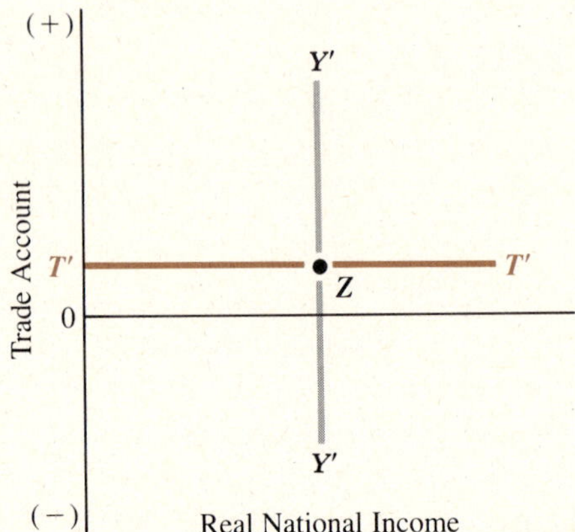

Internal and external balance are simultaneously attained at point Z. Internal balance is defined in terms of a target level of real national income and is depicted by the vertical line $Y'Y'$. External balance is defined in terms of a target level of the trade account and is depicted by the horizontal line $T'T'$. Only at the intersection, point Z, are both internal and external balance attained.

The Potential for Conflict Between Objectives

When policies used to move the economy closer to one objective move the economy further from the other objective, the objectives are said to be in conflict.

Policies to eliminate a recessionary gap will also influence the trade account by causing a movement along the net export function (which is negatively sloped). Whether there is a conflict between the objectives of internal and external balance depends on how the trade account and real national income compare to their target values.

For simplicity, we now make the assumption that the target level of real national income is the capacity level of output and that the target for the trade account is a zero balance.[2] Hence we can identify the initial situation relative to the targets simply in terms of the signs of the output gap and the trade account balance. There are four possible cases:

1. A trade account *deficit* combined with an *inflationary gap* poses no conflict, because the contraction of aggregate demand to eliminate the inflationary gap leads to a reduction in imports and hence reduces the trade deficit.
2. A trade account *deficit* combined with a *recessionary gap* does pose a conflict, because the expansion of aggregate demand to eliminate the recessionary gap leads to an increase in imports and hence a worsening of the trade deficit.
3. A trade account *surplus* combined with a *recessionary gap* poses no conflict, because the expansion of aggregate demand to eliminate the recessionary gap increases imports and hence reduces the trade surplus.
4. A trade account *surplus* combined with an *inflationary gap* does pose a conflict, because the contraction of aggregate demand to eliminate the inflationary gap leads to a reduction in imports and hence an increase in the trade surplus.

The four cases are depicted in Figure 42-2.

Conflict Cases

In case 2 in our list the trade account deficit calls for a decrease in national income, but the recessionary gap calls for an increase. In case 4 the trade account

[1] For example, a nation with a large undeveloped natural resource base may have a low current national income yet anticipate a high future national income when the resource base is developed. High current investment to develop the resource base and high current consumption in anticipation of that high future income will together lead to high imports and a trade account deficit. Hence the *target* trade account in such a circumstance may well be a deficit. (See also the discussion in Box 40-1 on page 886–887.)

[2] We emphasize that this assumption is made only to simplify the discussion and that the actual targets may often differ from these. The same principles apply regardless of the actual values of the targets.

FIGURE 42-2 Conflicts Between Internal and External Balance

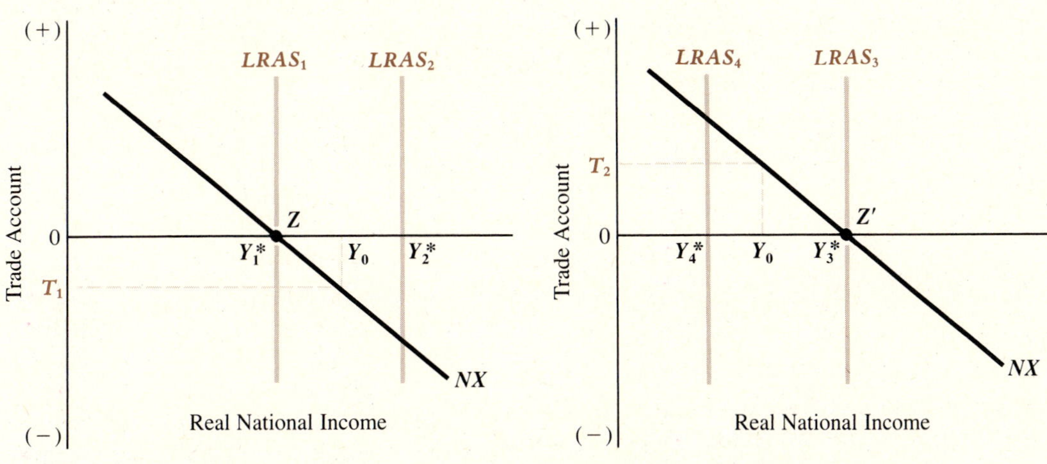

(i) A trade account deficit

(ii) A trade account surplus

Of the four different possible combinations of signs of the output gap and the trade account, only two pose conflicts. In both parts of the figure, the net export function, which relates the trade account to real national income, is shown by the black line labeled *NX*. The actual level of income is given by Y_0, so in part (i) there is a trade account deficit of T_1, while in part (ii) there is a trade account surplus of T_2.

In part (i), if potential output is given by Y_1* so there is an inflationary gap (case 1), there is no conflict, since adjustment of actual real national income to achieve one target will also achieve the other target, at point *Z*. However, if potential output is given by Y_2* so there is a recessionary gap (case 2), there is a conflict, since movement of actual real national income to achieve either target will cause a movement away from the other target.

In part (ii), if potential income is given by Y_3* so there is a recessionary gap (case 3), there is no conflict, since adjustment of actual real national income to achieve one target will also achieve the other target, at point *Z′*. However, if potential output is given by Y_4* so there is an inflationary gap (case 4), there is a conflict, since a change in actual real national income to achieve either target will cause a movement away from the other target.

surplus calls for an increase in national income, but the inflationary gap calls for a decrease.[3]

A conflict arises between the objectives of internal and external balance when the two call for opposite changes in the level of national income.

[3] Case 2 has traditionally attracted the most attention, perhaps because a trade deficit is generally viewed as being a more serious problem than a trade surplus, and—at least in the past—unemployment has been considered a more serious problem than inflation. Case 2 is often referred to as a situation in which there is a "balance-of-payments constraint" on domestic stabilization policy.

Basically, the conflicts arise from *movements along* the net export function; we now see that resolution of such conflict arises from *shifts in* the net export function.

Expenditure-changing and Expenditure-switching Policies

We start by repeating the basic equilibrium condition, that national income equal aggregate desired expenditure.

$$Y = C + I + G + (X - M) \quad [1]$$

The total $C + I + G$ is often referred to as domestic absorption, or simply absorption. This concept, which was discussed in Box 31-2 on pages 650–651, refers to total expenditure on goods for use in the economy. Denoting absorption by the letter A, we can rewrite the national income equilibrium condition as

$$Y = A + (X - M) \quad [2]$$

This condition states that equilibrium national income is equal to aggregate desired expenditure, which in turn is equal to domestic absorption plus net exports.

Equation 2 is useful in distinguishing between two types of policies that might be used to maintain internal and external balance. Policies that maintain the level of aggregate desired expenditure but influence its composition between domestic absorption and net exports are called **expenditure-switching** policies. Policies that change aggregate desired expenditure are called **expenditure-changing** policies.

Expenditure-changing policies involve moving along a given net export function, so changes in the trade balance and national income must be *negatively* related. If the initial situation calls for them to move in the same direction, the use of expenditure-changing policies necessarily involves a conflict.

The conflicts between the objectives of internal and external balance arise from the use of expenditure-changing policies.

An expenditure-switching policy shifts the net export function. As we shall see, this can lead to *positively* related changes in the trade balance and national income. Devaluation or revaluation of the domestic currency, restrictions on international trade such as tariffs or quotas, and domestic inflation or deflation relative to foreign conditions are all expenditure-switching policies.[4]

[4] When restrictions on international trade, such as tariffs or quotas, are used in this manner, they are referred to as *commercial policy*. Commercial policy may in some circumstances be useful for macroeconomic purposes, but it is never the case that commercial policy *must* be used; other expenditure-switching policies will have the same macroeconomic effects.

A Trade Account Deficit

As we have seen, a trade account deficit means that national income is less than domestic absorption. Now consider policies to eliminate the trade account deficit; to be successful, the policies must raise national income *relative* to absorption.

Case 1: A deficit combined with an inflationary gap: No conflict. If the economy already has an inflationary gap, national income should not be increased further. The trade account deficit indicates that domestic absorption is above the current level of national income and hence, by virtue of the inflationary gap, above the full-employment level. To eliminate the deficit, absorption must be lowered. In other words, if net exports are to rise, resources must be released through a reduction in domestic usage. This calls for *expenditure-reducing* policies such as reductions in the money supply, cuts in government expenditure, and increases in taxes. No conflict for expenditure-changing policies arises in this case, because the expenditure reduction cuts the inflationary gap and improves the trade account by inducing a movement along the net export function.

Case 2: A deficit combined with a recessionary gap: Conflict. When national income is below its capacity level, income can be expanded. But an expansion in national income with a fixed net export function would worsen the trade account, so expenditure-increasing policies are not appropriate. A reduction in national income to reduce the trade deficit would worsen unemployment, so expenditure-reducing policies are not appropriate. What is needed is a switch in expenditure away from foreign goods (thus reducing the trade deficit) and toward domestic goods (thus reducing the recessionary gap).

Policies to induce a *switch* of some expenditure from foreign goods to domestic goods—thereby *shifting* the net export function rightward and raising national income—will alleviate the conflict posed by a recessionary gap combined with a trade deficit.

Such policies include devaluation of the currency and protective measures such as tariffs and quotas. This is illustrated in Figure 42-3.[5]

[5] From the discussion in Chapter 40, it would appear that there should be two shifts in the *NX* function. The first is due to the switch in expenditure; the second, which will be in the opposite direction to the first, is due to the induced change in the price of domestic goods as national income changes. The analysis in Figure 42-3, and in this chapter, incorporates this second effect in the response of *NX* national income by using the *SRAS* curve to capture the price effect. **[54]**

A Trade Account Surplus

Cases 3 and 4 in our list both involve a trade account surplus. An expansion of national income will therefore cause a move toward external balance by raising imports. Hence in case 3, where there is a recessionary gap, no conflict arises, and expenditure-raising policies will lead to movement toward both targets. In case 4, where there is an inflationary gap, a conflict does arise; external balance calls for expenditure in-

FIGURE 42-3 A Trade Deficit and a Recessionary Gap

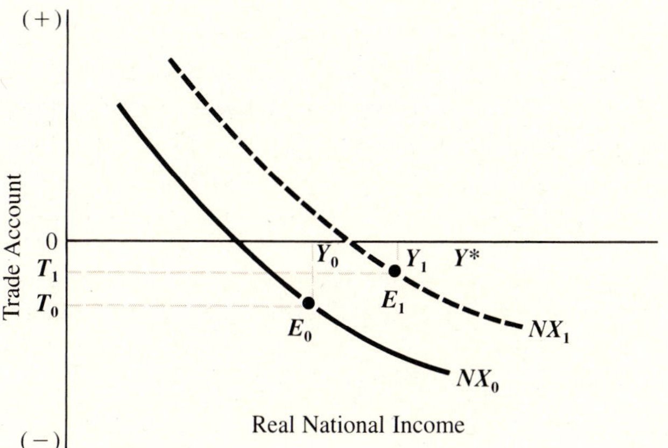

(i) Net export function

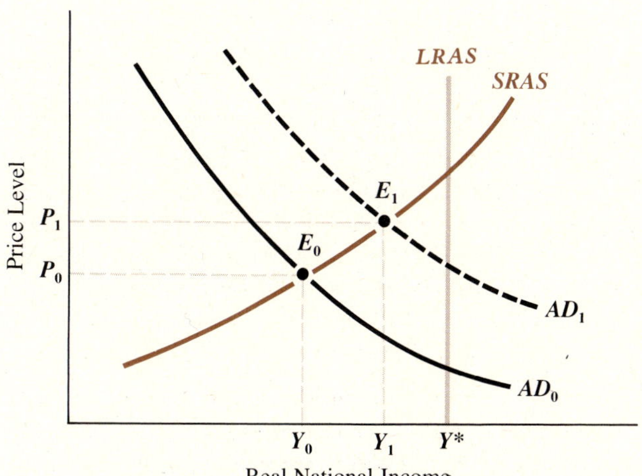

(ii) Determination of national income

A policy to switch expenditure away from foreign goods and toward domestic goods can be used to resolve the conflict posed by a trade deficit combined with a recessionary gap. Initially, the net export function is given by NX_0 in part (i), and aggregate demand is given by AD_0 in part (ii). Equilibrium is at E_0 with real national income equal to Y_0. There is a recessionary gap of Y_0Y^* and a trade deficit of T_0.

An expenditure-switching policy raises net exports at each level of income, so the net export function shifts right to NX_1 in part (i). The policy also raises aggregate demand, so the *AD* curve shifts right to AD_1 in part (ii). The new equilibrium is at E_1, with real national income of Y_1 and a trade deficit of T_1. Hence both the recessionary gap and the trade deficit are reduced.

creases, but internal balance calls for expenditure reduction. What is needed is a *switch* in expenditure away from domestic goods (thus reducing the inflationary gap) and toward foreign goods (thus reducing the trade account surplus).

Policies to induce a switch of expenditure from domestic goods to foreign goods—thereby *shifting* the net export function leftward and lowering national income—will alleviate the conflict posed by an inflationary gap combined with a trade surplus.

This is illustrated in Figure 42-4.

A General Statement

We have now seen the difference in the effects of the two types of expenditure policies in an open economy.

FIGURE 42-4 A Trade Surplus and an Inflationary Gap

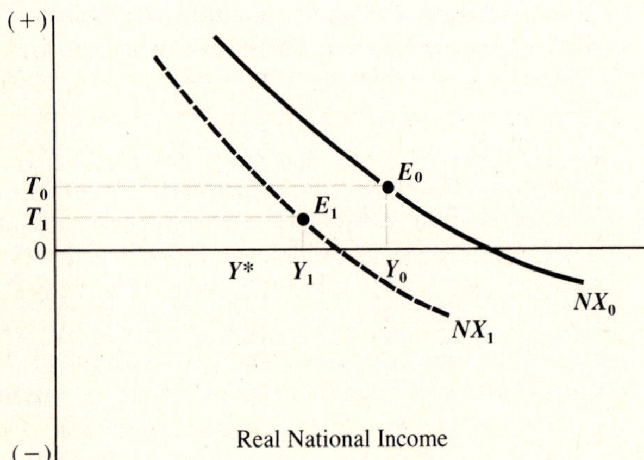

(i) Net export function

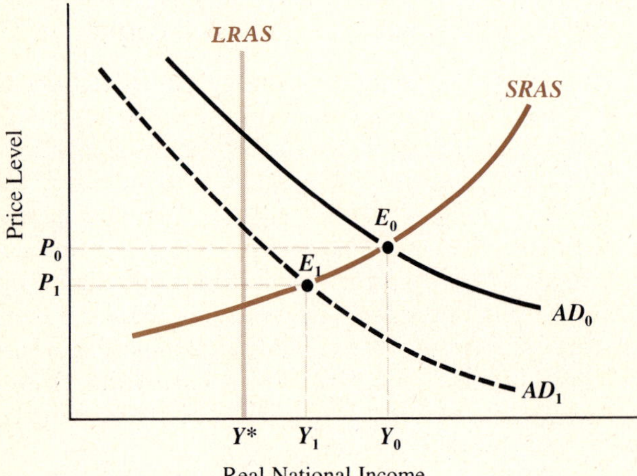

(ii) Determination of national income

A policy to switch expenditure away from domestic goods and toward foreign goods can be used to solve the conflict posed by a trade surplus combined with an inflationary gap. Initially, the net export function is given by NX_0 in part (i), and aggregate demand is given by AD_0 in part (ii). Equilibrium is at E_0 with real national income equal to Y_0. This is an inflationary gap of Y^*Y_0 and a trade surplus of T_0.

An expenditure-switching policy lowers net exports at each level of income, so the net export function shifts left to NX_1 in part (ii). The policy also lowers aggregate demand, so the aggregate demand curve shifts left to AD_1 in part (ii). The equilibrium moves from E_0 to E_1, real national income falls to Y_1, and the trade surplus falls to T_1. Hence both the inflationary gap and the trade surplus are reduced.

To achieve internal and external balance, a combination of expenditure-changing and expenditure-switching policies is generally required.

In the conflict situations, expenditure-switching policies will result in movement *toward* both targets. But they alone cannot be expected exactly to achieve both internal and external balance. Hence both types of policies are generally required. Expenditure-switching policies are necessary to shift the net export function in order to make the two objectives consistent. [In terms of Figures 42-3(i) and 42-4(i) this means that expenditure-switching policies should be used to ensure that the *NX* curve cuts the horizontal axis at Y^*. There is no assurance, however, that the effects of such policies on the aggregate demand curve will give rise to actual real national income of Y^*.] Then expenditure-changing policies—which shift the aggregate demand curve but not the net export curve—can be used to attain both internal and external balance simultaneously.

Some long-run aspects of such policies are taken up in Box 42-1.

Macroeconomic Policy and the Capital Account

The capital account of the balance of payments records international movements of investment funds. When foreign investors buy securities issued by Canadian corporations or governments or invest in Canadian industry, this capital inflow is recorded as a receipt in the balance of payments, because it gives rise to an increase in the amount of foreign currency offered for Canadian dollars in the foreign exchange market. Conversely, the acquisition of foreign assets by Canadians represents a capital outflow and is recorded as a payment because foreign currency is used up by such transactions.

The primary means by which capital flows can be influenced by the policy authorities is through domestic interest rates. International traders hold transactions balances just like domestic traders. These balances are often lent out on a short-term basis rather than being left idle. Naturally enough, holders of these balances will tend to lend them, other things being equal, in markets where interest rates are highest. If short-term interest rates are raised in Canada, this will induce an inflow of short-run capital to take advantage of the higher Canadian rates. A lowering of Canadian interest rates will have the opposite effect, as capital moves elsewhere to take advantage of the now relatively higher foreign rates.

Long-term capital flows are typically less sensitive to interest-rate differentials, but they are nevertheless likely to show some response. In particular, Canadian corporations and governments attempt to minimize the cost of long-term borrowing by selling bonds in foreign markets when the foreign interest rate is lower than the Canadian rate.

In discussing the trade account in the first part of this chapter, we did not distinguish between the effects of monetary and fiscal policy. However, capital flows respond to interest rates, and monetary and fiscal policies that have the same influence on income have opposite effects on interest rates. As we saw in Chapter 34, in a closed economy expansionary monetary policy exerts its influence on income by reducing interest rates. Fiscal policy influences aggregate demand directly, and fiscal-policy-induced increases in national income create an excess demand for money, which in a closed economy causes interest rates to rise. In discussing capital flows in an open economy it is therefore necessary to distinguish between the operation of monetary and fiscal policies.

Fiscal Policy and the Capital Account

The effects of fiscal policy on the capital account of an open economy are related to the interest-rate effects it would have in a closed economy. Expansionary fiscal policy, for example, leads to increased federal government borrowing in domestic capital markets. In a closed economy this forces interest rates up; in an open economy it forces other domestic borrowers to import their capital requirements from foreign financial centers. Many provincial governments finance their deficits by borrowing abroad themselves, thereby giving rise directly to a capital account surplus. In summary:

An expansionary fiscal policy will put upward pressure on interest rates and lead to an inflow

BOX 42-1

Expenditure-switching Policies in the Long Run

Use of expenditure-switching policies such as devaluation has often been very controversial. Supporters point to the increase in output and the reduction in the trade account deficit shown in Figure 42-3. Opponents focus on the inflationary impact indicated by the rise in the price level also shown in Figure 42-3. The controversy often hinges on disagreement about the relative size of these two effects. Some of the controversy can be defused by distinguishing between the long-run and short-run effects of such policies.

In the text we focused on the short-run effects of expenditure-switching policies, treating the *SRAS* curve as fixed and studying the shifts in the *NX* and *AD* curves. One alternative to using such policies is to do nothing, and let the monetary adjustment mechanism studied in Chapter 34 operate to eliminate the recessionary gap. (Similar automatic mechanism also exist that establish external balance in the long run.) Justification for using devaluation, for example, in the face of a recessionary gap and a trade deficit is that these automatic adjustment mechanisms are very slow to operate. Hence support for devaluation and other expenditure-switching policies focuses on their ability to influence output and the trade account *in the short run.*

Note, however, that such policies do not alter potential output (they do not shift the *LRAS* curve), and hence they have no effect on output in the long run. But by circumventing the monetary adjustment mechanism and stimulating aggregate demand, expenditure-switching policies ensure that when potential income is attained in the long run, the price level will be higher than it would have been in their absence. Opponents of such policies focus on this price-level effect, since that is the only long-run effect the policies have. Typically these opponents believe the automatic adjustment mechanisms are strong enough so that the long-run effect would be achieved fairly quickly without intervention or that devaluations set up expectations of price rises that quickly feed into wages and hence create very little real response of output and employment even in the short run.

The key policy implication of this debate is that devaluation and other expenditure-switching policies should be directed toward the external target, but they should be combined with expenditure-changing policies that focus on the internal target. In particular, a devaluation should be accompanied by expenditure-reducing policies to offset any inflationary gap caused by the devaluation in the short run and hence to avoid the price-level increase that would otherwise ensue in the long run.

of foreign capital, thereby moving the capital account toward a surplus. A contractionary fiscal policy will have the opposite effects.

Monetary Policy and the Capital Account

Since monetary policy influences interest rates in a closed economy, it will also influence the capital account in an open economy:

An expansionary monetary policy will put downward pressure on interest rates and lead to an outflow of capital, thereby moving the capital account toward a deficit. A contractionary monetary policy will have the opposite effects.

An Alternative Target for External Balance

So far in this chapter we have used *external balance* to mean achieving the target level of the trade account. Consideration of international capital flows suggests an expansion of this target to incorporate the capital account and interest payments on the foreign debt as well.

We now specify external balance in terms of a target level of the overall balance of payments.

For simplicity, we take external balance to mean a zero overall balance of payments so that any current account imbalance is exactly offset by capital account transactions.

Before turning to a discussion of how monetary and fiscal policy might be combined to achieve internal and external balance in this circumstance, it will be useful to examine the relationship between the money supply and the overall balance of payments.

The Balance of Payments and the Money Supply

Suppose that Canada is experiencing a balance-of-payments deficit and that the Bank of Canada intervenes in the foreign exchange market to maintain the value of the Canadian dollar. The Bank will be selling foreign currency in exchange for Canadian dollars and thereby running down its stock of official reserves. Payment for the foreign currency acquired by private participants in the market will normally be made in the form of a Canadian dollar cheque drawn on one of the chartered banks. This cheque will be cleared by reducing the deposits of the chartered bank at the Bank of Canada. These transactions are summarized in Table 42-1.

TABLE 42-1 Balance Sheet Changes Caused by a Sale of Foreign Currency by the Central Bank

Assets		Liabilities	
Nonbank private sector			
Foreign currency (equivalent value in Canadian dollars)	+100		
Deposits	−100		
Chartered banks			
Reserves (deposits with central bank)	−100	Demand deposits	−100
Central bank			
Foreign currency	−100	Deposits of chartered banks	−100

The money supply is reduced when the central bank sells foreign currency to maintain a fixed exchange rate when there is a balance-of-payments deficit. A deficit of 100 leads to an excess demand for foreign currency of 100, which is met by a reduction of official reserves by this amount. When the central bank receives payment in the form of a cheque drawn on a chartered bank, bank reserves fall by 100. There will then be a multiple contraction of deposit money through the process analyzed in Chapter 33.

If there are no offsetting transactions, a balance-of-payments deficit will lead to a decrease both in bank reserves and in bank deposits equal to the amount of foreign exchange sold by the central bank. A surplus will lead to an increase in bank reserves and deposits.

Thus a balance-of-payments deficit will lead to a contraction of the money supply. Of course, the central bank has the option of preventing this from happening by undertaking other offsetting transactions. For example, the decrease in bank reserves can be offset by an open-market purchase of bonds, which will have the effect of increasing bank reserves. This procedure of insulating the domestic money supply from the effects of balance-of-payments deficits or surpluses is known as **sterilization.**

Fixed Exchange Rates

Monetary Policy

To see the limitations of monetary policy under a fixed exchange rate, consider the following sequence of events. Suppose that interest rates in Canada are at levels similar to those in the rest of the world, and thus there is no inducement for large international movements of capital. Suppose now that the Bank of Canada, faced with a large recessionary gap, seeks to stimulate demand through an expansionary monetary policy. The Bank buys bonds in the open market, thereby increasing the money supply and reducing interest rates.

Lower interest rates stimulate an outflow of capital from Canada and thus a deficit on the capital account. To the extent that national income rises, movement along the net export function creates a deficit on the trade account. Thus the overall balance of payments moves into deficit. To maintain the fixed exchange rate, the Bank will have to intervene in the foreign exchange market and sell foreign currency. This will have the effect of *reducing* the money supply and thus *reversing* the increase brought about by the initial open-market operation.

If no other transactions are initiated by the Bank of Canada, national income and the money supply will fall and domestic interest rates will rise until they all return to their initial levels. Thus the deficit will be self-correcting, and the Bank's expansionary policy will be nullified.

Suppose now that the Bank of Canada attempts to sterilize the impact on the money supply of the balance-of-payments deficit. The difficulty with this strategy is that it can be continued only as long as the Bank has sufficient reserves of foreign exchange. If capital flows are highly sensitive to interest rates, as a great deal of evidence suggests is the case, these reserves will be run down at a rapid rate and the Bank will be forced to abandon its expansionary policy.

Under a fixed exchange rate, there is little scope for the use of monetary policy for domestic stabilization purposes because of the sensitivity of international capital flows to interest rates. The central bank will be forced to maintain domestic interest rates close to the levels existing in the rest of the world, and it will not be able to bring about substantial changes in the domestic money supply.

Fiscal Policy

Consider now the effectiveness of fiscal policy under fixed exchange rates. Suppose again that Canadian interest rates are in line with those of the rest of the world when an expansionary fiscal policy is introduced, aimed at reducing a large recessionary gap. The fiscal expansion raises the level of domestic interest rates and national income.

Higher interest rates stimulate a flow of capital into Canada, thereby leading to a surplus on the capital account. If the capital flows are large, as they are likely to be in Canada because of the close integration of Canadian and American capital markets, the surplus on capital account will exceed the current account deficit arising from the increased national income. Hence there will be an overall balance-of-payments surplus.

To maintain the fixed exchange rate, the Bank of Canada will have to intervene in the foreign exchange market and buy foreign currency. This will have the effect of increasing the money supply, thus reinforcing the initial fiscal stimulus.

Under a fixed exchange rate, interest-sensitive international capital flows stabilize the domestic interest rate and enhance the effectiveness of fiscal policy.

Combining Monetary and Fiscal Policy

Consider an attempt to increase employment with expansionary monetary policy that reduces interest rates and thereby stimulates investment and other interest-sensitive expenditure. The decline in domestic interest rates makes it more attractive to invest short-term capital abroad rather than at home. The outflow of short-term capital to be invested at more attractive rates in foreign financial centers worsens the balance of payments on the short-term capital account. Of course, if the expansionary policy succeeds in raising income, there will be additional strain on the balance of payments on current account as a consequence of the increased expenditure on imports caused by the rise in income.

In principle, the conflict can be removed by an appropriate combination of monetary and fiscal policy. Consider the country with full employment and a balance-of-payments deficit. It could eliminate the deficit by following a tighter monetary policy to increase domestic interest rates and attract short-term capital. At the same time, the contractionary effect of tight money on domestic expenditure and employment could be offset by raising government expenditures or cutting taxes. Thus the two goals can both be achieved through a combination of tight monetary policy and expansionary fiscal policy.

This strategy is unlikely to be a satisfactory solution to a persistent current account deficit. The country will find it increasingly difficult to maintain its exchange rate by importing short-term capital. Short-term international capital flows are extremely volatile, and they are particularly sensitive to shifts in expectations concerning exchange rates. If investors lose confidence in a country's ability to maintain its existing exchange rate, capital outflows will build up, and ultimately a devaluation will be required to reduce the deficit and restore confidence.

Flexible Exchange Rates

A major advantage of a flexible exchange rate is that it removes any conflict between domestic stabilization objectives and the balance of payments, because deficits or surpluses are automatically eliminated through movements in the exchange rate. In addition, a flexible rate often cushions the domestic economy against cyclical variations in economic activity in other countries. If, for example, the U.S. economy goes into a recession, the decline in U.S. income will lead to a reduction in demand for goods exported from Canada. The fall in exports will reduce income in Canada through the multiplier effect. But if the value of the Canadian dollar is allowed to respond to market forces, there will also be a depreciation. This fall in the external value of our currency will stimulate demand for our exports and encourage the substitution of domestically produced goods for imports. Thus the depreciation will provide a stimulus to demand in Canada that will at least partially offset the depressing effect of the U.S. recession.

Box 42-2 discusses some further aspects of fluctuating exchange rates.

Fiscal Policy

Suppose the government seeks to remove a recessionary gap by expansionary fiscal policy. An increase in government expenditures and/or a reduction in taxes will increase income through the multiplier effect and reduce the size of the gap. This will also tend to cause a movement along the net export function, leading to a deterioration of the trade account. However, this is not the whole story, for there will also be repercussions on the capital account and the exchange rate.

Capital flows and the crowding-out effect. In a closed economy, fiscal policy causes domestic interest rates to rise. This causes interest-sensitive private expenditures to fall, thus partially offsetting the initial expansionary effect of the fiscal stimulus. As we saw in Chapter 32, this *crowding-out effect* plays an important role in the analysis of fiscal policy in a closed economy. In an open economy the crowding-out effect will operate differently, due to international capital flows.

Higher domestic interest rates will induce a capital inflow and cause the domestic currency to appreciate. If capital flows are highly interest-elastic, the external value of the currency is likely to rise substantially. This will depress demand by discouraging exports and encouraging the substitution of imports for domestically produced goods. The initial fiscal stimulus will be *offset* by the expenditure-switching effects of currency appreciation.

Under flexible exchange rates there will be a strong crowding out of net exports that will greatly reduce the effectiveness of fiscal policy.

However, it is possible to eliminate the crowding-out effect by supporting the fiscal policy with an accommodating monetary policy. Suppose that the central bank responds to the increase in the demand for money induced by the fiscal expansion by increasing the supply of money so as to maintain domestic interest rates at their initial level. There will then be no capital inflow and no tendency for the currency to appreciate. Income will expand by the usual multiplier process.

The effectiveness of fiscal policy under flexible exchange rates can be enhanced by an accommodating monetary policy.

Monetary Policy

We have seen that there is little scope under fixed exchange rates for the use of monetary policy for domestic stabilization purposes. Under flexible exchange rates the situation is reversed, and monetary policy becomes a very powerful tool.

Suppose the Bank of Canada seeks to stimulate

BOX 42-2

Understanding Exchange Rate Changes

Since reaching a peak of over $1.05 U.S. in early 1976, the Canadian dollar has depreciated steadily, briefly falling below 70 cents U.S. in 1986 before rising again to around 76 cents U.S. by mid 1987. This fall, shown by the black line in the figure, has prompted news reports of a national crisis of disaster proportions and a source of national shame. Several considerations, however, help us put this slide in some perspective.

Currencies can appreciate or depreciate for many reasons. To take pride in the external price on one's currency is to commit oneself in advance to be proud of a great ragbag of events, some of which will seem undesirable to all reasonable people. Until the public and the media see the folly in viewing the value of a country's currency the way shareholders of a corporation view the price of its stock, there is little hope of a rational discussion of exchange rate policy.

In fact, the fall in the value of the Canadian dollar reflects a number of very different events, some with very different implications.

The fall in the early part of the period reflected higher Canadian inflation and was necessary to restore the competitive position of Canadian industry. Inflation was the problem; depreciation was part of the "solution."

The underlying trend value of the Canadian dollar in terms of the U.S. dollar changes as the Canadian price level changes relative to the American price level.* During the 1960s American inflation exceeded Canadian inflation, and the Canadian dollar rose above the U.S. dollar. From 1971 to 1976 Canadian inflation exceeded U.S. inflation, and the trend PPP value of the Canadian dollar fell steadily, reaching the range 89 to 91 units by the end of 1972. For a while capital flows and other events kept the value of the Canadian dollar above its trend rate, but in 1976 it fell rapidly toward its trend value. The actual value had to fall sooner or later to its trend value, and it is a good thing—it helped restore the international competitiveness of Canadian industry.

From 1981 through 1984 the fall in the Canadian dollar reflected different pressures. In 1980 tight monetary policy in the United States drove up interest rates in that country. As we saw in Chapter 41 (see especially page 902), this presented the Bank of Canada with a policy dilemma: Either let Canadian interest rates rise or let the Canadian dollar fall. The Bank tried to take a middle stance between these two, and

* Recall the discussion of the purchasing power parity exchange rate in Chapter 41, especially pages 900–901.

demand through an expansionary monetary policy. The Bank buys bonds in the open market, thereby increasing bank reserves and the money supply and reducing interest rates. Lower interest rates will cause an outflow of capital from Canada and thus a deficit on the capital account.

Under a fixed rate we saw that the Bank may be forced to reverse its policy in order to stem the loss of foreign reserves. Under a flexible rate, however, the Canadian dollar can be allowed to depreciate. This will stimulate exports and discourage imports so that the deficit on the capital account will be offset by a surplus on the current account.

Domestic employment will be stimulated not only by the fall in interest rates but also by the increased demand for domestically produced goods brought about by a depreciation of the currency. The initial monetary stimulus will be *reinforced* by the expenditure-switching effects of currency depreciation.

Under flexible exchange rates, monetary policy is a powerful tool for stabilizing domestic income and employment. If capital flows are highly interest-elastic, the main channel by which an increase in the money supply stimulates demand for domestically produced goods is a depreciation of the currency.

as a result the value of the Canadian dollar in terms of the U.S. dollar fell gradually between 1980 and 1986.

Is the Canadian Dollar Weak?

A related point is that over the period 1981–1985 the apparent weakness of the Canadian dollar actually reflects the strength of the U.S. dollar. This is shown by the colored line in the figure, where we plot the average or trade-weighted Canadian dollar exchange rate in terms of all Canada's trading partners. The divergent path, with the Canadian dollar falling against the U.S. dollar but rising against the rest of Canada's trading partners, results from the fact that the U.S. dollar was rising even more against European currencies and the Japanese yen during this period. From this perspective the widespread perception of a weak Canadian dollar in the 1981–1985 period was just wrong.

As noted, in early 1986 strong speculative pressures drove the Canadian dollar to just under 70 cents U.S., but later in the year and especially in 1987 the Canadian currency strengthened considerably in terms of the American. This meant that the large depreciation that the U.S. dollar experienced in terms of the offshore currencies did not lead to as large a depreciation of the Canadian dollar in terms of those currencies.

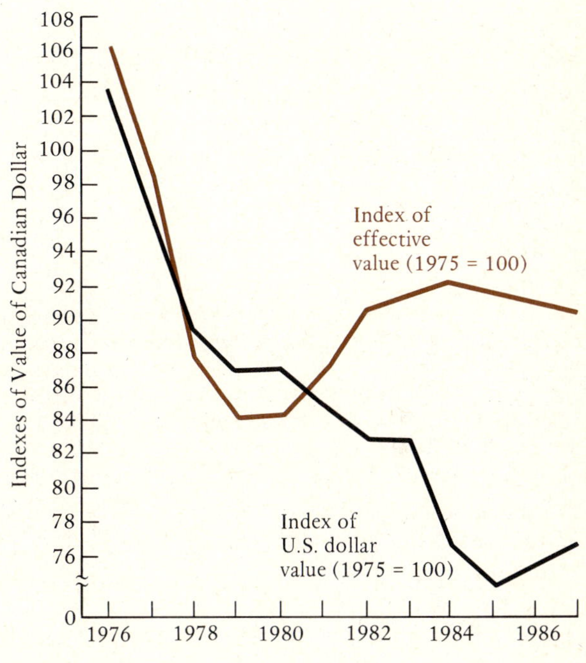

Canadian Stabilization Policy and External Balance

The foregoing arguments suggest that the choice between a fixed rate and a flexible rate can influence the operation of stabilization policy. It is instructive to examine recent Canadian experience from this perspective.

1950–1961: Introduction of Flexible Exchange Rates

Canada operated under a flexible exchange rate from 1950 to 1961. The one major cyclical fluctuation of the economy in this period began with the recovery from the mild recession of 1954.

The Canadian economy experienced large capital inflows during the period 1955 to 1961 in response to the attractive investment opportunities that existed in Canada. As shown in Figure 42-5, the price of one U.S. dollar remained below one dollar Canadian and at times fell to around 95 cents Canadian. By the end of 1957, however, the economy had turned down, and the unemployment rate rose sharply.

How did monetary policy respond to this serious recession? Although the money supply grew rapidly during 1958, the period 1959–1961 was characterized by a very restrictive monetary policy.

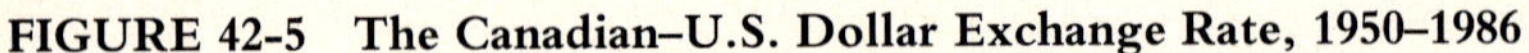

FIGURE 42-5 The Canadian–U.S. Dollar Exchange Rate, 1950–1986

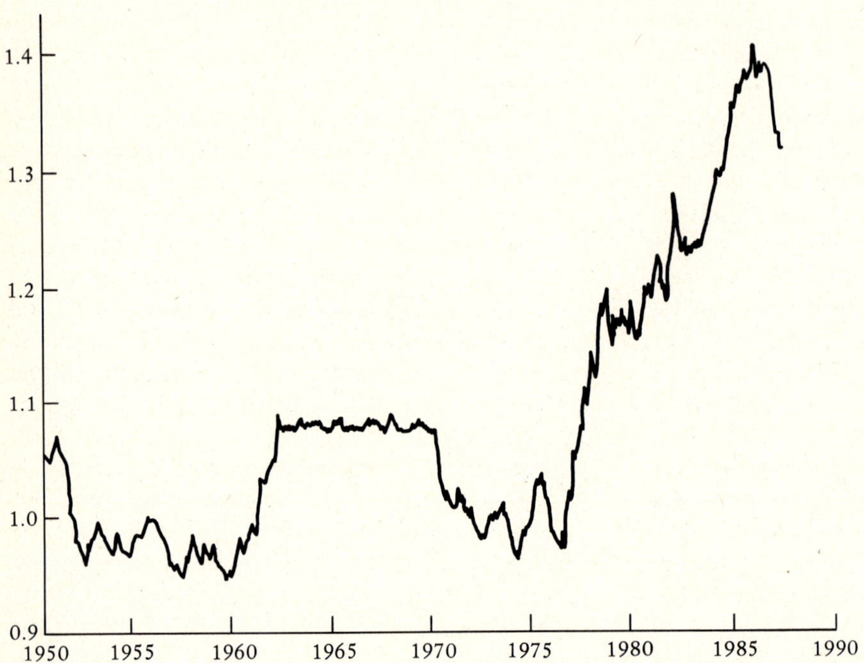

The price of a U.S. dollar has fluctuated from about $0.92 Canadian to over $1.40 Canadian. The exchange rate was determined largely by market forces during the 1950s, when flexible exchange rates were in use. During that period, the price of a U.S. dollar fluctuated from $1.08 Canadian to about $0.92 Canadian. From 1962 to 1970 the exchange rate was pegged in a narrow band around $1.08 Canadian. Since 1970 the exchange rate has again been largely market-determined. After an initial appreciation in the early 1970s, the Canadian dollar fluctuated around or above parity until 1976. From 1976 through 1986, the Canadian dollar steadily depreciated in terms of the U.S. dollar, as indicated by the rise in the price of the U.S. dollar. In 1986 and early 1987 the Canadian dollar appreciated somewhat.

As the theory outlined before indicates, what was needed was an expansionary policy that would have reduced interest rates and discouraged capital inflows. This would have caused the Canadian dollar to depreciate and stimulated the economy. Unfortunately, the advantages of a flexible exchange rate were not used to deal with the serious unemployment problem, and the hoped-for expansion of the money supply and depreciation of the Canadian dollar did not occur until 1961. This episode is discussed further in Box 42-3.

1962–1970: Fixed Exchange Rate

The exchange rate was pegged at $1.08 Canadian to the U.S. dollar throughout the period 1962–1970—that is, the Canadian dollar was worth 92.5 cents U.S. This period witnessed the buildup of boom conditions in the United States, fueled by government expenditures related to the Vietnam War. As is to be expected under a fixed exchange rate, the resulting rise in inflation in the United States spilled over into Canada. In the late 1960s the Canadian

BOX 42-3

The Coyne Affair

The late 1950s witnessed a high level of unemployment and a current account deficit in Canada. Part of the problem was that the U.S. economy was in a mild recession. Several Canadian economists maintained that the Canadian recession, in particular Canadian unemployment, was in fact being aggravated by the restrictive monetary policy pursued by the Bank of Canada. They argued that if monetary policy were loosened, aggregate demand would increase and unemployment would be reduced. They also argued that the current account deficit was primarily due to unusually low levels of exports caused by the U.S. recession; when the American recession ended, they contended, the current account would improve.

The governor of the Bank of Canada, James Coyne, argued that the current account deficit indicated that the Canadian economy was living beyond its means, financed by unusually large capital inflows. He defended the Bank's tight monetary policy on the grounds that if the money supply grew and interest rates fell, capital inflows would *increase.* This would cause an appreciation of the dollar and a further worsening of unemployment. Moreover, the increased current account deficit could be financed only by even larger capital inflows. Thus, in Coyne's view, an expansionary monetary policy would only exacerbate the problem, and contractionary policy was needed to restrain demand and eliminate the current account deficit.

After considerable controversy in academic and political arenas, the Bank of Canada's policies were repudiated. It was decided that expansionary policies were needed. Since he could not agree with these policies, Coyne was replaced as governor in July 1961, establishing the important precedent that in circumstances of fundamental disagreement, the governor of the Bank of Canada, an appointed official, must either agree to pursue the policies of the elected government as put forward by the minister of finance or resign.

The money supply began to expand. We saw in the text that expansionary monetary policy under flexible exchange rates will lead to a capital outflow, a currency depreciation, and effective expansion of aggregate demand. These predictions were all borne out by developments during this period. Unemployment began to fall almost immediately, and the recession was quickly ended. Downward pressure was put on the Canadian dollar, and in May 1962 the government pegged the Canadian dollar at 92.5 U.S. cents, lower than it had been throughout the previous 10 years.

---

government decided that control of inflation was its primary policy objective. Contractionary monetary policy was introduced, and the restriction in aggregate demand had the desired domestic result: By 1970 inflation had fallen to 3.3 percent. But unemployment had risen, reaching almost 6 percent.

As the analysis earlier in this chapter predicts, a tight monetary policy under fixed exchange rates led to a large balance-of-payments surplus. The Bank of Canada accumulated foreign exchange rapidly; it tried to sterilize the effects that its purchases of foreign exchange would otherwise have had on the domestic money supply, but it had only limited success. In the end, faced with the alternative of accepting a rapid rate of domestic monetary expansion or dropping the fixed exchange rate, the Bank chose the latter. On May 31, 1970, the Bank announced that it would no longer maintain the Canadian dollar at a fixed par value. Canada had reverted to a flexible exchange rate.

The attempt to inflate at a slower rate than the United States was incompatible with fixed exchange rates; in the face of a high balance-of-payments surplus, either the economy had to be allowed to expand faster or the exchange rate had to be freed. The latter course was chosen.

BOX 42-4

Foreign Inflation: Imported or Insulated?

Two distinct circumstances can lead to an appreciation of the Canadian dollar. One is a change in the price at which the Bank of Canada intervenes in the foreign exchange market; the other is a change in the foreign prices of traded goods in the absence of Bank of Canada intervention. The two circumstances have very different implications for the "competitiveness" of domestic industry. Many critics of Bank of Canada policy in the 1970s argue that the Bank has failed to recognize the distinction between the two cases. Let us examine this contention.

At given foreign-currency prices of traded goods, an increase in the foreign exchange value of the Canadian dollar as maintained by the Bank of Canada will lead to a reduction in the domestic price of traded goods. Output in both the export- and import-competing sectors will fall. In this case appreciation of the Canadian dollar *is* harmful to the international competitive position of Canadian industry, because it lowers the prices of traded goods relative to domestic costs.

At a given value of the exchange rate, an increase in foreign-currency prices of traded goods leads to an increase in exports and a reduction in imports. The first increases the supply of foreign exchange; the second reduces the demand for foreign exchange. As a result, the Canadian dollar appreciates.

This appreciation offsets the inflationary effects of the foreign-price rise on domestic prices and output. In this case appreciation of the Canadian dollar *is not* harmful to the international competitive position of Canadian industry; the appreciation is a response to foreign disturbances and is instrumental in the process that restores domestic costs and prices to their initial position relative to those of foreign industries.

Nevertheless, in the face of foreign inflation, increases in the value of the Canadian dollar are often opposed, and that opposition is sometimes strong enough to influence policy.

What happens when foreign prices increase and the Canadian dollar is not allowed to appreciate in the manner just outlined? The answer is simple: The Canadian price of traded goods must also rise. In the end, Canadian prices must equal foreign prices adjusted for the exchange rate. If the exchange rate does not change, Canadian prices must change. This is

1970–1975: Return to Floating

Once it was freed, the Canadian dollar rapidly rose in value almost to par with the U.S. dollar. The stage was now set for Canada to continue to pursue its policy of striving for a lower rate of inflation than that in the United States. If Canada were to achieve this goal, it would be necessary that the value of the Canadian dollar *continue to rise* at a rate approximately equal to the excess of the U.S. inflation rate over the Canadian inflation rate.[6]

However, the Bank of Canada, after adopting a flexible exchange rate in order to be able to pursue its anti-inflation policy, simultaneously adopted a more expansionary posture. In particular, it adopted a managed float, commonly referred to as a **dirty float.** A dirty float prevails when a central bank operates to regulate closely the foreign exchange value of the domestic currency without undertaking an explicit commitment to maintain it at or near a publicly announced value.

There are two ways to manage a dirty float. One is to intervene directly in the foreign exchange market to stabilize the exchange rate. A balance-of-payments surplus such as Canada was experiencing at the time would mean that the Bank of Canada would have to buy foreign exchange to keep the Canadian dollar from appreciating. Of course, the purchase of foreign exchange by the Bank of Canada would have meant that the supply of Canadian dollars would be rising.

The second method of managing a dirty float is to set domestic monetary conditions (rates of interest and rates of monetary expansion) so that the ex-

[6] The discussion of the PPP exchange rate on pages 900–901 could usefully be reviewed at this stage.

known as *imported inflation.*

Many economists argue that precisely such imported inflation occurred in Canada in 1974–1975. At that time OPEC price increases caused enormous increases in inflation in our major trading partners, in particular the United States. Canada then was basically self-sufficient in oil and hence was not adversely affected by the oil shock. The decrease in the relative price of Canadian goods resulting from the American inflation led to an increase in exports and a decrease in imports, causing upward pressure on the Canadian dollar.

The Bank of Canada met this by selling Canadian dollars, thereby stabilizing the exchange rate. Although Canada was on a de jure floating exchange rate at that time, the exchange rate did not in fact perform its "insulation" function because it was not allowed to float de facto. By fixing the exchange rate, the Bank of Canada allowed the rapid takeoff into double-digit inflation in the rest of the world to result in a similar inflation in Canada.

This policy error is not unique to the Canadian experience; it is similar to what has happened in other high-inflation countries such as Israel and Sweden. Attempts to protect domestic industry from the supposed ravages of appreciation end in a situation of imported inflation. But the *real* position of the domestic export sector is ultimately unchanged. Either the exchange rate adjusts, allowing domestic money wages and prices to remain constant, or the exchange rate is held constant and domestic inflation occurs. In the latter event, the inflation bids up domestic wages, causing the domestic price of traded goods to rise. The competitiveness of domestic industry remains the same as under the flexible exchange rate option, because in both cases the foreign-currency prices of our goods rise.

Similar arguments were being made when the United States inflation rate took off to 16 and 17 percent in early 1979; there was pressure on the Bank of Canada to intervene to prevent the Canadian dollar from appreciating. Fortunately, the high American inflation did not last very long, and the problem disappeared. But what would have happened had the U.S. inflation persisted? Have we learned, or will we repeat past mistakes?

change market clears at the desired exchange rate without substantial government intervention in the foreign exchange market. Essentially, this means adopting the monetary policy that would be consistent with fixed rates (and hence might better be termed a "dirty fix").

The Bank of Canada chose the second method, and it led to a more rapid expansion of the money supply than would have been consistent with the goal of reducing inflation. Indeed, it led predictably to a rate of inflation roughly equal to that in the United States and higher than the target rate that led to the monetary contraction of the late 1960s and the adoption of a flexible exchange rate in 1970. Indirectly, by maintaining policies consistent with a stable exchange rate, inflation was imported from the United States.

One reason often put forward to explain this apparent policy mistake is discussed in Box 42-4. Canadian export industries had a significant competitive advantage during the period of the late 1960s, when Canada was maintaining a fixed exchange rate and inflating more slowly than the United States, and this competitive advantage was reflected in the current account surplus experienced over that period. The revaluation that followed the floating of the exchange rate in June 1970 eroded much of the competitive advantage because Canadian costs in terms of U.S. dollars also rose.

As a result, further appreciation of the Canadian dollar was opposed on the grounds that it would further harm the competitive position of the export sector. As Box 42-4 emphasizes, this is not the case when the appreciation arises from a low domestic inflation rate relative to the foreign rate. Stabilizing the exchange rate merely led to increased domestic inflation with no gain in competitive advantage for the domestic export sector. Costs in terms of U.S. dollars still rose, not as a result of a rise in the value of the Canadian dollar but rather as a result of increased domestic factor costs, especially wages.

An alternative explanation or justification for the dirty float was that by the middle of 1970 unemployment had become so high that the government had decided it had become the most important problem. Accordingly, from 1970 through 1973, fiscal policy and monetary policy became expansionary.

In any event, Canada appears to have missed an opportunity to avoid at least some of the inflation that plagued the world economy in the 1970s. The full benefits of a flexible rate were not realized because the Bank of Canada resisted the appreciation of the Canadian dollar and permitted high rates of growth of the money supply. The experience of this period illustrates dramatically the futility of trying to protect Canada's export industries by holding the value of the Canadian dollar below its equilibrium level. This could only be done by increasing the rate of growth of the money supply, which had the effect of raising the domestic rate of inflation.

Whatever was gained by Canada's export industries from a lower Canadian dollar was subsequently lost through a higher rate of inflation. The nation's competitive position in world markets depends on its costs of production relative to those of other countries measured in terms of the same currency. The cost of production in Canada, measured in terms of, say, U.S. dollars, will rise as a result of either an appreciation of the Canadian dollar or an increase in domestic wages and prices. In view of the other undesirable effects of inflation, it seems clear that an appreciation of the Canadian dollar would have been less harmful to the Canadian economy.

1975–1980: Monetary Targeting

In 1975 the Bank of Canada began to follow policies that made use of the monetary independence created by flexible exchange rates. The Bank started announcing target rates of growth for the money supply. While on the surface this policy appeared to meet some of the earlier objections to the use of monetary policy under flexible exchange rates, most economists believed nevertheless that the policy was still one of a "dirty float."

In 1978–1979 a large number of wage contracts, following the unwinding of wage and price controls, were coming up for renewal. At the same time, the Canadian dollar was under substantial pressure. The Bank of Canada, worried that an inflationary surge coming from a depreciation would trigger an unacceptable increase in wages, intervened to support the dollar. However, many economists were skeptical of the importance of the direct influence of the exchange rate on wages; they believed that the harmful disruptions to financial markets caused by the uncertainty arising from the Bank's departure from its independent monetary stance were likely to be larger than any possible gains on the wage front. This experience was discussed in detail in Chapters 35 and 36.

1980–1983: Imported Monetary Restraint

In the early 1980s a problem for Canadian monetary and exchange rate management arose from the high average level and volatile behavior of interest rates in the United States. A rise in foreign interest rates leads, other things being equal, to large outflows of short-term capital and a depreciation of the domestic currency. Hence a rise in foreign interest rates such as occurred in the United States in 1980 and again in 1981 must be matched by a rise in Canadian rates, a depreciation of the Canadian dollar, or some combination of the two.

In the 1980 episodes Canadian interest rates rose, but by less than those in the United States. The resulting interest differential attracted capital to the United States, and as a result the Canadian dollar fell from a peak of 87 U.S. cents in July to 82.5 U.S. cents in December. When the next round of U.S. interest rate increases occurred in 1981, Canadian interest rates rose virtually as high as their U.S. counterparts, and the dollar remained relatively stable at around 83 U.S. cents. Again the Bank of Canada was criticized for pursuing a "dirty float."

Although nominal interest rates in the United States fell in 1983, real interest rates remained high. The Bank of Canada walked a middle ground between high Canadian real interest rates and depreciation of the Canadian dollar. While the value of the Canadian dollar fell slowly but steadily from 1982 on, it is widely agreed that the Bank of Canada acted to "protect the exchange rate" and that monetary policy in Canada was tighter than it would have been in the absence of the very tight U.S. monetary policy. This had benefits in the form of a substantial fall in inflation in the 1982–1984 period. It also had costs in terms of the severity of the 1982 recession and the persistent high unemployment of the 1983–1984 recovery.

1984–1987: Recovery and Stable Inflation

During the period 1984–1987 the Bank of Canada was able to reap the benefits of the monetary tightness that it pursued in the first years of the decade. The economy experienced a sustained recovery, inflation remained stable in the 4 percent range, and interest rates fell dramatically. As a result, the central focus of monetary policy was the re-entry problem discussed in Chapter 35—it had to accommodate the growth in the demand for real balance while not rekindling inflation. The exchange rate did not play a central role in the overall design or execution of monetary policy in this period, although exchange rate fluctuations were large and on occasion attracted the interest of the Bank and economic commentary.

The period was dominated by the dramatic fall in the value of the U.S. dollar in terms of the Japanese yen and the major European currencies. In late 1985 and early 1986 the Canadian dollar fell in terms of the U.S. dollar; during a brief period in January 1986 speculative pressures—apparently motivated by concern over Canada's large government budget deficit—drove the Canadian dollar below 70 cents U.S. The Canadian dollar thus experienced an even more dramatic depreciation in terms of the offshore currencies. The Bank of Canada took strong measures to counter the speculative attacks and kept to its medium-term goal of stabilizing the inflation rate. In late 1986 and early 1987 the market acknowledged its faith in these policies, and the Canadian dollar strengthened considerably in terms of the U.S. dollar, rising to around 74 cents U.S. This mitigated the depreciation experienced in terms of the overseas currencies, and the Canadian dollar stayed almost constant in terms of a trade-weighted average of all currencies.

Summary

1. Policymakers in an open economy are faced with policy targets or objectives relating to the foreign sector as well as to the domestic sector. Attainment of these targets is often called achieving external and internal balance, respectively. When policies to move the economy toward one target cause it to move away from the other, the targets are said to be in conflict.
2. Expenditure-changing policy used to control the level of national income will also influence the trade balance by altering imports. There will be a conflict of objectives if there is a trade account deficit and a recessionary gap or if there is a trade account surplus and an inflationary gap. Expenditure-switching policies that shift the net export function can be used to deal with conflict situations.
3. In general, both expenditure-switching and expenditure-changing policies are needed to attain internal and external balance.
4. The capital account is influenced by both fiscal and monetary policy because both influence domestic interest rates.
5. Under a fixed exchange rate, there is little scope for the use of monetary policy for domestic stabilization purposes. Because of the

sensitivity of international capital flows to interest rates, the central bank will be forced to maintain domestic interest rates close to the levels in the rest of the world, and it will not be able to bring about substantial changes in the domestic money supply.

6. Under a fixed exchange rate, capital flows will act to reinforce the effectiveness of fiscal policy.
7. Under a flexible exchange rate, fiscal policy actions will be offset by a crowding-out effect unless they are accompanied by an accommodating monetary policy that prevents changes in interest rates and the exchange rate.
8. Under a flexible exchange rate, monetary policy is a powerful tool. When capital flows are highly interest-elastic, the main channel by which an increase in the money supply increases demand for domestically produced goods is a depreciation of the exchange rate.
9. During the period 1950–1961 Canada was on a flexible exchange rate. The Bank of Canada failed to use monetary policy effectively to deal with a serious unemployment problem. In the late 1960s Canada was on a fixed exchange rate that prevented the authorities from avoiding the rising inflation rates experienced by other countries.
10. The floating of the Canadian dollar in 1970 did not remove the inflationary pressure coming from abroad because the Bank of Canada permitted excessively high rates of growth of the money supply during the period 1971–1975.
11. From 1975 to 1980 the Bank of Canada followed a policy of controlling the rate of growth of the money supply. Nevertheless, there were episodes in which a "dirty float" was maintained.
12. From 1980 to 1983 the Bank of Canada has tried to defend the value of the Canadian dollar. Nevertheless, high U.S. interest rates have led to both tight monetary policy in Canada and some depreciation of the Canadian dollar. Since 1984 monetary policy has been focused on maintaining economic recovery combined with stable inflation, with occasional focus on the exchange rate.

Topics for Review

Internal and external balance
Conflicts between objectives
Expenditure-changing and expenditure-switching policies
Monetary and fiscal policy under fixed exchange rates
Sterilization
Monetary and fiscal policy under flexible exchange rates
Dirty float

Discussion Questions

1. Explain how a country can influence the external value of its currency by (a) direct intervention in the foreign exchange market, (b) fiscal policy, (c) monetary policy.

2. One message of this chapter is that despite a formal commitment to flexible exchange rates, central banks often try to stabilize the exchange rate and to "mimic" policies of major countries' policies. Why might a central bank oppose both a depreciation and an appreciation of its currency? How has Canadian monetary policy performed in this respect in the past two or three years?
3. In a speech in December 1980, Bank of Canada governor Gerald Bouey stated that "the rapid run-up of U.S. short-term [interest] rates is bound to have a major impact on Canada through increases in interest rates here or through a fall in the foreign exchange value of the Canadian dollar, or some combination of the two." Why must one of these responses occur? What policies can the Bank of Canada follow in order to influence which of the possible responses occurs? Which is preferable?
4. In his annual report for 1977, Bank of Canada governor Gerald Bouey said: "If we in Canada continue our progress towards better control of our prices and costs we shall unquestionably benefit from higher levels of employment and output than would otherwise be possible. Better price performance will improve the competitive position of Canadian suppliers in foreign markets and in relation to foreign goods in Canadian markets." Why should Canada be concerned with its competitive position under a flexible exchange rate? In what other ways might a lowering of the rate of inflation lead to increased employment?
5. Which of the following pairs of policy goals can be reached simultaneously using an appropriate macroeconomic policy, and which involve conflicting objectives? Indicate the policies you would advocate in each case.
   a. Lower rate of inflation and a reduced trade deficit
   b. Elimination of an inflationary gap and a trade deficit
   c. Lower rate of unemployment and a reduced trade deficit
   d. Lower rate of unemployment and a reduced overall balance-of-payments deficit
6. Explain why the use of monetary policy for domestic stabilization is limited under a fixed exchange rate.
7. A country that maintains a fixed exchange rate will have to allow its inflation rate to adjust to the level occurring in the rest of the world. Is this inconsistent with the theories of demand-pull and expectational inflation discussed in Chapter 36?

Mathematical Notes

1. Since it is impermissible to divide by zero, the ratio $\Delta Y/\Delta X$ cannot be evaluated when $\Delta X = 0$. But the limit of the ratio as ΔX approaches zero can be evaluated, and it is infinity.

$$\lim_{\Delta X \to 0} \frac{\Delta Y}{\Delta X} = \infty$$

2. Many variables affect the quantity demanded. Using functional notation, the argument of the next several pages of the text can be anticipated. Let Q^D represent the quantity of a commodity demanded and

$$T, \overline{Y}, N, Y^*, p, p_j$$

represent, respectively, tastes, average household income, population, income distribution, its price, and the price of the jth other commodity.

The demand function is

$$Q^D = D(T, \overline{Y}, N, Y^*, p, p_j),\ j = 1, \ldots, n$$

The demand schedule or curve looks at

$$Q^D = q(p) \Big|_{T, \overline{Y}, N, Y^*, p_j}$$

where the notation means that the variables to the right of the vertical line are held constant.

This function is correctly described as the demand function with respect to price, all other variables held constant. This function, often written concisely as $q = q(p)$, shifts in response to changes in other variables. Consider a change in average income. If, as is usually hypothesized, $\partial Q^D/\partial \overline{Y} > 0$, then increases in average income shift $q = q(p)$ rightward and decreases in average income shift $q = q(p)$ leftward. Changes in other variables likewise shift this function in the direction implied by the relationship of that variable to the quantity demanded.

3. Quantity demanded is a simple, straightforward, but frequently misunderstood concept in everyday use, but it has a clear mathematical meaning. It refers to the dependent variable in the demand function from note 2:

$$Q^D = D(T, \overline{Y}, N, Y^*, p, p_j)$$

It takes on a specific value, therefore, whenever a specific value is assigned to each of the independent variables. A change in Q^D occurs whenever the specific value of any independent variable is changed. Q^D could change, for example, from 10,000 tons per month to 20,000 tons per month as a result of a *ceteris paribus* change in any one price, in average income, in the distribution of income, in tastes, or in population. It could also change as a result of the net effect of changes in all of the independent variables occurring at once. Thus a change in the price of a commodity is a sufficient reason for a change in Q^D but not a necessary reason.

Some textbooks reserve the term *change in quantity demanded* for a movement along a demand curve, that is, a change in Q^D as a result of a change in p. They then use other words for a change in Q^D caused by a change in the other variables in the demand function. This usage gives the single variable Q^D more than one name, and this is potentially confusing.

Our usage, which corresponds to that in all intermediate and advanced treatments, avoids this confusion. We call Q^D *quantity demanded* and refer to *any* change in Q^D as a *change in quantity demanded.* In this usage it is correct to say that a movement along a demand curve is a change in quantity demanded. But it is incorrect to say that a change in quantity demanded can occur only because of a movement along a demand curve (since Q^D can change for other reasons, for example, a *ceteris paribus* change in average household income).

4. Continuing the development of note 2, let Q^S represent the quantity of a commodity supplied and

$$G, X, p, w_i$$

represent, respectively, producers' goals, technology, the products' own price, and the price of the ith input.

The supply function is

$$Q^S = S(G,X,p,w_i),\ i = 1, 2, \ldots, m$$

The supply schedule or supply curve looks at

$$Q^S = s(p) \Big|_{G,X,w_i}$$

This is the supply function with respect to price, all other variables held constant. This function, often written concisely $q = s(p)$, shifts in response to changes in other variables.

5. Continuing the development of notes 2 through 4, equilibrium occurs where $Q^D = Q^S$. *For specified values of all other variables,* this requires that

$$q(p) = s(p) \qquad [1]$$

Equation 1 defines an equilibrium value of p; hence although p is an *independent* variable in each of the supply and demand functions, it is an *endogenous* variable in the economic model that imposes the equilibrium condition expressed in Equation 1. Price is endogenous because it is assumed to adjust to bring about equality between quantity demanded and quantity supplied. Equilibrium quantity, also an endogenous variable, is determined by substituting the equilibrium price into either $q(p)$ or $s(p)$.

Graphically, Equation 1 is satisfied only at the point where demand and supply curves intersect. Thus supply and demand curves are said to determine the equilibrium values of the endogenous variables, price and quantity. A shift in any of the independent variables held constant in the q and s functions will shift the demand or supply curves and lead to different equilibrium values for price and quantity.

6. The definition in the text uses finite changes and is called *arc elasticity*. The parallel definition using derivatives is

$$\eta = \frac{dq}{dp} \times \frac{p}{q}$$

and is called *point elasticity*. Further discussion appears in the Appendix to Chapter 5.

7. The propositions in the text are proven as follows. Letting TR stand for total revenue, we can write

$$TR = pq$$

$$\frac{dTR}{dp} = q + p\frac{dq}{dp} \qquad [1]$$

But from the equation in note 6

$$q\eta = p\frac{dq}{dp} \qquad [2]$$

which we can substitute in Equation 1 to obtain

$$\frac{dTR}{dp} = q + q\eta = q(1 + \eta) \qquad [3]$$

Because η is a negative number, the sign of Equation 3 is negative if the absolute value of η exceeds unity (elastic demand) and positive if it is less than unity (inelastic demand).

8. The axis reversal arose in the following way. Marshall theorized in terms of "demand price" and "supply price," these being the prices that would lead to a given quantity being demanded or supplied. Thus

$$p^d = D(q) \qquad [1]$$

$$p^s = S(q) \qquad [2]$$

and the condition of equilibrium is

$$D(q) = S(q)$$

When graphing the behavioral relations expressed in Equations 1 and 2, Marshall naturally put the independent variable, q, on the horizontal axis.

Leon Walras, whose formulation of the working of a competitive market has become the accepted one, focused on quantity demanded and quantity supplied *at a given price.* Thus

$$q^d = q(p)$$

$$q^s = s(p)$$

and the condition of equilibrium is

$$q(p) = s(p)$$

Walras did not use graphical representation. Had he done so, he would surely have placed p (his independent variable) on the horizontal axis.

Marshall, among his other influences on later generations of economists, was the great popularizer of graphical analysis in economics. Today we use his graphs, even for Walras' analysis. The axis reversal is thus one of those historical accidents that seem odd to people who did not live through the "perfectly natural" sequence of steps that produced it.

9. The relationship of the slope of the budget line to relative prices can be seen as follows. In the two-commodity example, a change in expenditure (ΔE) is given by the equation

$$\Delta E = p_C \Delta C + p_F \Delta F \qquad [1]$$

Along a budget line, expenditure is constant, that is, $\Delta E = 0$. Thus, along such a line,

$$p_C \Delta C + p_F \Delta F = 0 \qquad [2]$$

whence

$$-\frac{\Delta C}{\Delta F} = \frac{p_F}{p_C} \qquad [3]$$

The ratio $-\Delta C/\Delta F$ is the slope of the budget line. It is negative because with a fixed budget, to consume more F one must consume less C. In other words, Equation 3 says that the negative of the slope of the budget line is the ratio of the absolute prices (i.e., the relative price). While prices do not show directly in Figure 7-3, they are implicit in the budget line: Its slope depends solely on the relative price, while its position, given a fixed money income, depends on the absolute prices of the two goods.

10. The distinction made between an incremental change and a marginal change is the distinction for the function $Y = Y(X)$ between $\Delta Y/\Delta X$ and the derivative $\frac{dY}{dX}$. The latter is the limit of the former as ΔX approaches zero. Precisely this sort of difference underlies the distinction between arc and point elasticity, and we shall meet it repeatedly—in this chapter in reference to marginal and incremental *utility* and in later chapters with respect to such concepts as marginal and incremental *product, cost,* and *revenue*. Where Y is a function of more than one variable—for example, $Y = f(X, Z)$—the marginal relationship between Y and X is the partial derivative $\frac{\partial Y}{\partial X}$ rather than the total derivative.

11. The hypothesis of diminishing marginal utility requires that we can measure utility of consumption by a function $U = U(X_1, X_2, \ldots, X_n)$ where $X_1, \ldots, X_n$ are quantities of the n goods consumed by a household. It really embodies two utility hypotheses. First, $\frac{\partial U}{\partial X_i} > 0$, which says that for some levels of consumption the consumer can get more utility by increasing consumption of the commodity. Second, $\frac{\partial^2 U}{\partial X_i^2} < 0$, which says that the marginal utility of additional consumption is declining.

12. Because the slope of the indifference curve is negative, it is the absolute value of the slope that declines as one moves downward to the right along the curve. The algebraic value, of course, increases. The phrase *diminishing marginal rate of substitution* thus refers to the absolute, not the algebraic, value of the slope.

13. Marginal product as defined in the text is really incremental product. More advanced treatments distinguish between this notion and its limit as ΔL approaches zero. Technically, MP measures the rate at which total product is changing as one factor is varied. The marginal product is the partial derivative of the total product with respect to the variable factor. In symbols,

$$MP = \frac{\partial TP}{\partial L}$$

14. We have referred specifically both to diminishing *marginal* product and to diminishing *average* product. In most cases, eventually diminishing marginal product implies eventually diminishing average product. This is, however, not necessary, as the accompanying figure shows.

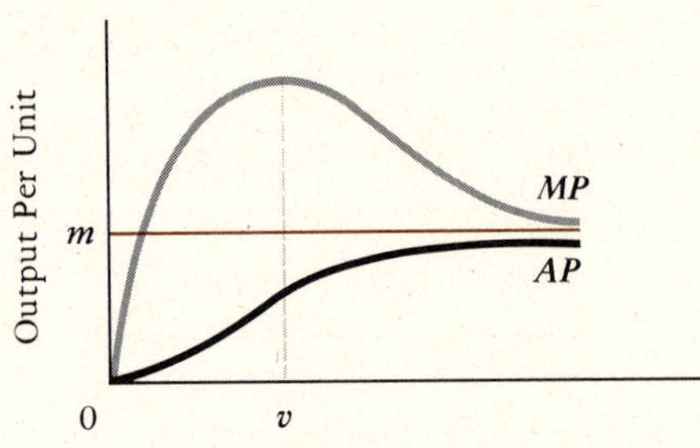

In this case marginal product diminishes after v units of the variable factor are employed. Because marginal product falls toward, but never quite reaches, a value of m, average product rises continually toward, but never quite reaches, the same value.

15. Let q be the quantity of output and L the quantity of the variable factor. In the short run

$$TP = q = f(L) \qquad [1]$$

We now define

$$AP = \frac{q}{L} = \frac{f(L)}{L} \qquad [2]$$

$$MP = \frac{dq}{dL} \qquad [3]$$

We are concerned about the relation between these two. Whether average product is rising, at a maximum, or falling is determined by its derivative with respect to L.

$$\frac{d\frac{q}{L}}{dL} = \frac{L\frac{dq}{dL} - q}{L^2} \qquad [4]$$

This may be rewritten:

$$\frac{1}{L}\left(\frac{dq}{dL} - \frac{q}{L}\right) = \frac{1}{L}(MP - AP) \qquad [5]$$

Clearly, when MP is greater than AP, the expression in Equation 5 is positive and thus AP is rising. When MP is less than AP, AP is falling. When they are equal, AP is at a stationary value.

16. The mathematically correct definition of marginal costs is the rate of change of total cost, with respect to output, q. Thus $MC = dTC/dq$. From the definitions, $TC = TFC + TVC$. Fixed costs are not a function of output. Thus we may write $TC = K + f(q)$, where $f(q)$ is total variable costs and K is a constant. From this we see that $MC = df(q)/dq$. MC is thus independent of the size of the fixed costs.

17. This point is easily seen if a little algebra is used:

$$AVC = \frac{TVC}{q}$$

but

$$TVC = L \times w$$

and

$$q = AP \times L$$

where L is the quantity of the variable factor used and w is its cost per unit. Therefore

$$AVC = \frac{L \times w}{AP \times L} = \frac{w}{AP}$$

Since w is a constant, it follows that AVC and AP vary inversely with each other, and when AP is at its maximum value, AVC must be at its minimum value.

18. A little elementary calculus will prove the point.

$$MC = \frac{dTC}{dq} = \frac{dTVC}{dq}$$

$$= \frac{d\,(L \times w)}{dq}$$

If w does not vary with output,

$$MC = \frac{dL}{dq} \times w$$

But, referring to note 15, Equation 3,

$$\frac{dL}{dq} = \frac{1}{MP}$$

Thus

$$MC = \frac{w}{MP}$$

Since w is fixed, MC varies inversely with MP. When MP is at its maximum, MC must be at its minimum.

19. As we saw in note 18

$$MC = \frac{dTVC}{dq}$$

If we take the integral of the MC from zero to q_0 we get

$$\int_0^{q_0} MC\, dq = TVCq_0 + K$$

The first term gives the area under the marginal cost curve and hence the total variable cost of producing q_0 units; the second term, the constant of integration, is total fixed cost.

20. Strickly speaking, the marginal rate of substitution refers to the slope of the tangent to the isoquant at a particular point while the calculations in Table 11A-1 refer to the average rate of substitution between two distinct points on the isoquant. Assume a production function

$$Q = Q(K, L) \quad [1]$$

Isoquants are given by the function

$$K = I(L, \overline{Q}) \quad [2]$$

derived from Equation 1 by expressing K as an explicit function of L and Q. A single isoquant relates to a particular value ($\overline{Q}$) at which Q is held constant. Define Q_K and Q_L as an alternative, more compact notation for $\partial Q/\partial K$ and $\partial Q/\partial L$, the marginal products of capital and labor. Also, let Q_{KK} and Q_{LL} stand for $\partial^2Q/\partial L^2$ and $\partial^2Q/\partial K^2$, respectively. To obtain the slope of the isoquant, totally differentiate Equation 1 to obtain

$$dQ = Q_K dK + Q_L dL$$

Then, since we are moving along a single isoquant, set $dQ = 0$ to obtain

$$\frac{dK}{dL} = -\frac{Q_L}{Q_K} = MRS$$

Diminishing marginal productivity implies Q_{LL}, $Q_{KK} < 0$ and hence, as we move down the isoquant of Figure 11A-1, Q_K is rising and Q_L is falling, so the absolute value of MRS is diminishing. This is called the *hypothesis of a diminishing marginal rate of substitution*.

21. Formally, the problem is maximize $Q = Q(K, L)$ subject to the budget constraint

$$p_K K + p_L L = C$$

To do this, form the Lagrangean

$$Q(K, L) - \lambda(p_K K + p_L L - C)$$

The first-order conditions for finding the saddle point on this function are

$$Q_K - \lambda p_K = 0; \; Q_K = \lambda p_K \quad [1]$$

$$Q_L - \lambda p_L = 0; \; Q_L = \lambda p_L \quad [2]$$

$$-p_K K - p_L L + C = 0 \quad [3]$$

Dividing Equation 1 by Equation 2 yields

$$\frac{Q_K}{Q_L} = \frac{p_K}{p_L}$$

that is, the ratio of the marginal products, which is (−1) times the MRS, is equal to the ratio of the prices, which is (−1) times the slope of the isocost line.

22. For this note and the next two it is helpful first to define some terms. Let

$$\pi_n = TR_n - TC_n$$

where π_n is the profit when n units are sold.

If the firm is maximizing its profits by producing n units, it is necessary that the profits at output q_n are at least as large as the profits at output zero. If the firm is maximizing its profits at output n, then

$$\pi_n \geq \pi_0 \quad [1]$$

The condition says that profits from producing must be greater than profits from not producing. Condition 1 can be rewritten

$$TR_n - TVC_n - TFC_n \geq TR_0 - TVC_0 - TFC_0 \quad [2]$$

But note that by definition

$$TR_0 = 0 \quad [3]$$
$$TVC_0 = 0 \quad [4]$$
$$TFC_n = TFC_0 = K \quad [5]$$

where K is a constant. By substituting Equations 3, 4, and 5 into Condition 2, we get

$$TR_n - TVC_n \geq 0$$

from which we obtain

$$TR_n \geq TVC_n$$

This proves Rule 1.

On a per unit basis it becomes

$$\frac{TR_n}{q_n} \geq \frac{TVC_n}{q_n} \quad [6]$$

where q_n is the number of units.

Since $TR_n = q_n p_n$, where p_n is the price when n units are sold, Equation 6 may be rewritten

$$p_n \geq AVC_n$$

23. Using elementary calculus, Rule 2 may be proved.

$$\pi_n = TR_n - TC_n$$

each of which is a function of output q. To maximize π it is necessary that

$$\frac{d\pi}{dq} = 0 \quad [1]$$

and that

$$\frac{d^2\pi}{dq^2} < 0 \quad [2]$$

From the definitions

$$\frac{d\pi}{dq} = \frac{dTR}{dq} - \frac{dTC}{dq} = MR - MC \quad [3]$$

From Equations 1 and 3 a necessary condition of maximum π is $MR - MC = 0$, or $MR = MC$, as is required by Rule 2.

24. Not every point where $MR = MC$ is a point of profit maximization. Continuing the equations of math note 23,

$$\frac{d^2\pi}{dq^2} = \frac{dMR}{dq} - \frac{dMC}{dq} \quad [4]$$

From Equations 2 and 4 a necessary condition of maximum π is

$$\frac{dMR}{dq} - \frac{dMC}{dq} < 0$$

which says that the slope of MC must be greater than the slope of MR. Taken with the previous result, it implies that for q_n to maximize π, $MR_n = MC_n$ at a point where MC cuts MR from below.

25. Marginal revenue is mathematically the rate of change of total revenue with output, dTR/dq. Incremental revenue is $\Delta TR/\Delta q$. But the term *marginal revenue* is loosely used to refer to both concepts.

26. To prove that for a downward-sloping demand curve, marginal revenue is less than price, let $p = p(q)$. Then

$$TR = pq = p(q)q$$

$$MR = \frac{dTR}{dq} = q\frac{dp}{dq} + p$$

For a downward-sloping demand curve dp/dq is negative by definition, and thus MR is less than price for positive values of q.

27. The case of the linear demand curve is easily studied using calculus. Let $p = a - bq$, which is the general equation for a downward-sloping straight line ($b > 0$). Then

$$TR = pq = aq - bq^2$$

and

$$MR = \frac{dTR}{dq} = a - 2bq$$

More generally, the demand curve is $p = p(q)$ and total revenue is

$$TR = pq = p(q)q$$

So marginal revenue is

$$MR = qp'(q) + p(q)$$

and its slope is

$$p''(q) + p'(q)$$

We can infer nothing about the sign of this expression given only our knowledge that $p'(q) < 0$, given that the demand curve is negatively sloped.

28. A monopolist selling in two or more markets will set its marginal cost equal to marginal revenue in each market. Thus the condition $MC = MR_1 = MR_2$ is a profit-maximizing condition for a monopolist selling in two markets. In general, equal marginal revenues will mean unequal prices, for the ratio of price to marginal revenue is a function of elasticity of demand: The higher the elasticity, the lower the ratio. Thus equal marginal revenues imply a higher price in the market with the less elastic demand curve.

29. The marginal revenue produced by the factor involves two elements: first, the additional output that an extra unit of the factor makes possible and, second, the change in price of the product that the extra output causes. Let Q be output, R revenue, and L the number of units of labor hired. The contribution to revenue of additional labor is $\partial R/\partial L$. This in turn depends on the contribution of the extra labor to output $\partial Q/\partial L$ (the marginal product of the factor) and $\partial R/\partial Q$, the firm's marginal from the extra output. Thus

$$\frac{\partial R}{\partial L} = \frac{\partial Q}{\partial L} \cdot \frac{\partial R}{\partial Q}$$

We define the left-hand side as marginal revenue product, MRP. Thus

$$MRP = MP \cdot MR$$

30. The condition that for profit maximization MRP be downward sloping at the point where $w = MRP$ is just an application of the proposition (proved in math note 24) that for profit maximization MC must cut MR from below. Consider the output added by the last unit of the variable factor. Its marginal cost is w, and its marginal revenue is MRP. Thus w must cut MRP from below. Since W is a horizontal line, MRP must be falling.

Putting the matter in standard mathematical terms,

$$w = MRP \qquad [1]$$

is a first-order condition of *either* maximizing or minimizing. The second-order condition for maximization is

$$\frac{dw}{dq} > \frac{dMRP}{dq} \qquad [2]$$

Since

$$\frac{dw}{dq} = 0 \qquad [3]$$

the slope of MRP must be negative to satisfy Equation 2; that is, it must be declining.

31. The proposition that the marginal labor cost is above the average labor cost when the average is rising is essentially the same proposition proved in math note 15. But let us do it again, using elementary calculus.

The quantity of labor depends on the wage rate: $L = f(w)$. The total labor cost is wL. The marginal cost of labor is $d(wL)/dL = w + L(dw/dL)$. This may be rewritten $MC = AC + L(dw/dL)$. As long as the supply curve slopes upward $dw/dL > 0$, therefore $MC > AC$.

32. Let t be the tax rate applied to the profits, π, of the firm. Thus the after-tax profits are $(1 - t)\pi$, where π is a function of output, q. To maximize profits after tax requires

$$\frac{d(1 - t)\pi}{dq} = 0$$

or

$$(1 - t)\frac{d\pi}{dq} = 0$$

Dividing through by $(1 - t)$ we can see that $d\pi/dq = 0$ depends on the level of q but is independent of the tax rate.

33. Calculating the ratio of the cost of purchasing a fixed bundle of commodities in two periods is the same thing as calculating the percentage change in each price and then averaging these by weighting each price by the proportion of total expenditure devoted to the commodity. The following expression illustrates the equivalence of these two procedures for the two-commodity case:

$$\frac{q^A p_1^A + q^B p_1^B}{q^A p_0^A + q^B p_0^B} =$$

$$\frac{p_1^A}{p_0^A}\left(\frac{q^A p_0^A}{q^A p_0^A + q^B p_0^B}\right) + \frac{p_1^B}{p_0^B}\left(\frac{q^B p_0^B}{q^A p_0^A + q^B p_0^B}\right)$$

Each q is a fixed quantity weight, and each p is a price. The superscripts A and B refer to two commodities; the subscripts 0 and 1 refer respectively to the base period and some subsequent time period. The expression on the left is the fixed bundle q^A and q^B valued at given year prices divided by its value in base year prices. The first term in the expression on the right gives the ratio of the price of good A in the given year and the base year multiplied by the proportion of total expenditure in the base year devoted to good A. The second term does the same for good B. Simple multiplication and division reduce the right-hand expression to the left-hand one.

34. In the text we define *MPC* as an incremental ratio. For mathematical treatments it is sometimes convenient to define all marginal concepts as derivatives: $MPC = dC/dY_d$, $MPS = dS/dY_d$, and so on.

35. The basic relation is

$$Y_d = C + S$$

Dividing through by Y_d yields

$$Y_d/Y_d = C/Y_d + S/Y_d \text{ or}$$

$$1 = APC + APS$$

Next take the first difference of the basic relation to yield

$$\Delta Y_d = \Delta C + \Delta S$$

Dividing through by ΔY_d gives

$$\Delta Y_d/\Delta Y_d = \Delta C/\Delta Y_d + \Delta S/\Delta Y_d \text{ or}$$

$$1 = MPC + MPS$$

36. This involves using functions of functions. We have $C = C(Y_d)$ and $Y_d = f(Y)$. So by substitution $C = C[f(Y)]$. In the linear expressions used in the text, $C = a + bY_d$, where b is the marginal propensity to consume. $Y_d = hY$, so $C = a + bhY$, where bh is thus the marginal response of C to a change in Y.

37. The elementary theory of national income can be described by the following set of equations (or model).

$Y = AE$	(equilibrium condition)	[1]
$AE = C + I + G + (X - M)$	(definition of AE)	[2]
$C = a + bY$	(consumption function)	[3]
$M = mY$	(import function)	[4]
$Y_d = hY$	(disposable income)	[5]

where I, G, and X are all treated as constant. Substituting Equations 3, 4, and 5 and collecting terms in Y, we can obtain the aggregate expenditure function relating desired expenditure to income.

$$AE = (a + I + G + X) + (bh - m)Y$$

where the first term (in parentheses) is autonomous expenditure and the second term is induced expenditure. Using Equation 1, the equilibrium level of income can be derived by solving

$$Y = (a + I + G + X) + (bh - m)Y$$

to obtain

$$Y = \frac{1}{1 - bh + m}(a + I + G + X) \qquad [6]$$

The example in Table 28-6 has these values: $a = 100$, $I = 250$, $G = 170$, $X = 240$, $b = 0.80$, $h = 0.90$, and $m = 0.1$. Substituting into Equation 6 yields

$$Y = \frac{1}{1 - .72 + .10}(100 + 250 + 170 + 240)$$
$$= \frac{1}{.38}(760) = 2{,}000$$

38. The total expenditure over all rounds is the sum of an infinite series. Letting A stand for the initiating expenditure and z for the marginal propensity to spend, the change in expenditure is ΔA in the first round, $z\Delta A$ in the second, $z(z\Delta A) = z^2\Delta A$ in the third, and so on. This can be written

$$\Delta A(1 + z + z^2 + \cdots + z^n)$$

If z is less than 1, the series in parentheses converges to $1/(1 - z)$ as n approaches infinity. The change in total expenditure is thus $\Delta A/(1 - z)$. In the example in the box, $z = 0.80$; therefore, the change in total expenditure is five times ΔA.

39. As we saw in Box 28–2, the simple multiplier, K, is equal to the reciprocal of the marginal propensity not to spend, $1 - z$, also called the marginal propensity to withdraw, w.

$$K = \frac{1}{w}$$

In an open economy the marginal propensity to withdraw is equal to the sum of the marginal propensity to save, $1 - b$, plus the marginal propensity to import, m. Hence the multiplier in an open economy

$$K_o = \frac{1}{(1 - b) + m}$$

is less than that in a closed economy

$$K_c = \frac{1}{(1 - b)}$$

if the two economies had a common marginal propensity to consume, b. Note that the denominator of K_o can be written as $1 - (b - m)$ where $b - m$ is the marginal propensity to consume *home goods*.

40. Using the multiplier derived in math note 39, we see that an autonomous increase in exports leads to an increase in national income given by

$$\Delta Y = \frac{1}{(1 - b) + m}\Delta X$$

The resulting increase in imports is given by the marginal propensity to import times the change in national income.

$$\Delta M = m\Delta Y$$

Combining, we can calculate the change in the trade balance, $\Delta T = \Delta X - \Delta M$, as

$$\Delta T = \frac{1 - b}{(1 - b) + m}\Delta X = (1 - b)\,\Delta Y$$

which is positive since b is less than one.

41. The accelerator may be stated as a general macroeconomic theory. Define I_n as the volume of net investment this year and ΔY as the increase in national income from last year to this year. The accelerator theory is the relationship between I_n and ΔY.

Assume that the capital-output ratio is a constant

$$\frac{K}{Y} = \alpha, \text{ so } K = \alpha Y$$

If Y changes, K must be changed accordingly

$$\Delta K = \alpha\Delta Y$$

But the change in the capital stock (ΔK) is net investment, so

$$\Delta K = I_n = \alpha\Delta Y$$

42. This is easily proven. In equilibrium the banking system wants sufficient deposits (D) to establish the legal ratio (r) of deposits to reserves (R). This gives $R/D = r$. Any change in D of ΔD has to be accompanied by a change in R of ΔR of sufficient size to restore r. Thus $\Delta R/\Delta D = r$, so $\Delta D = \Delta R/r$, and $\Delta D/\Delta R = 1/r$.

43. Proof: Let r be the reserve ratio. Let $e = 1 - r$ be the excess reserves per dollar of new deposit. If X dollars are deposited in the system assumed in the text, the successive rounds of

new deposits will be X, eX, e^2X, e^3X. . . . The series

$$X + eX + e^2X + e^3X \cdots = X(1 + e + e^2 + e^3 + \cdots)$$

has a limit

$$X\left(\frac{1}{1-e}\right) = X\left[\frac{1}{1-(1-r)}\right] = \frac{X}{r}$$

44. Suppose that the public desires to hold a fraction, v, of deposits in cash. Now let the banking system receive an initial increase in its reserves of ΔR. It can expand deposits by an amount ΔD. As it does so, the banking system suffers a cash drain to the public of $v\Delta D$. The banking system can increase deposits only to the extent the required reserve ratio r makes possible. The maximum deposit expansion can be calculated from

$$r\Delta D = \Delta R - v\Delta D$$

which, collecting terms, can be written

$$(r + v)\,\Delta D = \Delta R$$

Hence

$$\Delta D = \frac{\Delta R}{r + v}$$

45. The argument is simply as follows, where prime marks stand for first derivatives:

$$M^D = F_1(T), \quad F'_1 > 0$$

$$T = F_2(Y), \quad F'_2 > 0$$

therefore,

$$M^D = F_1(F_2(Y)) = H(Y), \quad H' > 0$$

where H is the function of the function combining F_1 and F_2.

46. Let $L(Y, r)$ give the real demand for money measured in purchasing power units. Let M be the supply of money measured in nominal units and P an index of the price level so that M/P is the real supply of money. Now the equilibrium condition requiring equality between the demand for money and the supply of money can be expressed in real terms as

$$L(Y, r) = M/P \qquad [1]$$

or by multiplying through by P in nominal terms as

$$PL(Y, r) = M \qquad [2]$$

In Equation 1 a rise in P disturbs equilibrium by lowering M/P, and in Equation 2 it disturbs equilibrium by raising $PL(Y, r)$.

47. This is expressed in functional notation as

$$DE = f(Y - Y^*)$$

where the restrictions are (a) that $f(0) = 0$ so when $Y = Y^*$ there is no demand effect; and (b) $f' > 0$ so that as Y rises, the demand effect rises. Together (a) and (b) imply that $DE > 0$ when $Y > Y^*$ and $DE < 0$ when $Y < Y^*$.

Point 4 implies that $f'' > 0$; that is, that the Phillips curve gets steeper as Y rises.

48. The "rule of 72" is an approximation derived from the mathematics of compound interest. Any measure X_t will have the value $X_t = X_0e^{rt}$ after t years at a continuous growth rate of r percent per year. Because $X_1/X_0 = 2$ requires $r \times t = 0.69$, a "rule of 69" would be correct for continuous growth. The "rule of 72" was developed in the context of compound interest, and if interest is compounded only once a year, the product of $r \times t$ for X to double is approximately 0.72.

49. The time taken to break even is a function of the *difference* in growth rates, not their level. Thus had 4 percent and 5 percent or 5 percent and 6 percent been used in the example, it still would have taken the same number of years. To see this quickly, recognize that we are interested in the ratio of two growth paths: $e^{r1t}/e^{r2t} = e^{(r1 - r2)t}$.

50. The equation for the IS curve is given by

$$y = c(y - T) + I(r) + G \qquad [1]$$

where $c'(y - T) > 0$ is the marginal propensity

to consume $[c'(y - T) = b]$, $I_r < 0$ is the response of investment to a change in the interest rate, and T is taxes. Substituting $T = T_0 + ty$ into [1], and differentiating, we get

$$wdy = -b\,(dT_0 + ydt) + I_r dr + dG \qquad [2]$$

where w is equal to $[1 - b\,(1 - t)]$, the marginal propensity not to spend. The *IS* curve is drawn for $dT_0 = dt = dG = 0$. Its slope is therefore

$$\left.\frac{dr}{dy}\right|_{IS} = \frac{w}{I_r} < 0 \qquad [3]$$

The horizontal shift in the *IS* curve due to a change in any of the exogenous variables (T_0, t, or G) can be calculated from [2] by setting $dr = 0$. For example, a change in G shifts the *IS* curve by

$$\left.\frac{dy}{dG}\right|_{dr=0} = \frac{1}{w} > 0$$

while a change in tax rates causes a shift of

$$\left.\frac{dy}{dt}\right|_{dr=0} = \frac{-by}{w} < 0$$

51. The equation for the *LM* curve is given by

$$M = PL(y,r) \qquad [1]$$

where $L(y,r)$ represents the demand for real money balances which depends positively on income ($L_y > 0$) and negatively on the interest rate ($L_r < 0$). Differentiating Equation 1 we get

$$dM = L(y,r)dP + PL_y dy + PL_r dr \qquad [2]$$

The *LM* curve is drawn for $dM = dP = 0$. Its slope is therefore

$$\left.\frac{dr}{dy}\right|_{LM} = -\frac{L_y}{L_r} > 0 \qquad [3]$$

The horizontal shift in the *LM* curve due to a change in the money supply can be calculated from Equation 2 by setting $dr = 0$.

$$\left.\frac{dy}{dM}\right|_{dr=0} = \frac{1}{LP_y} > 0 \qquad [4]$$

52. Equations 2 from each of the two previous math notes can be combined to give two relationships between dy and dr. Solving them simultaneously we can derive the following expressions for the effects of monetary and fiscal policy on national income and interest rates. Restricting our analysis of fiscal policy to the effects of government expenditure (so $dT = dt = 0$), and holding $dP = 0$, these are as follows:

$$\frac{dy}{dM} = \frac{-I_r}{D} > 0 \qquad \frac{dr}{dM} = \frac{-w}{D} < 0$$

$$\frac{dy}{dG} = \frac{-PL_r}{D} > 0 \qquad \frac{dr}{dG} = \frac{PL_y}{D} > 0$$

where $D = -(I_r PL_y + wPL_r) > 0$.

53. The aggregate demand curve can be written by solving Equations 1 from each of the math notes 50 and 51 to eliminate the interest rate, thus leaving a relationship between P and y. The relationship between *changes* in P and y can be written

$$Ddy = I_r L(y, P)dP - PL_r dG - I_r dM \qquad [1]$$

where D is as defined in note 52.

The *AD* curve is drawn from $dG = dM = 0$, so its slope is given by

$$\left.\frac{dP}{dy}\right|_{AD} = \frac{I_r L(y, P)}{D} < 0 \qquad [2]$$

The horizontal shift in *AD* can be calculated from Equation 1 by setting $dP = 0$, so that the effects of monetary (dM) and fiscal (dG) policy with a constant price level can be written as follows:

$$\left.\frac{dy}{dM}\right|_{dr=0} = \frac{-I_r}{D} > 0$$

$$\left.\frac{dy}{dG}\right|_{dr=0} = \frac{-PL_r}{D} > 0$$

which, of course, are as in math note 52.

54. Net exports equals exports minus imports.

$$NX = X - M \qquad [1]$$

Exports depend on foreign income, Y^f, and on the terms of trade.

$$X = X_0 + m^f Y^f - b^f\left(\frac{P}{eP^f}\right) \qquad [2]$$

where X_0 is autonomous exports, m^f is the foreign marginal propensity to import, b^f is the response of exports to a change in relative prices, P is the domestic price level, e is the exchange rate, and P^f is foreign prices. Imports depend on domestic income and the terms of trade.

$$M = M_0 + mY + b\left(\frac{P}{eP^f}\right) \qquad [3]$$

Combining Equations 1, 2, and 3, we can write

$$NX = (X_0 - M_0) + m^f Y^f - mY - c\left(\frac{P}{eP^f}\right) \qquad [4]$$

where $c = b + b^f$. In Chapter 39 we considered this relationship in isolation and hence the slope of the NX curve when drawn against national income was taken to be $dNX/dY = -m$, where the other variables in Equation 4 were held constant. Now we have to take into account the fact that P changes as Y changes.

Writing the $SRAS$ curve as

$$P = g(Y),\ g' > 0 \qquad [5]$$

and substituting Equation 5 into Equation 4, we eliminate P to yield

$$NX = (X_0 - M_0) + mY^f - mY - c\left(\frac{g(Y)}{eP^f}\right) \qquad [6]$$

The slope of the NX curve is now given by

$$dNX/dY = -(m + cg') < 0 \qquad [7]$$

Hence as Y rises, NX falls both because of the marginal propensity to import and because of substitution away from domestic goods as P rises.

Glossary

absolute advantage The advantage one nation has over another in the production of a commodity when the same amount of resources will produce more of the commodity in that nation than in the other.

absolute price The amount of money that must be spent to acquire a unit of a commodity. Also called *money price.*

acceleration hypothesis The hypothesis that when national income is held above potential, the persistent inflationary gap will cause inflation to accelerate; and when national income is held below potential, the persistent recessionary gap will cause inflation to decelerate.

accelerator The theory that relates the level of investment to the rate of change of national income.

actual GDP The gross domestic product that the economy in fact produces.

adjustable peg system A system in which exchange rates are fixed in the short term but are occasionally changed in response to persistent payments imbalances.

administered price A price set by the conscious decision of the seller rather than by impersonal market forces.

ad valorem tariff An import duty that is a percentage of the price of the imported product.

ad valorem tax See *excise tax.*

adverse selection Self-selection, within a single risk category, of persons of above average risk.

AE See *aggregate expenditure.*

aggregate demand Total desired purchases by all the buyers of an economy's output.

aggregate demand (*AD*) curve A curve showing the combination of real national income and the price level that makes aggregate desired expenditure equal to national income and the demand for money equal to the supply of money; the curve thus relates the total amount of output that will be demanded to the price level of that output.

aggregate demand shock A shift in the aggregate demand curve.

aggregate expenditure (*AE*) Total expenditure on final output of the economy; $AE = C + I + G + (X - M)$, representing the four major components of aggregate desired expenditure.

aggregate supply Total desired output of all the producers of an economy's output.

aggregate supply (*AS*) curve A relation between the total amount of output that will be produced and the price level of that output.

aggregate supply shock A shift in the aggregate supply curve.

allocation of resources The distribution of the available factors of production among the various uses to which they might be put.

allocative efficiency A situation in which no reorganization of production or consumption could make everyone better off (or, as it is sometimes stated, make at least one person better off while making no one worse off).

allocative inefficiency The absence of allocative efficiency. A situation in which either production or consumption could be reorganized so as to make everyone better off (or, as it is sometimes stated, make at least one person better off while making no one worse off).

annuity A given sum of money paid at stated intervals for a specific period of time or (in case of an *infinite annuity*) forever.

anticombine laws Laws designed to prohibit the acquisition and exercise of monopoly power by business firms.

appreciation A rise in the free-market value of domestic currency in terms of foreign currencies.

a priori Literally, "at a prior time" or "in advance"; knowledge that is prior to actual experience.

arc elasticity A measure of the average responsiveness of quantity to price over an interval of the demand curve. For analytical purposes it is usually defined by the formula

$$\eta = \frac{\Delta q/q}{\Delta p/p}$$

An alternative formula often used where computations are involved is

$$\eta = \frac{(q_2 - q_1)/(q_2 + q_1)}{(p_2 - p_1)/(p_2 + p_1)}$$

where p_1 and q_1 are the original price and quantity and p_2 and q_2 the new price and quantity.

With negatively sloped demand curves elasticity is a negative number. Sometimes the above expressions are therefore multiplied by -1 to make measured elasticity positive.

autonomous expenditure In macroeconomics, elements of expenditure that do not vary systematically with other variables, such as national income and the interest rate, but that are determined by forces outside of the theory. Also called *exogenous expenditure.*

autonomous variable See *exogenous variable.*
average cost (*AC*) See *average total cost.*
average fixed cost (*AFC*) Total fixed costs divided by the number of units of output.
average product (*AP*) Total product divided by the number of units of the variable factor used in its production.
average propensity to consume (*APC*) The proportion of income devoted to consumption; total consumption expenditure divided by disposable income ($APC = C/Y_d$).
average propensity to save (*APS*) The proportion of income devoted to saving; total saving divided by disposable income ($APS = S/Y_d$).
average revenue (*AR*) Total revenue divided by quantity sold.
average tax rate The ratio of total tax paid to total income earned.
average total cost (*ATC*) Total cost of producing a given output divided by the number of units of output; it can also be calculated as the sum of average fixed costs and average variable costs. Also called *cost per unit, unit cost, average cost.*
average variable cost (*AVC*) Total variable costs divided by the number of units of output. Also called *direct unit cost, avoidable unit cost.*

balanced budget A situation in which current revenue is exactly equal to current expenditures.
balanced budget multiplier The change in income divided by the tax-financed change in government expenditure that brought it about.
balance-of-payments accounts A summary record of a country's transactions that involve payments or receipts of foreign exchange.
balance of trade The difference between the value of exports and the value of imports of visible items (goods).
balance sheet A financial report showing a firm's assets and the claims against those assets at a moment in time.
bank notes Paper money issued by commercial banks.
barter A system in which goods and services are traded directly for other goods and services.
base control The use of the monetary base as the instrument by which the central bank attempts to influence its target variables. See also *interest rate control.*
base period A year or other point in time chosen for comparison purposes in order to express or compute index numbers or constant dollars. Also called *base year.*
beggar-my-neighbor policies Policies designed to increase a country's prosperity (especially by reducing its unemployment) at the expense of reducing prosperity in other countries (especially by increasing their unemployment).
blacklist An employer's list of workers who have been fired for union activity.
black market A situation in which goods are sold illegally at prices above a legal price ceiling.
bond An evidence of debt carrying a specified amount and schedule of interest payments and, usually, dates for redemption of the face value of the bond.
boom A period in the business cycle characterized by high demand and increasing production at a level that exceeds potential GDP.
boycott A concerted refusal to buy (buyers' boycott) or to sell (producers' or sellers' boycott) a commodity.
bread-and-butter unionism A union movement whose major objectives are better wages and conditions of employment rather than political or social ends.
budget balance The difference between total government revenue and total government expenditure.
budget deficit The shortfall of current revenue below current expenditure.
budget line Graphic representation of all combinations of commodities or factors that a household or firm may obtain if it spends a given amount of money at fixed prices of the commodities or factors. Also called *isocost line.*
budget surplus The excess of current revenue over current expenditure.
built-in stabilizer Anything that tends to adjust government revenues and expenditures automatically (i.e., without an explicit policy decision) so as to reduce inflationary and recessionary gaps whenever they develop.
business cycle More or less regular, long-term patterns of fluctuations in the level of economic activity.

C See *consumption expenditure.*
capacity The level of output that corresponds to the minimum short-run average total cost. Also called *plant capacity.*
capital A factor of production consisting of all manufactured aids to further production.
capital account A part of the balance-of-payments accounts that records payments and receipts arising from the import and export of long-term and short-term financial capital.
capital consumption allowance An estimate of the amount by which the capital stock is depleted through its contribution to current production. Also called *depreciation.*
capital deepening Adding capital to the production process in such a way as to increase the ratio of capital to labor and other factors of production.
capitalized value The value of an asset measured by the present value of the income stream it is expected to produce.
capital-labor ratio The ratio of the amount of capital to the amount of labor used by a firm, an industry, or the whole economy.

capital-output ratio The ratio of the value of capital to the annual value of output produced using it.
capital stock The aggregate quantity of a society's capital goods or the total of a firm's capital goods.
capital widening Adding capital to the production process in such a way as to leave factor proportions unchanged.
cartel An organization of producers who agree to act as a single seller, thus limiting competition among themselves, in order to maximize joint profits.
ceiling price See *price ceiling.*
central bank A bank that acts as banker to the commercial banking system and often to the government as well. In the modern world, usually a government owned and operated institution that controls the banking system and is the sole money issuing authority.
certificate of deposit (CD) A negotiable time deposit carrying a higher interest rate than that paid on ordinary time deposits.
ceteris paribus Literally, "other things being equal"; usually used in economics to indicate that all variables except the ones specified are assumed not to change.
change in demand An increase or decrease in the quantity demanded at each possible price of the commodity, represented by a shift in the whole demand curve.
change in quantity demanded An increase or decrease in the specific quantity bought at a specified price, represented by a movement along a demand curve.
change in quantity supplied An increase or decrease in the specific quantity supplied at a specified price, represented by a movement along a supply curve.
change in supply An increase or decrease in the quantity supplied at each possible price of the commodity, represented by a shift in the whole supply curve.
chartered bank Privately owned, profit-seeking institution that provides a variety of financial services, such as accepting deposits from customers, which it agrees to transfer when ordered by a cheque, and making loans and other investments.
classical unemployment See *real wage unemployment.*
cleared market A market in which buyers have been able to buy all they wish and sellers have been able to sell all they wish at the going price.
clearing house An institution where interbank indebtedness arising from transfer of cheques between banks is computed, offset against each other, and net amounts owing are calculated.
closed shop A place of employment in which a union has exclusive bargaining jurisdiction for all employees in a shop and only union members can be employed.
coefficient of determination (r^2 or R^2) A measure of how closely a relationship between two variables holds. A coefficient showing the fraction of the total variance of the dependent variable that can be associated with the independent variables in the regression equation; r^2 is used for two variables and R^2 for three or more variables.
collective bargaining The process by which unions and employers arrive at and enforce agreements.
collective consumption goods Goods or services that if they provide benefits to anyone, necessarily provide benefits to a large group of people, possibly everyone in the country.
collusion An agreement among sellers to act as though there were a single seller, for example, by setting a common price. Collusion may be overt or covert, explicit or tacit.
command economy An economy in which the decisions of the government (as distinct from households and firms) exert the major influence over the allocation of resources.
commercial policy Restrictions on the free flow of goods and services among nations.
commodities Items produced to satisfy wants. Commodities may be either *goods,* which are tangible, or *services,* which are intangible.
common-property resource A natural resource that is not privately owned and may be used by anyone.
common stock A form of equity capital usually carrying voting rights and a residual claim to the assets and profits of the firm.
comparative advantage The ability of one nation (region or individual) to produce a commodity at a lesser opportunity cost of other products foregone than another nation.
comparative statics Short for comparative static equilibrium analysis; the derivation of predictions by analyzing the effect of a change in some exogenous variable on the equilibrium position.
competitive devaluations A round of devaluations of exchange rates by a number of countries, each trying to gain a competitive advantage over the other and each failing to the extent that other countries also devalue.
complement Two commodities are complements when they tend to be used jointly with each other; the degree of complementarity is measured by the size of the negative cross elasticity between the two goods.
comprehensive income taxation (CIT) Use of a very broad tax base by defining taxable income to include income from most sources and thus eliminating most exemptions and deductions.
concentration ratio The fraction of total market sales (or some other measure of market occupancy) controlled by a specified number of the industry's largest firms, four-firm and eight-firm concentration ratios being most frequently used.
conglomerate merger See *merger.*
constant-cost industry An industry in which costs of the most efficient size firm remain constant as the entire industry expands or contracts in the long run.
constant returns A situation in which output increases

proportionately with inputs as the scale of production is increased.

consumerism A movement that asserts a conflict between the interests of firms and the public interest.

Consumer Price Index (CPI) A measure of the average prices of commodities commonly bought by households; compiled monthly by *Statistics Canada*.

consumers' durables See *durable good*.

consumers' surplus The difference between the total value consumers place on all units consumed of a commodity and the payment they must make to purchase the same amount of the commodity.

consumption The act of using commodities to satisfy wants.

consumption expenditure In macroeconomics, household expenditure on all goods and services except housing. Represented by the symbol C as one of the four components of aggregate expenditure.

consumption function The relationship between total desired consumption expenditure and all the factors that determine it; in a more specific sense, the relationship between desired consumption expenditure and disposable income.

corporation A form of business organization in which the firm has a legal existence separate from that of the owners and ownership and financial responsibility are divided, limited, and shared among any number of individual and institutional shareholders.

cost (of output) To a producing firm, the value of inputs used in producing output.

cost minimization An implication of profit maximization that the firm will choose the method that produces specific output at the lowest attainable cost.

Cournot-Nash equilibrium An equilibrium that results when each firm makes its decisions on the assumption that the behavior of all other firms will remain unchanged; also called the *non-cooperative equilibrium*.

CPI See *Consumer Price Index*.

craft union A union organized to include workers with a specified set of skills or occupations, regardless of where or in what industry they are employed.

cross elasticity of demand (η_X) A measure of the responsiveness of the quantity of a commodity demanded to changes in price of a related commodity, defined by the formula

$$\eta_X = \frac{\text{percentage change in quantity demanded of } X}{\text{percentage change in price of } Y}$$

cross-sectional data Several different measurements or observations made at the same point in time.

crowding out effect The offsetting reduction in private expenditure caused by the rise in interest rates that follows an expansionary fiscal policy.

current account A part of the balance-of-payments accounts that records payments and receipts arising from trade in goods and services and from interest and dividends earned by capital owned in one country and invested in another.

cyclically adjusted deficit (CAD) An estimate of the government budget deficit (expenditure minus tax revenue) not as it actually is but as it would be if national income were at its potential level.

day-to-day loan Loan made by a chartered bank to an investment dealer. Such loans make up part of the *secondary reserves* of the chartered banks.

debt Amounts owed to one's creditors, including banks and other financial institutions. That portion of a firm's money capital that has been borrowed from persons or institutions who are not owners of the firm.

decision lag The period of time between perceiving some problem and reaching a decision on what to do about it.

decreasing returns A situation in which output increases less than proportionately to inputs as the scale of production increases. A firm in this situation, with fixed factor prices, is an *increasing cost* firm.

demand The entire relationship between the quantity of a commodity that buyers wish to purchase per period of time and the price of that commodity.

demand curve The graphic representation of the relationship between the quantity of a commodity that buyers wish to purchase per period of time and the price of that commodity, other things equal.

demand deposit A bank deposit that is withdrawable on demand (without notice of intention to withdraw) and transferable by means of a cheque.

demand for money The total amount of money balances that the public wishes to hold for all purposes.

demand inflation Inflation arising from excess aggregate demand, that is, when national income exceeds potential.

demand schedule A table showing selected values of the quantity of a commodity that buyers wish to purchase per period of time and the corresponding price of that commodity, other things equal.

deposit money Money held by the public in the form of demand deposits with commercial banks.

depreciation (1) The loss in value of an asset over a period of time due to physical wear and tear and obsolescence. (2) The amount by which the capital stock is depleted through its contribution to current production. (3) A fall in the free-market value of domestic currency in terms of foreign currencies.

depression A period of very low economic activity with very high unemployment and high excess capacity.

derived demand The demand for a factor of production that results from the demand for products it is used to make.

differentiated product A product sufficiently distinguishable from others within an industry that the producer of each has some power over its own price; the products of firms in monopolistically competitive industries.

diminishing marginal rate of substitution The hypothesis that the marginal rate of substitution changes systematically as the amounts of two commodities being consumed vary.

direct investment In balance-of-payments accounting, foreign investment in the form of a takeover or capital investment in a branch plant or subsidiary corporation in which the investor has voting control.

dirty float See *managed float.*

discount rate (1) In the United States, the rate at which the central bank is prepared to lend reserves to commercial banks. (2) More generally, the rate of interest used to discount a stream of future payments to arrive at their present value.

discouraged workers People who would like to work but have ceased looking for a job and hence have withdrawn from the labor force, because they believe that no suitable jobs are available.

discretionary fiscal policy Fiscal policy that is a conscious response (not according to any predetermined rule) to each particular state of the economy as it arises.

disembodied technical change Technical change that raises output without the necessity of building new capital to embody the new knowledge.

disequilibrium The absence of equilibrium. A market is in disequilibrium when there is either excess demand or excess supply.

disequilibrium price A price at which quantity demanded does not equal quantity supplied.

disposable income (Y_d) The income that households have available for spending and saving; GDP minus any part of it not actually paid to households minus personal income taxes paid by households.

distributed profits Profits paid out to owners of a firm. For incorporated firms the distributed profits are called *dividends.*

dividends That part of profits paid out to shareholders of a corporation.

division of labor The breaking up of a production process into a series of repetitive tasks, each done by a different worker.

dollar standard A system under which countries hold reserves in and settle debts with U.S. dollars, but the dollar is not backed by gold or any other physical source of monetary value.

domestic absorption (A) Total demand for goods for use by domestic residents; equal to the sum of $C + I + G$.

double counting In national income accounting, adding up the total outputs of all the sectors in the economy so that the value of intermediate goods is counted in the sector that produces them and every time they are purchased as an input by another sector.

dumping In international trade, the practice of selling a commodity at a lower price in the export market than in the domestic market for reasons not related to differences in costs of servicing the two markets.

duopoly An industry that contains only two firms.

durable good A good that yields its services over an extended period of time. Often divided into the subcategories *producers' durables* (e.g., machines, equipment) and *consumers' durables* (e.g., cars, appliances).

dynamic differential A difference in factor prices caused by disequilibrium that will tend to lead to corrective movements of resources and will be eliminated in equilibrium. Also called *disequilibrium differential.*

economic growth Increases in real, or constant dollar, potential GDP.

economic profits or **losses** The difference between the revenues received from the sale of output and the opportunity cost of the inputs used to make the output. Negative economic profits are economic losses. Also called simply *profits* or *losses.*

economic rent That part of the payment to a factor in excess of its transfer earnings.

economies of scale Reduction of costs per unit of output resulting from an expansion in output; a negatively sloped *LRAC* curve over a range of output.

economies of scope Economies achieved by a firm that is large enough to engage efficiently in multi-product production and associated large-scale distribution, advertising, and purchasing.

economy A set of interrelated production and consumption activities.

effective rate of tariff The tax charged on any imported commodity expressed as a percentage of the value added by the exporting industry.

effluent charge A fee, fine, or tax on a producer for polluting activity, usually on a per unit basis.

elastic demand The situation in which for a given percentage change in price there is a greater percentage change in quantity demanded; elasticity greater than unity.

elasticity of demand (η) A measure of the responsiveness of quantity of a commodity demanded to a change in market price, defined by the formula

$$\eta = \frac{\text{percentage change in quantity demanded}}{\text{percentage change in price}}$$

With negatively sloped demand curves, elasticity is a negative number. Sometimes the above expression is multiplied by -1 to make measured elasticity positive. Also called *demand elasticity, price elasticity.*

elasticity of supply (η_s) A measure of the responsiveness of the quantity of a commodity supplied to a change in the market price, defined by the formula

$$\eta_s = \frac{\text{percentage change in quantity supplied}}{\text{percentage change in price}}$$

embodied technical change Technical change that can be utilized only when new capital, embodying the new techniques, is built.
employment The number of adult workers (15 years of age and older) who hold jobs.
endogenous expenditure See *induced expenditure.*
endogenous variable A variable that is explained within a theory.
entry barrier Legal or other artificial impediment to entry into an industry, such as patents, economies of scale, and established brand preferences.
envelope curve Any curve that encloses, by being tangent to, a series of other curves. In particular, the *envelope cost curve* is the *LRAC* curve, which encloses the *SRAC* curves by being tangent to each without cutting any of them.
equalization payments Transfers of tax revenues from the federal government to the low-income provinces to compensate them for their lower potential per capita tax yields.
equilibrium condition A condition that must be fulfilled if some market or sector of the economy or the whole economy is to be in equilibrium.
equilibrium differential A difference in factor prices that would persist in equilibrium, without any tendency for it to be removed.
equilibrium inflation The rate of inflation that arises when there is no shock inflation, when output is held at potential so there is no demand inflation, and when there is monetary accommodation of expectational inflation.
equilibrium price The price at which quantity demanded equals quantity supplied.
equity capital Funds provided by the owners of a firm the return on which depends on the firm's profits.
error term The difference between the measured value of a variable and the value as predicted by some theoretical or statistical relation.
excess capacity The amount by which actual output falls short of capacity output (which is the output that corresponds to the minimum short-run average total cost).
excess capacity theorem The proposition that equilibrium in a monopolistically competitive industry will occur where each firm has excess capacity.
excess demand A situation in which, at the given price, quantity demanded exceeds quantity supplied. Also called a *shortage.*
excess reserves Reserves held by a chartered bank in excess of the legally required minimum.
excess supply A situation in which, at the given price, quantity supplied exceeds quantity demanded. Also called a *surplus.*
exchange rate The price of one currency in terms of another.
excise tax A tax on the sale of a particular commodity; may be a *specific tax* (fixed tax per unit of commodity) or an *ad valorem tax* (fixed percentage of the value of the commodity).
execution lag The time it takes to put policies in place after the decision is made.
exogenous expenditure See *autonomous expenditure.*
exogenous variable A variable that influences other variables within a theory but is itself determined by factors outside the theory. Also called *autonomous variable.*
expectational inflation Inflation that occurs because decision makers raise prices (so as to keep their relative prices constant) in the expectation that the price level is going to rise.
expectations augmented Phillips curve The relationship between unemployment and the rate of increase of money wages or between national income and the rate of increase of money prices that arises when the demand and expectations components of inflation are combined.
expenditure-changing policies Policies that change the level of aggregate desired expenditure.
expenditure-switching policies Policies that maintain the level of aggregate desired expenditure but change the relative proportions of its components, domestic absorption, and net exports.
external balance A situation where the balance of payments accounts, or some subset of them, are at their target levels.
externalities Effects, either good or bad, on parties not directly involved in the production or use of a commodity. Also called *third-party effects.*

factor markets Markets in which the services of factors of production are sold.
factor mobility The ease with which factors can be transferred between uses.
factors of production Resources used to produce goods and services; frequently divided into the basic categories of land, labor, and capital.
fair trade laws Laws permitting duties to be applied to goods being traded "unfairly" because, for example, of subsidies or the practice of dumping.
falling-cost industry An industry in which the lowest costs attainable by a firm fall as the scale of the industry expands.
favorable balance of payments A credit balance on some part of the international payments account (receipts exceed payments); often refers to a favorable balance on current plus capital account (that is, everything except the official settlements account).
federation In respect to labor unions, any loose organization of national unions.
fiat money Paper money or coinage that is neither backed by nor convertible into anything else but is accepted as legal tender.
final output Total output of goods and services exclud-

ing what is sold to other firms for use as a component in producing their output; sometimes called *final goods.*

financial capital The funds used to finance a firm, including both equity capital and debt. Also called *money capital.*

fine tuning The attempt to maintain national income at or near its full-employment level by means of frequent changes in fiscal or monetary policy.

firm The unit that employs factors of production and produces goods and services to be sold to households, other firms, or the government.

fiscal drag The tendency for an output gap to open up because tax revenues rise faster than government expenditure as full-employment income rises due to economic growth.

fiscal policy The use of the government's revenue-raising and spending activities in an effort to influence the behavior of such macro variables as the GDP and total employment.

fixed cost A cost that does not change with output. Also called *overhead cost, unavoidable cost.*

fixed exchange rate An exchange rate that is maintained within a small range around its publicly stated par value by the intervention of a country's central bank in foreign market operations. Also called a *pegged rate.*

fixed factor An input that cannot be increased in the short run.

fixed investment Investment in plant and equipment.

flexible exchange rate An exchange rate that is left free to be determined by the forces of demand and supply on the free market with no intervention by the monetary authorities. Also called *floating exchange rate.*

floating exchange rate See *flexible exchange rate.*

floor price A minimum permitted price.

foreign exchange Actual foreign currency or various claims on it, such as bank balances or promises to pay, that are traded for each other.

45° line In macroeconomics, the line that graphs the equilibrium condition that aggregate desired expenditure should equal national income ($AE = Y$).

fractional reserve system A banking system in which chartered banks are required to keep only a fraction of their deposits in cash or on deposit with the central bank.

freedom of entry and exit The absence of legal or other artificial barriers to entering into production or withdrawing assets from production.

free good A commodity for which the quantity supplied exceeds the quantity demanded at a price of zero; therefore a good that does not command a positive price in a market economy.

free-market economy An economy in which the decisions of individual households and firms (as distinct from the government) exert the major influence over the allocation of resources.

free trade The absence of any form of government intervention in international trade, which implies that imports and exports must not be subject to special taxes or restrictions levied merely because of their status as "imports" or "exports."

frictional unemployment Unemployment caused by the fact that it takes time for labor to move from one job to another.

fringe benefits Compensation other than wages for the benefit of labor, such as company contributions to pension and welfare funds, sick leave, and paid holidays.

full-cost pricing Setting price equal to average total cost at normal-capacity output plus a fixed markup.

full employment Employment sufficient to produce the economy's potential output; all unemployment is frictional and structural.

function Loosely, an expression of a relation between two or more variables. Precisely, Y is a function of the variables $X_1, \ldots, X_n$ if for every set of values of the variables $X_1, \ldots, X_n$, there is associated a unique value of the variable Y.

functional distribution of income The distribution of income among major factors of production.

G See *government expenditure.*

gains from trade The increased national income that results from specialization and trade as opposed to self-sufficiency.

GDP deflator See *implicit GDP deflator.*

Giffen good An inferior good for which the negative income effect outweighs the substitution effect so that the demand curve is positively sloped.

gold exchange standard A monetary system in which U.S. currency is directly convertible into gold and other countries' currencies are indirectly convertible by being convertible into the gold-backed U.S. dollar at a fixed rate.

goods Tangible commodities, such as cars or shoes.

government All public officials, agencies, and other organizations belonging to or under the control of state, local, or federal government.

government expenditure Includes all government expenditure on currently produced goods and services and does not include government transfer payments. Represented by the symbol G as one of the four components of aggregate expenditure.

Gresham's law The theory that "bad," or debased, money drives "good," or undebased, money out of circulation because people keep the good money for other purposes and use the bad money for transactions.

gross domestic product (GDP) National income as measured by the output approach; equal to the sum of all values added in the economy or, what is the same thing, the values of all final goods produced in the economy.

gross investment The total value of all investment

goods produced in the economy during a stated period of time.

gross national expenditure (GNE) National income as measured by the expenditure approach; equal to the sum of expenditures on consumption, investment, government production and net exports.

gross national product (GNP) National income as measured by the income approach; equal to the sum of all factor incomes earned plus depreciation plus (to get the valuation at market prices) indirect taxes minus subsidies.

gross return on capital The receipts from the sale of goods produced by a firm less the cost of purchased goods and materials, labor, land, manager's talents, and taxes.

homogeneous product In the eyes of purchasers every unit of the product is identical to every other unit.

horizontal equity Focuses on differences that may arise among individuals or families with the same income levels but different circumstances.

horizontal merger See *merger.*

household All the people who live under one roof and who make, or are subject to others making for them, joint financial decisions.

human capital The capitalized value of productive investments in persons; usually refers to value derived from expenditures on education, training, and health improvements.

hypothesis of diminishing returns The hypothesis that if increasing quantities of a variable factor are applied to a given quantity of fixed factors, the marginal product and average product of the variable factor will eventually decrease. Also called *law of diminishing returns, law of variable proportions.*

hypothesis of equal net advantage The hypothesis that owners of factors will choose the use of their factors that produces the greatest net advantage to themselves and therefore will move their factors among uses until net advantages are equalized.

I See *investment expenditure.*

implicit deflator An index number derived by dividing national income measured in current dollars by national income measured in constant dollars and multiplying by 100. In effect, a price index with current-year quantity weights measuring the average change in price of all the items in national income.

import quota A limit set by the government on the quantity of a foreign commodity that may be shipped into that country in a given period.

import substitution industry Domestic production for sale in the home market of goods previously imported; usually involves some form of protection or subsidy.

imputed costs The costs of using factors of production already owned by the firm, measured by the earnings they could have received in their best alternative employment.

income-consumption curve A curve drawn on an indifference curve diagram and connecting the points of tangency between a set of indifference curves and a set of parallel budget lines, showing how the consumption bundle changes as income changes, with relative prices held constant.

income effect The effect on quantity demanded of a change in real income.

income elasticity of demand A measure of the responsiveness of quantity demanded to a change in income, defined by the formula

$$\eta_Y = \frac{\text{percentage change in quantity demanded}}{\text{percentage change in income}}$$

incomes policy Any direct intervention by the government to influence wage and price formation.

income statement A financial report showing the revenues and costs that arise from the firm's use of inputs to produce outputs over a specified period of time.

increasing returns A situation in which output increases more than in proportion to inputs as the scale of a firm's production increases. A firm in this situation, with fixed factor prices, is a *decreasing cost* firm.

incremental cost See *marginal cost.*

incremental product See *marginal product.*

incremental revenue See *marginal revenue.*

indexing The automatic change in any money payment in proportion to the change in the price level.

index number An average that measures changes over time of variables such as the price level and industrial production; conventionally expressed as a percentage relative to a base period assigned the value 100.

indifference curve A curve showing all combinations of two commodities that give the household an equal amount of satisfaction and between which the household is thus indifferent.

indifference map A set of indifference curves based on a given set of household preferences.

induced expenditure In macroeconomics, elements of expenditure that are explained by variables within the theory. In the aggregate desired expenditure function it is any component of expenditure that is related to national income. Also called *endogenous expenditure.*

industrial union A union organized to include all workers in an industry, regardless of skills.

industry A group of firms producing similar products.

inelastic demand For a given percentage change in price there is a smaller percentage change in quantity demanded; elasticity less than unity.

infant industry argument for tariffs The argument that new domestic industries with potential economies of scale need to be protected from competition from established low-cost foreign producers so that they can grow large enough to achieve costs as low as those of foreign producers.

inferior good A good for which income elasticity is negative.

inflation A rise in the average level of all prices. Sometimes restricted to prolonged or sustained rises.

inflationary gap A negative output gap, that is, a situation in which actual national income exceeds potential income.

inflation rate Percentage change in some price index from one period to another.

infrastructure The basic installations and facilities (especially transportation and communications systems) on which the commerce of a community depends.

injections Income earned by domestic firms that does not arise out of the spending of domestic households and income earned by domestic households that does not arise out of the spending of domestic firms.

innovation The introduction of an invention into methods of production.

inputs Materials and factor services used in the process of production.

interest The payment for the use of borrowed money.

interest rate The price paid per dollar borrowed per year; expressed either as a fraction (e.g., 0.06) or as a percentage (e.g., 6 percent) See also *real interest rate.*

interest rate control The use of the interest rate as the instrument by which the central bank attempts to influence its target variables. See also *base control.*

intermediate goods All outputs that are used as inputs by other producers in a further stage of production.

intermediate targets Variables that the government cannot control directly and does not seek to control ultimately, yet that have an important influence on policy variables.

internal balance State of the economy when real national income is at its target level.

invention The discovery of something new, such as a new production technique or a new product.

inventories Stocks of raw materials, goods in process, and finished goods, held by firms to mitigate the effect of short-term fluctuations in production or sales.

investment expenditure Expenditure on the production of goods not for present consumption.

investment goods Goods produced not for present consumption, i.e., capital goods, inventories, and residential housing.

invisible account A form of balance-of-payments account that records payments and receipts arising out of trade in services and the use of capital. Also called *service account.*

involuntary unemployment Unemployment due to the inability of qualified persons who are seeking work to find jobs at the going wage rate.

isocost line See *budget line.*

isoquant A curve showing all technologically efficient factor combinations for producing a specified output.

isoquant map A series of isoquants from the same production function, each isoquant relating to a specific level of output.

jurisdictional dispute Dispute between unions over which has the right to organize a group of workers.

Keynesians A label attached to economists who hold the view, derivative from the work of John Maynard Keynes, that active use of monetary and fiscal policy can be effective in stabilizing the economy. Often the term encompasses economists who advocate active policy intervention in general.

Keynesian short-run aggregate supply curve A horizontal aggregate supply curve indicating that when national income is below potential, changes in national income can occur with little or no accompanying changes in prices.

***k* percent rule** The proposition that the money supply should be increased at a constant percentage rate year in and year out, irrespective of cyclical changes in national income.

labor A factor of production consisting of all physical and mental contributions provided by people.

labor boycott An organized attempt to persuade customers to refrain from purchasing the products of a firm or industry whose employees are on strike.

labor force The total number of people either employed or actively seeking work.

labor union See *union.*

Laffer curve A graph relating the revenue yield of a tax system to the marginal or average tax rate imposed.

laissez faire Literally, "let do"; a policy advocating the absence of government intervention in a market economy.

land A factor of production consisting of all gifts of nature, including raw materials and "land" as conventionally defined.

law of demand The proposition that market price and quantity demanded in the market vary inversely with one another, that is, that demand curves slope downward.

law of diminishing returns See *hypothesis of diminishing returns.*

law of variable proportions See *hypothesis of diminishing returns.*

legal tender Anything that by law must be accepted for the purchase of goods and services or in discharge of a debt.

less-developed countries (LDCs) The lower-income countries of the world, most of which are in Asia, Africa, and South and Central America. Also called *underdeveloped countries, developing countries,* the *South.*

life-cycle hypothesis (LCH) A hypothesis that relates the household's actual consumption to its expected lifetime income rather than (as in early Keynesian theory) to its current income.

lifetime income See *permanent income*.

limited liability The limitation of the financial responsibility of an owner (shareholder) of a corporation or a limited partner to the amount of money he or she has actually made available to the firm by purchasing its shares.

limited partnership This is an ordinary partnership with the addition of one or more limited partners who do not participate in management while their personal liability for the debts of the firm is limited to the amount each has invested.

liquidity The degree of ease and certainty with which an asset can be turned into the economy's medium of exchange.

liquidity preference (*LP*) function The function that relates the demand for money to the rate of interest.

lockout The closing of operations by an employer during a bargaining dispute; the employer's equivalent of a strike.

logarithmic scale A scale in which equal proportional changes are shown as equal distances (for example, 1 inch may always represent doubling of a variable). Also called *log scale, ratio scale*.

long run A period of time in which all inputs may be varied, but the basic technology of production cannot be changed.

long-run aggregate supply (*LRAS*) curve The curve indicating total supply that is forthcoming when all wages and prices have adjusted; a vertical line at $Y = Y^*$.

long-run average cost (*LRAC*) curve The curve showing the least-cost method of producing each level of output. Also called *long-run average total cost (LRATC) curve*.

long-run Phillips curve (*LRPC*) The relation between national income and the price level when all goods and factor markets are in long-run equilibrium.

Lorenz curve A graph showing the extent of departure from equality of income distribution.

lower turning point The bottom point of the business cycle where a contraction turns into an expansion of economic activity.

Lucas aggregate supply curve A curve expressing the hypothesis that national output varies positively with the ratio of the actual to the expected price level.

M Imports; a country's total expenditure on imports.

M1 Currency plus demand deposits.

M1A M1 plus chequable savings deposits plus nonpersonal notice deposits.

M2 M1A plus personal savings and fixed-term deposits.

M3 M2 plus nonpersonal fixed-term and foreign-currency deposits.

macroeconomics The study of the determination of economic aggregates and averages, such as total output, total employment, the price level, and rate of economic growth.

managed float Intervention in the foreign exchange market by a country's central bank to respond to particular circumstances in pursuit of an unofficial exchange rate target, but not to maintain an announced par value. Also called *dirty float*.

marginal cost (*MC*) The increase in total cost resulting from raising the rate of production by one unit. Mathematically, the rate of change of cost with respect to output. Also called *incremental cost*.

marginal efficiency of capital (*MEC*) The marginal rate of return on a nation's capital stock. The rate of return on one additional dollar of net investment, i.e., an addition of one dollar's worth of new capital to capital stock.

marginal efficiency of capital schedule A schedule relating *MEC* to the size of the capital stock.

marginal efficiency of investment (*MEI*) The function that relates the quantity of investment to the rate of interest.

marginal net private benefit (*MNPB*) The difference between the contribution of a unit of production to a firm's revenue and its contribution to the firm's cost.

marginal net social benefit (*MNSB*) The difference between marginal social benefit and marginal social cost.

marginal physical product (*MPP*) See *marginal product*.

marginal product (*MP*) The change in quantity of total output that results from using one unit more of a variable factor. Mathematically, the rate of change of output with respect to the quantity of the variable factor. Also called *incremental product* and *marginal physical product* (*MPP*).

marginal productivity theory of distribution The theory that factors are paid the value of their marginal products so that the total earnings of each type of factor of production equal the value of the marginal product of that factor multiplied by the number of units of that factor that are employed.

marginal propensity not to spend The fraction of any increment to national income that is not spent on domestic production (1 − the marginal propensity to spend; i.e., $1 - \Delta AE/\Delta Y$).

marginal propensity to consume (*MPC*) The change in consumption divided by the change in disposable income that brought it about; mathematically, the rate of change of consumption with respect to disposable income ($MPC = \Delta C/\Delta Y_d$).

marginal propensity to save (*MPS*) The change in

saving related to the change in disposable income that brought it about; the rate of change of saving divided by disposable income ($MPS = \Delta S/\Delta Y_d$).

marginal propensity to spend The fraction of any increment to national income that is spent on domestic production; it is measured by the change in aggregate expenditure divided by the change in income ($\Delta AE/\Delta Y$).

marginal rate of substitution (*MRS*) (1) In consumption, the slope of an indifference curve, showing how much more of one commodity must be provided to compensate for the giving up of one unit of another commodity if the level of satisfaction is to be held constant. (2) In production, the slope of an isoquant, showing how much more of one factor of production must be used to compensate for the use of one less unit of another factor of production if production is to be held constant.

marginal revenue (*MR*) The change in a firm's total revenue arising from a change in its rate of sales by one unit. Mathematically, the rate of change of revenue with respect to output. Also called *incremental revenue.*

marginal revenue product (*MRP*) The addition of revenue attributable to the last unit of a variable factor. $MRP = MP \times MR$. Mathematically, the rate of change of total revenue with respect to quantity of the variable factor.

marginal social benefit The contribution of a unit of production to social welfare.

marginal tax rate The amount of tax a taxpayer would pay on an additional dollar of income, i.e., the fraction of an additional dollar of income that is paid in taxes.

marginal utility The additional satisfaction obtained by a buyer from consuming one unit more of a good; mathematically, the rate of change of utility with respect to consumption; also called *marginal value.*

marginal value See *marginal utility.*

margin requirement The fraction of the price of a stock that must be paid in cash, while putting up the stock as security against a loan for the balance.

market A concept with many possible definitions. (1) An area over which buyers and sellers negotiate the exchange of a well-defined commodity. (2) From the point of view of a household, the firms from which it can buy a well-defined product. (3) From the point of view of a firm, the buyers to whom it can sell a well-defined product.

market-clearing price Price at which quantity demanded equals quantity supplied so that there are neither unsatisfied buyers nor unsatisfied sellers; that is, the equilibrium price.

market economy A society in which people specialize in productive activities and meet most of their material wants through exchanges voluntarily agreed upon by the contracting parties.

market failure Failure of the unregulated market system to achieve optimal allocative efficiency or social goals because of externalities, market impediments, or market imperfections.

market sector That portion of an economy in which commodities are bought and sold and in which producers must cover their costs from sales revenue.

market structure Characteristics of market organization that affect behavior and performance of firms, such as the number and size of sellers, the extent of knowledge about each other's actions, the degree of freedom of entry, and the degree of product differentiation.

markup The amount added to cost to determine price.

medium of exchange Anything that is generally acceptable in return for goods and services sold.

merchandise account See *visible account.*

merger The purchase of either the physical assets or the controlling share ownership of one company by another. In a *horizontal* merger both companies produce the same product; in a *vertical* merger one company is a supplier of the other; if the two are in unrelated industries, it is a *conglomerate* merger.

microeconomic policy Activities of governments designed to alter resource allocation and/or income distribution.

microeconomics The study of the allocation of resources and the distribution of income as they are affected by the workings of the price system and by government policies.

minimum efficient scale (*MES*) The level of output at which long-run average cost is at a minimum. The smallest size of firm required to achieve the economies of scale in production and/or distribution.

minimum wages Legally specified minimum rate of pay for labor in covered occupations.

mixed economy An economy in which some decisions about the allocation of resources are made by firms and households and some by the government.

monetarists A label attached to economists who stress monetary causes of cyclical fluctuations and inflations and who believe that an active stabilization policy is not normally required. Often the term encompasses conservative economists who oppose active policy intervention in general.

monetary base The sum of currency in circulation plus reserves of the chartered banks.

monetary equilibrium A situation in which the demand for money equals the supply of money.

monetary policy An attempt to influence the economy by operating on such monetary variables as the quantity of money and the rate of interest.

money Any generally accepted medium of exchange.

money capital See *financial capital.*

money income Income measured in monetary units per period of time.
money rate of interest See *interest rate.*
money substitute Something that serves as a temporary medium of exchange but is not a store of value.
money supply The total quantity of money in an economy at a point in time.
monopolistic competition (1) A market structure of an industry in which there are many sellers and freedom of entry but in which each firm has a product somewhat differentiated from the others, giving it some control over its price. (2) More recently, any industry in which more than one firm sells differentiated products.
monopoly A market situation in which the output of an industry is controlled by a single seller.
monopsony A market situation in which there is a single buyer.
moral hazard A situation in which an individual or firm takes advantage of special knowledge while engaging in socially uneconomic behavior.
multilateral balance of payments The balance between one country's payments to and receipts from the rest of the world.
multiple regression analysis See *regression analysis.*
multiplier The ratio of the change in national income to the change in autonomous expenditure that brought it about.

Nash equilibrium See *Cournot-Nash equilibrium.*
national debt The current volume of outstanding federal government debt.
national income In general, the value of total output and the value of the income generated by the production of that output.
national income accounting The set of rules and techniques for measuring the total flow of output produced and incomes generated by this production.
natural monopoly An industry characterized by economies of scale sufficiently large that one firm can most efficiently supply the entire market demand.
natural rate of unemployment The rate of unemployment (due to frictional and structural causes) consistent with potential national income (Y^*). It is the rate of unemployment at which there is neither upward nor downward demand pressure on the price level.
natural scale A scale in which equal absolute amounts are represented by equal distances.
near money Liquid assets that are easily convertible into money without risk of significant loss of value and can be used as short-term stores of purchasing power, but are not themselves media of exchange.
negative income tax (NIT) A tax system in which households with incomes below taxable levels receive payments from the government based on a percentage of the amount by which their income is below the minimum taxable level.
net domestic income (NDI) at factor cost The sum of the four components of factor incomes (wages, rent, interest, and profits).
net exports Total exports minus total imports. Represented by the expression $(X - M)$ as a component of aggregate expenditure, where X is total exports and M is total imports.
net investment Gross investment minus replacement investment.
net national product (NNP) at market prices Sum of wages, rent, interest, profits, and indirect taxes minus subsidies.
net private benefit (*NPB*) The difference between private benefits and private costs.
net social benefit (*NSB*) The difference between social benefits and social costs. Where private production produces externalities, it is net private benefit plus external benefits and minus external costs.
net unborrowed reserves The total reserves of the commercial banking system minus required reserves minus the reserves that have been borrowed from the central bank.
neutrality of money The doctrine that the money supply affects only the absolute level of prices and has no effect on relative prices and hence no effect on the allocation of resources or the distribution of income.
newly industrializing countries (NICs) Formerly underdeveloped countries that have become major industrial exporters since World War II.
nominal GDP See *nominal national income.*
nominal national income Total output measured in dollars; the money value of national output. Also called *money national income* or *current dollar national income.*
nominal rate of interest See *interest rate.*
nominal rate of tariff The tax charged on any imported commodity.
nonmarket sector That portion of an economy in which commodities are given away and producers must cover their costs from some source other than sales revenue.
nonprice competition Competition by sellers for sales by means other than price cutting, such as advertising, product differentiation, trading stamps, and other promotional devices.
nontariff barriers to trade Restrictions, other than tariffs, designed to reduce the flow of imported goods.
normal capacity output The level of output that a firm hopes to maintain on average over the business cycle; typically, somewhat less than full capacity output.
normal good A good for which income elasticity is positive.
normal profits A term used by some economists for the imputed returns to capital and risk taking just necessary to keep the owners in the industry. They are included in what most economists, but not all businessmen, see as *total costs.*

normative statement A statement about what ought to be, as opposed to what is, was, or will be true.
note See *treasury bill.*

oligopoly A market structure in which a small number of rival firms dominate the industry.
open market operations The purchase and sale of securities on the open market by the central bank of securities (usually short-term government securities).
open shop A place of employment in which a union represents its members but does not have bargaining jurisdiction for all workers in a shop and membership in the union is not a condition of getting or keeping a job.
operating regime The combination of intermediate targets and policy instruments used to achieve those targets selected by a central bank in order to reach its policy goals.
opportunity cost The cost of using resources for a certain purpose, measured by the benefit given up by not using them in their best alternative use.
organization theory A set of hypotheses that predicts that the substance of the decisions of a firm is affected by its size and form of organization.
output gap The difference between total output that could have been produced at the potential level and what is actually produced; that is, potential GDP minus actual GDP.
outputs The goods and services that result from the process of production.

Pareto-efficiency See *Pareto-optimality.*
Pareto-optimality A situation in which it is impossible by reallocation of production or consumption activities to make all consumers better off without simultaneously making others worse off (or, as it is sometimes put, to make at least one person better off while making no one worse off). Also called *Pareto-efficiency*.
partnership A form of business organization in which the firm has two or more joint owners, each of whom is personally responsible for all of the firm's actions and debts.
paternalism Intervention in the free choices of individuals by others (including governments) to protect them against their own ignorance or folly.
pegged rate See *fixed exchange rate.*
per capita GDP GDP divided by total population.
perfect competition A market structure in which all firms in an industry are price takers and in which there is freedom of entry into and exit from the industry.
permanent income The maximum amount that a household can consume per year into the indefinite future without reducing its wealth. (A number of similar but not identical definitions are in common use.) Also called *lifetime income.*
permanent-income hypothesis (PIH) A hypothesis that relates actual consumption to permanent income rather than (as in the original Keynesian theory) to current income.
personal income Income earned by individuals before allowance for personal income taxes on that income.
petrodollars Money earned by the oil-exporting countries and held by them in short-term, liquid investments.
Phillips curve Originally, a relation between the percentage of the labor force unemployed and the rate of change of money wages. Now often drawn as a relation between the percentage of the labor force employed and the rate of price inflation or between actual national income and the rate of price inflation.
picket line Striking workers parading at the entrances to a plant or firm on strike; a symbolic blockade of the entrance.
point elasticity A measure of the responsiveness of quantity demanded to price at a particular point on the demand curve. The formula for point elasticity of demand is

$$\eta = \frac{\Delta q}{\Delta p} \times \frac{p}{q}$$

With negatively sloped demand curves elasticity is a negative number. Sometimes the above expression is multiplied by -1 to make elasticity positive.
point of diminishing average productivity The level of output at which average product reaches a maximum.
point of diminishing marginal productivity The level of output at which marginal product reaches a maximum.
policy instruments The variables that the government can control directly to achieve its policy objectives.
policy variables The variables that the government seeks to control, such as real national income and the rate of change of the price level.
political business cycle Cyclical swings in the economy generated by fiscal and monetary policy for the purpose of winning elections.
portfolio investment In balance-of-payments accounting, foreign investment in bonds or a minority holding of shares that does not involve legal control. See also *direct investment.*
positive statement A statement about what is, was, or will be true, as opposed to what ought to be.
potential GDP (Y^*) The real gross domestic product the economy could produce if its productive resources were fully employed at their normal intensity of use.
potential income See *potential GDP.*
potential national income See *potential GDP.*
poverty level The official government estimate of the annual family income required to maintain a minimum adequate standard of living.

precautionary balances Money balances held for protection against the uncertainty of the timing of cash flows.

preferred stock A form of equity capital with a preference over common stock to receipt of dividends up to a stated maximum amount; may be voting or nonvoting.

present value (*PV*) The value now of one or more payments to be received in the future; often referred to as the *discounted present value* of future payments.

price ceiling A maximum permissible price.

price-consumption line A line connecting the points of tangency between a set of indifference curves and a set of budget lines where one absolute price is fixed and the other varies, money income being held constant.

price control policy Any government policy that regulates the price at which a commodity can be bought and sold; often used to refer to the imposition of maximum prices on one or more commodities.

price discrimination The sale by a single firm of different units of a specific commodity at two or more different prices for reasons not associated with differences in cost.

price elasticity of demand See *elasticity of demand.*

price floor A minimum permissible price.

price index A number that shows the average percentage change that has occurred in some group of prices over some period of time; price indexes can be used to measure the price level at a given time relative to a base period.

price level The average level of a broad group of prices; it is usually measured by an index number.

price taker A firm that can alter its rate of production and sales without significantly affecting the market price of its product.

principle of substitution The implication of cost minimization that as the relative prices of the inputs vary, the proportions in which various inputs are used will vary so as to use relatively more of the cheaper inputs.

private cost The value of the best alternative use of resources used in production as valued by the producer.

private sector That portion of an economy in which the organizations that produce goods and services are owned and operated by private units such as households and firms.

producers' durables See *durable good.*

producers' surplus The difference between the total amount producers receive for all units sold of a commodity and the total variable cost of producing the commodity; it can be calculated by finding the difference between the marginal cost and marginal revenue associated with the production and sale of each unit of output and summing over all units of output.

product differentiation The existence of similar but not identical products sold by a single industry such as the breakfast food and the automobile industries.

production The act of making commodities.

production function A functional relation showing the maximum output that can be produced by each and every combination of inputs.

production possibility boundary A curve that shows which alternative combinations of commodities can just be attained if all available productive resources are used; it is thus the boundary between attainable and unattainable output combinations.

productive efficiency Production of any output at the lowest attainable cost for that level of output.

productivity Output produced per unit of resource input; frequently used to refer to *labor productivity,* measured by output per hour worked or per worker employed.

product markets Markets in which outputs of goods and services are sold.

profit (1) In ordinary usage, the difference between the value of outputs and the value of inputs. (2) In microeconomics, the difference between revenues received from the sale of goods and the value of inputs, which includes the opportunity cost of capital, so that profits are *economic profits.* (3) In macroeconomics, profits exclude interest on borrowed capital, but do not exclude the return to owner's capital.

progressive tax A tax that takes a larger percentage of income the higher the level of income.

progressivity of taxation The ratio of taxes to income as income increases. If the ratio decreases, the tax is *regressive;* if it remains constant, *proportional;* if it increases, *progressive.*

proportional tax A tax that takes a constant percentage of income at all levels of income and is thus neither progressive nor regressive.

protectionism Government intervention to provide partial or complete protection of domestic industries from foreign competition in domestic markets by use of tariff or nontariff barriers to trade.

proxy A document authorizing someone to exercise the voting rights of a stockholder in a corporation.

proxy fight A struggle between competing factions in a corporation to obtain the proxies for a majority of the outstanding shares.

public sector That portion of an economy in which production is owned and operated by the government or bodies appointed by it such as crown corporations.

public utility regulation Regulation of such things as prices and profit rates in industries that have been deemed to be natural monopolies.

purchase and resale agreement (PRA) An arrangement by which the Bank of Canada makes short-term advances as a lender of last resort to investment dealers. Government securities are sold to the Bank with an agreement to repurchase them.

purchasing power of money The amount of goods and services that can be purchased with a unit of money. Decreases in the purchasing power of money are measured by increases in a price index. Also called *value of money.*

purchasing power parity (PPP) exchange rate The exchange rate between two currencies that adjusts for relative inflation rates.

pure rate of interest The rate of interest that would rule in equilibrium in a riskless economy where all lending and borrowing are for investment in productive capital.

pure return on capital The amount capital can earn in a riskless investment; hence the transfer earnings of capital in a riskless investment.

quantity actually bought The amount of a commodity that households succeed in purchasing in some time period.

quantity actually sold The amount of a commodity that producers succeed in selling in some time period.

quantity demanded The amount of a commodity that households wish to purchase in some time period. An increase (decrease) in quantity demanded refers to a movement down (up) the demand curve in response to a fall (rise) in price.

quantity exchanged The identical amount of a commodity that households actually purchase and producers actually sell in some time period.

quantity supplied The amount of a commodity producers wish to sell in some time period. An increase (decrease) in quantity supplied refers to a movement up (down) the supply curve in response to a rise (fall) in price.

random sample A sample chosen from a group or population in such a way that every member of the group has an equal chance of being selected.

rate base The total allowable investment to which the rate of return allowed by a regulatory commission is applied.

rate of return The ratio of return to capital earned by a firm to total invested capital.

rate of return on capital Sometimes used synonymously with *rate of return.* Frequently used to refer to a specific capital good; the annual return to capital produced by a capital good, expressed as a percentage of the price of the good.

rational expectations The theory that people understand how the economy works and learn quickly from their mistakes, so that while random errors may be made, systematic and persistent errors are not made.

ratio scale See *logarithmic scale.*

real capital Physical assets of a firm, including plant, equipment, and inventories. Also called *physical capital.*

real income A household's or firm's income expressed in terms of the purchasing power of the income, that is, the quantity of goods and services that can be purchased with the income; it can be calculated as money income deflated by a price index.

real national income Total output measured in prices prevailing in some base year; changes in real national income reflect only changes in quantities produced. Also called *constant dollar national income.*

real product wage The proportion of each sales dollar accounted for by labor costs (including the pre-tax nominal wage rate, benefits, and payroll taxes).

real rate of interest The money rate of interest corrected for the change in the purchasing power of money by subtracting the inflation rate.

real wage unemployment Unemployment caused by too high a real product wage. Also called classical unemployment.

recession In general, a sustained downswing in the level of economic activity.

recessionary gap A positive output gap; that is, a situation in which actual national income is less than potential income.

regression analysis A quantitative measure of the relationship between two or more variables. *Simple regression* concerns the relation between Y and a single independent variable, X_1; *multiple regression* concerns the relation between Y and more than one independent variable, $X_1, \ldots, X_n$. Also called *correlation analysis.*

regression equation An equation describing the statistically determined best fit between variables, or best estimate of the average relationship between variables in regression analysis.

regressive tax A tax that takes a lower percentage of income the higher the level of income.

relative price The ratio of the money price of one commodity to the money price of another commodity; that is, a ratio of two absolute prices.

replacement investment The amount of investment that just maintains the existing capital stock intact.

required reserves The minimum amount of reserves a bank must, by law, keep either in currency or in deposits with the central bank.

reserve currencies Currencies (such as the U.S. dollar) commonly held by foreign central banks as international reserves.

reserve ratio The fraction of its deposits that a bank holds as reserves in the form of cash or deposits with a central bank.

resource allocation The allocation of an economy's scarce resources among alternative uses.

retained earnings See *undistributed profits.*

return to capital The total amount available for payments to owners of capital; the sum of pure returns to capital, risk premiums, and economic profits.

rising-cost industry An industry in which the minimum cost attainable by a firm rises as the scale of the industry expands.

rising supply price A rising long-run supply curve, caused by increases in factor prices as output is increased or by diseconomies of scale.

risk premium The return on capital necessary to compensate owners of capital for the risk of loss of their capital.

sample A small number of items, chosen from a larger group or population, that is intended to be representative of the larger entity.

satisficing A hypothesized objective of firms to achieve target levels of satisfactory performance rather than to *maximize* some objective.

saving All disposable income that is not spent on consumption.

savings deposit An interest-bearing deposit legally withdrawable only after a certain notice period. (Savings deposits were common prior to recent revisions in the Bank Act.)

scarce good A commodity for which the quantity demanded exceeds the quantity supplied at a price of zero; and therefore a good that commands a positive price in a market economy.

scatter diagram A graph of statistical observations of paired values of two variables, one measured on the horizontal and the other on the vertical axis. Each point on the coordinate grid represents the values of the variables for a particular unit of observation.

search unemployment Unemployment caused by people continuing to search for a good job rather than accepting the first job they come across when unemployed.

secondary reserves Interest-earning liquid assets held by banks. For purposes of the minimum ratio to deposits imposed by the Bank of Canada, secondary reserves are defined as holdings of *treasury bills, day-to-day loans,* and *excess cash reserves.*

sectors Parts of an economy.

securities market See *stock market.*

sellers' preferences Allocation of commodities in excess demand by decisions of those who sell them.

service account See *invisible account.*

services Intangible commodities, such as haircuts or medical care.

short run A period of time over which the quantity of some inputs cannot, as a practical matter, be varied.

short-run aggregate supply (*SRAS*) curve A relation between the price level of final output and the quantity of output supplied on the assumption that all input prices (including wage rates) are held constant.

short-run equilibrium Generally, equilibrium subject to fixed factors or other things that cannot change over the time period being considered. For a competitive firm, the output at which market price equals short-run marginal cost; for a competitive industry, the price and output at which industry demand equals short-run industry supply and all firms are in short-run equilibrium.

short-run Phillips curve (*SRPC*) A relation between unemployment and the rate of wage inflation or between national income and the rate of price inflation, drawn for a given state of expectations about the future rate of inflation.

short-run supply curve A curve showing the relation of quantity supplied to prices, when one or more factor is fixed; it is the horizontal sum of marginal cost curves (above the level of average variable costs) of all firms in an industry.

simple multiplier The ratio of the change in equilibrium national income to the change in autonomous expenditure at a constant price level.

single proprietorship A form of business organization in which the firm has one owner, who is personally responsible for all of the firm's actions and debts.

size distribution of income The distribution of income among households by amount, without regard to source of income or social class of households.

slope The ratio of the vertical change to the horizontal change between two points on a straight line.

Snake An agreement among the countries of the European Community (except the U.K.) to fix exchange rates among their own currencies and then let their joint rate float against the dollar.

social cost The value of the best alternative use of resources available to society as valued by society. Also called *social opportunity cost.*

special drawing rights (*SDR*s) Financial liabilities of the IMF held in a special fund generated by contributions of member countries. Members can use SDRs to maintain supplies of convertible currencies when these are needed to support foreign exchanges.

specialization of labor An organization of production in which individual workers specialize in the production of particular goods or services (and satisfy their wants by trading) rather than produce everything they consume (and satisfy their wants by being self-sufficient).

specific tariff An import duty of a specific amount per unit of the product.

specific tax. See *excise tax.*

speculative balances Money balances held as a hedge against the uncertainty of the prices of other financial assets.

stabilization policy Any policy designed to reduce the economy's cyclical fluctuations. Attempts by the government to remove inflationary and recessionary gaps when they appear.

stagflation The coexistence of high rates of unemployment with high, and sometimes rising, rates of inflation.

sterilization Operations undertaken by the central bank

to offset the effects of the money supply of balance-of-payments surpluses or deficits.

stockholders The owners of a corporation who have supplied money to the firm by purchasing its shares.

stock market An organized market where stocks and bonds are bought and sold. Also called *securities market.*

strike The concerted refusal of the members of a union to work.

strikebreakers Nonunion workers brought in by management to operate the plant while a union is on strike (derisively called *scabs* by union members).

structural unemployment Unemployment due to a mismatch between characteristics required by available jobs and characteristics possessed by the unemployed labor.

substitute Two commodities are substitutes for each other when both satisfy similar needs or desires; the degree of substitutability is measured by the magnitude of the positive cross elasticity between the two.

substitution effect A change in quantity of a good demanded resulting from a change in its relative price, eliminating the effect on real income of the change in price.

supply The entire relationship between the quantity of some commodity that producers wish to make and sell per period of time and the price of that commodity, other things being equal.

supply curve The graphic representation of the relation between the quantity of some commodity that producers wish to make and sell per period of time and the price of that commodity, other things being equal.

supply of effort The total number of hours of work that the population is willing to supply. Also called *total supply of labor.*

supply of money See *money supply.*

supply schedule A table showing for selected values the relation between the quantity of some commodity that producers wish to make and sell per period of time and the price of that commodity, other things being equal.

tacit collusion The adoption, without explicit agreement, of a common policy by sellers in an industry. Also called *conscious parallel action.* See also *collusion.*

takeover bid See *tender offer.*

tariff A tax applied on imports.

tax base The aggregate amount of taxable income.

tax expenditures Tax concessions, such as exemptions and deductions from taxable income and tax credits, designed to induce market responses considered to be desirable. They are called expenditures because they have the same effect as having no concessions and then spending money on subsidies and other transfers to the groups getting the concessions.

tax incidence The location of the burden of a tax; that is, the identity of the ultimate bearer of the tax.

tax-related incomes policy (TIP) Tax incentives for labor and management to encourage them to conform to wage and price guidelines.

tax-rental arrangements An agreement by which the federal government makes a per capita payment to the provinces for the right to collect income taxes.

tender offer An offer to buy directly some or all of the outstanding common stock of a corporation from its stockholders at a specified price per share, in an attempt to gain control of the corporation. Also called *takeover bid.*

term See *term to maturity.*

term deposit See *savings deposit.*

terms of trade The ratio of the average price of a country's exports to the average price of its imports.

term to maturity The period of time from the present to the redemption date of a bond. Also called simply the *term.*

third-party effects See *externalities.*

time deposit An interest-earning bank deposit, legally subject to notice before withdrawal (in practice the notice requirement is not normally enforced) and until recently transferable by cheque.

time-series data A set of measurements or observations made on some variable at successive periods (or moments) of time. Contrasted with *cross-sectional data.*

total cost (*TC*) The sum of the opportunity costs of the factors used to produce that output, it can be divided into total fixed costs and total variable costs of producing at a given level of output.

total fixed cost (*TFC*) Total costs of producing that do not vary with level of output.

total product (*TP*) Total amount produced during a given period of time by all the factors of production employed over that time period.

total revenue (*TR*) Total receipts from the sale of a product; price times quantity.

total utility The total satisfaction resulting from the consumption of a given commodity by a consumer in a period of time; also called *total value.*

total value See *total utility.*

total variable cost (*TVC*) Total costs of producing that vary directly with level of output.

trade account See *visible account.*

trade union See *union.*

transactions balances Money balances held to finance payments because payments and receipts are not perfectly synchronized.

transactions costs Costs incurred in effecting market transactions (such as negotiation costs, billing costs, and bad debts).

transfer earnings That part of the payment to a factor in its present use that is just enough to keep it from transferring to another use.

transfer payment A payment to a private person or institution that does not arise out of current productive activity; typically made by governments, as in welfare payments, but also made by businesses and private individuals in the form of charitable contributions.

transmission mechanism The channels by which a change in the demand or supply of money leads to a shift of the aggregate demand curve.

treasury bill The characteristic form of short-term government debt. A promise to pay a certain sum of money at a specified time in the future (usually 90 days to 1 year from date of issue). Although they carry no fixed interest payments, holders earn an interest return because they purchase them at a lower price than their redemption value. Also called *treasury note*.

undistributed profits Earnings of a firm not distributed to shareholders as dividends, but retained by the firm. Also called *retained earnings*.

unemployment The number of persons 15 years of age and older who are not employed and are actively searching for a job.

unemployment rate Unemployment expressed as a percentage of the labor force.

unfavorable balance of payments A debit balance on some part of the payments accounts (payments exceed receipts); often refers to the balance on current plus capital account (that is, everything except the official settlements account).

union An association of workers authorized to represent them in bargaining with employers. Also called *trade union, labor union*.

union shop A bargaining arrangement in which the employer may hire anyone at union wages, but every employee must join the union within a specified period of time (often 60 days).

unit costs Costs per unit of output, equal to total cost divided by total output. Also called *average cost*.

upper turning point The top point of the business cycle where an expansion turns into a contraction of economic activity.

utility The satisfaction that results from the consumption of a commodity.

value added The value of a firm's output minus the value of the inputs that it purchases from other firms.

value added tax (VAT) A multi-stage tax collected on the value added to goods as they progress through the production and distribution systems.

value of money See *purchasing power of money*.

variable A magnitude (such as the price of a commodity) that can take on a specific value, but whose value will vary with time and place.

variable cost A cost that varies directly with output. Also called *direct cost, avoidable cost*.

variable factor An input that can be varied in the short run.

velocity of circulation National income divided by quantity of money.

vertical equity Focuses on comparisons among individuals or families with different levels of income.

very long run A period of time in which the technological possibilities open to a firm are subject to change.

visible account A form of balance-of-payments account that records payments and receipts arising from the import and export of tangible goods. Also called *trade account* and *merchandise account*.

voluntary export restriction (VER) An agreement by an exporting country to limit the amount of a good exported to another country.

wage and price controls Direct government intervention in wage and price formation with legal power to enforce the government's decisions on wages and prices.

wage-cost push inflation An increase in the price level caused by increases in labor costs that are not themselves associated with excess aggregate demand for labor.

wealth The sum of all the valuable assets owned minus liabilities.

windfall profit A change in profits that arises out of an unanticipated change in market conditions such as a sudden increase in demand. Negative windfall profits are sometimes called *windfall losses*.

withdrawals Income earned by households and not passed on to firms in return for goods and services purchased, and income earned by firms and not passed on to households in return for factor services purchased.

X Exports; the value of all domestic production sold abroad.

X-inefficiency The use of resources at a lower level of productivity than is possible, even if they are allocated efficiently, so that the economy is at a point inside its production possibility boundary.

$X - M$ See *net exports*.

Index